THE
CITY
OF
ORPHANS

For Sean,

Nora

THE CITY OF ORPHANS

Relief Workers, Commissars and
the "Builders of the New Armenia"

Alexandropol/Leninakan
1919–1931

NORA N. NERCESSIAN

THE CITY OF ORPHANS
Relief Workers, Commissars and
the "Builders of the New Armenia"
Alexandropol/Leninakan
1919–1931

By Nora N. Nercessian

Copyright © 2016 Nora N. Nercessian
All rights reserved
No part of the material may be used or reproduced in any manner whatsoever without written permission of the author and the publisher.

Cover & Book Design by
Arrow Graphics, Inc.
info@arrow1.com

ISBN: 978-1-884186-61-5 (hc)
ISBN: 978-1-884186-60-8 (pb)
Library of Congress Control Number: 2016933267

Printed in the United States of America

Hollis Publishing
95 Runnells Bridge Road
Hollis, New Hampshire 03049
603.889.4500 • puritancapital.com

In Honor of

All Orphans, Within and Without the Gates of

The City of Orphans

&

My Grandfather Paul Boghos Nercessian

Cherished Teacher of Birds' Nest Orphanage

Byblos, Lebanon

From 1921–1925

"GATES TO HAPPINESS"
Children Gathered Behind the Gates of Kazachi Post
Front Cover, *The New Near East*, March 1922.

CONTENTS

Dedication	v
Acknowledgements	xi
INTRODUCTION: *"The Amazing, Stupendous Spectacle…"*	xiii
Abbreviations	xxi
Transliteration and Standardization of Names	xxiii

Part One
THE MAKING OF THE CITY OF ORPHANS

Chapter One: FROM BARRACKS TO ORPHANAGE — 3

The Changing Landscape of Alexandropol	3
Relief and Retreat	12
"The Slough of Despond"	15
The Meeting of May 17, 1919: A Question of *"Dignity"*	19

Chapter Two: ALEXANDROPOL AS THE *"SHOW DISTRICT"* — 24

The Return of ACRNE/NER: Restructuring	24
The Appeal of the Barracks	27
A Second Exodus	33
Concentration Resumed	36
Apprehension over Concentration	47

Part Two
THE CITY OF ORPHANS UNDER TWO FLAGS

Chapter Three: EXODUS — 57

Exodus from Alexandropol to Kars	57
"To Abandon Is a Crime…"	64
Exodus from Kars to Alexandropol: *"Packed into Boxcars Like Sardines in a Can, Only Worse"*	66
Return to Alexandropol: *"No Food at Any Price"*	71

**Chapter Four: COMMISSARS, RELIEF WORKERS,
AND THE PARAMETERS OF REDEMPTION**   82

    "America's Answer"   88
    The Limits of Redemption   96
    Mandates, Revisions, and Liaisons   100
    Adoption Revisited   107
    The Matter of Rare Books, Manuscripts, and Used Clothes   109
    "A State Within a State"…and Its Challenge(r)s   113
    An *"Extraordinary Meeting"*: New York, Summer 1923   120

**Chapter Five: CEREMONIES, PHOTO-OPS,
AND MOVING PICTURES**   124

    "I Showed Them We Are Men of State"   126
    Alice in Hungerland   129
    "A Gigantic Pageant"   132
    "Uncle America Sees It Through"   137
    An Evening of *"Internationale"*   139
    Senators and Congressmen   146
    Alexei Rykov, Georgy Chicherin, and Fridtjof Nansen   150

**Chapter Six: *"THREE SUBURBAN TOWNS OF SIX TO SEVEN
THOUSAND CHILDREN EACH"***   154

    Transfer from Yerevan to "Alekpol"   154
    Kazachi Post   159
    The Polygon   161
    Severski: *"The Largest Children's Hospital in the World"*   167
    Cleveland House and the School for the Blind   172
    Mens Sana in Corpore Sano: Sports, Athletics, and Boy Scouts   174
    Recreation and Culture   179
    "When the Sun Comes Out…" Yeghishe Charents at the Polygon   181
    Visiting Armenian Artists and the Armenian Debut of *Sasuntsi Davit*   182

Chapter Seven: EDUCATION FOR CITIZENSHIP   185

    Academic Instruction   186
    An Inexhaustible Labor Force: Industrial Training   191
    The Agricultural Program and the NER Institute of Agriculture   208
    Model Villages   215
    The Edith Winchester School of Nursing   216
    The Teacher Training Program   221
    Educational Priorities in 1924:
       Paul Monroe and Nshan Hovhannisyan   223
    The Elusive Phantom of (Un)Happiness   229

Chapter Eight: CHARACTER BUILDING FOR WORTHY CITIZENSHIP — 234

"*Perfect Little Spartans*": Order and Discipline — 236
"*The Errant Lambs of Christ*": Religious and Ethical Instruction — 240
Punishment for "*Incorrigible Mischief Makers*" — 244
The Meandering Path of Character Building: "*Oriord Sandukhd,*" "*Miss Maka*" and "*Mister Vord*" — 251
Satik, or Orphan #4654 — 257

Chapter Nine: OUTPLACEMENT, DOWNSIZING, AND THE RESHAPING OF THE CITY OF ORPHANS — 260

"Liquidation," or Outplacement — 261
"*Where There Is No School, nor a Student Body…*" — 268
Outplacement to Points North and Comrade Nurichanyan's Report on Orphans Outplaced in Abkhazia — 270
Staff Reorganization, Budget Cuts and Labor Unions — 284
"…*Something of the Spirit of America…*" — 289

Part Three
THE END OF AN ERA

Chapter Ten: THE POLYGON: "*ONCE GREAT IN NUMBERS, TODAY GREATER IN INFLUENCE…*" — 295

"*Strictly Confidential*" — 295
The Battle over Severski — 297
The Quest for Permanency — 305
Retrospective (and Prospective) at the Polygon: December 3 & 4, 1927 — 311
Permanency and Polygon's Core Group — 317
Democlean Sword and an Ultimatum — 322

Chapter Eleven: EGRESS — 327

Deliberations in New York and Leninakan — 327
Asset Liquidation — 331
The Final Withdrawal — 335
Reward and Retribution — 340

Chapter Twelve: APOCRYPHA — 349

Part Four
THE COMMUNITY OF THE CITY OF ORPHANS
1919–1931

A. Listing of Orphans (Incomplete)	375
B. Listing of American and Armenian Employees According to Department and Position (Incomplete)	479

APPENDIX
Diary of an Anonymous Relief Worker	521

ENDNOTES   549

SOURCES   597

ACKNOWLEDGEMENTS

The topic of this volume was suggested to me in Yerevan in summer 2012. The research necessary in its preparation charted my path to a large number of colleagues and friends to whom I owe a debt of gratitude that can hardly be expressed through the ritualistic gesture of acknowledgments. Their guidance and insights, which touch the pages in this book in various ways, is deeply appreciated, as is the support so generously and consistently extended to me over the last three years in Yerevan, Gyumri, New York and Cambridge, Massachusetts. It is my privilege to thank all the institute directors, archivists, scholars and researchers who took time from their busy schedules to contribute their perspectives and knowledge: at the Armenian Genocide Museum and Institute in Yerevan, Dr. Hayk Demoyan, Mrs. Gohar Khanumyan, and Mrs. Tatev Ghaltakhchyan; at the National Library of Armenia, Dr. Tigran Zargaryan, Mrs. Alisa Adamyan, Mrs. Lucine Hakobyan, and Mrs. Yebraxya Tchekelezyan; at the National Archives of Armenia, Dr. Amatuni Virapyan, Dr. Sonya Mirzoyan, Mrs. Marine Martirossyan, and Mrs. Gohar Avagyan; at the Academy of Sciences of the Republic of Armenia, Mrs. Anahit Mirzoyan; at the History Museum of Armenia, Dr. Anelka Grigoryan and Mrs. Seda Galstyan; at the Matenadaran, Dr. Shushanik Khachikyan; at the Institute of Archeology and Ethnography, Dr. Gayane Shagoyan and Dr. Hranush Kharatyan-Araqelyan; at the Hovhannes Shiraz House-Museum in Gyumri, Dr. Ara Papanyan and Mrs. Narine Khachatryan; at the Center for Armenological Research of Shirak Province in Gyumri, Dr. Sergei Hayrapetyan and Dr. Karine Aleksanyan; at the Shirak Province Historical Preservation Service in Gyumri, Mr. Avedik Melik-Sargsyan; at the Rockefeller Archives Center at Sleepy Hollow, New York, Dr. Jack Meyers and Ms. Nancy Adgent; at the Special Collections and Archives of Mount Holyoke College in South Hadley, Massachusetts, Ms. Leslie Fields; Mr. Shant Mardirossian, Chairman of the Near East Foundation, New York; and at the Harvard University Archives, Ms. Michelle Gachette.

My gratitude is also extended to many individuals whose assistance in the preparation of this book was invaluable: Dr. Suren Avetisyan, Yerevan; Dr. Paul Barsam, Belmont, Massachusetts; Ms. Dzovinar Derderian, Ann Arbor, Michigan; Ms. Satenik Faramazyan, Yerevan; Mr. Armen Ghazaryan, Yerevan; Mr. Gevorg Ghazaryan, Yerevan; Mr. Vahe Habeshian, Lowell, Massachusetts; Mrs. Margarita Hakobyan, Gyumri; Ms. Tsovinar Hambardzumyan, Yerevan; Ms. Hasmik Harutyunyan, Yerevan; Ms. Karine Harutyunyan, Yerevan; Mr. Mushegh Hunanyan, Yerevan and Gyumri; Mrs. Byurakn Cheraz Ishkhanyan, Yerevan; Dr. Mariam Kirakosyan, Yerevan; Dr. Asbed Kotchikian, Belmont, Massachusetts; Ms. Nora Lessersohn, Cambridge, Massachusetts; Ms. Marina Nercessian, Montreal, Canada; Mr. Raffik Papoyan, Gyumri; Mr. Hayk Sahakyan, Yerevan; Dr. Vahe Sahakyan, Ann Arbor, Michigan; Mr. Ruben Shugarian, Wellesley, Massachusetts; Dr. Hamo Sukyasyan, Yerevan; and Mr. Stepan Ter-Margaryan, Gyumri.

Last, but not least, I thank my family for their patience and forbearance during my odyssey of the last three years.

In many ways, this volume represents the cooperative and cumulative effort of many, but all errors and shortcomings are my responsibility alone.

Nora N. Nercessian
Cambridge, Massachusetts
December 2015

Partial view of children's assembly.
(RAC NEF Photos Box 145)

INTRODUCTION

"The Amazing, Stupendous Spectacle…"

When Dr. Mabel Elliott of Benton Harbor, Michigan, got off her wagon at the Alexandropol train station, the largest and once prosperous city in Russian Armenia had become host to the biggest orphanage in the world.

It was October 1921. As her carriage rattled up a small hill on the outskirts of Alexandropol, she could see rows of abandoned buildings that suggested—but just barely—that at some point in the not too distant past they had been populated by families, schoolchildren, and businesses large and small. Now, they looked eviscerated. Their new inhabitants, the vestiges of human carnage that had been crossing the border in waves for the past few years, had turned sections of the buildings into temporary living spaces covered with flattened out Standard Oil cans. A handful of buildings were still standing, though, displaying the red flag of the Soviet Socialist Republic of Armenia (SSRA). There were also a few shops selling some fruits, cigarettes, and used American clothing. The newest addition to the landscape of desolation was the statue of Karl Marx, which seemed to rise from the rubble that choked the once thriving metropolis.

Dr. Elliott's carriage reached the top of the small hill to a series of long barrack buildings, the Caucasus headquarters of Near East Relief (NER) and Dr. Elliott's first stop. The dozens of two-storied barracks, known as the Kazachi Post, were made of black volcanic rock, once roofed with red tiles. They sprawled along the railroad track and further away, in groups of four or six. Together they enclosed acres and acres of open space, at the corner of which stood a Russian church.

Situated at the south end of Alexandropol, the Kazachi was one of the three military posts that encircled the city. Of the other two, the Severski sat about 1.3 miles away, on the southwestern edge, while the Polygon, at 2.25 miles from the Severski, sat on the north. The three posts, combined, boasted more than 170 barrack buildings. Most of the barracks were two storied and if arranged in a continuous line, they would measure over two miles. All three posts were equipped with immense spaces for military drills, kitchens, bakeries, mess halls, outhouses, washing areas, sleeping quarters, warehouses and artillery sheds for the use of the Czar's Cossack, Dragoon, and Artillery Regiments, and their support staff.

In the fall of 1921 the Czar's soldiers were no longer at the Kazachi or at the other two posts. The last of the Russian forces had deserted or retreated *en masse* very soon after the Russian Revolution, taking with them much of their military arsenal. In summer 1918, within months of their retreat, many of the barracks echoed the devastation in the city they encircled. And within the year, refugees and orphans, survivors of the massacres and deportations of Armenians in what has since been recognized as genocide, had crossed the border into Russian Armenia in search of safe haven and filled many of the barracks. And now, in 1921, after two wars that had immersed Alexandropol into sheer devastation, the barracks were being repaired and refitted to become the home of more than 20,000 Western Armenian orphans who needed shelter, nourishment, clothing, and medical attention.

The cost of the repairs, along with the care of the army of orphans, was being underwritten by NER, with funds and provisions collected from the American public. A U.S. based humanitarian organization founded to provide relief to the victims of WWI in the Near East, NER had evolved from its predecessors—The American Committee for Armenian Relief (September 16, 1915, to November 20, 1915), The American Committee for Armenian and Syrian Relief (November 20, 1915, to June 27, 1918), The American Committee for Relief in the Near East (June 27, 1918, to August 6, 1919)—and incorporated as Near East Relief by an act of the U.S. Congress on August 6, 1919. NER was not only the first U.S. international humanitarian relief effort on such a scale, but the systems it put in place in the U.S. and internationally, would become the model for much of modern humanitarian fundraising.

A few dozen American relief workers represented NER in Alexandropol in fall 1921. Some of them also belonged to other organizations such as the Young Men's Christian Association (YMCA), the American Women's Hospitals (AWH), the American Board of Commissioners for Foreign Missions (ABCFM), the American Red Cross, etc. In Alexandropol, however, now the headquarters of NER's Caucasus branch with administrative offices at the Kazachi, they were all part of, and represented NER. Dr. Elliott was one of those Americans; she had come to reorganize medical services in Armenia, sent by AWH—a women's medical institution formed in the U.S. during WWI and run exclusively by American women—to organize and assume full responsibility for the medical care of 40,000 orphaned children, some 15,000 of whom lived outside the walls of orphanages.

A seasoned physician, administrator and relief worker with years of experience in war zones and with refugees, Dr. Elliott was not a woman to be easily impressed. But the sight of the "...amazing, stupendous spectacle of summer noon or evening..." had impressed her, as she watched thousands of young children pour out of buildings into the vast open space where the Czar's infantry had once drilled and paraded. "There can be no other sight like it in the world," she wrote,

> ...the earth becomes alive with little white figures...long lines of them cross and crisscross, linking the buildings together...from them all rises a sound, too widespread to be called a clamor, too light to be called a roar, too sharp to be

a murmur—thousands upon thousands of children's voices, laughing, crying, singing, talking, shouting, calling…

…at the dining rooms the beat of gongs marshals the ranks, and the kitchens sound like factories with the rattle of spoons. But unless you are close to one of these noises, you hear none of them. All are submerged and lost in the sound of children's voices…

In 1919, two years before Dr. Elliott arrived, NER had decided that the military barracks of the Kazachi, the Polygon, and the Severski were ideally suited for its mission of orphan care, where all Armenian orphans in the Caucasus could be concentrated. The sheer size and number of the buildings available to NER offered a unique opportunity to realize the momentous task of sheltering the large orphan population it had agreed to care for. The outcome, as it took shape during the decade of the 1920s, was the formation of the largest orphanage NER operated in the Near East, portrayed in newspapers and journals in the West as the City of Orphans.

The maintenance and mission of the City of Orphans, both in terms of its orphan population and facilities, necessitated a large force of workers, American and Armenian, quite possibly the largest group of workers among other NER orphanages in the Near East. Together with the orphans, they constituted a new community, radically different in its mission from the military community it replaced. With the exception of only a handful, the workers had all converged on the City of Orphans from different countries and continents and carried with them experiences as varied as they could possibly be. For over a decade the lives and aspirations of the members of this community intersected and evolved in ways fundamentally different from those of the previous occupants of the posts. Here were American men and women who had come from Massachusetts, California, Georgia, Michigan, South Dakota, New Hampshire, Maine, Ohio, New York, Texas, Kansas, Nebraska and other states. Here, also, were Armenian men and women most of whom had arrived in Alexandropol as refugees from Van, Tiflis, Kars, Mush, Sassun, Erzurum, Istanbul, Baku, Shushi, to name but a few, hoping to find safe haven in Russian Armenia. None of the American relief workers had been in Alexandropol before, and the majority spoke neither Russian nor Armenian. Most had been screened, hired, and assigned to their posts by NER headquarters in New York, and who, together with thousands of Armenian employees and scores of thousands of Armenian orphans would stay, in diminishing numbers, until 1931.

Among the caregivers, Armenians constituted the largest group. They were employed by NER's administration in Alexandropol as orphanage managers, assistant managers, teachers, principals, nurses, doctors, interpreters, cooks, bakers, washerwomen, doormen, barbers, charwomen, masons, water carriers, hewers, ironsmiths, hospital cleaners and guards. Among them were men who had received their university education in Paris, Berlin, Leipzig, Vienna, Petrograd or Moscow, and a large number of farmers and craftsmen. There were also some former army officers who had served in the Czar's army, and later in the army of the First Republic of Armenia (1918–1920.) Many received housing at the barracks.

American relief workers, native or naturalized, represented the smallest group of caregivers—but only in terms of numbers. This group oversaw the budget, negotiated with the authorities, deliberated on organization and operations, and hired local personnel to care for the needs of the children and their future. Here were director generals, assistant directors, secretaries, nursing directors, chief physicians and surgeons, accountants, agricultural experts, managers, mechanics, and engineers. Some stayed a few months; others were there for years. Some were seasoned relief workers, others learned on the job.

The children represented by far the largest and most diverse group of the new community. They spoke in a great number of dialects that differed from the Armenian spoken by Russian Armenians. More, they harbored customs and traditions of their ancestral villages and towns in Western Armenia, but which now survived in their minds as fragments of memories of home and family, vineyards and schools, songs and dances, all of them intermingled with their most recent memories of loss and perilous journeys which had made them members of the City of Orphans. More often than not, they had spent months or years of their young lives wandering alone or in bands, in fields, on mountains or on the streets, subsisting on grass and whatever they could steal, covered only in tattered rags and watchful of all predators—animal and human. Some were in their early teens, others much younger. Stories of survival differed among the children; but now, in Alexandropol, they were all residents of the City of Orphans—strangers in a strange land with adults they had not seen before.

Beginning in 1919 and through the first half of the decade of the 1920s, the new community within the somber barracks would be the subject of numerous articles in English and Armenian journals, books, and newspapers. The narratives that described the City of Orphans were justifiably dramatic. The sheer size of the orphan population alone, the largest concentration of Armenian orphans among all orphanages under NER's care, coupled with the equally striking size and character of the structures that housed them, was indeed nothing less than dramatic. In the early 1920s professional American photographers from the U.S. would travel to Alexandropol on NER's behest to capture the stunning sights that became currency in the West, while film crews would return to the U.S. with reels ready to be shown to large audiences from Hawaii to New York and Washington, DC.

Yet the situation on the ground was even more dramatic than words or moving pictures could hope to portray. Set in a devastated environment gripped by famine and shortages of every kind, relief would have to be imported in massive quantities from U.S. shores. Access to Armenia was by land only, and only through grueling efforts relief loaded on ships in U.S. ports—New York, New Jersey, New Orleans—or in Constantinople, could reach their destination. Cargo would be unloaded in the port of Batum on the Georgian Black Sea. From there it would proceed to Tbilisi by train, and thence on trains, if not disrupted by wars or political bartering, the cargo would arrive at the train station in Alexandropol and finally at the central warehouses of the Kazachi. Delays in provisions meant loss of lives on a large scale. For such a large dependent group, the collection of provisions, clothing, and medical necessities had to be conducted on a regular basis by armies of volunteers across the U.S., who would gather the essential foodstuff, clothing and medication, oversee the packing and loading in the U.S.

The staggering effort required for the collection and delivery of provisions of every type was only one of the components of the drama that underlined the singularity of the City of Orphans. Equally, if not more dramatic, were the complex political realities during which the City of Orphans was created and operated, and the unique mission it was assigned. Neither NER nor the leaders of Armenia—both of the First Republic and the SSRA—fully agreed on the substance of that mission. The drama was played out through the decade of the 1920s as the claims of two ideologically polar opposites—NER and SSRA—inevitably intersected at the City of Orphans. For both NER and SSRA recognized the special significance of the City of Orphans for the future of the country and both assigned to the diseased, traumatized, and starved orphans gathered there the responsibility of building a bright, new Armenia over the pyre of ashes it had become. It followed that the City of Orphans was not merely a sanctuary where homeless orphans could be sheltered, fed, healed, educated, and discharged when they reached the age of 16 or 17. Rather, it was invested with the unique mission of transmuting the orphans of Turkish Armenia into citizens capable, and worthy of, building the new Armenia.

For about a decade, NER and SSRA disagreed sharply on the type of citizen that would emerge from behind the walls of the City of Orphans and on the agency that would control their rite of passage from orphan to citizen. Would, or could, NER raise them as the bearers of an Armenian legacy redefined through Bolshevism, proudly marching toward a socialist state, as Soviet Armenia contended? Or, were the impressionable young children to be brought up as the loyal harbingers of American values capable of leading Armenia toward a progressive American way of life?

This volume tells the story of the City of Orphans in four parts. Part One looks at events that led up to its formation in Alexandropol at a time when the city was experiencing a radical human and physical transformation under military imperatives; the initial organization of relief and orphan care; the first exodus of relief workers in early spring 1918 and their return about one year later; initial efforts for, and concerns over the concentration of orphans in Alexandropol; NER's second, and sudden exodus from Armenia in May 1920, and its subsequent return a few months later. Part Two, which spans the decade of the 1920s, continues with NER's mistreatment by the local Revolutionary Committee in Alexandropol in fall 1920 followed by a third exodus, this time to Kars in December 1920 under the protection of Mustafa Kemal; the subsequent expulsion of 6,000 to 7,000 orphans from Kars to Alexandropol in the dead of winter 1921; NER's return to Armenia in response to SSRA's earnest pleas; the early phase of negotiations and cooperation between the leaderships of NER and SSRA, indicating that the policies of the early leaders of Soviet Armenia were more nuanced than is often projected. Part Two continues with the completion of concentration and the trajectory of expansion in NER's programs in Alexandropol, renamed Leninakan in 1924 in honor of Russian revolutionary and Bolshevik Party founder Vladimir Lenin; SSRA's policies with respect to orphan education and upbringing; and ends with the sharp reduction of the orphan population of the City of Orphans. Part Three covers the reconfiguration and retrenchment of the City of Orphans into the Polygon; the growing estrangement between NER and SSRA, followed by NER's final withdrawal from Armenia in spring 1931. The final chapter in Part Three consists of cursory glances at the lives of a handful of orphans and orphanage workers after they had joined the world outside the City of Orphans. Part Four shows two lists, both incomplete, which together provide a glimpse of the community of orphans and employees of the City of Orphans. The first list is a compilation of the names, place and date of birth of over 11,500 orphans. The list was compiled around the year 2000 and resides in the National Archives of Armenia in Yerevan. The second list carries the names of 705 Americans and Armenians who worked at the City of Orphans between 1919 and 1931. The list has been compiled from a large variety of archival documents, newspapers, journal articles, memoirs, letters, and autobiographies. While it remains incomplete, it has been included to project the tremendous labor required to operate an institution that at its peak most probably cared for over 25,000 orphans, and by way of acknowledging the contributions of all those who were part of the City of Orphans, from the washerwoman to the director general.

The Appendix presents the hitherto unpublished anonymous diary of a relief worker in the collections of The Armenian Genocide Museum-Institute in Yerevan, Armenia, transcribed by this author with minimal editing. While the anonymous writer of the diary spent only a short period of time in Alexandropol and left Armenia in May 1920, her narrative provides valuable insights into events in Yerevan, Kars, Karakilisa, and Alexandropol.

Primary sources dominate the information on which this volume is based, brought together from published and unpublished correspondences, memoirs, diaries, autobiographies, biographies, interviews with orphans and their descendants, official and institutional reports, reports by eyewitnesses, journalists and official visitors which appeared in newspapers, journals and periodicals in Armenia and the U.S. between 1919 and 1933.

This volume has benefited greatly from the recent contributions in Armenia on the study of refugees, orphans and orphanages that cover the period from 1918 through the decade of the 1920s. Of the studies during the last ten years the works of Karine Aleksanyan, Suren Avetisyan, Marine Martirosyan and Mariam Kirakosyan among others were valuable sources for understanding general issues related to orphans and refugees in the First and Soviet Armenian Republics, the nature and contributions by NER and other benevolent organizations that had been active in Armenia, as well as the intricate relationships that followed humanitarian assistance.

The present volume, however, tells the story of the City of Orphans only, where by the end of 1923, from the total number of Armenian orphans NER cared for in its orphanages throughout the Near East, over 56% were concentrated. Such a large concentration of orphans that lived within the enclosed walls of the barracks raises issues in which the story of the City of Orphans is anchored: when, how and why was it deemed advantageous to collect orphans from scores of orphanages throughout Armenia and assemble them in the military posts of Alexandropol; what did it take to tend to the needs of such a large army of children? What were the policies and educational programs that guided the shaping and reshaping of the City of Orphans? What were the issues and the outcome of years of cooperation, negotiations and posturing between NER and the SSRA? And, finally, but equally importantly, what were the rites of passage through which an army of children new to their surroundings, passed through as they grew into adulthood. These and related issues spanning the period between 1919 to 1931 are traced and reconstructed, so far as sources allow, through various prisms—the voices of orphans, relief workers, and officials from within and without—that together tell the story of the City of Orphans.

A special effort has been made in the present volume to bring into a single narrative context the voices of American relief workers and administrators, Armenian teachers and managers, and, the orphans themselves. Frequently these narratives diverge from each other in their perceptions and impressions, perspectives, predispositions, and expectations. But at the end, voices from all sides, from within and without the City of Orphans, intertwine into a wedge of history where courage and fear, generosity and indolence, malice and kindness intersect in a human drama that lasted until 1931. It was within that environment that—for better or for worse—the lives of scores of thousands of children, the builders of the new Armenia, were shaped and developed. Bewildered and traumatized when they first entered life within the barracks, they were given a number etched into a metal piece to be carried on their persons. Thousands died and were buried in cemeteries or in large pits not far from the train station in Alexandropol, but most were nursed back to health. Yet the sense of loss and pain and the need for affection remained ever present in all, throughout their institutionalized years and beyond.

This book is an attempt to honor a generation of children who had the tenacity to endure and the determination to survive their rites of passage, in one way or the other.

ABBREVIATIONS

ABCDFM	American Board of Commissioners for Foreign Missions
ACRNE	American Committee for Relief in the Near East
AGMI	Armenian Genocide Museum and Institute
ARA	American Relief Administration
ARF	Armenian Revolutionary Federation
AWH	American Women's Hospitals
HUA	Harvard University Archives
NAA	National Archives of Armenia
NEF	Near East Foundation
NER	Near East Relief
RAC	Rockefeller Archive Center
REVKOM	Revolutionary Committee
TSFSR	Transcaucasian Socialist Federative Soviet Republic

TRANSLITERATION AND STANDARDIZATION OF NAMES

The transliteration of place and individual names in this volume follows the table below. In documents and other original sources the names of individuals and places frequently appear in multiple permutations, depending on the author's background, nationality, and date of the document. To avoid such permutations, they have been standardized in the form in which it appears most frequently as, for example, Jalaloghli, Jalaloghlu, Djalal Oghlu, which has been standardized in this volume as Jalaloghli; or Sargsyan, Sarkissian, Sarkisyan, Sarkissyan, which has been standardized as Sargsyan. In direct quotes, however, the original spelling has been kept intact. Exceptions have been made in the names of a few individuals, as in the case of published authors, in which case the spelling used by the individual has been maintained.

Ա	A	Մ	M
Բ	B	Յ	Y
Գ	G	Ն	N
Դ	D	Շ	SH
Ե	E, Y	Ո	O, VO
Զ	Z	Չ	CH
Է	E	Պ	P
Ը	U (if at the beginning of a name)	Ջ	J
		Ռ	R
Թ	T	Ս	S
Ժ	ZH	Վ	V
Ի	I	Տ	T
Լ	L	Ր	R
Խ	KH	Ց	TS
Ծ	C	Ու	U
Կ	K	Փ	P
Հ	H	Ք	K
Ձ	DZ	և	EV, YEV
Ղ	GH	Օ	O
Ճ	CH	Ֆ	F

Part One

The Making of the City of Orphans

Children walking toward and away from dining hall.
(*The New Near East*, December 1926: 4)

CHAPTER ONE

FROM BARRACKS TO ORPHANAGE

The Changing Landscape of Alexandropol

Not long before the Kazachi, Severski, and the Polygon barracks were filled with the community of orphans and caregivers, they had been the essential components of an extensive military enclave that, in the latter half of the 19th and early 20th centuries, had caught the attention of the international press. Next to the old town of Gyumri renamed Alexandropol by Czar Nikolas I in 1837, the enclave had grown in size and prominence through the 19th century, in tandem with the Russo-Turkish wars. It included a large fortress, set on the western, highest end of the city, and several towers; the two most gigantic towers were the Black Sentry (*Sev Ghul*) and the Red Tower, the latter being strategically aligned along the Severski—Polygon axis, projecting a continuous line of defense. Toward the end of the 19th century, the full military installation could accommodate a fighting force of about 90,000 of the Czar's Cossack, Dragoon, and Artillery Regiments, and their support staff. The military installation that became interchangeable with the city of Alexandropol was part of a trajectory that joined the fortified cities of Sarikamish and Kars to the southwest; the three together defended hundreds of kilometers of Russian frontier with the Ottoman Empire.

The military power exuded by Alexandropol's enclave was commented on worldwide, especially in connection with the 19th century Russian military campaigns against the Ottoman Empire where Alexandropol was described as "the central and most important fortress," "one of the strongest in the whole empire of the czar," and the key to the Transcaucasian territory. The large fortress, together with the Red and Black Towers flanking it, were heavily mounted with guns. During the 1853–1856 Russo-Turkish war, for instance, the fortress had 150 cannons mounted on the walls and an immense store of arms and ammunition. It was built, reportedly, on

> ...the dividing line of the two empires. From the stream a mountain rises abruptly, with rugged sides and broad, level summit. On this lofty plain are reared the walls of the fortress. They are of vast extent, in some places raised from their native bed by the derrick, and swung into position on the walls. These are of remarkable thickness, and held to be secure against escalade. They are arched, and connected through their whole extent by a casemated gallery. Thus the cannon can be turned against the interior should an enemy effect an entrance.[1]

Coverage of Alexandropol in the western media increased during the 1877–78 war when Kars, Artahan, Sarikamish, Olti and Batum were annexed to Russia. *The Otago Witness* of New Zealand on May 5, 1877, reported on the fighting force amassed in Alexandropol:

> The Russians have entered the Turkish districts of Akalzik and Kars in Trans-Caucasia...The point at which the Russians crossed the frontier is at the Russian town and fortress of Gumri or Alexandropol, from which the celebrated fortress of Kars is about 45 miles W.S.W.[2]

"The great majority of the inhabitants of the new city and fortress of Alexandropol," *The Otago Witness* continued,

> ...built by the Russians on the old Turkish town of Gyumri, on the left bank of the Delhi Chai, a few miles above its junction with the Arpa—are Armenians. At Alexandropol a Russian army, under the command of Lieutenant-General Lorisamenskey,[3] comprising 115,000 men, or 90,000 fighting men, with 35 batteries of field artillery and 250 big guns, have been stationed for months past...

Ralph Meeker, a correspondent of *Harper's New Monthly Magazine* in New York, was one of the many Western correspondents who rushed to the battlefield in 1877 to report on the war.[4] He had landed in Odessa in June 1877 and had made his way to Kars, through the Transcaucasus. Along the way, between Vladikavkaz and Alexandropol he saw "artillery wagons and the great siege-guns that thundered against Kars. More than two thousand vehicles were moving, some were loaded with powder and shells, others carried clothing and medical supplies..."[5] In his reports on the war in Kars, Meeker drew attention to the magnificent grandeur of nature that surrounded the theater of war:

> Mountains, rivers, and plains mingled in silent grandeur. Ararat gleamed on the horizon beyond the spires of sacred Alaghez; and nearer Ani, the capital of the Georgians, showed its lonely ruins...

But the setting of grandeur had become the backdrop for the "horrors of war."

> ...the Russian batteries were throwing three thousand shells a day against Fort Kars, and its mighty guns answered continuously...mutilated forms from the forts, where death and destruction held sway, were brought upon a stretcher. Many soldiers were killed every day by bursting shells...In the evening, when funeral guns were fired at the graves of the dead, the Grand-Duke's imperial band played airs from Offenbach, while his elegantly dressed officers talked politics over their champagne.[6]

"It was curious to watch," Meeker wrote,

> ...the mongrel crowd that swarmed the sutler-shop bazars...There were Armenians, Circassians, reformed Bashi-Bazouks, Arabs, Tartars, Germans, Frenchmen, Italians, Greek confectioners, interpreters from Trieste, and near them, the camp restaurant, Russian princes, dukes, counts, barons and other men of birth and education, who spoke English and many other languages, and had travelled in America, dined at Delmonico's, and were enthusiastic about the Beauties of the Hudson.[7]

During his stop in Alexandropol, Meeker saw "Russian officers arriving and departing every hour," clouds of dust following the "immense cannons being dragged through the streets," as the "military wagon trains passed on their way to Kars."[8] Alexandropol had become, as *The Washington Post* described, "the largest and most powerful fortress and the principal arsenal in Transcaucasia."[9]

By the early 20th century, references also included descriptions of the city's prosperity and opulence. Italian diplomat, historian, and traveler Luigi Villari, for instance, commented on Alexandropol's "atmosphere of solid unromantic prosperity" during his visit to that city in 1905–1906:

> The houses are all of solid stone, dark grey or red in colour, usually two stories high, disposed in a regular plan, the straight streets crossing each other at right angles. There are a few public buildings…and near the post-office the no less inevitable town garden…[10]

Imperial military ambitions and the city's opulence were related phenomena. In fact, the wars of the 19th century had been essential prerequisites of the city's trajectory from an insignificant village to a major military and business hub, in large part due to the large remittances that the maintenance of the sizeable corpus generated for businessmen, large and small. Alexandropol's prominence and opulence had grown noticeably with the opening of the railway as the 19th century drew to a close. The first train from Tiflis, modern Tbilisi, made its debut in Alexandropol, on February 7, 1899; three years later the railroad had extended from Alexandropol to Yerevan and Kars, and by 1906, to Julfa and Tabriz. Although the rail system was meant to facilitate troop movements between various Russian garrisons, it nevertheless transformed Alexandropol into an important trade hub, whose railway station included a customs house that ensured steady revenues to the city coffers. The new rail connection and its far-reaching consequence were covered in the West in some detail and in official Consular Reports arriving in Washington. From information gathered from London, *The Minneapolis Journal* reported in its May 10, 1902, issue:

> It is officially announced in St. Petersburg that the new Alexandropol-Erivan railway will be completed and ready for traffic in August. The line is considered by the Russian war office as of first class strategic importance. It has a total length of 141 versts [93.5 miles], and consists of two sections—the first running from the fortress center of Alexandropol to the frontier river of Arpatchai, and the second from the little village of Uluchany, on the same stream, to Erivan, thus connecting in a closely linked chain the three chief Caucasian fortresses of Kars, Alexandropol and Erivan. On the completion of the new line, it is now definitely stated, the construction of the permanent way from Erivan to Djulfa, on the Persian frontier, will be immediately proceeded with…[11]

By then, there were over 400 shops and several manufacturing centers involved in export, and a 26.5-kilowat transformer. To travelers and visitors, Alexandropol offered a choice of several hostels and hotels, among them the "France Hotel," the "England Hotel" and the "Italia"; restaurants, cafes, beer stands and taverns; and recreational parks for the elite imitating the etiquette of the Russian aristocracy. In 1913, the city's bank could claim assets reaching 193,680 rubles.[12]

The Red, or Northern Tower. ("View of the North Tower/ Fortress," *The Archipelago of Holy Russia. Album of the Alexandropol Detachment, 1877–1878.* https://fotki.yandex.ru/next/users/humus777/album/432880/view/1068144)

The Black, or Southern Tower in 2013. (Photo by author)

"The Hill of Honor" where homage was paid to the officers who had fallen on the battleground during the imperial campaigns, was established after the 1853–54 Russian-Turkish War. (*Gyumri*, 2009: 43)

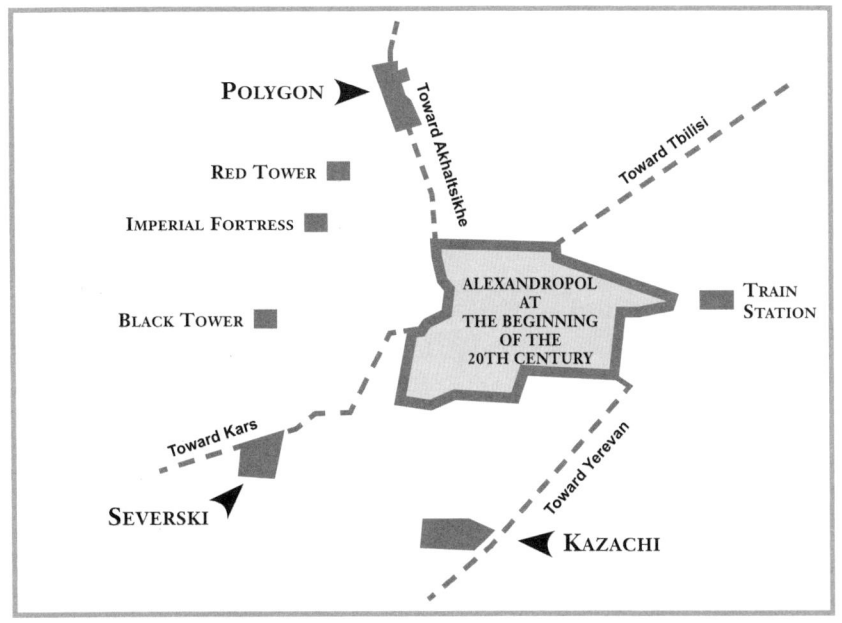

The Polygon, Severski and the Kazachi Barracks enclosing Alexandropol from the north, southwest and south, respectively. (Adapted from a schematic drawing by Stepan Ter-Margaryan, Gyumri)

Partial views of barracks, early 1920s. (RAC NEF, Photos Box 145. Detail)

Public Garden in Alexandropol. Early 20th century. (*Gyumri*, 2009: 64)

FROM BARRACKS TO ORPHANAGE 7

Artist's Reconstruction of Alexandropol. (Photo courtesy of Ashot Mirzoyan, Gyumri.)

Alexandropol's population had grown in tandem during the 19th century. If in 1826, the old town of Gyumri had 7,300 inhabitants, in the next 22 years the number increased by about 64%, with Armenians comprising 95.5% of the total; by 1897, and despite significant human losses during the Russian campaigns in which Armenians had participated, the population had reached 30,616. Now Armenians constituted 71% of the population, among them 1,111 members of the nobility, 302 members of the clergy, 363 businessmen, 20,240 tradesmen and small businessmen, and 7,999 villagers. The rest of the population consisted of 20 different backgrounds and nationalities.[13] Russians constituted the next largest group after Armenians, at 13.2%, most of them members of the Russian military. In 1916, fully into WWI, the image and presence of the Russian military, according to the Englishman Thomas D. Heald, was a dominant element in Alexandropol:

> …Big Russian official and school buildings dwarf the smaller Armenian homes…
>
> …the dominant element is the Russian military, and a large fortress and arsenal, defended by considerable earthworks, mark the importance of the place.[14]

Heald also made reference to the growing disturbances in the city, largely due to the increasing numbers of Russian soldiers in Alexandropol, many of them deserters from the Persian and Erzurum fronts:

> Every train brought back large numbers of fully-armed soldiers, who merely dumped themselves down and assumed a right to live without the least personal exertion of their own.

At first, Heald wrote, this element only crowded the town, but eventually it became very dangerous:

> Robberies frequently took place. Murders ceased to be rare. Even in open daylight a small party of these Russians would enter a bazaar stall, demand from the owner his possession, and on the slightest show of refusal either put a bullet through the man or knife him. The city authorities became helpless in face of this menace to good order, for the soldiers were always armed and supported one another.[15]

Other changes in Alexandropol's demographics had also started by 1916, with the arrival of an Armenian population group different from the native population. These were the refugees and orphans from Western Armenia, who were and remained for some time, a foreign element in the demographics, homeless and dependent on charity, but who would forever transform the human landscape of the prosperous city. They had begun to cross into Russian Armenia in late 1914, among them large numbers of unattached orphans who needed shelter and nourishment.[16] To care for orphans, the first of eight orphanages opened in Alexandropol in November 1915 and sheltered 30 children between the ages of three and five; seven more orphanages were added by 1917, altogether caring for 500 Western Armenian children. Orphanages also grew across the country as a whole, supported by lay and ecclesiastical authorities and community leaders in Armenia, the Caucasus, and Russia, while large numbers remained on the street.[17]

Supported by various lay and ecclesiastical organizations, many of the orphanages were disorganized and lacking in basic facilities. Conditions in some orphanages differed only slightly from each other. For instance, according to one orphanage director in Alexandropol, Tigran Mandakuni, the orphanage he directed in July 1916 was located in a large courtyard where the orphans lived with the landlord and two other families. The door of the stable opened into the courtyard, passing foul smells to the courtyard. The orphanage had seven rooms, four of which were used as bedrooms while the remaining rooms were used as a director's office, a dining room and a kitchen, which also served as storage space for wood and coal. There was no washing area. Two women worked in the orphanage; the establishment had no cook or male servant. The children themselves cleaned the toilets. The orphanage had opened on June 8, 1916, with 22 orphans; by June 29, the number of the orphans had reached 47.

Some orphanage directors had at first been willing to personally cover orphanage expenses, often using their good name in the community to secure needed supplies until monthly remittances arrived from headquarters—Tiflis, Moscow or Etchmiadzin—but had eventually resigned amidst recriminations and gossip. Such was the case with Father Hakob Khachvankyan, who served as the president of the Alexandropol branch of the Armenian Benevolent Society of the Caucasus. He had borrowed 12,000 rubles on his own credit to cover orphan needs. In his resignation letter, dated Alexandropol, October 2, 1916, he reminded the Council that he had obtained the advance on his personal responsibility and his good name. But, he wrote,

> Despite my letters and many telegrams…I have received no answer from you. I therefore ask the council, in the name of friendship, honor, justice to immediately find someone who will be in Alexandropol on the 8th of this month…to…liberate me from unnecessary attacks and gossip to which I was subjected for not listening and obeying the will and wishes of a few parasites. They now have comfortable positions in the orphanages with salaries, of course, and only God knows what else is going on there. Those types of people are always rewarded by honors and respect because our reality likes laziness and empty words better than hard toil and work without praise.[18]

The debts were still outstanding on November 21, 1916, and debt holders threatened to involve the chief of police in Alexandropol.

Set against dwindling economic resources in a volatile political climate of revolution and war, many orphans remained outside orphanages succumbing to starvation and disease in untold numbers, with the death rate remaining consistently high—around 75 per day. Centering attention on the growing numbers of orphans across the country and their treatment were various newspapers calling on national leaders to improve the conditions under which the orphans lived, because, they maintained, it was those orphans who would rebuild the nation from ruins.[19] The message in one newspaper read:

> Those remnants of the Turkish Armenian masses who reached us wretched and begrimed, left to the care of the nation a few thousand orphans who are our hope, by the way, and the source of our optimism. It is they who will become the steely foundations of those haloed ruins, [it is they] who are the anchors of our national existence, therefore the objects of our worship.[20]

In September 1916 a newly minted 31-year-old PhD from Europe, Gurgen Edilyan, submitted a thoughtful and thorough report on the condition of orphanages in Armenia, including those in Alexandropol.[21] Edilyan's professionally designed report, entitled *Gaghtakanakan vorbanotsner* [Orphanages for the Refugees], appeared in Tiflis in 1917, and was based on personal observations and meetings at 55 orphanages throughout Armenia.[22] It revealed uneven approaches to orphan care in terms of nutrition, clothing, health, hygiene and living areas, as well as in education and upbringing. He further went on to state that benevolent associations that had assumed the care of orphans often worked independently of each other without oversight by experts; that communication between the headquarters of a single association and its branches was lacking; and that the incessant transfers of orphans from one orphanage to another prevented the children from building stable relationships. Edilyan concluded that the public in general had not been prepared to face the needs of a large orphan population and lacked the necessary experience to organize orphanages in general, at a time when the one thing all orphanages had in common was the increase in their orphan population.[23]

Edilyan was especially concerned about the inadequate educational levels among many orphanage staff and directors, and the marked hierarchy he observed where the majority of directors and teachers were often semi-literate Russian Armenians, while more qualified Turkish Armenians were placed in the roles of cooks, servants, and charwomen. He urged the appointment of a larger percentage of Turkish Armenians as directors not only because they would be in a better position to relate to the Turkish Armenian children and understand their dialects, but also because resentment had already built up in the Turkish Armenian intelligentsia.

It is unclear if and the extent to which Edilyan's recommendations were enforced since alarms continued to sound by teachers and directors about the unattended needs of the orphans, and most disturbingly, about the cruel treatment of Western Armenian orphans by Russian Armenian teachers and directors. The situation had reached a critical level in Alexandropol in 1917, prompting an ultimatum from the Administration of the Alexandropol Teachers' Union. The ultimatum was sent to the headquarters of the Western

Armenian Union of Teachers in Tiflis, which in turn forwarded it in summary form to the Armenian Central Committee in Tiflis on March 28, 1917:

> Summary of the letter from Alexandropol: First, they speak of a Russian Armenian teacher by the name of Vardapetyan, who smashes the heads and teeth of the students, and is rewarded with the rank of senior teacher by the Educational Council of Tiflis…
>
> Another teacher by the name of Grigoryan Mihran is also on a similar harsh course; he punishes students by pitting their heads against each other.
>
> The female teachers in the orphanage school call the orphans of Sassun, who are unable to control their coughs during class in the wintertime… "son of an ass," "son of a Kurd," and by other inappropriate terms. Unable to endure the inadequate nutrition, clothing and beds, 12 orphans have escaped to the villages.
>
> Because he had no socks, the feet of Levon from Kelekuzan [a village in Sassun] had no skin left on them.
>
> In Orphanage No 6, two orphans share one dirty cover. Hungry orphans are compelled to steal bread to satisfy their hunger.
>
> Fifteen to 20 little children with scabies from Orphanage N. 4 are sent to the hospital each month, because of the prevailing filthy and lice-ridden conditions in the orphanage. None of the orphans have taken a bath in three months…[24]

At the end of the accompanying note, the Turkish Armenian Union of Teachers warned the Armenian Benevolent Central Committee of Tiflis that should the latter fail to act on the issues raised by Alexandropol, the letter and other similar ones would be submitted to the press.

As the stream of orphans and refugees into Alexandropol continued, by 1917 a total of 85,000–95,000 refugees from Western Armenia had crossed the border into the province.[25] Many continued north, but 25,754 stayed. Those who remained were not tradesmen, businessmen, members of the aristocracy or of the military; this group consisted mostly of destitute children, followed by women and a minority of able-bodied men. By 1917, the native population of Alexandropol was no longer able or inclined to care for the growing numbers of the destitute.[26] Pleas for assistance were frequently directed to the Holy See of Etchmiadzin, itself besieged by requests from around the country. On September 20, 1917, two representatives of institutions involved in the care of orphans and refugees in Alexandropol, Simon Ter-Grigoryan and Smbat Boroyan, petitioned Catholicos Gevorg V for additional funding. The request was being made because of the dwindling support from the population and the increasing numbers of refugees and orphans. "While the wave of refugees was new," the petition read,

> …the heart of the residents of the Caucasus and especially of the Armenians in the Caucasus was sympathetic toward the noble task of fraternal assistance. But the unspeakable decline and crisis of the economy day by day blurred the idea of fraternal assistance and the charm of helping refugees in the eyes of the community.

> ...these circumstances inevitably became the reason for the gradual decrease in donations; and lately there have been almost no donations...
>
> ...the district of Alexandropol has hosted and provided financial assistance to 85–95 thousand refugees, most of them having come and departed like a flowing river. Refugees move constantly, like flowing water, but for almost a year now, there have been 25,754 refugees, and a new wave of refugees has resumed from the country and different parts of the Caucasus.
>
> ...Refugees who have found shelter here are exclusively the relics of poor and destitute villages of Turkish Armenia...[27]

In Alexandropol, the authors of the petition continued, there were 4,231 children between the ages of one and 14 and an additional large number of orphans in orphanages. Could the Catholicos spare some of the resources under His disposition to "at least minimally cover" their nudity? And, could His Holiness order a holy encyclical to be prepared so that they, Ter-Grigoryan and Boroyan, under the leadership of a bishop, may raise funds from wealthy Armenians in Russia and the Caucasus for Turkish Armenian refugees? The answer from the Holy See, while sympathetic, pointed out that the needs were great all over the country, and that regrettably, the limited funds in the Church's coffers did not allow them to care for all refugees. The decision was to forward the amount of 5,000 rubles to be distributed only among the neediest. As for the requested encyclical for fundraising, the appeal would have to be made "in the name of the Catholicos," and, the amount raised could not be used for refugees and orphans in Alexandropol exclusively. Rather,

> ...the amount raised should enter the central coffers of Etchmiadzin, to benefit the work of rehabilitating the refugees in general.[28]

About a week later, on October 2, 1917, the Catholicos had asked the Chancery in Etchmiadzin to transfer the amount of 10,000 rubles to Alexandropol.[29]

Relief and Retreat

Earlier that year, in January 1917, 40 orphans from Sassun between the ages of eight and 12 had found refuge in the "Robinson" orphanage in Alexandropol, so named in honor of its benefactor, Emilia Robinson of the London Red Cross. The orphanage was supported by funds from the London based "England for Armenian Refugees" committee, an organization of several English unions, among them the "Armenian Society" founded by Emilia Robinson, the "Lord Mayor's Fund" and the "Women's Organization of Manchester," operating since 1915. The initial amount of 4,600 rubles expended to the orphanage in January had been spent by March 14, 1917.[30]

Contributions from the United Kingdom were made to other refugee centers in the country until mid-1920s. But meanwhile, more extensive and longer-lasting assistance had begun by a group of Americans who by 1917 had established workshops for the preparation of wool and cotton, weaving, and carpentry; provided subsidies for orphans placed in families in the amount of

Ernest Yarrow with son and wife on horseback before an orphanage in Yerevan. (RAC NEF Box 140)

ten rubles a month; monthly stipends for the aged infirm and needy widows with dependent children; medical assistance; cash support to local benevolent organizations;[31] and soup kitchens, which provided the only source of sustenance to the majority of the refugees and orphans.[32] Representing the New York headquartered American Committee for Armenian and Syrian Relief (ACASR), the precursor of the American Committee for Relief in the Near East (ACRNE) and subsequently Near East Relief (NER), this group was under the leadership of Ernest Yarrow, a missionary with many years of service to the Armenian communities in the Ottoman Empire, particularly in Van.[33] Yarrow, who would play a central role in the creation of the City of Orphans three years later, had arrived with his family in Russian Armenia in 1916. They had set sail in July, traveling north of England to escape mines and submarines, landing in Bergen, Norway, and continuing by train across Norway and Sweden down through Russia and to the Caucasus. Among the group working with Yarrow were Samuel Wilson, also a missionary; F.W. MacCallum of the Constantinople Mission; George F. Gracey of Urfa; George C. Raynolds, and Rev. and Mrs. Harrison A. Maynard of Bitlis. Some were sent from the U.S. by way of the Pacific and Siberia to help with relief work and others had come from Turkey, where their missions had closed. Among the group also were Thomas D. Heald of the English Society of Friends and Dr. Kennedy of the Lord Mayor's Fund of London, along with other workers, who had joined the Americans. In support of the group was U.S. Consul Samuel G. Wilson in Tiflis.

The goal of the early group of Americans was to deliver immediate relief, but there had been little time to develop a coherent program. And before a more organized plan could be put in place, in March 1918, the U.S. Consul in Tiflis, concerned over Russia's separate peace with Germany at the Treaty of Brest-Litovsk and the advance of German forces toward the oil fields of Baku, ordered all American relief personnel to evacuate. After an initial resistance, the relief workers eventually left with Ernest Yarrow on March 19, 1918.[34]

A few months earlier, at the end of October 1917, the new Soviet government in Moscow had decided to withdraw from WWI. Fighting was to stop immediately and Russian military bases were to be evacuated. Oksen Teghtsoonian, a refugee from Van, was at that time employed by ACASR in Yerevan, and witnessed the returning Russian soldiers pass through Armenia:

> ...long columns of soldiers with their horses and camels arrived from the Persian-Turkish frontier through Julfa and left, heading north. Similar detachments of deserting soldiers were leaving the Turkish front and arriving from Erzurum and Kars. Fear gripped everyone. When the last of these Russian soldiers was gone, the Turks would arrive...[35]

For Alexandropol, the evacuation of the city's military complex would be the portent of the next stage in the radical transformation of the once opulent city's human and physical landscape. It was in progress on December 1, 1917, when missionary Carl C. Compton arrived in Alexandropol with his wife. "The city was in chaos," he wrote,

> The Russian army was withdrawing from the nearby Turkish front, and a hastily organized volunteer Armenian army was rushing to the front to try to hold back the advancing Turkish army...the Russians were carrying with them all of their war materials, leaving the Armenians with almost nothing with which to fight. To make matters worse, the city was full of Armenian refugees who had fled from their homes in Turkey...[36]

By early 1918, the Kazachi, Severski, and Polygon had been abandoned by the Russian army. And, in a matter of months, the city's prosperity, born of the military imperative, would vanish as events that began to unfold in rapid succession dramatically stripped Alexandropol of its accumulated wealth.

At the retreat of the Russian soldiers, units of Armenian volunteer fighters now filled Alexandropol's military posts,[37] but were initially unable to resist the Turkish offensive into Russian Armenia. Turkish forces occupied Sarikamish on April 4, 1918, followed by Kars on April 28, and Alexandropol on May 11. When Armenia declared independence on May 28, 1918, Alexandropol was under Turkish occupation, and would remain so for the next seven months.

A month later, of the 93 orphanages operating in Armenia, only 35 had survived; the orphans in the orphanages of Alexandropol, Dilijan, Jalaloghli and Karakilisa had scattered, and many had not survived. Of the 850 orphans in the Dilijan orphanages, for example, only 300 had survived; of the 1,200 orphans in the orphanage at Jalaloghli, only 250 remained, and the number of survivors in the Alexandropol orphanages is unknown.[38]

Simon Vratsian, who would serve as the fourth and last Prime Minister of the First Republic of Armenia (1918–1920), poignantly described the predicament of orphans during the months that followed in a letter to a friend.[39] He had attended an Armenian Christmas Eve dinner at an orphanage in Yerevan, he wrote, organized by the Women's Society in Yerevan on January 5, 1918, with then Prime Minister Hovhannes Katchaznuni:

Along with Katchaznuni I attended the New Year's Eve dinner of the orphans that had been prepared by the women's society of Yerevan. Rows of long and bare tables had filled the large hall of the gymnasium. The meal was offered in copper plates: boiled red beans, a small piece of cheese, a few dried apricots, a few raisins and I don't know what else, a piece of bread made of barley flour and something like tea in blue copper cups.

It was impossible to watch without being moved when the orphans, boys and girls from five and six to fifteen and sixteen years old, began to enter the hall. They were dressed in uniforms made of dark and coarse cotton cloth produced in state factories. Thin, skin and bones, with big staggered eyes, as if they were shadows descended from the other world. They entered silently and sat where directed, their expressionless stares directed at the food on the table. Dinner, after the prayer, proceeded without any sound. Can you imagine a few hundred children around tables, without making a sound…!

Following dinner Kajaznuni tried to make a short speech to the children. Hardly a few words into his talk, he stopped; he began to sob like a child. The impact was devastating: the aging prime minister was crying, unable to speak, and hundreds of children's eyes watching him with indifferent, uncertain looks…

This is how many thousands of orphans in many parts of Armenia—it would not be an exaggeration to say the whole population of Armenia—greeted Christmas this year.

"Christ was supposed to have come to earth for the poor, the oppressed and the exploited," Vratsian remarked,

> Is it possible to find in any place any people poorer, more oppressed and more exploited than the Armenian people…?

The next day, he had attended dinner at the Holy See of Etchmiadzin, where, it seemed, he had received his answer:

> The next day, New Year's Day, I went to Etchmiadzin and attended the dinner of the brotherhood. There was plenty of food on the tables, and wine, and fruits. There were speeches made over the course of the dinner and toasts were emptied. Now we know who Christ came to earth for…[40]

"The Slough of Despond"

During the course of Alexandropol's seven-month occupation by Turkish forces, more than 45,000 people escaped the province, many in the direction of Tiflis.[41] Among those who fled the city were the wealthy, whose homes were now occupied by Turkish officers and soldiers. When the occupiers were forced to leave the province following the Armistice, the total population of the district had decreased by 38%: from 245,980 individuals in 1915, there were now 152,414. By contrast, the refugee population had registered an increase of 9,171 individuals from the 1915 figure of 22,818, bringing the total number of the district's refugee population to 34,361. Within this group, 2,372 were from other provinces of Russian Armenia and 31,989 from Turkish Armenia.[42]

Refugees passing through Alexandropol. (Barton 1930: facing page 84)

Orphans near the fortifications of Alexandropol. (*The Wide World Magazine*, October 1919: 506)

Before Turkish forces left Alexandropol, they had confiscated and transported to Turkey more than 50,000 large antlered animals, 100,000 heads of sheep, 5,000 horses, 2.5 million poods or 90,282,500 pounds [1 pood=36.113 lbs.] of wheat, one million poods of barley and various types of other provisions. They had also taken with them agricultural tools, spades, and 80% of the carts in the province to prevent the future cultivation of lands to replace the wheat and barley the province had been stripped off. Stores were robbed, large quantities of furniture from homes were taken, and rugs and carpets along with large panes of glass, doors, window jambs and roofing had been stripped off houses and carted off to Turkey. And, 12,000 individuals had been taken as slaves.[43]

If carts were now seen on the streets of Alexandropol, more often than not they were busy transporting decaying bodies to mass graves. The Minutes of the Committee on Refugees in Alexandropol, which met at least 26 times between December 10, 1918, and April 2, 1919, show that recurrent topics of discussion included the corpses that needed burial but often remained on the streets due to an insufficient number of death carts to carry the dead to burial pits. Lacking also was sufficient space for burial pits and gravediggers who could prepare the pits. Nor were there enough priests to perform the last rites for the dead. The Committee on Refugees anticipated that the situation would only worsen due to the growing number of refugees.[44]

Mortality rates remained especially high among unattached orphans. The February 24, 1919, meeting of the Committee included a report about one of the orphanages in Alexandropol where sick and healthy children lived together, with

16 THE CITY OF ORPHANS

no medical help in sight. The committee members had noticed that in a room of one orphanage, 25 corpses of orphans had been piled one on top the other.[45]

Nor were the military installations of Alexandropol or the abandoned barracks spared the destruction that swathed the city. Many of the barracks had been damaged during the war and stood in semi-ruinous states, echoing the state of their new inhabitants, the masses of traumatized, hungry, diseased children, women and men who had somehow survived the long marches and continued to arrive in an unending stream. By early January 1919, the posts were full of refugees, and conditions in Alexandropol had reached a critical stage. Typhus was wide spread, the daily mortality was high.

It is doubtful that as they designed the barracks, the Czar's military architects envisioned that not too far in the future, the instruments of war they had designed would become a vast repository of the victims of war and planned destruction. That was the scene that struck *The National Geographic Magazine* photographer and writer Melvin Chater when he visited the Polygon a few months after the Armistice. "Refugees whose numbers had grown in six weeks from 26,000 to 50,000 and in ten days from 50,000 to 58,000," he wrote,

Orphans collected in Alexandropol. (*The National Geographic Magazine*, 1919: 409. Detail)

…filled the Russian barracks, where they were massed like bees in swarming time. As we walked through those dark, cell-like rooms of shattered windows and smoked ceilings, not a bed or chair was to be seen, but only groups of wretched humanity, huddled together on their common bed of dank flagstones.

Through the dimness we could see a multitude of hands stretched despairingly forth, and again that low drone of "Bread, Bread, Bread!" shook us as we passed. Those who were strong enough

The Death Cart in Alexandropol. ("*Asia. The American Magazine on the Orient*, January-December, 1922: 273)

A section of the physical and human landscape of Alexandropol. (Paul Barsam Private Collection)

FROM BARRACKS TO ORPHANAGE

Refugees at the Polygon circa 1920. (AGMI Collection)

stumbled up and followed us out into the sunlight—an unforgettable throng of waxen faces and of wasted bodies that streamed with rags...[46]

"There were no human beings in those refugee camps," wrote thirty-two-year-old relief worker Elsie Kimball, the daughter of U.S. Senator Fred H. Kimball, to her family on November 25, 1919,

> —only beasts. Long ago these people ceased to be human. Men, women, and children by the score were huddled together in each room, and in the middle of the floor was a feeble fire, around which as many people as possible gathered for warmth.

The refugees received bread and soup once a day, continued Kimball, and tea and bread twice a day:

> This suffices to keep the body together, but the soul doesn't exist any longer. Women were lying on the hard floor all around us, almost too weak to move. And then there were tiny babies who were mere scraps of skin and bone.[47]

Alexandropol and the once imposing barracks reminded Chater of *The Slough of Despond*, a deep boggy pit of despair and hopelessness in John Bunyan's classic allegory of *The Pilgrim's Progress*. "Utter silence brooded over Alexandropol," he wrote:

> —a silence profound and sinister, as if the whole town were muffled out of respect for continuous burial. We found no violence, no disorder. The people showed the gentle somnolence of lotus-eaters, as they sat there in the long sunbathed streets, feeding on hope.
>
> Alexandropol is a blasted town (the handiwork of the Turk upon retreating,) with streets like the Slough of Despond: low, flat houses; long lines of sack clothed people sitting, lying, dozing, and dying, all in the spring sunlight; not a laborer at work, not a wheel turning save those of the wretched droshky [a low, four-wheeled carriage used especially in Russia] which we commandeered.
>
> ...The country through which we were passing revealed neither sowed acres nor cattle, nor sheep at graze; for seed, agricultural implements, and all else had been swept away by the enemy.[48]

The first people Chater met on his arrival in Alexandropol were children. They had gathered around his car, curious about the American flag that flew on his car. "I say children," he wrote

> but I really mean wizened and ancient dwarfs, with wrinkled foreheads and those downward cheek creases which deepen when one smiles. Not that they were smiling, however; they had forgotten the way of that, long ago. Occasionally, I saw them stoop, reclaim something, and masticate... I asked [the doctor] "What are those children eating?"

"Candle grease," he answered gruffly.

The Meeting of May 17, 1919: A Question of *"Dignity"*

In early spring 1919, John Elder, who had remained in Armenia after the American group had left, now represented ACRNE. He and Armenia's Minister of Care and Labor Sahak Torosyan negotiated a plan whereby orphan care would be transferred to ACRNE. The government of Armenia and the benevolent organizations had been able to shelter less than half of the growing army of orphans now in the territory of Armenia; the remaining orphans, three times larger in size, lived on the streets, where untold numbers of them died each day.[49] On March 2, 1919, the parliament had voted to accept ACRNE's offer for the care of orphans. ACRNE had been prepared to care either for orphans or refugees, and the government had opted for the first, because sustaining orphans until they reached maturity required a larger budget.

Torosyan and Elder arrived at an agreement on April 12, 1919, according to which the care of orphans and orphanages would be transferred to ACRNE on May 1, 1919.[50] The terms of the agreement stipulated that ACRNE would care for and educate all orphans in Armenia, including those in state orphanages and hospitals, as well as all orphans living on the streets, within or without the territory of Armenia, irrespective of their numbers. The upbringing and education of the orphans, Torosyan and Elder agreed, would follow the plan as developed by the Ministry of Education of Armenia.

The other points of the agreement stipulated that the furniture of orphanages and hospitals would be transferred to ACRNE; that large government buildings where orphanages, shelters, and children's hospitals were located would be put at the disposal of ACRNE free of rent; that to the extent possible, the government of Armenia would allow the use of buildings which ACRNE deemed suitable for orphanages; and that ACRNE was obligated to care for and educate the orphans of Armenia until such time as another, mandated organization could assume responsibility or when the government was in a position to undertake the care and education of orphans. However, in the event that ACRNE stopped its humanitarian work or returned the orphanages, the furniture and all possessions of the orphanages would be placed at the disposal of the government. Finally, the government of Armenia, through the Ministry of Care, reserved the right of moral supervision over the orphanages, shelters, and hospitals under the care of ACRNE, but without the right to interfere in their internal affairs.

The date when the transfer was scheduled for was May 1, 1919, until which time orphanages were the responsibility of the government of Armenia. Included in the list of orphanages, shelters and hospitals that would be transferred to ACRNE were those under the care of the Armenian Benevolent Association of the Caucasus, the Moscow Armenian Committee, and other benevolent organizations. ACRNE would not interfere in the internal affairs of these orphanages, but would hold the right for supervision and receive regular reports on expenditures. It was also noted that the benevolent organizations could reclaim their orphanages if they wished to maintain them through their own means.

Three days after the agreement, on April 15, Minister of Care Torosyan informed the Council of Ministers of Armenia that ACRNE members who had arrived in Yerevan, had raised an objection to one of the points of the agreement. The objection had to do with the stipulation that while ACRNE would finance the orphanages under the care of benevolent organizations, it would have no control over them except to ask for financial accounting. "Now," the Minister wrote,

> ...the American Committee [ACRNE] requests that that point be changed in the sense that those orphanages as well be placed under the complete direction of the American Committee.[51]

The government's decision to allow ACRNE to care for the orphans had been based on the realization that without outside assistance, the lives and future of the thousands of orphans was in jeopardy. Regardless, it met with strong opposition from some Armenian community and public leaders, newspapers and benevolent associations, at times culminating in heated debates and recriminations, and demands that the government amend the agreement. The issues came to a head at a meeting that lasted over four hours on May 17, 1919, in the home of Ministry of Care representative D. Davitkhanyan in Tiflis.[52] The Minutes of the meeting indicate that Dr. Saghyan, Director of Orphanages in Armenia and D. Davitkhanyan explained to the attendees, among them representatives of benevolent associations, the Armenian Women's Association and newspaper editors, that the reason orphanages were being transferred to the ACRNE had been financial. The number of orphans had increased from 2,500 to 15,000 in Yerevan and environs, but it had been possible to clothe only 11,000 of them. A budget of 120 million rubles was needed to care for the 15,000 orphans in Armenia and the 3,000 in Georgia, but the government did not have that amount at its disposal. Additionally, if all the orphans were to be gathered from the streets, the numbers would probably soar to anywhere from 30,000 to 35,000 and the budget would be doubled.

Those present were told that the decision to hand over the orphanages to the Americans had been reached at the Council of Ministers, that ACRNE had been willing to care either for orphans or refugees, and the government had opted for the first because sustaining orphans until they reached maturity required a larger budget. The attendees were also told that the upbringing and education of the orphans by the Americans would be conducted according to the program developed by the Ministry of Education of Armenia. In this way, the only responsibility required of the government would be moral supervision over the orphanages. Mr. Davitkhanyan then reported on his conversation with Miss Allen of ACRNE who had stated that the orphans would be given religious instruction: they would receive their religious education during the week from a Gregorian priest appointed by the Catholicos and attend the Armenian Apostolic church service on Sundays.[53] At the same time, the orphans would also take part in Protestant worship, where the Gospels would be read to them. Once they reached a certain age, the orphans could choose to follow their own credo—Protestant or Armenian Apostolic. Elder had given assurances that the intention was not to bring up Protestants at the orphanages but to prepare good citizens of Armenia. In preparation for the transfer, ACRNE representatives had visited orphanages and were making arrangements; and Captain Elder had asked that the transfer be delayed by one month to give ACRNE a chance to get better organized, although it would provide interim relief. Miss Allen had also told Mr. Davitkhanyan that ACRNE would assume the care of all the orphans in government orphanages, but if the benevolent organizations did not accept ACRNE's condition of total control of their orphanages, ACRNE would only provide them with free bread.

Of the host of questions and admonitions from the attendees, the most passionate centered on the upbringing of orphans. Although Dr. Saghyan assured the attendees that ACRNE had no hidden agenda, few of those present were convinced. It was asserted that Armenia's government should hold complete control over the orphanages, and not just the educational program of the orphans; that the public should stand by its orphanages; that the Americans and the British, who showed no regard toward Armenian social institutions thinking that Armenians were useless and inept, should be better informed of such institutions; that the government of Armenia should protect the orphans from all danger, including the Americans; and that a protest be registered against ACRNE to show that Armenians were capable of taking care of their own. One attendee went so far as to say that turning the orphanages over to the Americans constituted an immoral act on the part of the government of Armenia and an insult to their dignity because by such act Armenians proved that they were needy. Another attendee suggested that the estimated three million dollars should be given to the existing Armenian benevolent associations who were, after all, more familiar with orphanage work.

The minutes of that meeting do not reveal specific solutions whereby all orphans, within and without orphanages, could be accommodated when the state did not have the necessary funds to do so. Nor was there any clarification as to whose "dignity" was at stake—the dignity of those present at the meeting or that of the orphans. At the end, the attendees resolved that orphan education and upbringing should be in the hands of the government and managed by special councils whose membership would include representatives of ACRNE, the government of Armenia, and benevolent associations to ensure the protection of the unique culture of the Armenian people.

The public debate over the control of orphan upbringing and education did not ebb for some time. While some were satisfied with the quality of care orphans received in American orphanages,[54] ceding full control over orphans to "foreigners" remained unacceptable to others:

> Are we going to allow various irresponsible organizations to shape their [orphans'] hearts, souls and reason...? It is we who should take those orphans in our hands and give them proper nutrition and education, to receive from them tomorrow the authentic Armenian, the true Armenian...[55]

Running counter to that argument was the opinion that

> As necessary as young people with an Armenian heart are for us, it is equally and more important to have strong citizens...[56]

On May 22, 1919, Alexandropol Mayor Levon Sargsyan transferred ten orphanages and one orphan hospital in Alexandropol, with all their furniture, employees and orphans to ACRNE's local representatives Myrtle O. Shane, Lillian O'Neil, and Edwin K. Mitchell, Jr.[57] Soon, the Ministry of Care and Labor asked Elder to vacate the school buildings in Yerevan and relocate the orphans to Kazachi, so as to allow time to prepare the buildings for the coming academic year:

> In compliance with the decision of the Council of Ministers, all school buildings should be vacated so that orderly preparations can be made for the coming academic year. By informing you about this [decision] I ask that you undertake appropriate measures to relocate your orphanages and hospitals from the school buildings to Alexandropol, Kazachi post.[58]

The condition of Alexandropol's orphans and orphanages turned over to NER was recorded in a report by Dr. H. M. Marvin, who arrived in Alexandropol on May 24, 1919, two days after the agreement signed between Mayor Levon Sargsyan and Myrtle Shane and her colleagues.[59] According to the report, Myrtle Shane, on behalf of ACRNE, had taken over some 1,200 children whom government officials had gathered in 11 buildings scattered over the city, and 300 sick children had been gathered into two buildings, which "had been dignified by the name of 'hospital.'"[60] Although the buildings had windows, roof and floors,

> ...it would be difficult to conceive more abject filth or more revolting conditions than those obtained in the wards. Each bed consisted of an iron frame, partially covered in two planks over which a straw mattress was stretched, and on this the patient lay. Some of the children were clothed in little undershirts and drawers; some of them were entirely nude. From one to four patients were in each bed.

Marvin also made special note of the unsanitary contiditons in which the sick children were allowed to exist, and the indifference shown by the Armenian attendants in charge:

> There was a bathroom in each building but the doors were locked and the keys lost...A filthy attendant in each ward part of the time slept in a corner while the children starved for the food she was stealing. There were tin bed pans in several wards but they were never used as it was easier for the children to soil the mattress which was seldom changed. There was a small toilet in each building but the floors were so frightfully soiled with excretory matter that the ambulatory children used the ground as their toilet, so that at first it was almost impossible to talk through the yard. The superintendent spent his time in fighting with the

physician in chief, and in stealing for his personal use the food intended for the patients…the children were dying at the rate of seven a day.[61]

Within a week after Dr. Marvin's arrival, the entire administration of the hospital was revamped, the buildings thoroughly cleaned, windows opened and nailed open, bathrooms opened and cleansed, new mattresses made of flour sacks and hay, the children were fed at least three meals a day, barbers found and each child had been shaved and bathed at least once. By August 1919, the sick children were moved to the hospital at Kazachi, which consisted of two large, two-storied buildings and two smaller, one-story buildings, with accommodations for 1,230 patients. Medical supplies arrived the following month, and a dental clinic was established. A month later, NER established a receiving hospital in the city where children from the streets were taken in, bathed, fed and given a medical examination before being sent either to the orphanage or to hospital. In his report, Dr. Marvin wrote that credit for the improvements were in large part due to Janet MacKaye, the chief nurse.[62]

Discussions on orphan upbringing and education continued between June and December 1919,[63] and some orphanages and hospitals were reclaimed from ACRNE which, in August 1919 was renamed Near East Relief (NER). Thousands of orphans changed hands, moved from one orphanage to another against a background of disagreements over their upbringing and increasing political instability in the region.[64] It was not long before most of the benevolent associations caring for orphans had exhausted their resources and turned their orphanages over to the government or to NER. In September 1919 there were 25 orphanages and 11,029 orphans supported by NER in four major orphanage centers at Yerevan, Alexandropol, Karakilisa and Kars. At the end of December 1919 the number of orphans under NER's care in Armenia had reached 15,094. Sheltered in government orphanages, at the end of 1919 were 8,868 orphans, bringing the total number of orphans within the boundaries of Armenia under the care of the government and NER combined to 23,962. Outside the boundaries of Armenia, there were an additional 5,367 orphans, of whom 2,817 were under NER's care in orphanages in Tiflis, Akhalkalak and Baku. The remaining 2,550 were under the care of the government in Tiflis, Gandzak, Akhalkalak and Baku. None of the figures included the thousands outside orphanages. By fall 1920, NER had the largest group of orphans—19,896—with the largest concentrations in Alexandropol, followed by another 6,000 in Kars, where NER had assumed the care of orphans in government orphanages in spring 1920. A few months later, in early October 1920, there were 3,338 children left in the government orphanages, many of who had been moved to Jalaloghli and Kars.[65] A note from the director of the Kars orphanage indicated that conditions were so deplorable in Kars that "of the 1500 orphans, 1,200 are completely naked and have no beds."[66]

Chapter Two

ALEXANDROPOL AS THE *"SHOW DISTRICT"*

The Return of ACRNE/NER: Restructuring

General relief of thousands of tons of provisions, milk and quinine had begun to arrive in Armenia while negotiations on orphan care were in progress. And, it was not unusual to see "nervous little Ford cars, their tonneaus heaped high with Washburn-Crosby sacks, carrying flour rations to outlying villages, or the slow moving bullock cart drawing 'Pillsbury's Best' through zigzag mountain cart ruts overshadowed by ruins of ancient fortresses."[67] A significant portion of the relief was from the American Relief Administration (ARA) chaired by Herbert Hoover, with contributions from the Rockefeller Foundation, the American Red Cross, the Commonwealth Children's Fund, etc. But now, in charge of the administration and distribution of relief—the sole authority over the matter—were a corps of U.S. officers under the command of Colonel William Haskell, U.S. Army. Haskell held the titles of Interallied High Commissioner to Armenia and Director General of ACRNE's Caucasus Branch, with headquarters in Tiflis. The main office of ARA operations in Armenia was in Yerevan, and was already in operation in July 1919 under Major S. Forbes, when Haskell arrived. In his memoirs, Herbert Hoover, then head of the ARA in Europe—and future U.S. president—referred to the strong suggestion his Constantinople representative Howard Heinz had made, that due to the scope of the need and mismanagement issues he had seen, it would be best for the ARA to take full charge of relief administration and distribution in Armenia:

> The American Near East Relief Committee…announced they would look after Armenia…We assisted that Committee by looking after their shipping and diverting to them some cargoes en route…Five or six weeks later, Mr. Heinz at Constantinople informed me of rumors that "things had gone to pieces" in Armenia and that the Near East Committee's work had broken down.

> …Their report to me pictured an incredible state of affairs both as to the Near East Committee staff and the condition of the Armenians. Although some thousands of tons of food, clothing and medicine had been landed at Batum on the Black Sea for the Committee, only a part had ever reached the Armenians. Thousands of tons had been sold in Georgia and Azerbaijan, where there was no need of relief.

"The corruption and thievery were beyond belief," wrote Hoover:

> I instantly demanded the removal of the local American Director of the Committee and subsequently we had nearly every member of their business staff arrested. Some were convicted and others required to disgorge.

The director was replaced by Ernest Yarrow, "an able and devoted man," Hoover noted, and "for the sake of America's good name, I made no public remark on the episode."[68]

Haskell arrived in Yerevan in August 1919, and by October 1919, he had restructured the administration of relief with the help of his officers' corps and civilian NER personnel.[69] Accordingly, general relief in Armenia was divided into districts with each district headed by a group of U.S. officers' corps. Alexandropol was one of the districts Haskell had identified for relief distribution, and would be directed by Major L. K. Davis, Lt. Col. D. A. Robinson, Captain Soucy, and Captain Warner as Director of Orphanages and warehouses. The other designated districts and their directors were: Karakilisa, under Dr. Pratt, and Majors C. Livingston and McAlbin; Kars, under E. Fox, and director of orphanages V. Arcruny; Sarikamish, under Captain Kinne; Yerevan, under Colonel C. Telford, Lieutenant Colonels R. A. Dunford and H. W. Stephenson, Major E. L. Dyer, Captains J. Dangerfield, Jr., D. F. McDonald, and L. O. Fossum, Dr. C. D. Ussher of the ABCFM, and Director Major S. Forbes. All officers reported to ARA headquarters in Tiflis where Chief of Staff J. Rhea ran the office, succeeded later by E. L. Daley and Major J. C. Green of the ARA. Alexandropol was also designated, along with Yerevan and Kars, as one of three main receiving depots in the country, where refugees and orphans were examined, bathed, fed, clad, received medical treatment and hospitalized if needed. Each depot had a section for the examination and classification of all refugees; a section for medical treatment and conduct of baths; a section for the distribution of old clothes; and a section for the conduct of soup kitchens.[70]

In his regular reports on conditions in Armenia, Haskell pointed out that the "situation in the Caucasus was worst in the world," and pressed for the immediate shipment of necessities: 7,000 tons of wheat flour per month; child-feeding supplies for 150,000 children; clothing for men, women and children; and 10,000 square feet of window glass especially for hospitals.[71]

Relief provisions and relief workers assigned to ACRNE relief centers in the Near East and in Armenia continued to arrive with food, clothing, medical supplies, hospital units, and ambulances. On the USS *Pensacola*, sailing toward the end of January, were 40 relief workers, all men, taking with them food, clothing, medical supplies, hospital units, ambulances, and other necessities. In the group was Dr. Clarence Ussher. Ussher had spent many years at the Van Mission, and now, after an absence of three years spent in the U.S., he was on his way back, this time for the Caucasus. While in Constantiople, Clarence Ussher was interviewed by *Ashkhatank* reporter Onnik Mkhitaryan, where he described the hospital equipments, medication, and provisions that had already arived in Batum. There were more than 30 relief workers with him destined for the Caucasus, he said, and a request had been made for an additional 100 relief workers from the U.S.[72] The SS *Leviathan* sailed in February 1919 with more relief workers, doctors, nurses, expert agriculturists, mechanics, sanitary and civil engineers, and other technically trained men and women, teachers and orphanage workers, among them Myrtle O. Shane, formerly of the mission in Bitlis, all intended for Armenia.[73] The ships *Caesar*, the *Western Belle* and *the Newport News* followed in quick succession. From January 1919 to July 1920 total relief distributed in Armenia and the Caucasus amounted to 135,764 metric tons, with a value of $28,795,426.[74]

Ernest Yarrow had arrived with an expanded group of civilians to work alongside the U.S. Army officers,[75] among them

> An additional ten doctors and nurses [from Constantinople]...and we have telegraphed the Trebizond unit which is on the Black Sea to go on to Tiflis with all its personnel and supplies. This will make between forty and fifty workers in that region.[76]

In his October 1919 cable from Tiflis to the Department of State in Washington, Haskell explained that the personnel of the NER consisted of "11 regular officers, 14 demobilized officers, 20 men and 25 women."[77]

An especially useful commodity being transported to Armenia as to other NER orphanages in the Near East was the used clothing donated in the thousands of tons by the American public during major drives NER held throughout the U.S. These were shipped in bales across thousands of miles and distributed to refugees and orphans and remained in demand for several years to come. Used clothing and shoes donated in the U.S. were often repaired and adjusted at the orphanages. In one instance, a shoe manufacturer offered NER a consignment of mismatched shoes. The shoes were shipped to Yerevan where orphan boys trained in shoe repair refit the shoes for orphans.[78] The bales of old clothes were used in exchange for provisions and other commodities as livestock, butter, eggs, to supplement the foodstuffs being shipped in by NER,[79] and distributed to refugees at designated stations. According to a letter written by a young NER worker in Yerevan, among those waiting in line to receive used clothing was Prime Minister Hamo Ohanjanyan. As the young NER worker was trying to find appropriate clothing for a long line of people, she was suddenly startled by a "suave and unusually musical voice" asking, in perfect English, for a suit of the largest available underwear. She looked up to see "a very tall and very dignified gentleman arrayed in a greenish black, rather frayed Prince Albert, which he wore with the air of the proverbial Prince gracing rags." Then,

> To her surprise he offered her in payment the equivalent of thirty-eight cents in American money. Involuntarily she protested but he reassured her in his gracious tones: "Really, Madam, I have plenty, you know. You forget I receive the quite remarkable salary of twenty dollars a month."

> The little relief worker looked again and this time with dawning recognition. The gentleman she had not had the honor of meeting, but his picture was as familiar as that of Woodrow Wilson. He was none other than H. Ohanjanyan, the President [of the Council of Ministers] of the Republic of Armenia.[80]

The Appeal of the Barracks

NER's return to Armenia in 1919 signaled a new and comprehensive phase of relief operations that would soon center on orphanages and the barracks in Alexandropol as the principal, and eventually exclusive, center of orphan care.[81] Haskell's cables routinely updated NER and Washington about conditions in Armenia. In one message, addressed to NER Treasurer Cleveland H. Dodge, Haskell reported on the condition of orphans in Yerevan, Kars and Alexandropol:

> …Tiny children wear only the shreds of filthy rags, and crouch on the streets, numb with cold, whimpering with pain. Often, they are compelled to fight off the hungry pariah dogs which, driven by hunger, attack any living thing…[82]

In his report to Herbert Hoover in April 1920 Haskell had been candid about the benefit orphan care would have in deterring Bolshevism in Armenia, quite apart from the humanitarian dimension, and believed that "a direct relationship between hunger and Bolshevism existed, and therefore the child feeding work would have an effect upon the political life of the country."[83] Haskell believed that the average worker drifted towards Bolshevism as he saw the prospect of supporting and maintaining his family becoming more and more difficult. Ernest Yarrow, for his part, had drawn attention to the political significance of attending to the situation in Armenia and the Caucasus earlier in his essay published in the *Journal of International Relations* in 1919, where he had expressed the firm conviction that while the Caucasus seemed like an unimportant place on earth, neglecting its problems would create larger problems for the world in the future:

> …If America does not lend her influence, financial, political, and military…I firmly believe that before many years she will be reaping the whirlwind of her folly. This is a question of politics rather than of relief; and any careful student can see certain world principles at stake in this region, which if ignored will almost inevitably lead to a future world cataclysm.[84]

By distinction from the other two main receiving depots of Kars and Yerevan, Alexandropol was the most central and significant in Armenia, thanks to the large number of barracks, and the huge warehouses of the Kazachi post where vast quantities of cargo brought into Armenia could be stored and subsequently distributed to other relief districts. An equally important factor was that a spur of the railroad extended to the Kazachi warehouses making it easier to unload and load cargos under Captain Warner's supervision.

While Alexandropol's advantages in terms of transportation and storage made it an attractive choice for relief operations, the vast accommodations it offered at the Kazachi, Severski, and Polygon were also ideally suited for William Haskell's idea of concentrating all orphans in close proximity. In fact, by mid-March 1920, Haskell recommended that NER end activities by harvest time, namely August 1, except for orphanages and hospitals, which could be run for about $100,000 per month.[85] Haskell then proposed that the best course of action for NER would be to:

> Concentrate all orphanages and hospitals now scattered throughout Armenia, at one central point, where large public buildings are available without rent and where transportation costs will be cut to a minimum, and where the personnel may be combined.

The location Haskell favored was Alexandropol, which, he wrote,

> ...is the first large city in Armenia, on the railway from Georgia, [and] there exist large public buildings, formerly Russian barracks, where we now house about five thousand orphans and where additional space now exists for about ten to fifteen thousand more orphans. This is also a railroad junction and has unlimited storehouses of excellent character. Over twenty thousand refugees were formerly housed at this point, in addition to the orphans already there. This space is now vacant, due to the placing of refugees in villages, and makes these buildings available for the concentration of orphanages, with necessary hospitals, school buildings, industrial training plants, storehouses, et cetera.[86]

Haskell's other recommendations included reducing the American personnel in the Caucasus by 50% as soon as the concentration was completed, and maintaining an office in the port of Batum but,

> make our principle effort at Alexandropol; and maintain at Kars, Erivan and other former relief centers, a small organization for emergency relief, and for receiving such orphans as it might be later desirable to transfer to our great center at Alexandropol.[87]

By April 7, the concentration of orphanages had begun in earnest. Collection in one area would make it easier to attend to and sustain the needs of such a large orphan population, ran the overarching argument. By contrast, the District of Yerevan, by far the largest field of NER operations representing roughly 35% of the Caucasus branch activities with 11,000 children in orphanages, lacked proper housing, and of the available buildings, many were unsuitable.[88]

The list of reasons favoring Alexandropol as the major orphan depot was longer. Political conditions throughout the Transcaucasus were unstable and large-scale relief work gathered in one area had a greater chance of success and degree of security than if conducted at various widely scattered locations. And, should it be necessary, access to Tiflis and Kars was assured since Alexandropol was the junction point of railways. By way of explaining the reasoning behind such a major change of plans, Ernest Yarrow explained that he had personally toured most of the districts where NER operated in 1919, and was convinced that Alexandropol was best suited because of the "wonderful housing possibilities" available at the Russian barracks, and once all activities in orphan care were concentrated at the three posts, they would constitute NER's "show district."

Yarrow had been equally impressed with the receiving hospital in Alexandropol, which would facilitate the appropriate processing of incoming orphans:

> The receiving hospital in the city is another splendid institution. Here the children are received off the street, heads clipped, bathed, clothed as far as our meager supplies will allow, fed, and put to bed. They are kept for 24 hours and then given a thorough medical examination and then distributed either to orphanage

or hospital, thus this receiving station has a new set of inmates every day and there are never any empty beds.[89]

The decision to concentrate orphan care in Alexandropol, explained Yarrow, had been made by Haskell, who had found that under the uncertain political conditions of the Caucasus, it would be easier to care for a large orphan population. "Due to disturbing political conditions throughout Trans-Caucasus," he wrote,

> and the uncertainty as to the complete safety of this relief work if conducted on a large scale at various widely scattered points, recently it was found advisable by Colonel Haskell to arrange for the concentration of most of the orphans in that area at one single point. The city of Alexandropol was selected because of its exceptional situation, both as to climate and as the junction points of railways, and also because in Alexandropol there are huge barracks and other buildings formerly used by the Russian Army, which are now available for the Near East Relief at little or no expense.
>
> At Alexandropol there are concentrated now approximately 20,000 of the 75,000 orphan children for whom Near East Relief is responsible in the Caucasus area, and others are coming there daily, so that before winter sets in orphanages at other points, such as Erivan, Kars and Karaklis, will be used only as places for collecting the waifs as they come in and attending to their first needs as to food, clothing and cleanliness, including the very essential delousing and freeing from scabies and other skin diseases, after which they will be sent up to Alexandropol where they can be safer and have better care.[90]

Rumors that orphanages in Yerevan would close and orphans would be transferred to Alexandropol were circulating in late spring 1920, wrote NER employee Oksen Teghtsoonian in Yerevan:

> Rumors began to circulate that Near East Relief was planning a drastic new reorganization of its activities in Armenia, concentrating all their work in Alexandropol, and closing their Erevan orphanages and hospitals. I didn't pay much attention to these rumors; but very soon, early in the summer, these changes began to take shape...[91]

In the new plan, the Kazachi, Severski, and the Polygon would constitute the main center of orphan care and the two other sites to the south and southwest—Kars and Sarikamish—would serve as auxiliary locations connected to Alexandropol. During his tour, Yarrow had been impressed with the potential offered by Kars and Sarikamish, not far from Alexandropol by train. Like Alexandropol, Kars had spacious barracks and could "allow of transporting many hundreds of orphans and refugees from other congested districts such as Erivan."[92] In addition, it was connected via railway with Alexandropol to the north, and with the "large sub-station in Sarakamish" to the southwest. The expanded accommodations would soon become necessary, Yarrow explained, to house additional Armenian orphans scheduled to be transferred from neighboring republics because, noted Yarrow,

> all three of the republics [Georgia, Azerbaijan and Armenia] are trying to get rid of their surplus alien population and the Georgians' request for the removal of these people from Tiflis was considered reasonable and the transfer was undertaken by the Near East Relief.[93]

"Before spring [1920]," Yarrow estimated,

> we shall probably have in American institutions in the Caucasus between 30 and 35,000 orphan children. These institutions will have to be continued from five to seven years and their natural locations are Alexandropol, Kars, and Sarakamish.[94]

In the plan that evolved over the next several months, all orphans within and without Armenia would be concentrated along a corridor in the northwest. Three orphan cities, connected by railway would form a unique group, each one based in former Russian military bases, and each populated by children. Along that arc would be cared for and tutored the future builders of Armenia. In his September 1920 report, Yarrow had plans to transfer some orphans from Kars to Sarikamish to relieve the situation at Kars. "We have lately," he wrote

> …acquired a complete system of modern Russian barracks at Sarakamish with a view to establishing there eventually a school for five thousand boys.[95]

The grand plan of concentrating the orphans in one area was as much a novel idea as it was ambitious. It meant relocating thousands of children from orphanages across the country and the Caucasus, providing sufficient provisions when most of these would have to be shipped in through arduous treks and irregular train transportation. Twelve-year-old orphan Nishan S. Abrahamyan from Van remembered his transfer from Yerevan:

> They moved us to Alekpol by train. The train was very slow. We would go a short distance, and then we would get off the train, gather wood to burn and move the train.
>
> I was in orphanage #5. My number was 1899.[96]

Repairs on the Kazachi barracks had been in progress since early spring 1919 as negotiations over orphan care were conducted in Yerevan. "We began early in the spring [1919]" wrote Yarrow,

> to put in order a group of buildings known as Kazachee Post, a work which is now practically completed. There are about 40 substantial, dignified, stone houses which are surrounded by extensive fields.
>
> In the vicinity of Kazachee Post are situated the large central warehouses of the Near East Relief in Armenia. From this station is distributed the flour and other supplies on which the lives of so many thousands depend, a spur track of the railroad to the very doors of the warehouses makes the question of transportation quite simple…I might state here that the work itself is exceedingly nerve racking [sic] but the constant worry over additional funds and supplies adds to the burden a thousand fold.[97]

By the end of June, four of Kazachi's barracks had been renovated at the cost of 200,000 rubles and by December 1919 about 5,000 orphans were sheltered as more buildings were gradually repaired. The Armenian newspaper *Haraj* lauded the work that was taking shape in Alexandropol:

> The orphanages of Kazachi Post, where 5,000 orphans are now living, constitute the largest focus of care by the Americans. This is a beautiful and clean city of

children, which has its separate hospital, storage areas, railroad, ovens, baths and washrooms.[98]

Repairs and renovations of the posts, which were to continue for some years to come, were no simple tasks. Many of the barrack buildings were stark structures without roofs, floors, window frames and panes, or doors. Bathrooms had to be built on ground from which human corpses and debris from fallen buildings had to be cleared first; roofs had to be laid, windows and doors made and fitted; stoves would be made from oilcans in blacksmith shops, once the shops were built and equipped.

The plan now was that before winter 1920, orphanages as those in Yerevan, Kars, and Karakilisa would be used only as orphan collection sites, attending to their immediate needs as to food, clothing and medical care, including delousing,[99] treatment of scabies and other skin diseases, after which the orphans would be centralized in Alexandropol. Medical services, dispensaries, and clinics would be continued at all points where NER workers still carried on their work with orphans and refugees until centralization was complete.

Conducting repairs at the Polygon proved to be far more problematic. The Polygon had become a refugee camp, where denizens waited to return to their homes. Initially, Yarrow wrote, Haskell had intended to prepare the barracks to accommodate 50,000 or 60,000 refugees. But before the work was underway, 20,000 had "piled in with almost no warning." Only a single American officer was in charge of the 20,000, who "had to arrange for the feeding, bathing,

The account of Lt. Col. Robinson on the problems of vacating the Polygon. (NAA 205/1/634 Pt.1/f. 33 recto & verso)

washing, clothing, cooking, repairs on buildings, sanitation, water supply, policing, hospitalization, education for the children, and employment for the men and women."[100]

The relocation of the Polygon refugees was delayed for months. In February 1920, the government sent two representatives to assess their condition and relocation plans, which meant being sent to the abandoned villages around Kars and Alexandropol. The representatives arrived in Alexandropol on February 18 and submitted a comprehensive report on March 24, 1920. The first item of the report had to do with the Polygon, where they had found 24,000 refugees "the poorest relics of Turkish Armenia":

> This huge number of the Polygon refugees was left in cold stone buildings, which, with no exceptions, had absolutely no means of protecting the nakedness of thousands of refugees against the total cold of Alexandropol…in the last four or five months in the Polygon, an average of 15–20 people died per day.
>
> …the refugees were fed with bread only, receiving ¾ funt [1 funt= 409.51718 grams] daily…due to extreme poverty and innumerable privations, begging and the evil of moral degeneration has burrowed and grown in our people. At the same time, that mute and tragic mass has often served as a source of exploitation in the hands of Armenian and foreign adventurers.[101]

Most of the refugees had felt that, the abandoned villages were vulnerable, and had refused to leave. To protect them from the on-going attacks, self-defense units were designated to villages that were the most vulnerable, while Colonel Robinson and General Andranik provided the necessary attire for the guards.

Relocation was completed by March 24, despite obstacles in transportation, and only after much misunderstandings, misgivings, accusations, and negotiations. On April 10, Minister of Care Artashes Babalyan informed Haskell, among other things, that

> …the Polygon of Alexandropol…after being freed by the refugees the buildings were transfered [sic], as it is not unknown to Colonel Robinson and colonel Telford, to the Ministry of Care, in order that the latter keeps the buildings and makes room for the orfans [sic] of the Government from Erivan, Tiflis and Azerbaidjan. Already we have sent there orfans [sic] from Erivan. It is clear that it is not possible to leave our orfans in Tiflis and Azerbaidjan; the only building suitable for the orfanage [sic] use at the present time is the Polygon of Alexandropol.[102]

Five days later, on April 15, 1920, Yerevan District Commander Lt. Col. Telford informed the Minister of Care and Reconstruction of Armenia that NER wished

> to convert the Polygon at Alexandropol into a large orphanage. It is estimated that from twelve to fourteen thousand orphans can be accommodated there.
>
> …the concentration of orphans will be a great advantage, since it will simplify the problem of supply and the care of the orphans. It will be more economical and therefore more can be accomplished with the relief funds.

And once in their possession, explained Telford, NER proposed to repair all the buildings and put them into "first class shape like the buildings at Kazachi Post":

> This is all to be done with Near East Relief funds. It will be a distinct advantage for Armenia to have this large Army post repaired and reconstructed by the Near East Relief. I therefore request that the Polygon at Alexandropol be turned over to the Near East Relief for the above purpose.[103]

A Second Exodus

But even as orphan relocations were in full swing, repairs at the Kazachi and the Polygon were interrupted on April 29, 1920, when Haskell, from Tiflis, ordered most of his officers and NER male relief workers, together with all American women civilian personnel, to evacuate to Batum. His personal secretary at the time, Elsie Kimball, described the sudden decision to her family in the U.S.:

> There was a heap of excitement in the air that twenty-ninth day of April…particularly in colonel Haskell's office. We had heard, the previous evening, that the Bolsheviks had taken Baku…and naturally this news created a tremendous sensation in Tiflis. It meant…that our turn would come next…but it came much sooner than we had anticipated…[104]

At the end of the workday on April 29, Haskell had asked all the personnel to come to his living room where he announced the immediate evacuation of the women to Batum:

> We gathered in the Colonel's living room in stately array—about thirty-five of us, and he broke the news without flickering an eyelid. "The time has come," he said (pause), "when it is necessary to send you women from the Caucasus. We have received information of a grave nature today, and it means that you have _got_ to leave tonight, whether you want to or not—every last one of you—and let me tell you this, that if one of you refuses to leave, then she will lose her transportation back to the states, all salary due her, and all connection with the Near East Relief. I want no words—you have no choice—you are going, and you will have to be ready to leave here in two hours…All arrangements have been made for your transportation to Batoum and you will leave on a private train tonight, at ten, for Poti, and from there you will be taken by a U.S. destroyer to Batoum…AND REMEMBER—if you are not at the station at 8.00 o'clock, you no longer belong to this organization…That's all—there is no time to talk…Above all, say nothing to anybody whom you meet, on the street or elsewhere, about your going, for the safety of the women in the districts depends on your silence. We will get all the women out as fast as we can, and two officers have already left, today, for Armenia, to bring back the rest of the personnel…"
>
> Only four men accompanied us on that exodus of ours; the others remained in Tiflis until the personnel from Armenia had been conducted safely to Batoum.[105]

Haskell explained the new developments in a cable received by the ARA on May 11, 1920, and NER headquarters on May 13, 1920. It read:

> Baku occupied by Soviet troops two days ago. No opposition. Council defense organized Georgia. Tiflis declared in state siege. Fortunately practically all Near East supplies in Armenia. None whatever in Poti or Batum. Small quantity in Tiflis awaiting permission council defense to move it. Moved all American women in Tiflis to Batum and endeavoring to withdraw all American women from Armenia. Anticipate no trouble. Will wire when accomplished. Continuing relief work in all districts with skeleton personnel and will hold women at Batum until situation clears and is perfectly safe for them return to their work.[106]

A few days later, another cablegram from Haskell, now in Batum, announced that the "Bolsheviks" had taken Alexandropol and held control over NER property, warehouses, and personnel:

> ...tried to reach Erivan and Kars but no train has moved in Armenia for ten days. Impossible by automobile...Bolsheviki hold Alexandropol railroad center while Armenian government troops hold Erivan and Karakilisa. Garrison Alexandropol now Bolshevik and fighting government troops from Erivan. Armored train in Bolshevik hands controls situation. Delivered largest train of flour to Alexandropol. All our big warehouses Alexandropol held by Bolshevik. Our guards replaced by Bolsheviks. Our Personnel House occupied by Bolshevik. My representative practically a prisoner operating at Bolshevik dictation.[107]

The situation was tense in Tiflis. Haskell wrote that he had begun preparations to liquidate NER assets, and added that he was "selling Near East Stock at Tiflis rapidly" to prevent possible later loss, and was considering selling the cargo to be delivered on the SS *River Araxes* and SS *Sheaf Mead*, unless the situation showed signs of improvement:

> I have men representatives all stations but powerless supply them with flour or money due no communication. All stores are delivered in Armenia including Commonwealth child feeding supplies. Nothing at Batoum or Poti. Those at Tiflis mostly donated Red Cross supplies. Fear further delivery cannot reach men...Armenian Bolshevik situation might clear but even then no fuel oil exists in Armenia...

But, he reported, he had

> ...stocked every orphanage and hospital with six months supply essential articles food except Kars and Erivan where all foodstuffs on hand. Also plenty at Alexandropol in Armenian hands if they would stop civil war and distribute. *Kickapoo* cargo all delivered at Alexandropol.[108]

When Haskell cabled again from Tiflis on May 22, he had better news to relay:

> Situation improving. Armenian Government troops have retaken Alexandropole. Our warehouses returned. Our provisional government has opened communication between Batoum and Tiflis. We now need flour urgently.[109]

And, reversing his earlier order, Haskell now asked not to divert the SS *Sheaf Mead* and the SS *River Araxes* on their way to Batum, but

> On contrary expedite both...If SS *Poldenis* is ahead of SS *Sheaf Mead* send her *Batoum* instead of *Sheaf Mead* but must have one of them. My requirements therefore include *Lake Fiscus Jomar River Araxes* and either *Sheaf Mead* or

Poldenis...No flour received since *Chincha* which arrived first March and carried only 1,000 tons for Armenia...communication open with Armenia. I leave for Alexandropole and Erivan tomorrow.[110]

Haskell's orders and the sudden retreat had been compelled by an attempted coup d'etat that had followed the Bolshevik demonstration against the government in Yerevan on International Workers' Day on May 1st. The demonstration had eventually escalated to the successful, albeit short-lived, takeover of Alexandropol, Kars, and Sarikamish by a Revolutionary Committee (RevKom) of Armenian Bolsheviks. Their commander, Sargis Musayelyan, had declared Armenia a Soviet State from Alexandropol where the underground Armenian Communist Party had been founded in January 1920 to fight against the Allied Powers and the ruling Dashnaktsutyun (Armenian Revolutionary Federation, (ARF) party.

A glimpse of the urgency with which NER's American staff left Armenia is gleaned from the unpublished anonymous diary of a young female relief worker who had been transferred from Karakilisa to Kars just a week earlier, only to be ordered to Alexandropol, and thence to evacuate to Batum:

> I had been transferred to that [Kars] station just a week...when Col. Wright came down to take us all out of Armenia. The evening he came we knew something was wrong but they told us nothing until 7 o'clock the next morning (Sunday) when we were around and asked to "report" to the living room as soon as possible. There we were told that we must get our baggage to be ready at 12am and be ready to depart on the two o'clock train. Quietly and without even letting the servants know, we got out in a boxcar, straddling baggage. We carried seven days' ration with us. At Alexandropol we were to stay for 2 days where the Erivan crowds were also to report. From there a special train was to carry us to Tiflis...Beds, tables, stools, supplies, toilets were put in the cars where we were to live we knew not how long.[111]

As they were trying to leave at the Alexandropol train station on May 4, the Bolshevik Commander Captain Musayelyan had held the NER train back and NER representative Telford had been forced to sign a document in the name of the American government stating that America would continue to send wheat and would cooperate with the Soviet authorities in Armenia. Although Lt. Col. Telford was not authorized to do so, he signed the paper in order to get the group out of Armenia, and the party was allowed to continue on their journey to Batum, from where they reported to U.S. High Commissioner Rear Admiral Mark Bristol in Constantinople. The skeleton personnel left behind in Armenia was to continue the distribution of relief until the supplies were exhausted.[112]

Despite Haskell's orders to evacuate all women relief workers, Myrtle Shane had decided to disobey[113] the order and remained in Alexandropol with Elmer Eckman, the Director of Transportation and Purchase and now in charge of distribution of relief until the stocks were exhausted. Eckman's letter to his brother in North Dakota detailed the events that transpired at Alexandropol. With him, he wrote, was one American male civilian and "one American woman who had been a missionary, and refused to leave, saying she would die with her children." The warehouses contained vast amounts of food supplies, and his orders had been to continue work, if possible. Eckman had doubled the guards "to three hundred men all around, with a few machine guns and hand grenades," and had been able to organize a "working force among trusted Armenians, some Poles, and Russians." Then, just as things were running smoothly, "the Bolsheviki" had surrounded the post [most likely the Kazachi], requesting Eckman to turn the employees and the supplies over to their control:

> One bright morning, the advance guard of Bolsheviki officers slipped through our guard at daybreak, and walked right into the post and into my house. I was in bed and was summoned to appear in the sitting room. There I sure faced a mob, very respectful but meaning business. The chief commissar stepped out of the crowd and served notice on me to surrender all my men and all property in my possession; the notice had a nice little twister on the end of it, to the effect that should anything be missing or held out, my life, mentioning my name, would be forfeited. When I asked about this, he passed it off saying that it was merely a form similar to those served upon all people in authority.

As they were talking, the post "was suddenly surrounded by infantry, artillery, cavalry, and a Bolsheviki armored train," and all the "guards had simply vanished with their guns and all." Eckman then discussed the matter with the other Americans who had stayed with him and returned to continue his discussion with the occupiers of the post:

> I told them that as far as the supplies were concerned, they were not mine to turn over, as they belonged to the people of the United States.
>
> They had a long conversation over this, and finally agreed to leave the control of it all in my hands. They placed their own guards and comisars [sic] around the place, but allowed me to have my own agents, to see that nothing was touched. If the movement had succeeded of course they would simply have grabbed everything in sight and paid no attention whatever to us.[114]

The occupiers had kept the post under their control for six days until "driven out by government troops" that had reached Alexandropol on May 13 under the command of General Sepuh Nersesian. The rebels had left the next day and the government forces established order in the city. The leaders of the revolt were arrested and the Communist Party was banned in Armenia. None of the American relief workers had been harmed. One of their interpreters, however, had not been as lucky. *The Washington Post* reported that a certain Eugene Bakhmeteff, the brother of Boris Bakhmeteff, Ambassador of the Russian Provisional Government to the U.S., had been shot during the events of May 1920.[115]

Concentration Resumed

Ernest Yarrow and NER relief workers began to return to Alexandropol in early July. However, following directives from the War Department, Haskell and the U.S. military corps left Armenia permanently.[116] With Azerbaijan turning Bolshevik in April 1920 and the growing influence of Bolshevism in the Caucasus, there was concern whether Armenia and Georgia would be able to defend their independence. To avoid possible international complications, Haskell and his staff of U.S. army officers withdrew to Constantinople.[117]

Correspondence between Armenian government officials and the U.S. military staff reveals that despite the deep gratitude the government felt and expressed for the rescue efforts of Colonel Haskell and his staff, disagreements, at times verging on open confrontations, had surfaced on a variety of issues. Frequent pleas from the Minister of Care to district committees to be kind, friendly, and honest with the Americans who had come from far away to help Armenia, not to voice dissatisfaction, and to solve problems through mutual agreements and verbal negotiations rather than written complaints, had not helped.[118] Problems and disagreements had continued regarding areas of responsibility and jurisdiction assigned to each party, the cost of transportation of provisions, reimbursements, misinformation, misappropriation of relief, and mistreatment of orphans and personnel by some American officers.[119] The responsibility for the repairs of the barracks in Alexandropol was one of the issues revisited between the government of Armenia and NER. In a memorandum dated March 31, 1920, from Maxon S. Lough, Major Infantry to D. A. Robinson, Lieut. Col., Cavalry, requested funds for the repair of orphanages in Alexandropol from the Minister of Care in Yerevan. The amount requested was 400,000 Rubles. The request was submitted together with a cover letter dated April 6, 1920, signed by C. Telford, Lt. Col. G. S. "I am enclosing a letter to you," wrote Telford,

> ...from the American representative at Alexandropol asking for an allotment of four hundred thousand (400,000) roubles for repairs to buildings belonging to the Armenian government and in use by the NER as orphanages at Alexandropol.

The enclosed requisition, from D. A. Robinson, Lt. Col. Cavalry, and signed by Maxon S. Lough, Major Infantry, was "for the repair of permanent buildings belonging to the Armenian Government but now being used by the N.E.R. Orphanage" of the district of Alexandropol:

1. I request that the following amounts be appropriated for the repair of permanent buildings belonging to the Armenian Government but now being used by the N.E.R. Orphanage of this District:

a.	Labor	100,000 Rs.
b.	Materials	250,000
c.	Emergency Repairs	50,000

    Total . . . . 400,000 Rs.

2. These repairs are urgent and the period covered by this requisition is 15th March to 15th April.
3. A requisition for such materials as can be supplied from the Armenian Army Warehouses has been submitted.[120]

One of the significant disagreements earlier, in February 1920 involved Captain Warner, in charge of the orphanages and the warehouses at Kazachi and the Commander of the Alexandropol Garrison. An incident that had taken place at the post between officers of the two armies—Armenian and U.S.—had compelled the Prime Minister to lodge a complaint against Captain Warner. The Prime Minister of Armenia accused Captain Warner of forcibly taking over some buildings and showing conduct unbecoming an officer. He found Captain Warner's conduct "intolerable" and by order of the Minister of War requested that Warner return the barracks which he had "illegally" and "violently" seized, to the Armenian Garrison Commander. Telford's response arrived two days later, on February 20, 1920, with a copy sent to Lt. Col. Robinson in Alexandropol, stating that the matter had been referred to Colonel Haskell for his action. A much longer letter, dated Alexandropol, February 25, 1920, signed by Lt. Col. Robinson, addressed Haskell's Chief of Staff in Tiflis. Robinson explained that he had discussed the matter with Captain Warner, but neither understood what the complaint was based on:

> Neither Captain Warner, I, nor any other official of the Near East Relief, since I have been here, has occupied forcibly or otherwise any building belonging to the Alexandropol Garrison, nor have we forcibly occupied any building of any nature whatever belonging to anybody. We have occupied no buildings at Kazatchi Post or Kazatchi depot except those originally assigned to the Near East Relief by the government.
>
> No complaint of this nature has ever been made to me by the Commanding General, Alexandropol Garrison, the Quarter Master General of the Army nor the Armenian Supply Officer at Kazatchi Post, although I have interviews with them almost every week. Since my tour of duty here began no building has been occupied without my knowledge or direction, and then only through legal and proper methods…

The letter ended with the request that the Prime Minister clarify and identify specific complaints, provide the names of the officers who had lodged the complaint and the date when the incident was supposed to have taken place. "In the meantime," Robinson continued,

> I beg leave to point out the impropriety of the Prime Minister's stigmatizing the conduct of any American officer on duty in Armenia as "intolerable," "illicit," "illegal," or "violent," without presenting any evidence to support such expressions, and before the officer concerned has had a chance to be heard. However, this may have been the fault of the translator of the Prime Minister's letter and he may not have intended his communication to convey the meaning that it does in the translation I have before me.[121]

Yarrow Residence, Kazachi Post, 1920. (*The Friend*, November 1920: 285)

With the departure of U.S. officers in July 1920, relief operations were transferred to NER's civilian personnel with Ernest Yarrow at the helm, as NER Director General of the Caucasus Branch. By early summer Yarrow had taken up residence at the Kazachi, and moved the headquarters of NER's Caucasus Branch from Tiflis to

38   THE CITY OF ORPHANS

Alexandropol. In August, his wife Jane and their three younger children had joined him. "I am in charge of the Caucasus Branch of the Near East Relief," Yarrow explained in a letter on July 15, 1920,

> ...and immediately on taking charge moved the headquarters into Armenia and located at Alexandropol. There we live in a sort of fool's paradise, far from the rumors and scandals of the maddening crowd, and the political news which seeps into us is so old that it has lost its significance!

"The Bolsheviks," he wrote in his letter,

> ...are strongly entrenched in Azerbaijan, and the question is whether they are satisfied with their wonderful haul of the oil fields of Baku, or whether they wish to keep on until they have retaken all of the former Russian territory.

"If I were a Bolshevik," he continued, "and had as much wisdom as I have now,"

> I would call a halt, temporarily, at least. They would find nothing but pain in Armenia, and Georgia can be used as a sort of doorway from Russia to the outside world. This would establish trade for Russia, and I imagine would be welcome to the European nations, as in this way they could indirectly touch the Bolshevik kingdom, at the same time not committing themselves until they saw which way the cat was going to jump...

> I presume there has been a great deal of misinformation as to what has happened in the Caucasus. The Bolsheviks were let into the Republic of Azerbaijan by the front way. The Georgians fought them to a standstill on their border and have made a semi-fluid peace with them. Armenia shackled the hands of her own nationals who were Bolshevikally [sic] inclined and is now living in an immunity which is real if not permanent.

And, he added,

> The center of interest for the Near East Relief in this region, of course, is Armenia, since her condition gives the only pretext for our functioning here.[122]

Soon after Yarrow had assumed his position as Director General, issues came to a head at the Kazachi hospital. One specific incident that had taken place between an American physician and the Armenian medical staff at the Kazachi hospital on August 13, 1920, gave way to a barrage of complaints by the hospital staff, a list of which was sent to Ernest Yarrow and Prime Minister Hamo Ohanjanyan. The incident in question involved "Dr. Hodor," most likely a permutation of NER physician Dr. Hawthorne, who had physically and verbally abused the sick orphans in the hospital and some of the Armenian medical staff. This had not been an isolated incident but the final blow and had ultimately propelled Alexandropol's Union of Physicians and the Executive of the Red Cross to meet and lodge an official complaint against the doctor, demanding his immediate removal from Kazachi. The description of the incident and resolutions reached, dated August 18, 1920, were signed by Dr. A. Grigoryan and Dr. Drampyan-Manukyan in lieu of the secretary, and addressed the Prime Minister of Armenia:

18 August 1920
Alexandropol

The Union of Physicians of Alexandropol and the members of the Executive of the "Red Cross," convening with participation of the Vice President of the Central Executive of the "Red Cross," V. Arcruni, in an extraordinary meeting on August 15, 1920 to examine the detestable incident that took place on the 13th of this month at the Kazachi Post and determining that

1. On the 13th of this month physician Hodor working in the Alexandropol Medical Section of the NER has beaten with his hand held whip without mercy the orphans of the hospital, leaving many of them bloodied; and considering the fact that he has displayed such behavior in the hospitals of the Polygon as well as that of the Kazachi Post subjecting [the orphans] to cruel beatings;

2. During the same incident a few of the nurses of the hospital were subjected to insults and lewd comportment for the simple reason that they attempted to defend the children who were being beaten and because they invited the attention of Captain Dangerfield on the sad and savage behavior; and that [Hodor and Dangerfield] wanted to have one of the nurses put in jail by the police under the order of Captain Dangerfield;

3. Hospital physician Altunyan was subjected to severe beating by the whip receiving a wound on his forehead also because he defended the orphan children;

4. The whole staff of the hospital—nurses, custodial staff, sisters of charity, witnessing these savageries—was compelled to intervene,

The meeting decided

(a) That Doctor Hodor, as a psychologically unstable official cannot remain in a position of such responsibility, tarnishing the name of the great and humanitarian American people;

(b) That Captain Dangerfield, by his rude and impolite behavior toward the sisters of charity, has insulted the whole organization of the sisters of charity who, with selfless [devotion] and at the risk of their lives has labored in the weighty task of caring and educating the orphans;

(c) The meeting expresses its indignation toward the other doctors in the hospital for the uncaring attitude they displayed toward the orphans and toward the doctor, a sick man, who was torturing those orphans.

The meeting decided to forward this resolution to the head of the American mission, Mr. Yarrow, to the government of Armenia and if we do not hear from those, to the humanitarian American government in Washington.[123]

It is unclear if Yarrow answered the letter; he did, however, receive a second copy of the complaint a few days later, this time from the Ministry of Foreign Affairs, accompanied by a note dated August 30, 1920:

> Dear Sir,
>
> Forwarding You herewith enclosed a copy of the communication received by the Ministry for Foreign Affairs from the Medical Union of Alexandropol, which must have been sent to You, too. I have the honor to request your informations what steps have been taken by You relative to that matter.
>
> Truly Yours,
> General Secretary A. Ter-Akopian.[124]

It is unknown what steps the Director General took, if any. Dr. "Hodor" was still in Alexandropol three months later.

Overseeing the transfer from Haskell's military administration to Yarrow's civilian administration was Harold Barton, nephew of Clara Barton. Harold Barton had arrived with Haskell's relief mission to Armenia, and to him and another officer, Haskell had entrusted the task of transferring the organization to the civilian Near East Relief. A graduate from the Harvard College Class of 1909, Barton wrote in his 25th Harvard Class Report that "After the Bolsheviki seized Baku in 1920 the Colonel decided hastily to withdraw, leaving me and another officer to transfer our vast organization to the civilian Near East Relief."[125]

Barton remained in Armenia as Director of Schools, Orphanages and Hospitals until November 1920. "In addition to large scale organization and administrative work," he wrote,

> This position involved important negotiations with the Armenian National Government at Erivan, and later with their successors the Turkish Army of the Orient. When the Russian Red Army invaded Georgia to destroy the Georgian National government I was one of the few Americans remaining in Tiflis.

Upon his return to the U.S. Barton had reported to Washington, and was then sent back to Tiflis, on an unofficial mission:

> After the Soviet subjection of the Caucasus had been completed and the situation quieted down, I returned to Washington to report. I was immediately put through special civil service examinations and was sent back to Tiflis as a Trade Commissioner on an unofficial mission to ascertain if the Bolsheviki meant what they said about developing normal trade and investment relations with the capitalist powers in the Transcaucasian Corridor. After six months of unexpectedly happy relations with the Georgian Commissars, political and economic scandals broke out, the new doctrine of "economic espionage" was proclaimed and Washington eventually ordered me out.[126]

Consistent with plans to centralize orphan care in Alexandropol, special trains relocated orphans from Baku, Tiflis, Ghamarlu, Darachichak, Nor Bayazet, and other areas to Alexandropol, and by summer 1920, according to NER General Secretary Charles Vickrey, over 10,000 orphans had been gathered at Alexandropol. "Since the withdrawal of Colonel Haskell and the American military mission relief work continues under civilian direction of Captain Yarrow and strong American civilian personnel." Moreover, Vickrey added,

These orphaned boys and girls constitute the hope of the future for the near east. American philanthropy through Near East Relief is rendering inestimable service in promoting good will and international friendship. A few millions of dollars today in the form of food, education and industrial training for these orphans may save billions of dollars tomorrow in warfare and international strife.[127]

While the concentration of orphans to the northwest of the country proceeded, Oksen Teghtsoonian was transferred to Alexandropol in early August 1920 to arrange the logistics for the teachers NER was recruiting for the orphanage schools. "My job was at the Kazachi Post," wrote Teghtsoonian,

> …Three large buildings with a few dozen rooms were at my disposal to be cleaned and furnished for the arriving teachers. As a result of advertisements placed in the Armenian newspapers of Erevan, Tiflis, and Baku by the Americans, literally hundreds of teachers rushed to Alexandropol to enlist in this educational enterprise.

The job seemed easy at first, because "the warehouses were chock-full of the materials needed to furnish the buildings," wrote Teghtsoonian, but

> …in practice, it turned out to be quite difficult. All day long I would rush from office to office and warehouse to warehouse in order to procure a few beds or mattresses, some chairs and tables, oil lamps and linen. Despite all the red tape I succeeded in furnishing a good many rooms for the arriving teachers, most of them single men and women, though a few brought wives and children.[128]

By fall 1920, cargoes were being rushed to the warehouses at the Kazachi with hundreds of tons of food and clothing supplies. One such shipment carried, among other things, 5,813,000 pieces of old garments and shoes weighing 250 tons, 5,220 bags of rice weighing 210 tons, 1,680 bags of sugar weighing 75 tons, and 260 tons of soap. That was followed in early December 1920 by 1,000 tons of wheat flour, 400 tons of rice and 100 tons of sugar.[129]

The posts, renovated at NER's expense, had schoolrooms of different sizes, offices, administrative areas, hospitals and clinics, storage facilities, kitchens, bakeries, washing areas and bathrooms. Some facilities were large enough to allow for 1,500 children to be present in a dining room at the same time and for 450 to be washed at one time. Evacuation of orphanages was in full force especially in Yerevan, where the target evacuation date from Kanaker was set for September 10. In his memorandum of August 25, 1920, Yerevan District Commander L. O. Fossum,[130] informed the Minister of Care, that

> Following instructions received from NER Headquarters, Alexandropol, we are preparing for a complete evacuation of all buildings now occupied by the N.E.R. at Kanakir.

Although the target date of no later than September 10 was in force,

> …owing to the unsettled condition of the Rail-road, difficulty in securing cars, etc., we can set no definite date.

And, he added,

> As soon as practical we will move all N.E.R. equipment, and notify your office at once.[131]

In tandem with the renovations of the barracks in Alexandropol, NER had been preparing Kars to receive orphans. By summer 1920, NER operated seven orphanages in Kars—four in the city and the remaining three in a valley nearby.[132] Just a year earlier, when *Saturday Evening Post* reporter Eleanor F. Egan visited Kars, she had described the American relief headquarters in Kars as "an avalanche of woe," with one Armenian doctor temporarily in charge of the place:

> He was a graduate of Harvard University and had practiced medicine somewhere in New England—I forgot where…my mind was not registering such details: it was busy trying to associate him with Harvard. He was dirty beyond belief. Even his face was dirty—dirt-encrusted—and to shake hands with him heartily and naturally was a test of one's self-control. His hands—well, you see, there was no soap—absolutely none; no fuel with which to produce hot water…

> …He had gone back years ago, was practicing medicine in Turkish Armenia and prospering, but he got caught in the terrible drive against his people and fled with other refugees to Russian Armenia…He belonged to the group that moved northeastward from Erzurum and Kars; he was carried with the surging throng back to Kars—and there he was. An American relief officer found him and put him in charge of the hastily established headquarters while he hurried back to Alexandropol to get help and accumulate some supplies…[133]

The doctor had wished to show the American visitors the hospital under his charge:

> …It was not exactly a hospital, he said, but it would be as soon as the Americans arrived with the necessary supplies. In the meantime they had been building some wooden bedsteads and had got out of a deserted military barracks some old iron beds that were better than nothing. But they had no bedding of any kind; no blankets, no sheets, no mattresses, nothing—absolutely nothing!

Egan had then been taken to the children's ward:

> …The little people were more pitiable than the adults. They were in what was referred to as the children's wing…The ward, if I may call it that, had in it not one stick of furniture of any kind and the children were all lying on the dusty and rubbish-strewn floor with nothing under them and no covering save the rags they wore. A little dying person in a corner seemed not to bother anyone much. He was breathing his last.[134]

Conditions had much improved since Egan's visit, but with the arrival of thousands of orphans, available space had run out by summer 1920.[135] Additional buildings were now being prepared to accommodate more than a thousand orphans scheduled to arrive from Yerevan. Of the seven NER orphanages, six housed Armenian orphans while the seventh sheltered 150 Muslim orphans.

After the children had been moved from Yerevan to Kars or Alexandropol, NER had left some of their furniture behind in Yerevan, so that the government would be able to fill those buildings with the growing number of orphans who still roamed the streets. However, the government was in no position to provide clothing or food to all. In a letter from the Ministry of Care to NER dated August 23, 1920, the Minister asked if clothing could be provided from NER warehouses,[136] in answer to which L. Fossum informed the Minister that due to the large numbers of orphans now gathered in Alexandropol and Kars, NER could no longer accede to the needs of other orphanages:

1. At the present time it is an impossibility for the NER to issue anything in line of orphan's clothing.

2. Due to the concentration of such a large number of orphans, both at Alexandropol and Kars, every piece of material we now have is in great demand, and after making up this present issue our Ware-houses [sic] will be practically empty.[137]

The evacuations from Yerevan to Alexandropol and Kars allowed the consolidation of 26 NER orphanages in Yerevan into seven. About a year earlier, in June 1919, Armenia's Minister of Care had been concerned that schools in Yerevan were being used as orphan shelters, and had wished to expedite the process of transfers to ready schools for the upcoming academic year. In this regard, Minister Torosyan had suggested to John Elder that orphans sheltered in schoolhouses and children's hospitals in Yerevan be transferred to the Kazachi Post in Alexandropol. Torosyan had based his request on the unavailability of appropriate buildings in Yerevan and the government's lack of funds to repair existing ones.[138] However, repairs in Alexandropol and Kars were not yet completed when the government began moving orphans out of Yerevan to Alexandropol and Kars. In a memorandum dated October 9, 1919, William Haskell's Chief of Staff Lonergan in Tiflis had urged the Armenian National Council there to stop the relocations until NER was ready. He had just been informed, he noted in his memorandum, that the government of Armenia had sent 300 orphans from Yerevan to Kars and was planning to relocate another 400 in the near future. Lonergan had asked that the relocations stop because there were already a large number of orphans in Kars, more than NER could care for, reassuring the Council that,

> The NER in not too distant future will be in a position to care for a much larger number of orphans in Alexandropol. When that becomes a possibility, I will let you know so as you may transfer the orphans from Yerevan to Alexandropol.[139]

Nevertheless, requests for orphan transfers continued in summer 1920: buildings used as orphanages in Yerevan were needed for the military, and those in Etchmiadzin were needed for educational purposes. But with the transfer of other orphans form Akhalkalak and Tiflis, by early fall 1920 Kars and Alexandropol were at capacity and Yarrow decided to stop the transfers from Yerevan for the time being. Instead, he extended NER's work in Yerevan through the winter until Alexandropol would be able to receive more orphans. He explained to the Minister on September 8, 1920:

Excellency,

…We are not in position at the present time to accept any new orphans. Later, when we have more space available and our Orphanage Department is fully organized, it may be possible. In the event of our being able to increase the number of orphans cared for by us I shall be pleased to let you know.

I take this opportunity to renew to Your Excellency the assurances of my esteem.[140]

About one month later, on October 12, 1920, H. B. Barton had to explain again to the Minister of Care that NER was making every effort to expedite the relocation of children from Yerevan and Etchmiadzin, but circumstances beyond their control had delayed the process. Barton's note read in part:

> You are perhaps aware that we are making a sincere effort to release to the Armenian Government and ecclesiastical authorities, the buildings at Knikir [Kanaker] and Etchmiadzin which are urgently needed for the military and educational purposes. It is indeed our desire to comply with the needs and desires of the Government authorities in so far as we are able to do so. This whole policy, however, is conditioned by the progress of construction at the Polygon in Alexandropol, and by the availability of transportation for transferring our children from one place to another.[141]

Compounding the problem was a new difficulty that had slowed down, or stopped the relocations. This was the Turkish occupation of Sarikamish at the end of September, where the 600 boys from Yerevan's orphanage No. 5 were slated to be moved. In his note Barton explained that while NER was fully aware that the military needed the space occupied by orphanages and was trying its best to move the orphans out of Yerevan, the recent occupation of Sarikamish had disrupted the process. As a result, Barton wrote, the boys in Yerevan's orphanage No. 5 could not be moved as yet:

> As regards our orphanage Number 5 in the city of Erivan, which we are aware the military authorities need badly, unhappily the temporary occupation of Sarikamish by the Turks has interrupted our preparations in that place for the reception of the 600 boys who occupy the Number 5 orphanage.

As he tried to explain NER's best intentions about vacating some of the buildings, Harold Barton assured the Minister that as soon as Armenian forces retook possession of Sarikamish, NER would immediately resume preparations. "We have confidence," he wrote,

> …that the Armenian army will soon be once again in possession of Sarikamish and it is our intention to proceed immediately to the preparation of buildings to receive boys from Erivan and from Kars. The military authorities in the latter place are also very desirous that we should evacuate certain buildings in the city necessary to the military organization. We wish to assure you that in every way possible we are disposed to remove ourselves as obstacles to the development of your institutions.[142]

Another policy that needed clarification was NER's stoppage of general relief and its new focus on orphan care alone. The change created confusion as well as disappointment. Barton now explained the policy change in the Yarrow administration to the Minister of Care on Sept. 18, 1920:

To His Excellency,
The Minister of Care
Armenian Government.

Alexandropol, Sept. 18, 1920

Your Excellency: –

I had the honor some few weeks ago to define to you the transition that is taking place in the Near East Relief from the Haskell regime of comprehensive relief work to the Yarrow regime of intensified education and character building in our orphanages.

This transition has entailed the carrying over from the Haskell regime of certain branches of our work growing out of the relief of refugees last winter. It is clear to you that for the time being the Near East Relief is concerning itself only with the 20,000 orphans whom we inherited from the life-saving of last winter, and I know that you can understand clearly how the introduction of extraneous elements into this work impeded the progress of work which is vital to the coming generation.

Barton went on to explain that NER would not be transferring the children at the blind school in Etchmiadzin to Alexandropol and hoped that the government would now assume their care. Because, he added, NER planned to open a school in Karakilisa for the blind orphans in NER's orphanages:

During the period of great distress last winter, the Near East Relief assumed the responsibility for a home for the blind established at Etchmiadzin. Not only has the Near East Relief discontinued its work with adults, turning the same over to the proper Government authorities, but we are also in the process of evacuating as soon as possible, the District of Etchmiadzin. Therefore, it is requested that you provide for the taking over of this blind home, either by the Armenian Government authorities or by some private agency which is interested in the care of the blind. The blind orphans of the Near East Relief orphanages are being concentrated in a home and school for the blind which is in the process of being occupied at Karaklis at the present time.[143]

The future of the blind children was resolved by the end of September, as a committee in Etchmiadzin assumed jurisdiction over the home for the blind.[144] There was also the matter of the "abnormal" children:

We have in our institutions a certain number of abnormal children afflicted with insanity and epilepsy. We assume that the Government has already taken into consideration the need for an institution to care for these afflicted members of society, and we would request that you inform us at your earliest convenience of what facilities the Government has at its disposal for caring for these unfortunates.

I avail myself of this opportunity to renew to Your Excellency the expression of my profound respect and esteem.[145]

H. B. Barton
Director of Orphanages
And Hospitals

Apprehension over Concentration

Not all were enthusiastic about the idea of transferring orphans to Alexandropol. Some orphans had relatives living near the Yerevan orphanages and would occasionally visit the children. At issue were the separation of the children from their families, and the impersonality of the new environment where they would become just another number among thousands. Teghtsoonian explained:

> This idea the Americans had of concentrating the many thousands of poor orphans into these camps was very practical from their point of view in terms of running the operation at a reduced cost, but it had a traumatic effect on the kids. The small, scattered orphanages, schools, and hospitals in Erevan and the surrounding towns and villages were in the same area where most of the refugee families were living, so that close relatives and widowed mothers could visit the kids there to comfort them, and give them some feeling of love and belonging; in the remote and isolated camps they were totally lost.[146]

There had been other problems as well:

> The clever Americans who had dreamed up this orphan town had figured that it would work smoothly and efficiently like an American mass-production factory. But they hadn't thought about the climatic difference between the Erevan region and the plateau of Shirak…
>
> …The sharp chilly days of early October caught the management of the orphan town by surprise. It was found that these thousands of kids had no shoes and no warm clothes, and that there was no wood for the stoves in the buildings. It was pitiful to see the kids marching single file from one building to another, on their way from dormitories to dining rooms or classrooms, barefoot and shivering, dressed in flimsy summer clothes…
>
> …Drastic measures were taken to remedy the situation and dozens of seamstresses and shoemakers were put to work.[147]

The apprehensions in some official circles were for the most part based on the difficulties such a distance from the capital might pose in the supervision and control of the upbringing and education such a large segment of the future generation would be exposed to. In a note to the Council of Ministers, dated July 22, 1920, Minister of Care Artashes Babalyan reported that NER had recently been reducing its activities except in Alexandropol and Kars where it was concentrating NER orphanages, and that NER offices in Yerevan and Tiflis were being relocated to Alexandropol. "It is therefore necessary," he wrote

> …that the internal and educational life of those orphanages be under the supervision of the government. At the same time it will be necessary to negotiate with the central administration of the [American] Committee about various issues, which will be difficult to do from Yerevan…

He proposed that the provincial government of the Shirak province appoint a representative to act as liaison between the government and NER, to facilitate the transmission of requests and communication from the government to NER.[148]

The Ministry of Public Education revisited the issue of the education and upbringing of the orphans under NER care on August 14, 1920.[149] By December 1919, began the letter from the Ministry, NER and the Ministry of Education had agreed on a number of principles. Since then, the Ministry had acquainted itself with the work conducted during the preceding school year, and had arrived at some conclusions. It was understandable, read the letter, that in the early stages of its humanitarian work NER had been preoccupied with sheltering and feeding the orphans. Regrettably, the government had not been able to contribute adequately to the effort due to financial difficulties, nor had it been able to follow the education of the orphans. But now that the orphans were well cared for, and, in view of the fact that the work of education and upbringing of the orphans was not satisfactory, the government found it necessary to revisit the issue in greater detail.

Next followed a summary of the points of the agreement of December 1919: NER was given the leadership in orphan education; NER would invite supervisors and teachers in accordance with the policies of the Ministry of Public Education; NER orphanages would follow the curriculum used by state schools; the Ministry of Public Education would pay the salaries of 130 teachers and try to provide books and stationary supplies; and that the representatives of the Ministry held the right to be acquainted with NER's educational program and would have free access to the orphanage schools.

Acknowledging the terms of the December agreement, the Ministry now wanted to add a few amendments to the original agreement, whereby it reserved the right for general supervision of the educational program and the right to confirm the suitability of teachers and senior masters hired by NER. The Ministry also stated that NER could change the curriculum of its schools only after receiving permission from the Ministry of Education, that NER was obligated to submit a copy of its reports to the Ministry, and that NER would have to follow all directives published by the Ministry for the country's schools.

The Ministry's request to revisit the educational program was not made because the schools lacked an academic curriculum, but in part because that curriculum had remained largely on paper alone.[150] Ernest Yarrow's answer, dated September 6, 1920, was as compassionate as it was direct and terse.[151] He informed the Minister that a Director of Education had been appointed by headquarters in New York and was expected to arrive soon. In the meantime, Yarrow offered the general policy as developed by NER's leadership. "As you know," he wrote,

> ...in the activities of the Near East Relief are concentrated the sympathies and desire to help Armenia of the whole American people. It is the wish of the Near East Relief to make a definite contribution to the future Armenian nation...

> We do not wish in any way to alienate the children from their race and government, but we do wish to train them in such a way that they will have obtained the best

elements in American education, which has done so much toward making America one of the foremost countries of the world.

But to reach that goal, it was

> ...absolutely necessary that we be able to work in our education departments with the same freedom as that enjoyed by similar educational institutions in America. In America there are both Governmental and private institutions. The former are of course in their smallest details under Governmental supervision; and those run by private individuals or organizations are allowed a great deal of freedom in their internal life.

Of the two types of schools, Yarrow believed, the most successful and useful were those run by private organizations or individuals. He believed that in Armenia NER orphanage schools corresponded to the second type, although they would work in "very close cooperation and harmony with the Government," but that they would remain absolutely free from actual control by the Government. He then addressed the amendments proposed by the Ministry, which he found "entirely unacceptable":

> The changes which you propose in the present agreement between the N.E.R. and the Armenian Government are such as to be entirely unacceptable to the Near East Relief. These include the following:
>
> 1. The Minister of Education reserves the right to supervision and control.
> 2. Only such teachers shall be employed by the N.E.R. as are approved by the Minister of Education.
> 3. Changes in the curriculum shall be made only after receiving the approval of the Minister of Education.

Yarrow then clearly and emphatically told the Minister:

> I can assure you that the Near East Relief will not, either at this present time or at any time in the future, accept any one of the above three suggested principles. If the Armenian Government plans to insist on any one of them, either now or at any future time, I would request that such statement be put in writing so that I may forward it to New York headquarters and settle, once for all, this very important question...

At the end of his letter, Yarrow explained that NER would follow the official curriculum of the Armenian Government schools as closely as possible, but wished to draw the Minister's attention to some differences between ordinary day schools and orphanage schools. In the first, the student came from established homes where the parents could take care of the child until the age of 21 or older. By contrast, students in the second category were discharged from the orphanages at the age of 15 or 16 and would have to earn their own living. Therefore, they would need to be trained in skills in different trades, which meant that the hours the orphan spent in the classroom would have to be shorter to allow time for such training.

The response to Yarrow's letter from the Ministry still revealed concerns over the pedagogical methods being practiced by NER:

September 1920,
Yerevan

We are in receipt of your letter of September 6.

It appears that our previous note N 3412 did not sufficiently clarify our Ministry's position regarding our mutual relations.

Being well aware that it is your purpose as well as that of the government's—which has now assumed the role of parents—to provide the orphans such an education that can be useful in practical life, and to become patriotic, good citizens. We believe that, from the onset, there should not be any unclear issues in our relations, in order to avoid misunderstandings later.

The Ministry wished to set the record straight, and pointed out the "fatherly responsibility" the state felt toward the orphans:

You write in your note that you should be free in the area of education planning just as is the case at private schools in America. If our Ministry writes that changes in the educational curriculum must be subject to the approval of the Ministry, that does not mean that our official school program must in its entirety be transplanted into the orphanage schools without any changes. We have already had the opportunity to assure you that in the opinion of our Ministry, classes devoted to practical training should have priority; it is therefore self-evident, that the Ministry could not have opposed those changes that aim to provide a practical education. On the other hand, being accountable to the people for the future of the orphans, the Ministry cannot remain indifferent to the way in which the orphans' education and upbringing are being conducted. That is the fatherly responsibility, which, in America affords parents the possibility of oversight in the lives of private schools and to choose the school of their choice. It is that responsibility that compels us to reserve the right of oversight and of approval of changes in programs.

The letter from the Ministry also questioned the quality of some of the teachers NER had hired, and the concern that NER might inadvertently engage teachers who campaigned against the government, referring to Bolshevik sympathizers:

As regards our supervision, that, too, derives from the same general principle that the State must have oversight over the lives of schools. Second, as it appears from last year's reports of our regional directors, there were some unqualified teachers in the American schools who had no educational training. The State also cannot ignore the fact that the list of teachers may include such individuals known to be engaged in a campaign against our State, for example Bolsheviks.... The Committee [NER], unaware of local conditions and the public, may fall into errors that would harm school life. We feel the responsibility for supervision of your educational life in order to prevent such mistakes. These are the circumstances, which, we believe, will convince you as to the necessity of government supervision.[152]

The debates and negotiations over the control of orphans sheltered in NER orphanages were soon eclipsed by events that unfolded between September 28 and November 6, 1920, when all three cities where the future builders of Armenia would reach adulthood, fell under Turkish occupation. Four divisions from the XV Army Corps of Karabekir Pasha swept through the Armenian border. Sarikamish, about 15 miles from the Turkish border, fell first. Despite concerns following the fall of Sarikamish, NER staff in Kars decided, to the last person, to stay with the orphans, among them a certain Mr. Crane, a wealthy American, who worked without salary and each month spent tens of thousands of dollars from his own funds.[153] In gratitude for their dedication, Armenian Prime Minister Hamo Ohanjanyan wrote Yarrow on October 12, 1920, to thank the Americans in Kars. The letter read in part:

> …the attitude shown by the personnel of the Near East Relief toward danger compels me, in the name of the Government of Armenia, to express our profound gratitude and congratulations to them for their humane and noble conduct.
>
> I understand that among your personnel were certain individuals whose contracts were ended and who had completed their service with the Near East Relief and were about to start home to America. When danger threatened the children for whom they had been working, they decided to remain until the crisis was past.
>
> I have been informed that the American personnel were divided among the various orphanages, and they all decided to remain and protect the children at the risk of personal danger if the enemy approached.
>
> Their actions fill me with admiration at the courage and bravery shown.
>
> Again accept my thanks, and kindly express to all the Near East Relief personnel the appreciation of the Armenian Government.[154]

The fall of Kars came at the end of October, two weeks after the Prime Minister's letter. The number of orphans sheltered in NER orphanages in Kars at the time of the attack, according to James Barton, was around 10,000. The young American women who stood by their wards did so despite clear and present danger that erupted during the largest battle of the Turkish-Armenian War. With pandemonium and carnage outside the orphanage walls, terrified orphans watched as their guardians repelled threats. Elsie Kimball, Cora Beach, and Elizabeth Anderson hovered over the orphans and hospitals like anxious mothers. Cora Beach guarded her one thousand orphan boys with a large club in her hand threatening all Turkish soldiers who strayed her way.[155] At one point, when Turkish soldiers had smashed the windows with their bayonets and entered the orphanages, she approached them with bread and salt, and the American flag, as 12-year-old Azniv Aslanyan from Van, who had been transferred from Yerevan, watched the scene:

> …The Turks were breaking the window glasses with their bayonets…Our American woman principal raised the American flag and went forward with bread and salt towards the Turks and said it was an orphanage.[156]

Elsie Kimball had discovered about twenty Kurds reaching through the orphanage windows for blankets. She had dashed at them, waving a whip and shouting "*Heidy.*" All but one man, who was trying to take a blanket from the orphan on the other side of the window, went away only after Elsie Kimball had raised her whip.[157]

Elizabeth Anderson's[158] contract with NER was due to expire on September 30, 1920, but she had decided to stay:

> We had heard rumors that things were not going well, but at that time we looked upon the "war" as something rather amusing, and not likely to affect us at Kars. With the capture of Sarakamish, however, things began to look serious…
>
> …all our fuel was brought by rail from Sarakamish…and then, suddenly, on September 28, the Turks captured Sarakamish, an important strategic stronghold on the Armenian frontier, about sixty versts [1 verst =0.6629 mile] from Kars.

Then,

> On the night of the twenty-eighth [October], the Turks cut the railroad to Alexandropol. This was the most serious thing that had yet happened, for it broke our communication with the outside world; and it looked as if we were in for a long siege. At that time we had only about a month's supply for the children.

On the morning of October 30, when Kars was occupied, Anderson was moving wagons of milk and flour to the city hospitals from the warehouse. She had delivered ten loads by 11 o'clock in the morning and was returning to the warehouse for more, when

> …hell suddenly broke loose in the city. People poured from the houses; the streets became jammed with ox-carts, horses, soldiers, dogs, sheep, and animals of every description, with bedding hastily strapped on their backs…A pandemonium of excitement, which reminded me of the great movie scene in *The Last Days of Pompeii*.

She galloped to Hospital No. 2, only to find it flooded by refugees and retreating Armenian soldiers:

> It was the first American building in the path of the refugees and soldiers and they were pouring into it through the doors and windows they had broken…I screamed in Armenian that this was a children's hospital and that soldiers must not take refuge there…I saw that it was hopeless to attempt to stop them. I decided to get the children out and up to Hospital No. 1 on the hill. They were not bed-patients, but were all suffering from favus, the scalp disease…I gathered up the babies and gave them to the bigger girls to carry, then began to strip blankets and sheets from the beds, intending to lock them in the storeroom…
>
> Suddenly a new sound was added to the din—the crack and crash of bullets breaking glass. One, two, three whizzed. I knew it would be madness to attempt to move the children under rifle-fire, so I told them to lie flat on the floor while I hurried down to the door.
>
> Everything was silent in the building now; the people had stopped their moaning and had sunk into dumb terror…From the height across the river came the rhythmic tat-tat-tat of a machine gun, and I drew back as a bullet whistled uncomfortably close to my ear…
>
> …All I can remember is the husky breathing of the dying child at my feet. I looked out of the window, and on the crest of the hill opposite I saw a column of men marching as if on parade. At the head of the column was a red flag bearing the star and crescent.

> I have never felt so alone, so entirely helpless and so thoroughly frightened. I picked up the American flag…and stepped to the door. It was a little homemade flag, with just ten stars on it, but to me it felt like armor.
>
> Through the half-open door came a bayonet—slowly, cautiously, about on a level with my stomach. Behind it appeared a face—drawn, sweaty, eager, mean.
>
> "American!" I quivered; trying to say it with a Turkish accent, and holding out my flag. Up went the bayonet, and off went the gun right over my head. It made a terrible explosion in the narrow little entry. I staggered against the doorframe and said, "American," again, rather feebly.
>
> I think the Turk smiled. He lowered his bayonet and backed me into the room…[159]

It was estimated that within thirty minutes 30,000 people had evacuated the city, but the orphans and their caretakers had stayed in their orphanages.

The third, and largest orphan city, Alexandropol, fell one week later. NER Caucasus Director General Ernest Yarrow had been concerned over the unstable political situation even as the City of Orphans was taking shape in the summer, and had cautioned in early September 1920, that there was still potential danger in the political situation in the Caucasus. But, he had announced,

> …No matter what the situation is there is nothing to do but continue work until further activity is impossible. Enough flour is on hand to assure the lives of every Armenian until harvest. We have supplies enough for the orphanages to last six months.[160]

Yarrow's position, as well as those of the 37 American staff in Alexandropol, remained the same even after the fall of Sarikamish and Kars, after the arrival of trainloads of new refugees in Alexandropol at the end of September, the arrival of new Armenian fighter units and military leaders, and the pronouncement of martial law in the city. The military leadership, among them General Silikyan, now congregated at the Astoria Hotel in Alexandropol, the Armenian headquarters during the Turkish-Armenian War.[161] On November 4, 1920, three days before the city fell, Yarrow cabled from Alexandropol that NER's 37 American workers in Armenia had decided to stay despite the imminent attack by Turkish forces:

> Kars fell Oct. 30, before Turkish advance. Rumors that Turks are already half way to Alexandropol. All Near East Relief personnel were given choice of withdrawing, but all decided to remain…[162]

NER General Secretary Charles V. Vickrey explained to *The New York Times* that the reason behind the decision to stay was that NER had nothing to fear from Turkish forces:

> Our experience in connection with the Near East during the last five years has been that orphanages, hospitals and other similar institutions under control of the Near East Relief have been free from molestation by the Turks and others when these institutions have been administered by American Relief workers, in whose unselfishness and altruism the Turks, Kurds and Tartars, as well as the Armenians, have complete confidence.[163]

Cable dispatches from NER offices in Tiflis informed headquarters in New York that Alexandropol had been taken and communications between Alexandropol and Kars cut. The news was covered extensively in the U.S. and in some detail, but Charles V. Vickrey assured *The New York Times* on November 10, 1920, that

> ...Part at least of the needs...in the Caucasus had already been anticipated by the Near East Relief and that cargoes are now on the seas bound for Batum consisting of 5,813,000 cases and bales of old clothing and shoes, 5,200 bags of rice, 1,680 bags of sugar and 260 tons of soap and other supplies.

The assurances that NER relief workers were safe did not apply to the Armenian relief workers in Alexandropol. Four days before Vickrey's interview had appeared in *The New York Times*, the Armenian workers in Alexandropol were paid a month's salary and told that NER could not assure their safety. In fact, about one month earlier, on October 7, Oksen Teghtsoonian had been instructed by the main office to pay one month's salary to the Armenian teaching staff,

> ...and tell them that they were free to look after themselves since the Americans were not in a position to assure their safety. A sackful of paper money was brought to me and I began to pay all the teachers their wages, using one of our restaurant tables as an office. It took three or four hours to finish this job and then, after our last luncheon together, we stood outside of our building in a confused and frightened state.[164]

"Being very busy in our daily work and rather isolated in our camps," recalled Teghtsoonian,

> ...we were cut off from the outside world and its happenings. In early October rumors spread that a Turkish army was making threatening movements toward the border of the Armenian Republic...

> Refugee caravans of oxcarts and straggling men, women, and children now appeared in large numbers, passing through Alexandropol in their search for safety. Complete chaos and anarchy reigned in the city, and it was every man for himself.[165]

The subsequent occupation of Alexandropol lasted until April 22, 1921, during which time the city was designated as the headquarters of the Turkish forces. It was the second Turkish offensive and occupation of the city in less than three years. But this time, occupation was over a district that had the largest concentration of refugees—115,000 Turkish-Armenian and 2,000 Russian Armenian refugees—and, the largest concentration of orphans.[166]

Part Two

The City of Orphans under Two Flags

Children of Orphanages I, II, III.
(RAC NEF Photos Box 145)

Chapter Three

EXODUS

Exodus from Alexandropol to Kars

In the months following the fall of Kars and Alexandropol at the end of October and early November 1920, respectively, NER continued its work in Kars and Alexandropol under Turkish occupation. In both settings Turkish authorities assured NER that they would neither interfere in nor impede NER's mission in orphan care. But as the next few months showed, events did not go as expected either for NER, or for the orphans: by November 1920, all NER American relief workers, with the exception of a few men, evacuated Alexandropol in a mass exodus to Kars, to continue orphan care there. Plans would be disrupted, again, when two months later, NER would embark on yet another exodus—from Kars back to Alexandropol—that lasted until early April 1921. But this time, the exodus included not only relief workers but also thousands of orphans from Kars, many of whom had just been transferred there from other orphanages in Armenia.

The exodus from Alexandropol to Kars took place less than a month after the Turkish occupation. It was not, however, propelled by the Turkish headquarters in Alexandropol—at least not directly—but by a local Revolutionary Committee, a RevKom, installed and controlled by Karabekir Pasha's headquarters in Alexandropol.[167] Spurred by Turkish authorities, the local RevKom in Alexandropol had early on adopted an adversarial position against NER in Alexandropol. After a number of confrontations and intimidations during November, Ernest Yarrow had decided to leave Alexandropol for Kars in late November, together with NER's Alexandropol staff. Since the move was expected to be permanent, NER took along much of the supplies in the Kazachi warehouses for use in its orphanages in Kars, with the assistance and support of the Turkish army now camped in Alexandropol. For the more than 10,000 orphans NER had concentrated in Alexandropol during the preceding year, and who would remain in Alexandropol, a supply of two months was left in the warehouses of the City of Orphans.[168]

In his cable dated November 30, U.S. High Commissioner Rear Admiral Mark Bristol informed the U.S. Secretary of State in Washington that Americans were "all safe within the Turkish lines."[169] Four days later, on December 4, U.S. Consul in Tiflis Charles K. Moser provided the Department of State with additional details, stating that Director General Yarrow had found it impossible to proceed with relief work and had secured Turkish military protection to move the entire Near East personnel and stores to Kars:

> Finding it will be impossible to proceed with the work or to receive assurance of safety under the Bolshevik regime, Director General Yarrow has secured Turkish military protection and is removing entire Near East personnel and stores to trains going to Kars. Thus he is forced to abandon orphans and American relief work of five years. Relief work in Armenia proper no longer possible but Yarrow hopes under the protection of Turks to continue relief of Armenians in Turkey and to obtain communications and supplies through Erzurum and Trebizond.[170]

The news and details of the exodus were carried in newspapers in the U.S. and Turkey at some length. A December 19 report in *The New York Times* was headlined "Near East Relief Workers Leave Armenia: Sent by Kemal Pasha to Kars, Where They Continue to Aid 7,000 Orphans":

> The American Near East Relief workers in Armenia have been evacuated under the personal supervision of Mustafa Kemal Pasha, the Turkish Nationalist leader, and have arrived safely in Kars, Transcaucasia, according to advices from Kars…
>
> …Mustapha Kemal has placed the Americans under the protection of the Turkish army occupying Kars.[171]

One week later, on December 27, *The New York Times* cited headlines that had appeared the same day in the press in Ankara entitled "American Soliciting Protection from Turks" quoting an excerpt from Director General Ernest Yarrow's letter to the Turkish military commander on the eastern front:

> Owing to the impossibility of the Near East Committee's workers continuing relief work in Alexandropol, I request you, on behalf of the committee, to offer them the protection of the Turkish Government and nation against the Bolsheviki, and also the evacuation of their supplies and medical comforts to Kars.[172]

At the departure of Alexandropol's NER, Clarence Ussher, working in Yerevan but not as a member of NER, had remained behind. Also remaining in Yerevan were three NER staff members: Yerevan District Commander James Dangerfield and relief workers Ralph Thistle and Charles Pierce. All three had remained at their posts in Yerevan, *The New York Times* reported, despite the establishment of a Bolshevik regime in Armenia on December 2, followed by the arrival of the RevKom three days later, and of Felix Dzerzhinsky's Cheka, the Soviet state security agency, the next day.[173] U.S. newspapers continued to cover the transfer of power in Armenia, the Sovietization of the Caucasus, its significance to the Allies and various predictions of the imminent collapse of communism.[174]

Upon arrival in Kars, Ernest Yarrow designated Kars as the new headquarters of NER's Caucasus Branch, replacing Alexandropol, and was given assurances that NER's work in orphan care would go forward as usual in Kars under Turkish occupation.[175] Yet no sooner had Yarrow settled in Kars, when on December 14, 1920, he received an official "Act," signed by the Armenian RevKom President Kasyan and People's Commissar of Foreign Affairs Bekzadyan, and delivered to Yarrow by NER Yerevan relief workers Dangerfield and Thistle.[176] The "Act" was an official invitation to NER to return to Armenia with full guarantees for their safety. It read, in part:

Yerevan, 14 December 1920

Finding the work of the American Near East Committee [NER] in Armenia useful and indispensable in the area of public assistance, the Revolutionary Committee of the Soviet Socialist Republic of Armenia considers the continuation and development of the work of said Committee very desirable.

To this effect, the Revolutionary Committee promises its aid and assistance, offers guarantees against expropriations, and invites the Soviet Military and Civil authorities of the Republic to accord aid and assistance to the leaders of said Committee in the performance of their duties.

The President of the Revolutionary Committee
   Signed: Kassian

The People's Commissar for Foreign Affairs
   Signed: A. Bekzadian

The Director of the Office
   Signed: Sarbeyan

Authentication: A. Tcherpashian
Authentication by the Secretary of the Plenipotentiary Representation of the S.S.R. in Georgia
   [signed] E. Assribec...ian]

Yarrow's answer came on January 4, 1921, from Kars,[177] detailing the reasons for which the NER had left Alexandropol, albeit unwillingly:

Dear Sir: In reply to your letter of recent date, I wish to thank you, on behalf of the Near East Relief, for your expression of sympathy and respect for the activities which we have been carrying on. I can assure you that it was with the greatest regret that our Committee felt itself compelled to withdraw from Alexandropol. This action was decided upon after due consideration, in which all the American personnel shared, and it was practically the unanimous opinion of all concerned that it would be impossible for us to continue and do any good under the conditions laid down before us.

Yarrow next listed the specific circumstances that had led to the decision to retreat from Alexandropol:

Our decision was made after the first conference with you, but it was delayed in execution, hoping that there might be some modification of your attitude which would make possible the continuance of our care for the orphans; but after the third conference it was decided that it would be impossible for us to remain.

In order that there may be no doubt as to the reasons for our withdrawal I shall state them briefly. You will find all of them formulated and clearly defined in the discussions at the three conferences we had.

First: There was a persistent and almost violent expression of suspicion regarding the purpose for which the Near East Relief had come to Armenia. It was continually hinted that the plain humanitarian motives actuating us were simply a cloak for some deep and sinister political intrigue. In answer to this point I state at once that the Near East Relief has not now, nor has it ever had, any connection with any political body, or even officially with the American Government except in so far as the American Government shows a friendly and helpful interest in any American activity, whether carried on at home or abroad, which is regulated by the fair laws of our land. During Colonel Haskell's regime there was a semi-official connection between the N.E.R. and the American Government, but this was not of a political nature, Colonel Haskell only acting as the agent of the American Government in the loan of $50,000 worth of food supplies to the Armenian Government.

Second: All the money expended by the N.E.R. was collected from the American people by individual contributions. Many of those contributing were children and people of the poorer classes who made a great personal sacrifice in giving. Those of the Near East Relief who were administering these funds in the Caucasus felt that a very sacred trust had been imposed upon them in properly distributing the money and supplies sent to them from America. In Alexandropol we were threatened with the seizure by force of these supplies sent for a definite purpose, and with the probability of their being used for other purposes. Our very self-respect demanded that we do everything in our power to safeguard these supplies and the interest of the Americans who had contributed them, and had made us their trustees.

Third: In the third conference the American personnel was actually threatened with forcible retention in Alexandropol, and subjection to the indignities of prison and enforced labor. We Americans had to come to the Caucasus to try to save a nation which was rapidly being decimated by starvation. This was accomplished, and then we turned our attention to the caring for and rearing of 20,000 orphan children, the plan being to carry them on for about ten years until the Armenian nation could get on its feet and take over the responsibility. You can imagine the shock that it was to us all when, instead of receiving a grateful acknowledgment for the work we were doing, we were faced with the possibility of being placed in restraint and of being punished if our actions were not pleasing to the Government.

But Yarrow was willing to put the guarantees being offered to the test, and planned to send two volunteers—Milton Brown and Clark Martin—to Alexandropol, and had already sent a group to Tiflis to receive directions from New York:

> I am sending back Mr. Brown and Mr. Martin, who have volunteered, under your guarantees, to carry on the activities at Kazatche Post until such time as a general understanding shall have been arrived at and a permanent policy decided upon regarding operations in your territory. You probably know that I have sent a Commission to Tiflis to get in touch with our New York Headquarters and with the Bolshevik representatives. When this commission has finished its sessions and has reported back to these Headquarters I can then let you know what our policy will be hereafter.

Your attitude toward the Near East Relief during the coming days will undoubtedly have its effect upon the decision in Tiflis.

Yours truly,
E. A. Yarrow

The two volunteers, Milton Brown and Clark Martin, had in fact planned to return to Alexandropol with or without NER's blessing, if necessary, and were in Alexandropol by January 9, 1921.[178]

Some personal details and interpretations of events Yarrow had described in his letter slowly found their way in the U.S. press. Administrator and missionary Harrison Maynard gave his account in a letter to his sister in Topeka, Kansas. The contents of the letter were summarized and quoted in *The Albuquerque Journal*:

> …Mr. Maynard wrote that they did not leave their posts until attempts to negotiate with the Reds failed and he and his family were placed under arrest…

> Mr. Maynard wrote: "It seems that the Armenians called in the Bolsheviks to save them. They came and had enough influence to keep the Turks from claiming the country as their own and from following the claim with their customary brutalities."

> "But they did not have enough strength or perhaps the truth is that they did not see it to their advantage to drive the Turks out. The result was that the surrounding region was occupied by Turkish troops while an Armenian-bolshevik government pretended to rule."

Maynard's letter to his sister had also contained details of the behavior of Turkish soldiers and the local RevKom in Alexandropol:

> …the Turkish soldiers individually relieved the citizens of their shoes and coats as they needed them,

while "the bolshevik government,"

> …was composed of youthful swollen heads, who straightway undertook to bolshevize our goods and institutions. They were insulting; threatening and acted like madmen.

Maynard had further added that,

> No one wanted to desert the good work for the orphans, but the bolsheviks were making that work impossible. As I said before a bolshevik is near akin to a madman. One morning they sent soldiers to assist us. The Turks drove them away with bayonets. During the day we were taken on in our own coaches to Kars. All the girl orphans there were to be looked after as long as possible and our great supplies were to be sent on to Kars where we had 6,000 orphans also. Two months' supplies were left at Polygon to let the bolsheviks see what they could do for the orphans.[179]

A second official memorandum from Soviet authorities, dated January 15, 1921, responded to the charges Yarrow had raised in his letter of January 4. The memorandum, issued by the representative of the Soviet Socialist Republic of Armenia (SSRA) in Tiflis was addressed to Ernest Yarrow with copies to American Counsel Moser in Tiflis; NER Tiflis representative Mr. Elmer; NER Istanbul representative Dr. MacCallum; NER New York Representative Mr. Vickrey; and NER Central Committee Representative Mr. Jaquith. It was signed by Daniel Shahverdyan, People's Commissar of Foreign Affairs and

Plenipotentiary Representative of the SSRA in Georgia, and SSRA Special Envoy and NER liaison Varazdat Deroyan, then in charge of NER's refugee department.[180] The signatories began with an affirmation of the Armenian RevKom's desire for NER's continued activities in Armenia, offering full guarantees that such activities would not meet a single obstacle or impediment:

> Considering the continuation of your Committee's work in Armenia most desirable, the RevKom of the Socialist Soviet Republic of Armenia has exerted every effort to ensure that no disruptions are introduced in its life and normal development.

The reason NER had been treated as it had been, they explained, was that while Alexandropol was under Turkish occupation, the Armenian RevKom's authority had been limited to Karakilisa, Etchmiadzin and Yerevan only. As evidence of good will toward NER, they pointed to the fact that they had helped James Dangerfield and Ralph Thistle travel from Yerevan to Alexandropol and Kars, sending with them the Act of December 14:

> …being completely cut off from Alexandropol, the RevKom was able to effectuate its position in practice only in Yerevan, Karakilisa and Etchmiadzin; and aiding in the travel of Captain Dangerfield and Mr. Thistle to Alexandropol and Kars, [the RevKom] sent with them the Act [adopted] on December 14, 1920 sent to NER General Director Captain Yarrow, a copy of which is attached.

As more evidence of good will towards NER, the signatories pointed out that they had extended financial assistance to NER's Yerevan orphanage in the amount of 50 million rubles:

> As evidence of such a [positive] disposition on the part of RevKom [toward NER], we can mention the fact that the British orphanage in Yerevan, abandoned by its leaders, was turned over to the local branch of NER and 50 million Armenian rubles were released to support its operational expenses.

More,

> …NER schools have been listed as schools exempt from the general law on the state takeover of all schools.

With respect to the confrontations and intimidations NER had experienced in November, the signatories continued, these had not been the work of the RevKom now in power in Yerevan, but by a local group of communists in Alexandropol that had acted without a mandate from the central government. The government had sent a delegate to Kars to clarify the situation to Yarrow in December, but the delegate had not been allowed to enter Alexandropol, and as a result, a delegation was sent to Tiflis to meet with NER officials there:

> During the transitioning days of the Turkish invasion and change of regime there occurred incidents in Alexandrabol that had an overwhelmingly local character, [and] did not correspond either to general Soviet policies or to the dispositions of the newly instituted authorities, and [those incidents] were caused by such personalities who had no mandate to speak in the name of the authorities.

To dissipate these misunderstandings and to reinstate the truth, at the end of December the People's Commissariat for Foreign Affairs of the S.S.R.A. sent a delegate to the General Plenipotentiary [of NER]; however this delegate returned from Alexandrabol since he was unable to get permission from the Turks to go to Kars.

On January 6 of the current year the People's Commissariat of Foreign Affairs sent a delegation to Tiflis to perform the same duties regarding the NER with the local plenipotentiary of the NER.

The memorandum also pointed out that the Polygon had been taken over not by the SSRA RevKom, but by the "personalities who had no mandate to speak in the name of authorities," referring to the local Communists in Alexandropol. The official delegation sent to Tiflis on January 6 was empowered by the legitimate RevKom to offer many guarantees and incentives, among them the guarantee that NER orphanages would be kept intact with their name, flag, and organization to return them to NER. The delegation was also empowered to grant any new requests and enter into new negotiations with NER, but asked that the meeting not be held in Kars, to which they had no access. According to the letter, the delegation was "empowered to declare there and everywhere,"

1. The December 14, 1920 ACT. [Declaration]

2. The RevKom of the SSR of Armenia has received nothing from the NER nor has it taken anything from the NER.

3. On the contrary, it has contributed to the expansion of NER's activities, [and] to its normal functioning and security.

4. The takeover of the Alexandrabol orphanages known as the "Polygon" by the local RevKom has been done without the knowledge of the SSRA RevKom, a circumstance which is explained solely by the abnormal situation and the lack of communication between Alexandrabol and Yerevan.

5. These orphanages will be preserved as they are, with their name, flag and organization until the first opportunity when these can be turned over to the NER.

6. In no place in Armenia have the activities of the NER been ended. In Yerevan the [NER] work is being led by Dr. Ussher and Mr. Pierce, in Karakilisa by Captain Grant, all members of the NER, and are happy to continue their work.

7. The delegation is empowered to make new proposals, to bring to a satisfactory conclusion the unpleasant events that have occurred, and to conduct negotiations for the purpose of meeting any demand or wish, with the NER plenipotentiary representative sent from New York or Istanbul by [NER] Caucasus General Representative Captain Yarrow for that purpose, in a convenient place, because the Turks do not provide any possibility to conduct negotiations in Kars.

In communicating all the above, we have the honor of waiting for a response, and for the opportunity to reach an agreement with your representative regarding the venue and timing of such a meeting.

Plenipotentiary Representative of the Soviet Socialist Republic of Armenia in Georgia,
/Daniel Shahverdian/

SSRA Special Envoy to NER
/Varazdat Deroyan/

[Seal of the SSRA Plenipotentiary Representation in Georgia]

"To Abandon Is a Crime..."

Clarence Ussher had remained in Yerevan when NER had withdrawn. He had continued to work independently of the NER and had also agreed to look after the British orphanage and hospital, when British Committee representative H. Harcourt had fled the country in early November.[181] For a few weeks, Ussher hosted the Englishman Oliver Baldwin, who had in August 1920 been invited by Prime Minister Alexander Khatisian to help train the Armenian Army. Baldwin had chosen to stay on after Armenia's Sovietization, and was a guest of Clarence Ussher's for a few weeks, and during that time he had helped Ussher run NER's orphanages in Yerevan, with a few hundred orphans in each. "Our staff consisted of Armenian doctors and managers, many of whom had been educated in American missionary schools in Turkey or in the United States," Baldwin wrote, but

> Had doctor Ussher not stepped into the breach and taken over from those Americans who fled the country, the orphans would have starved, the stores been pillaged by the Red troops and the prestige of America sunk as low as that of Great Britain.
>
> For all in despair, for all true patriots, for all Social Revolutionaries, that faded American standard over his house meant the corner-stone of kindness and courage.[182]

After Armenia's sovietization Clarence Ussher enjoyed the protection of the SSRA government and received, on December 15, written guarantees that American property would remain intact. He was deeply concerned, however, that the imminent winter would wreak havoc on the isolated population of Alexandropol, and appealed to both the Soviet authorities in Armenia and NER. On December 17, 1920, he urged Commissar of Foreign Affairs A. Bekzadyan to grant extraterritoriality to Americans and American institutions, to arrive at some agreement with NER, to publicize it, and thereby enable the continuation of relief. "Honorable Sir," he addressed Bekzadyan,

> Permit me to express my thanks to you and the Bolshevik Government of Armenia for the courtesies and consideration shown to Americans and American institutions in Armenia and especially for the written guarantees of the inviolability of American property received from the present Government on the fifteenth instant.
>
> Americans working in Turkey have enjoyed extraterritoriality for many years without abusing their privilege as guests of the Government. This extraterritoriality has done much to encourage the American people to contribute generously toward the development of the country and the existence of its most needy

people. In this days [sic] of revolution and change with consequent interruption of communication it is natural that friends in America should have some anxiety as to the welfare of Americans and of the benevolent institutions to which the proletariat of America has contributed with considerable sacrifice. Anything which will tend to reassure them will encourage further benevolence and strengthen the friendship which has always existed between America and Great Russia of which Armenia is a sister Republic. If some such agreement could be made officially with the American Government and given wide publicity it might prove of benefit to both countries.[183]

Ussher also pled with NER's leadership in Tiflis, Istanbul, and New York, urging continuance of relief. NER headquarters in New York heard from Dangerfield on December 27 that the "Erivan Government shows highest consideration to Americans and gives us written guarantees to assist us and never to requisition our supplies."[184] For his part, Ussher explained to U.S. Ambassador Moser in Tiflis and NER headquarters in New York on December 26, that Yarrow and the NER staff were in Kars, that they had been invited back through written guarantees but that Yarrow had blocked NER's return. In Yerevan, he continued, the current government was doing its best to safeguard the Americans remaining in Yerevan and treated them with great affection. "The new government," reported Ussher, had been different from what had been expected, and "has been very moderate." Ussher was sure that if the moderate attitude continued, the country would soon be satisfied with the new government.[185] With the predicament of thousands of orphans and refugees becoming direr, Ussher insisted, on January 5, 1921, that it was

> …necessary that the NER negotiate with the government…The continuation of assistance and continuation of orphanage care in Erivan, Alexandropol and Karakilisa is imperative…[186]

Baldwin recalled that NER headquarters in New York had remained silent, and that he had told Ussher "it was useless to expect further help," but to which Ussher had always said "I can never believe that my countrymen would desert Armenia in her difficulties. Help will come."[187]

Ussher's pleas came amidst newspaper reports in the U.S. about the worsening refugee situation. On January 15, 1921, *The New York Times* reported that "more than 200,000 Armenian refugees between Kars and Alexandropol" were dying due to lack of food and fuel. Transportation had ceased entirely, the article continued, "anarchy stalks," and famine was inevitable unless shipments continued.[188] Ussher's pleas to headquarters were urgent. The orphans in the Caucasus were in more need than ever, thousands of refugees in Alexandropol were starving, he cabled on February 2, 1921, and added

> The soviet authority help in a friendly fashion. To abandon is a crime…Yarrow has left us. Encourage us.[189]

Recalling the predicament of orphans who had remained in Alexandropol when NER had retreated to Kars was one of those orphans, 13-year-old Ghazar Gh. Gevorgyan. "The orphanage," he recalled during an interview decades later,

> ...was sponsored by the American Relief Committee and the manager was Mr. Earo [Yarrow] an American, who went away with some American men and women, when Soviet power was established in Armenia...
>
> We, the orphans, were deprived of our guardians. We wandered in the fields looking for mouse nests which we destroyed, hoping to find some wheat there; these mice carried the typhus infection, so many of us got infected.[190]

Also pleading for assistance from NER and British officials in Tiflis was Varazdat Deroyan. The substance of Deroyan's meeting with a British official in Tiflis was received at the Foreign Office in London on February 1, 1921:

> An Armenian named Deroyan formerly working for Near East Relief and well thought of by them who is continuing relief work under Bolshevik auspices has come to Tiflis to beg us and the Americans to continue relief.

The author of the memo noted that in the area of Alexandropol, "the Turks" were "showing signs of intention to curtail relief work" and were "making increasing demands on relief supplies for their troops." Conditions in the part of the country controlled by soviet authorities differed, ran the report:

> In Bolshevik half of Armenia, Armenian Bolsheviks in power have so far displayed moderation, have committed no excesses and have permitted relief work to continue at Erivan and Karakilisa...allotting 50 million roubles for relief at Erivan. They have officially written to American Near East Relief begging them to continue work and promising protection. They offer same to Harcourt.[191]

The report ended with the recommendation to resume relief in the form of provisions and clothing. About two weeks later, on February 17, *The New York Times* summarized the report sent to the Foreign Office, adding that the forces of Mustafa Kemal Pasha had occupied the refugee camps at Alexandropol and were demanding orphanage supplies for their troops.[192]

Exodus from Kars to Alexandropol: *"Packed into Boxcars Like Sardines in a Can, Only Worse"*

During December 1920 and January 1921, amidst negotiations, cable dispatches and official letters between Tiflis, New York, Kars and Yerevan, the NER staff in Kars waited for a decision from New York, as it continued its work under increasing duress.[193] As in Alexandropol, the early protection and freedom promised by Turkish forces in Kars had been short-lived. Turkish authorities had soon mounted pressure on NER's administration in Kars with requests for provisions and supplies reserved for the orphans in the Kars warehouses, part of which they had helped NER transport from Alexandropol. At that time, watching the assistance of the Turkish army in expediting the transfer of supplies from Alexandropol to Kars, Elsie Kimball and a few NER staff members had been suspicious of Turkish helpfulness:

> All the remaining supplies have been brought to Kars for our orphans here, and the Turks helped to get them here. Some of us said at the time that there was method

in the efforts to assist us—that probably, just as soon as the supplies reached Kars, the Turks would commandeer them for their own use. And it certainly looks suspicious…[194]

Apart from demands on the supplies and provisions in the orphanage warehouses, Turkish officials interfered in the management and operations of the orphanages through restrictions. Elsie Kimball described some of them in her letter of Dec. 15, 1920, to her family in New York:

> …We serve only two meals a day, and even those two are very scanty and very poor in quality. So the orphans are in excellent condition for the development of disease…Besides, they haven't enough to wear…

> …We are carrying on our work under tremendous handicaps. Not only is there a lack of supplies of food, but there is a shortage of wood and water…everything depends upon the cooperation we get from the Turks in that direction. They do what all conquering armies do—grab everything that they can lay their hands on.

And, she continued,

> …the little wood that we had laid by, they have forbidden us to use, except in small doses which they dole out to us. They put seals on our wood warehouses and refuse to let us take out a single armful without first going through a whole lot of red tape with the government. Since they captured Kars, our water supply has been cut off, either because the men whom they have put in to operate the machinery that pumps the water don't know how to do the thing, or because there is a scarcity of water and they wish to divert it for their own use, leaving us without a drop.

And, although "the Pasha has forbidden any more looting,"

> …his soldiers, or other raiders, continue to go to our city orphanages and force the orphans to pass blankets, sheets, food—anything they want—out through the windows…

So you see, everything is in a mix-up…[195]

Kimball's letter a few weeks later, dated January 9, 1921, revealed that NER's stay in Kars was soon to come to an end since "the Turks are constantly asking Mr. Yarrow when he is going to move the orphans."[196] At the same time, NER was requested to provide provisions from NER warehouses for the 2,000 Turkish orphans to be transferred from Erzurum to Kars:

> The Turks have 2,000 orphans (Moslems) down in Erzeroum whom they are moving up here to Kars, and the other day Kasim [Kazim Karabekir] Pasha, the Commanding General here, asked Mr. Yarrow and Mr. White for supplies to care for these children. Mr. Yarrow replied that the commodities of which we have a surplus, the Turks might use, but before we could give up any of our other supplies, of which we have only enough, at present, to carry our orphanages over until spring, it would be necessary to receive the approval of the central office in New York.[197]

In reply, the Pasha had suggested that, Kimball wrote,

> ...under such circumstances, we could move out 2,000 of our orphans and send them to Alexandropol or elsewhere. Then we could care for the 2,000 Turkish orphans that are beginning to arrive in Kars.[198]

The orphans, wrote Kimball, were receiving two scanty meals a day and looked "just as emaciated as when they were first taken over, after the massacres," and the death rate was high. Then she added,

> I could give you many instances of their ravenous hunger. Here is one: Two days ago, when I went into the kitchens, I saw three boys kneeling down on the floor with their noses in a pile of dirt, in which they were madly groveling for a few crumbs of bread which had been swept there by the girl who takes care of the corridors. When this girl saw me coming, she said, "Quick, get up! Here comes Miss Kimball." But they paid no attention to her, and when she tried to pull them away, they crawled back on their hands and knees and snatching a handful of dirt, ran away with it, crunching as they went.

> We have so little water that we can bathe the children only once a month, or perhaps not so often as that, and we haven't sufficient clothes to go around...Every drop of water we get has to be drawn in buckets from the river, and it is a long hard climb over steep hills, in freezing weather...[199]

In view of the difficult circumstances, added Kimball,

> ...Mr. Yarrow announced yesterday that he would permit anybody to leave today—anybody who did not care to remain longer...I haven't had time yet to transcribe the rest of my letter relating to the Turkish invasion...I am writing this letter reservedly, for it may be censored...

Quite apart from inconveniences NER staff had to endure, they were also compelled to provide entertainment to Turkish officers who frequently visited the American staff and wanted to learn American-style dances. Among the officers, wrote Kimball, was Nuri Pasha, the brother of fugitive Enver Pasha:

> Quite frequently we have two or three celebrities here at the house, in the evening. Nuri Pasha and Kemal Bey, two Turks high in the ranks...visit us very often and they are learning to dance American style. Nuri Pasha is brother of the world-famous Enver Pasha, who is being sought everywhere by the Allies. Enver is somewhere in this country, cleverly evading the Allies, and never remaining in one place long enough to get caught...[200]

In fact, Nuri Pasha was the stepbrother of Enver Pasha, and a general in the Ottoman army, who during WWII would be the founder of the Turkestan Legion of the *Schutzstaffel*, or the *SS*, the special police force in Nazi Germany established as personal bodyguards of Adolf Hitler in 1925 and which during WWII would administer the concentration camps.

Despite restrictions and mounting demands, NER continued orphan care in Kars until the final order from Turkish officials at the end of January that NER move all the orphans out of Kars to Alexandropol, effective immediately. "Then began a conjecture as to what we—the American personnel—should do," wrote Elsie Kimball. But it was just at that time that Harold Barton arrived in Kars to discuss the future with the American staff:

> ...Mr. Barton arrived Wednesday morning, we had our conference that noon, and he told us then that the New York office had, through its representative, Mr. Jaquith, who was just out here a short time ago, instructed us that we were not to function under the Bolsheviks.[201]

Barton had told the staff that funds were

> ...difficult to secure and the Caucasus Branch of the N.E.R. must cease to operate. Therefore, we are going to leave Kars just as soon as we can get the children moved. The Bolsheviks will have to take care of the orphans, in Armenia.[202]

Since they couldn't stay in Kars, Kimball continued, and because "working under the Bolsheviks" was not an option, the orphans would have to be moved to Alexandropol "as rapidly as possible" and then the staff would leave for Constantinople for reassignment to duty elsewhere. She estimated that it would take about six weeks to complete operations, but longer, should there be difficulties in transportation.

By February 1, many of the personnel, including Ernest Yarrow and his family, had left for Constantinople, leaving 13 Americans, including Elsie Kimball, to carry on the work to a finish, following which they would leave by way of Erzurum and Trebizond. No plea or counterargument about the difficulties involved in moving children in the middle of winter changed the Turkish position.

At the end, the children were moved to Alexandropol during the months of February and March, on a journey that was perilous to all and fatal to many, especially the younger ones. "It was night and raining heavily," remembered 12-year-old Araksi Pluzyan who was among the children:

> Barefooted, with one shirt on, we were running toward the railroad at Kars. Our leader was Miss Beach. She was constantly calling, "don't fall behind, just run." [But] Turkish bands attacked the fleeing children and kept taking away the older girls and boys.

It was midnight when the train arrived, Pluzyan continued, and the children, drenched and shivering, were finally loaded on the train to Alexandropol:

> The train moved toward Leninakan [at that time still Alexandropol]. After we passed one station, Turkish bandits attacked the train, battered the doors and pulled away many of the boys and girls who had been sitting close to the doors and took them away in the dark of night. I remember the bitter cries and screams for help from those children like it was today... But somehow, the train moved on to Leninakan.[203]

Also on one of the trains transporting the children to Alexandropol was nine-year-old Heghine (Elena) Abrahamyan:

> They brought us in freight wagons. It was a few hour's way, but it took us several days. The wagons were sealed from outside; we were inside. The small ones could not bear all that suffering from hunger and thirst. They kept dying. The corpses were thrown out of the window for fear of infection.[204]

By April 5, NER had evacuated Kars completely, except for one member, Captain Dangerfield, who stayed behind for a few weeks longer to attend to final details. Two of the relief workers—Caroline Silliman and Myrtle Shane—returned to Alexandropol, and eight left for Constantinople via Trebizond. It had taken two months to move the children and the 1,200 Armenian personnel from Kars to Alexandropol. The May 14 issue of *Near East Relief*, edited by NER and printed in Constantinople for private circulation, announced that some American relief workers had left Kars for Constantinople, via Sarikamish, Erzurum, and Trebizond and had enjoyed the warm hospitality from Turkish officials on the way:

> ...The trip by narrow gauge railroad from Sarikamish to Erzeroum over the snowclad mountains was very beautiful. In Erzeroum, the Turkish officials treated the Americans as the guests of the town, showing the party every courtesy. The trip from Erzeroum to Trebizond was by wagon with Turkish guards assigned for protection. Telegrams were sent ahead, and at each point the party was received by officials who had been notified of their approach. These officials did everything in their power to make the party comfortable...[205]

There was no mention of the treatment NER and the orphans had been subjected to in Kars.

Among the group on their way to Constantinople was Elsie Kimball. "We're on our way again," she wrote from Trebizond on April 25, 1921,

> ...The Americans in the Caucasus are as nomadic as the Kurds...The Turks ordered us to send our six thousand Armenian orphans (1,000 had died during the winter after the Turks came in) to Alexandropol, which, by that time...[was] ruled by the Turks...

> So we spent two months evacuating the children and the Armenian personnel—who numbered about twelve hundred—and in shipping supplies to Alexandropol, closing accounts, etc. Each train that went out carried an average of six hundred children and personnel—packed into boxcars like sardines in a can, only worse.[206]

When NER had begun to move the supplies back to Alexandropol, it had encountered obstacles:

> We had troubles galore, especially in getting our supplies, which the Turks wanted for themselves and which they continually requisitioned for their army or their schools or their hospitals or their institutions...You simply can't imagine the difficulties that we encountered from October 30, the day the Turks entered Kars, until April 5, when we left Kars...

> It was a winter that none of us can ever forget...

> ...the orphans are in a very weakened condition, owing to a lack of proper nourishment during the last few months when we have been trying to conserve food and make it stretch out to the time when we should be able to get more. Just a little while ago, the children were dying in Alexandropol at the rate of twenty a day, and now the death rate must be even worse.

And yet, she added, more adversities awaited the orphans in Alexandropol:

And these hardships are not ended, either, for in Alexandropol, at this very moment, are 18,000 orphans and many Armenian personnel facing starvation and suffering from disease on account of the lack of supplies, which, we understand are plentiful in Constantinople, but which cannot be shipped...[207]

Return to Alexandropol: *"No Food at Any Price"*

As in Kars, conditions in Alexandropol had been deteriorating since November. A peace treaty had been signed between the Armenian government and Turkish commander Karabekir Pasha, and following the terms of the treaty, Armenian forces had withdrawn from Alexandropol by November 7. The treaty had also stipulated that Turkey would protect Armenia, help its development and safeguard its sovereignty.[208] But written guarantees had been reneged on almost immediately. Two days later the Pasha had requested a list of all the civil and government warehouses and their contents in Alexandropol, and within days, warehouses were emptied and their contents removed to Turkey. Next had followed the removal of all transportable goods such as roofs, window frames and panes, doors, etc., and their passage to Turkey, along with the province's cattle, horses, sheep, plows and anything that could be transported, for the second time in less than three years.[209]

Looting became prevalent in Alexandropol and its province. According to a March 19, 1921, report from the Chief of Police in Alexandropol addressed to the Mayor of the city, looting and crime by Turkish soldiers by day or by night had become uncontrollable:

> The soldiers break doors, windows, they even break through walls, and rush inside and loot; if rebuked, they kill. During the day they enter homes, pull people out and take them away as laborers, take off their clothes, beat them, and then they set them free...
>
> ...We ask that you enter negotiations with the Turkish authorities to put an end to these incidents, because of which the city's inhabitants live in a state of horror...[210]

The condition in the villages of the province was worse. The chief of Chorlu village about 15 miles north of Alexandropol, for example, reported that

> ...all the villages have been looted, there are no goods, no seeds nor clothing nor fuel. The streets of the villages are full of corpses, and to top it off famine and the cold...claim victim after victim. The situation becomes even more unbearable when Turkish soldiers and mobs mock their victims, brutalize them in even more horrifying ways, force parents to hand over their daughters and sons to them so they can be raped and killed. Turkish soldiers take away women and girls under the age of 40, and deport the males to areas around Kars, Sarikamish and Erzurum..."[211]

When Oliver Baldwin toured Alexandropol in the first week of March, the city was

> ...almost empty of inhabitants. Here and there an aged Armenian tailored for the Turkish soldiery or baked Turkish cakes or cobbled shoes, but the rest of the population were scattered, massacred, or living in caves by the side of Alagöz,

waiting for death. The silence of the town was enhanced by the snow in the streets, and our rumbling wheels were the only sounds, except for the soft patter of a Turkish soldier's feet on the pavement.

And, he continued,

The selling of blankets carried out by the N.E.R. in exchange for sheep had certainly transformed the Turkish soldiery, for in the place of ragged military uniforms or civilian clothes were now neatly-fitting khaki jackets of American blanket cloth.[212]

After his tour of the city, Baldwin had visited with Milton Brown and Martin Clark, and the three had stayed up late into the night. Brown had read excerpts from Madame Captanian's *Les memoirs d'une deportée Arménienne*. Brown had next spoken of how an Armenian translation of Homer had been discovered half completed in the ruins of Erzurum, how Kars had fallen, and how NER women had stayed at their posts in Kars after the Turkish occupation.[213]

The events of those months had been predicted, at least in part, by some observers of the Caucasus. Paxton Hibben, once an NER supporter who later distanced himself from the organization, had warned that the peace agreement "the Armenian Government was forced to sign with the victorious Turks," simply meant that

... the one great railway junction of Armenia, without possession of which Armenia can neither be fed, armed or defended, is to remain in Turkish hands, together with the central storehouses, not only of the Armenian Army, but of the American Near East Relief Committee...

"This means, also," Hibben had warned further,

... that the former Russian barracks that once quartered 90,000 Russian soldiers and that now houses 10,000 Armenian children under the care of the American women workers of the Near East Relief, become Turkish property...[214]

Soon after the withdrawal of Turkish forces from the provice of Alexandropol on April 22, 1921, a special committee of the Armenian RevKom compiled a full inventory of material and human loss incurred by the province while under occupation. According to the findings of the committee, between November 1920 and April 1921, 34,000 had died of starvation; 50,000 had been violated, among them 20,000 girls; 60,000 had been killed; and 8,000 had been enslaved. Of the province's large and small corneous animals 105,000 heads, along with agricultural implements and products in the value of 143,416,500 rubles worth of goods, had been taken south.[215]

In her letter home in June 1921, Elsie Kimball, who had returned to Armenia, described the vestiges of one incident, the massacre of 3,000 women and children. These were discovered by some American NER workers in late spring 1921, who

... came upon a gorge, not a great distance away, where three thousand Armenian women and children had been massacred by the Turks last November, when Kars and Alexandropol were taken... When the snows melted and the ice broke in the spring, the discovery was made by two or three of our American men. Hundreds of bodies were seen floating down the river; others were half buried in the banks, legs, arms and heads sticking out everywhere as evidence of the hurried attempt of the turks [sic] to conceal their victims. The indications are that these Armenians were herded together in Alexandropol or some town close by, driven out to this spot, about twelve miles away, and then shot or stabbed by Turkish soldiers. All this simply serves to reinforce the opinion of the Americans in Kars and Alexandropol that a great many more Armenians were massacred than we were aware of at the time.[216]

A few months later, Kimball noted that one could "scarcely move about this country without seeing signs of destruction, either of life or of property."[217]

The day after the Turkish forces had left, the American relief workers received their first letters from home. On that day, Milton Brown received 12 letters from his parents in Malden, Massachusetts, and replied with a long letter of his own, dated April 22, 1921, excerpts of which appeared in *The Boston Daily Globe* on July 17, 1921.[218] Written candidly and with immediacy, Brown's letter spanned the events that befell the orphans and NER relief workers in Kars and Alexandropol and offered insights into a complex situation that is largely absent from available official NER reports and publications:

> Dear Mother and Father—Today we received the first letters from the outside world for over four months. The Turkish occupation has shut us off completely from any communication, with Tiflis, even…So much has happened since I last wrote you that I would better repeat myself a bit than to omit, as I know that you must be interested in the situation here.

Brown began his narrative with NER's encounters with the local Alexandropol group that Karabekir Pasha had installed on November 17:

> …we were carrying on with little difficulty under the Turks when I last wrote, but the Bolsheviki had just been installed locally, under the guidance of the Turks, and we had been through the usual process of being arrested, etc. all of which seems now like a grand farce.

Brown continued his narrative with the events after NER's relocation to Kars; orders from Turkish authorities in Kars to move the orphans from Kars to Alexandropol; his return to Alexandropol with Clark Martin; and preparations in Alexandropol to receive the orphans arriving from Kars. He explained to his parents that the reason the children "were ordered by Kaisin [sic] Pasha to be sent to Alexandropol" was so that

> …the Turks might say at the Moscow peace conference that there were absolutely no Armenians, children or otherwise, in Turkish territory.

> So we had to move those poor, little freezing kiddies in freight cars as best we could with what supplies the Turks chose to let come with them to Alexandropol, and endeavor to house these additional 6,000 with the 11,000 already there.

He and Martin Clark, Brown explained, had been in Alexandropol preparing for the arrival of the orphans from Kars:

> Our warehouses had been turned literally over night into dormitories, and while we had no wood to build fires, we had plenty of blankets and a few extra mattresses. We figured by putting four small children in one bed that we could house them.

Brown also referred to the orders issued by NER headquarters for a total evacuation from the Caucasus when Armenia was Sovietized:

> ...we received word that the Near East must quit its activities at once in this now Bolshevik country—that the United States and its people didn't intend to send relief to any such parts.

> ...This certainly looked pretty cruel, with over 17,000 little mouths waiting to be fed by the Americans, and no Government in Alexandropol excepting the Turks, to turn them over to.

Acting on orders from headquarters in New York, where it had been decided to end all NER work in the Caucasus, H. C. Jaquith, then NER Assistant General Secretary, had sold the few reserve supplies remaining in NER's warehouses in Batum. The orders to stop all work in the Caucasus had put the American personnel in a quandary, Brown continued. "What to do we did not know," but at the end,

> It was finally decided that the game was up and we should have to abandon the children to sure death. Telegrams were sent, but never reached their destinations, begging that we be allowed to continue at least to distribute the food and clothing already on hand.

Brown explained that he and Martin had been determined to return to Alexandropol, and had asked Yarrow

> ...if we might sever our official connection with the Near East Relief and remain with the children as ordinary civilians, merely to supervise the distribution of supplies, and as possible moral effect on the native personnel in our employ.

> They [the native personnel] had told us that if we left they would be forced to abandon their work for fear of the Turks. I am not writing this with any idea of self-inflation, but merely to show how much the Armenians counted on the American influence over the Turks.

Yarrow had agreed and without the least hesitation had said, "Go ahead and stay for a few days until I can get to Tiflis myself, and I'll give you final orders from there." Their act had been crucial in sparing the lives of the thousands of orphans who had remained in Alexandropol. Oliver Baldwin who had passed through Alexandropol on his way to Kars, noted that

> ...only the presence of the NER saved a massacre of all the children, which would have resulted in Turkey saying to the world: "There is no reason to give back Alexandropol to the Armenians: it is a Turkish town. Besides, there are no Armenians in Alexandropol."[219]

When they had heard from Yarrow, a month later, the instructions were "to continue the work if we were still alive." Yarrow's message also included a change in policy from headquarters, informing them

> ...that our New York office had changed its decision, and wanted above everything, Bolshevik Government or not, to keep these children alive.

The reversal in NER's policies to resume relief work in Armenia was in contrast to its decision a few weeks earlier when it had decided to stop all relief work in Soviet Armenia. In a letter dated January 4, 1921, to Boghos Nubar

Pasha, President of the Western Armenian National Delegation in Paris, NER General Secretary Charles Vickrey had found it interesting

> ...that the position which you [Boghos Nubar Pasha] take...with reference to Turkish Armenia, as the center or heart of the new Armenian State, is the same position that Mr. Montgomery [Secretary of the Armenia-America Society] has been taking...

And, he had added,

> We were greatly disturbed here in the States, by the political change which in the eyes of the general public, obliterated the Armenian republic...We are inclined with you to take the position that Turkish Armenia must now be recognized as the Armenian Nation...[220]

As he concluded his letter, Milton Brown described the explosion that shook orphans and relief workers alike just before Turkish forces left:

> ...the Turks have taken their departure to their new boundary lines, after a terrible explosion in the fortress, which blew every pane of glass in the town and our orphanage to bits. Lucky Spring is here. They didn't leave as a result of the explosion, either. I shall write you details later...

The detonation had been set at the arsenal of the city by the Russian fortress, not far from the Polygon. Myrtle Shane, who had returned from Kars, was inspecting the orphanages at the Polygon when she

> ...glanced up and right there before my eyes was the grandest sight I ever expect to witness,- seemingly just beyond our farthest building. I cannot describe it, one great mass of rose-colored flame, a mass not yet burst. I was transfixed, could not utter a sound...A moment later the sound of the explosion reached my ears and then I screamed...and started to run...The cry of the children brought me to my senses and I set to work to stop the stampede. But...I discovered that they were stampeding the other direction to see the cause of it all, and since there were other powder houses in the fort where the explosion had occurred, some little distance from our building, but in plain view, the danger was not yet over. Finally we got them all corralled and at the other end of the premises...All our windows were smashed...[221]

Among the children running toward the explosion was 13-year-old Mihran Hovhannisyan:

> ...A black cloud engulfed our orphanages. We were all running towards the hills...It was only Dr. Yerznkyan who made us turn back saying "I am with you, don't be afraid." He gathered all the orphans around him and brought them back to the orphanages...[222]

As the transfer of orphans to Alexandropol was completed, supplies and provisions were running dangerously low. Alexandropol and its province had been under siege for months, no new supplies had been allowed to enter the City of Orphans, and Turkish authorities had used some of the supplies to maintain the Turkish army. When Milton Brown cabled headquarters on April 8, 1921, it was to ask for urgent necessities for an orphanage of more than 17,000 children.[223] "Our ration is now so small," he explained, "that all orphans and workers are underfed." Topping his list was flour: the orphanage needed 2,300 sacks per month, but at the time of the writing there was only 10 days' supply left. Next on the list was lard, of which 40 barrels were used per month, and the six barrels that remained were being used for the treatment of scabies, only; there was no milk for general orphan use, and the small amount of evaporated milk at hand was being used to make yogurt for enteritis cases and for the very small children; there were no vegetables; fresh meat had not been available since January 1, and of the other food items—rice, sugar and beans—there was either a very small amount left or none at all. "With no fat, no meat, no milk, and a scarcity of flour," he warned, "healthy children would be a miracle." To his list of necessities, Brown added a medical report from Dr. Russell B. Main: mortality rates were currently very high in Alexandropol. The chief underlying causes were severe enteritis, malnutrition amounting to semi-starvation, and exposure to damp and cold. There was also a mild epidemic of typhus and some cases of smallpox.[224]

Dr. Main had returned to Alexandropol sometime in early March 1921 and was the only American physician in charge at the time. Oliver Baldwin described him as a "delightful" man who consistently fought many diseases among the orphans:

> With him I went to round the hospitals. Hundreds and hundreds of Armenian orphans were being cared for here, and the strange diseases they suffered from beggar description…every disease that starvation, exposure, dirt and fatigue can cause was found amongst the patients: alopecia, anaemia, cankers, many forms of ringworm, oedema, ophthalmia, consumption, catalesy, pleurisy, rickets, cataract, erysipelas, chlorosia, worms: all were present, and sometimes a mixture of many, and at other times a disease that baffled. Against these diseases Dr. Mayne [sic] consistently fought.[225]

During the months of isolation, with no new supplies coming in, the death toll among the orphans had soared. According to one souce, an average of 10 children died at the Polygon from disease and lack of food during NER's absence.[226] The employees at the Kazachi orphanages had held a mass meeting and selected a committee to inform Milton Brown that they preferred to donate the amount of their salaries to help support the orphans. "Also a great thing," added Brown, further praising the generosity of the Armenian employees, was that

> …they voluntarily cut down their food ration in half. This was entirely the idea of the employees themselves.
>
> Owing to the impossibility for some time to move supplies forward to Alexandropol, the question of food for the thousands of orphans became very grave, and this generous act on the part of the native workers was a great help at a very trying time.[227]

But still, the children "were living on cocoa and one-fourth fruit for breakfast, bean soup with five or six beans apiece, and one-half fruit and bread for dinner and no supper."[228] Cables to headquarters in New York followed one another in rapid succession in April and May, sounding the alarm of imminent danger from starvation. MacCallum's cable from Constantinople to NER headquarters in New York was direct and to the point:

> ...Total orphans Alexandropol 18,000. Supplies Alexandropol allow half-rations April three to April thirty.
>
> After May first nothing.[229]

Ernest Yarrow's cable, published in the April 23, 1921, issue of *The New York Times* highlighted the urgent need for additional shipments. Complete freedom of operation and full guarantees had been pledged to NER, the cable read, and 32 Americans had returned to the Caucasus. Yarrow found the terms offered by the new government "satisfactory" and such that would make NER operations "easier than formerly." The relationship with the new government was "friendly and helpful," but, he urged,

> Near East Relief food supplies are exhausted...
>
> Situation in Armenia very critical. Send food supplies to Batum immediately. Vessels will be granted free passage.

Then he added:

> This is an opportunity for Near East Relief to establish relations between Russia and the rest of the world should this prove desirable.[230]

Informing the U.S. Department of State of the guarantees offered was U.S. Ambassador to Italy Robert Underwood Johnson, in his cable of April 19, 1921:

> Foreign Office informs me that the following telegram has been received from the Italian Minister to the Armenian Republic now residing at Tiflis:
>
> "The commander in chief of the Russian forces of the Caucasus has assured me in the most formal manner and has urgently begged me to inform the persons concerned that the supplies forwarded by the American Government or any other government to Armenia will be scrupulously forwarded in their entirety to Erivan by direct trains from Batum upon their arrival without subtracting anything therefrom on account of restrictions or for other purposes. Armenia is really in an unfortunate and piteous condition beyond any belief. Humanitarian measures are necessary, everything is lacking. The following are of especially urgent necessity: flour to make bread, sugar, preserves, new or old clothing, underwear and medical supplies."[231]

To put the guarantees of safe passage to test, the relief ship *Quequen* sailed from Constantinople carrying 350 tons of flour, rice, beans, and milk. This was a trial ship to see if, after such a long interval, transportation was still possible from Constantinople to Batum, and its arrival date was unknown.[232] But, "on the morning of April 22," wrote relief worker Veronica Harris,

> ...we had one-half day's ration of flour for the orphanages and a few beans and rice. It was not possible to further reduce the ration. We simply had to issue it and then, for the following day, we planned to use for the children what American personnel commissary supplies we had left and after that—nothing.

That day, Harris had gone to find the mayor of the city to see if he could suggest anything:

At the mayor's office we were informed that he was at the station; that the Turks had withdrawn in the night and that the Bolsheviks from Russia were sending a train in, the first trainload of Russian Red soldiers. We started down to the station but could not find the mayor, so we waited for the train. When it drew in there were only five cars, all decorated with branches of trees, and with Russian soldiers all over the cars.

We had speculated whether there might possibly be a case or two of supplies for us, praying that the impossible would happen.

Then,

A man in American uniform appeared at the door of a car, and when he saw us he jumped off, saluted, and said in a matter of fact tone, "I have two cars with supplies for the Near East Relief." I am ashamed to say that being a woman, I cried.[233]

MacCallum's cable from Constantinople dated April 28, 1921, confirmed that the *Quequen* had arrived safely, that he had purchased $80,000 worth of flour and milk and the balance of the supplies weighing 1,700 tons would be shipped that week, along with nine women relief workers.[234] "Not much for 17,000," Brown commented in his letter to his parents, "but we are thinking of the five loaves and two fishes and the next lot of supplies which Capt. Yarrow promises within a short time." Jaquith, in turn, cabled headquarters on April 22:

NEAREST NY
250 Rush shipload corn products especially cornmeal as American answer Cable 249. Famine will increase in geometrical proportion with lapse of time. This is first opportunity since November sixth to transport food from Batoum to Alexandropol and Erivan.[235]

On the same day, April 22, Charles Vickrey cabled Constantinople:

Neareast Constantinople
…Expect ship first week in May one thousand tons rice onethousand tons wheat-flour sixhundred tons cornmeal cornflour hominy thirtytons sugar fivehundred tons beans fivethousand cases cornsyrup from New York and New Orleans direct Batoum subject your instruction at Constantinople additional thousand tons wheatflour from Pacific Coast June First.[236]

Then, on May 3, 1921, Jaquith cabled to confirm the arrival of some supplies and to relay positive news about the Soviet authorities:

Immediate transport saved 18,000 orphans seven Americans at Alexandropol where food arrived same day last half-rations exhausted. Soviets guarantee near east unrestricted access to Georgia, Armenia and Azerbaijan. With absolute protection and direction of orphanages and supplies, latter duty free. Soviet Transcaucasian policy surprisingly moderate, apparently wishful…[237]

In the meantime, back in Yerevan, Clarence Ussher had been working in isolation. News from him had been scarce, but resumed in early April. In the first communication from Ussher on April 1st, he reported on acute starvation. "The prospect is dark," he wrote, "I am alone now." In his second communication, dated April 7th,

Mr. Barton, Capt. Yarrow's representative came in last night by auto to put Erivan again in touch with the Near East Relief. He brought a considerable package of letters but so far I have only time to open the most important business communications.

Mr. Barton is leaving and I have no time for more. I shall carry on here.[238]

In his annual report to Congress for the year ending December 31, 1921, NER General Secretary Charles Vickrey described the year as "one of the most trying situations which the medical staff of the Near East had to meet during the year. Six thousand children had to be transported in the dead of winter from Kars to Alexandropol in unheated railroad trains, spending two or three days and nights en-route across snow covered plains with no warm food."[239] Vickrey's report to Congress did not include additional details. In effect, between November 1920 and April 1921 children in Alexandropol and Kars had paid with their lives for the political, ideological, and military imperatives and bartering that evolved in a small area of the Caucasus within a period of five months. The stretch of the southern Caucasus from Sarikamish to Alexandropol, lauded only a short time ago for its housing possibilities and impregnable fortresses that would ensure the safety of the children, turned into a graveyard for thousands of young lives that had only recently, and just barely, escaped the perils of deportations and massacres.

According to James Barton, there had been 10,000 orphans in the NER orphanages in Kars at the time of the Turkish invasion,[240] but in the end, only 6,000 children arrived in Alexandropol in April 1921.[241] The difference may be explained through deaths, as recorded by Elsie Kimball, during the winter months from malnutrition and disease, and orphan casualties during the invasion of Kars. Relief worker Elsie White, for instance, wrote about how in one incident, 12 children had been killed and 60 struck by stray bullets:

> The children suffered much those days. They were in poor physical condition anyway, and all the strain tolled heavily on them…Our American nurse was talking to one of our Armenian doctors when a bullet came through the window striking and mortally wounding him so that he died in a few hours. About ten or twelve children were killed, and sixty struck by stray bullets.[242]

There had also been abductions following the Turkish occupation of Kars. Although no specific numbers have survived, Reverend Father Goryun Kotanchyan, the senior priest of the Holy Illuminator Church of Kars, mentioned in his report to the Catholicos the loss of large numbers of orphans through abduction or shooting over a period of several months:

> Every night, soldiers went to the orphanage, uncontrolled, chose beautiful virgins and took them away. The same fate befell the older girls in the orphanage.

To avoid abduction, the priest continued,

> …many of those who remained at the orphanage, apprehensive that a similar bitter fate awaited them, began to escape in the dark of night, in groups, through various impassable mountain paths. Some of them were saved, but some were shot midway by their pursuers.[243]

Abductions had continued during the transfer of orphans to Alexandropol, on the way to the train station in Kars and en route to Alexandropol, as the testimonies of Araksi Pluzyan and Heghine (Elena) Abrahamyan have revealed.

At the end, from the 10,000 children in Kars, only around 60% arrived in Alexandropol. Upon their arrival in Alexandropol, many more of the orphans from Kars succumbed to disease and starvation. Writing about "the children from Kars" at the Kazachi Post on April 22, 1921, Myrtle Shane commented that 108 children had died during the preceding week:

> …many of them especially from hospitals, have not been able to get over the effects of the difficult journey from Kars. Some of them were on the way as long as three days, although it is ordinarily only a three or four hour trip…the death rate, especially at Kazachi Post, where the sick children were kept, has been very great. One hundred and eight died last week…[244]

The death toll in the City of Orphans remained high in 1921. According to Vahan Cheraz, who had entered the employ of the Kazachi in spring 1921 as chief of guards,[245] the total number of deaths in 1921 had amounted to around 4,000. Francis Spencer Duryea, who had been part of the 31-member commission to visit Alexandropol in the summer of 1921, placed the number of deaths at over 3,000 during an interview with *The New York Times* in September 1921.[246] A third source, a report from the city health department provided additional and more specific details for each month of 1921.[247] Accordingly, the numbers of sick and diseased had risen sharply during the months of March and April, as the children from Kars had arrived, amounting to 1,007 deaths in March. The heaviest death toll had been in April, when out of 1,840 hospitalized children, 819, or about 45%, had died. In the following month, in May, of the 1,920 hospitalized children 708 had died, bringing the total number of deaths in the City of Orphans in the months of March, April and May alone to 1,715. There were an additional 330 deaths in June, out of 1,115 hospitalized patients, with the numbers of death ebbing gradually from July to December 1921, as the number of children in the hospital had dropped to 590, and the number of deaths to ten.

Causes of illness and death included tuberculosis, enteritis, malnutrition and meningitis. Contagious diseases were also rampant among those who had survived. By fall 1921, 14,000 children were infected with trachoma and the number of scabies cases at the Kazachi alone had reached 3,129.[248] And, according to at least one source, soon after returning to Alexandropol, NER hastened to open a special hospital for orphan girls who had contacted syphilis during the Turkish occupation.[249] It is not known how many of the orphan girls had contacted the disease and what percentage were treated successfully.

However, none of the above sources included the decaying corpses of orphans in the city's shelters and orphanages.[250] Excluded from the sources also were the fatalities among those children who lived on the streets. For every orphan sheltered within the orphanage in Alexandropol, there were at least two who remained outside. Among those children the daily death toll was about 20, and was expected to increase in the winter. Their bodies were loaded

The document, signed by Dr. Roland Blythe, lists the names of five children who had died between May 21 and May 25, 1922. The information by each name includes date of death, location, gender of the child, age, cause of death, the name of the physician signing the death certificate and place of interment. All five deceased orphans were girls between the ages of three and ten: Arakse Hovhannisyan, Paykar [surname unknown], Balasan Khachatryan, Nazan V(Z?)agaryan, Nvard Nikolyan. Their death certificates had been signed by Drs. Altunyan, Voskerichyan and Ter-Grigoryan. All five children had died in the Kazachi hospital and buried in the fraternal cemetery of Alexandropol. (NAA 131/2/35/f. 18)

on wagons that continuously made rounds of the streets, and took them to the great trenches dug near the railway track for burial, without ceremony.[251]

The number of deaths continued to ebb in 1922, registering 122 deaths. One partial set of death certificates at the Kazachi alone from the end of February to mid-June, 1922, signed by Kazachi Medical Chief Dr. Rowland P. Blythe, showed 36 incidences of death. The causes of death were tuberculosis, enteritis, nephritis, pneumonia, and meningitis. All were girls, ranging from infancy to age 14.[252]

The condition of children outside the City of Orphans remained unchanged in spring 1922. A cable entitled "Alexandropol," dated April 2, 1922, and addressed to Charles Vickrey in New York informed headquarters that NER Superintendent of General Relief Kenneth Downer had toured 20 villages with a total population of 25,000 for five days in early spring 1922. Downer had reported that one-fourth of the adults were incapacitated and bedridden and only one in fifty of the population was normal. In one family, reported Downer, of the 15 members of a month earlier, only three remained; the dead included all the male members of the family. With respect to the children in the 20 villages, Downer reported that there were 1,500 orphans who would have to be removed immediately if they were to live, and even in small villages the weekly death list included ten children.[253]

Exodus

CHAPTER FOUR

COMMISSARS, RELIEF WORKERS, AND THE PARAMETERS OF REDEMPTION

The City of Orphans experienced its most significant expansion in terms of the number of relief workers, Armenian employees, its orphan population, and in the range and outreach of its programs during the first few years following NER's return to Armenia in 1921. This was due, in large part, to the leadership of the new Armenian RevKom (Revolutionary Committee), whose moderate policies persuaded NER that notwithstanding profound ideological differences, an American organization could work, and would be welcome in a Soviet state. Differences between two ideological opposites were eclipsed by the imperative of sheltering, healing, feeding, and educating thousands of orphans, the future citizens of Armenia.

The new RevKom was led by 35-year-old Alexander Myasnikyan, also known as Alexander Myasnikov and his penname A. Martuni, who arrived in Yerevan on May 4, 1921, to replace the first RevKom that had been established earlier when the Red Army had occupied Yerevan in early December 1920, and to amend the latter's policy of war communism. Myasnikyan arrived with a mandate from Lenin to assume the leadership of a new, moderate policy of a more gradual transition to communism, replacing the harsh and fanatical first RevKom that had created a strong reaction from many segments of the population, and to begin the daunting task of rebuilding the devastated country. A graduate of the Faculty of Law at Moscow University, Myasnikyan had proven his organizational and leadership skills in Belarus and Moscow during the Russian Revolution. By May 21, he was Chairman of the Council of People's Commissars and Military Affairs of the new RevKom of Armenia with a new cast of Commissars. Among them were Sergei Lukashin, First Secretary of the Communist Party of Armenia and Commissar of Economy; Askanaz Mravyan, Commissar of Foreign Affairs; Artashes Karinyan, Commissar of Justice; Aramayis Yerznkyan, Commissar of Agriculture; and Sargis Hampardzumyan, Commissar of Health.[254] All of them would work with and support NER's activities.

The hallmark of Myasnikyan's moderate policies was toleration, which extended from his introduction of the New Economic Policy (NEP) allowing greater freedom to farmers, to issuing pardons to those who had fled the country during the months of war communism, and inviting artists and intellectuals to come to Armenia.[255] To provincial RevKoms, Myasnikyan advocated and stressed the importance of flexibility, which he felt was a sign of strength rather than weakness. "Information is being received," he wrote in one of his circulars sent to provincial RevKoms in May 1921, "about conflicts between the population and government organizations" regarding confiscations, and urged the exercise of "extreme caution" in dealing with the population. Henceforth, confiscations, searches, aggravations of the population should stop, the circular read, and insisted that Provincial RevKoms were obligated to explain the new parameters to all local government organs "with no exceptions."[256]

Myasnikyan's policy of toleration was especially manifest in the government's attitude toward NER. Within one week of his arrival, he had signed a mandate allowing wide-reaching privileges, freedoms, exemptions and guarantees to NER, its personnel and its operations in Armenia.[257] The mandate, co-signed by Foreign Affairs Commissar Askanaz Mravyan was translated and sent to the Secretary of State in Washington, DC, by U.S. High Commissioner Admiral Mark Bristol in Constantinople. It read:[258]

> Sir: In my dispatch No. 191, of May 10, 1921, I communicated to the Department the text of an agreement between the Georgian Soviet Government and the Near East Relief for the distribution of Near East Relief supplies in the Caucasus. I now have the honor to enclose a copy of a statement signed by representatives of the Soviet Armenian Republic recognizing the Near East Relief and giving them certain privileges for their work in that area.
>
> [Enclosure—Translation]
>
> Mandate from the Socialist Soviet Republic of Armenia to the Near East Relief
>
> The Revolutionary Committee of S[ocialistic] S[oviet] A[rmenian] R[epublic] fully sympathizing with the aims of the Near East Relief in the Caucasus certifies that the Soviet Government of Armenia is willing to proffer all the necessary help to the N.E.R. in its work of organizing orphanages for homeless children and supplying the needy population with food, medicaments, shoes, etc.
>
> 1. In view of the above stated the Government of the S.S.R.A. guarantees freedom of travel both coming and leaving Armenia at their convenience without any hindrance to all citizens of the United States working in the N.E.R.
>
> 2. Recognises [sic] the right of the N.E.R. to distribute its supplies to the population according to its own decision or to control such supplies it has delivered to some local organization.
>
> 3. All supplies shipped to Armenia consigned to N.E.R. are to be free of customs, railway charges and all other taxes.
>
> 4. The property of the N.E.R. is entirely free from requisition.
>
> 5. Free export of N.E.R. goods to Georgia and Azerbaijan is guaranteed.
>
> 6. The N.E.R. is granted the right to prepare and transport charcoal and firewood from the woods in Armenia for the needs of the N.E.R. work, from those districts and places it finds convenient which will be approved by the Government.[259]

7. The Government guarantees entire freedom of action to the N.E.R. promising not to meddle in the internal administration of the organization or any interference on the part of its members and officials.

8. The Government also guarantees that no demand whatever on its part or any public organizations or authorities will be addressed to the N.E.R. except through the Commissary of Foreign Affairs or his agents.

MYASNIKOFF, *Chairman of the Revkom*
MRAVIAN, *Commissioner [Commissar] of Foreign Affairs*

Six months later, at the First Congress of Armenian Soviets in January 1922, Myasnikyan praised NER before a nation-wide audience of communist officials. "In a country like Armenia," he stated, the NER had an "extraordinary significance," because vast numbers of orphans and refugees were still unattached to land or industry and needed significant assistance. "To care for the orphans," he continued

> ...we have hosted the Americans, who are energetic, active people; they are indeed doing great work here; they do not occupy themselves with politics and deserve our encouragement.[260]

In the resolution passed at the end of the Congress genuine gratitude was expressed to the American people for their assistance to orphans and refugees of Armenia.

To facilitate communication between NER and government bodies and to find efficient and timely resolutions for requests from NER, on October 12, 1921, Myasnikyan appointed Sargis Abovyan as government liaison with NER. As representative of the government Abovyan was authorized by the Council of People's Commissars to resolve any and all issues NER might raise.[261]

Not unusual under Myasnikyan were personal contacts with and favors for NER. In a note dated October 4, 1921, Myasnikyan's chief of staff informed Milton Brown that Myasnikyan had placed his personal wagon at Brown's disposal while traveling to Batum:

> Herewith I communicate to you for your information that proper arrangements have been made by the President of the Council of People's Commissars Comrade Myasnikyan, so that his special wagon # 62 will be at your service for your departure to Batum tomorrow.[262]

NER's administrators often wished to discuss outstanding issues and problems with Myasnikyan directly. On October 11, 1921, NER's Yerevan Acting District Commander Dudley Lewis invited "Comrade Myasnikyan" to an informal dinner at his residence to discuss some problems. The other guests would be Mr. Aroyan[263] and Mr. Evangulian.[264]

As the leader of a devastated country, Myasnikyan's attention was focused on its reconstruction, and within weeks of his arrival a roadmap was in progress for irrigation canals to cultivate larger areas of land, hydroelectric plants, and improvement in literacy. Significant economic assistance came from Moscow in cash, provisions, fuel, agricultural implements, animals, telephone and telegraph equipment, and medications valued in the millions of rubles.[265] Soviet

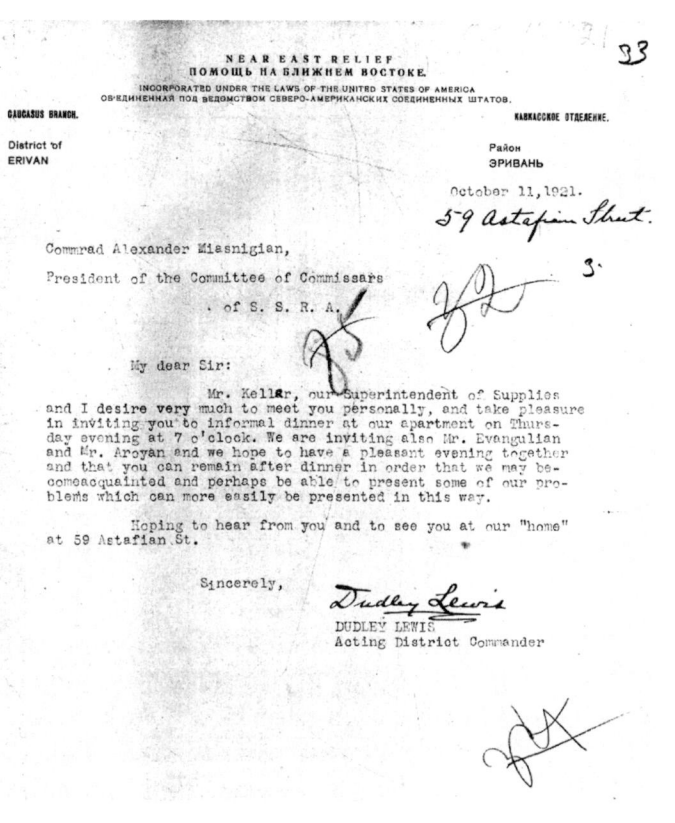

Russia also sent military uniforms and 10 planes. The task ahead was daunting, wrote Myasnikyan in November 1921, in *Khorhrdayin Hayastan* [Soviet Armenia]:

> Soviet Armenia has acquired a population of refugees and indigent people. This is not an exaggeration; it is a fact. [Soviet Armenia] has acquired an army of one hundred thousand orphans and skeleton-shaped children. Our country is a piece of the earth housing orphans and refugees. It is a pervasive hell of woes, tears, and sufferings.

But, he promised,

> The Armenia of the working people will, no matter what, transform that hell into [a place worthy of] human existence.[266]

A year later, when NER headquarters approved a policy to reduce the budgets for all NER orphanages in the Near East by 25% due to lack of funds, Myasnikyan wrote an open letter to U.S. President Warren Harding, to thank him and to plead against budget reductions in the orphanages in Armenia. The letter is reproduced below, in full:[267]

Dinner invitation from Dudley Lewis to Alexander Myasnikyan. (NAA 113/38/10/f. 33)

> Open Letter to President Harding
>
> From the President of the Council of People's Commissars of the Armenian Soviet Socialist Republic
>
> Dear Mr. Harding!
>
> On behalf of my people and personally I wish to thank you and, through you, the American people for the numerous charitable donations made by America to help Armenia. Tens of thousands of Armenians have survived and are alive today due to the American assistance sent in recent years. We shall never forget it.
>
> The American Committee for Relief in the Near East helped to bring thirty thousand Armenian orphans under the loving care of Americans. It is the ongoing donations by Americans that in the present day have helped support the lives and upbringing of these thirty thousand orphans.
>
> It has come to my attention that recently the donations for these orphans have been in constant decline forcing the American management of the Orphanage to reduce the daily rations in order to save for the future. If it is in your power, Mr. President, or, if you think there is anything I must do to reinvigorate the interest of the American society in the children they have adopted, it is my conviction we should spare no effort toward that end. At stake is the future of the Armenian Republic, which depends on the wellbeing and proper upbringing of these children.

> Our country is as yet very poor. However, we hope that the richer harvest this year will pave the way for radical changes in our living conditions this coming June or July. We have much commitment and determination to reach our goals. Our people never shy away from hard work. If consistent effort and perseverance prove successful, Armenia will live on and become stronger.
>
> I am confident, Sir, that you support us with your heart and soul. I am confident that your people wish us well. We are trying to be worthy of your compassion and your support, doing everything we can. The thirty thousand orphans sheltered by Americans will perpetually bond our two countries in an unbreakable friendship.
>
> With respect,
>
> President of the Council of People's Commissars

An inscription in the top left corner of the letter may suggest that the letter was not sent. It reads: "Not accepted." The date below the note is May 12, [1922], and is signed "Mravyan," then serving as People's Commissar of Foreign Affairs.

In March 1922, Myasnikyan had become Chairman of the Transcaucasian Soviet Federative Socialist Republic (TSFSR) that included Armenia, Georgia and Azerbaijan. When he left for Tiflis, his policies were continued by his successor as Chairman of the Council of People's Commissars, moderate Sergei Lukashin (Srapiyonyan) who assumed the leadership of SSRA in May 1922. A lawyer and communist organizer like Myasnikyan, Lukashin had spent a year in Germany, France and Switzerland, studying industrial production and economy, and had arrived in Armenia with Myasnikyan.

When Lukashin addressed the 2nd Congress of Soviets in Armenia on November 29–30, 1922, he thanked NER, as had his predecessor 11 months earlier, for its "significant" assistance to the orphans:

> The American Committee has nearly 30,000 orphans under its care, for whom it spends approximately six million gold rubles annually. From February to October 1 of this year, it has received up to 1,900 wagons of goods, which is a considerable assistance, and we must express our gratitude to the American Committee working in Armenia. If we consider that they collect large amounts, kopek-by-kopek, from the schoolchildren of America for the children of Armenia, then the size of the assistance the American Committee brings to Armenia will be evident.

At the same time, Lukashin continued,

> …we tell them that the American Committee must conform to the laws and order in Armenia both in the education and upbringing of children, and in the area of relations between their bodies and our workers' organizations. In this connection, there were some conflicts in the beginning. Our People's Commissariat of Enlightenment had not paid attention to the schools of the American Committee, but now their scholastic plans conform to the spirit of the plans and directives of the People's Commissariat of Enlightenment. In this area the American committee does not show opposition.

Lukashin then expanded on the types of concessions being made to the American Committee, including the government's payment of about six million gold rubles for the transportation of goods from Batum to Yerevan. "After all this," Lukashin concluded,

> ...they will have to understand that in Armenia they must submit to the existing workers' legislation and not be led by the laws of America.[268]

Gratified with the support NER enjoyed from the top leadership and other government officials,[269] Yarrow voiced his support for the young communists now leading Armenia and the newly formed TSFSR:

> ...Such Bolshevist theories as are being tried are entirely subordinated to the primary task of pulling the country together again after seven years of war and terrible economic disruption.

> ...the three republics, apparently so full of discordant racial and religious elements, have achieved a real federation. They have pooled some of the most important executive functions in a council of representatives from the three governments [of Azerbaijan, Armenia and Georgia] and the new chairman of that council, the executive head of the Caucasus, is now the Armenian leader, Miasnigian, in whose sincere purpose and general ability I have entire confidence.[270]

The congenial relations and gratitude from Armenians were passed along in Vickrey's report to the U.S. Congress:

> ...The gratitude of all classes is most pronounced and heartening. Whether in conversation with the Catholicos at Etchmiadzin, with the patriarch at Constantinople, with representatives of the exiled Dashnakzagan [ARF] government at Geneva, the *de facto* soviet government in Erivan, or with the representatives of the common people...the expressions of appreciation and of life-indebtedness for American relief are essentially the same.[271]

Some NER members and visitors to Armenia were surprised, and impressed by, the new generation of Armenian leaders now at the helm of the government, who, as Dr. Esther Lovejoy, the president of the American Women's Hospitals remarked during her visit in 1922, "were not the dreamy idealists we read about, but young Armenian university and business men."[272] Mabel Elliot had met one of those men earlier, the young chairman of the Economic Council of Alexandropol, when she visited him in his office in 1921. She did not mention his name, but described him as a "new type of Armenian...thin, earnest, with deep-set eyes in which burned a flame." "There could be no question of his sincerity or devotion," she wrote,

> He worked hard, ten to fourteen hours a day; he received a salary of eight dollars a month, and certainly did not spend more on his way of living; one glance at his face showed that he needed better food than he was eating. His office was a bare room, furnished with an unpainted, rough table and chairs.

But she had noticed with amazement how "the walls of his office were lined with maps and charts," and

> On the windowsill was stacked a file of home-study courses from Cornell University. How they had found their way here I do not know. In the outer office, a secretary was translating into Armenian a Cornell pamphlet on farm soils.[273]

The new leadership of Armenia was equally surprising to Barclay Acheson, in charge of NER's overseas programs and a leading figure in the organization. It "was something of a shock" to him that some of "these Bolsheviks" were well-educated cosmopolitans.[274]

"America's Answer"

In spring 1921, many of the barracks were roofless and in semi-ruinous states. NER was now faced with the staggering task of repairing and refitting the stone buildings into orphanages with a growing orphan population. And this time, repairing barracks destroyed a second time during the Turkish occupation of Alexandropol required greater effort and significant investment in infrastructure and would become NER's "largest single unit of relief work."[275] It was also necessary to refit and remodel buildings originally intended for a military community into a functional habitat for the new community of orphans, which meant refurbishing the barracks as dormitories, workshops, classrooms, and offices. It also meant improving the sanitary environment, such as building sewers, bathrooms and laundry facilities. The vast majority of the orphan population was afflicted with some type of contagious disease, most commonly scabies, favus and trachoma, and treating them required sizable hospitals, clinics and isolation wards. When children were first selected or picked up from the streets, nurses with their sleeves rolled-up and with basins of antiseptics, undressed them. The rags they had on were tossed into a fire with tongs. The child was given a bath; the head was shaved then passed on to a nurse who dressed the child's sores, and placed in the appropriate orphanage if no hospitalization was needed. More often than not, medical treatment

NER representative selecting orphans to be admitted to the orphanage. (*The New Near East*, December 1922: 14)

continued at the orphanage and became as important as nutrition. Daily treatments in the thousands were given at the Kazachi, Polygon and Severski and followed strict schedules, announced by the ringing of the bell and the call of the bugle.

The City of Orphans occupied a central place in the countless pleas in NER's fundraising campaigns, press releases and public presentations, detailing the needs involved in caring for such a large congregation of orphans.[276] Essays in *The New Near East*, as other media outlets, especially highlighted the fact that violence and war had not ceased and that the number of orphans increased by the day:

> War does not allow the condition of things in the Near East to better themselves. There are certain fortunate thousands of children within the orphanages of Near East Relief to whom the generosity of the American people continues to give the necessities of life and an elementary education. But the story which we must continue to tell, until peace is brought into Transcaucasia and Asia Minor, is the story of the starving thousands of little children outside the orphanage gates, human progeny yet victims of pitiless humanity.[277]

The message remained the same in 1922. NER's "largest single unit of work," as NER General Secretary Charles Vickrey pointed out in his annual report to NER's Board of Trustees for the year 1922 was "…the Armenian Republic of the Russian Caucasus and has remained undisturbed." Vickrey went on to say that there were approximately 1,300,000 Armenians in this area," and that "the Russian Soviet Armenian Republic, with serious and economic problems of its own, is giving every possible cooperation in the care and support of these visitors from across the Turkish border." And while, Vickrey continued, NER had adopted the policy of limiting relief efforts to the care of orphans exclusively, in practice, the implementation of that policy had proven difficult to uphold during 1922:

> We have earnestly endeavored to discontinue all general or adult relief, but the country as a whole is not as yet economically self-supporting…
>
> To avoid the recurrence of wholesale starvation, Near East Relief was again obliged to give out general relief, either in return for labor to construct roads and rebuild irrigation ditches or in the form of seed grain (in the value of $61,000).[278]

American commissions and NER officials began to arrive in Armenia in the summer of 1921 and in 1922. Reports were prepared for distribution to NER headquarters in New York, for the U.S. news media and the public. One of the members of the American commission to arrive in Alexandropol in summer 1921 was John Finley, New York State Commissioner of Education and later editor of *The New York Times*, whose observations were published in *The American Review of Reviews*[279] and the *Kindergarten-Primary Magazine*[280] soon after his return. There he described what the 1921 commission saw as they arrived at the train station in Alexandropol:

> As the American party descended from its train at Alexandropol, the old Russian garrison town and railway center of Transcaucasia, they stumbled across the dead

body of a little boy, lying on the tracks. A grown man, livid with cholera, starting towards their car to ask for a bit of bread, fell dead at their feet...[281]

Finley went on to say, "For every child inside an orphanage there is at least one outside, without shelter or food or friends." NER with its limited budget could barely provide them with shelter and food, and as a result,

> In nearly all of the centers, the industrial work, which promised so much, has had to be discontinued for lack of room, lack of materials and lack of skilled workers to carry it on. Education is being given up, reluctantly, but of necessity, in many of the larger orphanages. And worst of all, every day dozens, even hundreds of children are being turned away from the orphanages to wander the streets, hungry and half naked.[282]

Outside the orphanages, NER fed thousands of children one meal a day and provided them with clothing sent over from America. The meal consisted of a bowl of soup and a piece of bread, which was enough to keep the children from starvation, but not for long, wrote Finley:

> All this was in August, when the danger from cold and exposure was at a minimum. Even then the toll of deaths was twenty or more in one city alone each day. What it must be now that the snow is on the ground can only be imagined.[283]

Urgent appeals continued with Charles Vickrey's interviews and reports. In the October 1921 issue of *The Literary Digest*, he described Armenia as "A Vast Orphan Asylum," the direct result of the Turkish invasion of Alexandropol. But such statements from Vickrey and others countered the position held by Admiral Mark Bristol, who criticized NER for believing false reports about Turkish atrocities in the Caucasus. In one of his letters to James Barton, dated March 28, 1921, Admiral Bristol had objected to NER's continued reports about losses in Armenia, which made his "blood boil":

> I see that reports are being freely circulated in the United States that the Turks massacred thousands of Armenians in the Caucasus. Such reports are repeated so many times it makes my blood boil.[284]

"In addition to the reports from our own American Relief workers that were in Kars and Alexandropol," wrote Admiral Bristol,

> and reports from such men as Yarrow, I have reports from my own Intelligence Officer and know that the Armenian reports are not true.[285]

The Admiral characterized "The circulation of such false reports in the United States," as "an outrage" which did the "Armenians more harm than good." James Barton, on May 6, 1921, agreed, at least partially, with Bristol, even at a time when Alexandropol had reached its nadir and orphan mortality under NER had reached astronomical proportions, and wrote:

> With reference to the false reports that come through reporting massacres of the Armenians by the Turks, there is no one who can deprecate this more than I do.[286]

Barton continued to explain that NER found itself in a difficult position because of "a brilliant young Armenian, a graduate of Yale University, by the name of Cardashian," who was a lawyer in New York and claimed to have "the latest and fullest information out from Armenia," and, a close associate of

Senator Lodge, the President, the State Department and others in Washington. Cardashian, explained Barton,

> ...is constantly reporting atrocities which never occurred and giving endless misinformation with regard to the situation in Armenia and in Turkey. We do not like to come out and attack him in public. That would injure the whole cause we are all trying to serve, because people would say that we are quarreling among ourselves and would lose confidence in the whole concern. We have tried in New York Office to give publicity to nothing we did not have every reason to believe to be correct. We are therefore trying to keep controversial matters out and only keep before the public the actual needs in Armenia."

To the Admiral's chagrin, NER's campaigns continued. With almost no exception, conditions in Armenia were described as the direst in NER's field of operations in the Near East, and almost all addressed the thousands of orphans who could not be accommodated by NER. In Alexandropol, wrote Sherman L. Divine, Pastor of the First Presbyterian Church of Spokane, Washington, there were three children outside for every child who had been given shelter in the orphanage,[287] while NER national field director John W. Mace commented:

> Armenia is the land of the living nightmare. We thought we had become pretty well hardened to suffering after seeing the refugee camps in Constantinople and Batoum, but Armenia brought nothing but an uninterrupted series of sights at the memory of which one sickens.[288]

In a land of living nightmare, gratitude for America was widespread, wrote Julian Zelchenko of *The Newark Evening News*,[289]

> Women kissed my hands and even my clothing when they learned I was from America. The greatest thing in Armenia is the American flag and the song I heard most frequently was "My Country 'tis of Thee.'"

Children waiting for admission by the gates of the City of Orphans. (*The New Near East*, January 1923, cover page)

At public presentations, former NER workers described the condition of orphans, focusing on those who begged admission into the City of Orphans. One such presentation, delivered by Mabel Farrington to audiences in Maui, Hawaii, in early January 1922 was covered in the semi-weekly *Maui News*:

> ...one of the most difficult tasks she [Mabel Farrington] was asked to undertake in Armenia was to go to the gate of one of the orphanages and face a hundred children assembled there, and tell them that there was vacancy which would admit one of them.
>
> She says that when she finally screwed up her courage enough to tell the youngsters the news there was a feeble shout of joy and then a silence as each famished child looked at its neighbor.

After deliberating on who among them would fill the vacancy, the children had arrived at a decision:

> Miss Farrington was surprised to see them pushing the strongest boy in the lot toward the gates. The others explained that he was the most likely to live of any of them and that they wished him to grow up to be a strong, healthy Armenian.[290]

The response from much of the American public was overwhelming. Local committees and volunteers cooperated in the staggering effort for the collection of donations from different states and loading of relief ships in the U.S. headed to points in the Near East. The "*Clontare*," for instance, was filled through the cooperation of five states: Tennessee, Indiana, Michigan, Louisiana and New York. A large cargo of corn grits, flour and clothing was assembled at New Orleans; 700 bales of clothing, 35,000 pounds of cocoa, 25,000 pounds of which were donated by the Hershey Company were added in New York; 800 bushels of seed wheat and 200 bushels of barely, rye and millet, 3,500 cases of condensed milk, a carload each of canned goods from Chattanooga, Tennessee, and Fort Wayne, Indiana; 40,000 unbreakable soup bowls and agricultural implements and harness, and flour from Michigan. The steamship sailed from New York on February 20, 1922, for Constantinople and Batum, and from there, to Alexandropol and Yerevan.

Loading the *Leise Maersk*[291] began in New Orleans on April 7 with 57 tons of canned goods and clothing from Tennessee; 175 tons of beans from Colorado; 600 tons of wheat flour from the Midwest; 607 tons of wheat flour from Canada, and $200,000

The *Datchet* being unloaded in Batum. Capacity cargo included 4,500 tons of flour, rice, beans, etc. (*The New Near East*, January 1922: 18)

worth of surplus army medical supplies donated by the U.S. government in Charleston, South Carolina. The final loading took place in New York, with supplies ranging from tractors to condensed milk. There were ten tractors purchased by the Near East Relief, 1,500 cases of canned milk from the school children of the state of New York and Ohio, several hundred bales of clothing, 1,700 tons of commodities from the Pacific Coast including canned salmon, dried fruit, wheat flour, beans and clothing.

The *Leise Maersk* left New York on Saturday, May 20, 1922, for Constantinople. About 1,200 tons of its cargo was dropped off at Derindje in Constantinople for orphanages there and the remainder proceeded to the Caucasus. The *Coeur d'Alene* was scheduled to sail on Monday from Constantinople for the Caucasus with 1,000 tons of supplies, only four days after the SS *Deep Water* had sailed from Constantinople for the Caucasus on Thursday, May 18, with 5,000 tons of corn grits, cereals and medical supplies.[292]

The *Saugus* sailed from Newark on June 20, carrying 60 carloads of foodstuffs, arriving in Alexandropol in August 1922. The goods were first distributed to one of the Polygon buildings called *"New Jersey House."* Among the goods were seven cases of phonographs, the personal gift of Thomas A. Edison, and half a million units of canned goods, the gift of school children in New Jersey,[293] including two classes of crippled children at the Belmont Avenue School in Newark, New Jersey.[294] Children at the Peddie School for Boys at Hightstown, New Jersey, had collected $45.41 after hearing NER volunteer Elizabeth Pashayan talk to them about Armenia,[295] and three crisp $10 bills had been raised by children in St. Paul's school in New York. From the bed-ridden children of Ward 6 of Bellevue Hospital in New York arrived $3.62,[296] and from school children in Nampa, Washington, came foodstuff.[297] To ease some of the problems of transportation of supplies to the orphanages, NER purchased 40 mules from the British in Constantinople and shipped them from Constantinople to Batum by boat.[298] Relief ships continued into 1923, with the reconditioned USS *Leviathan*, sailing from New York Harbor on July 4th 1923, carrying provisions and seven relief workers destined for Alexandropol.

The *Leise Maersk* being loaded in New York with 4,000 tons of foodstuff, medication and farm equipment. (*The New Near East*, June 1922, cover page)

Used Clothes from Michigan being transported to New York for shipment to the Near East.
(*The New Near East*, May 1922: 7)

Used clothes being packed into bales by volunteers in NER's New York warehouse.
(*The New Near East*, May 1921: 14)

Used shoes.
(Barton 1930: facing page 211)

Christmas Gift for Armenia from the Baltimore Ford Dealers.
(*The New Near East*, January 1921:22)

Food gifts from the crippled children of the Belmont Avenue School in Newark, NJ.
(*The New Near East*, June 1922: 15)

94   THE CITY OF ORPHANS

↑
Flour supplies being moved to the Kazachi.
(*The New Near East*, February 1922: 14)

↑
One of 40 mules being loaded on a ship to be transported to Alexandropol.
(*The New Near East*, September 1921: 7)

↑
Transporting supplies in the Caucasus.
(*The New Near East*, December 1920: 25)

→
Case Tractors crated for shipment to Armenia.
(*The New Near East*, March 1922: 5)

COMMISSARS, RELIEF WORKERS... 95

The Limits of Redemption

Despite official Yerevan's cooperation with NER, some local authorities had taken a critical, and at times hostile, stance toward NER, occasioning circulars from the People's Commissariat of Internal Affairs instructing all provincial revolutionary committees to create the necessary conditions to enable NER's work without any impediments or obstructions.[299] Regardless, challenges to the government's cooperative stance continued to be reported by NER. One instance was the confiscation of NER property under the American flag in Yerevan. C. D. Ussher complained to the Commissar of Foreign Affairs, in July 1921, that such arbitrary acts went against the spirit of cooperation, and that

> If the Acts, mandates and documents of the RevKom of Armenia are to be respected only by the President of the RevKom and the Commissaire [sic] of Foreign Affairs we cannot but look with apprehension at the prospects of other nationals attempting relief or business in Russian territory…
>
> As Americans working in the Caucasus and guests of the government we desire to be as helpful as possible and to do all in our power to strengthen the bonds between this country and America. Misunderstandings and irregularities are liable to occur on both sides in transition periods but we trust nothing will mar the friendship which is traditional between the Americans and the Armenians and in fact the whole Russian people.[300]

The regional RevKom in Alexandropol also remained uncooperative at times. In December 1921 Askanaz Mravyan had to caution the Alexandropol RevKom that the representatives of the American Committee had complained that the RevKom had seized their farms, refusing to return them, which kept them from sowing. Mravyan's order was to return the farms and smooth out misunderstandings.[301] This was followed by a circular of January 6, 1922, this time from the People's Commissariat of Internal Affairs, instructing all leaders of Soviet institutions to refrain from such acts. Should such incidents occur, the circular read, severe punishments would be imposed.[302]

One of the most flagrant deviations from the government's policies of cooperation took place in Karakilisa in mid-May 1922, where things had come to a head between NER and army personnel. Milton Brown had received a letter from NER Karakilisa District Commander J. D. McNabb, dated May 16, 1922, where the latter detailed events that had transpired at Karakilisa following killings in the town.[303] The complaint, addressed to NER in Tiflis, had to do with the demand of the chief of the local Cheka—State Security police with extraordinary powers, the precursor of the KGB—to use one of the rooms in the "American House," which NER had denied:

> …he [the Cheka agent] came and informed us that we had four empty rooms at the American House and that he desired one of them. I began to inform him that we have three extra rooms; one guest room, a parlor and a dining room and that we must have extra space for visiting or travelling personnel, when he sprang from his seat, apparently in a rage, and rushed from the room. Since that time we have been subjected to numerous indignities and annoyances.

A series of accusations had been hurled at the American personnel, who were then taken to the local Political Bureau where they were questioned and threatened, then finally released. But later, all were ordered to report to the Cheka for "investigation," and their rooms had been searched in their absence. One of the employees, Mrs. Brown, was not allowed to leave the building after her investigation, but had been forced to stay

> ...in a filthy room with a lot of soldiers, subjected to leers and apparently jeering remarks in regard to the "Americans." She was offered a chair by a soldier; before she could sit down it was snatched by some kind of an under officer who immediately sat upon it himself, Mrs. Brown being compelled to stand for more than an hour.

Intimidations had continued during and after the so-called investigations, with armed agents of the Bureau invading the hospital. In addition, many of the Armenian employees—the hospital manager, the purchasing agent, the head of construction and repairs, an orphanage inspector, a bookkeeper, two warehousemen and a number of laborers—had been arrested. McNabb then concluded:

> I wish to protest officially for the Near East Relief at Karakilis and for the American Personnel against the treatment we have received, the insolent manner in which the investigations have been made, the lack of cooperation in our work for the Armenia Children and poor as indicated by arrest of necessary personnel without intimation to us as to probable length of their detention or any apology for upsetting our organization: against the intimation that we are suspected criminals and against the surveillance of our house and daily life.

> We all consider that it is practically impossible to carry on our work for the Armenians here if we are to be subjected continually to insult, indignity, suspicion, lack of co-operation and petty annoyances.

> I respectfully suggest that these matters be taken up with Mr. Maesnikian [Myasnikyan] "President" of Armenia, whom I understand is now in Tiflis.

Recriminations were reciprocal, at times pointing to exclusionary and disrespectful attitudes on the part of some American relief workers toward their Armenian colleagues. One of the earliest complaints was dated May 28, 1921, and addressed to the SSRA People's Commissar of Health. The author of the report was Dr. Melkumyan, Director of Alexandropol's Health Department, whom Myasnikyan would appoint Liaison officer between NER and the government in Alexandropol in December 1921.[304] In his angry report, Melkumyan related what he characterized as undue restrictions and disrespectful behavior toward the Armenian employees at Kazachi post. "After the establishment of Soviet rule in Armenia," he began,

> the Americans turned the Kazachi Post into an "untouchable fortress" with restrictions on free entry and exit.

> The Kazachi is completely surrounded by boy scouts, who do not allow free entry and exit from 7 in the morning until 6 in the evening, without the permission of the Americans.

The staff of the orphanages and hospitals at the Kazachi, he continued, felt as though they were in prison, citing specific examples where the wife of one of the physicians, Dr. Papikyan, had needed to send for a midwife from the city but was not allowed to because the Americans were not there to give permission. The wife of another doctor, Dr. Harutyunyan, was nearly beaten because she had gone over the other side of the fence for a walk. In addition to these acts of disrespect, the report stated, Armenian employees leaving work to go to their homes in the city were subjected to body searches:

> Every day, before leaving for the city, the staff is searched. Every day the nurses, doctors and other staff are subjected to such types of searches, even taking off their underwear. The medical staff has come to me, asking to be freed of their service to the Americans, which I couldn't allow without your arrangements and because the children would be left without a medical staff.

Complaints to the Americans had yielded no results. Dr. Melkumyan had not wished to interfere in the "internal affairs of the Americans,"

> ...because they are "autonomous." Today I received a telegram where it is said that the American doctor Main [Dr. Russell B. Main], who had sided with the removal of that aspect of the regime, has been let go and that the entire medical staff of Kazachi Post wishes to leave their work. Please hasten to make arrangements and give instructions, so that I may know how to act in the future.[305]

It appears that at least one of the problems was that among the Armenian personnel NER had hired were those who were openly critical or hostile to the new regime. In an effort to alleviate the problem, Milton Brown, at the time serving as Yerevan District Commander, signed a general order on December 21, 1921, informing all NER staff that anyone making critical statements about the government would be turned over to the Cheka.[306]

Nonetheless, a few days later a newspaper in Alexandropol published an article attacking the remnants of the former government who worked in NER's orphanages, their counter-revolutionary stance, and their attempts to turn the Americans against Soviet authorities. A copy of the article, which had first appeared in Yerevan on December 24, 1921, had reached Ernest Yarrow in Tiflis, who had it translated into English and sent it to Milton Brown for action. Entitled *"They Suck and Oppress Under the American Flag,"* it read, in part:

> ...To-day, most of our children and youth are orphans, and live in orphanages.

> Most of those orphanages are under the care of the American Committee of Relief. They are altogether cut off and isolated from the Government.

General order from Milton Brown to NER employees. (NAA 113/38/14/f. 56)

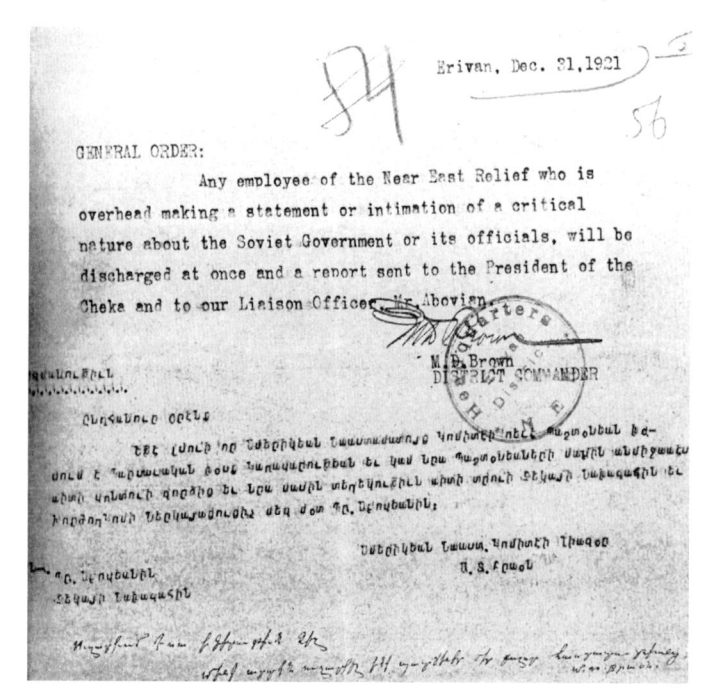

98 THE CITY OF ORPHANS

Now the question rises: if Relief Work is the sole object, why have those orphanages and other departments become nests of counter-revolutionaries? Why is it that the employees thereof are either Generals, Officers, Members of Parliament, Zangezur "heroes," mercenaries, traders without shops, or scoutmasters?

…The place swarms, in the true sense of the word, with counter-revolutionary elements of every class and every description.

…Is Relief Work only a veil to such activities? Should the clothes and supplies, which come from far away America in the name of orphans and the destitute, belong in the end to such gentlemen-adventurers?…Those persons are busy all day with self-provisioning, looting, rapine, evacuation of warehouses and sale on the market of property belonging to the destitute.

Their pocketsful of Dollars are a proof to the fact. It does not please them to live in the Armenia of the Soviets, so they sneak away to America, riding and relying on their Dollars…

…The organ [official newspaper] of our government is despised in the office…Whose work is it? People think it's the Americans. But they are terribly mistaken, for in the office sit the Tashnak Chiefs and the General, by whose instigation the Americans are induced to strain relations with the government.

The orphanages are oppressed under frightful methods. Who is to blame? Again, the Americans know nothing, because therein reign as kings the scoutmaster tyrants, the Onniks and Tcherazes, who have reduced the youthful little boys to slave hood…Keep them breadless for days, crucify them with their "Rise-Raise!" Poor bare-footed and half-naked adolescents, who have already been crucified by fate, who have suffered, who are destitute and persecuted!

…Until when? [307]

On January 5, 1922, Brown forwarded the article, along with his own terse note, to Sargis Abovyan:

We have received from Captain Yarrow the enclosed translation of an article which appeared in the Soviet Journal in Alexandropol. It is practically the same article which appeared in the Erivan newspaper some time ago, about which we had a discussion when Captain Yarrow was here.

Captain Yarrow makes the following statement: "If the Government does not take immediate and strict measures against the publication of articles detrimental to the Near East Relief, the cordial relations which at present exist between the Near East Relief and the Government will certainly be strained, if not entirely broken. Such practice is wholly uncivilized."

On his part, Brown added:

I cannot understand why your government allowed this article to be republished in Alexandropol on December 24th after the painful conference, which you and Captain Yarrow had on this matter in the entresol of my house. I presume it is another mistake and I can assure you that a repetition of such mistakes will result in something pretty serious.[308]

Challenges to NER's privileges continued on the regional level in Alexandropol, with the Executive Committee of the provincial RevKom occasionally reminding NER of its limits. Between March and August 1922 two disputes had to do with NER's jurisdiction over its native employees and its practice of posting guards on lands surrounding the posts, designated for cultivation. In a note dated March 29, 1922, assistant to the Superintendent of General Relief Kenneth A. Downer informed the provincial RevKom that should any NER employee be found guilty of a crime, the RevKom should first notify NER, and only through NER should the guilty party be handed to the court.[309] The answer from the RevKom was curt and to the point. NER was somewhat mistaken, stated the note; that in fact it would have to be just the opposite. "Under no circumstances," the note read, was NER's position acceptable, and pointed out that being an NER employee should not be interpreted as a privilege that placed them above the law of the land, and seek "protection under the flag of the United States of North America." "For your information," the note concluded, "in the event of proof of criminality, any native NER employee would be arrested and tried as a citizen of SSRA, whether or not they were NER employees." NER would be notified of the fact in due time and whenever possible.[310]

The second dispute involved NER's right to plant vegetable seeds in the arable land around the Severski, which, NER believed, had been handed over to them along with the Severski barracks.[311] The provincial RevKom disagreed, maintaining that NER had rights on the land around the Polygon only. The note that Alexandropol's RevKom sent the Chief of Police informed the latter that NER had rights over the Polygon lands only, where it posted guards. But should the police notice that NER had posted guards on other lands stating that it belonged to them, the guards should be disarmed and arrested immediately, and the Executive Committee notified of each incident.[312]

Mandates, Revisions and Liaisons

The agreement of May 7, 1921, was the first of several that would be signed during the decade of the 1920s, and one of the most generous in the privileges extended to NER operations. In the agreements and mandates that followed Armenia's entry in the TSFSR—in August 1922, November 1922 and January 1923[313]—the sweeping privileges granted to NER were subjected to revisions and modifications, with the clear understanding that all future mandates would have to be approved by the government of the TSFSR and not Armenia alone. The mandate signed between NER and Soviet Armenia in August 1922, for instance, was voided in Tiflis on the grounds that Armenia had acted independently of the TSFSR[314] and was subjected to revisions in Moscow and Tiflis. A new mandate had still not been finalized on January 13, 1923, when Charles Vickrey wrote to Chairman of the Council of Commissars Sergei Lukashin from Constantinople. In fact, Vickrey wrote two letters to Lukashin on that day, in both of which he regretted that he had been "so close as Constantinople" yet unable to come to the Caucasus "to renew personal acquaintance," that "the recent upheavals in connection with the Greco-Turkish War" had "thrown upon our hands a very large additional number of Armenian orphans and refugees," and that he would have liked to have shown Lukashin "a number of pictures we took last summer in some of which you and your colleagues appear."[315] The wording of the two letters is identical with the exception that in one, he inserted three additional paragraphs that referred to the delay of the new mandate:

> I of course have been deeply disappointed to learn that both the mandate, which was signed in Tiflis last August, and the later mandate, which was signed in Moscow for some reason, have not yet become effective. This naturally leaves us in a very uncertain position as to where we stand and as to whether the Government really desires to co-operate with us in the child-welfare work and in the general industrial and agricultural reconstruction that our program entails.
>
> I feel that you and most of the Armenian friends sincerely appreciate the effort that we are making to help you in building up the resources of the country, but that some influences which I do not fully understand are working against co-operation with us.

Vickrey then added that the delay would have serious consequences in NER's fundraising efforts in America and therefore future assistance from the American public:

> This, of course, makes it very difficult indeed for us in America to secure funds for continuation of our purely relief work, much less for adequate agricultural and industrial development, for the average American citizen naturally argues that if the government of the country does not give every possible assistance there is little reason why America should make sacrifices to support any child-welfare or other developments within the country when of course there is no thought or possibility of any financial, political or other benefit to the American contributor.[316]

It is unclear which of the letters Vickrey eventually sent, but a mandate was finally signed in Tiflis on February 10, 1923.[317] In broad terms, it upheld the guarantees offered to NER in earlier agreements, but added a number of restrictions and limitations not found in the mandate of 1921. It stated that NER desired to care for 25,000 orphans and provide them with food, clothing and medicine, and that from the remaining donations it would care for children and adults who were still not cared for, regardless of nationality or religion; and that NER would organize the work of reconstruction through agricultural machinery and equipment introduced into Armenia.

As an organization, continued the mandate, NER and its American staff were exempt from taxation. NER would pay no taxes on all goods related to relief work in the TSFSR, and the cost of transporting relief and related goods in the territory of TSFSR would be free of charge. Goods would be forwarded after customs inspection. The government guaranteed the safety of the American staff and their freedom of movement within the territory of the TSFSR, and would provide them with certificates, free of charge. Free of charge also were the facilities used by NER currently or in the future and the use of telephone and telegram for official business.

On the other hand, the mandate found it necessary to state that NER's activities should be strictly limited to humanitarian work and that under no circumstances could it have a political, religious or business dimension. Furthermore, none of the goods and objects imported by NER for humanitarian purposes could be sold or exchanged by NER for other goods in the internal markets of the TSFSR or SSRA, either directly or through individuals, without prior authorization. And, should any of its foreign officials violate those rules, NER was obligated to expel, and if necessary, remove such officials from the boundaries of TSFSR. All of NER's native employees were subject to the laws of the country and all foreign nationals working for NER were subject to the laws operating in the SSRA, with permissions and limitations pertaining to foreigners. Additionally, all relations between NER and its native employees, such as vacation time and work hours, were to be governed by the country's labor laws.

The limitations continued with the stipulation that NER facilities could be inspected by representatives of the government but only in the presence of a liaison appointed by the TSFSR to facilitate communication between the authorities and NER. As for NER's mail, outgoing mail would be inspected by representatives of the government in Tiflis and sealed with NER's seals and the seal of the liaison, and then sent to Batum for shipment outside TSFSR. NER's incoming mail would be sealed while still on board ship, by the representatives from NER and the liaison's office and then forwarded to Tiflis. There, the seal would be broken and the mail inspected by the liaison, after which it would be handed over to NER's representative for distribution.

One of the most significant limitations in the February 1923 agreement had to do with the education and upbringing of the thousands of orphans under NER's care, who in the near future would be entering Soviet society. In no uncertain terms, the mandate stated that the education and upbringing of the children would be conducted under the supervision of the People's Commissariat of Enlightenment, that all curricula used in NER schools and kindergartens should correspond to those used in state schools, and that the teaching faculty would be accountable to the Commissariat of Enlightenment.

The issue of children's education and upbringing had been discussed earlier, in 1922, when the Commissariat of Enlightenment had reminded NER's Director of Education that while the instruction of the English language was allowed because European languages were taught in Soviet schools,[318] NER would have to refrain from teaching morality or ethics to the children. The People's Commissariat of Enlightenment had at that time also pointed out that NER school curricula would have to correspond to the curriculum used in state schools. More, the people's Commissariat of Enlightenment was authorized to confirm the appointment of supervisors and teachers before they were hired.

NER's obligations in the area of orphan education and upbringing were revisited two months after the February 1923 mandate by People's Commissar of Enlightenment Askanaz Mravyan of Armenia.[319] According to the agreement signed between NER and TSFSR, Mravyan wrote, the upbringing and education of orphans in all NER orphanages should proceed under the supervision of the Commissariat of Enlightenment. To ensure the normal course of education and upbringing, to regulate supervision and to preempt possible misunderstandings in the future, Mravyan wished to familiarize NER's Director of Education with the approach that the Commissariat would apply. Areas touched by the new regulations included schools, orphanages, workshops, and boy scout organizations. Instructors were obligated to ensure that the curricula and statutes of state schools were applied and when necessary to make observations and comment on them. To imbue the work of upbringing and education with the dignity it deserved, Mravyan continued, instructors appointed by the state would organize courses, conferences, lectures and exhibits, and come to an agreement with NER on the expenses involved. Mravyan then suggested that it was important to open technicums for agriculture and organize trade workshops. In other words, NER was now obligated to ensure that the education and upbringing it provided the army of orphans would help them transition, in the near future, into young Soviet, socialist citizens.

In 1923, the City of Orphans was no longer under the exclusive purview of NER. In the course of additional changes and restrictions that ensued in the months and years to come, NER's sovereignty was slowly but irrevocably diminished. Local unions would be established in NER's orphanages; in the hiring of new employees, NER would be obligated to do so through institutions qualified to provide workers, subject to all regulations announced by the People's Commissariat of Labor; and NER could not keep personnel who were of draft age. NER had the right to have guards to protect its institutions, but they could be armed only with the types of guns allowed by the state and with the proviso that the total number of guns in each NER establishment did not exceed the number of guns in the possession of the city police. The Military and the Cheka, if warranted, had the right to search NER premises and make arrests, but only after notifying NER's administration which would then be allowed to be present during those operations, if they so desired. Finally, NER would have to be diligent in registering deaths and births. As specific areas of NER's jurisdiction were formulated, by 1923 NER was also told, again, to end the teaching of religion in its schools and that missionaries were barred from working in Armenia.[320]

Writing seven years after the February 1923 mandate, James Barton referred to the "increasing co-operation from the Soviet officials," which within a year after NER's return to Armenia had resulted in an agreement that "gave the Committee [NER] concessions and privileges not accorded to any other foreign company or organization."[321] He considered the conclusions to be of "such importance and showed the influence of the humanitarian work on the Soviet government" that he quoted "the most significant items from the agreement" that had been entered into in 1922.[322] However, the 22 provisions of the agreement he published in 1930 focused exclusively on the concessions and privileges extended to NER. None of the restrictions and limitations of the February 1923 mandate were included in his account.

Along with the growing control over NER's activities also grew the role of the office of the liaison, or representation office, to facilitate the flow of communication between NER and Soviet authorities, and, to keep the authorities abreast of the world within the walls of the orphanages. Myasnikyan had appointed Sargis Abovyan as liaison in October 1921 to facilitate communication between the SSRA government and NER[323] followed, in November, by the appointment of Dr. Melkumyan, who had been in NER's employ the year before, as liaison officer between NER and the SSRA government in Alexandropol. Milton Brown, signing as the personal representative of the Director General, had expressed his gratitude to Myasnikyan for Melkumyan's appointment.[324] By 1923, among the liaisons were Georgy Sargsyan, representing the People's Commissars in Alexandropol and Nariman Ter-Ghazaryan, representing the TSFSR to all foreign humanitarian organizations. Their responsibilities included the regularization of channels of communication; handling of all requests, complaints, instructions and resolutions from the government and the NER; ensuring that relief work proceeded smoothly and that directives and policies developed in Yerevan or Tiflis were applied. The issues that reached the liaison included requests from NER for suitable orphanage buildings in Yerevan,[325] requests from NER for building material for the orphanages,[326] requests for loans in guns and ammunitions from the government,[327] requests to purchase telephones,[328] request to use the tennis court in Yerevan,[329] requests for the exemption of NER's Armenian employees from military service, the latter being one of the most frequent,[330] and complaints about NER from various districts.[331]

Two pages of the questionnaire signed by NER relief worker Lila Stanley in 1923. (NAA 131/3/20/f. 65)

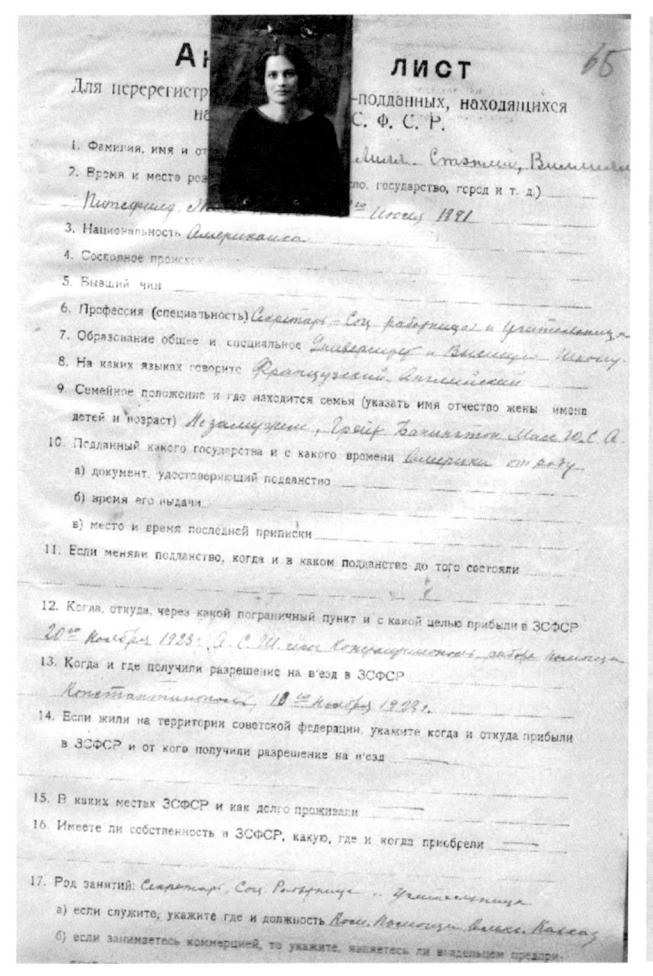

Liaisons sent frequent reports to Yerevan or Tiflis updating Soviet authorities on relief activities. One comprehensive report dated May 26, 1923, shows the extent to which the liaisons followed the affairs of the NER within the City of Orphans.[332] Prepared by N. Ter-Ghazaryan, the report described the positive impact and success of the expanded liaison's office, and the close attention liaisons paid to the employees of the NER, local or foreign. Until 1922, it read, NER had 4,500 native employees who were selected primarily from the refugees and from the former military and intellectual class. About 80–90% of them were not members of labor unions and there were no representatives of the local labor unions in any of NER's institutions. Before the liaison or representation system had taken shape, NER and its employees had functioned independently in the area of orphan education and upbringing. Older pedagogical methods were used and the laws of God were taught. And although NER's highest administration had tried to block changes requested by Soviet authorities and had threatened to leave the Transcaucasus, changes had nevertheless been applied at NER schools and orphanages. Now, the People's Commissariat of Enlightenment ensured that the education of orphans corresponded to the programs and the standards of state schools.

With respect to relations with governmental bodies and until the establishment of the system, Ter-Ghazaryan continued, NER had dealt with and related to all governmental, professional, public and private institutions directly, which had

> …created the impression that the NER was a completely autonomous institution, a type of state within a state. The NER flag could be seen flying everywhere, and foreign mail passed without supervision or being sealed. From the first day of the existence of the representation, the NER was told to stop direct dealings with governmental bodies,

and to broach issues through the liaison only. This provided the opportunity for the representation office

> …to be informed of the progress of NER's work and to liquidate all the misunderstandings and conflicts between the NER and governmental bodies, as well as trade and public organizations.

The next area regulated through the liaisons, continued Ter-Ghazaryan, was the hiring and firing of employees, which NER had conducted single-handedly, hiring the most backward thinking employees. The representation intended to collect information on all 4,500 employees through questionnaires, a copy of which would be kept at the office of the Cheka. With respect to foreign personnel, the liaison's

Front page of NER Ophthalmologist Russell Uhls's personal certificate issued in 1922. (NAA 131/1/104/f. 1)

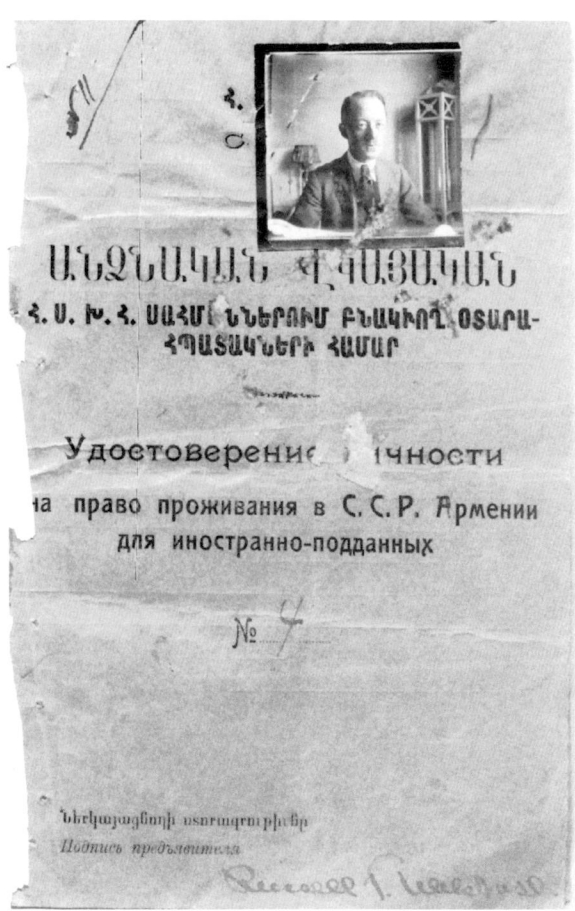

role included protecting their rights and freedom of movement, their right to receive passports from the outside, and their exemption from taxes on personal packages from outside. The liaison kept regular communication with NER through daily meetings with the Chief Director, and additionally, the liaison was now empowered to fire employees who did not perform their responsibilities appropriately.

Other changes included the liaison's involvement in NER's conduct in commercial operations through state and economic bodies; in the distribution of relief which was no longer to be the purview of the NER alone; in the inspection of NER's foreign mail, together with the Transcaucasus Cheka, which regularly inspected NER's mail, and then resealed it. The representation's office, the report continued, was now involved in the accounting of freight from the outside and use of credit for railroad expenses. Now, through regular inspections, all freight addressed to foreign organizations was accounted for, and a detailed accounting was requested on how the railroad credit was used. For the transportation of freight, the liaison had given NER 148,171 rubles and 65 kopeks between January 1 and May 26, 1923, and the cost of NER's utilities, post and telegram expenses had amounted to 4,464,750 rubles. For the third quarter of 1923, the Sovnarkom, the Council of People's Commissars, had appropriated 80,000,000 rubles for transportation of provisions and other material.

At the end of the report, Ter-Ghazaryan commented that the British Mission, which was limited to Armenia, was insignificant by comparison to NER. The British Mission had only two orphanages, in Yerevan, where 99 girls and 61 boys were housed, but who were being educated at NER's schools. He noted that NER's activities had decreased since January 1923, and that no new orphans were being accepted. Finally, he explained that there were two different opinions at NER about their future activities: one group wished to continue work in the Transcaucasus while the other wished to move operations to Persia, Turkey and Greece. In view of the importance of foreign relief for Armenia, certain complications could arise, cautioned Ter-Ghazaryan, should foreign relief organizations decide to withdraw from Armenia.

The increased watchfulness over NER had to do, at least in part, with the protection NER's Armenian employees enjoyed as members of an American organization. In 1922, Lukashin had alerted Myasnikyan of the problem and stated that steps were being taken. "The American Committee," he had written to Myasnikyan,

> ...nurtures counter-revolutionary organizations. By the decision of the Central Committee, it has been decided to disarm the militia of the American organization; to appoint governmental commissars in the main institutions of Amerkom [American Committee, NER]; to register all employees and pass them through the filter of the unions; and to cleanse Karakilis of the American institutions and give their buildings to the headquarters of the Armenian brigade leaving a small area of Karakilis to Amerkom.
>
> We ask that you inform Ter Ghazaryan to raise all these issues in Tiflis and to obtain Yarrow's permission.[333]

Adoption Revisited

Another change of policy introduced after Armenia's Sovietization related to the adoption of Armenian orphans by Americans in the U.S. The change in policy did not apply to NER's sponsorship program whereby Americans in the U.S., among them President and First Lady Harding and President and First Lady Wilson, would support one or more children in the orphanage in Armenia through monthly or annual stipends.[334] Rather, the policy change related to the earlier practice of sending orphans for adoption in the U.S., which according to the new regulations, was categorically forbidden. This was a departure from the early years of NER's relief operations in Armenia when trainloads of children were sent to Batum and from there by ship to ports in the U.S. It is not clear how many shiploads of children were sent to the U.S. nor has a record of the exact number of orphans, their names or their locations in the U.S. been available. There exists, however, some episodic information about the process of orphan selection that has emerged during interviews with former orphans and their descendants. It can be inferred from these recollections that the process took careful planning and deliberation, and was highly selective.

Circumstances under which orphans were selected seem to have lingered on for decades in the memories of some former orphans. In young Gohar, the older sister of Hovhannes Shiraz, it was a story she often told her granddaughter, Mrs. Narine Khachatryan, a musician and a docent at the Hovhannes Shiraz House Museum in Gyumri.[335] "When I was a young girl," Mrs. Khachatryan recounted to this author in October 2013,

> I often stayed over at my grandmother's home...in the evenings she liked telling me stories about her childhood...

> Some of the stories brought back painful memories to her. The cruelest of her memories were of her years in the orphanage...I remember that there was one specific incident which was especially painful for her, but which she would retell often:

>> One day when we woke up, they told us to wash up quickly...then they bathed a few of the orphans, put clean clothes on them and made them stand in line. We were waiting for a guest, we were told. I don't remember how long we waited, but we were tired when the guests came.

> Among the guests was a grey-haired woman, and

>> ...In the hands of the grey-haired woman was a measuring tape. The guests all went into the nurses' office and began calling us in one by one. Each orphan who came out looked at the rest of us with astonished eyes, and none of them answered any questions.

>> Then it was my turn. I went in. They began to measure first my height, then the length and width of my limbs. First the measurement around the thumb, then the wrist, then the neck, the waist, the distance between the eyes, the distance between the temple to the nose, between the nose and the mouth and the shape of the face. The shape of the nose was especially

> noted. I, too, like all the rest, was surprised, but didn't ask any questions, and left the room.
>
> A few weeks went by, and one morning they woke us up early again, made us wait in line and began to read names. The orphans whose names were announced stepped away from the line.
>
> Etched in my memory is the beauty of those girls: they were all of the same height, same facial shape, and same beauty. They put them all in a car and took them away. We found out later that they took them all to the U.S.

My grandmother would talk about this episode very often and would become visibly unhappy. One day, with my child's curiosity, I asked her why they had not taken her. My grandmother answered:

> I was short, and Manik (my grandmother's sister) was too tall. That is why they didn't take us. They had chosen only the girls who fit the required norms [of beauty] and intelligence.

Surprised, I asked what the standard proportions were. My grandmother explained that if the thumb measured 8cm, then the forearm should be 16cm, and the neck 32cm, the waist 64cm. These were considered the ideal proportions of physical beauty.

The required norms of beauty had at times caused the separation of siblings if only one of them was accepted for adoption in the U.S. This was the case with the two Sukyasyan sisters—Armenuhi and Amalya—at the Severski, when only the younger sister, Amalya, was accepted for adoption. Armenuhi was not chosen, Amalya explained decades later, because

> …she had a big nose; they used to say she was bad; that's why they didn't take her. But the teachers liked her because she was so vivacious…

Armenuhi, said Amalya, "wanted to go to America," but when one day the children

> …had been divided into two or three groups, and they were making the selections…
>
> …Armenuhi would run and stand among those who had been selected. They would take her by the arm and take her back to her place. And this went on a few times. At the end, when they saw that there was no way out, they left us both here.
>
> …Healthy and beautiful boys and girls were sent to America…they would fill entire trains and send them off…[336]

Adoption in America was brought to an end early in the Soviet period. A cable from Yerevan ordered the immediate return of the last trainload of children just as the train had reached Batum and preparations were being made to board the ship for the U.S. And when the question of adoption in the U.S. reemerged later on, SSRA policy consistently opposed it. One communiqué for instance, dated October 10, 1925, from Georgy Sargsyan, inquired whether the Council of People's Commissars would agree to the adoption of children overseas:[337]

> The NER receives applications from American citizens abroad to adopt Armenian children in the orphanages. Is it possible to send the children abroad for that purpose and by which procedure can that be done?

The answer came on November 9, 1925, from the *Gaghtni Bazhin* [Secret Department] of the government, quoting Mravyan:

> If the adoption of the orphans by the Americans is associated to the children leaving for America—the People's Commissariat of Enlightenment is opposed to it.[338]

Another note, from Nariman Ter-Ghazaryan to A. Mravyan at the People's Commissariat of Enlightenment, dated October 28, 1925, Leninakan, inquired regarding the policy on overseas adoptions:

> The NER has come to us many times, asking permission to allow citizens of the Northern United States of America to adopt children from the NER orphanages. For that reason I wish to ask if it is acceptable to send Armenian orphans to be adopted by citizens of the Northern United States, and if so, to instruct us about adoption procedures.[339]

The decision remained the same: If the adoption of the children by Americans depended on the children leaving for America, the People's Commissariat of Enlightenment is opposed to it. Still, requests for adoption had reemerged in February 1926.[340]

The Matter of Rare Books, Manuscripts and Used Clothes

Myasnikyan's government launched efforts to collect, centralize, and preserve all archival material and museum objects related to the history of Armenians under the auspices of the state. The laws that were passed in this respect were publicized in the January 7, 1922, issue of *Khorhrdayin Hayastan*, strictly banning the destruction of archival papers by individuals or institutions. Two months later, on March 6, 1922, Myasnikyan endorsed a mandate by Commissar of Enlightenment Poghos Makintsyan, asking all institutions in the Russian Socialist Federation to use all possible ways to transfer all archival material, antiquities, and museum objects in their possession related to Armenia, to the government of SSRA as soon as possible.[341]

One year after the law had been announced, NER and liaison Ter-Ghazaryan exchanged letters and admonitions, spurred by an article published in the Armenian newspaper *Joghovurdi dsayn* in Constantinople on March 15, 1923. The article was entitled "The American Committee Protects Armenian Antiquities" and drew attention to NER's practice of buying rare books and manuscripts in exchange for used clothes so as to save them. It read, in part:

> The employees of NER were able to save from spoilage 30,000 biblical manuscripts decorated with garlands and illustrations. Those books were obtained as a result of the exchanges with used clothes. The Americans…are trying, as much as possible,

to preserve old Armenian traditions by gathering the classical works of Armenian writers.

About two weeks later, on April 5, 1923, Ter-Ghazaryan's office issued a terse note to NER's Tiflis Director.[342] The letter quoted the announcement in *Joghovurdi dzayn*, and continued:

> By informing you about it, I ask that you do not refuse to provide written answers to the following questions posed by the government of Soviet Armenia:
>
> 1. By whose arrangement and from which area have the above-mentioned books been collected?
>
> 2. At the same time, what measures have been taken on your part to prevent similar purchases in Armenia without obtaining the appropriate permission from governmental bodies? And,
>
> 3. For what reason have the above-mentioned antiquities not yet been presented to the museum of the government of Armenia?

It is unclear if NER was aware of the laws publicized one year earlier. The response from Mr. Marden of the NER office in Tiflis came on April 16, 1923, and was a protest against citizen Ter-Ghazaryan's inferences:

> In answer to your letter…I [wish to] inform you, that the article published in *Joghovurdi dzayn* is significantly exaggerated.
>
> One year ago, before Captain Yarrow left, an attempt was made to save large quantities of Armenian books by paying needy people with used clothing; and in that way to preserve that Armenian literature which would otherwise be lost. They are still being protected by the committee [NER], and after Captain Yarrow returns I suggest that you discuss their final disposition with him.[343]

The letter was evidently forwarded to Lukashin, who in his handwritten note at the top of the letter specified the next step to be taken:

> Instruct Ter-Ghazaryan and Abovyan to ascertain the quantity, list and suggest returning [them to] the museum…SL [Sergei Lukashin] June 12, 1923.

The last word in the hand-written note reads: "Accomplished."

A few months after the controversy over the manuscripts, the SSRA and NER signed a contract on September 1, 1923, in Alexandropol, regulating the distribution and sale of used clothes.[344] According to the terms of the contract NER could sell used clothing in American packaging of a certain size, each of about 5 poods [about 82 kilos] at the price of $80 per package, calculated in American currency or NER checks, according to the day's rates. The government agreed to buy 1,000 poods of used clothing from NER, payable on or before the 15th of each month. The exchange would take place in either Alexandropol or Tiflis, so long as the cost of transportation was undertaken by TSFSR. In the event that used clothes were of inferior quality, had been damaged while in transit, or if the packages were not of the appropriate size, NER would repackage them such that each would weigh about 5 poods. The

Hay and livestock exchanged for used clothes bales. (*The New Near East*, March 1922: 11)

two sides also agreed that if the conditions of the agreement were not met by the government or if the government, for any reason, could not deliver on its obligations, then NER would be permitted to sell the used clothes in the open market to cover its needs in the Caucasus, as had hitherto been the practice, without any interference.

Collected from American citizens of almost every state of the Union, the thousands of tons of used clothing had been, and continued to be, through the 1920s, a currency sometimes more trusted than the ruble. In the early years of NER operations old clothes bales had proven their indispensable value in clothing thousands of refugees and orphans and routinely used as a commodity in exchange for labor, as barter for hay, firewood and foodstuff for the orphanages.[345] In its September 1923 issue, *The New Near East* announced that in the preceding six months of that year, the Purchasing Department in the Caucasus area had been able to pay "all but $10,000 of the $85,000 expenditures" with American old clothes. Of the remaining $10,000 in expenditures, $5,000 was made with corn grits and only $5,000 was paid out in cash.[346] The terms of the September 1 agreement now placed the right to exchange old clothes from the U.S. into official channels, aiming to put an end to the exchange of old clothes by what one document of May 9, 1923, called "speculating individuals" who sold the goods in the open markets with significant profit, particularly since excise tax was not paid on relief.[347]

The rare manuscripts and books remained with NER until July 1924, when acceding to the government's request Ernest Yarrow formed a committee led by Varazdat Deroyan to receive from NER, and transport to the manuscript repository of Etchmiadzin a number of old Armenian rare books and manuscripts, together with an iron safe to keep them secure.[348] In total, Deroyan transferred 82 manuscripts and 300–400 publications in classical

Armenian. Ernest Yarrow described the transfer in his letter of July 4, 1924, addressed to Lukashin:[349]

> Mr. Sarkis LUKASHIN,
> President of the Council of Commissars
> of the People of Armenia
>
> It is with the greatest pleasure that I wish today to acquit myself of a duty towards Armenia, by turning over to the Library of Etchmiadzin, through your intermediary, our modest collection of manuscripts and rare publications.
>
> The Near East Relief has not only endeavored to care for orphans and refugees in Armenia, to save them from famine and disease, but has also tried to accomplish another task, besides and within its regular duties.
>
> It does not behoove me to quote and commend our work of the past and of the present. But whoever assumes to record our achievements in this country, surely will not overlook the modest token of today.
>
> There was a time when ancient Armenian culture and literature were also homeless and unprotected, as the thousands of children in our orphanages. It is very fortunate that they have found for the first time protecting parents in the persons of yourselves and the Armenian Government, and the fact leads us to believe that the day is near when our children, too, will be able to flourish without any parents.
>
> A happy coincidence will afford me the possibility of sending to you one of our collaborators, Mr. V. Deroyan, who personally directed the work of salvaging these manuscripts in time, and who is also appointed to handle the details of their transfer to you.
>
> With friendliest regards,
> [signed] E. A. Yarrow

In the document that was signed on July 4, 1924, the collection was described as a gift from NER to the SSRA. The signatories were E. A. Yarrow, M.D. Brown and V. M. Deroyan representing NER, and the "Representative of the Council of Commissars of the People of Armenia."[350] The agreement included a total of nine clauses, which stated that the collection was a gift of the Near East Relief to the Library of Etchmiadzin and would "not be reattributed"; that the gift was to be accepted as a token of Armenian and American friendship; that the state would respect "the desire of the Near East Relief, by safe-keeping the collection in the Library of Manuscripts at Etchmiadzin for all time"; and that both sides could publish the agreement in any daily newspaper in Yerevan and New York. Clause #4 of the document read:

> The Near East Relief also presents to the LIBRARY [Etchmiadzin] a metal Book Case with the following inscription in Armenian & English:

A GIFT
FROM THE NEAR EAST RELIEF
TO THE LIBRARY OF ANCIENT MANUSCRIPTS AT ECHMIADZIN
JULY 4, 1924
E. A. YARROW

It appears from the Agreement that NER had at one time considered publishing a catalog of the collection, as inferred from clause #7, which read:

> The same Party [Council of People's Commissars] also engages itself to allow free disposal of the Collection to any one member of the First Party [NER] when the Near East Relief decides to realize its desire, that is the publication of the scientific and illustrated catalog of the collection.

"A State Within a State"... and Its Challenge(r)s

If TSFSR and SSRA would introduce restrictions on NER's privileges and regulate its activities, they would still have to continue the policy of cooperation for the time being because, as Ter-Ghazaryan cautioned, "certain complications could arise, should foreign relief decide to withdraw from Armenia." After all, there were still thousands of orphans whose future without NER's support could be uncertain, at best. Besides, NER was not a negligible relief operation; it was the largest of all philanthropies operating in the Near East after WWI, with an impressive and unprecedented infrastructure of networks in the U.S. The organization had been able to put in place a system of fundraising in the U.S. that involved almost every element of the American public with thousands of volunteers from Hawaii to New York, Maine to Georgia, and had been able to raise millions for relief work.[351] The material that volunteers had at their disposal touched the hearts and souls of the U.S. public from school children and prisoners in state penitentiaries to mothers and grandmothers, women in high society and churchmen, senators to presidents and university presidents, influential newspaper editors and businessmen. Almost always, national, regional and local committees were chaired by city, state and federal officials, men and women who held influential positions in media outlets, political circles, financial establishments and industry.[352] And, it enjoyed the support of U.S. presidents. H. C. Jaquith, who served as NER Director in Greece and Turkey declared in 1924 that NER's character and mission were unlike any other U.S. organization's:

> The position of this organization is unique. Groups of Americans have long maintained organizations abroad; commercial organizations, such as the Standard Oil and the American Tobacco Company; humanitarian relief organizations, the Red Cross, the Friends, the Y.M.C.A. and many others. But the exigencies of the situation in the Near East have made the Near East Relief almost a nation in itself—a nation without a country, a power without an army, a responsibility without any tangible resources, a weight in international councils. The mere creation and existence of this organization, with its influence as a factor in the Near Eastern situation, have made it important in any consideration of that situation.[353]

The significance of Jaquith's characterization of NER was not lost to Soviet officials. Liaison Ter-Ghazaryan had described NER as "a state within a state," in 1923, just as People's Commissar of Agriculture Aramayis Yerznkyan thought that NER, in many ways, was a "government within a government." In large part, this was due to the amount of relief it distributed in Armenia, vastly superior to the British or the Norwegian missionary Bodil Biørn, in terms of duration and sheer quantity. NER's uniqueness was also predicated upon the fact that it had been incorporated by the U.S. Congress on August 6, 1919, and enjoyed special, official approval of its efforts to organize food and medicine shipments to the Near East. In Armenia, particularly in Alexandropol, the "power without an army" was physically anchored in monumental structures that had once exuded the formidable power of the Czar. Even in their dilapidated and ruinous state in 1922, according to the American artist and journalist John dos Passos, "the great rows of gray barracks" were "the most outstanding buildings" in Alexandropol.[354]

When Barclay Acheson saw the buildings for the first time, he remarked that structures that once housed the Czar's soldiers now epitomized "America's answer" to the challenge of thousands of Armenian orphans:

> ...In Czarist days the great stone barracks that stretched along the roads for miles, like sentinels, housed some of the proudest crack troops of the Russian Empire. Polygon, a group of over eighty large buildings, housed the officers, men, horses, and guns of an artillery regiment. Severski and Kazachi were even more imposing. The first was built for the cavalry, the second for the infantry. But all the swaggering men in gray uniforms were gone. They and their Czar were dead, and their empire and the world they frequented had perished with them.[355]

Most of the buildings, he continued, had been partially destroyed but "American money had again put most of them in repair. Around the buildings,

> ...the trench-scarred artillery range was being plowed by a great line of American tractors. The level parade grounds had become truck gardens, weeded by children in cheap white uniforms made by themselves. The new government had given the buildings and land to house and feed the greatest concentration of defenseless children the world has ever seen. American personnel and American dollars organized it and provided for its maintenance.[356]

NER's vision of activities was wider and encompassed more than Armenia or the Caucasus. Already in the summer of 1921 NER's leadership had begun cultivating relations in the Russian Federation and in August 1921, it had sent a commission to report on the Volga region. The commission consisted of Albert A. Johnson (Chairman), Director of the New York State Institute of Applied Agriculture; Paxton Hibben (Secretary), Secretary of the U.S. Embassy in Petrograd from 1905–1906 and Fellow of the Royal and the American Geographical Societies; Ernest Yarrow (Treasurer), Director General of NER Caucasus Branch; Frank Connes, official interpreter of the Supreme Court of the State of New York with service in the American Red Cross in Russia during WWI; and John R. Voris, NER Associate General Secretary. To proceed to the Volga region for observation of conditions, permission was sought from the authorities of the Georgian SSR, Russian Socialist Federated Soviet

Republic representative Boris Legrand, and Chief of the political section of the 11th Russian Army Morris Lisofsky on August 4, 1921, in Tiflis.[357] The group, known as *The Russian Commission of the Near East Relief* was organized on August 12, 1921, and left Tiflis on August 16, returning on September 12, 1921. The Georgian government had supplied a private car at no cost to NER, for a tour that covered 4,863 miles. During the tour, the commission visited Stavropol, Kuban-Black Sea, Don, Kharkov, Voronezh, Tambov, Ryazin, Moscow, Penza, Simbirsk, Samara, Saratov, Tsaritsyn, Astrakhan, etc. It also met a number of high officials, among them Lev Kamenev, Leonid Krasin, Georgy Chicherin, Vladimir Sokolsky, Budu Mdivani, Gregory Weinstein, and others. The information the commission gathered was published in a booklet and made available for sale in the U.S. The results of the discussions as well as the group's observations and conclusions had been cabled to New York and to Herbert Hoover periodically, but the latter had never once replied to NER's cables.[358]

In Armenia, relations were routinely cultivated with successive Chairmen of the People's Commissars—Sergei Lukashin, Sargis Hambardzumyan, Sahak Ter Gabrielyan—and various Commissars, by leading NER representatives as Charles Vickrey, Ernest Yarrow, and Barclay Acheson. Director General Yarrow would confer regularly with SSRA government officials, among them Alexander Myasnikyan.[359] Enjoying respect within and without Armenia, on May 5, 1922, Ernest Yarrow met Armenian representatives in Constantinople and outlined the situation in Armenia, NER's efforts there, and praised the government of SSRA, especially Alexander Myasnikyan, who was "doing his utmost to really help the people."[360] In 1923, Yarrow was involved in discussions with the government on issues beyond those immediately related to the orphanage he directed. One such issue was the proposed transfer of orphans from orphanages in the Middle East to Armenia and NER's orphanage at Alexandropol, on which Yarrow consulted with several government members in Yerevan, including Lukashin and produced a road map. The text was sent to NER's European Representative Gordon Berry in Geneva, Switzerland and a copy to Sergei Lukashin. There, Yarrow detailed a comprehensive approach covering the core problems that were at the basis of the future of the orphans:

> If Armenians living in foreign countries desire to cooperate with this government, they must do so in a whole-hearted and sincere spirit, accepting its authority and in general becoming loyal to its principles.

But this was not so easy, because

> At present there are various committees or organizations, which represent themselves as the mouthpiece of the Armenian people. I believe there is still a remnant of the old Caucasus Armenian government who call themselves national representatives of the Armenian people. Everyone knows that this has become simply an empty term, but these people must recognize the fact that there is only one Armenian government and only those who have been officially delegated by this government can speak in its behalf. During this past winter there has been a great deal of agitation regarding settling of Armenian refugees in various parts of Russia, and also Armenia, but I doubt whether the Armenian government has been requested to delegate a representative to take part in these negotiations.

Yarrow next broached the subject of financial support to Armenia:

> It is understood here that there are several legacies which have been left by wealthy Armenians for the purpose of furthering the interests of the Armenian nation. There seems to be no effort on the part of those who control these funds to make them available for the development of the only country in which there is a real Armenian life and national existence. If the present Armenia is to progress, it is in need, and very urgent need, of all the possible funds it can get at its disposal. Therefore, the government here feels that if prominent Armenians in different parts of the world have a real interest in the Armenian national existence, they ought to take all necessary steps to make these legacy funds available at once.

Yarrow realized that the transfer of funds could meet legal difficulties especially in terms of applying the funds to Armenia, but felt that those legal difficulties could be overcome, and continued:

> My personal recommendation would be, if these funds can be made available, to form a mixed commission consisting of three persons to administer these funds, one from the present government, one selected by Armenians outside of Armenia, and the third an American who has had close contact with both parties and who is also familiar with the situation here.

For the American component of the committee, he offered his own services:

> It is far from my thoughts or desire to seek added responsibility, but I would be willing to act on such a commission if deemed advisable, believing that I would have the confidence both of the government here and of Armenians in various parts of the world. Of course, this commission would have to act in every case with the approval of the government…

Having had multiple discussions with the government of Soviet Armenia about the transfer of orphans, Yarrow summarized:

> The government is willing to accept children from outside up to the capacity of the land available, but it must have absolute guarantees that these children will not be simply dumped onto this country and the support withdrawn. They would wish that the general responsibility would be assumed by the Near East Relief, which is an organization of somewhat permanent character, although the details of the transfer and maintenance could be carried on by the societies providing the funds…[361]

On January 23, 1924, two days after Lenin's death, Yarrow hastened to write a letter of condolences to Ter-Ghazaryan. Copies of the letter were also forwarded to Lukashin, Dr. Melkumyan in Alexandropol, the Central Government at Moscow and to the President of the Transcaucasian Government. "We hasten to express through you to the government of the Union of Socialist Soviet Republics our sympathy in this your loss," he wrote and added:

> However great difference of opinion may exist in the world outside of Russia as to some of the policies experimented with during the past years of transition and crisis, all thinking people conversant with the world's history will agree that Comrade Lenin will go down in history as one of Russia's greatest leaders…as well as one of the world's greatest statesmen produced during the period of the world war.

Propose "International Peace Park" at Mount Ararat

Photo of Ernest Yarrow mounted against Mount Ararat. (*The Elyria Chronicle Telegram*, September 13, 1924)

Yarrow praised "Comrade Lenin" for his "protest against an intolerable autocracy and championship of the rights of the laborer," and assured Ter-Ghazaryan that

> The Near East Relief joins with all true citizens of the world in its appreciation of the character of your lamented leader...[362]

A few months later, a significant number of U.S. newspapers carried a photograph of Ernest Yarrow appended below a photograph of Mount Ararat, above which was printed "Propose 'International Peace Park' at Mount Ararat." The caption under the photograph read:

> Proposals have been made by Armenia, through E. A. Yarrow, head of the Near East Relief, to interest Americans in a plan to establish an "international peace park" on the border of Turkey and Armenia, including the whole of Mount Ararat, upon which Norah's Ark is supposed to have grounded when the flood waters began to recede...[363]

NER's relations with SSRA included gifts for members of the government, secular and lay. NER gifted the Catholicosate in Etchmiadzin and the government with several American cars. The NER had adjusted, at least on the surface, to government regulations. The Norwegian missionary Bodil Katharine Bjørn who had founded *Lusaghbyur*, a small orphanage in a former luxurious villa in Alexandropol for about 30 of the weakest orphans, did not enjoy a similar relationship with the authorities. Bjørn had emphasized the importance of a home atmosphere and personalized care. But the numbers were never over thirty at any given time. With the growing intolerance of the state toward Christian teaching, an aspect of care Biørn did not wish to exclude from her orphanage, the authorities eventually closed down the orphanage in 1925 and the orphans were transferred to NER. Her pleas to the authorities to reverse the decision were unheeded.[364] A year later, the British Committee also stopped relief and orphan care in Armenia.

Barclay Acheson was especially active in the mid and latter half of the 1920s in meetings with government officials with whom he enjoyed cordial relationships. His letter to Lukashin from Batum on August 12, 1924, reflected the personal relationships he cultivated with SSRA's leadership. Before leaving the Caucasus, Acheson wrote,

> …Will you permit me to express to you personally, my genuine pleasure in your acquaintance. My stay in the Caucasus has been a pleasant one. Plans have been inaugurated and problems solved. I am convinced that the outcome will be an improved program for our Near East Relief institutions, and an improved citizenship when the orphans are discharged into normal life. Your continued cooperation and assistance in that sense is important for success. I am very glad that you hold the position you do and are so deeply interested in the future of these children. Your many efforts to improve the environment within which the children will live out their lives, including irrigation projects, educational efforts, etc. will be a source of great encouragement to that segment of the American public which has invested so much in these children and which is so genuinely and sympathetically interested in the future of the Armenian Republic.
>
> Permit me again to thank you for the kind hospitality that I have enjoyed and particularly for the assistance which you gave me in my trip to Tabriz. Your kindness on that occasion will always be remembered.
>
> I look forward with pleasure to seeing you again in six months. I am now on my way for America, where I will do everything that I can to encourage and strengthen the growing friendship between the United States and Russia.[365]

On the home front, Acheson highlighted the positive changes in Soviet Armenia and addressed NER's justification for continued cooperation with Bolsheviks. In his essay entitled "An Emerging Russia," Acheson tried to dispel the negative image the Bolsheviks had acquired in the U.S.:

> The Bolshevist government has been in control in Armenia for about four years. During that time there have been innumerable prophecies of disintegration and counterrevolution, but throughout Russia the present government is probably stronger today than ever before. One of the causes of its strength and long continuance in office is the fact that the present government officials are more nearly practical politicians than theorists. They have set out to make a profession of politics.[366]

He had been especially impressed with Sergei Lukashin:

> I have met Lukashin, President of the Armenian Republic…born leader, but of the practical man-of-affairs type. I was impressed by…his grasp of local, national and international affairs…
>
> There is also a selective and training process going on that is improving the caliber and efficiency of government personnel. This, taken with the patient character of the people, is likely to mean the perpetuation of the present regime for an indefinite time. It may result in complete stabilization.

But, he added:

> At present the government could not undertake the completion of the work of Near East Relief in the Caucasus. Public utilities, such as railroads, telegraph, etc., are in good condition. Outworn equipment is being replaced, the service is being improved and the management and organization seem competent. The new currency is above par. Little progress has been made as yet, however, in establishing new industries…

NER's unique relationship with the Soviet government was announced in many circles and in the U.S. media. At the October 1923 meeting of The National Council of Congregational Churches in Springfield, Massachusetts, James Barton declared:

> The Soviet Government, we were told would confiscate our property and stop our work. But they have not done so. On the other hand they have encouraged us by giving free transportation for both our workers and supplies on the government railroads. Dr. Finley visited this orphanage last summer and was greatly impressed by the work being done. He described the twelve thousand children as the most moving sight in his whole life.[367]

Nevertheless, U.S. public perception of NER's work in Soviet Armenia was divided between those who criticized the organization for working and complying with Soviet authorities and those who felt that NER was delivering an indispensible service to humanity and Christendom. NER relief workers, the latter group felt, were ambassadors of good will and in the absence of official diplomatic relations with Russia, NER had filled a vacuum. Those opposing the first view remained, however, deeply skeptical. *The Chicago Daily Tribune*'s December 15, 1924, issue, for example, reported that for the first time "this American organization has been attacked" by the Cheka:

> The position of the near east relief in the soviet republic of Armenia has become critical.
>
> The cheka has just arrested three principal Armenian teachers in an orphanage in Alexandropol on a charge of counter-revolution and the whole Armenian staff has fallen under suspicion. The fate of the three teachers is unknown. It is the first time the cheka has attacked this American organization, which is caring for 17,000 Armenian orphans in the Caucasus.

The arrest of the teachers had "thrown the near east work under grave suspicion," continued *The Chicago Tribune*, and predicted that "if the cheka interferes further the Americans will practically be forced to get out of Russia."

The article also went on to announce that "Bible teaching is forbidden" and that orphans cared for by NER were being taught communist doctrine and atheist viewpoints:

> …The teaching of communist doctrines to the orphans was one of the essential conditions in the agreement with the soviets. The officials justify this on the ground that as the orphans are going to live in Russia, they should clearly understand the theories and doctrines of the present Russian government.

> ...one or two leading Armenian communists lecture daily to the children on communist doctrines and use official soviet government school books, which treat everything from a communist and atheist viewpoint.

But, *The Tribune* continued, some teachers had not sat idly by, and had

> ...torn out some of the worst pages of the schoolbooks...

Inquiries about the sagacity of NER's expenditures were also raised by some of its supporters. In Denver, Colorado, for instance, one NER supporter had asked Charles Vickrey to account for expenditures:

> Will you kindly explain the press dispatch from Moscow that Near East Relief assisted in building the new irrigation canal near Mount Ararat, which was opened by the Bolshevist premier and other officials a few days ago? I should like to know if Near East Relief contributions are being used to help the Soviet.[368]

In defense of NER was *The Denver Times* editor George Sanford Holmes. He acknowledged that

> The principles of communism espoused by Russia are repugnant to America and the acts of many of its leaders revolting. The face of the American public, as a whole, is set like steel against Bolshevism, its teaching and its methods.

But, he added:

> That the Russian peasant or worker, however, is a beast with horns, a sort of a bogie man, is a popular impression shared by the thoughtless only or those whose prejudices have caused them to lose sight of the fact that human nature is much the same the world over and that the individual Russian is probably but little different from the same person of any country.

NER had understood that, the defense ran, and deserved only praise for its work, which represented "one of the most highly organized and efficient programs of relief in the history of international relations," and it was hardly surprising

> ...that some of its acts have from time to time aroused the criticism of those who have been misinformed in regard to the actual nature of its work and the conditions confronting it abroad, where much of its activity has had to be carried out in close contact with the Soviet government of Russia.[369]

An *"Extraordinary Meeting"*: New York, Summer 1923

Despite divided public opinion in the U.S., NER continued its activities in SSRA. But by 1923, it had also accepted the additional care of Greek and Armenian refugees fleeing the Smyrna catastrophe in September 1922, which demanded large amounts of additional funding. NER's expenditures rose dramatically, just as contributions were ebbing. Some sectors of the U.S. public were tired of giving for a cause that seemed to get only more complicated, and others were impacted by the deflationary depression in the U.S. in 1920 and 1921. In addition, U.S. policy was shifting away from Armenia in large part due to U.S. High Commissioner Rear Admiral Mark Bristol, who opposed NER's public campaigns in support of Armenia and Armenians.

By summer 1923, many contributors had quit, and others were dropping each month. Without an endowment, NER's Executive Committee had taken measures in the hope of curtailing its financial problems and had decided on February 9, 1922, to reduce the budget appropriations of all its institutions in the Near East by 25%. Administrative expenses at Alexandropol, with the free use of extensive barrack buildings conservatively valued at over $5,000,000 were minimal. Still, by summer 1923 the coffers in New York were empty and "the word 'bankruptcy' stalked like a ghost," wrote Acheson in his unpublished manuscript. "If we failed,"

> …what could we possibly do with the 60,000 children then in our orphanages—children we had taken into foreign lands upon which they had no claim; children who would have to be turned out into refugee camps, to wander in packs like the wild children of Erivan, in overpopulated countries where hundreds of thousands of adults could not find employment.[370]

To prevent total bankruptcy, a hasty emergency meeting of a select few had first convened in Boston in summer 1923 followed, a few days later, by an extraordinary meeting of NER's Executive Committee at an aristocratic and exclusive club in New York City, frequented by the leadership of Wall Street.[371] In the committee rooms of the club, wrote Acheson, occurred "many a piece of skullduggery in high finance," and it was in the same "unhallowed rooms that this little group of idealists" who gave national leadership to the Near East Relief, met each month for fifteen years."[372] The circumstances that led up to that extraordinary meeting had begun during the summer, when the Executive Committee did not hold its regular monthly meeting:

> With little warning, the Chairman of the Executive Committee, the Chairman of the Board of Trustees, and the Treasurer, were called together and told that the bank balances of their organization were down to less than $100,000 and that over $600,000 in outstanding drafts might be presented for payment at any moment.[373]

An appraisal of the situation during the meeting concluded that NER was technically bankrupt and that it would probably be one million dollars in debt by October. At that point, wrote Acheson,

> The Treasurer, Mr. Cleveland H. Dodge, pressed his cigarette into an ash tray with bony fingers, turned a rugged but kindly face on the rather frightened executive officers, and inquired: "How much immediate credit do you think you need?"

He was told that they needed somewhere between a minimum of $500,000 and a maximum of $1,200,000 [the equivalent of $6,890,000 and $16,536,000 in 2014, respectively] to carry the relief program until the fall months when receipts would probably again exceed expenditures. "Well," Dodge had answered, without criticizing the Trustees,

> …I have some securities that I'm not needing just now. I'll turn over $500,000.00 worth of them to the bank to guarantee our credit." There was a breathtaking silence before the chairman, Mr. Edwin M. Bulkley, spoke: "But, Mr. Dodge, I do not believe that it is right to let you assume this responsibility personally. What will happen if, instead of the minimum, the maximum estimate of our deficit should turn out to be correct?" Mr. Dodge peered around the circle. "Well—in that case, I suppose I'll just have to put up some more securities."[374]

The meeting of the full Executive Committee of the Board of Trustees that took place in the fall, was "like a funeral," recalled Acheson. The members were pensive,

> ...burdened with thoughts that caused their faces to tighten as they had never done when personal fortunes were in jeopardy. They shook hands stiffly, and solemnly took their places around the luncheon table. It was like a funeral...the lives and morals of 60,000 children depended on this same fickle public at a time when foreign nations were repudiating their debts and our own statesmen were jeering at American generosity, saying that we were playing Santa Claus to an unappreciative world. The tide was against us.[375]

James Barton, who had opened the meeting with a prayer, "was not quite ready to believe in victory, although he was ready to endure failure courageously." "The luncheon was an excellent one," Acheson continued, but there was no appetite because "the ghosts of hungry children were in the room." Then, suddenly,

> Mr. Dodge laid down his napkin, pushed back his chair, and started talking as he rose to his full six feet of bony height. "What you men need is faith...there is no better way of raising money than to let people know that you need money. Let's take the American public into our confidence. There are many thousands of good people in the United States.

"It was interesting to watch their keen faces—some intellectual, some rugged and practical, some scholarly and saintly," observed Acheson:

> They lighted up at the first sound of his [Dodge's] voice. "Some of you clergymen know more about faith than I do," he continued, "but what I do know is that those who have faith usually succeed, while those without it always fail..." he smiled whimsically, "But I know that we have no reason for all this gloom. Let's sing a hymn. Come on, get up—you, too, Morgenthau."[376]

"It would be interesting," concluded Acheson, "to know what happened to the financial plotting in the adjoining rooms," but in their own group the atmosphere had changed, and all were prepared to battle the grim year ahead as they decided to borrow more money and adopted a budget that would make it unnecessary to turn a single child away from any orphanage. Because, Acheson wrote, "a single leader had not faltered in a crisis. If he had, within an hour they would probably have been laying plans to liquidate the work."[377]

There had been expectations, at least on the part of Ernest Yarrow, that Armenians living outside Armenia might help in the reconstruction of Armenia. But none of the legacies left behind by wealthy Armenians outside Armenia, Yarrow had lamented, had been made available for Armenia.[378] In August 1924, NER began fundraising locally in Leninakan and asked for shop space in the center of town, free of charge, where they could display and sell some of the items orphans had made.[379] Two months later, in October 1924, Theodore Elmer, the Chairman of the Administrative Committee in Leninakan asked Sergei Lukashin's support in observing the Golden Rule Sunday, a fundraising program NER had launched in 1922. In this program, individuals and families around the world who wished to participate, were asked to replace their customary Sunday meal in December with an orphanage meal of bread, stew, cocoa and some fresh vegetables, and donate the difference in cost between the frugal orphanage meal and their customary Sunday dinner to NER for the benefit of the starving Armenians. The purpose of Elmer's letter to Lukashin was

> ...to urge upon you our hope that the S. S. R. of A. might show its appreciation of our work for its orphans and at the same time provide some additional funds for those orphans not at present cared for by uniting with the various countries of the world who are to observe Golden Rule Sunday by a common meal...

Elmer went on to explain that a proclamation asking the citizens of Armenia to eat an orphan meal and donate the savings to help homeless orphans would be a significant message to the world, and should Lukashin agree with the plan,

> ...it would encourage us here with the thought that we are united in a common cause, it would draw the attention of the people to the need and opportunity as nothing else would, and it would show the world that Armenia sympathizes with our efforts and is doing her best to help her own orphans.[380]

The Golden Rule Sunday was still being observed at NER's orphanages in Leninakan in 1926, attended by 5,000 children and 600 guests, as described by NER nurse Inez Webster:

> We were all up at dawn hurrying about, getting our homes in perfect order, fixing ourselves as neat as possible, then rushing tables and benches out on the field, finding our best sheets to use as table cloths, scouring our spoons until they shone, arranging the bowls, cutting the bread and setting the tables.

Everything had been in readiness when the clock had struck 12:

> The band played, the children fell into line, and with joy in our hearts and gratitude to those who made our lives possible, we started our triumphant march around the Post. We stopped for our Managing Director, who joined the throng, our guests fell into line, the band played a little louder, and to its music we all reached our tables.

Once at the tables, everyone stood at attention as the national anthem of Armenia was played, followed by the "Star Spangled Banner." The thrill of the day, wrote Webster,

> ...for us Americans was that noon dinner with our children and our guests, but the thrill for the children came with our night meal, when every one of those 5,000, whom generous people are providing for, had their turn in sacrifice and the privilege of helping someone else. They chose to have only bread for supper, going without their cacao and thereby saving $145, their contribution toward helping someone else less fortunate than themselves.[381]

Chapter Five

CEREMONIES, PHOTO-OPS, AND MOVING PICTURES

To bring the U.S. public closer to an understanding of its humanitarian mission, NER produced extensive visual material especially in the form of photographs and motion pictures, some of them produced by the Swedish-American photographer Carl E. Wallin. NER relief worker Elsie Kimball, then private secretary to Colonel Haskell in Tiflis, described Wallin's work in a letter to her family on March 2, 1920:

> The big excitement today is that we had our pictures taken by the moving picture man who was sent out here from New York by the International Film Corporation. Now, these pictures will appear in different movies in New York City and elsewhere, all over the country, around the first of May…Mr. Wallen [Wallin], the movie man, may reach New York a little earlier than May first…or perhaps later, but watch out for him…you would be interested to see these pictures of the Near East—and especially those taken this afternoon of all of us Americans in Tiflis. You will see us walking down the steps of Colonel Haskell's house, in the rear courtyard, and as I was the only one who wore a service cap (such as the soldiers wear, you know), you can pick me out quickly…Also, you will see a picture of Colonel Haskell and his staff, as well as one of Mrs. Haskell…[382]

Photographer helping orphan girl pose for the camera. (RAC NEF Photos Box 139)

124 THE CITY OF ORPHANS

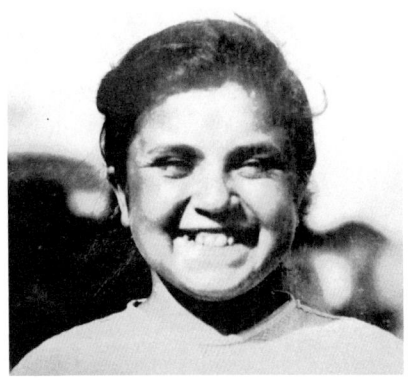

Orphan girl poses for the camera.
(RAC NEF Photos Box 138)

Two girls from Severski posing with Barclay Acheson.
(RAC NEF Photos Box 140)

Many of the scenes in the films and photographs shot in Armenia were staged at the City of Orphans. Children posed for photographers and filmmakers in small groups or in the thousands in various formations, sorted by size, by age and by gender, wearing white, often bare-foot and bare headed. They marched ceremoniously in honor of visitors from the U.S., Commissars, and ecclesiastical authorities from Etchmiadzin, including the Catholicos. Before they appeared in front of such august audiences, they would rehearse for weeks on the vast open spaces by the barracks, ideally suited for such panoramic displays of Armenia's future generation.

Professional photographers and filmmakers needed little more to produce the most striking testimonials of NER's staggering work; all they needed to add to the theatrical and cinematographic venues before them was imagination and a camera lens to transmit the singularity of the spectacle to audiences thousands of miles removed from Alexandropol. The message the children sent to all those who viewed them through the lens, was obvious: the little people were not just the relics of carnage; they were the future of the country and, as *The New York Times* declared in its August 5, 1923, issue, the "builders of the new Armenia."[383] They were the agents of progress and peace, although it was not clear which agency would bring them about—Soviet or American. Nevertheless, thousands of children expressed their gratitude to the generous American public through photographs and films, as they posed for cameras or in formations that spelled "Thank You America" and "NER," sang the *Stars and Stripes* to commissars and American dignitaries, or bowed down to their waists as they received the blessings of ecclesiastical authorities.

"I Showed Them We Are Men of State"

High ranking U.S. and Soviet delegations were usually welcomed at the train station in Alexandropol by key members of the American staff, by groups of orphans and their orchestra, and at times by representatives of the government, before proceeding to their tour of the City of Orphans and to private meetings.

A courtesy SSRA extended to NER was a private coach on the train. The coach, used regularly by NER personnel and visitors, carried NER's name, and was

> ...attached to the train, free of charge, a half-sized coach that was once the private property of Grand Duke Nicholas, a toy presented to him on his birthday by Queen Victoria.[384]

One of the early ceremonies in Alexandropol occurred on August 8, 1921, in honor of the arriving American delegation headed by Charles Vickrey. Among the more than 30-member delegation were John R. Voris, NER Associate General Secretary from New York; California State Assemblyman Frank R. Buckalew, from Berkeley, California; New York businessman Conrad Henken; NER Women's Organizations president Mrs. Florence Spencer Duryea from New York; New York State Institute of Applied Agriculture Director Albert A. Johnson, from Farmingdale, New York; New York State Commissioner of Education and later Editor of *The New York Times* John Finley, from New York; former U.S. Embassy Secretary in Petrograd (1905–1906) and Fellow of the Royal and American Geographical Societies Paxton Hibben; and Frank Connes, official interpreter of the Supreme Court of the State of New York who had served in the American Red Cross in Russia during WWI. The commission also included photographers and filmmakers.

The event was to mark, among other things, the official transfer of the military posts in Alexandropol to NER and was met by an official delegation representing the government of SSRA. A representative of the government, who subsequently reported to SSRA People's Commissar of Foreign Affairs Askanaz Mravyan in some detail, was one of the officials who met the group. According to the report, the visitors were met at the train station by

> ...a group of orphans from our state run orphanages in Alexandropol and a group of scouts; there was an orchestra and an honor guard of the Armenian Red Army.

"In a short speech," he reported to Mravyan,

> I welcomed them on behalf of the RevKom and [offered] wide-ranging assistance in the realization of their objectives. In response,

NER private wagon, marked in Russian "General Director American Comittee." (RAC NEF Photos Box 136)

Vickrey stressed that he had heard of the favorable attitude of the Alexandropol RevKom while in Istanbul and hopes that the same relationship continues in the future.

The ceremonial parade of the orphans, scouts and honor guard was filmed for a movie. It was a novelty for the Americans that we pay so much attention to our children, and [they] marveled at our orphans, scouts, orchestra—and that all of them were organized by the state.

The next day, August 9th holiday, they [the commission] were in their orphanages. Vickrey had sent a special messenger to invite me. As a representative of the government, they photographed me with Vickrey a few times, [including] a scene where an American woman is applauding the representative of the government.

He realized, the author continued, that such photographs with manifestations of affection had their negative sides. But he felt that they also held a positive significance, since through those photographs the opinion of the majority in America would change toward the positive. The author continued to report on the delegation's visit to nearby villages with "their well-known agronomist and two engineers," who had been impressed with what they had seen. The intention of the visit, wrote the author, was to emphasize the reconstructive work the government had begun and, "to show that we are not so impoverished." Then he continued to report on his discussion with Vickrey:

> Yesterday, on the 10th, Vickrey came to see me personally and asked that we go to the Severski post. I had already told them about the contents of your cable regarding the posts, that they could consider it theirs. He liked the construction work…that day they also visited our orphanages, with which he was quite satisfied.[385]

Among those who had met and praised the visiting committee, and possibly the author of the report to Mravyan, was Deputy Commissar of Foreign Affairs Artashes Karinyan. His speech, later quoted by Conrad Henken in the October 21 issue of *The Watchman Examiner* in New York and reprinted in the November 1921 issue of *The New Near East*, was a moving tribute to the assistance of "America and the Near East Relief," in whose glory a monument would be built in the hearts of the orphans:

> The best friend is he who comes to assistance in dark and black days. In all of our history we have lived through its darkest pages in these last few years…By their love of work this nation has built itself out of these difficulties through similar days in our history, and there is no reason to get discouraged now; especially since with such friends as the Americans, we are sure to come out of this present difficulty in the shortest possible time. The darkest days are passed and some day the sun will shine again. On that day we will build a monument. That monument will be to the glory of the work of America and the Near East Relief, and it will be set up in the hearts of these little orphan children. That will be in a very short time.[386]

When the commission had arrived at the Kazachi, welcoming them were Kazachi's boy scouts, of whom their scoutmaster Vahan Cheraz was very proud. "Yesterday," he wrote to a friend on August 7, "an important American mission on its way to Yerevan stopped at the Kazachi Post for a few minutes. My boys had gone to meet them and were photographed many times."[387]

Also in honor of the visiting Americans, and for the cameras, five thousand children posed in a formation that spelled "N E R" and the sign of the star, against a backdrop of barrack buildings. "Into the magic letters 'N E R' and the 'Star,'" read *The New Near East* article describing the event,

> ...these little wards of America...poured all their heartfelt appreciation of what those symbols meant to them. Back of those symbols stood their friend, America, and the visitors were America's representatives...

Five thousand children pose to form the letters N E R and the star symbolizing the Near East Relief, Kazachi Post, August 1921. (*The New Near East*, December 1921: 18)

The ceremony took place on what had been the parade ground outside Kazachi Post, once a Russian barracks and now housing Near East Relief orphans. In the background are some of the orphanage buildings. If all the orphanage buildings at Alexandropol were placed end to end they would stretch a distance of three miles.

Three miles of orphans in one town![388]

At the end of the visit, while saying goodbye at the train station, Charles Vickrey had asked the author of the report about the best way in which NER's work could be organized in order for it to yield the most benefits. The author's reply:

> I said that first, the main attention should be directed at the assistance being organized in the small districts, and second, parallel to that to put the peasantry to work and provide them with the opportunity so that in a short time, being freed of parasitism, they may live by the outcome of their labor. To the question of how many needy people there were in our province, I gave them the figure of 100,000 and promised to send him data about our province today.

> In general, during the whole meeting I showed that we are men of state; we have the strength to work courageously during times of crises, and we have our perspective on economic reconstruction, etc.

The author ended the report by urging the government to finalize the transfer of the Severski to NER:

> Now it is important that we form the contract for the Severski post,[389] and give them a significant part of the land around it, so that they may organize their work. It is important to expedite this so that they may begin their initial work.

> The RevKom will decide on the boundaries of the land, but the contract, a copy of which I am sending to you, should be signed and returned while I am still here.[390]

The author cautioned, however, that Americans should not be allowed to pull down whichever building they chose to. He suggested that decisions as to which buildings were unusable and subject to demolition be made by a joint commission. A few days later, on August 13, 1921, the Soviet government officially handed over the city of orphans with its 20,000 orphans to NER.

Alice in Hungerland

While members of the commission were busy with agreements and inspections, the film crew that had accompanied them in August 1921 was busy shooting scenes for a movie that would soon become a favorite among U.S. schoolchildren. Entitled *Alice in Hungerland*, it was an obvious reference to the popular children's adventure tale *Alice in Wonderland*, where a little girl named Alice falls into a rabbit hole and thence into a journey of fantasy and strange creatures. The *Hungerland* version was about the adventures of Alice in the Near East. In this version, Alice was a pretty American girl in a nice white dress, whose father was a relief worker in the Near East. One day, she decided to see with her own eyes the people for whom her father worked. She concealed herself in one of the rescue ships headed for the Near East and finally reached her father in Constantinople. Together, they continued on to Batum and on to Armenia. Her journey, in the course of which she saw dirty, starving, naked, dying children, eventually brought her to the City of Orphans in Alexandropol. Alice was saddened by much of what she saw, and especially troubled by scenes of children outside the orphanage gates waiting for admission.

As she entered the City of Orphans, she realized that the children there were very different from those outside: they were healthy; they happily went to classes and workshops. They were simply happy. Only when she saw the dormitories where two or three children shared a single cot, she understood why there was no room for the ones outside the gates. Then, Alice noticed truckloads of flour entering the compounds and wondered why, with such quantities of food available, there was none left for the children outside the gates—until she saw what it took to feed the thousands within the gates. Still, she occasionally managed to distribute bread to the hungry children she had met, fully aware that all her efforts were inadequate.[391] As the film came to an end, a scene showed a large group of little children in rags pleading for help with outstretched hands.

The silent film *Alice in Hungerland* in three reels was written by Emerson D. Owen, a newspaper editor in Scranton, Pennsylvania, who had been among the visitors in Alexandropol in summer 1921 as the publicity director of the tour,[392] and was produced with the assistance of William Selig, the producer of *"Ravished Armenia"* in 1919. But unlike the latter, the primary focus of *Alice in Hungerland* was on the lives and predicament of orphans and their needs, within and without the orphanage. In the U.S., *Alice in Hungerland* attracted large audiences, especially children, and was widely shown across theaters from New Hampshire to Hawaii. *The Washington Post* announced on December 11, 1921, that the first showing of the film in Washington, DC, was to be on December 17, 1921, at Keith's Theater at noon and that immediately before the showing, at 11:45 a.m., the Marine band would give a concert, followed by

Alice (left) with Ambassador Morgenthau. (*Signs of the Times*, May 30, 1922: 16)

Alice of Hungerland. (RAC NEF Staff Photos Acheson Box 142)

Mrs. Florence Spencer Duryea. (RAC NEF Staff Photos Acheson Box 142)

an address by Commander Brokenshire of the Navy. The same program would be repeated at Howard's Theater at 3:00 p.m., on the same day.[393]

Showings of *Alice in Hungerland* continued across the country—Maui, Hawaii; Ontario, Oregon; Ogden Utah; Dakota City, Nebraska; Kingman, Arizona; New York City, New York; Manchester, New Hampshire; Lyonsville, Illinois, to name a few—throughout 1922,[394] and was endorsed by some of the most influential men in the world of business, including steel magnate Charles Schwab.[395] Local NER committees ensured that *Alice in Hungerland* was shown to as many audiences as possible, regardless of the size of the town or potential audience. The town of Lyonsville, Illinois, for instance, where the film was to be shown, was too poor to have electric light. In order to show it to its 200 inhabitants, it was necessary to transport a Delco light plant from a distance of 12 miles to Lyonsville. Following the showing, the sum of $500 was raised on the spot.[396]

Accompanying many of the showings was Mrs. Florence Spencer Duryea, president of NER's Women's Organizations bureau in New York. The showing in Manchester, New Hampshire, was especially memorable for her because the schools in that city had initially resisted the idea of collecting money from schoolchildren, but had eventually made an exception. Five thousand children had come to watch and left determined to help:

> The picture of the adventures of "Alice" struck a responsive chord in the hearts of those children, just as they had been thrilled by the adventures of "Alice in Wonderland." But "Alice in Hungerland" did something to them that the other Alice could never do. However they might thrill and laugh with Lewis Carroll's little heroine, when the book was closed they knew the story was ended, that it was not true anyway, and therefore, if they would, it was not necessary to help Alice with her troubles.
>
> With "Alice in Hungerland" it was different. They saw a child like themselves, happy and well cared for, in a land whose children and their pitiful condition were incomprehensible to her. They saw her trying to help them by giving bread to the ragged, hungry hordes.

They went home from seeing that film determined, like Alice, to help. They have gone into their schools, asking their teachers if they may not be permitted to bring to the schools, as collecting places, money to buy food and clothes for the hungry children of Armenia.[397]

In the role of little Alice was not a movie star but an actual 12-year-old orphan girl by the name of Esther Razon, who had been selected from an orphanage in Constantinople by Mrs. Florence Spencer Duryea for the part. Under Mrs. Duryea's care, Alice had accompanied the commission's visit to Armenia in summer 1921 to shoot the film. But when the commission had completed its work and was ready to return home, Mrs. Duryea had realized that she had become attached to the little girl and adopted her as her foster child, giving her the name Alice Duryea.[398]

Alice asks: Are you children? (*The New Near East*, January 1922: 12)

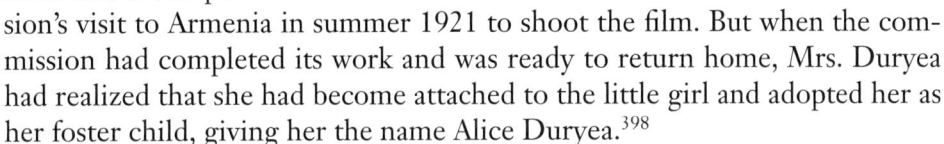

As the film toured the country, a complication surfaced about the identity of the young girl. Rabbi Stephen S. Wise of New York, who had established that Alice was a Jewess, had obtained a writ of *habeas corpus* in the Supreme Court on April 27, 1922, directing Mrs. Duryea to produce her adopted daughter in court. The Rabbi stated that the girl known as Alice Duryea was in fact Esther Razon, and that she was not Armenian, but Jewish, adopted from a Jewish orphanage in Constantinople. The Rabbi pointed out that when Mrs. Duryea had adopted the girl, she had promised to rear her as a Jew. Rabbi Wise had received a statement to that effect from the authorities of the orphanage in Constantinople, and upon hearing that Esther was now being raised as a Christian, he had cabled Mrs. Duryea requesting her to surrender Esther to Dr. Wise. Mrs. Duryea had refused the request, causing the Rabbi to resort to *habeas corpus* proceedings.[399] The story was carried in newspapers in New York for several weeks, usually showing scenes of Alice or Esther in court, accompanied by NER's endorsement of Mrs. Duryea's character and financial standing, as the lawyers of each party negotiated behind the scenes.[400]

Orphan girls dance for Alice, who stands behind the musicians. (*The New Near East*, June 1922: 16)

CEREMONIES, PHOTO-OPS... 131

At the end, Alice remained with Mrs. Duryea, and when her name reappeared in the news again, in 1939, it was to announce that "Miss Alice Duryea" was engaged to be married,[401] and later, that "Miss Alice Duryea" had wed a certain John Kinney,[402] and that she had given birth to a daughter, Elisa, in December 1944.[403]

"A Gigantic Pageant"

In summer 1922, while Alice's fate was being debated in the courts of New York, the ceremonies and pageantry in honor of visiting delegates from the U.S. at the City of Orphans assumed epic proportions. In the delegation were U.S. filmmakers and photographers, and Barclay Acheson, whose candid and detailed descriptions of events help recreate the full spectacle that unfolded on the Kazachi parade grounds in the summer of 1922. When their train arrived in Alexandropol, wrote Acheson,

> We learned at once that the moving picture squad had been busily at work during our absence [in Yerevan.] In fact, it was these energetic photographers who invited the government officials who had been with us in Tiflis and on the return journey to remain for the night and participate in the gigantic pageant to be staged on the parade grounds the next day.[404]

Acheson wrote that everyone was working hard, and there was excitement and enthusiasm everywhere, with the exception of a few relief workers who objected to the interruptions in the children's schedules for clinic and classroom. But those who understood the importance of the movie for NER's fundraising campaign with U.S. contributors agreed that everything should be pushed aside for the picture. The scenes already taken, Acheson remarked, were sufficiently authentic and convincing, but all agreed that the movie still needed a photographic climax, a grand finale, which would prove that large numbers of children still depended on the U.S. for "life itself." [405]

As he reconstructed the day in some detail some years later, Acheson began with the arrival of the first group of guests at the Kazachi, which included the Catholicos and his entourage from Etchmiadzin in an American car:

> The great day dawned bright and clear, and our important visitors began to arrive early. Among the first was the Catholicos from Etchmiadzin, head of the Armenian Church. He arrived in one of our American automobiles, accompanied by several church dignitaries.

The group from the Holy See had retired to refresh themselves after the drive from Etchmiadzin. When they had reappeared, they wore their ceremonial robes, complete with miters and dazzling gold chains, ready for the ritual ahead:

> They retired "to shake off the dust" and soon reappeared, resplendent in miters, gold chains, long flowing black robes, and colorful vestments, to take their places on the improvised platform.

The next group to arrive was the government officials and commissars. Their youth and simple apparel set a sharp contrast to the older and sumptuously dressed clergy. The government officials, wrote Acheson,

> ...wore simple uniforms with caps and buttons ornamented with hammer and sickle. Most of them were young, almost boyish, in contrast with the gray-bearded and very dignified ecclesiastics.[406]

On the platform also were the resident American relief workers, the regional director, doctors, department heads, nurses, a delegation of important local employees from nearby posts, and, the visiting Americans, who were the honored guests. The photographers and film crew were busy taking close-up shots of various groups—the mayor of the city welcoming the Catholicos, the Catholicos greeting the regional director—and all meeting each of the members of the American delegation.

At this point, Acheson interrupted his narrative to make some observations. It would be difficult, if not impossible, he reflected, "for anyone living in the United States to imagine the intense drama going on behind the scenes, a drama that could not be photographed." There were several enactors in that behind-the-scenes drama. One group were those NER employees who belonged to the old aristocracy:

> Many of our most competent local employees were of the old aristocracy. Some of them learned what they knew of welfare work while supervising schools, hospitals, or soup kitchens that they were once able to support with their own private funds.[407]

Gathering of orphans for ceremonies before the Russian church at Kazachi. Summer, 1922. (RAC NEF Photos Box 153)

Detail of ceremony before the church at Kazachi. (RAC NEF Photos Box 153)

CEREMONIES, PHOTO-OPS... 133

And, he thought, with some regret, the Soviet government had at times unfairly lodged complaints against NER for offering them employment:

> Government officials sometimes accused us of favoritism or of sheltering the enemies of the common people. The fact, however, was that they were employed and retained because they were the most competent people available. They spoke English; they had the educational and cultural background necessary to the competent management of our most important departments. But they were bourgeoisie, or worse, to the Communists. For instance, the man in charge of one of our warehouses was once a famous general, and our best veterinarian was a woman who once had a string of racehorses of her own.[408]

Acheson then returned to the pageant, to the presence of church dignitaries and government officials in close proximity with each other, but who, despite deep animosities, at times managed to smile to each other:

> When the Church dignitaries shook hands with government officials they recalled churches made into communist clubhouses, with the cross on the steeple replaced by the hammer and sickle in great electric signs, and they knew that these same officials were probably atheists who had often called the church "the opiate of the people." They also remembered that sons and daughters of priests had been forced to disavow their fathers' religion as a condition of admission to the government-controlled labor unions…

At the same time, Acheson understood the risk that government officials were taking by appearing with the clergy:

> The government officials were also in a difficult position. Here they were meeting these traditional enemies of the revolution in a friendly way in public—it would be hard to explain that to the party members.

But, he concluded,

> The children—and the need of telling the story of the children to the American public—were the one thing that could have brought this group together on the same rostrum at a public function.[409]

Included in the pageantry was the march of the children in columns, led by boy scouts. Other boy scouts "stood stiffly at attention, like human signposts, to mark the area where each unit of five hundred was to assemble," and then,

> …bugles sounded, and the seemingly endless lines of well-disciplined children came marching into the parade ground from every direction. Although bare-legged and bare-headed, they were washed and starched until their homespun garments made a gallant spectacle as they marched down the improvised aisles and took their appointed places before the dignitary-laden rostrum.[410]

As a gesture of respect to the American audiences and donors, each boy scout leading columns of marching children held an American flag. The boys were on the right, the girls on the left, with the babies in front and the older children and orphanage employees in the background. The spectacle united all, friend and foe alike:

As that throng of 17,000 children who had experienced the utmost of tragedy, suffering, and human beastliness assembled, the gray-bearded churchmen, the youthful communist officials, and the remnants of the old aristocracy united in a salute to their stout hearts and youthful courage.[411]

"They were a sturdy lot," observed Acheson, "because the weaklings had been ruthlessly weeded out," and only the mentally alert and the physically strong had survived." Then the camera turned to the rostrum and began to film the Chairman of the Council of Commissars, as he thanked the Americans:

> ...the President of the Commissar's Council of Armenia was speaking. With a voice that shook with emotion he talked of the "great change"; for everyone present remembered these same children "before the Americans gathered them into this great institution and thus expressed the most extraordinary instance of mass neighborliness the world has ever seen."

The Catholicos was the last to speak. In his message he reminded the 17,000 children how tragic their lives had been, how they had been called back from the grave and been reborn through NER's efforts:

> You have been rescued, called back from the grave. You live by a new spirit that has recently come to this tortured world. Human kindness is not new, but human kindness on such a vast scale for unknown people in a distant land has never been seen before on this earth. I am old and spent with suffering, but I thank God that at least I have seen this miracle. This new spirit has touched your dying bodies with a magic wand. You have been twice born, and we pray that this new life that is yours may be lived in a new world of brotherhood and understanding. May it encircle the earth.[412]

As the ceremony closed, the orphanage bands first played the Armenian national anthem, followed by *The Stars and Stripes Forever*. Finally, the band led the long, winding columns of children down the road and across the fields back to their respective dormitories. The gigantic pageant, which the film crew would use as the photographic climax for a movie they were preparing, was to be shown at fundraising events in the U.S.

The commission's stay came to an end soon and preparations were made to leave Alexandropol. "It was hard to go," wrote Acheson,

> Begging for money at home seemed like a prosaic task in comparison with the great adventure on the foreign field. But the Americans who stayed behind felt otherwise. They longed for home. Not that they were quitters—never that. Theirs was the natural longing for loved faces and familiar scenes. They faced the hard task of fighting famine and epidemics with inadequate equipment and money. If

"Bon Voyage" to the visiting American delegation, early 1920s. (RAC NEF Box 144)

CEREMONIES, PHOTO-OPS...

only those iron gates could be opened and no one turned away! But we parted gaily on the station platform. The orphanage band played "The Star Spangled Banner" as the train pulled out—and we waved good-bye until we were out of sight.[413]

Formation of orphan boys with the American Flag. (*The New Near East*, (December 1921: 13)

Formation of orphan girls with the American flag. (RAC NEF Photos Box 145)

From the behind the scenes moments during the various "shoots" taken in summer 1922, the one Acheson was to remember for a long time to come was the one that showed

> ...the pinched faces and withered limbs of children who stood in the dust at the iron gates, hoping for admission. They were the damned. With claw-like hands they picked at festering sores or scratched incessantly beneath vermin-infested rags. They had gnomes' faces, gray and drawn, that pressed against those iron bars each day.
>
> It was there, while the camera clicked, that we gave the beggars bread on condition that they "go away." We watched the forlorn and ragged groups as they walked away in the sun and dust, reluctantly, aimlessly—until a bend in the road took them out of sight. One of them looked back at us so hopefully, thinking we might relent, but our hands were tied. Who could explain those iron gates to him?

That scene in our movie, although "staged," showed exactly what would happen in a few short weeks to the rescued thousands within the gates if cash receipts decreased suddenly in America, or ceased altogether.[414]

The photographers and filmmakers who accompanied NER commissions to Armenia in the first half of the 1920s were professionals charged with capturing dramatic scenes and translating them into pictorial expressions of gratitude at fundraising appeals in the U.S. It was in keeping with that tradition that on March 1923, a certain Mr. Bardeau, a photographer, was sent by NER headquarters in New York to collect photographs and news articles "that when made public in America would stimulate interest in the work in the Caucasus" and increase donations from organizations and individuals.[415] Bardeau had wished to personally meet with Sergei Lukashin but had failed to do so since the latter had been absent from Yerevan. But before leaving, Bardeau had left a statement at the President's office for him to sign if he deemed it appropriate:

> The statement has been translated and is herewith presented for your consideration. In the event that you consider it unwise to present the request to the president please return it to this office, but if in your judgment there is no reason to prevent it, do so, with the understanding that it can be altered, if necessary, in any way desired: the form presented being but a general idea of what is desired.
>
> Please understand that a statement of this kind will be of the utmost value to the organization, in its effort to raise funds…[416]

"Uncle America Sees It Through"

Alice in Hungerland was only one piece of the visual material that brought the orphanage at Alexandropol to the U.S. for fundraising purposes. Another such film was *"Uncle America Sees it Through"* about which NER announced in January 1921. Other films NER produced and showed across the U.S. included *"One of These Little Ones,"* and *"What the Flag Saw,"* all featuring NER's orphanages throughout the Near East including Armenia. But to date only a very short clip of seven seconds is available on line, showing children running around on the Kazachi grounds.[417]

"Uncle America Sees It Through" was shot in the summer or fall of 1922. Present during the filming was Dr. Esther Pohl Lovejoy, president of the American Women's Hospitals, who had come to visit Dr. Elliott in Armenia in summer 1922.[418] In the role of "Uncle America" was an NER worker who had never before been an actor, but was willing to act the part for the sake of the children. The film makers drove from place to place to get special features for the story, as groups of visitors watched the children assembled from the different posts being drilled in preparation for the motion picture. Children under their own leaders were so well trained, wrote Esther Lovejoy,

Announcement on visual material available for presentations. (*The New Near East*, January 1921: 11)

Movies and Lantern Slides

Practically all state officers of Near East Relief have available a new motion picture reel, "CHILDREN OF SORROW," and sets of exquisitely colored LANTERN SLIDES for use in popular meetings and in Sunday schools.

These reproductions of recent scenes in Armenia are authentic and educational.

Write to your state office and date up the pictures early in the year.

that they marched and counter-marched, forming the most intricate figures with little apparent effort. Most of the filming had taken place on the parade grounds of the Kazachi:

> Day after day, the children were assembled for practice on this great square. There was a pulpit in front of the Russian Church facing the grounds, on which a priest, in picturesque vestments, was to be "shot" blessing the children. When the stage was finally set, and the children at attention, after days of intensive training, the priest ascended the pulpit and "registered" in accordance with instructions. "Shoot!" came the startling command, and it is a good thing the poor old man did not understand our language, for even those of us who knew what it was all about, were relieved to see him descending from the pulpit quite uninjured, with a childlike smile on his venerable face.[419]

Dr. Lovejoy had been especially impressed with the endurance of 5,000 children, all under the age of eight. "The making of this picture was an exhausting task," she wrote, "even for those who rode in automobiles—and the children had to walk." "The endurance of the children,"

> …was beyond understanding. About five thousand little boys, none of whom were more than eight years old, lived at Polygon Post, where I was staying. They were perfect little Spartans. Their rations were simple, containing the proper proportions of the different kinds of food necessary for normal development. Their lives were absolutely regular. They arose, ate, went to school, to work, and to bed by the sound of the bugle.[420]

Everyday, the little children would walk the distance from the Polygon to the Kazachi, where they were drilled and prepared for the ceremony:

> …These little tikes walked in their bare feet, drilled most of the day in the hot sun, without food and with very little water, and marched back in the evening, as chipper as though nothing had happened. I thought surely some of them would be sick, but they seemed to enjoy the experience…[421]

Young children marching in pairs. (RAC NEF Photos Box 138)

The film *"Uncle America Sees it Through"* opened in New York and was subsequently shown across the country, especially in the Midwest. Announcements were made in numerous newspapers in large and small cities, previewing the film, where a special appeal was made for the collection of grain. *The Rushville Daily Republican* in Rushville, Indiana, announced that *"Uncle America Sees it Through"* was the "most graphic portrayal of the Near East situation ever produced, one scene alone showing 15,000 orphans in formation" and would be shown at the Princess Theater on April 4 and 5 [1923]. The children of the largest orphanage, read the article, referring to the City of Orphans, called the United States their "uncle country," and went on to say that

Film Announcement. (*The Winslow Mail*, October 5, 1923)

> Mass pictures of this great city of children show 15,000 in a grand review, assembling, marching and disbanding in one scene that for general proportions probably outdoes anything of the kind ever thrown on the screen. There is action and pep with plenty of color throughout the picture and after the three reels have been given audiences usually wish there was more of it.[422]

One of the audiences was a group of 1,000 inmates of the Federal Penitentiary in Atlanta, Georgia. They had sat hushed before the spectacle of 18,000 children streaming across the great parade ground of the armies of the Czar at Alexandropol. This was the first time that an NER motion picture was shown in a prison. The prisoners became so interested in NER's relief, it was reported, that they asked to have *The New Near East* placed on the exchange list of their newspaper, *Good Words*.[423] Another convict, in a Virginia prison, had sent 25 cents to NER. The amount represented the wages for two and a half day's hard labor on the Virginia roads.[424]

An Evening of *"Internationale"*

On the day before the commission left Alexandropol in 1922, Dr. Lovejoy wrote,

> The children at the orphanages had sung the *"Star Spangled Banner"* for the American visitors and we were thrilled. They sang it in our language as a performance for our entertainment.

The children, according to another member of the visiting committee, had been eager to learn not only the Star Spangled Banner but also Yankee Doodle.[425]

That evening, the government had regaled 50 Americans—the visiting Americans and some of the American personnel in Alexandropol—through a program of art, entertainment and speeches. A theatrical performance and a concert had followed a reception, and finally, a dinner:

> The President of the Federation of Georgia, Armenia and Azerbaijan, the members of the Economic Council, and other officers of the Soviet Government,

received us in the official reception room, which had formerly been used by the representatives of the Russian Empire. The pictures of the Czar, Czarina, and members of the royal family, had been replaced by those of Lenin, Marx, Trotsky and other men...[426]

The theatrical performance and concert

...was manifestly an exhibition of native culture for the benefit of the Americans and it certainly was edifying. First they sang the *"Internationale"* and they put so much temperament into it, that we could feel the meaning although we did not understand their language:

> Arise you pris'ners of starvation! Arise ye wretched of the earth, for justice thunders condemnation, a better world's in birth.

The dinner was the climax of the evening:

There was plenty of good food, stirring speeches and an excellent interpreter. As an introduction, the band played the *"Internationale"* and we all stood at respectful attention, just as we would have done in any country while listening to the national hymn.

The President of the Economic Council, a youth consecrated to Communism, delivered an address of welcome supplemented by an impassioned exposition of the living principles of the U. S. S. R. [Union of Socialist Soviet Republics], after which the band played the *"Internationale"* and we all stood at respectful attention again.

Charles Vickrey had been the guest of honor that evening, and had spoken of

...Universal brotherhood and the work of the Near East Relief, and the band repeated the *"Internationale"* while we all stood at attention as before.

In fact, the *"Internationale"* was played throughout the evening:

After each speech, American or Soviet, the band played the *"Internationale"* and we all responded respectfully whether we wanted to or not. The Bolsheviks were beaming...this was the first opportunity of trying it on so large a company of outsiders. At least fifty Americans were present. In addition to field personnel, there were Near East home workers from many of the states between New York and California, and to see them moving up and down to the tune of the *"Internationale"* was an inspiring spectacle to the Communists...

There were at least 12 dinner speakers, wrote Esther Lovejoy, herself being the last:

The Soviet representatives seemed particularly interested in what I had to say, although I was merely telling the story of the work of the American Women's Hospitals in their own territory. This was the only field in which we did not negotiate directly with government officials, and, for this and diverse reasons, the work did not seem like our work in other countries.

"Bravo! Bravo! Bravo!" cried the Bolsheviks, time after time, and especially when I sat down...Surely those musicians would play the *"Star Spangled Banner"* for a change and as a farewell courtesy to their American visitors. But...the band struck up the *"Internationale"* and we all stood at respectful attention until the last note had died away, after which we departed in peace.[427]

Map outlining NER centers in the Near East, formed by 4,200 girls of the Severski. The title, "Near East Relief" at the top is formed by boys from the Polygon. All are under 12 years of age. (AGMI Collection)

The Biblical verse "Of Such is the Kingdom" from the Gospel of Saint Mathew (19:14) as formed by 1,200 younger girls at the Severski. (AGMI Collection)

CEREMONIES, PHOTO-OPS... 141

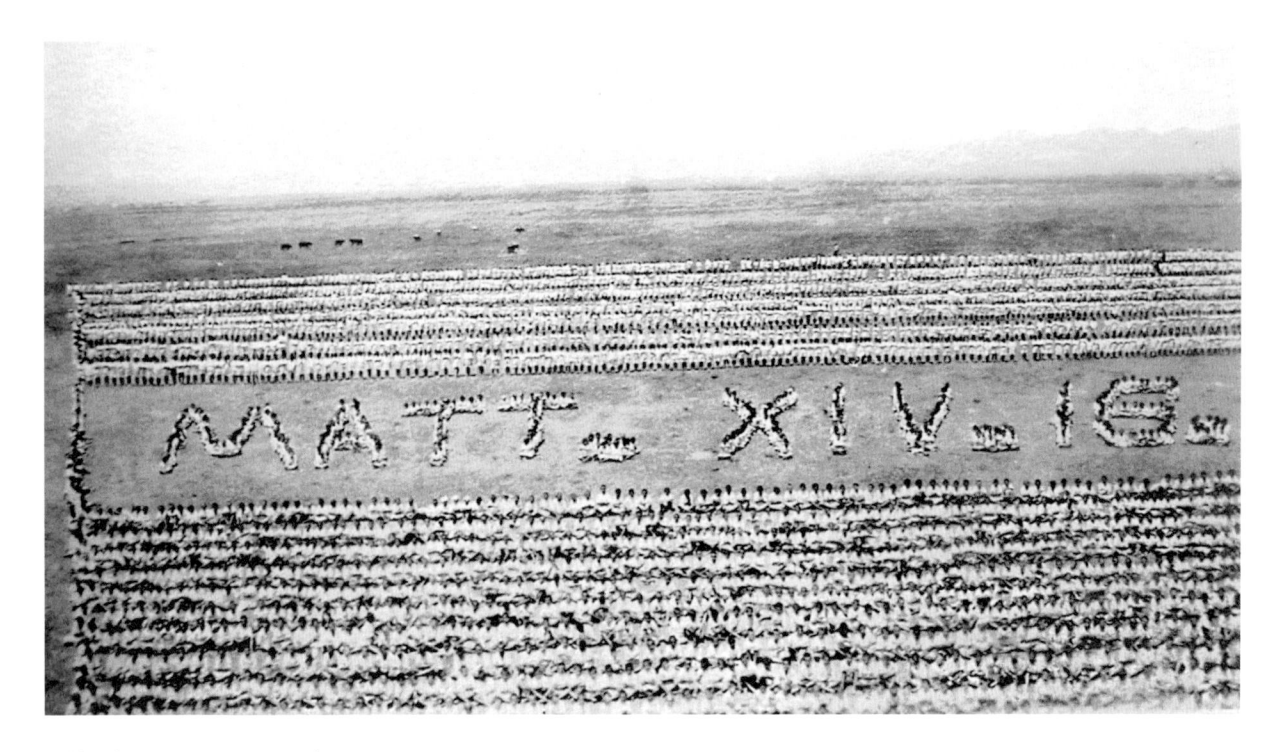

Biblical verse in Saint Matthew
(14:16) referring to Jesus feeding
the 5,000 is formed by 5,000
boys at the Polygon.
(AGMI Collection)

"America We Thank You"
formed by 2,000 orphan girls.
(RAC NEF Photos Box 153)

The phrase "Golden Rule Children of the Near East" is formed by 2,500 children at the Polygon. (AGMI Collection)

"Fill the Empty Bowl" formed by children at the Polygon. (RAC NER Box 133)

THE 35,000 children now under the care of the Near East Relief form a bowl into which 27,825,000 meals must be poured within the year. An even larger number of additional orphans, half-orphans and destitute children in broken families and refugee camps should be fed. Large numbers of these will die this coming winter when the temperature descends below the zero mark if additional relief is not forthcoming.

You have saved them thus far.

Shall they have food in their bowl tomorrow?

Measure your gift to them by the Golden Rule.

THE children who form the words of the Golden Rule in this photograph are some of the 5,000 children in the Polygon Orphanage at Alexandropol. The Director of this orphanage wrote on Golden Rule Sunday of last year: "It is warmer to night,— only twenty-five degrees below zero. There is ten feet of snow on the ground, and the wolves can be heard at night. The children have no means to dry their wet feet. *Under these conditions, can you imagine what it means for them to give up voluntarily, as they have just done, nearly fifty per cent of their bread ration for use among needy children in the refugee camps?"*

CEREMONIES, PHOTO-OPS...

Children on the
Polygon grounds.
(AGMI Collection)

Five thousand children spell "Whatsoever Ye would that Others Would do Unto You, Do Ye Even So to Them" from the Gospel of St. Mathew 7: 12. (AGMI Collection)

Children marching.
(RAC NEF Photos Box 145)

144 THE CITY OF ORPHANS

Drills, circa 1922.
(Lovejoy 1927: facing page 116)

Massed Drill at the Polygon, 1925.
(Barton 1930: facing page 22)

Seversky girls performing gymnastics before Fridtjof Nansen and visiting guests, June 1925.
(The National Library of Norway, Photo Collection of Fridtjof Nansen 6d144)

CEREMONIES, PHOTO-OPS...

Drills in winter.
(RAC NEF Photos Box 153)

Children's assembly before visitors.
(Barton 1930: facing page 125)

Senators and Congressmen

In the first half of the 1920s the City of Orphans hosted a number of notable U.S. representatives who accompanied NER, as well as Soviet commissars and official figures from Yerevan, Tiflis and Moscow. Among the senators and congressmen who arrived in Alexandropol in September 1923 were Senator E. F. Ladd of North Dakota, Senator W. H. King of Utah, Congressman James A. Frear of Wisconsin, and Kansas Governor and later U.S. Senator from Kansas Henry J. Allen. The primary mission of the group had been the investigation of conditions in Russia, but when they had stopped in Tiflis, Ernest Yarrow had suggested that they also make a stop at Alexandropol.

The visit had created much excitement among the American relief workers in Alexandropol. "The chief item of interest this week," wrote Elsie Kimball to her family,

> is the visit of the Congressional party, which included the famous Senator King of Utah, Senator Ladd of North Dakota and Congressman Freer of Wisconsin,

146   THE CITY OF ORPHANS

as well as such lesser lights as Professor Johnson, manager of the party, Dr. Bowen, a protégé of William Randolph Hearst, sent by him to study conditions in Russia, and Mr. Connes, official interpreter for the U.S. Supreme Court. They arrived at ten o'clock Thursday morning and four or five of us went down to meet them. They had a special engine bring them down from Tiflis and Captain Yarrow, who went up there to meet them when they arrived from Moscow, accompanied them to Alexandropol.[428]

The first order of business had been a tour of the posts, continued Kimball:

> Immediately after the party arrived at Kazachi Post, automobiles took them for a hurried visit over each Post—Kazachi, Severski and Polygon…We had the jolliest time, and Senator King, who at first seemed to me very haughty and distant, forgot his reserve and waxed jovial with all the rest of us.

The inspection tour had been followed by a parade of orphans:

> In the afternoon, a parade of orphans was given in honor of the guests and this apparently impressed them exceedingly. Ten thousand children marched past the grandstand where the Senators sat to review them.

The group had been feted in the evening by government officials:

> …in the evening a number of us attended a banquet given by the Bolshevik officials in the city. Including the Americans and the Bolsheviks, there were about forty people there, all told. It was a splendid dinner and the toasts were excellent…Senator King was Toastmaster.

In his detailed account published in February 1924, the commission's secretary George L. Bowen, explained the commission's purpose and the cities it visited. Because "reports from Russia had been highly conflicting," he began, and since the foreign policy of the United States was yet unclear, some members of Congress had formed an unofficial commission to embark on an inspection tour of Russia "with the frankly avowed purpose of getting at the truth of the Russian situation."[429] The commission's tour, which covered several thousand miles of Russian territory, had been financed privately and not by the U.S. government. After visiting cities in Russia and spending a week in Moscow,

> We chartered for ninety dollars a day, a big Russian Pullman car, formerly the property of the Minister of Railroads under the Czar, and with our 700 pounds of American canned goods and a couple of servants to look after our car for us and to do our cooking, we started on our trip through the interior.[430]

Ernest Yarrow, in Tiflis at the time, had arranged for their visit to Alexandropol. "We arrived in Alexandropol in the morning," wrote Senator Ladd later, describing their arrival at the train station,

The Honorable Henry J. Allen with a girl scout and an orphan to be admitted to the orphanage. (*The New Near East*, July 1923: 3)

> ...and here a real thriller was in store. When the train pulled in we had many American workers there to greet us, and a band playing "The Stars and Stripes forever."

From the train station the group was taken to the orphanages by car and in keeping with earlier traditions, watched the orphans parade before them:

> We got into American automobiles and sailed away toward the orphanages where later over ten thousand Armenian orphans paraded for us...[431]

Another member of the commission, Governor and later Senator from Kansas Henry J. Allen, had been equally impressed by the spectacle of the City of Orphans. When back in the U.S., he made several public appearances to speak about the commission's tour of Russia, with references to Alexandropol. At the Fifth Avenue Presbyterian Church in New York on June 10, he described Soviet Russia as "the industrial paradise of idleness," but where one of the hopeful signs that normal conditions might return was that the peasants were "flocking back to the church." He regretted, however, that at the orphanage in Alexandropol religion was not being taught and had been replaced by the teaching of Ethics:

> At Alexandropol, where the Near East Relief provides for 17,000 Armenian children in an orphanage, religious instruction has ceased because of the ruling. The good men and women there have substituted the teaching of ethics, and I am hopeful that their instruction will develop a leadership that will bear fruit in the future.[432]

Senator Allen's article "New World Ideals and the Future Near East" appeared in *The New Near East* in the summer of 1923.[433] The Editor's note above the article read:

Visiting American Commission. (RAC NEF Photos Box 138)

The following paragraphs are excerpts from an address made in New York on June 8 by the Hon. Henry J. Allen, ex-Governor of Kansas, immediately upon his return from the Near East where he made a three-months' survey as an act of public service after consultation with the State Department and others interested in Near East Relief.[434]

For the Senator, possibly the most interesting country in all the Near East was the "Transcaucasian portion of Russia," where he found NER's work to be remarkable. In Alexandropol, the barracks had been roofless and every stick of wood had been used for fuel when the refugees had found shelter there, he said. But NER had put roofs on the buildings and had turned them into "what is probably the greatest orphanage the world ever saw," caring for 15,000 children. And, he added,

> The great keynote of our work is in impressing upon the refugee children of these Armenians the American program…,

which was fundamental, and where real hope rested.[435] The children were all learning some type of trade, the Senator said, and he was sure they

> …would bring into the industrial and agricultural life of Armenia a new leadership and they will plant there a picture of America that could not have been planted in any other way.[436]

Senator William H. King of Utah, the third U.S. official of the 1923 commission, was the guest of honor at NER's Annual Dinner in October 1923, in New York. In the excerpts of his speech published in *The New Near East*,[437] the Senator praised NER's work and America's role in helping "distracted nations of the world in hours of peril," which

> …because of its [America's] proud position morally, and may I say, financially, is the nation of all nations that is competent to be a leader among the nations of the earth today.

During the trip through Russia, said the Senator,

> …With my associates (Senator Ladd, Congressman Frear, Professor Albert A. Johnson) I had the opportunity of going through Russia. We traveled perhaps ten or fifteen thousand miles, went over into Siberia, then down the Volga, passed through the Caucasus Mountains to the Trans-Caucasian republics, visiting Georgia, and the Armenian Republic. We went and looked at the little children there, examined the work that was being done and made as careful an investigation as our limited time permitted…

He admitted that at first he had been against granting NER's request for a charter from the U.S. Congress in 1919:

> May I say that when a charter was sought in Congress for this organization I at first opposed it, not that I didn't sympathize with the object of it—quite the reverse, but I felt it wasn't the province of the government to grant private charters to corporations; that corporations asking for charters from the Federal Government should be federal corporations, they should serve a governmental and a federal purpose, but upon investigation I permitted myself to be persuaded to support the scheme…

And now, the Senator was convinced that it was imperative that NER continue its work in Russia, because

> No matter what the desires may be of the Bolshevik government, its resources are so exhausted, its power for support of the people of Russia is so limited, that it is almost humanly impossible for them to care for the thousands and hundreds of thousands of homeless children that you find in every part of Russia... In the famine districts in Armenia you will find greater suffering and greater poverty and more orphan children than you will in any other part of Russia.[438]

Alexei Rykov, Georgy Chicherin, and Fridtjof Nansen

Among the high-ranking Soviet officials to visit the City of Orphans were Alexei Rykov, then Chairman of the Council of People's Commissars of the Russian SFSR and Georgy Chicherin, People's Commissar for Foreign Affairs. *The New York Times* covered the story in its March 12, 1925, issue, under the heading "Soviet Chiefs Laud Near East Relief Work." *The New York Times* reporter had been invited to accompany the high-ranking Soviet officials to Leninakan, where opening ceremonies for the irrigation canal were to take place. On Ernest Yarrow's invitation, they had also visited the City of Orphans. The story was wired to New York and appeared the next day:

> Mr. Rykoff, Mr. Tchicherin, and other members of the Central Government, accompanied by M. Loukaseen, Premier of the Armenian Republic, visited the headquarters of the Near East Relief today and inspected 8,000 orphans, assembled on the plain adjoining the orphanages. He was introduced by Captain Ernest Yarrow.[439]

Alexei Rykov, read the article, had kissed several of the children assembled to honor the visitors:

> In perfect Armenian language, M. Rykoff addressed the children, telling them they were victims of the imperial war and national strife and will therefore enjoy the protection of the Free Soviet Federation where they will no more be subjected to atrocities. He kissed several children, expressing satisfaction with the work of the Near East Relief.[440]

When the group had arrived at the Leninakan train station, a crowd of more than 50,000 people, thousands of them from the outlying villages, had gathered to greet them at the station, reported *The New York Times*, and a grand parade and demonstrations had been held. After inspecting the orphanages, the party went out in American cars to inspect the irrigation work.

> ...The Shiraksy [Shirak] Canal, built during the last two years, is forty miles long with a two-mile tunnel through rocky mountains. It will irrigate 15,000 acres. The opening ceremony greatly impressed the Armenian peasantry. Mr. Rykoff operated a sluice and as the water rushed in the "*Internationale*" was sung.

"Armenia has made wonderful progress since its Sovietization," *The New York Times* concluded, and "Americans living and working there during the last six years testify that Armenia is now unrecognizable." In honor of the visiting Soviet officials, NER gave a large banquet at the "American Club" of the orphanage, *The New York Times* reported, attended by NER personnel and high-ranking officials of the government. One of the speakers at the banquet was NER Managing Director General Joseph Beach, who delivered a brief history of NER.

Present also at the opening of the new canal were Ernest Yarrow, and members of the League of Nations, headed by League of Nations High Commissioner for Refugees and well-known Norwegian polar explorer and scientist Fridtjof Nansen.[441] At the opening ceremonies, Nansen wrote,

> Together with the President of Armenia and the Commissar for Agriculture and a number of others, including Mr. Yarrow, of the Near East Relief, I was asked to cross the suspension bridge to the sluice at the mouth of the tunnel. At a given signal the President and several members of the Government… began raising the huge sluice-gate in front of the tunnel, amid enthusiastic shouts of applause… I had to lend a hand with the windlass, together with my friend the Commissar for Agriculture… Mr. Yarrow took his turn at it, too, and several public officials. Gradually the opening became large enough down below for us to see the redeeming water flow through…[442]

Soviet delegation addressing the crowd in Leninakan. The visible wording of the banner reads, "Greetings to the Proletariat Revolution." (RAC NEF Photos Box 153)

Crowd gathered to hear the Soviet Delegation in Leninakan. (RAC NEF Photos Box 145)

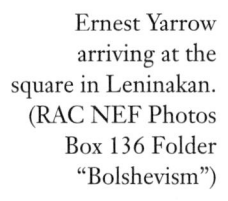

Ernest Yarrow arriving at the square in Leninakan. (RAC NEF Photos Box 136 Folder "Bolshevism")

CEREMONIES, PHOTO-OPS… 151

Fridtjof Nansen and Ernest Yarrow on the suspension bridge over the newly opened water canal near Leninakan, June 1925. (The National Library of Norway, Fridtjof Nansen Photo Archives 6d139)

Nansen welcomed at the Severski by Janet MacKaye, June 1925. (The National Library of Norway, Fridtjof Nansen Photo Archives 6d094)

Nansen had spent two days at the City of Orphans and visited all three of the posts. There was no heat even in the wintertime, wrote Nansen, but he was full of praise for the cleanliness he observed everywhere, the long halls with double-decker beds with clean linen, the nursing school, and especially the strict discipline with which the children marched in groups to the dining room. Among some of the other aspects that impressed Nansen were the surgical work being conducted at the Kazachi hospital, which not only treated the orphans but their relatives as well. He also noted the 4,000 girls gathered around Janet MacKaye at the Severski; the physical exercise classes he saw being held everywhere; the Polygon orphanage where 3,500 boys and 1,500 girls lived; the kindergarten; and workshops for the older orphans. Here, the boys had planted small gardens and were waiting for the water to reach their gardens but not sure if it would. But,

> The water began to flow in the little canals built earlier and became stronger. Elation was boundless. The boys immediately began to fill their tin bowls with water. One boy found out that they could open smaller branches, and everyone began doing the same thing.[443]

At the Polygon, Nansen had been impressed with the school for the blind where among other objects, the children made combs and brushes. He received a gift of two brushes from the children—one for his clothes and the other for his hair. Decades later, Zvart Muradyan, née Nacharyan, a blind orphan girl of 12, remembered Nansen's visit, and how Nansen had stroked her hair and given her chocolates.[444] Before he left Armenia, Nansen and the other members of his delegation paid a short visit to Jalaloghli.[445]

Apart from official delegations the City of Orphans hosted individual dignitaries, at times on the occasion of holidays observed in the U.S., such as Washington's Birthday. In February 1924, for instance, in addition to the

152   THE CITY OF ORPHANS

Ethnographic Day organized at the Polygon by NER, featured orphans dressed in different national costumes. Seated in the middle, third from the left, is Nshan Hovhannisyan, Superintendent of Polygon schools. (The National Library of Norway, Fridtjof Nansen Photo Archives 6d002)

American relief workers in Tiflis and Stepanavan who had come to celebrate Washington's Birthday at the City of Orphans, the guests included the Italian and German consuls and their coterie, as well as a few Russian singers who would be entertaining the guests on that day.[446] On Thanksgiving Day, 1923, among the guests, according to Elsie Kimball, was the Persian Consul in Tiflis, whose wife was an American woman from Boston. Among the guests for Thanksgiving were also two British women, Mrs. Harrison and her daughter, the family of Mr. Harrison, the head of the Indo-European Telegraph Company in Tiflis.[447] Earlier, in summer 1923, according to Kimball, an Italian nobleman had been a guest of the City of Orphans:

> An Italian Prince named Pinyatelli [Pignatelli], cousin-in-law of the King's daughter, has been visiting the Americans here recently…His office is located [in Moscow.] I think he does diplomatic work.
>
> Count Albezzi, who was here in the Caucasus during my first year and who married one of the American N.E.R. girls, is his cousin.[448]

By the mid-1920s, the City of Orphans had indeed become the "Show District" Ernest Yarrow had envisioned five years earlier. Of the various qualities that afforded the City of Orphans its singularity was the fact that it represented the only enclave in the Soviet Union where American traditions were so openly upheld, the Red, White and Blue was displayed and *Stars and Stripes Forever* could be sung, in the presence of official delegations and dignitaries—Soviet, American or European. The vast army of orphans impressed the august visitors with their choreographed parades and performances, but when visitors had left, when they no longer were called upon to perform, life for the children would return to its regulated schedule of work and study.

Chapter Six

"THREE SUBURBAN TOWNS OF SIX TO SEVEN THOUSAND CHILDREN EACH"

Transfer from Yerevan to "Alekpol"

The relocation of orphans to Alexandropol or "Alekpol" did not always proceed smoothly, especially in Yerevan, where within six weeks, between April 1 and May 18, 1923, the orphan population in NER's orphanages there had decreased by 1,744 and the hospital reduced in size and services.[449] Of those, 646 orphans were transferred to Alexandropol, while the others were either discharged or transferred to the government. A month earlier, NER had been asked to transfer 400 boys and 100 girls "not less than fifteen years old," to the government along with their clothing, shoes, winter and summer underwear, as well as towels, blankets, bedding, etc. The full list of items NER sent with the children included furniture and objects for use by the children.[450]

Miscommunications and resistance were not unusual. In one incident, as Yerevan District Commander Dr. John Evans was preparing to transfer "three cars boys, all ages, favus cases" to Alexandropol, a May 21, 1923, order from Chairman of People's Commissars Sergei Lukashin asked that the transfer be temporarily postponed.[451] Evans wrote the "Responsible Representative for Armenia" in Yerevan on the same day to explain that it was not possible to cancel the transfer already scheduled, but that subsequent transfers would resume after instructions from NER's Tiflis office:

1. In reference to the request of the President of Armenia, that the Near East Relief temporarily postpone the further transfer of orphans from this district to Alexandropol, that you transmitted to me verbally this morning, permit me to explain that the transfer of three or four cars of favus cases was arranged prior to this request and cannot be postponed at this time without considerable loss and confusion.

2. The above mentioned children will go tomorrow but further transfers will be postponed subject to direction from my Headquarters, who have been informed of the request.

3. This letter is to explain the sending of the orphans tomorrow to avoid the possible misunderstanding that this office is failing to regard the request of the President.[452]

In a second note the following day to the "Responsible Representative in Erivan," Evans revisited the issue. Since arrangements had already been made for the group of orphans with favus, he planned to go ahead with the transfer. However, in compliance with the order of the Chairman of the Council of People's Commissars further orphan transfers to Alexandropol would be postponed. And, he added in the P.S.:

> The group of orphans with favus transferred today, May 22, 1923, will not exceed 150 and in all probability will be approximately 125. Exact figures of actual transfers are impossible to obtain until time of transfer owing to parents and relatives withdrawing their children at unexpected times.[453]

Three days later, on May 24, 1923, Evans tried to clarify NER's on-going plans for consolidation in Yerevan:

> On or before July 1, 1923, it is the present policy of this organization to consolidate this district to a great extent. The permanent status on that date will consist of not over 200 children in orphanages, about 100 on the farm areas, and approximately 700–800, "home placed."[454]

The next day, on May 25, Evans inquired if there would be any objection to the transfer of some 35 children hospitalized with chronic and incurable diseases to Alexandropol, where they would receive better care.[455]

Additional clarification and modification came from NER Caucasus Branch Acting Director General Marden in Tiflis, on May 25, 1923. NER's Administrative Committee, it read, had decided to support 500 children in the government vocational school in Yerevan until February 10, 1924, and that currently they were maintaining 1,000 home orphans. Furthermore, the NER was preparing to open two large shelters, one for boys and the other for girls, for 200–300 orphans. In other words, he wrote, they anticipated maintaining at the end of the academic year in Yerevan, from 1700 to 1800 children, transporting the rest to Alexandropol. This was being done out of financial considerations, hoping to coordinate the educational work there in the best possible way. At the end of his letter Marden added that he hoped the explanations would help alleviate objections from the government.[456]

Orphan transfers out of Yerevan had resumed about a week later, when Evans wrote to the "Responsible Representative for Armenia, Erivan" on June 4, 1923, that

> With the authority of the above arrangement please be informed that on Wednesday, June 6, 1923, this district plans to transfer 35–40 orphans who are suffering with chronic diseases, to the hospitals at Alexandropol.

Evans also pointed out that,

> ...in conference, June 2, 1923, between President of Armenia, Director General and Assistant Director General of the Near East Relief, and the District Commander of Erivan District, it was arranged that the Near East Relief would continue the transfer of orphans to Alexandropol or other districts at its pleasure, with the understanding that employees will in the future be released at the rate of not exceeding 100 per month, for the months of June, July and August...

but that at the end of the school year,

> ...all teachers in this district will be liquidated without regard to the numbers involved, and that this agreement terminates by September 1, 1923.[457]

It appeared, however, that the discussion in Lukashin's office had created some confusion. On June 6, John Evans revisited the matter of transfers to provide his own understanding of the issues:

1. Your letter No. 74, June 5, 1923, states the agreement as to the transfer of orphans from this district to Alexandropol, arrived at in conference between the Director General and the President of Armenia, on June 2, 1923, differently from what I understand it, though I was present at the conference.

2. It is not my understanding that the Near East Relief <u>obligates</u> itself to maintain in orphanages any specific number of children, though the statement was made that it was our <u>policy</u> to have a small number of orphans in Near East Relief orphanages, a certain number home placed, and others on the farms.

   I fear that some confusion in this matter has arisen through misinterpretation, and have asked my headquarters to specifically state their understanding of this agreement, that no further trouble may arise.[458]

The following day, on June 7, 1923, Evans notified the government that in compliance with prior agreements, 125–150 orphans would be transferred to Alexandropol and added that "...unless the policy of the organization changes, this should complete the transfers for the present, the balance remaining until the end of the school year.[459] Three days later, on July 10, he informed the "Responsible Representative for Armenia" that in compliance with instructions from Near East Relief Headquarters, on July 10, 1923, 140 orphan girls would be transferred from Yerevan to Jalaloghli.[460]

With large numbers of orphans now evacuated from Yerevan, A. Mravyan asked Abovyan on June 8, 1923:

> As a result of the transfer of some orphans to Alekpol, certainly a large number of beds are not being used, the need for which we feel in the government orphanages.
>
> Would the NER agree to give those beds to the commissariat?
>
> Please inform us of the outcome.[461]

Although the SSRA government and NER had reached an agreement on the transfers, the decision continued to be challenged by some. One challenge came from the president of the trade union organized by NER's employees in Yerevan, who wrote to Lukashin on July 16, 1923, asking that the transfers out of the orphanages cease. They had failed to change NER's decision to transfer orphans to Alexandropol, he wrote, describing that decision as a "capricious whim" which could not withstand a logical critique. The transfers were harmful to the orphans, he argued, because the orphans often had relatives or friends in Yerevan to whom they were attached and were reluctant to part from. Most orphans had been transferred against their will, as a result of which they had escaped during the transfers and now lived on the streets:

...the majority of the orphans who are being moved, weeping and wailing, have escaped en route and live today in the marketplace in Yerevan where they spend their lives stealing, begging...and other disgusting means. In this way, the moral and financial effort the NER has spent in the last 5–6 years is deteriorating, as is the new generation.[462]

One of the escapees was Pyurastan Harutyunyan, who had run away from Kazachi to find her brother in Yerevan. NER Regulating Officer Harrison Maynard had fed her, but failing to find her brother, had sent her to the "Responsible Representative, Sovnarcom," so that she may be placed in a government orphanage. It seems the "Responsible Representative" had not acceded to the request and sent her back to Maynard. Maynard, in his turn, reminded the "Responsible Representative" of NER's rule prohibiting escaped orphans from reentry into the orphanage, and sent the child back.

Note from H. Maynard regarding Pyurastan Harutyunyan. (NAA 113/38/33/f. 17)

Second note from H. Maynard about Pyurastan Harutyunyan. (NAA 113/38/33/f. 15)

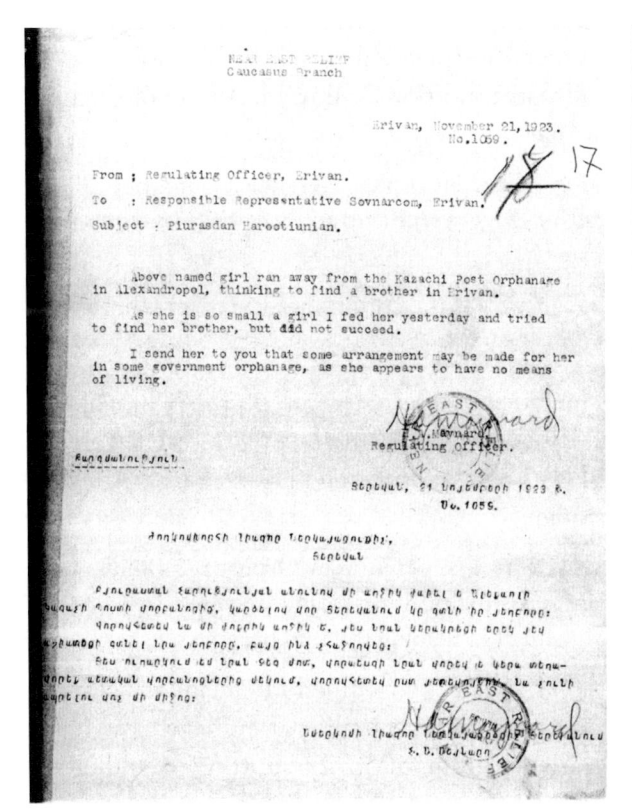

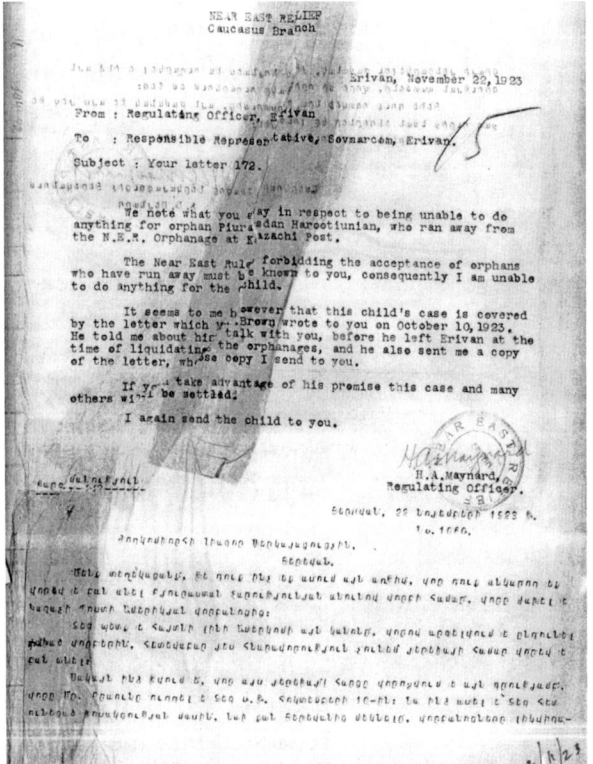

A memorandum from the Administrative Office of Orphanages in Yerevan showed that in August 1923, 200 children lived on the streets; their numbers would doubtless double in the fall:

> At night, multitudes of "street children" sleep on the streets of Yerevan, in the park, gardens, squares and covered areas. Some of them are the orphans who escaped from Amerkom [American Committee]...it is necessary to gather these children from the streets and shelter them...[463]

The president of the trade union had another objection: by closing down NER's orphanages in Yerevan, its employees, who in the cumulative provided a living for close to 2,500 people, would be left without an income. This factor, according to the writer, was as important as the separation of orphans from their loved ones. The president of the trade union ended his letter by asking Lukashin to appeal to Charles Vickrey, who was expected to meet with Lukashin in the near future, confident that Vickrey would stop the transfers.

Nevertheless, transfers out of Yerevan continued. On September 29, 1923, Milton Brown, then in Yerevan, asked Sergei Lukashin for a train of 15 wagons to transport 400 orphans out of Yerevan:

> We are prepared to make this transfer whenever we receive word from you that the train is at our disposal.
>
> It will be very convenient for the N.E.R. if this transfer can be accomplished during the coming week.[464]

By October 13, 1923, Yerevan orphanages #8, #2 and former orphanage #9 had been evacuated, with further evacuations planned for all NER buildings, "as rapidly as transportation and railroad conditions" allowed. A note of October 1923 informed the government that

> ...on account of the liquidation of Erivan orphanages, the Committee [NER] cannot hereafter furnish bread to the government and we will make necessary arrangements to issue flour instead.[465]

In 1924 there remained in Yerevan only "an employment station where they kept from one to two hundred children."[466]

Consolidation plans also included the evacuation of the Darachichak orphanage, which was achieved by May 3, 1923.[467] However, as NER Yerevan Superintendent of Agriculture F. P. Freeman informed liaison Sargis Abovyan on June 14, 1923, NER had arranged

> ...to leave twelve older orphans with a supervisor in Orphanage Building #2, furnishing them equipment and seeds for cultivating land previously used by the Near East Relief, for their own benefit in helping them to become self sustaining.

"The local government of Akhta [Hrazdan]," continued Freeman, had allowed them the use of this land already sown in wheat and barley," and now NER requested that the government give written authority allotting "Building #2 to the exclusive use of the Darachichak Land Colony." Already two families had moved into "this small building and it is requested that this grant for the building be given as soon as possible to forestall further difficulties."[468]

The orphan population now amassed in Alexandropol was distributed in groups to the north, west and southwest corners of the city, which NER relief worker Pauline Jordan of Welchville, Maine, described as

> ...three suburban towns of six to seven thousand children each...Each of these orphanage towns is directed by a group of five or six Americans. Their task is the general supervision of the large staff of Armenian doctors, nurses, teachers and helpers who are in immediate charge of the children.[469]

Many of the barracks had been refitted to serve the needs of an army of orphans. About one third of the total number of barracks served as dormitories, the rest as bathrooms, kitchens, bakeries, dining rooms, classrooms, workshops, staff residences, offices, clinics and hospitals, and, according to *The New Near East*, if all the orphans in all three posts were to sit at table together, the length of the table would exceed 15 miles.[470] In one of the dining rooms, 1,500 children could eat and in one of the baths 450 children could bathe at the same time.[471] To maintain the grounds and orphanages, and attend to all the needs of the children, NER employed a large force of Armenian employees, including physicians, teachers, accountants, etc.[472]

In 1922, it cost NER $89,000 per month to maintain the City of Orphans, or $1,201,283.51 in 2014 dollar value.[473] According to the April 1923 issue of *The New Near East*, in the summer of 1922 the minimum monthly needs for the entire complex of orphanages—the Severski, Polygon and Kazachi—included:

> 111,134 cans of milk, 183 tons of flour, 88 tons of grits, 8 tons of sugar, 44 tons of beans, 4 tons of cocoa, 12 tons of oil, 8 tons of raisins, 32 tons of rice, 6 tons of fruit, 4 tons of soap, 5 tons of nuts, 8 tons of candles, 1¼ tons of tea, 90 tons of meat.[474]

Kazachi Post

The Kazachi, the administrative center of NER's Caucasus operations, sheltered in its barracks 6,400 orphan girls by the end of 1921, and offered basic necessities to an additional 3,000 girls in the city of Alexandropol. In his report to Congress for the year ending December 31, 1921, Charles Vickrey had put the value of the Kazachi property at $3,000,000 (or $36,038,505.15 in 2014 dollar value), used by NER free of rent.[475]

The post in 1922 had an Armenian employee force of 1,133 individuals.[476] Each day at the Kazachi a minimum of 5,750 pounds of bread was consumed, for which 4,000 pounds of flour were used. Twenty-nine men hired exclusively for the job of baking bread operated eight ovens, each oven with the capacity of baking 75 loaves of bread at the same time, each loaf weighing 10 pounds. In addition, about 36 pounds of bread were toasted for the hospital patients each day. The ovens were heated by mazut[477] and wood. In late 1921, for instance, a total of 70 trainloads of wood were received at Kazachi, representing only a portion of the 4,000,000 pounds needed in the winter season.

To give a more comprehensive picture of necessities required to run basic operations at the Kazachi, Vickrey's report for 1921 detailed some of the items actually used every month at the post in 1921. The monthly list included: 2,300 sacks of flour; 40 barrels of lard; 1,875 cases of milk; about 3,000 poods of beans; about 1,000 poods of sugar; and about 1,700 poods of rice. Meat had been extremely scarce, and none was given to the orphans; vegetables were needed badly and would not be available till harvest time. Vickrey's list also included items needed from the U.S.: bully beef [corned beef], sewing needles, of which only 30 were left including those brought

A section of the Kazachi, circa 1920. (*The Military Surgeon*, February 1921: facing page 150)

from Kars; leather, needed to make shoes for winter and for which no cattle were left in that part of the country; paint for the tin roofs of both the Kazachi and the Polygon to prevent deterioration; and glass panes for windows.[478]

The Kazachi had its own electric-lighting plant, a 32-horsepower engine and a 220-voltage dynamo capable of providing for 600 electric lamps and a telephone line with an extension running to the Polygon district.[479] Of the infrastructure, miles of underground pipes had been repaired to ensure the purity of the water supply whose source was in the nearby mountains; the sewer system was greatly improved over the existing one but would be replaced by a newer system in the spring; and roads within and between posts were being repaired. Transportation within and without the post was mostly by mule and horse, although at times cars and trucks were used as well. Local women working at the post did the general laundry by hand, but a new central laundry equipped with washing machines, a drier, and motor were planned for. The older orphan girls did most of their own laundry; they also sewed, cooked and kept their orphanages in order, which helped lower the cost of running the orphanage.[480]

Skilled and unskilled laborers on staff at Kazachi's workshops had made much of the repairs and refitting. Masons and carpenters were responsible for building roads, bridges, sheds, general maintenance, such as plastering and whitewashing, as well as making mazut tanks and ox-carts. Using a turner lathe, carpenters made all the tables, benches, stools, black-boards, shelves, doors, window frames, wash tubs, bakery tubs, wooden beds, tool handles, filing cases, etc.[481]

The blacksmiths and mechanics made the keys, locks, hooks, hinges, workmen's tools, knives, car-springs, and repaired automobiles and mazut burners. Tinsmiths made stoves, pipes, soup bowls, tin dishes, cups, showers for the bath-house, oil cans, tanks, ID tags worn by orphans, sewer covers and tin roofs, and were responsible for the repairs of the stoves. The plumbing workshop repaired and equipped a central bathhouse that made it possible to bathe 1,200 children daily. The plumbers were also in charge of the water pipes on the post.[482]

In 1921, the Kazachi was one of the biggest businesses in the area.[483] While much of the food supplies for the post were received from the U.S., large quantities of wood, vegetables, hay, meat, butter, eggs, and fruit were purchased locally, when and if available, usually through the exchange of used clothing:

> People from the surrounding villages come in daily with products on a small scale, but these taken as a whole, amount to a large quantity. The Near East Relief deals

with as many as 1,500 people daily in this way. Most of the products are paid for with articles of clothing.[484]

Hospitals at the Kazachi spread over two main buildings, medical and surgical, in addition to an open-air tuberculosis hospital, a nursery for infants up to three years old, a maternity ward, an isolation ward for contagious diseases in two buildings, and ambulatories in four of the barrack buildings. A convalescent hospital cared for patients for one week or 10 days before they were returned to the orphanages. The hospital buildings were equipped with electric lights, replacing candles and smoky tin lamps.[485] The chief surgeon at the Kazachi was Dr. Rowland Blythe of Cranford, New Jersey, a young man in his early 30s. He had sold his house and according to his sister, he was in Alexandropol "in Russian Caucasus, Bolshevik territory" at the end of June.[486] He was back in practice in New York in January 1925.

The schooling Kazachi's children received were equivalent to the elementary and grammar schools of America.[487] Due to their large numbers, the 4,384 school-aged children were spread over ten schools, each having anywhere from 300 to close to 700 children, who were educated in shifts.[488]

The Polygon

A detailed account of the Polygon as it stood in summer 1921 emerges from Father Grigor Nzhdehyan's report of July 1921, addressed to the Reverend Father Artak, Prelate of the Diocese of Shirak, to whom he intended to provide a comprehensive picture of the orphanage. Father Grigor Nzhdehyan had been invited by the administration of the Polygon to serve as priest and instructor in ethics/morality for the Polygon orphans,[489] and had begun work on June 2, 1921.

The polygon was beautiful, wrote Father Grigor. In July 1921 there were 4,772 orphans in the Polygon, all boys; the orphan population had grown when orphans from Kars had been transported there in March 1921, and was likely to grow further since the flow of orphans had not yet stopped. The Americans, he wrote, had a temporary orphanage in the city where new orphans were collected and sheltered until more buildings at the Polygon were repaired. The girls lived at the Kazachi Post by the city cemetery south of the city, and were greater in number.

Polygon Office. (RAC NEF Photos Box 153)

The bell structure built by NER at the Polygon. (RAC NEF Photos Box 1530)

The 4,772 boys at the polygon between the ages of four and 17 were grouped according to age and housed in six buildings, on both floors. Nutrition, clothing, and bedding had been scarce during the preceding winter when the Americans had escaped. As a consequence, there had been various illnesses due to lack of food and other necessities and mortality had soared. In the absence of the Americans, an average of ten children had died daily at the Polygon. But since the Americans' return and under their organized and caring administration the situation had improved significantly. The children now received one meal per day, which included meat, rice, beans, sweet buns and tea in the morning and one funt [1 funt=about .9 lb.] of bread. The clothes and bedding of the orphans were very good, and always clean. Every two weeks the children received a bath and a change of clothing, including underwear.

Four physicians staffed the hospitals of the Polygon, whose cleanliness and orderliness were exemplary. The Polygon had four hospitals. In one were the very sick children with various diseases caused by the conditions under which they had lived; the second hospital was for children with scabies and favus; the third was for convalescing children; and the fourth was exclusively for patients with eye problems, especially trachoma. At the time of Father Grigor's writing, there were about 1,100 patients, exclusive of those in the eye hospital. His numbers were not exact, he wrote, since some orphans were discharged, new ones were admitted, and others died, the latter group averaging about four boys per day in June 1921. Mortality had decreased in July, which was due, according to Father Grigor, to the care of a young physician by the name of Dr. V. Yerznkyan, who maintained high standards of care. He was the only member of the staff at the Polygon who had declined a salary and received his daily food only.

In the remainder of the detailed report Father Grigor described the various departments of the Polygon. Mr. Margerum, who had recently arrived from America and replaced Mr. Johnson, supervised Polygon's Administrative Department. Mr. Margerum was a "real American," extremely nice, a real Christian and church lover, an honest man, dedicated to his work. He had applied strict order. He had given up his factory in America, Father Grigor wrote, and had donated his profits to the care of the orphans in Armenia. Mr. Margerum oversaw a few assistants, interpreters, an accountant, and a chief of finance. Eight other departments reported to the Administrative Department. One of these was the Department of Reconstruction with 107 employees, who erected new buildings and restored the destroyed ones, supervised by engineer Mikayelyan. This department was also responsible for all the warehouses, with 14 workers. The Department of Transportation with 18 workers; the section on ovens, with 23 workers; distribution stations with two workers; a dining room with 13 employees for the staff and the Americans, and other departments and sections were all under the Administrative Department.

The second department was the Orphanage Department, directed by Miss [Myrtle] Shane, who for more than two years had dedicated herself at Kars and at the Polygon to the education of Armenian orphans. To Miss Shane reported a staff of 160. Miss Shane had witnessed the events in Kars and had returned to Alexandropol where she worked passionately. The Department was responsible for all issues relating to orphans, including the hiring and firing of orphanage staff.

One of four dining rooms at the Polygon. (Paul Barsam Private Collection)

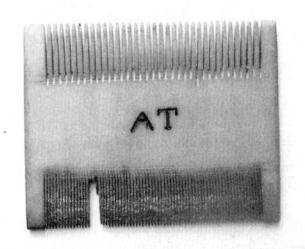

Delousing comb. (AGMI Collection)

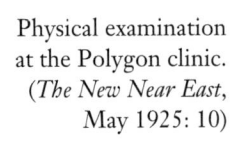

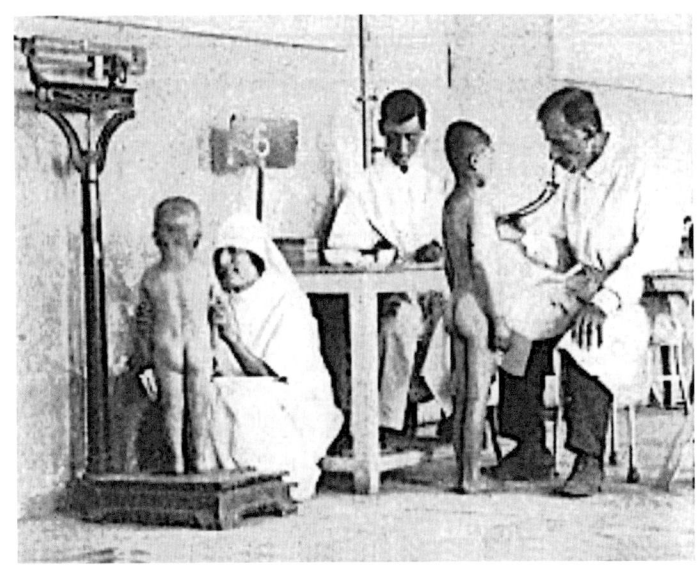

Physical examination at the Polygon clinic. (*The New Near East*, May 1925: 10)

Caroline Silliman, who spoke Armenian fluently and had dedicated her life to Armenian orphans, the report continued, directed the Department of Education. She supervised 37 employees of whom 32 were teachers and there were plans to increase the teaching staff for the upcoming academic year. Included in the education department were sewing workshops for women with 29 employees.

The Hospital Department, wrote Father Grigor, included ambulatory care, dentistry and pharmacy and was directed by the American Miss Thom (she was actually a Canadian), who had been in Armenia since summer 1920. She had first come to Alexandropol, then had left for Kars, then later returned to Alexandropol. She was responsible for the hospitals, 147 nurses, and the cleanliness of the washing areas.

Mr. Ogden, who specialized in Agronomy, Father Grigor continued, directed the Industrial Department. This section was in charge of nine office workers, 31 different workshops, 46 militia and about 70 older orphans who stood guard at the Polygon. In the workshops, orphans learned sculpting or etching with two teachers; drawing with one teacher; carpentry with two teachers; sewing and tailoring with nine teachers; shoe repair with seven teachers; tinsmithing with one teacher; book binding with one teacher; hair cutting with one teacher; blacksmithing with one teacher; locksmithing with one teacher; pottery with one teacher, etc. The products that came out of these workshops made by the orphans were used exclusively for the needs of the orphanage.

Turkish Armenian and Russian Armenian staff and older orphans ran the Department of Enlightenment. It had a Theater Section that had been formed by a group of theater lovers, and a suitable building, but lacked the necessary costumes and other essentials. During the winter, 13 theatrical presentations, three lectures and four or five events had taken place there. Another section in this group published newspapers. With Mr. Johnson's support, this section had begun to publish the collotype weekly papers titled *Huys* (Hope) and *Kayc* (Sparkle). Although both had been temporarily discontinued, efforts were being made to resume their publication. *Hope* had been published in 50 or 60 copies and sent to the Kazachi Post as well as to other places in the city and to Istanbul and America.

The Literary Association had been established with the goal of organizing lectures, providing support to the Theater Section as well as building a library/reading room, although the latter was still work in progress. There was one library with approximately 700 books, some in duplicate, and while most were children's literature, orphans of all ages used them as well. Efforts were underway to increase the number of books but the high cost of books and irregular transportation were obstacles. At the time of writing, three large buildings were being repaired to serve as classrooms and library/reading room.

Religion and instruction in ethics were Father Grigor's purview. He lectured on religion and morality to orphans of all ages. Projected plans included liturgy classes, especially for Saturday evenings and Sundays, and a prayer book, with the hope of having an altar to administer mass to the orphans and the staff. Although the American staff practiced a different creed, they spared no effort to support the Armenian liturgy, which would help connect the orphans to their traditions. Father Grigor was especially gratified that the Americans valued and loved the liturgy of the Armenian Church, and pleased that the American administration encouraged the teaching of religion and morals to the orphans. He regretted, however, that he lacked the necessities for the proper performance of the liturgy and asked the help of the higher spiritual authorities. Still, he had plans to begin a Sunday school to teach literacy to the workers, organize lectures beneficial to the orphans and anyone willing to attend.

Father Grigor then turned to the cemetery. He was delighted with Mr. Margerum's design for a new and beautiful cemetery that would have a chapel in the center surrounded by graves set in a circular pattern, which would allow for future expansion. The new cemetery design had paths running between each two rows of graves and one wide and direct path to the center. When first designed, the direction of the graves had been such that the dead would be buried on a north to south axis, which ran counter to the traditions of the Armenian Church according to which the dead were buried on a west to east axis. But the design had been adjusted to fit the Armenian tradition. They planned to begin work after the harvest, when the crops on the land adjoining the cemetery would be harvested and the land freed. In addition, Dr. Yerznkyan had suggested that the present cemetery, which was quite spacious, be surrounded by barbed wire, for which purpose a large quantity of barbed wire had been acquired.

In summation, Father Grigor's report mentioned that each employee received daily bread and other provisions and twice a year they received winter and summer clothing. "Beyond these," he continued,

> ...I find it necessary to state here that the conduct of the Americans and their intense program for our orphans, their care, education, to teach intellectual and various beneficial knowledge, in one word, their efforts to prepare a cultured generation is above all praise. Self-sacrificing, kind and honest and perfect humanitarians, in the truest sense of the word...[490]

Their work should serve as an example for all, he wrote, and if, he added, from time to time unpleasant things happened in the isolated world of the orphanage,

Children on their way to the Kazachi church. (Barton 1930: facing page 142)

Polygon dormitory.
(Barton 1930: facing page 134)

and of course there were exceptions, those were due to the low level of education of some of the Armenian staff and their lack of dedication to saving the remnants of the nation. He regretted that such people left a negative impression on the Americans, who had come to help, through heroic efforts and at enormous self-sacrifice.

According to Father Grigor, more than 650 individuals holding various responsibilities were employed at the Polygon in summer 1921. Yet with the exception of Dr. Yerznkyan, his report makes no reference to the Armenian employees by their names, by contrast to the extensive details it provides about the operations of the Polygon and the American staff. Nor does Father Grigor elaborate on the condition of the thousands of orphan boys, except minimally and then chiefly with reference to their mortality and morbidity.

A few months after Father Grigor's report, the orphan population at the Polygon had increased, and double-decker beds were made to provide room for 6,000 children.[491] Dr. Elfie R. Graff of the American Women's Hospitals reported in September 1921 that about 20% of the boys were infected with trachoma, and that they were getting very good medical care from the native doctors:

> I find that the Polygon orphanages are being well taken care of medically by the native doctors. I have been looking over their work and find it very good. As soon as we obtain scales, we are going to make a study of the nutrition values.[492]

By 1922, several more of the Polygon barracks had been repaired and many of them dedicated to various states in the U.S., as Massachusetts, Washington and Connecticut:

> "Massachusetts House" is a dormitory for 350 boys, and one of a group of 15 such houses. The state was represented at the ceremonies by Mrs. R. R Uhls of Fitchburg [Massachusetts]. "Connecticut House" is a hospital with 300 beds under the direction of Miss Elizabeth Thom, of Chicago. The medical and nursing staffs are entirely Armenian. Connecticut was represented on dedication day by Miss Caroline Silliman of New Canaan. "Washington House" named after the state of Washington, is designed as the residence of the American personnel. The state was represented at the dedication ceremonies by Alfred D. Merritt, of Tacoma.[493]

And it was expected that in the future,

> ...the more important of the many stone buildings scattered over its 200 acres will hereafter bear the name of an American state.[494]

Indeed, by April 1, 1922, 44 buildings were named after a state in the United States.[495]

Polygon Administrative Director Fred Margerum, of whom Father Grigor had spoken so highly, stayed in Armenia less than seven months.[496] In a letter to the President of the Executive Committee of the Alexandropol RevKom,

Margerum explained that he had been ordered to leave the Polygon, he knew not why:[497]

> Polygon, Alexandropol, Jan. 28, 1922
>
> My dear Sir,
>
> It is with a sick heart that I tell you I have been ordered to leave my boys at the Polygon. I do not know the reason. I do know that I have done my best. I want to thank you, my comrade, for your kindnesses to me. I want to wish you good health and success in your efforts to help in the cause of bringing about a more equitable distribution of the good things of this life, in the effort to improve the conditions of the poor, to educate the masses, to afford labor its rightful dignity and to spread democracy.
>
> There was a time when I regarded the doctrines of the present leaders of Russia as those of fanatical dreamers uselessly trying to bring about Utopian conditions on earth but after being better informed, I feel that much good must come from the movement with which you are identified.
>
> Again thanking you for the happiness that has been mine through my association with you, I beg to remain,
>
> Very sincerely yours,
> Fred P. Margerum [Signed]

Earlier, on May 28, 1921, another NER staff member, Dr. Russell Main, had also been fired. According to a letter from Dr. Melkumyan, the Director of Alexandropol's Health Department, Dr. Main had been fired because he had protested against NER's strict discipline of body searches to which Armenian employees were subjected upon leaving work in the evening.[498]

Severski:
"The Largest Children's Hospital in the World"

In her reorganization of medical care at the City of Orphans in 1921 and 1922, Dr. Elliott designated the Kazachi as the surgical center headed by Dr. Blythe, and the Polygon hospitals as the center for medical cases under her leadership.[499] The 200 tuberculosis patients were moved to the new tuberculosis center just opened in Dilijan, under the supervision of Dr. Graff and nurse Katherine Pellow.[500] The dental care of the orphans was entrusted to two local dentists who had access to a recently purchased complete line of dental supplies and equipment from Tiflis.[501] For the major and one of the most pervasive health problems, trachoma, Dr. Elliott suggested the use of much of Severski post, with over 40 barracks, which was officially turned over to NER

View of Trachoma Hospital with the long line of children in line for treatment. (Lovejoy 1927: between pages 122 and 123)

"Three Suburban Towns..." 167

Detail of the Trachoma Hospital at Severski.

in summer 1921. In view of the extremely infectious nature of the disease and the vast number of orphans inflicted with it, the best approach, she thought, would be the concentration of all trachoma treatment at the Severski. The Trachoma Hospital was placed under Dr. Uhls, an eye specialist who arrived in spring 1921 with his wife, Florence.

Repairs started in August 1921. By December 15, four buildings were completed and occupied by 1,633 orphans, and by January 1st another 1,000 orphans were accommodated as repairs were conducted on additional barracks.[502] Referring to the acquisition of the Seversky by NER and the decision to house trachoma patients in the new setting, *The Indianapolis Star* in its November 20, 1921, issue announced:

> The new system of buildings to which Capt. Yarrow has just fallen heir known as the "seversky," or north barracks has just been turned over to the Americans by the Armenian government in time to take in several thousand more tots before winter. The three systems of ex military barracks [Kazachi, Polygon and Severski] cover several square miles of space and form the apices of a triangle with the city of Alexandropol in the center.
>
> Although the buildings are in a bad state of disrepair, Capt. Yarrow reported work has already been commenced under the direction of Byron D. MacDonald of Dorranceton, Pa [Pennsylvania] to put them in condition.
>
> The new barracks will be used as a kind of hospital orphanage and devoted especially for the care of trachoma sufferers...which will be placed in charge of Dr. Russell Uhls...

The decision to turn the Severski into a trachoma hospital was made during the course of negotiations between Dr. Elliott and Ernest Yarrow, where it was agreed that for one full year the American Women's Hospitals would organize, direct, and pay for the American and Armenian staff salaries. In a letter dated March 7, 1922, to her colleague Dr. Esther Lovejoy, Elliott wrote:

> ...we have at least 15,000 cases of trachoma under our care...
>
> We have here at the present time a trachoma specialist, Dr. Uhls, and a very good surgeon, Dr. Blythe, and I will do the medical work. There are three nurses (American) at this post (Severski), one at Polygon Post and two at Kazachi Post. I will bring down both my nurses from Erivan and may transfer one from here if we find we don't need these.
>
> However, I will start immediately to establish our training school for nurses on a proper basis...Our Erivan class of nurses has just been capped.

In another letter 10 days later to Dr. Lovejoy, she provided more details:

The Alexandropol work will be tremendous when we get it organized; it is almost unbelievable the "medical factory" that will be in operation...I am personally examining all the children's eyes for trachoma here, as we find the native doctor's tendency is to give the child the benefit of the doubt and call the case negative when the trachoma is slight. To-morrow I am going to Darachichak to examine the eyes of children and arrange the medical program, for we shall be sending children there soon, and I want to be sure that they are all trachoma-free.

It is an awful job getting these children changed about. We have sent 400 trachoma cases to Alexandropol; cleaned and fumigated two buildings, and made them safe for trachoma-free children...

Then the terrific job will begin of getting enough personnel to treat thousands and thousands of eyes daily at Alexandropol.[503]

In charge of repairs at the Severski was also N. H. Anderson of Bridgeboro, New Jersey, a former champion athlete of Wesleyan University in Connecticut and a shot-putter.[504] To equip the hospital, NER decided to open a sewing shop in Alexandropol. It was expected that the work would occupy several hundred women until spring, when it was hoped that most of the women would find work in the fields. When the news that a sewing shop would be hiring refugee women to make thousands of mattresses, bed sheets and clothing, a mob of women gathered before daylight to apply for jobs. The morning when Pauline Jordan arrived to open the shop, she was pulled from her horse and her clothing almost torn to bits as the women surged about her, kissing her hands, clutching and kissing her skirt, and falling on their knees before her as they begged for work.[505]

The enormity of the patient population and the efforts required to prepare the hospital became the subject of numerous articles in nursing and medical journals in the U.S. for the next few years.[505] One article in *The American Journal of Nursing* in 1922 detailed how the 40 barracks at Severski were repaired and the hospital set up:

Children gathered for treatment at Severski Post. (NEF Photos Box 138)

Deciding on the need for such a hospital was simple,—getting it ready for occupancy was quite another matter. There stood the forty stone buildings, given by the Armenian government, with strong solid walls, but with leaking roofs and not a door or window or bit of woodwork left intact. Near by was the town of Alexandropol full of starving refugees, able to supply an infinite amount of labor, but almost nothing in the way of materials. To get things into condition in Armenia was not a question, as it would be in America, of stepping to the telephone and ordering so many doors and window frames, so many mattresses and blankets. But soon 400 refugees under American supervision were at work repairing the buildings. Very ingenious they showed themselves at making something out of nothing, straightening pieces of bent tin for roofing, improvising window catches out of lengths of wire; and one by one the buildings were made ready.[507]

Few of the 30 buildings in use had beds; mattresses were laid on the stone floor, wrote Pauline Jordan. In the schoolrooms there were no desks and chairs and the pupils squatted

> ...upon straw mattresses, which are placed around on the cold flooring. Pencils and paper are too scarce for common use, so each child uses a slate made of tin. Their clothing is just as rough-and-ready as the schoolroom equipment. Near East Relief orphans being clad in American cast-off garments, of which non-descript and often ill-fitting raiment they are inordinately proud. Meals consisting of such staple foods as bread, corn-grits, stews of potatoes, onions and beans, are served from the United States—our daily menu is cut close to absolutely scientific requirements, figures in calories.[508]

The trachoma hospital opened in early 1922 with 2,700 beds and by June 1922, 6,000 worst trachoma cases had been gathered at the Severski.[509]

Dr. Uhls remained in Armenia until 1924. "The whole plant is one vast hospital," he wrote, "which will have a greater number of patients than any institution known to the writer," and added:

> Never has there been such an opportunity for research. Thousands of cases are under absolute control, and daily observation...
>
> Send to these suffering children a research worker with the power to discover the cause of trachoma.[510]

Dr. Uhls and nurses administering trachoma treatment at the Trachoma Hospital. (*The New Near East*, September 1923: 15)

His full report of that year on conditions at the Severski detailed the progress made in three years.[511] According to his report, over 14,000 cases of the malignant, malicious, virulent, contagious eye disease were found initially, out of a total of 25,000 orphans.[512] The hospitals were taxed to capacity with general diseases with no means for isolation; there were no properly trained doctors or nurses, and supplies and equipment were lacking. With the reorganization began the intensive work of giving 98,000 treatments in one week:

> Doctors were given special instructions; a training school for nurses recruited from our own orphanages was opened; operating rooms began functions, and out clinics were established wherever necessary. Every child with a Trachoma diagnosis received a daily treatment. At one time 98,000 treatments were given weekly. It was remarkable how soon the Armenian girl nurses learned to treat deftly and quickly. Generations of rug weaving have given nimble fingers.

Dr. Uhls next described the treatment method:

> …The most practical position for an eye treatment where large numbers are concerned, speaking particularly of the application of the copper stick, is for the child to place his head in the nurse's lap, sitting on a low stool at her feet. The patient is comfortable, the nurse is comfortable, and it is much easier to perform the irrigation.
>
> We consider two nurses necessary to properly apply the copper stick—one to overt the lid over a cotton tipped applicator, the other to apply the stick. It is not possible to reach the cul-de-sac in any other manner. The stick is rubbed lightly across the everted lid twice, and an irrigation with normal salt follows. This is done for the first few applications until a tolerance is established for the copper sulphate.
>
> …Cotton tipped applicators are prepared in advance, one for each patient to be examined. Small cards are prepared with the various diagnoses printed on them.
>
> The examiner puts on a rubber apron, a rubber glove on his left hand, and a Turkish towel across his left knee. A nurse is behind him ready to hand him the applicators one at a time as the patient steps up. A bowl of weak Bichloride solution is at the examiner's left side. The examiner seizes an applicator with his towel (which is frequently changed), grasps the lashes and quickly reverts the lid over the applicator. He calls out the diagnosis and the proper card is given to the child, who marches in the line to the recorder, who takes the card to be used over again.
>
> This method is not ideal, but it is surely an improvement over the examinations of school children usually in vogue in our own United States schools.
>
> We did not put forth any special propaganda for the prevention of blindness in Armenia, but we trained doctors and nurses to fight Trachoma, and 25,000 children know that Trachoma can be cured.[513]

Each child had an applicator assigned to him or her. Part of the process was automatic, as each child picked up his applicator and moved down the line toward the physician or nurse. The process only took a few seconds, but the treatments had to be kept up, in many cases a few times a day, day after day, for months and years. The rest of the day, the children went to school.[514]

Dr. Uhls's report also included general remarks about the health condition of the orphans. There was improvement in the general health conditions of 25,000 children in Near East Relief institutions in the Caucasus; the death rate for the 12-month period [1924] just ended was 8.6 per thousand, that is, 215 orphan deaths in 1923, but two-thirds of the deaths had been due to causes originating prior to the admission of the children into the orphanages. These were largely children who had been unable to recuperate from prolonged periods of starvation.[515] Another decline was registered in favus, the contagious disease which robbed the orphans of their hair.[516] The improvement was attributed to NER's introduction of treatment by X-ray, which reduced the incidence of favus by 96%.[517] This had revolutionized the earlier method of coating the child's head with a tar cap and then freeing the scalp of its diseased hair by tearing off the cap. Additional steps were taken in 1924 to improve health conditions by establishing at the Polygon a department to train children in basic public health, but which, as Barclay Acheson explained, was mired in difficulties:

> In order to understand the difficulties that must be overcome in securing the cooperation of the children in the simple subjects of personal cleanliness and sanitation, one should know that at present the children are without tooth brushes and handkerchiefs and that it would cost from $15,000 to $20,000 a year to provide them with handkerchiefs alone. Bathing is difficult, toilet paper is unknown, and in the past there have been times when there was not even a sufficient supply of soap.[518]

Cleveland House and the School for the Blind

Under Dr. R. T. Uhls's direction at the Severski was also the school for blind children, established in summer 1922.[519] According to information released in the U.S., it was the first of its kind in Armenia, and was to be operated in connection with the Trachoma Hospital. And since the city of Cleveland, Ohio would be providing for its maintenance, the school would be called "Cleveland House." NER reported that the school was dedicated in summer 1922 in the presence of "the Ministers of Education and Social Welfare of Armenia," with photographer and relief worker Jane Hardcastle representing the city of Cleveland.[520] A year later, *The New Near East* announced in its October 1923 issue that the only school for the blind in Armenia celebrated its first anniversary. The School, it was stated, was being

> …operated under the direction of Miss Pauline Jordan, a Near East Relief worker in charge of education at the Seversky orphanage. Among its accomplishments during the period of its existence have been the organization and training of a blind orchestra, and the training of seven blind teachers, who will be used to establish other blind schools in Armenia and Georgia. Weaving and brush making are being taught in an effort to make the school and its pupils self-supporting.[521]

The 150 blind orphans, between the ages of five to 14, would be taught the usual elementary school studies by native teachers, with an emphasis on teaching marketable productive skills, such as mat and basket weaving and making brushes.[522] By 1925, 80 blind orphans at the school were producing a record number of 8,000 brushes per month. A year later, *The New Near East* announced that Geneva Hammond, also a relief worker, had transcribed Mabel Elliott's *Beginning Again at Ararat* into Braille.[523] There had been no textbooks for the blind available in Armenia when Pauline Jordan had first arrived in Alexandropol, but she had fashioned the first textbooks in braille ever to be made in Armenian, using crude pieces of cardboard and a hatpin.[524] NER also stated that in addition to teaching orphans to read in braille, Pauline Jordan had organized a training center for teachers and an orchestra for the blind, which was one of the best in the country.

The testimony of Zvart Muradyan, one of the blind orphans at Alexandropol, adds a perspective that differs somewhat from NER accounts.[525] She had lost her sight at the age of five, and had been taken by her parents to the "American Orphanage" in Karakilis to save her from starvation, whence she was transferred to the City of Orphans in 1922. At about that time, according to Zvart Muradyan's account, the blind Armenian composer and ethnomusicologist Nikoghayos Tigranyan, had adapted the braille technique to the Armenian alphabet, which he used at the school for the blind he opened in Alexandropol.[526] A native of Alexandropol and blind from the age of nine, Nikoghayos Tigranyan had completed his studies at the Vienna Institute for the Blind (1873–80), and studied piano and compositional theory, later continuing his studies in 1893 at the St. Petersburg Conservatory under Rimsky-Korsakov, among others. Tigranyan had settled in his native Alexandropol in 1921, where he established a school for the blind. He was reportedly the first to introduce the Braille System in Armenia at the music school he founded in Alexandropol. Zvart Muradyan recalled that Tigranyan had heard of the blind children at the NER orphanage and asked the orphanage administration to allow him to organize a school for the blind at the orphanage. Tigranyan taught 45 boys and 40 girls in braille, Zvart Muradyan among them. Tigranyan, stated Muradyan, directed the School for the Blind.

In 1925, NER asked the Soviet Armenian government to assume the responsibility of the school for the blind. The People's Commissariat of Enlightenment accepted the responsibility in view of the fact that being the only blind school in the country it had a significance on the state level, but on condition that NER would secure provisions for the school for two more years.[527]

By 1923, the world outside the City of Orphans had improved, wrote Elsie Kimball—now assigned to the Kazachi—to her family on June 10, 1923:

> Here we are, all safe and sound…Things have changed a lot…The Bolsheviks were most chivalrous to us…Alexandropol is different now. The city has been built up a lot, the streets have been repaired, there is scarcely any disease, people are much better dressed and the refugees are well cared for.[528]

And, she added, tennis was "currently the big game" at the posts: two courts had been built at the Kazachi, one at the Polygon, and one at Severski. But according to SSRA People's Commissar of Health Lazaryan, two diseases from which the City of Orphans had been spared, continued to pose a threat to the general population in Armenia. In his update of 1924, Lazaryan listed malaria as the most prevalent and harmful, present in all its forms and varieties. In general, 45% of the country was infected with malaria; but the rate of infection rose to 85% among the population of the fertile lowlands. Insufficiency of funds had prevented the government from performing the necessary drainage of these lands, as a result of which only preventive and curative means were now being used.[529] The Commissar then briefly reported on the second "disaster," which was

> ...syphilis, most prevalent in those sections of the country that had been occupied by Turkish solders. For its treatment at least 50 kilograms of Neosalvarsanis were required yearly, and the necessary equipment for six Venereal Medical Stations.[530]

Mens Sana in Corpore Sano: Sports, Athletics, and Boy Scouts

While athletic education and a boy scout program existed in the Republic of Armenia, a more comprehensive and nationwide effort took shape with the arrival of three scoutmasters—Vahan Cheraz, Onnik Yazmajian, and Tigran Khoyan—from Constantinople.[531] The three men left Constantinople on the Italian steamship *Semiramis* on July 26, 1920, arriving in Batum on July 30. From there, they boarded the train on August 9 and arrived in Alexandropol on August 13. In their wagon were a few refugees and the 20-year-old Arshavir Shirakian.[532] Shirakian was the executioner who would later assassinate Said Halim Pasha in Rome on December, 1921, Mehmed Jemal Azmi in Berlin in April 1922 and mortally wound Behaeddin Shakir Bey in Berlin, all three of whom had been found guilty of crimes against humanity by Ottoman courts during what became characterized as the Genocide of the Armenians.

Cheraz and his companions chose Alexandropol as the center of physical education in Armenia and for the scout movement:

Scouts of the Kazachi Post. (*The New Near East*, October 1921: 7)

> After our first visit, it became clear to us that the center of the physical education movement in Armenia should be Alexandropol, and only Alexandropol...Alexandropol is spacious, healthy...The physical education movement here is the most wide spread...the vast masses of the orphans are here and the rest are in Kars, four hours away.[533]

Especially important in the choice of Alexandropol was the fact that there were already 600 boy scouts in the city. Weighing on the side of Alexandropol, also, was the fact that there were several thousand orphans there who could be trained, along with thousands more in Kars, only a few hours away by train. More, the fields in Alexandropol—as those by the Kazachi and Severski—were suitable for athletic games.

The three scout masters decided that Yazmajyan would work in Yerevan, Khoyan would work in Kars, and Cheraz in Alexandropol. But plans were interrupted when war broke out in fall 1920. In a letter from Alexandropol dated September 28, 1920, Cheraz spoke about the unsettled state of the program, the deplorable condition of the orphans, the news that Olti had already fallen and of the refugees from Sarikamish who had begun to arrive in Alexandropol.[534] In October 1920, as the danger of war drew close, Cheraz resigned from his mission of educating boy scouts to join the Armenian Army fighting in Kars, leaving the boy scouts to his friend Tigran Khoyan.[535] For the war effort, the Armenian military now asked Khoyan's help. The latter tells of an incident when he was requested to see General Araratyan of the Armenian Army in Alexandropol and asked to provide 21 older scouts to report to the fortress for immediate training on the cannons. The scouts were happy to accede and reported to the fort the following day.[536]

The Polygon football team in 1921. Top row, left to right: Armenak Sargsyan, Yenok Gyurjyan, Tsolak Haykazyan, Sedrak Torosyan, Tigran Grigoryan. Second row, seated: Ruben Gasparyan, Mkhitar Harutyunyan, Nshan Hovhannisyan (Polygon educational superintendent and team president), Gaspar Sedrakyan, Gaspar Hakobyan, Markos Sahakyan. First row, seated, Hayk Hakobyan. (Aghababyan and Sahakyan 2004: 25)

Cheraz resurfaced in Alexandropol in early spring 1921 and following a meeting with Kazachi District Commander Milton Brown, became the chief of guards at Kazachi. The warehouses of the Kazachi, which served all three orphanages, were being looted and large quantities of food, clothing, and shoes had disappeared. Cheraz was hired to stop the looting; it was not long before he tightened security around the post and instituted strict procedures for entry and exit, a move not appreciated by all:

> Our duteousness, by which we have turned the Kazachi Post inaccessible to internal and external thieves and speculators has upset a class of people so much that they speak with us with their hands on their guns…the RevKoms are tensely disposed toward us, but they can't [act] without proof, since we are in American employ…[537]

The Kazachi soon became the primary area of Cheraz's activities in sports, physical education, and the organization of boy scouts.[538] But for Cheraz, the primary mission of physical education, and particularly the scout movement, went far beyond the standard scout formation: that mission was to transform the orphans into strong, worthy and honorable citizens of Armenia, who would eagerly participate in its rebuilding as future leaders, soldiers, and citizens.[539] As far as possible, he wrote, "the boys are being educated,"

> …according to the standard scout laws and regulations, aiming to make them bodily and mentally strong and instructing them to become useful future men, soldiers or citizens.

The games he taught the orphans included middle and long-distance running, long, triple and high jump, archery, discus throwing, shot put, javelin, swimming, boxing, basketball, volleyball, weight lifting, diving, and football (soccer). Some sports were more popular than others. Boxing and wrestling were among the most popular, for which a special ring was built. In 1921 two American boxers showed boxing techniques as well as free style wrestling and baseball to the orphans. Basketball by the second half of the 1920s would also flourish at the Polygon whose team members frequently met with the city basketball team, known as the *Karutsoghner* (Builders). The latter would also frequently visit the Polygon to watch the Polygon team play against the American staff trainers, and learn their technical and tactical moves.[540]

The most popular game among the orphans was soccer.[541] The teams formed at the orphanages gained renown not only in Armenia but in the Caucasus as well, and the best players in Armenia came from the City of Orphans.[542] The posts had their own soccer teams and trainers: the Severski team was formed by the Polish engineer Vladimir Soldan; the Kazachi team through the efforts of Vahan Cheraz; and the Polygon team, never defeated during its eight years of existence, was formed through the support of Polygon school principal Nshan Hovhannisyan. The main players at the Polygon were Tzolak and Trchnak Haykazyans, "Jab" or Gevorg Abrahamyan, Paghtik Movsesyan, and Serop Temirjyan,[543] also known by the nickname of Malagan Serob. Soccer games took place on the fields of the Kazachi, Polygon and Severski, although the field favored above all was the one at Kazachi. During the Olympic games the bleachers around the field were filled with spectators, and near the field white ribbons outlined the word USA, with orphan girls filling the letter outlines. The music bands, in unison, played the American anthem, as about 1,600 boy scouts stood at attention.

Above and beyond the athletic program Cheraz instituted at the Kazachi, it was to the scout movement and the scouts he trained with Milton Brown's full support, that Cheraz dedicated himself—body and soul. Brown had been a scoutmaster like Cheraz and unconditionally supported Cheraz's efforts. In his report to headquarters in New York in late 1921, Brown referred to the scouts, divided into six troops of thirty scouts each and their duties:

Scout training at Kazachi Post.
(Paul Barsam Private Collection)

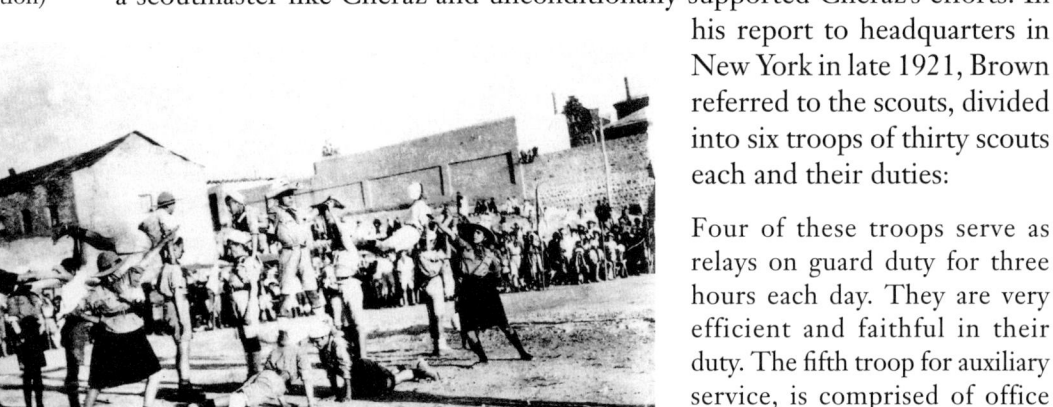

Four of these troops serve as relays on guard duty for three hours each day. They are very efficient and faithful in their duty. The fifth troop for auxiliary service, is comprised of office boys, messengers, telephone boys, mess servants, artists, boys on ambulance and sanitary duty, etc. The sixth troop is comprised of workshop apprentices.[544]

The boys were being educated, continued Brown,

The boy scout motto "Rise and Raise," above the tribute to Milton Brown.
(*The New Near East*, April 1923: 15)

...according to the regular scout laws and regulations, aiming to make them bodily and mentally strong and instructing them to become useful future men, soldiers or citizens.

In addition to their regular school work,

> ...they receive lectures on various subjects and instruction in English. In their quarters are reading rooms and libraries which the boys put to good use.

Particular attention was paid to the scouts' development:

> ...Measurements of the boys are taken upon their admittance to the Scout organization and every two months following. The results are astonishing. The organization owes its success and popularity to the untiring efforts and interest of the instructor, Mr. Tcheraz.[545]

The scouts enjoyed special privileges. The Kazachi workshops prepared their clothing, socks, ties, hats and belts, as well as their sports equipment; they were always clean and well dressed; they had their own music band, and a diary was kept which noted the daily activities of each scout. Those who excelled were given the honor of being called "*Ari*" or brave. On Saturday evenings the scouts marched through the Kazachi—an event that was the source of great excitement around the post.[546] The acclaim of Kazachi's scouts, wrote Cheraz in May 1922,

> ...grows by each passing day. Mr. Horn [successor to Ernst Yarrow] has become an unconditional supporter. Everything is OK. It has been decided to increase the number of boys to 250, and it has already reached 210...[547]

"We have expanded into the back area of our building," Cheraz reported "to build an indoor gymnasium and workshop, and to open a reading room where I will give English language classes and lectures.[548] In 1922, the scouts began to build

> ...a large swimming pool, 40 meters long and 20 meters wide. It requires 150 barrels of cement, but Horn is so certain of approval from Tiflis that the boys have already started work, and their impatience has no bounds.[549]

Among the scouts were Gurgen Achemyan, later Gurgen Mahari, whose poem *The Song of the Scout* Cheraz sent to Constantiople for publication,[550] Soghomon Tarontsi, and Mkrtich Armen, among others. All three would become prominent writers later in life.

Milton Brown, Cheraz's enthusiastic supporter, left Alexandropol toward the end of 1922. On that occasion, Cheraz and his scouts presented Brown with a badge and a moving tribute in Armenian and English, which read in part:

> The boy scouts in particular have been the object of your special and kindly attention, so that in a very short time, those boys of poor physique and unsteady morality, thanks to your unreserved patronage and prodigal encouragement, have attained the much coveted honor of becoming Scouts...

> Meeting in solemn assembly and perfect accord, we have passed a resolution whereas we wish you to accept the title of Honorary Chief Scout of Kazatchi Post. Acknowledging you as our chief, despite the distance between us, we add a new link to the bonds which bind us to your memory and the duties we have accepted to perform...

> And now, good-bye and God-speed…
> On behalf of the Boy Scouts of Kazatchi post,
> Vahan Cheraz, Chief Scout
> And by name, the Assistant, Teacher, Sargeant,
> Patrol leaders and Tramps' Squad Leader.[551]

Cheraz's vision of the boy scout movement and for the Armenia the boy scouts were to build met with persistent resistance from the SSRA, one of the early expressions of which was registered in August 1922. Following the celebration of Armenian actor Armen Armenyan's jubilee at the Polygon on August 19, 1922, Cheraz had told the attendees to rise to their feet while they sang *"Mer Hayrenik"* (Our Fatherland), the national anthem of the former government. The letter of protest that came to the Kazachi three days later was from the Alexandropol Provincial RevKom, addressed to "Mister Rankin," District Director of the Polygon. The Provincial RevKom called Rankin's attention to the unacceptability of such songs in the SSRA and curtly advised Rankin to ban the hymn from the orphanages. The Provincial RevKom also requested that the scoutmaster [Vahan Cheraz] be fired immediately. "According to our information," the note read,

> …the counter-revolutionary hymn *"Mer Hayrenik"* is sung during various formal events at the Polygon and in general. Likewise, on the evening of August 19 when Actor Armenyan's jubilee was being celebrated, *"Mer Hayrenik"* was being sung and your scoutmaster even had the audacity to ask that those present rise to their feet during the singing of the hymn…
>
> Until now, presuming that the NER, through you, would eventually have paid attention to the oft-recurring phenomenon in the above mentioned NER institution [Polygon], we had not invited your attention to it.[552]

However, the letter ran, in view of the incident on August 19, the RevKom was now instructing NER to relieve the scoutmaster of his duties immediately, and inform the Executive Committee of the RevKom when the task had been done. Beyond that, NER was requested to put an end to the singing of such songs, which were altogether unacceptable to the government in power and would heretofore be construed as a rebuff against it, replete with all its attendant consequences. It is not clear if Cheraz was fired by NER, but the following year he was not in Alexandropol, but was put in charge of 100 NER orphans, busily planning a village he named *Ariashen*, near Sardarapat, for the future use of the orphans.[553]

A few days earlier, on August 6, a complaint had been lodged against Onnik Yazmadjian, who had lost his job as scoutmaster with the NER in Yerevan. The complaint was not lodged by the SSRA government but by Yerevan District Commander John H. Evans, whose memorandum to the "Responsible Representative for Armenia, Erivan" read, in part:

> Recently it is frequently reported to me that Onnig Yazmadjian a Scout Master, released from duty with the Near East Relief, in passing these headquarters, makes insulting remarks to different officials of the organization. This occurrence was again called to my attention this day by an official report of the Chief of the Inspection Department…

While this seems a small matter to take official notice of, permit me to explain that these actions seriously disturb the relations of the organization with its employees, who look to us to protect them from insults of this kind....

The matter is brought to your attention in the hope that some official action can be taken which will prevent such occurrences in the future, for in the lack of this of necessity the matter will have to be referred to Near East Relief Headquarters for such action as they consider wise. It would seem to me preferable to settle the affair without reference to superior authority, if such is possible. The Near East Relief has no desire to persecute any individual, but on the other hand feels that it is our right to be protected from insult and herewith appeals to you to take such action as will protect our employees from this annoyance.[554]

According to Cheraz, NER had fired Onnik Yazmadjian because the latter's scouts had assaulted an American.[555]

Recreation and Culture

Attempts were made early on to ease the effects of institutional life on the orphans through music, theater, community singing, summer camps on the shore of the Arpachai,[556] film showings and various entertainment programs and games.

Music at the City of Orphans was provided by student orchestras, among them the boy scout orchestra, the Brass Orchestra of the Polygon, and Severski's Blind Orchestra. Polygon's brass orchestras included children of various ages as well as some teachers. Gurgen, the younger son of NER employee Lucine Aghayan and one of the younger members of the Brass Orchestra, would become a well-known trombonist. He graduated from the brass division of Yerevan's Komitas Conservatory, and beginning in 1936 worked at the capital's Spendiaryan Ballet and Opera Theater for decades. "Maestro Gurgen" also produced a generation of musicians.[557]

The Blind Orchestra consisted of string, brass and keyboard instruments, played by 30 blind children. Zvart Muradyan recalled that it had been formed by a Polish composer whom Nikoghayos Tigranyan had invited to Alexandropol. Under Tigranyan's tutelage, the children learned to play piano pieces by Beethoven and other works of classical music.

A theater club organized by a group of Kazachi's Armenian personnel in 1921 met in the dining room of the hospital. During performances by orphans and Armenian personnel and, on occasion, professional actors from Yerevan, a stage would be improvised for musical numbers or dramatic pieces, as *Mecapativ muratskanner* [Honorable Beggars] and *Paghdasar aghbar* [Brother Baghtasar]—both popular works by 19th century Western Armenian satirist Hakob Paronyan—and performed before a packed audience.[558] Theatrical performances had become frequent by 1924. In the fall semester of 1924 alone at the Polygon, students staged several plays, in Armenian translation, with the support and encouragement of superintendent Nshan Hovhannisyan and a teacher of the theatrical arts. These included Oscar Wilde's *The Star Child*, performed for the younger children seven times; *The Happy Prince*,

The Brass Orchestra. (Lucine Aghayan Collection, AGMI. Gurgen Aghayan stands in the third row from bottom, second from the right)

The Blind Orchestra. (Minasyan 1980: 55. Drawing attributed to Marietta Shahinyan, 1926, Leninakan)

performed twice, also for the younger children. Performances for older orphans included Friedrich Schiller's *The Robbers*, staged twice; several of Uriel Acosta's works; Armen Tigranyan's *Anush* opera, staged four times; Molière's *The Imaginary Invalid*; William Shakespeare's *Tempest*, and others.[559]

On most Saturday evenings in 1924, different groups of older girls hosted a party where among the invitees were former orphans who lived close by. The cost to NER per gathering was $2.80. This was seen as a novelty and an attempt on the part of NER's administration to develop wholesome relationships on the model of boys and girls in America.[560]

Film showings were frequent, almost every evening in 1926, wrote NER employee Harutyun Alpoyachyan, when the whole Polygon had electricity. The events were encouraged by NER's administration and took place in the large stadium at the edge of the Polygon. Of the 50 films available, a few were about tourism, one was about the Swiss Alps, a few dwelled on the life of orphans, and the rest were on agriculture.[561] One film, shown only a few times at the orphanage, wrote Alpoyachyan, was about the life and progress of "the American millionaire Ford," which showed Ford's rise from a simple laborer to a millionaire. The film disappeared, added Alpoyachyan, when the upper echelons asked to review the film and never returned it.[562]

Armenian Christmas, celebrated on January 6, was a special day for the orphans in the early 1920s. On that occasion, the children received new shoes and stockings, extra food, and a handkerchief full of nuts, raisins, an apple, candy, and cake. At night, a Christmas tree was lit; the children danced around the tree, heard recitations, and various kinds of entertainment.[563]

There were also some unusual forms of entertainment. Alpoyachyan writes that one time NER staged a live chess game at the Polygon. The game was played by actual human beings dressed as soldiers with actual guns in their hands, with king and queen, small cannons, and had lasted a few hours. Alpoyachyan also referred to entertainment by groups of dwarfs NER had invited to the Polygon. They had arrived in two cars and performed in the sports arena at the Polygon.[564]

"When the Sun Comes Out…"
Yeghishe Charents at the Polygon

Children at the Polygon had been familiar with the name and works of Yeghishe Charents since 1922. Armenian language and literature teachers as Nikoghayos Kirakosyan and Karapet Apinyan often read Charents's *Danteyakan araspel* [Dantesque Legend], *Ambokhnere khelagarvac* [The Frenzied Masses], *Soma*, and other works, as examples of classical poetry. Charents's *Amenapoem* [Poem for All] and *Depi apagan* [Toward the Future], were frequently recited on the stage. Around the time of Lenin's death, Kirakosyan gave a long lecture on Charents to the teachers and employees of the Polygon, declaring Charents as the greatest poet of Armenia.[565] "I was so raptured by Charents's poetry," wrote Khachik Dashtents, the future famed writer, then known as Khachik Tonoyan, an orphan boy at the Polygon, "that I, too, read a lecture to the students and employees of the Polygon on two of Charents's collections of poetry." Dashtents was 15 years old when Charents visited the Polygon in 1925:

> In the fall of 1925 Charents came to the Polygon. The tempestuous reception he found among our students and teachers was a sight to behold. Other well-known proletarian writers had come before. But Charents's magnetism was different.

At one point during Charents's lecture, one of the orphans, Soghomon Movsisyan, the future Armenian writer Soghomon Tarontsi, addressed the audience and declared:

> When the sun comes out, all the stars are eclipsed.

Charents's speech, delivered with great emotion, had been interrupted by long and recurring bursts of applause and ecstatic exclamations. When it was over, 15-year-old Dashtents was asked to go on stage to meet Charents. "They have told me about you," said Charents to the young boy and told him to rewrite his poems in a notebook and present it to him. "All that happened so fast," recalled Dashtents decades later, "that I didn't know how I fled the stage, with my face flushed."[566] In April 1926, Dashtents met Charents in Yerevan. The class that would soon be graduating from the Polygon, among them Dashtents, was taken on an excursion to Yerevan and Etchmiadzin, and one chilly evening, young Dashtents attended the meeting of the "Noyember" [November] literary group that was headed by Charents. Dashtents was the youngest member of the group gathered there. "I sat in a corner like a shy boy," he wrote, "with the orphan's sorrow on my forehead, and watched

Charents the entire time." At the end of the meeting, Charents gave him a gilded red membership card with his own signature, admitting the boy into the "Noyember" literary group.[567]

Visiting Armenian Artists and the Armenian Debut of *Sasuntsi Davit*

There were other visiting artists, writers and composers at the Polygon in the mid-1920s. Alpoyachyan made references to the Armenian poet and writer Hakob Hakobyan who had come twice, and to the well-known cellist, composer, and conductor Artemi Ayvazyan, who in 1938 founded the Armenian Jazz Orchestra. Ayvazyan was in fact a friend, and frequent visitor of one of Polygon's directors, Miss Mays, and performed at the Polygon on several occasions.[568]

Two other artists who visited the orphanage in the mid-1920s were composer, ethnomusicologist, and pianist Nikoghayos Tigranyan and singer Tigran Nalpantyan. The two artists had come to the Polygon to choose orphans with good voices and musical talent to offer them training. One of the children they heard was Shoghik H. Mkrtchyan, who would emerge a few years later as one of Armenia's most popular singers. "One day," Mkrtchyan recounted in an interview decades later,

> ...news had spread that they had come to select children who had good voices, in order to take them to the city to study. I was thirteen or fourteen years old then; the composer Nikoghayos Tigranyan and the well-known singer Tigran Nalpantyan wanted to hear me sing in the office of the orphanage director.
>
> I sang with emotion and with tearful eyes, recalling my lost parents and our home. "My daughter," Nalpantyan asked "why are you here?"
> "I have no one" I said, "I am an orphan."

One year later, she was in Yerevan studying at a music school, and later at the Conservatory in Yerevan. By 1926 she was a popular singer on Yerevan radio.[569]

At the Polygon, one of the most memorable events was the concert given by Alexander Spendiaryan, who had arrived soon after Kalinin and Lukashin had visited the Polygon. Spendiaryan at the time was already well known as a composer and conductor and as the founder of Armenian National Symphonic Music. Alpoyachyan, as the electrician in charge at the Polygon, was asked to increase the lighting in the hall where visiting artists were to hold performances. Only later did Alpoyachyan realize that the increase in the lighting was in anticipation of Spendiaryan's visit. True to their custom of inviting artists, wrote Alpoyachyan, the Americans had invited him for a performance at the Polygon. "Spendiaryan came with 15–20 musicians and musical instruments," remembered Alpoyachyan:

> It was a wonderful concert...they played *Yerevan Etudes*, *Three Palms*, etc.[570]

Of special significance for the orphans was the visit of prominent Armenian actor and theatrical director Armen Armenyan in the early 1920s, who became a popular figure at the Kazachi for a few months. Originally from Constantinople, Armenyan, born Ipekyan, had been applauded for his performances in the Near East, Europe, and the Caucasus for his roles as Franz Moor in Schiller's *The Robbers*; as Iago and Shylock in Shakespeare's *Othello* and *The Merchant of Venice*, respectively; as Harpagon in Molière's *The Miser*, and as the Baron in Pushkin's *The Covetous Knight*. While on tour in Tiflis, the Armenian Commissariat of Enlightenment had invited Armenyan to revive the once famous theater in Alexandropol, now in a semi-ruinous state. Armenyan had acceded to the invitation and left for Alexandropol in March 1921. While busy with the reconstruction of the theater, Alexandropol's NER administration had invited Armenyan to hold recitation classes for the children at the Kazachi and the Polygon. "A few times a week after lunch," wrote Armenyan in his memoirs,

> ...I would go and spend two hours with the boys and girls at the Kazachi Post and the Polygon.
>
> Naturally, they had no idea about the theater, so at the beginning, I would hold simple discussions with them about theater and what it meant; about actors, their creative work and plays.[571]

It was a pleasure, he wrote, to work with such bright children. Armenyan first taught the orphans to do monologues and short dialogues, and gradually introduced them to short scenes, which the children relished:[572]

> At class time, they would wait impatiently by the door; as soon as they saw the carriage which the director had put at my disposal appear, they would begin to greet me from afar with hand gestures and joyful yells. I would jump out of the carriage and shout:
>
> "Hello, my children"
> "Hello, father," they would reply.

When the children asked to attend some performances in the city, Armenyan asked the director's permission to take groups of 10 or 12 older orphans to the theater in Alexandropol where he performed on Saturday and Sunday evenings. It was not long before the younger children wanted to be included in the weekend sorties as well. The children also suggested that a performance could be staged at the orphanage, with the orphans as actors. When the children suggested the idea, he wrote, "I found the idea an attractive one, but which piece to choose? Where?" The piece would need to include as many people as possible, and it would need to be comprehensible to the orphans and interesting enough to the spectators. He finally decided on one of the scripts he had with him—the Armenian epic story of David of Sassun—that included songs and dances and large numbers of actors. But such a complicated piece needed an expansive, tiered setting like an amphitheater set in the bosom of nature. It was the director of the orphanage who found the ideal setting at the southwestern end of Kazachi Post [currently the site of cemetery #2 in Gyumri] and invited Armenyan to accompany him to the location:[573]

...One day, when I had come out of class and was getting ready to get into the carriage, he [the director] took my arm and said, "I think I have found the amphitheater you wanted. If you would like, let us go together to see it. It is not far from here."

We went to the valley to the southwest of the Kazachi Post. The place was truly very appropriate...

Optically it was very suitable, but the acoustics...?

The director jumped, ran and climbed the hill facing us and began to speak. The acoustic was fantastic—every word was audible...

And now, that which remained was to actualize our "miracle," get my little "actors" ready and give an open-air dramatic performance.

As soon as I got home, I sat down and occupied myself all night with the plans for preparation and presentation. The next day I invited voice teachers Daniel Ghazaryan[574] and Kolya Alavertyan and instructed them to form music for soloists and the chorus...

Once Armenyan chose his "little actors," he worked with them on monologues, then dialogues, and then finally full scenes. Daniel Ghazaryan and Kolya Alaverdyan worked with soloists and the chorus. After working for about two months they began to rehearse on location. This part of the work was extremely consuming. "Can you imagine?" Armenyan wrote,

> I stood on one side of the hill with my loudspeaker and little "signalist" flags and on the other side, the actors...and when the screaming and loudspeaker didn't help, I would go down, then climb towards them, then descend again, only to ascend yet again to my place. So many times, perhaps five, ten times...[575]

The first performance took place at 6 p.m. on July 8, 1922. It was attended by orphans and staff from all three posts, by students from the city schools and by local government officials—a total of 10,000 spectators. The spectators were seated on the ground while music was provided by the Brass Orchestra of the orphanage, standing on the little hill. All the scenes were performed by orphans—about 150 children of different ages—many of them victims of atrocities in Sassun. Armenyan noted in his autobiography that newspaper reviews had especially praised the battle scenes where Sassuntsis hurled stones at the enemy, the performance of Sassuntsi group dances and the songs of Sassuntsi women. An encore performance was scheduled for July 30, 1922.

Chapter Seven

EDUCATION FOR CITIZENSHIP

Both governments of Armenia and the NER agreed that the path to the orphans' future citizenship was through education, and that only through education would the illiterate, diseased, and hapless orphans be remade into productive and self-sufficient citizens. All agreed, also, that orphan schooling had to differ from the schooling of children who were growing up in a home environment. The orphans' stay at the orphanage was short-term. At age 16 or 17 they would have to enter the world outside the walls of the orphanage where, in the absence of parental support, they would need to be self-sufficient. For that, orphans would have to be taught a skill through which a livelihood could be assured.

In charting the path for the education of Armenia's future generation, a responsibility it had assumed in April 1919, NER put a premium on education in the practical trades and industries. To that end, it refitted many of the barracks of the City of Orphans to accommodate large and small workshops where the orphan, beginning at age 11 or 12 or sometimes as early as age six or seven years, would spend at least half a day learning a useful industrial skill. And it was in those workshops that a generation of seamstresses, lace makers, carpenters, tailors, shoemakers, ironsmiths, tinsmiths, barbers, bookbinders, knitters, potters, housekeepers, locksmiths, and mechanics were to be trained to replace those who had perished during the preceding years of war, starvation, and depopulation.

Beyond the industrial skills taught in workshops, NER instituted three other programs. The first, and possibly the earliest, was the nursing program, one in each of the three posts, to prepare nursing help for the hospitals. In 1924, the three nursing schools merged into a single, revamped School of Nursing named after Edith May Winchester, whose graduates supplied nurses for the government in villages and towns. The second, and most extensive, was the program in agriculture, begun in late summer 1921 and expanded beyond the barracks in Alexandropol to the towns of Jalaloghli (Stepanavan, after 1923) with a subdivision at Karakala, possibly modern Noramut,[576] both in the adjacent province of Lori. By 1923, the agricultural program, named the NER Institute of Agriculture, included animal husbandry and apiary. The third, and smallest, was the teacher-training program, begun at the request of the Soviet Armenian government, to prepare much-needed teachers for the country.

In the larger educational vision for the orphans, academic instruction was largely eclipsed by the emphasis on the practical education of the child. At times, the special talents or preferences of some orphans were subsumed in the workshops and especially in the fields and in the farms. One reason for the emphasis on agricultural education had to do with the fact that 98% of the orphans were the children of peasants and farmers, which meant, so the reasoning went, that about 95% of the children should or would prefer to follow the paths of their parents, in which case they needed no more than a primary education.[577]

Academic Instruction

One of the earliest reports on academics instruction at the City of Orphans covers the 1919–1920 academic year at the Kazachi.[578] It is a 20-page detailed description, in Armenian, of the disorganized and neglected condition of classes and classroom instruction when the school had first opened in October 1919, and the difficulties by which desks, chairs, books, and blackboards were finally obtained through personal initiatives. Instruction had finally begun in February 1920. According to the report, boys and girls were at first placed together in a small building regardless of age, under unsanitary and crowded conditions. There were a few frayed textbooks and a small number of writing pads, but no desks or blackboards, or a curriculum of any kind. The students were brought to school to dance and sing and then returned to the orphanages. Compounding physical difficulties was the internal bickering among the "ignorant Armenian" teachers and staff, which had been detrimental to the education of orphans.[579] The children, stressed the report, had expressed a special interest in reading, but there were no books for the 7,000 orphans. Requests for assistance were made of the Ministry of Education, but none were heeded. With support from the community, some copybooks, pens, pencils, "*Lusaber*" II and III textbooks, etc., had been acquired and with the help of NER relief worker Olivia Hill, the school had been organized. There had been 2,153 students, who came to class in two shifts—one group in the morning and the other after lunch—each shift supplementing the day with work in the workshops. But another group of 1,323 students had been denied classroom instruction because of space shortages and other technical issues. Then, of the 2,153 students 913 had been transferred, leaving 1,240 students, of whom 466 suffered from favus and other illnesses and were sent to the hospital. Several dozens of children worked in the vegetable garden next to the school, but a larger number had expressed the wish to join them. Between February 15 and June 30, the report continued, 117 days had been devoted to schooling. There had been no school on Saturdays and Sundays since the children were bathed on those days.

At the end of his report the author emphatically urged that the government attend to the education and upbringing of the orphans, and to do so even before attending to the needs of children in the regular schools of the country. True, he wrote, the orphans received adequate nourishment and clothing, but because of the lack of attention to their education and upbringing, theft, slothfulness and roguishness had taken root in them and they lacked in independent thinking and initiative. If serious attention were not paid to their upbringing, those orphans, "the hope of our future," would grow up to be a criminal generation. The author hastened to add that those orphans who had attended school were deeply attached to the school, which was proof that if the methods used were well thought out, the orphans could be reformed, and the goal of preparing worthy citizens of Armenia would be reached. But now, in the absence of a coherent educational program, the children roamed idly in the fields, ate grass or chewed on bones. Inattention to the future of the orphans, the author repeated in conclusion, was tantamount to the worst of crimes, and suggested in the strongest terms, a total overhaul of the schools at the Kazachi and the Polygon.[580]

The educational program of the City of Orphans was revisited when NER returned from its last exodus in spring 1921, against the background of the high morbidity and mortality of 1921, and the flow of new orphans from the countryside. The approach that emerged for the academic instruction of orphans by 1922 aimed to provide, as Kazachi teacher Madame Romanoff described, only a primary education. "Armenian children," she began, "are naturally bright and have a keen desire to learn. Speaking generally, they are easy to teach and make very satisfactory pupils." But few of the children, she continued, had received any schooling before coming to the orphanages; there were girls of 12 or 13 who were just beginning to read, and 5,000 of the 6,000 girls were in elementary classes equivalent to the first, second or third grades in the American school system. She observed that although most of the girls she taught were the daughters of peasant farmers "they were particularly good at figures and mastered elementary arithmetic courses quickly." And, she added

> …they could go on to higher mathematical work if there were any opportunity for them to acquire or use this knowledge.

But since there were no prospects for higher mathematical work, the girls were directed toward manual training and learning to become good housewives:

> We do not try to teach advanced subjects. We wish, above all, to equip these girls with a type of education, which will be most useful to the life which they will lead in the new Armenia. Handicraft seems to us at present more important than book learning, so we let the class-room work rest with elementary subjects and transfer the pupils as early as possible to manual training classes, where they learn sewing, knitting, weaving and other things which will enable them to become useful housewives and practical self-supporters in the new Armenia.[581]

Knitting was especially important, thought Madame Romanoff, because refugee life had left the children "with a curious inability to devote their attention solely to one task," and besides, she thought, knitting was "one of the best treatments for this mental attitude, and all the girls learn to knit. It helps to bring back their minds into an orderly track." [582]

The academic curriculum included Russian and Armenian, since those were the two languages in use in the Caucasus. English was reserved for the brighter children, added Madame Romanoff, although "all of them wish to learn English, for they have a profound reverence for America, which they call their 'Uncle-country.'" Classroom instruction, in the absence of blackboards, textbooks or furniture, was very difficult, she said, but the lack of such basic needs had not diminished the children's eagerness to learn, which she sometimes found "pathetic":

> Our teaching is done under great difficulties. The buildings are huge stone barracks which formerly housed the soldiers of the Czar. They are cold and very difficult to heat in winter. There are no desks or benches, so the children sit tailor-fashion on straw mattresses spread over the floor. We are short of schoolbooks, blackboards and other equipment. Usually the teacher is the only one who has a textbook, and lessons are learned mostly by repeating over and over what the teacher reads from the book. Yet with all our difficulties, these little children, refugees from the hills and villages, learn to study with an eagerness which is sometimes pathetic.[583]

The children were taught by 90 teachers, continued Madame Romanoff, referring to the teaching staff of the Kazachi, and almost all of the 90 teachers in charge of about 6,000 girls were Armenian. They represented some of the "brightest men and women of old and new Armenia, and several have studied in the U.S. or in American Colleges in the Near East." There were a few Russian teachers, like Madame Romanoff herself. The Superintendent of the school was "an American, Roy Davis of Monticello, Arkansas, and his assistant, Mr. John Mejloomian [Hovhannes Mechlumyan]" was a distinguished Armenian educator, a graduate of Leipzig University.[584]

Love of learning was not limited to the girls at the Kazachi. Polygon's Director of Education Caroline Silliman described her students in one of her letters home in late summer 1921. "Our children," she wrote,

> ...are so anxious to learn, that some of them actually cry to go to school. And they are not bluffing, either...

> They had had such an interrupted year, poor little tads, they didn't want to stop when they had the chance. Most of our children are between eight and twelve years old. Very few of them can read or write with any degree of ease. If only the troubled waters will quiet, that will not be true a year from now.[585]

Describing the school at Severski was another Russian NER employee, Nina Brailovskya, an interpreter who had begun to work in 1921. "There are now 1,500 children in our school at Severski," she wrote:

> I have been with them since the beginning of the school and have come to love them very much...

> Our school is in a big old stone building, formerly the barracks for a thousand of the Czar's hussars. It is a cold building and of bare furnishings. The school children have neither desks nor benches. Until desks and benches can be provided, they sit on mattresses of straw spread out atop the cold stone floor, while the teacher stands in front of the class and teaches the lesson.[586]

There were 30 native teachers at the Severski and the classes averaged about 50 very young children, whose daily schedules included games and songs interspersed with simple arithmetic and language classes:

> The arithmetic class is assembled around a small stove in a rather cold corner of one of the larger rooms. No text-book is used, for books are scarce in Armenia since the war. Arithmetic is taught with a large "abacus" on which the children learn to do addition, subtraction and even multiplication and division…
>
> There is a sewing-class in another corner of the big arithmetic room. Here, some of the children sit on a broad window-ledge, dangling their feet half way to the floor as they knit or sew. Other children are winding thread, which is made from unraveling the fibers carefully saved from every waste piece of cloth. Thread is precious in this country and while we get a good deal of spooled thread from America, we need more than we can import, and the children learn economy by making their own thread from these ravelings.[587]

Beans were used for counting and arithmetic, and sometimes a blackboard could be a section of the wall, painted with black dye.[588] Conditions in the kindergartens were no different. There were no benches, no little tables and chairs or equipment of any kind. The children sat in a circle on little grass mats on the floor. They had rough wooden blocks from the carpenter shops, a few colored pencils, perhaps one pair of scissors they used in turn, and bits of colored paper saved from packages. A ball or a skipping rope was a thing to be treasured. Here, the little ones also learned to sew, braid mats, and weave.[589] Heating in the schoolrooms, continued Nina Brailovskya, was provided by "little round iron stoves," topped by "a pitcher of water, which helps to keep the air of the school room moist and warm."[590]

The educational curriculum took shape gradually in the early 1920s but with increasing intervention by the SSRA government, which insisted that NER's orphanage schools would need to follow guidelines developed by the Commissariat of Enlightenment for all schools in Armenia. In line with that expectation was the request for the exclusion of classes in religion from the curriculum. In answer to the latter, NER replaced religious instruction by a course in Ethics. Roy Davis, writing from Alexandropol on September 29, 1922, informed the "Commissar of Education" that:

> In keeping with the understanding we had in my recent conversation with you, the curriculum of the N.E.R. schools has been made [to] conform with that of the Government schools except in the matter of English language and Ethics. We are giving some English in the upper classes for the purpose of training some students for usefulness in our own offices and a course in Ethics for the purpose of giving our orphan students something in the way of ethical and moral training to supply the lack of home training which it is impossible to give them in large orphanages such as ours.[591]

Providing additional information on the new Ethics course, Davis added, would be Mr. Melik-Adamyan, the Supervisor of the course on Ethics, who was carrying the letter to Yerevan.

A few months later another report, dated February 8, 1923, this time from NER Caucasus Branch Director of Education Ernest Partridge assured the "Commissar of Education" that religious instruction had been eliminated from the curriculum of NER's schools and that:

> The schools of normal-aged students were directed by the program of your governmental schools. A different program was made out for our school of subnormal aged students, though this program also was approximated to this of yours. The teaching of religion was taken out of the school program since the second half of the first half-year. By the reports of our head teachers the school program of this half-year is said to be accomplished.[592]

Partridge also reported that some Severski buildings had been restored for school purposes, that a "great number of school desks had been made" during the first semester and concluded with the names of the principals of the six NER schools, who were:

> "G. Edilian (Kazachi): H. Mejloomian (Alexandropol): T. Ter-Meliksetyan (Severski); N. Hovhannesian (Polygon); S. Tigranian (Yerevan); H. Hovhannesian (Jalaloghli)." [593]

Partridge then provided details on the number of students and academic schedule. During the first term, from August 15 to January 13, there had been regular studies of 22 weeks or 106 days, and thus far the work had run under normal conditions and the schools were at all times supplied with a sufficient amount of school books and other necessities. The statistical sheet he attached to his report included the specific numbers of students in each of the posts.[594] The school at Kazachi taught a total of 4,544 students in morning, afternoon, and night classes. Of these, 4,255 were girls, 289 were boys, and 137 were non-orphans. In terms of distribution, 322 were in kindergarten, 2,159 in first grade, 968 in second, 455 in third, 319 in fourth, 173 in fifth, and 65 in sixth grade. They had had 2,739 instruction periods taught by 98 teachers and 15 other employees. Absenteeism had been 7% and there had been 57 instances of tardiness.

At the Polygon, of the total of 4,814 students, 2,294 attended classes in the morning, 2,289 in the afternoon, and 231 at night; of this group 12 were non-orphans, 4,743 were boys and 71 were girls. In terms of class distribution, 526 were in kindergarten, 1,760 in first, 1,193 in second, 742 in third, 306 in fourth, 123 in fifth, and 61 in sixth grades. They had had 2,651 instruction periods and had been taught by 91 teachers and 5 other employees. There had been 1% absenteeism and no tardiness.

At the Severski, from a total of 2,431 students 1,117 received instruction in the morning, 870 in the afternoon, and 444 at night. Here, there were 279 boys and 2,152 girls; 56 were non-orphans. The class distribution represented the following picture: 166 in kindergarten, 1,570 in first grade, 336 in second, 232 in third, 87 in fourth, and 40 in fifth grade. They had had 2,164 instruction periods taught by 72 teachers and 9 other employees. There had been 402 instances of tardiness and 4% absenteeism.

A total of 11,994 students—5,311 boys, 6,478 girls, and 205 non-orphans—studied at the three posts. Partridge's list included statistics from other NER orphanages in Armenia. Accordingly, there were a total of 2,434 orphans (1,081 boys and 1,353 girls) in Stepanavan, 192 in Darachichak, and 4,124 in Yerevan. American teachers were manufacturing textbooks with typewriters and duplicating machines and were scouring the country for books. One outcome of the effort was the establishment of bookbindery workshops to restore old textbooks to a useable condition.[595]

Six months after Partridge's report, the July 8, 1923, issue of *Khorhrdayin Hayastan* carried an article by People's Commissar of Enlightenment A. Mravyan entitled "The Problem of Orphan Education," where the Commissar stressed the urgency of training the children in agriculture and trades. At the same time, he continued,

> ...the orphans should be trained to be cultured farmers...not like American farmers or ranch owners; rather of the communal, communist type.[596]

This was not because of abstract economic reasons, Mravyan explained, but because economically it would be less expensive to organize large communal farms for such large numbers of orphans than small private farms.

Two months later, in September 1923, the People's Commissariat of Enlightenment informed NER that Hovsep Karakhanyan, Director of the Technical School in Alexandropol, was appointed as the Commissariat's representative to NER. Karakhanyan was to be acquainted with the program of education and upbringing in the orphanages, schools and vocational schools under NER, and NER was kindly requested to extend him the necessary assistance so that he might accomplish his task.[597]

An Inexhaustible Labor Force: Industrial Training

If the SSRA government objected to the teaching of religion, it supported and encouraged NER's program in industrial training. Here, too, progress had been slow at first because the most basic tools and raw material had been lacking, and most tools would first have to be produced and raw material brought in from elsewhere.[598] Industrial training was especially important because data gathered by NER in early 1922 showed that in some parts of Armenia orphan children outnumbered the able-bodied adults, a phenomenon most conspicuous in Alexandropol, Jalaloghli, and Karakilisa. In Alexandropol, for instance, there were 31,000 orphans while the able-bodied adult male population numbered less than 3,000.[599] Charles Vickrey explained that in providing industrial training to the orphans NER was supporting SSRA's efforts in reconstruction. At the same time, by providing industrial training, NER helped

> ...the development of the orphans of the Near East into a practical and self-respecting manhood and womanhood,[600]

who would then become

> ...productive citizens, industrial leaders and ambassadors of friendship, good will and peace to all men.[601]

For the young children, the path to "practical and self-respecting manhood and womanhood" was mapped by hard work. Beginning sometimes as early as at the age of six or seven, children strong enough to work were trained in some type of skill in the large workshops of the barracks, where they spent at least half of each day. And orphan productivity, usually under the supervision of instructors, was staggering.[602] Even while learning skills, the sheer numbers of children represented an inexhaustible labor force, capable of producing much that was needed to maintain the City of Orphans. This meant, among other things, that the children's labor ensured that the orphanages would be run at a minimal cost. "Industrial education," wrote *The New York Times* editor and leading NER supporter John Finley in 1922,

> ...served not only to train the children and teach them self-reliance and independence, but it has enabled the organization to run its establishments on a most economical basis. With the children making their own clothes, their own furniture and doing most of the work about the grounds, the institutions are run at a minimum cost to the Near East Relief treasury.[603]

Initially, industrial education had developed as much out of educational policies as out of the necessity for the repairs, cleanup and remodeling of the barracks. During the two wars and occupation of Alexandropol, many of the buildings had collapsed or were on the verge of collapse, and window glasses had been shattered, the latter during the explosion of the nearby fortress on the day of the Turkish evacuation in April 1921. Helping with the clean up and repair were the boys healthy enough to do so, and who played a significant role in turning the Polygon into a habitable environment. By 1923 and 1924, children began to replace the adult native workers of the City of Orphans. Barclay Acheson had observed that

> Over three thousand children were learning to make clothing and shoes, both for themselves and for the little ones too young to master a needle. One group was having a wonderful time packing clean straw into new mattresses. Like ants, they carried the great bundles away to the double-decker beds in their crowded dormitories. That group must have been in the orphanage for a year or more—long enough to forget—for they were actually laughing!

> ...Two great buildings were filled with hand-looms and sturdy homespun was being woven. Every effort was being made to use the willing childish hands to produce their own food and clothing and to care for themselves, because that would reduce costs. Everyone knew that reducing costs meant admitting more of the starving, ragged children that stood forever at the gates—and it must be done quickly or they would die.

At the girls' orphanage,

> The great masses subdivided themselves into little groups, supervised by older children who mothered the little tots, combed their hair, washed their faces, dressed them properly, and saw that they got to the clinic for trachoma treatment, or to the classroom to study, on schedule. Soon we learned that even smaller groups, called "families," were made up of very interesting little individuals.

> On a bench in the shade of a building we saw a beautiful girl comforting a child who had torn her dress, and with skillful fingers patching the little garment "so that it was better than new."[604]

Acheson had also observed the dining rooms, where older children served the younger ones, often as many as 2,000 at the same time.

Much of the program of the industrial education designed for the girls consisted of skills that would prepare them to be future housewives and mothers, and included sewing, knitting, mattress making, and weaving classes. The sewing class employed 15 instructors for 300 girls in the morning and for another 300 in the afternoon. Between September 3 and November 26, 1921, orphan girls had made 5,724 dresses, 3,341 underskirts, 3,250 undershirts, 2,287 under drawers, 995 coats, 649 laborer's aprons, 500 sheets, 1,344 quilt covers, 236 pillow cases, 2,487 towels, 400 pairs of cloth slippers, 170 boy scout suits, and 170 boy scout overcoats. All the underwear was made of Red Cross pajama suits, and some 2,000 dresses and 400 coats were made from the old clothes that had been donated by the American public.[605]

In December 1921, 15 sewing machines were introduced at the Kazachi, and within a few weeks, orphans had produced 1,915 caps, 13,803 stockings, and 1,307 sweaters. All the clothes sewed were used for the 6,000 children at Kazachi Post and almost all of the 3,000 children in the city of Alexandropol.[606] Each week 18,000 pairs of socks were mended and used clothing from the U.S. was refitted into clothing. This included 300 suits of underwear per day, darning 400 stockings, and refilling 48 mattresses daily.

In the knitting classes 16 instructors taught a total of 1,200 girls;[607] in the mattress making class one teacher taught 50 girls in the morning and another 50 in the afternoon. One group combed the wool for the mattresses, quilts, and pillows, while a second group sewed them. In 1921, orphan girls had produced 832 mattresses, 1,765 wool quilts, and 332 pillows. The weaving class, which had been in operation for one month at the time of the report, had six looms in operation, all of them made by the construction department. There were a total of 100 students in the class with eight teachers and plans were developed to begin dye works and adding four looms for making rugs and *kilims*.[608] Twenty more looms were built in January 1922, which would provide work for another 1,000 children.[609] The looms were set up in the Kazachi Post where Byrtene Anderson supervised the work. This was a long, low building, where 1,000 girls between the ages of ten and 15 sat on low benches around long tables cutting garments that would then be sent to the machine sewers. The first 1,000 girls would work in the morning and study in the afternoon, while another thousand would replace them at the looms.[610]

Industrial education for the boys meant teaching them to be carpenters, ironsmiths, tinsmiths, shoemakers, mechanics, bookbinders, brick makers, tailors, ditch diggers, road pavers, printers and masons.[611] The orphans in the blacksmith and mechanic shops learned to make hinges, locks, workmen's tools, knives and car springs; they repaired automobiles and mazut burners. These shops were equipped with drill stands, a three-horsepower engine, and other equipment. In the tinsmith workshops the boys learned how to make stoves, pipes, showers for the bathhouse, oilcans, tanks and registration tags; they repaired tin roofs, stoves, and sewer covers. They also made soup bowls, dishes, spoons and cups from the 10,000 empty milk tin cans that had

Approximately 10,000 empty condensed milk tin cans at the Kazachi dump. (*The New Near East*, February 1922: 5)

been tossed in a dump at the Kazachi.[612] NER's Northwest area chairman Sherman L. Divine, from whose region the mills of Washington State, Idaho, Utah and Montana had supplied large amounts of condensed milk to Armenia, was at Alexandropol in 1921 and witnessed how flour sacks and milk tins had found additional uses:

> ...the milk tins were fashioned by the rescued children into cups for the orphanages, hospitals and clinics of Near East Relief [and] the flour sacks became their own new "spring suits." It was a simple operation, requiring only the cutting and hemming of a hole in the bottom for the head to stick through; cutting off the corners and sewing meal sack sleeves to them. Rather breezy and not very stylish, but warmer and far better in every way than the filthy rags in which they were found starving in the streets.[613]

In the machine workshops, where repairs were made on gymnastic and agricultural equipment using old piping, boys had put together a complete machine shop using the metal scraps discarded by the Russian armies. A particularly impressive achievement by the boys was the rebuilding of an old American tractor.[614] In the carpenter shops, orphan boys made and repaired benches, chairs, and tables. In some shops the boys had become expert enough that outside orders had come to them for hand-carved furniture.[615] In the shoemaking workshops, the boys did all the leather repair work for the post, such as sandals for scouts and for the hospitals, belts, saddles, bridles, harness, etc. Each shoemaker repaired an average of 20 pairs daily. In the tailor shops at the Polygon, boys produced 400 garments and 90 pairs of stockings daily,[616] but this quantity still fell short of the demand for the 8,000 orphan boys sheltered at the Polygon.[617]

The industrial education at the city of Orphans was covered in several U.S. industrial journals during 1922. The reuse of empty tin cans at the City of Orphans was the subject of an article in *The Canning Age*,[618] while ironsmithing was covered in *American Blacksmith and Motor Shop*.[619] The latter highlighted the necessity of educating blacksmiths since not only had most of the blacksmiths been killed, but because the country had been stripped of even basic tools; new blacksmiths were needed to make anything from hammers to axes to shoes for ox teams that transported wood for the orphanage. NER had been able to find a few blacksmiths to teach the boys, and organized a smithy for the older boys. Six months of apprenticeship qualified a boy to shoe an ox.

Another article, by Barclay Acheson, appeared in *American Industries*, and highlighted how orphan boys adapted shoes rejected in the U.S. for the orphan population in Alexandropol:

> Shoeing 18,000 children...was also solved by the boys. From a shipment of hides from America the required shoes were fashioned under the direction of refugee boot makers. In another shipment came a consignment of...mismatched samples an American manufacturer had offered to the Near East Relief...Boys went to work with a will on the task of producing a right for every left and in a short time the shoes were ready for the wearer.[620]

The orphans, Acheson continued, had learned to do practically everything for themselves: from making their shoes and clothing to building furniture, creating household utensils and repairing the buildings. And, he added,

> ...Armenian children are ambitious and quick to learn, once their bodies become normal, and they take to American methods very readily, even to the introduction of American hygiene. When these boys grow up and prosper there is going to be a great demand for American bathtubs and other sanitary appliances, judging by their delight in American baths.

> ...they set about their tasks with considerable vim and enthusiasm. That is probably why they become skilled workers in so short a time. There are boys and girls in NER orphanages who are qualified artisans at twelve.[621]

And, added Acheson, nothing was wasted in "Hungerland." It was among the 18,000 children in those barracks, the childhood of 400,000 refugees who had fled from Van, Erzurum, Trebizond and Bitlis, where craftsmanship had developed further than any of the other NER institutions in the Near East.

Articles on industrial education at the City of Orphans and orphan productivity continued to appear in 1923 in newspapers in the U.S. and elsewhere. These revealed, unwittingly, that being an orphan in the City of Orphans meant hard labor. The article that ran in a newspaper in New Zealand was not unique:

> The place is a little city in itself...

> From breakfast until luncheon the young Armenians get a bit of schooling...It is in the afternoon, however, that the Alexandropol orphanage takes on perhaps its most interesting aspect. Then it becomes an industrial centre with textile factories, tailor shops, tin and metal works, carpenter establishments, shoe manufactories, plumbing and masonry schools...

> The garments made from home woven cloth may not be models of style and elegance, but they serve their purpose...And what are styles compared with matters of real interest, such as gardening and laying walks, digging ditches, cleaning yards, and mending windows, doors, and casements? The children are engaged in everything that there is to be done in connection with running a small city.[622]

The industrial workshops were working at full pace when Barclay Acheson visited the Polygon in the summer of 1924. He was impressed by the Polygon's buildings, "arranged with military precision along a refugee-built road," but more impressed by

> the activity of the place, the buzz of work surrounding the central repair shop and the boys' industrial shop, which are run in affiliation, the medical clinic, the model farm and the unimposing but important little soap factory. This last-mentioned innovation is the outgrowth of a soap famine. It now manufactures tons of soap of exactly the right quality to meet the various needs,

and produced it "more cheaply than we can secure it elsewhere." The workshops, wrote Acheson, had had their origins in the scattered repair shops of the Polygon which once repaired cars and tractors, shod horses and made furniture, bolts, hinges, and other necessities. Now they were consolidated, better organized, and successfully reduced NER's overhead. Acheson then mentions that a year earlier, in 1923, he had witnessed a fourteen-year-old orphan build a car:

> Last year a fourteen-year-old boy, now working full time in this shop, actually made an automobile. He still has it. It stands about four feet high and resembles a hand-made, narrow gauge model of a Ford runabout. It is in no sense an assembled affair. Practically all the parts were actually made by hand. Its one-cylinder engine, transmission, steering apparatus, two gears and rope tires are mysteriously and wonderfully made. When the young, unheralded genius who made it put a teacupful of gasoline into the tin-can tank, started the motor and stepped into the seat, the thing actually started and nearly ran over us. I would have saluted reverently a coming Edison if I had not been convulsed with laughter.[623]

A teenager builds a car out of metal scraps. (RAC NEF Photos Box 136)

Working in the industrial workshops was tiring for the children, and sometimes hazardous to their health. When Araksi Pluzyan was 12 years old she entered the third grade. In view of her talent in needlework, she was placed in the needlework workshop for girls. But, she wrote,

> ...after working for a long time, my eyesight began to suffer and I could not see well after dusk. After work, they used to take me by the hand and lay me down. A few other children had the same problem...after some treatment I got better.

By 8th grade, Araksi was not doing needlework any longer.

THE CITY OF ORPHANS

She was assigned to do laundry after school, in addition to her other chores. Her director was Mrs. Shushanik:

> She was a kind woman, she would often say to me "Araksi, you're a nice girl, you do those chores," I would get tired from all the work. But what could I do? If I didn't do the work I would have been told to leave the orphanage and I had no one. Where would I go? And I hadn't finished school either, to be able to earn my daily bread.[624]

A humble laborer's daughter from Van, young Araksi had shown talent in acting. In her memoirs she recounts an encounter she had in the mid-1920s when she was in 8th grade with actor Armen Armenyan:

> Our literature teacher was Comrade Kirakossyan, a rather tall man, a graduate from Germany…Our lesson that day was "Anush." He asked me to recite a passage…

After listening to the young girl, the teacher asked her with tearful eyes:

> "My girl, who do you have?" I said, "The Turks killed them all, I have no one, I am alone." He then chose different passages and told me to recite, which I did.

> "Artistic talent lives in you," he said. After lunch, you should study at the Theatre/Fine Arts School."

> Blushing, I replied: "No, I am not free after lunch. I do laundry in the laundry room after lunch."

> My teacher wiped away his tears and said, "I will take care of that." Two days later, two actors came to our school—Armenyan and Pisheryan. They met me, got to know my abilities, and I was freed from the laundry room.

> After school, I used to study with Armenyan and acted in several major roles: as Margarit in *Patvi Hamar*; as Sona in the *Evil Spirit*; as Magda in *Jrasuzi Zenk*; as Astghik in *Gomsomoli Astghik*; and as Amalya in *Sasune Ayrvum e*.[625]

The greatest threat to the City of Orphans in 1923 was a fire that threatened the warehouses and orphanage buildings in March. The incident was reported by Reuters on April 31, 1923, and caught the attention of several U.S. and international newspapers for the next few days.[626] One of the first to cover the story was *The New York Times*,[627] followed by *The Hawera & Normanby Star*,[628] published in Taranaki, New Zealand, and *The Barrier Miner*, published in New South Wales, Australia, with reports that the fire had destroyed "one of the immense warehouses used by the Near East Relief Committee at Alexandropol where thousands of children were housed."[629] The papers reported that the fire had ruined a 1,000 ton warehouse, and menaced several of the orphanage buildings. Further damage had been prevented by "a bucket brigade of two thousand children and a battalion of Soviet Armenian soldiers, all working together with NER relief worker Janet MacKaye. The brigade's equipment consisted of four large hand pumps and a motor truck converted into a water carrier. The children, *The New York Times* reported, had saved the orphanages.

Orphan boy learning bookbinding.
(*The New Near East*, October 1923: 10)

Cap making.
(*The New Near East* (October 1923: 11) →

Washing butter in the creamery at Karakala or Kazachi.
(*The New Near East*, June 1925: centerfold) →

Ironsmithing at the Polygon.
(*The New Near East*, June 1925: 10) ↓

198 THE CITY OF ORPHANS

Shoemaking class.
(*American Industries*,
June 1922: 38)

Tinsmithing, using
empty tin cans of milk.
(*The New Near East*,
January 1925: 11)

Carpentry workshop.
(Barton 1930: facing page 304)

Pottery class.
(*The New Near East*,
March 1922: 7)

EDUCATION FOR CITIZENSHIP

↑
Orphan boys learning to drive tractors.
(*The New Near East*, June 1923: 13)

"Hans" the Simmental bull with an orphan boy.
(RAC NEF Bound Volumes Box 134) ↓

↑
Animal Husbandry, Karakala or Jalaloghli.
(Barton 1930: facing page 305)

↑
Lesson in Animal
Husbandry.
(*The New Near East*,
December 1924: 17)

Preparation of honey
in Stepanavan.
(*The New Near East*,
June 1926: 11) ↓

Apiary at Stepanavan.
(*The New Near East*,
January 1923: 15) ↓

EDUCATION FOR CITIZENSHIP 201

Gardening in Alexandropol. (*The New Near East*, June 1923: 13) →

↑ Farmland in Stepanavan or Alexandropol cultivated by orphans. (Barton 1930: facing page 304)

↑ Kazachi orphans picking potatoes. (*The New Near East*, June 1925: 11)

Cutting hay for the winter. (Barton 1930: facing page 304) →

↑
Soup poured into pails to be served in the dining rooms.
(*The New Near East* June 1925: 4)

Cooking class for girls. (RAC NEF Bound Volumes Box 134) ↓

←
Dining room girls slicing bread. Each girl cut 2,000 portions of bread for every meal.
(*The New Near East*, June 1925: 5)

EDUCATION FOR CITIZENSHIP 203

Girl hanging her wash to dry. (RAC NEF Photos Box 145) ←

Girl cobbler. (*The New Near East*, October 1924: 7) ↓

↑
Girl bookbinder. (*The New Near East*, October 1924: 7)

Making lace. (*The New Near East*, October 1923: 11) →

↑
Sewing class.
(*American Industries*,
June 1922: 40)

Dressmaking class.
(*The New Near East*,
October 1924: 6) ↓

Orphan girls working
at spinning wheels.
(RAC NEF
Photos Box 153) ↓

EDUCATION FOR CITIZENSHIP

In the classroom.
(RAC NEF
Photos Box 153)
←

Class at Polygon, with
Caroline Silliman
and a translator.
(*The New Near East*,
February 1923: 6)

Arithmetic class.
(*The New Near East*,
June 1925: 4.
The description under
the photo reads:
"Little Davitian Marian
estimates the number of
meals needed every year
at Kazachi Post.") →

206   THE CITY OF ORPHANS

↑
Braille class.
(*The New Near East*,
September 1922: 16)

Blind orphan
girl learning to
read in Braille.
(*The New Near East*,
April 1923: 10) ↓

Blind boy
playing the *oud*.
(*The New Near East*,
April 1923: 11) →

←
Canning class for
blind orphans.
(*The New Near East*,
September 1922: 16)

↑
Music practice.
(RAC NEF
Photos Box 153)

EDUCATION FOR CITIZENSHIP

The Agricultural Program and the NER Institute of Agriculture

In a country where the memory of starvation remained vivid for some time, preparing the future farmers of Armenia was considered an especially urgent task for NER and SSRA alike. NER's program in agriculture, by far the most comprehensive of its programs, was designed to improve productivity and deter future famines. Early plans in 1921 had consisted of the cultivation of 50 acres of land by the Polygon and 25 acres at the Kazachi, but progress had been slow in the absence of oxen, mules and horses.

A much greater variety of seeds, agricultural implements and tractors began to arrive in late 1921 and 1922, as part of NER's program in agriculture.[630] Conducted with the blessing and encouragement of the government of Soviet Armenia, the agricultural program evolved over the next few years into an expansive program that spread over two additional sites in the adjacent Lori region: Jalaloghli or Stepanavan, at a distance of about 50 miles from Alexandropol, and Karakala, about another hour and a half from Stepanavan on horseback. To launch the program, NER needed land to plant wheat, fruits and vegetables. The government was happy to accommodate and granted thousands of acres of land, totaling 17,600 in 1921, for the "free use during operations of Near East Relief."[631] In June 1923, *The New Near East* reported that in Jalaloghli and Karakala 6,000 desiatines [1 desiatine = 2.70 acres] of pasture land and 40 desiatines of vegetable land were made available to NER, with 800 desiatines of grain land and 15 desiatines of irrigated vegetable land in and around Alexandropol, totaling to approximately 18,500 acres of land in Alexandropol, Jalaloghli and Karakala.[632]

At least three main benefits were foreseen in the program. The first was that it would supply NER with meat, grains, varieties of foodstuffs and raw industrial materials such as cotton, sheepskins, leather, and wool for use in the orphanages. The program would also demonstrate to Armenian farmers how better farming methods and improved livestock, coupled with modern agricultural machinery, would more rapidly improve conditions in the country. The third benefit of the program was that it would train orphans to become the future farmers of the country, familiar with modern techniques of agriculture.[633]

The expansive program exacted significant investments on the part of NER. It involved the participation of expert American agriculturalists to design and execute the program, and the importation of tractors, agricultural implements and seeds from ports in the U.S. to the Caucasus by ship and train. Among the earliest American agriculturalists to reach the region were Sam and Ethel Newman who sailed from Seattle, Washington, arriving in Alexandropol in summer 1921.[634] By late 1921, they had moved to Jalaloghli. "The government has promised us all the land we want," wrote Ethel Newman to friends in Oregon

> And—well, it looks as though there are great big things ahead, and my, how the work grips one...we are teaching thousands of boys modern farming, producing food for thousands more, and incidentally the peasants are taking lessons."[635]

"It is wonderful," wrote Sam Newman a few months later,

> ...to see the eagerness of the homeless, ragged and half famished people to aid in this constructive plan...They [the Armenians] have great reverence for anything American, and in the big agricultural project undertaken by the Near East Relief they see a glimmer of hope for their much-persecuted race.[636]

When the Newmans had first arrived at Jalaloghli, the orphanage there sheltered only 400 boys and girls, wrote Ethel Newman:

> There were 1,000 in this lot last spring, but because of malnutrition and sickness, 600 of them died during the summer, so the Soviet officials had only 400 left to turn over to us.

But, she added,

> Enough have been brought down from the over-crowded orphanage at Alexandropol to make 2000 here...It is wonderful to see how the wretched, dirty, starved little newcomers begin to blossom and grow as soon as they have been bathed, clothed and given a few rations of wholesome food."[637]

The next group of agriculturalists sailed for Alexandropol on February 3, 1922. Among them were Leonard Harthill, Chairman of the Department of Horticulture of the New York School of Applied Agriculture,[638] and agriculturalists H. A. Hall and J. A. Cronin.[639] Harthill would remain a full year, to conduct an experiment to determine the most useful adaptation of modern farming methods to conditions in Armenia.[640] Hartill was appointed director of the experiment, reports of which would determine NER's full-scale agricultural program. The special train on which they arrived carried 36 carloads of American agricultural machinery—tractors, gangplows, modern agricultural implements—and bushels of seed for wholesale farm production. The first 1,000 acres were plowed in eleven days by ten American tractors.

In summer 1922 Leonard Harthill cabled New York with the good news that 91% of American seed grain sown in Armenia had sprouted and promised a record crop.[641] He estimated that if American methods were adopted in the country as a whole, cereal production could increase by as much as 300% in fall 1922.[642] The results in Alexandropol alone were remarkable. Two thousand acres of land had been plowed by 22 American tractors and had produced 22 bushels of barley per acre, far above the 10 bushels an acre produced by native methods.[643] In addition, the Alexandropol region furnished around 3,500 poods of meat, which lowered the cost of meat consumed at the City

Tractor shed. (RAC NEF Photos Box 153)

of Orphans where 2,000 poods of meat were consumed each month. Land in Alexandropol had been seeded, and an additional 1,000 acres had been ploughed ready for sowing in the spring. It was estimated that if the season were normal there would be at least 60,000 poods of grains. There would also be a sufficient amount of feed for a herd of cattle in the winter season capable of furnishing the necessary meat at the Alexandropol posts during the winter and spring, and the organizational and preparatory work done during 1922 would yield even greater results in 1923.[644]

Indeed, by mid-1923, the area of Alexandropol had produced 9,682 poods of barley, 6,310 poods of wheat, and 1,300 poods of linseed. The yield at Karakala and Stepanavan had included 3,180 poods of vegetables and 5,000 poods of potatoes. In addition, Karakala and Stepanavan had produced about 3,500 poods of meat and by-products of livestock, 1,150 sheepskins, 400 cowhides and 60 poods of mutton fat, which were delivered to Alexandropol.[645] By September 1924, twelve new types of vegetable seeds were imported into Armenia,[646] yielding an annual production in vegetables and cereals of 180 bushels of cucumbers, 500 bushels of beans, 720 bushels of cabbage, 3,572 bushels of potatoes, 3,600 bushels of beets, 1,322 bushels of rye, 1,438 bushels of oats, 3,334 bushels of wheat, and 7,458 bushels of barley. Among the achievements were the production of 24-pound turnips, 20-pound beets, and 400 bushels of potatoes per acre.[647]

The summary of achievements of 1922 was presented at the Annual Meeting of NER's Board of Trustees in New York, and highlighted the agricultural program as a worthwhile investment, especially since the thousands of orphans being trained would one day become the future leaders in their country and the investment may

> ...in future years prove a blessing to both America and Russian Armenia by promoting mutually helpful and friendly trade relations.[648]

Based on the results of the 1922 experiment, NER proceeded with the establishment of the Institute of Agriculture. Among other things, the Institute aimed to leave a permanent contribution to the economic life of Armenia when relief work ended. The program operated at Jalaloghli, Karakala and Alexandropol, with Jalaloghli designated as the centerpiece of the Institute. The physical plant at Jalaloghli consisted of the 36 buildings of former military barracks, given to NER free of rent, where NER had installed drainage and sanitation systems, a bakery, a laundry and a water-driven electric station from an old watermill, to provide electricity to the institute.[649] It had hundreds of acres of land under cultivation, grazing land and barns to house cattle for breeding and dairying purposes. In 1925, NER imported 5,000 poplar trees from different parts of Russia for the reforestation of the acres around the farm school.[650]

In the fall of 1924, Samuel Newman, directing NER's Institute of Agriculture, reported that there were 684 boys and 463 girls in Stepanavan learning to be farmers. Their ages varied: 40 were 12 years old; 400 were 14 years old; 547 were between the ages of 14 and 16; and 160 were above 16 years old.[651] The Institute's faculty consisted of 33 American and Armenian academic and agricultural instructors.[652] All department directors had their offices in the main Administration building, a two-story, stone building called the Gulbenkian Hall, named after the businessman and philanthropist naturalized British citizen of Armenian origin.[653] Operating expenses for the quarter ending September 30, 1924, totaled $34,692.91; it was anticipated that the total for the following month, October 1 through 31, 1924, would amount to $10,808.75.[654]

By September 1924 Stepanavan had become a strictly Agricultural School. Each boy and girl was given a small tract of land for the season with a specific crop and taught how to plant, cultivate and follow plant growth through various stages until harvest. Subjects taught included: soils; plant life; field crops, home gardening; fruit gardening; floriculture, beekeeping, poultry, animal husbandry, animal feeding, animal breeding, and dairying. The Farm-Mechanics Department included courses in farm machinery, carpentry, blacksmithing, harness making, and a home economics section that included cooking and sewing. Each department combined theoretical and practical work.

Classes in poultry included demonstrations in the use of incubators, and the apiary department, launched in the spring of 1924, was bound to become, Sam Newman thought, one of the most important contributions since Armenia, and especially the Lori region, was noted for its honey. Repairs were also well underway at Stepanavan:

Sam Newman (left), Barclay Acheson (center) and Ernest Yarrow (right), consulting. (*The New Near East*, October 1924: 5)

> …About the first of August we began the repairs and reconstruction necessary on our school building: Our plant is fairly ready and that means that we have about as complete an Agricultural plant as the average school in America.
>
> Our school building has sufficient class-rooms and a large assembly hall which will seat at least 500 children and is ideal for educational movies[655] or lectures. The rooms include three rooms, which are being equipped for a practical laboratory to be used in connection with the class work. We are having some difficulty in getting the necessary equipment but everyone is contributing until we are getting a well-equipped laboratory. Dr. Evans has helped most by giving us a large amount of equipment from the medical supplies.[656] We have a fairly good library with a large reading room in connection, which is used during free time and is a very popular place.
>
> …We are planning to take over all orchards which adjoin our land, and begin to set a couple of acres of trees and bushes for the Fruit Gardening department. We have started to prepare the soil for the Fall planting of trees. This branch of the work will include simple forestry, a study which is sorely needed in Armenia. This will include very practical suggestions for the improvement of the Armenian forests. We have now a plan ready to present to the government asking that certain mountain sides where young timber has started be protected from animals and that such places be withheld from pasture grants. Such simple precautions will tremendously increase Armenia's timber resources in a few years.

One of the most successful components of the program in Jalaloghli, reported Newman, had been the Home Gardening program where each orphan was given a plot of land to cultivate vegetables. The orphans had produced potatoes, cabbage, carrots, beets, and other vegetables for their own consumption, but would also provide Leninakan with cabbage and "all the beets and carrots they can use."[657]

In charge of the Institute's orphanage department and girls' education in Stepanavan in 1925 was Elsie Kimball. "I am teaching the girl *tastiaraks* [group leaders or home room teachers] English" she wrote,

> ...it is fun to teach these Armenian girls English, for they love nothing so much as to study. I never saw any people so eager to learn as the Armenians are, and for that reason it is easy to teach them. Armenian children think more of their books than of their play, and there is no punishment so great for them as to be obliged to stay out of school for a day.[658]

And, she continued,

> ...this morning I went into the regular day school and visited a room that is used only for study purposes. The children all stood up, as they invariably do when one of the Americans enters a room where they are, and then immediately sat down and paid no more attention to me, but simply glued their eyes to their books and began to buzz their lessons out loud. American children...would have glued their eyes on the visitor and have been glad of an excuse to stop studying.[659]

"All day long," she explained to her family in another letter from a camp she had organized near Stepanavan,

> I play with the orphans...The big girls and I play volleyball two or three hours a day...With the smaller girls I dance (much to their amusement) and play light games...

> I am sitting out under the trees in a most delightful spot ten miles from Djalal Oghlou. Five little girls are sitting with me, three of whom are the cutest rascals you could possibly imagine...They are learning Armenian dances and I never in this whole country ever saw such exhibitions of skill along this line. If I were to take them to New York and they were to dance before the most select public, they would bring the house down. American children certainly haven't any talent whatsoever in this direction, compared with the Armenian children. The Armenians are the very personification of grace, and some of our children in the orphanage are perfect wonders in ballet, etc.[660]

She was especially close to three little girls—Haigush, Khorsik and Emmik—who

> I think the world of, and they also seem to think the world of me...This morning when I was looking through a magazine they sat beside me and gazed at the pictures with deepest interest. One of these pictures was a girl at some summer camp in America, and I said, "See, here is a picture of Miss Kimball." Immediately they seized the magazine and kissed the girl furiously and repeatedly![661]

The smaller ranch at Karakala, about 12 miles from Stepanavan, specialized in stockbreeding and dairy, and boasted of stone barns large enough to house 1,000 heads of cattle under one roof. Repairs were conducted on 17 buildings of which 14 were used as stables, one as a milk factory, one as a warehouse, and one as living quarters. The milk factory, which produced butter and cheese, had not been possible to modernize.[662] Once the property of the Grand Duke Nicholas of Russia, Karakala was acquired by NER to help increase the livestock production in Armenia and to teach orphan boys modern American methods of stockbreeding. Among the animals imported for cross breeding were thoroughbred pigs, hogs and chickens, and

> …seventy-eight head of cattle of Swiss blood, one-third larger than native stock into Russian Armenia for dairying and breeding purposes.
>
> …The organization [NER] had the dual purpose of encouraging efforts to make up for heavy losses in the cattle industry in the Russian Caucasus during the World War and during the invasions and famine in the years following the War, in addition to the educational value in its own school work. This effort was justified by the immediate economic returns to the orphanages of Near East Relief.[663]

The high-grade bulls were purchased, in part, from the $5,000 donation made to NER by Armenians in California.[664]

The ranch at Karakala was run by Russian refugee "Madame Zonia Tsendorf" whom NER appointed as chief veterinarian and director of stock farming in Armenia in summer 1922.[665] "On our largest American ranch," she wrote, "we have room for nearly 5,000 animals. We shall devote some attention to the development of new types of stock and to the raising of horses and mules. The American mule, used by the American Army in France, has a great future in Armenia."[666] By early 1926, additional areas were being established for cows, and the herd of selected grade milking cows had reached 360.

Sam Newman left Stepanavan, and NER, in the summer of 1925, and for a while Stepanavan and Karakala were directed by Alfred G. Smaltz, a native of Le Mars, Iowa, who had come to the Caucasus as a member of The American Friends (Quakers) Relief and Reconstruction Mission to Russia. The following year Smaltz was in Samara, Russia, involved in the agricultural relief and reconstruction of the area. Upon return to the U.S., Smaltz spoke at public gatherings about the progress he had seen in Russia, improvements in agriculture and the lives of the Russian peasantry. The illustrated lecture he gave at the Mt. Sinai Temple in Le Mars, about his personal experiences in Armenia and Russia, was summarized in *The Sioux City Journal*:

> American interests are awakening to the resources of Russia, and are stationing representatives in important commercial centers…
>
> Despite current press reports to the contrary, the political situation in Russia is quiet, the government is becoming more conservative and is considerate in its treatment of the peasant classes…[667]

Karakala made the news in *The New York Times* in July 1926. The headline ran "American Battles Tartar Raiders All Day, Till Cavalry Saves Near East Relief Ranch," and told the story of how Karakala superintendent Paul W. Phillips and his wife, both from Seattle, Washington, had been woken up by orphans crying one night that Tartar [a term used at times for Muslim

Azerbaijanis] tribesmen from Azerbaijan had crossed the mountains in the night and were raiding the ranch. Paul Phillips, who had often had to ward off cattle thieves in the American Northwest, had

> ...picked up his rifle and hurried out, to see the Tartars driving away prize Swiss stock... Thinking to frighten the thieves, he opened fire, but the raiders, numbering from twenty to thirty, made a stand behind the rocks and returned the fire.[668]

The fighting had continued through the day and ended, *The Hamilton Evening Journal* reported, only when

> One of their orphans escaped on horseback and brought Cronin [William Cronin] and his aids from over a mountain...[669]

The raiders had been repelled, but Mrs. Phillips had been severely beaten by one of the tribesman.

In 1925, the Institute's program included outreach, consisting of the distribution of seeds at no cost to villagers and the free use of the Swiss and Simmental bulls for crossbreeding purposes. The average calf born through crossbreeding at the age of eight months was larger than the native cow mother.[670] As an educational effort, the Institute also hosted teachers from other schools in the area. On one occasion in 1925, 40 teachers arrived "from the primary and secondary government schools of Armenia to the Farm School of Near East Relief at Stepanavan" for demonstrations and lectures. Demonstration of farming techniques were also made for representatives of the Agricultural Bank of Yerevan, which on one occasion had resulted in the purchase of 10,000 tractors:

> Conducted a demonstration at its Farm School of American tractors on June 18th for representatives of the Agricultural Bank of Erivan, which led to the importation of 10,000 tractors from America into the area (Russia) as a part of the effort by that country to increase its production, following famine years.[671]

NER had not intended to be an agent for the sale of American equipment or commercial relations, it was stated, and the purchase had come as a natural consequence:

> Although the Near East Relief as a philanthropic organization had no relationship to the commercial phases of this very considerable transaction, it had originally introduced the use of American tractors as a part of its Farm School work and had taken into the Russian Caucasus for the first time one of the better known types of American tractors, in addition to other American tractors and machinery. The organization avoided the effect of being an advance agent for American equipment but this result came naturally from the increased production demonstrated by using motor equipment.[672]

The same year the Institute's staff organized a large stock show, the first of its kind in the Caucasus since WWI, with an exhibition of 41 high-grade animals:

> To stimulate country-wide interest the organization's agricultural staff arranged for a procession of high-grade animals, both horses and cattle, covering 34 miles, led by a Semintal bull, weighing 2,232 lbs., which crossed a mountain 8,000 ft.

in altitude to become the chief center of interest at the show and to receive the Armenian Government's leading award, "The Certificate of Highest Praise."

And,

> The Government Ministry of Agriculture stated at the show there was "not the least doubt but that these imported Swiss and Semintal breeds will greatly improve the inferior cattle now in the Russian Caucasus."[673]

NER's investment in the agricultural program, as well as the tremendous effort it took to plan and implement it, was deeply appreciated by SSRA officials.[674] By 1925, the result had exceeded expectations in production, orphan education, and benefits to the country. In fact, the Soviet Armenian government had hired all of the 200 boys who had learned to operate tractors and one of them was hired as advisor to the Agricultural Bank's representative.[675]

The Institute's program was guided by an agricultural advisory committee in the U.S. whose members included Senator Arthur Capper of Kansas and Professor O. S. Morgan, Chairman of the Department of Agriculture at Columbia University. The latter served as vice chairman of the committee and spent most of his sabbatical year preparing textbooks on the various phases of animal husbandry, agriculture, and horticultural work. Within a few years, American agricultural experts working in Armenia had been able to establish a remarkable program against great obstacles. Yet to a large extent, the success as well as the benefits the agricultural program yielded hinged on the free labor provided by the unnamed thousands of young orphans,[676] who worked in the fields and gardens, cared for the animals, milked the cows, cleaned the cowsheds, and prepared butter and honey. The value of their labor far surpassed the monthly cost of $2 to feed a child in Stepanavan.[677]

Model Villages

Even before the full agricultural program had been put in place, orphans had begun to plow land for cultivation around the posts. They had attached an iron plow to a pair of wheels from an abandoned ammunition cart and harnessing themselves to it, had plowed the beds for seeding. But water had been scarce. To remedy the situation, the boys built a dam across one of the roadside ditches through old tin cans, leaky pails and broken crockery to make a reservoir to catch rainwater.[678] The radishes, corns, turnips, beets, cabbages, and sunflowers they grew had provided for some of the needs of the orphans and staff. To keep watch over their gardens, by early 1922, the boys also built small, flat-topped huts of stone or sheet-iron, of which there was a great amount lying around the barracks. The gardens themselves were enclosed in sheet-iron, wire or even stonewall and attended by the boys.[679]

From the small huts had grown the model villages, as part of the larger industrial and agricultural programs. Essentially, these were "suburbs" of small homes the orphans built near their vegetable gardens. Eventually, it was hoped, these small homes would serve as models for village communities, to be populated by NER orphans when discharged from the City of Orphans and married. The orphan girl would perform the chores of home life and apply her knowledge of sanitation, animal care, personal care, infant care, and basic first aid.[680]

When Barclay Acheson visited the Severski in the summer of 1924, a small model village had already developed at the edge of the post near a large truck garden where vegetables were being raised. "The model village," Acheson explained, "was composed of a group of small stone buildings,"

Orphan boy building a model home.
(RAC NEF Photos Box 139)

A "home" built by orphans at the Polygon.
(RAC NEF Photos Box 145)

…resembling those of a native village…The model village points the way to improved village life…

A small garden is planted with flowers and trees. One cow and several sheep are in the shed. In the rooms of the little flat roofed houses are demonstrated butter and cheese making, proper location and operation of looms, good ventilation and lighting, the care of babies—in fact, all the home industries of native life plus modern methods of sanitation and hygiene. It is a practical, inexpensive contribution to an improved rural life.[681]

The Edith Winchester School of Nursing

The Edith Winchester School of Nursing was founded in 1924, when the preexisting smaller nursing schools in the three posts were consolidated. Before the consolidation, 26 nurses had graduated from the Severski nursing school, almost all of whom worked in the hospitals and clinics of the City of Orphans under the supervision of Red Cross nurse Grace Blackwell.[682] The nursing schools at the Polygon and the Kazachi were directed by Gertrude H. Legge and Mrs. Russell T. Uhls, both from Worcester, Massachusetts.[683]

As the orphan girls graduated from nurse training, they replaced paid native nurses at NER hospitals, and worked in exchange for room and board and a small wage.[684] Their services were requested at state run hospitals and clinics. In 1923, for instance, Dr. Kamsarakan, head of the University Hospital at Yerevan and Chairman of the Armenian Red Cross, asked that as many of the graduating classes as could be spared, be sent to the University Hospital in Yerevan as instructors.[685] In a note to Dr. Kamsarakan in April 1924, Grace Blackwell listed the names of the first two years' graduates from the Severski nurse training program all of whom, except for one nurse, worked in the City of Orphans. According to Blackwell's note, the nursing graduates on October 26, 1923, were: Bambich Ter-Grigoryan, (?)ura Kaladelchik, Lusya Aslanyan, Mariam Eramlyan (?), Tsedik Manukyan (?), Zabel Amiryan, Tigranuhi Barkhudaryan, Azniv Hakobyan, Goharik Karapetyan, Yelena Ter-Tateosyan, Vardush Manukyan, Vardush Galustyan, Kalipse Poghosyan, and Astghik Hakovbyan. Graduates on April 19, 1924, were: Lusya Sargsyan, Arcvik Hakobyan, Marine Harutyunyan, Vardanush Movsesyan, Satenik Ghazaryan, Haykanush Sargsyan, (?)achatar Khorenyan, Deghtsanik Petrosyan, Yeghis Hakobyan, Astghik Nshanyan, Viktor Minasyan, and Mariam Kyantaryan.[686]

The Edith Winchester School of Nursing, named in honor of a young American Red Cross nurse who had died of typhus four months after arriving in Yerevan in 1919, was located at the Kazachi.[687] It had a rigorous program lasting three years, or six semesters, each semester consisting of 4.5 months.[688] Theory classes were held six days a week and offered instruction in Professional Ethics, Personal Hygiene, Bacteriology, Anatomy and Physiology, Pharmacology, Surgical Nursing, Gynecology, Obstetrics, Internal Medicine, Physical Therapy, Skin and Urinary Tract Diseases, Nutrition, Public Health, Psychology, Child Rearing/Nutrition, and Russian.

Practical training took place during rotations at clinics and hospitals in the orphanages and in the city. These included the hospital and clinics at Lukashin Post (formerly the Kazachi), the polyclinic at the Polygon, and the Second Soviet Hospital in the city. Nurse trainees worked in patient rooms and isolation rooms, operating and postoperative rooms, labs, and pharmacies. Special groups of student nurses also spent additional hours in nutrition classes held in the kitchen and bacteriology classes, which met in the laboratory. Not all nurse trainees, however, were given the opportunity to gain practical training at the Second Soviet Hospital's obstetrical department. While the physician in charge of obstetrics, Dr. Yuzpashyan, allowed the trainees to work in the wards, he did not allow them to personally deliver babies. Elsie Jarvis, then Director of the Edith Winchester School of Nursing, complained to the Director of the Leninakan Health Department on March 1, 1928, that nurse trainees had enough preparation to perform deliveries and that excluding them from the process hindered their education.[689] Practical training continued through the year, except for a 15-day vacation in the summer. Vacations were short mainly because the nurses in training were orphans and had no parents or families to spend time with outside.

Edith May Winchester. (*Team Work*, June 13, 1924: 63)

CZAR'S OLD BARRACKS USED TO TRAIN NURSES IN NEAR EAST

MRS RUSSELL T. UHLS   **MISS GERTRUDE H. LEGGE**

Military structures which the Russian Czar built in Alexandropol, Russian Armenia, to train his men for war, are now being used by Mrs Russell T. Uhls and Miss Gertrude H. Legge, two Worcester County nurses, to train orphan girls as nurses, according to word reaching the Near East Relief office here. The two nurses are in charge of two of the three Near East Relief training centers in the Armenian city.

Former elaborate barracks have become stations for equipping orphan girls to fight typhus, cholera and other plagues in the Armenian famine area.

The girls are selected from those over 14 years of age among the 20,000 children in American orphanages in Alexandropol. Their eagerness to join the Americans in the hospital work and to train for the nursing profession has aroused favorable comment among medical heads of the relief organization. Some of them may later be selected for additional training in America in order that they may return to their native land as leaders in their profession. There is a lack of nurses throughout the Caucasus.

Mrs Uhls, who was Miss Pearl Larson of Fitchburg, is the wife of the physician in charge of the Near East Relief Trachoma Hospital in Alexandropol. She is a graduate of the Worcester City Hospital Training School.

Miss Legge is a graduate of the Worcester Memorial Hospital. Prior to her enlistment with the Near East Relief she served in Serbia with the American Women's Hospital. She is a native of Oxford and a sister of Mrs. T. E. Harrington of Wrentham. Prior to her overseas service she was engaged in work for the Visiting Nurses' Association of Spencer.

The Boston Daily Globe, August 30, 1922.

The Edith Winchester School was meant to lay the foundations of the nursing profession in Armenia, as the Institute of Agriculture had done for agriculture, with the full support and endorsement of the government. This was to be a permanent teaching institution where nurses could be trained to serve in any capacity required of them in their professional field. By the end of 1926, the Winchester School had graduated around 100 nurses, all of whom eventually entered government service.[690]

In 1925, one year after its foundation, the Winchester School received international recognition from the International Council of Nurses, through the support of Dr. Uhls. The latter summarized the discussion he had held with the Secretary of the Council in a note dated September 11, 1924, addressed to his colleague Dr. Kamsarakan:[691]

Dear Doctor,

At a conference with the Secretary of the International Council of Nurses today, I took up the question of recognition of the Near East Relief Training School for nurses at Alexandropol.

Recognition of the school by the International Council would mean that graduates would have a definite standing in any country which affiliates with this organization and this includes practically all the civilized countries.

The Secretary was of the opinion that the Near East Relief School would have no trouble in gaining recognition and will present the application for consideration at the next meeting of the International Council which will be held in Helsingfors [Helsinki] in July, 1925...

I do not know the progress your school in Erivan is making, but you would do well to closely model it after the training school at Alexandropol which conforms to the strict requirements of the International Council...

The New York office is considering the establishing of two scholarships for graduate nurses. If this can be arranged, two of the most capable and intelligent nurses will be sent to America for one year, one to take a course in the teaching of nursing, and the other a course in Public Health nursing. They will then be returned to Armenia and should be given positions as teachers in your Erivan Nurses Training School.

Mrs. Uhls is well and joins me in regards to you and all of our Erivan friends.

Nurses at the Severski.
(*The American Journal of Nursing*, July 1922: 830)

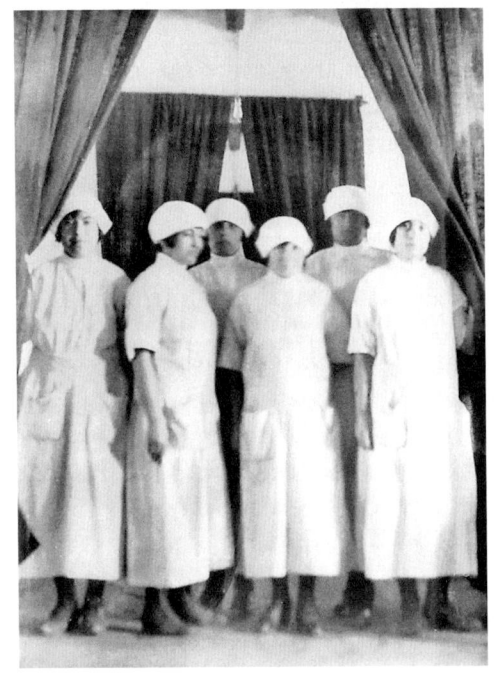

Winchester School Nurses.
(RAC NEF Photos Box 138)

Elizabeth Jarvis and an Armenian physician as interpreter, with the class at the Winchester School.
(*The American Journal of Nursing*, April 1926: 285)

The Winchester School was recognized by the Council the following year, and a December 1925 report announced that "an American nurse and her Armenian nurse assistant" had represented the school at the annual congress at Helsinki and that the Council had designated the Armenian graduate nurse, "Satenik Kalmanian as permanent representative on the Council for Transcaucasia." This was especially significant, the report continued, because "the entire country of Russia, with its 132 million population, was not represented on the Council. At the occasion, NER headquarters in New York designated an insignia to be worn by the graduate nurses, which showed the white star of NER and the name of the school." [692]

Occasionally, NER accommodated specific requests from the Armenian government. In 1926, the government asked for fifteen graduate nurses to help in a program of malaria prevention near Yerevan.[693] The following year, NER was asked that the school place additional emphasis on obstetrical training, so that nurses could be sent to remote villages after graduation and attend to obstetrical patients. Acceding to the request, NER added an obstetrical ward of 18 beds to the nurses' training program, along with a nursery attached to it in 1927,[694] and appointed the first Public Health nurse at the school.[695]

Elsie Jarvis was the director of the school when a powerful earthquake shook Leninakan and surrounding areas on October 22, 1926.[696] A second earthquake, five times stronger than the first, had followed the first shock, dislocating all electric and gas mains, and tremors had continued intermittently for 42 days, coupled with a blizzard that descended on the ravaged area a week later. The series of shocks had disrupted the cemeteries as well, where corpses spewed from their graves were scattered about. The damage to property and human loss was monumental. When the tremors finally ended, two-thirds of the population of Leninakan and those of 23 villages around the city were homeless, and martial law had been proclaimed throughout the earthquake zone.[697]

At the time of the earthquake there were 20 American personnel at the City of Orphans. At the first sign of the earthquake NER relief workers Janet MacKaye and Belle Bass had mobilized the terrified children and instructed the older ones to sing Armenian folksongs as they marched them all to safety, as Dorothy Stratton had led a group of blind and deaf children to safety. By the time the second earthquake shook Leninakan the children, partly clothed, were out of the buildings.[698]

Help arrived soon from many directions. The government of Armenia and the Soviet republics of Georgia and Azerbaijan rallied to help the victims of the quake with financial assistance and supplies, Red Cross trains of doctors and nurses, and battalions of soldiers and firemen.[699] The October 26, 1926, issue of *The Miami Daily News and Metropolis* reported that the Soviet government in Moscow donated $250,000 for Relief and NER agreed to provide up to 20,000 rubles to help the Armenian Red Cross continue its work. A sum of $5,000 was cabled immediately and a nation-wide appeal for aid was made to all NER state committees. Assistance also arrived from 600 Armenian orphans who had been sent from NER's orphanages in the Near East to farms and industrial plants in France as laborers. Their contribution was in the amount of 5,000 francs to be used for the victims of the earthquake. *The New York Times* reported that the boys, who earned an average of $6 to $8 a month, had volunteered to raise the amount.[700]

One week after the earthquake, *The Los Angeles Times* stated that the earthquake had ushered into the world 72 babies, of whom "Twenty-eight, including two sets of twins, were born in the American tent hospital," and that "a second hospital under canvas has been opened to care for maternity cases."[701] The nurses had christened the first child born in the tent hospital "Grace Coolidge Dubenkian" in honor of U.S. First Lady Grace Coolidge. There had also been one set of triplets, whom the nurses christened "Faith," "Hope," and "Charity."[702]

Four Red Cross nurses, Elsie L. Jarvis, Laura MacFetridge, who later succeed as the school's director, Edna Steiger, and Janet MacKaye together with 75 graduates of the School worked with surgeons and NER Chief

Surgeon Walter Sisson for days, over improvised operating tables in the open air outside the posts.[703] Within a week, 130 operations were performed by candlelight by surgeons and nurses. The three city hospitals in Leninakan had been razed to the ground. To accommodate their patients, NER workers evacuated the 200 patients from their hospital into tents to make room for the injured population of the city and villages. And due to the shortage of food in the city, NER turned its bakery over to the government.[704]

The barracks were not spared the destruction that covered the region. Many of the barracks at the Severski and Polygon were damaged and the houses where the American relief workers lived had become uninhabitable. Children and personnel lived in the open for days under winter weather conditions, but there had been no deaths either among the orphans or the staff.[705] The Soviet Armenian government voiced special appreciation of the nurses and medical staff. Aramayis Yerznkyan, the Minister of Agriculture and Chairman of the Government's Relief Commission, expressed the heartfelt appreciation of the Armenian people and Government for American help:

> Through all the tragic days and nights of succeeding earthquakes, America was the only foreign country that thought of us. Your charity has touched our hearts, kindled our souls. No Armenian can ever forget those noble and unselfish American nurses who bound up our wounds and assuaged our anguish. Every one of our 10,000 orphans is a living expression of gratitude for all America's goodness to us.[706]

The nurse trainees of the Edith Winchester School were especially praised in *The American Journal of Nursing*, for their "invaluable aid to the doctors and the American nurses in the makeshift hospital."[707] A few months later, Edna F. Steiger acknowledged the important role the graduates of the Winchester School played in the lives of orphans, especially in keeping epidemics out of the orphanage, in *The American Journal of Nursing*:

> …So far we have had only one [epidemic], measles—which however we have succeeded in keeping out of the orphanage. This I attribute to the help I am getting from our native nurses who have graduated from our own training school. I have appointed a public health nurse for the post and as this is the first appointment of this kind with the organization, she is quite proud of her position, and is certainly a wonderful help to me. She was, as are most of our nurses, a former inmate of the orphanage and then graduated from our training school. When we see results of this kind, it helps to realize that our efforts are not in vain.
>
> Edna F. Steiger, Leninakan.[708]

The Teacher Training Program

The teacher-training program was put into operation about the same time as the Edith Winchester School of Nursing. In accordance with NER's educational policy, 5% of the orphans each year were selected from among the bright students for a special program to prepare future teachers. The select group received an additional two years of education and one year

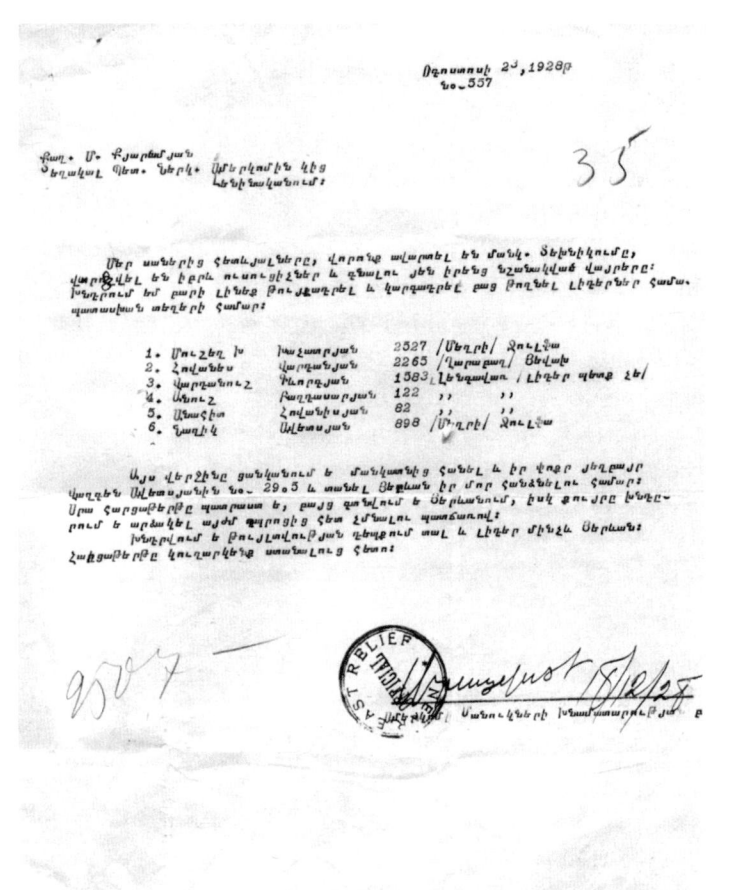

Note asking Citizen Melik Karamyan to provide leaders to accompany graduates of the Pedagogical Technicum to different regions of Armenia where they were scheduled to begin teaching in fall 1928.
(NAA 39/1/5/f. 35)

of practical teaching. This meant that if the children's education ended at the 7th grade, the brighter ones were offered instruction in the 8th and 9th years, which were the same as those planned for the last two years of high school in government schools. Subjects offered during the 8th and 9th years included Armenian Language and Literature, Russian and English languages, History, Economics, Government Law, Economic Geography, Drawing and Singing, Auditorium, General Biology, Physiology and Hygiene, Physics, Chemistry, Astronomy, and Mathematics. The third year's subjects included Psychology, Pedagogy, and Methods and Practice of Teaching.[709] At the end of the program, students were examined on Armenian Literature, Social Science, Russian language, Physics, Anatomy, Physiology, Mathematics, and History of Education.[710]

The first year's graduating class in June 1925 had 27 students, all of whom were subsequently employed as teachers in government schools. The group had received their additional schooling after they had left the orphanage and held jobs in the city. They would walk the distance to the Polygon at night, even at -20 °C temperatures and despite the danger of attacks by wolves. Nonetheless, they had been able to complete the 18 months' course in nine months.[711]

NER explained that the program in teacher training had been initiated at the request of the government to prepare students as future teachers "owing to a serious shortage of teachers in the public schools of Alexandropol, Armenia,"

> ...the government has asked Near East Relief to prepare older orphan boys and girls to supply the deficiency. These children have been trained in the orphanage schools by American methods, with which Armenian educators have been impressed and which they believe will more than offset their youthfulness.[712]

"The Commissar of Education," NER's annual report for 1926 read, "has indicated that he could use several hundred such teachers"[713] and that once an emergency refugee-feeding organization, the NER was now "the largest single nongovernmental educational organization in the Near East. The Armenian government especially, and other governments to a lesser extent," the report added, "are bidding eagerly for graduates from our normal courses to take positions as teachers in government and other schools."[714]

Educational Priorities in 1924:
Paul Monroe and Nshan Hovhannisyan

Of the periodic reviews of NER's educational program, one of the most comprehensive was conducted by Paul Monroe, a prominent U.S. educator and Director of Columbia University's Teacher's College. After spending four months in NER relief operations in the Near East in 1924, including NER's major efforts in Armenia, Monroe believed that industrial education should be the most important part of the orphan's education.[715] He urged NER's Board to ensure that each child was given a definite training in some specific industry, and recommended that industrial education "be given every week of every year to every child." Monroe further recommended that the children's industrial education should begin earlier than NER's practice at 10 or 11 years old, preferably after the child reached the age of 6 or 7. This would be easily accomplished with the girls, he wrote, because they could be taught sewing and embroidery at that age, and could do

> ...housework in the dormitories and personnel houses.[716]

In the area of agriculture, Monroe found Stepanavan and Karakala to be the most promising. However, those locations could only accommodate about a thousand children at a time. Monroe approved of the agricultural training of the smaller children in Alexandropol, but felt that these could never be more than school gardens. Monroe approved of the nursing and teacher training programs, but suggested that greater numbers of nurses and teachers be trained to meet the needs of the country, and that a public health component be added to the nursing program. With respect to teacher training, he felt that classes of 30 or 40 students were not enough, especially since the government had indicated the need for 800–1,000 teachers. On the other hand, he continued,

> ...the training is not of sufficiently practical character to justify any great increase in effort or numbers unless such practical training which would afford a demonstration of American ideals is established.[717]

Monroe had heard from the staff that the SSRA government presented "unsurmountable difficulties," to which he responded,

> Against this view may be urged the statement made everywhere by government and school officials that their ideal is to introduce American educational purposes, methods and organization...In other words they are requested to train as many of the boys and girls of the orphanage for the teaching profession as can be prepared for it. Within the limits of funds available I would urge that this be done...

One of the older orphans who taught class half a day and studied during the second half. (*The New Near East*, October 192: 15)

EDUCATION FOR CITIZENSHIP

Monroe's argument for increasing the number of teachers in training was also based on other considerations. Larger numbers of students in the teacher training program would not only supply much-needed teachers for the country, but would offer the additional advantage of replacing paid teachers with unpaid student teachers:

> The pupil teachers could be used quite extensively to teach the children in the orphanages thus reducing the expense of the education work and contributing quite as much as do the post orphans in industry to the support of their training.

Monroe's proposal to replace teachers by student teachers was also based on the argument that trained in the orphanages, student teachers

> ...would more readily adapt themselves to American educational purposes and methods than do those trained under the traditional methods.[718]

Among the student teachers was Araksi Pluzyan, who had graduated in 1926. During her last year at the Polygon, she was given two classes to teach in the primary school, in exchange for room and board. She would study at the Polygon in the mornings and teach the younger children in the afternoon. Like other graduates of the teacher-training program, after leaving the orphanage, Araksi was assigned to teach third grade at the Noradagh village in New Bayazet and at Sarmsakhli village in Kirovakan.[719]

With respect to the Armenian teaching staff, Monroe had observed that the teachers were well educated and experienced and many of the orphanage schools were better than some in the U.S., especially those in rural areas. As for NER's American personnel, whom he held in high esteem, Monroe commented that many of them did not have sufficient or minimal experience

Group photograph showing Polygon Schools superintendent Nshan Hovhannisyan in the center, possibly surrounded by a group of young student teachers, mid-1920s. (AGMI Collection)

224 THE CITY OF ORPHANS

in the areas they were held responsible for, and had had to learn it the hard way. He further observed that only a very small number of the personnel had direct contact with the orphans and spent most of their time with office work.[720]

In his report, Monroe referred to Stepan Lisitsyan, a noted Armenian educator who had completed studies in Europe and returned to the Caucasus, and to Lisitsyan's approach to education. He agreed with "Dr. Lisitsyan of Tiflis" on all his points except with Lisitsyan's statement that more attention should be paid to the teaching of the sciences and that the amount of apparatus needed for science classes should be greatly increased:

> I do not agree with him on this last point. His view is due to the methods of teaching science in the schools throughout this entire area and in Europe in general. This is usually by demonstration by means of complex and valuable apparatus in the hands of the teacher. Usually it is by the lecture method with perhaps some co-operation on the part of the pupil.

Instead, Monroe felt that

> …it would be far better to manufacture simple and perhaps crude apparatus or to find the illustrative materials in the ordinary industrial, mechanical, household and farm operations around them. A few simple microscopes and similar instruments would be the most that is needed. The handicraft work in the shops could well be directed to make most of the necessary apparatus. It can be done. However it cannot be done by the teachers now in charge. If they cannot be shown by someone now on the field and interested in the handicraft work it should be done by some science teacher or an American instructor who know [sic] how.[721]

When in Leninakan in summer 1924, Paul Monroe had been accompanied by Barclay Acheson and Tigran Margaryan, the director of one of Moscow's experimental schools. The three had held meetings with Polygon schools superintendent Nshan Hovhannisyan, during which suggestions had been made that there should be "little work inside the classroom and a lot of work outside the classroom," for "games in the open-air and awareness and practice of hygiene," and for replacing the term "orphanage" with "Polygon Children's Workshop."[722] By the end of the fall semester, on December 26, 1924, Nshan Hovhannisyan produced a detailed mid-year report of 20 typewritten pages covering every aspect of the schools at the Polygon. He thanked the group for their valuable input and assured them that their suggestions would be followed as much as possible[723] and that every effort would be made to address the shortcomings they had identified.[724]

Hovhannisyan then proceeded with a full and detailed description of the academic curriculum and extracurricular activities, including excursions to factories and city offices; lectures and performances; student self-government; teacher self-improvement programs; and evening classes, attended mostly by workers where teaching was conducted primarily by former students of the Polygon, and added that in general, 34% of the teaching faculty were former orphans of the Polygon.[725] The report also included a description of how the orphans' days were planned at the Polygon from six in the morning when the orphans woke up, washed, tidied their bedrooms and had breakfast, through supper time and bed, punctuated by workshops, classrooms, games, and time in the library reading room. According to Hovhannisyan's report, there were a total of 5,121 students at the Polygon in December 1924 of whom only 121, or 2.3% were ill. Of the student group, 322 boys and girls worked in the tailor shops, 360 boys in joiners' shops, 133 boys in shoemaking shops, 156 boys in tinsmith shops, 87 in ironsmith shops, 47 boys in locksmith's shops, 42 boys in painters' shops, 49 boys in the bindery, 7 in the ceramics shops, etc. Thirty-five boys and 47 girls worked as instructors; 49 boys and 22 girls were group leaders; 85 boys and 22 girls worked in NER offices, and 20 girls worked in the hygiene department. In the area of the creative arts, 92 boys and 6 girls studied music, 20 boys and 30 girls studied dance, 38 boys and two girls studied drawing, and 22 boys and 19 girls studied theater. These students were above 12 years of age, of which age group there were 1,717.

With respect to the teaching faculty, the 1924–25 academic year had started with 62 male and 24 female teachers, but at the end of the year there were 70 male teachers and 24 female teachers, most of them young. In terms of faculty salaries, these varied from $15.75 per month to $24.15 per month, depending on the level of education, responsibility, and seniority. Among the teachers, 38 could read and write Russian, 25 English, 12 French, 5 German, and 18 Turkish.

In terms of the expenses of the educational department, Hovhannisyan mentioned that the main expense items were salaries, renovations, utilities (heat, electricity, water), transportation, textbooks, and scholastic needs. The total expenses for the first semester, from September to December 1924 when 5,050 students had been educated, had amounted to $14,257.03. Of that amount, $9,950 was spent on salaries, $725.62 on reconstruction, $350 on utilities, $337.68 for repairs, $2,760.93 for textbooks and stationary supplies, and $132.80 for transportation. This meant, Hovhannisyan pointed out, that it had cost $2.82 to educate each child for one semester, or about 70¢ per month, per child.[726]

Many open-air games and excursions into the world outside the orphanage had been integrated into the children's daily schedule to broaden their practical knowledge, wrote Hovhannisyan, and children over the age of eight spent half of their working hours in workshops learning trades. But by contrast to Monroe's vision of orphan education, Hovhannisyan's report reveals a pronounced preference for a well-rounded and balanced education. Children were offered music, theater, art, a library and a reading room—whether they were the sons and daughters of farmers or not. A Pedagogical Museum, while still inadequate, was formed during the 1924–25 academic year and featured maps, photographs of plants and animals, photos and models of anatomy, and basic equipment to conduct experiments in chemistry and physics.

The theatrical work, according to Nshan Hovhannisyan, was adequate. There was a teacher who taught theater arts and there were various theatrical groups. In the fall 1924 semester, performances had included, among others, Oscar Wilde's *The Star Child* and *The Happy Prince*, Friedrich Schiller's *The Robbers*, works by Uriel Acosta, Armen Tigranyan's *Anush Opera*, Molière's *The*

Imaginary Invalid, William Shakespeare's *Tempest*, and others. There was an adequate amount of theatrical props and conveniences.

Polygon's building No. 18, where the secondary school was located, housed a library and a reading room, the Pedagogical Museum, the Theater, and the Art Studio. The latter had begun in 1921, and had talented students. General art classes were conducted in classrooms for the general student population, but students who attended the studio were especially talented. The library had 11,291 books, of which 705 were in foreign languages and the rest in Armenian. In the first semester, books had been checked out 12,557 times, and 5,870 books were read in the reading room.

The differences between the positions held by Monroe and Hovhannisyan on orphan education was especially evident in the area of women's education. If for Monroe six- or seven-year-old girls could be put to work cleaning personnel houses or dormitories to prepare them for family life and motherhood, for Hovhannisyan the road to an improved family life and especially motherhood, would need to be demarcated through education. To that end, he strongly suggested extending the educational experience, especially for orphan girls, beyond the existing system. After all, he argued, girls would eventually become mothers, and educated mothers would raise a generation that would benefit the Armenian nation.[727]

The orphanage, for Monroe, was not a place for a well-rounded education for orphans, nor a place where love of learning and school could be nurtured, although many relief workers had praised the love of learning they observed in the orphans. That characteristic, so pronounced in the children, had not ebbed in 1927. Everett Gunn, who had joined the NER staff a few years after Monroe's report, wrote in his college class report:

I never saw people so hungry for education…

…thousands of people are in night schools as well as children enrolled in classes during the day…

…More than ever is the observer convinced that free education is the basis of progress…[728]

By summer 1926, when Educator George Wilcox spent three months in Armenia to study the educational system, he reported that NER's schools followed the septennial school model set by the government, which offered three years above the elementary school.[729] The difference was that English was not taught at the government schools but that the government had approved the teaching of English in NER's schools because it considered "English the most useful international language."[730] Wilcox wrote that there were two grades of vocational schools: a three-year lower vocational school for children between the ages of 12 and 15, and a four-year technical school or Technicum, backed by the government's consistent emphasis on vocational education throughout the system.[731] Wilcox was especially impressed with the government's efforts to eradicate illiteracy, encouragement of young men and women to enter the teaching profession, and determination to establish teachers' institutes for professional self-development. Wilcox had also been impressed with the "Commissar of Education and his able assistants."[732]

The Polygon library in 1927 could boast of being one of the largest elementary school reference libraries in the world. Its acquisitions had reached 11,543 reference books in 1927, 10,970 of which were in Armenian. Most had been obtained through the exchange of old clothes, some had been produced by NER, and still others, such as agricultural books were brought through specific programs. But there was still a paucity of textbooks. To remedy the problem, some NER teachers had worked out courses in the sciences in mimeograph for classroom instruction with the view of later printing them for general use in Armenia. "Aside from the training of teachers," NER General Secretary Charles Vickrey reported for the year ending December 31, 1926,

> ...an important contribution is being made in the preparation of textbooks primarily to meet the imperative requirements of our own educational classes, but at the same time serving the wider educational interests of the Near East. We have in large part been obliged to create and produce our own textbooks in the Armenian language, the excellent and adequate books of pre-war time having disappeared or become obsolete.[733]

The list of books by the end of 1926, included, Vickrey continued:

> *Methods of Teaching Armenian*, by Doctor Edilyan, 300 pages, 1,000 copies. A valuable textbook for teachers of Armenian language in use in all our schools
>
> *Practical Gardening Manual*, by Mr. Hartill, printed in Leninakan, 60 pages, 2,000 copies
>
> *Practical Nursing*, a textbook for the Nurses' Training School, 40 pages
>
> *Materia Medica*, another textbook for the Nurses' Training School, 70 pages
>
> *Hygiene*, printed for the department of education of Near East Relief, 170 pages, 3,000 copies
>
> *Obstetrics*, printed in Constantinople for the Nurses' Training School, 270 pages, 500 copies
>
> *Soils and Plant Life*, a new textbook for agricultural training just being printed, 3,000 copies
>
> *Farm Tractors, Farm Machinery, and Field Operations with Farm Machines*, three textbooks on farm machinery by Prof. A. A. Stone, Head of the Farm Mechanics Department, State Institute of Applied Agriculture, Farmingdale, Long Island
>
> *How to Teach Field Crops*, by Prof. H. W. Nisonger, Assistant Professor of Agricultural Education, Ohio State University, Columbus, Ohio
>
> *Lessons in Practical Poultry Husbandry*, by Prof. C. E. Lee, Head of the Department of Poultry Husbandry, State Institute of Applied Agriculture, Farmingdale, Long Island

Beekeeping, by Prof. George C. Horton, Instructor in Beekeeping, University Extension, Columbia University, New York City

NER's overall educational plan was met with criticism by some of the Armenian employees, among them its closest supporters Vahan Cheraz and Varazdat Deroyan. Cheraz described NER's vision and operations in Leninakan as being inattentive to the orphans, which were presumably the very reason of NER's existence in Armenia. He called NER's efforts "uneven, monotonous, contradictory, forward or backward in education, sometimes successful, often unsuccessful attempts."[734] Varazdat Deroyan, like Cheraz a long time friend of the NER, wrote that NER did not place a premium on education and that well trained native teachers were not allowed to have a voice in the decision making if they could not communicate in English. In 1924, he wrote, the Armenian staff had hoped that Acheson would look into their complaints on educational problems, but to no avail; things had remained the same.[735] The chaotic existence of the schools, Deroyan wrote, only illustrated the disorganized state of the entire institution,[736] which was neither Soviet nor American.[737]

The Elusive Phantom of (Un)Happiness

Among Paul Monroe's recommendations was the expansion and upgrading of the play program, especially free play and games, and its integration in the orphan's educational life. Play, according to Monroe, would offset the harrowing experiences that orphans had lived through, and help them not to "always look upon the world with fear and terror." Play would teach the children cooperation and self-reliance, and would allow freedom of expression. Although some elements of a play program already existed in the orphanages, it did not seem to Monroe that it was sufficiently developed:

> In two or three instances there were play experts at work but the number of children was so great that the program did not seem to get over. On the afternoons free from shop and school it seemed odd to see the children by hundreds take to sewing and knitting and practically none of them to play.[738]

NER's efforts to teach children to play had started several years earlier, with a special early effort made at Kars in summer 1920. But after much effort it had been declared a failure. Elizabeth Anderson, who had been a member of NER's relief activities in Kars, wrote of the director's decision "that something must be done to make the listless, morbid children more like human beings," who "roused themselves only to eat":

> So he designed merry-go-rounds, swings, and seesaws; and for weeks went to the orphanage and demonstrated the broad jump, high jump, quoits, and blind man's buff. The children loved to watch him and would mechanically do as they were told; but immediately afterward would sink back into their lethargy. The teachers were ordered to *make* the boys play; and so each in turn was forced to swing or seesaw or something, for five minutes at a time. They looked so thoroughly miserable...at last the playground was admitted a failure...[739]

The children's indifference to play, and their listlessness were attributed to the traumas they had experienced before arriving at the orphanage, and was a major concern to observers. "A smile never appears" on the faces of the children, wrote James Barton,

> ...The children did not weep or moan or beg for anything—they simply sat about for days with a look of despair upon their faces, with no interest in their companions, no curiosity—an entire absence of normal childhood.[740]

To remedy the situation, NER instituted a "Play" program in Alexandropol that in 1922 was taught by Mary Davis. She observed that on sunny days, the kindergarten children went out into the playground to be taught how to play. But the fact that they did not know how to play was not surprising, she added, "since how could they know how to play, these tragic little waifs, whose brief lives have been spent in crowded refugee camps, or wrecks of mud huts, or in some corner of a ruin by the roadside...?" At the same time, she had been surprised that as soon as they gathered on the playground

> ...they form into little groups, singing in their piping voices, clapping their hands and weaving back and forth in the most intricate steps that would puzzle many an experienced dancer of another race, with a zest that makes their eyes shine and brings the color to their cheeks.[741]

In 1924, following Monroe's recommendation to integrate play into the daily lives of the orphans, NER made plans to restructure the play program and sent Columbia University Teachers' College graduate Helen Mays to teach the orphans "how to laugh and romp to help them get ready to play the larger games of life later on."[742] The move was most enthusiastically supported by Barclay Acheson, who felt that a good play program would help counter the monotony of institutional life and offset the children's tragic histories. Acheson was also convinced that the program would teach the traumatized child the

Teaching children to play.
(Barton 1930: facing page 318)

importance of teamwork which, he thought, was lacking in such an individualistic race as the Armenians, but was an essential attribute "if ever the Armenians are to be welded into one racial unit."

Acheson was aware that the children were excited about sports games, especially soccer, and loved to dance Armenian folk dances to Armenian music. But, he felt, all Armenian music was in a minor key and often evolved around tragic scenes or laments. He asked that songs with happier lyrics be translated from English into Armenian, and games from Bancroft, Thomas, Curtis and Angell, be translated and taught to the children in groups of fifty. Acheson further asked that in their spare time, native workers translate simple plays for theatrical performances into the Armenian language, because, as he explained, Armenian plays were tragic rather than amusing. A translated play was to be performed every Saturday evening under the supervision of the local personnel.[743]

Dolls made by orphans using pieces of their own clothing and hair. (AGMI Collection)

Official NER publications praised the outcome of the measures taken to ensure the transformation of the orphans into happy children. Secretary of the Armenia-America Society in New York, George R. Montgomery, returned from a visit in Armenia to say that the "little, old, deformed men and women" had become happy children.[744] In fact, the very first thing Montgomery had announced upon his return from Alexandropol had been: "The children are happy!" He was hopeful that the future of the youth in the Caucasus would soon improve and "that the boys and girls of the Caucasus may be as successful in achieving future happiness as the boys and girls of America."[745]

The Merry-Go-Round. (RAC NEF Photos Box 153)

EDUCATION FOR CITIZENSHIP

It is difficult to determine the long-lasting impact the "Play" program had on the children. The games introduced to turn the children into carefree and happy beings seem to have engaged the children only in part, by contrast to the children's love of their native songs and dances. One assessment, published in the journal *The Playground* in 1927, showed that while there had been some improvement, problems in children's behavior still lingered on. Play, the article stated, was one of the best psychological and physical remedies and taught the children self-support. This was especially important for "The Armenian,"

> because the Armenian...is naturally serious, his folk songs are serious, his national anthem is a dirge.

> He can watch a thrilling event and make no sound of excitement. When to their native suppressions are added the depressions following upon disaster it requires a real making-over to permit expression. Near East Relief tried to bring about that making-over. One of its methods was by introducing both organized and free play, games and sports. The individualistic child who had been fending for himself for months, sometimes for a year or two, needed to have his heart opened to others, to learn team work. Trained recreation teachers set themselves to the task and taught the native teachers who passed on the lore...

> ...in former cavalry barracks at Leninakan, the thousands of children were organized with play captains and assistant captains, group leaders and assistant leaders for every twenty children. With the huge parade ground to perform upon the 68 games, which they learned, might all be going at once if it was desired. Prize flags were used to arouse competition.

But,

> There is still no shouting on the sidelines, incredible as it seems to us shouters of the Western World. That is the last step to be achieved in the teaching of play securing an expression of pleasure.[745]

Reflecting on the Play program some years later, Acheson had doubts about the effectiveness of the program to transform the listless orphans into happy children. The change in his position had followed an encounter with a 12-year-old boy in the City of Orphans. The 12-year-old had accompanied Acheson on his tours and had carried Acheson's heavy 4X5 Graphlex camera for days:

> He trudged along sturdily, nor would he surrender his heavy load to any other. He could not understand a word we said, but somehow he always managed to have the camera ready and at my elbow when it was needed.

It was on the last day of his visit in Alexandropol, when he wanted to thank the boy, that Acheson realized that none of the measures put in place could satisfy the one need the orphans had. He had wanted to thank the boy with a gift:

> I showed him my jackknife, and when he displayed slight interest I emptied my pockets and spread all my treasures before him—a gold pencil, a fountain pen, a tricky steel tape. I even suggested that if there was anything in the canteen on

which he had set his heart, I would buy it for him gladly, because he had been so useful and I wanted to have something "for memory's sake."

But the boy did not want a gift, wrote Acheson. Instead,

> He picked up the camera rather formally and handed it back to me, for his job was done.
>
> Then two little hands gripped mine, and with trembling lips and tear-filled eyes he said something passionately. "He says that all he wants is to be loved," said the interpreter, turning his face away and crying openly... Then he led the little boy away, and I was left alone.
>
> Here was a hunger that American dollars could not satisfy. It walked and slept with every one of the 17,000 children in Alexandropol constantly.[747]

Chapter Eight

CHARACTER BUILDING FOR WORTHY CITIZENSHIP

The ultimate goal of the various educational programs was to teach the children skills by which they could earn a living when they joined citizens outside the walls of the barracks. But was learning a skill sufficient for them to qualify for citizenship worth its name? Within the walls of the barracks most disagreed; they believed that greater challenges would need to be faced and conquered before full citizenship could be awarded. The reasoning seemed to be straightforward: the horrors of months and years of survival under perilous conditions, dislocation from their ancestral homes, and the loss of all that they held dear, had not only traumatized the children but had developed in them undesirable character traits. Those undesirable traits needed to be erased and the children would have to be re-educated with a code of ethics that would transform them into worthy citizens. That transformation could not be achieved overnight and needed sustained effort, NER believed.[748] After all, as Senator Henry J. Allen had commented, Armenians had for centuries been "hounded from pillar to post" and had not had "much time to spend in developing character, preoccupied as they had been with survival." "The greatest work Near East Relief is doing today" the Senator had declared, was that it was

> …planting in the hearts and in the minds of these children of Armenians a new picture of brotherhood, a new interpretation of that which is fundamental in the character of manhood and womanhood.[749]

The "new interpretation" of character, or character building, as James Barton explained in his chapter by the same title, was central to NER's educational vision. The struggle for survival had made "little animals" of the orphans, believed Barton, and had developed in them "the animal instinct of self-preservation without moral restraint."[750] The NER believed, and Barton agreed, that the mission of the orphanages was to transform the untutored, undisciplined child through relief workers:

> Starved, diseased, unschooled children formed the raw material that had to be remolded and remade…
>
> …Underneath the animal instincts of self-preservation, beneath the diseased, underfed body and forbidding exterior, there lay hidden the potentialities of youth to be nourished and trained for leadership…

This was the task to which the relief workers devoted themselves: feeding the body back to normal, training the mind into ways of usefulness and building character for the purposes of life. The tragic past had to be effaced by new activities.[751]

Inevitably, the substance of the "new interpretation," or the new ethical code, together with the methods by which it was transmitted to the future citizen, became the subject of protracted debates and confrontations between the authorities of SSRA and NER. During the First Republic of Armenia impassioned voices had argued that left to its own devices, NER would produce a generation of young Armenians without a uniquely Armenian national identity, traditions, or religious doctrine. With the SSRA government, the debates were predicated on political doctrine and lasted for nearly a decade, growing in intensity in the second half of the 1920s in tandem with Stalin's ascendancy. At no time was there complete agreement about the path the orphans would have to follow on their way to citizenship, nor did either party completely relinquish its exclusive right to chart their path. Each side wished to raise the future builders of Armenia in its own image: NER saw in them the apostles of Western values that would civilize the Near East, while the SSRA government envisioned the children as future Soviet citizens baptized in the doctrines of socialism, eager to build a soviet, socialist, progressive society.

It is doubtful that the children, whose characters were to be restored, were aware of the on-going debates between NER and government officials. What mattered to them, and what they experienced and witnessed without understanding the political or ideological underpinnings, were the implementation of such measures on their bodies and souls, experiences some orphans would remember well into their later life. Some former orphans would speak of these experiences during short or long interviews, others would record them in autobiographical memoirs which would either be published when such publications were allowed toward the end of the 20th century, or would remain among the family papers. Still others would record in the literary medium of short and long novels and poems, their experiences on the path toward worthy citizenship, and their experience with the relief workers who guarded that path.

This chapter comprises excerpts of varying lengths that relate to and present glimpses of what former orphans remembered and how they perceived of the process through which their character was to be formed and reformed at the City of Orphans. Among them are the memoirs of Khachik Dashtents (Khachik Tonoyan), born in the village of Dashtadem in Sassun in 1909 to a shepherd's family, written in Moscow in 1935, which Dashtents tentatively titled *De Profundis*;[752] the autobiography of Mihran Hovhannisyan, born in the Khastur village of Alashkert in 1908, entitled *Kensagrutyunner, kentsaghayin-sovorutyunner, hishoghutyunner, yeghelutyunner* (Biographies, Lifestyles-Habits, Recollections, Events);[753] an essay, *Mi petur im arciv kyankits* [A Feather from My Eagle Life], and a poem entitled *Im unker Lorike* [My Friend Lorik] by Hovhannes Shiraz (Onnik Karapetyan), born in Alexandropol in 1915; the autobiography of Garnik Stepanyan (Garnik Ter Stepanyan), born in Mamakhadun village of Yerznka in 1909 to a tailor's family, titled *Mghdzavanjayin orer,* [Nightmarish Days]; the autobiographical novel *Skaut*

#89 [Scout #89] by Mkrtich Armen (Mkrtich Arutyunyan), born in 1906 to a poor tradesman's family in Alexandropol;[754] and the autobiography of Araksi Pluzyan, born in an artisan's family in Van in 1909, entitled *Im kyanki patmutyune* [The Story of My Life].[755] Of the group, the memoirs of Khachik Dashtents, Mihran Hovhannisyan, and Araksi Pluzyan remain unpublished to date. Mkrtich Armen's autobiographical novel *Skaut #89* was published in 1933;[756] Garnik Stepanyan's *Mghdzavanjayin orer* was published in 2009;[757] and Shiraz's *Mi pedur im arciv kyankits* and *Im unker Lorike* appeared in 1984 and 1960, respectively.

Four of the above—Dashtents, Shiraz, Stepanyan and Armen—were well-known in later life: Dashtents as one of Armenia's premier literary figures; Shiraz as one of Armenia's beloved anti-establishment poets; Stepanyan as a prolific literary and art critic, playwright, and lexicographer; and Mkrtich Armen, whose popularity in large part came from his novel *Heghnar aghpyur* [Heghnar Fountain] published in 1935, and which in the early 1970s was made into a black and white film. Armen's *Skaut #89*, which is the longest account of life in the City of Orphans in the early 1920s, was regarded by some as ideologically biased and non-factual. More recent writings, however, consider it an accurate reflection of actual historical events, albeit with some exaggerations.[758] In addition to the above, this chapter also includes excerpts from interviews conducted with former orphans Vardges Aleksanyan,[759] Arusyak Hovhannisyan (Israyelyan),[760] and Aharon Manukyan.[761]

Taken together, these memoirs and short recollections speak of three broad and interrelated categories of measures designed to replace "undesirable" characteristics in the orphans with "desirable" ones: order and discipline; religious and ethical instruction and special punishment for the incorrigibles, often comprising physical and emotional abuse. The substance of the memoirs and the intensity of recollections depended in large part on the period of time at the City of Orphans and even more directly, on the particular teachers and relief workers with whom the orphan came in contact.

"Perfect Little Spartans": Order and Discipline

Strict order and discipline would bring much-needed structure and order to the life of the children, it was believed, and were made to permeate almost every aspect of life in the posts. One of the most poignant descriptions of the impact of order and discipline in the City of Orphans was written by Derenik Demirchyan in 1925. His essay entitled "A Great City of Little Children," appeared in *The New Near East*.[762] Demirchyan, a well-known poet, novelist, translator, and playwright who had attended the University of Geneva in the early 1900s, had been sent by the SSRA government in 1925 to inspect the City of Orphans. Demirchyan was overcome by the image of the army of children who seemed to him an "…overflowing sea of life packed into row after row of barracks." Demirchyan was especially struck by the strict order and symmetry that pervaded the City of Orphans and expanded on it throughout his report:

Children march in ranks in a long line to the dining hall, passing another long line on its way back from the dining hall. These are very little children, whose eyes have been opened on the world only for a few years. An Armenian nurse, red-cheeked and kindly, is holding one of them by the hand and the others are following her. They march behind her under the impulse of some instinct, silent and obedient, cheerful and happy.

On the endless rows of tables in the dining hall were "dishes all alike arranged symmetrically on the tables, endless rows of spoons and chunks of bread," where "child waiters bustled about, arranging everything." In the kitchens,

> …children at work again. Huge boilers, all alike, in which savory soup is boiling. Big tubs full of great quantities of sliced potatoes and cabbage, all alike and evenly cut. Every odd corner packed with supplies.

There were endless lines of beds in each dormitory and "endless lines of towels, one to each bed. First one dormitory; then another; then still another; endless lines of dormitories, full of beds," and each bed was numbered:

> Numbers everywhere,—on the bed, on the towel, on the child.
>
> But not, I think, on the child's soul.

Each one of the 11,000 young souls had a story, he wrote, and

> …each one of them *is* a story. You would like to know each story, if that were possible. You would like to stop and study each one, to see and know each little soul, but it is not possible. They are too many."

It was not a fairy tale, he added,

> …nor yet a dream. It is life. It is the future of Armenia.[763]

The outcome of such order and discipline, the spectacle of endless rows of children marching from dormitory to dining room, to class, to workshop and everywhere else in between, at the call of the bugle and the bell, had become the hallmark of the City of Orphans and had caught the attention of the international press. In March 1923, two years before Demirchyan's essay appeared in *The New Near East*, *The Hawera & Normanby Star* in New Zealand would write that only through discipline could the large orphan population in Alexandropol, "picked up from the highways and byways, from the gutters and alleys of Asia Minor" be so well organized:

> …When the rising bell sounds, 20,000 little heads are raised from their straw pillows and 20,000 little bare feet land with a thud on the floor. Unwashed faces and unmade beds are not permitted even in this family of 20,000. At the sound of the breakfast bell they must be ready to file in ranks of two across the compound to the dining halls, where at long wooden tables they have their bread and tea or bread and cocoa, the morning ration in all Near East orphanages.[764]

And discipline had its rewards, the paper continued. At the end of each week, the table showing the best etiquette would be rewarded by the privilege of displaying the American flag:

> Nor are table manners neglected. Each table is in competition with the other for neatness and order. If native teachers have not a watchful eye out, then the captain of the table spies a breach of etiquette. For each week the table is presented with

an American flag, a prize which incites even the youngest to heroic efforts at deportment.

Those disciplined children, the paper concluded, were the future of Armenia:

> Twenty thousand boys and girls are not many compared to the millions in America. But these overseas American wards are a nation of children—the hope, the nucleus of a new Armenia. And reared according to American ideals, these future citizens of a war-ravaged country are the hope of a better world over there.

Especially noticeable were disciplined children under eight years old, of whom Dr. Esther Lovejoy had spoken in 1922:

> ...They were perfect little Spartans. Their rations were simple, containing the proper proportions of the different kinds of food necessary for normal development. Their lives were absolutely regular. They arose, ate, went to school, to work, and to bed by the sound of the bugle.[765]

During photo-ops and filming sessions, wrote Lovejoy, groups of visitors were always watching the children assembled from the different posts drilling for the pictures, commenting, with some irony, that

> ...No group of children in the world are better prepared for communistic life than these children raised like Spartans in the American orphanages of Armenia...these children are not only physically and mentally, but psychologically equipped for service in the Union of Socialist Soviet Republics.[766]

Admiration of the disciplined children would only grow. While at the Polygon in 1924, Barclay Acheson watched the children when,

> At the sound of the dinner bell sturdy, bare-legged lads—5,600 of them—came swarming from every direction...so many of them were *little* chaps.

Dinner, as all meals, was eaten while standing:

> They gathered in the enormous dining-room and stood along the bare board tables in the unadorned halls and ate a thick vegetable soup from earthen bowls or munched the coarse brown head,

and, as the visitors passed by them,

> ...Literally hundreds of them, with wooden spoons held level with waiting mouths, would pause, as we passed, for a friendly grin of welcome to the "visitors from America."[767]

If discipline were to eradicate old habits, it would have to be consistent and could not show mercy, even to the hungry child. It would have to teach lessons that would not be easily forgotten, especially the lesson that they could no longer forage for food in trash piles, as they had done in the past for survival. It mattered not if they were left hungry after a meal—foraging was not allowed in the City of Orphans. Vardges Aleksanyan remembered in his advanced age that the child who had been caught foraging for food would be punished by being made to sit in a corner and watch the others eat while he remained hungry.[768] The lesson Mihran Hovhannisyan recorded in his autobiography involved an incident at the Polygon where a hungry orphan boy had picked up a discarded fish head from the kitchen floor. Before he could eat it, "Mishe"

[Miss Shayne] had spotted the boy and began to run after him. The boy had escaped, but

> "Mishe" was very angry; she declared that all the orphans would be denied food for a whole day and for the entire day she did not give us food or bread...[769]

And for a whole day, orphans were confined to their barracks.

The incident Mihran Hovhannisyan recounted about Myrtle Shayne was not singular. Arusyak Hovhannisyan (Israyelyan), remembered that

> One day an American director, Miss Shayne, saw a few of the orphans searching for food in the trash bins. To punish them, she denied everyone their daily food, and threw away that day's food. We stayed hungry an entire day.[770]

Mihran Hovhannisyan. (Hovhannisyan Family Private Collection)

Present at one such incident was Shushanik Ter-Grigoryan, one of the Armenian managers at the Polygon. Distraught by the cruelty of the punishment for such a petty misdoing, Ter-Grigoryan had entered a heated argument with an American administrator, and told her not to set foot in the orphanage again. "The children are ours," she had said, "You have come here and help us; you give us food and clothing. [But] their souls are ours; it is we who will bring them up.[771] Ter-Grigoryan tendered her resignation from her position in June 1921, and returned only after Myrtle Shane had left Alexandropol a few months later.[772]

The extent to which discipline was upheld at the Polygon emerges in one of the autobiographical sketches of Khachik Dashtents. On a spring day with nature in full bloom, an orphan nicknamed "the gravedigger" and known for his irreverence toward authority, had led a few of the hungry boys to dig up roots. Thirty minutes later, their faces were covered with green foam. They had returned to their orphanage before sunset with bloated bellies only to be met on the doorstep by disciplinarian Paron Yenok [Mr. Yenok], himself an orphan, who was taken aback by their appearance. By then the boys' behavior was odd and Paron Yenok concluded that they had eaten the wrong roots and had gone mad. Next follows a scene in Dashtents's memoir where all the boys are tied to the tree at Yenok's orders and "Miss Mann," their religion teacher, appears with her dog Jack on her way to the pool. The scene of the boys with foaming mouths tied to the tree terrifies Miss Mann:

Khachik Dashtents as a village teacher in the 1930s. (Anahit Dashtents Turabian Private Collection)

> "What is this that I see? Why have you tied them up?
> "They have gone mad," said disciplinarian Yenok.
> "Mad?" "Why have they gone mad?"
> "They ate wild grass..."
> "That is sad. This is the first time in my life that I see such a scene. This one, I think, had written that he wanted to be a poet," says Miss Mann pointing to Dashtents. "In my opinion, going mad is not a sign of becoming a poet."
> Looking at Miss Mann, Dashtents giggled...
> "Among these was someone who had written that he wanted to be a

CHARACTER BUILDING... 239

priest. Where is that boy?"

"He has gone mad, too…"

"What is in their bags?" asks Miss Mann.

"Grass."

"In their bellies?" asks Miss Mann again.

"Likewise grass."

"Children," said Miss Mann addressing the boys who had gone mad, "Are you not having enough to eat? But we have brought sweetened milk for you from America."

With that, Miss Mann smiled and calling Jack, calmly went her way.[773]

Oriord [Miss] Sandukhd, who had earned the less than endearing epithet of "Oriord Andund" [Miss Abyss] because of her stern adherence to discipline and the special zeal with which she applied it on the children, was the Armenian manager of Polygon's orphanage #2. She could not remain so passive as Miss Mann. Her anger exploded in a string of choice expletives and cusswords hurled at the boys:

> …you rebels, moths of our orphanage! You disgraced my name! Was I not saying that at an opportune time you would all be brigands?…I am terrified of your eyes and your gazes.

Oriord Sandukhd then looked at them threateningly, wrote Dashtents, and continued:

> How I yearn to beat your bodies, stomp you into smithereens under my feet, so that you will cease to exist, disappear from the face of the earth. What kind of opinion will a person form about our country after looking at you?…You take religion classes. You have gospels…!

> This is the time to study and not the time to go mad. Do you understand? Your manager is talking with you; you stone heads, heels of Satan, rebels, thieves of our orphanage, future assassins. How will I account for you before God, before Jesus Christ? Won't they say from your orphanage come assassins? They'll blame this poor guy [disciplinarian Yenok] because of you.

In the end, the boys are subjected to additional disciplinary measures: they are taken to the cold, semi-dark room in the cellar under the school, reserved by Mr. Morris for the confinement of rebellious children, and locked inside.[774]

"The Errant Lambs of Christ": Religious and Ethical Instruction

Mihran Hovhannisyan had entered the Polygon when he was about eleven years old. The days at the Polygon, he wrote, began with religious instruction where they were taught various prayers and the Ten Commandments. Those who did well in the class were awarded the "excellent" mark; those who did not, were punished. After they had woken up and washed in the mornings, they would say their first prayer, followed by another prayer before breakfast, and a third one after breakfast. And, every Saturday and Sunday they were taken to church for worship and more prayers.[775]

Hovhannisyan was transferred to Jalaloghli, very unwillingly; but still in some ways he had been relieved because, he thought, he would no longer have to be near "Mister Ogden" [Lester Ray Ogden], one of the directors at the Polygon. It was not long, though, before Mister Ogden appeared at Jalaloghli, as its director, bringing with him his strict observance of religious instruction for which he was known at the Polygon. One day, in protest against religious strictness imposed on them, the orphans decided to eat their meals without first saying a prayer. The defiance was reported by Armenian manager Paron Vahan [Mr. Vahan] to Mr. Ogden, who called a general meeting of orphans and staff and reprimanded them in a long-winded speech, all the while cracking his whip:

> You eat our American bread, and don't want to be subjected to us? Well, I'll show you, etc., etc.…![776]

Following the meeting, Armenian regional government leaders had come

> …and explained to us in detail that we should heed and be subjected to all the rules and laws of the Americans. They convinced us by saying "No matter what they expect you to do, you are obliged to do it." And once again, we became docile, praying three times a day…[777]

References to religious instruction at the Polygon occur several times in Dashtents's memoirs. One such episode begins on the day he first saw the barracks of the Polygon to which, he wrote, "were consigned an enormous army of Armenian orphanhood."[778] It was a cold September morning when the children had been made to stand by the walls, waiting to be registered. The process had continued till late evening, when they were finally assigned to various buildings according to their age, with about 700 children in each building. He was placed in the orphanage where the notorious Oriord Sandukhd reigned supreme.

Very soon after his arrival, a large church bell was brought and hung amidst the gray buildings. Then, one morning the orphans were told,

> With the tolling of this bell you must feel the dawning of the sun, and with the tolling of this bell you should wake up. Each peal of the bell should be a compass to you and each peal, a prayer. You must pray to God when you go to eat and you must pray when you go to sleep.

> And that morning at sunrise pealed the first toll of the bell and beneath its peal we learned to pray…

> And we entered the dining room in rows and ate our first meal under that same prayer.

Then, continues Dashtents, a church with no dome was built facing the bell, and a priest arrived with cymbals and incense. One morning the children were told:

> You must read the Gospels every Saturday at school, and every Sunday you must go to church, because you are little sinners and God must forgive you your sins.

> You must come down on your knees in the church, and you must pray on your knees and cross your faces, because you have all strayed and you must come out of your errant ways.

That Sunday,

> ...they took us to church in rows and the priest, burning the incense toward us, said:
>
> "You, the errant lambs of Christ...Where are your parents?"
>
> We crossed our faces and with our hats in hand, our heads bowed, docile and submissive, we left the church.

Then, continued Dashtents,

> ...they brought 50 militias. They gave them guns and said:
>
> "Encircle the Polygon, stand alert at your posts, each of you in one corner, and keep watch such that neither the bird on this side can leave nor the bird on the other side can come in..."
>
> Then they wove a thick, long rope and tied it along the length of the main entrance on the street side, and said to us: "Your fatherland is here, and your horizon ends here, where the rope begins..."
>
> ...And so began our life at the Polygon—on that gray and monotonous military plain, where only the sun used to console our sorrow and only the sun used to cherish us...[779]

Dashtents's narrative on religious education includes a description of the first class in religious instruction that took place immediately after breakfast. The teacher, Paron S. [Mr. S], enters the room, takes out his small gospel book, presses it against his breast and fixing his eyes toward the ceiling says a prayer. He next introduces himself to the children, asks them to place their gospels on their desks, and asks:

> "Children, do you know what the world is made of?"

The gravedigger raises his hand:

> "Why wouldn't we know?" says the gravedigger, raising a bony forefinger.
> "What is it made of, my son?"
> "The world, Paron S., is made of...a coffin."
> "My son...!"
> "No, No, Paron S. the world is a graveyard."
> "My son...! Listen, my sons, listen! I will now tell you what the world is made of. The world, my sons, is made of prayer. The world is the house of God; the world is a big steeple. We all come, toll the bell in turn and pray for God to hear. Whoever is just, God calls him to heaven, whoever in unjust, to hell. Is it clear, children?"
> "It is clear, it is clear," call the children in one voice, "there is only one thing that is not clear."
> "If there's anything left unclear, let me know, and I will clarify it."
> "You say the world is the house of God, Paron S., but why is there so little food in that house? Corpses are strewn everywhere; people are eating grass and going

> mad; children are grazing like lambs. God lives in heaven. He…doesn't have anything to do…"
>
> "My son, my son, shut your mouth. Atone, you have sinned against God."

Next, Baron S. moves on to the subject of arithmetic:

> "Now, children, I want to know whether you know how to count or not."
> "Why not, Paron S.," answers the gravedigger in a loud voice, buoyant.
> "So, who can present a multiplication problem?"
> "Let me say it, Paron S. Five coffins multiplied by six equal 30 coffins."
> "My son, you speak of a coffin again?!"
> "Say 'dead,'" suggests Ishkhanik, busy with his sketching, to the gravedigger.
> "Very well, Paron. There were ten dead in the poorhouse at the graveyard. On each of the dead there were five buttons. How many buttons total?"
> "There were a total of 50 buttons," answers Ishkhanik from where he was sitting, as he continues to sketch.
> "Children, my sons, let go of the dead and the coffins. I will ask you another question. Who is the greatest multiplier?"
> "It is Cacao, Cacao," answers Avag, nicknamed the cook.
> "That is wrong, the biggest multiplier is a man's belly," says Moses, nicknamed 'the general.'
> "Relax, children. If you don't know, let me say it. The biggest multiplier is God. God is the denominator and man is the numerator."
> "And who is Jesus Christ?"
> "Jesus Christ lives in heaven."

The bell rings, and the first class in religion ends with the teacher cautioning the children:

> Children, this is our first class in religion, and I say to you on behalf of God, be good, be obedient. Do not sin against God. Do not question that which should not be questioned. Evil is found outside the fence, on the other side, and good is found within the fence, on this side.[780]

Another scene from Dashtents's memoirs, which takes place at the gravedigger's funeral, highlights the imperative of the orphans' absolute submission to religious injunctions. Two evenings before the funeral, Oriord Sandukhd had punished the gravedigger especially severely for having listened to a recitation of Armenian mythology. There is no indication of where that recitation took place or by whom, but in the morning the gravedigger was the only one in the barrack to remain in bed after the sound of the bell. Oriord Sandukhd had arrived on the scene still seething with anger from the evening before, and seizing the boy's ankles, had pulled him down from the second tier of the bunk bed. The boy lay on the floor inert and unconscious. He was pronounced dead and his burial was scheduled for the following day. The funeral procession was led by Father Hyusik, with a Bible in hand and a cross hung around his neck. Behind the coffin marched the children from Oriord Sandukhd's orphanage, while the gravedigger's close friends took turns carrying the coffin. At the graveyard behind the hospital, Father Hyusik begins the last rites and then, picking up a handful of earth, strews it over the open grave. The next scene becomes dramatic: just as the coffin is slowly lowered into the open grave, the lid begins to move from the inside, and, in the next second it flies off, revealing the gravedigger in his underwear. The boy sits up, and looks angrily around him. The children are terrified and begin to step back from the grave. Father Hyusik is dumbfounded and orders the lid closed:

"Sleep, my son, sleep; earth you were, earth you shall become."

The gravedigger ignores the priest's exhortations and jumps out of the coffin. Still, the priest continues,

"My son, my son! Mea Culpa, my God! The dead are resurrecting! My son, come back and lay down in the coffin. Baron S., catch him. Earth you were, earth you shall become, my son; earth you were, earth you shall become…"

The gravedigger is incredulous:

"Woe, Father Hyusik, you want to bury me alive!
I spit on your gospel, on your cross, on your censer, on your god…Boys, push Father Hyusik into the hole."

Then, the gravedigger picks up a handful of earth, strews it on the priest and says,

"Earth you were, earth you shall become, from earth you were, dust you shall become, Father Hyusik! Jesus Christ! Jesus Christ!!"

The episode ends as the gravedigger turns to Baron S. and says:

"Baron S., did I not tell you that the world is made of a coffin?[781]

Dashtents's friend the gravedigger would meet an inglorious end. When the news of the gravedigger's "resurrection" and verbal exchanges with the priest spread through the orphanage, the medical committee, chaired by Dr. Johnson, decided that the gravedigger suffered from a disease that had caused a temporary stoppage of breathing. But the medical reason notwithstanding, the gravedigger from thereon was dubbed a rebel who had dishonored the Gospels and God. One week after his "resurrection" he had stolen one kilogram of wafers from Father Hyusik's stack of bread hidden behind the altar, planning to distribute the bread to his friends. But on his way out of the church the guards had caught him. The following day he was sentenced to spend his nights in the cellar under the school, his feet in shackles. The following week, the police took him away from the orphanage as a rebel, an atheist and a future thief.

Punishment for *"Incorrigible Mischief Makers"*

In the minds of those determined to reform lost souls, punishment was a necessary measure that included corporal as well as verbal abuse. The deeds that merited severe corporal punishment covered a wide spectrum, from listening to recitations of Armenian mythology, as was the case with the gravedigger, to foraging for food and stealing bread when the child was hungry. Corporal punishment was applied frequently and with special vehemence by some employees of the City of Orphans who carried with them whips and bullwhips at all times. The Armenian director of orphanage #9 at the Polygon, for example, was especially notorious for his ardent zeal for punishment with the use of a whip, for which the boys had nicknamed him "Gnut Artashes," [Whip Artashes]. Mihran Hovhannisyan recalled that Gnut Artashes

> …was a thin, tall fair-haired man…He…used to beat and punish the orphans a lot…the boys used to call him Gnut Artashes…because he often punished the boys with his whip.[782]

Of the 29 pages of Mihran Hovhannisyan's memoirs pertaining to life in various orphanages, a significant number relate directly to his experiences at the Polygon and Jalaloghli. He refers to "Mister Ogden" and "Dr. Hodor" (possibly Dr. Jefferson Hawthorne) with regard to the degree of cruelty they were each capable of. "They were cunning and tyrants," Hovhannisyan wrote:

> Every morning, Mr. Ogden used to go around the buildings and courtyards of the orphanages with a bullwhip in his hand. When he saw a child he did not like, he would whip the child so hard that the child would become unconscious.[783]

Hovhannisyan had observed that Ogden

> …wore boots, summer or winter, and always wedged in his boots was his whip; when he spotted a naughty child, he would whip the child.[784]

"Dr. Hodor," the Kazachi physician against whose repetitive abusive behavior toward orphans and colleagues a letter of protest had been written in the summer of 1920, had a different approach. He would go around the buildings and courtyards on his horse with binoculars hanging from his neck,

> …He would look through his binoculars to see which child was being naughty, then he would drive his horse at the child, throw him under his horse's hoofs and beat him with his whip.[785]

The methods used during corporal punishment at the Polygon were not limited to whipping the children unconscious. Hovhannes Shiraz, who was at the Polygon from around the age of five till about eight, had experienced several of them personally and described their application in a prose laced with bitterness and pain.[786] The orphanage, he wrote, "was a true hell":

> It was called the Polygon orphanage, where from the bud of my childhood was to bloom the flower of my youth. I remember the life of that orphanage; it was a vision of death, a dark journey of torture. A small mischief, a small misstep, and beatings were sure to come on the pathetic, half-starved child. They would strip the child naked; they would make him kneel all day long, naked, until evening.
>
> Oh, how many times have I stood, I mean, knelt, naked on those pebbles on a child's knees; but for which of my sins? I don't even remember it now. It was a sin that a butterfly would commit with a flower.
>
> But the horrible was yet to come.[787]

The beatings and kneeling became sweet memories for Shiraz after relief worker Joseph Beach established a particularly severe

Hovhannes Shiraz as an orphan. (Narine Khachatryan Private Collection. Photo also on exhibit at the Hovhannes Shiraz House Museum in Gyumri)

type of punishment for the "Incorrigible Mischief Makers." This particular form of punishment involved throwing a healthy child into a tub of yellow sulfur compound typically used at that time in the treatment of children with scabies. This measure would be used if the misdeed

> ...was very big, as for example, if they had stolen bread, a shoe, or a bed sheet. If the orphan was accused of theft, they would send him to the bathhouse. But what was that bathhouse...was that punishment? Oh, it was indeed punishment, an incredible thing. Those bathhouses were reserved for those who suffered from scabies. Healthy children were mixed with those who were being treated with a solution of sulfur...
>
> They twice threw me in that yellow hell...and even now, when I remember it, it is as if the smell of sulfur rises from my memories...
>
> I remember many, many things from that cruel hell...[788]

But, he wrote, addressing his reader,

> I do not wish to offend your feelings because I think you have not been an orphan and gone to such bathhouses...[789]

The future poet had been punished especially for escaping from the orphanage. But it was worth it, Shiraz wrote:

> ...from that dark and black hell I would often abscond and escape to the fields; others escaped to the city, toward the marketplace; but I used to escape to the green bosom of the valleys...until evening; and tired and hungry, I would return to my lair...[790]

He had known the consequences well. He would be beaten each time, but would do it again and again.

Relief workers and Armenian employees who had continuously inflicted physical pain on a child inevitably left lasting memories which did not diminish in old age: "Oriord Andund," "Gnut Artashes," Joseph Beach, "Dr. Hodor," "Mishe" and "Mister Ogden." One of the most feared was Ogden, who was transferred to one of NER's orphanages in Greece in the mid-1920s, where he was feared as much for his choice of punitive measures as for the enjoyment he received from the administration of such punishments. Garnik Stepanyan was among the boys in NER's orphanage in Oropos, Greece, where Ogden became director. Some details from Stepanyan's autobiography are excerpted below since they also relate to Ogden's approach to character building and behavior in Armenia.

Leonard Ogden had first impressed the children as a quiet, gentle, and soft-spoken man who visited their dormitories, the hospital and the classrooms, and shared their meals. All of that had endeared Ogden to the orphans. The orphans felt especially close to Ogden because they knew he had been in Armenia, had walked the streets of Yerevan and Alexandropol. They, the orphans, had only heard of Armenia, sang songs in Armenian, but had never been there. But Ogden had, and that made Armenia real for them. Soon, as Ogden had taken over the administration, he had begun to develop "strange habits, which surprised us, but gave him indescribable pleasure." "Those who disturbed discipline," wrote Stepanyan, Ogden subjected

> ...to indescribable physical punishment. Paron Sahak [one of the Armenian teachers at the orphanage] used to say in a voice trembling with fury, that such inhuman punishment was given only in the Middle Ages by the Catholic Inquisitors, without explaining to us what the Inquisition was.

Ogden derived pleasure when he saw two children fight, Stepanyan continued:

> ...Ogden would appear out of nowhere. He would stop the fistfight. He would not try to find out who was guilty and who was innocent. He would have two pairs of boxing gloves brought to him, put them on their hands, explain the rules of boxing through an interpreter, and about the parts of the body they should hit and the parts they should not, and why. He would then distance the opponents from each other, and would give the signal to strike.

> The harder they hit each other, inflicted pain [on each other], the greater was the gratification of the American...He showed absolutely no sign of a conscience, even when one of the opponents who had a weak stature, was being beaten brutally while the other remained unharmed. When the match was over with the defeat of one side...he would approach the fighters, take off their gloves, cool them with a towel, and would ask them to shake hands and reconcile.[791]

Garnik Stepanyan in 1928. (Stepanyan 2009)

The fighters would do as they were told but only for Ogden's benefit. "Such boxing punishments,"

> Were held in public...so that they would have a didactic significance. While he calmly watched the cockfight, we orphans would feel sorry for the victim even if he was not our friend. On occasion, we cried and were filled with hatred toward Ogden.

> ...At night he had the habit of walking through our bedrooms, unseen by us. When he caught someone being disorderly, he would appear immediately, and say very calmly: "Come here..."[792]

In Stepanyan's account of life in the Greek orphanage, over 50 pages evolve around "Mister Ogden" and events associated with him. Ogden had organized a camp in August 1925, where he continued the method he used in Alexandropol, of gathering the children to listen to his lessons on morality every day. At first Ogden announced that for the first of their sessions, he would speak on any subject the boys asked him to. The answer from the boys was unanimous: Armenia. At that,

> Mister Ogden smiled, bent his head and uttered two words: O, Armenia, Armenia...There is no Armenia...

Ogden had uttered the last phrase in Armenian—*Chka*, it does not exist. Then, Ogden's

> facial expression changed...He said that our Armenian teachers had given us the wrong education and continued to do so, by constantly talking to us about an imaginary Armenia.

"Armenia," Ogden continued:

> ...does not exist...There is a country that used to be called such, a country, where widespread poverty, squalor, backwardness reign, which is filled with orphans, the diseased, thieves and bandits. People there are godless, they even rebel against their benefactors...And where there is no God, there cannot be moral comprehension, kindness, loyalty.[793]

Ogden advised the children not to be carried away by such reveries but learn only that which was necessary to make an honest living.

The topics Ogden discussed in other sessions covered health and hygiene, which Stepanyan felt would have been valuable for the children in later life, except that Ogden often discussed it by bringing examples from the Alexandropol orphanages and always in a negative sense. Ogden also gave the boys lessons on sex education, especially focusing on the evils of diseases transmitted through sexual activity, and led to inevitable death. To ensure that the boys understood the dire consequences of the sexual instinct, Ogden put in circulation the Armenian translation of a book entitled *Gerezman yeritasardats* [Grave of the Youth], which he had asked to be sent to him from Athens.

An especially painful event had to do with the summer camp where Stepanyan spent some time in August 1925, when Ogden's extreme use of physical punishment had resulted in the death of a Greek orphan boy by the name of Banayit. When Stepanyan and his friends arrived at the scene, Banayit was being punished publicly for stealing three clusters of grapes, for which he was to receive 40 lashes. On the faces of the orphans gathered there, wrote Stepanyan,

> ...was the expression of terror. Banayit, the most intelligent, shiest and disciplined orphan, a Greek boy, had been tied to the tree with a thick rope, naked to the waist.
>
> Standing next to him was Mister Ogden, impassive, calm, with three clusters of grapes by his feet...
>
> Mister Ogden arranged for a fresh branch from a willow tree to be brought to him. He took off the leaves, straightened the stick on his knees and swung it in the air a few times...
>
> He gave the stick to an older orphan and ordered him to lash Banayit's naked back and legs forty times...The boy was hesitating. It was not a pleasant task. The translator explained that it was meaningless to refuse.
>
> We did not see the first strike. As soon as the stick went up in the air, we instinctively shut our eyes. We only heard Banayit scream "O, Mother" in Greek.
>
> Poor boy, what mother! We had been denied a mother's tenderness a long time ago, but each time we were in a difficult spot, we used to yell "O, Mother."[794]

Banayid had lost consciousness after the twentieth strike of the lash. But still the lashing had continued.[795] Banayit's face had turned the color of lead and the impressions of the rod on his back had increased. Ogden was

> ...watching the red stripes on Banayit's back...no sign of a conscience could be seen on Ogden's face. His blue eyes were sparkling.

After the 20th lash Banayit could no longer scream; he was unconscious...his head hung to his shoulder like a ripe poppy bud. His face had changed; it had become the color of lead. We could no longer look at him now. Only Mister Ogden was looking at him...

The beating ceremony was over. They cut Banayit's rope. Unconscious, he fell under the tree. The cluster of grapes he had stolen was next to his face. We were all in trepidation. We wanted to come to his help, do something. [But] We dared not.

Mister Ogden sat next to him, ordered for water to be brought. He calmly held Banayit's arm, touched his pulse. He sprinkled water on his face, rubbed his temples.

Banayit slowly opened his eyes, looked at Ogden...The American stroked his head, coddled his hair, his cheeks, and then said, through an interpreter, that there is nothing worse in this world than stealing, and nothing more beneficial than the beatings given for it, which hurts the body, but heals the soul, purifies it...

He carefully put Banayit's head on the green grass. He called for the interpreter again. He whispered something into his ear. The interpreter stood up and spread out his arms. We understood...[796]

An oppressive mood had persisted in the orphanage in the next days. The boys wandered if Mister Ogden had committed the same brutalities in Armenia. One orphan was sure it would have been impossible: "There, it is Armenia, they wouldn't let him do what he wanted, to torture innocent boys like that." Nevertheless, the orphans had decided to ask Hakob, Ogden's interpreter. Hakob confirmed that Ogden had used the same extreme punishments in Armenia, that he had brutalized many of the orphans and that at the end, a group of orphans unable to bear his severe methods, had escaped from the orphanage. The interpreter then recounted an incident where Ogden had heard that one of the orphans in the Polygon had stolen a loaf of bread and distributed it among his fellow orphans and had punished the orphan with his rod. But that had not been sufficient punishment: Ogden had arranged that the boy would spend the night under the eave of the roof in -30 degree temperature, with only one cover. Unable to endure the cold, the boy had cut up the cover, turned it into a rope, climbed down from the roof and had disappeared in the dark of night.[797] Hakob also told the orphans, very cautiously, that a few older orphans had one day overcome Ogden and beaten him up severely. It was following that incident that Ogden had left Armenia.

It is unclear if Barclay Acheson was familiar with the details of Ogden's treatment of orphans, but he was not, Acheson wrote in his diary in 1927, "very much in sympathy with Ogden's tattletale methods of discipline":

> We have always been conscious of his devotion to the boys and the effect of his work, but I really fear that he is a little cracked—at least he has a persecution complex.[798]

It is unclear, however, when and if Ogden was released from NER service.

Physical punishment in NER orphanages remained in practice in the latter half of the 1920s. A note dated February 23, 1925, from SSRA Liaison Georgy

Sargsyan cautioned Citizen Brown (Milton Brown, Director of Orphans in Alexandropol) that Armenian government bodies had frequently received complaints about orphanage managers Smbat and Sandukhd Kyalashyan, and teachers Mariam, Gohar and Heghush. These complaints, Sargsyan continued, had caught the attention of the Commissariat of Enlightenment, which in turn had no choice but to instruct the appropriate governmental bodies to conduct an investigation into the allegations. The investigation had shown, Sargsyan explained, that without a doubt, the aforementioned individuals practiced severe physical punishment with the children, such as beatings or locking them up in cold rooms. As a result, children escaped from the orphanages and spread all kinds of stories about the orphans' lives in the orphanages. Keeping such employees at the orphanage, concluded Sargsyan, served as an encouragement to others, and served neither the best interests of NER nor of the State. Sargsyan asked that Brown release them from their employment and send them to his office.[799]

Sandukhd Kyalashyan had evidently not been fired from her position because an inquiry from Deputy Commissar Yaghupyan, dated November 18, 1926, directed G. Sargsyan to investigate complaints that had arrived in his office. Sargsyan's answer came on December 18, 1926.[800] The subject of the report was a young man of 23, Levon, a former orphan, who now held the position of manager at orphanage #8. Levon was known for his use of severe punitive measures to maintain discipline in the orphanage. Sargsyan had met with a number of orphans and concluded that complaints about disciplinary methods were not groundless. While such measures as beatings and internment were not lacking at the orphanages in general, Levon and his colleague Sandukhd Kyalashyan exercised these measures systematically and with particular fervor. And should there be a decision to begin legal procedures, suggested Sargsyan, the two should appear in court together. Sargsyan reported that in his meetings with the administration at the orphanage, he had been told that strict punitive measures practiced at the orphanage were in part due to the fact that the staff was overworked and tense. But Sargsyan thought that to be a mere excuse. He argued that rather than using severe measures to discipline the children, managers should find alternative pedagogical methods to help orphans develop intellectually and emotionally. The methods used currently, he believed, only reinforced negative characteristics in the orphans, such as subservience and perversion. Much of what transpired in NER's orphanages, he added, was still unknown, and much of the internal life of the orphanage was shrouded in secrecy. He suggested that first, the Commissariat of Enlightenment should tighten supervision over the orphanage, and second, that it should infuse the orphanages with Pyoner [Pioneers]—communist youth between 10 and 12 years of age—organizations. That, he added, would be a better approach than discipline by beatings.

Sargsyan ended his report by bringing in another, but in his mind, a related issue. It is not possible not to mention another circumstance here, he wrote, that most of the older girls discharged from the NER orphanage have lost their virginity.[801] A special physical examination conducted on orphan girls as prospective workers at the textile factory in Leninakan, had revealed that 33%

of the girls were not virgins. He urged a special investigation at the orphanage to determine the circumstances that had led to that situation, and added that he had already designed a basic plan for that purpose.

Equally noted for his use of physical punishment had been Joseph Beach, who in 1926 was the Managing District Commander. In December 1928, Beach sent a memo, dated December 15, to Caleb Flagg, later the Acting Managing Director, detailing an incident that had occurred in his office. The memo, which was to be disseminated among the Polygon personnel, explained how Beach had personally delivered corporal punishment to 14-year-old Aristakes Hayrapetyan because the latter had disobeyed Beach's order to clean the cowshed, insisting that his responsibility was to milk the cows only. Beach explained that the punishment had taken place in his office on December 12, described how the punishment had been delivered, and outlined the additional punishment that was to be upheld by the staff:

> I slapped his face three times, and then, put him on a chair and struck his backside eight times...
>
> Because he refused to follow exact orders, he must be punished in the following way:
>
> 1. He is forbidden to attend school for one month, or until such time that through his good behavior, he earns permission to attend school.
> 2. He will work in the cowshed for one whole day.
> 3. In the orphanage he must be punished by receiving water and bread only for three days.
>
> I ask each of you to follow through so that his punishment is carried in full.[802]

The Meandering Path of Character Building: *"Oriord Sandukhd," "Miss Maka"* and *"Mister Vord"*

At the City of Orphans, the children's pathway to "worthy citizenship" was neither coherent nor uniformly applied. This had to do, in large part, with the fact that it was predicated on individuals from widely varying backgrounds in education, religious faith and pedagogical approach. One approach that stood in sheer contrast to Oriord Sandukhd's was the one that was typified by Janet MacKaye, who spent almost the entire decade of the 1920s working with the orphans. In the early 1920s, the group of orphans at the Severski—all less than eight years old—lived under her care in an oasis of love. Her wards were known as *The Blue Babies*, so called because they all wore little dresses and baby-boy suits of blue chambray with white collars and trimmed with bits of embroidery on the pockets, all made possible through Miss MacKaye's friends and her personal resources. The building they lived in at the Severski had a playroom that differed from the bare rooms of the other barracks: pictures were hung on the walls, there were toys in play-pens for the youngest children, and a small phonograph, gifts sent by Miss MacKaye's friends. Janet MacKaye was, wrote

Mabel Elliot, "the point in Seversky where emotion breaks through routine"[803] and not only because of what the children wore or their unique surroundings. "A hundred times a day," Elliott continued, "in all the posts, a child timidly touched your skirt and searched your face with eyes hungry for a smile that would be all her own. They waved and called "Good Night" to any passing American, asking for attention and affection." But not Miss Mackay's *Blue Babies*:

> ...The Blue Babies did not ask for your interest and affection; they took them, happily, expecting them from you because they had always had them from Miss MacKaye.[804]

If Janet MacKaye's orphans at the Severski felt assured of her love, some orphans at the Polygon had a different perspective: that the orphan's life was not valued even as much as a dog's. The sense of worthlessness blares through Hovhannes Shiraz's poem *Im unker Lorike*, dedicated to Shiraz's friend Lorik, an orphan boy who had lost his parents during the deportations from Van and had eventually found shelter at the Polygon.[805]

Lorik's story begins on a hot summer day when the orphans escape to the fields to cool themselves down in the Arpachai River, knowing full well that they would be punished if "Mister Vord," the bespectacled director of their orphanage were to catch them. Shiraz does not remember the latter's full name, only that it was mister something or other, ending in "vord," and in his poem, dubs him "Mister Vord." Mister Vord was sometimes nice, other times hateful, but for the slightest mischief he would pull an orphan's ear so hard that it turned deep red, and then would mockingly cry "Look, the orphan's ear turned as red as my dog's tongue."

While playing in the fields one day, Shiraz and his friends get a whiff of meat being barbequed nearby. "There's a feast!" they cry and run toward the aroma. This was not the first time that they followed the aroma of barbequed meat. The aroma told them that there was a feast somewhere; they would find it and then stand around, looking pitiful and sad, until the guests got drunk enough to throw them a few morsels. As they approach the feast this time, they suddenly turn ashen, horrified: they had spotted Mister Vord seated at a table among some wealthy guests, enjoying food and drinks. Then they overhear part of the conversation at the table:

> "This is our last feast…"
> "Don't speak, my heart is full."
> "I will take the orphans away."
> "Take them, you'll be doing good, if they allow you…"
> "Who are they not to allow me…!?"

Gingerly, the boys begin to backtrack like lambs that had just spotted the wolf. But just then, Mister Vord looks in their direction. The orphans now begin to run in the direction of the river but are intercepted by Mister Vord and his dog and chased to the Arpachai. In the final scene in the narrative, Lorik and Mister Vord's dog are in the river fighting an undercurrent. Lorik's friends urge him to come out of the water, but Lorik is busy trying to save the dog. The dog is saved but Lorik is unable to resist the undercurrent and drowns.

Mister Vord spares no effort to save the dog, and pulls it out of the water into safety. As the orphans search for Lorik, Mister Vord tells them to go clean up so he can take them to America. And, he says, whoever doesn't come, "I will beat him up, and send him to Lorik." At that point, the orphans, screaming and crying, begin to hurl rocks at Mister Vord, who runs away together with his dog. From that night on, the orphans do not return to the orphanage. They live on the streets and survive as beggars and petty thieves and by selling water.

Equally inconsistent were the approaches evident in the Boy Scout program—the one under Vahan Cheraz at the Kazachi, and the other under Ray Ogden at the Polygon. While both aimed to restore character, they were based on disparate perceptions of the children under their care and the mission they each ascribed to their scouts. For Cheraz, who believed in strict discipline, his job was nothing less than the preparation of a strong, self-confident and healthy generation of Armenians whom he would train morally, physically and intellectually. His mission, Cheraz felt, was unlike any other. In the orphanages, he wrote, "there is a huge mass of thousands, with no names, pale, without smiles, but nevertheless precious…"[806] The negative characteristics they now had were not innate but had been acquired during their traumatic young lives. With the proper training and guidance, all orphans had the potential to soar above the depths of their existence, to become strong men and women, with self-dignity and purpose in life, all wrapped in unconditional love from him, their scoutmaster. In his letters to friends in Istanbul and France, Cheraz often described the scouts as "lion cubs," who were

> …the glory and honor of Kazachi Post…[807]
> Can anyone call my boys orphans now? They're pashas, princes, angels, lions but not orphans.[808]

In the fall of 1922, Cheraz assigned to his boy scouts an unusual responsibility: to stand guard by the orphanages occupied by the older girls at the Kazachi. The new assignment came immediately after Cheraz confirmed rumors that large quantities of aborted fetuses were buried under the mounds around the girls' latrines. Wishing to confirm or dispell the rumors once and for all, he had decided to investigate and had sent an NER messenger to his friend Onnik Yazmajyan to join him in the investigation, post haste.[809] Yazmajyan, who would recount the incident some years later,[810] had arrived at the Kazachi scout house at 9:30 in the evening to find Cheraz on his bed, terse and uncommunicative. "Untill 11pm that night" Yazmajyan wrote, "Cheraz answered my questions with the silence of a stone. Then, all of a sudden, rising to his feet, he ordered the scouts, boys and girls, to gather around and bring with them shovels and pickaxes." The group moved in silence to a remote area within the Kazachi compound, where Cheraz ordered the scouts

> …to dig a hole three meters wide in diameter and 1.5 meters in depth. The hole was ready in a few minutes.
>
> We set out again, and without a sound surrounded a former barrack assigned to orphan girls.

> We entered the orphanage with about 50 girl scouts; Cheraz ordered the toilets to be opened wide…
>
> He [Cheraz] was the first to step into the sewer…

Yazmajyan next described how the group returned to the pit they had dug earlier to bury the remains of unborn fetuses collected from the sewer:

> Using the handles of two shovels, Cheraz prepared a cross, slipped a note into an empty bottle and threw it in the pit with the aborted fetuses.

The funeral ceremony ended with prayers as the scouts covered the pit with earth. That same night, Cheraz issued an order to have the female Armenian manager of the orphanage building where the fetuses had been discovered, arrested and taken to jail. Yazmadjian's account does not include the manager's identity nor any details about the circumstances whereby the sewers had been filled by unborn fetuses. It does, however, mention that from then on, scouts guarded the orphanages of the older girls, day and night.

Across town at the Polygon, Leonard Ray Ogden felt that his task was a difficult one because the children were "not very promising material from which to make upright citizens." His solution was to experiment with small groups of about two hundred at a time by taking them to a camp away from the orphanage where they would have no communication with the world outside. Every evening at the campsite, Ogden would gather his scouts around the campfire, and would teach the boys lessons from the Bible. He would also frankly tell the boys that he had heard people say:

> …Armenians are a crafty, dishonest, lying people. It infuriates them. I've seen the whole hundred around a camp fire, so angry that they choked when they tried to speak…I tell them that people are justified in having a low opinion of Armenians, because there are Armenians who *do* lie and cheat and steal. They all know it. I say that as long as their own people disgrace them, they have no right to resent others having a bad opinion of them. It is up to them to clean their own house, if they want other people to take off their shoes when they come in…

Ogden was especially annoyed that many of the orphans bore a grudge against humanity for the cruel hardships they had endured, and during his talks around the campfire he taught the boys to liberate their "warped little minds from grudge":

> Many of these warped little minds have to be freed of "grudge." Some have to be untangled from a web of thought that has led them to feel that the world owes them something and consequently that they owe the world little. Many have bent under the weight of the very word "orphan" and feel they cannot surmount the stigma that attaches to it…

His teachings, Ogden believed, had given a few hundred boys fine ideals of manhood and of service, and prepared the leaders for the new Armenia.[811]

Added to the mix of contradictory, if not mutually exclusive approaches to character formation was the insistence of the Soviet Armenian government that character building and upbringing should be anchored in socialist ideology. People's Commissar of Enlightenment A. Mravyan had cautioned

NER in April 1923 that to avoid future misunderstandings, it was to be clearly understood that all NER schools and kindergartens were obligated to follow the educational vision of the government, the most important goal of which was to promote socialist principles among the young generation.[812] Watchful over the process of character building, liaison officers frequently reported that older pedagogical methods continued to be practiced at the City of Orphans and that foreign missionaries and members of the former military and intellectual class of Armenia taught the laws of God.[813] In his July 17, 1924, report to Lukashin, for example, Sargsyan suggested that to change the existing practices, especially in orphan upbringing, it was necessary to closely supervise the Armenian teachers NER hired, because

> …The task of upbringing has been turned over to adventurers or religiously inclined elements, which secure their careers by flattery and through other turpitudes before the high-ranking American staff.
>
> This issue is not secondary for us; it is similar to slow death.

Sargsyan's suggestion was to more closely and systematically scrutinize the current teachers and those who would be hired in the future:

> It is necessary to carefully verify the teaching cadres before the 1924–25 academic year and to remove all those who are unacceptable to us, in accordance with the agreement with NER. But that should be done without delay…because the *post-factum* verification of lists of teachers does not yield desirable results and would only cause complications with NER, as the past years have shown. The best thing would be for the People's Commissariat of Enlightenment to send a special person here for that purpose.[814]

A week later, July 24, 1924, the Commissariat of Enlightenment had taken action. To ensure that state guidelines were being followed, Tigran Musheghyan, representing the Commissariat of Enlightenment, was sent to Leninakan on the suggestion of Sergei Lukashin. In a note marked "Secret," Sargsyan was informed of Musheghyan's upcoming visit and was asked to facilitate the latter's mission in Leninakan. Musheghyan, the note read, would also be conducting a purification of NER's Armenian teachers and employees.[815]

The SSRA government also resorted to another intervention of the "new interpretation" of manhood and womanhood, by recruiting young

Note about Musheghyan's mission at the City of Orphans marked "Secret." (NAA 113/38/42)

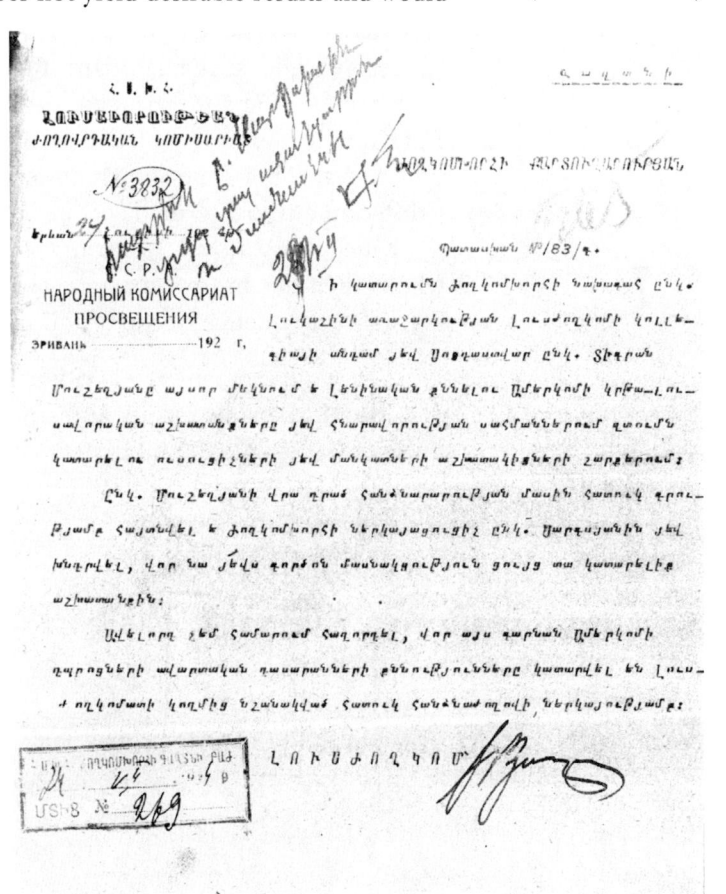

boys to secretly infiltrate the American orphanages and establish secret cells of Patkoms or Boy Communists. The first association of Patkoms in Armenia had been established in Yerevan on June 15, 1921, and the one in Leninakan a month later, on July 15.[816] Ideologically opposed to the boy scouts being formed concurrently at the Kazachi, the Patkoms had been raised in the spirit of Communism, and their assignment was to infiltrate, report on, and eventually destroy Kazachi's boy scout program. In their official organ, *Patkom*, the scouts were painted as the personification of all that was evil, against whom the Patkoms were to wage merciless battle.[817] In 1924, *Patkom* called on the young communists to convert the orphans in the American orphanages to communism:

Patkoms of Leninakan and Stepanavan!
Contact the orphans of the American Committee [NER],
Contribute to their Leninian education[817]

Mkrtich Armen. (http://nakhshkaryan.blogspot.com/2012/12)

Among the earliest to infiltrate the ranks of the scouts at Kazachi in 1921 was 15-year-old Mkrtich Armen [Mkrtich Arutyunyan] whose 228-page long illustrated autobiographical novel *Skaut #89* [Scout #89], is by far the most detailed narrative about the Kazachi to date. The narrative begins in early May 1921, when Armen enters the Kazachi, and flows through experiences, incidents and acquaintances he makes, much of which increase his resolve against the rampant injustice, excessive corporal punishment, and discrimination at the Kazachi, all of which he duly reports to the provincial RevKom in Alexandropol. He is told from the beginning that Kazachi Post is not Armenia, but America, that there, a different set of rules were in place and a different authority ruled.

Much of the novel is devoted to the success of the young communist cells, whose membership grows by each passing day and which #89 explains as a natural consequence of the brutal treatment of orphans.[819]

Skaut #89 being shown his bed. (Armen 1933: 16. Sketch by Sh. Hovhannisyan)

The scout movement was officially banned in SSRA in 1923. As the nucleus of a future nationalist army and a progeny of bourgeois society it was by definition unacceptable by the tenets of socialism. And now the scouts, along with a growing number of orphans, had entered the ranks of young communists. They met secretly in the remote areas of the City of Orphans, in the open air, away from the eyes of their American benefactors. But to do so in the winter months, the young communists occasionally asked for, and received support from an employee, despite the administration's strict regulations. One such employee was Mariam Margaryan, manager of Polygon's orphanage #8. In her short, unedited, and unpublished autobiography written years after the Americans had left, she described the secrecy that had shrouded their meetings:

> There was an underground young communists' organization in the Polygon. The Americans were very watchful, so as to catch the organization's members, as a result of which it was very difficult for the organization to hold meetings in the orphanages. In the summer, they somehow managed to meet outside, between rocks, in the fields, but during the winter months, that was altogether impossible.

One day,

> Being certain that I would accept and help them in every way so that they would hold their meetings in a normal way, the children took a risk and asked if they could hold their young communists' meetings in my room at certain times of the night.
>
> Their surprise was great when, without hesitation, I acceded to their request, especially since I knew that in the event of a small suspicion, the Americans would fire me from my job within the hour.

"To this day," she added in her autobiography, "the children of Orphanage #8, especially the young communists, remember my deed with gratitude."[820]

Satik, or Orphan # 4654

Mkrtich Armen's novel carries an obvious ideological bias against Americans and openly distrusts the American "uncles" and "aunts." Armen's primary targets, however, are not the Americans, but the counter-revolutionary Armenian staff of the orphanages—especially Vahan Cheraz—that catered to the Americans, and were sanctioned by them.[821] Although *Skaut #89* was not Mkrtich Armen's most popular novel, he returned to the same theme 21 years, in 1954, and published an expanded, 458-page long version entitled *Karmir yev kapuyt poghgapner* [Red and Blue Neckties]. When he again revisited *Skaut #89* in 1971, it was in an article entitled *Amerkomi gorcuneyutyune Hayastanum*[822] [The Activities of Amerkom in Armenia], where he insisted that the incidents he had revealed in *Skaut #89* were based on facts and not calculated to stir up agitation among its readers, as his critics had maintained. Just as a black and white film of his most popular novel *Heghnar aghbyur*[823] premiered in Yerevan, Armen redirected his readers' attention to the brutalities perpetrated at the Kazachi. He now maintained that NER had fed, sheltered, and clothed thousands of orphans and refugees, and that this was made possible by the generosity of the American people who had helped Armenia in its time of need. But, he insisted, there could be no doubt about the injustices and severe punishment inflicted on what had remained of the nation. He was sure that some of the American relief workers dealt in their own "small businesses" by exchanging precious objects with used clothes donated by the generous American people; that as an organization, NER was in the region to secure the business interests of the U.S. government, especially in the oil wells of Baku; and that when the Soviet Union collapsed, as many believed it would, the U.S. government would have a foothold in the Caucasus through NER. Nowhere in the article, however, does he mention Scoutmaster Vahan Cheraz, in whose eventual demise he may have played a role.

Armen died one year after he had published his final defense of *Skaut #89*. Despite its ideological bias, much of the feelings and observations recorded by Armen correspond to those recounted by orphans who carried no ideological or doctrinal biases, then or later. The exception is a singular episode about 14-year-old Satik, whose fate deeply embitters #89, and reveals the worthlessness of an orphan, in this instance an orphan girl. "My name is Satik," she says, when they first meet by chance in a small room by the belfry of the Kazachi church where #89 was on guard duty:

> "You won't forget?" Satik asks.
> "Why would I forget?"
> "Satik. You say 'Tatik,' and it will come to you."
> "Yes, it will come to me."
> "Scout, would you like us to be friends?"

The scout nods. Satik reaches into her blouse, and pulls out a round, metal piece and says:

> "Now that we're friends, take my number and keep it with you—4654…And your number…eighty nine?…Fine, I'll remember it…"

Scout #89 puts the metal piece with Satik's orphanage number in his pocket and looks at her, smiling. Satik smiles back. Then, covering her face, she says:

> "Scout, come and kiss me so that we won't forget each other."

Laughing, #89 puts his wooden stick down, moves closer to Satik, and kisses her.[824] But the budding first love is interrupted in the following days when Satik disappears. #89 searches for her everywhere, but to no avail. Finally, some time later, while parading with other scouts in front of the "House of the Americans," he spots Satik and steps out of the parade:

> "Satik…?" he asks, incredulous.

Satik is shaken. She stops and looks around:

> "Eighty nine?!"…She exclaims.
> "Where have you been, Satik jan? Where have you been…?
> "You have changed so much, you've filled in, gotten darker…" says Satik with admiration, without answering his question.
> "Satik," asks 89 impatiently, "tell me about yourself…Was that you last Saturday night standing by the door of the Americans?"
> "It was I…"
> "What are you doing here…?"

Satik lowers her head and shrugs her shoulders:

> "I don't know," she says under her breath, a little while later.
> "You don't know what you're doing here…?" Eighty-nine asks, surprised.
> "No."
> "You don't want to say it…"

Satik is fearful; she looks around her:

> "Let's move a little to that side. The Americans will see from the window…"
> "Do you want to go to the room by the belfry?" suggests eighty-nine.
> "Let's go. I'll tell you everything, scout…"[825]

But barely have they taken two steps when all of a sudden, Mr. Nonse steps before them. Swearing at #89 in English, Mr. Nonse takes Satik back to the house of the Americans.[826] Satik's story ends when the same American to whom she had been made to provide her services gives Satik away in marriage to a man who had come to fetch a bride from the orphanage. As marriage negotiations are in progress, "Mister Nonse" asks Satik:

> "Do you want to get married?"

Satik looks at him with hatred in her eyes and says calmly:

> "It's all the same to me…"
> "Satik, what do you mean it's all the same?" screams #89.

Satik taken away by "Mister Nonse." (Armen 1933: 133. Sketch by Sh. Hovhannisyan)

It is then that Satik realizes #89 had been privy to the negotiations. Her eyes fill with tears, but she says nothing. Mister Nonse laughs at #89, eyeing him with contempt, then invites the groom-to-be to the administration office to finalize arrangements. Before he leaves, he turns to one of the orphan girls standing next to #89:

> "And you, Arshaluys, you come to my room starting tomorrow…"[827]

The groom-to-be leaves with Satik. They have gone a short distance when Satik looks back and calls: "Farewell, eighty-nine…" The episode ends as Satik reaches into her pocket and pulls out a handkerchief. Satik is crying.

How close the frequently contradictory approaches came to charting the way to an exemplary manhood and womanhood is difficult to assess. But by the mid-1920s, new plans for recasting the mission of the City of Orphans were in progress, creating along the way additional problems for the government of SSRA, NER, and above all for the children of the City of Orphans. The new plans involved a sharp reduction of the orphan population of the City of Orphans—a mass disbursement—that did not stop till summer 1929.

Chapter Nine

OUTPLACEMENT, DOWNSIZING, AND THE RESHAPING OF THE CITY OF ORPHANS

Not long after orphan concentration had concluded, the orphan population of the City of Orphans began to decline—at first gradually, then sharply beginning in 1924, when NER launched a program of reducing the orphan population as quickly as possible.

The gradual decline was evident earlier, as significant numbers of families, now in a better position to provide for their children, reclaimed them from the orphanage. Reclaiming had been especially noted in 1923, when NER announced that orphanages in Yerevan would be closed and the children transported to Alexandropol. At that time, to prevent the possible exploitation of the children by imposters posing as parents or relatives, Chairman of the Council of Commissars Sergei Lukashin and Director of Orphanages Milton Brown had agreed on procedures that would ensure the child's safety.[828]

Other factors that had contributed to the decline of the orphan population were predicated on the rule that children who had reached the age of 16 or 17 would be discharged from the orphanage. Some of those discharged had been hired as employees in the office, or as teachers and laborers by NER. A few hundred had been employed at the new textile factory in Alexandropol and some of the older girls had been given in marriage to suitors seeking wives. Another factor that contributed to the attrition had been the hundreds who had escaped from the orphanage in the course of relocations from Yerevan to Alexandropol, and more would follow suit in the years to come. One memorandum, for instance, dated November 24, 1925, stated that in just the preceding two months, 98 orphans, all of them over the age of 12, had escaped from the orphanage. Of them, 86 had been girls.[829] In the memorandum, signed by the Secretary of the Council of People's Commissars and the Director of the Secret Department, NER was asked to undertake means so as to deter such frequent occurrences.

Another factor in the gradual depletion of the orphan population in the early 1920s was NER's outplacement program whereby children were placed with families in village communities. In August 1923, for instance, 1,341 children were outplaced, mostly with refugee farmers during harvest season.[830] But still, according to figures NER published in November 1923 there were 17,000 at the orphanages.[831]

As the orphan population at the City of Orphans grew older, so did concerns over the future of thousands who would soon be discharged at the age of 16 or 17, and expected to earn their living using skills they had learned at the orphanage. But employment opportunities were scarce, if existent at all, especially in the province of Alexandropol where, close to 85,000 of the population were on the verge of starvation.[832] The concern over the children's future reached critical levels in 1924, as the number of children who became or who would soon become of discharge age in NER orphanages reached 8,275. Among them were 1,671 boys and 3,052 girls between the ages of 14 and 16, and 1,649 boys and 1,903 girls between the ages of 16 and 17. In the state orphanages, there were a total number of 816 children, of whom 366 boys and 194 girls were between the ages of 14 and 16, and 141 boys and 115 girls between the ages of 16 and 17.[823]

The deep concern, shared by the Soviet Armenian government and NER alike, had to do with the fear that once discharged, and in view of the scarcity of jobs, many of the orphans would ultimately join the boys and girls who already called the street their home, and survived through illegal means. In fact, reports from the Commissariat of Enlightenment showed that court cases involving theft by individual orphans or groups, many of them skilled shoemakers, weavers and tailors, had increased with the growing number of discharged orphans. Over 50% of the cases involved orphan girls.[834]

Joining the chorus of alarms about the bleak future of the orphans was liaison Georgy Sargsyan. In his report to Lukashin on July 17, 1924, Sargsyan urged immediate action from the government to protect discharged children from undesirable consequences. It was understandable, he wrote, that NER did not wish to keep orphans beyond the age of 17, but it was imperative

> …to undertake extraordinary measures and of the kind that would yield real results both for the country and for the children. One such means could be to give part of the future textile factory including electricity, to the NER for one year so that NER would assume the responsibility of teaching weaving to a few hundred of our orphans. I am currently in negotiations with Yarrow, who has agreed in principle, but I foresee complications when the issue of the building comes up, for which it will be necessary to spend a sum of money on renovations.[835]

"Liquidation," or Outplacement

Further aggravating the situation was NER's announcement in 1924 that due to financial limitations it had no recourse but to dramatically reduce its operations and begin an accelerated discharge program of orphans regardless of age. The policy was in line with Paul Monroe's recommendation in 1924, when he had advised that orphan outplacement should be at the center of NER's future plans, and should proceed on a more accelerated pace. "Two and a half years ago," he wrote, there had been "25,000 orphans with the organization and "now [1924] the number in institutions is about 14,500," with about 6,000 "receiving out relief." The plan was to outplace another 2,500 or 3,500 within a few months:

It is expected by September 1st, 1924, to reduce the former number to 12,000, possibly to 11,000 and the number of out relief to 1,000.

A good solution for the boys, Monroe suggested, was to place them in the half deserted Armenian villages with some subsidy from NER, if necessary, because

Such a plan would contribute to the economic rehabilitation of the country; would provide for a normal absorption of the boys; would afford opportunities for co-operation of the Near East Relief with central and local authorities and organizations and would be an excellent educational program. Some such plan would seem to afford the largest possibilities for the orphans in Armenia.[836]

Indeed, in February 1925, the orphan population of the City of Orphans had dropped to 11,000.[837] A more accelerated outplacing, while desirable for Monroe, was not possible in Armenia because of conditions in the country.[838]

While Monroe believed that outplacing orphans into family environments would spare them the negative effects of institutional life, he also believed that such measures were an equally important prerequisite for NER's transition from its emergency phase of pure relief to a new "Constructive Phase," which hinged on general and specialized education rather than relief. For the transition to the next phase, the orphans would need to be outplaced as rapidly as possible and on a large scale, even before they reached the accepted discharge age. They were to be placed with relatives if no immediate family members were found, or in foster homes where they would temporarily receive a small stipend from NER. Foster parents could either adopt the children or take them in as laborers to help with chores around the house or in the fields. Before handing the children to foster parents, however, a thorough background check of the prospective foster family would need to be conducted to ensure the safety and well being of the child, and NER would need to maintain close supervision of outplaced orphans.[839]

The process of outplacements invited much criticism since established procedures were not always followed. Georgy Sargsyan reminded Ernest Yarrow that families claiming their children out of orphanages should first apply for permission at his office, located in building 86 on 23rd street in Leninakan, and only after receiving permission should they proceed to the appropriate office at the orphanage. He brought up the serious problem he had noticed, he said, whereby children were signed out without a proper background check of those claiming to be relatives. As a result, many children had been exploited and then thrown back on the streets when their usefulness was over. Sargsyan suggested that a special committee consisting of him and NER representatives should look closely into the circumstances the family lived in. These precautions were necessary to prevent large groups of homeless children on the streets, especially since the Soviet government was most interested in the fate of the future Soviet citizens, now in the orphanages. "I assume," he added at the end, "you will take measures to immediately stop the current system of unloading the orphanages and adapt the process to the suggested plan."[840]

In his report to Sergei Lukashin and the Secret Department of the People's Council of Commissars, dated July 17, 1924, Sargsyan pointed out that 5,413 children had been liquidated from all American orphanages in Armenia by the end of 1923, followed by 4,324 children in the first six months of 1924 alone:

> If we look at the numbers, one thing becomes clear, that the discharging of this year is being done in the same way as last year. The lists I have in my hand indicate the following numbers: From all the American orphanages in Armenia, 5,413 children were liquidated in 1923. In the first six months of 1924, 4,324 children were liquidated.
>
> It must be admitted, however, that during the last two months more order is noted in the discharging process than before. But, unfortunately, with one novelty, that is, sending groups of children to cities and villages, to look for their parents…[841]

Sargsyan blamed Varazdat Deroyan for the "novelty," and claimed that Deroyan had "forced" the children to look for their parents at a time when few parents came to reclaim their children. Deroyan, he wrote, did not "inspire trust" in him:

> Deroyan: that is the name of that director, who had made it his purpose to reduce, at any cost, the number of children in the orphanages…determined to meet the daily quota of reduction…
>
> …Deroyan continues to discharge children every day, and now in small groups, and forces them to roam in the villages and search for their relatives. Some of the children are lost from sight, and some return empty-handed.
>
> …It is not right to allow the children to walk all over the country in the heat and rain, looking for their relatives…[842]

At a meeting held on September 6, 1924, the Provincial Executive Committee of Leninakan passed a resolution to form a committee that would look for job opportunities in state institutions and to give priority to orphans discharged from NER orphanages.[843] The meeting had been occasioned by a note in August 1924 from Georgy Sargsyan addressed to the Provincial Executive Committee of Leninakan alerting the members that the time had come to seriously think about placing orphans in jobs. There were scores of boys and girls, Sargsyan wrote, who had been discharged because they had reached the age of 16, and now surrounded his office asking for jobs. "Some are hungry and homeless," Sargsyan continued.

> …they resort to extreme measures, on account of which a more serious issue stands before the Executive Committee—the liquidation of crime and prostitution.

And added,

> I am not convinced that nine out of ten girls who have been subjected to liquidation from NER are not practicing immorality, and I exhort you to pull them out of their wretched profession. In the future, the number of orphans subjected to liquidation will grow in geometric progression…[844]

The annual report to NER's Trustees for the year 1924 stated that the general policy during the year had been reduction of relief operations to a minimum, necessitated by financial restrictions. In the interest of economy, it read, orphanages had been consolidated in most areas, the size of the American staff had decreased with additional responsibilities being relegated to the remaining American staff, and older orphans had begun to replace adult native employees. The task of outplacement, it continued, had not been easy and some overseas workers thought it had been too drastic for the good of the children.[845]

The wording of the report Sargsyan submitted to the "Central Executive Committee of Armenia" was more explicit and detailed. "Concomitant with the liquidation of orphans from NER orphanages," he wrote on January 19, 1925, the number of homeless children has increased dramatically. "In the last few months," he continued,

> ...the representation has tried all possible means so that the orphans being liquidated from NER orphanages would not add to the rise in the number of homeless on the streets. The measures tried with that in mind have tended to deprive all those who used to go to NER orphanages to take children out by illegal means and after they carried out their intentions, were throwing them back on the street. But until we began to apply measures, many children had been signed out of NER orphanages without any questions, with a naïve belief in all those who said they wished to care for orphans. And taking advantage of this type of friendliness, looking to find workers for their summer work...many individuals had succeeded in having their distant relatives signed out from the orphanage, intending to throw them back on the streets.[846]

To decrease the number of homeless children, concluded the report, it was necessary to decree that only close relatives be allowed to claim the children. This would prevent NER, he added, from signing the children out at the first possible opportunity. In the absence of such a decree NER's orphanages could become an endless source of homeless children on the street.[847]

Further alarms in 1925 were triggered by another announcement made by "Citizen Yarrow and Citizen Acheson," that in 1925 NER planned to outplace 3,000 to 4,000 more children within the boundaries of Armenia due to lack of funds.[848] In response to NER's 1925 announcement for additional outplacements, liaison N. Ter-Ghazaryan drafted two options to prevent a recurrence of the situation of 1924.[849] The first option stipulated that NER would hand over all responsibility for one of the posts with a large number of children—the Polygon or the Kazachi—to the Council of People's Commissars with the proviso that it would be obliged to pay a monthly stipend of $7 for the care of each child during 1925. The monthly cost would drop to $6 per child in 1926, and to $4 per child in 1927. NER would maintain the right to ensure that the funds were used for their intended purposes; NER would hold the right to withdraw support in the event of misspending; and, it would not be obligated to sustain a child if he or she left the post. In addition, a detailed listing of all orphans being transferred to the care of the government would need to be compiled, and the transfer would be made between March 15 and April 1, 1925. NER's responsibilities would stop at the end of 1927, at which time the Council of the People's Commissars would be obligated to care for all children who remained in the barracks transferred to them.

Certain that NER would prefer to relocate the children to the villages as temporary labor, Ter-Ghazaryan offered a second option which would be effective on June 1, 1925. This option stipulated that NER would be obligated to present a detailed list of all children under its care no later than March 15, 1925, indicating the conditions in which the children's relatives or friends lived in, their exact address, and the children's gender and age. NER would also have to conduct a thorough investigation of the physical environment where the children would be sent before signing them out of the orphanage. Once the list was prepared, children who had immediate family members would be transferred to their families on condition that NER would give the child, upon leaving the orphanage, the child's underwear, bed, the blanket used by the child while in the orphanage, along with two months' provisions for the child as well as for the child's relatives, the amount of which was to be decided between NER and the Council of People's Commissars by separate contract. Finally, a permanent and authoritative Liquidation Committee composed of members of NER and SSRA would have to be formed to oversee the process of outplacement and to keep constant watch over the children relocated to villages. Without the Liquidation Committee, NER would have no right to liquidate even a single child. Attached to the options was a summary statistic showing that on December 1, 1924, there were 11,039 orphans in NER's orphanage. On March 30, 1925, Ter-Ghazaryan reported that NER Director Beach was in full agreement with the creation of a committee to oversee the liquidation process, to develop a coherent plan, and begin an inspection of those areas where the children would be relocated.[850]

The minutes of the meeting held in the office of A. Mravyan on April 27, 1925, then serving as Deputy Chairman of the SSRA Council of People's Commissars, show that the issue of "liquidating" 3,000 children and 500 orphan employees from the NER orphanages was discussed and a number of resolutions made. According to the resolutions, Sargsyan and Ter-Ghazaryan would request certain information from NER. The requested information would include: detailed data about children slated for outplacement, including their gender, age, health condition, level of literacy, etc.; the number of children who had been signed out to their families and relatives; the length of time NER was willing to support the outplaced children and by how much; and the number of children who could be placed with villagers. NER would also be asked what they intended to do with the 500 orphan employees who would be released from their jobs. The minutes also stipulated that the School for the Blind would be transferred to the government if NER would subsidize it for two years.[851]

The Liquidation Committee was established in May 1925. By October 30, 1925, 75% of the 3,000 orphans slated for liquidation for that year had been discharged and many had been released to their families and relatives. NER and the liaison's office had cooperated in the effort, reported Georgy Sargsyan on October 30, 1925, and the process had moved along without the previous year's unpleasant incidents. It was expected that the quota of discharges would be met by early December.[852]

During the year 1925 parents and relatives had claimed 2,446 children; 265 orphans had run away from the orphanage; and 22 orphans had died.[853] By January 1, 1926, according to the accounting of the Commissariat of

Enlightenment, there were 8,234 orphans left in NER's orphanage. By the end of the year, on December 31, 1926, the orphan population had shrunk to 5,563—approximately 20,000 had been reclaimed, adopted, outplaced, escaped, or died in less than four years. At native institutions and refugee families, NER subsidized 3,883 children in 1926.[854] Monthly subsidies paid for each child were from $1.50 to $2, in addition to a monthly allowance of 45¢ to $1 for the medical supervision of each child.[855]

With outplacements in progress, a December 1925 NER report titled *Institutions and Industries by Areas*, highlighted the advantages of placing orphans in homes. Outplacement "encouraged initiative" in children, it meant that the orphan was offered "elements of home life," "prevented the effect of isolation from the outside world," and "avoided the paralyzing effect of mass orphanage life." And most of all, the report pointed out, outplacements allowed the important new benefit of disseminating western ideals on a scale larger, and over a population wider than those in the orphanages alone. The dissemination would be through the outplaced child, who would take with him or her the ideals learned in the orphanage to his or her new environment, and in that way "western ideals" would get "under the skin of the Near East":

> It will be obvious that the American stimulus was therefore reaching an entire home in each case instead of only the child formerly in the orphanage...[856]

In sharp contrast to NER's characterization of the orphan as an agent of western ideals were the plans proposed about six months earlier at the Commissariat of Enlightenment titled *"The Economic Future of Armenia's Orphans."* The proposal characterized the children as "an extremely useful category" for the strengthening of the greater glory of socialism.[857] Thousands of orphans in the state and NER orphanages were near discharge age, among them children soon to reach the ages of 16 and 17, and even 14 and 15, since NER was now trying to discharge younger children as well. To leave them to their fate, read the proposal, would be tantamount to the creation of prostitution houses and street gangs, who would not only harm themselves but would present a horrible social danger to the community and the state. Those perils had to be prevented and wide avenues developed for a solution for the future of the orphans. The solution would be to enlist the army of orphans in the process of shaping the socialist basis of the country. And the best avenue for that would be to attach them to the land, forming agricultural communities based and inspired by Communist ideals, namely, turn the orphans into Village Communists. Such transformation would be easy because the children were already used to the collective life of the orphanage and to a certain degree could care for their needs such as mending their own socks, cleaning after themselves, etc. This important aspect, the author believed, should be capitalized in future plans regarding orphans.

As evidence that the orphans presented a fertile soil for the foundation of a communist generation was the tremendous success of the Patkom [Boy Communists] and Komerit [Young Communist] movements among the orphans. Among the boy communists, 75% of the leaders were orphans, and the former orphans had proven to be the best workers among the communist youth groups. In the Communist

Party too, former orphans stood out for their intelligence and readiness for self-sacrifice. It was clear from these data, ran the argument, that orphans were ideal material for the propagation of the new socialist economic order.

The orphans also represented free labor, the proposal continued, and in the thousands. Once they were organized in village and agricultural communities, they could be put to work on the irrigation of thousands of Armenia's un-irrigated desiatines. And, the thousands of desiatines of marshes, once drained, would allow the relocation of agricultural colonies on the lands, and the cultivation of cotton and tobacco. Armenia's Alpine desiatines, too, were perfect for dairy farming, and thousands of orphans could be put to work on those farms—all of which would become showcases for the new Armenia. Such a roadmap also included the gathering of orphans around industrial and trade workshops from where would emerge a generation of locksmiths, carpenters, tinsmith, ironsmiths, etc., who would help Armenia's development in the technical sphere.

It was recommended that these suggestions be put in place *posthaste*, since there were already 9,081 orphans between the ages of 14 and 17 who expected the government to direct their fate and their future, and that the number would only grow when a new army of orphans, now between the ages of 12 and 14 soon joined them. And each year, in successive new units that army would pound on the government's door for a solution. And, since Soviet Armenia's paltry budget was already being supplemented by the resources of the Transcaucasus Federation and could barely cover its own expenses, it would be wise to ask assistance from the Soviet Union; without that possibility, a viable solution to the orphan problem would be difficult to arrive at.[858]

Yet the roadmap so defined did not include girls. The future of orphan girls, the author suggested, presented a particularly thorny problem, more so, since three fifths of the orphans nearing discharge age were girls. At NER as well as at state orphanages, groups of girls were already learning tailoring and basket weaving, but job opportunities in these trades could not possibly accommodate thousands of working hands. A large industrial project alone, such as the weaving factory of Alexandropol, could offer employment for the multitudes.[859]

Not all orphans had looked forward to village life or life in a factory. Some hoped to get further educated, a prospect that was not always within reach. A group of three orphans in 1924, for instance, had tried and failed, and, eventually resorted to writing to the President of the Council of Commissars for guidance. The three—Hayastan Hakobyan, Zagar Sahakyan and Hrand Chuduryan—identified themselves as "We the American Orphans of Leninakan," and recounted how they had successfully passed exams in Leninakan and on that basis had sold everything and spent the money with the hope that they would continue their education in Yerevan. But they had been asked to take additional exams in Yerevan, and had failed. The three signatories had no one to go to and now appealed to the Council of Commissars to help them find jobs. As if the years of oppression were not enough, they wrote, now they roamed the streets of Yerevan, alone and defenseless. "Therefore you, the Soviet authorities," they wrote, "are our hope,"

> ...we ask you to secure us, to free us from all stings, from claws. We await your assistance; show us a path through which we can free our young lives from an unbearable predicament. We remain hopeful.[860]

As outplacements continued, NER's vision of a "Constructive Phase" gradually became a reality, albeit of some concern to Barclay Acheson who feared that the American public may not be inclined to fund NER's constructive activities:

> Take the refugee out of those squalid camps and put them into pleasant villages, and the melodramatic tragedy that the public loved would be gone. Empty those barracks-like orphanages and place the children with simple, kindly, but crudely primitive foster-parents, and the satisfaction that both an individual and a nation derive from playing god disappears...

As a result, continued Acheson,

> ...We would lose the fiction that these children were going to modernize the Near East and the sob-stories that arouse emotions and raise money.[861]

"With a few exceptions," Acheson reflected,

> ...an audience if asked to give money to buy dolls for tiny tuberculosis victims who were about to die, would wallow in an emotional debauch—imagine emaciated little hands, soon to be stilled in death, caressing a brand-new doll on Christmas Eve—and give enough money to buy quintuplets for every child. They might even give enough to build a new hospital. But if that same audience were asked to give a fraction of that amount to prevent several times as many children from ever contracting tuberculosis, the appeal would fall on deaf ears, because the appeal lacked the melodramatic...[862]

In November 1925, NER had signed a mandate to continue the care of the children now in orphanages for three more years.[863] The new cotton mills in Leninakan had given Acheson hope when he visited them in July 1926. He was impressed by the number of former NER orphans working there, and hoped that when the projected larger plant opened, NER ex-orphans would be given positions as supervisors. Mayor Yesayan of Alexandropol, elected to the position at the age of 22, had especially impressed Acheson. He described Yesayan as a young man of about 25, who was responsible for much of the progress in the city. During one of their conversations, Yessayan had remarked that people trained in the building trades—ironworkers and mechanics able to handle engines—were most needed in the country. Yessayan had also pointed out to Acheson that the NER had trained too many shoe makers, etc., and that currently in Armenia there was a demand for stenographers and general office help.[864]

"...Where There Is No School, nor a Student Body"

Not all shared NER's positive assessment of orphan outplacements. School principals bitterly complained of disruptions and uneven approaches to education and educational planning due to outplacements. Disruptions had been especially felt during the mass outplacements 1924 and 1925, when academic planning for the education of the remaining children had been challenging at best.

As the orphan population decreased, so did the number of schools in the posts. In his mid-year report, Polygon Schools Superintendent Nshan Hovhannisyan spent some time in describing the administrative difficulties the Polygon faced at the beginning of the semester, due to outplacements from the Polygon and the closing of the schools at Kazachi post:

> We began the 1924–25 academic year by accepting new elements, new students. The closing down of the Kazachi post gave us more than 1,300 female students, most of them under the age of 11, and a small portion of the older girls who were sent to us to conduct orphanage work and study in the secondary school.[865]

The addition of 1,300 girls from the Kazachi to the existing 4,545 students at the Polygon, Hovhannisyan wrote, would have brought up the total number of students at the beginning of the 1924–24 academic year to 5,845 students. But in fact, there were only 5,185, since some students were transferred to the agricultural school in Stepanavan and others were outplaced during the summer vacation. As a result, the number of schools had been reduced from ten to seven.

Writing six months earlier, Kazachi Schools Superintendent Hayk Hovhannisyan described in his annual report the negative effect the 1924 outplacement had had on the academic program. "The past academic year," began his report dated July 18, 1924,

> ...would have been the most productive for the schools at the Kazachi Post and their orderly closing a day of victory in the history of the educational work conducted by the NER. But such an unexpected liquidation, realized with such speed, of the afore mentioned schools turned everything upside down and placed us before a sad *fait accompli*.
>
> Under such circumstances, where there is no school, nor a student body, each academic report, especially with the idea of benefiting from it in the future, loses its purpose...[866]

Throughout his report Hayk Hovhannisyan brings up the impact of continuous changes on the student body during the 1923–24 academic year, when new students were transferred from Jalaloghli and Batum, and others were "liquidated." Then there had been the transfer of the Kazachi kindergarten to the Severski on March 1, 1924, and the transfer of the epileptic students from the city to the Kazachi. In November 1923, he wrote, there had been a total of 4,450 students, which at the end of the academic year had been reduced to 3,453 in eight schools. Furthermore, he continued,

> It is not clear to me where our students have gone. How many to the Severski? How many to the Polygon? How many were placed out? I do not know. I now feel like the captain who reports to his commander when there is no army.[867]

At the end of the academic year 1923–24, there were a total of 89 teachers at the Kazachi schools, he reported, and nine student teachers whom he found unmotivated, fatigued, and lacking in pedagogical skills.[868]

Disruptions peaked following additional outplacements and a drop in the orphan population at the Polygon to 1,103 boys and 1,670 girls. By 1928 chaos and disruption were rampant and were particularly severe during the first semester of the 1927–1928 academic year. Academic reports from Polygon superintendents and teachers reflect the depth of the growing disorderliness in and outside classrooms. One report stated:

> Disorderliness in our schools has reached extremes. Classes #4, #7, #14 and recently #18 stand out especially for their disorderliness. It can be stated without reservations that in the first three groups no work is being done, and if done, it is unproductive…Noise, uproar, absenteeism, commotion, capricious and arbitrary attitude toward work, lack of attention, indifference; in one word, chaos, neglect.
>
> I will mention two classes—#7 and #14—where students often get into fights, break each other's noses and head, and get bloody. And if the highest administration does not take drastic measures, serious consequences may occur in the future.
>
> It is at once natural and understandable that the work conducted under these circumstances cannot yield any results and if we insist that it can, we would have been busy with self-delusion.[869]

Not a day passed that this or that teacher did not send a student, or take the student over, to see the director, or call the director to restore order in the classroom. "The classroom," the report read,

> …has become a type of former police station; and the director, rather than occupy himself with administrative and pedagogical matters, is mostly busy investigating incidents.[870]

Outplacement to Points North and Comrade Nurichanyan's Report on Orphans Outplaced in Abkhazia

Olivia Hill was assigned to the task of outplacing the children. She would need to meet a certain quota each year, would need to make "strenuous efforts to outplace the less desirable children,"[871] and supervise those already outplaced. In that context, Hill reported to Acheson that

> …a number of the outplaced children are diseased, ragged and unhappy, but in spite of this when she first goes to the village they hang back and are reluctant to meet her because they fear she has come back to take them to the orphanages. When they find out that she has simply come to inquire into their welfare they are very talkative and happy to see her.[872]

Olivia Hill had also suggested that she would like to have a traveling hospital with her, along with a barber, a nurse, and other help to clean the children. Acheson, on his part, wanted to encourage the children in their new settings and way of life and suggested that a few prizes be given to those children who had contributed something to their community. The primary purpose would be to help children think of themselves as community servants rather than the recipients of unearned help.[873]

In the massive outplacement program that continued through 1929, children of various ages were sent to Baku, Yerevan, and Tiflis but with a larger number to the Northern Caucasus and the Black Sea Region. Outplacement locations to points north included Vladikavkaz (North Ossetia), Krasnodar (Russia), Batum (Georgia), Sukhum (Georgia), Grozny (the capital of the Chechen Republic of the Russian Federation), Adler (Russia), etc.,[874] and often to areas where Turkish Armenian refugees had settled. Within two years, 1,844 children had been sent north, many of them underage.[875] A relatively small number were adopted,[876] the majority was placed in homes as foster children, and many more were signed out as permanent or temporary laborers. To coordinate the process, NER sent a few of its employees to points north to open and man a local NER office.

Once or twice a month lists of orphans slated for outplacement were prepared at the City of Orphans. Usually accompanied by a staff member from the orphanage, the group would first be sent to Tiflis in a train car that was always reserved for the NER, and from there to Batum.[877] Accompanying one such group of 30 orphans to Adler, was Polygon employee Harutyun Alpoyachyan. Upon arriving in Batum, he wrote,

> …we were met by the manager of the American office in Batum, an Armenian general of the czar's army by the name of Shelkovnikov…Then we boarded a ship and went to Adler, where we were met by the representatives of the [NER] office directed by Hambaryan…At the office in Adler there were lists of people who wanted to adopt an orphan, specifying the age and sex of the orphans they wanted.[878]

A sampling of the lists of orphans sent north reveals that although outplacements were continuous throughout the year, requests peaked during the spring months of April and May and then again in September and October, corresponding to the months when villagers sowed or harvested their lands.

A medical examination to establish that the child was able to perform tasks expected of him or her was required before leaving the orphanage. One of the lists compiled on April 26, 1927, shows the names of 126 orphans aged 16 and 17, who had undergone physical examinations and had been found healthy enough for work.[879] On the same day, and again two days later, 59 children were sent to Adler and Sukhum.[880] A sampling for the following month shows that on May 27 alone 42 children were sent as laborers to Adler.[881]

Although discharge and outplacement protocols had been put in place, it appears that at times they remained on paper alone. In 1928, the Soviet Armenian government sent A. Nurichanyan to visit villages where the children had been outplaced and to assess the condition of orphans NER had outplaced in Abkhazia and who were reportedly neglected. The 12-page detailed report Nurichanyan submitted on October 31, 1928, was based on his meetings with various government officials, conversations with the orphans themselves, and personal observations.[882] He could get little or no information from state or local officials, he wrote, since most of them were not even aware that orphans had been transferred to their area, or how and when they had arrived. In the absence of the necessary information from state officials, he had next gone to NER's Sukhum office, where he had inquired about the process by which an orphan was relocated to Abkhazia. There he was told that outplacement to the region had begun in 1926, at which time NER had established the office of a permanent representative in charge of child placement. As a general rule, he was told, the process began when the village councils in Abkhazia informed NER's local representatives that they wished to take in orphans. The village council was then required to guarantee, in writing, that the requestor was financially secure, that the members of the family were healthy and enjoyed a good reputation in their village. The list would then be forwarded to Leninakan for approval by liaison G. Sargsyan. Once Sargsyan approved the list, the requested number of children would be scheduled for transfer to Abkhazia in a special convoy. The process was completed when NER representatives in Sukhum sent a follow-up report to Leninakan, indicating how many of the children had been adopted, how many had been signed out as peons and laborers, and their locations.

In general, explained Nurichanyan, in rural economies the child was taken into a family in one of two ways: either as temporary help where the child provided free labor in return for food and shelter, or adopted as a family member. The adopted child was usually young and was to have the same rights and privileges of a biological child of the family: he or she would be given his portion of land, be cared for medically and not be asked to do work above his strength level. Were these procedures followed? Asked Nurichanyan. Not always, was the answer. He had been in villages where official papers for orphan-laborers did not even exist, and there were cases where the children

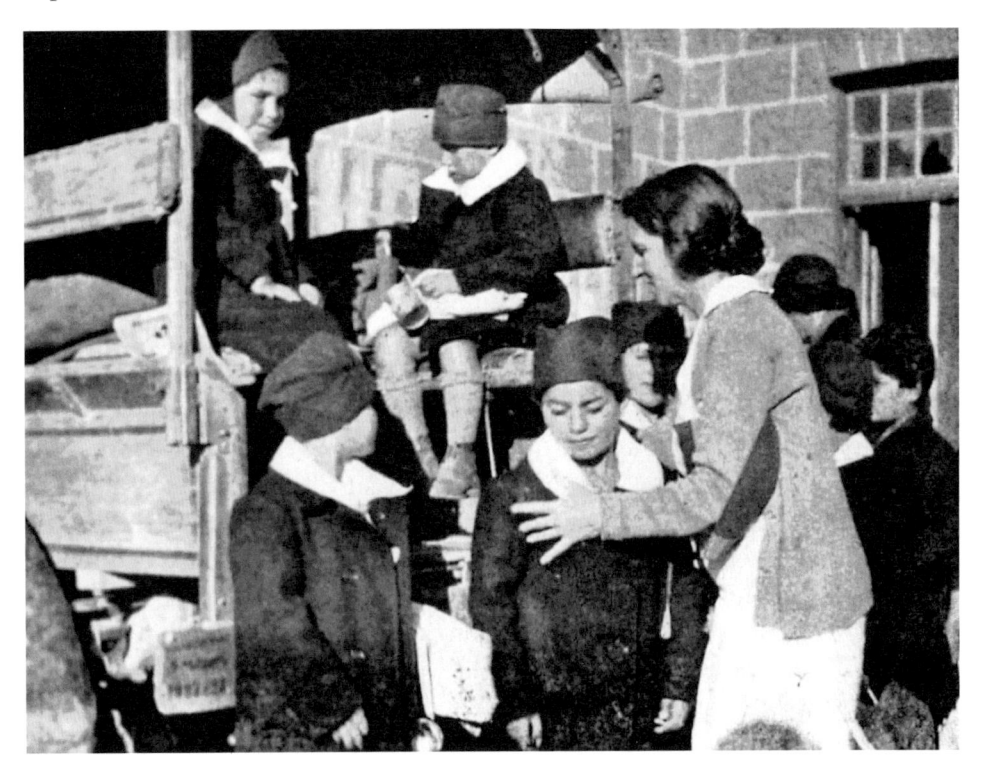

Children boarding a truck for their journey to Sukhum for adoption or labor. (Barton 1930: facing page 333)

were handed over to villagers without the knowledge of the village council, or due process, and cited an example:

> When they were passing by Novy Afon, an Armenian approaches the NER representative in Abkhazia, Comrade Garnik Hyusyan, and asks that an orphan be sent to him. The latter takes down the citizen's address, promises to send him an orphan.[883]

In conversations with orphans, Nurichanyan had discovered that most children outplaced in rural economies did not know if they were foster children or adopted. The situation was the same in many villages in the Northern Caucasus:

> …all the orphans there think they have been adopted, although the agreements signed in many of the rural economies has been for welfare.[884]

But, he remarked, the child's status was actually irrelevant, because regardless of their status, the children did the same amount of work. And, if there wasn't enough work, the children were let go "without any difficulties and sent back to the NER office in Sukhum":

> …The other side bears no legal responsibility…At each step, at whim, the child is let go if he or she cannot help at home or take part in rural work.

> …The orphan adopted as a son is proscribed from the rural economy or community with no difficulties and sent to the NER office, which places him, under the same terms, in another rural community.[885]

According to Nurichanyan's report, the first group sent to Abkhazia, in 1926, had consisted of 110 orphans who were placed in the Sochi region as laborers and peons. Of that group, 66 were girls, 20 of whom had later married and nine had returned to Armenia. The rest of the orphans continued to work as laborers, cooks, and cobblers. Job security or contracts for these children were not enforced because the government in Abkhazia did not want to interfere with NER orphans. When Nurichanyan had asked an older orphan in a village of the Northern Caucasus what his salary was, the orphan said he did not know and that Nazar (NER representative in Sochi) would know. The orphan did not know how much he made or when he would receive his wages.

In 1927, 361 older orphans had arrived in Abkhazia as laborers. A few of the girls had returned to Armenia, and the rest worked as servants in private homes. The following year, in 1928, 617 orphans were sent from Leninakan and were distributed among 38 Armenian villages of the region. Of the group, 33 were older orphan boys and girls, and the rest were between the ages of 14 and 15. Of the younger group, some were temporarily placed in homes, some had disappeared without a trace, others were adopted, but two boys and 10 girls had returned to Armenia with NER's knowledge. In the same year, 124 orphans had been sent to the Sochi Region as laborers. Twenty-one had relocated to Abkhazia, 13 had returned to Armenia, six had gone to Rostov to continue their education, and two were in the Northern Caucasus doing their own work. Of the older girls in the group, 11 had married, four had been adopted, and the rest continued as laborers. A year later, 534 orphans had been sent to the Sochi region. Of this group, 460 were under age: 392 girls and

68 boys had been adopted, 74 were taken as foster children in 20 Armenian villages, and three had returned to Armenia with NER's knowledge. In total 1,844 orphans had been sent to Abkhazia and the Northern Caucasus.[886]

Concerning the education of outplaced orphans, most of the adopted children attended village schools; but those taken in as laborers did not. With respect to work hours, there were no set hours and depending on the season, the children worked as much as the villagers they were staying with. The girls worked at home cleaning the house, baby-sitting and cooking, as well as working in the field, and harvesting tobacco. The laborers, boys and girls, rested only on Sundays, and many were not paid salaries. According to protocols, NER representatives would have to meet the children and talk to them, and nurses would have to go through the villages and check on the children's health and provide free medication, if needed. Yet when Nurichanyan had visited villages in the Abkhazia and Sukhum region with NER physician Sargsyan, an examination of the children conducted in his presence revealed that 90% of the children placed around the black sea suffered from trachoma and 50% from malaria. NER, he was told, was trying to move those orphans to the mountainous areas. The younger children harvesting tobacco were in a particularly unhealthy state. Local authorities were aware of the situation, but because the children had been placed by NER, they did not wish to interfere.[887]

Refugees from Turkish Armenia, who had arrived in 1914 or earlier, Nurichanyan explained, populated the villages in Abkhazia and Sochi. Many of them did not have children and had adopted orphans and treated them as their own. Others, however, in the guise of adopting an orphan, exploited them as servants and would throw them out if they could not perform their chores, even if they were adopted. Tobacco farmers in particular, preferred to take in Armenian orphans rather than employ Russian laborers, because the children represented free labor. He ended the report by saying that NER did not keep in touch with the local authorities in Abkhazia, which is why the local bodies were not aware of the children who had been sent there from Leninakan.

Some orphans had had difficulty adjusting to their new environments. Siranush Shahinyan had passed her medical examination and sent to work in the home of Melik and Mariam, originally from Van and now in Sukhum, as indicated in a document dated June 17, 1927.[888] By early September, however, she had returned to the Polygon, because, as Olivia Hill explained to G. Sargsyan in a note dated September 2, 1927,

> …during two months, after changing 11 homes, she [Siranush] had finally declined to work because she is inept, and has come here.

Hill continued to explain that the girl had a mother in Yerevan, who was not in a position to help her, and she would be placed under the care of a sister and brother-in-law.

Other orphans had refused to go where NER planned to send them, as, for example Avdal Simonyan, who categorically refused to be sent anywhere NER had assigned him to. In fact, he signed a declaration where he stated that he "personally will find a job suitable for myself and am leaving the orphanage voluntarily."[889]

Another orphan, Manuk Gasparyan had gone to great lengths to avoid transfer to Sukhum, as Olivia Hill recounted to G. Sargsyan:

> Manuk Gasparyan, approximately 19–20 years old, is one of our Polygon boys. We wanted to send him to the Sukhum area to work, but in the last minute, he painted his mouth and nose pretending to be sick. We sent him to the hospital for a medical examination; they found him to be completely healthy. But from his manners I suspected that he might not be normal. In view of the fact that sending such types of boys to Sukhum area is not beneficial, and would leave a very bad impression on the population, I ask that you do not refuse to mediate to have him accepted at the weaving factory. It is awkward to send him elsewhere for work.[890]

Olivia Hill's note about Siranush Shahinyan. (NAA 39/1/8/f. 10)

Some orphans were afraid of adoption. In the fall of 1927, 14-year-old Aghasi Karoyan had been sent for adoption in Talin, less than 34 miles south of Leninakan:

> A man from Talin, who had no child of his own, had expressed the wish to adopt a child from the orphanage. A boy from Talin, who had been with me at the orphanage earlier, had told the man about me, that I had no close relatives, and that he could take me.

Karoyan recounts that the man had then written a letter to the orphanage in Leninakan stating that Aghasi was his brother's son, and that he wished to adopt him and bring him to Talin. The search for a boy by that name at the orphanage yielded no results. But, continued Aghasi Karoyan,

Statement of Avdal Simonyan. (NAA 39/1/3/f. 30) ↓

> They gathered all the boys by the name of Aghasi, questioned each one, and then focused on me. In the fall of 1927, they put me in a cart with other children, and brought us to Talin. There, I noticed that a man approached the head of the group and asked who Aghassi was. I felt that he was not our relative. I was very scared…I did not go. I said: "He is not my uncle." I raised such a commotion in Talin…that the group leader also realized it was impossible to break my will; he had no choice but to take me back to the orphanage in Leninakan."[891]

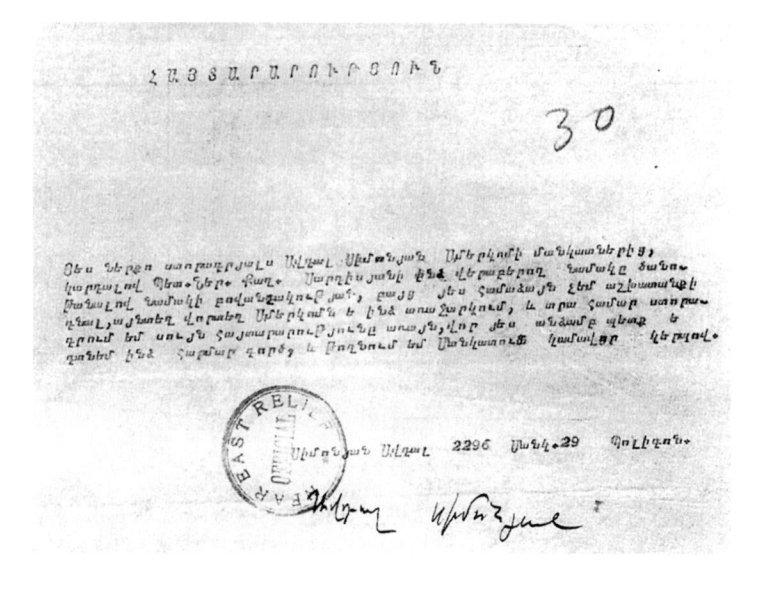

OUTPLACEMENT, DOWNSIZING… 275

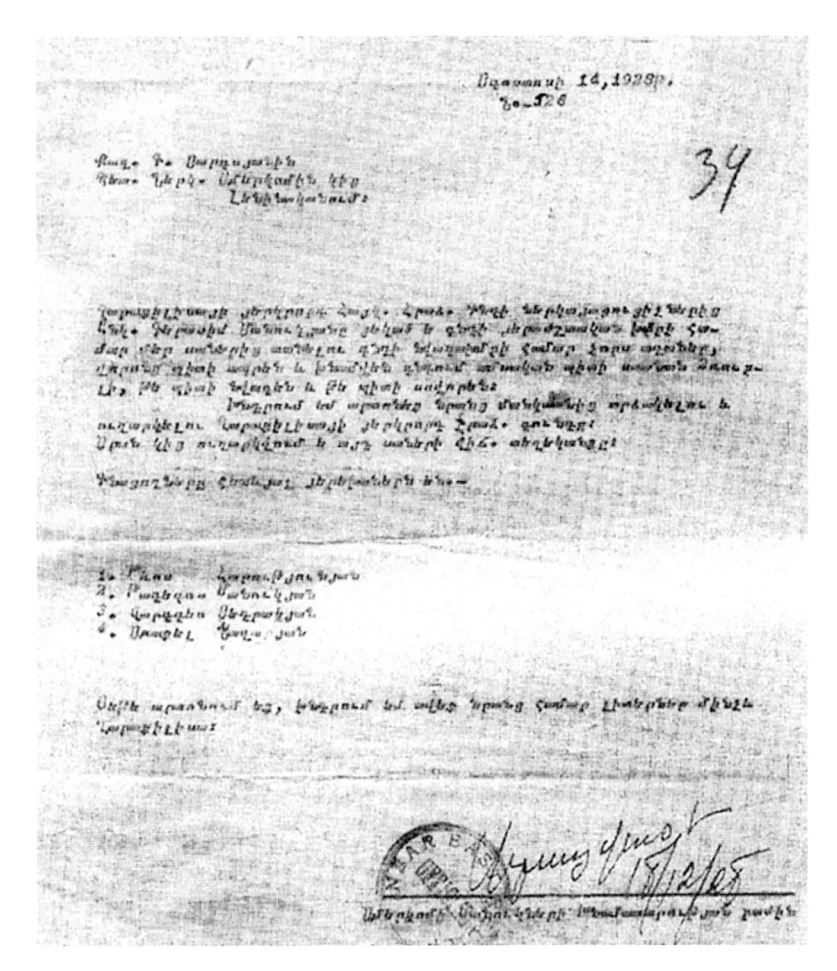

NER request for permission to send four boys to Karakilisa. (NAA 39/1/5/f. 34)

Groups of orphans were also sent to the copper mines in Ghapan, in the south of the republic, while others were sent to Karakilisa to join the orchestra of the Second Armenian Rifle Regiment in that city "at the request of Gerasim Manukyan, representing the Regiment."[892]

The pace of outplacement to the north increased significantly during 1928 with groups being sent for adoption or labor on an almost daily basis during the spring months.[893] But on November 5, 1928, five days after Nurichanyan submitted his report, the SSRA Central Executive Committee met for its 58th session to hear about the condition of NER orphans in Abkhazia and the Northern Caucasus and decided to ask the Executive Committee of the People's Commissariat of Enlightenment to increase supervision over outplaced NER orphans in the region; to stop transferring orphans to Abkhazia; and, to issue a series of instructions to NER and local bodies in Abkhazia to improve supervision over orphans already transferred there.[894] Discussion of outplaced children in the rural economies of Abkhazia and the Northern Caucasus reemerged during the January 3, 1929, meeting of the People's Commissariat of Enlightenment. It was decided that the TSFSR representative N. Ter-Ghazaryan would ask NER to stop relocating children to villages in Abkhazia,[895] because of the high incidence of malaria reported in children sent there.[896]

In its annual report to the U.S. Congress for the year 1928, NER described its policy for 1928 as "…one of constructive liquidation, with emphasis on the word 'constructive.'"[897] It also pointed out that the reduction of operations, while "somewhat rapid," had been "scientifically directed."[898] It did, however, acknowledge some of the difficulties encountered by outplaced children: in 1925 relatives "of some sort or another" had been found for 80% of the outplaced children but in 1928, only 15% had been outplaced with relatives. As a result, the report continued,

> The children…go into strange homes under strange conditions, many of the homes barely able to make a living. The malaria scourge along the Black sea shore

276   THE CITY OF ORPHANS

has made especially difficult the satisfactory welfare of 1,500 boys and girls placed among Armenian farmers in the tobacco district of Abkhazia.[899]

The report went on to praise Janet MacKaye who had attended to the children's health in health wagons with graduate nurses. But post-orphanage work, to ensure that the children were well rooted in their new locations to the extent that the economic conditions of the country generally permitted, had been costly and had increased NER's expenditures. Nonetheless, it was a tremendous job,

> ...being better done every month as the organization changes into an agency, not only completing its orphanage responsibility, but fully serving its obligation to the safety of the children placed out until they are old enough to carry on by their own efforts.[800]

Under the sub-heading "Constructive Reduction of Operations," the report reviewed in some detail the benefits of the "scientific" outplacement of orphans, which had helped reduce NER's operational budget—in the Caucasus as in all of its orphanages in the Near East, by 30%:

> ...A reduction of 30% in our overseas operations during the year brought about largely by the scientific outplacing of children from our orphanages in homes or supervised employment and by the progress of children already so outplaced into full self-support.[901]

Open-air mobile clinic organized by Janet MacKaye. (*The Huntington Daily News*, March 3, 1930)

Village Mobile Clinic. (*An Investment that Will Endure*: 4)

Մայիս 27 1927

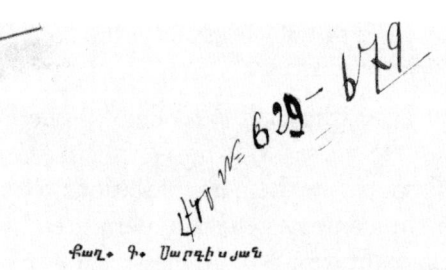

Թ. 278

Քաղ. Գ. Սարգսյան

Պետ. Լեբ. Ամերիկույեն կից Լենինականում

Հետևյալ շափաս յերեխաները ուղարկվելու են Ադլերի շրջան աշխատանքի, նրանց անունները քժական անկանցուցակուն կան խնդրում եմ տալ ԼԻՏԵՐՆԵՐ Լենինականց մինչև ԲԱՔՈՒՄ վաղ յերեկոյան գնացով.

1.	Մուրադյան	Զիշակ	Սալվե	Մանուկ	Աշրակ
2.	Ղազարյան	Հագոպորդ	Ջորջաբ	Մանուկ	Ալաշկերտ
3.	Կարապետյան	Կալիքսեն	Իանում	Գասպար	Շին Բաժազդ
4.	Երեսյան	Միրանոշ	Սարքար	Երեսա	Վան
5.	Իաչատուրյան	Վարսենիկ	Յեվա	Իաչատուր	Ղարս
6.	Մինասյան	Յեվգենիա	Հայկուշ	Մինաս	Մուշ
7.	Ավետիսյան	Մարգարիտ	Սալվե	Ավետիս	Խնուս
8.	Գալստյան	Արաքսի	Հայկանոշ	Հարություն	Լենինական
9.	Շառոյան	Քրիստինե	Գայանե	Պետրոս	Մուշ
10.	Դանիելյան	Շուշանիկ	Ռոս	Դանիել	Բուլանդ
11.	Կարապետյան	Անգին	Արմաշաս	Գրիգոր	Երզնկա
12.	Իսրայելյան	Մերանուշ	Մարիամ	Մամբրե	Բուլանդ
13.	Արզականյան	Իանում	Մարիամ	Արշակ	Ղարս
14.	Ալեքսանյան	Թամարա	Գեղանուշ	Մարտիրոս	Դարաբաղ
15.	Մարտիրոսյան	Զալուր	Իակուշի	Մարտիրոս	Բասեն
16.	Ակոբչյան	Պաճառ	Առլեա	Մկայան	Ալաշկերտ
17.	Իաչատուրյան	Հայկանուշ	Յեվա	Իաչատուր	Ղարս
18.	Մուրադյան	Ջանո	Եվնիկ	Վանեն	Վան
19.	Շմավոնյան	Եվորդ	Եվրան	Հարություն	Վան
20.	Իաչատուրյան	Քավական	Անուշ	Արշակ	Նոր Բաղեզդ
21.	Մուրադյան	Վարդանոշ	Մարիամ	Վարդան	Վան
22.	Ավետիսյան	Միրանոշ	Վարդանոշ	Ավետիս	Վան
23.	Պետրոսյան	Իակուշի	Ռոսուն	Մանուկ	Վան
24.	Վարդանյան	Վարդանոշ	Մարիամ	Դաշար	Բուլանդ
25.	Երեսյան	Չրութ	Զազա	Ավետիս	Թերջան
26.	Մամիկոնյան	Բութոշ	Սերոշ	Ղուկաս	Ալաշկերտ
27.	Մարիբրոշյան	Յեզսիկ	Անգին	Մարտիրոս	Վան
28.	Հովհաննիսյան	Ռոսիկ	Արուսիակ	Յերան	Ղարս
29.	Մաթևոսյան	Վիկտորյա	Նարկիզ	Յերանոս	Յանսի շեվան
30.	Իաչատուրյան	Շուշանիկ	Մաքրուշի	Կարապետ	Ղարս
31.	Ղարիբյան	Յեզսիկ	Աթթանաս	Հովհաննես	Ալ Ջավաղ
32.	Պողոսյան	Ֆերազ	Մարգարիտ	Պողոս	Խնուս
33.	Թումասյան	Արեքի	Գյուլզազ	Սերակ	Ղարս
34.	Հարությունյան	Բաղդշի	Կարգիզ	Հարություն	Վան
35.	Սարգիսյան	Սերոբ	Իաթուն	Սարգիս	Բիթլիս
36.	Կարապետյան	Աղթիկ	Տախկին վորբ անգործ մնացած Լենինականում.
37.	Ավետիսյան	Բաղրատ	Գյուլզազ	Ավետիս	Ղարս

Ռ.Մ.ՀԵԼԼ

Շարունակություն

38.	Մինասյան	Հայկանուշ	Մրոս	Դենազ	Բայանդուր
39.	Մելիքյան	Սուլթան	Սանամ	Մելքար	Այնթաբ
40.	Սարգսյան	Միրանոշ	Կդղան	Կարապետ	Կողպ
41.	Ամբայան	Յուզբեք	Զորան	Ամբատ	Ղարս
42.	Մինասյան	Համբիկ	Զատանչեմ	Որայջ	Իզմիր
43.	

Ռ.Մ.ՀԵԼԼ

Ամերիկի Մանուկներրի Խնամատուցյան Բաժին

List of children being sent to Adler as laborers. (NAA 39/1/4/ff. 8 and 9)

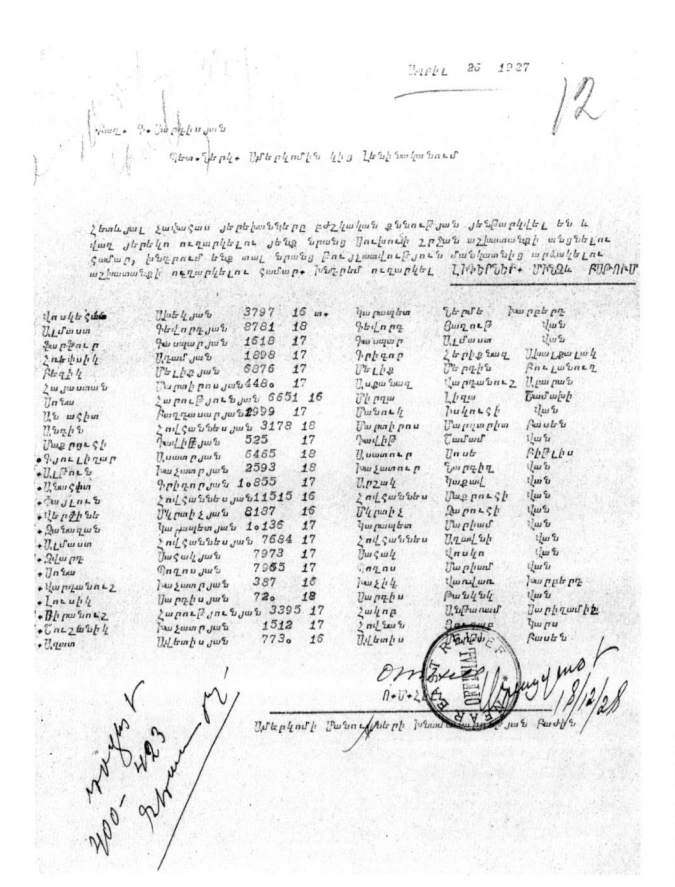

List of children who had passed physical examination and were being sent to Sukhum.
(NAA 39/1/6/f. 12)

List of foster families in Sukhum and children in their care.
(NAA 131/3/558/f. 69)

Lists of individuals wishing to take children for adoption and as temporary student-agriculturalists, and list of orphans who had volunteered. (NAA 39/1/7/ff. 22, 23)

List of children who had been transferred to Sukhum and Adler.
(NAA 31/3/555/f.231)

List of children being transferred to Sukhum.
(NAA 131/3/593/f. 3)

List of children who had passed medical examination and found fit for labor or adoption.
(NAA 39/1/6/ff. 20–23)

Name		#	Home	age	Remarks
Vartkes	Mardirosian	1	X	17	✓
Krikor	Karabetian	2780	III	17	✓
Mirak	Khosrovian	5443	IX	16	✓
Chougas	Nshanian	360	IX	17	✓
Baghdasar	Krikorian	2762	IX	17	✓
Enouk	Davitian	3117	IX	18	dumb. shoemaker Reg 5
Haroutiun	Mardirosian	2918	IX	17	✓
Azad ✗	Avedisian	7730	III	16	lame (Special Order)
Aram	Hakopian	3608	29	16	✓
Galoust	Davitian	54	X	16	✓
Babgen	Vartanian	7038	X	15	small
Mugrdich	Simonian	2024	X	16	✓
Alexan	Avedisian	1454	X	15	small
Kegham	Mouradian	5784	X	17	✓
Saro	Torosian	1729	IX	15	small
Markos	Vartanian	7458	IX	11	"
Khoren	Torosian	3571	X	16	✓
Movses	Krikorian	7576	X	17	Shoemaker Reg 5
Daniel	Hakopian		XII	16	
Torkom	Torkomian		X	15	small
Bakrad	Avedisian	5402	XII	15	"
Vachagan	Mekhakian	1444	III	15	"
Anoushavan	Vanetzian	1044	IX	15	"
Haykaz	Vartanian	2473	IX	15	"
Ardavazd	Sarayan	1029	IX	15	"
Hampartzoum	Khachadorian	7177	III	18	✓
Khachadour	Haroutiunian	1156	X	17	✓

Name		#	Home	age	
Soultan	Mekhitarian	306	XV	16	✓
Louisik ✗	Sarkisian	720	"	17	✓
Vartouch ✗	Khachadourian	389	"	16	✓
Anahid ✗	Krikorian	10855	"	17	✓
Piloun ✗	Hovhanesian	10515	"	17	✓
Zvart ✗	Sahakian	7973	"	16	✓
Almast ✗	Hovhanesian	7684	"	16	✓
Zanazan ✗	Karabedian	10136	"	17	✓
Verdjine ✗	Mardichian	8187	"	16	✓
Atour ✗	Khachadourian	2593	"	17	✓
Arghik	Sarkisian	1386	"	17	✓
Siran	Avedisian	9221	"	16	✓
Gulizar ✗	Asadrian	6466	"	17	✓
Anahid ✗	Baghdasarian	9999	"	16	✓
Un king ✗	Hovhanesian	3178	"	17	✓
Araxi	Hakopian	1095	"	16	✓
Makrouhi ✗	Davitian	525	"	16	✓
Hasmik	Stepanian		"	17	
Siran	Khachadourian	976	"	16	
Siran	Hovhanesian	4739	"	17	
Mariam	Davitian	2585	"	16	
Migar	Mekhitarian	3683	"	17	
Arousiak	Panosian	9944	XI	16	
Yughaper	Hakopian	3850	"	17	
Azik	Khachadourian	4137	"	17	
Shoushanik	Ghazarian	11273	"	17	
Zvart	Sarkisian	6147	"	17	
Siroush	Markarian	10113	"	16	
Youghaber	Melkonian	9986	"	17	
Manoushak	Manoukian	3162	20	17	
Soultan	Mesropian	8747	XVIII	16	
Hazmvart	Ghazarian	12035	"	17	

Staff Reorganization, Budget Cuts, and Labor Unions

During his trips to Leninakan in the latter half of the decade of the 1920s, Barday Acheson was busy restructuring and downsizing the staff and budget of the City of Orphans. Neither the increased responsibilities NER had assumed with refugees in Greece nor the economic problems at home had been advantageous to NER's coffers in New York, making it necessary to revisit its institutions in the Near East and the Caucasus and plan for the future. As the Director of Overseas programs, it was Acheson who would execute the changes. His diaries and book typescript, the latter never completed, yield much valuable information about the events that would change the shape and direction of the City of Orphans in the latter 1920s.

Acheson did not believe that the "mild form of recession" of 1923 was the only reason the American public had gradually withdrawn its support. True, it was easier in an uncertain financial climate "to economize on the food and clothing of refugees on far-distant doorsteps."[902] But the business recession, Acheson wrote, had been accompanied by "a kind of moral recession" in the U.S. leadership:

> …Our leaders told us that we had a pretty good thing in our broad acres, our limitless resources, and our teeming industrial centers, and that we had better keep it for ourselves and let the rest of the world go hang…In other words, idealism also suffered from the disillusionments of post-war treaty-making.[903]

Nonetheless, during the difficult years when U.S. "emotional generosity had dried up," NER had enjoyed the support of thousands of citizens who were "made of sterner stuff" and who believed that

> …after saving children from death a nation is under obligation, even at a sacrifice, to perform the less melodramatic task of giving them enough moral training and enough income producing skills to prevent them from becoming a social menace. It was these who resisted the post-war moral retreat, who still clung to the wartime heights of world citizenship…[904]

Through summer 1926 Acheson, with Yarrow's help and support, developed an Organizational Manual and a list of new assignments for the American staff with a view of consolidating responsibilities to reduce expenses and install new policies.[905] One of the chief changes he planned was to reorient the orphanage from being simply a feeding and clothing station to a nurturing home environment:

> …Our policy and ambition was to have the Americans know the children and take an interest in their development and future lives. For instance, if an American were put in charge of the newspapers, the object would not be to produce better newspapers, they are good enough now, but it would be an opportunity for contact between the Americans and the children that should result in an improved character of the children.[906]

It is unclear which, if any specific, "newspapers" Acheson was referring to, but the goal was to make one-to-one contact between Americans and orphans part of the routine. Reorganization of the American personnel at the City of

Orphans included grouping all business activities and concerns under a single business manager to free department heads and experts from business or administrative duties thereby allowing them to devote their time to their specialties, be it in agriculture, industrial education, or recreation.[907]

Among the American staff Acheson found Caroline Silliman, Helen Mays, and Janet MacKaye especially valuable. But meetings with the three women revealed that all three were unhappy with the leadership of Joseph Beach and questioned Acheson's decision to bring Beach back to the Caucasus as Managing Director. Yarrow and Wilcox, the latter one of the educators at the Polygon, had also questioned the wisdom of Beach's return.[908] Acheson himself had doubts about Joseph Beach and recognized that Beach was a difficult person to handle. Still, there were some advantages to Beach's appointment, he thought, because while Beach had "never succeeded in riding the horse himself," he had been able to keep some NER field personnel, such as Ernest Yarrow, "out of the saddle."[909] Acheson acknowledged that Yarrow "was a real help," and

> ...probably the strongest man that we have ever had in the Caucasus. On the other hand I will never be entirely free from anxiety as long as he is in the Caucasus and Shelkovnikoff is at Batoum. The alternative is that he might be made into a very active and vindictive enemy that would utterly ruin our work if he was not handled properly.[910]

Regardless of the complaints, Acheson was resolute and told Beach's critics that

> ...the personnel in the Caucasus had made it impossible for one director after another; first Yarrow, then Horn, then Mr. Marden and then Yarrow again, and now Mr. Beach; that I did not propose to have this procession of martyrs continue.[911]

Recasting the enormous relief center into a new vision and adjusting it to a much smaller orphan population was not an easy task, and one that would continue over the summer of 1927 when Acheson looked at other avenues to reduce the budget. Continuing his review of the faculty, Acheson now urged further expansion of the practice of replacing local teachers by older orphans. This would not only offer the child the opportunity to gain practical experience but would also help reduce NER's payroll. The same principle of reducing expenses by hiring orphans was applied to general maintenance. By

Armenia's First Traveling Hospital

The first traveling clinic ever seen in Armenia, while Miss Janet McKay and a student starting off to make the rounds of Leninakan district where there are several thousand out-placed children. Miss McKay is director of the only training school for girl nurses in the Caucasus conducted by Near East Relief.

Janet MacKaye and a nurse on the traveling hospital. (*The Taylor Daily Press*, May 28, 1928)

the end of July 1927, many of the orphans had replaced adult local teachers and employees. Twenty boy bakers had replaced all the employees except two managers and the bookkeeper in the bakeries. In transportation, all wagon drivers had been replaced by boy drivers; in the construction department, only the foremen remained to direct the work of boy whitewashers, stone workers, carpenters, and others; 15 tractor drivers and mechanics in agricultural work were replaced by boys who also ran a sawmill. Other orphan boys were now hospital attendants, ambulatory workers, and storage keepers in the hospital. Older boys were also in charge of the bread and meat stations, the bathhouse was run entirely by boys and former orphan boys managed five of the 16 orphanage buildings. And, a list of employees at the Polygon from the late 1920s shows that out of 39 employees, 25 were orphans, of whom 13 were washerwomen.[912] In the classrooms, nineteen boys from the teacher training school, called "dastiarags"[913] (group leaders or home room teachers), served as teachers and, finally, of the daily English class for 20 advanced students, some students worked as office help, interpreters, and translators. Boys who were not naturally skilled filled in where needed.

But the task of staff reorganization was more complicated than replacing paid workers with older orphans. When Acheson analyzed the departmental budgets with Joseph Beach on July 25, 1927, to estimate future reductions, he concluded that the biggest problem was the extremely high native staff payroll, amounting to 50% of the total expenditures, mostly due to union laws.[914] While the salaries of the American staff were decided in New York, those of the Armenian staff were dictated by the labor unions in Armenia, with which NER's relations had been strained since 1923.[915] One complaint the labor unions had registered in 1923 involved the one-month vacation NER allowed native employees, as opposed to two months vacation per year according to labor laws. In his letter to the President of the Professional Unions of Armenia, "Mr. Gasparian," dated July 9, 1923, NER Director of Personnel Fred G. Lange had explained that the shorter vacation time had to do with the fact that since orphans had no homes to go to during the vacation period they needed continuous supervision throughout the year.[916] But, Lange added, referring to an earlier discussion, supervision of the children in the summer months was different from that of the regular year and consisted mostly of recreational supervision, and therefore the teachers could well view it as a type of vacation:

> …the change from ordinary class-room work to the supervision of recreational activities in itself constitutes a change for the teachers which would serve in a fair measure the same purpose as a vacation, and considering that the teachers have in addition to this a full month's vacation free of all duties, we feel that their physical needs are fully cared for. We again wish to repeat and emphasize these considerations and to affirm that a ruling such as you propose would be very detrimental to the progress and best interests of the children for whom we are all working.

Another item Lange raised in his note referred to regulations regarding the termination of employment at the orphanage:

> ...in full compliance with the provisions of our Mandate, we shall pay the teachers whom it may be necessary to liquidate, on the following basis:
>
> a. Where two weeks notification has been given of intent to liquidate, no liquidation pay will be given. Where no such notification has been given two weeks pay will be given.
>
> b. Those of our employees who have been in the service six months or more shall receive a two weeks vacation, which if not taken will be paid for.[917]

Some of the rulings on salaries by the labor unions had cost NER $10,000 per month for 10 months in 1926 and 1927. At his meeting with Ter-Ghazaryan in July 1927, Acheson pointed out that funds raised in America were intended for relief purposes only:

> I told Ter-Ghazaryan that I was not going to fight over these questions—that I would simply order all the American personnel to Batoum some sunshiny morning and leave them holding the sack unless a greater degree of cooperation was secured.[918]

Acheson was convinced that NER was being extorted and had in fact given serious thought to "dismissing all the children to relatives" and giving them subsidies, but he was not quite ready to endanger relations he had worked so hard to build:

> I am convinced that we are being gouged by the labor unions, and yet I am not quite willing to smash into the intricate relationships that have built up through months of negotiation.[919]

Acheson next brought up the issue of labor unions with Artashes Karinyan, then chairman of the Communist Party Central Executive Committee of Armenia.[920] Karinyan first asked Acheson to convey his regards to Vickrey, Barton and MacCallum, and then the two men discussed the question of NER extending its mandate for another year. If NER were inclined to renew the mandate, said Acheson, it would be impossible to do so, unless some degree of cooperation was secured from the labor unions. Karinyan was very much in support of the extension and promised to look into the problem. Karinyan felt that agricultural work was the prime need of the country, encouraging NER to continue its agricultural program. A day later, on July 29, 1927, Acheson brought up the subject again with Ter-Ghazaryan. He very much feared, he said, that the salaries the labor unions dictated for NER's local employees in Leninakan might very soon force NER out of business in Leninakan:

> I think we are spending more money on the labor unions than on the children right now. Last winter, we had to pay something like $3,000 or $4,000 a month as salaries for teachers that we did not need for nine months because of union rules. This waste of American funds is outrageous.[921]

Two days later, on August 1, 1927, Acheson had an extended discussion with the labor unions in Leninakan. Present were the secretary of the combined labor unions, representatives of four major unions, and Georgy Sargsyan. All agreed that the percentage of the total budget now spent on wages was indefensible, and Acheson on his part asked the labor union leaders to help the Americans understand Armenian laws and work together with the Americans to solve problems locally. The labor unions expressed the wish to cooperate, with Acheson warning them "not to kill the goose that lays the golden egg."[922]

Acheson's careful review of expenditures in 1926 and 1927 included consolidating various functions of the physical plant. Consolidating the warehouses was an obvious way of reducing cost, as was improving the system of ordering supplies, inventorying existing supplies, etc.[923] Each department would now have to limit all buildings and construction of every type within a total appropriation of $15,000, of which $1,000 was to be used to complete repairs on personnel houses and the remaining $14,000 on building water lines and renovations in all departments, including the farm. In addition, wood would have to be rationed, equipment that had been thrown all around the place should be placed under lock, and finally, since there were too many on the payroll, personnel would need to be cut by one-third.

The budget review in summer 1927 showed that it had cost NER an average of $84,321 per month to run the Polygon from January to June 1927. To come within budget, a reduction of $139,000 in total expenditures would have to be made in the next six months.[924] In his diary entry for July 20, 1927, Acheson wrote, "We are still carrying the machinery of an organization intended to support 40,000 children."[925] Acheson had to remind the staff that the orphanage was now operating for 3,500 children and should be managed on a budget of $40,000 to $50,000 per month,[926] and repeating his statement of a year earlier, he told the American staff to get away from the idea of orphanage and think of school. But Acheson wasn't hopeful that all the American staff could make such a transition. "I do not feel," he wrote,

> ...that our Americans are working very hard or that they have much enthusiasm for their work. They are simply carrying on by the day.[927]

The hospital and the nursing school incurred a disproportionate part of the total monthly expenditures—$11,000 per month. He had been aware of the situation during the preceding summer and had thought that expenditures on health were the main obstacles to an economic reduction of costs.[928] He had also felt then, that "our doctors have been much more interested in operations than they have been in cleaning up the common diseases of the children." The medical department would need to change course from doing chiefly surgery and concentrate on preventative medicine, and medical care to the community outside the orphanage would have to be limited only to the number of patients needed for nurses' clinical training.[929] Part of the medical expenditures had to do with the continuing treatment of trachoma. Dr. Dudley C. Kalloch, who had succeeded Dr. Uhls as the resident ophthalmologist, had discovered in 1926 that in NER's clinic in the city of Leninakan where children outplaced from orphanages were seen, 69 of the 284 children, or about 24.3%, were infected with trachoma. The disease was far more prevalent among the children still living in the orphanage, where 3,868 children out of 5,220, or 74.1% were still infected with the disease and explained it as a result of the close contacts that were inevitable in orphanage life. Kallogh's findings and the various approaches he took using treatment methods in practice in the U.S. at the time, appeared in the *The Journal of the American Medical Association* while he was still in Leninakan.[930]

During further discussions with the medical staff and nurses, it was decided to keep only a small hospital of 150 beds, which was all that was needed for the children and for nurses' training.[931] To reduce the medical budget further, and with the backing of Dr. Sisson, the surgeon, Acheson stated that there had been too much operating in the hospitals and not enough attention paid to the medical requirements of the children.[932] He then encouraged Winchester Nursing School Director Elsie Jarvis to instill the idea of social service in her nurses and insisted "nurses have got to go to the towns of Armenia to make our investment in them worth while."[933] There was now also a Junior Service Corps, who had been taught hygiene and simple health principles, to enable them to follow the home-placed orphans being subsidized by NER.[934]

"...*Something of the Spirit of America*..."

In April 1926, three months before Acheson's arrival in Armenia, the headline "Armenian Wealth Grows, Envoys Say" in the April 25, 1926, issue of *The New York Times* announced the arrival of a commission from Soviet Armenia in New York. The commission to New York, read *The New York Times* article, included "Dr. S. Kamsarakan, President of the Armenian Red Cross; Krikor Vardanyan and Karen Mikaelyan, well-known publicists in their own country." They planned to stay for three months, and had been sent to interest Americans, especially those of Armenian descent, in "the development of the new Armenian Homeland in the Caucasus." They had come, *The Times* reported, quoting Karen Mikaelyan, "not to arouse sympathy, but to give to the outside world a better idea of the new Armenian nation, which is now alive and flourishing, under the aegis of Soviet Russia."

Mikaelyan had been surprised to discover that only a few Americans realized that there was such a thing as a Republic of Armenia and that most Americans believed that all the Armenians either perished in the last great massacres or were scattered to the four corners of the earth. But, Mikaelyan had stated,

> We now have our own nation, one which fulfills most of the ardent dreams of Armenian nationalists...
>
> Although our nation is only five years old, there is already a national university at Erivan, with a library of 200,000 volumes and four separate Faculties—in medicine, agriculture, political and social science and pure science.
>
> ...We are very proud of our university—proud of what it has accomplished in five years. We think of it as a symbol of Armenia's rebirth and revival.

Mikayelyan had also highlighted the cultural interests of the new Armenia:

> ...Americans will be interested in our National Theatre of Erivan, which produces "Othello" and "Hamlet" and "The Merchant of Venice" in the Armenian language, with great success. Shakespeare is as great a favorite with the Armenian lovers of literature as he is with the English or Germans.

In their public appearances, Mikayelyan and the other envoys had praised NER's ongoing efforts and thanked the American people and NER:

> Americans are always popular in Armenia. The Armenian people can never forget what American help accomplished during the darkest days. The Near East Relief organization is still doing a great work, caring for 10,000 or the 15,000 orphans in the country.

The commission's visit was also covered in the September 1926 issue of *The New Near East*, where Dr. Kamsarakan was quoted as saying through an interpreter "All three envoys personally owed their lives to American relief work."[935] On that note, Charles V. Vickrey had commented on the "unique" relationship that had evolved between the peoples of Armenia and America, which was based purely on humanitarian interest of one nation in another. Vickrey had added that the uniqueness would be ever lasting because it was between peoples and not governments:

> This has not been a movement of governments, but of peoples. There is scarcely an American to whom the idea of Armenia is not familiar, and there is no Armenian who does not know that the American flag means help in trouble and safety in danger...The bond between America and Armenia is one proof that the world is really growing better.

> The Armenians are now a part of Russia. Another chapter in their long history has begun. Armenia will live, for its roots are deep and they refuse to die...Now they have a new sap—something of the spirit of America. Fifty thousand children, nearly five per cent of the population, have grown up under American care. Tomorrow they will be the leaders of their country. We are very proud of the fact that something of America has been planted there, something that will grow.

In his Report to Congress for the Year Ending 1926, Vickrey went further in his assessment of the future that awaited orphans in whom "something of America had been planted." He believed that orphans who had grown up in the City of Orphans were destined to lead Armenia to a happier future, just as in 1860 Abraham Lincoln had come "out of a log cabin in the unpromising rural districts of Illinois to lead our Nation through its great crisis." The children from the City of Orphans, he stated, would take their leadership positions not only in Armenia but also in the vast expanses of Russia, which were,

> ...open to the children from our orphanages in Armenia as the business offices of New York City and the congressional halls of Washington are to the school boys of Illinois and California. They have perfect freedom of intercourse between Moscow and Alexandropol. Moreover, one is impressed with the increasingly large numbers of officials and educational and commercial leaders in Moscow, Tiflis, and other government centers who are Armenians from the south.[936]

Orphan outplacements would continue through 1929, but in the summer of 1926 Acheson was busy planning a radically new configuration of the City of Orphans. According to the new plan as it ultimately emerged, the work in Karakala and Stepanavan would cease altogether and their programs, along with the orphans, would be transferred to the Polygon, and many would be outplaced. Simultaneous with that move would be the transfer of the work and the orphans from the Severski and the Kazachi, to the Polygon. With all programs, orphans and staff gathered at a single post, the Polygon would signal the beginning of the new "Constructive Phase" of NER's activities in Armenia, and the arena where the last phase of NER's activities would play out in dramatic interludes.

The first issue of the student weekly paper "Nor Ughi" [New Path], published by Severski students, Saturday, July 4, 1925. (NAA 1387/1/284/f. 1) Below is the translation of the editorial column on the left.

The "New Path"

Dear reader, today marks the appearance of our student newspaper "New Path" that has arrived to state to us that we are no longer the ignorant and backward orphans that we were only a few years ago. This paper is telling us, orphans, that it is enough to have groped in ignorance and in the dark, that it is necessary to emerge into the lighted world and to understand and comprehend all that which had been dark and incomprehensible.

The "New Path" will be opening to us a new world where with every footstep we will be encountering people who are better informed, more active, [people who] have a better understanding [of things], [the ones who] will be establishing the foundations of a new structure for our destitute orphan lives.

Therefore it is the moral responsibility of each one of you to show active and fervent support to our beloved "New Path" newspaper.

Long live the "New Path" and [long live] our orphanhood that has already matured and is self-aware.

Ed[itor], G[N?]ar-Mut

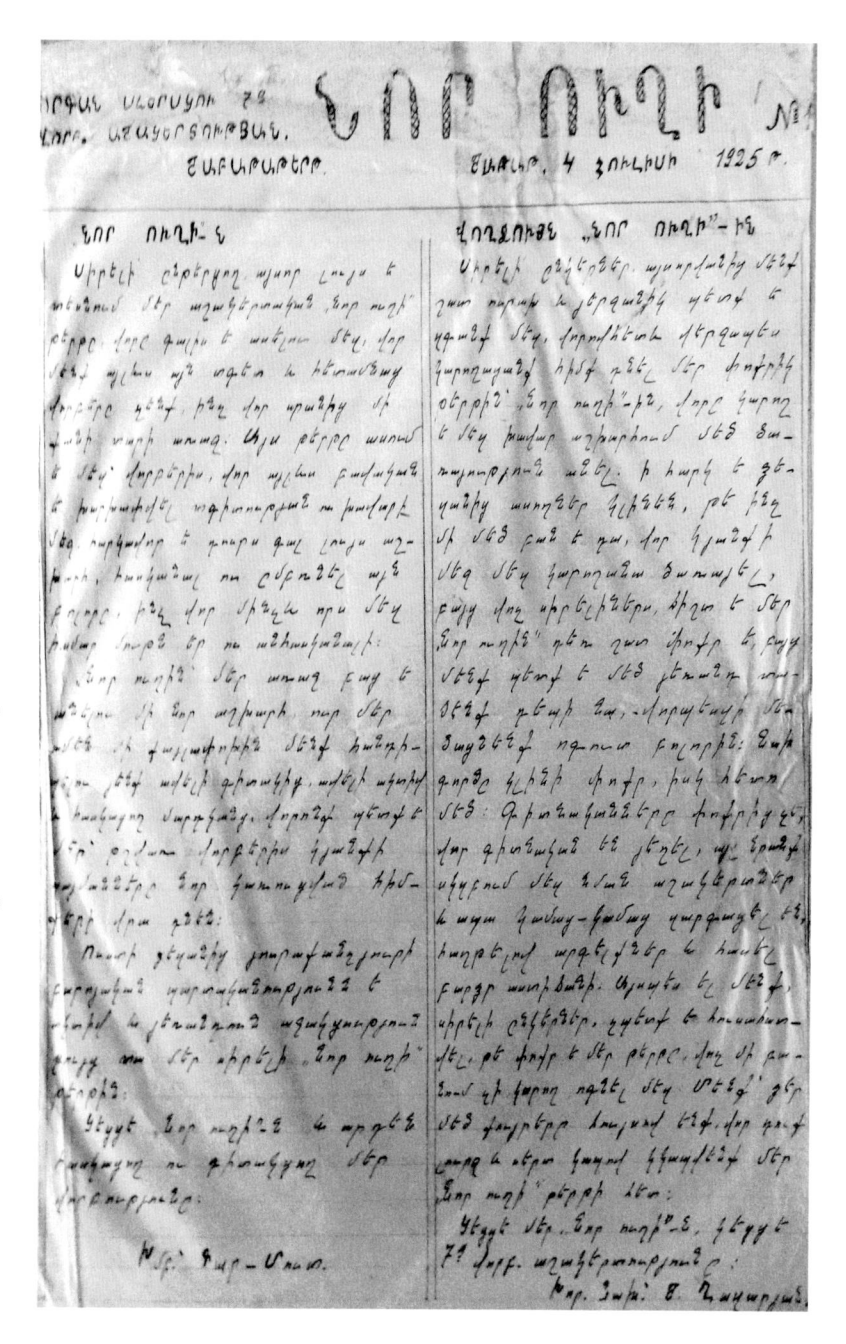

Part Three

The End of an Era

CHAPTER TEN

THE POLYGON: "ONCE GREAT IN NUMBERS, TODAY GREATER IN INFLUENCE..."

"Strictly Confidential"

With more than half the orphan population gone and funds running low, plans were put in place in Leninakan in summer 1926 to reconfigure the City of Orphans and concentrate all functions and assets into a single post—the Polygon. From NER's perspective, the reconfiguration would take a year, and the best approach would be to first return Stepanavan, Karakala, and Kazachi post to the government over summer 1926. NER would continue its use of Severski till spring 1927, during additional projected outplacements, at which time all NER operations would be concentrated in the Polygon, permanently. And there, at the Polygon, the NER would launch its next, and "Constructive Phase." The move would mark

> ...the beginning of a new chapter—one of constructive helpfulness through education to those who sit in the ancestral house of Christendom that new woes may be prevented.[937]

Yarrow, who had arrived in Leninakan in 1926 at Acheson's invitation to help him launch the new plans, supported the projected changes.[938] A tour of all three posts was conducted and the assets of each inventoried. The Polygon had orphanages, stables, agricultural buildings, vocational schools, clinic, laundry, schools, etc., but many of the buildings needed repairs. The Kazachi, renamed Lukashin Post, had warehouses, the nurses' residence, hospitals, and a section for the "feeble-minded." But there were no orphans at the Kazachi; they had been outplaced or transferred to the other posts. As for the Severski, it had orphanages, industrial rooms, and a model village. The farm at Karakala, while ideally suited for stockbreeding, needed an additional investment of $50,000 to $100,000 to maintain it, for which no provision had been made in the budget. Besides, 90% of the training in stockbreeding and dairying could be secured at a lesser cost and for a much larger number of students if the main idea behind the work could be transferred to the Polygon. The agricultural school at Stepanavan was also ideally located, but it, too, like Karakala, was isolated. The school could be transferred to Leninakan, especially since the new irrigation canal launched under Myasnikyan and completed under Lukashin provided ample irrigation to the area.[939]

The goal was concentration, which was as important for financial reasons as for efficient administration, and "would save at least $10,000 to $15,000 per month.[940] The government was kept abreast of NER's plans through numerous meetings with NER administrators and with Acheson, in particular. Acheson laid down his plans in a preliminary memorandum dated July 20, 1926, marked "Strictly Confidential." Here, he formulated the general approach, analyzed the issues, proposed solutions and outlined his steps toward a reconfiguration of NER's work in Armenia.[941] The main issues he raised dealt with outplacement, which he regretted had not proceeded as fast as he had hoped it would; with the persistence of trachoma within the orphanages necessitating proper isolation areas; the large hospital at the Kazachi which was now too large for current needs and needed to be replaced by a smaller one; and NER's budgetary constraints. Also discussed in the memorandum was the transfer of the agricultural, stockbreeding, and dairying programs from Karakala and Stepanavan to the Polygon.

Acheson then laid out the schedule: Karakala would be returned to the government before January 1, 1927, followed by Stepanavan when the equipment needed for the installation of the agricultural program at the Polygon and other logistical details were resolved, and the Kazachi would be returned once details of medical work and warehouses had been worked out. The next step would be the return of the Severski to the government. This would take place on July 1, 1927, after which all NER activities would be concentrated at the Polygon. Acheson had given much thought to the plan, he wrote, and felt that it would best conserve the resources of the NER and lay the groundwork for a permanent educational program in Armenia. As Acheson noted in his diary in 1926, his plan would

> …promote the educational program that it [NER] contemplates and provide for leaving a permanent institution in Armenia that will perpetuate its memory and assist in solving the agricultural, medical and trade training problems of the country.

NER could do this because

> …Near East Relief is in the best position that it has been in during its history in this country for effecting this program, and its plan during the past two years have been directed toward the accomplishment of this purpose. It therefore would be very unfortunate if circumstances prevented the materialization of this plan.[942]

But the events of the next few weeks upset Acheson's schedule and threw him into a whirlwind of meetings and negotiations in the summer of 1926 in Leninakan, Yerevan, and Tiflis. The cause was the urgent, and persistent request of the military for the immediate release of the Severski. Acheson had been informed of the military's request in a cable from NER's Tiflis headquarters, even before he had arrived in the Caucasus. Upon arrival in Tiflis, liaison Ter-Ghazaryan had reopened the topic and advised him to acquiesce.[943] But Acheson had refused, quoting the stipulation in NER's mandate whereby no buildings or property could be taken away from NER without the latter's consent. NER's investments in repairs and equipment at the Severski alone, he wrote, had cost an estimated $250,000 and had been made with that stipulation in mind:

> When NER took over Seversky practically every building was a complete ruin, without roof, windows or floors. And NER made an enormous investment (estimated at $250,000.00 in this Post) with the understating that it was to have full use of the Post until its own best interests caused it to return it to the Government.[944]

The issues were discussed at a meeting in the office of Chairman Sargis Hambardzumyan of the Council of People's Commissars on July 22, 1926, in Yerevan with NER staff and Acheson present, and at a second meeting on the next day, July 23, at 3pm. "I told the President," wrote Acheson in his diary, that

> ...we felt it best to retain Polygon and Seversky—Polygon permanently and Seversky until spring (June 15). If this were agreed to we would consider releasing Kazachi, Kara Kala and Stepanavan now. We would then concentrate stock breeding, Ag[riculture], Nurses Training, etc. in an institution that could be made permanent in the future if desired. He seemed to be impressed but the Gov[ernment] is evidently not anxious to concede Se[verski] even for a few months longer.[945]

NER's preferences—and the consequences should these be ignored—were summarized in a letter from Ernest Yarrow to Chairman Hambardzumyan, and amounted to a roadmap of NER's future work in Armenia.[946] His letter, began Yarrow, had been written in an "entirely unofficial and personal manner," and, he continued,

> I am certain...that you will accept the fact that in any suggestions I make to the Near East Relief, I keep fully in mind the interests of the Armenian Government with which I have had such cordial relations for so many years.

The first of several interrelated issues was a proposal to establish a progressive educational program as a permanent institution:

> The Near East Relief is in a position as never before, to put into effect a progressive educational program. They are ready to put this program into effect if it meets the approval of the government and the government gives its full cooperation.

The second item was a clarification of NER's financial status, and an attempt to correct the misconception that the organization was in financial difficulty:

> The question of financial difficulty during the past year was due largely to misunderstanding and largely without the knowledge of Mr. Acheson. If the present plans of the Near East Relief are accepted, I feel certain that this situation will not arise again, and also that there will be an end of the liquidation of excessive surplus supplies.

The Battle over Severski

The third, and "vital concern" that called for "<u>immediate</u> decision," Yarrow continued, concerned the military's request for the use of the Severski, which could unhinge the future of the progressive program:

> No progress can be made in reconstruction plans until this is settled, and the need for immediate decision is apparent from the fact that all transfers and changes should be completed before September so as to enable the schools to begin in permanent surroundings, with their permanent program.[947]

NER's staff had all agreed, continued Yarrow, that

> ...one of the posts, Stepanavan, Seversky, or Polygon can be immediately released. The number of children remaining in the orphanages is entirely too large at present to be accommodated in any one post, so there is no question but that two posts will have to be retained until next spring at least.

Yarrow then suggested that

> ...the interests of both the civil Government and the Near East Relief will be best conserved by giving up Stepanavan immediately and centering the work in Leninakan. The seven or eight hundred children can be distributed between Seversky and Polygon, making hardly any impression on these posts.

In this plan, the Severski would be released in spring 1927, by which time

> ...the number of children would be so decreased...that Seversky could then be released and the whole work concentrated at the Polygon.

At that time, also, the NER would launch the work of building permanent institutions:

> During the next two years institutions could be built at the Polygon which would be a permanent contribution to the educational and economic life of the country, and at the same time serve as a fitting memorial to the long term of Near East activities here and the lasting friendship which it symbolizes of the American people toward the Armenian people.

While Yarrow recognized the military's needs as "just and reasonable in itself," he believed that it was in conflict with "the immediate best interests of the orphans and the future cultural progress of the country":

> If the civil authorities could persuade the military authorities to defer their demand until next June, and in the meantime make the Stepanavan barracks accessible for their temporary occupation during the winter, I believe the widest interests of the country could be conserved.

Then Yarrow pointed out, in no uncertain terms, that in the event NER's plan was rejected, the NER would withdraw from Armenia:

> It is my personal opinion, and I have so advised Mr. Acheson, that if this arrangement of retaining Seversky for the winter cannot be made, there is no use of the Near East Relief concerning itself with founding permanent institutions or putting into effect a progressive program.

In which case, NER

> Would simply send the children out as fast as possible and close the work with dignity and honor, without making any effort to make any contribution to the institutional life of the country.

He ended his letter by reiterating that what he had written was entirely his personal viewpoint and was not to be interpreted as Acheson's views, although he hoped that the Chairman

> ...would be able to come to a helpful understanding, and I take this opportunity of again expressing my respect for the Government you represent and the hope that I will again have been able to have served both the Government and the Near East Relief, even in a small degree.[948]

Regardless, the military remained intransigent: Severski was to be evacuated immediately. For the next several weeks, Acheson protested to liaisons and high-ranking government officials in Yerevan, Leninakan, and Tiflis against the illegality of the act, pointed out the inevitable consequences should NER be forced to evacuate the Severski, with repeated reminders of the assistance NER had brought to Armenia in general, and the amounts spent on repairing the Severski, in particular. On numerous occasions he reminded the authorities that the mandate was effective for two more years, that no property held by NER could be taken away without its consent, and that the demand for Severski's immediate release would cause NER to disobey the government's own stated requirement of a certain number of cubic square feet necessary for each child in a dormitory or school. The NER could not conform to that law, Acheson argued, unless it retained both posts for the coming year.[949]

The debates, often cordial, at times harsh, turned into intense bartering sessions where each party tried to extract an advantage in return for concessions. Terms and demands of negotiations proposed at different times and in different combinations included the acquisition of sufficient land for the projected permanent Agricultural Institute at the Polygon; assurances that the Polygon would be made into a cultural center for all time without which there would be no particular point in NER developing a permanent school;[950] responsibility for expenses involved in building repairs; the immediate transfer of all "deficient children such as the blind, epileptic" and "sub-normal" to the government, which was "almost obligatory to the Government."[951]

At his meeting with Yerznkyan in Yerevan, wrote Acheson,

> Erzinkian was his usual friendly self and appeared to be anxious to have the plan as outlined realized. He promises that there would be no difficulty whatever concerning the liquidation or transfer of our stock and equipment at Kara Kala and Stepanavan.[952]

With Mravyan, Acheson had discussed the need for retaining the Severski for another year because of the yet unresolved trachoma situation:

> I outlined the whole case to him—emphasizing in particular the trachoma situation and the need of sufficient room for isolation, during the coming year.[953]

Once, on his way from Yerevan to Leninakan with Georgy Sargsyan, the latter had told Acheson that he felt NER personnel were not interested in the activities of the government. Acheson's reply was that NER was keeping out of the affairs of the government because they felt that they were not really welcome. Sargsyan then urged that NER familiarize itself with the various committees, organizations and methods of operation and assured Acheson that the government desired it. "It looks to me," wrote Acheson, "as though each of us had been feeling somewhat put out when in reality we did not correctly understand the other's attitude."[954]

During his stay in Tiflis, Acheson had met with Mamia Orakhelashvili, Deputy Chairman of the USSR Council of People's Commissars and First Secretary of the Transcaucasian Communist Party Committee in Tiflis and one of the most influential Soviet officials in the Caucasus. Acheson had strongly protested the government's actions and reneging on the written agreement in the mandate:

> President O. stated that the reason for the government's embarrassment was that the GOVT. had taken action turning back all military posts to the military. Heretofore the army had been quartered on a war basis; that is, in tents and temporary quarters. The Govt. now feels that it must look after the interests of the army and provide them with permanent quarters.

The government had also assumed that

> ...owing to our liquidation we are in position to release Seversky—and on this basis official and final action had been taken by the Government.

In the course of the meeting Orakhelashvili had also remarked that "while the work of the NER had been appreciated," he believed that

> ...we should look toward the time that the Government would be able to discharge its own responsibility to these children,

to which Acheson had responded:

> Our responsibility was that having brought the children into this country our obligation was training them so that they would be good citizens; otherwise it would have been better for the country if the children had perished.[955]

At the end of an hour, when no progress had been made, Acheson had stated that unless the government could advance some arguments that he had not heard before or did not withdraw its request for Severski, he would be "compelled to withdraw the entire program," that he would regard himself as entirely free from all commitments. "Orakhelashvili," wrote Acheson,

> ...tried to jolly me out of this position by proposing a hunting trip, and I stated that if the children had to be turned out of Seversky I wanted the Government officials to come down and do it personally.[955]

At the end, Orakhelashvili had promised to appoint a commission that would give the matter full consideration.

Acheson had also met with Sergei Lukashin while in Tiflis. NER, he told Lukashin, was being coerced into an unreasonable decision and found itself morally responsible to expend the funds it had raised for the good of the children in the Severski barracks, and that the government's actions, for all intents and purposes, constituted a breach of contract. To that,

Cit. Lookashin stated that if NER withdrew the children would not suffer, although it would probably be true that other government departments would not have funds equal to their duties, but that NER had volunteered to care for the children for an additional three-year period and that the Government desired them to do so.[957]

During the meeting, Acheson also offered his help in the acquisition of machinery for the textile factory:

> I stated...that if the Government desired to purchase machinery in America I would be willing to take supplies for certain of our needs and pay cash in America. The figure of $100,000 was suggested.[958]

The round of meetings in Tiflis and Yerevan were interrupted when Acheson began a tour of Russia—on a path similar to that taken by NER's Russian Commission in 1921—visiting Vladikavkaz, Rostov, Novgorod, Kazan, Samara, Saratov, Astrakhan, Leningrad, Moscow and Petrovsk, arriving in Tiflis at midnight, via Baku, on September 13, 1926. Immediately upon his return to Tiflis, Acheson resumed his meetings on the Severski. More arguments were proposed by Acheson, but to no avail. The committee appointed by Orakhelashvili to assess the Severski situation had passed a decision that supported the government's position and urgently requested the return of the Severski. In reality, wrote Acheson, "the request was...an ultimatum..."[959] In meetings and letters, Acheson repeated the significant investment NER had made in Armenia and the Caucasus amounting to $25,000,000, including $250,000 for the repairs of the Severski. He felt a moral responsibility to the American public with regard to the quarter of a million dollars relief money that had been spent on the Severski barracks, and which were now to be used for military purposes:

> ...NER had spent millions of dollars and that it was practically being kicked out of buildings contrary to mutual agreements and contract and that such an act could not be concealed from the American public.[960]

"This puts me and the men I represent," Acheson explained on various occasions,

> ...in a hole with the American Public as we can not possibly explain why buildings we have payed [sic] so much money for should be recalled particularly as we have always had the agreement that blds. [buildings] we repaired should remain in our hands until we were through with them.[961]

Acheson met with liaisons Sargsyan and Ter-Ghazaryan the day after he returned from his tour, and showed them the cables he had received from New York on the Severski situation and told them that he wished to be completely free of all obligations in the Caucasus. This was not due to any lack of sympathy for the children, he said, but due to the fact that by its actions, the government had damaged NER's ability to raise funds for work in Russia. But Ter-Ghazaryan was not swayed, and at the end, prevailed: despite very real concerns for the children's welfare, at least part of the Severski would have to be returned by October 15.[962]

Realizing that further discussion would cause greater problems for the coming year, Acheson suggested that they would accommodate as many children as possible in the Polygon and leave the rest at Severski. The Severski would then be turned over to the government on October 15 with the remaining children. "This gave Mr. Ter Ghazaryan deep concern," Acheson wrote,

> ...but I stated that I was not willing to spend the extra funds that would be required on any program other than that of a concentrated unit; however, if the Government chose to take charge of the repairs of the buildings I would be willing to move the children as rapidly as the Government was able to prepare the buildings for their habitation. Mr. Ter Gazarian was unwilling to undertake this contract and I, therefore, again stated that we would put whatever children we could in Polygon and leave the rest in Seversky for them to handle in any way that they saw fit.[963]

After the meeting, Acheson cabled Constantinople and asked them to hold all information concerning the Severski negotiations confidential.

The next day, September 15, Acheson had two meetings, both with Lukashin. One agenda item was unrelated to the Severski and had to do with legal procedures against NER. Some employees, who had been released from their jobs at NER, had opened court procedures against it; Acheson asked Lukashin to "squelch" them, lest they serve as precedents.[964] Lukashin told Acheson that NER was protected in the same sense and in exactly the same way that the Government was protected in such matters and that he would see to it that NER's rights were preserved.[965]

The next issue on the agenda was NER's future program. Lukashin's position had been that if NER wished to retain the Polygon their rights would not be challenged, so long as they had at least 1,000 children on the post. Lukashin had also explained that only serious military necessity had caused the government to request the use of the Severski and was not a reflection of an unfriendly act, and that the matter had been under discussion for three years. He had felt then that the needs of the children took precedence over the military but that when Severski was taken over by NER it was understood and definitely stated that if it were required for military necessity it would have to be returned.[966] Lukashin also assured Acheson that NER would enjoy the government's cooperation so long as its activities were not of a missionary nature.[967] Acheson then wanted assurances of government cooperation if NER was to establish a cultural center at the Polygon, to which Lukashin stated that NER need have no concerns. The next item of discussion was the cotton machinery where Lukashin explained that the cotton mill machinery discussed earlier had already been purchased, but that they were planning to buy two or three more units in the future and deeply appreciated the effort Acheson had made in securing the information he had requested. At the end, Lukashin assured Acheson of the good will of the SSRA government toward NER and its wish to cooperate with NER in every practicable way.[968]

Although NER's rights over the property were defensible on legal grounds, being the consummate negotiator, Acheson felt that he had pushed as far as he could:

>...I am convinced that our friends in Government circles are very genuinely impressed by the situation...
>
>I regard the whole situation as extremely serious as over-insistence on our part will undoubtedly jeopardize our relationships with certain influential leaders, while on the other hand the reality of our moral obligations to the giving-public of America and the inevitability of the press getting wind of the situation makes me feel that I can do no less than defend our interests to the utmost.[969]

Back in Leninakan, on September 17, 1926, Acheson and the American staff worked out a tentative schedule for the concentration at the Polygon. Accordingly, the farm school at Stepanavan would be moved to the Polygon on Wednesday, September 22, followed by the transfer of the herd and personnel from Karakala to the Polygon on Thursday, September 23. As for the Severski, 1,200 children of the Severski Primary Department would start school in Severski on September 21 and continue until after the hospital had been moved to the Polygon and the buildings at Kazachi Post were made ready to receive them, presumably between October 15 and November 1. It was also decided that the Severski kindergarten would be moved to the Polygon on the 20th or 21st of September, and the Severski Vocational Group would be moved to the Polygon and resume its activities there on Sept. 27. Finally, the local personnel of the Severski would be moved to the Kazachi, allowing the transfer of all 1,200 children from the Severski to the Polygon.[970] A week later, the decision was to leave the hospital at the Kazachi and move the epileptic, tubercular and subnormal children—but not the blind—to Severski, to be left there until the Government took them over, releasing space for the local personnel. That evening the orphan group leaders at the Polygon gave a party they had organized entirely by themselves, and Acheson gave out whistles to group leaders.[971]

To ensure the timely relocation and to "place the responsibility for any delays where they belong," the group in charge of the scheduling met with Sargsyan at 5:30 in the evening of September 27 and outlined the areas Sargsyan would be responsible for during the anticipated relocations. These included: the Polygon water supply; irrigation water supply for farming; allocation of about 10,000 poods of hay a year from Karakala for the Polygon herd; making 25,000 rubles available for the construction work at the Polygon; securing an adequate number of men and materials for repairs at some of the Kazachi buildings where the local personnel would be moved; the immediate building of two tennis courts at the Polygon; confirmation of the date of transfer of epileptic, tubercular, and chronic medical cases on October 1 whose care NER would assume for the month of October; housing arrangements and care of 200 older children who would begin work at the textile mills; the arrangement of 25 train cars for the morning of September 22 for the transport of children from Stepanavan to the Polygon; military guards for and during all transfers and for the protection of vacated property; and finally, securing transport from the army to move the equipment from Severski to the Polygon. Sargsyan agreed to attend to all requests.[972]

At the end of September, Acheson informed the government that the Severski had been vacated at the request of the government and on their terms, but NER's Executive Committee in New York reserved the right, without prejudice or commitment, to review the Severski incident and reach such conclusions concerning it as they saw fit.[973] Despite the difficulties he faced in the summer of 1926, Acheson continued to cooperate with government officials and representatives. When, for example, Leninakan's Cheka called on him he was happy to oblige:

> The first assistant to the chief of the Cheka called just as I was starting for lunch, in regard to some automobile tires they wanted. The matter was easily arranged...It is necessary for us to exchange courtesies with these government officials as we frequently are in need of gasoline, tires, etc. ourselves, and at a very recent date have received a similar courtesy to that which the cheka is requesting today.[974]

Acheson also felt, as did some of the American staff, that the government was doing everything within its means to reconstruct the country but that their efforts were not being acknowledged in the U.S.:

> The chief injustice that has been done to the present Gov. by the publicity that has been current in America is the constant statement that this Gov. is responsible for the conditions that existed when they took controll [sic]. It is quite obvious that they were not the cause of those conditions and moreover that there has been a very marked improvement in every way since they took controll [sic].[975]

"I am," he wrote, "constantly impressed with the way every one looks and the general air of prosperity.[976]

During his tour of Russia in the summer of 1926, Acheson had hoped to meet with Georgy Chicherin, in charge of Soviet foreign policy from 1918 until 1928, to discuss the question of vagrant children in Russia. He had hoped to discuss American and Russian cooperation in solving the problem and then bring a group of influential Americans into Russia the following year. But due to the inaction of the Caucasus representative in facilitating the meeting, he had not been able to achieve his goal.[977]

Acheson met with the local personnel at the Severski on Sept. 27, 1926, to inform them, that "...we were not releasing Severski because we wanted to but because of the urgent demand of the government," and that they should expect changes in the personnel as well:

> ...we would retain in our employ the best personnel, whether they were at Polygon or Seversky, and that it was their duty and privilege to perpetuate the spirit of Seversky in their new quarters in Polygon.[978]

Acheson had a similar meeting with the Polygon personnel the same day. His message was that the reorganization was being carried out—in the areas of nurses' training, agricultural work, stockbreeding, trade school, etc.— to respond to the needs of Armenia, and that NER would retain the best and release the least efficient personnel. He also announced that the local personnel would be moved to Kazachi.[979] That same evening Acheson had a long meeting with Vahan Cheraz, the former scoutmaster at Kazachi, who had recently returned from exile and needed employment. After their long meeting, Acheson wrote in his diary:

> His experiences were very unpleasant and he thinks that they were directed against the NER and Brown in particular. I told him that in this he was mistaken and that his chief difficulties had grown out of communications from the outside concerning his lack of sympathy with the present government.[980]

Acheson had also told Cheraz that

> …it would be foolish for us to try to give him substantial aid as such aid would immediately prove to those who were suspicious that we were showing favoritism toward him.

Acheson then added in his diary:

> I got one point worth jotting down from my conference with him, i.e., that those hostile to the N.E.R. claim that it is a haven for the enemies of the Government, meaning by this that we have in our employ large numbers of the old aristocracy and former intellectuals.[981]

Two days later, Acheson wrote,

> …My idea is that we should give him [Cheraz] temporary employment as often as possible.[982]

The temporary jobs Cheraz was given at NER did not appeal to him, as he explained in one of his letters dated January 26, 1927:

> I have found temporary employment again. Work has lost all its charm…and all…moral gratification…It is the Augean Stables [the fifth labor of Heracles], or the Temple where the moneychangers have built a nest. Unfortunately, there is neither Heracles nor Christ to purify them with their blessed brooms in their hands. Poor orphans…[983]

When he wrote his friends again in February 19, 1927, he was unemployed:

> …These last few days my work was again thwarted by a command from high up, and I am left without a job, or even the hope of being employed.

> …A few days ago they told me that I have to leave this job, and needless to say, they did not offer me a new job.[984]

The Quest for Permanency

When he returned to the Caucasus in summer 1927, Acheson broached two related topics with the TSFSR leadership in Tiflis: the extension of NER's mandate, due to expire in 1928, and the idea of establishing permanent institutions in Armenia. Both topics were discussed with Shalva Eliava, Chairman of the TSFSR Council of People's Commissars and Sergei Lukashin, with the latter at two separate meetings on July 21, 1927.[985] Eliava had no objection to the extension of the mandate. Acheson, however, was not prepared to commit himself as yet and wanted to have "a few of the most important leaders consider the matter preparatory to a fuller consideration of it later." At his meeting with Lukashin, Acheson explained that he did not wish to come to the end of the present NER mandate without knowing what would follow next, and wished to have the option of continuing under the present mandate in the event that NER's work was not completed by 1928. Lukashin, wrote Acheson,

> ...was in a very friendly humor, and we had quite an extended and jovial conversation, during which he said that he would like to come to New York and I said I would like to show him around. We took up the question of extending the Mandate, my position being that I did not wish to go to the end of our present Mandate without understanding what was to follow, and that, while I was not sure that we would need more time than the present amount of time allotted to complete our work, I wanted to have an option of continuing under the existing Mandate if, in our judgment, it should be necessary.

Lukashin had then answered that

> ...there was no objection whatever to our continuing under our present Mandate and that the matter should be regarded as settled in principle, the only question being the length of time that would be required. We estimated that there would be between 2,000 and 2,500 children under our care in November 1928.[986]

Acheson also asked about the future of Lukashin Post, referring to Kazachi's new designation, and whether any consideration had been given to making it a cultural center:

> He said that they wanted to bring in additional children that are being cared for elsewhere; that is, orphans now under the care of the Government. The idea of making it a cultural center does not seem to be very popular...[987]

Acheson next raised the subject of permanency:

> I asked him about a continuing piece of work here and he said that as far as he could determine there would be a very welcome attitude toward any continuing piece of work that Near East Relief wishes to propose and finance.

But, Acheson added in his diary:

> It was not said at this time, but I have it on good authority that the one thing that the Government considers most seriously in matters of this kind is the question of espionage. Evidently, our purpose and intentions are now well understood and appreciated by higher government officials.[988]

Back in Yerevan, Acheson met with Artashes Karinyan, at the time serving as chairman of the SSRA Central Executive Committee, on July 28, where he brought up, among the many topics under discussion, the arrests of 28 Armenian employees and teachers at the Polygon. The news had been broadcast in the U.S., and carried in some detail in *The Los Angeles Times* and *The New York Times* in similar articles in their September 29, 1927, issues, both based on an Associated Press release.[989] Releasing details on the arrests to *The New York Times* was NER's Director of Foreign Department Laird W. Archer in New York, who stated that he had received the news that 28 Armenians had been "detained for interrogation." Archer expressed regret at the occurrence, but said,

> …it was not a situation in which the American relief directors could interfere, as the arrests were in all probability political, and the Near East Relief never intruded in political matters.

Laird W. Archer reassured the public "We have never had any American workers arrested by the Soviet authorities":

> Among the 1,000 native relief workers employed by us," said Mr. Archer "there are undoubtedly many who belonged to the old Russian regime. The twenty-eight, or some of their number, were possibly caught spreading anti-Soviet literature or sending anti-Soviet propaganda out of the country. That explains why they are being "detained for interrogation."

The New York Times article ended with a brief history of how NER had "saved a million lives." *The Los Angeles Times*, which had also used the Associated Press release, cited additional thoughts from Director Archer. "These people," Archer had said referring to the arrested Armenian employees,

> …were among a large number of other persons called up for interrogation on suspicion of having to do with a revolutionary movement. They were not called up in connection with our work…they are all local Armenians out of 1000 employed by us,

and, he had added,

> The soviet action does not affect our work and we have not been disturbed by it. The Russian government has approved our mandate for another year.

The arrests, according to Archer, had spread out over a period beginning in June 1927 and while he did not mention the arrested employees by name, among them may have been 14 teachers and employees that SSRA State Political Affairs Department Chief Melik-Osipov had wished to be fired from NER's staff. Melik-Osipov's list of NER teachers "who are considered anti-Soviet elements" and dated May 18, 1927, included: Sirakan Tigranyan, Zaven Ter-Mateosyan, Mikayel Ayvazyan, Gurgen Khazhakyan, Nshan Hovhannisyan, Artashes Darbinyan, Abraham Melik-Janyan, Artashes Badalyan, Barunak Harutyunyan, Israyel Ter-Abrahamyan, Artak Melyan, Azniv Maylamazyan, Mesrop Avetisyan, and Bagrat Hakobyan.[990] All were suspected of counterrevolutionary activities and of association—past or current—with the Dashnaktsutyun, or ARF, the party that had established and governed the First Republic of Armenia in 1918 until the Communist takeover in 1920. Melik-Osipov had alerted the Leninakan liaison's office, that

> According to our information, they [NER] are going to make severe reductions in the NER teaching staff. For that reason, by attaching the list of NER teachers with anti-Soviet dispositions, we ask that you take timely means so that they [individuals mentioned above] will be included in the cutbacks. We specifically insist that Nshan Hovhannisyan be dismissed…[991]

The entry under Nshan Hovhannisyan's name pointed out that he was a Western Armenian, a former member of the ARF party, and a fanatical Protestant who hated Soviet rule. Hovhannisyan, according to the entry, taught religion to the students and tried to educate them in a chauvinistic and anti-Bolshevik spirit. He was, Melik-Osipov wrote,

> ...considered the most loyal and dedicated personality to the Americans. The latter respect him and assist him in every way. He keeps close relations with the Dashnaks, and enjoys great reputation among the teachers...[992]

During his meeting with Karinyan on July 28, Acheson had assured him that NER maintained neutrality and that

> ...we made no pretensions of interfering with the way the existing government dealt with its subjects...

And he had

> ...stated frankly that we unintentionally had become a refuge for people that were not members of the political party now in power. I said that this was due primarily to the fact that we desired employees who could speak English, but that it was not our intention or desire to have enemies of the Government in our organization, and that, as far as I knew, those who had been employed were not hostile to the existing government—in fact, some of those arrested had spoken vigorously in behalf of the Government.

Acheson had been interested to know if

> ...the arrest of these employees was an attempt to investigate our organization and its purpose and program. I stated that, if the Government had any doubt as to our non-political and friendly purpose, we would remove ourselves from their boundaries within thirty days...

In answer to Acheson's query,

> Cit. Karinian stated emphatically and repeatedly that the Government had no thought whatever of investigating Near East Relief and that members of his own staff in his own office had been arrested simultaneously.[993]

In the course of the meeting Karinyan had mentioned that his brother was planning to come to the U.S. for training as a practical engineer, and Acheson had offered to help him in every way possible.[994]

Nshan Hovhannisyan, one of the most popular teachers at the Polygon and an ardent supporter of NER, was at the Cheka when Acheson met with Karinyan. Acheson mentions that detail in his diary entry of July 30, two days after his meeting with Karinyan, and depicts Hovhannisyan as having fallen from grace with some NER directors. These issues had emerged in a meeting between Acheson and NER Education Director Allen:

> ...I discussed Miss Silliman and her work with Allen. He volunteered the recommendation that she be placed in charge of the Normal School. Baron Nishan was given much leeway and many responsibilities by Miss Silliman. I am convinced that, after Miss Silliman left, he took advantage of her absence and

Allen's lack of familiarity to give his relatives and friends work and privileges. As a result, Allen lost confidence in him. He [Hovhannisyan] is now in the Tcheka [Cheka], and this makes it easier to place Miss Silliman in charge of the Normal School, although I think Miss Silliman also understands that Nishan has fumbled an opportunity.[995]

Aboard ship from Batum to Constantinople on August 4, 1927, Acheson noted in his diary that on the whole, the work and the financial situation in the Caucasus were sound. There had been reports of NER's dwindling income in U.S. newspapers in 1927,[996] but during Acheson's negotiations with Ter-Ghazaryan on the sale of used clothes in July, on August 2nd,[997] and August 3rd it had been agreed that the government would accept 4,000 bales of old clothes at $70 per bale for the next year, which would provide a total income of $280,000 for NER.[998] Acheson had agreed to the price although he knew, he wrote, that various departments of the government sold them at $130 or $140 per bale.[999]

With respect to the American staff, Acheson's chief criticism was that nothing was done for the children after they had been outplaced in homes, and that

> The whole organization is held at a low standard of efficiency and at a low standard of attainment by the general low standards of the community in which they are working.[1000]

With respect to the government, Acheson felt that the Caucasus was now stable and considerable progress had been made in the development of natural resources. But there was general hostility from the government and labor unions toward the few who had had cultural advantages in the past. And, he wrote,

> I feel that this government will evolve into different forms, but that its essential characteristics—emphasis of the evils of capital, unearned increment, inherited wealth, etc.—would not change in his lifetime.[1001]

Acheson would return to the Caucasus and to Armenia a few more times. But not Ernest Yarrow, who returned to the U.S. in 1926, where until 1929 he was on NER's staff of speakers to raise money for NER's work. Before leaving Armenia in 1926, Yarrow had met the Catholicos at Etchmiadzin and the two had discussed the possibility of modernizing the Armenian Church. His Holiness had told Yarrow, wrote Acheson,

> ...that this was not an opportune time for the free, quiet and prolonged discussion that would be necessary if the church was to give consideration to the question of a modernizing revision of its dogma. In other words, the time is not yet ripe for this step.[1002]

On the other hand, His Holiness had been willing, continued Acheson,

> ...to change the <u>methods</u> of church service,—our interpretation of this being that he would welcome catechism classes, young peoples organizations and other adaptations of methods that have been developed in the Western church.

Acheson and Yarrow also understood from the discussion that the Holy See had the authority to start a school for theological training, but it did not have the means to do so and would welcome outside aid. The church had been ready to welcome teachers from "non-conformist sects," but only

> ...on condition that these individuals would pledge themselves not to disturb the unity of the old church or work against its organization.[1003]

As Yarrow and Acheson discussed the issue in New York on January 7, 1927, both agreed that the proposal from the Catholicos was untenable:

> The genius of the Eastern peoples is toward centered church authority, and any non-conformist movement, at best, would reach a comparatively small minority of the peoples, and according to present outlook, the bulk of the people would still remain in the old church...

> No organization up to the present has gone into these eastern countries with the stated policy of helping the old church to a high spiritual state and at the same time guaranteeing that nothing should be done to disturb its authority.[1004]

Beyond that, there was also the matter of the government's position toward religion that needed to be taken into account. While "in Russia today the government is opposed to religion," they gave "freedom of worship"

> ...to all churches, and especially do they encourage the establishment of non-conformist sects, there being a law that any ten people can band together and receive authority for organizing a church, on condition that the principles of the church are moral and not contrary to the political principles of the government...

At the end, the matter had been dropped because

> ...any seeming success on the part of Protestant organizations would be largely obtained with the aid of the government which is professedly and avowedly irreligious...[1005]

About three years later, Moscow-based International News Service Correspondent Edward Deuss had visited the Catholicos. "The Episcopal palace," Deuss wrote,

> ...had been taken over by the government. The 82-year-old Catholicos lived in the cloisters of the monastery.

> We came into a long bare room with arched windows along one side. At the far end in a high armchair behind a simple modern desk sat the aged ruler in a black silk robe with a black silk skull cap...

> He held out his wrinkled hand, palm downward, as if he intended it to be kissed, but when I stooped as if to kiss the hand, he jerked it away with a smile.

> "I came to your holiness and convey most cordial good wishes," I said in Russian.

> The old man's eyes twinkled.

"Thank you," he said. "I know many Americans, and am extremely fond of them. There have been many of them here in the last ten years, and many have come to see me."

They chatted a few more minutes, and then the interview was over. "One was impressed," wrote Deuss,

> …with the restraint of the old father. He had suffered so much, been imposed upon so much, that he kept his thoughts to himself.

Once outside the cloister, accompanied by archbishops,

> …a man came out of the army barracks, moved up slowly and photographed us.[1006]

Retrospective (and Prospective) at the Polygon: December 3 & 4, 1927

With NER operations now centered exclusively at the Polygon, Managing Director Joseph Beach organized an open house at the Polygon for December 3 and 4, 1927, to celebrate 11 years of NER presence and contributions to Armenia, seven years of which had been under Soviet rule. The official invitation, dated November 26, 1927, was addressed to Citizen Karakhanyan and explained:

> On Saturday, December 3, from 10 in the morning to five in the evening, all our departments will be open for guest visits. The main areas to visit that day will be the following: the central exhibit room where NER's past and current activities will be exhibited; the schools of the educational department, including the pedagogical and seven year schools where classes will be in progress; the vocational school where the work will be in progress; the clinics, hospital and Nursing School; the exhibit of animals that have been cared for especially, where also will be exhibited the result of five years of veterinary work with Caucasian, Russian, Swiss and Semintal cows, as well as sheep, birds, barns, milking shed, etc.; fifteen orphanages where 3,150 orphans live.[1007]

The celebration would continue the following day, December 4, which in America, Beach pointed out, was Golden Rule Sunday, when a special effort would be made to collect contributions for orphans under NER care. Then, he continued,

> At 9:30 in the morning, a general meeting will be held in the Physical Education hall of building #57, where various individuals, as well as the representatives of our students, will deliver speeches. Golden Rule Sunday dinner will take place at 12noon, with the participation of orphans and guests.

During dinner, designated groups would sell tickets, the revenues to be used for improvements in the life of orphans. There was no fixed price assigned to the tickets, wrote Beach. Then would follow,

> …at one in the afternoon (or immediately after dinner) an exhibition of the physical education classes in the southern part of building #29, or, in the physical education hall of building #57, depending on the weather.

At the end of the celebrations, orphan girls of the "Comrade Rykov Club" would invite the guests for tea in the orphanage building, "named after Comrade Alexei Rykov."[1008]

In substance and approach, the exhibit was in line with, and featured NER's new vision as it summed up its past achievements and projected the permanent institutions of the future. At the time of the retrospective the components of the agricultural program were a general laboratory, a museum, two classrooms for practical work, 40 cows, 4 bulls, 30 hogs, calves, horses, a greenhouse, and a dairy plant.[1009] The subjects taught included animal husbandry, agronomy, general agriculture, chemistry, Armenian language and literature, Russian and English languages, geography, economic geography, singing and drawing, biology, hygiene, physics, mathematics, and crafts.[1010] Two hundred and ninety three boys and girls between the ages of 11 and 17[1011] had cultivated over 500 acres of land. According to Alpoyachyan this was the stretch of land from Leninakan to Jajur, where orphans worked all day long. New farm machinery arrived in 1928, which Alpoyajyan was asked to assemble, a challenging task because there were neither manuals nor instructions included with the pieces.[1012] When the assembly work was completed and the machine began to collect, thrash, clean, and put the wheat in bags, villagers from everywhere, wrote Alpoyachyan, came to watch the work, in total amazement. Also watching the work were representatives of the government.

Symbolizing NER's achievements and now its headquarters, the Polygon was poised as a world apart, and distinct from the other two posts. It signaled NER's new, "Constructive Phase" and the hope that in their aggregate, its past achievements would be a permanent monument and NER's legacy in the SSRA. NER's Report to Congress for the year 1928 highlighted the potential of the new phase as projected through the Polygon, now described as "the great center…once great in numbers" but "today greater in influence than it ever was, and unquestionably greater in importance," where "the selective results are conspicuous…"[1013] There were also references to the "high grade" care the remaining orphans received, now that there were fewer of them. This made it "possible to divide the orphanages into units of children's homes, with an American director for each group."[1014] Reference was also made to the special kitchens and a new course for the girls. The new course had at first been named "Home Economics," but after objections from the authorities to the use of the word "home" in the title, the course had been renamed "Expert Culinary Course," a new addition to the vocational school. The course included instruction in cooking, food purchasing, and dietetics. Although originally established for girls, the course was later attended almost entirely by boys and men who were being trained as managers of collective farms.[1015]

Represented in the new setting of the Polygon also were the programs NER had developed in the past five years, but with some modifications, especially in the Agricultural and Industrial programs. The curriculum of the Industrial School had changed. It no longer pushed production for the sake of reducing costs, but aimed to familiarize students with practical application and project work to learn skills at a level higher than basic manual labor.

The Agricultural and Farm School, now conducting its work on 500 acres of land, featured an abridged version of the curricula of Stepanavan and Karakala. The comprehensive program of three years, offered by the Institute of Agriculture, was replaced by courses lasting from three to six months, since Acheson had felt that

> ...boys can take a three months or a six months course before they are liquidated and that if that course is complete within itself their training will be profitable, whereas children who take only one preliminary year of a three year course will find it practically useless.[1016]

A new feature, introduced by superintendent Paul H. Phillips of Pullman, Washington, was dry farming.[1017]

NER was especially proud of the achievements of its graduates. By 1928 it had graduated 62 students, 14 of whom were chosen to work in the new government agricultural commune of Aleksandrovka[1018] where they were placed in charge of 150 acres.[1019] The Edith Winchester School of Nursing, long a supplier of nurses to the country, had graduated 126 nurses by 1927, of which 70 were already in government service.[1020] The Teacher Training School had begun to supply teachers for the government schools in 1926 and student teachers for the orphanage earlier, and by 1929, a total of 220 young men and women had graduated, many of who were teaching in village schools.[1021]

Reorganization and downsizing had continued at the Polygon as more children were signed out for adoption, as laborers and student-agriculturists on a permanent or temporary basis.[1022] The orphan population of the Polygon dropped to 1,103 boys and

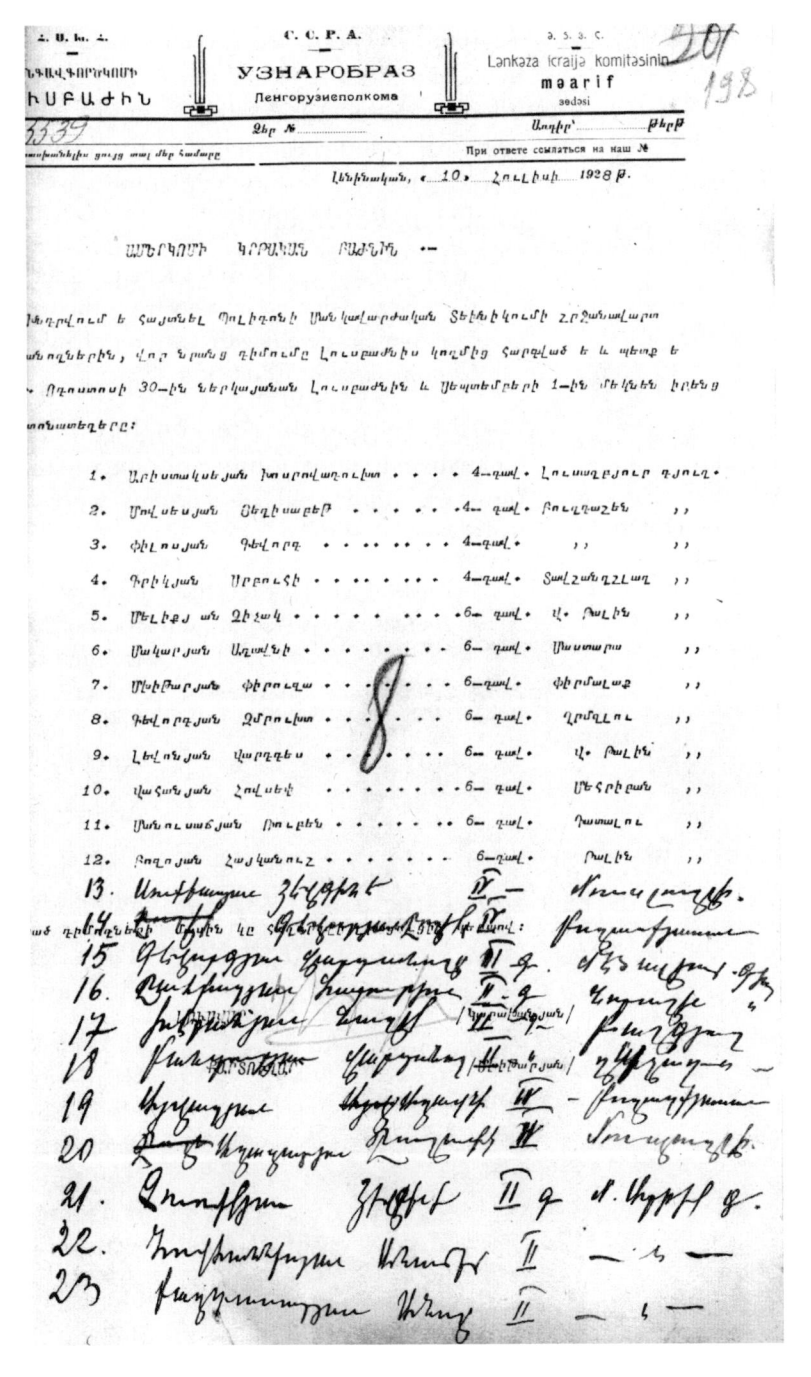

The document lists the names of graduates from Polygon's Pedagogical Technicum scheduled to begin teaching in the villages on September 1, 1928. (NAA 131/3/558/f. 198)

1,670 girls, necessitating additional reorganizations at the end of the 1927–28 academic year.

Writing on June 10, 1928, Managing District Commander Joseph Beach presented the educational plan for the upcoming 1928–1929 academic year explaining that due to the rapid rate of outplacements in progress, students in the Primary school would be divided into a total of 10 groups. The reduced teaching staff NER wished to retain at the Primary School for the academic year 1928–1929 included one principal, one head teacher, and nine teachers from the existing teaching staff.[1023] The name of long-time educator and mentor Nshan Hovhannisyan was conspicuously absent from the list. In the Septennial School, the students would be gathered into five groups only. The new configuration would need one principal, one head teacher, and five teachers. The Agricultural school would have six or seven groups and needed one principal, one head teacher, and seven teachers; the Pedagogical Technicum would have five groups with one principal and ten teachers. In his closing paragraph, Beach added:

> In all schools the Government program of education will be followed. In case there is any slight variation from the regular Government program this will be discussed in detail with Cit. Karahanian [Karakhanyan], representative of the Commissariat of Education.[1024]

About six weeks later, on July 27, 1928, NER Education Committee Chairman Everett Gunn announced that the situation had changed since June, and additional adjustments were now to be made due to new orders from New York:

> Because of recent orders from the New York Headquarters for the Near East Relief to increase the speed of liquidation of Polygon children and because the budget is much reduced it is necessary to inform you that we wish to revise the teachers list for Industrial School, Agricultural School and Primary School sent to you on June 10.

Adjustments included the merger of the

> …Agricultural School and the Industrial School into one school known as Vocational-Agriculture…

The teaching staff Gunn proposed to keep for the Vocational-Agriculture School was:

> Ishkhan Shindian, Principal; Tachat Ghemoian, Head-teacher; Mkrtich Sanoian, Soghomon Melik-Shahnazarian, Sahad Movsisian, Galoost Baghalian, Armenak Sarkissian, Ohan Kiandarian, Heghine Isahakian as teachers, with Toros Jamagotchian [Jamgotchian] as substitute and secretary.

Gunn added that adjustments were made in the staff at the Primary School as well. Now,

A graduate of the Winchester Nursing School in charge of a village clinic.
(*An Investment That Will Endure*: 12)

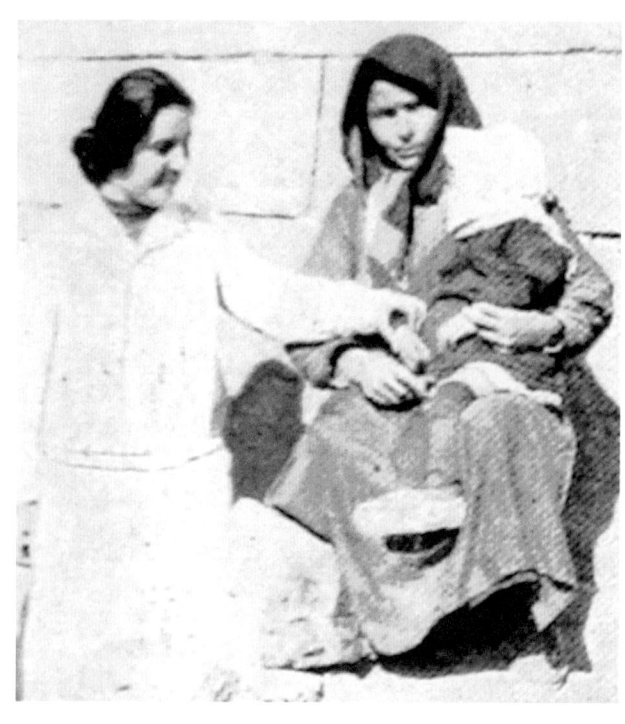

only six teachers would be needed, in addition to a principal, head-teacher and substitute teacher/secretary, for two groups in each grade. The final list consisted of:

> Haik Hovhannissian, Principal; Bagrat Toomanian, Head-teacher; Ashkhen Alvardian, Israel Ter-Abrahamian, Hakop Tovmasian, Vardges Ter-Hovhannisian, Makroohy Ter-Mardirosian, Parooir Babaian, Arpiar Safrastian, Shahbaz Shahbazian as teachers.[1025]

So far as the Technicum was concerned, it was

> ...as yet a little indefinite except if continued as now outlined we will have not over five groups and not less than four. We would also like to recommend Haik Hovhannessian to serve as head-teacher of Technicom [Technicum] as well as principal.

The Technicum teaching faculty would consist of 12 teachers:

> Sirakan Tigranian, Moorad Azatian, Gevork Brootian, Nicola Kirakosian, Mambre Mkerian, Karabed Papian, Hovhannes Ter-Mirakian, Grigor Ter-Boghosian, Isahak Zakarian, Benjamin Aghoian, Vagharshak Davtian, Mikayel Ayvazyan.

In addition, he added in a note, "a good teacher of Russian will be needed."[1026]

Frank S. Buckalew had been Director of Finance when the transition to the Polygon had been made. His letter to his father describing the changes at the City of Orphans appeared in the June 4, 1928, issue of *The Berkeley Daily Gazette*:

> Leninakan...has a population of around 30,000 and its buildings range from earthquake refugee dugouts to two story buildings. Just beyond the outskirts of the city are three army posts—one or two miles apart, which were built in 1905 by the Tsar...
>
> At one time the Near East Relief occupied all three posts and some buildings in the city with the care of over 20,000 orphan children. Today, we occupy Polygon, the old artillery post and a small part of Kazachi, the cavalry post; Seversky, the infantry post, where Miss Janet McKay had her wonderful girls orphanage has been returned to the government.

About two-thirds of the approximately 3,000 orphans, he explained, were girls, and although it was "a small family now," it still presented "a big work with many ramifications." There was, first of all, the kindergarten orphanage:

> There are less than 200 of these little tikes now and they are a cute bunch of kids. During the day they have their kindergarten school under the sole supervision of an Armenian teacher who lives in the orphanage home to care for them. They have their regular hours for clinic and bath and what fun they have in the recreational building with their dances and games. I used to have my fun with them just at bedtime, which is always at nightfall. They love to get bounced into bed or carried about on one's shoulders. They are hungry for affection and for treasures. Any little thing looms large in their world. A picture from a magazine, the lining from my letters, an empty match box each attracted the attention of covetous eyes.

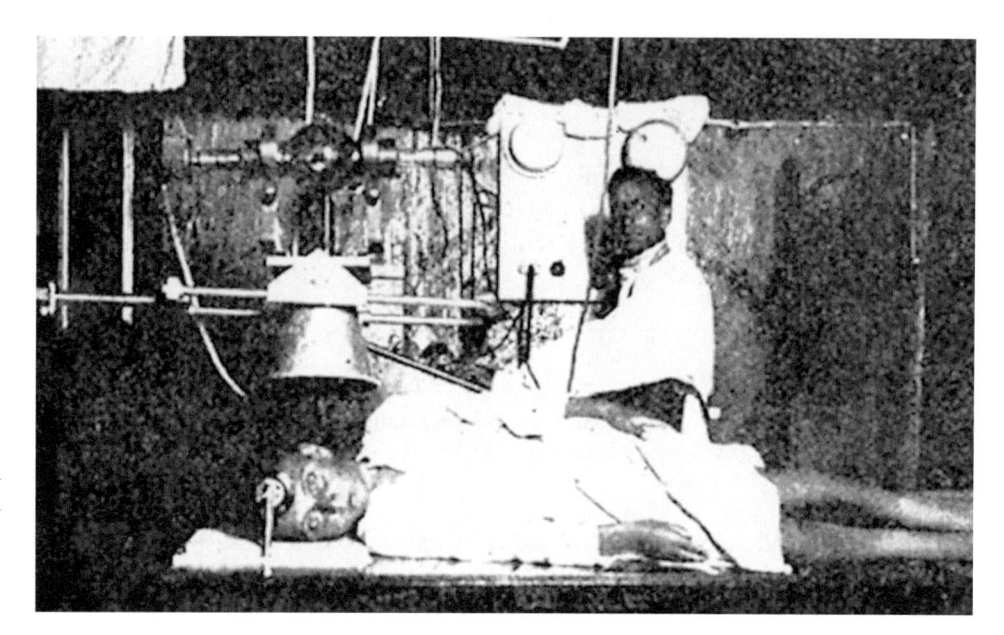

Orphan boy receiving X-Ray treatment for favus. (*The New Near East*, June 1926: 11)

Buckalew continued to say that favus and trachoma still persisted at the Polygon. But now, favus was being treated by the new X-Ray method, and trachoma by the more successful electric or diathermy treatment, under the supervision of Dr. Kalloch. In the new setting of the Polygon, the orphans were divided into Boys' and Girls' Homes. An Armenian employee, under the supervision of an American, lived in each home. The homes took pride in the appearance of their rooms, and in some, older girls had hemstitched and embroidered some of the pillow and table covers. All the children went to school, which conformed to government guidelines in all respects, and those who had shown special aptitude received additional education in the normal school. This latter group, added Buckalew, "were hustled away" by the government to teach in village schools:

> ...The last time I was with this group was on January 6, which is their Christmas time. They were having a party and what fun they did have. If you have never been to an Armenian dance you cannot know, for I cannot describe the procedure to give an inkling of its entertaining features.

Most of the children received half a day's training in the vocational school, made their own clothing and shoes, and, added Buckalew "repaired the stoves needed for our 70 or 80 buildings. Bear in mind that this last winter reached 40 below Fahrenheit..." The agricultural school that was attended by many children had a large practical outlet: a good-sized dairy, horses, mules, chickens, pigs, sheep, etc., where the children raised vegetables for fall and winter use. A new feature was the installation of two subterranean silos by Paul Phillips, who had

> ...filled them with silage cut from the products grown on the farm. This is the first demonstration of silage in Armenia and is proving a great aid in the winter feeding of our stock. Phillips is a wonderful fellow. He is very capable in his chosen work but also has a very keen interest in his employees and in the children especially. He organized an indoor baseball competition which lasted from spring until the

snow came. It always drew a large gallery of children and the enthusiasm and good feeling created was of inestimable value.

The first of the last two items Buckalew brought up were summer camps, which were being continued but now under the direction of Education Director Helen Mays, who was regarded highly by the government in Yerevan:

> Last summer Miss Mays... ran a wonderful camp with the aid of an interpreter and the older boys whom she is training for recreational leadership. In this capacity she is highly respected by the central government who have asked her to lecture at the University at Erivan and to help them plan the program for future work...

The second item was the Edith Winchester School of Nursing, maintained at the Kazachi hospital, whose graduates were sought by the government for health work in the villages.

Permanency and Polygon's Core Group

When Acheson returned to the Caucasus in summer 1928, there were approximately 1,600 children left at the Polygon, whose outplacement would be determined by the final outcome of Acheson's negotiations for permanency. On his way to Leninakan, Acheson had met with TSFSR Council of People's Commissars Chairman Shalva Eliava in Tiflis on July 21 and verbally presented the scenario he had in mind. A week later, in Leninakan, Acheson described his vision to Eliava in a long and detailed letter dated July 22.[1027] There he explained that while NER's Executive Committee and Board of Trustees had accepted that NER activities would soon cease, many of the members wished it would not. His own position about the immediate liquidation of NER activities had also changed, Acheson added, after he had returned and had personally examined the work that was being done. This change of position compelled him first to further accelerate the liquidation of the current work, but at the same time, to ascertain the government's position with regard to NER's idea of establishing permanent educational institutions in the Caucasus. He hastened to add that his proposal would have to be approved by New York's Executive Committee, but regardless of the outcome, liquidation would continue.

In the remaining pages of his letter Acheson presented an analysis of the orphan population as of July 15, 1928, NER's financial situation, the mandate, and the question of permanency. In reference to the orphan population, he explained that there were approximately 1,600 children. Of that number, 813 suffered from favus, trachoma, and physical defects. For example, he elaborated, 93 of them limped or were slightly disabled; 45 were blind in one eye; 40 had heart defects; 19 were intellectually inferior, etc. But the illnesses or defects these children had did not mean that they could not lead an ordinary life, with the exception of the 19 who would be considered chronically incurable. In fact, three hundred had already been cured of favus and were being kept under observation for two or three months, and the medical department assumed that more than 400 would be completely cured in the next three months.

The remaining 800 children, continued Acheson, were completely healthy physically, and could be liquidated gradually in the next 12 months, which meant that they would be placed in homes and villages.[1028]

Acheson planned to liquidate and end orphanage work by September 1, 1929. To that end, he presented a schedule of liquidations by groups. In the first group would be 350 children who were not completely healthy and were in the hospitals, but had taken part of orphanage activities and education, and should not be considered defective. These children had incurable chronic diseases and would not benefit from staying at the Polygon any longer and could be more appropriately and easily placed in some of the schools run by the government, and eventually find their place in life. These 350 children would be transferred to government institutions by the following schedule:

> September 1: 100 children (19 chronically ill; 19 mentally inferior; and 62 as selected by NER
> October 1: 100 children, as selected by NER
> November 1: 100 children, as selected by NER
> December 1: 50 children, as selected by NER[1029]

To help the government with the transferred children, NER would provide supplies and equipment in the value of 120,000 rubles. But, he added, if the government institutions in which those children would be placed actively sought to place them with relatives, then only a very small number would remain in the government institutions.

The second group consisted of 400 children who were under medical care but were expected to recuperate fully in the next few months, and would be outplaced. The third group consisted of 400 healthy children who had completed their education and were ready for outplacement, for which effort Acheson hoped to enlist the government's help.

The fourth, and last group at the Polygon consisted of 400 to 500 children who were the healthiest and the brightest. These, Acheson characterized, as "The Core Group" for whom an additional year of education at the Polygon would be offered. "Most of those children, so far as we know have no family," he explained and added:

> ...we think that the "Core Group" could be the nucleus for the proposed future work of the NER, should there be mutual agreement on that work.[1030]

The idea of a core group had been discussed among NER's leadership two years earlier, in summer 1926, in the context of outplacements and had been supported by Charles Vickrey who had been in Leninakan for a few days. "Mr. Vickrey," Acheson had noted in his diary,

> ...favors outplacing the less receptive children; in other words, he favors the policy, as previously announced in Syria, Greece and now in the Caucasus that we spend our money on the children that are more likely to take places of leadership.[1031]

At that time, in summer 1926, the staff had begun classifying the children into groups so that when the time came, there would be "a wisely selected group that will form the backbone of the educational work and an emphasis on outplacing the less desirable of the children."[1032] Acheson had been pleased with the idea:

> We have developed the idea of a corps of the most responsive children, our idea being that the outplacing Department shall put pressure on disposing of the subnormal groups. This may be done either by active effort to move them or increasing subsidy for those who will care for them or transferring them in units to Government institutions as we are now doing with the blind, epileptic, etc.[1033]

Acheson had presented, and had received approval for the idea of the Core Group during his speech before the Board of Trustees in New York on January 18, 1927, and stated that NER would educate the "most responsive" of the children for another year, to prepare them for leadership in its permanent institutions. Trained and reared in the best American traditions, these children would then serve as the agents of change for a new, progressive world in Armenia, and of world peace.[1034]

In his letter to Eliava, Acheson explained that apart from the four groups still at the Polygon, there was a group of 5,000 outplaced children who had not received sufficient attention to date. These children had experienced serious problems of adjustment to the new economic and social conditions and it was now necessary to attend to their needs. He was concerned that without the proper adjustment, those children might be alienated from their environments and become vagrants, and a problem for the state:

> We can prove with pride, added Acheson, that 90% of the 40,000 children who have passed through our institutions, have taken root in their new environment after being placed out, and as positive elements.

Acheson then offered an additional year of supervision for the children outplaced in Abkhazia:

> For the 2,000 children who had been received with open arms in Abkhazia another year's supervision and follow up would be needed to ensure that they were rooted in their new environment.

"Otherwise," he wrote, "they would be living criticism of NER's work.[1035] To achieve its intentions to properly distribute the promised assistance to the government and provide supervision, Acheson suggested that NER continue operations for another year. He expressed gratitude for the exceptional support NER had received from government representatives and institutions, without which the colossal results NER had achieved and continued to achieve would have been impossible, and hoped for similar cooperation from the government now.

The last section of Acheson's lengthy communiqué to Eliava was devoted to finances. To support the plans as outlined, Acheson wrote, NER would like to continue to take full advantage of the arrangement for the sale of used clothing, and import another 2,000 bales for one year beginning November 30, 1928, terms and prices of used clothes to be decided by mutual agreement. In addition, Acheson asked that NER be allowed to sell, at a maximum price, surplus goods and foodstuff in its warehouses, which were spoiling and losing value. For these, he set a price of approximately 200,000 rubles. These sales would not impact the needs of the orphans, he added, since even after the sale of surplus goods, by June 30, 1929, NER would still have 200,000 rubles worth of clothes, foodstuff, permanent furniture, and animals for use in its warehouses to secure the needs of the coming academic year.

The last item in Acheson's communiqué had to do with NER's permanent work. He raised the issue of the existing mandate, due to expire in one year. NER hoped that they would be able to move on to a more permanent work, and therefore proposed and asked that the current mandate be extended for an indefinite period of time but with the proviso that either party can void it at any time, with a six-month notice.[1036] Having faith in the significance of traditions of friendship between peoples, he wrote, and in the fact that traditions of friendship and mutual understanding are consolidated through permanent and temporary joint undertakings such as NER's practical assistance in the Caucasus, and further believing that the permanent programs NER now proposed would contribute to the development of Armenia, he asked that the government express its views about the idea of permanent work and ways in which it could be implemented. Additional details could wait, he added, until the government's position on the issue was known. Acheson would bring the government's response to NER's Executive Board, and in the course of the following year he would return with a specific proposal from New York, convinced that plans now being formed would be mutually acceptable. To further clarify his point, Acheson proposed an institution that would offer practical education for peasant youth as its main direction; those with average abilities would become village chiefs and the brighter ones would receive scholarships to continue in the government's institutions of higher education. And of course, as guests and friends of the government, NER had in mind such plans that would be fully loyal to the interests of the Soviet Union. Acheson concluded his letter with expressions of gratitude to Eliava and to the government for their continuing assistance and friendship.[1037]

Shalva Eliava's reply of August 6, 1928, was transmitted through Ter-Ghazaryan, who was instructed by Eliava to relay the decisions of the TSFSR Council of Commissars to Acheson.[1038] The TSFSR government had agreed to NER's plan for the final liquidation of orphans under its care during the coming year, and to that end, the agreement between the government of TSFSR and NER was extended until November 1, 1929. Accepted also were NER's proposal for the sale of used clothes, surplus goods and foodstuff, and, the transfer of 250–400 children to the SSRA government. Details would be worked out and registered on paper between Ter-Ghazaryan and NER. NER's proposal for permanency, on the other hand, would need to be studied further:

> Concerning the permanent work of the NER, the government of Transcaucasia, although well-disposed to the Committee's proposal... finds it necessary to submit that proposal to detailed research, especially since its final decision depends on the discussion of the Executive Committee in New York.

Eliava concluded his letter by asking Ter-Ghazaryan to

> ...transmit to cit[izen] Acheson and the foreign staff of the NER the best wishes of the government of Transcaucasia, for their fruitful work in the assistance to the orphans.[1039]

Acheson, now in Batum, replied on August 12, 1928. He would take Eliava's letter to the Executive Committee in New York, he wrote, and report their detailed discussions to his colleagues. He was sure the Executive Committee would be interested in the attitude of the Transcaucasus government about permanent work, and was truly certain that on the basis of the trust established through their eight-year-old cooperative work, some type of creative endeavor would be agreed upon, and concluded:

> Before I leave the Caucasus, I wish to express, through you, my gratitude to Cit. Eliava for all the friendliness they showed me during the time I was there, and to express to you my best wishes for the future.[1040]

The "defective" children were transferred to Stepanavan, and schedules and subsidies were detailed in a formal Agreement in Tiflis on September 24, 1928. The signatories of the Agreement were NER Managing Director Joseph Beach with Controller of Supplies Caleb B. Flagg on the one side, and Transcaucasian Sovnarkom Representative Nariman Ter-Ghazaryan and SSRA People's Commissar of Social Insurance Effendieff, on the other.[1041] The terms would be in force until November 1, 1929, the date when NER's work within the boundaries of TSFSR would stop. But conditions at the farm school in Stepanavan, now under government control, were dire, with many buildings in disrepair, several of them lacking roofs. Rehabilitating the buildings to accommodate the needs of "defective" children would cost the Council of People's Commissars of Armenia 16,247 rubles and 18 kopeks.[1042] Presenting the figures was Citizen B. Effendieff, who asked for a loan of 10,000 rubles from the Council of People's Commissars to prepare the buildings on time. The loan would be paid off immediately after receiving some of the commodities promised by NER. But it appears that conditions in Stepanavan had not yet improved by March 7, 1929, when Sargsyan wrote the Council of Peoples' Commissars castigating the Commissariat of Social Welfare for neglecting its obligations to provide care for the "defective" children at Stepanavan. To care for those children, Sargsyan wrote, the People's Commissariat of Social Welfare had

> ...received and continues to receive from NER $68,000 worth of goods to ensure their care, and whose value in the market is no less than 250,000 rubles. After all this it would have been reasonable to expect that the People's Commissariat of Social Welfare would have created conditions more or less tolerable so that they [the children] would live and be educated at the orphanages in Stepanavan...

But because of the inattentiveness of the Commissariat of Social Welfare, the flow of orphans escaping from Stepanavan to Leninakan had continued, wrote Sargsyan, flooding the streets of the city and adding to the number of homeless already on the streets. Not a week passed, continued Sargsyan, when groups of children who had been transferred to Stepanavan did not appear on the streets, or asked NER to take them back to the Polygon, or gone to the city officials in Leninakan for help. Already three groups of children had been taken back to Stepanavan, accompanied by militia or NER employees, yet despite official requests from Sargsyan and Ter-Ghazaryan, no steps had been taken to improve conditions at Stepanavan. Because the Commissariat of Social Welfare had ignored such requests,

> ...the number of homeless children on the streets increase at a time when the state is seriously struggling against it, and, the prestige of the People's Commissariat of Social Welfare is falling before the NER, which can justifiably think that the amount of $68,000 is not being used to care for its orphans.

"It is incomprehensible to us," Sargsyan concluded,

> ...through which moral right the Commissariat of Social Welfare disperses the orphans placed under their care, when it has received $68,000.00 from NER specifically for their care. Just today a group of five escaped orphans was returned to Stepanavan.[1043]

A partial list of the homeless, compiled for the period from June 10 to November 28, 1928,[1044] showed 45 boys between the ages of 12 to 18, mostly from Turkish Armenia, Kars, Leninakan and Karabagh. Many cited the street as their address, and the majority had no family and a large number had one family member in another city. Under the heading of "Occupation" descriptions included "pickpocket," "thief," "student," and "ragtag"; and, several had been arrested for petty crimes. Another partial list from the same period consisted of 13 names, all of them girls between the ages of 13 and 22, almost all had at least one relative who lived elsewhere, and all were engaged in prostitution. About 50% had been arrested and had served time. Six of the girls—two of them 14 years old, three of them 16 years old, and a 17-year-old—had contracted gonorrhea. Six girls listed the street as their homes; six had been working as prostitutes since the ages of 13, 14, 15 and 16, and one had started at the age of 20; the 22-year-old was married, but her husband was in prison.[1045]

Democlean Sword and an Ultimatum

Concurrent with outplacements, discussions on mandate extensions and permanency, tensions were mounting in Leninakan with Managing District Commander Joseph Beach occupying pride of place in complaints sent to the SSRA government. Criticism of Joseph Beach's actions had peaked in 1928 when he was openly and personally criticized for defying government requests and for resorting to severe punitive measures with the children. To look into grievances against Beach and to develop a unified plan that would facilitate the orphans' transition to active citizens of Soviet society, Tigran Musheghyan, representing the People's Commissariat of Enlightenment, returned to the Polygon at the beginning of the 1928–29 academic year to meet with Beach. During their meeting, Beach reassured Musheghyan that conditions would change and promised to develop a unified and coherent educational program.

Some teachers warned Musheghyan that forming a unified program was extremely challenging when educational work was organized such that the staff of one department was not allowed to be involved in another department, even for good reason. But the major obstacle was Beach, and his unwillingness to implement suggestions made by government representatives. NER routinely agreed to follow government directives, Musheghyan was told, but reneged on their promises after government representatives had left and continued in the same unsystematic, random, and isolated fashion as before.[1046]

Additional details of Joseph Beach's behavior followed on January 14, 1929, from the Pedagogical Council of the agricultural school president Shindyan, submitted to the secretary of the Leninakan liaison office, Babanyan. Shindyan's five-page report stood in sheer contrast to Buckalew's description of the kind and undisturbed world the orphans enjoyed at the Polygon, published in *The Berkeley Daily Gazette* only about six months earlier. In Shindyan's report the Polygon was the venue of continuous physical and verbal abuse, where Joseph Beach and his close associates threatened orphans and teachers who questioned his orders, an act that in Beach's mind was tantamount to treason and ingratitude. Shindyan explained that the situation had deteriorated especially after Musheghyan had left Leninakan. Beach, wrote Shindyan, had always been suspicious of Soviet education, and more, he believed that NER's responsibility was to ensure only the physical well being of the orphans. That is to say, he was willing to educate the children only such that they would be able to identify the alphabet. If any type of education had been offered beyond that level, Beach had done so with the gnashing of his teeth. Beach was especially infuriated that the teachers had complained to Musheghyan about him and now wanted to take revenge against them and against the orphans.[1047] At several meetings with teachers, in November and December 1928, the report continued, Beach had emerged as a person who hated the local teachers and the students. Beach's pedagogical methods were based on humiliations, beatings, imprecations and threats to keep the orphans hungry, wrote Shindyan, and his words addressed to the orphans had been:

> Who gave you that shoe to wear? Whose are those clothes? Who feeds you? Do you know how much money has been spent on you?

The person in charge of the agricultural program and held in high esteem by Beach and all the Americans, the report continued, was a woman by the name of E. Kuznetsova, who had begun to work for NER at Karakala. Her assistant, Barsegh, held the students of the Agricultural School in terror, and did not spare cusswords and severe beatings. Rather than follow a well-defined program in farming, the students were forced to follow orders, often arbitrary. And if the student refused, he would be cussed at, beaten, and threatened. There had been problems between the students and the department personnel whereby disobeying students would be sent to the American director, resulting in heavier work responsibilities in the cowsheds, listing their names in the black book and, possibly, expulsion from the school. Pleas from the students had occasioned further insults from Joseph Beach who had characterized the orphans as lazy and ungrateful. Beach had called disobedient orphans to his office and had beaten, threatened, and humiliated them all. For three days, reported Shindyan, Citizen Beach's office had turned into an inquisition room, where independent-minded orphans who refused to be subjugated and bow their heads like paupers, were insulted and beaten. Shindyan concluded that only a man filled with vile hatred was capable of such hostility and derision and that his hatred toward orphans had long been in his heart. At the present time, Shindyan added, Beach's anger and the danger of the schools being shut down hung like a democlean sword over their heads.

About a week before Shindyan's report, liaison Georgy Sargsyan had sent an angry note to the Council of the People's Commissars with a copy to the Commissariat of Enlightenment, recounting an incident that had taken place at the Polygon on January 5, 1929.[1048] That day, he had officially informed Joseph Beach that he wished to gather the older students of the Polygon and speak with them on the occasion of the holidays, although he does not specify which holiday. But Joseph Beach had not only brusquely refused his proposal, saying that anti-religious discussions were not allowed within the boundaries of the Polygon, but had also refused to allow the students to participate in discussions taking place at the city schools. Furthermore, Beach had refused Sargsyan's official request that by the laws of the State, Sunday, January 6 [Christmas Day in the Armenian Calendar] was not to be observed as a holiday, and that work should continue as usual. Consequently, Sargsyan had,

> ...officially protested against that type of behavior on the part of NER, which is diametrically opposed to the general policy of Soviet authority with respect to religion, and told him that I would write to you about it.

Beach's blatant posturing had infuriated Sargsyan. He now insisted that the Council of People's Commissars issue an ultimatum to Beach:

> In view of the fact that NER's *modus operandi* can under no circumstance be tolerated within the boundaries of Soviet Armenia any longer, at a time when there are only 480 orphans left in its orphanages, I ask that you categorically request citizen Beach to execute the representation's proposals in full and without any objection; to put into practice the policy of the Soviet authorities regarding religious and other issues in its schools and among its staff; and in general, to strictly follow the conditions signed between the Soviet authorities and NER...

And, since NER was not an extraterritorial organization but a private enterprise, concluded Sargsyan,

> ...I ask that you protest against the attitude of citizen Beach mentioned above in an ultimatum.

Beach had subsequently met the Chairman of the People's Commissars in Yerevan since a note labeled "Secret" from Yerevan to Sargsyan read:

> We inform you that citizen Beach, the Managing Director of NER, has met with the Chairman of the Council of Peoples' Commissars about his violations of the decisions of the government and has given his explanations, following which the matter may be considered closed.[1049]

On the basis of Sargsyan's letter, on February 1, 1929, the Secreteriat of the Communist Party of Soviet Armenia resolved that the Council of the People's Commissars, through their appropriate bodies, should stop NER from violating Soviet law. The letter was signed by the Second Secretary of the Communist Party, Aghasi Khanjyan.[1050] Nine days after the resolution, the February 10, 1929, issue of the Leninakan newspaper *Banvor* carried an article titled "*Banvor* is banned from the Polygon."[1051] The article announced that a committee of *Banvor* editors had visited the Polygon on February 4, 1929, to see which newspapers were made available for the students. In the course of their visit the committee had discovered that *Banvor* was banned from the Polygon because it had recently carried a report about the bestial treatment of an orphan by an NER staff member. A few days later, on February 12, 1929, Citizen Dr. Melik-Karamyan of the Leninakan liaison's office inquired of Joseph Beach if *Banvor* had indeed recently been banned because of the unfavorable article against one of NER's employees. If the ban did indeed exist, Melik-Karamyan wrote, it was necessary to lift it.[1052]

Beach's letter of protest came one week later, on February 19, 1929.[1053] There, Beach avowed that all allegations were false and that *Banvor* had never been banned from the Polygon. Furthermore, Beach added, the appearance of such articles in the newspaper was an unfriendly act toward NER and should be penalized by the government, especially since the same article had been reprinted in Yerevan. They were all total lies, he wrote, but as a result, NER's work had been devalued by 50–75%.

Beach's note occasioned a terse response from Melik-Karamyan on February 23. Melik-Karamyan's reply, a copy of which was sent to the Council of People's Commissars, did not address the virtues or vices of *Banvor*, but focused on Beach's "arrogance" and "obduracy" to accept any criticism, even when it was constructive.[1054] Beach's letter had caused him "pain," Melik-Karamyan wrote, and held that all newspapers in Armenia published critical articles about state and public institutions so that they would benefit from the critique and thereby promote the reconstruction of the country. In the process, he conceded, editors at times exaggerated issues and strayed from reality, while other times there were personal reasons for such exaggerations. But, Melik-Karamyan added, NER need not be concerned about any loss in the value of its work:

> Fortunately, your fear that the value of NER's work is devalued by 50–75% in the eyes of the masses of Armenian workers because of published rebukes is not valid. If we approach the issue from that angle, then we should have closed a significant part of our institutions by now, about which, as I said above, more articles of a critical nature appear every day in our newspapers...[1055]

Typically, Melik-Karamyan continued, institutions criticized by papers either publicly denied accusations if they were unfounded, or tried to improve if the criticism was valid, and in my opinion, he wrote,

> ...the most logical step for NER as well, would have been to refute the articles in *Banvor* if they did not correspond to reality. Naturally, the representation

will also take measures so that various individuals, should there be any, do not take advantage of the situation to raise their personal dispositions toward your organization.[1056]

Melik-Karamyan then reminded Beach that *Banvor's* criticisms did not relate to NER as an organization but to this or that of its employees who had mistakenly found employment at NER and had failed to remain at the height of their calling. He suggested that the publication of such articles might be beneficial to NER because now it could free itself from employees whose harmful activities may actually cause a real depreciation of the value of NER's work.

Chapter Eleven

EGRESS

Deliberations in New York and Leninakan

In tandem with official negotiations on the one hand, and disputes on the local level in Leninakan on the other, NER's Conservation Committee in New York continued deliberations on the possibility of installing permanent institutions at the Polygon. The Conservation Committee had been formed in 1928, with Cleveland E. Dodge, the son of NER's first Treasurer and prominent American philanthropist Cleveland H. Dodge, as chair and Barclay Acheson as secretary. The Conservation Committee was charged with the task of developing ways in which opportunities that had evolved from 12 years of NER activities in the Near East and the Caucasus could be conserved and translated into permanent or semi-permanent institutions.[1057] To that end, NER's available assets and existing opportunities in the field would be assessed, a sample study of donor attitude in the U.S. be conducted, and ways in which permanent programs could be built on the foundations of NER's earlier relief programs be developed. At the Conservation Committee's February 14, 1929, meeting, O. S. Morgan, who had accompanied Barclay Acheson during the latter's Caucasus tour, was "firmly of the opinion that the perpetuation of a program along the general lines and in accordance with the principles of our present work was highly desirable," because

> (a) We have a large potential in stores, plant, and good-will centered in Armenia. Widely distributed in other parts of the Caucasus this potential consists of our ex-orphans and favorably contacted officials and peasant families.
>
> (b) We embody charitable, constructive American philanthropy, to Armenia, the Caucasus and to Russia. While Government maintains justifiably a watchful-waiting policy, we maintain the open-door.
>
> (c) We have a contributing constituency in America that has generously supported the work in the Caucasus sector. If they have a continuing interest great enough to warrant us in undertaking a peasant-youth school program for a five-year (as a minimum) period, then we should go ahead.[1058]

At the end of the meeting the committee voted that as "an expression of the favorable attitude toward the negotiations now in process in the Caucasus," and looking toward "the establishment of a semi-permanent peasant-youth school," funds should be made available "for scholarships to be given to needy and deserving Near East Relief ex-orphans for education" in the event that preliminary negotiations "develop favorably." For the fiscal year June 30, 1929, to June 30, 1930, the available amount would not exceed $95,000.[1059] The committee also voted that should agreement be reached over "the semi-permanent peasant-youth school in the Caucasus," it would be "on a demonstration basis and shall become completely indigenous as quickly as possible."[1060]

The committee reiterated its commitment two months later at its April 12, 1929, meeting, but was unanimous on the proviso that

> ...no continuing work should be undertaken in Russia, unless there was a sincere desire on the part of the government officials to cooperate with the proposed undertaking.

"In other words," read the Minutes of the meeting,

> ...the committee did not wish to be merely tolerated but would prefer to withdraw unless the presence of an American institution and American work in the Caucasus was sincerely desired.[1061]

While the committee members acknowledged the fact that "a situation of this kind could not be properly and fully appreciated by anyone not actually on the ground," they nevertheless hoped that Acheson and Monroe, who would be conducting negotiations in the Caucasus in spring 1929, would "avoid any premature commitments." At the same time, if during negotiations Acheson and Monroe felt that insistence on a one year program "would jeopardize the chances of obtaining, for the next year's work, all the available facilities as are within the power of the Transcaucasian government," they were authorized to proceed with discussions on a five-year plan of no more than $100,000 per year. The final confirmation of the five-year plan would be deliberated upon in New York.[1062]

In July 1929, the Conservation Committee heard Barclay Acheson's preliminary report of discussions held with the Soviet Transcaucasus leadership, a major item of which was that 50% to 75% of the operating costs in the Caucasus would be covered through the sale of old clothes and surplus supplies which were no longer needed following the wholesale outplacements of orphans. The Committee then voted to accept the Caucasus Mandate until June 1, 1930, and to "reaffirm our policy of programizing our work in the Caucasus along lines of vocational agriculture to benefit the mass of peasant youth rather than developing highly technical training for teachers only." Of the other items voted on was the approval to close down the Winchester School of Nursing and transfer it to the medical school and the Armenian Red Cross in Yerevan, where it would be supervised during the first few months by Leninakan Nursing Director Laura MacFetridge. The Committee also voted to approve the report on the closing of the Normal School and the transfer of the undergraduate students to the Government School at Leninakan. The vocational and agricultural programs remained at the Polygon.[1063]

Agreement between NER and the Armenian Red Cross for the transfer of the Edith Winchester School of Nursing to Yerevan. (NAA 154/3/7/ff. 214–215)

The Conservation Committee was still interested in continuing its activities in the southern Caucasus, and Armenia in particular, at its November 14 meeting, especially since they felt that

> …there was particular value in maintaining work in Southern Russia, as no other American work is welcome in this field.[1064]

When the committee met three months later, on February 10, 1930, it found the results of the preceding six months, on the whole, encouraging and voted that Acheson and Monroe be authorized to

> …proceed with negotiations upon their arrival in the Caucasus, with the understating that they had discretionary authority to develope [sic] a program in the Caucasus that would involve an expenditure of $100,000 a year for five years after June 30, 1930, this expenditure to be in excess of the expense connected with the field supervision of the outplaced wards of Near East Relief…it being understood that all contracts and agreements contain the usual clauses providing that the American organization is not obligated to spend funds in the Caucasus unless its American constituency is willing to contribute the funds required.[1065]

In the course of the meeting on February 10, 1930, the members heard a cable from Joseph Beach, paraphrasing Ter-Ghazaryan's reply with respect to the proposed agricultural school. It read, in part:

> WE HAVE ON OUR PART MANY TIMES EMPHASIZED OUR MOST CORDIAL ATTITUDE TOWARD THE NEW ACTIVITIES OF NEAREAST IN CONNECITON WITH EDUCATION CHILDREN ALONG AGRICULTURAL LINES. PROGRAM

> OUTLINED YOURSELF AND REPRESENTATIVES NEAREAST REGARDING AGRICULTURAL EDUCATION AND FOR THE JOINT ARRANGEMENT ALL DETAILS FUTURE WORK OF NEAREAST HERE HAVE BEEN NOTED WITH SATISFACTION.

Ter-Ghazaryan had also asked Beach to transmit "highest appreciation" for the work done by NER in "liquidating homeless and orphan problem in Transcaucasia," and added,

> IN VIEW CLOSING RELIEF WORK WE ARE GLAD TO NOTE READINESS AND DESIRE OF NEAREAST TO CARRY OUT ON NEW BASIS THE PROPOSALS SUGGESTED BY NEAREAST TO GOVERNMENT ALONG LINES WORKED OUT BY GOVERNMENTS SPECIAL COMMITTEE,

Hoping that when Mr. Acheson arrived,

> WE SHALL BE ABLE TO ARRANGE FINALLY ALL CONDITIONS FOR DEVELOPMENT OF SUCH AN IMPORTANT INSTITUTION AS THE AGRICULTURAL SCHOOL AND THUS GUARANTEE ITS CONTINUED EXISTENCE WITH THE MUTUAL SUPPORT OF THE NEAREAST AND THE GOVERNMENT.

At the end of the meeting, the Committee authorized Acheson and Monroe to continue negotiations upon arrival in the Caucasus to finalize a five-year program that would begin after June 30, 1930.[1066]

A month later, in March 1930, Joseph Beach sent an encouraging report about his trip to Sukhum and meetings in Yerevan.[1067] Beach recounted his experiences and observations, detailing how he had been received in Sukhum with great warmth by village chiefs and outplaced orphans alike, and had heard nothing but praise and deep appreciation for NER's agricultural work in Armenia. Beach had also been to Yerevan to follow up on the visit of government officials to the Polygon earlier, and "to discuss with the Commissar of Education the general principles that should underlie the work of the agricultural school for the coming year":

> We had a most satisfactory conference with Cit. Yeghiazarian, a young man who had succeeded Cit. Moravian [Mravyan] as Commissar of Education. During the two-hour conference we outlined the main principles that should underlie our work for next year and Cit. Charakchian, who had been a member of the brigade to visit Polygon earlier in the month, was appointed as one of a committee of two to visit us again in early April and reduce the plan for next year's work to a concrete written outline to be submitted to the Narcompros [People's Commissariat of Education] and to Mr. Acheson, as a tentative basis for our agricultural school work next year. We found everyone in Erivan most cordial indeed and particularly these members of the Educational Department.

During his visit to Yerevan, Joseph Beach had also inspected the nursing school recently relocated to Yerevan, and noted with great satisfaction that his visit to the lectures and the practical work of the nurses in the hospital had convinced him that the work in Yerevan was being carried out exactly along the lines that Laura MacFetridge had laid down:

> Every one of the things she [Laura MacFetridge] had been insisting upon during the months of her stay in Erivan have been carried out, and it is clear that the hospital and medical department, and Red Cross leaders are accepting entire our theory for the training of nurses. This change of attitude indicates really a marked achievement on the part of Miss MacFetridge who, by quiet good humor, patient tact, and firmness when necessary, had carried through in spite of her severe illness…the very things that will make nurses' training, in my opinion, one of the most important parts of our activities in the Caucasus.

While in Yerevan Beach had also met with Chairman S. Ter-Gabrielyan of the Council of People's Commissars for one and one half hours:

> Mr. Gunn was with me, and it was most opportune that he and Mr. Gunn should meet. The conference took on an atmosphere quite unofficial and friendly…

> We discussed agricultural questions for a long while and Mr. Gunn was able to be most helpful. We reported the various phases of our activity at Leninakan. I reported quite fully upon my trip to Soukhoum. President Ter Gabrielian indicated that he was awaiting with keen interest Mr. Acheson's visit, and I gave assurance that Mr. Acheson would be here in early May.[1068]

Everett Gunn, Beach reported, had been convinced that there were real opportunities for constructive service in Armenia, just as he was certain that during his upcoming visit Mr. Acheson would find attitudes toward the NER to be even friendlier and more favorable than during his last trip.

Yet when Acheson returned to the Caucasus in May 1930 expecting to finalize the proposal for an outlay of $500,000 to be spent over five years for the agricultural school at the Polygon, events took an unexpected turn. Rather than the favorable disposition promised in Beach's report, Acheson's proposal was rejected outright. The reason was that the military now demanded the use of the Polygon buildings as well. Nor was any offer made on the part of the government to provide NER with new buildings.

However, during the negotiations a new idea had developed. This was a consultancy program where a few NER personnel would be appointed as advisors in agriculture and would work with Soviet Armenian officials. On that occasion, Everett Gunn was appointed consultant to the Agricultural and Farm school, or as it was then called, the Polygon Agricultural Technicum. The mission of the Agricultural and Farm School, to be maintained by the Near East Foundation, the successor of Near East Relief, and announced in newspapers in the U.S., would be to "help combat the deplorable conditions of the country" by training leaders who would consist of:

> …a core group of boys and girls, 100 from Near East Relief orphanages and 150 selected with government aid from improverished families in the villages…[1069]

Asset Liquidation

But Acheson was not entirely satisfied with the new idea. He deferred his consent, saying that he needed a few more months to give the Executive Committee in New York the opportunity to deliberate on the new proposal.

In the meantime, NER staff in Leninakan was occupied with the liquidation of NER's assets that had accrued during years of relief work. The vast organization that had been put in place to care for an army of orphans was no longer needed. Acheson's discussions with, and letter to TSFSR Council of People's Commissars Chairman Shalva Eliava in May 1930, had led to the formulation of a contract specifying the terms and conditions of the liquidation of assets NER no longer needed, to take place between August 1 and December 31, 1930.[1070]

The terms of the agreement signed between Ter-Ghazaryan and Acheson were detailed, with the main stipulations being that NER's property was entirely at its own disposal and that NER could distribute or sell them as it saw fit; that proceeds of sales were to be used for operating costs within the Transcaucasus or distributed as gifts to organizations of NER's choice in the Transcaucasus; that NER was free to transfer such of its own supplies and equipment as it wished to other areas, up to a maximum valuation of $10,000; that NER was allowed to take out of the Transcaucasus all accounting records, documents, and archives relating to its work in the Transcaucasus; and that NER's American personnel were free to export their household effects and personal property, "including the two Ford automobiles owned by Mr. Collins and Mr. Gunn," but personal property purchased within the Soviet Union was subject to the usual export regulations of the Union. Finally, during the liquidation period, NER personnel in the SSRA would have access to a sufficient number of buildings at the Polygon, including the garage and warehouses, and that NER would have to officially announce its liquidation in the newspapers and request all institutions and individuals who had any claims on it to present their claims through the representative of the TSFSR Commissars. After October 15, 1930, all claims upon the Near East Relief would be considered invalid.[1071]

Parts of the Polygon were gradually returned to the authorities, some temporarily. On August 18, 1930, NER temporarily placed Building #57 and other buildings connected with the farm school, at the disposition of the People's Commissariat of Agriculture, so that the Government would manage the Polygon Agricultural Technicum.[1072] In progress was an inventory of the farm equipment. Flagg's note dated August 29, 1930, informed Dr. Melik-Karamyan that the inventory was almost complete:

> This is to advise you that Mr. Gunn has been busy assisting Cit. Korkmazian in getting the farm machinery ready for silo filling, etc., and our work of pricing the lists has been somewhat delayed. The pricing has been completed and the lists are now ready to be typed. We hope to have them finished in the next two or three days. As soon as ready we will forward a copy to Cit. Ter-Ghazaryan and a copy to your office.[1073]

Also returned in August, and also temporarily, was the Polygon bakery located in building #75. For such facilities as were turned over to the government, NER's proviso was that "if requested by the Near East Relief, all of the buildings, etc., may be returned intact to the Near East Relief for the purpose of again administering the technicom," and that the diesel needed "for the heating of the ovens" should be purchased from the Near East Relief until "the Near East Relief supply was exhausted."[1074] In the same note, Flagg responded to Melik-Karamyan's request about purchasing American auto-parts, and to say that NER did not have those parts. The request was one of several concerning the purchase of auto parts or American cars NER had brought to Armenia, some of which it had given as gifts to government and ecclesiastical officials, and others for use by the staff. Another inquiry had to do with Dodge Car #5, sold to a German subject by the name of Cit. Fritz Midtzler.[1075] Answering Dr. Melik-Karamyan's inquiry, Flagg wrote that he personally knew nothing of such a sale but that he had learned through their garage personnel that the sale had been made in 1923 or 1924, and since the case was very old, he promised to search for any documents they might still have on the sale.

Ter-Ghazaryan, too, inquired about a car, specifically the car used by NER Director of Finance and Supplies Lowell B. Collins. The car in question was not for sale, explained Flagg on September 3, and was being used by Collins. Flagg then reminded Ter-Ghazaryan that according to the contract that he, Ter-Ghazaryan, had signed with Acheson, NER was free to export the cars used by Mr. Collins and Mr. Gunn:

> In the conversation in your office August 8th between yourself and Mr. Acheson, regarding your request for two Ford Cars and five Nash Cars to complete the automobile purchases for the Government, Mr. Acheson suggested the possibility, should New York so decide, of using these two cars to apply on your request for the purchase of two Ford Cars.
>
> Before his departure, Mr. Acheson gave me instructions that these two cars should not be disposed of, but should be held pending the receipt of his instructions as to their disposition.
>
> ...Mr. Gunn's car is being retained for his use, as he has been appointed "consultant" to the Polygon Agricultural Technicom.[1076]

Flagg then concluded:

> I would also restate that in accordance with my instructions from Mr. Acheson, no cars whatsoever will be sold prior to November 1st, and also that it is very probable that the cars in question will be exported abroad...[1077]

As for the Polygon library, especially rich in the subject of agriculture in the Armenian and English languages, the decision was to leave it in Armenia. But, Flagg explained to Ter-Ghazaryan, the arrangement was temporary and that it was to be used exclusively for the agricultural school. Furthermore, the library was to be kept intact and at the first request from NER, it would be returned to NER in its entirety:

> In accordance with Mr. Acheson's instructions the Near East Relief library, which is a part of the Agricultural Technicom, has been placed on the loan list and turned to the custody of the Narcomzem [People's Commissariat of Agriculture] who are this year conducting the Polygon Agricultural Technicom. In our agreement with the Narcomzem it is understood that they are to keep this library intact, using it

for the school purposes, and to return it to the Near East Relief at such time as we may request.

It therefore seems to me that under Cit. Korkmazian, the administrative head of the school, the custodianship of the library is adequately taken care of.[1078]

With regards to the medical supplies, NER wished to give them to the Armenian Red Cross, which was headquartered in a rented space in NER's Yerevan property in 1928.[1079] But when local authorities in Leninakan reviewed the list, they deleted three items—a typewriter in English, four flour warehouse platform scales, and some food supplies—from the list of items NER wished to donate to the Armenian Red Cross. But after some negotiations, Flagg was able to reinstate them back on the list, and informed Dr. Kamsarakan of the Armenian Red Cross, that all the items would be shipped on November 24, 1930.

Some of the inventory of surplus provisions at the Polygon were sent to NER's Tiflis division for distribution. These included 10 boxes of concentrated milk, one sack of sugar, five boxes of soap, one box of tea, one box of Macaroni, five parcels of blankets, linen and fabric, five boxes of shoes, one box of vegetable oil and cacao, and one case of laundry detergent.[1080]

By June 30, 1930, as it had been agreed, all relief activity had stopped. But still, two months later Dr. Melik-Karamyan had referred a woman by the name of Arevahat Madoian, to the Polygon. The assistance Matoian asked for was turned down, resulting in an unpleasant scene at the Polygon, and a meeting with NER's lawyer. Flagg was compelled to explain the situation to Melik-Karamyan in a letter dated August 29, 1930:

> In agreement reached between Mr. Acheson and Cit. Ter Gazaryan it was distinctly stated that all forms of relief work theretofore carried on by the Near East Relief were to cease as of June 30th. This agreement was reached in May 1930. Accordingly we have discontinued all assistance to various cases in Batoum, Tiflis and Leninakan, since that date.
>
> This woman, Arevahad Madoian, came to Polygon on August 28th, and we examined her case and refused to give her further rations. This decision was reached on the basis of the agreement stated above, and also on the basis that her case was one of some years standing, that she had not received any rations since August 1929, and that she was properly a social insurance case. This was evidently before she made a visit to your office. I wonder if she told you that she had already been to Polygon and had been refused.
>
> Again on the morning of August 29th she came to Polygon with your letter and we explained to her again our decision. She displayed considerable temper and threatened to get the Near East Relief into trouble. We asked her to step into another office and had her talk with our lawyer who is here.[1081]

Asset liquidation was accompanied by staff reduction. Thirteen Armenian employees were discharged in May 1930: NER Sukhum nurse Mariam Shahinyan who had been attending to the medical needs of orphans outplaced in area villages; Polygon agronomist Ishkhan Shindyan; typist and translator Margarite Seilanoff at the Nurses Training School in Yerevan; Polygon Chief

Accountant Alexander Kharazoff; Polygon secretary Nvard Karaseferyan; Polygon cook Margarite Kirakosyan; Polygon charwoman Varinka Stebanyan; Polygon dentist Tamara Merkurova; Polygon nurses Djantaz Torosyan, Sophia Tokmachyan and Tigranuhi Gevorgyan; and, Polygon pharmacist Ruben Vasilyan.[1082]

By spring 1930, all but six of the American employees had left permanently.[1083] By June, Joseph Beach and his family left Leninakan via Tiflis, Moscow and Berlin, leaving Caleb Flagg as Acting Managing Director.[1084] With Flagg at that time were Elizabeth Mayston, as his secretary, Everett Gunn as Consultant in Agriculture; Adela Chickering, in charge of the Expert Culinary Course, and L. B. Collins as Director of Finance. By the end of September 1930, Elizabeth Mayston and L. B. Collins had left, leaving behind Caleb Flagg, Everett Gunn, and Adela Chickering, all three of whom would stay until spring 1931.

The Final Withdrawal

The last chapter of negotiations on continued work in Leninakan and NER's final withdrawal, came soon after Laird Archer's visit in February 1931. Archer, who had succeeded Acheson as NER's Executive Secretary of Overseas Programs, had arrived in Leninakan to resume negotiations. Flagg had announced Archer's expected arrival to Ter-Gabrielyan a few weeks earlier, in a letter reproduced in full, below:

On January 31, 1931

Dear Cit. Ter-Gabrielian:

I am sure you will remember very clearly the friendly talks and conferences which you had last August with Mr. Acheson, Executive Secretary of the Near East Relief.

Before leaving Mr. Acheson promised to again present the question of continued work in Trans-Caucasus to the Executive Committee of the Near East Relief in New York.

Mr. Acheson is now in New York and Mr. Laird W. Archer, who has for years been connected with our New York Office, is this winter taking Mr. Acheson's place as Executive Secretary on the Foreign Field with Headquarters in Athens. After a month's delay the visa has been granted for Mr. Archer to come to the Caucasus. According to cable advice he sailed from Athens two days after the receipt of visa. He is coming prepared to continue Mr. Acheson's discussion of last August in accordance with the decision of the Executive Committee in New York.

We expect Mr. Archer to arrive in Leninakan about February 10th and between February 10th and 15th we propose to come to Erivan for the purpose mentioned above. As soon as Mr. Archer arrives we will send you a telegram asking for an appointment which will be most convenient to you.[1085]

Archer's meetings, however, went awry and negotiations collapsed altogether. Archer then returned to Greece from where he sent reports to New York, precipitating an Inter-State communiqué from Acheson to all field directors. The communiqué, dated March 10, 1931, announced NER's immediate withdrawal from Armenia and Georgia, detailing the circumstances that had led to NER's final withdrawal from the region.[1086] Since the document clarifies the sudden turn of events and provides details about NER's final days in the SSRA, large sections of the communiqué are reproduced below. It began:

> You are somewhat familiar with the situation in the Caucasus as a result of the February conference. Since then we have received a cabled report from Mr. Archer who has just returned to Greece from the Caucasus. As a result of his [Archer's] cabled reports we will withdraw from Armenia and Georgia at once.

Acheson instructed field directors to abstain from any statements to the press, at least until the American personnel were safely out of Armenia, after which "it is important for us to protect the lives and well-being of the local personnel who must remain. They have helped us courageously during all the years of our work in Russia." Statements to the press would be made, the communiqué continued, through the New York office:

> Carefully considered statements will be issued by the national Office; therefore, no statements other than those issued by the national office should find their way into the papers of the United States. The nature of the official statements will be considered by our Board of Directors and by the Executive Council, and you will be asked to cooperate later if Area statements are desired.

To further emphasize the urgency of his request, Acheson added:

> …you should know that Mr. Archer reports that thirty of our personnel have been arrested recently and that either four or six have been shot.[1087]

Following the preamble, Acheson next addressed the reasons NER had not withdrawn earlier and traced the steps that had led to the eventual decision to do so. "We decided to remain in the Caucasus last summer," he wrote, "for two reasons":

> A. To Dispose of our Assets
>
> It was important for us to supervise the expenditure of the rouble balance that had accumulated in Russian banks as a result of the sale of old clothes and equipment, and to dispose of supplies, farm equipment, herd and other assets in a way that was in keeping with the intention and purpose of the contributors when the funds were provided for these purposes. This administrative problem was an important one, as the total assets in the Caucasus last summer were variously estimated as worth from $250,000 to $500,000. None of them could be withdrawn from the country.
>
> B. To test the value of Consultants
>
> Only time could test out the value of a proposed program of assisting the Armenian Government through counselors or consultants. Mr. Archer found that the bulk of the supplies and rouble balance had been disposed of in accordance with our instructions and that the balance could be wisely turned over to the Armenian Red Cross for the purpose of the completion of certain parts of our work, particularly those connected with the Nurses Training School; and the consultant relationship was not desirable, partly because of the Government's attitude, partly because of

the isolated position in which it placed our personnel, and partly because of the anti-American sentiment that has developed in Russia since the notorious trial that was fully reported in the newspapers.[1088]

Acheson expected that the American personnel would be out of the Caucasus by April first, and NER's work in the Caucasus would end by the end of the fiscal year, or June 30, 1931. "It will, therefore," he pointed out,

> ...be entirely correct to let people [in the U.S.] pay the balance of the pledges made for the support of students in the Caucasus for the present school year, as we are turning over supplies and cash to the Polygon School and the Armenian Red Cross Nurses Training School in excess of the sums represented by these scholarships.[1089]

Next Acheson turned to the events that had led up to NER's withdrawal, in chronological order:

> 1. We proposed an expenditure of $500,000 during a period of five years, beginning June 30, 1930, for the Polygon School. This proposition was made in May. It was not regarded as acceptable by the Government because the military authorities demanded the use of the Polygon buildings for military purposes and refused to provide new buildings. At this time the Stalin faction of the Communist party were in the ascendancy.

In view of the situation, wrote Acheson, NER had begun to develop a substitute program, but no longer in Armenia:

> 2. We decided that we could accomplish more good with this fund elsewhere; therefore, we arranged to transfer funds and personnel to the other areas, particularly Albania and Bulgaria. Between May and July of 1930, negotiations were begun and commitments made with the Beirut University, International College at Smyrna, the Albanian Government, Haskell's school in Bulgaria, Black's college in Sofia, etc. This was the substitute program. I am sure that you will agree with the administration that it was a better investment of the available funds.

But, Acheson went on to explain:

> 3. When we returned to the Caucasus, we found that a compromise arrangement had been made between the two factions of the Communist party, and the Government offered to build the buildings for us if we could renew the original proposition.

Yet this time it was NER that had declined the offer:

> This we declined to do, stating that we had decided to withdraw. Out of these negotiations grew the suggestion of consultants.

At the same time, Acheson had realized that

> ...we had to leave a few of our personnel in the Caucasus in order to dispose of the assets that we held in a way that would be satisfactory to our contributors.

"We therefore," he continued,

> ...stated that it would take us several months to re-analyze the situation and report back to New York on the possibility of maintaining a program through consultants.

Stalling for time had been necessary for two other reasons as well:

> ...for the purpose of giving our local personnel a chance to find other positions, and partly because we honestly wished to test out the possibilities of this arrangement.[1090]

But plans had been upset when, "during the fall and winter months, the Stalin faction of the communist party had again regained power." The communists had

> 4. ...staged the trial in Moscow with which you are all familiar, and this resulted in a great wave of hostility toward all foreign organizations. The central authority at Moscow apparently decided to disavow many of their previous arrangements with the semi-independent Caucasus Governments and to dominate more completely Caucasus affairs. This led to the removal of some of our closest friends in high positions and reduced the effectiveness of our proposed consultant relationships.

Nevertheless, the delay

> ...did give us a splendid opportunity of disposing of our assets in a satisfactory way and accomplished all that we had hoped for it.[1091]

He was convinced, wrote Acheson, that under the circumstances, the consultancy program would not have been a good investment, and that

> ...even though we should decide to have some work in the Caucasus in the future, we would be more likely to have a favorable opportunity for such work if we withdrew in a dignified and becoming manner than if we attempted to carry on with the unfavorable public sentiment which now exists.[1092]

> To summarize: The time has come to withdraw; the work that we undertook has been splendidly accomplished; and the assets entrusted to our administration have been wisely disposed of. None of them have been allowed to fall into the hands of any faction that would use them for purposes other than those for which they were contributed.

Acheson ended his communiqué by praising the American personnel Flagg, Chickering, and Gunn and the local personnel, for having stayed the course and for having handled the difficult circumstances of NER's last days in Armenia successfully. And now,

> Polygon school has been turned over to the Educational Department and will be continued as an agricultural school for peasant youth. The nurses training work has been turned over to the Armenian Red Cross and will be carried forward under their administration and with their own funds. The children have all been outplaced—most of them in rural villages; moreover, they have been supervised for nearly two years—many of them for a longer period. Thus they have been given a chance to root themselves into the existing social structure to the best advantage possible under existing conditions.

The local personnel had been protected as long as possible, and the majority had good employment. But, he added with regret,

...[a] few have apparently paid a heavy price for their loyalty to our organization. This fact is the deepest injustice and the most keenly felt reflection on our humanitarian effort. It can in no way be charged to any fault of the Americans who lived in the Caucasus or to the organization we represent. It can only be accounted for by the unreasoning prejudices now rampant in Russia and their fears and suspicions against all foreign agencies. It in no way represents the deep-rooted feeling of the peoples we have served, or the officials with whom our organization has come directly in contact.[1093]

One of the last institutions to be turned over to the government was the Expert Culinary Course run by Adela Chickering. During the last six months of instruction, 20 men had attended her course from the various collective farms in the district. "The leader was a big six-footer with enormous mustache," said Chickering, "tall hat, long red native coat and boots. He was married and the father of a family, but he was one of my best pupils."[1094] Chickening's course was turned over to the authorities on March 31, 1931, and in the following weeks NER left Leninakan for ever, taking with them much of their archives, and depositing the rest at the liaison's office in Leninakan. Caleb Flagg was in Tiflis when he wrote his farewell letter to Ter-Gabrielyan in June:

Tiflis, Georgia.
June 15, 1931.
Cit. Ter-Gabrielian
President of S.S.R. of Armenia
Erivan, S.S.R.A.

My dear Cit. Ter-Gabrielian:-

Notwithstanding the negotiations and discussions which took place between yourself and Mr. Acheson in Erivan, and between cit. Eliava and other government officials with Mr. Acheson in Tiflis, on Mr. Archer's visit to the Caucasus in February of this year, the proposition of a cooperative work on the basis of consultants furnished by the Near East Relief was rejected by the Trans-Caucasian Government. Thereupon Mr. Archer instructed me to completely liquidate the property of the Near East Relief and, therefore, the organization withdraws from further work in the Soviet Union.

To all of those who were interested in the discussions of a year ago this decision came as a great disappointment. We remember the interest shown and the cordial expressions of invitation to continue a bond of friendship between our two countries as expressed in a cooperative work and cultural relations.

In liquidating the property of the organization it has been distributed to different organizations, the three receiving the larger gifts being the Armenian Red Cross, the Narcomzem Technicom at Polygon and the Didubey Trade School in Tiflis.

The last of the American Personnel are now in Tiflis en route to Batoum and we are concluding our last business matters with the Government Representation. Before the organization is actually closed, I wish to send you this letter of appreciation and farewell.

In the twelve years of its work in Armenia the various personnel of the Near East Relief have seen wonderful changes and marked progress in the condition of the country. We are glad to feel that the work which we have done has been some contribution to this progress. In the early days we were able to preserve the lives of many of the inhabitants. Thereafter during most of the period we have cared for and educated thousands of children who have now gone out into normal life in Armenia or the surrounding Republics of the Soviet Union. We are gratified to feel that the majority are healthy active young people and we trust that notwithstanding that their childhood was spent under institutional conditions they have the foundation for the making of good citizens of the Soviet Union.

The work which we have been permitted to accomplish we could not have carried through alone. We are greatly indebted to the helpful suggestions of the various Government officials and to the cooperation of governmental departments. Because of the size of the work, we owe a great debt of appreciation to the faithfulness and ability of our employees who are natives of this country.

To you and your associates and to the Armenian Sovnarcom I would express the appreciation of the Near East Relief and of its personnel as individuals for your many courtesies and cooperation. Our best wishes are with you for the future of the Republic and we trust that the momentum gained during the past ten years will enable you not only to fulfill your plans, but to exceed them in building up a happy prosperous Republic and people.

Very truly yours,

C. B. Flagg (signed)
Acting Managing Director,
Caucasus Area - N.E.R.[1095]

Reward and Retribution

During and after NER operations, several American relief workers received well-deserved medals and recognition internationally or in their hometowns, while articles in U.S. publications paid homage to the valor they had displayed at trying times.

For their courage and commitment, Charles Vickrey had awarded the gold medal to Elizabeth Anderson, James Errol, Nelson Meeks, and Olive Smith on January 9, 1922.,[1096] One week later, on January 16, *The Boston Globe* announced the names of relief workers to whom James Barton awarded distinguished service medals in the Council Chambers of Boston's State House. Among them were Harold Barton and Dr. Jefferson Hawthorne. Also awarded for distinguished service to Armenia were Veronica Harris and Ernest Yarrow, each of who were bestowed The Order of Saint Gregory the Illuminator by Gevorg V Catholicos of the Armenian Church.[1097] The latter had also been awarded the Order of the Lion and the Sun by the Persian government for his relief efforts in that region, and medals from the Soviet leadership in Moscow. Veronica Harris, according to *The Reno Evening Gazette*, had married a Georgian prince, Nicolai Alexandrovitch, in Constantinople on December 26, 1922.[1098]

Milton Brown received the Near East Relief Medal for Service in the Council Chamber of the State House in Boston in April 1923.[1099] The Soviet government in Moscow decorated NER Chief Surgeon Dr. Walter Sisson of Wauseon, Ohio, for opening seven casualties clearing stations in the earthquake area in Leninakan and for operating continuously for 72 hours after the first shock, during which he had performed 85 amputations and 76 other operations on injured peasants.[1100] Dr. Sisson was also awarded with a gold medal struck especially for him, by the Armenian Surgeons Society and three other American physicians—Mabel E. Elliott, Roland P. Blythe and Russell T. Uhls—were made honorary members of the Armenian Medical Society in recognition of their work in Armenia.[1101] For her work during the earthquake in Leninakan, Laura MacFetridge was awarded a medal in 1926 by NER[1102] and a school in Philadelphia was named in her honor. Bell Bass and Elsie Jarvis received the Cleveland H. Dodge medal for distinguished service in 1927.

Elsie Kimball had left NER's service in early 1926, disappointed that rather than orphanage work which she preferred and was promised by successive directors, she had been placed in a series of secretarial positions. She had finally lost hope of doing what she loved most when Joseph Beach was in charge and accepted a position in the Georgian Manganese Company Limited in Tchiatouri, Georgia in February 1926.[1103] Nevertheless, NER awarded her a medal soon after she had returned home permanently, in 1928. Also working at the Georgian Manganese Co. was Sam Newman, once the Dean of NER's Agricultural program. He had left NER with his wife in July 1925, and worked as the head of Property and Supply Department.[1104] Commended also were Maytie Johnson, in May 1930,[1105] and Dorothy Sutton of Montclair, New Jersey, who was decorated with NER's Distinguished Service Medal.

In the 1930s and until his death in 1957, Barclay Acheson rose into prominence as a national figure in the U.S. A charismatic public speaker, Acheson appeared before numerous audiences representing the Near East Foundation, the successor of Near East Relief, and later as the founder of *Reader's Digest*, at home and internationally. His audiences included national clubs such as the Rotary and Lions Clubs, universities, church groups and general audiences. He brought to them the experiences and knowledge he had gained first hand during

NER women honored with the Distinguished Service Medal. (*The Monroe News Star*, January 11, 1928)

Brings Message to President Hoover From King Fuad I. of Egypt

Left to right: Barclay Acheson, Mrs. Barton, H. C. Jaquith and James Barton aboard the SS *Lafayette* in early January 1931. (*The Mount Pleasant News*, January 7, 1931)

his travels around the world, captivating audiences around the country on issues of peace, international cooperation, freedom, and progress.[1106] Acheson was awarded the rank of Commander of the Order of the Redeemer by the Greek government, and among his acquaintances and friends were King Boris of Bulgaria, King Zog of Albania, King Fuad I of Egypt, King Faisal of Iraq, and Allen W. Dulles, the Director of the Central Intelligence Agency.

Janet MacKaye left the Polygon in 1929, and soon after her return to the U.S. she, too, was honored for her many years of service.[1107] But these were eclipsed by the greater honors she had received even before she had left Leninakan. At the farewell dinner given in her honor, attended by officials from every department of the government, MacKaye was regaled by praises. On that occasion also, a street in Leninakan was named after her. The story was carried in several U.S. newspapers soon after she had returned:

> No name is brighter in the relief work of the little land [Armenia] where Noah's Ark grounded, than that of Miss McKay [MacKaye]. One of the streets of this city has been named for her and when she was guest of honor at a farewell dinner, every department of the government was represented. Speakers from all walks of life lauded her self-sacrificing labors.[1108]

U.S. newspapers also wrote about the mobile village clinics MacKaye had established. "These clinics," one newspaper stated, "serve 810 villages, averaging 16,500 treatments a year among people with whom 12,200 children from the American orphanages have been outplaced.[1109]

No medals or awards were forthcoming to NER's Armenian employees in Armenia. Many were arrested, exiled or executed, some for their loyalty to NER, as Acheson had acknowledged in his communiqué. Some, like Lucine Aghayan, as recounted by her granddaughter Tereza Aghayan, "was persecuted for the very reason that she had worked with the Americans" and, despite the fact that she had been highly educated, spoke six languages and had much to offer her fatherland, she was subsequently refused employment.[1110]

Vahan Cheraz, the founder of the boy scout movement, had been arrested and exiled in late 1924 and returned some months later. After six months of unemployment he had sought employment from Acheson during the latter's visit in 1926.[1111] Two months later, liaison Sargsyan had informed then NER Director General Eastman that Cheraz should have no employment, however meager, at the orphanage, and Cheraz had lost his job. His last, and final arrest followed soon, a few months after his daughter Byurakn's birth. Lavrentiy Beria, Stalin's close associate, executed Cheraz in January 1928 while a prisoner at the notorious Medekh prison in Tiflis. During his interrogation Cheraz had openly admitted that he had been a close associate of "The American Brown [Milton Brown] of the Leninakan NER" from 1921 to 1924, who, the interrogator added, was "known to us as an American spy."[1112]

Harutyun Alpoyachyan, who had worked at the Polygon for five years in different capacities, was arrested at the end of December 1930. No reasons were given for his arrest and imprisonment at various Cheka prisons in Leninakan and Yerevan, or at the Medekh prison in Tiflis. Soon after his arrest the Cheka had expropriated and carried off everything in his room, among them four cameras, two of which belonged to him and the other two he kept for Everett Gunn. Evidently, after Alpoyachyan was arrested, Gunn had asked that the Cheka return his cameras:

One day it was my turn to be interrogated…

…After a long silence one of the Chekists asked how many cameras I had in Leninakan. I said four, of which two were mine, and the other two belonged to the American Mister Gunn. I also gave them the make of the cameras.

I learned later that Mister Gunn had gone to the Cheka and asked that his cameras be returned; they had called me in to verify if Mister Gunn was telling the truth.

Anyway, Mister Gunn's cameras were returned to him.[1113]

During multiple interrogations Alpoyachyan was offered his freedom in exchange for false testimony against his friends and colleagues at the Polygon, which Alpoyachyan categorically refused. He was sentenced to exile in Siberia.

Nshan Hovhannisyan was no longer the Superintendent of Education at the Polygon after 1927. A note from Melik-Osipov had specifically requested that Hovhannisyan not be employed by NER.[1114] The circumstances under which Hovhannisyan left Armenia are unclear, but he was subsequently in France, then in Syria where he held a teaching position in an Armenian school. He had tried to return to Armenia without success and was for many years a teacher at the Melkonian School in Cyprus.[1115]

14 AMERICANS GIVEN MEDALS

Women Play Prominent Part in Near East Relief Work In Russia, Turkey and Greece.

New York.—(*P*)—Hardships in the disease-infested, revolution-torn Near East are all things of the past for 14 Americans who have returned to their homes for leaves of absence from the ranks of the Near East Relief.

In recognition of their services in Russia, Turkey, and Greece, these 14 were given the Distinguished Service Medal of the organization at the annual meeting here.

Seven of the workers are women whose official report in the Near East Relief office reads like a war record. Famines, massacres, earthquakes, disease, allwere experiences from which they say they have just come back ome "for a rest."

Miss Dorothy Stratton of Norwalk, Conn., lived through 72 days of earthquake last year in Armenia and had thousands of orphans under her care in the two institutions in the affected area. After this disaster she was transferred to Leninakan in the Caucausus mountains, where the Near East Relief operates prehaps the largest orphanage in the world.

Miss Agnes Evon of Pittsfield Mass., was cited for her heroism in the Smyrna disaster in 1922 where she was responsible for giving aid to thousands of women and children. Her own life was saved by a United States marine who carried her bodily from the scene of action. Last year she was in Beriut where she had charge of all the relief work in Syria and was the founder of a maternity hospital.

Miss Jennie Ryan, of Malone, N. Y., was in Asia Minor during a devsisted typh astating typhus epidemic. She assisted in the removal of 22,000 people from the central part of the country to the coast during the periods of deportation and massacre of the Turkish minorities.

Miss Elsie Kimball, of Mount Vernon, N. Y., spent five years in the midst of starvation and epidemic in southern Russia and was at Kars at the time of the massacres there in 1922.

Others who were given recognition of their work in these desolated regions during the last five or six years are: Frank America, Buffalo, N. Y.; Mrs. Carlotta Wells, Briggs, New York; Gertrude Coit, New London, Conn; Captain and Mrs. Wilfred H. Day, Pelham, N. Y.; Rose Ewad, Yonkers, N. Y.; Harry A. Eastman, Cleveland; Charles Fowle, Providence, R. I.; and Charles Morris, New York.

Americans recognized for service by NER. (*The Biloxi Daily Herald*, January 16, 1928)

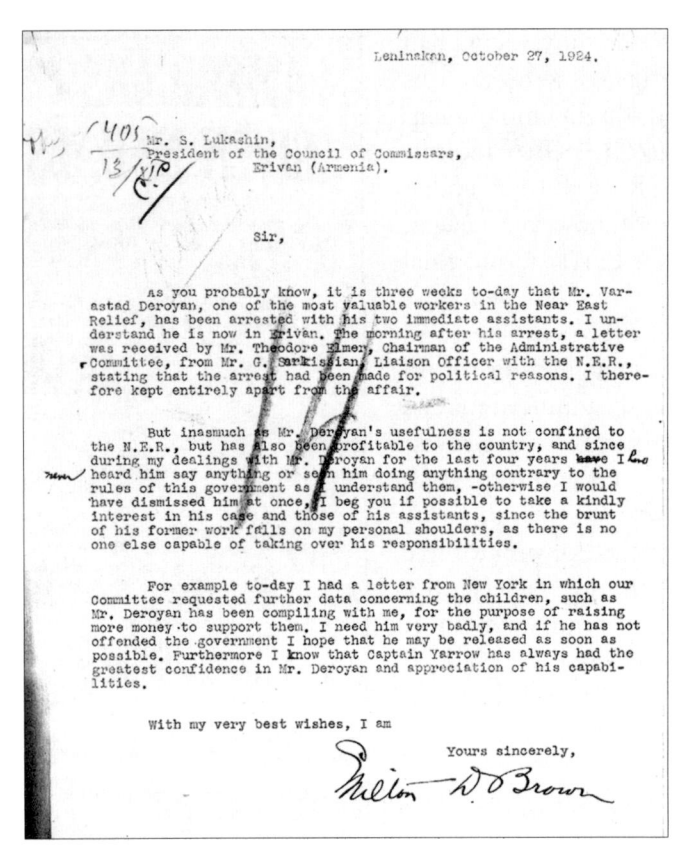

Note from Milton Brown to Sergei Lukashin about Varazdat Deroyan's arrest in 1924. (NAA 113/3/174/f. 48)

Varazdat Deroyan, one of the mediators for NER's return to Armenia in 1920 and the holder of various positions at NER's institutions in Tiflis, Yerevan and Leninakan, was arrested four times by the Cheka—in 1922, 1924, 1931 and 1935. He had been released following interventions from influential friends in government after the first three arrests, but when arrested again in 1935, his supporters had themselves lost their positions or had been purged. Deroyan was sentenced to hard labor in Siberia, where he died in a concentration camp.[1116] During his interrogations by the Cheka in September 1931, he had insisted that NER, as an organization, was not engaged in espionage but if there were spies among them they worked on their own initiative.[1117] In the course of his interrogations Deroyan had praised several of NER's leaders, including Dangerfield, whom he described as an archeologist and art appreciator interested in monasteries and old manuscripts, and who, as an individual (like Telford) deserved the highest respect.[1118] The same was true of Milton Brown who, much like Telford and Dangerfield, liked antiques.[1119] Regarding Fothergill, Deroyan said he had stayed in Armenia from 1922 until 1931, and that he was a business-minded naturalized British citizen, fluent in Russian and German. As such, he had served as the main interpreter to NER directors after Yarrow.[1120]

There were more arrests of NER's Armenian employees after NER withdrew. Gurgen Edilyan, who as a young PhD from Europe had surveyed the condition of orphans in 1916, then served as principal of the Kazachi schools and subsequently as Dean of the Pedagogical Faculty of Yerevan State University, was purged in 1937. Sirakan Tigranyan, once the Minister of Public Education and Art and a high official under the First Republic of Armenia and later Director of the Polygon Pedagogical Technicum, had been arrested in 1924, then again in 1933 and 1937 and executed in 1937. Davit Barnasyan, Director and Supervisor of Polygon's student self-government section, was arrested in 1933 on charges of being a French agent. Vardan Maksapetyan had begun teaching at the Polygon in 1924 but was arrested one year later, released and arrested again in 1937; Polygon Zoology and Animal Husbandry teacher Shahen Shirakuni was arrested in 1927 and exiled until 1933, and then arrested again in February 1935. Also arrested in 1937 were Polygon Mathematics and German teacher Hovhannes Mechlumyan, and Physics, Mathematics, Geography and Armenian Language teacher Artavazd Mikayelyan, while Vahram Terzipashyan's arrest came in 1949, when he was charged with being an anti-Soviet agitator.[1121] Lieutenant General Movses

Silikyan, one of the highest officers in the army of First Republic of Armenia, who had worked for NER from 1923 to 1929, was arrested in 1921, 1927, 1935, then arrested again in 1937 and executed at the age of 74. Among those arrested in the next decade was Anushavan Gevorgyan-Harutyunyan, an interpreter at the City of Orphans from 1922–1924. Born in the Akhuryan village of the province of Alexandropol, he had left for the U.S. in 1911, at the age of 18, and had worked, among other places, at the Riverside Cement Company in Los Angeles, California. He had returned to Armenia in February 1917 and taken up residence in Alexandropol the following year, working first as an interpreter for the British Relief Committee and then for NER. In 1949, he was accused of being a member of the Dashnak Party and together with his entire family, was exiled to Siberia.[1122] Records of interrogations and verdicts of these employees have been preserved in the National Archives of Armenia in a section entitled the "Wrongfully Condemned."

Moderate government officials were among those who were summarily purged or imprisoned. Chairman of the Council of People's Commissars Sergei Lukashin was executed in 1937; Chairman of the Council of People's Commissars Sahak Ter-Gabrielyan, it was reported to Stalin, had committed suicide by throwing himself from the window of his third floor prison cell in 1937; Poghos Makintsyan, Commissar of Internal Affairs under Myasnikyan, was arrested in 1937 and executed in 1938; Commissar of Agriculture Aramayis Yerznkyan was arrested and died in prison; and Commissar of Foreign Affairs Alexander Bekzadyan was executed in 1939. Alexander Myasnikyan had been killed in March 1925, about a year after Lenin's death, when the plane he was on exploded in mid-air, in what is generally agreed to have been an assassination engineered by Laurenti Beria. In Tiflis, Mamia Orakhelashvili and Shalva Eliava were both executed in 1937. Alexei Rykov was purged in 1938. All, and many more were accused of being enemies of the people; and all had been supporters of NER's relief activities in Armenia.

Among NER staff arrested during the notorious purges of 1937 was also Vardanush Cheraz who had married Vahan Cheraz in 1924, and worked as a manager of the Polygon kindergarten. She was arrested on charges of counter-revolutionary activities. She and her 10-year-old daughter Byurakn lived in the city when on October 7, 1937, young Byurakn woke up at 2 o'clock in the morning to see her mother standing by the door, ashen, while a few officers of the Cheka turned their home upside down. One of them, a woman, was conducting a body search on her mother. In 2012, 75 years later, she, Mrs. Byuragn Cheraz Ishkhanyan, recalled the scene of her mother being dragged away in the middle of the night:[1123]

Vardanush and Byuragn. (Vahan Ishkhanyan's https://vahanishkhanyan.wordpress.com/2014/05/04/gnd/)

Mrs. Byurakn Cheraz Ishkhanyan before a bust of her father, on the occasion of the opening of a hall dedicated to Vahan Cheraz at the Pedagogical Institute in Gyumri in 2014. ("Untanekan Alpom. Vahan Cheraz." https://vahanishkhanyan.wordpress.com/2014/06/10/cheraz/photo by Shaghik Arcruni)

> On that nightmarish night…they took my mother away. Wearing only a nightgown, barefeet, I began running after the car. Then I didn't see them any more…I don't know how they got me home…
>
> I did not go to school for several days…when I did summon enough courage to go, I saw that my photograph had been taken off the wall of honor students. The space where my photograph had hung was conspicuously blank…I was the daughter of an enemy of the people. My friends stopped talking to me…

The ten-year-old used to go to jail to see her mother and bring her some food. But,

> I would wait in line for hours, and when my turn came, they would tell me there was no one there by that name and that I should go to the Cheka. I would go to the Cheka, wait in line again, and when my turn came they would say "she's not here." I was never able to bring anything to my mother.
>
> Then, after a delay of two months, I got a note from my mother asking for warm clothes. We went to the jail, but there, they told us she was no longer in Leninankan, and that she had been sentenced to 10 years of exile without the privilege of correspondence.

Vardanush Andreasian Cheraz was executed in November 1937. Her daughter was adopted by her uncle, whose wife changed Byuragn's last name to Andreasian over concerns that the name Cheraz would create problems for them.[1124]

So ended a decade of NER activities in SSRA. Many men and women, American and Armenian, most of them young, had had the courage to step into, and the tenacity to endure, a particularly unstable political situation. It was their efforts, at times convergent, often at odds with each other that had transformed the mortar and stone left behind by the czar's armies into human habitats. While their memories would remain in the minds and souls of the thousands they had helped, in official circles, in the U.S. or the SSRA, the memory of their achievements would grow dim. In Soviet Armenia, NER would be vilified and those associated with the institution, would remember it only in the privacy of their thoughts.

In the U.S., official circles seemed to be oblivious to the monumental effort it had taken to care for the thousands of orphans. When the United States recognized the Soviet Union in 1933, *The New York Times* published an editorial in its November 16, 1933, issue, hailing the raising of the American flag in Moscow, for the first time, it said, since 1918. There was no mention of NER's decade-long work in the Soviet Union, nor of the American flag that had flown over the City of Orphans, or the frequent chanting of *Stars and Stripes Forever* by thousands of barefooted children. *The New York Times* editorial drew a terse response from Barclay Acheson:

> On your editorial page today it is stated, "With the arrival of Ambassador Bullitt in Moscow our flag has been raised for the first time in that city since 1918." The writer goes on to say, "Less formally, one imagines, the American flag must have occasionally been seen in Soviet Russia later than that," and says specifically that the American Government was very much in touch with the Soviet Government during the famine years 1921–1923, when the American Relief Administration was operating in Russia, and that it spent something like $60,000,000 or $70,000,000 for food and medical relief.

Acheson then reminded the editor that

> American workers under the white star of the Near East Relief entered the Russian Caucasus in 1919 and unfurled there the red, white and blue emblem of their country. That emblem continued to proclaim to Russia the friendliness of America until 1931. Under its protection hundreds of thousands of lives were saved. During one Winter, 500,000 people were clothed. In great hospitals, orphanages, and farm and vocational schools some 30,000 children were made well and strong, were tenderly sheltered and were prepared for self support in Soviet Russia. In one orphanage alone, at Leninakan, formerly Alexandropol, 23,000 children were gathered into what was known as the "Orphan City." The last service rendered to Russia by American workers there was the demonstration of a model farm, on which the remaining orphans were trained to aid their country in rural development, together with boys and girls chosen from surrounding villages by government officials, so that they, too, might share with the orphans a knowledge of Western methods.

> I would like to add that the American flag flying officially in Russia today will be none the less welcome because of the friendly service given to Russia by American workers under their flag, which flew less formally, a service in which was expended for the relief and the regeneration of a famine-ridden and poverty-stricken people a very fair proportion of the $125,000,000 administered by the Near East Relief in the Near Eastern countries.[1125]

Reflecting with hindsight on NER's work in Armenia years later, Acheson felt that when NER was feeding the hungry and healing the diseased, communist officials had found it easy to cooperate with NER. But as the emergency had passed, fundamental differences had become increasingly apparent and had given way to an ever-widening difference of judgment:

> The increasing age of the children brought up the question of what they were going to be like and what they were going to do with their lives after they graduated from our orphanage schools. We did not fully comprehend the radical differences between our American ideals and communist social doctrines until after we had spent months and years discussing this question. For example, we differed concerning property rights, home life, the value of self-reliance and individual initiative, and concerning religious training.[1126]

Some party members had been deeply interested in the children's welfare, others more so in "One Million Dollars" worth of American supplies in old clothes," but that did

> ...not mean that the Russian officials were tricky or vicious or that they did not wish to do the best possible for our children from their point of view.

It had meant, however, that

> It took ten years of conflict over what that best really was to reveal how profound our differences really were. We finally concluded that the ideals of self-government by a free people and the beehive social concept of Stalin were antagonistic, irreconcilable and mutually destructive.

The earlier atmosphere of cooperation and understanding had deteriorated over time with the increasingly autocratic regime that had made it virtually impossible to function:

> It was the little official, the subordinate, advanced as a reward for his zeal, who was most exasperating. He was determined to apply his new-found doctrines to every department within the orphanage… the worst for us and for Russia happened as the more tolerant and democratic members of the Communist party were eliminated by execution or exile. This process was gradual but it continued until Stalin and his henchmen controlled Russia completely, and all hope for the enfranchisement of the 160,000,000 people living in Russia had to be abandoned.[1127]

Chapter Twelve

APOCRYPHA

By spring 1931 the Polygon, the last reminder of the City of Orphans, was vacated of its benefactors and beneficiaries. All the somber barracks where thousands of children had been healed and fed, had learned to farm, to teach, embroider, make shoes, raise animals and nurse the sick, had reassumed their original destiny in the service of the military. The respite from the military imperative was a thing of the past and the "amazing, stupendous spectacle" that had so impressed Dr. Mabel Elliott in 1921 was replaced by the sound of military drills and soldiers marching under the flag of the Red Army.

The vast warehouses where NER had stored provisions, equipment and furniture, used clothes and medicines, were also emptied. Some of the equipment and property had been liquidated and the remaining provisions and goods donated and exchanged. But not the renovations and upgrading the American public, through NER, had invested in the barracks. They were there to stay and became the property of the armed forces of SSRA and the Soviet Union. Among these was the large hospital NER had renovated and refurbished at the Severski, which remained in use as a military hospital until it was destroyed by the earthquake of 1988 in Leninakan.[1128]

The American benefactors had returned to their homes, to their families and loved ones. Of the Armenian employees, some had found jobs elsewhere, others remained unemployed, and a number of them were in exile or had been purged.

And what of the orphans, the very population group around whom so many negotiations had been conducted for so many years, and about whom so much had been written in papers and journals in the U.S., Armenia, and elsewhere? Where was "home" for them? Once the citizens of the City of Orphans, they were now scattered in different parts of the world. "Home," for some, was the Northern Caucasus; for others it was further north in Russia; for many it was Georgia, where they made a living as laborers, temporary or permanent. There was also the other group, of unknown numbers, for whom "home" was in North America, where they had been shipped leaving only a dim trace behind them. For the majority, however, home was Soviet Armenia, not their towns and villages in Kars, Van, Erzurum, Mush or elsewhere; they did not return to their ancestral hearths and extended families, the orchards and brooks where they had played and whose memories still lingered in their minds. They were now citizens of the SSRA, the new, socialist Armenia, which they would help build by tilling the land or working in factories, and for which they would die. After all, they were now young Communists, and everything else, including their lives in the City of Orphans, would have to be eclipsed by their new identity. But memories could not be so easily erased or dismissed—they never are. There was so much to talk about, to process, to share, so much of which sense had to me made. But all of that would have to wait for several decades, until Stalin was no more, until the Cold War had ebbed and Armenia would become independent again.

Even before they had left the barracks to enter life in Soviet Armenia, the state had mounted rigorous efforts to erase and degrade the memory of the American orphanages, efforts that intensified with Stalin's rise to power. The American orphanages were painted as the lairs of counterrevolutionary Armenian teachers, the devils incarnate, who had abused and enslaved vulnerable orphans. One such effort was the publication of a booklet by M. Abgar entitled *Gyanke Dashnaktsakan vorbanotsnerum*, [Life in the Dashnak Orphanages], published in 1931, the year NER left Armenia. The 22-page booklet had been sponsored by the Armenian Central Committee of the All-Union Leninist Communist Youth League, the Communist Party organization for young people aged 14 to 28 to spread Communist teachings and prepare future members of the Communist Party.

Abgar's booklet addressed Armenia's communist youth organizations where a large number of former orphans held memberships, and is a bitter incantation against NER orphanages, especially its Armenian teachers and employees. The American orphanages, where cruelty and slavery reigned supreme, declared Abgar, were full of Dashnaks who had sold their souls and their dignity to the Americans and made lavish use of the whip on orphans. He especially targeted the scouts, both under Ogden and Cheraz, whose preferential treatment of a select few was to be expunged by "the birth of a new life," the life offered by the Communist youth organization, dedicated to the building of a bright, socialist Armenia. Nothing positive could be said about NER's orphanages or its employees, Armenian or American.

In the ensuing decades, discourse, especially in public, remained limited to a select and trusted few, and memories would have to be locked for the time being, in fact for several decades, as Hranush Kharatyan-Araqelyan argues,[1129] within the individual as she or he grappled with his or her lot. Inevitably, such memories became muted Apocrypha, excluded from the canons of Stalin's bible. When memories of the past, including the years at the City of Orphans were "unlocked," accelerating after the collapse of the Soviet Union, former orphans still alive now shared their experiences in public—in autobiographies, documentary collections, and newspapers. Amidst accounts of persecution, loss and survival, surfaced fragments of reminiscences of the City of Orphans in varying lengths, their contents dependent on the years they were at the orphanage and the adults they had had the fortune, or misfortune, to come in contact with. Now well into their 80s and older, the former orphans spoke: there were "Mister Yaro's [Yarrow] big round chocolates;'[1130] there were a few words of English remembered from their American benefactors—"open the door," "close the door," "goodbye."[1131] There were favorites among the American relief workers: "Miss Kimball," "Mister Nelson," "Mister Brown"—

and the song about "Mister Brown" that Makruhi Sahakyan[1132] remembered circulating in the orphanage:

> They sent a telegram to America
> Mister Brown came,
> He gathered all the orphans
> No one was left homeless or unprotected

Acts of kindness, cherished secretly for decades, emerged from a maze of experiences. Azniv Aslanian remembered that the day she was "leaving them for good, the Americans, Miss Mary, Miss MacKaye, Miss Hill...kissed me."[1133] She had learned embroidery and sewing at the Kazachi, and when she left in 1929 she could also speak English and type. A special episode of kindness Lyudvik Yeghyazaryan remembered concerned an orphan named Yango who played the Armenian stringed instrument *tar*.[1134] Yango had damaged his arm muscles when dynamite had accidentally exploded near him. To restore Yango's impaired arm, an American relief worker had volunteered to be a transplant donor. The American surgeon had successfully performed the operation and Yango was able play the *tar* again. But Yango's right arm, unlike his left, was freckled:

> ...the freckles were constant reminders of the American man who did not spare his own body part for a stranger. He was truly one in a million.

But above all, there was "Miss Maka," (Janet MacKaye) Yeghiazaryan said, "just saying her name brings me to tears. She was the kindest person I have ever met."

Acknowledgments of association with the Americans had been especially perilous under Stalin. Lyudvig Yeghiazaryan had feared alienation and was imprisoned for having been in an American orphanage. He had left the Polygon in 1927 and worked in the Leninakan textile factory until 1933 when he was recruited into the Armenian Division of the Soviet Army. His Division was based at the Polygon, not far from the building where he had grown up. He left the Polygon when he was demobilized in 1935, only to return in 1941 as part of the Leninakan counter-intelligence unit when WWII had erupted. A year later, he was expelled from the Communist Party and sent to prison for having made what was perceived as a deleterious remark during Stalin's long speech on the radio, on the occasion of the 25th anniversary of the October Revolution. But, he said during an interview in April 2010, at the age of 101:

> I am sure that the main reason for my imprisonment was having been raised in an American orphanage.
>
> I am also glad that now I can express my deep gratitude to the American people, as before I was not allowed. I was even repressed for having been in an American orphanage...[1135]

Despite anathemas and arrests, memories of some Americans proved impossible to erase. The memory of "Miss Maka," whom many in Leninakan referred to as "the Mother of Armenia,"[1136] was passed down to the next generation and outlasted the Soviet Union itself. In 2004, 75 years after Janet

Aznviv Hakobyan. (Tikin Margarita Private Collection, Gyumri)

Photograph of Janet MacKaye and the table clock in the home of Tikin Margarita in Gyumri in 2004. (Alexandropol Digital Archive I.D. 0460)

MacKaye left Leninakan, now renamed Gyumri, her photograph stood on a table in the home of Gyumri resident Tikin [Mrs.] Margarita, the daughter of Azniv Hakobyan, a former student of Janet MacKaye's. Displayed next to the photograph in 2004, was a table clock Tikin Margarita's mother had received as a gift from Janet MacKaye in 1927. The photo next to it was one of a large stack of photographs Azniv had kept hidden in the house. Miss Maka had been away from Leninakan when Azniv was given in marriage.[1137] Upon her return, she had found her student living in a cellar and pregnant with child. She had returned with clothing, a baby's crib, food, and, a table clock as a wedding gift. Tikin Margarita explained that during the Stalinist era, her mother would secretly retrieve the photographs in the dark of night to look through them, remembering happy times. She would then return them to their secret hiding place.[1138]

Devotion to Janet MacKaye was shared by many of the orphans in her charge. When she had returned from her vacation in 1926, the children had stood by the road waiting to welcome her back, wrote Robert Buckalew:

> …She knew hundreds of these children by name and many from babyhood. They wouldn't go to school nor move from the road until the old Dodge had gone by bringing them [Janet MacKaye, Caroline Silliman and Helen Mays] from the station and what an ovation. Just picture it, 5000 children cheering for joy because their friend, their mother, had come back to them.[1139]

Armenuhi Sukyasyan had been another one of Janet MacKaye's students. She was 12 years old when she was admitted to the Severski, and remembered her first Christmas with Miss Maka:

> The first year, Miss Maka told us to weave a sock. I was inexperienced at the beginning, and made a small sock. Then I saw that they stuffed the New Year's presents in the socks, and I only got a few presents. The next year, I wove a sock so long—about my height—that Miss Maka would take it and wrap it around her neck and would laugh…they filled it to the hilt with fruits, candy…We lived well…

Armenuhi remembered how Miss Maka had intervened when her younger sister Amalya was to be sent, together with the "…healthy and beautiful boys and girls…to America":

> They used to fill entire trains and take them away. They wanted to take my younger sister away too, but I cried loud, hard, and long. I said "I won't let you; either you take me too, or leave both of us here. I don't have any other relatives but her. Miss Maka loved me very much; she saw how hard I was crying, [and] she did not let them take my sister away, saying, 'if you're not taking her, let her sister stay, too.'"[1140]

Barclay Acheson had repeatedly encouraged the American relief workers to spend more time with the orphans than in their offices, but only a handful had heeded his pleas for direct contact with the orphans. Inevitably, the orphans' more frequent contacts were with the Armenian teachers and managers—and there was plenty of them to remember. For Makruhi Sahakyan, they were "Tikin Taguhi, Tikin Nvard, Oriord Makruhi, Oriord Shushanik, Gohar, all of them from Van";[1141] for Vardges Aleksanyan it was "Varzhapet [teacher] Sahak,"[1142] father of the well-known future writer Soghomon Tarontsi; for Arusyak Hovhannisyan (Israyelyan) it was Shushanik Ter-Grigoryan, Dr. Satyan, Tigranuhi Nersisyan, Ashkhen Dustrikyan, and Vardanush Andreasian (Cheraz) and Vahan Cheraz,[1143] who were not only their teachers but their mothers and fathers as well, and would remain "unforgettable throughout our lives…" Mihran Hovhannisyan's two favorite teachers were Mkrtich Aylamazyan, who married another one of his beloved teachers, Oriord Satenik; both treated the children like their own."[1144] As he was being transferred to Stepanavan Mihran Hovhannisyan had cried when saying good-bye to his beloved teachers and kissed their hands. He would meet Mkrtich Aylamazyan again 12 years later in Yerevan, where the latter worked as a physician. That would be their last meeting.[1145]

Skills taught at the orphanage, such as needlework and typing, enabled orphans to support their families in later life. Needlework had helped Rehan M. Manukyan to secure her family's livelihood:

> I, as many, many others, am grateful to the Americans because we owe our lives to them. Beyond that, I learned embroidery at the American orphanage, with which I was later able to provide a living for my family.[1146]

Azniv Aslanian[1147] had married and had three children. She had learned English and typing at Polygon's Pedagogical Technicum and found a position at the Matenadaran as a bibliographer.

Zvart Muradyan, one of the blind children, remembered her braille teacher and composer, Nikoghayos Tigranyan, at her 100th birthday. Tigranyan, she said,

> …formed a large orchestra. We played everything. I was his student and learned to play Beethoven, Mozart, and Tchaikovsky under him.[1148]

Zvart Muradyan. (*Aravot*, October 9, 2010)

Zvart Muradyan with her husband and children. (Frame from Video made on the occasion of Zvart Muradyan's 100th birthday. https://www.youtube.com/watch?v=vi2RtHnvu-U.)

She was happy she grew up in the orphanage, she said, because otherwise she would not have received an education:

> There were many like me in the orphanage. The older

> children helped the younger ones. I didn't feel that I was blind...we didn't feel we were orphans.
>
> ...the older girls, the seeing, used to knit. At that time there were neither needles nor thread. So in spring and summer we used to gather long blades of grass and twigs, and use them in place of thread and needle.[1149]

When she left the orphanage, she married another blind orphan, and had four children. She had a busy life: besides working at various factories, to secure a living for her family, she wrote books in braille, and with her husband became one of the founders of the first Association for the Blind in Armenia, and played an active role in its growth. Her message on her 100th birthday was:

> If all four of my children were alive now [two of the boys had died], I would be the happiest person in the world...Even now, I will leave this world a happy person. I am content with the life I've lived...One should be an optimist...hope is life...

Shoghik Mkrtchyan. (Petrosyan 1991: cover page)

Memories of friendships forged at the City of Orphans were prevalent, and vivid. Lyudvig Yeghiazaryan spoke of his best friends Onnik (Hovhannes Shiraz) and Soghomon Tarontsi.[1150] Shoghik H. Mkrtchyan, known at the City of Orphans as "*Shoghshoghun Shoghik*" [Radiant Shoghik] remembered "Shiraz, Khachik Dashtents and others," with whom she "grew up...half-starving."[1151] She married *kamancha* player Gurgen Mirzoyan, the director of the ensemble of folk musical instruments of the Armenian Philharmonic. In her lifetime, Shoghik sang for poets Yeghishe Charents and Avetik Isahakyan, Communist Party leader Aghasi Khanchyan, the linguist/philologist Hrachya Acharyan, all of who helped her in various ways. Her songs had especially touched Hrachya Acharyan, who visited Shoghik at the radio station where she sang to meet her in person.[1152] He saw her dressed in a tattered dress and worn out men's shoes. From that day, he adopted Shoghik as his godchild and from time to time would help her with clothes and money.

Shoghik's first solo concert, in Yerevan, was with composer and conductor Daniel Ghazaryan, who played the musical accompaniment. Just as her first song "*Lanjer-Marjan*," was followed with enthusiastic applause, Shoghik withdrew behind the curtain and refused to come out again. "I won't go back on stage," she said, "I'm afraid." "Who are you afraid of?" asked the composer, surprised, "the audience applauds you, and you are afraid!?" Eventually, she returned to the stage to finish the concert, only to meet a large crowd of admirers gathered outside the hall to thank her. All her life she resisted pressure to become an opera singer, preferring to sing folk songs, as she had for the orphans at Kazachi and Polygon when barely a teenager.[1153] In 1929, she won first prize at the first national Art Olympics, and a few years later would sing at the Kremlin for Stalin and Anastas Mikoyan.[1154]

Nshan Abrahamyan had been part of the brass band in Alexandropol. He was transferred to Stepanavan in 1924, where he met Sirush, writer Derenik Demirchyan's niece:

…we liked each other. After the Technicum, in 1929, they appointed us to the animal husbandry farms created by the Americans. Sirush left agriculture and worked in the local kindergarten. I was drafted into the army and went to Kirovakan. In 1931 I was accepted in the Geology department at the university…Sirush and I got married. For the first time a jazz band was formed in the city…I became their trumpeter. In 1936, when Moscow Cinema opened, we used to play there.[1155]

Romantic relationships among the orphans were not rare. Adel and Gurgen had met at the City of Orphans when they were both 15 years old; she became a nurse and he a driver. After they left the orphanage they married and had 12 children and named them after lost family members. At her death, Adel still had the pair of small high-heeled shoes she had with her when she had entered the orphanage.[1156] Harutyun Azoyan and Herignaz Karapetyan, both from Kars, were married in 1922, at the age of 19. At about that time, they realized that their teacher at the orphanage, Marine Azizyan, was alone with no one in the world, and invited her to come and live with them. Teacher and students lived together for 25 years, and when the teacher died, she was buried in the Azoyan family grave. The couple had nine children, of whom four survived and were cared for by the teacher.[1157] Harutyun Azoyan became a goalie in one of the earliest football teams in Alexandropol and his photograph is preserved at the museum of the Football Federation of Armenia.

Avetis Poghosyan and Hayastan Grigoryan had met at the Polygon and married. A July 1926 certificate indicates that Avetis had completed his studies and had gained skills in animal husbandry, tinsmithing, and carpentry in

Avetis Poghosyan's Certificate of Employment and Certificate of Graduation from Stepanavan. (Avetis Poghosyan Collection, AGMI)

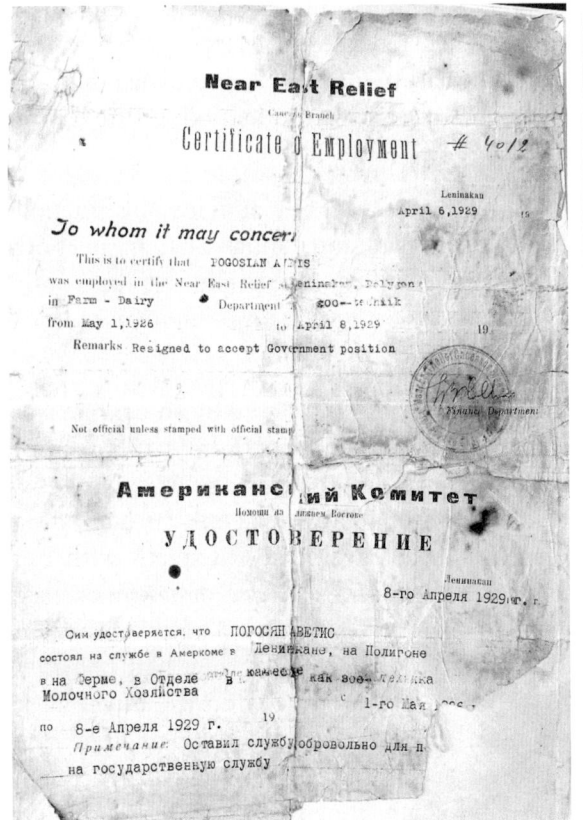

Hayastan and Avetis Poghosyan in later life. (Avetis Poghosyan Collection, AGMI)

Ekaterina Mkrtchyan and Gohar Shagaryan. (Photos courtesy of their grandson Mr. Armen Ghazaryan)

Hayastan, seated, left. (Avetis Poghosyan Collection, AGMI)

Stepanavan. Another document states that he had been employed by NER in the Farm-Dairy Department in Leninakan from May 1926 to April 1929, at which time he had resigned to accept a government position. A third document, dated August 1929, indicates that the couple had started a family, and Hayastan was to be praised for having taken proper care of her child.

There were also instances when former orphans would meet again, now as in-laws, as with Ekaterina Mkrtchyan and Gohar Shagaryan, both born in Kars. Ekaterina lived into her 90s; Gohar died at the young age of 34. Their common legacy is their grandson Armen Ghazaryan of Yerevan.[1158]

One of the most precious moments remembered by an orphan was reunion, sometimes unexpectedly, with a parent, family member or close friend. In her account of her grandmother Lucine Aghayan's life, Teresa Aghayan described such a reunion in some detail.[1159] According to that account, Lucine Aghayan had entered the Kazachi with her two youngest sons, Vardan and Gurgen, and the two daughters of her sister-in-law, who were contemporaries of her sons. The two girls had found their way to the U.S., but before they left they had halved a towel from the orphanage into two. Printed in red on the towel were the words: "MEDICAL-U.S.A.-DEPARTMENT." They kept one half of the towel and gave the other half to their cousin Gurgen. Each half was to be kept so that if, and when, they met again in the future, the two halves would help them recognize each other. Almost 40 years later, the husband of one of the girls visited Armenia and met Gurgen, by then a well-known musician at the Spendiaryan Opera and Ballet Theater. The towel halves were presented and made whole again.

The two halves of the towel sewn in the center. (Lucine Aghayan Collection, AGMI)

Reunion with mothers was especially precious and unforgettable. Shahen Sargsyan, later known as Armenia's beloved Gusan (minstrel) Shahen, had been discovered by his mother as he sang in the Church of Seven Wounds of the Holy Mother of God, now the Cathedral of St. Astvacacin, in Alexandropol. He had been sure that he had witnessed his mother's murder and had mourned her for days. He and other homeless orphans had been gathered from the streets of Alexandropol and brought to the Polygon, where his injured foot was operated on:

> I remember how the American physician completely healed my foot…Gangrene had set in, but the American physician immediately operated on my foot and healed it in such a way that a few months later I did not limp anymore. I was saved.[1160]

His talent as a singer was discovered early on at the Polygon and he was placed in the children's chorus that sang hymns during the celebration of the Armenian liturgy on Sundays and High Holidays. Then, on a warm, sunny spring Sunday, as the children sang to a packed congregation that spilled outside the church, they were interrupted by a woman's scream and the commotion that followed at the door. The children had immediately been escorted out and taken back to the Polygon, where he heard that the commotion had been caused by a woman who had screamed and then collapsed on the steps of the church. The woman, he soon found out, was his own mother. She had been told her son had been killed and buried in a mass grave and had come to the church where Shahen sang to pray for his soul. Instead, she had recognized her son's shrill voice that used to rise over the chorus reverberating on the walls of the church, and had fallen unconscious. Without losing time and with the help of a sympathetic orphanage guard, his mother had taken Shahen out of the orphanage under the cover of night.[1161]

Gusan Shahen at the age of 28. (Shahen 2011)

Shahen had met his friend "Ono" (Hovhannes Shiraz) at the Polygon. Like Shiraz, he would often slip out of the Polygon during the day, and together they would go to the market in Alexandropol,

Shiraz with a friend from the orphanage during a visit to Leninakan. (House Museum of Hovhannes Shiraz, Gyumri)

The Alexander Martuni (Myasnikyan) Polygon football team in 1927. Left to right, Aghen Hovhannisyan, Tonakan Galstyan, Tsolak Haykazyan, Onik Chakhoyan, Hakob Minasyan, Tadevos Karapetyan, Gevorg Abrahamyan, Rafael Manukyan, Baghtasar Movsisyan. (Aghababyan and Sahakyan 2004: 26)

then return to the Polygon at night. Shiraz was often seen at the market place, stealing food and selling water to passers by. On one occasion, one of his customers had taken the water from him, then pulled the boy's cap over his eyes, and run off without paying him. Shiraz would meet that customer during a visit to Leninakan decades later when he was already acknowledged as one of the most important poets of his time. From the large crowd who had come to greet the poet, an old man pushed his way through and said to Shiraz, "I owe you money." "You owe me nothing," Shiraz answered, surprised. "Ah, but I do," said the old man, "When you were a boy I stole water from you and did not pay," and reaching into his pocket he put ten kopeks in Shiraz's hand. Shiraz, in turn, gave the elderly man ten rubles, even though he lived a meager existence.[1162]

Hovhannes Shiraz's reunion with his mother had also taken place in the marketplace, as he had tried to steal a loaf of bread from an elderly woman. The woman had turned around, shocked, only to see her own son trying to snatch the loaf of bread from her. In tears, she had embraced him and kissed his dirty face.

Shiraz, who remained an anti-establishment poet during his lifetime, would often recall his childhood as an orphan and a homeless young boy in his poems. His works were translated into 50 languages, and the large profit of one of his collection of poems, *"Peace Be To All,"* he donated to the orphans of USSR veterans of the Vietnam War.

Of special renown at the Polygon was its football team. The team played against the *Arsenal* of Tiflis and *Progress* of Baku, and in seven years, it had only allowed two goals to penetrate its defenses.[1163] By 1927, the Polygon team was renamed Alexander Martuni, in honor of Alexander Myasnikyan who had penned many essays under the pseudonym Alexander Martuni.

At least one member of the Alexander Martuni football team, Tatevos Karapetyan,[1164] continued his education at Yerevan State University to become a prominent member of the faculty and administration of the Department of Geography and Geology.[1165] Karapetyan's colleague Kirakos Ohanyan in the department of Geography and Geology had also grown up in the City of Orphans.

Polygon football team leading member and founder Tsolak Haykazyan had been one of the 6,000 orphans transferred from Kars to Alexandropol, and one of Ray Ogden's scouts at the Polygon. After graduation in 1924, he had stayed at the Polygon as an employee, working as a secretary and teacher of Armenian language and geography. He was drafted

THE CITY OF ORPHANS

into the Soviet Army in 1928 and began his military service in the First Yerevan Regiment, only to be ejected from military service one year later, for reasons unknown to him. Still, he was mobilized in the Soviet Army in 1941, and taken prisoner of war by the Germans. When back in the SSRA after the war, he was arrested in May 1949 as an ARF party member, but released in October of the same year due to the absence of evidence.[1166]

A leading organizer of the secret Pyoner groups at the Polygon was Heciyê Cindî, an orphan from Kars of Yezidi ancestry. Among his papers, now at the National Archives of Armenia, are lists and photographs of some of the members of the Polygon Pyoner groups, as well as circulars signed by him.[1167]

Cindî graduated from Polygon's Pedagogical Technicum in 1929. Eight years later, in 1937, he was arrested on charges of spying and nationalism and sent to prison, but released one year later following a campaign for his release mounted by Armenian intellectuals. Cindî would become a linguist and after 1959, a researcher in the Oriental Department of the Armenian Academy of Sciences where he directed the Department of Kurdish studies and lectured on Kurdish Literature and Language. For one year he served as the head of the cultural section of the Kurdish newspaper *Riya Teze*, and subsequently as anchor in the Kurdish section of Radio Yerevan.

Like Heciyê Cindî and scores of other orphans, Araksi Pluzyan was sent to villages to teach in village schools after graduating from the Polygon. Away from a familiar and sheltered environment, she felt "helpless, almost blind about life," she wrote in her memoirs, and vulnerable, because she was an

Kirakos Ohanyan. ("History of the Faculty," Yerevan State University Website, http://ah.do.am/mer_masin/nshanavor_demq/ohanyan_kirakos_ohani.htm)

Tatevos Karapetyan. ("History of the Faculty," Yerevan State University Website, ahttp://ah.do.am/mer_masin/nshanavor_demq/karapetyan_tadevos_harutyuni.htm)

Pyoner group at Polygon, Heciyê Cindî as director, fourth from left, top row. (NAA 883/1/509 Heciyê Cindî photo collection)

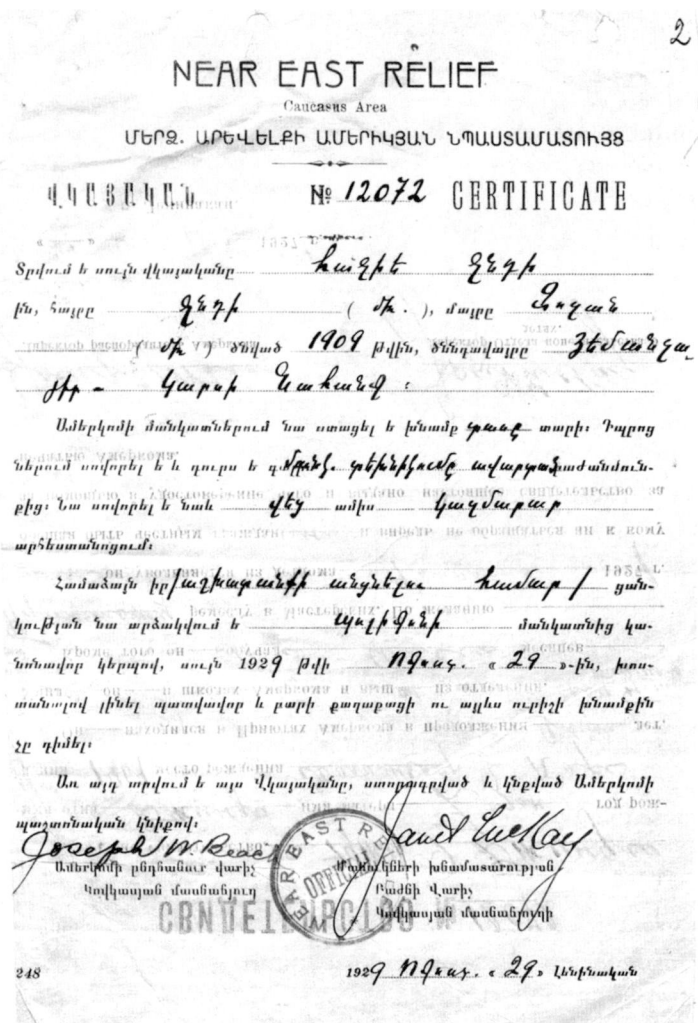

Heciyê Cindî's Certificate of Graduation, August 9, 1929. (NAA 883/1/289/f. 2)

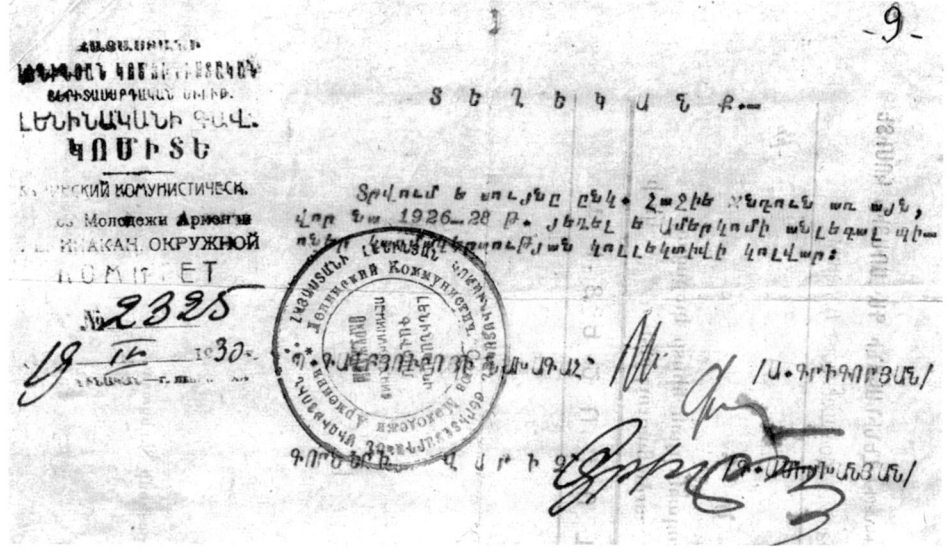

Bulletin affirming that Heciyê Cindî had been the director of the illegal Pyoner organization at the Polygon from 1926–1928. (NAA 883/1/289/f. 9)

orphan. When teaching in a village in Vanadzor, a "Comrade Kishmishyan" of the Commissariat of Enlightenment had come to her school and observed her classes. She was trembling like a leaf, she wrote, fearful that if they did not approve of her teaching, she would be out of a job. But to her surprise, two days later the school had received orders to send Pluzyan to Yerevan to attend university. She entered the university during the academic year 1930–31 with maximum privileges, and was registered in the pedagogical department, where she met and worked with its first dean, Gurgen Edilyan. Unlike other orphans, she never once mentions friends she had made at the orphanage or later on in life in her memoirs. She is admired for her punctuality and ability for hard work, but the pages of her autobiography are filled with that which she remembers most—a deep sense of loss and vulnerability. She never married or had a partner in her life. Many men had wanted to take advantage of her loneliness and wanted to have "secret relationships" with her, she wrote, and many had tried to "steal her honor" by force, but they had come face to face with an impregnable moral fortress which they had been

Graduating Class in 1929 in Joseph Beach's garden. Heciyê Cindî stands in top row, third from the left. (NAA 883/1/509 Heciyê Cindî photo collection)

Polygon graduates in Soghutly, 1928 or 1929. Ghazar Avetisyan is third from the left, bottom row, seated; Heciyê Cindî is fifth from the right, top row; Khachik Dashtents is fourth from the right, third row from the top. (Anahit Dashtents Turabyan Private Collection.)

unable to conquer. Alive in her memory is Voskan, a little boy with whom she grew up in Van, with whom she picked flowers and fruits from the orchards, built nests for the birds, and swam in the brook by her house. Voskan is part of a sweet moment of childhood encased in her memories. "My life passes like a dream," she wrote, "I am alive one day, and in the earth the next…" and ended,

> Although my mind thinks about many things, my hands are lonely…How many flowers should have grown on this soil but did not…[1168]

APOCRYPHA 361

Arpik Vardapetyan. (Hayk Khachatryan 1975: 720)

Ruben Gharibyan. (Hayk Khachatryan 1975: 436)

Aghavni. (Hayk Khachatryan 1975: 23)

Vahan Grigoryan. (Hayk Khachatryan 1975: 159)

The list of former orphans who became writers, editors, poets and translators after they left the City of Orphans is significant. Almost all were members of the Writers' Union founded by the government in 1934, where the earlier groups as "Hoktember" [October] and "Noyember" [November] had been absorbed. Among the members who had been at the City of Orphans were: Arpik Vardapetyan, the niece of Vahan Teryan, who had joined the newspaper *Ranchpar* as editor and in 1941 graduated from the Department of Western European Literature and Languages of Yerevan State University, and served on the editorial board of "Haypedhrat," the state publishing company.[1169]

Ruben Gharibyan had been transferred from Yerevan to Leninakan, then to Stepanavan and back to Leninakan. When he left the City of Orphans in 1928, he moved to Yerevan and worked at tobacco and canning factories and eventually at the *Pyoner* monthly magazine.[1170]

Aghavni (Aghavni Grigoryan), poet, essayist and translator, a graduate of the Polygon Pedagogical Technicum, had later served on the editorial boards of the *Pyoneri Kanch* [Call of the Pioneer] and *Sovetakan Hayastan* [Soviet Armenia], among other newspapers. She was also an editor of radio broadcasts and a prolific writer and translator. Her first poem had appeared in 1928, in Leninakan's *Banvor* paper.[1171]

Vahan Grigoryan had been educated at Leninakan and Jalaloghli until 1924. In 1933, he graduated from the Moscow Institute of Cinematography, and went on to serve in the Red Army. In 1934–35, he directed the Association of Soviet Writers of Armenia, organized to help the Army and Navy of the Red Army. From 1938 to 1948 he was deputy editor of the monthly *Sovetakan grakanutyun yev arvest* and later an editor of *Hayastan*.[1172]

After he left Kazachi Post in 1923 and for the next two years, Mkrtich Armen was an instructor to Young Communist groups in Leninakan, and subsequently a teacher in various village schools and cultural and proletarian institutions and associations.[1173] He graduated from the State Cinematography Institute in Moscow in 1932, and three years later, in 1935, published his most popular novel, *Heghnar Aghbyur*. Two years later Armen was arrested and sentenced to exile as an enemy of the people. His sentence was exculpated eight years later.

Sarmen (Armenak Sargsyan) had graduated from the Polygon in 1924, but had stayed on two additional years as a teacher before leaving for Yerevan. He graduated from the linguistics department of Yerevan State University in 1932 and would become a renowned poet. Among his works are the lyrics of the anthem of Soviet Armenia, which remained in use from 1944 to 1991.[1174]

Khachik Dashtents (Khachik Tonoyan), like many of his contemporary writers in the 1930s, would be targeted as a nationalist and anti-Soviet element who had joined, as one of his "critics" declared in 1937, "the army of enemies of the proletariat and of our people," and who was the spiritual son of "nationalistic dregs," which referred, among others, to Yeghishe Charents, Vahram Alazan, and Gurgen Mahari.[1175] The defamatory criticism had been occasioned by the publication of Dashtents's collection of poems in Moscow in 1936, where Dashtents had been studying English at the Institute of Foreign Languages. The volume was titled *Bots* (Flame). Dashtents continued his studies in Moscow until 1940 and was able to elude the destructive environment of the Writers' Union in Yerevan and the rampant persecutions, exiles and executions that befell the "nationalistic dregs" in 1937. When he returned to Yerevan in 1940, he occupied himself primarily with translations of English poets and writers into Armenian, most notably the works of William Shakespeare, Henry Wadsworth Longfellow, George Gordon Byron, Edgar Allan Poe, and Oscar Wilde. In 1933, Dashtents had been especially encouraged by Charents to translate Wilde's works into Armenian. Shakespeare and Byron were great, Charents had said to him, but suggested that the young man translate Oscar Wilde into Armenian. At that time, young Dashtents was familiar with Wilde's *The Picture of Dorian Gray*, and offered to translate it into Armenian. Charents hesitated. "Perhaps *De Profundis*?" Wilde's meditations in prison, asked Dashtents. Not that either. The most appropriate, in Charents's opinion, was Wilde's *The Ballad of Reading Gaol*,[1176] about the crushing unremittingness of prison life which destroyed the souls and bodies of its inmates and any chance of rebirth. Dashtents translated the poem with his friend Sargis Alemyan, also once an orphant at the City of Orphans. A few years later in Moscow, Dashtents wrote his memoirs with extensive references to his life at the Polygon and entitled it *De Profundis*, or, From the Depths.

Sarmen. (Film clip Habeckian 2010, *Im hin unkernere* [My Old Companions]. (https://www.youtube.com/watch?v=ZvXcMTsjJD0)

Top row, left to right: Khachik Dashtents, Martiros Kyureghyan, (XX). Seated, left to right, (XX), Armenak Asatryan, (XX), Grigor Donoyan (older brother of Khachik Dashtents), as university students in Yerevan, in October 1930. (Photo courtesy of Mrs. Rima Arakelyan and Mr. Armen Ghazaryan)

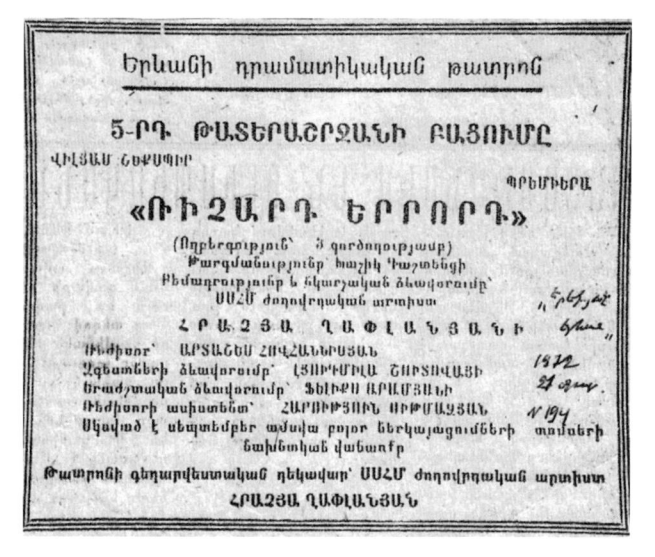

Announcement for Shakespeare's Richard III theatrical performance at the Dramatic Theater of Yerevan as it appeared in *Yerekoyan Yerevan*, August 21, 1972. The play was translated by Khachik Dashtents. (Anahit Dashtents Turabian Private Collection)

Khachik Dashtents and Hovhannes Shiraz, Yerevan, June 1960, detail. (Anahit Dashtents Turabian Private Collection)

Gurgen Mahari, 1930s. (Antonina Mahari Private Collection)

Soghomon Tarontsi, 1945. (https://charkhchyan.wordpress.com, November 12, 2013)

Soghomon Tarontsi (Soghomon Movsisyan) had graduated from the Polygon in 1926 and from the Historiography Department of Yerevan State University in 1930 to become a productive writer and translator.[1177] He had received his early education from his father, Sahak, a cherished teacher at the City of Orphans. Like Dashtents, for many years he occupied himself with translations, in addition to writing his books and poems.

Soghomon Tarontsi and many of the illustrious poets of Armenia were embroiled in the destructive atmosphere that ruled within the Writers' Union in the 1930s, orchestrated it is believed, primarily by Nayiri Zaryan and Hrachya Kochar. Once close friends with Gurgen Mahari, Zaryan is also believed to be responsible for Mahari's exile. After spending some time at the Kazachi,[1178] as one of Cheraz's scouts, Mahari had joined Zaryan in Yerevan, where they were both *Dastiaraks* (home room teachers or group leaders), at NER's orphanage #5 in Yerevan. Mahari published his first book in verse titled *Titanik* in 1924. His autobiographical trilogy on *Mankutyun* [Childhood] and *Patanekutyun* [Adolescence] were his first works in prose published in 1930. The third volume of the trilogy, *Yeritasardutyan semin* [On the Threshold of Youth], appeared in 1956, after he had returned from his second exile. He had been arrested on charges of plotting an assassination against Laurenti

364 THE CITY OF ORPHANS

Beria, Stalin's henchman, and sentenced to ten years of exile in Siberia in 1936. Mahari had returned in 1947, but had been sent back in 1948, finally returning only after Stalin's death in 1953. Together, the three parts of the trilogy recount the story of his ancestral home, his family, orphanhood, and survival. Although he makes no specific mention of the City of Orphans, his writing resonates with the experiences of thousands of his generation.[1179]

Also exiled in 1937 was Vahram Alazan (Vahram Gabuzyan), who had been at the Polygon in the early 1920s.[1180] He had returned from his exile in 1954 but for the remainder of his life was bed-ridden due to illnesses incurred while in exile.[1181] Alazan had been the first to discover and encourage Shiraz's talent.[1182] Like his contemporaries, Alazan had believed in the promise of the revolution and had supported it, but also like many of his contemporaries, he became the victim of persecutions during the Stalinist period.

Nairi Zaryan emerged as one of the most controversial figures in Armenia during the Stalinist period and is considered to be responsible for the persecution and arrest of several of the progressive and talented writers in the 1930s.[1183] A faithful devotee of Stalin, he reached prominence in the Writer's Union and within party ranks, eventually controlling the Writers' Union.

Andranik Markosyan's discharge papers to study in Yerevan. (NAA 39/1/8/f. 14)

Sargis Aleksanyan's discharge paper to study in Yerevan. (NAA 39/1/8/f. 14)

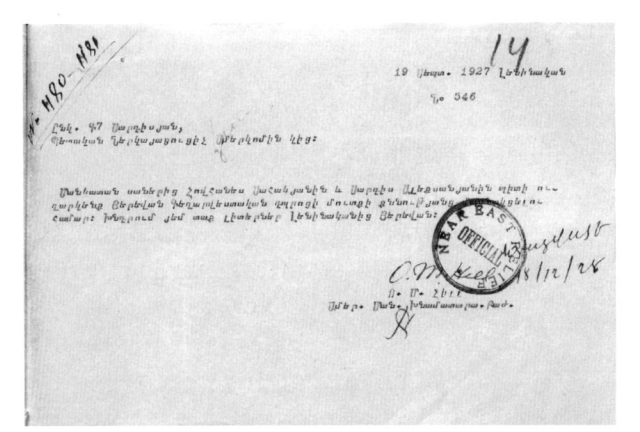

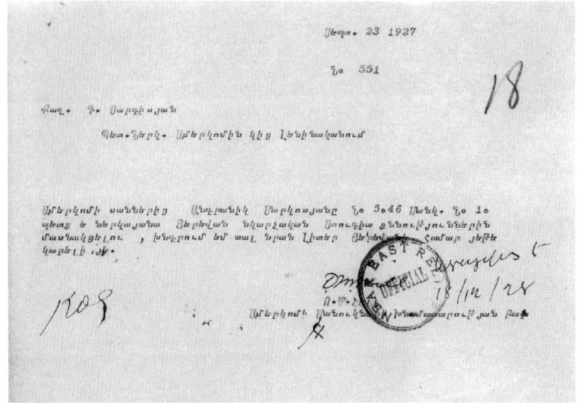

First row, left to right: Paghtasar Mesropyan, Koryun Simonyan, Nerses Israyelyan(?), Andranik Markosyan, Hmayak Avetisyan, (XXX), (XXX.); Second row, left to right: (XXX), Shavarsh Vagharshakyan, teachers Mamikon Panosyan, Stepan Altunyan, Armenak Kyulnazaryan, Petros Rashoyan, (XXX); Top row, standing, left to right: Sargis Aleksanyan, Levon Tonakanyan, (XXX), Vanik Karapetyan, (XXX), (XXX). Alexandropol, 1921. (Arakelyan 2007: 18)

Left to right: Levon Tonakanyan, Sargis Aleksanyan and Vanik Karapetyan. (Grigoryan 1989: 128)

Zaryan's novel *Paron Petros u ir nakhararnere* [Mr. Petros and his Ministers] first published in 1958, is an unequivocally critical depiction of an orphanage in Yerevan, and is considered to be autobiographical. The protagonist is a young orphan by the name of Aram Alanagyan who undergoes a profound ideological change and becomes a Communist. He enlists in the *Sbartak* young Communist organization, and penetrates the American orphanages.

From Polygon's art studio for the especially talented would emerge several of the best-known artists, nurtured in their formative years by Stepan Altunyan. They would continue their education in art after Altunyan's studio at the Geghard Technicum in Yerevan, at that time the only place where advanced art studies were offered, and subsequently in Leningrad or Moscow.

Among the young orphans were Koryun Simonyan, Nerses Israyelyan, Andranik Markosyan, Hmayak Avetisyan, Sargis Aleksanyan, Levon Tonakanyan, and Vanik Karapetyan.[1184]

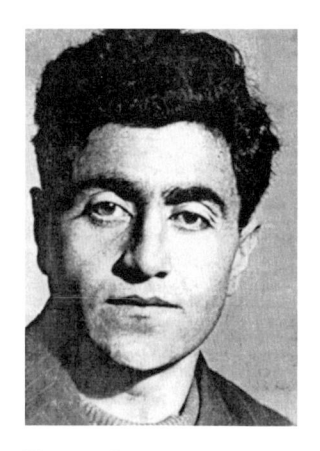

Koryun Simonyan. (Arakelyan 2007: 28)

Sargis Aleksanyan. (Arakelyan 2007: 100)

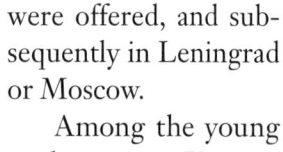

Andranik Markosyan. (Arakelyan 2007: 110)

Vanik Karapetyan. (Arakelyan 2007: 66)

Levon Tonakanyan. (Arakelyan 2007: 86)

Nerses Israyelyan. (Grigoryan 1989: 132)

Jonik Zakaryan. (Arakelyan 2007: 150)

But the artistic careers of several of the group of orphans from the Polygon were cut short when WWII erupted, where they fought valiantly in defense of the Soviet Union, not unlike the older orphan boys among the boy scouts who had been enlisted in defense of the fatherland during the Armenian-Turkish War in 1920.[1185] During World War II, former orphans, now of age to be drafted into the army, provided a ready source of soldiers for the Red Army. Among the large number of those who fought—and paid the supreme sacrifice—for the defense of the Soviet Union were: Koryun Simonyan, Sargis Aleksanyan, Andranik Markosyan, Vanik Karapetyan, Levon Tonakanyan, Nerses Israyelyan, all of them members of Stepan Altunyan's studio, and another, younger former orphan of the City of Orphans, Jonik Zakaryan. Levon Tonakanyan (born in Artahan, 1911) died on the battlefield at Krivoy Rog in 1941; Sargis Aleksanyan (born in Erzurum, 1910) fell in May 1942; Koryun Simonyan (born in Kars, 1910) was mortally wounded and died in 1943; Jonik Zakaryan (born in Alexandropol, 1916) was lost in action during the battle of the Kertch peninsula in

Hmayak Avetisyan. (Grigoryan 1989: 101)

Hmayak Avetisyan. Self-Portrait with the corpse of his mother. (Film clip, Movsesyan January 2013, https://www.youtube.com/watch?v=7sJ3z46mpI4)

Nrank Chveradartsan [They Did Not Return], 1975 by Hmayak Avetisyan. (Grigoryan 1989: between pages 96 and 97)

Portrait of his future wife Araksya, by Hmayak Avetisyan. (Film clip, Movsesyan: January 2013, https://www.youtube.com/watch?v=7sJ3z46mpI4)

APOCRYPHA 367

1942; Andranik Markosyan (born in Mush, 1913) was wounded but returned to the battlefield and killed in December 1944, during the last stage of the battle for Smolensk; Nerses Israyelyan (born in Van, 1907) was wounded in both legs in 1943, but returned to the battlefield in March 1944 to fight his final battle in Vyazma encircled by the Wehrmacht's 3rd and 4th Panzer divisions; Vanik Karapetyan (born in Moks, 1910), the only survivor of his family, died in the first year of fighting in the Finnish-Russian War. In his backpack were found colored pencils, sketches, his self-portrait, and the photograph of a young woman.

Karapetyan, Markosyan, and Aleksanyan were 31 years old; Simonyan was 33, Israyelyan 37, and Zakaryan 26. Many of their canvases are preserved at the National Gallery of Armenia in Yerevan and in private collections.

Hayk Khachatryan. (Grigoryan 1989: 249)

Hmayak Avetisyan had survived. While in Leningrad, he had met and married Araksya, an orphan from the Polygon. He was one of the few of the original group who returned from the battleground and would become a prominent artist. Among his canvases is a large posthumous oil painting of his orphanage friends who had fallen on the battleground. Measuring five feet by four and one half feet, the painting is titled *Nrank Chveradartsan* [They Did Not Return].

Hayk Khachatryan (born in Mush, 1908) had chosen acting as a career, and had appeared in a variety of roles at the Mravyan Theater in Leninakan after he had left the City of Orphans. During WWII, he fought in the battlefields of Ukraine, Belarus, and Poland. His last letter, dated January 20, 1945, was addressed to his wife, when his unit was 30 kilometers from Berlin:

> …With Sasha and Andrei we drank to our families on New Year's Eve…Vardush jan, tonight we attack to occupy Berlin. There are 30 kilometers left. If by the luck of my children I remain alive, we shall see each other. If not…
> Well, they're calling us. With the 30 rubles I am sending you, buy the children copybooks, so that they may learn [be educated] well.
> I embrace you all with boundless yearning.
> Good night.[1186]

While saying goodbye to his son at the train station in Leninakan, he had made a promise that he would be back before the boy began second grade at school. But Hayk Khachatryan was not able to keep his promise to his son.

Helping in the war effort was Azniv Parnasyan who had graduated from the Edith Winchester School of Nursing in 1928. She worked as a nurse at the Polygon until 1941, at which time she was drafted into the Red Army's Crimean Front as a nurse. She was wounded a year later and with other casualties had been taken prisoner by the Germans, but had been able to escape to Armenia in 1947. She had tried to explain to the authorities in Armenia that she had been kept in the Crimea against her will and had been a prisoner of war. But Stalin's dictum, made early during WWII that "deserters" and prisoners of war would be punished severely, was maintained and she was arrested in 1949.[1187]

Polygon orphans, 1921–1922. Ghazar Avetisyan is first from the left, top row, standing. (Ghazar Avetisyan Collection, AGMI)

At least one former orphan from the City of Orphans—Ghazar Avetisyan—reached Berlin. He had graduated from the Polygon Pedagogical Technicum in June 1927 and taught in villages from 1928 to 1932, followed by six years of studies at the Karl-Marx Polytechnic Institute in Yerevan, graduating as an engineer. He was among the 300 Armenian soldiers who entered Berlin in May 1945. He died of natural causes in 1988.[1188]

Few, if any, of the orphans are alive in 2015. Some of the buildings they lived in were occupied by the residents of Leninakan/Gyumri, especially following the earthquake of 1988.

In 2003, one of the barracks at the Severski was renovated and refurbished as an orphanage. It opened its doors as the Terchoonian Home Orphanage, through a donation of the family of Vahan Terchoonian who once was an orphan there.

An inhabited barrack. (Photo by author, October 2013)

APOCRYPHA

The Kazachi Church. (Photo by author, October 2013)

View of a few of the Polygon barracks. (Photo by author, October 2012)

The Polygon barracks and some of those at the Severski are for the most part occupied by the soldiers of the Russian Federation.

The Armenian armed forces occupy parts of the Kazachi barracks, but the Russian church, once the focal point of moving pictures and momentous ceremonies viewed by audiences around the world, lays in semi-ruin.

Newspapers fell silent about the City of Orphans after NER had withdrawn from Leninakan. There were no more success stories about orphans, stories of the singularity of the phenomenon called the City of Orphans, nor inquiries about the destiny of the thousands of children who once lived there. International News Service Correspondent Edward L. Deuss stationed in Moscow, summarized the reason, in the January 20, 1930, issue of *The Huntingdon Daily News*. For the past ten years, Deuss wrote, NER had saved 22,000 orphans and finally, in fall 1929, had placed the last of them in good homes or jobs. Most of the barracks had been returned to the government, which was building up "a strong Red Army post...close to the Turkish border." The task had been tremendous, Deuss continued, but now many of the orphans were in government technical schools, or working in farms and factories. At the new textile factory 80% of the workers were former NER orphans. They had proven, the director of the new textile factory in Leninakan had told the visiting Americans, to be exemplary and well-disciplined workers. The reason for that, Deuss declared, was

> ...that they are American trained...
>
> The workers were trained for the future by Americans who have prepared them to play a leading role in the socialization and industrialization of their country...
>
> They are all members of the Communist youth organizations, the Pioneers and Comsomols. This is the nucleus of the future proletarian state of Armenia. It is on this American trained youth that the Soviet Government will depend to carry on the work of communal farming and industrialization, to lead the fight against old customs, old religion, for Communism.

The story of the City of Orphans was eclipsed, it seems, by reports on the political realities of the 1930s and the 1940s, chief among them Stalin's rise to power and the purges that became the hallmark of his reign, discussed in innumerable articles in the U.S. media. One such article published in April 1938 entitled "Armenia Dances as Moscow Plays," denounced the wholesale execution of Armenian government members, especially the ostensible "suicide" of Armenian Communist Secretary Aghasi Khanchyan, the "uncompromising enemy of Nationalist or anti-Communist elements in Armenia and a most loyal Stalinist."[1189] The article went on to comment that Khanchyan's "suicide" had been "the first awakening shock" to Armenians who had been "assiduous to please Moscow." But Armenia's attitude toward Moscow was understandable, the article continued, because as a "very small Christian nation embedded in the very midst of alien and hostile Mohammedan peoples and with fear of a Turkish invasion hanging over them," Armenia did everything to please Moscow, lest Moscow's protection be withdrawn.

In the following decades, the city of Leninakan would be mentioned in U.S. newspapers from time to time. In October 1950, for instance, numerous papers covered reports issued in Kars that Russia was "massing troops on her frontier with Turkey and Iran," and that six divisions "from Leninakan in Soviet Armenia were drawn up along the Turkish border just east of Kars."[1190] Eight years later, in September 1958, headlines described an international incident that had taken place south of Leninakan on September 2, 1958. On that day, two pairs of Soviet MIGs had intercepted and shot down a United States Air Force C130 "Hercules" military transport aircraft because the latter had "violated Soviet air space." All six members of the aircrew were killed. Officials from Leninakan had escorted their bodies to the border where they were received by Col. John Chalfont, U.S. Air Attaché in Ankara, and from there taken to the hospital morgue in Kars.[1191] In a later incident, in 1970, two U.S. Army generals, their Turkish escort officer and their pilot were seized when their plane had strayed across the heavily fortified Soviet Turkish border in stormy weather and landed near Leninakan. The passengers and the pilot had been taken into custody in Leninakan for having violated Soviet air space.[1192]

But stories of epic proportions, of American relief workers and orphans were heard no more. The silence over the City of Orphans outside Armenia, coupled with the dangerous consequences of references to it or to the Americans who had served in Armenia, ultimately dimmed the memory of the once unique institution. Inevitably, the story of an extraordinary undertaking that was the City of Orphans was preserved only in fragments, as personal experiences, in the minds of relief workers and orphans. Its history of over ten years was strewn in various archives, newspapers, memoirs and autobiographies around the world. The integral whole had been obliterated.

In the minds of the former orphans, however, the fragmented memories of the City of Orphans came to life, when they returned to the place of their childhood from time to time, to reminisce about their friends, their teachers and the years they spent at their orphanage—the good and the bad.

Reunion at the Polygon, 1960s–1970s. Ghazar Avetisyan is third from the right, second row from the top; Hmayak Avetisyan is seated, first from the right, first row. (Ghazar Avetisyan Collection, AGMI)

PART FOUR

The Community of the City of Orphans

1919–1931

LISTING OF ORPHANS (Incomplete)

To date, the definitive number of the children who entered the City of Orphans remains unavailable. Estimates in official and unofficial sources vary from 23,000 to 40,000 and more. At the same time, it is unclear if any of the estimates include those children who escaped from the orphanage or the thousands who died while in the orphanage.

Thanks to the generosity of the National Archives of Armenia, it has been possible to include at least a partial list, of over 11,500 orphans, who were residents of the City of Orphans between 1919 and 1931.

The original system of alphabetization by the child's first name has been maintained in order to preserve the integrity of the archival documents. Each entry carries the place and date of birth of the orphan, with the first name followed by the father's name and the child's last name, in that order. Frequently, however, and possibly because the child's last name could not be confirmed, the father's name was added in parentheses in the form of a last name, to which was appended the "yan" ending. Place of birth usually includes the name of the village, town, region, or country. The archival spelling and designation of the child's place of birth have been maintained using the transliteration key at the beginning of this volume, with a few exceptions: Kars is used instead of Ghars; Etchmiadzin and not Ejmiacin; Karabagh, and not Gharabagh. The names of regions and countries have been transliterated from the original, except in a few cases, as Russia, Persia, Georgia, Turkey, and Northern Caucasus, which have been replaced by current convention. To keep the integrity of the original documents, place names that appear in different forms, such as Sogyutli, Sogudli, Syogutli, have been kept intact. Finally, the silent Armenian syllable "e" (Ը) in place names or individuals' names is represented by "U" when it appears at the beginning of a name, examples being Undzak and Uznaberd.

Abet Galusti Barseghyan, Kars, Nakhijevan, 1913 ◆ Abet Ghukasi Ghevondyan, Akhalkalak, Olaverd, 1913 ◆ Abet Hovsepi Hovhannisyan (Churukhanyan), Akhalkalak, Marjakhet, 1914 ◆ Abet Mkrtchi Ghazaryan, Leninakan, Chrpli, 1912 ◆ Abet Nazari Manukyan, Leninakan, Paltli, 1916 ◆ Abet Yeghishi Saghatelyan, Akhalkalak, Vachian, 1911 ◆ Abet Zakari Zakaryan, Kars, Koghb, 1914 ◆ Abgar Arshaki Arshakyan, Akhta, Zenjelu, 1913 ◆ Abgar Artushi Hovhannisyan, Sarighamish, Shatevan, 1910 ◆ Abgar Geghami Harutyunyan (Geghamyan), Mush, Hartirt, 1912 ◆ Abgar Hovhannesi Khachatryan, Basen, Chibuk, 1914 ◆ Abgar Hovhannesi Sarafyan, Bitlis, Baghesh, 1916 ◆ Abgar Petrosi Petrosyan, Basen, Armtlu, 1915 ◆ Abgar Smbati Smbatyan, Gharakilisa, 1916 ◆ Abgar Smbati Torosyan, Alekpol, Kotigegh, 1908 ◆ Abgar Vanoyi Yeghoyan, Kaghzvan, Chankli, 1907 ◆ Abgar Yeremi Bisharyan, Mush, Ardirt, 1914 ◆ Abraham Gevorgi Martirosyan, Sarighamish, Gholakilise, 1913 ◆ Abraham Gevorgi Nalbandyan, Akhalkalak, 1911 ◆ Abraham Grigori Tonoyan, Bitlis, Khulik, 1910 ◆ Abraham Hovhannesi (Hovhannisyan) Melkonyan, Alashkert, Hamat, 1911 ◆ Abraham Hovhannesi Mkhitaryan, Kars, Agrak, 1914 ◆ Abraham Khachaturi Baroyan, Erzrum, Akh-kilisa, 1910 ◆ Abraham Khachaturi Kirakosyan, Bulanagh, Shirvanshikh, 1912 ◆ Abraham Kirakosi Khachatryan, Kotayk, Bash-gyugh, 1916 ◆ Abraham Mambrei Dokhikyan, Van, Moks, 1911 ◆ Abraham Manasi Aleksanyan, Van, Teghut, 1912 ◆ Abraham Samveli Samvelyan, Kharberd, Sarighamish, 1914 ◆ Abraham Sargsi Manukyan (Sargsyan), Van, Psandasht, 1908 ◆ Abraham Sedraki Mkrtchyan, Khud, 1916 ◆ Abraham Sedraki Sedrakyan, Khnus, Berdam, 1912 ◆ Abraham Serobi Danielyan (Serobyan), Sarighamish, 1904 ◆ Abraham Stepani Carukyan, Shirak, Toparlu, 1910 ◆ Abraham Stepani Stepanyan, Shirak, Kosaghbyur, 1912 ◆ Abraham Stepani Stepanyan, Tiflis, 1913 ◆ Abraham Zakari Simonyan (Zakaryan), Yerevan, Tezkharab, 1910 ◆ Abris Hayrapeti Hovsepyan, Shamakhi, Zarkaran, 1912 ◆ Acho (Margarit) Ghazari Margaryan, Hin Nakhijevan, Batuml, 1908 kam 1911 ◆ Acho Khachaturi Khachatryan, Kars, 1919 ◆ Acho Zibili Zibilyan, 1920 ◆ Adam Aghoyi Yervandyan, Pambak, Ghaltaghchi, 1916 ◆ Ade Hovhannesi Melik Adamyan, Goghtan, Agulis, 1910 ◆ Adibeg Avoyi Avoyan, Daralagaz, Basargechar, 1912 ◆ Agapi Aleksani Karapetyan, Alekpol, Jalab, 1914 ◆ Agapi Arami Aramyan, Shirak, Samrlu, 1917 ◆ Agapi Arshaki Poghosyan, Bitlis, 1911 ◆ Agapi Azizi Karapetyan, Bulanakh, Kharaghl, 1910 ◆ Agapi Grigori Grigoryan, Manazkert, Berd, 1910 ◆ Agapi Karapeti Bluzyan, Van, 1914 ◆ Agapi Martirosi Ghukasyan, Erzrum, Narman, 1911 ◆ Agapi Mkrtchi Karapetyan, Kars, Dolbandlu, 1916 ◆ Agapi Petrosi Voskanyan, Ardahan, 1909 ◆ Aghabeg Sargsi Nalchajyan, Kars, Zarishat, 1910 ◆ Aghabek Harutyuni Melik-Sargsyan, Kars, Bazrgyan, 1913 ◆ Aghabek Karoyi Hovhannisyan, Alekpol, Parni, 1912 ◆ Aghabek Markosi Harutyunyan, Leninakan, Toparlu, 1907 ◆ Aghabek Sargsi Kirakosyan, Leninakan, Horom, 1909 ◆ Aghabek Sargsi Sargsyan, Aparan, Gharakilisa, 1914 ◆ Aghabek Serobi Serobyan, Gharakilisa, 1918 ◆ Aghabek Vasili Grigoryan, Aparan, Samadarvish, 1914 ◆ Aghajan Khurshudi Khurshudyan, ◆ Aghasi Aghiki Sargsyan, Khnus, Gharagarpu, 1914 ◆ Aghasi Aleksani Hovhannisyan, Shirak, Khligharakilisa, 1911 ◆ Aghasi Arakeli Arakelyan, Alashkert, Ahmat, 1912 ◆ Aghasi Arshaki Ghaltakhchyan, Kars, Khasnigyugh, 1911 ◆ Aghasi Arshaki Sahakyan, Kars, Cbni, 1912 ◆ Aghasi Arshaki Sargsyan, Alekpol, Chorli, 1913 ◆ Aghasi Danieli Danielyan, Akhalkalak, Sulda, 1918 ◆ Aghasi Gevorgi Atoyan, Kars, 1909 ◆ Aghasi Gevorgi Gevorgyan, Van, 1913 ◆ Aghasi Gevorgi Karapetyan, Manazkert, Norali, 1910 ◆ Aghasi Grigori (Grigoryan) Hovhannisyan, Leninakan, Mec Kiti, 1918 ◆ Aghasi Gyulbanki (Arakeli) Sukiasyan, Sarighamish, Armtlu, 1913 ◆ Aghasi Hakobi Avagyan, Alekpol, Ghonakhstan, 1914 ◆ Aghasi Hakobi Hakobyan, Alekpol, 1913 ◆ Aghasi Hakobi Sahakyan, Sarighamish, Chrasun, 1913 ◆ Aghasi Hambardzumi Hambardzumyan, Kars, Zachi, 1914 ◆ Aghasi Hambari Sargsyan, Kars, Dolbandli, 1912 ◆ Aghasi Harutyuni Vahanyan, Kars, Parket, 1909 ◆ Aghasi Hovhannesi Grigoryan, Leninakan, Imirkhan, 1917 ◆ Aghasi Hovhannesi Hovhannisyan, Van, 1913 ◆ Aghasi Hovhannesi Natanyan, Van, Shaghpaz, 1912 ◆ Aghasi Kamsari Hovhannisyan, Ghazakh, Atun, 1916 ◆ Aghasi Karapeti Sahakyan, Kars, Ghapanlu, 1914 ◆ Aghasi Khachaturi Zakaryan, Kars, 1908 ◆ Aghasi Melkoni Ghasabyan, Kars, Mazaray, 1910 ◆ Aghasi Minasi Ginosyan (Asatryan), Alekpol, Imrkhan, 1909 ◆ Aghasi Mkhitari Aghajanyan, Kars, Badlamad, 1913 ◆ Aghasi Mkrtchi Harutyunyan, Akhalkalak, Dolukhan, 1918 ◆ Aghasi Mnatsakani Shahbazyan, Alekpol, Toparli, 1912 ◆ Aghasi Movsesi Grigoryan, Kars, 1912 ◆ Aghasi Mukoyi Arakelyan, Kars, Bekliahmed, 1914 ◆ Aghasi Musheghi Hamazaspyan, Akhalkalak, Gemirda, 1916 ◆ Aghasi Musheghi Petrosyan, Kars, 1914 ◆ Aghasi Musheghi Poghosyan, Shirak, Tafshanghshlagh, 1910 ◆ Aghasi Nazari Astvacatryan, Kaghzvan, Chankli, 1911, 1909 ◆ Aghasi Petrosi Ghazaryan (Petrosyan) Kars, 1911 ◆ Aghasi Piloyi (Piloyan) Antonyan, Shirak, Syogutli, 1914 ◆ Aghasi Sahaki Gevorgyan, Sarighamish, Ktan, 1913 ◆ Aghasi Sakoyi Avoyan, Kars, Nakhijevan, 1907 ◆ Aghasi Sargsi Sargsyan, Basen, Krbabash, 1917 ◆ Aghasi Sargsi Sargsyan, Kars, Baglamat, 1914 ◆ Aghasi Saroyi Hayrapetyan, Darachichak, Karvansara, 1914 ◆ Aghasi Sedraki Izmiryan, Erzrum, 1911, 1910 ◆ Aghasi Serobi Serobyan, Shirak, Chorli, 1917 ◆ Aghasi Varosi Khachatryan, Kars, Ughuzli, 1914 ◆ Aghasi Vasili Isahakyan (Vasilyan), Yerevan, Darachichak, 1912 ◆ Aghasi Yeghishei Galstyan, Alekpol, Toparlu, 1910 ◆ Aghasi Yeranosi Ayvazyan, Karin, Nkar, 1912, 1911 ◆ Aghasi Yervandi Nersisyan, Leninakan, Horom, 1914 ◆ Aghavard Margari Margaryan, Van, 1908 ◆ Aghavard Muradi Muradyan, Etchmiadzin, Haytagh, 1915 ◆ Aghavard Serobi Ghazaryan, Van, Nor gyugh, 1911 ◆ Aghavart Asaturi Grigoryan, Van, 1911 ◆ Aghavni (Asanet) Baghdasari Movsisyan, Van, Archesh, 1908 ◆ Aghavni Aleksani Aleksanyan,

Gharakilisa, Hajighara, 1914 ◆ Aghavni Arakeli Khachatryan, Kaghzvan, 1909 ◆ Aghavni Arami Movsisyan, Bitlis, 1914 ◆ Aghavni Arshaki Arshakyan, Van, Yerimer, 1914 ◆ Aghavni Arshaki Poghosyan, Alekpol, Horom, 1915 ◆ Aghavni Asaturi Hovhannisyan, Manazkert, 1913 ◆ Aghavni Avetisi Avetisyan, Alashkert, 1914 ◆ Aghavni Avetisi Avetisyan, Bitlis, 1917 ◆ Aghavni Avetisi Avetisyan, Van, 1909 ◆ Aghavni Avetisi Avetisyan, Van, Berkri, 1910 ◆ Aghavni Danieli Hayrapetyan, Basen, Dalibaba, 1913 ◆ Aghavni Daviti Davtyan, Van, Karchkan, 1908 ◆ Aghavni Davti Gevorgyan, Leninakan, Duzkharaba, 1917 ◆ Aghavni Galusti Galstyan, Basen, Khosroveran, 1912 ◆ Aghavni Gevorgi Ayvazyan, Kars, 1911, 1910 ◆ Aghavni Gevorgi Tonoyan, Kars, Arazgyugh, 1910 ◆ Aghavni Ghazari Makaryan, Mush, 1910 ◆ Aghavni Ghazari Simonyan, Van, 1909 ◆ Aghavni Ghukasi Ghukasyan (Aghanents), Alekpol, Samrlu, 1916 ◆ Aghavni Grigori Grigoryan, Gharakilisa, 1917 ◆ Aghavni Grigori Grigoryan, Karin, Khnzr, 1912 ◆ Aghavni Grigori Harutyunyan, Yerevan, 1908 ◆ Aghavni Grigori Yeghiazaryan, Aparan, Blkhera, 1917 ◆ Aghavni Hakobi Abrahamyan, Bitlis, 1912 ◆ Aghavni Hakobi Chitaghyan, Basen, Bashgyugh, 1912 ◆ Aghavni Hakobi Hakobyan, Tiflis, 1915 ◆ Aghavni Hakobi Hakobyan, Van, Haventstimar, 1910 ◆ Aghavni Hakobi Sargsyan (Hakobyan), Van, Aljavaz, 1912 ◆ Aghavni Hambardzumi Margaryan, Pambak, Hajighara, 1914 ◆ Aghavni Haruti Petrosyan, Kars, Pirvali, 1911 ◆ Aghavni Harutyuni Sargsyan, Van, Shatagh, 1909 ◆ Aghavni Harutyuni Simonyan, Van, Avants, 1911 ◆ Aghavni Hayrapeti Hayrapetyan, Alashkert, Pokr Gharakilisa, 1911 ◆ Aghavni Hmayaki Aleksanyan, Shirak, Mets Kyapanak, 1909 ◆ Aghavni Hovakimi Aleksanyan, Yerevan, Gharakhach, 1912 ◆ Aghavni Hovakimi Stepanyan, Alekpol, Chiftali, 1914 ◆ Aghavni Hovhannesi Gevorgyan, Akhalkalak, Khorenia, 1911 ◆ Aghavni Hovhannesi Ghazaryan, Van, Alur, 1912 ◆ Aghavni Hovhannesi Hovhannisyan, 1917 ◆ Aghavni Hovhannesi Hovhannisyan, Alashkert, 1914 ◆ Aghavni Hovhannesi Sargsyan, Kars, Araz gegh, 1909 ◆ Aghavni Hovhannesi Tumasyan, Van, Ashogh, 1914 ◆ Aghavni Hovsepi Hakobyan, Basen, Jrasan, 1911 ◆ Aghavni Hovsepi Ter-Hovhannisyan, Khut, Piko, 1911 ◆ Aghavni Karapeti Karapetyan, Erzrum, Abdndi, 1909 ◆ Aghavni Kerobi Mkrtchyan, Shirak, Kyavtarlu, 1911 ◆ Aghavni Khachaturi Hakobyan, Kars, Gharamamed, 1910 ◆ Aghavni Khachaturi Karapetyan, Erzrum, Targuni, 1908 ◆ Aghavni Khachaturi Karapetyan, Kars, Pirvali, 1910 ◆ Aghavni Manuki Grigoryan (Manukyan), Echmiacin, Khatunarkh, 1915 ◆ Aghavni Margari Margaryan, Mush, Aghaghbyur, 1912 ◆ Aghavni Martirosi Avetisyan, Kars, Bayburt, 1914 ◆ Aghavni Martirosi Ayvazyan, Kars, Ughuzlu, 1914 ◆ Aghavni Matosi Martirosyan, Van, Shitan, 1908 ◆ Aghavni Mesropi Movsisyan, Leninakan, Kaftarlu, 1911 ◆ Aghavni Mheri (Gevorgi) Muradyan, Alashkert, Uzkilisa, 1913 ◆ Aghavni Minasi Mkrtchyan, Kars, 1914 ◆ Aghavni Mkhitari Hovhannisyan, Malaskert, Latara, 1912 ◆ Aghavni Mkrtchi Mkrtchyan, Shatakh, 1912 ◆ Aghavni Mkrtchi Mkrtchyan, Van, Havants, 1914 ◆ Aghavni Movsesi (Vardani) Vardanyan (Movsisyan), Van, 1909 ◆ Aghavni Movsesi Janoyan, Van, Kec, 1908 ◆ Aghavni Musheghi Musheghyan, Khnus, Ghavurma, 1910 ◆ Aghavni Nazari Nazaryan, Khnus, 1912 ◆ Aghavni Nersesi Nersisyan, Alashkert, Gharakilis, 1910 ◆ Aghavni Nikoghosi Babagyulyan, Nakhijevan, Gulibekdiza, 1914 ◆ Aghavni Petrosi Ghukasyan, Van, Mokhraberd, 1908 ◆ Aghavni Petrosi Grigoryan, Van, Aygatan, 1908 ◆ Aghavni Petrosi Kostanyan, Kars, Gharamamed, 1914 ◆ Aghavni Petrosi Vardanyan, Bitlis, 1908 ◆ Aghavni Poghosi Poghosyan, Van, Mokhraberd, 1911 ◆ Aghavni Safari Vardanyan, Kars, Kyuragdar, 1909 ◆ Aghavni Sahaki Sahakyan, Sharur, Khanlukhlar, 1915 ◆ Aghavni Sargsi Muradyan (Sargsyan), Kars, Blden, 1911 ◆ Aghavni Sargsi Sargsyan, Kharberd, 1914 ◆ Aghavni Saribeki Hakobyan, Kars, Gharaghala, 1911 ◆ Aghavni Sedraki Luroyan, Bitlis, Prkhus, 1910 ◆ Aghavni Sedraki Sedrakyan, Alashkert, 1914 ◆ Aghavni Simoni Simonyan, Igdir, 1912 ◆ Aghavni Sipani Sipanyan, Bitlis, Caghkunk, 1910 ◆ Aghavni Sirakani Sirakanyan, Echmiacin, Sardarapat, 1914 ◆ Aghavni Stepani Nahapetyan, Alekpol, Bandivan, 1911 ◆ Aghavni Stepani Stepanyan, Yerevan, 1917 ◆ Aghavni Torosi Badalyan, Igdir, Surmalu, 1914 ◆ Aghavni Vahani Altunyan, Akhalkalak, Vachian, 1917 ◆ Aghavni Vardani Ghazaryan, Van, Shatakh, 1905 ◆ Aghavni Vardani Mesropyan, Van, Aygestan, 1909 ◆ Aghavni Vardani, Hakobyan, Yerevan, Ghamarli, 1915 ◆ Aghavni Zakari Martirosyan, Kars, 1912 ◆ Aghavni Zakari Zakaryan (Asatryan), Basen, Ishkhan, 1913 ◆ Aghavni Zohrabi Manukyan, Tiflis, 1918 ◆ Aghavnik Allahverdi Ghazaryan, Bitlis, Shengyugh, 1914 ◆ Aghavnik Bagrati Yeghiazaryan (Bagratyan), Yerevan, Sardarabad, 1914 ◆ Aghavnik Hovhannesi Rustamyan, Akhalkalak, Karcakh, 1914 ◆ Aghavnik Mekhaki Galstyan, Pambak, Ghshlagh, 1915 ◆ Agho Hakobi Safaryan, 1914 ◆ Aghun Musheghi Musheghyan (Sargsyan), Pambak, Mec Parni, 1918 ◆ Aghunik (Aghavni) Avetisi Hovakimyan, Darachichak, Verin Akhta, 1916 ◆ Aghunik Adami Davtyan, Alekpol, Bandrvan, 1915 ◆ Aghunik Aghabeki Stepanyan, Kars, Ghzlchakhchakh, 1914 ◆ Aghunik Aleki Karapetyan, Leninakan, Ghanlija, 1909 ◆ Aghunik Aleksani Movsisyan, Leninakan, 1914 ◆ Aghunik Andoyi Petrosyan, Kars, 1914 ◆ Aghunik Arami Aramyan, Kars, 1918 ◆ Aghunik Arshaki Melkonyan, Kars, Jorkhana, 1914 ◆ Aghunik Avetisi Avetisyan, Kars, Ghapanda, 1912 ◆ Aghunik Avetisi Margaryan (Avetisyan), Bulanakh, Yonjali ◆ Aghunik Badali Badalyan, Kars, Ughuzli, 1914 ◆ Aghunik Daviti Davtyan, Tifliz, 1916 ◆ Aghunik Daviti Davtyan, Van, Atan, 1914 ◆ Aghunik Davti Gevorgyan, Shirak, Duzkharaba, 1914 ◆ Aghunik Fidani Hambaryan, Leninakan, Sariar, 1914 ◆ Aghunik Galusti Galstyan, Kars, Chal, 1912 ◆ Aghunik Gaspari Manukyan, Hin Bayazet, 1918 ◆ Aghunik Gevorgi Barseghyan, Van, Moks, 1910 ◆ Aghunik Gevorgi Ghazaryan (Terzyan), Kaghzvan, 1911 ◆ Aghunik Gevorgi Tigranyan, Leninakan, Mahmuchugh, 1915 ◆ Aghunik Grigori

LISTING OF ORPHANS

Makyan, Lori, Urut, 1916 ♦ Aghunik Harutyuni Harutyunyan, Van, Tiramer, 1914 ♦ Aghunik Hovakimi Yeghoyan, Leninakan, Ortakilisa, 1912 ♦ Aghunik Hovhannesi Hovhannisyan, Basen, Tarkhuj, 1914 ♦ Aghunik Hovhannesi Vardanyan, 1914 ♦ Aghunik Hovsepi Hovhannisyan, Van, Mortaberd, 1905 ♦ Aghunik Hovsepi Hovsepyan, Leninakan, Gharakilisa, 1918 ♦ Aghunik Karapeti Hovhannisyan, Shirak, Dyuzinarab, 1914 ♦ Aghunik Khachaturi Ghazaryan, Shirak, Alikhan, 1913 ♦ Aghunik Knyazi Knyazyan, Leninakan, Gharakilisa, 1920 ♦ Aghunik Margari Zakaryan, Akhalkalak, Dabish, 1913 ♦ Aghunik Martirosi Tarzyan, Kars, 1911 ♦ Aghunik Mesropi Karapetyan, Erzrum, Toti, 1912 ♦ Aghunik Miaki (Misakyan) Ghazaryan, Alekpol, Mets Kapanak, 1912 ♦ Aghunik Mikayeli Gevorgyan, Kars, Beyliahmat, 1917 ♦ Aghunik Minasi Manukyan, Yerznka, Berkri, 1910 ♦ Aghunik Misaki Avetisyan, Leninakan, Chrakhli, 1914 ♦ Aghunik Mkrtchi Mkrtchyan, Van, 1914 ♦ Aghunik Mkrtchi Mkrtchyan, Van, 1914 ♦ Aghunik Mnatsakani Harutyunyan, Kars, Byurakdar, 1914 ♦ Aghunik Mnatsakani Sargsyan, Kars, 1913 ♦ Aghunik Movsesi Hambardzumyan, Alekpol, Ghapul, 1913 ♦ Aghunik Movsesi Movsisyan, Van, 1913 ♦ Aghunik Movsesi Torosyan, Gharakilisa, Hajighara, 1912 ♦ Aghunik Mukuchi Mkrtchyan, Alekpol, Chiftali, 1918 ♦ Aghunik Muradi Muradyan, Alashkert, Ahmat, 1911 ♦ Aghunik Nahapeti Sargsyan, Van, 1910 ♦ Aghunik Nersesi Hakobyan (Haroyan), Kars, Berna, 1912 ♦ Aghunik Nikoli Khosrovyan, Kars, Bashshoragal, 1917 ♦ Aghunik Petrosi Petrosyan, 1918 ♦ Aghunik Petrosi Poghosyan, Bitliz, 1913 ♦ Aghunik Pilosi Aslanyan, Kars, Mazra, 1909 ♦ Aghunik Rafayeli Baghdasaryan, Alekpol, Svanverdi, 1914 ♦ Aghunik Samsoni Asatryan, Bulanagh, Kop, 1912, 1911 ♦ Aghunik Sargsi Harutyunyan, Kars, 1911 ♦ Aghunik Sargsi Karapetyan, Kars, 1913 ♦ Aghunik Saroyi Hakobyan, Alekpol, Ghonakhghra, 1916 ♦ Aghunik Saroyi Karoyan, Shirak, Samrli, 1914 ♦ Aghunik Sedraki Gasparyan, Shirak, Ghzlghoch, 1913 ♦ Aghunik Smbati Sahakyan (Torosyan), Kars, Aghjaghala, 1917 ♦ Aghunik Soghomoni Sargsyan, Alekpol, Ghonakhghran, 1915 ♦ Aghunik Soghomoni Soghomonyan, Daralagyaz, Mokhradasht, 1917 ♦ Aghunik Soghomoni Tumasyan (Soghomonyan), Kars, Uzunkilisa, 1918 ♦ Aghunik Tatosi Martirosyan, Kars, 1910 ♦ Aghunik Tatosi Misakyan, Akhalkalak, 1918 ♦ Aghunik Tigrani Ghandilyan, Alashkert, Iritso, 1914 ♦ Aghunik Tigrani Khachatryan, Kars, Mazra, 1918 ♦ Aghunik Tonoyi Hovhannisyan (Tonoyan), Vardov, Gyandemir, 1912 ♦ Aghunik Vardani Harutyunyan, Basen, Archarak, 1911 ♦ Aghunik Vardani Mkrtchyan, Kars, Chirgha, 1911 ♦ Aghunik Vardani Yengoyan, Alekpol, Horom, 1910 ♦ Aghunik Yeghiazari Manukyan, Kars, Paldrvan, 1913, 1912 ♦ Aghunik Yeghiazari Sahakyan, Van, Harbints, 1909 ♦ Aghunik Yeghoyi Harutyunyan, Alashkert, Gharakilisa, 1914 ♦ Aghunik Yervandi Simonyan, Alekpol, Mahmudjugh, 1919 ♦ Aghunik Zakari Hambaryan, Akhalkalak, Mec Kentira, 1913 ♦ Aghunik Zakari Sahakyan, Van, Pokr gyugh, 1908 ♦ Aghvan Arami Grigoryan, Alashkert, Gharakilisa, 1913 ♦ Aghvan Arami Hayrapetyan, Alashkert, Iritsu gyugh, 1917 ♦ Aghvan Arseni Grigoryan, Leninakan, Toros gyugh, 1917 ♦ Aghvan Artaki (Sedraki) Manasyan, Alekpol, Bandrvan, 1914 ♦ Aghvan Barseghi Barseghyan, Kars, Bayburt, 1915 ♦ Aghvan Hakobi Hakobyan, Alekpol, Svanverdi, 1917 ♦ Aghvan Harutyuni Meloyan, Alekpol, Horom, 1913 ♦ Aghvan Khachaturi Khachatryan, Mush, Alashkert, 1915 ♦ Aghvan Khachaturi Khachikyan, Karvansara, 1918 ♦ Aghvan Mesropi Torgomyan, Akhalkalak, Gandza, 1916 ♦ Aghvan Misaki Sahakyan, Kars, Byurakdara, 1915 ♦ Aghvan Rafayeli Hovhannisyan, Leninakan, Julab, 1916 ♦ Aghvan Tadevosi Manukyan, Leninakan, Illi, 1911 ♦ Aghvan Vardani Mkhitaryan, Kars, Bashshoragal, 1913 ♦ Aghvan Yeghoyi Yeghoyan, Shirak, Ghrkh-Dagirman, 1915 ♦ Agika Ismayili Ismayelyan, Etchmiadzin, Chotankar, 1916 ♦ Agnes Vardani Vardanyan, Alashkert, Khoyanay, 1911 ♦ Ago Aloyan (Karapetyan) ♦ Aharon Gevorgi Khudaverdyan, Van, 1908 ♦ Aharon Grigori Barseghyan, Nakhijevan, Znjrlu, 1910 ♦ Aharon Manuki Manukyan, Van, Kindanas, 1915 ♦ Aharon Movsisyan ♦ Aksen Avetisi Grigoryan, Lengavar, Illi, 1916 ♦ Alek Hovhannesi Hakobyan, Kars, Gyoleban, 1913 ♦ Alek Makari Poghosyan, Alekpol, Chorlu, 1913 ♦ Aleko Barseghi Barseghyan, Alekpol, Baytar, 1913 ♦ Aleksan Abrahami Aleksanyan, Igdir, 1912 ♦ Aleksan Aharoni Aharonyan, Nor Bayazet, Vordaklu, 1916 ♦ Aleksan Aleksanyan, 1920 ♦ Aleksan Andreasi Arushanyan, Shamakhi, Kysylij, 1911 ♦ Aleksan Avagi Avetisyan, Alashkert, Mzri, 1907 ♦ Aleksan Hakobi Aleksanyan, Kars, 1919 ♦ Aleksan Hakobi Davtyan, Kars, 1910 ♦ Aleksan Hanesi Martirosyan, Leninakan, 1915 ♦ Aleksan Haruti Hakobyan, Shirak, Baghdashen, 1910 ♦ Aleksan Harutyuni Martirosyan, Olukh, Akrak, 1910 ♦ Aleksan Hovasapi Minasyan, Shirak, Chosli, 1911 ♦ Aleksan Hovsepi Grigoryan, Leninakan, Ghazanchi, 1911 ♦ Aleksan Karapeti Ghevondyan, Shamakhi, Zarkhi, 1912 ♦ Aleksan Karapeti Karapetyan, Van, Tagh, 1913 ♦ Aleksan Khachaturi Baroyan, Basen, Chrasun, 1911 ♦ Aleksan Khachaturi Tumasyan, Leninakan, Ortakilisa, 1909 ♦ Aleksan Kirakosi Kakoyan, Kars, Yagrag, 1911 ♦ Aleksan Kostani Kostanyan (Araksyan), Lori, Uzundara, 1916, 1915 ♦ Aleksan Manasi Aleksanyan, Bitlis, Teghut, 1913 ♦ Aleksan Markosi Markosyan, Van, Surb Sahak, 1914 ♦ Aleksan Mikayeli Mikayelyan, Hamamlu, Chotur, 1912 ♦ Aleksan Misaki Misakyan, Leninakan, Aleksandrovka, 1913 ♦ Aleksan Mkrtchi Grigoryan, Mush, Bostakand, 1912 ♦ Aleksan Mkrtchi Ter-Hakobyan, Kars, Ardahan, 1906 ♦ Aleksan Mnatsakani Khachatryan, Alekpol, Ghulichan, 1910 ♦ Aleksan Nikoli Muradyan, Kars, Dashkov, 1914 ♦ Aleksan Petrosi Avetisyan, Alashkert, Mollaslima, 1912 ♦ Aleksan Poghosi Simonyan, Kars, Pirvali, 1915 ♦ Aleksan Polei Ghazaryan, Kars, Karmir vank, 1914 ♦ Aleksan Saribeki Alekyan, Gharakilisa, Ghshlagh, 1912 ♦ Aleksan Simoni Aghajanyan, Kars, Mazra, 1912 ♦ Aleksan Sukiasi Sukiasyan, Basen, Chrason, 1913 ♦ Aleksan Torosi Torosyan, Akhalkalak, Mets Khanchallu, 1915 ♦ Aleksan Vardani Avagyan, Alekpol,

Aghin, 1911 ◆ Aleksandr Mkhitari Mkhitaryan (Mkheyan), Alashkert, Khayabek, 1909 ◆ Aleksandr Muradi Arshakyan (Muradyan), Van, Khachan, 1906 ◆ Aleksandr Sargsi Sargsyan, Basen, Khoshgeldi, 1914 ◆ Aleksandr Tovmasi Asatryan, Sasun, Manrdzor, 1911 ◆ Aleksandria Konstandini Achemyan, Lori, Selim, 1908 ◆ Aleksi Meliki Hovhannisyan, Shirak, Toros gyugh, 1915 ◆ Alichka Kostani Karapetyan, Losi, Matan, 1918 ◆ Alina Khachaturi Galoyan, Van, 1909 ◆ Alkhatun Gevorgi Sargsyan, Van, 1913 ◆ Almaghan Madoyi Khachatryan, Alekpol, Sogyutlu, 1913 ◆ Almast Ayvazi Avdalyan, Mush, Gharaghala, 1911 ◆ Almast Badali Badalyan, Van, 1916 ◆ Almast Gaspari Gasparyan, Erzrum, Kyoghk, 1914 ◆ Almast Geghami Geghamyan, Bulanagh, Shekhaghup, 1914 ◆ Almast Gevorgi Gevorgyan, Van, Janik, 1909 ◆ Almast Gevorgi Gevorgyan, Van, Kochanis, 1912 ◆ Almast Gevorgi Hovhannisyan (Gevorgyan), Van, Marmara, 1909 ◆ Almast Gevorgi Khachatryan, Bitliz, Khart, 1910 ◆ Almast Ghazari Aleksanyan, Basargechar, N.Zaden, 1909 ◆ Almast Ghunkanosi Harutyunyan, Basen, Gomadzor, 1913 ◆ Almast Ghurshudi Ghurshudyan, Erzrum, Vardanlu, 1911, 1912 ◆ Almast Grigori Hovhannisyan (Grigoryan), Julmali, 1917 ◆ Almast Hakobi Alemyan, Kharberd, Berdak, 1910 ◆ Almast Hambardzumi Hambardzumyan, Erzrum, 1916 ◆ Almast Hambardzumi Hambardzumyan, Khnus, Elpis, 1909 ◆ Almast Hmayaki Palanjyan, Kaghzvan, 1911 ◆ Almast Hovhannesi Afrikyan, Kaghzvan, 1910 ◆ Almast Hovhannesi Hovhannisyan, Maku, 1915 ◆ Almast Hovhannesi Hovhannisyan, Tiflis, 1918 ◆ Almast Hovhannesi Martirosyan, Turkey, Van, 1910 ◆ Almast Hovhannesi Martirosyan, Van, Berkri, 1913 ◆ Almast Karapeti Antrevelyan, Mush, Khasgyugh, 1912 ◆ Almast Karapeti Karapetyan, Alashkert, Khazlu, 1908 ◆ Almast Kirakosi Grigoryan, Motkan, Shen, 1913 ◆ Almast Mamikoni Mamikonyan, Basen, Gomadzor, 1916 ◆ Almast Manuki Manukyan, Karin, Khnus, 1912 ◆ Almast Manuki Manukyan, Van, Artashat, 1913 ◆ Almast Meliki (Asaturyan) Astvacaturyan, Kars, Bayburd, 1910 ◆ Almast Meliki Melikyan, Van, Karvansara, 1916 ◆ Almast Misaki Harutyunyan, Erzrum, Hoghek, 1911 ◆ Almast Poghosi Poghosyan, Alashkert, Uchkilisayi vank, 1910 ◆ Almast Poghosi Yekeyan, Khnus, Garachoban, 1908 ◆ Almast Sargsi Gasparyan (Sargsyan), Van, Kharakants, 1909, 1911 ◆ Almast Sargsi Sargsyan, Sanahin, Manes, 1915 ◆ Almast Tumasi Tumasyan, Shirak, Mavrak, 1913 ◆ Almast Vardani Avetisyan, Hin Bayazet, Arcani, 1912 ◆ Almast Yepremi Davtyan, Bayazet, Igdir, 1916 ◆ Altun Asaturi Asatryan, Kharberd, 1915 ◆ Altun Daviti Davtyan, Van, 1911–1917 ◆ Altun Grigori Aleksanyan, Alashkert, Koshk, 1910 ◆ Altun Knyazi Knyazyan (Ghazaryan), Manaskert, 1912 ◆ Altun Melkoni Grigoryan, Kars, Bashkyadiklar, 1913 ◆ Altun Mnatsakani Mnatsakanyan, Van, Shatagh, 1912, 1914 ◆ Altun Vardani Zatoyan, Van, Hayots dzor, 1909 ◆ Alura Makverdich, Leninakan, 1927 ◆ Amalia Eloyan, Kaghzvan, 1918 ◆ Amalia Movsesi Sargsyan, Kars, Pervali, 1916 ◆ Amalia Mukuchi Mukuchyan, Leninakan, Ortakilisa, 1917 ◆ Amalia Sargsi Sargsyan, Leninakan, Ghapli, 1916 ◆ Amalya Abgari Grigoryan, Igdir, Surmala, 1907 ◆ Amalya Arami Marunukyan, Leninakan, 1911 ◆ Amalya Avetiki Hovhannisyan, Leninakan, 1908 ◆ Amalya Avetiki Kirakosyan, Alekpol, 1914 ◆ Amalya Bagrati Kostanyan, Kaghzvan, 1919 ◆ Amalya Gevorgi Ayvazyan, Kars, 1912 ◆ Amalya Hajibadi Mkrtchyan, Kars, 1911 ◆ Amalya Hakobi Arakelyan, Nor Bayazet, 1912 ◆ Amalya Hakobi Hovhannisyan, Nukhi, Akhpilakand, 1913 ◆ Amalya Hamazaspi Vardanyan, Kharberd, Berdak, 1909 ◆ Amalya Hovhannesi Hovhannisyan, Leninakan, 1921 ◆ Amalya Hovhannesi Petrosyan, Bulanakh, Teghut, 1911 ◆ Amalya Karapeti Avagyan, Van, 1913 ◆ Amalya Margari Darbinyan, Van, 1910 ◆ Amalya Mikayeli Mikayelyan, Alekpol, Khligharakilisa, 1914 ◆ Amalya Nazari Gyulambaryan, Nakhijevan, Akulis, 1913 ◆ Amalya Sedraki Harutyunyan, Leninakan, 1912 ◆ Amalya Serobi Serobyan, Igdir, Dalburun, 1915 ◆ Amalya Sirakani Sirakanyan, Leninakan, Dashkend, 1917 ◆ Amalya Vahani Piloyan, Kars, 1915 ◆ Amalya Zohrabi Aghakhanyan, Leninakan, 1912 ◆ Amasia Gabrieli Barinyan, Kars, Kaghzvan, 1914 ◆ Amirbek Karapeti Gevorgyan, Shirak, Chzkhlar, 1919 ◆ Anahit Aleksani Hovakimyan, Leninakan, Babul, 1912 ◆ Anahit Aleksani Melkonyan, Kars, Digor, 1911 ◆ Anahit Aleksani Mkoyan, Akhalkalak, Satgha, 1913 ◆ Anahit Aleksani Vardanyan (Poghosyan), Kars, Ghanshi, 1910 ◆ Anahit Andreasi Hambardzumyan, Daralagyaz, Gurzubilak, 1910 ◆ Anahit Arami Tigranyan, Tiflis, 1909 ◆ Anahit Arshaki Arshakyan (Yeghoyan), Alashkert, 1916 ◆ Anahit Arshaki Arshakyan, Mush, Teghut, 1908 ◆ Anahit Arshaki Avetisyan, Polis, 1908 ◆ Anahit Arshaki Grigoryan, Van, Ishkhan, 1910 ◆ Anahit Bagrati Aghajanyan, Tpkhis, 1912 ◆ Anahit Bagrati Bagratyan, Kars, Parker, 1911 ◆ Anahit Barseghi Barseghyan, Hin Nakhijevan, 1912 ◆ Anahit Danieli Danielyan, Yerevan, Getashen, 1914 ◆ Anahit Eghoyi Papikyan, Alekpol, Aghin, 1913 ◆ Anahit Esayi Minasyan, Leninakan, Duzkharaba, 1913 ◆ Anahit Gaspari Gasparyan, Alashkert, Ghonjali, 1904 ◆ Anahit Gaspari Martirosyan, Alashkert, 1916 ◆ Anahit Gevorgi Baghdasaryan, (Gevorgyan), Bulankh, Kop, 1911 ◆ Anahit Gevorgi Harutyunyan, Yerevan, 1906 ◆ Anahit Gevorgi Knyazyan, Alekpol, Horom, 1913 ◆ Anahit Gevorgi Safaryan (Gevorgyan), Surmalu, Igdir, 1909 ◆ Anahit Gevorgyan, Leninakan, Kosaghbyur, 1916 ◆ Anahit Grigori Arzumanyan, Kars, Voghuzla, 1914 ◆ Anahit Grigori Baghdasaryan, Tiflis, 1911 ◆ Anahit Grigori Grigoryan, Leninakan, Ghanlika, 1918 ◆ Anahit Grigori Harutyunyan (Grigoryan), Alekpol, Jajur, 1913 ◆ Anahit Grigori Mikayelyan, Shirak, Adigaman, 1911 ◆ Anahit Grigori Poghosyan, Kars, Kyurakdara, 1916 ◆ Anahit Grigori Tarumyan, Batum, 1915 ◆ Anahit Hakobi Avetisyan, Akhalkalak, Chandura, 1913 ◆ Anahit Hakobi Hakobyan, 1920 ◆ Anahit Hakobi Hakobyan, Persia, Seydakar, 1908 ◆ Anahit Hakobi Hakobyan, Van, 1914 ◆ Anahit Hakobi Sargsyan, Leninakan, Tashghala, 1914 ◆ Anahit Hakobi Zakaryan, Kars, Bangihamat, 1913 ◆ Anahit Hambardzumi Nikoghosyan, Erzrum, Arjabad,

1914 ♦ Anahit Harutyuni Gasparyan, Sarighamish, 1917 ♦ Anahit Harutyuni Harutyunyan, Akhalkalak, Pokr Benduray, 1915 ♦ Anahit Harutyuni Harutyunyan, Van, Khachan, 1914 ♦ Anahit Harutyuni Karapetyan, Alekpol, Gheghach, 1917 ♦ Anahit Harutyuni Karapetyan, Kars, Zrchi, 1917, 1912 ♦ Anahit Harutyuni Melik sargsyan, Kars, Bazrgyan, 1912 ♦ Anahit Harutyuni Melkonyan, Yerevan, Davalu, 1913 ♦ Anahit Hmayaki Barseghyan, Echmiacin, 1913 ♦ Anahit Hmayaki Serobyan, Leninakan, Tashkhalu, 1915 ♦ Anahit Hovhannesi Hovhannisyan, Dilijan, 1916 ♦ Anahit Hovhannesi Hovhannisyan, Mush-Khut, Voshut, 1909 ♦ Anahit Hovhannesi Muradyan, Kars, Sogutlu, 1912 ♦ Anahit Hovhannesi Poghosyan, Akhalkalak, Mrakol, 1910 ♦ Anahit Hovsepi Avetisyan (Hovsepyan), Van, Kem, 1909 ♦ Anahit Israyili Chakhoyan, Kars, 1910 ♦ Anahit Karapeti Baghdasaryan, Van, Shah-bagh, 1910 ♦ Anahit Khachaturi Barseghyan, Igdir, 1914 ♦ Anahit Khachaturi Gharafyan, Bulanagh, Yonjalu, 1909 ♦ Anahit Khachaturi Khachatryan, Etchmiadzin, 1915 ♦ Anahit Khachaturi Khachatryan, Ghamarlu, Tokhanshalu, 1913 ♦ Anahit Khachaturi Khachatryan, Nukhi, 1911 ♦ Anahit Khachaturi Mkrtchyan, Alekpol, Ghapli, 1914 ♦ Anahit Khachaturi Vardanyan, Bitliz, 1912 ♦ Anahit Kostani Adamyan, Alekpol, Khli Gharakilisa, 1912 ♦ Anahit Levoni Khachatryan, Yerevan, Ghamarlu, 1913 ♦ Anahit Manuki Baghdasaryan, Van, 1912, 1910 ♦ Anahit Manuki Manukyan, Shirak, Mastara, 1915 ♦ Anahit Margari Arzumanyan, Igdir, Tashbaran, 1910–1915 ♦ Anahit Margari Karapetyan, Alekpol, 1910 ♦ Anahit Martirosi Hambardzumyan, Tavriz, Vinay, 1911 ♦ Anahit Martirosi Martirosyan, Kharberd, Mazra, 1911 ♦ Anahit Martirosi Simonyan, Kars, Kyoragdar, 1912 ♦ Anahit Martirosi Torosyan, Alashkert, 1916 ♦ Anahit Melkoni Melkonyan, Yerevan, Sardarapat, 1917 ♦ Anahit Mkrtchi Gasparyan, Van, Sevan, 1909, 1908 ♦ Anahit Mkrtchi Gharibyan, Kars, Bashkadiklar, 1909 ♦ Anahit Mkrtchi Safaryan, Leninakan, Dzityankov, 1912 ♦ Anahit Movsesi Movsisyan, Gharakilisa, Hamamlu, 1915 ♦ Anahit Musheghi Chatajyan, Akhalkalak, Vachian, 1911 ♦ Anahit Musheghi Musheghyan, Pambak, Parni, 1914 ♦ Anahit Nazari Manukyan, Kaghzvan, 1914 ♦ Anahit Nersesi Sargsyan, Kars, Bashkyatiklar, 1914 ♦ Anahit Nikolayi Melkonyan, Surmali, Igdir, 1910 ♦ Anahit Nikolayi Nazaryan, Nakhijevan, Yanjezi, 1911 ♦ Anahit Petrosi Meloyan, Kars, Paldrvan, 1912 ♦ Anahit Petrosi Petrosyan, Sarighamish, Hopveran, 1909 ♦ Anahit Poghosi Grigoryan, Kars, Hamzakarak, 1908 ♦ Anahit Rabsi Rabsinyan, Ghurdughuli, Gechrlu, 1916 ♦ Anahit Sahaki Manukyan, Van, Batakants, 1909 ♦ Anahit Sahaki Sahakyan, Kars, 1918 ♦ Anahit Sargsi Badalyan, Pambak, Sarumsakhlu, 1908 ♦ Anahit Sargsi Bastrmajyan, Trapizon, 1916 ♦ Anahit Sargsi Gevorgyan, Nor Bayazet, Solak, 1912 ♦ Anahit Sargsi Harutyunyan, Alekpol, 1912 ♦ Anahit Sedraki Sedrakyan, Echmiacin, 1916 ♦ Anahit Sedraki Sedrakyan, Leninakan, Ghzlkilisa, 1913 ♦ Anahit Sedraki Setoyan, 1918 ♦ Anahit Sinekerimi Firjalyan, Van, 1908 ♦ Anahit Smbati Sargsyan, Leninakan, Mets Kiti, 1914 ♦ Anahit Stepani Gasoyan, Akhalkalak, Olaver, 1915 ♦ Anahit Stepani Stepanyan, Trapizon, 1913 ♦ Anahit Tadevosi Sahakyan, Leninakan, Tashlanghshlagh, 1912 ♦ Anahit Tatosi Astvacaturyan, Yerevan, Kanaker, 1914 ♦ Anahit Tigrani Tarzyan (Tigranyan), Leninakan, 1913 ♦ Anahit Torosi Mutafyan, Akhalkalak, 1912 ♦ Anahit Torosi Torosyan, Kars, Behliaverdi, 1914 ♦ Anahit Tumasi Melkonyan, Kars, Tikniz, 1913 ♦ Anahit Vahani Gevorgyan, Van, 1910 ♦ Anahit Vanoyi Hakobyan, Alekpol, Parni gyugh, 1918 ♦ Anahit Vardani Hakobyan (Vardanyan), Ghamarlu, Khatunarkh, 1918, 1920 ♦ Anahit Vardani Hovhannisyan, Yerevan, Dzoragyugh, 1913 ♦ Anahit Vardani Khachatryan, Sasun, Taghavank, 1911 ♦ Anahit Vardani Vardanyan, Yerevan, Khatunarkh, 1914 ♦ Anahit Varosi Shahbazyan, Kars, Khani-gyugh, 1913 ♦ Anahit Yeghiki Yeghikyan, Kars, Chala, 1915 ♦ Anahit Yepremi Movsisyan, Sharur, Norashen, 1912 ♦ Anahit Yeranosi Arakelyan, Sasun, Sheniar, 1910 ♦ Anakhas Hakobi Grigoryan, Hin Bayazet, Arcap, 1910 ♦ Anakhas Hameti Hametyan, 1917 ♦ Anakhas Hovhannesi Avetisyan, Khnus, 1912, 1911 ♦ Anakhaz Hovhannesi Hovhannisyan, Manazkert, Noratin, 1915 ♦ Anastas Karapeti Khachoyan, Zangezur, Agarak, 1914 ♦ Anastasia Mikayeli Mikayelyan, Madan, 1916 ♦ Anatolia (Anahit) Yeknoyi Aleksanyan, Pirvali, 1915 ♦ Anatolia Levoni Mikayelyan, Ghamarlu, 1914 ♦ Andranik (Hovhannes) Sargsi Hovhannisyan, Van, Aygestan, 1910 ♦ Andranik Abeli Abelyan (Virabyan), Nakhijevan, Dznaberd, 1913 ♦ Andranik Abgari Jalalyan, Pambak, Gharakilisa, 1914 ♦ Andranik Abrahami Abrahamyan, Tiflis, 1915 ♦ Andranik Abrahami Avetisyan, Alekpol, Shoragyal, 1912 ♦ Andranik Aghabeki Hartinyan, Akelpol, Illi, 1912 ♦ Andranik Aleki Manukyan, Leninakan, Bandrvan, 1916 ♦ Andranik Aleki Yeghiazaryan, Gharakilisa, Parni gyugh, 1913 ♦ Andranik Aleksani Khurshudyan, Kars, 1914 ♦ Andranik Aleksani Mkrtchyan, Bulanagh, Kaparlu, 1913 ♦ Andranik Arakeli Ghazaryan (Arakelyan), Alashkert, 1913 ♦ Andranik Arakeli Malkhasyan, Alekpol, Sogyutli, 1914 ♦ Andranik Arakeli Varzhapetyan, Leninakan, Aghin, 1917 ♦ Andranik Arami Aramyan, Khnus, 1911 ♦ Andranik Armenaki Amirkhanyan, Bulanagh, 1915 ♦ Andranik Armenaki Harutyunyan, Basen, Khzveran, 1913 ♦ Andranik Arshaki Arshakyan (Hakobyan), Erzrum, Hekipat, 1911 ♦ Andranik Arshaki Arshakyan, Alekpol, Pokr Keti, 1914 ♦ Andranik Arshaki Baghdasaryan, Akhalkalak, Dilif, 1912 ♦ Andranik Arshaki Galstyan, Kars, Bashkyadiklar, 1910 ♦ Andranik Arshaki Nahapetyan, Kars, Mec Parket, 1909 ♦ Andranik Artushi Mihranyan, Sarighamish, 1919 ♦ Andranik Asaturi Margaryan, Khnus, 1912 ♦ Andranik Asaturi Vardanyan, Kars, Gyulagarak, 1918 ♦ Andranik Aslani Aslanyan, Alashkert, Yonjalu, 1908 ♦ Andranik Avetiki Hovsepyan, Van, Lanjars, 1908 ♦ Andranik Avetisi Avetisyan, Kars, Blbul, 1914 ♦ Andranik Avetisi Kamalyan, Van, Kozer, 1911 ♦ Andranik Bagoyi Varosyan, Ghzlghoch, 1908 ♦ Andranik Bagrati Harutyunyan, Akhalkalak, Merenia, 1914 ♦ Andranik Barseghi Barseghyan, Kars, Paldrvan, 1919 ♦ Andranik Danieli Danielyan,

Kars, Dorbandlu, 1917 ♦ Andranik Danieli Karapetyan, Alashkert, Mankasar, 1912 ♦ Andranik Daviti Karapetyan, Kars, 1917 ♦ Andranik Daviti Tadevosyan, Alekpol, Uzunkilisa, 1909 ♦ Andranik Davti Gevorgyan, Shirak, Duzkharaba, 1916 ♦ Andranik Gabrieli Baghoyan, Kars, Bayburt, 1913 ♦ Andranik Gabrieli Grigoryan, Kharberd, 1913 ♦ Andranik Gaspari Kirakosyan, Alashkert, Gharakilis, 1911 ♦ Andranik Gaspari Martirosyan (Vagharshakyan), Alashkert, Deghin-tapa, 1911 ♦ Andranik Geghami Geghamyan, Mush, Avzut, 1914 ♦ Andranik Gevorgi Baghdasaryan, Bayazet, 1914 ♦ Andranik Gevorgi Baghdasaryan, Bulanakh, Takarlu, 1913 ♦ Andranik Gevorgi Gevorgyan, Bulanagh, Shekh haghab, 1911, 1912 ♦ Andranik Gevorgi Nazaryan, Derjan, Chkhnlu, 1912, 1910 ♦ Andranik Gevorgi Sargsyan, Alekpol, Ghonaghran, 1915 ♦ Andranik Gevorgi Sargsyan, Alekpol, Kapanak, 1913 ♦ Andranik Gevorgi Sargsyan, Alekpol, Mahmajugh, 1910 ♦ Andranik Gevorgi Shahnazaryan, Kars, Baklamat, 1914 ♦ Andranik Gharibi Garibyan, Bitlis, 1909 ♦ Andranik Ghazari Arshakyan, Bitlis, Manazkert, 1914 ♦ Andranik Grigori Faljyan, Nukhi, Nizh, 1913 ♦ Andranik Gulani Gulanyan, Khnus, 1907 ♦ Andranik Gurgeni Gurgenyan, Vladikavkaz, 1914 ♦ Andranik Hakobi Adamyan, Etchmiadzin, Javarabad, 1911 ♦ Andranik Hakobi Sargsyan, Basen, Cholakhli, 1911 ♦ Andranik Harutyuni Harutyunyan, Alekpol, Imrkhan, 1916 ♦ Andranik Harutyuni Hovhannisyan, Shirak, Taparli, 1910 ♦ Andranik Hayrapeti Ghazaryan, Hin-Nakhijevan, Gladzor, 1912 ♦ Andranik Hipoyi Stepanyan, Kars, Aghjala, 1910 ♦ Andranik Hmayaki Mikayelyan, Akhalkalak, Mec Kyandira, 1914 ♦ Andranik Hovakimi Baghdasaryan, Erzrum, Basen, 1914 ♦ Andranik Hovhannesi Hakobyan, Mush, Bostakand, 1909 ♦ Andranik Hovhannesi Hovhannisyan (Mkhitaryan), Erzrum, Gomadzor, 1912, 1911 ♦ Andranik Hovhannesi Hovhannisyan, Bulanagh, Khataghlu, 1906 ♦ Andranik Hovhannesi Hovhannisyan, Kars, Bashgyugh, 1913 ♦ Andranik Hovhannesi Hovhannisyan, Sarighamish, 1908 ♦ Andranik Hovhannesi Poghosyan, Basen, Archarak, 1910, 1911 ♦ Andranik Hovhannesi Zhamkochyan, Van, Kusubash, 1910 ♦ Andranik Hovsepi Yeghoyan, Nakhijevan, Sultanbek, 1912 ♦ Andranik Karapeti Andreasyan, Kars, Aksi-Ghaz, 1909 ♦ Andranik Karapeti Avetisyan, Alekpol, Sogutli, 1914 ♦ Andranik Karapeti Khachatryan, Kars, Pirvali, 1910 ♦ Andranik Karapeti Sahakyan, Kars, Ghapanli, 1917 ♦ Andranik Khachaturi Khachatryan, Yerevan, Arinj, 1911 ♦ Andranik Khachiki Ghukasyan, Manazkert, Terek, 1909 ♦ Andranik Khlghati Sargsyan, Khnus, Gobal, 1908 ♦ Andranik Khurshudi Poghosyan, Bulanagh, Khabaghl, 1910 ♦ Andranik Levoni Grigoryan, Yerevan, 1918 ♦ Andranik Manuki Hambardzumyan, Leninakan, Taknalu, 1910 ♦ Andranik Manuki Hovsepyan, Alekpol, Jalab, 1912 ♦ Andranik Manuki Manukyan, Kars, Bashkyadiklar, 1920 ♦ Andranik Manuki Sahakyan, Van, Aljavaz, 1907 ♦ Andranik Margari Margaryan ♦ Andranik Margari Martirosyan, Alekpol, Dashkhala, 1914 ♦ Andranik Martiki Martirosyan, Alekpol, 1915 ♦ Andranik Martirosi Hakobyan, Akhalkalak, Goman, 1911 ♦ Andranik Meliki Asoyan, Leninakan, Ghonakhran, 1918 ♦ Andranik Meliki Astoyan, Kars, Bayburt, 1913 ♦ Andranik Meliki Hovhannisyan, Alashkert, Katisan, 1909 ♦ Andranik Meliki Karapetyan, Alchavaz, Kochir, 1908 ♦ Andranik Meliki Melikyan, Basen, Jeghan, 1913 ♦ Andranik Melkoni Ghazaryan, Etchmiadzin, VaKarshapat, 1912 ♦ Andranik Minasi Barseghyan, Kars, Nakhijevan, 1914 ♦ Andranik Minasi Hovhannisyan, Leninakan, Ghanlija, 1916 ♦ Andranik Misaki Misakyan, Kars, Tiknis, 1914 ♦ Andranik Mkrtchi Aghekyan, Leninakan, 1908 ♦ Andranik Mkrtchi Harutyunyan, Leninakan, Svanverdi, 1914 ♦ Andranik Mnatsakani Mnatsakanyan, Alashkert, Maymanjugh, 1912 ♦ Andranik Mnatsakani Mnatsakanyan, Alekpol, Songyurli, 1913 ♦ Andranik Mnatsi Tonoyan, Alekpol, Mahmudjugh, 1912 ♦ Andranik Movsesi Abrahamyan, Van, Van, 1916 ♦ Andranik Movsesi Barseghyan, Mush, Hamzashen, 1910 ♦ Andranik Mukuchi Torosyan, Kars, Hamzyakyarak, 1910 ♦ Andranik Muradi Hakobyan, Mush, Bulanagh, 1909 ♦ Andranik Muradi Sargsyan, Kars, Dolbandlu, 1916 ♦ Andranik Musheghi Markosyan, Manazkert, Berd, 1912 ♦ Andranik Musheghi Tumoyan (Musheghyan), Akhlat, Vorsadzor, 1901 ♦ Andranik Nazari Asatryan, Kaghzvan, Chankli, 1908 ♦ Andranik Nazari Khachatryan, Kaghzvan, Gharavank, 1911 ♦ Andranik Nazari Tonoyan, Bulanagh, Shirvanshen, 1912 ♦ Andranik Papiki Paikyan, Van, Ozm, 1912 ♦ Andranik Petrosi Hovhannisyan, Kars, Berna, 1912, 1910 ♦ Andranik Petrosi Nersisyan, Shamakhi, 1915 ♦ Andranik Poghosi Hakobyan, Basen, Arjakrak, 1914 ♦ Andranik Poghosi Khachatryan, Alekpol, Ghoshavank, 1910, ♦ Andranik Poghosi Minasyan, Basen, Dalibaba, 1912 ♦ Andranik Poghosi Nersisyan (Poghosyan), Yerevan, Makravank, 1909, 1911 ♦ Andranik Poghosi Sargsyan, Karin, 1912 ♦ Andranik Poghosi Simonyan, Van, Archesh, 1913 ♦ Andranik Safari Mkrtchyan, Khnus, 1909 ♦ Andranik Sahaki Kerobyan, Basen, Chrason, 1912 ♦ Andranik Sahaki Muradyan, Van, Atanan, 1908 ♦ Andranik Samsoni Rafayelyan, Ardvin, Tandzut, 1910 ♦ Andranik Sargsi Davtyan, Erzrum, 1914 ♦ Andranik Sargsi Ghevondyan, Akhalkalak, Karzakh, 1914 ♦ Andranik Sargsi Muradyan, Erzrum, Gomadzor, 1910 ♦ Andranik Sargsi Sargsyan, Kars, 1918 ♦ Andranik Sedraki Karapetyan, Khnus, Burnaz, 1911 ♦ Andranik Sedraki Sedrakyan, Kars, Hamzakyarak, 1912 ♦ Andranik Sergoyi Sevoyan, Alekpol, Gharakilisa, 1917 ♦ Andranik Serobi Martirosyan, Basen, Aghjaghalar, 1914 ♦ Andranik Serobi Vardanyan, Basen, Hovasun, 1916 ♦ Andranik Soghomoni Sargsyan, Kaghzvan, 1916 ♦ Andranik Srapi Kirakosyan (Srapyan), Erzrum, Terjan, 1908 ♦ Andranik Srapioni Heghtaryan, Kars, Gharaghala, 1911 ♦ Andranik Srgeyi Srgeyan, Khut, Grichonq, 1911 ♦ Andranik Tadevosi Tadevosyan, Surmalu, Khoshkhabar, 1912 ♦ Andranik Tepanosi Avetisyan, Lori, Bado, 1913 ♦ Andranik Tigrani Hakobyan, Leninakan, Sirvan chugh, 1911 ♦ Andranik Tigrani Petrosyan, Kars, 1914 ♦ Andranik Tonoyi Tonoyan (Hovhannisyan), Alekpol, Servanjukh, 1913 ♦ Andranik Tonoyi

Tonoyan, Kars, Aghamardzag, 1915 ♦ Andranik Vanoyi Mardoyan, Alekpol, Tashtan-ghshlagh, 1917 ♦ Andranik Vardani Gevorgyan, Persia, Maku, 1911 ♦ Andranik Vardani Ter-Simonyan, Manazkert, 1906 ♦ Andranik Vardani Vardanyan, Van, Avan gyugh, 1912 ♦ Andranik Vasili Vasilyan, Igdir, Alichan, 1915 ♦ Andranik Yeghiazari Jiloyan, Ardahan, Shafsh, 1915 ♦ Andranik Yepremi Torosyan, Kars, Dolpantli, 1911 ♦ Andranik Yervandi Martirosyan, Kars, Melikkoy, 1910 ♦ Andranik Zakari Aboyan, Erzrum, Narman, 1912, 1911 ♦ Andranik Zakari Yeghishyan, Leninakan, Ateyaman, 1916 ♦ Andranik Zakari Zakaryan, Erzrum, 1908 ♦ Andranik Zohrabi Margaryan, Nor Bayazet, Veri Gharanlagh, 1912 ♦ Andreas Gevorgi Gevorgyan, Nakhijevan, 1918 ♦ Andreas Meliki Grigoryan, Kars, Pirvali, 1911 ♦ Andreas Navasardi Nahapetyan, Bayazet, Mosun, 1912 ♦ Andreas Sargsi Hayrapetyan, Igdir, Punik, 1909 ♦ Anghalat Petrosi Petrosyan, Kars, 1914 ♦ Angin Abrahami Sargsyan, Yerevan, Caghkunk, 1913 ♦ Angin Adami Khachatryan, Gavmas, Gabs, 1916 ♦ Angin Aleksani Grigoryan, Alekpol, Ghonakhghra, 1913 ♦ Angin Andraniki Grigoryan, Yerevan, Aghavnatun, 1913 ♦ Angin Andraniki Serobyan, Karabagh, 1916 ♦ Angin Arakeli Arakelyan (Yenovkyan), Alashkert, Bagnots, 1914 ♦ Angin Arseni Arsenyan, Alekpol, Avanverdi, 1917 ♦ Angin Arshaki Grigoryan, Zangezur, 1915 ♦ Angin Arshaki Harutyunyan, Kar, Mavrak, 1912 ♦ Angin Asaturi Amirkhanyan, Yerevan, Davalu, 1912, 1911 ♦ Angin Avagi Adamyan (Avagyan), Kars, Gorkhana, 1916 ♦ Angin Avetisi Avetisyan, Bitliz, Tighut, 1911, 1909 ♦ Angin Avetisi Harutyunyan, Bitlis, Meck, 1907 ♦ Angin Balabeki Sargsyan, Leninakan, Bandrvan, 1910 ♦ Angin Barseghi Mikayelyan, Kars, Bayraghdar, 1915 ♦ Angin Galoyi Simonyan, Leninakan, Imrkhan, 1911 ♦ Angin Gaspari Gasparyan, Kars, 1916 ♦ Angin Gaspari Ghazaryan, Alekpol, Hajinazar, 1918 ♦ Angin Gevorgi Avoyan, Leninakan, Sarhat, 1917 ♦ Angin Gevorgi Ter-Hovsepyan, Ardahan, Drabat, 1913 ♦ Angin Grigori Ghazaryan, Yerevan, Molaghasm, 1914 ♦ Angin Grigori Karapetyan, Erzrum, 1912 ♦ Angin Haruti Avetisyan, Kars, Uzunkilisa, 1909 ♦ Angin Harutyuni Harutyunyan, Sasun, Shikalen, 1913, 1911 ♦ Angin Hayrapeti Davtyan, Erzrum, Dali baba, 1912, ♦ Angin Hayrapeti Hayrapetyan, Yerevan, Gharakhach, 1911 ♦ Angin Hovhannesi Hovhannisyan, Ardahan, 1914 ♦ Angin Hovhannesi Hovhannisyan, Van, Bozania, 1918 ♦ Angin Hovhannisyan, Zangezur, Zargyaran, 1909 ♦ Angin Manuki Hovhannisyan, Basen, Krdabas, 1912, 1909 ♦ Angin Martirosi Harutyunyan, Kars, Berni, 1912 ♦ Angin Mikayeli Hakobyan, Kars, Kagizman, 1911 ♦ Angin Minasi Minasyan, Van, Mokhraberd, 1912 ♦ Angin Misaki Misakyan, Alashkert, Yernjalu, 1909 ♦ Angin Mkrtchi Martirosyan, Alekpol, Ghzlghoch, 1911 ♦ Angin Mkrtchi Mkrtchyan, Shirak, Bandrvan, 1913 ♦ Angin Mkrtchi Tonoyan, Shirak, Ghapra, 1918 ♦ Angin Mnatsakani Mnatsakanyan, Yerevan, Davalu, 1913 ♦ Angin Ohannesi Vardanyan, Kaghzvan, Yenghidju, 1911 ♦ Angin Petrosi Muradyan, Bitlis, Bkhus, 1908 ♦ Angin Piloyi Zakaryan, Leninakan, Khligharakilisa, 1911 ♦ Angin Sakoyi Sakoyan, Leninakan, Ghaplu, 1917 ♦ Angin Sargsi Arakelyan, Karabagh, Vanashen, 1914 ♦ Angin Sedraki Sedrakyan, 1918 ♦ Angin Shaheni Shahinyan, Mec Gharakilisa, Avdibek, 1912 ♦ Angin Tigrani Saroyan, Alekpol, Hajinazar, 1913 ♦ Angin Vahani Khachatryan, Alekpol, Tomardash, 1913 ♦ Angine Sargsi Minasyan, Archesh, Soskan, 1918 ♦ Anichka Aghabeki Dilanyan, Lori, Gyulagarak, 1914 ♦ Anichka Aleksani Karapetyan, Kars, Kaghzvan, 1920 ♦ Anichka Gaspari Muradyan, Bulanagh, Kopeti, 1907 ♦ Anichka Gevorgi Gevorgyan, Leninakan, 1916 ♦ Anichka Yervandi Aleksanyan (Yervandyan), Jalaloghli, 1919 ♦ Aniko Semuili Mkrtchyan, Igdir, Tashburan, 1911 ♦ Aniko Varazi Varazyan, Surmalu, 1915 ♦ Anna Arshaki Arshakyan, Gharakilisa, Vardanlu, 1914 ♦ Anna Avetisi Avetisyan, Bulanagh, Yonjali, 1910 ♦ Anna Avetisi Torosyan, Erzrum, Kepbrikkov, 1911 ♦ Anna Avoyi Sargsyan, Kaghzvan, 1913 ♦ Anna Gabrieli Grigoryan, Kharberd, 1912, 1910 ♦ Anna Gaspari Harutyunyan, Sarighamish, Shadivan, 1910 ♦ Anna Gevorgi Gevorgyan, Tpkhis, 1919 ♦ Anna Grigori Manukyan, Akhalkalak, Sulda, 1911 ♦ Anna Hamoyi Sukiasyan, Erzrum, Dzaghan, 1912 ♦ Anna Harutyuni Mikayelyan, Kharberd, Bashaghag, 1907 ♦ Anna Karapeti Caghikyan, Kaghzvan, 1914 ♦ Anna Karapeti Hovhannisyan, Hasanghali, Kyoprkoy, 1912 ♦ Anna Karapeti Manukyan, Kars, 1913 ♦ Anna Karapetyan ♦ Anna Khachaturi Khachatryan, Erzrum, Bakarjeti, 1910 ♦ Anna Manuki Harutyunyan (Manukyan), Kaghzvan, Karabagh, 1906 ♦ Anna Markosi Khevoyan, Akhalkalak, Aragal, 1918 ♦ Anna Martirosi Ghazaryan, Karin, 1910 ♦ Anna Mnatsakani Mnatsakanyan, Erzrum, Gomadzor, 1909 ♦ Anna Nikoyi Nikoyan, Erzrum, Bayburt, 1908 ♦ Anna Petrosi Abrahamyan, Basen, Hori, 1909 ♦ Anna Petrosi Petrosyan, Alashkert, Khznakar, 1911, 1910 ♦ Anna Sargsi Stepanyan (Simonyan), Nukhi, Japaravan, 1911 ♦ Anna Sergeyi Gabrielyan, Nukhi, Chardar, 1910 ♦ Anna Simoni Poghosyan, Kars, Mazra, 1909 ♦ Anna Stepani Vahradyan, Akhalkalak, 1913 ♦ Anna Tigrani Avetisyan, Alekpol, Dzithankov, 1910 ♦ Anna Trdati Holoyan, Akhalkalak, Abul, 1917 ♦ Anna Yervandi Petrosyan, Shirak, Mastara, 1913 ♦ Annakhas Grigori Manukyan (Grigoryan), Bulanagh, Latar, 1917 ♦ Annichka Derdzakyan Kars, 1918 ♦ Annik Abrahami Shahinyan, Nukhi, Tarak, 1908 ♦ Annik Aghabegi Aghabegyan, Kharberd, Penik, 1908 ♦ Annik Grigori Grigoryan, Van, 1919 ♦ Annik Khachaturi Khachatryan, Van, Avrasha, 1913 ♦ Annik Nikoghosi Poghosyan, Kars, Chirik, 1911 ♦ Annik Simoni Ghukasyan, Nukhi, Tarakend, 1912, 1911 ♦ Annik Soghomoni Khachatryan, Tiflis, 1915 ♦ Annik Tovmasi Hovhannisyan, Nukhi, 1910 ♦ Annman Asaturi Ghandilyan, Tiflis, Calka, 1910 ♦ Annman Atami Khachatryan, Shirak, Kapo, 1914 ♦ Annman Avetisi Avetisyan, Yerevan, Bashaparan, 1916 ♦ Annman Gevorgi Hayrapetyan, Kars, Kyurakdar, 1912 ♦ Annman Grigori Melkonyan, Basen, Chrason, 1914 ♦ Annman Hambardzumi Sahakyan, Kars Cpni, 1906 ♦ Annman Meliki Melkonyan, Shirak, Duzkhabara, 1911 ♦ Annman Mikayeli Avetisyan,

Kars, Dashkov, 1909 ♦ Annman Mkhitari Grigoryan, Alekpol, Mets Kiti, 1915 ♦ Annman Sargsi Arakelyan, Akhalkalak, Poka, 1912 ♦ Annman Tigrani Aghajanyan, Alekpol, Zalab, 1912 ♦ Antanaz Knyazi Muradyan, Aparan, Samadarvish, 1913 ♦ Antanes Avoyi Avoyan, Aparan, Tavjlu, 1914 ♦ Antanis Yeghoyi Ghazaryan, 1912 ♦ Antaram Abrahami Abrahamyan, Alashkert, 1914 ♦ Antaram Avetisi Avetisyan (Baghdasaryan), Kars, Ortakilisa, 1915 ♦ Antaram Beniamini Karapetyan, Olti, Akrak, 1909 ♦ Antaram Hakobi Harutyunyan, Van, Janik, 1909 ♦ Antaram Hovhannesi Hovhannisyan, Van, 1909 ♦ Antaram Hovhannesi Muradyan, Bulanagh, Kop, 1910 ♦ Antaram Karapeti Karapetyan, Salmast, Khoy, 1912 ♦ Antaram Khachaturi Gevorgyan, Bulanagh, Kop, 1910 ♦ Antaram Knyazi Knyazyan (Gasparyan), Bulanakh, Shirvanshikh, 1908 ♦ Antaram Meliki Hakobyan, Talin, Gozlu, 1915 ♦ Antaram Meliki Kurghinyan, Leninakan, Horom, 1911 ♦ Antaram Mnatsakani Mnatsakanyan, Van, Hater, 1912 ♦ Antaram Petrosi Petrosyan, Khnus, Khotoy, 1914 ♦ Antaram Tigrani Tigranyan, Van, Sosbat, 1913 ♦ Antaram Torosi Muradyan, Archish, Akants, 1910 ♦ Antaram Vardani Avetisyan, Van, Manushak, 1911 ♦ Antaram Yeghiazari Yeghiazaryan, Van, Ishkhan, 1909 ♦ Antaram Yeghiazari Yeghiazaryan, Van, Khadankonis, 1913 ♦ Antaran Hakobi Martirosyan, Shirak, Dzithankov, 1912 ♦ Antevan Avetisi Tovmasyan, Bulanagh, Shirvan-shekh, 1912 ♦ Antevan Sargsi Khlghatyan, Bulanagh, Harndzor, 1914 ♦ Anton Aleki Nahapetyan, Shirak, Imrkhas, 1913 ♦ Anton Grigori Hambaryan, Kars, Mavrak, 1917 ♦ Anton Sedraki Sedrakyan, Alashkert, 1917 ♦ Anton Tadevosi Tadevosyan, Hin Nakhijevan, 1916 ♦ Anush Abrahami Abrahamyan, Hin Nakhijevan, 1912 ♦ Anush Armenaki Grigoryan, Hin Bayazet, Arcap, 1912 ♦ Anush Arshaki Arshakyan, Leninakan, Ghanlija, 1913 ♦ Anush Arshaki Manukyan, Van, Nor gyugh, 1918 ♦ Anush Aruti Ilikyan, Akhalkalak, Gandza, 1912 ♦ Anush Asaturi Mkrtchyan, Mush, Mushughshen, 1913 ♦ Anush Asoyi Asoyan, Leninakan, Gyulli, 1917 ♦ Anush Astvacaturi Mkrtchyan, Shirak, Illi, 1916 ♦ Anush Avetisi Karapetyan, Akhalkalak, Mets Gyondura, 1910 ♦ Anush Avetisi Minasyan (Avetisyan), Leninakan, Taknali, 1912 ♦ Anush Ayvazi Ayvazyan (Avetisyan), Nakhijevan, Zarnji, 1908 ♦ Anush Ayvazi Kirakosyan, Sarighamish, Dalibaba, 1909 ♦ Anush Daviti Barseghyan, Olti (Kars), Agrag, 1911 ♦ Anush Ervandi Mkrtchyan, Surmala, Evjilar, 1915 ♦ Anush Galusti Karapetyan (Abrahamyan), Basen, Hekipar, 1911 ♦ Anush Gevorgi Eloyan (Gevorgyan), Alashkert, Yekhntapa, 1913 ♦ Anush Gevorgi Gevorgyan, Erzrum, Injal, 1913 ♦ Anush Gevorgi Melkonyan, Igdir, Mollaghamar, 1910 ♦ Anush Ghazari Hovhannisyan, Nakhijevan, Khatatasht, 1912 ♦ Anush Ghazari Sargsyan, Hin Nakhijevan, Ghazanchi, 1910 ♦ Anush Grigori Grigoryan, Kars, Ghani, 1914 ♦ Anush Hakobi Alaverdyan, Pambak, Dostlu, 1917 ♦ Anush Hambardzumi Grigoryan, Kars, Ghzl-chakhchakh, 1913 ♦ Anush Hayrapeti Hovhannisyan, Hin Nakhijevan, Ghazanchi, 1908 ♦ Anush Hovhani Gasparyan, Batum, Tandzut, 1909 ♦ Anush Hovhannesi Hovakimyan, Kars, Ardahan, 1917 ♦ Anush Hovhannesi Hovhannisyan, Khnus, Berd, 1915 ♦ Anush Karapeti Andreasyan, Basin, Dalibapay, 1909 ♦ Anush Karushi Tadevosyan, Yerevan, Dashlanghshlagh, 1921 ♦ Anush Martirosi Martirosyan, Kars, Gitalu, 1912 ♦ Anush Martirosi Vardanyan, Aparan Imuli, 1912 ♦ Anush Meliki Melikyan, Van, Archegh, 1907 ♦ Anush Mikayeli Hakobyan, Nakhijevan, Norashen, 1908 ♦ Anush Mkrtchi Grigoryan, Kars, Pirvali, 1910 ♦ Anush Mkrtchi Hakobyan, Surmalu, Blur, 1909 ♦ Anush Movsesi Movsisyan, Van, 1912 ♦ Anush Nikoli Yeghiazaryan (Nikolyan), Darachichak, Kaghot, 1911 ♦ Anush Nshani Martirosyan, Karin, Agrak, 1910 ♦ Anush Poghosi Poghosyan, Bulangh, Hognuk, 1912 ♦ Anush Safari Poghosyan, Bulangh, Rostom-Gyodak, 1910 ♦ Anush Sargsi Sargsyan, Khnus, Aros, 1909 ♦ Anush Sedraki Sedrakyan, Mush, Krdagom, 1915 ♦ Anush Sirakani Manukyan, Nor Bayazet, Kyosamahmed, 1913 ♦ Anush Smbati Mkrtchyan, Alekpol, Illi, 1916 ♦ Anush Smbati Stepanyan, Yerevan, Nakhijevan, 1912 ♦ Anush Soghomoni Soghomonyan (Martirosyan), Alashkert, Gharakilisa, 1909 ♦ Anush Stepani Stepanyan, Van, 1911 ♦ Anush Stepani Vardanyan, Nakhijevan, Shekhmahmud, 1912 ♦ Anush Stepanyan, 1922 ♦ Anushavan Arami Aramyan, Shirak, Toros gyugh, 1916 ♦ Anushavan Arami Hakobyan (Ustyan), Kars, Pirvali, 1909 ♦ Anushavan Arami Khashkalyan, Kars, Uzunkilisa, 1913 ♦ Anushavan Arshaki Arshakyan, Shirak, Daharlu, 1915 ♦ Anushavan Arsheni Khachatryan, Alekpol, 1908 ♦ Anushavan Bakhshii Arzumanyan, Karabagh, Shushi, 1916 ♦ Anushavan Gevorgi Ghazaryan, Hin Nakhijevan, Noragjugh, 1915 ♦ Anushavan Ginosi Khachatryan, Kars, Kaghzvan, 1911 ♦ Anushavan Grigori Grigoryan, Leninakan, Jalab, 1917 ♦ Anushavan Grigori Grigoryan, Leninakan, Saribash, 1918 ♦ Anushavan Hakobi Baghdasaryan, Shamakhi, 1912 ♦ Anushavan Hakobi Mikayelyan, Lori, Haghpat, 1913 ♦ Anushavan Hamboyi Hambaryan, Alekpol, Bangivan, 1916 ♦ Anushavan Harutyuni Malazyan, Van, 1911 ♦ Anushavan Karapeti Kirakosyan, Alekpol, Maymajugh, 1909 ♦ Anushavan Karoyi Karoyan, Gharakilisa, Parni gyugh, 1916 ♦ Anushavan Khachaturi Vardevanyan, Kars, Cbni, 1911 ♦ Anushavan Kirakosi Barseghyan, Kars, Hamzakarak, 1912 ♦ Anushavan Madoyi Martirosyan, Akhalkalak, Chzghlar, 1912 ♦ Anushavan Manuki Vanecyan, Kaghzvan, 1912 ♦ Anushavan Martirosi Martirosyan, Nakhijevan, Parabar, 1915 ♦ Anushavan Martirosi Sahakyan, Nakhijevan, 1913 ♦ Anushavan Meliki Hayroyan, Shirak, Boghazkan, 1914 ♦ Anushavan Mesropi Aramyan (Artavazyan), Van, 1915 ♦ Anushavan Mesropi Sargsyan, Surmalu, Taghburun, 1909 ♦ Anushavan Mkrtchi Hakobyan (Mkrtchyan), Alekpol, Ghapli, 1914 ♦ Anushavan Mkrtchi Hayrikyan, Shatakh, 1914 ♦ Anushavan Mkrtchi Mkrtchyan, Gharakilisa, Chotur, 1916 ♦ Anushavan Mkrtchi Tadevosyan, Leninakan, Ghonakhran, 1913 ♦ Anushavan Nazari Torosyan, Hin Nakhijevan, 1914 ♦ Anushavan Petrosi Gevorgyan, Van, 1909 ♦ Anushavan Petrosi Petrosyan, Leninakan, Sogyutli,

1912 ♦ Anushavan Sahaki Sahakyan, Tavriz, 1916 ♦ Anushavan Samsoni Serobyan, Kars, Voghuzli, 1915 ♦ Anushavan Sedraki Galstyan, Alekpol, Ghzlghoch, 1914 ♦ Anushavan Sedraki Vardanyan, Kars, Kyodaklar, 1914 ♦ Anushavan Simoni Simonyan, Aparan, Ghashchi, 1912 ♦ Anushavan Smbati Karapetyan, Alekpol, Svanverdi, 1914 ♦ Anushavan Stepani Hovhannisyan, Van, Nor gyugh, 1912 ♦ Anushavan Sukiasi Gevorgyan, Aleksandropol, Svanverdi 1914 ♦ Anushavan Tadevosi Yeghiazaryan, Sardarabad, 1914 ♦ Anushavan Tatosi Davtyan, Shirak, Haji nazar, 1911 ♦ Anushavan Tovmasi Sahakyan, Van, Boghazkyasan, 1912 ♦ Anushavan Vagharshaki Smbatyan, Nakhijevan, Noso, 1911 ♦ Anushavan Vahani Vahanyan, Kaghzvan, 1913 ♦ Anushavan Vardani Vardanyan, Etchmiadzin, Inakli, 1910 ♦ Anushavan Yeghiazari Martirosyan, Bitlis, Mush, 1907 ♦ Anushik Avetisi Sahakyan, Kars, Bagrahan, 1914 ♦ Anushik Avetisi Shakaryan, Van, 1913 ♦ Anushik Mamikoni Hakhnazaryan, Surmali Igdir, 1915 ♦ Anushik Mkrtchi Hovhannisyan, Kars, Pvik, 1912 ♦ Anushka Torosi Ghambaryan, Kars, Ghorkhana, 1914 ♦ Anzhel Khachiki Petrosyan (Khachikyan), Van, 1913 ♦ Anzhel Tigrani Tigranyan, Van, 1914 ♦ Anzhela Ispiryan, 1920 ♦ Apreshum Garegini Gareginyan (Apreshumyan), Bulanagh, Koghak, 1912 ♦ Aprshum Amirkhani Amirkhanyan, Mush, Aghzud, 1912 ♦ Ara-Geghetsik Ghevondi Ispiryan, Akhalkalak, Satkha, 1915 ♦ Arabi Karapeti Manukyan, Kars, Chala, 1910 ♦ Arabkhan Arami Voskanyan, Erzrum, Dzandzakh, 1912 ♦ Arakel Avetisi Tigranyan, Van, 1908 ♦ Arakel Baghdasari Tovmasyan, Bitlis, Yekmal, 1913 ♦ Arakel Barseghi Manukyan, Sarighamish, Charasun, 1910 ♦ Arakel Gaspari Manukyan, Alashkert, Hin Bayazet, 1912 ♦ Arakel Gaspari Poghosyan, Manazkert, Berd, 1912 ♦ Arakel Gevorgi Gasparyan, Akhalkalak, Gandza, 1914 ♦ Arakel Ghambari Depoyan, Alekpol, Gharamahmad, 1914 ♦ Arakel Ghukasi Ghukasyan, Van, 1911 ♦ Arakel Harutyuni Muradyan, Mush, Bostankand, 1911 ♦ Arakel Hghlati Muradyan, Mush, Hamzashen, 1908 ♦ Arakel Israyeli Petrosyan, Bitlis, Karmnjlu, 1908 ♦ Arakel Karapeti Baghdasaryan, Alchavaz, Fazokh, 1907 ♦ Arakel Khachaturi Poghosyan, Manazkert, Sultanlu, 1910 ♦ Arakel Khosrovi Kosrovyan, Bitliz, 1913 ♦ Arakel Misaki Misakyan, Erzrum, Kopal, 1910 ♦ Arakel Mkhitari Sargsyan (Manukyan), Bulanagh, Gharaghl, 1909, 1907 ♦ Arakel Mkrtchi Mkrtchyan, Mush, Gomer, 1914 ♦ Arakel Musheghi Tonoyan, Bulanagh, Gharaghl, 1912 ♦ Arakel Nazareti Nazaretyan, Khnus, Yayi, 1912 ♦ Arakel Sahaki Arakelyan, Kars, Khaschifrlik, 1912 ♦ Arakel Sargsi Sargsyan, Archesh, Kozer, 1913 ♦ Arakel Sargsi Sargsyan, Mush, Yaragh, 1916 ♦ Arakel Soghomoni Martirosyan (Soghomonyan), Alashkert, Mangasar, 1910 ♦ Araks Barseghi Petanyan, Akhalkalak, Karcakh, 1910 ♦ Araks Tadevosi Gasparyan, Alekpol, Khli Gharakilisa, 1916 ♦ Araks Yenoki Minasyan, Gharakilisa, Darband, 1914 ♦ Arakse Aleki Ghazaryan, Alekpol, Gyuli budagh, 1910 ♦ Araksi (Anush) Martirosi Melikyan, Kars, Kyurakdar, 1911 ♦ Araksi Abgari Afrikyan, Kaghzvan, 1908 ♦ Araksi Abrahami Abrahamyan (Avgalyan), 1913 ♦ Araksi Abrahami Madoyan, Kars, Kyadiklar, 1914 ♦ Araksi Aleksani Grigoryan (Aleksanyan), Shirak, Ghonakhghran, 1914 ♦ Araksi Andreasi Seyranyan, Karabagh, Shushi, 1911 ♦ Araksi Arakeli Arakelyan, Alashkert, Bastur, 1917 ♦ Araksi Arami Harutyunyan, Van, 1909 ♦ Araksi Aristakesi Hovhannisyan, Kars, Syogutlu, 1912 ♦ Araksi Arshaki Hambaryan, Shirak, Chrakhli, 1914 ♦ Araksi Arshaki Minasyan, Sarighamish, 1913 ♦ Araksi Arshaki Vardanyan, Kars, Aksi Ghaza, 1912 ♦ Araksi Artashi Harutyunyan, Kars, Bash-Katiklar, 1915 ♦ Araksi Avagi Avetisyan, Kars, Tazakyand, 1911 ♦ Araksi Avetisi Grigoryan, Kars, Uzunkilise, 1915 ♦ Araksi Baghdasari Baghdasaryan, Van, 1915 ♦ Araksi Baghdasari Muradyan, Tokat, 1912 ♦ Araksi Barseghi Movsisyan, Akhalkalak, Dadez, 1912 ♦ Araksi Elbaki Hakobyan, Kars, Gorkhana, 1912 ♦ Araksi Gabrieli Sargsyan, Alekpol, Horom, 1912 ♦ Araksi Galusti Galstyan, Lori, Sanahin, 1918 ♦ Araksi Gevorgi Gevorgyan, 1914 ♦ Araksi Gevorgi Hunanyan, Russia, Tsaritsin, 1912 ♦ Araksi Gevorgi Shakhbazyan, Kaghzvan, 1912 ♦ Araksi Ghazari Zakaryan, Kars, Pokr Parkir, 1919 ♦ Araksi Grigori Grigoryan, Van, 1909 ♦ Araksi Grigori Sargsyan, Kars, Ghzlchakhchakh, 1914 ♦ Araksi Hakobi Gapoyan, Ardahan, 1915 ♦ Araksi Hakobi Hakobyan, Alekpol, Bashgegh, 1914 ♦ Araksi Hakobi Hakobyan, Alekpol, Bozyokhush, 1914 ♦ Araksi Hakobi Hakobyan, Kars, Pirvali, 1912, 1911 ♦ Araksi Hakobi Harutyunyan, Leninakan, 1911 ♦ Araksi Hakobi Karapetyan, Kars, Sarighamish, 1915 ♦ Araksi Hakobi Vonopyan, Akhaltsikhe, 1910 ♦ Araksi Hambardzumi Hakobyan (Hambardzumyan, Alekpol, Ghzlghoch, 1917 ♦ Araksi Hambardzumi Hakobyan, Igdir, Margare, 1912 ♦ Araksi Hambari Avoyan, Leninakan, Bandivan, 1911 ♦ Araksi Harutyuni Galstyan, Alekpol, Kharkov, 1910 ♦ Araksi Harutyuni Harutyunyan, Erzrum, Dali-baba, 1916 ♦ Araksi Harutyuni Harutyunyan, Tpkhis, 1915 ♦ Araksi Hmayaki Sukiasyan, Akhalkalak, 1913 ♦ Araksi Hovhannesi Hovhannisyan, Alekpol, Ghaplu, 1918 ♦ Araksi Hovhannesi Karapetyan, Kars, Ghzl-chakhchakh, 1909 ♦ Araksi Hovhannesi Yeghiazaryan, Yerevan, 1918 ♦ Araksi Karapeti Nazaryan, Kars, Bashshoragal, 1911 ♦ Araksi Karapeti Vardanyan, Van, Shushants, 1907 ♦ Araksi Khachaturi Karapetyan, Kars, Pervali, 1907 ♦ Araksi Khachaturi Khachatryan, Leninakan, Gheyghach, 1914 ♦ Araksi Kyureghi Kyureghyan, Akhalkalak, Hoshtaver, 1916 ♦ Araksi Maksimi Hovsepyan, Baku, Karabagh, 1911 ♦ Araksi Malkhasi Malkhasyan, Kars, Gharkhana, 1913 ♦ Araksi Manuki Ghazaryan, Kars, Agarak, 1917 ♦ Araksi Manuki Minasyan, Kars, Berna, 1916 ♦ Araksi Manuki Sahakyan, Erzrum, Ishkha, 1912 ♦ Araksi Manuki Yeghoyan (Manukyan), Leninakan, Pokr Beti, 1917 ♦ Araksi Margari Martirosyan (Torosyan), Sarighamish, Armtlu, 1916 ♦ Araksi Martirosi Ghazaryan, Gharakilisa, Aghbuagh, 1915 ♦ Araksi Martirosi Martirosyan, Hin Bayazet, Arcap, 1910 ♦ Araksi Martirosi Sargsyan, Leninakan, Kyorakdar, 1912 ♦ Araksi Martirosi Yeghiazaryan, Sarighamish, Bashgyugh, 1909 ♦ Araksi Matevosi Matevosyan, Alekpol, Tashlaghshlagh, 1909 ♦ Araksi

Matiki Ghazaryan, Alekpol, Ghonaghlran, 1909 ♦ Araksi Meliki Ispiryan, Alekpol, Mahmudjugh, 1913 ♦ Araksi Meliki Melikyan, Alekpol, Aghghula, 1917 ♦ Araksi Misaki Khachatryan, Kars, Gorkhana, 1914 ♦ Araksi Misaki Misakyan, Alekpol, Mastara, 1916 ♦ Araksi Mkrtchi Ayvazyan, Kars, Kyatiklar, 1911 ♦ Araksi Mkrtchi Mkrtchyan, Leninakan, Norashen, 1914 ♦ Araksi Mnatsakani Mnatsakanyan, Erzrum, 1909 ♦ Araksi Movsesi Kostanyan, Kars, Oghzlu, 1912 ♦ Araksi Nikoli Margaryan, Nor Bayazet, Pashakend, 1914 ♦ Araksi Nikoli Nikolyan, Alekpol, Sirvangjugh, 1916 ♦ Araksi Petrosi Manukyan (Petrosyan), Yerevan, Bzhni, 1910 ♦ Araksi Petrosi Papikyan, Leninakan, Gharakilisa, 1916 ♦ Araksi Poghosi Poghosyan, Akhta, Makravank, 1914 ♦ Araksi Rubeni Ghazaryan, Kars, Bashkadiklar, 1912 ♦ Araksi Rubeni Pluzyan, Van, 1909 ♦ Araksi Sahaki Karapetyan, Lori, Bzovdara, 1914 ♦ Araksi Sargsi Khachatryan, Shirak, Tagmalu, 1919 ♦ Araksi Sargsi Sargsyan, Leninakan, Duzkharaba, 1912 ♦ Araksi Sargsi Sargsyan, Vagharshapat, Voghakan, 1914 ♦ Araksi Saroyi Sargsyan, Alekpol, Babslu, 1917 ♦ Araksi Sergoyi Khachatryan, Kars, Parker, 1913 ♦ Araksi Sergoyi Kondyan, Akhalkalak, Mets Khanchalu, 1911 ♦ Araksi Serobi Manukyan, Kaghzvan, 1910 ♦ Araksi Shavarshi Ghukasyan, Pambak, Taparlu, 1912 ♦ Araksi Simoni Asatryan, Akhalkalak, 1913 ♦ Araksi Simoni Karapetyan, Kars, Ughuzlu, 1911 ♦ Araksi Smbati Pepoyan, Nakhijevan, Tazakand, 1916 ♦ Araksi Tigrani Karapetyan, Kars, Paldrvan, 1912 ♦ Araksi Torosi Tonakanyan, Akhalkalak, Dilif, 1912 ♦ Araksi Vahani Gevorgyan, Leninakan, Chzghlar, 1913 ♦ Araksi Volodyayi Avetisyan, Alekpol, Aghin, 1910 ♦ Araksi Yegori Yegoryan (Mkrtchyan), Alekpol, Samrlu, 1917 ♦ Araksi Yenoki Pilosyan, Kars, Mec Parker, 1910 ♦ Araksi Yeremi Movsisyan, Igdir, 1914 ♦ Araksi Yervandi Hakobyan, Kars, Pirali, 1911 ♦ Araksi Yervandi Nikoghosyan, Sarighamish, Armatli, 1908 ♦ Araksi Zakari Hovhannisyan, Kars, Perval, 1909 ♦ Araksi Zohrabi Manukyan, Alekpol, Ghighaj, 1912 ♦ Araksia Gogori Zakaryan, Leninakan, Ghanlika, 1915 ♦ Araksia Hamayaki Serobyan, Alekpol, Takghala, 1913 ♦ Araksya Arshaki Minasyan, Alekpol, Yeganlar, 1911 ♦ Araksya Shoghakati Davtyan, Alekpol, Hajinazar, 1913 ♦ Aram Abrahami Shahbazyan, Shirak, Bandrvan, 1913 ♦ Aram Arakeli Arakelyan, Mush, Kop, 1911, 1909 ♦ Aram Arakeli Mnatsakanyan, Karen, Yeghan, 1911 ♦ Aram Arakeli Petrosyan (Arakelyan), Basen, chorasan, 1914 ♦ Aram Arshaki Arshakyan, Van, Berkri, 1914 ♦ Aram Arshaki Petrosyan, Shirak, Ghoshavank, 1912 ♦ Aram Artashesi Hovhannisyan, Sarighamish, Shadivan, 1914 ♦ Aram Aspoyi Aspoyan, Van, Dzkor, 1912 ♦ Aram Avetisi Hakobyan, Zangezur, Goris, 1912 ♦ Aram Avetisi Mkrtchyan, Kars, Baglamar, 1909 ♦ Aram Avetisi Papovyan, Kars, Kaghzvan, 1912 ♦ Aram Ayvazi Harutyunyan, Shirak, Gheghaj, 1912 ♦ Aram Baghdasari Poghosyan, Gandzak, 1916 ♦ Aram Danieli Kirakosyan, Khlat, Prkhus, 1912 ♦ Aram Gabrieli Ferjulyan, Van, 1910 ♦ Aram Garegini Gareginyan, Van, Birdak, 1911 ♦ Aram Gevorgi Arakelyan, Alashkert, Ghayabek, 1910 ♦ Aram Gevorgi Damurjyan (Minasyan), Van, 1912 ♦ Aram Ghazari Ghazaryan (Mosoyan), Mush, Khut, 1911 ♦ Aram Ghazari Harutyunyan,Van, Karkar, 1910 ♦ Aram Ghukasi Ghukasyan (Muradyan), Bulanagh, Teghut, 1912 ♦ Aram Grigori Grigoryan, Kars, Kars, 1916 ♦ Aram Grigori Melkonyan, Basen, Chrason, 1914 ♦ Aram Grigori Nikoyan (Eloyan), Basen, Dali-baba, 1914 ♦ Aram Grigori Vardanyan, Kars, Kadiklar, 1912 ♦ Aram Hakobi Galstyan, Van, Bozer, 1912 ♦ Aram Hakobi Khlghatyan, Basen, Akrak, 1912 ♦ Aram Hakobi Mkrtchyan, Erzrum, Basghojay, 1914 ♦ Aram Hambardzumi Grigoryan, Nakhijevan, Gyumri, 1914 ♦ Aram Hamzaspi Grigoryan, Alekpol, Bashkadiklar, 1914 ♦ Aram Hazroyi Sargsyan, Akhlat, Khyartak, 1912 ♦ Aram Hmayaki Khachatryan, Alekpol, 1913 ♦ Aram Hovakimi Davtyan, Van, Norduz, 1911 ♦ Aram Hovakimi Hovakimyan, Daralaghyaz, Sultan Bek, 1912 ♦ Aram Hovhannesi Gevorgyan, Erzrum, 1914 ♦ Aram Hovhannesi Hovhannisyan, Van, Urants, 1912 ♦ Aram Hovhannesi Mikayelyan, Baku, Gandzak, 1913 ♦ Aram Hovhannesi Mkrtchyan, Alekpol, Maymujagh, 1912 ♦ Aram Hovhannesi Muradyan, Kars, 1911 ♦ Aram Hovsepi Saratyan, Bitlis, Baghesh, 1914 ♦ Aram Karapeti Barseghyan, Kars, 1911 ♦ Aram Karapeti Muradyan, Sasun, Hazlo, 1912 ♦ Aram Karapeti Parikyan, Van, 1914 ♦ Aram Karapeti Sahakyan, Zangezur, Alkhadia, 1917 ♦ Aram Khachaturi Arakelyan, Alekpol, Aghin, 1912 ♦ Aram Khachaturi Khachatryan, Erzrum, Kyoprikey, 1914 ♦ Aram Khachaturi Khachatryan, Van, Andzav, 1914 ♦ Aram Khachaturi Musheghyan, Sarighamish, Agarak, 1912 ♦ Aram Levoni Saponchyan, Akhaltsikha, Tsurghut, 1914 ♦ Aram Makari Gevorgyan, Alekpol, Tiknis, 1913 ♦ Aram Manuki Asaturyan, Van, 1911 ♦ Aram Manuki Bashgarontsyan, Van, 1913 ♦ Aram Manuki Manukyan, Basen, Armtlu, 1916 ♦ Aram Manuki Torosyan (Hovhannisyan), Kars, Bayburt, 1912 ♦ Aram Matosi Mkrtchyan, Alekpol, Bashgyugh, 1911 ♦ Aram Melkoni Davtyan, Shirak, Ortakilisa, 1913 ♦ Aram Melkoni Melkonyan, Manazkert, Rostom-Kedak, 1910 ♦ Aram Mikayeli Hovhannisyan, Leninakan, Hachikhalil, 1912 ♦ Aram Misaki Danielyan, Erzrum, Kghi, 1914 ♦ Aram Misaki Melkonyan, Kars, 1912 ♦ Aram Mkhitari Stepanyan (Mkhitaryan), Van, Moks, 1907 ♦ Aram Mkrtchi Grigoryan (Mkrtchyan), Van, Sevan, 1912 ♦ Aram Mkrtchi Martirosyan, Alekpol, Bozdoghan, 1912 ♦ Aram Movsesi Movsisyan, Kaghzvan, 1916 ♦ Aram Muradi Muradyan, Bitliz, 1910 ♦ Aram Muradi Muradyan, Van, 1912 ♦ Aram Musheghi Musheghyan, Yerevan, Makravank, 1911 ♦ Aram Nahapeti Sakoyan, Kars, 1917 ♦ Aram Nersesi Mikayelyan, Kars, 1914 ♦ Aram Nikoli Khachatryan, Alekpol, Sariar, 1916 ♦ Aram Petrosi Barseghyan (Petrosyan), Van, Mokhraberd, 1912, 1911 ♦ Aram Petrosi Hakobyan, Van, Norshnjgh, 1911, 1916 ♦ Aram Petrosi Hovhannisyan, Bitlis, Khushik, 1911 ♦ Aram Petrosi Nersisyan (Petrosyan), Darachichak, Makravank, 1911 ♦ Aram Sahaki Hovhannisyan, Leninakan, Aghin, 1910 ♦ Aram Sargsi Tonoyan, Kars, Bashkadiklar, 1905 ♦ Aram Sedraki Melkonyan, Akhalkalak, Vareva, 1912,

1911 ♦ Aram Shaheni Shahinyan, Van, Kaskas, 1912 ♦ Aram Smbati Grigoryan, Alekpol, Bayandur, 1912 ♦ Aram Smbati Karapetyan, Alekpol, Ghoshavank, 1913 ♦ Aram Tatosi Sargsyan, Archesh, Ktrackar, 1912 ♦ Aram Torosi Khachatryan, Kars, Ghoshavank, 1911 ♦ Aram Tovmasi Tovmasyan, Sasun, Spghank, 1909 ♦ Aram Tukhoyi Tukhoyan, Van, Akhorik, 1913, 1911 ♦ Aram Vanoyi Simonyan, Van, 1911 ♦ Aram Vardani Sheroyants (Malkhasyan), Shirak, Melikkyand, 1912 ♦ Aram Yeghoyi Yeghoyan, Van, Norashen, 1910 ♦ Aram Yeremi Melkonyan, Gharakilisa, Spitak, 1912 ♦ Aram Zakari Zakaryan, Kars, Syogutlu, 1917 ♦ Aramayis Andreasi Poghosyan, Etchmiadzin, 1913 ♦ Aramayis Arshaki Mkrtchyan, Shirak, Kyalal, 1812 ♦ Aramayis Artashesi Harutyunyan, Alekpol, Svanverdi, 1911 ♦ Aramayis Avetisi Ter-Arakelyan, Kaghzvan, 1912 ♦ Aramayis Badoyi Minasyan, Alekpol, Jajur, 1914 ♦ Aramayis Garegini Baghdasaryan, Van, 1910 ♦ Aramayis Geghami Hovhannisyan, Talin, Mastara, 1915 ♦ Aramayis Geghami Khachatryan, Yerevan, Narvzlu, 1912 ♦ Aramayis Gharakhani Azoyan, Basin, Kotanlu, 1916 ♦ Aramayis Grigori Grigoryan, Mets Gharakilisa, 1914 ♦ Aramayis Grigori Grigoryan, Yerevan, 1914 ♦ Aramayis Hakobi Hakobyan, Igdir, Alkzl, 1912, 1911 ♦ Aramayis Hakobi Hakobyan, Jalaloghli, Ashkyorpi, 1914 ♦ Aramayis Hambardzumi Hovhannisyan, Igdir, Alighamur, 1911 ♦ Aramayis Harutyuni Garunyan (Karanyan), Alekpol, 1912 ♦ Aramayis Hmayaki Hamoyan, Alekpol, Ghpchakh, 1912 ♦ Aramayis Hovhannesi Mikayelyan, Kars, 1918 ♦ Aramayis Hovhannesi Stamboltsyan, Akhalkalak, Khanchal, 1911 ♦ Aramayis Karapeti Khachatryan (Karapetyan), Etchmiadzin, Mastara, 1911 ♦ Aramayis Khachaturi Khachatryan, Kars, 1914 ♦ Aramayis Knyazi Simonyan, Erzrum, 1914 ♦ Aramayis Kvoyi Kvoyan, Bulanakh, Yonjala, 1918 ♦ Aramayis Matevosi Gevorgyan, Kars, 1909 ♦ Aramayis Misaki Bezhanyan, Gyokchay, Ghalagoz, 1914 ♦ Aramayis Mkrtchi Baghdasaryan, Kars, 1911 ♦ Aramayis Nikoli Melkonyan, Alekpol, Ghrkhtagerman, 1914 ♦ Aramayis Sahaki Sahakyan, Kotayq, Bash, 1913 ♦ Aramayis Sargsi Minasyan, Alashkert, Yonjalu, 1912 ♦ Aramayis Sargsi Mkrtchyan, Yerevan, Darachichak, 1909 ♦ Aramayis Saroyi Harutyunyan, Shirak, Svanverdi, 1912 ♦ Aramayis Simoni Avagyan, Darachichak, Solak, 1912 ♦ Aramayis Simoni Baghdasaryan, Kars, 1911 ♦ Aramayis Smbati Karapetyan, Alekpol, Svanverdi, 1913 ♦ Aramayis Smbati Shekoyan, Jajur, 1914 ♦ Aramayis Stepani Simonyan, Kars, 1912 ♦ Aramayis Tadevosi Tadevosyan, Alekpol, Toros gyugh, 1912 ♦ Aramayis Tigrani Tigranyan (Manukyan), Nakhijevan, 1917 ♦ Aramayis Vagharshaki Kirakosyan, Alekpol, Givlibulagh, 1913 ♦ Aramayis Varagi Gevorgyan, Alekpol, Ghazarapat, 1915 ♦ Aramayis Yeghiazari Yeghiazaryan (Sargsyan), Surmalu, Koghb, 1913 ♦ Aramayis Yeghishei Mkrtchyan, Bulanagh, Kop, 1918 ♦ Aramayis Yeremi Mkrtchyan, Echmiacin, Byurakan, 1912 ♦ Aramayis Zakari Hovhannisyan (Zakaryan), Kars, Pirvali, 1917 ♦ Aranas Simoni Simonyan, Akhalkalak, Diliska, 1914 ♦ Araqsi Karapeti Manukyan, Kars, 1919 ♦ Ararat Arshaki Ginosyan, Alekpol, Taliboghli, 1912 ♦ Ararat Hakobi Hovhannisyan, Alekpol, 1912 ♦ Ararat Hovhannesi Kocharyan, Leninakan, Dzithankov, 1914 ♦ Ararat Hunani Manukyan, Alekpol, Mahmatjugh, 1912 ♦ Ararat Mikhaili Sargsyan, Leninakan, Gharakilisa, 1913 ♦ Ararat Mkrtchi Avetisyan, Hin Bayazet, 1912 ♦ Ararat Mkrtchi Choloyan, Shirak, Syogutli, 1914 ♦ Ararat Mkrtchi Martirosyan, Kars, Gharaghala, 1910 ♦ Ararat Nazareti Nikoghosyan, Shirak, Toros, 1911 ♦ Ararat Soghomoni Barseghyan, Kars, Svanverdi, 1913 ♦ Ararat Toni Abrahamyan (Khachatryan), Nor Bayazet, Basargechar, 1908 ♦ Arcrun Garegini Vardanyan, Ghamarlu, Aligamar, 1917 ♦ Arcruni Galusti Galstyan, Alashkert, 1918 ♦ Arcvik Danieli Grigoryan (Karapetyan), Manazkert, Gharaghala, 1908 ♦ Arcvik Droyi Iashakyan, Surmalu, Igdir, 1913 ♦ Arcvik Grigori Manukyan, Akhalkalak, Suldar, 1916 ♦ Arcvik Khachaturi Barseghyan, Surmalu, Igdir, 1914 ♦ Arcvik Poghosi Poghosyan, Kaghzvan, 1918 ♦ Arcvik Stepani Hambardzumyan, Persia, Gharadagh, 1917 ♦ Arcvik Stepani Ter-Mkrtchyan, Goghdan, Akulis, 1914 ♦ Ardar Sargsi Sargsyan, Erzrum, Terjan, 1914 ♦ Areg Khachaturi Khachatryan, Ghamarlu, Tapabash, 1914 ♦ Areg Setoyi Grigoryan, Mush, Mgragom, 1914 ♦ Aregnaz Abeli Abelyan, Van, Baykhnir, 1910 ♦ Aregnaz Abraham Sahakyan, Kars, Paldrvan, 1912 ♦ Aregnaz Abrahami Sargsyan, Archesh, 1908 ♦ Aregnaz Aleksani Aleksanyan, Shirak, Gizlu, 1909 ♦ Aregnaz Aleksani Mkrtchyan, Yerevan, Alapars, 1911 ♦ Aregnaz Anushavani Abrahamyan (Anushavanyan), Kaghzvan, Karabagh, 1913 ♦ Aregnaz Arakeli Barseghyan, Kars, 1907 ♦ Aregnaz Arshaki Pashayants (Arshakyan), Kokhi, 1913 ♦ Aregnaz Danieli Poghosyan, Bulanagh, Rustam-gedak, 1909 ♦ Aregnaz Davti Davtyan, Gharakilisa, Ghshlagh, 1917 ♦ Aregnaz Galusti Abrahamyan, Kars, Nakhijevan, 1908 ♦ Aregnaz Galusti Galstyan, Basen, Dali-baba, 1914 ♦ Aregnaz Galusti Galstyan, Sarighamish, Gharakilisa, 1909 ♦ Aregnaz Gayanei (Khosrovi) Sargsyan, Van, Avirak, 1910 ♦ Aregnaz Gevorgi Gevorgyan, Khnus, 1910 ♦ Aregnaz Gevorgi Gevorgyan, Van, Jank, 1913 ♦ Aregnaz Ghazari Poghosyan, Basen, Izviran, 1914 ♦ Aregnaz Grigori Amirkhanyan, Bayburt, 1912 ♦ Aregnaz Hakobi Hakobyan, Van, 1910 ♦ Aregnaz Harutyuni Avetisyan, Alekpol, Illi, 1913 ♦ Aregnaz Harutyuni Baloyants, Kars, Marza, 1908 ♦ Aregnaz Hovhannesi Asatryan, Kars, Pirvali, 1910 ♦ Aregnaz Hovhannesi Ghazaryan, Manaskert, Noradi, 1912 ♦ Aregnaz Hovhannesi Hovhannisyan, Khnus, Berd, 1912 ♦ Aregnaz Hovhannesi Hovhannisyan, Shirak, Gharakilisa, 1914 ♦ Aregnaz Hovhannesi Sirakanyan, Alekpol, Svanverdi, 1915 ♦ Aregnaz Hovsepi Grigoryan, Van, Aljavaz, 1914 ♦ Aregnaz Karapeti Aharonyan, Karabagh, Shushi, 1911 ♦ Aregnaz Khachaturi Alaverdyan (Khachatryan), Kars, 1911 ♦ Aregnaz Khachaturi Sarukhanyan, Nakhijevan, Damrzdan, 1915 ♦ Aregnaz Makari Avetisyan, Sasun, Kajaran, 1907 ♦ Aregnaz Manuki Mkrtchyan, Alashkert, Khazlu, 1909 ♦ Aregnaz Meliki Dalukyan, Mec Gharakilisa, Hajipar, 1915 ♦ Aregnaz Mikayeli Mkhitaryan, Kars, Uzunkilisa,

1909 ◆ Aregnaz Mkhitari Avetisyan, Leninakan, Arkhvali, 1913 ◆ Aregnaz Mkhitari Hovhannisyan, Khnus, 1914 ◆ Aregnaz Mkrtchi Markosyan, (Manukyan), Kars, Nakhijevan, 1912 ◆ Aregnaz Mkrtchi Martirosyan, Kars, Bazrgyan, 1908 ◆ Aregnaz Mkrtchi Mkrtchyan, Basen, Yaghan, 1917 ◆ Aregnaz Mkrtichi Sargsyan, Nakhijevan, 1908 ◆ Aregnaz Nersesi Nersisyan (Manukyan), Leninakan, Boghazkyasan, 1910 ◆ Aregnaz Papiki Gasparyan, Alekpol, Bozyoghash, 1913 ◆ Aregnaz Petrosi Grigoryan (Petrosyan), Erzrum, 1908 ◆ Aregnaz Petrosi Muradyan, Bitlis, 1911 ◆ Aregnaz Petrosi Petrosyan, Kars, Bagara, 1912 ◆ Aregnaz Poghosi Poghosyan, Manazkert, 1915 ◆ Aregnaz Sahaki Elbakyan, Basen, Stahan, 1912 ◆ Aregnaz Sahaki Sahakyan, Persia, Salmast, 1910 ◆ Aregnaz Sargsi Muradyan, Kars, Paldrvan, 1912, 1910 ◆ Aregnaz Sedraki Grigoryan, Kars, Dirbandl, 1911 ◆ Aregnaz Sedraki Vardanyan, Alashkert, Chldrghan, 1912 ◆ Aregnaz Serobi Hovhannisyan, Bitlis, 1909 ◆ Aregnaz Smbati Manukyan, Kars, Kotiksatlmish, 1916 ◆ Aregnaz Tatosi Tumasyan, Kars, Bagrahamat, 1915 ◆ Aregnaz Vahani Madoyan, Alekpol, Dashlaghshlagh, 1912 ◆ Aregnaz Vardani Zakaryan, Kars, Tazakand, 1910, 1909 ◆ Aregnaz Vasili Vasilyan, Dilijan, Jarkhet, 1912 ◆ Aregnaz Yeghiazari Gevorgyan, Alekpol, Aghin, 1909 ◆ Aregnaz Yeghiki Margaryan, Kars, Berni, 1912 ◆ Aregnaz Abrahami Shahbazyan, Alekpol, Paldrvan, 1911 ◆ Aregnazan Antoni Ghazaryan (Antonyan), Leninakan, Bandrvan, 1915 ◆ Aregnazan Armenaki Sahakyan, Kars, Bakldahmat, 1917 ◆ Aregnazan Avetisi Ghazaryan, Basen, Archarak, 1914 ◆ Aregnazan Baghdasari Baghdasaryan, Mokac, 1913 ◆ Aregnazan Barseghi Sargsyan, Kars, Chermali, 1910 ◆ Aregnazan Gevorgi Gevorgyan, Nor Bayazet, Norataz, 1913 ◆ Aregnazan Ghazari Minasyan, Mush, Taghavni, 1910 ◆ Aregnazan Harutyuni Harutyunyan, Ballanakh, Hatkon, 1916 ◆ Aregnazan Hovhannesi Abrahamyan, Mush, Bulanagh, 1916, 1914 ◆ Aregnazan Hovhannesi Hovhannisyan, Kars, 1921 ◆ Aregnazan Khachaturi Khachatryan, Van, Kozak, 1914 ◆ Aregnazan Melkoni Hovhannisyan, Mush, Badnoc, 1909 ◆ Aregnazan Mesropi Mesropyan, Mush, Khas-gyugh, 1912 ◆ Aregnazan Misaki Misakyan, Sarighamish, 1914 ◆ Aregnazan Musheghi Musheghyan, Bulanagh, Khoshgyaldi, 1914, ◆ Aregnazan Sargsi Sargsyan, Bulanagh, Kop, 1911 ◆ Aregnazan Saroyi Saroyan, Kars, Bashshoragyal, 1918 ◆ Aregnazan Sedraki Avagyan, Erzrum, Krtabaz, 1914 ◆ Aregnazan Sivkeuzi Manukyan, Kars, Mazra, 1913 ◆ Aregnazan Smbati Kirakosyan, Sarighamish, Sthan, 1911 ◆ Aregnazan Sukiasi Sahakyan, Manazkert, Rostamgidak, 1913 ◆ Arestak Hovhannesi Gevorgyan (Hovhannisyan), Kars, Baghliahmat, 1916 ◆ Arestak Karapeti Petoyan, Kars, Ghzlchakhchakh, 1911 ◆ Arestak Sargsi Sargsyan, Shahnazar, 1919 ◆ Arestak Srapioni Harutyunyan, Surmalu, Evchilar, 1912 ◆ Areti Filayi Kachikov, Lori, Alaverdi, 1912 ◆ Arev Karoyi Harutyunyan, Leninakan, Kefli, 1913 ◆ Arevaluys Astvacaturi Grigoryan, Mush, Hasnav, 1911 ◆ Arevaluys Sedraki Barseghyan, Alashkert, Gharakilisa, 1911 ◆ Arevaluys Tigrani Tigranyan, Bulanagh, Mashtlu, 1913 ◆ Arevhat Abrahami Torosyan, Alekpol, Chiftali, 1912 ◆ Arevhat Aleksani Antonyan, Akhalkalak, Diliska, 1913 ◆ Arevhat Aleksani Gasparyan, Alekpol, Chotur, 1914 ◆ Arevhat Aleksani Harutyunyan, Kars, Mec Parker, 1911 ◆ Arevhat Aleksani Manukyan, Shirak, Chrakhli, 1914 ◆ Arevhat Antuani Gasparyan, Alashkert, Yeghantapa, 1913 ◆ Arevhat Armenaki Gevorgyan, Sarighamish, Baglamad, 1916 ◆ Arevhat Arseni Hovhannisyan, Julfa, 1912 ◆ Arevhat Arshaki Arshakyan, Igdir, 1917 ◆ Arevhat Arshaki Kirakosyan, Kars, 1911 ◆ Arevhat Artashesi Stepanyan, Bandrvan, 1912 ◆ Arevhat Avagi Gevorgyan, Kars, Baylamat, 1913 ◆ Arevhat Ervandi Gharagyozyan, Kars, 1914 ◆ Arevhat Galusti Poghosyan, Shirak, Leninakan, 1908 ◆ Arevhat Gevorgi Gevorgyan, Karabagh, 1915 ◆ Arevhat Gevori Gevorgyan, Leninakan, Ortakilisa, 1914 ◆ Arevhat Ghazari Ghazaryan, Yerevan, 1918 ◆ Arevhat Ghazari Yazgulyan, Ardahan, 1913 ◆ Arevhat Ghukasi Zazyan (Ghukasyan), Kars, Kyurakdara, 1912 ◆ Arevhat Grigori Grigoryan, Daralagyaz, 1914 ◆ Arevhat Grigori Grigoryan, Leninakan, Chrakhli, 1914 ◆ Arevhat Grigori Hayrapetyan, Alashkert, 1915 ◆ Arevhat Grigori Mshetsyan, Akhalkalak, Karcakh, 1916 ◆ Arevhat Hakobi Hakobyan, Alekpol, Gharakilisa, 1920 ◆ Arevhat Hakobi Hakobyan, Ashtarak, 1918 ◆ Arevhat Hakobi Hakobyan, Turkey, Bulanagh, 1916 ◆ Arevhat Hakobi Ivanyan, Aleksandropol, Shishtpya, 1914 ◆ Arevhat Hakobi Karapetyan, Nakhijevan, Khachikilisa, 1916 ◆ Arevhat Hakobi Markosyan, Alekpol, Tilif, 1909 ◆ Arevhat Hambardzumi Hakobyan, Kars, Baglamat, 1917 ◆ Arevhat Hambardzumi Yayloyan, Alekpol, Sariar, 1906 ◆ Arevhat Harutyuni Arakelyan, Kars, Paldrvan, 1910 ◆ Arevhat Harutyuni Davtyan, Yerevan, Bashnazet, 1916, 1917 ◆ Arevhat Harutyuni Margaryan, Ashtarak, Mastara, 1913 ◆ Arevhat Harutyuni Sargsyan, Kars, Ghzlchakhchakh, 1910 ◆ Arevhat Hayki Avetisyan, Kars, Kaghzvan, 1913 ◆ Arevhat Hovhannesi Gharibyan, Alashkert, Berd, 1909 ◆ Arevhat Hovhannesi Harutyunyan, Kars, Byurakdara, 1914 ◆ Arevhat Hovhannesi Hovhannisyan, Akhalkalak, Sulda, 1915 ◆ Arevhat Hovhannesi Khachatryan, Kars, Gharamahmat, 1908 ◆ Arevhat Hovhannesi Petrosyan, Kars, Ghoshavanq, 1911 ◆ Arevhat Hovhannesi Satoyan, Lengavar, Kharkul, 1916 ◆ Arevhat Hovhannesi Shatoyan, Kars, Mazra, 1907 ◆ Arevhat Karapeti Tobilyan, Alekpol, Mec Artik, 1913 ◆ Arevhat Khachaturi Mkrtchyan, Kaghzvan, 1915 ◆ Arevhat Khlghati Manukyan, Kars, Bashkyatiklar, 1912 ◆ Arevhat Manuki Manukyan, Alashkert, Piran, 1912 ◆ Arevhat Martirosi Martirosyan, Kars, Gyurmlu, 1914 ◆ Arevhat Meliki Mclikyan, Leninakan, Duzkharaba, 1916 ◆ Arevhat Meliki Melikyan, Leninakan, Sarhat, 1917 ◆ Arevhat Minasi Minasyan, Leninakan, Samedlu, 1913 ◆ Arevhat Mkrtchi Harutyunyan, Alekpol, Norashen, 1913 ◆ Arevhat Mkrtchi Torosyan, Alekpol, Ghanlicha, 1907 ◆ Arevhat Mkrtchi Yeghiazaryan, Nakhijevan, 1912 ◆ Arevhat Mukayeli Gevorgyan, Alekpol, Gharakilisa, 1916 ◆ Arevhat Mukayeli Tadevosyan, Nakhijevan, 1915 ◆ Arevhat Muradi (Levoni) Muradyan, Akhalkalak, Chantura, 1912 ◆ Arevhat

Musheghi Movsisyan, Akhalkalak, Vachian, 1916 ◆ Arevhat Nazareti Hakobyan, Alekpol, Chorli, 1911 ◆ Arevhat Nikoli Nikolyan, Leninakan, Pokr Keti, 1916 ◆ Arevhat Petrosi Grigoryan, Leninakan, Imrkhan, 1911 ◆ Arevhat Petrosi Poghosyan, Yerevan, Bashaparan, 1915 ◆ Arevhat Poghosi Arakelyan, Alekpol, Aghin, 1912 ◆ Arevhat Poghosi Poghosyan, Kars, Ghzlkhach, 1909 ◆ Arevhat Poghosi Poghosyan, Vedi Basar, Kashka, 1918 ◆ Arevhat Samsoni Unusyan, Alekpol, Khli-Gharakilisa, 1918 ◆ Arevhat Sargsi Haykazyan, Baku, 1918 ◆ Arevhat Sargsi Sargsyan, Akhalkalak, Gimbirda, 1916 ◆ Arevhat Sargsi Sargsyan, Kars, Nakhijevan, 1910, ◆ Arevhat Saribeki Mnatsakanyan, Ashtarak, Byurakan, 1916 ◆ Arevhat Saroyi Avagyan, Leninakan, Saribash, 1911 ◆ Arevhat Sedraki Sedrakyan, Alekpol, Duzkend, 1914 ◆ Arevhat Serobi Petrosyan, Etchmiadzin, Gyozlu, 1910 ◆ Arevhat Sirakani Manukyan, Nor Bayazet, Kyosamahmed, 1913 ◆ Arevhat Stepani Stepanyan, Ghamarlu, Davalu, 1912 ◆ Arevhat Tadevosi Gevorgyan (Tadevosyan), Shirak, Ortakilisa, 1911 ◆ Arevhat Tatosi Hovhannisyan, Alekpol, 1914 ◆ Arevhat Tevosi Tevosyan, Yerevan, 1916 ◆ Arevhat Torosi Torosyan, Leninakan, Svanverdi, 1916 ◆ Arevhat Vardani Khachatryan, Nakhijevan, Shikhmahmut, 1913 ◆ Arevhat Vardani Muradyan, Alekpol, Babslu, 1912 ◆ Arevhat Vardani Sargsyan, Kars, 1908 ◆ Arevhat Vardani Vardanyan, Kars, Sogyurlu, 1915 ◆ Arevhat Vasili Vasilyan, Kars, Marza ◆ Arevhat Yeghishi Mikayelyan, Kars, Kyadiklar, 1914 ◆ Arevhat Yepremi Harutyunyan, Yerevan, Aylabat, 1908 ◆ Arevik Mukayeli Grigoryan, Mec Gharakilisa, Chotur, 1914 ◆ Arevshat Meliki Melikyan (Asatryan), Mush, Arkavank, 1912 ◆ Argish Gevorgi Gevorgyan, Tiflis, 1917 ◆ Arika Hovhannesi Hurikhanyan, Kars, Katigyugh, 1914 ◆ Aris Grigori Gyurjyan (Ghazaryan), Van, Berkri, 1914 ◆ Aristak Hakobi Hovhannisyan, Mush, Ardon, 1914 ◆ Aristakes Aleki Mnoyan, Kars, Aksi-ghazli, 1912 ◆ Aristakes Antoni Ghazaryan (Antonyan), Alekpol, Bandrvan, 1910 ◆ Aristakes Galusti Broyan, Akhalkalak, Satkha, 1912 ◆ Aristakes Gaspari Gasparyan, Van, Hermer, 1912 ◆ Aristakes Grigori Baboyan, Hin Bayazet, 1911 ◆ Aristakes Grigori Yeghiazaryan, Kars, Gedaksatrmish ◆ Aristakes Hakobi Poghosyan, Kars, 1910 ◆ Aristakes Harutyuni Simonyan, Kars, Ughuzlu, 1912 ◆ Aristakes Meliki Gevorgyan, Alashkert, Monchalu, 1911 ◆ Aristakes Minasi Hovhannisyan, Alekpol, Ghanlija, 1914 ◆ Aristakes Mkrtchi Tevanyan, Leninakan, Paltlu, 1914 ◆ Aristakes Nikoli Baghdasaryan, Kars, Tashkov, 1917 ◆ Aristakes Petrosi Petrosyan, Van, Moks, 1912 ◆ Aristakes Sargsi Hakobyan, Van, Janik, 1913 ◆ Aristakes Sargsi Hayrapetyan, Igdir, Panik, 1914 ◆ Aristakes Tadevosi Pahlevanyan, Akhalkalak, Gyumrdi, 1911 ◆ Armaghan Arshaki Arshakyan, Kars, Hamzakarak, 1912 ◆ Armaghan Gaspari Gevorgyan, Ghamarlu, Janguli, 1912 ◆ Armaghan Nahapeti Stepanyan, Kars, Aghjaghala, 1914 ◆ Armaghan Petrosi Petrosyan, Batum, 1913 ◆ Armaghan Tadosi Aghajanyan, Kars, Mazra, 1913 ◆ Armaghan Vardani Vardanyan, Tiflis, Samadarvish, 1915 ◆ Armanush Aleksani Virabyan, Kars, 1917 ◆ Armanush Avetisi Avetisyan, Nakhijevan, 1912 ◆ Armanush Avetisi Ter-Hovhannisyan, Kars, Tigos, 1913 ◆ Armanush Galusti Sahakyan, Kars, Asgghaza, 1915 ◆ Armanush Hakobi Hakobyan, Kars, Bayburt, 1915 ◆ Armanush Hovhannesi Yaralyan, Alekpol, Talanghshlagh, 1912 ◆ Armanush Khachaturi Vardanyan, Etchmiadzin, 1915 ◆ Armanush Mkrtchi Vardanyan, Igdir, Koghb, 1913 ◆ Armanush Tumasi Tumasyan, Kars, Baygharay, 1914 ◆ Armavir Hakobi Nazaretyan, Akhalkalak, Bandur, 1912 ◆ Armaz Khanumi Makaryan, Karin, Hin Bayazet, 1911 ◆ Armenak Abeli Amatunyan, Kars, Gidalu, 1912 ◆ Armenak Aghabeki Martirosyan, Kars, Aghjaghala, 1910 ◆ Armenak Aleksani Aleksanyan (Charchoyan), Basen, Gomadzor, 1911 ◆ Armenak Antoni Antonyan, Erzrum, Tedeveran, 1912 ◆ Armenak Antonyan, 1916 ◆ Armenak Arami Fahradyan, Erzrum, Grdabaz, 1912 ◆ Armenak Armenakyan, Kars, 1917 ◆ Armenak Arseni Nazaryan, Baku, Yermankyanr, 1911 ◆ Armenak Arzumani Arzumanyan, Yerevan, Aghbash, 1914 ◆ Armenak Avetisi Avetisyan, Bulanagh, Hotnzor, 1915 ◆ Armenak Avetisi Mkrtchyan, Erzrum, Juzveran, 1910 ◆ Armenak Barseghi Petrosyan, Van, Armizan, 1913 ◆ Armenak Fidoyi Srveyan, Khut, Pichank, 1916 ◆ Armenak Galusti Mkrtumyan, Lori, Ashot Yerkati berd, 1913 ◆ Armenak Garegini Gaboyan, Archesh, Haspistan, 1912 ◆ Armenak Gevorgi Avoyan, Shirak, Sarhat, 1912 ◆ Armenak Gevorgi Galstyan, Moks, 1909 ◆ Armenak Gevorgi Gevorgyan, Mush, Bosdakand, 1908 ◆ Armenak Gevorgi, Arakelyan (Gevorgyan), Mush, Kop, 1912 ◆ Armenak Grigori Grigoryan, Kars, Gyoran, 1918 ◆ Armenak Grigori Grigoryan, Nukhi, Sapatu, 1913 ◆ Armenak Grigori Grigoryan, Sasun, Girmav, 1910 ◆ Armenak Grigori Kochoyan, Mush, Liz, 1909 ◆ Armenak Grigori Sargsyan, Kharberd, Nor-gyugh, 1910 ◆ Armenak Gurgeni Gurgenyan, Shoragyal, Bashshoragyal, 1916 ◆ Armenak Hakobi Baboyan, Ardahan, 1912 ◆ Armenak Hakobi Grigoryan, Darachichak, Taycharukh, 1913 ◆ Armenak Hakobi Guvaryan, Leninakan, Horom, 1913 ◆ Armenak Hakobi Hakobyan, Van, Berkri, 1914 ◆ Armenak Hakobi Martirosyan, Hin Nakhijevan, Marza, 1911 ◆ Armenak Hambari Hambaryan, Alekpol, Bandivan, 1913 ◆ Armenak Harutyuni Ghazaryan, Kars, 1910 ◆ Armenak Harutyuni Harutyunyan, Shirak, Armatlu, 1913 ◆ Armenak Harutyuni Mkrtchyan, Akhalkalak, Sulta, 1910 ◆ Armenak Harutyuni Sargsyan, Aljavaz, 1908 ◆ Armenak Hayrapeti Arzumanyan, Nakhijevan, Damurchi, 1913 ◆ Armenak Hovhannesi Hovhannisyan, Erzrum ◆ Armenak Hovhannesi Torosyan, Erzrum, Krtabaz, 1910 ◆ Armenak Hovhannesi Tovmasyan, Mush, 1911 ◆ Armenak Hranti Hrachyan, Khnus, Khlat, 1916 ◆ Armenak Karapeti Karapetyan, Erzrum, 1911 ◆ Armenak Karapeti Karapetyan, Sasun, Hazzo, 1908 ◆ Armenak Karapeti Manukyan, Khnus, Goghanduk, 1910 ◆ Armenak Khachaturi Petrosyan, Leninakan, Jajur, 1916 ◆ Armenak Kirakosi Barseghyan, Erzrum, Appantlu, 1913 ◆ Armenak Knyazi Simonyan, Erzrum, 1912, 1911 ◆ Armenak Manuki Batasyan, Basen, Keprikoy, 1908 ◆ Armenak

Matevosi Ghazaryan, Erzrum, Totik, 1914 ♦ Armenak Melkoni Melkonyan, Van, 1909, 1912 ♦ Armenak Misaki Ghazaryan, Khnus, Dzaha, 1907 ♦ Armenak Mkrtchi Mkrtchyan, Sasun, Dngetk, 1913 ♦ Armenak Mkrtichi Mkrtchyan (Tarlanyan), Van, Khachan, 1913 ♦ Armenak Mnatsakani Artashyan, Echmiacin, Oshakan, 1913 ♦ Armenak Movsesi Gevorgyan, Basen, 1914 ♦ Armenak Movsesi Kirakosyan, Alashkert, Chlkani, 1910 ♦ Armenak Movsesi Mkhitaryan, Bulanagh, Liz, 1908 ♦ Armenak Movsesi Movsisyan, Khnus, 1914 ♦ Armenak Muradi Muradyan (Tarloyan), Bulanagh, Konchalva, 1908 ♦ Armenak Musheghi Asatryan, Mush, 1906 ♦ Armenak Nersesi Harutyunyan, Bulanakh, Kop, 1917 ♦ Armenak Ohani Yeroyan, Kars, Ortakilise, 1914 ♦ Armenak Papiki Mkrtchyan (Papikyan), Basen, Gomadzor, 1912, 1914 ♦ Armenak Petrosi (Ohani) Petrosyan, Khnus, Labutagh, 1910 ♦ Armenak Petrosi Azizyan, Van, Narekgyugh, 1908 ♦ Armenak Poghosi Khurshudyan, Mush, Khasgyugh, 1905 ♦ Armenak Poghosi Poghosyan, Mush, Khasgyugh, 1913 ♦ Armenak Sahaki Sahakyan, Yerevan, Shirazlu, 1915 ♦ Armenak Santriki Manvelyan, Shamakh, Kyolluj, 1911 ♦ Armenak Sargsi Sargsyan, Van, Bakhvants, 1904 ♦ Armenak Serobi Serobyan, Van, Archesh, 1909 ♦ Armenak Shamirei Lusyan, Terjan, Ghachagh, 1908 ♦ Armenak Smbati Petrosyan, Leninakan, Illi ♦ Armenak Stepani Abrahamyan, Shirak, Shish-tapa, 1910 ♦ Armenak Stepani Mikayelyan, Shirak, Kosaghbyur, 1916 ♦ Armenak Tatevosi Stepanyan, Shirak, Illi, 1911 ♦ Armenak Tigrani Baghdasaryan, Mush, Liz, 1911 ♦ Armenak Torosi Poghosyan (Torosyan), Bitlis, Gozaldara, 1908 ♦ Armenak Vanoyi Parunakyan, Leninakan, 1913 ♦ Armenak Varosi Karapetyan, Kaghzvan, Zochi, 1908 ♦ Armenak Yeghiazari Gasparyan, Van, Gyavash, Paykhnir, 1914 ♦ Armenak Yepremi Hovhannisyan, Van, Shatvan, 1913 ♦ Armenuhi (Armaghan) Avetisi Avetisyan, Van, 1911 ♦ Armenuhi Aleki Ghazaryan, Alekpol, Gyulibulagh, 1912 ♦ Armenuhi Arami Gyodakyan, Yerevan, 1911 ♦ Armenuhi Armenaki Poghosyan, Alekpol, 1914 ♦ Armenuhi Avetisi Avetisyan, Van, Hangshtan, 1907 ♦ Armenuhi Bagrati Poghosyan, Kars, 1913 ♦ Armenuhi Gevorgi Gevorgyan, Van, Avan, 1908 ♦ Armenuhi Ghazari Tarjumanyan, Kaghzvan, 1914 ♦ Armenuhi Ghukasi Khachatryan, Akhalkalak, Chandura, 1911 ♦ Armenuhi Grigori Grigoryan, Alashkert, Bulanakh, 1914 ♦ Armenuhi Grigori Torgomyan, Akhaltsikha, 1912, 1911 ♦ Armenuhi Hambardzumi Mutafyan, Baybert, 1911 ♦ Armenuhi Hunani Hunanyan, Kaghzvan, 1913 ♦ Armenuhi Khachaturi Baghdasaryan, Leninakan, Khli Gharakilisa, 1912 ♦ Armenuhi Khachaturi Kocharyan, Kars, Kaghzvan, 1915 ♦ Armenuhi Knyazi Khachatryan, Kars, 1914 ♦ Armenuhi Knyazi Knyazyan, Kars, Araz gegh, 1913, 1912 ♦ Armenuhi Margari Margaryan (Avaryan), Van, Sevan, 1910 ♦ Armenuhi Matevosi Gurgenyan, Leninakan, Bashshoragal, 1916 ♦ Armenuhi Mesropi Mikayelyan, Kars, Bayrakhtar, 1911 ♦ Armenuhi Minasi Minasyan, Van, Gurupagh, 1910 ♦ Armenuhi Nshani Antiazyan, Akhalkalak, 1910 ♦ Armenuhi Petrosi Muradyan, Van, 1910 ♦ Armenuhi Poghosi Avagyan, Nakhijevan, Taza gyugh, 1916 ♦ Armenuhi Poghosi Tumanyan, Van, 1911 ♦ Armenuhi Sahaki Khachatryan, Kars, Tigor, 1914 ♦ Armenuhi Sedraki Ter-Mkrtchyan, Basen, Khz-Viran, 1911 ♦ Armenuhi Senekerimi Hovhannisyan, Van, Cvstan, 1907 ♦ Armenuhi Soghomoni Ter-Matevosyan, Kars, Kyurak-dara, 1911 ♦ Armenuhi Sureni Muradyan, Akhalkalak, Chandura, 1912 ♦ Armenuhi Tadevosi Poghosyan, Kars, 1918 ♦ Armenuhi Tatosi Gasparyan, Alekpol, Gharakilisa, 1910 ♦ Armenuhi Vahani Vahanyan, Nakhijevan, Khalfalu, 1916 ♦ Armenuhi Vahani Vahanyan, Van, 1911 ♦ Armenuhi Yeghiazari Khachatryan, Kars, Banglahamar, 1914 ♦ Armenuhi Zohrabi Zohrabyan (Yagulbyan), Yerevan, Davalu, 1915 ♦ Armik Tigrani Dulgaryan, Shamakhi, Madrasa, 1914 ♦ Armine Stepani Sukiasyan, Shirak, Alekpol, 1912 ♦ Arpenik Adami Gevorgyan, Leninakan, Kefli, 1913 ♦ Arpenik Aghaloyi Smbatyan, Zangezur, Shnatagh, 1919 ♦ Arpenik Aleksandri Babajanyan, Nukhi, 1911 ♦ Arpenik Aleksani Andoyan, Alekpol, Chchlghlar, 1914 ♦ Arpenik Aleksani Khachatryan, Leninakan, Ghazarabad, 1915 ♦ Arpenik Aleksani Varosyan, Kars, Cmni, 1908 ♦ Arpenik Arakeli Madoyan, Basen, Gyolantav, 1909 ♦ Arpenik Armenaki Bozikyan, Van, Arcap, 1911 ♦ Arpenik Armenaki Rostomyan, Igdir, 1915 ♦ Arpenik Arshaki Gharibyan, Sarighamish, Armtlu, 1911 ♦ Arpenik Arshaki Mkhitaryan (Arshakyan), Manazkert, 1912 ♦ Arpenik Arshaki Mkhitaryan, Basen, Bashgyugh, 1909 ♦ Arpenik Artashi Sardaryan, Kars, Gorkhana, 1915 ♦ Arpenik Artuni Arshakyan, Kars, Ughuzlu, 1914 ♦ Arpenik Artushi Harutyunyan, Stepanavan, Gyargyar, 1910 ♦ Arpenik Astvacaturi Sahakyan, Van, Andzav, 1912 ♦ Arpenik Avagi Avagyan, Daralagyaz, Khachik, 1915 ♦ Arpenik Avetisi Avetisyan, 1920 ♦ Arpenik Avetisi Hakobyan, Kars, 1913 ♦ Arpenik Avetisi Manukyan, Kars, Aksighaz, 1916 ♦ Arpenik Avetisi Stepanyan, Alekpol, Kefli, 1911 ♦ Arpenik Avetisi, Torosyan, Nakhijevan, Yarmej, 1915 ♦ Arpenik Begoyi Mnoyan, Alekpol, Taparlu, 1912 ♦ Arpenik Danieli Danielyan, Gharakilisa, Parni gyugh, 1914 ♦ Arpenik Davti Hovhannisyan, Kars, Bayburt, 1916 ♦ Arpenik Gabrieli Gabrielyan, Alekpol, Gorghan, 1916 ♦ Arpenik Galusti Varosyan, Kars, Chala, 1911 ♦ Arpenik Gevorgi Biatyan, Darachichak, Zanjrlu, 1913 ♦ Arpenik Gevorgi Gevorgyan, Nakhijevan, Kntonner, 1914 ♦ Arpenik Gevorgi Hovhannisyan, Salmast, Alighzl, 1913 ♦ Arpenik Gevorgi Markosyan, Basen, Armtlu, 1912 ♦ Arpenik Gevorgi Mkrtchyan, Kars, Berni, 1914 ♦ Arpenik Gevorgi Poghosyan (Harutyunyan), Beghazlu, 1914 ♦ Arpenik Ghazari Petrosyan, Kars, Diku, 1911 ♦ Arpenik Ghevondi Ter-Mesropyan, Kars, Nakhijevan, 1910 ♦ Arpenik Ghukasi Ghukasyan, Kars, Gharakilise, 1915 ♦ Arpenik Ghukasi Vardapetyan, Akhalkalak, P. Kendur, 1912 ♦ Arpenik Grigori Grigoryan, Kars, Hamzakar, 1912 ♦ Arpenik Grigori Hakobyan, Kars, 1913 ♦ Arpenik Grigori Harutyunyan (Khachatryan), Alekpol, 1912, 1910 ♦ Arpenik Hakobi Hakobyan, Alekpol, Jalab, 1914 ♦ Arpenik Hakobi Hambardzumyan, Igdir, 1911 ♦ Arpenik Hakobi Sargsyan, Kars,

Ghzlkilisa, 1914 ◆ Arpenik Hakobi Ter-Hakobyan, 1919 ◆ Arpenik Hakobi Vanopyan, Akhaltsikha, 1912 ◆ Arpenik Harutyuni Avetisyan, Alekpol, Alekpol, 1914 ◆ Arpenik Harutyuni Gabrielyan, Leninakan, Khligharakilisa, 1907 ◆ Arpenik Harutyuni Grigoryan, Kars, Krmtlu, 1912 ◆ Arpenik Harutyuni Harutyunyan (Ghazaryan), Karabagh, Shirvan, 1914 ◆ Arpenik Harutyuni Harutyunyan, Leninakan, Aghin, 1909 ◆ Arpenik Hayrapeti Ghukasyan (Sukiasyan), Akhalkalak, Bzarvet, 1918 ◆ Arpenik Hayrapeti Simonyan, Yerevan, Yuva, 1912 ◆ Arpenik Hovaki Sukiasyan, Akhalkalak, Satkha, 1913 ◆ Arpenik Hovhannesi Antonyan, Dilijan, Akhtam, 1915 ◆ Arpenik Hovhannesi Asatryan, Echmiacin, Aylanlu, 1914 ◆ Arpenik Hovhannesi Danielyan, Nakhijevan, Aylabad, 1911 ◆ Arpenik Hovhannesi Ghazaryan, Lori, Urut, 1916 ◆ Arpenik Hovhannesi Grigoryan, Leninakan, Ghrkh, 1908 ◆ Arpenik Hovhannesi Hakobyan, Akhalkalak, 1914 ◆ Arpenik Hovhannesi Hovhannisyan, Alekpol, Boztoghan, 1914 ◆ Arpenik Hovhannesi Hovhannisyan, Darachichak, Karvansara, 1915 ◆ Arpenik Hovhannesi Hovhannisyan, Kars, 1908 ◆ Arpenik Hovhannesi Hovhannisyan, Shirak, Gharamahmed, 1911 ◆ Arpenik Hovhannesi Hovhannisyan, Yerevan, Khashli, 1914 ◆ Arpenik Hovhannesi Khachatryan, Kars, Bash-kadiklar, 1912 ◆ Arpenik Hovhannesi Mkrtchyan, Kars, Baglamar, 1909 ◆ Arpenik Hovhannesi Poghosyan, Kars, Uzunkilisa, 1912 ◆ Arpenik Hovhannesi Stepanyan, Kars, Mazra, 1915 ◆ Arpenik Hunani Vardanyan, Kars, 1911 ◆ Arpenik Jangirovi Gevorgyan, Karabagh, Akhlatia, 1913 ◆ Arpenik Karapeti Apanyan, Kars, 1914, 1912 ◆ Arpenik Karapeti Hovhannisyan, 1912 ◆ Arpenik Karapeti Karapetyan, Igdir, Surmalu, 1914 ◆ Arpenik Karapeti Khachatryan, Leninakan, Daharli, 1910 ◆ Arpenik Kerobi Muradyan, Kars, 1916 ◆ Arpenik Kerobi Tevrizyan, Kaghzvan, 1912 ◆ Arpenik Khachaturi Gevorgyan, Pambak, Chotas, 1915 ◆ Arpenik Khachaturi Khachatryan, Spargert, Uruk, 1915 ◆ Arpenik Khachaturi Markosyan, Yerevan, Kyulali, 1916 ◆ Arpenik Khachaturi Trdatyan, Shirak, Duzkharaba, 1912 ◆ Arpenik Khachaturi Varatyan, Kars, Beyliahmet, 1911 ◆ Arpenik Khnkoyi Harutyunyan, Leninakan, Toros gyugh, 1911 ◆ Arpenik Kolyayi Stepanyan, Baku, 1910 ◆ Arpenik Levoni Ghazaryan, Kars, 1911 ◆ Arpenik Markosi Hakobyan, Shirak, Chalab, 1914 ◆ Arpenik Martirosi Asoyan, Shirak, Bayandur, 1914, 1915 ◆ Arpenik Martirosi Saroyan, Kars, Chala, 1910 ◆ Arpenik Martirosi Stepanyan, Alekpol, Dzithankov, 1912 ◆ Arpenik Mekhaki Mesrobyan, Akhalkalak, 1910 ◆ Arpenik Meliki Khachatryan, Basen, Gomadzor, 1913 ◆ Arpenik Melkoni Barikyan, Kars, 1911 ◆ Arpenik Mesropi Mesropyan, Kars, Bayrakh-tar, 1916 ◆ Arpenik Mikayeli Avetisyan, Kars, Berni, 1911 ◆ Arpenik Mikayeli Mikayelyan (Nersisyan), Van, Archesh, 1910 ◆ Arpenik Mikayeli Mkrtchyan, Shirak, Parni gyugh, 1914 ◆ Arpenik Minasi Dilanyan (Muradyan), Kars, Bajamat, 1910 ◆ Arpenik Misaki Harutyunyan, Kars, Vosghuzlu, 1912 ◆ Arpenik Misaki Mkrtchyan, Kars, Sarighamish, 1914 ◆ Arpenik Misaki Poghosyan, Kars, Chala, 1911 ◆ Arpenik Misaki Sahakyan, Alekpol, Gharakilisa, 1910 ◆ Arpenik Mkhitari Gasparyan, Alekpol, Aghin, 1911 ◆ Arpenik Mkrtchi Hakobyan, Kars, Bayraghdat, 1909 ◆ Arpenik Mnatsakani Hovhannisyan, Igdir, Khalfali, 1914 ◆ Arpenik Nazareti Soghomonyan, Leninakan, Ghligharakilisa, 1914 ◆ Arpenik Nazari Nazaryan, Kaghzvan, 1914 ◆ Arpenik Nikoli Nikolyan, Leninakan, Sogyutli, 1913 ◆ Arpenik Nshani Komisaryan (Kamsaryan), Erzrum, Ghtadzor, 1916 ◆ Arpenik Petrosi Petrosyan Chakhoayn, Alekpol, Chiktali, 1916 ◆ Arpenik Petrosi Petrosyan, Mets Gharakilisa, Parni, 1918 ◆ Arpenik Poghosi Harutyunyan, Leninakan, Khapli, 1913 ◆ Arpenik Poghosi Poghosyan, Nor Bayazet, Dali ghardagh, 1914 ◆ Arpenik Sahaki Baghdasaryan, Kars, 1911 ◆ Arpenik Sahaki Hovsepyan (Sahakyan), Yerevan, 1918 ◆ Arpenik Sahaki Jotyan, Pambak, Parni gyugh, 1914 ◆ Arpenik Sahaki Yeghiazaryan, Kars, Aski-Ghaza, 1913 ◆ Arpenik Sakoyi Manukyan, Kars, Gyodakdara, 1911 ◆ Arpenik Sakoyi Minasyan, Kars, Paldrvan, 1912 ◆ Arpenik Sargsi Aghajanyan, Kars, Ghzl-chakhchakh, 1914 ◆ Arpenik Sargsi Hovhannisyan, Nor Bayazet, Tuskulu, 1912 ◆ Arpenik Sargsi Manukyan, Kaghzvan, 1911 ◆ Arpenik Sargsi Sahakyan, Shirak, Jajur, 1914 ◆ Arpenik Sashayi Hambardzumyan, Karabagh, Shushi, 1914 ◆ Arpenik Sedraki Harutyunyan, Kars, 1914 ◆ Arpenik Sedraki Hovsepyan, Ghamarlu, Oghorbash, 1914 ◆ Arpenik Sedraki Melkonyan, Yerevan, Ashtarak, 1911 ◆ Arpenik Sedraki Sedrakyan, Bitlis, 1910 ◆ Arpenik Sedraki Tumasyan, Kars, Chormali, 1912 ◆ Arpenik Sedraki Yatrjaryan, Etchmiadzin, Haytaz, 1914 ◆ Arpenik Shmavoni Gyulazyan, Yerevan, Norashen, 1915 ◆ Arpenik Simoni Azizyan, Van, Norduz, 1914 ◆ Arpenik Simoni Gabrielyan, Gharakilisa, 1918 ◆ Arpenik Simoni Sargsyan, Leninakan, Jalabtsi, 1920 ◆ Arpenik Sisaki Danielyan, 1913 ◆ Arpenik Smbati Torosyan, Leninakan, Mets krdi, 1913 ◆ Arpenik Soghomoni Sargsyan, Karabagh, Pirjamal, 1914 ◆ Arpenik Sosi Pashikyan, Pokr Gharakilisa, 1908 ◆ Arpenik Stepani Harutyunyan, Leninakan, Ghanlija, 1913 ◆ Arpenik Sukiasi Ghazaryan, Leninakan, Chzghlar, 1910 ◆ Arpenik Tadevosi Manukyan, Leninakan, Toros gyugh, 1914 ◆ Arpenik Tigrani Baboyan, Nakhijevan, Kyaltapu, 1913 ◆ Arpenik Tigrani Gevorgyan, Leninakan, Mastara, 1914 ◆ Arpenik Torosi Torosyan, Shirak, Chorli, 1914 ◆ Arpenik Tovmasi Sargsyan, Alekpol, Mec Kiti, 1913 ◆ Arpenik Vaghinaki Karapetyan, Ghamarlu, Chidamlu, 1916 ◆ Arpenik Vardani Hovhannisyan, Akhalkalak, Abul, 1914 ◆ Arpenik Vardani Vardanyan, Leninakan, Ortakilisa, 1915 ◆ Arpenik Yeghiazari Petrosyan, Ghamarlu, 1909 ◆ Arpenik Yeghoyi Yeghoyan, Alekpol, Kiti, 1911 ◆ Arpenik Yegori Gabrielyan, Surmalu, Koghb, 1906 ◆ Arpenik Zakari Martirosyan, Igdir, 1910 ◆ Arpik Atanesi Aghajanyan, Echmiacin, 1915 ◆ Arpik Avagi Avagyan, Aparan, Damerlu, 1914 ◆ Arpik Avetisi Khachatryan, Alekpol, Bash gjugh, 1918 ◆ Arpik Geghami Geghamyan (Varosyan), Kars, Paldrvan, 1915 ◆ Arpik Ghazari Arzumanyan (Tarjumanyan), Kaghzvan, 1911 ◆ Arpik Ghukasi Ghukasyan,

Kars, Bayburt, 1916 ♦ Arpik Hakobi Hakobyan, Kars, Bayburt, 1919 ♦ Arpik Mnatsakani Mnoyan, Shirak, Bashgegh, 1915 ♦ Arpik Movsesi Khachatryan, Igdir, 1913 ♦ Arpik Nersesi Jangiryan, Tpkhis, 1918 ♦ Arpik Poghosi Poghosyan, Akhalkalak, 1915 ♦ Arpik Poghosi Poghosyan, Bulanagh, 1916 ♦ Arpik Samsoni Arakelyan, Nor Bayazet, 1916 ♦ Arpik Sedraki Arshakyan, Yerevan, 1916 ♦ Arsen Aleki Varosyan, Kars, Ghzlchakhchakh, 1913, 1912 ♦ Arsen Azati Barseghyan, Zangezur, Sevakar, 1910 ♦ Arsen Baboyi Petrosyan, Derjan, Khachghyaz, 1909 ♦ Arsen Galusti Tadevosyan, Kars, Ghzlchakhchakh, 1913 ♦ Arsen Grigori Mkrtchyan, Vaspurakan, Aminashat, 1909 ♦ Arsen Harutyuni Makaryan, Kars, Agarak, 1910 ♦ Arsen Hayrapeti Davtyan, Shamakhi, Madras, 1912 ♦ Arsen Hovhannesi Hovhannisyan, Bitlis, Akhlat, 1913 ♦ Arsen Karapeti Mirzoyan (Karapetyan), Van, Amenashat, 1910 ♦ Arsen Karapeti Ter-Vardanyan, Nakhijevan, Azo-Ter, 1910 ♦ Arsen Mattsi Matevosyan (Mattsyan), Kars, Bashgegh, 1913 ♦ Arsen Meliki Sargsyan, Kars, Ghzlchakhchakh, 1914, 1913 ♦ Arsen Mikayeli Hovhannisyan, Shirak, Dadalu, 1914 ♦ Arsen Minasi Tonoyan, Basen, Shatevan, 1914 ♦ Arsen Mkrtchi Serobyan, Basen, Talibaba, 1911 ♦ Arsen Petrosi Simonyan (Petrosyan), Kars, Derbandlu, 1913 ♦ Arsen Sargsi Sargsyan, Archesh, 1912 ♦ Arsen Serobi (Aro) Aboyan, Leninakan, Tashkhala, 1915 ♦ Arsen Simoni Muradyan, 1916, 1913 ♦ Arsen Zakari Gevorgyan (Zakaryan), Alashkert, Yonjalar, 1907 ♦ Arshak (Hambari), Hambardzumi Avagyan, Alekpol, Mastara, 1912 ♦ Arshak Aghaloyi Smbatyan, Zangezur, Shnatagh, 1911 ♦ Arshak Arakeli Hakobyan, Karabagh, Kyuratagh, 1914 ♦ Arshak Arami Khachatryan, Shirak, Pirvali, 1918 ♦ Arshak Asaturi Sahakyan, ♦ Arshak Avetisi Asatryan, Shirak, Chchkhlar, 1911 ♦ Arshak Baghdasari Sukiasyan, Archesh, Judka, 1912 ♦ Arshak Galusti Grigoryan, Leninakan, Toros gyugh, 1917 ♦ Arshak Gaoyi Gevorgyan, Shirak, Syogutli, 1918 ♦ Arshak Hakobi Hovhannisyan, Mush, Cghaka, 1913 ♦ Arshak Harutyuni Petrosyan, Shamakh, Kragand, 1916 ♦ Arshak Hayrapeti Vanetsyan, Kars, Ortaghala, 1914 ♦ Arshak Hovsepi Ter-Samvelyan, Mush, Shirvanshigh, 1909 ♦ Arshak Karapeti Hovhannisyan, Kars, Bvek, 1907 ♦ Arshak Karapeti Karapetyan, Van, 1912 ♦ Arshak Khachaturi Mesropyan, Mush, Arkavank, 1912 ♦ Arshak Khurshudi Khurshudyan, Mush, Mishtlu, 1913 ♦ Arshak Manuki Hakobyan, Shirak, Paltli, 1914 ♦ Arshak Manuki Manasyan, Manazkert, Norashen, 1911 ♦ Arshak Marati Ghukasyan, Khnus, Krt, 1912 ♦ Arshak Mkrtchi Petrosyan, Kars, Tekor, 1915 ♦ Arshak Movsesi Serobyan, Alashkert, Yonjalu, 1914 ♦ Arshak Nersesi Jhangiryan, Tiflis, 1914 ♦ Arshak Petrosi Hakobyan, Alekpol, Jajur, 1914 ♦ Arshak Poghosi Grigoryan, Nor Bayazet, Gandza, 1910 ♦ Arshak Poghosi Poghosyan, Alchavaz, Khoran, 1914 ♦ Arshak Sahaki Sahakyan, Lori, Shahnazar, 1917 ♦ Arshak Sahaki Sahakyan, Mush, Drmet, 1911 ♦ Arshak Simoni Simonyan, Yerevan, 1911 ♦ Arshak Tadevosi Nazaretyan, Nakhijevan, Shekhmahmud, 1911 ♦ Arshak Yervandi Yeranosyan, Yerevan, Oshakan, 1914 ♦ Arshaluys (Khosrovi) Abgaryan, Akhaltskha, 1913 ♦ Arshaluys Aleksani Aleksanyan, Nakhijevan, Alashkert, 1916 ♦ Arshaluys Aleksani Khurshudyan, Kars, Kars, 1910, 1908 ♦ Arshaluys Arami Ghazaryan, Kars, 1917 ♦ Arshaluys Armenaki Baghalbashyan, Leninakan, 1911 ♦ Arshaluys Avagi Hakobyan, Khnus, Khnus-ghala, 1911 ♦ Arshaluys Avagi Martirosyan, Nukhi, 1908 ♦ Arshaluys Avdali Avdalyan (Baghdasaryan), Khnus, 1915 ♦ Arshaluys Avetisi Babayan, Akhaltskha, Goru, 1913 ♦ Arshaluys Budaghi Topchyan, Nakhijevan, Tumbul, 1913 ♦ Arshaluys Gabrieli Gabrielyan, Koghb, 1914 ♦ Arshaluys Gabrieli Harutyunyan, Nakhijevan, Ghazanchi, 1913 ♦ Arshaluys Galusti Papikyan, Leninakan, Nor Artik, 1915 ♦ Arshaluys Gaspari Hakobyan, Kars, Bayburt, 1912 ♦ Arshaluys Ghazari Yeghoyan, Karabagh, 1915 ♦ Arshaluys Hakobi Harutyunyan, Tpkhis, 1913 ♦ Arshaluys Hakobi Harutyunyan, Van, 1914 ♦ Arshaluys Hambardzumi Sahakyan, Van, Shatakh, 1912 ♦ Arshaluys Harteni Kashagorcyan, Bitlis, 1920 ♦ Arshaluys Harutyuni Avetisyan, Surmalu, Aghveris, 1916 ♦ Arshaluys Harutyuni Harutyunyan, Gyokzay, Pataklu, 1912 ♦ Arshaluys Harutyuni Harutyunyan, Nukhi, Tashbulagh, 1913 ♦ Arshaluys Hayrapeti Arzumanyan, Karabagh, 1912 ♦ Arshaluys Hovhannesi Hovhannisyan, Nakhijevan, Akulis, 1915 ♦ Arshaluys Hunani Hunanyan, Kars, Aghuzum, 1914 ♦ Arshaluys Karapeti Karapetyan, Nor Bayazet, 1917 ♦ Arshaluys Karapeti Petrosyan, Shushi, 1914 ♦ Arshaluys Khachaturi Baghshetsyan, Tiflis, 1913 ♦ Arshaluys Khachaturi Gorinyan, Igdir, Koghb, 1911 ♦ Arshaluys Khachaturi Karapetyan, Manazkert, Ghasmik, 1912 ♦ Arshaluys Khurshudi Abrahamyan, Baku, 1917 ♦ Arshaluys Lazari Aghamiryan, Karabagh, Shushi, 1908 ♦ Arshaluys Manuki Manukyan, Tiflis, 1914 ♦ Arshaluys Matevosi Dinoyan, Van, 1916 ♦ Arshaluys Matsaki Sargsyan, Kars, 1914 ♦ Arshaluys Misaki Baghdasaryan, Alashkert, Gharakilise, 1911 ♦ Arshaluys Mkhitari Amirkhanyan, Kars, 1916 ♦ Arshaluys Mkhitari Mkhitaryan, Mush, Vardo, 1911 ♦ Arshaluys Mnatsakani Nersisyan, Nakhijevan, 1914 ♦ Arshaluys Movsesi Movsisyan, Erzrum, Teteveran, 1913 ♦ Arshaluys Nahapeti Nahapetyan, Van, 1913 ♦ Arshaluys Nshani Sofyan, Van, 1911 ♦ Arshaluys Petrosi Panosyan, Van, Ardzak, 1907 ♦ Arshaluys Petrosi Petrosyan, Alashkert, Berd, 1909 ♦ Arshaluys Poghosi Savoyan, Kars, Berna, 1908 ♦ Arshaluys Sahaki Sahakyan, Vaspurakan, Van, 1913, 1911 ♦ Arshaluys Sargsi Tumanyan, Bayburt, Blur, 1912 ♦ Arshaluys Sedraki Sedrakyan, Basen, Yaghuts, 1914 ♦ Arshaluys Sukiasi Poghosyan, Alashkert, Khastur, 1912 ♦ Arshaluys Tadevosi Tadevosyan, Van, Patik, 1915, 1913 ♦ Arshaluys Tigrani Avetisyan, Kars, Mets Parkit, 1913 ♦ Arshaluys Tigrani Barseghyan, Van, 1909 ♦ Arshaluys Tigrani Tigranyan, Mush, 1914 ♦ Arshaluys Torosi Torosyan, Basen, Hekebad, 1914 ♦ Arshaluys Vardani Vardanyan, Van, Khashun, 1915 ♦ Arshaluys Yeghishi Yeghishyan, Alashkert, Ahmat, 1915 ♦ Arshaluys Yeghoyi Hayrapetyan, Etchmiadzin, Khatunarkh, 1913 ♦ Arshaluys Yesayi Stepanyan, Igdir, Alikamar, 1914 ♦

Arshaluys Zakari Mazmanyan, Ardahan, Hrapat, 1911 ♦ Arshavir Abrahami Arakelyan, Kaghzvan, Pirs ♦ Arshavir Arami Khachatryan, Kars, Jrji, 1914 ♦ Arshavir Danieli Mnatsakanyan Yerevan, Artashat, 1913 ♦ Arshavir Maghaki Stepanyan, Batum, Tandzat, 1908 ♦ Arshavir Margari Israyelyan, Surmalu, Mola-Ghamar, 1912 ♦ Arshavir Matosi Matosyan, Koghb, 1915 ♦ Arshavir Misaki Bejanyan, Gyokcha, Ghalagoz, 1912 ♦ Arshavir Misaki Misakyan, Kars, Ghapanlu, 1908 ♦ Arshavir Movsoyi Ter-Sargsyan, Kars, 1912 ♦ Arshavir Nersesi Amirkhanyan, Akhalkalak, Satgha, 1913 ♦ Arshavir Sargsi Sargsyan, Baku, 1917 ♦ Artash Aghajani Antonyan, Yerevan, Pokr Shahriar, 1916 ♦ Artash Apikoni Adamyan, Shirak, Mastara, 1911 ♦ Artash Arami Hakobyan, Kars, Karmalu, 1911 ♦ Artash Arshaki Ghukasyan, Kars, Bashgegh, 1913 ♦ Artash Barseghi Barseghyan, Kars, Nakhijevan, 1914 ♦ Artash Gaspari Vardanyan, Khnus, Ghayghavush, 1914, 1913 ♦ Artash Khachaturi Khachatryan, Basen, Kyorpukoy, 1913 ♦ Artash Manuki Eloyan, Alashkert, Yeghntap, 1914 ♦ Artash Petrosi Gevorgyan, Kars, Jalal, 1916 ♦ Artash Saroyi Shaboyan, Kars, 1913 ♦ Artash Yepremi Artashesyan, Nakhijevan, 1915 ♦ Artashes Adibeki Manukyan, Nor Bayazet, Khul-ali, 1915 ♦ Artashes Aleksani Hovhannisyan, Leninakan, Khli Gharakilisa, 1914 ♦ Artashes Aleksani Tarbashyan, Alekpol, Aghin, 1912 ♦ Artashes Armenaki Atoyan, Kars, Mets Parkid, 1909 ♦ Artashes Armenaki Kalashyan, Kars, Jirmalu, 1912 ♦ Artashes Arseni Sargsyan, Nakhijevan, Sers, 1911 ♦ Artashes Avagi Sahakyan, Aparan, Blkher, 1910 ♦ Artashes Danieli Asatryan, Kars, Ghzl-chakhchakh, 1912 ♦ Artashes Davti Tukhikyan (Davtyan), Van, Pakhner, 1909 ♦ Artashes Galusti Galoyan, Leninakan, Goshavank, 1912 ♦ Artashes Gaspari Khachatryan, Alashkert, Yeghntap, 1905 ♦ Artashes Gilbangi Sukiasyan, Sarighamish, Armtlu, 1911 ♦ Artashes Grigori Grigoryan, Van, Nor-gyugh, 1908 ♦ Artashes Hakobi Malkhasyan, Kars, Uzunkilisa, 1912 ♦ Artashes Hakobi Tovmasyan, Van, Maltak, 1912 ♦ Artashes Hakobyan Artashes Hovhannesi Melikyan, Igdir, Koghb, 1912 ♦ Artashes Hovhannesi Tiftikchyan, Yengyuri, 1911 ♦ Artashes Karapeti Tovmasyan, Etchmiadzin, 1912 ♦ Artashes Khachaturi Galakyan (Harutyunyants), Kars, Kyodak-dara, 1913 ♦ Artashes Khachaturi Khachatryan, Nakhijevan, Kakhanov, 1910 ♦ Artashes Khurshudi Mkhitaryan, Bitlis, Shina, 1913 ♦ Artashes Margari Margaryan, Van, 1912, 1911 ♦ Artashes Martirosi Aghababyan, Kars, 1911 ♦ Artashes Martirosi Manusajyan, Akhalkalak, Goman, 1908 ♦ Artashes Mekhaki Karapetyan, Kars, 1915 ♦ Artashes Meliki Danielyan, Akhalkalak, Vachian, 1913 ♦ Artashes Meliki Ter-Poghosyan, Tiflis, 1913 ♦ Artashes Mikayeli Revazyan, Ghzlar, 1913 ♦ Artashes Misaki Koshtoyan (Gevorgyan), Kaghzvan, 1908 ♦ Artashes Mkrtchi Grigoryan, Kars, 1908 ♦ Artashes Mkrtchi Mkrtchyan, Van, 1912 ♦ Artashes Mkrtchi Serobyan, Erzrum, Ghshlagh, 1909 ♦ Artashes Nazari Aslanyan, Salmast, 1911 ♦ Artashes Nazari Saroyan, Alashkert, Gharabek, 1907 ♦ Artashes Ohanjani Ohanjanyan, Kars, 1917 ♦ Artashes Papiki Hakobyan, Erzrum, Yughviran, 1912, 1913 ♦ Artashes Paskevichi Grigoryan, Julfa, 1912 ♦ Artashes Petrosi Simonyan, Van, 1907 ♦ Artashes Petrosi Tazagyulyan, Ardahan, Volti, 1913 ♦ Artashes Sahaki Sahakyan, Basen, Jrashen, 1915 ♦ Artashes Sargsi Ghazaryan, Akhalkalak, Orjar, 1911 ♦ Artashes Sargsyan, 1919 ♦ Artashes Sedraki Sargsyan, Kars, Chorkhana, 1911 ♦ Artashes Soghomoni Shahbazyan, Kars, Tekniz, 1916 ♦ Artashes Stepani Manvelyan Stepanyan, Kars, Shavghi, 1912 ♦ Artashes Tovmasi Vardanyan, Julfa, 1914 ♦ Artashes Yervandi Sargsyan, Alekpol, Duskharaba, 1912 ♦ Artashes Yervandi Sargsyan, Kars, Mets Parkit, 1911 ♦ Artashes Yesayi Melikyan, Igdir, 1910 ♦ Artavazd Abeti Maloyan, Leninakan, 1913, 1911 ♦ Artavazd Aghasu Mnoyan, Kars, Chala, 1912 ♦ Artavazd Arakeli Arakelyan, Nakhijevan, Guznud, 1910 ♦ Artavazd Arakeli Hovhannisyan, Kars, Uzunkilisa, 1912 ♦ Artavazd Arami Fahradyan, Basen, Krtabas, 1914 ♦ Artavazd Arami Hakobyan, Alekpol, Toparlu, 1913 ♦ Artavazd Arami Poghosyan, Yekaterinbad, 1912 ♦ Artavazd Arshaki Arshakyan (Harutyunyan), Alekpol, Bashgegh, 1916 ♦ Artavazd Arshaki Arshakyan, Shirak, Daharli, 1912 ♦ Artavazd Avagi Antonyan, Ardahan, 1914 ♦ Artavazd Bagrati Galstyan (Galtyan), Kars, 1909 ♦ Artavazd Bagrati Sargsyan, Kars, Derbend, 1918 ♦ Artavazd Daviti Danielyan, Gharakilisa, Hamamlu, 1914 ♦ Artavazd Geghami Margaryan, Kars, Ghapanlu, 1911 ♦ Artavazd Gevorgi Khachatryan, Akhalkalak, 1918 ♦ Artavazd Gevorgi Poghosyan, Leninakan, Alaverdi, 1912 ♦ Artavazd Gevorgi Tadevosyan, Kars, Paldrvan, 1914 ♦ Artavazd Ghazari Khachatryan, Kars, Aghazum, 1912 ♦ Artavazd Grigori Israyelyan, Kars, Kars, 1917 ♦ Artavazd Grishi Armenakyan, Alekpol, 1914 ♦ Artavazd Hakobi Nersisyan, Sharur, Khanakhlar, 1915 ♦ Artavazd Hakobi Tadevosyan, Kars, Zarishat, 1910 ♦ Artavazd Hakobi Torosyan, Kars, 1915 ♦ Artavazd Hambardzumi Aghajanyan, Kars, Shatevan, 1909 ♦ Artavazd Hovhannesi Mkhitaryan, Kars, Berni, 1913 ♦ Artavazd Karapeti Aslanyan, Kars, Ughuzlu, 1910 ♦ Artavazd Karapeti Karapetyan, Shamakhi, 1913 ♦ Artavazd Karapeti Musheghyan, Mush, Ereshter, 1912 ♦ Artavazd Karapetyan, Van, 1913 ♦ Artavazd Khachaturi Petrosyan, Leninakan, Babul, 1912 ♦ Artavazd Khachoyi Martirosyan, Kars, Aksighachi, 1917 ♦ Artavazd Makari Nersisyan, Kars, Gyarmlu, 1914 ♦ Artavazd Markosi Mkrtchyan, Leninakan, Chzghlar, 1912 ♦ Artavazd Martirosi Khachatryan, Akhalkalak, 1919 ♦ Artavazd Mheri Muradyan, Kars, Ghzlchakhchakh, 1910 ♦ Artavazd Mkhoyi Gasparyan, Surmali, Koghb, 1912, 1911 ♦ Artavazd Mkrtchi Hakobyan, Basen, Patzhvan, 1915, 1914 ♦ Artavazd Mkrtchi Harutyunyan, Alekpol, Svanverdi, 1912 ♦ Artavazd Mkrtchi Movsisyan, Alekpol, Ghanlicha, 1914 ♦ Artavazd Mkrtchi Nahapetyan, Leninakan, 1911 ♦ Artavazd Mkrtichi Ayvazyan, Alekpol, Boghazkasan, 1912 ♦ Artavazd Mukayeli Pilosyan, Kars, Shadivan, 1912 ♦ Artavazd Musheghi Mkrtchyan, Persia, 1914 ♦ Artavazd Nikoli Ghazaryan, Imrkhan, 1912 ♦ Artavazd Petrosi Hambardzumyan, Akhalkalak, Chanjgha, 1914 ♦ Artavazd Petrosi Matevosyan, Kars, 1914 ♦

Artavazd Petrosi Sargsyan, Kars, Ghzlchakhchakh, 1914 ♦ Artavazd Sargsi Ghandilyan, Kars, 1912 ♦ Artavazd Sargsi Movsisyan, Alekpol, Gzl-chakhchak, 1910 ♦ Artavazd Sargsi Muradyan, Lori, Gyulagarak, 1917 ♦ Artavazd Sargsi Pambughjyan, Kars, Bagliahmat, 1914 ♦ Artavazd Senekerimi Artoyan (Artavazdyan), Alekpol, Gharakilisa, 1919 ♦ Artavazd Sergoyi Hakobyan, Alekpol, Paldrvan, 1911 ♦ Artavazd Serobi Manukyan, Kars, Ghapanlu, 1913 ♦ Artavazd Simoni Minasyan, Ardahan, Shashvet, 1912 ♦ Artavazd Stepani Antonyan (Stepanyan), Shirak, Bandrvan, 1912 ♦ Artavazd Stepani Stepanyan, Basen, Arjarak, 1919 ♦ Artavazd Sureni Karapetyan (Aslanyan), Akhalkalak, Namzara, 1915 ♦ Artavazd Tigrani Saroyan, Kars, Chala, 1910 ♦ Artavazd Tigrani Vardanyan, Alekpol, Syogutli, 1913 ♦ Artavazd Torosi Nersisyan, Zangezur, Angeghadzor, 1915 ♦ Artavazd Vagharshaki Malkhasyan, Kars, Uzunkilisa, 1913 ♦ Artavazd Vahani Mkrtchyan, Hin Bayazet, 1912 ♦ Artem Harutyuni Gevorgyan, Kars, Mec Parket, 1912 ♦ Artem Hayrapeti Baloryan, Karabagh, Shushi, 1911 ♦ Artem Manuki Hovhannisyan, Ghamarlu, Artashat, 1914 ♦ Artem Stepani Gharibyan, Alekpol, Ghazarapat, 1907 ♦ Artem Tigrani Yeghoyan, Shirak, Sogyutli, 1914 ♦ Artemis Atoyi Atoyan, Kharberd, 1920 ♦ Arto Meliki Melikyan, Alekpol, Svanverdi, 1914 ♦ Artush Harutyuni Nazaryan (Harutyunyan), Surmalu, Koghb, 1911 ♦ Artush Martirosi Tadevosyan, Ghamarlu, Navruzlu, 1914 ♦ Artush Movsesi Movsisyan, Bulanagh, Mazra, 1914 ♦ Artush Poghosi Poghosyan, Nakhijevan, Norsi, 1915 ♦ Artush Sargsi Hakobyan, Kars, 1915 ♦ Artush Simoni Jalalyan, Alekpol, 1911 ♦ Artyom (Harutyun) Pilosi Aslanyan, Kars, Mazra, 1911 ♦ Artyom Grigori Mosinyan, Lori, Uzunlar, 1915 ♦ Artyom Nazari Sahakyan, Kars, Nakhijevan, 1917 ♦ Artyom Tatosi Galstyan, Shamakh, Zargaran, 1911 ♦ Arus Abrahami Abrahamyan, Gharakilisa, Dostlu, 1919 ♦ Arus Ghazari Hakobyan, Leninakan, Otakilisa, 1914 ♦ Arus Grigori Grigoryan (Gmriyan), Leninakan, Chrakhli, 1913 ♦ Arus Grigori Grigoryan, Yerevan, 1917 ♦ Arus Hovaki Hovakyan (Hovhannisyan), Shirak, Taknar, 1916 ♦ Arus Hovhannesi Hovhannisyan, Batu, 1917 ♦ Arus Hovhannesi Piloyan, Kars, Uzunkilisa, 1916 ♦ Arus Hovhasi (Vardani) Vardanyan, Leninakan, Mastara, 1918 ♦ Arus Khachaturi Hakobyan, Yerevan, 1919 ♦ Arus Minasi Minasyan, Nakhijevan, 1920 ♦ Arus Misaki Matevosyan, Kars, Ghoshavank, 1913 ♦ Arus Sakoyi Muradyan, Kars, Ortaghala, 1914 ♦ Arus Simoni Karapetyan, Kars, Oghuzlu, 1915 ♦ Arus Simoni Simonyan, Akhalkalak, Mets Khanchali, 1917 ♦ Arus Vahani Vardanyan, Leninakan, 1919 ♦ Arus Varosi Vardanyan, Leninakan, Zarnji, 1915 ♦ Arus Yeghiazari Yeghiazaryan, Erzrum, Alashkert, 1912 ♦ Arus Zakari Zakaryan, 1918 ♦ Arush Mkrtchi Mkrtchyan, Kars, Cbni, 1912 ♦ Arusik Misaki Minasyan, Van, Aljavaz, 1910 ♦ Arusyak Abdali Mkhitaryan, Kars, Torban, 1913 ♦ Arusyak Abrahami Manukyan, Kars, 1915 ♦ Arusyak Aghabeki Margaryan, Gharakilisa, Goran, 1915 ♦ Arusyak Aleksani Manukyan, Kars, 1915 ♦ Arusyak Andreasi Hambardzumyan, Ghamarlu, Godavlu, 1913 ♦ Arusyak Andreasi Hayrumyan, Karabagh, Shushi, 1913 ♦ Arusyak Arakeli Arakelyan, Olbi, 1909 ♦ Arusyak Arami Mikayelyan, Kars, 1918 ♦ Arusyak Armenaki Mirzoyan, Van, Hayots dzor, 1913 ♦ Arusyak Arseni (Baghdasari) Yeloyan, Leninakan, Kyapanak, 1920 ♦ Arusyak Arshaki Arshakyan (Karapetyan), Leninakan, Ghurtbulagh, 1911 ♦ Arusyak Asaturi Gevorgyan (Asatryan), Van, Kabapka, 1908 ♦ Arusyak Avagi Nersisyan, Leninakan, Khlli Gharakilisa, 1911 ♦ Arusyak Avagi Pashayan, Yerevan, Koghb, 1912 ♦ Arusyak Avagi Safaryan, Mush, 1911 ♦ Arusyak Avagyan, Kars, Mavrik, 1916 ♦ Arusyak Avetisi Avetisyan, Ahalkalak, 1915 ♦ Arusyak Avetisi Grigoryan, Van, Norashen, 1911, 1910 ♦ Arusyak Babajani Khachatryan, Yerevan, 1911 ♦ Arusyak Badali Badalyan, Bitliz, 1909 ♦ Arusyak Barseghi Avetisyan, Alekpol, Bashgegh, 1910 ♦ Arusyak Barseghi, Hovsepyan, Bulanagh, 1914 ♦ Arusyak Barsegi Karapetyants, Kharakilisa, Geran, 1914 ♦ Arusyak Bateki Khachatryan, Kars, Bagliahmed, 1908 ♦ Arusyak Gabrieli Sahakyan, Kars, Ortakilisa, 1912 ♦ Arusyak Galusti Galoyan, Badnoc, 1914 ♦ Arusyak Galusti Melkonyan (Galstyan), Ayntap, Batnots, 1914 ♦ Arusyak Galusti Papikyan, Alekpol, Ghzlghoch, 1912 ♦ Arusyak Galusti Tonoyan, Kars, Berni, 1910 ♦ Arusyak Ghazari Ghazaryan, Kars, 1910 ♦ Arusyak Ghukasi Hakhverdyan, Nakhijevan, Gznur, 1911 ♦ Arusyak Ghurshuti Manukyan, Khnus, Khlat, 1910 ♦ Arusyak Grigori Grigoryan, Kars, 1912 ♦ Arusyak Grigori Grigoryan, Kars, Hamzaketak, 1909 ♦ Arusyak Grigori Hayrapetyan, Shamakhi, Buzand, 1913 ♦ Arusyak Grigori Khachatryan, Leninakan, Ghutni ghshlagh, 1913 ♦ Arusyak Grigori Kirakosyan, Kars, Bulanagh, 1912 ♦ Arusyak Grigori Saghatelyan, Akhalkalak, Karzakh, 1910 ♦ Arusyak Grigori Vardanyan, Chanakhchi, Janjrlu, 1913, 1912 ♦ Arusyak Hakobi Ghalumyan, Ghazakh, Sevkar, 1912 ♦ Arusyak Hakobi Guzhyan, Tiflis, 1909 ♦ Arusyak Hakobi Hakobyan, 1909 ♦ Arusyak Hakobi Hakobyan, Leninakan, Ghurdbalagh, 1911 ♦ Arusyak Hakobi Harutyunyan, Kaghzvan, 1911 ♦ Arusyak Hakobi Harutyunyan, Sarighamish, Stan, 1918 ♦ Arusyak Hakobi Ohanyan, Kars, 1910 ♦ Arusyak Hardeni Grigoryan, Nakhijevan, Karchivan, 1913 ♦ Arusyak Harutyuni Avetisyan, Kaghzvan, 1916 ♦ Arusyak Harutyuni Budaghyan, Van, 1912 ♦ Arusyak Harutyuni Harutyunyan, Alashkert, Hamat, 1909 ♦ Arusyak Harutyuni Simonyan, Kars, Tezekbar, 1917 ♦ Arusyak Hayrapeti Gasparyan (Baghdasaryan), Kars, 1907 ♦ Arusyak Hovhannesi Grigoryan, Yerevan, Akhten, 1913 ♦ Arusyak Hovhannesi Hovhannisyan, Bulanagh, 1914 ♦ Arusyak Hovhannesi Hovhannisyan, Erzrum, 1913 ♦ Arusyak Hovhannesi Hovhannisyan, Kars, Jalsoy, 1915 ♦ Arusyak Hovhannesi Simonyan, Archesh, Kozir, 1908 ♦ Arusyak Hovhannesi Simonyan, Gori, Ghzlkilisa, 1914 ♦ Arusyak Hovhannesi Torosyan, Alekpol, Khli Gharakilisa, 1912, 1914 ♦ Arusyak Hovsepi Muradyan, Kars, Ughuzlu, 1908 ♦ Arusyak Karapeti Avagyan, Mush, Hamzashen, 1909 ♦ Arusyak Karapeti Karapetyan, Akhalkalak, 1917 ♦ Arusyak Karapeti Karapetyan, Basen, Yaghan, 1913 ♦

Arusyak Karapeti Karapetyan, Kars, Byurakdar, 1916 ♦ Arusyak Karapeti Karapetyan, Kars, Sogutli, 1907 ♦ Arusyak Karapeti Serobyan, Van, Nabar, 1917 ♦ Arusyak Karapeti Vardanyan, Nakhijevan, Aza, 1915 ♦ Arusyak Karoyi Khlghatyan, Kars, Paldrvan, 1909 ♦ Arusyak Kerobi Mikayelyan, Lori, Shahnazar, 1914 ♦ Arusyak Lyudvigi Tadevosyan, Yerevan, Nakhijevan, 1909 ♦ Arusyak Manuki Khachatryan, Kars, Paldrvan, 1911 ♦ Arusyak Margari Akulyan, Kars, Nakhijevan, 1911 ♦ Arusyak Markosi Ghandoyan, Akhalkalak, Merenia, 1911 ♦ Arusyak Martirosi Aharonyan, Erzrum, Khazar, 1910 ♦ Arusyak Meliki Melikyan, Aljavaz, Kojr, 1911 ♦ Arusyak Melikseti Carukyan, Kars, Pokr Parker, 1908 ♦ Arusyak Melkoni Hovhannisyan, Yerevan, Atma gyugh, 1911 ♦ Arusyak Melkoni Minasyan, Kars, 1916 ♦ Arusyak Mikayeli (Mukoyi) Khachatryan, Nor Bayazet, 1912 ♦ Arusyak Minasi Minasyan, Van, 1915 ♦ Arusyak Mirzajani Davtyan, Nakhijevan, Ghazanchi, 1913 ♦ Arusyak Mkhitari Baghdasaryan, Khnus, 1912 ♦ Arusyak Mkrtchi Hakobyan, Kars, Chala, 1912 ♦ Arusyak Mkrtchi Mkrtchyan, Bulanagh, Rostom Gedak, 1915 ♦ Arusyak Mkrtchi Mkrtchyan, Yerevan, 1918 ♦ Arusyak Movsesi Hakobyan, Alashkert, Amat, 1912 ♦ Arusyak Movsesi Hovhannisyan, Yerevan, Nork, 1910 ♦ Arusyak Muradi Muradyan, Kars, 1917 ♦ Arusyak Musheghi Avagyan, Ghamarlu, 1913 ♦ Arusyak Nazari Minasyan, Kars, Bvek, 1909 ♦ Arusyak Nersesi Avagyan (Zozanyan), Van, Noragyugh, 1912 ♦ Arusyak Nersoyi Aghanyan, Leninakan, Sariar, 1910 ♦ Arusyak Nikolayi Gyulnazaryan, Nakhijevan, Guzlut, 1912 ♦ Arusyak Nshani Okheyan, Van, Noragyugh, 1912 ♦ Arusyak Paveli Papikyan, Baku, 1909 ♦ Arusyak Petrosi Eloyan, Mush, Vardenis, 1909 ♦ Arusyak Petrosi Petrosyan, Kars, Gyuzlu, 1918 ♦ Arusyak Petrosi Ter-Manvelyan, Batum, Ardvin, 1908 ♦ Arusyak Poghosi Panosyan, Tiflis, 1911 ♦ Arusyak Sahaki Sahakyan, Van, 1913 ♦ Arusyak Sargsi Basentsyan, Alekpol, Ghoshavank, 1915 ♦ Arusyak Sargsi Ghazaryan, Akhalkalak, Vorghagyugh, 1911 ♦ Arusyak Sargsi Grigoryan, Shirak, Ghaltaghchi, 1914 ♦ Arusyak Sargsi Mukayelyan, Kars, Hamzakalak, 1910 ♦ Arusyak Sargsi Muradyan, Kars, Jalal, 1909 ♦ Arusyak Sargsi Sargsyan, Igdir, Kokhp, 1916 ♦ Arusyak Sargsi Sargsyan, Kars, Bashgegh, 1907 ♦ Arusyak Saribeki Martirosyan, Mush, Birmog, 1913 ♦ Arusyak Sedraki Avetisyan, Kars, Banglamar, 1911 ♦ Arusyak Sedraki Chakhoyan, Kars, Kaghzvan, 1910 ♦ Arusyak Serobi Hovsepyan, Alashkert, Hamad, 1910 ♦ Arusyak Shaheni Shahinyan, Alekpol, Avdibek, 1910 ♦ Arusyak Smbati Khachatryan, Alekpol, Bayandur, 1915 ♦ Arusyak Soghomoni Soghomonyan, Kars, Sogyudlu, 1914 ♦ Arusyak Sosei Shirinyan, 1919 ♦ Arusyak Stepani Harutyunyan, Akhalkalak, 1915 ♦ Arusyak Stepani Kocharyan, Gyakcha, Tobishen, 1914 ♦ Arusyak Stepani Poghosyan, Baku, Shamakh, 1911 ♦ Arusyak Tachati Muradyan, Akhalkalak, Chandura, 1913 ♦ Arusyak Tadevosi Hovhannisyan, Kars, Nakhijevan, 1908 ♦ Arusyak Tatosi Hakobyan, Ghamarlu, Chidamlu, 1915 ♦ Arusyak Tatosi Petrosyan, Baku, Shamakhi, 1909 ♦ Arusyak Tigrani Tigranyan, Igdir, Koghb, 1917 ♦ Arusyak Vanoyi Hakobyan, Gharakilisa, Parni gyugh, 1912 ♦ Arusyak Vanoyi Midoyan, Alekpol, Kh. Gharakilis, 1909 ♦ Arusyak Yeghiazari Aleksanyan, Kars, Baglamat, 1913 ♦ Arusyak Yeghiazari Manukyan, Yerevan, Etchmiadzin, 1909 ♦ Arusyak Yeghoyi Harutyunyan, Kars, 1912 ♦ Arusyak Yenkoyi Asatryan, Bulanakh, 1911 ♦ Arusyak Yeranosi Mkrtchyan, Nakhijevan, Karabab, 1911 ♦ Arusyak Yervandi Grigoryan, Akhalkalak, Mec Aragyugh, 1912 ♦ Arusyak Zadoyi Varosyan, Kars, Gorkhana, 1917 ♦ Arusyak Zakari (Zakaryan) Melikyan, Khnus, Burnuz, 1912 ♦ Arusyak Zakari Grigoryan, Leninakan, Jajur, 1911 ♦ Arusyak Zakari Mkrtchyan, Khnusbirt, 1908 ♦ Arusyak Zebeti Petrosyan, Gharakilisa, Ghshlagh, 1920 ♦ Arzakan Hakobi Hakobyan, Van, 1918 ♦ Arzukan Arshaki Arshakyan (Tatoyants), Yerevan, 1912 ♦ Arzukan Gevorgi Gevorgyan (Margaryan), Surmalu, Yevjilar, 1913 ♦ Arzuman Aleksani Varosyan, Pambak, Gharakilisa, 1909 ♦ Arzuman Barseghi Grigoryan, Alekpol, Boghaz-kasan, 1912 ♦ Arzuman Grigori Antonyan, Alekpol, Illi, 1917 ♦ Arzuman Hakobi Avetisyan, Leninakan, Ortakilisa, 1916 ♦ Arzuman Meliki Galstyan, Alekpol, Toros, 1914 ♦ Arzuman Meloyi Navoyan, Leninakan, Pokr Kiti, 1913 ♦ Arzuman Nersoyi Manukyan, Alekpol, Boghazkasan, 1909 ♦ Asanet Armenaki Mirzoyan, Bulanagh, Khoshgyardi, 1916, Asanet Grigori Grigoryan, Leninakan, Sirvangyugh, 1911 ♦ Asanet Hranti Hakobyan, Alashkert, Berd, 1913 ♦ Asanet Khachaturi Harutyunyan, Kars, Pokr Parket, 1908 ♦ Asanet Khachiki Zhamharyan, Bitlis, 1912 ♦ Asanet Manuki Knyazyan, Akhta, Alapars, 1914 ♦ Asanet Martirosi Danielyan, Alekpol, Khrmzlu, 1912 ♦ Asanet Martirosi Martirosyan, Basen, Gomadzor, 1912 ♦ Asanet Mikayeli Mikayelyan, Yerevan, Karvansara, 1915 ♦ Asanet Petrosi Poghosyan, Van, Voskerak, 1915, 1911 ♦ Asanet Sargsi Margaryan, Dilijan, Bozi gegh, 1919 ♦ Asanet Sedraki Papoyan, Alekpol, Duzkend, 1917 ♦ Asanet Tigrani Gharibjanyan, Alashkert, 1911 ♦ Asatur Avagi Manukyan, Mush, Khut, 1912 ♦ Asatur Hakobi Hmayakyan, Van, Bergri, 1909 ♦ Asatur Herosi Ishkhanyan, Van, 1912 ♦ Asatur Karapeti Karapetyan, Van, 1908, 1910 ♦ Asatur Karapeti Karapetyan, Van, 1912 ♦ Asatur Manuki Manukyan, Van, 1919 ♦ Asatur Misaki Margaryan, Khnus, 1913, 1910 ♦ Asatur Misaki Misakyan, Leninakan, Tashkhala, 1917 ♦ Asatur Movsesi Movsisyan, Van, Boghanj, 1911 ♦ Asatur Muradi Muradyan, Bayazet, Batnots, 1913 ♦ Asatur Nahapeti Gevorgyan, Bulanakh, Hamzashekh, 1908 ♦ Asatur Nshani Nshanyan, Van, 1914, 1913 ♦ Asatur Sahaki Sahakyan, Yerevan, Yuva, 1909 ♦ Asatur Sargsi Hovhannisyan, Bulanagh, Ghatar, 1911 ♦ Asatur Sargsi Karapetyan, Nakhijevan, Aza, 1909 ♦ Asatur Sedraki Hovhannisyan, Mush, Khasgyugh, 1915, 1914 ♦ Asatur Sergoyi Varosyan, Alekpol, Ghzlghoch, 1912 ♦ Asatur Sirekani Avetisyan, Akhalkalak, Aragal, 1915 ♦ Asatur Tadevosi Hovhannisyan, Kars, Ghzl-chakhchakh, 1916 ♦ Asatur Tigrani Paronyan, Bayburt, 1908 ♦ Asghik Smbati Smbatyan, Darachichak, 1915 ♦ Ashen Hovhannesi

Nalbandyan, Van, 1912 ♦ Ashkharabed Aghabeki Ter-Hovhannisyan, Igdir, Kulab, 1915 ♦ Ashkhen Aleki Alekyan, Alekpol, Torosgyugh, 1914 ♦ Ashkhen Aleksani Ayvazyan, Yerevan, Sardarabad, 1912 ♦ Ashkhen Arakeli Ghazaryan (Arakelyan), Akhalkalak, Ghrdbulagh, 1913 ♦ Ashkhen Arami Nersisyan, Akhalkalak, Lomaturtskh, 1915 ♦ Ashkhen Arseni Hovsepyan, Kars, Bayburt, 1912 ♦ Ashkhen Arseni Iskandaryan, Alekpol, Aghkilisa, 1911 ♦ Ashkhen Arseni Tonoyan, Yerevan, Abas-gol, 1914 ♦ Ashkhen Artashesi Sargsyan, Kars, Payghara, 1915 ♦ Ashkhen Avetisi Mkrtchyan, Basen, Yuzviran, 1914 ♦ Ashkhen Avetisi Zakaryan, Sarighamish, 1914 ♦ Ashkhen Danieli Maloyan (Danielyan), Kars, Bashshoragal, 1916 ♦ Ashkhen Daviti Panosyan, Hin Nakhijevan, Znaberd, 1912 ♦ Ashkhen Gabrieli Movsisyan, Kars, 1914 ♦ Ashkhen Galusti Galstyan, Kars, Paldrvan, 1916 ♦ Ashkhen Galusti Hovhannisyan, Shirak, Sarikar, 1912 ♦ Ashkhen Geghami Sukiasyan, Kars, Ortaghala, 1914 ♦ Ashkhen Gevorgi Gevorgyan (Serobyan), Kars, Birnay, 1910 ♦ Ashkhen Ghazari Ayvazyan, Nakhijevan, Norashen, 1914 ♦ Ashkhen Grigori Grigoryan, Shirak, Paldrvan, 1914 ♦ Ashkhen Grigori Grigoryan, Yerznka, Toros, 1910 ♦ Ashkhen Grigori Movsisyan, Kars, Mazra, 1909 ♦ Ashkhen Hakobi Hakobyan, Alekpol, Arkhvali, 1914 ♦ Ashkhen Hakobi Hakobyan, Basen, Yaghan, 1915 ♦ Ashkhen Hakobi Hakobyan, Lori, Shnogh, 1914 ♦ Ashkhen Hakobi Hakobyan, Shnogh, 1916 ♦ Ashkhen Hamazaspi Hovhannisyan, Kaghzvan, 1910 ♦ Ashkhen Hambardzumi Davtyan, Karabagh, 1914 ♦ Ashkhen Hambardzumi Hambaryan, Kars, Shativan, 1917 ♦ Ashkhen Harutyuni Sargsyan, Shirak, Jajur, 1911 ♦ Ashkhen Harutyuni Simonyan, Mec Gharakilisa, Parnigegh, 1911 ♦ Ashkhen Hasoyi Hasoyan, Etchmiadzin, Kuchak, 1914 ♦ Ashkhen Hayrapeti Hayrapetyan, Zangezur, Agarak, 1917 ♦ Ashkhen Hovaki Galstyan, Aparan, Ghotur, 1912 ♦ Ashkhen Hovhannesi Ghandilyan, Sarighamish, 1913 ♦ Ashkhen Hovhannesi Ghazaryan, Baghesh, Bkhus, 1909 ♦ Ashkhen Hovhannesi Hovhannisyan, Lori, Urut, 1918 ♦ Ashkhen Hovhannesi Hovhannisyan, Van, Ererin, 1909 ♦ Ashkhen Hovhannesi Sargsyan, Kars, Kyorakdar, 1912 ♦ Ashkhen Hovhannesi Ter-Aristakesyan, Kars, Byoragdara, 1913 ♦ Ashkhen Jallati Poghosyan, Karabagh, Shushi, 1910 ♦ Ashkhen Karapeti Barseghyan, Kars, 1909 ♦ Ashkhen Karapeti Danielyan, Kars, Ughuzli, 1911 ♦ Ashkhen Karapeti Ghazaryan, Kars, Bulanagh, 1911 ♦ Ashkhen Karapeti Hakobyan, Karabagh, Nukhi, 1904 ♦ Ashkhen Khachaturi Ghazaryan, Kars, Gharajugh, 1910 ♦ Ashkhen Khachaturi Ghukasyan, Leninakan, Ortakilisa, 1912 ♦ Ashkhen Khachaturi Mitilchyan, Gyumushkhan, 1909 ♦ Ashkhen Khachaturi Movsisyan (Khachatryan), Sarighamish, 1912 ♦ Ashkhen Khudaverdi Alaverdyan, Salmast, 1914 ♦ Ashkhen Kirakosi Grigoryan, Leninakan, Sariar, 1913 ♦ Ashkhen Manuki Gabrielyan, Sarighamish, Bashgegh, 1911 ♦ Ashkhen Margari Tadevosyan, Nor Bayazet, Dali ghardash, 1909 ♦ Ashkhen Markosi Markosyan, Hin Nakhijevan, Sultanbek, 1913 ♦ Ashkhen Martirosi Martirosyan, Shirak, Syogutli, 1909 ♦ Ashkhen Martirosi Martirosyan, Yerevan, Haytagh, 1915 ♦ Ashkhen Martirosi Sargsyan, Sarighamish, Bashgegh, 1910 ♦ Ashkhen Meliki Ghazaryan, Leninakan, Takarli, 1911 ♦ Ashkhen Meliki Martirosyan (Melikyan), Yerevan, Molla-Ghasm, 1913 ♦ Ashkhen Misaki Hovhannisyan (Barseghyan), Lori, Uzunlar, 1913 ♦ Ashkhen Misaki Sargsyan, Mush, Kronk, 1914 ♦ Ashkhen Mkhoyi Aloyan, Leninakan, Paltli, 1910 ♦ Ashkhen Mkoyi Hovhannisyan, Sarighamish, Bashgyugh, 1914 ♦ Ashkhen Mkrtchi Manukyan, Darachichak, Babakishi, 1908 ♦ Ashkhen Mkrtchi Mkrtchyan, Aparan, Bash-Aparan, 1914 ♦ Ashkhen Mnatsakani Mnatsakanyan, Yerevan, Akhta, 1909 ♦ Ashkhen Muradi Kirakosyan, Sarighamish, Armtlu, 1911 ♦ Ashkhen Muradi Mkrtchyan, Mush, Khazlu, 1911 ♦ Ashkhen Musheghi Musheghyan (Maksadyan), Mush, Bulanagh, Liz, 1907 ♦ Ashkhen Musheghi Petrosyan, Khnus, 1909 ♦ Ashkhen Nazari Mayesyan, Kars, 1911 ♦ Ashkhen Nikoli Danielyan, Kars, Nakhijevan, 1912 ♦ Ashkhen Petrosi Petrosyan, Kars, Berni, 1911 ♦ Ashkhen Poghosi Poghosyan, Alekpol, Aleksandrovka, 1910 ♦ Ashkhen Sahaki Antonyan, Akhalkalak, Aragyal, 1913 ♦ Ashkhen Sahaki Elbakyan, Kars, Stan, 1909 ♦ Ashkhen Sargsi Melkonyan, Akhalkalak, Vachian, 1917 ♦ Ashkhen Sargsi Sargsyan, Yerevan, 1913 ♦ Ashkhen Sargsi Torosyan, Alekpol, Ghazalghoch, 1913 ♦ Ashkhen Saroyi Grigoryan, Kars, Pokr Parker, 1915 ♦ Ashkhen Sedraki Barseghyan, Kars, Sarighamish, 1918 ♦ Ashkhen Sedraki Petrosyan, Alekpol, Paldrvan, 1912 ♦ Ashkhen Sedraki Sedrakyan, Van, Badnos, 1909 ♦ Ashkhen Sergoyi Khachatryan, Alekpol, 1914 ♦ Ashkhen Sergoyi Papikyan, Lori, Urut, 1913 ♦ Ashkhen Sergoyi Sargsyan, Gyokchay, Keghshurt, 1912 ♦ Ashkhen Shahbazi Mkrtchyan, Alashkert, Khazlu, 1912 ♦ Ashkhen Simoni Simonyan, 1917 ♦ Ashkhen Sirekani Sirakanyan, Kars, Bvek, 1916 ♦ Ashkhen Smbati Smbatyan, Igdir, Zakrlu, 1915 ♦ Ashkhen Soghomoni Soghomonyan, Van, 1915 ♦ Ashkhen Stepanosi Mikayelyan, Akhalkalak, Kyosaghbyur, 1912 ♦ Ashkhen Tadevosi Grigoryan, Karabagh, 1913 ♦ Ashkhen Tigrani Karapetyan, Kars, Paldrvan, 1913 ♦ Ashkhen Tigrani Nikoghosyan, Kars, Arcateli, 1914 ♦ Ashkhen Torosi Manukyan, Sarighamish, Kokhviran, 1910 ♦ Ashkhen Torosi Voskanyan, Leninakan, Sogudli, 1912 ♦ Ashkhen Tumasi Varzhapetyan, Kars, 1915 ♦ Ashkhen Vagharshaki Ter-Barseghyan, Kars, 1910 ♦ Ashkhen Vardani Aznavuryan, Akhalkalak, Chandura, 1911, 1910 ♦ Ashkhen Vardani Shahnazaryan, Yerevan, Zinjghlu, 1911 ♦ Ashkhen Vardani Vardanyan, Van, Nor gyugh, 1912 ♦ Ashkhen Vardani Vardanyan, Yerevan, 1918 ♦ Ashkhen Voskani Konyan, Sanahin, Vornak, 1916 ♦ Ashkhen Vostani Mirzoyan, Nakhijevan, Gyumri, 1913 ♦ Ashkhen Yenoki Yenokyan, Bulanagh, 1916 ♦ Ashkhen Zakari Amroyan, Nakhijevan, Gyumri, 1910 ♦ Asho Vardani Khachatryan, Kars, Ghzlchakhchakh, 1914 ♦ Ashot Abrahami Abrahamyan, Sarighamish, Cholakhli, 1909 ♦ Ashot Aleki Grigoryan, Kars, Hamzaparak, 1917 ♦ Ashot Aleksani Baghoyan, Kars, Bayburt, 1914 ♦ Ashot Aleksani Ghumashyan (Aleksanyan), Gharakilisa, Hajighara, 1917 ♦ Ashot Andreasi Melikyan,

Akhalkalak, Gandza, 1912 ♦ Ashot Arakeli Davtyan, Kars, Paldrvan, 1913 ♦ Ashot Arakeli Gevorgyan, Kars, 1908 ♦ Ashot Artashi Artashyan, Alekpol, Haji-Nazar, 1917 ♦ Ashot Ashoti Ashotyan, 1920 ♦ Ashot Avagi (Arshak) Gharajyan, Kars, Chirghan, 1908 ♦ Ashot Avagi Ashotyan (Izghatyan), Leninakan, Bashgegh, 1918 ♦ Ashot Avagi Avagyan, Sarighamish, 1916 ♦ Ashot Avetisi Varosyan, Kars, Kyuragdara, 1914 ♦ Ashot Baghdasari Vardanyan, Alekpol, Sirvangyugh, 1911 ♦ Ashot Bagrati Kostanyan, Kars, Kaghzvan, 1914 ♦ Ashot Barseghi Barseghyan, Basen, Adian, 1914 ♦ Ashot Daviti Avetisyan, Pambak, Gharakilisa, 1918 ♦ Ashot Gabrieli Pilrakyan, Javakhk, Aragova, 1910 ♦ Ashot Gaspari Gasparyan, Karabagh, 1915 ♦ Ashot Gaspari Mkrtchyan, Kars, 1912, 1914 ♦ Ashot Gevorgi Hovsepyan, Leninakan, 1914 ♦ Ashot Gevorgi Khumaryan, Kars, Kyatiklar, 1914 ♦ Ashot Gevorgi Sargsyan, Kars, Ghzlchakhchakh, 1912 ♦ Ashot Gevorgi Stepanyan, Kars, Baglamad, 1911 ♦ Ashot Gevorgi Vardanyan, Sarighamish, Cholakhlu, 1912 ♦ Ashot Ghazari Nasaryan, Dilijan, Paldrvan, 1919 ♦ Ashot Ghukasi Ghukasyan, Nakhijevan, Jalal, 1915 ♦ Ashot Grigori Grigoryan, Kars, Hamzakar, 1917 ♦ Ashot Hakobi Sargsyan, Sarighamish, 1911 ♦ Ashot Haruti Harutyunyan, Kars, Tglmet, 1914 ♦ Ashot Harutyuni Aramyan, Shamakhi, Madras, 1912 ♦ Ashot Harutyuni Hrachyan, Van, 1918 ♦ Ashot Harutyuni Melkonyan, Leninakan, Sogutlu, 1911 ♦ Ashot Hovhannesi Atoyan, Kars, Bayburd, 1914 ♦ Ashot Hovhannesi Gharakhanyan, Alekpol, Ghrnaghran, 1913 ♦ Ashot Hovhannesi Hovhannisyan, Akhalkalak, Kentra, 1913 ♦ Ashot Hovhannesi Melkonyan, Koghb, Koghb, 1913 ♦ Ashot Kakoyi Kakosyan, Gharakilis, Vordnav, 1914 ♦ Ashot Karapeti Kochoyan, Van, 1911 ♦ Ashot Karapeti Poghosyan, Kars, 1913, 1911 ♦ Ashot Karapeti Sargsyan, Van, 1913 ♦ Ashot Khachaturi Khachatryan, Kars, Cbni, 1912 ♦ Ashot Khachoyi Grigoryan, Kars, Ughuzli, 1911 ♦ Ashot Khachoyi Hovhannisyan, Nor Bayazet, 1913 ♦ Ashot Kochari Kocharyan, Mush, Prkhus, 1912 ♦ Ashot Macaki Harutyunyan, Alekpol, Sogatlu, 1912 ♦ Ashot Manuki Hakobyan, Kars, 1914 ♦ Ashot Maratyan, Kars, 1916 ♦ Ashot Markosi Markosyan, Akhalkalak, Korkh, 1914 ♦ Ashot Martirosi Grigoryan, Kars, Araz, 1913 ♦ Ashot Martirosi Sargsyan, Shirak, Karagdar, 1916 ♦ Ashot Meliki Arakelyan, Kars, Aghuzum, 1914 ♦ Ashot Meliki Sahradyan, Kars, 1916 ♦ Ashot Melkoni Tonoyan, Kars, Nakhijevan, 1913 ♦ Ashot Meloyi Khurshudyan, Kars, Bashshoragal, 1911 ♦ Ashot Misaki Khachatryan, Kars, 1913 ♦ Ashot Misaki Khachatryan, Kars, Gorkhana, 1911, 1910 ♦ Ashot Misaki Levonyan, Kars, Kaghzvan, 1910 ♦ Ashot Mkrtchi Baghdasaryan, Kars, 1911 ♦ Ashot Mkrtchi Hovakimyan, Gharakilisa, Hamamli, 1914 ♦ Ashot Mnacakani Mnacakanyan, Nakhijevan, 1914 ♦ Ashot Movsesi Movsisyan, Manazkert, Khotanlu, 1914 ♦ Ashot Mukayeli Ter-Gevorgyan, Kars, 1912 ♦ Ashot Nazari Khachatryan, Kars, Berna, 1911 ♦ Ashot Nikoli Simonyan, Kars, Ghoshavank, 1912, 1911 ♦ Ashot Petrosi Aregakyan, Ardahan, 1913 ♦ Ashot Petrosi Hakobyan (Petrosyan), Gharakilisa, Ghaltakhchi, 1916 ♦ Ashot Petrosi Muradyan, Kars, Berna, 1918 ♦ Ashot Poghosi Poghosyan, Yerevan, Noragavit, 1917 ♦ Ashot Poroyi Harutyunyan, Kars, Ghzl-chakhchakh, 1912, 1910 ♦ Ashot Sandroyi Mkrtchyan, Akhalkalak, Dadesh, 1916 ♦ Ashot Satoyi Martirosyan, Ardahan, 1915 ♦ Ashot Simoni Harutyunyan, Kars, Khani, 1916 ♦ Ashot Simoni Tonoyan (Aleksanyan), Leninakan, Kharkov, 1909 ♦ Ashot Sirakani Tumasyan, Kars, Pirvali, 1913 ♦ Ashot Stepani Voskanyan, Akhalkalak, Vachian, 1912 ♦ Ashot Tadevosi Gyulbazyan, Kaghzvan, 1912 ♦ Ashot Tadevosi Karanyan, Alekpol, 1914 ♦ Ashot Varosi Martirosyan, Alekpol, Norashen, 1910 ♦ Ashot Yeghiazari Adamyan, Kars, Zaim, 1908 ♦ Ashot Yegori (Nikoli) Barseghyan, Alekpol, Ghazarapat, 1914 ♦ Askanaz Arami Hakobyan, Sumarlu, Alighamar, 1910 ♦ Askanaz Hovsepi Matevosyan, Van, 1915 ♦ Askanaz Knyazi Harutyunyan, Alekpol, Svanverdi, 1912 ♦ Askanaz Petrosi Chakhoyan, Alekpol, Chiktalu, 1912 ♦ Askanaz Saroyi Harutyunyan, Shirak, Svanverdi, 1909 ♦ Askanaz Yepremi Vardanyan, Igdir, Najafal, 1912 ♦ Aslan Sargsi Khachatryan, Khnus, Berd, 1909 ♦ Aslan Sianosi Aslanyan (Sianosyan), Van, Tonia, 1907 ♦ Asli Barseghi Sargsyan, Kars, Chirmali, 1912 ♦ Asmar Baghdasari Baghdasaryan, Khnus, Khazchavush, 1911 ♦ Aso Gevorgi Funjyan, Leninakan, Ghapli, 1918 ♦ Astaf Karapeti Najiryan, Manazkert, Norashen, 1910 ♦ Astenik Poghosi Petrosyan, Van, Shatakh, 1908 ♦ Astghik Abgari Ter Davtyan (Abgaryan), Alekpol, Gyozlu, 1912 ♦ Astghik Aleksani Aleksanyan, Alashkert, 1917 ♦ Astghik Aleksani Hambardzumyan, Nakhijevan, Gumri, 1910 ♦ Astghik Aleksani Karapetyan, Shirak, Bashshoragyal, 1915 ♦ Astghik Aleksani Khachatryan, Kars, Mavrak, 1907 ♦ Astghik Arami Khachatryan, Alekpol, Ghanlija, 1912 ♦ Astghik Arami Khachatryan, Alekpol, Samrlu, 1912 ♦ Astghik Armenaki Papikyan, Kars, Nakhijevan, 1915 ♦ Astghik Arseni Arsenyan, Nakhijevan, Seys, 1914 ♦ Astghik Arseni Savayan, Kars, Berni, 1914 ♦ Astghik Arshaki Arshakyan, Ghazakh, Koghb, 1913 ♦ Astghik Arshaki Stepanyan, Aparan, Alikuchak, 1908 ♦ Astghik Asaturi Abalyan (Asatryan), Gharakilisa, Hajighara, 1915 ♦ Astghik Asaturi Ter-Ghazaryan, Gharakilisa, Parni gyugh, 1911 ♦ Astghik Asaturi Yeghyan, Karabagh, Shushi, 1915 ♦ Astghik Avetisi Avetisyan, Kars, Bagra, 1914 ♦ Astghik Avetisi Khachatryan, Nakhijevan, Aza, 1913 ♦ Astghik Avetisi Simonyan, Leninakan, 1916 ♦ Astghik Badali Karapetyan, Alekpol, Ghzlkilisa, 1916 ♦ Astghik Baghdasari Baghdasaryan, Kars, 1917 ♦ Astghik Barseghi Ter-Nikoghosyan, Sarighamish, Shativan, 1911 ♦ Astghik Gabrieli Minasyan, Van, Plavan, 1910 ♦ Astghik Gaspari Gasparyan, Khnus, Haramik, 1913, 1912 ♦ Astghik Geghami Stepanyan, Yerevan, Dashburun, 1914 ♦ Astghik Gevorgi Arakelyan, Pambak, Ghshlagh, 1910 ♦ Astghik Gevorgi Gevorgyan, Kars, 1916 ♦ Astghik Gevorgi Nersisyan, Kars, Bashgegh, 1917 ♦ Astghik Gevorgi Simonyan, Alekpol, Bayandura, 1912 ♦ Astghik Ghazari Zakaryan, Kars, Pokr Parkir, 1910 ♦ Astghik Grigori Grigoryan, Darachichak, Taycharukh, 1912 ♦ Astghik Grigori Grigoryan, Erzrum, 1916 ♦ Astghik Grigori

Hambardzumyan, Caghkadzor, Caghkunk, 1914 ♦ Astghik Grigori Karapetyan, Dilijan, Karvansara, 1915 ♦ Astghik Grigori Sahakyan (Grigoryan), Kars, 1909 ♦ Astghik Grigori Sirunyan, 1922 ♦ Astghik Hakobi Hakobyan, Echmiacin, Jafarabad, 1911 ♦ Astghik Hakobi Hakobyan, Maten, 1914 ♦ Astghik Hakobi Javadyan, Nakhijevan, Nukhi, 1912 ♦ Astghik Hakobi Karapetyan, Igdir, Koghb, 1913 ♦ Astghik Hakobi Margaryan (Hakobyan), Kars, Dolbandlu, 1914 ♦ Astghik Hamayaki Aghekyan, Alekpol, Ghzlghoch, 1913 ♦ Astghik Hambardzumi Babayan (Hambardzumyan), Nakhijevan, Ghazanchi, 1914 ♦ Astghik Harutyuni Barinyan, Kaghzman, 1912 ♦ Astghik Harutyuni Martirosyan, Alekpol, Ghzlghoch, 1912 ♦ Astghik Harutyuni Mirmanyan, Tiflis, 1914 ♦ Astghik Harutyuni Petrosyan, Karabagh, Keshshort, 1910 ♦ Astghik Hayrapeti Ghevondyan, Shamakh, Zarkho, 1909, 1908 ♦ Astghik Hayrapeti Hayrapetyan, Yerevan, 1914 ♦ Astghik Hayrapeti Manukyan (Hayrapetyan), Kars, Ortakhala, 1913, 1911 ♦ Astghik Hovaki Hovhannisyan, Ejmiacin, Ghariar, 1917 ♦ Astghik Hovhannesi Baghdasaryan, Nakhijevan, Duz, 1913 ♦ Astghik Hovhannesi Ghasabyan, Baku, 1909 ♦ Astghik Hovhannesi Ghevondyan, Vaspurakan, Van, 1909 ♦ Astghik Hovhannesi Hovhannisyan, Alekpol, Ghzlkilisa, 1915 ♦ Astghik Hovhannesi Hovhannisyan, Alekpol, Ojaghlu, 1918 ♦ Astghik Hovhannesi Hovhannisyan, Kaghzvan, 1914 ♦ Astghik Hovhannesi Hovhannisyan, Leninakan, Ghzlar, 1915 ♦ Astghik Hovhannesi Hovhannisyan, Persia, Gharadagh, 1913 ♦ Astghik Hovhannesi Kirakosyan, Kars, 1910 ♦ Astghik Hovhannesi Manukyan, Alekpol, Ghazarabad, 1911 ♦ Astghik Hovhannesi Nersisyan, Igdir, 1909 ♦ Astghik Hunani Sargsyan, Kars, 1914 ♦ Astghik Igiti Sargsyan, Kars, Araz, 1911–1912 ♦ Astghik Israyeli Hovoyan (Israyelyan), Bitliz, 1910, 1911 ♦ Astghik Karapeti Avetisyan, Alekpol, Sogutli, 1912 ♦ Astghik Karapeti Hovhannisyan, Kars, Aksighaz, 1912 ♦ Astghik Karapeti Karapetyan, Ghamarlu, Darghalu, 1913 ♦ Astghik Karapeti Karapetyan, Leninakan, 1917 ♦ Astghik Karapeti Khachatryan, Akhalkalak, Chantura, 1912 ♦ Astghik Khachaturi Avagyan, Daralagaz, Biralu, 1908 ♦ Astghik Khachaturi Hakobyan, Leninakan, Ghapli, 1909 ♦ Astghik Khachaturi Khachatryan, 1918 ♦ Astghik Khachaturi Khachatryan, Nukhi, Dashbulak, 1911 ♦ Astghik Khachaturi Khachatryan, Van, 1912 ♦ Astghik Khachaturi Papoyan, Kars, Mec Parket, 1912 ♦ Astghik Macaki Ghumalyan, Mec Gharakilisa, 1917 ♦ Astghik Makari Avetisyan, Leninakan, Bozdoghan, 1910 ♦ Astghik Margari Grigoryan, Van, 1910 ♦ Astghik Margari Margaryan, Kars, 1914 ♦ Astghik Margari Muradyan, Aziz gyugh, 1918 ♦ Astghik Martirosi Ghazaryan, Kars, Bayburt, 1908 ♦ Astghik Martirosi Kyureghyan, Kars, Jalal, 1915 ♦ Astghik Martirosi Martirosyan, Kars, 1917 ♦ Astghik Matevosi Aleksanyan, Lori, Kurtan, 1915, 1916 ♦ Astghik Matevosi Grishyan, Tifliz, 1913 ♦ Astghik Matevosi Matevosyan, Jalal oghli, Ordaklu, 1917 ♦ Astghik Matosi Antonyan, Akhalkalak, Ghulalis, 1914 ♦ Astghik Meliki Melikyan, Persia, Yenzeli, 1912 ♦ Astghik Meliki Melkonyan, Kaghzvan, 1918 ♦ Astghik Mesropi Mesropyan, Kars, Bayraktar, 1913 ♦ Astghik Misaki Khachatryan, Kars, Tiknez, 1915 ♦ Astghik Mkrtchi Arakelyan, Echmiacin, Gharkhar, 1916 ♦ Astghik Mkrtchi Cerunyan, Nakhijevan, Nors, 1911 ♦ Astghik Mkrtchi Hakobyan, Persia, Dizi, 1911 ♦ Astghik Mkrtchi Martirosyan, Akhalkalak, Abul, 1914 ♦ Astghik Mkrtchi Mnoyan, Akhalkalak, Smaverdi, 1911 ♦ Astghik Mkrtchi Stepanyan, Akhaltsikha, 1915 ♦ Astghik Mkrtichi Abrahamyan, Kars, Katiklar, 1908 ♦ Astghik Mnacakani Grigoryan, Shirak, Horom, 1911 ♦ Astghik Mnatsakani Petrosyan, Kars, 1913 ♦ Astghik Mnatsakani Sedrakyan (Ghazaryan), Basar, Garni, 1916 ♦ Astghik Mukayeli Muradyan, Basen, Atan, 1912 ♦ Astghik Muradi (Meliki), Shahinyan, Tiflis, 1914 ♦ Astghik Muradi Khurshudyan, Manazkert, 1914 ♦ Astghik Musheghi Hakobyan, Kars, Janjugh, 1910 ♦ Astghik Nazari Sahakyan, Alekpol, Mec Kiti, 1914 ♦ Astghik Nazari Ter-Harutyunyan, Kaghzvan, 1910 ♦ Astghik Nersesi Ishkhanyan, Karabagh, Rushanashen, 1912, 1909 ♦ Astghik Nikoghosi Babagyulyan, Hin Nakhijevan, Tiza, 1912 ♦ Astghik Nshani Avetisyan, Van, Shahbazi, 1906 ♦ Astghik Nshani Dilbabyan, Trapizon, Gyumurkhana, 1908 ♦ Astghik Parsami Harutyunyan, Leninakan, Armtlu, 1916 ♦ Astghik Petrosi Arakelyan, Baku, 1911 ♦ Astghik Petrosi Muradyan, Van, 1914 ♦ Astghik Petrosi Petrosyan, Batum, 1911 ♦ Astghik Petrosi Petrosyan, Van, Artamet, 1916 ♦ Astghik Sahaki Yeghoyan, Leninakan, Dyuzkhabar, 1913 ♦ Astghik Samsoni Samsonyan, Igdir, Arshamat, 1915 ♦ Astghik Sargsi Sargsyan, Koghb, 1907 ♦ Astghik Sargsi Soghomonyan, Kars, Ortakilisa, 1911 ♦ Astghik Sargsi Voskanyan, Kars, 1912 ♦ Astghik Sedraki Galstyan, Kars, Paldrvan, 1915 ♦ Astghik Serobi Movsisyan, Kars, Bashkadiklar, 1915 ♦ Astghik Sirekani Muradyan, Alashkert, Zetkan, 1912 ♦ Astghik Smbati Tadevosyan, Kars, Paldrvan, 1912 ♦ Astghik Smbati Vardanyan, Kars, Mets Parker, 1908 ♦ Astghik Sosi Avetisyan, Alekpol, Ghzl-kilise, 1915 ♦ Astghik Stepani Hayrapetyan, Leninakan, Gheghaj, 1910 ♦ Astghik Tadevosi Simonyan, Shulaver, 1909 ♦ Astghik Tatosi Torosyan, Kars, Parkit, 1915 ♦ Astghik Tevosi Hovhannisyan, Yerevan, Akhta, 1917 ♦ Astghik Tigrani Karapetyan, Alekpol, 1910 ♦ Astghik Tigrani Tigranyan, Manazkert, Berd, 1914 ♦ Astghik Vagharshaki Mirapyan, Kars, 1914 ♦ Astghik Vardani Mirzoyan, Hobarvet, 1916 ♦ Astghik Yenoki Yenokyan, Hin Bayazet, 1908 ♦ Astghik Yervandi Gharagyozyan, Kars, 1910 ♦ Astghik Zakarei Maghlushyan, Olti, 1909 ♦ Astghik Zakari Hambardzumyan, Nakhijevan, Sultanbck, 1914 ♦ Astghik Zohrabi Harutyunyan, Alekpol, Svanverdi, 1915 ♦ Astine Simoni Karapetyan, Van, 1912 ♦ Astvacatur Hasrati Ghazaryan, Bitlis, Armtlu, 1912 ♦ Asya Mkrtchi Asliyan, Kars, 1908 ♦ Atabek Hambardzumi Harutyunyan, Dilijan, Poghoskilisa, 1911 ♦ Atabek Misaki Misakyan, Yerevan, Taparlu, 1914 ♦ Atabek Vaziri Israyelyan, Nor Bayazet, N. Gharanlukh, 1914 ♦ Atlas Antoni Antonyan, Sarighamish, 1918 ♦ Atlas Baroyi Baroyan, Mush, Shekhaghub, 1909 ♦ Atlas Gaspari Petrosyan (Gasparyan), Lori, Haghpat, 1915 ♦ Atlas Israyeli

Asatryan, Khnus, Khalzav, 1916 ♦ Atlas Movsesi Alekyan, Alashkert, Khastur, 1915 ♦ Atlas Saroyi Mkrtchyan, Bulanagh, Hamzashen, 1909 ♦ Atlas Sukiasi Sukiasyan, Basen, Toti, 1912, 1911 ♦ Atlas Zakari Poghosyan, Mush, Bulanagh, 1910 ♦ Atlaz Gevorgi Khlghatyan, Kars, Dolbandlu, 1914 ♦ Atrash Karapeti Karapetyan, Kars, Ortakadiklar, 1915 ♦ Atrin Grigori Karslyan, Van, 1914 ♦ Atrine Petrosi Petrosyan, Van, 1912 ♦ Avag Arshaki Arshakyan, Alekpol, Zarnzi, 1914 ♦ Avag Arshaki Khachatryan, Shirak, Japlu, 1911 ♦ Avag Arshaki Tonoyan, Lori, Gyulagarak, 1914, 1915 ♦ Avag Azkanazi Madoyan, Aparan Sachlu, 1914 ♦ Avag Baghdasari Baghdasaryan, Van, Abagha, 1916 ♦ Avag Gabrieli Dallakyan, Pambak, Hajidara, 1910 ♦ Avag Galusti Hovhannisyan, Pambak, Sarmsakhlu, 1917 ♦ Avag Ghukasi Ghukasyan, Leninakan, Sariar, 1911 ♦ Avag Ghukasi Sargsyan, Nakhijevan, Laloyi-Mavruk, 1912 ♦ Avag Hovhannesi Baghdasaryan, Archesh, Bozer, 1912 ♦ Avag Hovhannesi Hayrapetyan, Yerevan, Davalu, 1913 ♦ Avag Hovhannesi Hovhannisyan, Kars, 1914 ♦ Avag Hovhannesi Hovhannisyan, Mush, Hovnar, 1909 ♦ Avag Hovhannesi Sargsyan, Khnus, Mjinkit, 1910 ♦ Avag Kerobi Martirosyan, Kars, Jalal, 1912 ♦ Avag Khurshudi Manukyan, Bulanagh, Gharaghala, 1906 ♦ Avag Knyazi Tumasyan, Kars, 1908 ♦ Avag Kuchaki Tonoyan (Kuchakyan), Mush, Gharaghl, 1912–1914 ♦ Avag Serobi Muradyan, Bitliz, Capor, 1910 ♦ Avag Soghomoni Khachatryan, 1918 ♦ Avat Gevorgi Khachatryan (Gevorgyan), Erzrum, Khnus, 1910 ♦ Avdal Aleksani Simonyan, Mush, Bostakand, 1911 ♦ Avetik Artashesi Grigoryan, Alekpol, Kaps, 1914 ♦ Avetik Avetisi Khurmajyan, Kars, 1919 ♦ Avetik Bagrati Avetisyan, Sarighamish ♦ Avetik Bagrati Avetisyan, Sarighamish, 1919 ♦ Avetik Barseghi Avetisyan, Alekpol, Bash-gyugh, 1914 ♦ Avetik Elbaki Sahakyan, Leninakan, Gyugh, 1912 ♦ Avetik Geghami Azizyan, Yerevan, 1914 ♦ Avetik Gevorgi Antonyan, Leninakan, Khli Gharakilisa, 1911 ♦ Avetik Grigori Madoyan, Kars, 1911 ♦ Avetik Haruti Mkhoyan, Paltlu, 1917 ♦ Avetik Harutyuni Avetisyan, Alekpol, Toparlu, 1911 ♦ Avetik Hovhannesi Hovekyan, Basen, Tzveran, 1913 ♦ Avetik Hovhannesi Sargsyan, Shirak, Sogyutli, 1914 ♦ Avetik Hovhannesi Ter-Asatryan, Hin Nakhijevan, Akulis, 1903 ♦ Avetik Hovhannesi Vardanyan, Van, Khums, 1909 ♦ Avetik Karapeti Avagyan, Alekpol, Alekpol, 1914 ♦ Avetik Khachaturi Khachatryan, Kars, Bulanagh, 1911 ♦ Avetik Khechoyi Matinyan, Lori, Kurtan, 1913 ♦ Avetik Misaki Yeritsyan, Basen, Ishkhi, 1910 ♦ Avetik Nikoli Nikolyan, Leninakan, Sarikar, 1916 ♦ Avetik Parsami Shiroyan, Shirak, Maymnjugh, 1912 ♦ Avetik Petrosi Torosyan, Alekpol, Jajur, 1912 ♦ Avetik Poghosi Harutyunyan, Yerevan, 1916, 1914 ♦ Avetik Serobi Serobyan, Shirak, Saral, 1914 ♦ Avetik Smbati Carukyan, Leninakan, 1911 ♦ Avetik Smbati Serobyan (Smbatyan), Nor Bayazet, Vordaklu, 1915 ♦ Avetik Tadosi Zakaryan (Tadosyan), Shirak, Sariar, 1914 ♦ Avetik Yeghishei Kirakosyan, Alekpol, 1914 ♦ Avetis Arseni Sargsyan, Kars, 1916 ♦ Avetis Barseghi (Barseghyan) Hakobyan, Shirak, Bandrvan, 1917 ♦ Avetis Gevorgi (Kocharyan) Gevorgyan, Leninakan, Gheghaj, 1914 ♦ Avetis Gevorgi Baghdasaryan, Shirak, Khalijan, 1917 ♦ Avetis Ghazari Ghazaryan, Bulanagh, Votnchor, 1911 ♦ Avetis Grigori Avetisyan, Lori, Urut, 1917 ♦ Avetis Grigori Grigoryan, Igdir, Panik, 1912 ♦ Avetis Grigori Hovhannisyan ·(Avetisyan), Shirak, Ortakilisa, 1919 ♦ Avetis Hakobi Arakelyan, 1918 ♦ Avetis Hakobi Hovsepyan, Basen, Yekebat, 1910 ♦ Avetis Hambriki Grigoryan, Bulanagh, Shrvanjugh, 1913 ♦ Avetis Harutyuni Baghdasaryan, Gamarlu, Arakzl, 1912 ♦ Avetis Harutyuni Harutyunyan, Vaspurakan, Shidan, 1909 ♦ Avetis Hmayaki Stepanyan, Leninakan, Gharakilisa, 1913 ♦ Avetis Hovasapi Avetisyan, Kars, Gyodukhatrich, 1910 ♦ Avetis Hovhannesi Harutyunyan, Alashkert, Ishkhan, 1914 ♦ Avetis Ivani Galstyan, Nakhijevan, 1909 ♦ Avetis Khachaturi Babayan, Yerevan, Verin Norashen, 1915 ♦ Avetis Khachaturi Yasaghultsyan (Hovhannisyan), Kars, Chala, 1909 ♦ Avetis Khachoyi Khachoyan, Pambak, Gharakilisa, 1918 ♦ Avetis Margari Avetisyan, Basen, Yaghan, 1912 ♦ Avetis Matevosi Khachatryan, Gharakilisa, Chotur, 1914 ♦ Avetis Melkoni Manukyan, Nakhijevan, Julfa, 1912 ♦ Avetis Misaki Avetisyan, Olti, 1908 ♦ Avetis Misaki Karapetyan, Basen, Armtlu, 1910 ♦ Avetis Mkrtchi Poghosyan, Mush, Krdakar, 1900 ♦ Avetis Navasardi Gasparyan, Yerevan, Arinj, 1914 ♦ Avetis Ohannesi Avetisyan (Ohanyan), Van, 1909 ♦ Avetis Rubeni Hovhannisyan, Kars, Baghli-ahmed, 1910, 1908 ♦ Avetis Safari Manukyan, Kars, Bulanagh, 1913 ♦ Avetis Sargsi Asatryan, Kars, Bashshoragal, 1916 ♦ Avetis Sargsi Ter-Ghukasyan, Kharberd, Balisher, 1911 ♦ Avetis Sedraki Aghamiryan, Norduz, Pervadalan, 1909 ♦ Avetis Sedraki Movsisyan, Basen, Hekepat, 1909 ♦ Avetis Stepanosi Aleksanyan, Leninakan, Ghris, 1909 ♦ Avetis Tigrani Ghazaryan, Shoragal, Haji khalil, 1913 ♦ Avetis Torosi Varderesyan (Torosyan), Alekpol, Svanverdi, 1911 ♦ Avetis Yeghoyi Muradyan, Van, Kerdz, 1911 ♦ Avetis Yeghoyi Yeghoyan, Aljavaz, Gazokh, 1909 ♦ Avetis Yeloyi Yeloyan, Kars, Bulankh, 1914 ♦ Avetis Yenoki Ghazaryan, Akhta, Yayji, 1910 ♦ Avetis Yeranosi Melkonyan, Leninakan, Ortakilisa, 1914 ♦ Avik Vardani Harutyunyan, Kars, Archarak, 1913 ♦ Aycem Tatosi Poghosyan, Kars, 1919 ♦ Aycemik Hakobi Petrosyan, Kars, 1914 ♦ Aycemik Martirosi Martirosyan, Yerevan, Chidamlu, 1913 ♦ Ayvaz Antoni Hovakimyan, Bandrvan, 1913 ♦ Azat Abrahami Abrahamyan, Mush, Drmert, 1913 ♦ Azat Aghajani Aghajanyan, Mush, 1916 ♦ Azat Aleksani Aleksanyan, Mush, Khosh-gyaldi, 1910 ♦ Azat Arakeli Gevorgyan (Arakelyan), Alashkert, Ghayabek, 1912 ♦ Azat Avetisi Avetisyan, Ijevan, 1911 ♦ Azat Avetisi Martirosyan, Moz, Khvnir, 1910 ♦ Azat Avetisi Melkonyan, Basen, Izveran, 1912 ♦ Azat Ayvazi Ayvazyan, Aljavaz, Arin, 1911 ♦ Azat Baghdasari Ayvazyan (Baghdasaryan), Manazkert, Derik, 1911 ♦ Azat Galusti Galstyan, Erzrum, Basen, 1914 ♦ Azat Gaspari Gevorgyan, Van, 1914 ♦ Azat Gaspari Kirakosyan, Mush, 1912, 1913 ♦ Azat Gevorgi Gevorgyan, Van, Hasan-Tamra, 1911 ♦ Azat Gevorgi Sargsyan, Mush, Kop, 1913 ♦ Azat Ghazari Muradyan,

Mush, Havatorig, 1910 ◆ Azat Ghukasi Abrahamyan, Kars, Chala, 1914 ◆ Azat Ghukasi Mkrtchyan, Bulanagh, Kokh, 1914 ◆ Azat Grigori Sirunyan, Kars, Bulanagh, 1911 ◆ Azat Hakobi Hakobyan, Khlat, Aghagh, 1912 ◆ Azat Hakobi Hakobyan, Van, Aljavaz, 1913 ◆ Azat Hakobi Hovhannisyan, Manazkert, Tondras, 1910 ◆ Azat Hakobi Movsisyan, Akhlat, Srbadzor, 1912 ◆ Azat Hambardzumi Simonyan, Kars, Bayburt, 1910 ◆ Azat Harutyuni Galstyan (Harutyunyan), Ayntap, Kosh, 1914 ◆ Azat Harutyuni Harutyunyan, 1919 ◆ Azat Hovhannesi Hovhannisyan (Manukyan), Khnus, Yenikoy, 1911 ◆ Azat Hovhannesi Hovhannisyan, Van, Tshod, 1909 ◆ Azat Hovhannesi Khachatryan, Bitlis, Topavank, 1909 ◆ Azat Hovhannesi Muradyan, Van, 1912 ◆ Azat Hovsepi Hovsepyan, Alashkert, Berd, 1913 ◆ Azat Khachaturi Aghababyan (Khachatryan), Basen, Alijagrak, 1910 ◆ Azat Khachaturi Martirosyan, Van, 1911 ◆ Azat Khachaturi Sargsyan, Van, Nor gyugh, 1909 ◆ Azat Knyazi Gasparyan, Mush, Kakarlu, 1912 ◆ Azat Manasi Hovakimyan, Akhlat, Khulik, 1911 ◆ Azat Manuki Avetisyan, Van, Vozim, 1912 ◆ Azat Manuki Badoyan, Mush, Khasgyugh, 1912 ◆ Azat Manuki Manukyan, Mush, Khasgyugh, 1913 ◆ Azat Manuki Vardanyan, Van, Veri-Sipan, 1911 ◆ Azat Margari Feroyan, Van, Aljavaz, 1912 ◆ Azat Margari Margaryan, Mush, Khasagyugh, 1913 ◆ Azat Martirosi Martirosyan, Bitlis, Kultik, 1916 ◆ Azat Martirosi Nalbandyan, Van, 1909 ◆ Azat Meliki Melkonyan, Bulanagh, Kop, 1910 ◆ Azat Mikayeli Ayvazyan, Alashkert, Berd, 1912, 1911 ◆ Azat Misaki Arakelyan, Mush, 1911 ◆ Azat Mkhitari Ghazaryan, Bulanagh, Yonjala, 1912 ◆ Azat Mkhitari Khachatryan, Bayburt, 1920, 1918 ◆ Azat Mkhitari Mkhitaryan, Yerevan, 1912 ◆ Azat Mkrtchi Khachatryan (Mkrtchyan), Alashkert, Khoshian, 1913 ◆ Azat Mkrtchi Mkrtchyan, Van, Grak, 1913 ◆ Azat Movsesi Katamyan, Van, Archesh, 1913 ◆ Azat Movsesi Tovmasyan, Baku, 1912 ◆ Azat Muradi Muradyan, Batnots, Marmus, 1911 ◆ Azat Musheghi Tumasyan, Alashkert, Shushan, 1912 ◆ Azat Petrosi Petrosyan, Akhlat, Jimalverdi, 1913 ◆ Azat Petrosi Petrosyan, Erzrum, Khnusghala, 1911 ◆ Azat Petrosi Petrosyan, Mush, Latar, 1909 ◆ Azat Poghosi Poghosyan, Mazkert, Ghasmera, 1912 ◆ Azat Sahaki Safaryan, Bitlis, Kalhog, 1910 ◆ Azat Sahaki Serobyan, Van, Alijavaz, 1912 ◆ Azat Sargsi Sargsyan, Kars, Pokr Pesrkit, 1919 ◆ Azat Sedraki Alanshints, Bulanakh, Dighut, 1911 ◆ Azat Sedraki Manukyan, Khnus, Kopal, 1912 ◆ Azat Sedraki Sedrakyan, Khnus, Berd, 1912 ◆ Azat Sedraki Vokhyan, Erzrum, Antasi, 1911 ◆ Azat Smbati Margaryan, Bulanakh, Teghut, 1912 ◆ Azat Soghomoni Manukyan (Soghomonyan), Mush, 1914 ◆ Azat Soghoyi Hakobyan, Mush, Khasgyugh, 1912 ◆ Azat Tachati Khachatryan, Van, 1912 ◆ Azat Yeghiazari Vardanyan, Van, Archesh, Irishtar, 1913 ◆ Azat Yeroyi Nushekyan, Hin Bayazet, Bayazet, 1911 ◆ Azat Yesayi Sahakyan, Van, Archesh, 1913 ◆ Azat Zakari Margaryan (Zakaryan), Bulanagh, Sheghaghup, 1912 ◆ Azat-Bek Melkoni Ishkhanyan (Sopoyan), Yerevan, Aparan, 1919 ◆ Azatuhi Harutyuni Harutyunyan, Van, 1916 ◆ Azatuhi Hovhannesi Khachatryan, Van, 1916 ◆ Azatuhi Karapeti Karapetyan, Van, 1918 ◆ Azatuhi Petrosi Petrosyan, Trapizon, 1912–1914 ◆ Azganush Arseni Arsenyan, Akhalkalak, Sulda, 1915 ◆ Azganush Asaturi Parsamyan (Asatryan), Baybert, Avarak, 1910 ◆ Azganush Avetisi Avetisyan, Kars, 1916 ◆ Azganush Daviti (Margaryan) Davtyan, Kars, Tekniz, 1916 ◆ Azganush Elbaki Minasyan, Alekpol, Bashshoragal, 1910 ◆ Azganush Galusti Galstyan, Leninakan, Taknalu, 1915 ◆ Azganush Gevorgi Gevorgyan, Igdir, 1914 ◆ Azganush Hakobi Hakobyan, Leninakan, Ghanliza, 1919 ◆ Azganush Hamazaspi Hamazaspyan, Kars, Araz, 1917 ◆ Azganush Hmayaki Hmayakyan, Alekpol, Svanvirt, 1914 ◆ Azganush Kirakosi Kirakosyan, Kars, Kyadeklar, 1916 ◆ Azganush Levoni Tadevosyan, Kars, Bazrgyan, 1915 ◆ Azganush Martirosi Azakyan, Igdir, Alghamar, 1911 ◆ Azganush Martirosi Martirosyan, Yerevan, Tegor, 1914 ◆ Azganush Matosi Matosyan, Leninakan, Bashshoragal, 1919 ◆ Azganush Misaki Khachatryan, Basen, Hekibad, 1913 ◆ Azganush Mkrtchi Avagyan, Alekpol, Ghazarapat, 1912 ◆ Azganush Mkrtchi Petrosyan, Kars, Tekor, 1912 ◆ Azganush Petrosi Petrosyan, Kars, Chala, 1917 ◆ Azganush Serobi Hovhannisyan, Alekpol, Svanverdi, 1911 ◆ Azganush Simoni Melkonyan, Kars, Ijos, 1910 ◆ Azganush Stepani Tukhikyan, Basen, Dali-baba, 1913 ◆ Azganush Vahani Khachatryan, Kars, Uzughli, 1917 ◆ Azganush Vahani Vahanyan, Kars, Uzunkilisa, 1916 ◆ Azganush Vanoyi Vanoyan, Shirak, Babalu, 1916 ◆ Azganush Yeghiazari Adamyan, Kars, Zaim, 1914 ◆ Azgi Tipani Tipanyan, Alekpol, Ghonakhghran, 1918 ◆ Azgil Hmayaki Melikyan, Kars, Aghuz, 1911 ◆ Azgin Knyazi Gevorgyan, Kars, Ghzl-chakhchakh, 1912 ◆ Azgo Arakeli Arakelyan, Leninakan, Toros gyugh, 1920 ◆ Azgo Haruti Sargsyan, Kars, Parket, 1918 ◆ Azgo Harutyuni Harutyunyan, 1919 ◆ Azgo Harutyuni Harutyunyan, Kars, 1919 ◆ Azgo Hovhannesi Filoyan, Kars, Uzunkilisa, 1913 ◆ Azgo Sedraki Sedrakyan, Leninakan, Gyuzli, 1917 ◆ Azgo Vanyayi Khachatryan, 1920 ◆ Azgo Yegori Yegoryan, Leninakan, Chrpl, 1918 ◆ Azgush Grigori Grigoryan, Alekpol, Ghaplu, 1915 ◆ Azgush Hakobi Abrahamyan, Basen, Chasason, 1913 ◆ Azgush Hovsepi Grigoryan, Baku, 1918 ◆ Aziz (Iskuhi) Hakobi Nersisyan, Nakhijevan, Sharut, 1915 ◆ Aziz Ghazari Melikyan, Khnus, Khayakopti, 1910 ◆ Aziz Hayrapeti Gevorgyan, Nor Bayazet, Khul ali, 1910 ◆ Aziz Hovhannesi Arshakyan, Akhalkalak, 1915 ◆ Aziz Hovhannesi Hovhannisyan, Bulanagh, Shekhazlu, 1911 ◆ Aziz Khachiki Hakobyan, Archesh, Blumak, 1911 ◆ Aziz Manuki Manukyan, Pambak, Gharakilisa, 1919 ◆ Aziz Misaki Grigoryan (Misakyan), Bitlis, Prkhus, 1910 ◆ Aziz Nazari Nazaryan (Melkonyan), Alashkert, Khastur, 1914 ◆ Aziz Poghosi Poghosyan, Leninakan, 1918 ◆ Aziz Zakari Hakobyan, Shirak, Boghazkasan, 1913 ◆ Azkanaz Kyureghi Zurnachyan (Kyureghyan), Alekpol, Duzkharab, 1912 ◆ Azniv Abrahami Abrahamyan, Alekpol, Armtlu, 1910 ◆ Azniv Aleksani Tashchyan, Kars, Khani gyugh, 1913 ◆ Azniv Antoni Khachatryan, Van, Khzhishk, 1914 ◆ Azniv Armenaki Davtyan, Kars, Beklemet, 1914 ◆ Azniv Armenaki

Muradyan, Bulanagh, Hamzashekh, 1913 ♦ Azniv Armenaki Nikoghosyan, Basin, Hasnakar, 1912 ♦ Azniv Arseni Arsenyan, Shirak, Svanverdi, 1911 ♦ Azniv Arshaki Ghukasyan, Ashtarak, 1918 ♦ Azniv Arshaki Harutyunyan, Kars, Ghoshavank, 1914 ♦ Azniv Asaturi Davtyan, Alekpol, 1908 ♦ Azniv Asaturi Mkrtchyan, Mush, 1909 ♦ Azniv Aslani Nikolyan (Aslanyan), Van, Aygestan, 1910 ♦ Azniv Avagi Gasparyan, Akhalkalak, Satgha, 1914 ♦ Azniv Avetisi Artenyan (Avetisyan), Manazkert, 1913 ♦ Azniv Avetisi Avetisyan, Turkey, Norashen, 1916 ♦ Azniv Avetisi Hakobyan (Avetisyan), Ayntap, Ghara-duz, 1915 ♦ Azniv Avetisi Manukyan, Alashkert, Berd, 1908 ♦ Azniv Avetisi Tigranyan, Van, Archesh, 1913 ♦ Azniv Babajani Maghakelyan, Baku, Shamakhi, 1913 ♦ Azniv Baghdasari Mnoyan, Bulanagh, Hamzashekh, 1909 ♦ Azniv Baloyi Khachatryan, Kars, Byazrgan, 1917 ♦ Azniv Daviti Aghajanyan, Kars, Ghzlchakhchakh, 1913, 1911 ♦ Azniv Gabrieli Gabrielyan, Leninakan, Ghazarabad, 1912 ♦ Azniv Gabrieli Gabrielyan, Manazkert, Derk, 1910 ♦ Azniv Galusti Galstyan, Kars, Chotakhli, 1910, 1912 ♦ Azniv Galusti Mikayelyan, Shirak, Gheghaj, 1913 ♦ Azniv Gaspari Gasparyan, Khnus, Gobal, 1909 ♦ Azniv Gevorgi Avetisyan, Techani, Khach, 1912 ♦ Azniv Gevorgi Gevorgyan, Alashkert, 1916 ♦ Azniv Gevorgi Gevorgyan, Kars, Hamzakalak, 1909 ♦ Azniv Gevorgi Hakobyan, Bitlis, Nela, 1910 ♦ Azniv Gevorgi Poghosyan, Mush, Artonk, 1911 ♦ Azniv Ghazari Bagasyan, Karin, Kerprukoy, 1904 ♦ Azniv Ghazari Harutyunyan, Erzrum, Dalibaba, 1909 ♦ Azniv Ghazari Karapetyan, Sarighamish, Shatrvan, 1910 ♦ Azniv Grigori Grigoryan, Alekpol, Mastara, 1914 ♦ Azniv Grigori Hayrapetyan, Yerevan, Aparan, 1913 ♦ Azniv Grigori Paronyan, Akhalkalak, Machatya, 1911 ♦ Azniv Grigori Petrosyan, Manazkert, Gharaghayil, 1908 ♦ Azniv Grigori Simonyan, Mush, Bulanagh, 1911 ♦ Azniv Grigori Stepanyan, Bayburt, Avarak, 1909 ♦ Azniv Hakobi Hakobyan, Basen, Tarkhocha, 1913 ♦ Azniv Hakobi Hakobyan, Van, Kem, 1913 ♦ Azniv Hakobi Hakobyan, Vaspurakan, Van, 1910 ♦ Azniv Hakobi Zakaryan (Hakobyan), Nakhijevan, 1915 ♦ Azniv Hambardzumi Hovsepyan, Van, Grapash, 1908 ♦ Azniv Harutyuni Harutyunyan (Baghdasaryan), Leninakan, Gyuzaldara, 1917 ♦ Azniv Harutyuni Harutyunyan, Gharakilisa, 1914 ♦ Azniv Harutyuni Harutyunyan, Van, Karzvan, 1909Azniv Harutyuni Hovsepyan, Kars, Paldrvan, 1908 ♦ Azniv Harutyuni Pilosyan, Kars, Kyurak-Dara, 1914 ♦ Azniv Harutyuni Safaryan (Harutyunyan), Bulanagh, Kharabshar, 1910 ♦ Azniv Harutyuni Tonoyan, Balanush, Shekhaghlu, ♦ Azniv Hovaki Korkotyan, Kars, Bangliahmat, 1909 ♦ Azniv Hovakimi Sargsyan (Ayvazyan), Ardahan, 1910 ♦ Azniv Hovakimi Vardanyan, Shatakh, Kaghpi, 1912 ♦ Azniv Hovhannesi (Vardani) Mkoyan, Van, Janik, 1913 ♦ Azniv Hovhannesi Adamyan, Mush, Bazlu, 1908 ♦ Azniv Hovhannesi Hovhannisyan, Alekpol, Mets Sariar, 1914 ♦ Azniv Hovhannesi Hovhannisyan, Basen, Yertapin, 1911 ♦ Azniv Hovhannesi Mkrtchyan, Kars, Bangliakhmet, 1912 ♦ Azniv Hovsepi Hovhannisyan, Bulanagh, Hamzashegh, 1912, 1911 ♦ Azniv Hovsepi Kakoyan, Leninakan, Muslughli, 1914 ♦ Azniv Hovsepi Khurshudyan, Mush, Mkragom, 1909 ♦ Azniv Hovsepi Sargsyan, Leninakan, Bayandur, 1911 ♦ Azniv Karapeti Karapetyan, Alashkert, Khastur, 1913 ♦ Azniv Karapeti Karapetyan, Shirak, Khaplu, 1913 ♦ Azniv Karapeti Karapetyan, Van, Sipan, 1909 ♦ Azniv Karapeti Tumasyan, Basen, Ajaraj, 1915 ♦ Azniv Karapeti Voskanyan, Erzrum, Vekikhas, 1917 ♦ Azniv Khachaturi Khachatryan, Basen, Kstapaz, 1914 ♦ Azniv Khachaturi Khachatryan, Karin, Khnus, 1906 ♦ Azniv Khachaturi Khachatryan, Khnus, 1912 ♦ Azniv Khachaturi Khachatryan, Van, 1910 ♦ Azniv Khachaturi Petrosyan, Basen, Badiveran, 1916 ♦ Azniv Khosrovi Khosrovyan, Zangezur, Nors, 1916 ♦ Azniv Knyazi Hovhannisyan, Leninakan, Jajur, 1911 ♦ Azniv Levoni Manukyan, Ardvin, Shavshir, 1916 ♦ Azniv Lorisi Avetisyan, Mush, 1911 ♦ Azniv Manuki Harutyunyan, Kars, Khabali, 1910 ♦ Azniv Manuki Manukyan, Mush, Khars, 1907 ♦ Azniv Manuki Manukyan, Van, Gusnents, 1907 ♦ Azniv Manuki Manukyan, Yerevan, Mastara, 1914 ♦ Azniv Margari (Hakobi) Movsisyan, Van, Archak, 1910 ♦ Azniv Margari Margaryan, Alashkert, Heghintapa, 1911 ♦ Azniv Margari Mkrtchyan, Khnus, Khozlu, 1908 ♦ Azniv Margari Sahakyan, Basen, Ishkha, 1912 ♦ Azniv Martiki Gasparyan, Yerznka, Chkhlnots, 1910 ♦ Azniv Masisi Harutyunyan, Van, 1909 ♦ Azniv Mataloyi Harutyunyan, Leninakan, Mastara, 1917 ♦ Azniv Matevosi Simonyan, Shirak, Tavshanghshlagh, 1909 ♦ Azniv Mikayeli Davtyan, Basen, Jrason, 1912, 1911 ♦ Azniv Misaki Khachatryan, Erzrum, Hekebar, 1914 ♦ Azniv Misaki Zakaryan, Manazkert, Derek, 1909 ♦ Azniv Mkhitari Sahakyan, Manazkert, Berd, 1908 ♦ Azniv Mkhitari Tonoyan, Alashkert, 1915 ♦ Azniv Mkhitari Tonoyan, Bitlis, Khachik, 1903 ♦ Azniv Mkrtchi Badalyan, Van, Mashtak, 1907 ♦ Azniv Mkrtchi Hambardzumyan, Erzrum, Arjarak, 1913 ♦ Azniv Mkrtchi Kapalyan, Erzrum, Khazlu, 1907 ♦ Azniv Mkrtchi Stepanyan, Alashkert, Berd, 1917 ♦ Azniv Movsesi Tumanyan, Van, Kharakonis, 1910 ♦ Azniv Nahapeti Nahapetyan, Alashkert, Gharakilisa, 1909 ♦ Azniv Nazari Nazaryan, Mush, Manazkert, 1915 ♦ Azniv Nazari Safaryan, Mush, Mirbran, 1911 ♦ Azniv Nazari Yekmalyan, Basen, Chyuruk, 1912 ♦ Azniv Nazari Zakaryan, Mush, 1912 ♦ Azniv Petrosi Petrosyan, Van, Bashkalan, 1913 ♦ Azniv Petrosy Manukyan (Petrosyan), Van, Archesh, Erishat, 1909 ♦ Azniv Poghosi Ayvazyan (Baghdasaryan), Kars, 1910 ♦ Azniv Poghosi Deghtrikyan, Van, 1911 ♦ Azniv Sahaki Mkhitaryan, Kars, Bernagyugh, 1912 ♦ Azniv Sargsi Martirosyan, Karin, Bayazet, 1909 ♦ Azniv Sargsi Martirosyan, Van, 1915 ♦ Azniv Sargsi Sargsyan, Archesh, 1915 ♦ Azniv Saroyan ♦ Azniv Sedraki Sedrakyan, Khnus, 1913 ♦ Azniv Serobi Petrosyan, Leninakan, Sirvangyugh, 1914 ♦ Azniv Sirakani Poghosyan, Akhalkalak, Aragal, 1912 ♦ Azniv Sukiasi Ayvazyan, Sarighamish, Bashgyugh, 1909 ♦ Azniv Sukiasi Hovsepyan (Sukiasyan), Van, Archis, 1916 ♦ Azniv Sukiasi Sahakyan, Mush, Rostom-gedak, 1907 ♦ Azniv Sukiasi Torosyan, Basen, Dot, 1908 ♦ Azniv Tachati Tachatyan, Alekpol, Ghoshavank, 1910 ♦

Azniv Tigrani Avetisyan, Alekpol, Tashlanghshlagh, 1913 ♦ Azniv Tigrani Tigranyan, Khnus, Haros, 1911 ♦ Azniv Torosi Varderesyan, Shirak, Svanverdi, 1911 ♦ Azniv Tovmasi Grigoryan, Bulanagh, Yonjalu, 1908 ♦ Azniv Tovmasi Tovmasyan, Alashkert, Khoshan, 1914 ♦ Azniv Tumasi Tumasyan, Chrasun, 1913 ♦ Azniv Vagharshaki Vagharshakyan, Erzrum, Chinis, 1914, 1910 ♦ Azniv Vardani Hovhannisyan, Akhalkalak, Chanchgha, 1914 ♦ Azniv Vardani Martirosyan, Bitlis, Prkhus, 1908 ♦ Azniv Yeghiayi Yeghiazaryan, Erzrum, Bayburt, 1912 ♦ Azniv Yervandi Yervandyan, Van, Aljavan, 1915, 1917 ♦ Azniv Zakari Harutyunyan, Alekpol, Syogutli, 1909 ♦ Azo Madoyi Martirosyan, Bashkert, 1916 ♦ Azo Sarsgi Karapetyan, 1919 ♦ Azo Varosi Martirosyan, Alekpol, Bughdashen, 1912 ♦ Babken Akribasi Karapetyan, Shirak, Chghzlar, 1917 ♦ Babken Armenaki Simonyan, Yerevan, Davalu, 1912 ♦ Babken Arshaki Tovmasyan, Yerevan, Oghobbaylu, 1914 ♦ Babken Avagi Hovhannisyan, Kars, 1912 ♦ Babken Balasani Davtyan, Igdir, Kulab, 1913 ♦ Babken Gabrieli Harutyunyan, Shirak, Bayandur, 1914 ♦ Babken Galusti Avagyan, Kars, Pirvali, 1916 ♦ Babken Galusti Ter-Martirosyan, Alekpol, Chrakhli, 1916 ♦ Babken Garegini Gareginyan, Surmalu, Igdir, 1912 ♦ Babken Gevorgi Aghoyan, Kars, 1916 ♦ Babken Harutyuni Khachatryan, Hamamlu, Tapanli, 1913 ♦ Babken Hayki Nersisyan, Kars, Bayrakhtar, 1909 ♦ Babken Hlghati Manukyan, Kars, Bashkadiklar, 1916 ♦ Babken Hovhannesi Matinyan, Kars, Bayraghdat, 1913 ♦ Babken Hovhannesi Melkonyan, Kars, Tigos, 1911 ♦ Babken Hovhannesi Simonyan, Leninakan, Maymatjugh, 1918 ♦ Babken Knoyi (Kocharyan) Gojoyan (Knyazyan), Shirak, Syogutli, 1917, 1916 ♦ Babken Manuki Melikyan (Kirakosyan), Kars, Chiftali, 1917 ♦ Babken Misaki Avagyan, Alekpol, Dzithankov, 1910 ♦ Babken Misaki Mkrtchyan, Alekpol, Kavtarlu, 1914 ♦ Babken Mkrtchi Araratyan, Tiflis, 1909 ♦ Babken Mkrtchi Harutyunyan (Mkrtchyan), Alekpol, Tavshanghshlagh, 1912 ♦ Babken Movsesi Shahinyan, Kars, Bashshoragyal 1911 ♦ Babken Nikoli Khachatryan, Kyavar, Ddmashen, 1911 ♦ Babken Rubeni Rubinyan, Hin Bayazet, Uzunkilisa, 1912, 1911 ♦ Babken Safari Vardanyan, Kars, Kyurakdar, 1910 ♦ Babken Samsoni Hovhannisyan, Ghamarlu, Artashat, 1911 ♦ Babken Senekerimi Mkrtchyan, Ardahan, 1913 ♦ Babken Simoni Poghosyan (Simonyan), Alekpol, Sariar, 1912 ♦ Babken Soghomoni Grigoryan, Kars, Ghoshavank, 1911 ♦ Babken Tadevosi Khachoyan, Leninakan, Mec Kapanak, 1916 ♦ Babken Yepremi Andreasyan, Gandzak, 1915 ♦ Babo (Asatur), Hovhannesi Hovhannisyan, Daralagyaz, Khachik, 1912 ♦ Badal Armenaki Grigoryan, Hin Bayazet, Arcap, 1911 ♦ Badal Harutyuni Khachatryan, Van, Utan, 1911 ♦ Badal Karapeti Shaboyan, Bitlis, Dabavank, 1908 ♦ Badal Manuki Manukyan, Akhlat, 1910 ♦ Badal Mikayeli Mikayelyan (Margaryan), Alekpol, Toparlu, 1910 ♦ Badal Poghosi Poghosyan (Petrosyan), Bulanagh, Labar, 1908 ♦ Badik Petrosi Begoyan, Yerevan, Alikzl, 1912 ♦ Baghdagyul Shmavoni Shmavonyan, Alashkert, Gharakilise, 1910 ♦ Baghdasar Abrahami Ter-Khachatryan, Persia, Tavriz, 1912, 1910 ♦ Baghdasar Aghajani Stepanyan, Bulanagh, Mashtlu, 1909 ♦ Baghdasar Aleksani Tonoyan, Mush, Norashen, 1911, 1909 ♦ Baghdasar Avagi Simonyan, Shirak, Pallanghshlagh, 1910 ♦ Baghdasar Avetisi Avetisyan, Alashkert, 1914 ♦ Baghdasar Avetisi Stepanyan (Avetisyan), Van, Alkev, 1911, 1910 ♦ Baghdasar Gaspari Melkonyan, Kars, Dashkov, 1914 ♦ Baghdasar Gaspari Mnoyan (Gasparyan), Kaghzvan, Changli, 1915 ♦ Baghdasar Gevorgi Baghdasaryan, Bulanagh, Latar, 1909 ♦ Baghdasar Grigori Hovhannisyan, Kars, 1914 ♦ Baghdasar Harutyuni Grigoryan, Kars, Karmlu, 1910 ♦ Baghdasar Hovhannesi Aslanyan, Nor Bayazet, Basargechar, 1918 ♦ Baghdasar Hovhannesi Melkonyan, Kars, Askighazi, 1912 ♦ Baghdasar Martirosi Grigoryan, Kars, Arazi, 1910 ♦ Baghdasar Melkoni Madoyan, Kars, Gharamahmad, 1913, 1912 ♦ Baghdasar Muradi Manukyan (Muradyan), Kars, 1916 ♦ Baghdasar Muradi Muradyan, Mush, Vostamkita, 1909 ♦ Baghdasar Zakari Mnoyan (Zakaryan), Kaghzvan, Chankli, 1910 ♦ Baghshi Sargsi Sargsyan (Baghdasaryan), Karabagh, Shushi, 1915 ♦ Bagrat Abrahami Hakobyan, Van, Archak, 1913 ♦ Bagrat Adami Poghosyan, Khnus, Gobar, 1912 ♦ Bagrat Arshaki Adamyan, Shirak, Mec Keti, 1912 ♦ Bagrat Arshaki Ayvazyan (Arshakyan), Khnus, 1912, 1911 ♦ Bagrat Avetisi Avetisyan, Basen, Gomadzor, 1916 ♦ Bagrat Avetisi Barseghyan, Kars, Getiksatlmsh, 1912 ♦ Bagrat Avetisi Hovhannisyan (Avetisyan), Kars, Syogutli, 1911 ♦ Bagrat Galusti Galstyan, Alashkert, Kamlipachakh, 1918 ♦ Bagrat Gevorgi Gevorgyan, Nor Bayazet, Noraduz, 1914 ♦ Bagrat Ghazari Sargsyan, Kars, Cbni, 1911 ♦ Bagrat Grigori Hambaryan, Leninakan, Mavrak, 1911, 1910 ♦ Bagrat Grigori Khachatryan, Kars, Kyulagdara, 1912 ♦ Bagrat Grigori Yeghiazaryan, Kars, Birnay gyugh, 1910 ♦ Bagrat Hakobi Haykyan, Alekpol, Gharakilisa, 1913 ♦ Bagrat Hamayaki Arakelyan (Hamayakyan), Leninakan, Mavrak, 1914 ♦ Bagrat Hovhannesi Hovhannisyan, Khnus, Yelpin, 1914 ♦ Bagrat Hovhannesi Hovhannisyan, Leninakan, Ghapli, 1914 ♦ Bagrat Hovsepi Hovsepyan, Kars, 1921 ♦ Bagrat Karapeti Poghosyan, Leninakan, Khli Gharakilisa, 1913 ♦ Bagrat Khachaturi Khachatryan, Kars, 1919 ♦ Bagrat Levoni Hovhannisyan, Alashkert, 1918 ♦ Bagrat Manuki Grigoryan, Kars, Ortaghala, 1912 ♦ Bagrat Manuki Manukyan, Kars, Paldrvan, 1913 ♦ Bagrat Margari Gyulgazyan, Kars, 1907 ♦ Bagrat Margari Petrosyan, Alashkert, 1911 ♦ Bagrat Martirosi Gasparyan, Gyokchay, Tobishen, 1913 ♦ Bagrat Martirosi Harutyunyan, Kars, Ghzlchakhchakh, 1915 ♦ Bagrat Matevosi Matevosyan, Bayazet, Mosun, 1912 ♦ Bagrat Matsoyi Khachatryan, Kars, Paldrvan, 1911 ♦ Bagrat Misaki Misakyan, Khnus, Khod, 1916 ♦ Bagrat Mkhoyi Davtyan, Manazkert, Noragyugh, 1917 ♦ Bagrat Mkrtchi Hovhannisyan, Bayazet, Korun, 1913 ♦ Bagrat Musheghi Sargsyan, Kars, 1914 ♦ Bagrat Nahapeti Mkhitaryan, Kars, Tekor, 1911 ♦ Bagrat Nazaryan, Tiflis, 1918 ♦ Bagrat Nersesi Babajanyan, Alekpol, Ortakilisa, 1910 ♦ Bagrat Pilosi Grigoryan, Kars, Mazra, 1912 ♦ Bagrat Poghosi Sargsyan

(Poghosyan), Kars, Bagliahmat, 1914 ◆ Bagrat Poghosi Serobyan (Poghosyan), Bitlis, Prkhus, 1909 ◆ Bagrat Prikazi Gevorgyan, Talin, Mastara, 1913 ◆ Bagrat Rubeni Movsisyan, Ghamarlu, Gharamzalu, 1914 ◆ Bagrat Sahaki Mkhitaryan, Alashkert, Gharakilisa, 1909 ◆ Bagrat Sargsi Vardanyan, Kars, Kyurakdar, 1912, 1911 ◆ Bagrat Stepani Sargsyan (Ikoyan), Kars, 1914 ◆ Bagrat Stepani Yevangulyan, Karabagh, Madras, 1913 ◆ Bagrat Tadevosi Melikyan (Tadevosyan), Alashkert, 1914 ◆ Bagrat Yeghishi Asatryan, Kars, Kars, 1910 ◆ Bagrat Yeghoyi Sargsyan, Kars, 1917 ◆ Bagrat Zakari Badalyan, Nakhijevan, Yarmnja, 1911 ◆ Bakhcho Khachaturi Movsisyan, Basen, Gomadzor, 1911 ◆ Bakhlagiz Smbati Harutyunyan, Alekpol, Ghanlija, 1915 ◆ Bako Musoyi Musoyan, 1914 ◆ Balabek Gabrieli Sardaryan, Kars, Gorkhana, 1908 ◆ Balabek Yeghiazari Gevorgyan, Gharakilisa, 1911 ◆ Balabek Yeghishi Mikayelyan, Kars, Orta Katiklar, 1914 ◆ Balas Haruti Harutyunyan, Kars, 1918, 1917 ◆ Balasan Arakeli Arakelyan, Alekpol, Bashgyugh, 1915 ◆ Balasan Arseni Harutyunyan, Alekpol, Aghin, 1907 ◆ Balasan Arshaki Bagratyan (Arshakyan), Sarighamish, Ghoshakilisa, 1917 ◆ Balasan Arshaki Mnoyan, Alekpol, Bozigyugh, 1913 ◆ Balasan Artashesi Mkrtchyan, Alekpol, 1914 ◆ Balasan Gevorgi (Garegini) Danielyan, Leninakan, Boghazkesan, 1919 ◆ Balasan Gevorgi Gevorgyan, Leninakan, 1915 ◆ Balasan Gevorgi Sahakyan, Kars, Mec Parket, 1911 ◆ Balasan Grishayi Manukyan, Kars, Mec Parket, 1913 ◆ Balasan Hambardzumi Martirosyan, Kars, Aghjaghala, 1914 ◆ Balasan Hamboyi Hamboyan, Shirak, Bandrvan, 1917 ◆ Balasan Harutyuni Harutyunyan, Leninakan, Ghanlich, 1914, 1912 ◆ Balasan Harutyuni Stepanyan (Harutyunyan), Alekpol, Chzghlar, 1912 ◆ Balasan Hovani Simonyan, Alekpol, Shishtapa, 1920 ◆ Balasan Hovhannesi Hovhannisyan, Kars, Mec Parker, 1915 ◆ Balasan Khachaturi Baghoyan, Kars, Bashkadiklar, 1914 ◆ Balasan Khachaturi Khachatryan, Kars, 1914, 1911 ◆ Balasan Matevosi Ghazaryan, Alekpol, Chzghlar, 1910 ◆ Balasan Mkrtchi Sargsyan, Leninakan, 1915 ◆ Balasan Mnoyi Mnoyan, Alekpol, Bashgegh, 1914 ◆ Balasan Safari Grigoryan, Kars, Paldrvan, 1915 ◆ Balasan Sergoyi Sergoyan (Vardanyan), Yerevan, Mastara, 1916 ◆ Balasan Shaheni Shahinyan, Gharakilisa, Adibek, 1913 ◆ Balasan Simoni Harutyunyan, P. Gharakilisa, 1914 ◆ Balasan Srapioni Ghazaryan, Kars, Uzunkilisa, 1911 ◆ Balasan Stepani Simonyan, Leninakan, Toparlu, 1914 ◆ Bale Sergoyi Muradyan, Khnus, 1914 ◆ Baniamin Hakobi Hayrapetyan, Shirak, Bughdashen, 1913 ◆ Baniamin Sakoyi Karapetyan, Kars, Cholakhli, 1913 ◆ Baregham Hakobi Navasardyan, Nakhijevan, Mazra, 1911 ◆ Bariptugh Hovhannesi Hovhannisyan, Van, Marmet, 1910 ◆ Barsegh Avagi Avagyan (Abrahamyan), Erzrum, 1912 ◆ Barsegh Beglari Ghazaryan (Beglaryan), Daralagyaz, Keshishveran, 1913 ◆ Barsegh Harutyuni Avetisyan, Nakhijevan, Badamlu, 1910 ◆ Barsegh Khachaturi Margaryan, Alekpol, Parni gyugh, 1912 ◆ Barsegh Khachaturi Vardanyan, Alekpol, Duzkharaba, 1903 (1908) ◆ Barsegh Margari (Khachaturi) Grchoyan, Alekpol, Bayandur, 1916 ◆ Barsegh Meliki Khachatryan, Aparan, Ghrkhdagirman, 1911 ◆ Barsegh Meliki Melikyan, Leninakan, Boghazkasan, 1916 ◆ Barsegh Petrosi Petrosyan, Mush, Shikhlan, 1914 ◆ Barsegh Poghosi Avetisyan (Poghosyan), Van, Mokhraberd, 1912 ◆ Barsegh Rafayeli Garoyan, Akhalkalak, Olaver, 1913 ◆ Barsegh Saroyi Manukyan, Kars, Tazakyand, 1912 ◆ Barunak Gaspari Vagharshyan (Ghazaryan), Alashkert, Yeghntap, 1916 ◆ Barunak Harutyuni Ghazaryan, Van, Berd, 1908 ◆ Basi Poghosi Poghosyan, 1913 ◆ Bavakan Abgari Hamazaspyan (Abrahamyan), Kars, Arazgyugh, 1917 ◆ Bavakan Antoni Aghajanyan, Lori, Gyargyar, 1910 ◆ Bavakan Arshaki Khachatryan, Nor Bayazet, 1912 ◆ Bavakan Avoyi Astoyan, Alekpol, Kharkov, 1912 ◆ Bavakan Daviti Davtyan, Leninakan, Alikhan, 1917 ◆ Bavakan Davti Davtyan, Karabagh, Nukhi, 1914 ◆ Bavakan Gaboyi Grigoryan, Leninakan, Gholghat, 1918 ◆ Bavakan Hambardzumi Galstyan, Kars, 1915 ◆ Bavakan Harutyuni Vardanyan, Persia, Tavriz, 1910 ◆ Bavakan Hovhannesi Badoyan (Hovhannisyan), Shirak, Tomartash, 1912 ◆ Bavakan Hovhannesi Kocharyan (Hovhannisyan), Nukhi, 1916 ◆ Bavakan Hovhannesi Manukyan, Nor Bayazet, 1910 ◆ Bavakan Khachaturi Grigoryan, Gharakilisa, 1916 ◆ Bavakan Khachaturi Musheghyan, Alekpol, Mastara, 1917 ◆ Bavakan Mkrtchi Sargsyan, Leninakan, Mastara, 1917 ◆ Bavakan Samsoni Samsonyan, Ashtarak, Arjavank, 1914 ◆ Bavakan Sargsi Margaryan, Lori, Bozigyugh, 1913 ◆ Bavakan Sargsi Petrosyan, Alekpol, 1912 ◆ Bavakan Sargsi Vardanyan, Dilijan, Poghoskilisa, 1915 ◆ Bavakan Vahani Ghabuzyan, Chzghlar, 1916 ◆ Bavakan Variki Hovsepyan, Kars, Bashkyadiklar, 1914 ◆ Bavakan Yeranosi Sahakyan, Kars, Oghuzli, 1917 ◆ Bayaz Galusti Sargsyan, Leninakan, Kaftarlu, 1914 ◆ Bayaz Ivani Gharibyan, Bitlis, Prpus, 1908 ◆ Bayaz Karapeti Vardanyan, Bitlis, Prkhus, 1908 ◆ Bayaz Mkrtchi Hovhannisyan, Khnus, Khlat, 1912 ◆ Bazik Hakobi Hakobyan, Igdir, Khalfali, 1915 ◆ Bazik Zohrabi Muradyan (Zoroyan), Bulanagh, Kop, 1916, 1914 ◆ Beko Grigori Pepoyan, Kars, Vorta, 1917 ◆ Beniamin Aleksani Aleksanyan, Alashkert, Iritsu, 1914 ◆ Beniamin Avetisi Avetisyan, Kars, Paldrvan, 1912 ◆ Beniamin Danieli Danielyan (Mkhitaryan), Alashkert, Khazlu, 1914 ◆ Beniamin Gaspari Hlgatyan, Alashkert, Irits gyugh, 1911 ◆ Beniamin Geghami Musheghyan, Kars, Bashkadiklar, 1912 ◆ Beniamin Khachaturi Muradyan, Leninakan, Kharkov, 1913 ◆ Beniamin Khachaturi Simonyan, Alekpol, Jajur, 1911 ◆ Beniamin Mesropi Avetisyan, Van, Berkri, 1913 ◆ Beniamin Mkrtchi Dovlatyan, Nor Bayazet, 1913 ◆ Beniamin Safari Davtyan, Khnus, Garakopri, 1907 ◆ Beniamin Sahaki Grigoryan, Basen, Hopviran, 1914 ◆ Beniamin Ter-Karapeti Ter-Karapetyan, Mush, Krdagom, 1914 ◆ Benik Amirjani Buniatyan, Nukhi, 1914 ◆ Benik Jafari Nikoghosyan, Shushi, Vardashen, 1913 ◆ Beno Vahani Gasparyan, 1917 ◆ Bersab Abrahami Simonyan, Kars, Kyadiklar, 1912 ◆ Bersab Aleki Aloyan, Alekpol, Paltlu, 1912 ◆ Bersab Karapeti Tovmasyan, Manazkert, Berd, 1912 ◆ Bersab Manuki Manukyan, Leninakan, Sirvan, 1913 ◆ Bersab Petrosi Sargsyan, Khnus, Kharakopri, 1908 ◆ Bersab

Smbati Grigoryan, Alekpol, Ghazarapat, 1918 ♦ Bersab Tigrani Ghandilyan, Alashkert, 1908 ♦ Bersabe Abgari Khachatryan, Akhalkalak, Bughashen, 1916 ♦ Bersabe Aleksani Martirosyan, Khnus, Khara joghan, 1907 ♦ Bersabe Arakeli Saroyan, Kars, Chala, 1913 ♦ Bersabe Arshaki Mkrtchyan (Arshakyan), Khnus, Gharakyopru, 1910 ♦ Bersabe Aveti Grigoryan (Hakobyan), Leninakan, Ilsiabi, 1920, 1918 ♦ Bersabe Barseghi Torosyan, Shirak, Ghalija, 1914 ♦ Bersabe Ghukasi Ghukasyan, Bulanagh, Kop, 1909 ♦ Bersabe Grigori (Poghosi) Hovhannisyan, Manazkert, Berd, 1912 ♦ Bersabe Grigori Hghlatyan, Kars, Koghb, 1912 ♦ Bersabe Kerobi Hakobyan, Mush, Apri, 1908 ♦ Bersabe Margari Margaryan, Van, 1914 ♦ Bersabe Meliki Melikyan, Alekpol, Ghzlkilisa, 1915 ♦ Bersabe Melkoni Melkonyan, Sharur, Norashen, 1914 ♦ Bersabe Minasi Kerobyan, Alashkert, Mankasar, 1909 ♦ Bersabe Mkhitari Hovhannisyan (Mkhitaryan), Manazkert, Gharaghala, 1909 ♦ Bersabe Movsesi Movsisyan, Mush, Maztlu, 1911 ♦ Bersabe Musheghi Movsisyan, Mush, Derek, 1913 ♦ Bersabe Petrosyan, Bulanagh, Shirvanshekh, 1912 ♦ Bersabe Poghosi Baghdasaryan, Khnus, Khosli, 1911 ♦ Bersabe Sahaki Avetisyan, 1915 ♦ Bersabe Sargsi Hovsepyan, Tpghis, Akhlkalak, 1917 ♦ Bersabe Sargsi Sargsyan, Alekpol, Syogutli, 1918 ♦ Bersabe Stepani Hambardzumyan, Persia, Gharadagh, 1914 ♦ Bersabe Tadevosi Tadevosyan, Leninakan, Tavshanghshlagh, 1916 ♦ Bersabe Torosi (Tadevosi) Mkrtchyan, Akhalkalak, Merenia, 1911 ♦ Bersabe Vardani Muradyan, Manazkert, Tapavank, 1912 ♦ Bersabe Vardgesi Mikayelyan, Akhalkalak, 1915 ♦ Bersabe Yeghoyi Khachatryan, Bulanagh, Kop, 1915 ♦ Berso Minasi Petrosyan (Minasyan), Shirak, Sariar, 1913 ♦ Bestam Vardani Sargsyan (Vardanyan), Bulanagh, Rostamgedi, 1910 ♦ Betghehem Aghabeki Aslanyan, Kars, Mazra, 1917 ♦ Betghehem Aleki Davtyan, Shirak, Khli Ghara, 1912 ♦ Betghehem Arshaki Arshakyan, Alekpol, Ghlighra, 1916 ♦ Betghehem Grigori Sahradyan, Kars, 1912 ♦ Bctghehem Sargsi Ghukasyan, Akhalkalak, Orujalar, 1916 ♦ Betghehem Stepani Balakyan, Alekpol, Tavshanghshlagh, 1913 ♦ Betghehem Vahrami Gevorgyan, Alekpol, Ghanlija, 1912 ♦ Betghehem Vardani Khachatryan, Kars, Ghoshavank, 1911 ♦ Betghem Mukuchi (Mkrtchi) Martirosyan, Shirak, Ghzlghoch, 1914 ♦ Betghem Safari Shahinyan, Kaghzvan, 1914 ♦ Betkhehem Aleki Petrosyan, Kars, Ghzlchakhchakh, 1915 ♦ Betkhehem Avetisi Ter-Antonyan, Akhalkalak, Goman, 1911 ♦ Betkhehem Barseghi Barseghyan, Alekpol, Poladlu, 1913 ♦ Betkhehem Elbaki Elbakyan (Ardinyan), Kars, Gorkhana, 1915 ♦ Betkhehem Gabrieli Grigoryan, Kars, 1911 ♦ Betkhehem Ghazari Simonyan, Kars, Gedaksatlmish, 1910 ♦ Betkhehem Hambardzumi Hambardzumyan, Leninakan, Chchzlar, 1913 ♦ Betkhehem Hovhannesi Grigoryan, Kars, Gharamahmat, 1910 ♦ Betkhehem Hrapi Muradyan, Leninakan, Ghonakhran, 1912 ♦ Betkhehem Karapeti Danielyan, Kars, Oghuzli, 1909 ♦ Betkhehem Khachaturi Hovhannisyan, Kars, Mec Parket, 1915 ♦ Betkhehem Sargsi Sargsyan, Jalaloghli, Shahnazar, 1915 ♦ Betkhehem Vahani Hambaryan, Leninakan, Ghanlija, 1912 ♦ Betkhem Gabrieli Ter-Gevorgyan, Kars, 1907 ♦ Betkhem Galusti Galstyan, Leninakan, Pokr Gharakilisa, 1913 ♦ Betkhem Grigori Ajanyan, Akhalkalak, 1913 ♦ Betkhem Grigori Hovhannisyan, Sarighamish, Churuik, 1915 ♦ Betkhem Hovhannesi Hovhannisyan, Leninakan, Koraghbyur, 1914 ♦ Betkhem Pilosi Madoyan, Leninakan, Sariar, 1914 ♦ Beybut Musheghi (Ghazari) Ghazaryan, Bashaparan, 1918 ♦ Bezek Yepremi Nikoghosyan, Yerevan, Yeghvard, 1915 ♦ Bezik Grigori Melkonyan (Hovhannisyan), Mush, Yonjalu, 1910 ♦ Bezik Meliki Melikyan, Kop, Terek, 1912, 1910 ♦ Bezik Musheghi Melkonyan, Bulanagh, Hachtlu, 1910 ♦ Bezo Karapeti Karapetyan, Nor Bayazet, 1917 ♦ Blbul Harutyuni Galstyan, Erzrum, Basen, 1911 ♦ Bohtan Rashoyi (Rashoyan) Stepanyan (Kotoyan), Bulanagh, Kop, 1913 ♦ Borik Aghajani Baghdasaryan, Karabagh, Hadrut, 1913 ♦ Boris Paveli Malchinyan, Tiflis, 1914 ♦ Bulbul Aleksani Mkrtchyan (Aleksanyan), Erzrum, Harsnikar, 1913 ♦ Bumaf Ghukoyi Aleksanyan, Kars, Teknis, 1915 ♦ Burastan Aleksani Barseghyan, Alekpol, Samrli, 1914 ♦ Burastan Arami Davtyan, Alekpol, Bandrvan, 1914 ♦ Burastan Arami Sargsyan, Kars, Ortakilisa, 1917 ♦ Burastan Arshaki Mnoyan, Kars, Chala, 1913 ♦ Burastan Bekoyi Karapetyan, Kars, Gorkhan, 1917 ♦ Burastan Elbaki Harutyunyan (Elbakyan), Kars, Uzunkilisa, 1911 ♦ Burastan Geghami Sukiasyan, Kars, Ortaghala, 1914 ♦ Burastan Grigori Muradyan, Kars, Aghjaghala, 1912 ♦ Burastan Hakobi Badasyan, Erzrum, Koprikoy, 1911 ♦ Burastan Hakobi Hakobyan, Kars, Mavrag, 1916 ♦ Burastan Hakobi Khalatyan, Kars, Bashkadilak, 1914 ♦ Burastan Hakobi Mkrtchyan, Kars, Kyurakdara, 1914 ♦ Burastan Hamayaki Hamayakyan, Alekpol, Babrlu, 1914 ♦ Burastan Haruti Harutyunyan, Baku, 1918 ♦ Burastan Harutiki Alaverdyan, Alekpol, Chorlu, 1913 ♦ Burastan Harutyuni Harutyunyan, Van, Khachyan, 1913 ♦ Burastan Hayrapeti Yenokyan, Igdir, Kulap, 1912 ♦ Burastan Hovhannesi Gaboyan (Khachatryan), Kars, Mec Parket, 1917 ♦ Burastan Hunani Hunanyan, Pambak, Avdibek, 1915 ♦ Burastan Karapeti Misakyan, Kars, Gorkhana, 1916 ♦ Burastan Khachaturi Armenakyan, Kars, Hamzakarak, 1915 ♦ Burastan Khachaturi Khachatryan, Kars, Mec Parket, 1913 ♦ Burastan Kostani Vardanyan, Kars, Ortakilisa, 1918 ♦ Burastan Misaki (Misakyan) Yengibaryan, Etchmiadzin, Dadali, 1915 ♦ Burastan Misaki Avagyan, Leninakan, Dzithankov, 1912 ♦ Burastan Mkuchi Kostanyan, Alekpol, Armtlu, 1912 ♦ Burastan Mnatsakani Arshakyan, Alekpol, Bashgyugh, 1914 ♦ Burastan Mnoyi Gevorgyan, Leninakan, Ghapli, 1915 ♦ Burastan Movsesi Shahinyan, Kars, Bashshoragyal, 1914 ♦ Burastan Nahapeti Galoyan, Sarighamish, Armtlu, 1911 ♦ Burastan Nersesi Sarukhanyan, Akhalkalak, Alasta, 1914 ♦ Burastan Petrosi Petrosyan, Van, Artamert, 1912 ♦ Burastan Sahaki Abgaryan, Shirak, Ghanlija, 1913 ♦ Burastan Sahaki Barseghyan, Sarighamish, Shativan, 1912 ♦ Burastan Sargsi Khachatryan, Alekpol, Taknali, 1916 ♦ Burastan Sargsi Sargsyan, Kars, 1917 ♦ Burastan Sedraki Amiryan, Kars, Ortizak, 1910 ♦ Burastan

Shavarshi Sargsyan, Alekpol, Ghli Gharakilisa, 1914 ♦ Burastan Simoni Simonyan, 1917 ♦ Burastan Tatosi Elbakyan, Kaghzvan, Khar, 1910 ♦ Burastan Tatosi Tatosyan, Alekpol, Illi, 1918 ♦ Burastan Tigrani Tigranyan, Van, 1912 ♦ Burastan Tigrani Tigranyan, Van, Hayots dzor, 1910, 1909 ♦ Burastan Torosi Ayvazyan, Basen, Armtlu, 1909 ♦ Burastan Vanoyi (Vahani) Barseghyan, Leninakan, Paltli, 1919 ♦ Burastan Vardani Hakobyan, Kars, Mavrak, 1914 ♦ Burastan Vardani Hakobyan, Kars, Paldrvan, 1916 ♦ Burastan Vardani Vardanyan, Alekpol, Jajur, 1912 ♦ Burastan Voskani Voskanyan, Leninakan, Ghazarapat, 1914 ♦ Burastan Yegori Yegoryan (Petrosyan), Leninakan, Danagirmaz, 1915 ♦ Burastan Yervandi Yervandyan, Kaghzvan, 1914 ♦ Burastan Zakari Manukyan, Kars, Ughuzli, 1911 ♦ Byureghik Poghosi Simonyan, Kars, Pirvalu, 1912, 1910 ♦ Caghik Abgari Grigoryan (Mirzoyan), Hin Nakhijevan, Taza gyugh, 1917 ♦ Caghik Abgari Manukyan, Akhalkalak, Khojabek, 1912 ♦ Caghik Arakeli Kostanyan, Lori, Uzunlar, 1915 ♦ Caghik Armenaki Mkhitaryan, Mush, Hamzashegh, 1908 ♦ Caghik Arshaki Arshakyan, Kars, 1921 ♦ Caghik Arshaki Khachatryan, Kars, Shirmalu, 1914 ♦ Caghik Arshaki Nikoghosyan, Yerznka, 1910 ♦ Caghik Avetisi Avetisyan, Darachichak, Karvansara, 1911 ♦ Caghik Danieli Danielyan (Hakobyan), Nukhi, Aghbalkand, 1913 ♦ Caghik Daviti Davtyan, Kars, Bashshoragyal, 1913 ♦ Caghik Gevorgi Gevorgyan, Van, 1915 ♦ Caghik Grigori Khachatryan, Van, Cucker, 1912 ♦ Caghik Grigori Ter-Stepanyan, Erzrum, Agrak, 1912 ♦ Caghik Hakobi Karapetyan, Nor Bayazet, Basargechar, 1915 ♦ Caghik Hakobi Sargsyan, Kars, Bangliahmat, 1912 ♦ Caghik Hambardzumi Hambardzumyan, Yerevan, 1914 ♦ Caghik Hambardzumi Khachatryan, Etchmiadzin, Mola Bayazet, 1914 ♦ Caghik Hovhannesi Aleksanyan, Kars, 1909 ♦ Caghik Hovhannesi Hovhannisyan, Yerevan, Bejghazlu, 1910 ♦ Caghik Hovhannesi Karapetyan, Kars, Tazakand, 1911 ♦ Caghik Hovhannesi Voskanyan, Nakhijevan, Martiros, 1911 ♦ Caghik Khachaturi Khachatryan, Shirak, Ghanlija, 1912 ♦ Caghik Khachaturi Khachatryan, Van, Aparan, 1914 ♦ Caghik Khachaturi Khachatryan, Yerevan, Ghurdughuli, 1915 ♦ Caghik Khachoyi Khachatryan, Kars, Bashkyadiklar, 1915 ♦ Caghik Khachoyi Soghomonyan, Kars, Uzunkilisa, 1918 ♦ Caghik Madatyan, 1917 ♦ Caghik Manuki Mnoyan, Van, Ghani, 1910 ♦ Caghik Manushakyan, 1918 ♦ Caghik Margari Margaryan Voskanyan, Grg-Bulagh, Aghazor, 1912 ♦ Caghik Misaki Misakyan, Akhta, Makravank, 1916 ♦ Caghik Mkrtchi Ghukasyan (Mkrtchyan), Kars, Agrak, 1914 ♦ Caghik Nshani Nshanyan, Van, 1912 ♦ Caghik Saroyi Karoyan, Leninakan, Samrlu, 1914 ♦ Caghik Saroyi Saroyan, Kars, 1916 ♦ Caghik Sedraki Sedrakyan, Yerznka, Piriz, 1917 ♦ Caghik Sergoyi Hovhannisyan (Sergoyan), Leninakan, Mastara, 1909 ♦ Caghik Smbati Alekyan, Alekpol, Illi, 1914 ♦ Caghik Smbati Harutyunyan, Kars, Bashshoragyal, 1916 ♦ Caghik Smbati Stepanyan (Smbatyan), Hin Nakhijevan, 1914 ♦ Caghik Yeghoyi Sargsyan, Daralagyaz, Yashghay, 1915 ♦ Caghik Yenoki Mkrtchyan, Vedi, Keshviran, 1910 ♦ Caghik Yepremi Yepremyan, Yerevan, Yeghvard, 1908 ♦ Caghik Yervandi Yervandyan, Yerznka, Gharatush, 1912 ♦ Caghik Zakari (Petrosi) Tevosyan (Tazagyulyan), Ardahan, 1911 ♦ Caruk Knyazi Torosyan, Kars, Jala, 1913 ♦ Catur Movsesi Poghosyan, Shamakhi, Khani shen, 1911 ♦ Chakhal Sedraki Manukyan, Leninakan, Bozdoghan, 1913 ♦ Chichak Hakobi Hovhannisyan, Leninakan, Khrgh, 1910 ♦ Chichak Manuki Muradyan, Kars, Agrak, 1910 ♦ Chichak Mikayeli Melikyan, Van, Archesh, 1911 ♦ Chichak Mkrtchi Mkrtchyan, Motkan, Mrtsank, 1914 ♦ Chichak Sargisi Hovoyan (Hovhannisyan), Bulanagh, Latar, 1909 ♦ Chichak Sargisi Sargsyan, Bulanagh, Koghb, 1910 ♦ Chicho Hambardzumi Sargsyan, Mush, Tiramer, 1913 ♦ Chinar Avagi Nersisyan, Leninakan, Khli Gharakilis, 1913 ♦ Chinar Baghdasari Levonyan, Van, Sevan, 1913 ♦ Chinar Dizini Aghababyan, Akhalkalak, Lomaturs, 1915 ♦ Chinar Gevorgi Torosyan (Gevorgyan), Kars, Jalal, 1914 ♦ Chinar Khachoyi Khachoyan, Alekpol, Emirkhan, 1917 ♦ Chinar Martirosi Martirosyan, Van, Ketsa, 1909 ♦ Chinar Meliki Shahinyan, Alashkert, Mankasar, 1913 ♦ Chinar Movsesi Movsisyan, Van, 1909 ♦ Chinar Petrosi Harutyunyan, Alekpol, Hamamlu, 1918 ♦ Chinar Poghosi Tevosyan, Igdir, Gyulija, 1912 ♦ Chinar Sedraki Melkonyan (Sedrakyan), Kars, Gorkhana, 1916 ♦ Chinar Sedraki Mikayelyan, Akhalkalak, Burnashet, 1915 ♦ Chinar Yeghiazari Adamyan, Kars, Zaim, 1917 ♦ Chino (Chinar) Vardani Yeghoyan, Akhalkalak, Diliska, 1915 ♦ Chino Arshaki Poghosyan, Tiflis, 1916 ♦ Chino Avetisi Serobyan, Akhalkalak, 1919 ♦ Chino Hovhannesi Hovhannisyan, Kars, Bashkyadiklar, 1914 ♦ Chino Khachaturi Khachatryan, Akhalkalak, 1917 ♦ Chino Poghosi Poghosyan ♦ Chnashkharhik (Arshaluys) Vardani Vardanyan, Igdir, Alija, 1914 ♦ Chnashkharhik (Chinastan) Garegini Petrosyan, Akhalkalak, Kendura, 1915 ♦ Chnashkharhik Arseni Melkonyan, Akhalkalak, Sulda, 1914 ♦ Chnashkharhik Harutyuni Berberyan, Akhalkalak, Vachyan, 1913 ♦ Chnashkharhik Khachoyi Yenokyan, Akhalkalak, 1914 ♦ Chnashkharhik Tevani Khachatryan, Akhalkalak, Abul, 1915 ♦ Chnashkharhik Yervandi Aristakesyan, Leninakan, Daharlu, 1909 ♦ Cilvan Martirosi Nalbandyan, Van, 1918 ♦ Covik Abrahami Abrahamyan, Kars, Bayghara, 1909 ♦ Covik Arakelyan, Nukhi, 1916 ♦ Covik Artashesi Sargsyan, Kars, Bayghar, 1912 ♦ Covik Gaspari Gasparyan, Van, 1915 ♦ Covik Harutyuni Barseghyan (Barsoyan), Kars, Dolbandlu, 1916 ♦ Covik Martirosi Baghdasaryan, Hin Nakhijevan, Didivar, 1912 ♦ Covik Martirosi Khachatryan, Kars, Berni, 1911 ♦ Covik Martirosi Petrosyan (Martirosyan), Kars, Nakhijevan, 1914 ♦ Covik Mihrani (Abrahami) Baghdasaryan, Kars, Bashgegh, 1917 ♦ Covik Musheghi Asatryan, Kars, Berna, 1910 ♦ Covik Nikoli Sahakyan, Kars, Paldrvan, 1916 ♦ Covik Sahaki Sahakyan, Kars, Agrak, 1913 ♦ Covik Smbati Smbatyan, Kars, Bagaran, 1916 ♦ Covinar Abrahami Barseghyan, Alekpol, Syogutli, 1915 ♦ Covinar Abrahami Karapetyan, Kaghzvan, 1913 ♦ Covinar Avagi Melkonyan, Kars, Bashkyadiklar, 1914 ♦ Covinar Badoyi Hovhannisyan, Kars, Ghzlchakhchakh,

1912 ♦ Covinar Harutyuni Harutyunyan, Akhalkalak, Orojalab, 1912 ♦ Covinar Kerobi Movsisyan, Erzrum, 1909 ♦ Covinar Petrosi Martirosyan (Petrosyan), Alekpol, Samrlu, 1912 ♦ Covinar Sahaki Sahakyan, Kars, Agrak, 1913 ♦ Covinar Tigrani Barseghyan (Yeghoyan), Alekpol, Syogutli, 1911 ♦ Covinar Tumasi Tumasyan (Arakelyan), Kars, Aksi ghaza, 1912 ♦ Covinar Zakeosi Maghlojyan, Olti, Agrak, 1911 ♦ Dalal Aloyi (Badalyan) Aloyan, Bulanagh, Yonjalu, 1913 ♦ Dalal Arseni Arsenyan, Manazkert, 1916 ♦ Dalal Aslani Madoyan, Lori, Marts, 1909 ♦ Dalal Avetisi Abrahamyan, Mush, Yonjala, 1912 ♦ Dalal Grigori Avagyan (Grigoryan), (Bitlis), Akhlat, Khuli, 1908 ♦ Dalal Manuki Khachatryan (Manukyan), Bulanagh, Votnchor, 1910 ♦ Dalal Martirosi Muradyan, Manazkert, Kanikosk, 1909 ♦ Dalal Mkhitari (Soghoyan) Mkhitaryan, Kars, Gyularin, 1914 ♦ Dalal Sargsi Sargsyan, Alekpol, Darlu, 1914 ♦ Daniel Gevorgi Poghosyan (Nalbandyan), Alashkert, 1912 ♦ Daniel Hakobi (Mkrtchyan) Hakobyan, Mush, Manazkert, 1910 ♦ Daniel Sargsi Sargsyan, Kars, Zrchi, 1913 ♦ Daniel Senekerimi Nazaryan, Van, Kuel, 1907 ♦ Daniel Stepani Harutyunyan, Kars, Gharaghala, 1912 ♦ Dasto Khachaturi Movsisyan, Basen, Gomadzor, 1914 ♦ Davit Armenaki Stepanyan, Aparan, Atma, 1908 ♦ Davit Asaturi Asatryan, Hayots dzor, Ker, 1906 ♦ Davit Danieli Manukyan, Kars, Khani gyugh, 1912 ♦ Davit Hovhannesi Bavoyan, Bulanagh, Kop, 1910 ♦ Davit Hovhannesi Hovhannisyan, Hasanghala, Hekibad, 1913 ♦ Davit Hovhannesi Hovhannisyan, Van, Aljavaz, 1917 ♦ Davit Karapeti Movsisyan (Karapetyan), Alekpol, Palutli, 1911 ♦ Davit Margari Margaryan, Hin Bayazet, 1915, 1913 ♦ Davit Mesropi Barseghyan, Bulanagh, Yonjalu, 1909 ♦ Davit Petrosi Davtyan, Chrason, 1920 ♦ Davit Petrosi Petrosyan, Van, Kendanants, 1912 ♦ Davit Sargsi Arshakyan, Sarighamish, Armtlu, 1916 ♦ Davit Sedraki Khachatryan, Shirak, Khli Gharakilisa, 1916 ♦ Davit Serobi (Davtyan) Serobyan, Leninakan, Bandivan, 1914 ♦ Deghdzanik Daviti Petrosyan, Van, Gandzak, 1906 ♦ Deghdzanik Gaspari Margaryan, Bulanagh, Hatkon, 1911 ♦ Deghdzanik Hovhannesi Hovhannisyan, Mush, Yershtir, 1915 ♦ Delibar Grigori Grigoryan (Nahapetyan), Khnus, Khlata, 1911 ♦ Demo Avetisi (Bozoyan) Avetisyan, Akhta, Karvansara, 1914 ♦ Derenik Arakeli Sargsyan, Khnus, 1918 ♦ Derenik Bagrati Manukyan, Kars, Pirvali, 1916 ♦ Derenik Hghlati Veloyan, Mush, Tsronk, 1912 ♦ Derenik Igiti Igityan, Shirak, Toparlu, 1914 ♦ Derenik Mkhitari Melikyan, Mush, Sokhkom, 1912 ♦ Dilbar Avetisi Stepanyan, Van, 1914 ♦ Dilbar Margari Svaryan (Margaryan), Van, Sevan, 1914 ♦ Dilbar Movsesi Vardanyan (Movsisyan), Leninakan, 1912 ♦ Dilbar Nersesi Melikyan, Akhlat, Matnivan, 1911 ♦ Dilbar Sargsi Sargsyan, Alashkert, Mankasar, 1908 ♦ Dilbar Tatosi Davtyan (Tadevosyan), Nakhijevan, 1914 ♦ Dilbar Ter-Gabrieli Dilbaryan (Ter-Gabrielyan), Erzrum, Dalibaba, 1911 ♦ Dilbo Martirosi Martirosyan, Yerevan, 1918 ♦ Dilbo Mkoyi Mkoyan, Sarighamish, Alicharak, 1909 ♦ Dimatevos Vardevani Dunkikyan, Erzrum, 1913 ♦ Dimitri Vardani Bagratyan, Akhalkalak, Karcakh, 1914 ♦ Donik Matsoyi Martirosyan, Kars, Aghjaghal, 1915 ♦ Drakhtuhi Abrahami Martirosyan, Ghamarlu, 1909 ♦ Drakhtuhi Torosi Torosyan, Igdir, Najafali, 1913 ♦ Drastamat Levoni Sargsyan, Leninakan, Duzkharaba, 1913 ♦ Drmo Hakobi Hakobyan, Kop, Rostamgedak, 1914 ♦ Dro Khoreni Gevorgyan (Khorenyan), Surmalu, Blur, 1915 ♦ Dukhik Abeti Tumasyan, Akhalkalak, Tadesh, 1914 ♦ Dukhik Avetiki Serobyan, Kars, Kharkov, 1913 ♦ Dukhik Gabrieli Sahakyan, Kaghzvan, 1912 ♦ Dukhik Ghazari (Ghazaryan) Gevorgyan, Bulanagh, Kharaghlu, 1912, 1909 ♦ Dukhik Grishayi (Grigor) Chomaryan, Akhalkalak, 1914, 1912 ♦ Dukhik Hakobi Karapetyan, Nakhijevan, Koghp, 1914 ♦ Dukhik Hayrapeti Ayvazyan, Kars, Koghp, 1913 ♦ Dukhik Khachaturi (Khachatryan) Sargsyan, Igdir, Blur, 1914 ♦ Dukhik Khachaturi Hakobyan, Sharur, Norashen, 1911 ♦ Dukhik Matosi Matosyan, Bulanagh, Malakyamb, 1917 ♦ Dukhik Meliki Khachatryan, Erzrum, Gomadzor, 1914 ♦ Dukhik Mkrtchi Hovhannisyan (Mkrtchyan), Leninakan, Tashkhalu, 1915 ♦ Dukhik Mkrtchi Karapetyan (Avetisyan), Kars, Dorbandlu, 1912 ♦ Dukhik Vanoyi Tonoyan, Pambak, Sarmusaghli, 1913 ♦ Dukhik Vardani Vardanyan, Basen, Hekibta, 1915 ♦ Dunba Mayisi Trikupova, Novo Nikolaevka, 1917 ♦ Dzyunik Aleksani Gasparyan, Bulanagh, Noratin, 1909 ♦ Dzyunik Hovhannesi Petrosyan (Hovhannisyan), Manazkert, Noratin, 1910 ♦ Dzyunik Kerobi Karapetyan (Yeghikyan), Bulanagh, Teghut, 1911 ♦ Edmond Khachaturi Khachatryan, Alekpol, Bashgegh, 1917 ♦ Eduard Arshaki Hovhannisyan, Khnus, Gharachoban, 1911 ♦ Eduard Hakobi Aghajanyan, Kars, 1914 ♦ Eduard Khachaturi Karapetyan, Alekpol, Sariar, 1910 ♦ Eduard Khachiki Grigoryan, Alashkert, Berd, 1914 ♦ Eduard Kristofori Stepanyan, Van, 1909 ♦ Eduard Margari Pashtoyan (Margaryan), Van, 1912 ♦ Elbak Arshaki Arshakyan, Alashkert, Iritsu, 1914 ♦ Elbek Galusti Stepanyan, Leninakan, Kefli, 1913 ♦ Elbis Abgari Aramyan, Basen, Dalibaba, 1911 ♦ Elbis Aslani Aslanyan, Sarighamish, Gyulantap, 1918 ♦ Elbis Hakobi Hakobyan, Basen, Koprikoy, 1911 ♦ Elbis Markosi (Kirakosi) Ter-Markosyan, Van, Shedana, 1910 ♦ Elbis Matosi Hovoyan, Kars, Bashkadiklar, 1916 ♦ Elbis Serobi Kandoyan, Van, 1911 ♦ Elibek Gharibi Mkoyan (Gharibyan), Kars, Kedaklar, 1915 ♦ Emil Galusti Torgomyan (Galstyan), Van, 1913 ♦ Emil Hovhannesi Melik-Adamyan, Hin Nakhijevan, Akulis, 1908 ♦ Emma Grigori Caturyan, Baku, 1908 ♦ Emma Karapeti Karapetyan, Yerevan, 1916 ♦ Emma Meliki Melikyan, Persia, Enzeli, 1914 ♦ Emma Mkrtchi Aslikyan, Kars, 1908 ♦ Emma Mnatsakani Gevorgyan, Alekpol, Mastara, 1912 ♦ Emma Stepani Tadevosyan (T. Mkrtchyan), Baku, 1912 ♦ Epraksi Nersesi Haroyan, Kars, Bern, 1914 ♦ Fahrat Poghosi Harutyunyan (Poghosyan), Kars, Ghzlchakhchakh, 1908 ♦ Falaknaz Mnatsakani Kerobyan, Basen, Gomadzor, 1914 ♦ Farfar Baghdasari Sargsyan, Van, Aljavaz, 1911 ♦ Farfar Gaspari Grigoryan (Gasparyan), Van, 1910 ♦ Farfar Gevorgi Martirosyan, Alekpol, Chorli, 1911 ♦ Farfar Gevorgi Sargsyan, Bulanagh,

LISTING OF ORPHANS

Votnchor, 1911 ♦ Farmo Petrosi Hovhannisyan (Petrosyan), Manazkert, 1912 ♦ Farmo Petrosi Hovhannisyan, Bitlis, Tundras ♦ Felek Baghdasari Khachatryan, Alashkert, Khastur, 1915 ♦ Fenik Aleksani Karapetyan (Hakobyan), Alekpol, Bozyoghash, 1914 ♦ Fiadro Arshaki Hakobyan, Igdir, 1912 ♦ Fidan Abrahami Abrahamyan, Manazkert, Gharaghala, 1910 ♦ Fidan Aghoyi Aghoyan, Bulanagh, 1915 ♦ Fidan Armenaki Abrahamyan (Armenakyan), Kars, Bulanagh, 1914 ♦ Fidan Arshaki Arshakyan, Van, 1913 ♦ Fidan Asaturi Asatryan, Manazkert, Tolaghbash, 1915 ♦ Fidan Grigori Aspaturyan (Grigoryan), Archesh, Gandzak, 1914 ♦ Fidan Haruti Harutyunyan, Mush, Haner, 1915 ♦ Fidan Harutyuni Harutyunyan, Mush, Hamzashekh, 1909 ♦ Fidan Hovhannesi Hovhannisyan, Manazkert, Marmus, 1912 ♦ Fidan Karapeti Karapetyan, Yerevan, 1919 ♦ Fidan Khurshudi Tadevosyan (Khurshudyan), Khnus, Krt, 1908 ♦ Fidan Margari Margaryan, Bulanagh, Piran, 1908 ♦ Fidan Mkhitari Amrzatyan, Manazkert, Berd, 1910 ♦ Fidan Poghosi Avetisyan, Mush, Agrak, 1912 ♦ Fidan Sargisi Ispindaryan (Grigoryan), Bulanagh, Hamzashekh, 1907 ♦ Fidan Stepani Hayrapetyan, Surmalu, Alija, 1912 ♦ Fido Anushavani Poghosyan, Dutagh, Batnots, 1910 ♦ Fido Stepani Poghosyan, Kars, Paldrvan, 1917 ♦ Filik Yeghoyi Yeghoyan, Bulanagh, Blur, 1914 ♦ Finja Bagrati Bagratyan, Leninakan, Gharakilise, 1917 ♦ Finjan Gaspari Gasparyan, Mush, Bulanagh, 1913 ♦ Finjo Hovhannesi Hovhannisyan, Mush, 1911 ♦ Firik Baghdasari Avdalyan, Kars, Gidala, 1911 ♦ Flit Manuki Asoyan (Manukyan), Alashkert, 1911 ♦ Flora Adami Avagyan, Kars, Ghzlchakhchakh, 1912 ♦ Flora Antoni Antonyan, Kars, Kyadiklar, 1912 ♦ Flora Arakeli Gasparyan (Arakelyan), Aparan, Mulk, 1914 ♦ Flora Arshaki Khachatryan, Kars, Voghuzlu, 1911 ♦ Flora Daviti Martirosyan (Davtyan), Basen, Chrason, 1912 ♦ Flora Garegini Petrosyan, Erzrum, Ishkhu, 1911 ♦ Flora Gevorgi Ghazaryan, Alekpol, Illi, 1912 ♦ Flora Hakobi Hakobyan, Alekpol, Shishtapa, 1916 ♦ Flora Hovhannesi Andreasyan, Kars, 1913 ♦ Flora Hovhannesi Hambaryan (Hovhannisyan), Kars, Bashshoragal, 1913 ♦ Flora Karapeti Gevorgyan, Bulanagh, Gharaghala, 1910 ♦ Flora Khachaturi Kirakosyan, Kars, Ghzlchakhchakh, 1913 ♦ Flora Melkoni Hovhannisyan, Badnots, 1913 ♦ Flora Minasi Vardanyan, Pambak, Ghshlagh, 1912 ♦ Flora Mkrtchi Mkrtchyan (Karapetyan), Mush, 1912, 1911 ♦ Flora Mkrtchi Mkrtchyan, Mush, Arinj, 1909 ♦ Flora Musheghi Andreasyan (Musheghyan), Bitlis, 1916 ♦ Flora Nikoli (Kolyayi) Ghazaryan, Lori, Shahnazar, 1917 ♦ Flora Petrosi Grigoryan, Leninakan, Imrkhan, 1910 ♦ Flora Simoni Mkhitaryan, Kars, Palutlu, 1912, 1910 ♦ Flora Soghomoni Hovhannisyan, Alekpol, Chorlu, 1914 ♦ Flora Sukiasi Voskanyan, Alashkert, Garasi, 1914 ♦ Flora Zakari Martirosyan, Kars, 1918 ♦ Florentsia Tatosi Ghazaryan (Zadoyan), Alekpol, Sariar, 1914 ♦ Fndgh Avetisi Sargsyan, Khnus, Berd, 1911 ♦ Fndgh Mkhitari Mkhitaryan, Khnus, Khut, 1909 ♦ Fndgh Muradi Sahakyan, Etchmiadzin, Noratin, 1915 ♦ Fransuhi Tigrani Shaljyan, Van, 1912 ♦ Frants Minasi (Sargis) Stepanyan, Basen, Chrason, 1910 ♦ Fros Saroyi Martirosyan (Sargsyan), Leninakan, Ghanlija, 1918 ♦ Gabriel Geghami Sirovanyan (Hakobyan), Yerevan, Gezrlu, 1914 ♦ Gabriel Markosi Markosyan, Van, Kendanants, 1912 ♦ Gabriel Mikayeli Gabrielyan, Kars, Parket, 1911 ♦ Gabriel Mkrtchi Hovakimyan, P. Gharakilisa, Hamamlu, 1913 ♦ Gabriel Petrosi Petrosyan, Van, 1912 ♦ Gabriel Saroyi Hovhannisyan, Kars, Uzunkilisa, 1914 ♦ Gabriel Vardani Mkrtchyan (Vardanyan), Aljavaz, Bargat, 1913 ♦ Gagik Arami Mikayelyan, Bayburt, 1914 ♦ Gagik Arshaki Sargsyan, Leninakan, Illi, 1914 ♦ Gagik Gabrieli (Mkoyi) Sargsyan, Kars, Pirvali, 1918, 1916 ♦ Gagik Nazareti Nazaryan, Igdir, 1914 ♦ Gagik Poghosi Hovhannisyan, Kars, Gedaksatlmish, 1912 ♦ Gagik Sedraki Carukyan, Kars, Pirvali, 1913 ♦ Gagik Serobi Sargsyan, Kars, Pirvalu, 1911, 1909 ♦ Gagik Zakari Martirosyan, Kars, 1916 ♦ Galust Arshaki Arshakyan, Leninakan, Ghurdbulagh, 1918 ♦ Galust Avetisi Hovhannisyan, Vaspurakan, Dzoravants, 1909 ♦ Galust Baghdasari Baghdasaryan, Van, 1916 ♦ Galust Baghdasari Hakobyan (Baghdasaryan), Mush, Khut, 1916 ♦ Galust Bagrati Hakobyan, Kars, Bayghara, 1914 ♦ Galust Caruki Markosyan, Alekpol, Badivan, 1910 ♦ Galust Daviti Davtyan, Erzrum, Khazgyugh, 1912, 1911 ♦ Galust Gaspari Gasparyan, Leninakan, Ojaghula, 1917 ♦ Galust Hambardzumi Khachatryan, Akhalkalak, Bzarvet, 1915 ♦ Galust Harutyuni Davtyan, Van, Noragyugh, 1906 ♦ Galust Harutyuni Muradyan, Van, Moks, 1909 ♦ Galust Markosi Galstyan, Alekpol, Illi, 1909 ♦ Galust Martirosi Martirosyan, Nor Bayazet, Basargechar, 1914 ♦ Galust Matsoyi Khachatryan, Leninakan, Ghulijan, 1913 ♦ Galust Meloyi (Melkoni) Gasparyan (Meloyan), Kars, Paldrvan, 1912 ♦ Galust Mkrtchi Kocharyan, Alekpol, Ghanlija, 1916 ♦ Galust Mkrtchi Vasilyan, Kars, Bazrgyan, 1912 ♦ Galust Mnatsakani Kharmandaryan, Kars, Bashshoragyal, 1908 ♦ Galust Movsesi Manukyan, Shirak, Dalband, 1911 ♦ Galust Pablei Grigoryan, Leninakan, Tashlaghshlagh, 1912 ♦ Galust Stepani Barseghyan, Alekpol, Chzghlar, 1911 ♦ Galust Stepani Harutyunyan, Pambak, Kurtan, 1918 ♦ Galust Tigrani Tigranyan, Etchmiadzin, Evjilar, 1913 ♦ Garan Khachaturi Khachatryan, Yerevan, Noragavit, 1905 ♦ Garan Saroyi Ter-Stepanyan, Alekpol, Illi, 1914 ♦ Garegin Agheki Khachatryan, Igdir, Dashburun, 1909 ♦ Garegin Aleksani Stepanyan, Kars, 1912 ♦ Garegin Arakeli Khachatryan (Arakelyan), Nakhijevan, Hajivar, 1914 ♦ Garegin Arami Aramyan, Kars, 1916 ♦ Garegin Arami Yeranosyan, Erzrum, Tedevan, 1914 ♦ Garegin Armenaki Hakobyan (Armenakyan), Alekpol, Toros gyugh, 1913 ♦ Garegin Arzumani Khachatryan, Caghkadzor, Ddmashen, 1912 ♦ Garegin Avagi Melkonyan, Chanakhchi, 1913 ♦ Garegin Avagi Sirekanyan, Basen, Hekepat, 1912 ♦ Garegin Avetisi Manukyan, Kars, 1909 ♦ Garegin Danieli Petrosyan (Danielyan), Alekpol, Illi, 1914 ♦ Garegin Daviti Davtyan, Erzrum, 1909 ♦ Garegin Gabrieli Amirkhanyan, Kars, Bashgegh, 1913 ♦ Garegin Gerasimi Harutyunyan, Van, Narek, 1911 ♦ Garegin Gevorgi Gevorgyan, Darachichak, Ddmashen, 1914

♦ Garegin Gevorgi Gevorgyan, Shirak, Ikhirabi, 1918 ♦ Garegin Gevorgi Ghazaryan, Leninakan, Illi, 1911 ♦ Garegin Gevorgi Harutyunyan, Basen, Armtlu, 1911, 1912 ♦ Garegin Gevorgi Harutyunyan, Leninakan, Khli Gharakilis, 1913 ♦ Garegin Ghzroyi Ghzroyan, Manazkert, Rostomgedak, 1913 ♦ Garegin Ginosi Antonyan (Ginosyan), Leninakan, Jajur, 1913 ♦ Garegin Grigori Martirosyan, Kars, 1908 ♦ Garegin Hakobi Hakobyan, Nakhijevan, Damrzndan, 1913 ♦ Garegin Hakobi Harutyunyan (Hakobyan), Kars, Aksighaz, 1912 ♦ Garegin Hakobi Mkrtchyan (Mkoyan), Alekpol, Merjegli, 1912 ♦ Garegin Harutyi Adamyan, Kars, Baktamat, 1912 ♦ Garegin Harutyuni Harutyunyan, 1914 ♦ Garegin Harutyuni Vardanyan, Kars, Gedaksatlmish, 1910 ♦ Garegin Hovakimi Shahinyan, Lori, Gyulagarak, 1908 ♦ Garegin Hovhannesi Avetisyan, Van, 1915 ♦ Garegin Karapeti Sargsyan, Gyokchay, Keshkhart, 1913 ♦ Garegin Kerobi Kerobyan, Kars, Dashkov, 1915 ♦ Garegin Levoni (Andranikyan) Levonyan, Hin Nakhijevan, Ijan, 1917 ♦ Garegin Madoyi Madoyan, Gharakilisa, Mec Parni, 1917 ♦ Garegin Makari Harutyunyan, Kars, Getiksatlmish, 1910 ♦ Garegin Manuki Manukyan, Van, Pagagyaduk, 1910 ♦ Garegin Manuki Simonyan, Kars, Derbandli, 1909 ♦ Garegin Manuki Stepanyan, Kars, Baglamat, 1914 ♦ Garegin Minasi Hovhannisyan, Igdir, Surmalu, 1916 ♦ Garegin Mkhitari Mkhitaryan, Bulanagh, 1912 ♦ Garegin Mkrtchi Elbakyan, Basen, Votkan, 1917 ♦ Garegin Mkrtchi Karapetyan, Leninakan, 1914, 1913 ♦ Garegin Mnatsakani Baghdasaryan, Kars, Bayraghdar, 1914 ♦ Garegin Movsesi Ghazaryan, Kars, Voghuzli, 1911 ♦ Garegin Movsesi Movsisyan, Van, Anggh gyugh, 1912 ♦ Garegin Muradi Simonyan, Sarighamish, Armtlu, 1911 ♦ Garegin Musheghi Harutyunyan, Kars, 1914 ♦ Garegin Nikoghosi Aloyan (Alaverdyan), Alekpol, Chodli, 1911 ♦ Garegin Nikolayi (Nikoghayosi) Baghdasaryan, Karabagh, Benakta, 1916 ♦ Garegin Rafayeli Tsolakyan, Darachichak, Taycharukh, 1911 ♦ Garegin Saghateli Davoyan (Davityan), Basen, Krtavzu, 1911 ♦ Garegin Sahaki Hovsepyan, Kars, Nakhijevan, 1909 ♦ Garegin Saribeki Shaboyan, Kars, 1914 ♦ Garegin Saroyi Aghababyan, Kars, Tazakand, 1910 ♦ Garegin Serobi Yeghoyan, Alekpol, Syogutli, 1912 ♦ Garegin Srabi Vardanyan, Kars, Batiklar, 1912 ♦ Garegin Srapioni Srapyan, Shirak, Sariar, 1919 ♦ Garegin Stepani Khachatryan, Kars, Tikniz, 1912, 1910 ♦ Garegin Tadevosi Sukiasyan, Mamakhatun, Kotiran, 1911 ♦ Garegin Tovmasi Grigoryan, Gokcha, Sataglu, 1910 ♦ Garegin Umrshati Mkhitaryan, Sasun, Khut, 1912 ♦ Garegin Vardani Knyazyan, Yerevan, Davalu, 1912 ♦ Garegin Vardani Sakoyan (Vardanyan), Alekpol, Kaps, 1908 ♦ Garegin Vardani Vardanyan (Mirzoyan), Shirak, Toparli, 1918 ♦ Garegin Zakari Movsisyan, Kars, Ghzlchakhchakh, 1906 ♦ Garnik Aleksani (Abgari) Abgaryan, Aparan, Gozli, 1913 ♦ Garnik Arshaki Arshakyan, Nakhijevan, 1916 ♦ Garnik Arshaki Harutyunyan (Arshakyan), Nakhijevan, Taza gyugh, 1917, 1914 ♦ Garnik Artushi Khachatryan (Arakelyan), Yerevan, Ghamarlu, 1912 ♦ Garnik Galusti Karapetyan, Alekpol, Taknali, 1911 ♦ Garnik Hambardzumi Hambardzumyan, Van, 1912 ♦ Garnik Hovhannesi Berberyan, Van, 1914 ♦ Garnik Hovhannesi Davoyan (Hovhannisyan), Aparan, Tanchrlu, 1911 ♦ Garnik Hovhannesi Hovhannisyan (Gevorgyan), Leninakan, P. Gharakilisa, 1918 ♦ Garnik Hovhannesi Hovhannisyan, Alekpol, Ghoshavank, 1912 ♦ Garnik Hovhannesi Hovhannisyan, Van, Koghbants, 1912, 1911 ♦ Garnik Hovhannesi Margaryan, Van, Kril, 1911 ♦ Garnik Hovsepi Hovhannisyan, Alashkert, 1908 ♦ Garnik Khachaturi Khachatryan, Yerevan, Chidamlu, 1913 ♦ Garnik Minasi Hovhannisyan, Igdir, Tashbura, 1911 ♦ Garnik Sahaki Sanragorcyan, Van, 1910 ♦ Garnik Tzhikyan ♦ Garnik Yeghiazari Yavudyan (Yeghiazaryan), Van, 1910 ♦ Garnik Yervandi Ghazaryan, Leninakan, Dharlu, 1916 ♦ Garnik Yesayi Badalyan, Van, Archesh, 1912, 1911 ♦ Garsevan Hambardzumi Petrosyan, Erzrum, Yaghan, 1911 ♦ Garsevan Nazareti Gevorgyan, Leninakan, Toparli, 1913, 1912 ♦ Garush (Karapet) Sergoyi Hakobyan (Sergoyan), Nakhijevan, Norashen, 1915 ♦ Garush Artashi Artashyan (Petrosyan), Basen, Hopveran, 1917 ♦ Garush Bagrati Mkrtchyan, Nakhijevan, Aylapat, 1912 ♦ Garush Petoyi Petoyan, Aparan, Bashaparan, 1917 ♦ Gaspar Abrahami Harutyunyan (Abrahamyan), Mush (Bulanagh), Hamzashekh, 1910 ♦ Gaspar Hakobi Hakobyan, Mush, Aliklpan, 1909 ♦ Gaspar Knyazi Sahakyan (Knyazyan), Mush, Gharaghl, 1907 ♦ Gaspar Manuki Manukyan, Mush, Kop, 1912 ♦ Gaspar Melkoni Gasparyan, Van, Hndstan, 1910 ♦ Gaspar Mkrtchi Hovhannisyan (Mkrtchyan), Mush, Khut, 1915 ♦ Gayane Abeli Zakaryan, Hin Nakhijevan, Gyumri, 1912 ♦ Gayane Abgari Ayvazyan, Akhalkalak, Vachian, 1912 ♦ Gayane Abrahami Abrahamyan, Van, 1914 ♦ Gayane Arami Khachatryan, Alekpol, 1913 ♦ Gayane Arami Poghosyan (Ghazaryan), Surmalu, Igdir, 1915 ♦ Gayane Arshaki Aghajanyan (Arshakyan), Leninakan, 1916 ♦ Gayane Arshaki Karapetyan (Muradyan), Kars, Berna, 1913 ♦ Gayane Avetisi Stamboltsyan, Akhalkalak, Khojaberd, 1912 ♦ Gayane Babayi Vardanyan, Zangezur, Tarashen, 1913 ♦ Gayane Baregi Vardanyan, Basen, Hopviran, 1913 ♦ Gayane Davti Nazaryan, Leninakan, Chiftali, 1912 ♦ Gayane Galusti Mikayelyan, Leninakan, Kaps, 1913 ♦ Gayane Ghazari Amroyan (Hovhannisyan), Ghazakh, Chanakhchi, 1915 ♦ Gayane Ghazari Torosyan, Akhalkalak, Samsar, 1916 ♦ Gayane Grigori Gevorgyan (Grigoryan), Berd, Van, 1910 ♦ Gayane Grigori Grigoryan (Vardanyan), Terjan, Mants, 1912 ♦ Gayane Grigori Grigoryan, Surmalu, Bangliahmat, 1916 ♦ Gayane Grigori Hovhannisyan (Grigoryan), Nakhijevan, Araz, 1917 ♦ Gayane Grigori Vardanyan, Surmalu, Igdir, 1915 ♦ Gayane Hakobi Sahakyan (Hakobyan), Basen, Chrasun, 1909 ♦ Gayane Hambardzumi Grigoryan, Bayburt, Averak, 1913, 1911 ♦ Gayane Hambardzumi Khalatyan, Nor Bayazet, 1907 ♦ Gayane Hovhannesi Tadevosyan, Erzrum, 1914 ♦ Gayane Martirosi Mkrtchyan, Alekpol, 1912 ♦ Gayane Martirosi Mkrtchyan, Kars, Bazrgyan, 1913 ♦ Gayane Mkrtchi Darbinyan, Akhalkalak, 1914 ♦ Gayane Mkrtchi Mkrtchyan, Lori, Ghshlagh, 1913

LISTING OF ORPHANS

♦ Gayane Mukayeli Trdatyan (Voskanyan), Kars, Mazra, 1909 ♦ Gayane Muradi Muradyan, Mush, Gemay, 1910 ♦ Gayane Poghosi (Sargsi) Sargsyan (Poghosyan), Alekpol, Koraghbyur, 1914 ♦ Gayane Sargsi Khachatryan, Leninakan, Kaps, 1911 ♦ Gayane Sargsi Poghosyan, Leninakan, Kaps, 1912, 1910 ♦ Gayane Sedraki Melkonyan, Van, Aljavaz, 1910 ♦ Gayane Shaheni Harutyunyan, Van, Berkri, 1913 ♦ Gayane Simoni Ishkhanyan, Van, Aygestan, 1906 ♦ Gayane Simoni Sargsyan, Kars, Pokr Parket ♦ Gayane Tachati Manukyan, Batum, Shavshert, 1910 ♦ Gayane Tadevosi Grigoryan, Erzrum, Vardik, 1913 ♦ Gayane Tatosi Varosyan, Kars, Bashagyugh, 1910 ♦ Gayane Voskani Arzumanyan, Shamakh, Kyavandi, 1919 ♦ Gayane Yeghoyi Aghayan, Nakhijevan, Julfa, 1914 ♦ Gayane Yenoki Manukyan, Nakhijevan, Birali, 1912 ♦ Gedevan Yepremi Yepremyan, Shirak, Ghazarabad, 1917 ♦ Gegeon (Peto) Misaki Manaseryan, Yerevan, Imanshalu, 1914 ♦ Gegham Akperi Gevorgyan, Etchmiadzin, Iktali, 1916 ♦ Gegham Aleki Aleksanyan, Alekpol, Arkhvali, 1912 ♦ Gegham Aleksani Harutyunyan, Leninakan, Ghazarabad, 1911 ♦ Gegham Arami Karapetyan, Leninakan, 1910 ♦ Gegham Arami Mamikonyan (Babajanyan), Lori, Mghart, 1914 ♦ Gegham Aristakesi Galoyan (Galstyan), Van, Yererin, 1912 ♦ Gegham Arshaki Arshakyan, Shirak, Gheghach, 1919 ♦ Gegham Baghdasari Kostanyan, Kars, Ughuzlu, 1911 ♦ Gegham Davti Karapetyan, Kars, Sogutlu, 1916 ♦ Gegham Davti Vardanyan, Alekpol, Chivtali, 1910 ♦ Gegham Garegini Musheghyan (Gareginyan), Mush, Bulanagh, 1913, 1910 ♦ Gegham Gevorgi (Gevorgyan) Tovmasyan, Yerevan, 1915 ♦ Gegham Gevorgi Grigoryan, Kars, Baglamat, 1913 ♦ Gegham Gulani Gulanyan, Khnus, 1910 ♦ Gegham Hakobi Hakobyan, Mush, Khutshin, 1910 ♦ Gegham Hakobi Melikyan, Mush, Unan, 1909 ♦ Gegham Hayrapeti Khochoyan (Yesayan), Zangezur, Agarak, 1920 ♦ Gegham Hovhannesi Hovhannisyan, Yerevan, Zinjilu, 1912 ♦ Gegham Hovhannesi Sargsyan (Hovhannisyan), Basen, Aljarak, 1916 ♦ Gegham Hunani Asatryan, Shirak, Syogutlu, 1911 ♦ Gegham Karapeti Hambaryan, Leninakan, Chiftalu, 1915 ♦ Gegham Kirakosi Muradyan, Sarighamish, Stahan, 1911 ♦ Gegham Mikayeli Mkhitaryan, Van, Archesh, 1910 ♦ Gegham Misaki Gevorgyan, Bulanagh, Hamzashen, 1910 ♦ Gegham Misaki Misakyan, Akhlat, Alashkert, 1916 ♦ Gegham Nikoghosi Hamayakyan, Gharakilisa, Aghbulagh, 1915 ♦ Gegham Papiki Petrosyan, Basen, Harsnkar, 1908 ♦ Gegham Petrosi Petrosyan, Van, Abagha, 1914 ♦ Gegham Petrosi Rashoyan, Vardo, Aner, 1912 ♦ Gegham Sargsi (Sargsyan) Sahakyan, Van, 1915 ♦ Gegham Sargsi Sargsyan, Khnus, Bamik, 1911 ♦ Gegham Stepani Piliposyan, Erzrum, Tarkun, 1911 ♦ Gegham Tovmasi Tovmasyan, Sarighamish, 1918 ♦ Gegham Varosi Harutyunyan, Kaghzvan, 1908 ♦ Gegham Varosi Mkhitaryan, Kars, Berna, 1912 ♦ Gegham Voskani Gasparyan, Leninakan, Kyapanak ♦ Gegham Yenoki Yenokyan, Van, Tazagyugh, 1914 ♦ Geghanush Batiki Aloyan, Bulanagh, Yonjalu, 1912 ♦ Geghanush Grigori (Misaki) Grigoryan (Misakyan), Bayburt, 1914 ♦ Geghanush Manuki Manukyan, Van, 1908 ♦ Geghanush Ohani Zakaryan, Shamakh, Ghajar, 1912, 1910 ♦ Geghanush Simoni Simonyan, Basen, Erzrum, 1913 ♦ Geghetsik (Gyulizar) Karapeti Karapetyan, Daralagyaz, 1913 ♦ Geghetsik Davti Tumasyan, Bitlis, Modkan-Mci, 1910 ♦ Geghetsik Gaspari Manukyan, Manazkert, Masmus, 1906 ♦ Geghetsik Hovhannesi Hovhannisyan (Hakobyan), Alekpol, Ghapli, 1911 ♦ Geghetsik Petrosi Petrosyan (Atoyan), Akhalkalak, Khospia, 1912 ♦ Gerasim (Drastamat) Serobi Serobyan, Archesh, 1911 ♦ Gerasim Aghabeki Soghomonyan, Karabagh, Arjadzor, 1908 ♦ Gerasim Armenaki Hunanyan, Etchmiadzin, Khatunarkh, 1914 ♦ Gerasim Arshaki Ginosyan, Alekpol, Talipoghli, 1917 ♦ Gerasim Arshaki Mkrtchyan, Leninakan, Kapanak, 1914 ♦ Gerasim Hovhannesi Margaryan, Shirak, Ghzlghoch, 1912 ♦ Gerasim Karapeti Karapetyan (Mkhitaryan), Kars, Ortakyadiklar, 1916 ♦ Gerasim Nikoli Nikolyan, Leninakan, Toros gyugh, 1918 ♦ Gerasim Sedraki Hovhannisyan, Ghamarlu, Vogharbekta, 1914 ♦ Gevorg (Goro) Nikoli (Goroyan) Nikolyan, Kars, 1916 ♦ Gevorg (Grigor) Stepanyan, Lori, Matan, 1918 ♦ Gevorg Abrahami Abrahamyan, Nukhi, Sabata, 1910 ♦ Gevorg Aleksani Aleksanyan, Shirak, Balutli, 1915 ♦ Gevorg Aleksani Buniatyan, Kaghzvan, 1912 ♦ Gevorg Aleksani Hunanyan, Alekpol, Ghapuli, 1910 ♦ Gevorg Antoni Minasyan, Kars, Zrchi, 1912 ♦ Gevorg Arakeli Terteryan, Kharberd, Lachvan, 1910, 1912 ♦ Gevorg Arakeli Zalibegyan, Yerevan, Ortajlu, 1914 ♦ Gevorg Arami Hovhannisyan, Leninakan, Ghoshavank, 1913 ♦ Gevorg Arami Karapetyan, Nor Bayazet, 1912 ♦ Gevorg Armenaki Yeloyan (Sedrakyan), Khnus, Khnusberd, 1912 ♦ Gevorg Arseni Hayrapetyan, Yerevan, Gheghach, 1916 ♦ Gevorg Arseni Yeghiazaryan, Kars, Berna, 1917 ♦ Gevorg Asaturi Hovhannisyan, Shirak, Jajur, 1914 ♦ Gevorg Asaturi Muradyan (Asatryan), Van, Moks, 1907 ♦ Gevorg Ashoti Ashotyan, Tiflis, 1916 ♦ Gevorg Ashoti Harutyunyan, Leninakan, Davalu, 1917 ♦ Gevorg Avagi (Avagyan) Manukyan, Erzrum, Derjanti, 1912 ♦ Gevorg Avagi Avagyan, Leninakan, 1913 ♦ Gevorg Avetisi (Avoyi) Shahinyan, Kars, 1912 ♦ Gevorg Baghdasari Melkonyan, Alekpol, 1913 ♦ Gevorg Bagrati Kostanyan, Kaghzvan, 1912 ♦ Gevorg Caruki Carukyan, Kars, Ortakyadiklar, 1913 ♦ Gevorg Daviti Hovhannisyan, Van, Ktrac kar, 1912 ♦ Gevorg Galusti Barseghyan, Kars, Hopviran, 1909 ♦ Gevorg Galusti Ghazaryan, Alekpol, Kefli, 1913 ♦ Gevorg Ghazari Hakobyan, Darachichak, Nerkin Paghsi, 1912 ♦ Gevorg Grigori Grigoryan (Chumaryan), Akhalkalak, 1915 ♦ Gevorg Gyanjoyi Gasparyan, Aljavaz, Norashen, 1908 ♦ Gevorg Hakobi Babayan, Kars, Ardahan, 1911 ♦ Gevorg Hakobi Hakobyan, Manazkert, Hekmal, 1914 ♦ Gevorg Hakobi Hakobyan, Van, 1912 ♦ Gevorg Hakobi Mkrtchyan, Alekpol, 1913 ♦ Gevorg Hakobi Ohanyan, Kars, 1912 ♦ Gevorg Hamayaki Abgaryan, Leninakan, Ghoshavank, 1913 ♦ Gevorg Hambardzumi Navoyan (Naroyan), Koghb, 1914 ♦ Gevorg Harutyuni Hakobyan, Akhalkalak, Khospia, 1912 ♦ Gevorg Harutyuni Harutyunyan, Akhalkalak, Karcakh, 1914, 1913 ♦ Gevorg

Hovhannesi Grigoryan (Mkhitaryan), Kars, 1917 ♦ Gevorg Hovhannesi Khachatryan, Alekpol, Ghapli, 1911 ♦ Gevorg Hovhannesi Tazviyan, Akhalkalak, Tatesh, 1916 ♦ Gevorg Hovsepi Yeghoyan (Yeghiazaryan), Mush, Shekhakhab, 1914 ♦ Gevorg Karapeti Barseghyan, Alekpol, Gyozli, 1913 ♦ Gevorg Karapeti Khachatryan, Batum, 1914 ♦ Gevorg Khachoyi Azoyan, Erzrum, Dzandzagh, 1916 ♦ Gevorg Khachoyi Khachatryan, Kaghzvan, 1911 ♦ Gevorg Khoreni Metsatunyan, Akhalkalak, 1916 ♦ Gevorg Kirakosi Kirakosyan, Kars, Begliahmet, 1915 ♦ Gevorg Levoni Ghazaryan, Yerevan, 1913 ♦ Gevorg Makari Gevorgyan, Shirak, Khaltagh, 1914 ♦ Gevorg Martirosi Ghazaryan (Martirosyan), Bulanagh, Hatkon, 1907 ♦ Gevorg Meliki Adamyan, Shirak, Babrlu, 1912 ♦ Gevorg Meloyi Antonyan, Alekpol, Tapadolak, 1917 ♦ Gevorg Misaki Hovhannisyan, Bulanagh, Yonjalu, 1918 ♦ Gevorg Misaki Misakyan, Erzrum, Bayburt, 1913 ♦ Gevorg Mkhitari Grigoryan, Kars, Bayburt, 1915 ♦ Gevorg Mkhitari Mkhitaryan, Manazkert, Rza agha ghasmi, 1912 ♦ Gevorg Mkrtchi Dovlatbekyan, Tiflis, 1914 ♦ Gevorg Mkrtchi Mkrtchyan, Yerevan, Aparan, 1914 ♦ Gevorg Mkrtchi Nikoghosyan, Shirak, Artik, 1915 ♦ Gevorg Mkrtchi Poghosyan, Sasun, Aghbik, 1909 ♦ Gevorg Mnatsakani Gevorgyan, Ashtarak, 1913 ♦ Gevorg Movsesi Asvaturyan, Alekpol, Aghin gyugh, 1911 ♦ Gevorg Muradi Mkhitaryan (Muradyan), Shirak, Tashkhalu, 1912 ♦ Gevorg Nikoghayosi Asatryan (Aslanyan), Alekpol, Azat, 1912 ♦ Gevorg Ohannesi Danielyan, Erzrum, 1910 ♦ Gevorg Paruyri Arshakyan, Leninakan, Kharkov, 1914 ♦ Gevorg Petrosi Petrosyan, Basen, Yuzveran, 1910 ♦ Gevorg Pilosi Barseghyan, Kars, Mazra, 1914 ♦ Gevorg Sargsi Safoyan, Kars, Bazrgan, 1914 ♦ Gevorg Sargsi Sargsyan, Tpkhis, 1913 ♦ Gevorg Sedraki Hakobyan (Sedrakyan), Mush, Tom, 1906 ♦ Gevorg Sedraki Yeghoyan, Alekpol, Adikaman, 1914 ♦ Gevorg Simoni Pilosyan, Kars, Ghoshavank, 1910 ♦ Gevorg Soghomoni Sargsyan, Leninakan, Syogutlu, 1912 ♦ Gevorg Soghomoni Ter-Gevorgyan, Van, Yeghegis, 1910 ♦ Gevorg Stepani Stepanyan, Kars, Paldrvan, 1921 ♦ Gevorg Voskani Danielyan, Kars, Mavrak, 1909 ♦ Gevorg Voskani Vardanyan, Alekpol, Maymajugh, 1917 ♦ Gevorg Yeghishi Avetisyan (Atoyan), Alekpol, 1912 ♦ Gevorg Yeghoyi Yeghoyan, Leninakan, Mastara, 1916 ♦ Gevorg Yegori Galstyan, Hamamlu, 1913 ♦ Gevorg Yenoki (Shirinyan) Martirosyan, Tirjan, Ghachagh, 1911 ♦ Gevorg Zakari Ter-Samvelyan, Bulanagh, Shirvanshegh, 1910 ♦ Ghalam Nikoli Davoyan, Alekpol, Boghazkasan, 1910 ♦ Ghalam Yegori Mukelyan (Yegoryan), Alekpol, Parni gyugh, 1914 ♦ Gharib Avetisi Asoyan, Sasun, Gerkhva, 1910 ♦ Gharib Khachatryan, Bulanagh, Kop, 1919 ♦ Gharib Tigrani Harutyunyan, Alekpol, Sirvangyugh, 1910 ♦ Gharib Tigrani Sakoyan (Tigranyan), Alekpol, Toros gyugh, 1908 ♦ Ghazal Hakobi Hakobyan, Alekpol, Ghazarapat, 1914 ♦ Ghazal Zakari Poghosyan, Mush, Yonjalu, 1908 ♦ Ghazar (Hazarapet) Vagharshaki Karapetyan, Nakhijevan, Dznaberd, 1913 ♦ Ghazar Arseni Ghazaryan, Leninakan, Gyulibulagh, 1916 ♦ Ghazar Arshaki Petrosyan, Kars, Dolbandlu, 1909 ♦ Ghazar Avetisi Ghazaryan (Avetisyan), Mush, 1910 ♦ Ghazar Avetisi Ghazaryan, Mush, Krdagom, 1910 ♦ Ghazar Harutyuni Martirosyan (Harutyun.), Karchkan, Vanik, 1912 ♦ Ghazar Harutyuni Petrosyan, Van, Pelva, 1911 ♦ Ghazar Harutyuni Yeghiazaryan, Kars, Berna, 1908 ♦ Ghazar Hmayaki Davtyan, Manazkert, Bagaran, 1912 ♦ Ghazar Hovhannesi Harutyunyan, Van, Mokhraberd, 1910 ♦ Ghazar Hovhannesi Hovhannisyan (Muradyan), Karchkan, Khums, 1911 ♦ Ghazar Karapeti (Mkrtchi) Yeghishyan, Etchmiadzin, 1916 ♦ Ghazar Khachaturi Khachatryan, Kharberd, 1905 ♦ Ghazar Levoni Simonyan (Levonyan), Leninakan, Ghonaghran, 1916 ♦ Ghazar Nahapeti Nahapetyan, Sarighamish, 1918 ♦ Ghazar Poghosi Gasparyan, Bulanagh, Kop, 1908 ♦ Ghazar Soghoyi Soghoyan (Soghomonyan), Leninakan, Chiftali, 1917 ♦ Ghazar Yervandi Yervandyan, Van, Kerc, Hayots dzor, 1911 ♦ Ghazaros Hovsepi Baroyan, Basen, Chrason, 1910 ♦ Ghazaros Manuki Hovhannisyan, Kharberd, Azar, 1909 ♦ Ghazaros Tigrani Jojoyan (Tigranyan), Van, Blten, 1914 ♦ Ghevond Ghazari Ghazaryan, Erzrum, Terjan, 1913 ♦ Ghevond Khachaturi Melkonyan, Kars, Mavrak, 1910 ♦ Ghevond Martirosi Avetisyan, Van, 1908 ♦ Ghevond Martirosi Martirosyan, Van, 1906 ♦ Ghevond Senekerimi Ayvazyan, Alekpol, Ortakyadiklar, 1916 ♦ Ghevond Yegori Movsisyan, Shirak, Chlokhan, 1909 ♦ Ghukas Gevorgi Gevorgyan, Leninakan, Toros gyugh, 1917 ♦ Ghukas Gevorgi Ghazaryan, Kars, Syogutli, 1913 ♦ Ghukas Khachaturi Avetisyan, Kars, 1908 ♦ Ghukas Nshani Nshanyan, Terjan, Priz, 1911 ♦ Ghukas Tigrani Tigranyan, Basen, Toti, 1909 ♦ Ghumash Avetisi Torosyan, Van, 1914 ♦ Ghumash Harutyuni Gasparyan, Sarighamish, 1910 ♦ Ghumash Minasi Manukyan (Minasyan), Van, Archesh, 1909 ♦ Ghumash Rafayeli Rafayelyan, Van, Hirana, 1909 ♦ Ghumash Yenoki Yenokyan, Ghamarlu, 1918 ♦ Ghumri Yeghiazari Khachatryan, Alekpol, Bozdoghan, 1910 ♦ Ghunki Vardani Melkonyan, Leninakan, Ghzlghoch, 1918 ♦ Ghurban Mahmati Mahmatyan, Ashtarak, Agarak, 1914 ♦ Ginevan Grigori Sahakyan, Alekpol, 1912 ♦ Ginevard Mukuchi Mukuchyan, Leninakan, Darband, 1916 ♦ Gino Antoni Grigoryan, Yerevan, 1916 ♦ Gino Galusti Galstyan, Leninakan, Hajinazar, 1914 ♦ Gino Khachaturi Khachatryan, Van, Karchkan, 1910 ♦ Gino Manuki Nahapetyan, Alashkert, Khastur, 1904 ♦ Gino Minasi Hovhannisyan, Alekpol, Danagirmaz, 1910 ♦ Gino Mnatsakani Mnatsakanyan, Leninakan, Babrlu, 1917 ♦ Gino Movsesi Movsisyan, Mush, Yerizak, 1910 ♦ Gino Sedraki Tumasyan, Leninakan, Ghazanchi, 1913 ♦ Ginovabe Ghazari Ghazaryan, Van, Voghkava, 1907 ♦ Ginovabe Samsoni Safaryan, Alashkert, Gharakilisa, 1912 ♦ Ginovaber Abrahami Sargsyan, Bitlis, 1911 ♦ Ginovaber Ayvazi Amirshatyan, Manazkert, Berd, 1910 ♦ Ginovabi Stepani Arakelyan, Nakhijevan, Aza, 1914, 1913 ♦ Ginovari Hovhannesi Karapetyan, Bulanagh, Kaghzvan, 1915 ♦ Gnel Khachaturi Martirosyan (Khachatryan), Basen, Dalibaba, 1911 ♦ Gnun Avetisi Barseghyan, Kars, Gedaksatli, 1915 ♦ Gohar Gevorgi Asoyan, Kaghzvan, 1909

♦ Gohar Gevorgi Manukyan, Igdir, 1913 ♦ Gohar Hamoyi Hamoyan, Kars, 1918 ♦ Gohar Harutyuni Harutyunyan, Kars, 1918 ♦ Gohar Poghosi Hovhannisyan, Yerevan, Khrkhbulagh, 1917 ♦ Goharik Abrahami Marmaryan, Kaghzvan, 1911 ♦ Goharik Antoni Khachatryan (Antonyan), Tiflis, 1918 ♦ Goharik Arami Aramyan, Igdir, 1918 ♦ Goharik Arshaki Tovmasyan, Yerevan, Ghamarlu, 1916 ♦ Goharik Avagi Avagyan (Harutyunyan), Leninakan, 1914 ♦ Goharik Avetiki Aslanyan, Alekpol, 1911 ♦ Goharik Avetisi Hakobyan, Kars, 1912 ♦ Goharik Bagrati Bagratyan, Alekpol, Ghanlija, 1918 ♦ Goharik Barseghi Barseghyan, Kars, Bashshoragal, 1913, 1914 ♦ Goharik Geghami Virabyan, Yerevan, Blur, 1911 ♦ Goharik Gevorgi Aslanyan, Kars, 1914 ♦ Goharik Ghukasi Ghukasyan, Kars, 1916 ♦ Goharik Hakobi Tadevosyan, Kars, 1918 ♦ Goharik Hamayaki Hakobyan, Surmalu, Igdir, 1913 ♦ Goharik Hamayaki Sedrakyan, Van, 1913 ♦ Goharik Hambardzumi Pashinyan, Gharakilisa, 1914 ♦ Goharik Harutyuni Arakelyan, Olti, 1910 ♦ Goharik Harutyuni Galstyan, Leninakan, 1913 ♦ Goharik Harutyuni Kirakosyan, Kars, 1914 ♦ Goharik Harutyuni Mosikyan, Leninakan, 1910, 1909 ♦ Goharik Hmayaki Melkonyan, Kars, 1911, 1912 ♦ Goharik Hovhannesi Hovhannisyan, Van, 1919 ♦ Goharik Hovhannesi Karapetyan, Kars, 1906 ♦ Goharik Hovhannesi Kirakosyan, Kars, 1915 ♦ Goharik Karapeti Karapetyan, Alashkert, Garasu, 1918 ♦ Goharik Karapeti Nalbandyan, Leninakan, Gharakilisa, 1908 ♦ Goharik Levoni Galstyan, Kars, 1915 ♦ Goharik Maghaki Stepanyan, Batum, Tandzut, 1908 ♦ Goharik Markosi Baloyan (Markosyan), Etchmiadzin, Khatunarkh, 1911 ♦ Goharik Martirosi Gharibyan (Martirosyan), Leninakan, 1914 ♦ Goharik Martirosi Hakobyan, Alekpol, 1914 ♦ Goharik Martirosi Hovhannisyan, Alekpol, 1912 ♦ Goharik Martirosi Ter Harutyunyan, Kharberd, 1921 ♦ Goharik Matsaki Mnatsakanyan, P. Gharakilisa, Chgdalar, 1918 ♦ Goharik Misaki Hovhannisyan, Kars, Mec Parket, 1917 ♦ Goharik Mkrtchi Bagratyan (Mkrtchyan), Kars, Norashen, 1914 ♦ Goharik Mkrtchi Karapetyan, Leninakan, 1917 ♦ Goharik Mnatsakani Harutyunyan, Leninakan, 1911 ♦ Goharik Mukayeli Varosyan, Alekpol, 1916 ♦ Goharik Mukuchi Khachatryan, Akhalkalak, 1918 ♦ Goharik Muradi Nersisyan, Kars, 1914 ♦ Goharik Nersesi Hovhannisyan (Nersisyan), Kars, Khuyujugh, 1913 ♦ Goharik Nersesi Nersisyan, Erzrum, Kharacha, 1911 ♦ Goharik Nikoghosi (Mkrtchi) (Nikoghosyan) Mkrtchyan, Surmalu, Khalfalu, 1914 ♦ Goharik Nikoghosi Nikoghosyan, Terjan, Bagarich, 1910 ♦ Goharik Piloyi Hovhannisyan, Kars, Hamzakarak, 1914, 1912 ♦ Goharik Poghosi Avetisyan, Van, Mokhraberd, 1908 ♦ Goharik Sahaki Mikayelyan (Sahakyan), Van, Heren, 1910 ♦ Goharik Sargsi Basentsyan, Leninakan, Ghoshavank, 1912 ♦ Goharik Sargsi Karapetyan, Kharberd, 1907 ♦ Goharik Sargsi Sargsyan, Khnus, 1920 ♦ Goharik Sargsi Sargsyan, Lori, Aghkorbi, 1918 ♦ Goharik Smbati Arakelyan, Kars, Paldrvan, 1912 ♦ Goharik Stepani Stepanyan (Manukyan), Van, Archesh, 1912 ♦ Goharik Tadevosi Astvacatryan, Yerevan, Kanaker, 1909 ♦ Goharik Tatosi Martirosyan, Kars, 1911 ♦ Goharik Torosi Shahinyan, Kars, Pirvalu, 1912 ♦ Goharik Vahani Gholdughchyan, Kars, 1910 ♦ Goharik Vardani Alaverdyan, Alashkert, Berd, 1911 ♦ Goharik Vardani Vardanyan, Karin, 1918 ♦ Goharik Vardani Vardanyan, Van, Khachakilisa, 1913 ♦ Goharik Yeghishi Mkrtchyan, Alekpol, 1912, 1908 ♦ Goharik Yenoki Yengibaryan, Igdir, 1911 ♦ Goharik Zohrabi Arshakyan, Tiflis, 1913 ♦ Gozal Misaki Khachatryan, Alashkert, Berd, 1912 ♦ Grab Grigori (Haroyi) Grigoryan (Harutyunyan), Kars, Gyamrlu, 1914 ♦ Grab Sedraki Avetisyan, Kars, Bangliahmat, 1913, 1911 ♦ Grab Stepani Galstyan, Kars, Akrak, 1915 ♦ Grabion Harutyuni Chaghalyan, Hin Bayazet, Musun, 1912 ♦ Grabion Shmavoni Gnunyan, Kars, Bashshoragyal, 1918 ♦ Grap (Brabion) Hakobi Hakobyan (Antonyan), Basen, Khoshgaldi, 1914 ♦ Grap Baghdasari Baghdasaryan, Khnus, Khozlu, 1915 ♦ Grap Hovhannesi (Hovhani) Sargsyan, Kars, Bayghara, 1915 ♦ Grapion Minasi Grigoryan (Minasyan), Kars, Shadigara, 1912 ♦ Grapion Vardani Melikyan, Alekpol, Ghanlich, 1913 ♦ Grigor (Grisha) Aghabeki Barseghyan, Karabagh, Sevakar, 1912 ♦ Grigor (Grisha) Arshaki Mkrtchyan, Alekpol, Kyapanak, 1913 ♦ Grigor (Grisha) Sargsi Hakobyan, Nakhijevan, Norashen, 1913 ♦ Grigor Abrahami Abrahamyan, Darachichak, Farugh, 1912 ♦ Grigor Aghajani Galstyan, Dirjan, Khotkhol, 1909 ♦ Grigor Aghasu Sanosyan, Akhalkalak, Ara gegh, 1916 ♦ Grigor Alaverdi (Avdali) Hovhannisyan (Avdalyan), Nor Bayazet, 1912, 1911 ♦ Grigor Andreasi Baroyan, Karabagh, Mushkapar, 1911 ♦ Grigor Andreasi Barseghyan, Bayburt, Averak, 1909 ♦ Grigor Arakeli Davtyan, Gyokcha, Kyalband, 1912 ♦ Grigor Arami Tutunjyan, Kars, 1914 ♦ Grigor Aristakesi Avdalyan, Kars, Hamzakar, 1900 ♦ Grigor Armenaki Ayvazyan, Erzrum, 1910 ♦ Grigor Arshaki Arshakyan, Shirak, Ortakilisa, 1919, 1918 ♦ Grigor Arshaki Ziroyan, Alekpol, Ojaghlu, 1914 ♦ Grigor Avetisi Gumriyan (Avetisyan), 1914 ♦ Grigor Baghdasari (Gaspari) Baghdasaryan (Gasparyan), (Kars) Basen, Dzandzakh, 1917 ♦ Grigor Balasani Grigoryan, Van, Khorgom, 1908 ♦ Grigor Barseghi Margaryan, Etchmiadzin, Hajighala, 1913 ♦ Grigor Dovlatyan, 1922 ♦ Grigor Galusti Martirosyan, Kars, 1917 ♦ Grigor Galusti Zhamharyan, Kars, 1910 ♦ Grigor Ghevondi Hambaryan, Sarighamish, Ghoshakilisa, 1913 ♦ Grigor Grishayi Gevorgyan, Yerevan, Arzakand, 1912 ♦ Grigor Habeti Muradyan, Kars, 1911 ♦ Grigor Hakobi Aghajanyan, Kars, 1911 ♦ Grigor Hakobi Aleksanyan (Hakobyan), Ghurdughuli, Ghazikidan, 1919 ♦ Grigor Hakobi Baghdasaryan, Kars, 1913 ♦ Grigor Hakobi Hakobyan, Van, 1917, 1915 ♦ Grigor Hakobi Poghosyan, Kars, 1916 ♦ Grigor Harutyuni Harutyunyan, Basen, 1914 ♦ Grigor Harutyuni Harutyunyan, Kars, Ghzlchakhchakh, 1912 ♦ Grigor Harutyuni Papoyan, Kars, Uzunkilisa, 1914 ♦ Grigor Harutyuni Vardanyan (Harutyunyan), Alekpol, Illi, 1914 ♦ Grigor Hayrapeti Stepanyan, Tavriz, 1914 ♦ Grigor Hovakimi Grigoryan, Etchmiadzin, Sardarabat, 1914 ♦ Grigor Hovhannesi Hakobyan

(Hovhannisyan), Kars, Cbni, 1913 ♦ Grigor Hovhannesi Harutyunyan, Mush, Khasgyugh, 1912 ♦ Grigor Hovhannesi Karapetyan, Leninakan, Aghin, 1916 ♦ Grigor Karapeti Baghdasaryan, Alekpol, 1911 ♦ Grigor Karapeti Karapetyan, Van, Khumar, 1911, 1910 ♦ Grigor Ketikchyan, Igdir, Surmalu, 1914 ♦ Grigor Khachaturi Abgaryan (Khachatryan), Van, Alkhur, 1910 ♦ Grigor Khachaturi Harutyunyan, Mush, Yamara, 1910 ♦ Grigor Khachaturi Khachatryan, Igdir, Panik, 1912 ♦ Grigor Khachaturi Khachatryan, Leninakan, Mahmatjugh, 1915 ♦ Grigor Khachaturi Martirosyan, Talin, 1913 ♦ Grigor Kirakosi Davtyan, Sasun, Hazva, 1914 ♦ Grigor Levoni Harutyunyan, Ghamarlu, Chidamlu, 1911 ♦ Grigor Makari Nazaretyan, Kars, 1915 ♦ Grigor Mambrei Hambardzumyan (Khangildyan), Igdir, Alighamar, 1916 ♦ Grigor Manuki Manukyan, Kaghzvan, Yendija, 1913 ♦ Grigor Margari Margaryan, Kharberd, Kalisher, 1909 ♦ Grigor Margari Sargsyan (Margaryan), Manazkert, Berd, 1912 ♦ Grigor Matevosi Hovhannisyan, Mush, Khasgyugh, 1913 ♦ Grigor Mecoyi Mecoyan (Mkrtchyan), Akhalkalak, Sulda, 1917 ♦ Grigor Mheri Martirosyan, Bulanagh, Blakar, 1911, 1910 ♦ Grigor Minasi Holoyan, Basen, Arjarak, 1912 ♦ Grigor Misaki Arakelyan, Alekpol, Svanverdi, 1912 ♦ Grigor Misaki Charchoghlyan, Mush, 1912 ♦ Grigor Mnatsakani Sargsyan, Etchmiadzin, 1912 ♦ Grigor Mukayeli Hovhannisyan (Mikayelyan), Alekpol, Artik, 1917 ♦ Grigor Nersesi Karapetyan (Nersisyan), Van, Nartagh. kanghar, 1907 ♦ Grigor Petrosi Grigoryan, Kaghzvan, 1911 ♦ Grigor Petrosi Hakobyan, Bulanagh, Blur, 1907 ♦ Grigor Petrosi Haykazyan, Van, 1911 ♦ Grigor Petrosi Hovsepyan (Petrosyan), Yerevan, Ghamarlu, 1912 ♦ Grigor Petrosi Mkrtchyan, Alekpol, Palkli, 1915 ♦ Grigor Petrosi Voskanyan, Kghi, Lchik, 1912 ♦ Grigor Poghosi Ghazaryan, Alashkert, Chedkan, 1908 ♦ Grigor Safari Vardanyan, Kars, Mazra, 1910, 1909 ♦ Grigor Sahaki Hakobyan, Yerznka, 1908 ♦ Grigor Sargsi Sargsyan (Zakaryan), Shirak, Daharlu, 1914 ♦ Grigor Sargsi Sargsyan, Baku, Ghlik, 1912 ♦ Grigor Sargsi Sargsyan, Kars, Paldrvan, 1914 ♦ Grigor Sedraki Aslanyan, Kars, Gharamahmat, 1912 ♦ Grigor Sedraki Grigoryan, Alekpol, Shishtapa, 1916 ♦ Grigor Sedraki Sedrakyan, Kars, 1918 ♦ Grigor Sergoyi Terteryan, Akhalkalak, Ikhtila, 1914 ♦ Grigor Simoni Geghamyan (Simonyan), Van, Zeynis, 1915 ♦ Grigor Simoni Muradyan, Aljavaz, Nor Shnjgh, 1910 ♦ Grigor Smbati Martirosyan, Alekpol, 1913 ♦ Grigor Srapioni Matsoyan, Leninakan, Ortakilisa, 1917 ♦ Grigor Tadevosi Arakelyan, Kaghzvan, Gharavank, 1911 ♦ Grigor Tadevosi Tarminyan, Lori, Uzunlar, 1914 ♦ Grigor Tatosi Manukyan, Kars, Cbni, 1916 ♦ Grigor Vardani Vardanyan, Alashkert, 1911 ♦ Grigor Vardani Yeretsyan, Akhalkalak, Mec Khanchali, 1915 ♦ Grigor Yegori Hovhannisyan, Alekpol, Sagud, 1915 ♦ Grigor Zadoyi Zadoyan, Van, Kharakants, 1908 ♦ Grigor Zakari Grigoryan (Zakaryan), Mush, Harterin, 1908 ♦ Grish Bareghami Hakobyan, Etchmiadzin, Evjilar, 1914 ♦ Grish Karapeti Karapetyan, Nakhijevan, Shekh-mahmud, 1914 ♦ Grish Tatosi Manukyan, Kars, Ghzlchakhchakh, 1916 ♦ Grisha Artemi Navasardyan, Karabagh, Shushi, 1912 ♦ Grisha Hakobi Balasanyan, Kaghzvan, Khab, 1913 ♦ Grisha Hakobi Hakobyan, Leninakan, Kyurakdar, 1912 ♦ Grisha Haruti Harutyunyan, Karabagh, 1917 ♦ Grisha Hayrapeti Sargsyan, Baku, Nukhi, 1913 ♦ Grisha Mamikoni Petrosyan, Etchmiadzin, Alibiklu, 1914 ♦ Grisha Martirosi Martirosyan, Leninakan, Bozi gyugh, 1914, 1915 ♦ Grisha Muradi (Smbati) Muradyan, Lori, Gharaghala, 1919 ♦ Gugush Gojoyi Sargsyan, Koghb, 1914 ♦ Gule Ghazari Makaryan, Mush, Mush cghak, 1914 ♦ Gulkhas Grigori Karapetyan, Leninakan, Ghskh-Dagirman, 1913 ♦ Gurgen (Movsesi) Movsisyan, Van, Aygestan, 1913 ♦ Gurgen Abgari Manukyan, Akhalkalak, Khojabat, 1915 ♦ Gurgen Aleki Minasyan, Basen, Khoshgaldi, 1911 ♦ Gurgen Arakeli Arakelyan, Leninakan, Chiftali, 1918 ♦ Gurgen Arami Groyan, Gharakilisa, 1915 ♦ Gurgen Arseni Savoyan, Kars, Berna, 1916 ♦ Gurgen Arshaki Mkhitaryan, Alashkert, Bashgyugh, 1910 ♦ Gurgen Artashesi Aghajanyan, Alekpol, Mastara, 1912 ♦ Gurgen Artyomi Boyajyan, Leninakan, 1912 ♦ Gurgen Asaturi Hovhannisyan, Yerevan, Ghamarli, 1912 ♦ Gurgen Avetisi Azizyan (Avetisyan), Van, Tok, 1909 ♦ Gurgen Baghdasari Avagyan, Van, Abagha, 1916 ♦ Gurgen Bagrati Khachatryan, (Baku), Igdir, 1912 ♦ Gurgen Barseghi Petrosyan, Igdir, Blur, 1914 ♦ Gurgen Beglari Beglaryan (Sargsyan), Leninakan, Ghoshavank, 1909 ♦ Gurgen Davti Hovsepyan, Nukhi, Tashbulagh, 1912 ♦ Gurgen Gabrieli Piltakyan, Akhalkalak, Aragova, 1918 ♦ Gurgen Garegini Gareginyan, Igdir, Mavi, 1916 ♦ Gurgen Gaspari Mkrtchyan, Kars, 1913 ♦ Gurgen Gevorgi (Garniki) Gevorgyan, Bitlis, Batnots, 1912 ♦ Gurgen Gevorgi (Nikitayi) Khachatryan, Alekpol, 1915 ♦ Gurgen Gevorgi Aghoyan, Kars, 1911, 1909 ♦ Gurgen Gevorgi Gevorgyan, Alekpol, Altakhji, 1916 ♦ Gurgen Gevorgi Gevorgyan, Van, 1909 ♦ Gurgen Gevorgi Martirosyan (Gevorgyan), Van-Shatakh, Patik, 1909 ♦ Gurgen Gevorgi Sargsyan, Basen, Cholakhlu, 1913, 1911 ♦ Gurgen Ghazari Zakaryan (Ghazaryan), Kars, Pokr Parket, 1912 ♦ Gurgen Ghevondi Gabrielyan, Kars, Uzunkilisa, 1917 ♦ Gurgen Ghukasi Chakhalyan, Kars, Zrchi, 1911, 1910 ♦ Gurgen Grigori Faroyan, Kharberd, 1912 ♦ Gurgen Grigori Gasparyan, Leninakan, 1917 ♦ Gurgen Grigori Grigoryan, Van, Chobanoghli, 1915 ♦ Gurgen Grigori Stepanyan, Kars, 1914 ♦ Gurgen Hakobi Hakobyan, Terjan, Mants, 1907 ♦ Gurgen Hakobi Sargsyan, Kars, Beglamar, 1910 ♦ Gurgen Hambardzumi Zakaryan, Akhalkalak, Gandza, 1915 ♦ Gurgen Harutyuni Sargsyan, Kars, Korkhan, 1912 ♦ Gurgen Haykazi Davtyan, Not Bayazet, Ghshli, 1916 ♦ Gurgen Hayki Kirakosyan, Alekpol, 1912 ♦ Gurgen Hayrapeti Babayan, Nakhijevan, Nazarapat, 1912 ♦ Gurgen Hayrapeti Gevorgyan, Mush, Bulanshogh, 1911 ♦ Gurgen Hovsepi Hovsepyan, Karabagh, Gandzak, 1911 ♦ Gurgen Hovsepi Khalatyan, Dilijan, Karvansara, 1914 ♦ Gurgen Karapeti Papikyan, Alekpol, Syogutlu, 1912 ♦ Gurgen Khachaturi Grigoryan, Van, Artamet, 1909 ♦ Gurgen Levoni Gevorgyan, Kars, Mavrak, 1914 ♦ Gurgen Lyudvigi Tatevosyan, Hin Nakhijevan, 1911 ♦ Gurgen

Makari Nazaretyan, Kars, 1912 ◆ Gurgen Manuchari Arzumanyan, Karabagh, Shushi, 1914 ◆ Gurgen Manuki (Mihrani) Manukyan, Van, Perkli, 1913 ◆ Gurgen Manuki Zakaryan, Akhalkalak, Tadish, 1914 ◆ Gurgen Margari Hovhannisyan, Kars, 1913 ◆ Gurgen Matsaki Matsakyan, Shirak, Ghzlkilisa, 1915 ◆ Gurgen Mikayeli Mikayelyan (Tokhmanyan), Van, 1909 ◆ Gurgen Minasi Barseghyan, Kars, Nakhijevan, 1911 ◆ Gurgen Minasi Margaryan, Kars, 1913 ◆ Gurgen Minasi Minasyan, Leninakan, Salut, 1917 ◆ Gurgen Misaki Arakelyan, Kars, Karmir vank, 1909 ◆ Gurgen Misaki Hovhannisyan, Leninakan, Dagali, 1911 ◆ Gurgen Misaki Simonyan, Alekpol, Chlokhan, 1912 ◆ Gurgen Mkrtchi Amiryan, Kars, Tikor, 1910 ◆ Gurgen Mkrtchi Grigoryan, Kars, Parket, 1914 ◆ Gurgen Movsesi Elibegyan, Akhalkalak, Sulda, 1911 ◆ Gurgen Movsesi Ter-Sargsyan, Kars, 1912 ◆ Gurgen Navasardi Ghazaryan, Yerevan, Kanaker, 1914 ◆ Gurgen Nazari (Mkrtchi) Mkrtchyan, Shirak, Khli Gharakilisa, 1912 ◆ Gurgen Nazari Mayasyan, Kars, Bvik, 1911 ◆ Gurgen Nikoli Hloyan (Khachatryan), Leninakan, Haji khalil, 1911 ◆ Gurgen Nikoli Nikolyan, Alashkert, 1915 ◆ Gurgen Petrosi Khachatryan (Petrosyan), Kars, Mavrak, 1914, 1913 ◆ Gurgen Petrosi Kurghinyan, Erzrum, Patshen, 1909 ◆ Gurgen Petrosi Manukyan, Kaghzvan, 1913 ◆ Gurgen Petrosi Sahakyan, Hin Bayazet, Masan, 1908 ◆ Gurgen Poghosi Poghosyan (Tadevosyan), Keshviran, Bulanagh, 1918 ◆ Gurgen Rafayeli Rafayelyan (Tovmasyan), Van, Ererik, 1912 ◆ Gurgen Sargsi (Sargsyan) Harutyunyan, Alekpol, Ghapli, 1915 ◆ Gurgen Sargsi Gevorgyan, Leninakan, Jajur, 1912 ◆ Gurgen Sargsi Navasardyan, Yerevan, Aghbash, 1913 ◆ Gurgen Sedraki Movsisyan, Basen, Hekibad, 1913 ◆ Gurgen Sedraki Poghosyan, Yerevan, Basargechar, 1913 ◆ Gurgen Sedraki Sedrakyan, Leninakan, Bozdoghan, 1912 ◆ Gurgen Sedraki Sedrakyan, Leninakan, Mejidlu, 1916 ◆ Gurgen Simoni Harutyunyan (Simonyan), Van, 1914 ◆ Gurgen Simoni Simonyan, Nakhijevan, Aprakunis, 1914 ◆ Gurgen Smbati Voskanyan, Nakhijevan, Yarmja, 1914 ◆ Gurgen Soghomoni Grigoryan, Khnus, Berd, 1910 ◆ Gurgen Soghomoni Poghosyan, Leninakan, Duzkharaba, 1911 ◆ Gurgen Tadevosi Adamyan, Kars, Kaghzvan, 1911 ◆ Gurgen Tadevosi Galstyan, Nakhijevan, Karatash, 1912 ◆ Gurgen Tadevosi Hakobyan, Alekpol, Pokr Kapanak, 1915 ◆ Gurgen Tigrani Grigoryan, Kars, Gedaksatlmish, 1910 ◆ Gurgen Tigrani Poghosyan, Van, Yanggh, 1912 ◆ Gurgen Trdati Hovhannisyan, Nakhijevan, Birali, 1914 ◆ Gurgen Unani Hakobyan, Mush, Votnchor, 1912 ◆ Gurgen Vahanyan, 1922 ◆ Gurgen Vardani Hovhannisyan, Surmalu, Tejrlu, 1916 ◆ Gurgen Varosi Baghdasaryan, Kars, Chala, 1912 ◆ Gurgen Voskani Grigoryan, Kars, Bagran, 1910 ◆ Gurgen Yegori Yegoryan, Shirak, Toros gyugh, 1913 ◆ Gurgen Yenoki Hovhannisyan (Yenokyan), Leninakan, Sogyutli, 1911 ◆ Gurgen Zakari T. Samvelyan, Mush, Shirvanshugh, 1909 ◆ Gurgen Zakari Tumasyan, Kars, 1911 ◆ Gyozal Arami Hovhannisyan, Shirak, Gyuli bulagh, 1912 ◆ Gyozal Avetisi Grigoryan, Alashkert, Ghazigyugh, 1911 ◆ Gyozal Baghdasari Baghdasaryan, Van, Noraduz, 1913 ◆ Gyozal Gaspari Hovhannisyan, Mush, Sardar, 1911, 1909 ◆ Gyozal Gevorgi Petrosyan (Gevorgyan), Van, Mandan, 1914 ◆ Gyozal Movsesi Haroyan (Movsisyan), Alashkert, Ghazi, 1908 ◆ Gyozal Musheghi Avetisyan (Baghdasaryan), Alashkert, Yonjalu, 1914 ◆ Gyozal Sargsi Hovhannisyan, Van, Cbni, 1913 ◆ Gyozal Tatosi Yeghiazaryan, Van, 1906 ◆ Gyozal Vardani Hovhannisyan (Sargsyan), Bitlis, Yeghegis, 1911 ◆ Gyozal Vardani Hovsepyan (Vardanyan), Van, Abagha, 1909 ◆ Gyule Karapeti Asatryan (Karapetyan), Basen, Archarak, 1914 ◆ Gyulgaz (Gyulizar) Kebuli Kebulyan, Leninakan, Gharakilisa, 1920 ◆ Gyuli Hakobi Hakobyan, Erzrum, 1912 ◆ Gyuli Samsoni Hovsepyan (Samsonyan), Kars, Kyurakdar, 1914 ◆ Gyulistan Karapeti Karapetyan, Van, Moks, 1913 ◆ Gyulistan Petrosi Petrosyan, Kharberd, Shapsharu, 1907 ◆ Gyulizar Abgari Manukyan, Basen, Tod, 1909 ◆ Gyulizar Arakeli Arakelyan, Ghamarlu, 1914 ◆ Gyulizar Asaturi Asatryan, Bitlis, Prkhus, 1912, 1909 ◆ Gyulizar Buniati Boyatyan, Persia, Khoy, 1912 ◆ Gyulizar Galusti (Galustyan) Torosyan, Aljavaz, 1909 ◆ Gyulizar Gaspari Hovhannisyan, Badnodts, 1914 ◆ Gyulizar Gevorgi Gevorgyan, 1918 ◆ Gyulizar Gevorgi Poghosyan (Gevorgyan), Bitlis, 1912, 1910 ◆ Gyulizar Ghazari Avetisyan (Ghazaryan), Nor Bayazet, Gori, 1908 ◆ Gyulizar Ghukasi Sargsyan, Bitlis, Tapavank, 1909 ◆ Gyulizar Goroyi Vozmanyan, Kars, Yamanchair, 1913 ◆ Gyulizar Grigori Grigoryan, Bulanagh, 1911 ◆ Gyulizar Hakobi Davtyan, Van, Kyoshk, 1914 ◆ Gyulizar Hakobi Harutyunyan (Hakobyan), Basen, Kadubaz, 1914 ◆ Gyulizar Hakobi Karapetyan, Yerevan, 1916 ◆ Gyulizar Hakobi Manukyan, Bitlis, Por (Volor), 1908 ◆ Gyulizar Hakobi Ter-Harutyunyan, Sarighamish, Aksi ghaz, 1910 ◆ Gyulizar Hambardzumi Hambardzumyan, Kars, Nakhijevan, 1909 ◆ Gyulizar Harutyuni Harutyunyan, Sasun, Maghen, 1914 ◆ Gyulizar Hasoyi Hasoyan, Alekpol, 1913 ◆ Gyulizar Hovhannesi Mkrtchyan (Hovhannisyan), Van, Andzav, 1909 ◆ Gyulizar Hovhannesi Sedrakyan (Hovhannisyan), Van, Gorcut, 1911, 1910 ◆ Gyulizar Hovsepi Hovsepyan, Van, Noraduz, 1911 ◆ Gyulizar Khachaturi Hovhannisyan, Kars, Gharamahmud, 1912 ◆ Gyulizar Manuki Davtyan, Van, Khachan, 1909 ◆ Gyulizar Mikayeli Mikayelyan, Nor Bayazet, 1912 ◆ Gyulizar Mkrtchi Mkrtchyan, Manazkert, 1908 ◆ Gyulizar Nahapeti Arakelyan (Martirosyan), Basen, Kachlu, 1913 ◆ Gyulizar Nersesi Melikyan, Akhlat, Matnavank, 1913 ◆ Gyulizar Petrosi Petrosyan, Kars, 1919 ◆ Gyulizar Poghosi Manukyan, Mush, Bulanagh, 1914 ◆ Gyulizar Sahaki Manukyan, Sasun, Hazari, 1914 ◆ Gyulizar Sargisi (Daviti) Davtyan (Sargsyan), Van, Karchkan, 1914 ◆ Gyulizar Sargsi Aramyan, Kars, Bulanagh, 1913 ◆ Gyulizar Sargsi Muradyan, Moks, Arinj, 1911 ◆ Gyulizar Sargsi Sargsyan, Gharakilisa, 1918 ◆ Gyulizar Sedraki Sedrakyan, 1913, 1911 ◆ Gyulizar Serobi Serobyan, Bitlis, Mtsik, 1917 ◆ Gyulizar Shmavoni Tadevosyan, Igdir, Evjilar, 1906 ◆ Gyulizar Simoni Stepanyan, Moks, Noravank, 1909 ◆ Gyulizar Vahani Hovhannisyan,

Mush, Kop, 1912 ◆ Gyulizar Vanoyi Tonoyan, Gharakilisa, 1916 ◆ Gyulizar Vardani Vardanyan, Alashkert, Chdkan, 1909 ◆ Gyulizar Yeghiazari Yeghiazaryan, Van, Pshavants, 1912 ◆ Gyulizar Yesayi Sahakyan, Van, Akants, 1911 ◆ Gyulizar Zakari Maghlchyan, Olti, 1910 ◆ Gyulkhaz Hakobi Vardanyan, Lori, Akori, 1912 ◆ Gyulnaz Karapeti Karapetyan, Bulanagh, Gyambu, 1911 ◆ Gyulperi Mkrtchi Mkrtchyan, Basen, Toti, 1911 ◆ Gyulvard Aleksani Barseghyan, Alekpol, Ghzlkilisa, 1910 ◆ Gyulvard Arakeli Sargsyan, Bulanagh, Prkashen, 1908 ◆ Gyulvard Movsesi Movsisyan, Van, Aljavaz, 1912 ◆ Gyulvard Sargisi Galoyan, Kars, Ghzlchakhchakh, 1913 ◆ Gyulvard Vasili Arsenyan, Yerevan, Tekrlu, 1914 ◆ Gyuzal Danieli Vardanyan (Danielyan), Bulanagh, 1910 ◆ Gyuzal Movsesi Movsisyan, Alashkert, Khazgyugh, 1908 ◆ Habet Ayvazi Ayvazyan, Basen, Bashgegh, 1913 ◆ Habet Barseghi Karapetyan, Alashkert, Chlkan, 1912 ◆ Habet Galusti Farhadyan (Aboyan), Kars, Nakhijevan, 1913 ◆ Habet Ghazari Vardanyan, Mush, Hartert, 1909 ◆ Habet Hakobi Minasyan, Kars, Ghzlchakhchakh, 1917 ◆ Habet Hovsepi Kirakosyan (Tovmasyan), Kharberd, Nor gyugh, 1909 ◆ Habet Khachaturi Khachatryan, Mush, Vardenis, 1914 ◆ Habet Maloyi Barikyan (Maloyan), Khnus, Kopala, 1910 ◆ Habet Mkhitari Poghosyan (Mkhitaryan), Khnus, Khlat, 1912 ◆ Habet Mkoyi Sargsyan, Kars, Khani, 1910 ◆ Habet Mkrtchi Mkrtchyan (Berberyan), Van, 1909 ◆ Habet Nikoghayosi Vardanyan, Leninakan, Mec Keti, 1912 ◆ Habet Sahaki Melkumyan, Sarighamish, Chrason, 1911 ◆ Habet Sedraki Saghoyan, Alekpol, Dzithankov, 1912 ◆ Habet Simoni Simonyan, Leninakan, Khoturbulakh, 1915 ◆ Hachi Serobi Janoyan, Basen, Ishkhu, 1911 ◆ Hachie (Jndi) Janoyi Tumoyan, Kars, Tikor, 1909 ◆ Hajibab (Sahak) Hovhannesi Carukyan, Erzrum, Aspavarak, 1910 ◆ Hakob (Hovhannes) Gevorgi Gevorgyan, 1918 ◆ Hakob (Sedraki) Hakobyan, Alekpol, Mec Keti, 1911 ◆ Hakob Arakeli (Galoyi) Arakelyan, Kars, Chankli, 1917 ◆ Hakob Arami Aramyan (Alemyan), Nakhijevan, 1916 ◆ Hakob Arshaki Arshakyan, Kars, 1920 ◆ Hakob Atoyi Karapetyan, Alekpol, Illi, 1910 ◆ Hakob Avetisi Sahakyan, Etchmiadzin, Nerkin Khatunarkh, 1910 ◆ Hakob Avoyi Vardanyan, Basen, Cholakhli, 1910 ◆ Hakob Azizbeki Yuzbashyan, Leninakan, Ghonaghran, 1913 ◆ Hakob Badali Badalyan (Sahakyan), Kaghzvan, Bagran, 1913 ◆ Hakob Badoyi Avetisyan, Basen, Chrason, 1912 ◆ Hakob Bagrati (Ghazari) Poghosyan (Pochikyan), Kars, 1912 ◆ Hakob Bagrati Stepanyan, Alekpol, Ghazarapat, 1911 ◆ Hakob Balasani Davtyan, Surmalu, Kulap, 1911 ◆ Hakob Barseghi Poghosyan (Barseghyan), Basen, Ekhibad, 1915 ◆ Hakob Daviti Hakobyan (Davtyan), Basen, Armtlu, 1915 ◆ Hakob Galusti Ter-Hakobyan, Leninakan, Daharli, 1914 ◆ Hakob Geghami Hakobyan, Sarighamish, Churukh, 1914 ◆ Hakob Gevorgi Gevorgyan, Shirak, Ortakilisa, 1916 ◆ Hakob Gevorgi Hakobyan, Leninakan, 1913 ◆ Hakob Ghazari Melkonyan (Ghazaryan), Kars, 1911 ◆ Hakob Ginosi (Smbati) Ginosyan, Shirak, Darband, 1917 ◆ Hakob Grigori Gasparyan, Tiflis, 1910 ◆ Hakob Grigori Khachatryan, Sarighamish, 1914 ◆ Hakob Grigori Sargsyan (Grigoryan), Akhalkalak, Machada, 1914 ◆ Hakob Grigori Yeghiazaryan (Grigoryan), Van, Archesh, 1910 ◆ Hakob Grigori Yeloyan (Muradyan), Kaghzvan, 1910 ◆ Hakob Hambardzumi Badalyan, Akhalkalak, 1908 ◆ Hakob Haroyi Haroyan, Basen, 1914 ◆ Hakob Harutiki Mikayelyan, Akhalkalak, Mec Gentura, 1911 ◆ Hakob Harutyuni Arakelyan, Olti, 1910 ◆ Hakob Harutyuni Gevorgyan (Harutyunyan), Bulanagh, Kop, 1915 ◆ Hakob Harutyuni Hakobyan (Shaghikyan), Akhalkalak, Abul, 1914 ◆ Hakob Harutyuni Sichenyan, Russia, Rostov, 1911 ◆ Hakob Hmayaki Hakobyan, Igdir, 1914 ◆ Hakob Hmayaki Mirijanyan, Kaghzvan, Khas, 1911 ◆ Hakob Hovhannesi Hakobyan (Manushakyan), Van, Hndzak, 1910 ◆ Hakob Hovhannesi Hovhannisyan, Erzrum, Jrason, 1913 ◆ Hakob Hovhannesi Mkrtchyan (Hovhannisyan), Igdir, Khalfalu, 1911 ◆ Hakob Hovhannesi Yeritsyan (Hovhannisyan), Gavash, Dshogh, 1910 ◆ Hakob Hovsepi Mkhoyan, Alekpol, Munjughli, 1911 ◆ Hakob Karapeti Danielyan, Alashkert, Khastur, 1913 ◆ Hakob Karapeti Harutyunyan (Karapetyan), Van, Chobanogh, 1911 ◆ Hakob Karapeti Karapetyan, Sarighamish, Khoshgyaldi, 1913 ◆ Hakob Karapeti Karapetyan, Surmalu, Blur, 1915 ◆ Hakob Khachaturi Hovhannisyan, Ghamarlu, Chidamlu, 1912 ◆ Hakob Khachaturi Khachatryan, Alashkert, Kyuja, 1907 ◆ Hakob Khachaturi Khachatryan, Alekpol, Choprlu, 1915 ◆ Hakob Khachaturi Margaryan, Yerevan, Davalu, 1911 ◆ Hakob Khachaturi Matinyan, Lori, Kurtan, 1912 ◆ Hakob Levoni (Khachaturi) Khachatryan, Van, 1913 ◆ Hakob Manuki Shahinyan (Manukyan), Van, Kachet, 1907 ◆ Hakob Markosi Sahakyan, Kars, Bayburt, 1910 ◆ Hakob Martirosi Martirosyan, Kharberd, 1912 ◆ Hakob Mekhaki Hakobyan (Khachatryan), Kars, 1919 ◆ Hakob Meliki Asoyan, Shirak, Ghonaghran, 1915 ◆ Hakob Meliki Melikyan, Leninakan, Ghanlija, 1918 ◆ Hakob Melkoni Melkonyan, Bulanagh, Kharabshat, 1913 ◆ Hakob Misaki Durgaryan (Misakyan), Shirak, Tavshanghshlagh, 1909 ◆ Hakob Misaki Saroyan, Kars, Gyamrlu, 1912 ◆ Hakob Mkrtchi (Hakobyan) Khachatryan, Akhalkalak, 1913 ◆ Hakob Movsesi Yeghiazaryan (Movsisiyan), Sarighamish, 1911 ◆ Hakob Nazareti Aslanyan, Leninakan, Mazra, 1908 ◆ Hakob Petrosi Boyajyan (Petrosyan), Svaz, Zimar, 1912 ◆ Hakob Petrosi Petrosyan, Leninakan, Aparan, 1912 ◆ Hakob Petrosi Sahakyan, Surmalu, Kulap, 1914 ◆ Hakob Poghosi Harutyunyan, Shirak, Aghin, 1911 ◆ Hakob Poghosi Nersisyan (Poghosyan), Akhalkalak, 1916 ◆ Hakob Sahaki Poghosyan (Sahakyan), Kars, 1915 ◆ Hakob Seroyi Manasyan, Shirak, Bandivan, 1916 ◆ Hakob Simoni Martikyan, Baybert, Lsonk, 1908 ◆ Hakob Smbati Tonoyan, Leninakan, Ghlli Gharakilis, 1914 ◆ Hakob Sukiasi Gevorgyan, Leninakan, Shuragyal, 1908 ◆ Hakob Sukiasi Manukyan (Sukiasyan), Basen, Toti, 1909 ◆ Hakob Tevosi Dikhtrikyan, Van, 1912 ◆ Hakob Tigrani Panosyan, Kars, 1914 ◆ Hakob Tigrani Tigranyan, Sarighamish, 1916 ◆ Hakob Vaghoyi Aleksanyan, Alekpol, 1910 ◆ Hakob Vardani Vardanyan, Leninakan, Bozyoghush,

1916 ♦ Hakob Yeghiazari Sargsyan, Kars, 1914 ♦ Hakob Yervandi Simonyan, Alekpol, Tekniz, 1918 ♦ Hakob Zakari Asatryan, Basen, Ishkhi, 1913 ♦ Hamas Arshaki Poghosyan, Alekpol, Ghrtbulagh, 1914 ♦ Hamas Karapeti Karapetyan, Van, Averak, 1914 ♦ Hamaspuyr Mesropi Mesropyan, Kars, 1912 ♦ Hamaspyur Abrahami Harutyunyan, Shirak, Bashgegh, 1913 ♦ Hamaspyur Aleksani Gasparyan, Surmalu, Evjilar, 1911 ♦ Hamaspyur Avetisi Avetisyan, Kharberd, 1913 ♦ Hamaspyur Baghdasari Baghdasaryan, Khnus, Khalchavush, 1914 ♦ Hamaspyur Barseghi Badalyan, Etchmiadzin, Khatunarkh, 1917 ♦ Hamaspyur Galusti Hakobyan, Kars, Khanigegh, 1914 ♦ Hamaspyur Garegini Gevorgyan, Khnus, Berd, 1910 ♦ Hamaspyur Hakobi Harutyunyan (Hakobyan), Alekpol, Artik, 1909 ♦ Hamaspyur Harutyuni Samvelyan, Kars, Mazra, 1913 ♦ Hamaspyur Hovakimi Danielyan, Kars, Tigos, 1915 ♦ Hamaspyur Hovhannesi Hovhannisyan, Bayazet, Gyol, 1914 ♦ Hamaspyur Hovhannesi Mkrtchyan, Alekpol, Kefli, 1914 ♦ Hamaspyur Hovsepi Mkrtchyan, Leninakan, Ghonaghran, 1911 ♦ Hamaspyur Kerobi Sargsyan, Sarighamish, Chivdali, 1914 ♦ Hamaspyur Khoreni Shazryan, Van, Kharakants, 1912 ♦ Hamaspyur Minasi Minasyan, Alashkert, Yonjalu, 1914 ♦ Hamaspyur Mkrtchi Janazyan, Koghb, 1917 ♦ Hamaspyur Mkrtchi Martirosyan (Mkrtchyan), Aljavaz, Arjra, 1910 ♦ Hamaspyur Mkrtchi Mkrtchyan, Daralagyaz, Ghakha, 1910 ♦ Hamaspyur Poghosi Gharibyan, Van, Noravan, 1909 ♦ Hamaspyur Simoni Gulikhanyan, Kars, Kyadiklar, 1910 ♦ Hamaspyur Simoni Hovhannisyan, Kars, Mavrak, 1914 ♦ Hamaspyur Smbati Mkrtchyan, Leninakan, Syogutlu, 1915 ♦ Hamaspyur Soghomoni Grigoryan, Ghazarapat, 1914 ♦ Hamaspyur Tigrani Tigranyan, Khastur, 1915 ♦ Hamaspyur Vardani Martirosyan, Akhalkalak, Padish, 1912 ♦ Hamaspyur Varosi Malkhasyan, Kars, Baglamar, 1911 ♦ Hamaspyur Varosi Varosyan, Kars, Zochi, 1911 ♦ Hamaspyur Zadoyi Khachatryan, Kars, Baglamat, 1911 ♦ Hamaspyur Zarmani Tadevosyan (Poghosyan), Kyamaghi, Tortun, 1909 ♦ Hamayak Abrahami Grigoryan, Kars, Baglamat, 1909 ♦ Hamayak Adami Virabyan, Kars, 1911 ♦ Hamayak Aleksani Venetsyan (Aleksanyan), Leninakan, Khlli Gharakil, 1914 ♦ Hamayak Arami Grigoryan (Aramyan), Van, Shatakh, 1914 ♦ Hamayak Arshaki Sukiasyan, Kars, Araz, 1911 ♦ Hamayak Barseghi Barseghyan, Leninakan, Talin, 1916 ♦ Hamayak Barseghi Hovhannisyan, Kars, Tigor, 1914 ♦ Hamayak Galusti Galstyan, Yerevan, Ddmashen, 1913 ♦ Hamayak Gevorgi Mkrtchyan (Gevorgyan), Kars, Bagliahmat, 1915 ♦ Hamayak Hakobi Torosyan, Kars, Bern, 1914 ♦ Hamayak Harutyuni Harutyunyan, Kars, Zochi, 1912 ♦ Hamayak Harutyuni Harutyunyan, Mush, Berd, 1913 ♦ Hamayak Harutyuni Khachatryan, Kars, Chala, 1916 ♦ Hamayak Hovhannesi Hovsepyan, Kars, Nerkin Kyadiklar, 1912 ♦ Hamayak Hranti Ghazaryan, Manazkert, 1913 ♦ Hamayak Khachaturi Tigranyan, Tiflis, Shulaver, 1912 ♦ Hamayak Madati Madatyan, Kars, Tigor, 1911 ♦ Hamayak Mekhaki Hovsepyan (Mikayelyan), Nakhijevan, Gharababa, 1911 ♦ Hamayak Melkoni Hambaryan, Aparan, Adiyaman, 1912 ♦ Hamayak Mkrtchi Karapetyan, Julfa, 1912 ♦ Hamayak Mkrtchi Khachatryan (Mkrtchyan), Kars, Uzunkilisa, 1915 ♦ Hamayak Movsesi Hovhannisyan, Alekpol, Aghin, 1908 ♦ Hamayak Nahapeti Nahapetyan, Kars, Tikor, 1914 ♦ Hamayak Nikolayi Khlghatyan, Leninakan, Khachakilisa, 1912 ♦ Hamayak Sedraki Gevorgyan, Kars, Cbni, 1912 ♦ Hamayak Sedraki Sahakyan, Kars, 1914 ♦ Hamayak Serobi Gasparyan, Turkey, 1916 ♦ Hamayak Serobi Serobyan, Darachichak, 1915 ♦ Hamayak Shamiri Hovhannisyan, Karabagh, Alkhata, 1910 ♦ Hamayak Smbati Mosoyan (Smbatyan), Alekpol, Illi, 1912 ♦ Hamayak Vardani Sargsyan, Kars, Kaghzvan, 1915 ♦ Hamazasp Abrahami Poghosyan, Khnus, Salvori, 1910 ♦ Hamazasp Armenaki Grigoryan, Alekpol, Khbchagh, 1910 ♦ Hamazasp Geghami Avetisyan, Nor Bayazet, 1910 ♦ Hamazasp Hakobi Mkrtchyan, Kars, Kyurakdara, 1911 ♦ Hamazasp Hakobi Petrosyan (Hakobyan), Van, Artamet, 1914 ♦ Hamazasp Hayrapeti Arakelyan (Hayrapetyan), Alashkert, Gharakilise, 1912 ♦ Hamazasp Hovhannesi Hovhannisyan, Alekpol, Gharakilisa, 1912 ♦ Hamazasp Khachaturi Khachatryan, Shirak, Chorli, 1917 ♦ Hamazasp Malkhasi Danielyan, Kars, Zhrshi, 1913 ♦ Hamazasp Margari Vardanyan (Margaryan), Khnus, 1912 ♦ Hamazasp Martirosi Martirosyan, Yerevan, Yuva, 1913 ♦ Hamazasp Mkrtchi Karapetyan, Persia, Julfa, 1913 ♦ Hamazasp Poghosi Poghosyan, Van, 1912 ♦ Hamazasp Poghosi Saroyan (Zadoyan), Bitlis, 1918 ♦ Hamazasp Rostomi Vardanyan, Koghb, Allizamar, 1911 ♦ Hamazasp Sergoyi Arakelyan, Yerevan, Eylar, 1914 ♦ Hambardzum Abrahami Mkrtchyan (Mirzoyan), Kars, Syogutli, 1912 ♦ Hambardzum Asaturi Muradyan (Asatryan), Berkri, Abagh, 1915 ♦ Hambardzum Avetisi Aspaturyan (Avetisyan), Van, Archesh, 1912 ♦ Hambardzum Avoyi Avoyan, Basen, Arjarak, 1912 ♦ Hambardzum Danieli Mkrtchyan (Danielyan), Igdir, Yeghvard, 1916 ♦ Hambardzum Gevorgi Khachtryan, Leninakan, Ortakilisa, 1913 ♦ Hambardzum Ghazari Ghazaryan, Terjan, Bulik, 1911 ♦ Hambardzum Grigori Ghazaryan (Grigoryan), Van, 1907 ♦ Hambardzum Grigori Khachatryan, Shirak, Ghzlghoch, 1913 ♦ Hambardzum Hakobi Gulanyan (Hakobyan), Van, Soskan, 1914 ♦ Hambardzum Hakobi Hakobyan, Leninakan, Ghzlghoch, 1915 ♦ Hambardzum Hamazaspi Hamoyan, Leninakan, Bandivan, 1912 ♦ Hambardzum Hovhannesi Hovhannisyan, Van, 1915 ♦ Hambardzum Hovhannesi Madoyan, Kars, 1910 ♦ Hambardzum Hovhannesi Nalbandyan, Kars, Byurakdar, 1914 ♦ Hambardzum Karapeti Grigoryan (Levonyan), Akhalkalak, Turs, 1917 ♦ Hambardzum Khachaturi Khachatryan, Van, 1908 ♦ Hambardzum Khachaturi Khachatryan, Van, Shidan, 1909 ♦ Hambardzum Khachaturi Tumasyan, Leninakan, Zarinja, 1910 ♦ Hambardzum Khachiki Igityan, Mush, 1919 ♦ Hambardzum Manuki Manukyan, Kars, Cbni, 1914 ♦ Hambardzum Martirosi Aghoyan, Kars, Kaghzvan, 1911 ♦ Hambardzum Martirosi Voskanyan, Kars, Cbni, 1911 ♦ Hambardzum Melkoni Samsonyan, Aparan, Byulichva, 1914

♦ Hambardzum Minasi Alopyan, Basen, Archak, 1913 ♦ Hambardzum Nazareti Vardanyan, Leninakan, Bozdoghan, 1914 ♦ Hambardzum Nersesi Ter-Grigoryan, Batum, Tandzut, 1912 ♦ Hambardzum Nikoghosi Nersisyan (Nersoyan), Kars, Bayburt, 1909 ♦ Hambardzum Nshani Guyumjyan, Kharberd, Berdak, 1906 ♦ Hambardzum Ohani Kelyan, Leninakan, Ghzlkilisa, 1916 ♦ Hambardzum Poghosi Poghosyan, Igdir, Blur, 1911 ♦ Hambardzum Sahaki Nazaryan, Lori, Ghotur, 1912 ♦ Hambardzum Sahaki Petrosyan, Baku, 1912 ♦ Hambardzum Sahaki Ter-Grigoryan, Batum, Tandzut, 1910 ♦ Hambardzum Smbati Grigoryan, Shirak, Daharlu, 1918 ♦ Hambardzum Smbati Harutyunyan (Smbatyan), Leninakan, Ghanlija, 1912 ♦ Hambardzum Stepani Bulukhyan, Ardahan, Shavshi, 1910 ♦ Hambardzum Stepani Harutyunyan, Pambak, Gyoran, 1918 ♦ Hambardzum Tonoyi Tonoyan, Basen, Vorghatli, 1914 ♦ Hambardzum Vardani Vardanyan, Van, Mashtak, 1911 ♦ Hamest Nshani Sofyan (Nshanyan), Van, 1908 ♦ Hamet Usufi Usufyan, Mush, 1907 ♦ Hammi Shaheni Shahinyan, Yerevan, 1915 ♦ Hamo Galoyi Mkrtchyan (Galoyan), Akhalkalak, Pokr Kendura, 1912 ♦ Hamo Saroyi (Sakoyi) Gevorgyan (Sakoyan), Leninakan, Jajur, 1916 ♦ Hana (Almast) Alii Aliyan, Yerevan, 1912 ♦ Harazat Aleki Melikyan, Kars, Bern, 1913 ♦ Harazat Hunani Hakobyan (Hunanyan), Bulanagh, Votnchor, 1914 ♦ Harut Mkrtchi Arshakyan (Mkrtchyan), Van, Aljavaz, 1914 ♦ Harut Nahapetyan, 1927 ♦ Harutik Melkoni Minasyan, Kars, Dolbandlu, 1917 ♦ Harutik Sedraki (Mghdoyan) Mkhitaryan, Akhalkalak, Dilif, 1917 ♦ Harutik Tigrani Panosyan, Kars, 1914 ♦ Harutyun (Hayrik) Sargisi Harutyunyan (Sargsyan), Salmast, Havtvan, 1911 ♦ Harutyun (Pilipos) Hovhannesi Piliposyan, Etchmiadzin, 1912 ♦ Harutyun (Shakroyi) Zakari Muradyan, Ardvin, Batum, 1918 ♦ Harutyun Abgari Gharibyan (Abgaryan), Kars, Zrchi, 1911 ♦ Harutyun Aghasi Galoyan (Aghasyan), Kars, Argina, 1912 ♦ Harutyun Aleksani Aleksanyan, Van, 1914 ♦ Harutyun Aleksani Alekyan, Basen, Hekibat, 1912 ♦ Harutyun Amirkhani Amirkhanyan, Nor Bayazet, Basargechar, 1913 ♦ Harutyun Armenaki Mkrtchyan, Sasun, Ishkhu, 1911 ♦ Harutyun Artashesi Tavrizyan, Akhalkalak, Tadesh, 1914 ♦ Harutyun Avetisi Nshanyan, Alashkert, 1914 ♦ Harutyun Galusti Galstyan (Ghazaryan), Akhalkalak, Duzkharaba, 1914 ♦ Harutyun Gaspari Hovhannisyan, Kharberd, Kharberd, 1913 ♦ Harutyun Gevorgi Gevorgyan, Leninakan, Mazar, 1912 ♦ Harutyun Hakobi Amirkhanyan, Shirak, Darlu, 1911 ♦ Harutyun Hakobi Khachatryan (Hakobyan), Basen, Koprikoy, 1912 ♦ Harutyun Hamayaki Amiryan, Alekpol, 1912 ♦ Harutyun Hambardzumi Hambardzumyan (Hakobyan), Bitlis, Teghut, 1914 ♦ Harutyun Harutyuni Safaryan, Erzrum, Agrak, 1910 ♦ Harutyun Hovakimi Hovsepyan (Hovakimyan), Hayots Dzor, Hermer, 1912 ♦ Harutyun Hovhannesi Ghazaryan (Hovhannisyan), Leninakan, Sariar, 1916 ♦ Harutyun Hovhannesi Harutyunyan, Etchmiadzin, Varmadar, 1919 ♦ Harutyun Hovhannesi Hovhannisyan, Alekpol, Sariar, 1921 ♦ Harutyun Hovhannesi Ter-Meliksetyan, Kars, 1913 ♦ Harutyun Hovhannesi Vardanyan, Erzrum, 1912 ♦ Harutyun Khachaturi Baghdasaryan, Kars, Kyadiklar, 1914 ♦ Harutyun Khachaturi Gasparyan (Khachatryan), Basen, Chrason, 1916 ♦ Harutyun Khachaturi Khachatryan, Shirak, Mec Keti, 1915 ♦ Harutyun Khachiki (Poghosi) Poghosyan, Mush, Amaran, 1913 ♦ Harutyun Levoni Galstyan, Kars, 1912 ♦ Harutyun Marati Muradyan, Van, Vazem, 1915 ♦ Harutyun Margari Tadevosyan, Kars, Cbni, 1911 ♦ Harutyun Markosi Markosyan (Harutyunyan) Leninakan, Imrkhan, 1912 ♦ Harutyun Markosi Markosyan, Yerevan, Khatunarkh, 1915 ♦ Harutyun Martini Sargsyan (Sakoyan), Kars, 1912 ♦ Harutyun Martirosi Martirosyan, Van, Kghzi, 1911 ♦ Harutyun Martirosi Shahbazyan, Van, Alyur, 1909 ♦ Harutyun Matevosi Karapetyan (Ghasabyan), Shamakhi, Madras, 1914 ♦ Harutyun Mekhaki Arshakyan (Karapetyan), Akhalkalak, Chandura, 1916 ♦ Harutyun Meliki Grigoryan (Melikyan), Alekpol, Ghanlija, 1911 ♦ Harutyun Melkoni Melkonyan, Van, Hayots dzor, 1910 ♦ Harutyun Mesropi Karapetyan, Kars, 1913 ♦ Harutyun Minasi Gasparyan, Baku, 1914 ♦ Harutyun Mkhitari Mkhitaryan, Kars, Kaghzvan, 1908 ♦ Harutyun Mkrtchi Kerobyan, Ardahan, 1913 ♦ Harutyun Mkrtchi Mkrtchyan, Van, Mokhraberd, 1912 ♦ Harutyun Movsesi Movsisyan (Abrahamyan), Erzrum, Asparak, 1911 ♦ Harutyun Movsesi Movsisyan, Leninakan, Ortkilisa, 1917 ♦ Harutyun Nersesi Simonyan, Kars, 1910 ♦ Harutyun Poghosi Mkrtchyan (Poghosyan), Sasun, Jlrtu, 1914 ♦ Harutyun Poghosi Poghosyan, Ardahan, Satler, 1910 ♦ Harutyun Saghateli Galstyan, Kars, Kaghzvan, 1910 ♦ Harutyun Sahaki Harutyunyan, Kars, 1914 ♦ Harutyun Sahaki Sargsyan (Sahakyan), Kars, Baglamat, 1913 ♦ Harutyun Sargsi Harutyunyants, Kars, 1913 ♦ Harutyun Sargsi Sargsyan (Yeranaosyan), Derjan, Yespirak, 1910 ♦ Harutyun Sedraki Sedrakyan, Basen, Hekibad, 1908 ♦ Harutyun Shavarshi Goljanyan, Alekpol, Khli Gharakilisa, 1913 ♦ Harutyun Sirasi Sirunyan, Bitlis, 1912 ♦ Harutyun Soghomoni Grigoryan (Soghomonyan), Van, Yar, 1911 ♦ Harutyun Stepani Khachatryan, Nakhijevan, Shekhmahmud, 1910 ♦ Harutyun Stepani Voskanyan (Yeghtaryan), Kars, Gharaghala, 1912 ♦ Harutyun Sukiasi Sargsyan, Sarighamish, Bashgyugh, 1913 ♦ Harutyun Tadevosi Shahbazyan, Kars, Gharamahmat, 1909 ♦ Harutyun Tatosi Grigoryan, Sarighamish, Cholakhlu, 1911 ♦ Harutyun Tatosi Harutyunyan (Tadevosyan), Akhalkalak, 1917 ♦ Harutyun Tatosi Tatosyan, Leninakan, Jajur, 1913 ♦ Harutyun Tovmasi Asatryan, Sasun, Lordnkor, 1909 ♦ Harutyun Vardani Vardanyan, Van, Vororan, 1912 ♦ Harutyun Yeghiazari Sargsyan, Van, Kharakonis, 1910 ♦ Harutyun Yeghiazari Saroyan, Mush, 1913 ♦ Harutyun Yegori Gasparyan, Kars, Mavrak, 1910 ♦ Harutyun Yenoki Varosyan, Leninakan, 1911 ♦ Hasan Huseini Husoyan, Yerevan, 1909 ♦ Hasmik Aghajani Aghajanyan (Karapetyan), Bayazet, 1910 ♦ Hasmik Aleksani Aleksanyan, Igdir, Arcap, 1913 ♦ Hasmik Armenaki Hovhannisyan, Bitlis, 1910 ♦ Hasmik Arseni Manukyan, Hin Bayazet, 1914 ♦ Hasmik Arseni Papikyan, Shirak, Khli Gharakilis, 1916

♦ Hasmik Ayvazi Sargsyan (Ayvazyan), Van, Archesh, 1914 ♦ Hasmik Daviti Davtyan, Van, Abagha, 1914 ♦ Hasmik Garsevani Nazaryan, Yerevan, 1913 ♦ Hasmik Gevorgi Gevorgya, Van, Aljavaz, 1912 ♦ Hasmik Grigori Sirakanyan, Nakhijevan, 1916 ♦ Hasmik Grigoryan, Batum, 1917 ♦ Hasmik Harutyuni Harutyunyan, Surmalu, Tashbura, 1916 ♦ Hasmik Harutyuni Harutyunyan, Van, Karchkan, 1914 ♦ Hasmik Harutyuni Karanyan, Leninakan, 1915 ♦ Hasmik Hovakimi Grigoryan, Etchmiadzin, Sardarapat, 1913 ♦ Hasmik Hovsepi Hovsepyan, Yerevan, 1916 ♦ Hasmik Khachaturi Stepanyan, Nakhijevan, Janbi, 1911 ♦ Hasmik Mamikoni Atanesyan, Yerevan, Margar, 1911 ♦ Hasmik Manuki Hovhannisyan, Shatakh, Tagh, 1907 ♦ Hasmik Manuki Vanetsyan, Kaghzvan, 1915 ♦ Hasmik Martirosi Martirosyan, Van, 1914 ♦ Hasmik Martirosi Martirosyan, Van, Astvatsaghin, 1908 ♦ Hasmik Mikayeli (Manuki) Manukyan, Van, Araz, 1914 ♦ Hasmik Mkrtchi Harutyunyan, Etchmiadzin, 1914 ♦ Hasmik Mkrtchi Mkrtchyan, Kars, 1913 ♦ Hasmik Musheghi Harutyunyan, Igdir, 1913 ♦ Hasmik Nadoyi Mkrtchyan, Mush, Bulanagh, 1913 ♦ Hasmik Nersesi Nersisyan, Sgherd, Vozim, 1913 ♦ Hasmik Norayri Minasyan, Surmalu, Igdir, 1911 ♦ Hasmik Sargisi Vardanyan, Alashkert, Mazra, 1909 ♦ Hasmik Sedraki Hovhannisyan, Erzrum, 1910 ♦ Hasmik Simoni Simonyan, Yerevan, Davalu, 1912 ♦ Hasmik Smbati Smbatyan, Kars, Paldrvan, 1920 ♦ Hasmik Tadevosi (Torosi) Zhamharyan, Pambak, Gharakilisa, 1919 ♦ Hasmik Zakari Zakaryan (Yeritsyan), Lori, Marts, 1915 ♦ Haso (Sargis) Gevorgyan, Yerevan, 1916 ♦ Hastat Gevorgi Avagyan, Basen, Krdavaz, 1917 ♦ Hato Khachaturi Khachatryan, Manazkert, Berd, 1915 ♦ Hayastan (Grigori) Zakari Zakaryan, 1919 ♦ Hayastan Abgari Hovhannisyan (Abgaryan), Kars, 1915 ♦ Hayastan Abrahami Harutyunyan, Kars, Araz, 1913 ♦ Hayastan Abrahami Manukyan, Kars, 1911 ♦ Hayastan Arakeli Arakelyan (Yeghiazaryan), Van, Archesh, 1908 ♦ Hayastan Arami Hovhannisyan, Alekpol, Ghzlghoch, 1912 ♦ Hayastan Arshaki Khachatryan, Nakhijevan, 1913 ♦ Hayastan Arshaki Khachatryan, Shirak, Khli Gharakilis, 1910 ♦ Hayastan Arshaki Manukyan, Kars, 1912 ♦ Hayastan Arshaki Margaryan (Arshakyan), Kars, 1910 ♦ Hayastan Asaturi Harutyunyan, Kars, 1910 ♦ Hayastan Askanazi Martirosyan, Aparan, Tazagyugh, 1910 ♦ Hayastan Askanazi Martirosyan, Mush, Allicha, 1911 ♦ Hayastan Avetisi Zakaryan, Sarighamish, Cholakhli, 1913 ♦ Hayastan Baghdasari Hakobyan, Kars, Gyamrlu, 1910 ♦ Hayastan Barseghi Barseghyan, Kars, Ortakilisa, 1912 ♦ Hayastan Barseghi Barseghyan, Kars, Ortakilisa, 1912 ♦ Hayastan Bekoyi Bekoyan (Hakobyan), Kars, Ortaghala, 1917 ♦ Hayastan Danieli Danielyan, Van, Aljavaz, 1911 ♦ Hayastan Gabrieli Vardanyan, Kars, Zrchi, 1912 ♦ Hayastan Gevorgi Gevorgyan (Mkhitaryan), Leninakan, Hajinazar, 1915 ♦ Hayastan Gevorgi Gevorgyan, Kars, 1918 ♦ Hayastan Ghukasi Ghukasyan, Jalal, 1919 ♦ Hayastan Grigori Grigoryan (Shakaryan), Alekpol, Ghonakhran, 1915 ♦ Hayastan Grigori Grigoryan, Alashkert, Gharakilisa, 1916 ♦ Hayastan Grigori Grigoryan, Kars, Uzunkilisa, 1916 ♦ Hayastan Grigori Proshyan (Grigoryan), Igdir, Panik, 1909 ♦ Hayastan Grigori Sirunyan - Grigoryan, Alashkert, Berd, 1914 ♦ Hayastan Hajibabi Ter-Matevosyan, Akhalkalak, Gimbirda, 1913 ♦ Hayastan Hakobi Hakobyan, Kars, Ghzlchakhchakh, 1913 ♦ Hayastan Hakobi Harutyunyan (Hakobyan), Nakhijevan, 1912 ♦ Hayastan Hamazaspi Hamazaspyan, Alekpol, Mec Keti, 1914 ♦ Hayastan Hambardzumi Mirzoyan (Hambardzumyan), Van, Archesh, 1908 ♦ Hayastan Harutyuni Harutyunyan (Ghazaryan), Kars, Shadivan, 1911 ♦ Hayastan Harutyuni Zhamkochyan, Basen, Kyoprkoy, 1913 ♦ Hayastan Hayroyi Harutyunyan, Alashkert, Uchkilisa, 1913 ♦ Hayastan Hmayaki Hovhannisyan, Aparan, Tamjlu, 1913 ♦ Hayastan Hovhannesi Alekyan (Badasyan), Kars, Chermalu, 1912 ♦ Hayastan Hovhannesi Hovhannisyan, Erzrum, Dalibaba, 1913 ♦ Hayastan Hovhannesi Nersisyan, Van, Pakhezik, 1912 ♦ Hayastan Hovhannesi Sargsyan (Kostanyan), Basen, Armtlu, 1913 ♦ Hayastan Hovsepi Torosyan, Kars, Derbandlu, 1915 ♦ Hayastan Hovsepi Torosyan, Leninakan, Darband, 1914 ♦ Hayastan Izabeki Simonyan, Kars, Mec Parket, 1913 ♦ Hayastan Karapeti Davoyan, Kars, Kyurakdar, 1916 ♦ Hayastan Karapeti Hakobyan, Kars, Gedaksatlmish, 1912 ♦ Hayastan Karapeti Karapetyan, Bulanagh, Shirvanshekh, 1914 ♦ Hayastan Karapeti Karapetyan, Gharakilisa, Adibeg, 1916 ♦ Hayastan Karapeti Karapetyan, Pambak, Gyoran, 1916 ♦ Hayastan Karapeti Karapetyan, Sarighamish, Ghoshakilisa, 1917 ♦ Hayastan Karoyi Harutyunyan, Shirak, Kapanak, 1913 ♦ Hayastan Khachaturi Barseghyan (Khachatryan), Van, 1904 ♦ Hayastan Khachaturi Khachatryan, Ortakilisa, 1914 ♦ Hayastan Mamikoni Gharibyan, Surmalu, Alijan, 1918 ♦ Hayastan Manuki Manukyan (Karapetyan), Kaghzvan, 1916 ♦ Hayastan Manuki Serobyan, Kars, Hopviran, 1911 ♦ Hayastan Margari Sandayan, Kars, Baglamat, 1917 ♦ Hayastan Martirosi Khachatryan, Shirak, Sariar, 1921 ♦ Hayastan Martirosi Martirosyan, Leninakan, Ghanlija, 1913 ♦ Hayastan Martirosi Martirosyan, Turkey, 1918 ♦ Hayastan Martirosi Vardanyan, 1917 ♦ Hayastan Minasi Arakelyan (Minasyan), Alekpol, Chrpuli, 1914 ♦ Hayastan Mkrtchi Sargsyan (Yeghikyan), Leninakan, 1908 ♦ Hayastan Mkrtchi Sargsyan, Kars, Bashkyadiklar, 1915 ♦ Hayastan Mnatsakani Hovhannisyan, Leninakan, Syogutli, 1914 ♦ Hayastan Movsesi Hakobyan, Alekpol, Syogutli, 1911 ♦ Hayastan Movsesi Vardanyan (Harutyunyan), Alekpol, Ghlli Gharakilis, 1912 ♦ Hayastan Muradi Hakobyan, Mush, Drmet, 1912 ♦ Hayastan Muradi Melikyan, Kars, Paldrvan, 1913 ♦ Hayastan Nazari Nazaryan, Kars, Bayram-pasha, 1916 ♦ Hayastan Sahaki Khachatryan, Alekpol, Horom, 1914 ♦ Hayastan Sakoyi Muradyan, Kars, 1910 ♦ Hayastan Samsoni Samsonyan, Yerevan, Anavanq, 1912 ♦ Hayastan Sargsi Sargsyan, Lori, Shahnazar, 1918 ♦ Hayastan Saroyi Sargsyan, Alekpol, Armtlu, 1914 ♦ Hayastan Saroyi Torosyan, Alekpol, Ghonaghran, 1918 ♦ Hayastan Senoyi Sargsyan, Leninakan, Mec Kyapanak, 1911 ♦ Hayastan Shaheni Gasparyan (Shahinyan), Erzrum,

Bulanagh, 1912 ◆ Hayastan Shahinyan, Leninakan, 1921 ◆ Hayastan Simoni Hovhannisyan (Simonyan), Van, 1907 ◆ Hayastan Simoni Simonyan, Pambak, Dzori Gharakilis, 1911 ◆ Hayastan Smbati Hambardzumyan, Yerevan, Noraduz, 1912 ◆ Hayastan Smbati Nazaryan, Alekpol, Mets Kapanak, 1913 ◆ Hayastan Sukiasi Ter-Hakobyan, Sarighamish, Churug, 1912 ◆ Hayastan Tadevosi Hovhannisyan (Tadevosyan), Yerevan, 1913 ◆ Hayastan Tatosi Grigoryan, Kars, Joji, 1911 ◆ Hayastan Tigrani Petrosyan, Kars, 1915 ◆ Hayastan Vardani Vardanyan, Leninakan, Aghin, 1917 ◆ Hayastan Varosi Hakobyan, Alekpol, Chorli, 1913 ◆ Hayastan Yeghiazari Arakelyan, Bulanagh, Yonjalu, 1912 ◆ Hayastan Yegori Bayrakhtaryan (Yegoryan), Kars, 1916 ◆ Hayastan Yenoki Vardanyan, Surmalu, Khalfalu, 1914 ◆ Hayastan Zakari Torosyan, Kars, Karmir vank, 1914 ◆ Hayastan Zakari Zakaryan, Mec Gharakilis, 1917 ◆ Haygyul Nasoyi Grigoryan, Nor Bayazet, Dalaghartash, 1915 ◆ Hayk Arakeli Jihanyants (Arakelyan), Surmalu, Blur, 1914 ◆ Hayk Arami Harutyunyan, Leninakan, Khlli Gharakilis, 1910 ◆ Hayk Arseni Khachatryan (Khachikyan), Akhalkalak, Baralet, 1916 ◆ Hayk Avetisi Khachatryan, Hin Nakhijevan, Aza, 1913 ◆ Hayk Avetisi Vardanyan, Basen, Dalibaba, 1911 ◆ Hayk Bagrati Galstyan, Yerevan, 1916 ◆ Hayk Bagrati Mkrtchyan, Hin Nakhijevan, Aylapat, 1913 ◆ Hayk Galusti Serobyan, Kars, Gharamahmat, 1913 ◆ Hayk Garegini Baghdasaryan, Van, Kharakonis, 1909 ◆ Hayk Gevorgi Gevorgyan, Aparan, Blkher, 1916 ◆ Hayk Gevorgi Gevorgyan, Yerevan, Ghazanchi, 1915 ◆ Hayk Ghazari Mikayelyan, Kars, Ghzlchakhchakh, 1917 ◆ Hayk Ghukasi Avetisyan, Nakhijevan, Aprugin, 1914 ◆ Hayk Grigori Sargsyan (Grigoryan), Erzrum, Tortan, 1911 ◆ Hayk Hambardzumi Nahapetyan, Kars, Cbni, 1911 ◆ Hayk Harutyuni Petrosyan, Shamakhi, Geghjurt, 1908 ◆ Hayk Harutyuni Sargsyan, Kars, Gorkhana, 1910 ◆ Hayk Hovhannesi Khachatryan, Alekpol, Ghzlghoch, 1912 ◆ Hayk Hovhannisyan, Nakhijevan, Alkhatan, 1915 ◆ Hayk Khachaturi Avetisyan (Khachatryan), Davalu, Gharakhach, 1912 ◆ Hayk Khachaturi Hovhannisyan, Gyokcha, Aza, 1914 ◆ Hayk Khosrovi Grigoryan, Kars, Araz, 1913 ◆ Hayk Madoyi Madoyan, Shirak, Khli Gharakilis, 1914 ◆ Hayk Mekhaki Tokmajyan, Kars, 1914 ◆ Hayk Mikayeli Nazaryan, Van, Krel, 1910 ◆ Hayk Mnatsakani Harutyunyan, Shirak, Chiftali, 1913 ◆ Hayk Mnatsakani Martirosyan (Markosyan), Alekpol, 1908 ◆ Hayk Nahapeti Harutyunyan, Khnus, Gobal, 1909 ◆ Hayk Rubeni (Simonyan) Rubinyan, Igdir, 1916 ◆ Hayk Sargsi Harutyunyan, Olti, Ardahan, 1909 ◆ Hayk Shamili Hovhannisyan, Zangezur, Akhlatyan, 1916 ◆ Hayk Simoni Vardanyan, Mush, 1909 ◆ Hayk Smbati Atashyan (Smbatyan), Alekpol, Ghzlghoch, 1915 ◆ Hayk Smbati Frankyan (Smbatyan), Igdir, Surmali, 1916 ◆ Hayk Tsolaki Chukhajyan, Bulanagh, Gharaghl, 1914 ◆ Hayk Vardani Hovhannisyan, Igdir, Tichrlu, 1912 ◆ Hayk Vardani Vardanyan, Van, 1908 ◆ Hayk Vasili Bozyan, Ghazakh, Koghb, 1912 ◆ Hayk Yervandi Poghosyan, Kars, Mec Parket, 1911 ◆ Hayk-Aram Aleksandri Manukyan, Alekpol, Chrakhlu, 1914 ◆ Haykanush (Azniv) Poghosi Poghosyan, Van, Pshavank, 1912 ◆ Haykanush Abeti Abetyan, Kars, Ghoshakilisa, 1914 ◆ Haykanush Abrahami Sargsyan, Kars, Orta-Ghala, 1911 ◆ Haykanush Adami Hovhannisyan, Yerevan, Norashen, 1911 ◆ Haykanush Adami Melkonyan, Kars, Ghazanchi, 1910 ◆ Haykanush Aghajani Aghajanyan, Mec Gharakilis, Adibek, 1915 ◆ Haykanush Aleki Darbinyan, Shirak, Syogutli, 1913 ◆ Haykanush Aleksani Minasyan, Kars, Bashshoragyal, 1916 ◆ Haykanush Antanasi Yavoyan (Antanasyan), Kars, Nakhijevan, 1910 ◆ Haykanush Arami Hakobyan, Kars, Pirvali, 1912 ◆ Haykanush Armenaki Shahnazaryan, Khnus, 1913 ◆ Haykanush Arseni Mkrtchyan, Nakhijevan, Aylapat, 1911 ◆ Haykanush Arshaki Ghadimyan (Arshakyan), Ghamarlu, Verin Daghralu, 1915 ◆ Haykanush Arshaki Ghazaryan (Arshakyan), Kars, Mavrak, 1915 ◆ Haykanush Arshaki Khachatryan, Shirak, Khli Gharakilis, 1914 ◆ Haykanush Artashesi Khachatryan, Aparan, 1914 ◆ Haykanush Artashi Abelyan, Igdir, Blur, 1912 ◆ Haykanush Asaturi Asatryan, Sarighamish, Shadivan, 1910 ◆ Haykanush Atabeki Martirosyan (Atabekyan), Koghb, Abazgyol, 1914 ◆ Haykanush Avetiki Khachatryan (Karapetyan), Alekpol, Chlokhan, 1914 ◆ Haykanush Avetisi Avetisyan, Bulanagh, Shirvanshekh, 1910 ◆ Haykanush Azizi Davtyan (Azizyan), Bulanagh, 1914 ◆ Haykanush Badali Fahradyan (Badalyan), Kars, Ughuzli, 1915 ◆ Haykanush Baghdasari Hakobyan, Bulanagh, Yonjalu, 1912 ◆ Haykanush Barseghi Mnatsakanyan, Persia, Tavriz, 1911 ◆ Haykanush Bebuti (Petrosi) Tarkhanyan, Nukhi, 1916 ◆ Haykanush Daviti Davtyan (Vardanyan), Tiflis, 1916 ◆ Haykanush Daviti Davtyan, Van, Irija, 1912 ◆ Haykanush Daviti Petrosyan (Davtyan), Kars, Tekniz, 1913 ◆ Haykanush Galoyi Martirosyan, Leninakan, Horom, 1913 ◆ Haykanush Galusti Hovhannisyan, Kars, 1919 ◆ Haykanush Gaspari Avagyan (Gasparyan), Manazkert, Blur, 1913 ◆ Haykanush Gaspari Gasparyan, Khnus, Sarlu, 1917 ◆ Haykanush Geghami Nahapetyan, Alekpol, Maymanjugh, 1913 ◆ Haykanush Gevorgi Aghajanyan, Kars, 1911 ◆ Haykanush Gevorgi Hambardzumyan, Shirak, Chzghlar, 1910 ◆ Haykanush Gevorgi Karapetyan, Kars, Kaghzvan, 1912 ◆ Haykanush Gevorgi Manukyan, Kars, Chala, 1914 ◆ Haykanush Ghazari Gevorgyan, Kars, Bagaran, 1914 ◆ Haykanush Ghazari Ghazaryan, Dirabak, 1907 ◆ Haykanush Ghazari Ghazaryan, Etchmiadzin, Ghosh, 1914 ◆ Haykanush Ghazari Ghazaryan, Van, 1915 ◆ Haykanush Grigori Arshakyan, Van, Noravan, 1906 ◆ Haykanush Grigori Grigoryan, Mush, Ardon, 1910 ◆ Haykanush Grigori Grigoryan, Van, Moks, 1913 ◆ Haykanush Grigori Grigoryan, Yerevan, Tashburn, 1919 ◆ Haykanush Grigori Hovnanyan, Van, Artamet, 1905 ◆ Haykanush Grigori Papikyan, Basen, Aygepat, 1910 ◆ Haykanush Hakobi Hakobyan (Varosyan), Alekpol, Bozdoghan, 1918 ◆ Haykanush Hakobi Hakobyan, Dilijan, 1917 ◆ Haykanush Hakobi Hakobyan, Mush, Bulanagh, 1916 ◆ Haykanush Hakobi Hovhannisyan, Basen, Yaghan, 1914 ◆ Haykanush Hakobi Hovhannisyan, Kars, Akrak, 1913 ◆ Haykanush Hakobi

Manukyan, Kaghzvan, 1915 ◆ Haykanush Hakobi Poghosyan (Hakobyan), Kars, Ghzlchakhchakh, 1912 ◆ Haykanush Hambardzumi Muradyan, Shamakhi, Madras, 1912 ◆ Haykanush Harutyuni Hakobyan (Ghalachyan), Erzrum, Kghi, Hosing, 1909 ◆ Haykanush Harutyuni Harutyunyan, Kars, Bayrakhtar, 1914 ◆ Haykanush Harutyuni Kamalyan, Moks, Arinj, 1908 ◆ Haykanush Harutyuni Sargsyan, Aljavaz, Archesh, 1911 ◆ Haykanush Harutyuni Ter-Poghosyan, Kaghzvan, Koghb, 1910 ◆ Haykanush Harutyuni Zohrapyan, Akhalkalak, Hamzar, 1914 ◆ Haykanush Hayrapeti Shahbazyan, Ghamarlu, 1910 ◆ Haykanush Hayrapeti Shahbazyan, Yerevan, Ghamarlu, 1910 ◆ Haykanush Heroyi Kocharyan, Kars, Bazrgan, 1913 ◆ Haykanush Hovakimi Hovakimyan, Van, Shatakh, 1908 ◆ Haykanush Hovakimi Petrosyan, Daralagyaz, Yelpin, 1916 ◆ Haykanush Hovhannesi Baghdasaryan, Nakhijevan, Chanakhchi, 1912 ◆ Haykanush Hovhannesi Hovhannisyan, Kars, 1910 ◆ Haykanush Hovhannesi Hovhannisyan, Kars, Pirvalu, 1919 ◆ Haykanush Hovhannesi Hovhannisyan, Mush, Irishtir, 1908 ◆ Haykanush Hovhannesi Sargsyan, Nakhijevan, 1913 ◆ Haykanush Hovhannesi Ter-Harutyunyan, Etchmiadzin, Parpi, 1913 ◆ Haykanush Hovnani Margaryan (Hovhannisyan), Alashkert, Gharakilisa, 1911 ◆ Haykanush Karapeti Ghayfajyan, Van, Khorkom, 1909 ◆ Haykanush Karapeti Ghazaryan (Karapetyan), Bulanagh, Kop, 1908 ◆ Haykanush Karapeti Karapetyan, Alekpol, Paltlu, 1908 ◆ Haykanush Karapeti Karapetyan, Alekpol, Psti Keti, 1912 ◆ Haykanush Karapeti Khachatryan, Nakhijevan, 1915 ◆ Haykanush Karapeti Manukyan, Aparan, Sachlu, 1912 ◆ Haykanush Karapeti Mayilyan, Dilijan, 1911 ◆ Haykanush Kerobi (Hovhannesi) Hovhannisyan (Kerobyan), Alashkert, Ziro, 1911 ◆ Haykanush Khachaturi Bozoyan, Leninakan, Horom, 1909 ◆ Haykanush Khachaturi Doshoyan (Poghosyan), Tiflis, 1913 ◆ Haykanush Khachaturi Khachatryan, Bitlis, 1914 ◆ Haykanush Khachaturi Khachatryan, Kars, Zarm, 1909 ◆ Haykanush Khachaturi Petrosyan (Khachatryan), Kars, Chala, 1911 ◆ Haykanush Khachaturi Saroyan, Leninakan, Chzghlar, 1914 ◆ Haykanush Kirakosi Safaryan, Bitlis, Totik, 1911 ◆ Haykanush Manaseri Gevorgyan, Van, Mkhkner, 1908 ◆ Haykanush Manuki Tadevosyan, Alashkert, Gharakilisa, 1908 ◆ Haykanush Margari Astvacatryan, Surmalu, Najabal, 1910 ◆ Haykanush Margari Sargsyan, Manazkert, Berd, 1909 ◆ Haykanush Margari Yeranosyan, Bulanagh, Agrak, 1906 ◆ Haykanush Martirosi Alikhanyan, Leninakan, Duzkharaba, 1911 ◆ Haykanush Martirosi Arakelyan (Hovhannisyan), Shirak, Aghin, 1913 ◆ Haykanush Martirosi Gasparyan (Martirosyan), Kars, Hamzakarak, 1911 ◆ Haykanush Martirosi Ghazaryan (Martirosyan), Alekpol, Horom, 1913 ◆ Haykanush Martirosi Hovhannisyan (Martirosyan), Leninakan, Mec Keti, 1913 ◆ Haykanush Martirosi Martirosyan, Van, Ishkhan, 1911 ◆ Haykanush Martirosi Papoyan, Alekpol, Pirvali, 1915 ◆ Haykanush Mekhaki Hakobyan, Kars, Tigor, 1914 ◆ Haykanush Meliki (Musheghi) Khachatryan, Kars, Ughuzlu, 1914 ◆ Haykanush Meliki Khechoyan, Mush, 1908 ◆ Haykanush Melkoni Melkonyan, Van, Archesh, 1913 ◆ Haykanush Melkoni Poghosyan, Surmalu, Blur, 1908 ◆ Haykanush Melkoni Sargsyan (Melkonyan), Archesh, Aghstav, 1912 ◆ Haykanush Minasi Arakelyan, Kars, Bangliahmat, 1911 ◆ Haykanush Minasi Grigoryan, Kars, 1919 ◆ Haykanush Minasi Minasyan, Kars, Khachizvan, 1914 ◆ Haykanush Minasi Movsisyan, Akhalkalak, 1914 ◆ Haykanush Misaki Sargsyan, Kars, Bayraghdar, 1910 ◆ Haykanush Mkrtchi Hovhannisyan (Mkrtchyan), Khnus, Khnus, 1909 ◆ Haykanush Mkrtchi Martirosyan, Kars, 1910 ◆ Haykanush Mkrtchi Mkrtchyan, Bayazet, 1910 ◆ Haykanush Mkrtchi Muradyan (Mkrtchyan), Van, Aljavaz, 1907 ◆ Haykanush Mkrtchi Muradyan, Aljavaz, 1909 ◆ Haykanush Movsesi Movsisyan (Melkonyan), Mush, Abul-bohar, 1909 ◆ Haykanush Movsesi Sukiasyan (Movsesyan), Alekpol, Gyullibulagh, 1913 ◆ Haykanush Muradi Muradyan, Tpkhis, 1914 ◆ Haykanush Musheghi (Suriki) Musheghyan, Bulanagh, Shekhmahmud, 1914 ◆ Haykanush Nazari (Yenoki) Enokyan, Etchmiadzin, Sharur, 1908 ◆ Haykanush Nersesi Manukyan, Igdir, Najafar, 1911 ◆ Haykanush Nersesi Nersisyan, Kars, Bern, 1910 ◆ Haykanush Nikoghosi Nikoghosyan, Erzrum, Mamakhatun, 1909 ◆ Haykanush Nshani Aghabalyan, Terjan, Belkli, 1911 ◆ Haykanush Nshani Manukyan, Van, 1909 ◆ Haykanush Nshani Mkrtchyan, Ardahan, Javshert, 1901 ◆ Haykanush Ohani Avetisyan (Ohanyan), Van, Moks, 1910 ◆ Haykanush Petrosi Aharonyan, Khnus, Khomkhaya, 1909 ◆ Haykanush Petrosi Davtyan (Petrosyan), Khnus, Huramik, 1913 ◆ Haykanush Petrosi Grigoryan, (Petrosyan), Van, Shatakh, 1909 ◆ Haykanush Petrosi Torosyan, Leninakan, Jajur, 1911 ◆ Haykanush Poghosi Aleksanyan (Poghosyan), Alekpol, Taknalu, 1913 ◆ Haykanush Poghosi Poghosyan (Vardanyan), Bulanagh, Latara, 1913 ◆ Haykanush Potiki Potikyan (Asatryan), Van, Aljavaz, 1909 ◆ Haykanush Safari Ghazaryan (Safaryan), Archesh, Motsa, 1912 ◆ Haykanush Sahaki Sahakyan, Van, Aljavaz, 1913, 1910 ◆ Haykanush Sahaki Shabanyan, Shamakhi, Sakhian, 1912 ◆ Haykanush Sargisi Baghdasaryan, Etchmiadzin, Shahriar, 1914 ◆ Haykanush Sargisi Sargsyan, Van, 1906 ◆ Haykanush Sargsi Hovhannisyan (Sargsyan), Manazkert, Tolaghbash, 1916 ◆ Haykanush Sargsi Karapetyan (Sargsyan), Aljavaz, Arcke, 1912 ◆ Haykanush Sargsi Piloyan, Leninakan, Chrplu, 1908 ◆ Haykanush Saroyi Minasyan, Alekpol, Sirvanjugh, 1914 ◆ Haykanush Serobi Poghosyan, Alekpol, Imrkhan, 1910 ◆ Haykanush Serobi Serobyan, Etchmiadzin, 1914 ◆ Haykanush Shavi Petrosyan, Kars, 1910 ◆ Haykanush Smbati Hakobyan, Surmalu, Igdir, 1913 ◆ Haykanush Smbati Sargsyan, Tiflis, 1915 ◆ Haykanush Soghomoni Gagikyan, Van, Hatanan, 1910 ◆ Haykanush Stepani Stepanyan (Movsisyan), Etchmiadzin, Ashtarak, 1917 ◆ Haykanush Tatosi Tadevosyan, Lori, Urut, 1916 ◆ Haykanush Ter-Garegini Meliksetyan (Gareginyan), Van, Aljavaz, 1914 ◆ Haykanush Tigrani Hachyan (Mecoyan), Leninakan, Svanverdi, 1910 ◆ Haykanush Tigrani Khachatryan, Leninakan, Gharakilisa, 1914 ◆ Haykanush Vahani Hakobyan,

Darachichak, Ddmashen, 1914 ♦ Haykanush Vahani Serobyan, Kars, Uzunkilisa, 1911 ♦ Haykanush Vardani Galstyan, Ardahan, 1917 ♦ Haykanush Yeghiazari Asatryan, Ayntap, Batnots, 1915 ♦ Haykanush Yeghishei Khachatryan, Alekpol, Toros, 1910 ♦ Haykanush Yeghishi Avetisyan, Akhalkalak, Dadesh, 1914 ♦ Haykanush Yeghishi Sahakyan (Yeghishyan), Khnus, 1910 ♦ Haykanush Yeghoyi Pnjoyan, Alekpol, Tavshanghshlagh, 1910 ♦ Haykanush Yervandi Mkrtchyan, Hin Nakhijevan, Jayri, 1913 ♦ Haykaram Abrahami Gaboyan, Yerevan, 1917 ♦ Haykaram Khachaturi Baghdasaryan, Kars, Kyadiklar, 1912 ♦ Haykaz Abrahami Gevorgyan, Basen, Khzveran, 1909 ♦ Haykaz Aghababi Davtyan, Erzrum, 1913 ♦ Haykaz Armani Martirosyan, Kars, Kaghzvan, 1910 ♦ Haykaz Arshaki Barseghyan, Akhalkalak, Karzakh, 1913 ♦ Haykaz Arshaki Harutyunyan, Alekpol, Syugutli, 1913 ♦ Haykaz Artashesi Poghosyan (Artashyan), Yerevan, Mastara, 1913 ♦ Haykaz Avetisi Gharagyozyan (Avetisyan), Alekpol, 1911 ♦ Haykaz Avetisi Varosyan, Kars, Kyurakdara, 1911 ♦ Haykaz Barseghi Barseghyan, Ghazakh, 1918 ♦ Haykaz Daviti Tunikyan, Yerevan, Mastara, 1914 ♦ Haykaz Galusti Papikyan, Basen, Yuzveran, 1912 ♦ Haykaz Galusti Petrosyan, Alashkert, Ghayabeg, 1914 ♦ Haykaz Gaspari Gasparyan, Alekpol, Gozlu, 1912 ♦ Haykaz Gaspari Vardanyan, Khnus, Ghal-Chavush, 1913 ♦ Haykaz Gevorgi Gabrielyan (Gevorgyan), Leninakan, 1916 ♦ Haykaz Gevorgi Melkonyan, Kars, Paldrvan, 1917 ♦ Haykaz Ghazari Karapetyan, Kars, 1916 ♦ Haykaz Grigori Melkonyan, Erzrum, 1909 ♦ Haykaz Hakobi Hakobyan, Van, 1915 ♦ Haykaz Hamayaki Manukyan (Bodoghyan), Akhalkalak, 1919 ♦ Haykaz Hamazaspi Madoyan, Basen, Bashgyugh, 1911 ♦ Haykaz Hambardzumi Simonyan, Basen, Sthan, 1910 ♦ Haykaz Hambardzumi Tazagulyants, Ardahan, Olti, 1916 ♦ Haykaz Harutyuni (Sahakyan) Hakobyan, Aparan, Gharabulagh, 1912 ♦ Haykaz Harutyuni Petrosyan, Alekpol, Kyadiklar, 1914 ♦ Haykaz Hovaki Knyazyan (Hovakyan), Yerevan, Mastara, 1914 ♦ Haykaz Hovhannesi Mkrtchyan (Hovhannisyan), Leninakan, Illi, 1911 ♦ Haykaz Hovhannesi Poghosyan, Van, Archesh, 1911 ♦ Haykaz Hunani Hunanyan, Igdir, Kharfali, 1914 ♦ Haykaz Karapeti Karapetyan, Akhaltsikha, Khorenia, 1918 ♦ Haykaz Kerobi Khachatryan, Basen, Dalibaba, 1909 ♦ Haykaz Khachaturi Hovhannisyan, Yerevan, Nor Bayazet, 1914 ♦ Haykaz Khachaturi Khachatryan, Leninakan, Atiyaman, 1914 ♦ Haykaz Khachaturi Navoyan, Alekpol, Khlli Gharakilis 1913 ♦ Haykaz Kolyayi Mikayelyan (Soroyan), Shamakhi, Madras, 1917 ♦ Haykaz Macaki Antonyan, Darachichak, Caghkunk, 1915 ♦ Haykaz Margari Margaryan, Mush, 1911 ♦ Haykaz Martirosi Hovhannisyan, Kars, 1913 ♦ Haykaz Martirosi Martirosyan (Arutyan), Kars, Tekniz, 1910 ♦ Haykaz Martirosi Martirosyan, Sarighamish, Bash gyugh, 1913 ♦ Haykaz Mikayeli Mikayelyan, Leninakan, Khrmzlu, 1914 ♦ Haykaz Movsesi Petrosyan, Karabagh, Sev gyugh, 1909 ♦ Haykaz Muradi Muradyan, Mush, Khnusghala, 1911 ♦ Haykaz Musheghi Musheghyan, Khnus, Berd, 1912 ♦ Haykaz Petrosi Avetisyan, Alekpol, Aghin, 1914 ♦ Haykaz Sahaki Mkhitaryan, Kars, Berna, 1913 ♦ Haykaz Tadevosi Tadevosyan, Basen, Hekibad, 1913 ♦ Haykaz Vardani Khachatryan, Kars, Uzunkilisa, 1911 ♦ Haykaz Voskani Vardanyan, Kars, Pirvali, 1912, 1911 ♦ Haykazun Saghateli Ter-Gevorgyan, Kars, Kyurakdara, 1913 ♦ Hayko Daviti Grigoryan (Ohanyan), Bulanagh, Yonjalu, 1918 ♦ Hayko Manuki Manukyan, Shirak, Paltlu, 1917 ♦ Hayko Mnatsakani Mnatsakanyan, 1918 ♦ Hayko Yeghishi Yeghishyan, Kars, 1918 ♦ Haykuhi Hovhannesi Guloghlyan (Galoyan), Van, 1912 ♦ Haykush Abrahami Vardanyan, Kars, 1914 ♦ Haykush Aghabeki Gharibyan (Aghabekyan), 1920 ♦ Haykush Aghasu Galstyan, Akhalkalak, 1918 ♦ Haykush Arakeli Arakelyan, Basen, Ishkhan, 1909 ♦ Haykush Arshaki Nazaryan, Yerevan, Nakhijevan, 1914 ♦ Haykush Avetisi Avetisyan, Etchmiadzin, 1915 ♦ Haykush Avetisi Avetisyan, Kars, Jala, 1916 ♦ Haykush Gevorgi Gevorgyan (Ispiryan), Alekpol, Ghonaghran, 1918 ♦ Haykush Gevorgi Gevorgyan, Pambak, Gharakilisa, 1917 ♦ Haykush Ghazari Yeritsyan, Basen, Yaghan, 1914 ♦ Haykush Ghukasi Ghukasyan, Kars, Bagran, 1914 ♦ Haykush Hakobi (Sayati) Navasardyan, Pambak, Gharakilisa, 1919 ♦ Haykush Hakobi Sukiasyan, Alashkert, Gharakilisa, 1916 ♦ Haykush Harutyuni Sargsyan, Kars, Gorkhana, 1919 ♦ Haykush Hmayaki Hamoyan, Talin, 1916 ♦ Haykush Hovhannesi Hovhannisyan, Van, Psti gyugh, 1910 ♦ Haykush Karapetyan, Shirak, Kaftarlu, 1920 ♦ Haykush Khachaturi Ghazaryan, Etchmiadzin, Aparan, 1914 ♦ Haykush Knyazi Harutyunyan (Minasyan), Alekpol, Bahandur, 1911 ♦ Haykush Matevosi Matevosyan (Martirosyan), Kars, Paldrvan, 1916 ♦ Haykush Meliki Melikyan, Kars, 1920 ♦ Haykush Misaki (Hovhannesi) Misakyan (Hovhannisyan), Bulanagh, Hamzashekh, 1914 ♦ Haykush Misaki Misakyan, Kars, 1915 ♦ Haykush Mukoyi Muradyan, Kars, Banglamat, 1915 ♦ Haykush Samsoni Papikyan, Basen, Gomadzor, 1913 ♦ Haykush Santoyi Ohanyan, Tiflis, 1907 ♦ Haykush Stepani Mejlumyan, Lori, Atan, 1915 ♦ Haykush Tigrani Malakyan (Shahbazyan), Alekpol, Mahmatjugh, 1918 ♦ Haykush Vardani Misakyan, Yerevan, 1918 ♦ Haykush Yeranosi Yeranosyan, Alekpol, Sarmtlu, 1917 ♦ Hayrapet Abrahami Khachatryan, Karabagh, Mzkit, 1915 ♦ Hayrapet Arakeli Khlghatyan (Arakelyan), Etchmiadzin, Shariar, 1910 ♦ Hayrapet Avetisi Sargsyan, Bulanagh, Tezuran, 1912 ♦ Hayrapet Gevorgi Hovhannisyan, Surmalu, Alkghzl, 1917 ♦ Hayrapet Karapeti Meloyan (Karapetyan), Leninakan, Bozdoghan, 1912 ♦ Hayrapet Nersesi Nersisyan (Simonyan), Surmalu, Alija, 1912 ♦ Hayrapet Sahaki Sahakyan, Bayburd, Hyuseynik, 1912 ♦ Hayrapet Samsoni Serobyan (Srapyan), Alashkert, 1918 ♦ Hayrik (Hakob) Movsesi Allaverdyan, Van, Caytar, 1910 ♦ Hayrik Armenaki Grigoryan (Armenakyan), Van, Herendin, 1911 ♦ Hayrik Avagi Sargsyan, Nakhijevan, Ghazanchi, 1912 ♦ Hayrik Gevorgi Khudaverdyan, Van, 1911 ♦ Hayrik Hovhannesi Hovhannisyan, Sasun, Taghavank, 1914 ♦ Hayrik Manuki Teloyan (Manukyan), Van, Armshat, 1911 ♦ Hayrik Mkrtchi Hovhannisyan, Hayots dzor, 1918 ♦

Hayrik Mkrtchi Panosyan, Van, Akhorik, 1912 ♦ Hayrik Petrosi Petrosyan, Van, 1914 ♦ Hayrik Simoni (Simonyan) Harutyunyan, Van, 1911 ♦ Hayrik Stepani Arakelyan, Nakhijevan, Aza, 1910 ♦ Hayrik Tonoyi Khachatryan, Manazkert, Khasmik, 1913 ♦ Hayrik Vardani Hovhannisyan, Van, 1914 ♦ Hazarapet Gevorgi Badalyan, Hin Nakhijevan, Demirzndan, 1911 ♦ Hazarapet Kyureghi Harutyunyan, Nakhijevan, 1910 ♦ Hazarapet Simoni Ghazaryan, Akhalkalak, Sultan, 1915 ♦ Hazarapet Zakari Zakaryan (Shahabuni), Nakhijevan, Noragyugh, 1913 ♦ Hazrvard Arshaki Arshakyan, Alashkert, Gharakilisa, 1915 ♦ Hazrvard Baghdasari Grigoryan (Baghdasaryan), Alashkert, Ghazi gyugh, 1912 ♦ Hazrvard Hovhannesi Torosyan, Kars, Ghapanlu, 1913 ♦ Hazrvard Manuki Ghazaryan, Alashkert, Hamat, 1909 ♦ Hazrvard Musheghi Davtyan (Musheghyan), Alashkert, Gharakilisa, 1911 ♦ Hazrvard Nikoli Grigoryan, Alashkert, 1915 ♦ Hazvard Serobi Serobyan, Alashkert, Iritsu, 1910 ♦ Heghinar Hovhannesi Asatryan, Alashkert, Gharakilisa, 1912 ♦ Heghinar Petrosi Hovhannisyan, Akhalkalak, 1907 ♦ Heghine (Heghush) Harutyuni Harutyunyan, Van, Hayots dzor, 1916 ♦ Heghine Abrahami Hambardzumyan, Van, Aljavaz, 1914 ♦ Heghine Aleksani Aghajanyan, Sisian, Tatev, 1908 ♦ Heghine Aleksani Hakobyan (Aleksanyan), Kars, 1916 ♦ Heghine Arshaki Tutunjyan, Kaghzvan, 1909 ♦ Heghine Daviti Hovsepyan, Nakhijevan, Karkhanbayla, 1911 ♦ Heghine Daviti Nersisyan, Van, Ikmal, 1908 ♦ Heghine Gabrieli Hovhannisyan, Kars, 1917 ♦ Heghine Galusti Ayvazyan (Galstyan), Ghamarlu, Spahan, 1912 ♦ Heghine Gevorgi Badalyan, Akhalkalak, Gandza, 1910 ♦ Heghine Ghazari Aghayan, Leninakan, Samrlu, 1914 ♦ Heghine Grigori Grigoryan, 1917 ♦ Heghine Grigori Grigoryan, Kaghzvan, 1914 ♦ Heghine Grigori Grigoryan, Kars, 1913 ♦ Heghine Grigori Grigoryan, Nakhijevan, Kznut, 1908 ♦ Heghine Grigori Grigoryan, Nor Bayazet, Basargechar, 1914 ♦ Heghine Grigori Petrosyan, Nukhi, Valakyand, 1910 ♦ Heghine Hakobi Aghajanyan, Kars, Kaghzvan, 1908 ♦ Heghine Hakobi Hakobyan, Mush, Bulanagh, 1916 ♦ Heghine Hakobi Hakobyan, Tigor, 1914 ♦ Heghine Hambardzumi Kirakosyan (Hambardzumyan), Basen, Dalibaba, 1912 ♦ Heghine Harutyuni Harutyunyan, Baku, 1915 ♦ Heghine Harutyuni Harutyunyan, Erzrum, 1915 ♦ Heghine Harutyuni Harutyunyan, Mush, 1912 ♦ Heghine Harutyuni Harutyunyan, Mush, Tevrjan, 1914 ♦ Heghine Harutyuni Topchyan, Shamakh, Gandzak, 1908 ♦ Heghine Hovsepi Arakelyan (Hovsepyan), Leninakan, Gozlu, 1908 ♦ Heghine Israyeli Arakelyan (Danielyan), Kars, 1915 ♦ Heghine Kerobi Kerobyan, Khnus, 1915 ♦ Heghine Khachaturi Baghshetsyan (Khachatryan), Nor Bayazet, Kyavar, 1915 ♦ Heghine Manuki Manukyan, Bulanagh, Votnchor, 1912 ♦ Heghine Manuki Yeghoyan, Shirak, Pokr Keti, 1911 ♦ Heghine Margari Sargsyan, Yerevan, Imanshalu, 1916 ♦ Heghine Matevosi Tankamyan, Akhalkalak, Gandza, 1909 ♦ Heghine Muradi Muradyan, Kop, Yonjalu, 1911 ♦ Heghine Nikoghosi Nikoghosyan, Erzrum, Bayburt, 1911 ♦ Heghine Nshani Ter-Ghazaryan, Van, Archak, 1912 ♦ Heghine Petrosi Grigoryan, Kaghzvan, 1910 ♦ Heghine Petrosi Jonoyan (Petrosyan), Leninakan, Jajur, 1913 ♦ Heghine Petrosi Petrosyan, Bulanagh, Yonjalu, 1911 ♦ Heghine Sahaki Shahbazyan, Etchmiadzin, Khatunarkh, 1913 ♦ Heghine Sargisi Antanosyan, Akhalkalak, Gandza, 1911 ♦ Heghine Simoni Ter-Karapetyan, Van, Archak, 1908 ♦ Heghine Soghomoni Sorsoryan, Shamakhi, 1914 ♦ Heghine Sosei Khachatryan, Alekpol, Bozdoghan, 1913 ♦ Heghine Tonakani Grigoryan, Kars, 1911 ♦ Heghine Vakhtangi (Vardani) Aznavuryan (Vakhtangyan), Akhalkalak, 1916 ♦ Heghine Vardani Stepanyan, Manazkert, Ghasmig, 1911 ♦ Heghine Vayradi Hakobyan, Kars, Bashkyadiklar, 1910 ♦ Heghine Yepremi Zakaryan, Nukhi, 1910 ♦ Heghnar Aghabeki Aghabekyan, Kars, 1918 ♦ Heghush (Sarukhani) Nersesi Sarukhanyan, Alastan, 1918 ♦ Heghush Abrahami Manukyan, Kars, Kyurakdara, 1909 ♦ Heghush Bagrati Ter-Mikayelyan, Kars, Hamzakyarak, 1916 ♦ Heghush Gevorgi (Gevorgyan) Khachatryan, Van, 1915 ♦ Heghush Gevorgi Abajyan, Leninakan, 1914 ♦ Heghush Grishayi Pahlevanyan, Akhalkalak, Satgha, 1915 ♦ Heghush Hambardzumi Ghabulyan, Gandzak, 1913 ♦ Heghush Hambardzumi Karapetyan, Leninakan, Tavshanghshlagh, 1909 ♦ Heghush Hovsepi Hovsepyan, Surmalu, Kulab, 1912 ♦ Heghush Khachaturi Khachatryan, Van, 1910 ♦ Heghush Khachaturi Khachatryan, Van, Kurubas, 1914 ♦ Heghush Maruti (Marutyan) Vardanyan, Van, Patakants, 1911 ♦ Heghush Melkoni (Tigrani) Melkonyan, Pambak, Gharakilisa, 1917 ♦ Heghush Mikayeli Sahakyan (Mikayelyan), Ghazakh, Sri, 1913 ♦ Heghush Poghosi Minasyan, Nakhijevan, 1912 ♦ Heghush Soghomoni Soghomonyan, Leninakan, Chlokhan, 1918 ♦ Heghush Sukiasi Sukiasyan, Sarighamish, 1908 ♦ Heghush Vardani Hovhannisyan, Kars, Paldrvan, 1918 ♦ Henrik Gokori Gokoryan, 1919 ♦ Henrik Grigori Derdzakyan, Van, 1910 ♦ Hergo Zakari Vardanyan, Ayntap, Terek, 1914 ♦ Herik (Tatsui) Gasparyan, Leninakan, Hajinazar, 1918 ♦ Herik Hovhannesi Antonyan, Ghazakh, Aghdam, 1917 ♦ Herik Vahani Ghazaryan, Kars, 1918 ♦ Heriknaz (Sahaki) Abgari Abgaryan, Kars, Gyamrlu, 1916 ♦ Heriknaz (Yerinaz) Kochoyi Melkonyan, Khnus, 1913 ♦ Heriknaz (Yerinaz) Musheghi Musheghyan, Khnus, Khalil-Chavush, 1915 ♦ Heriknaz Antoni Eloyan, Koghp, 1910 ♦ Heriknaz Arami Yasagelyan, Khnus, Gharakyopr, 1909 ♦ Heriknaz Arshaki Arshakyan (Safaryan), Alashkert, Mankasar, 1914 ♦ Heriknaz Arshaki Gasparyan, Kars, Mazra, 1913 ♦ Heriknaz Avetisi Stepanyan, Leninakan, Kifli, 1912 ♦ Heriknaz Avetisi Vardanyan, Sarighamish, Ghoshakilisa, 1914 ♦ Heriknaz Galusti Hovhannisyan, Alekpol, Mec Sariar, 1915 ♦ Heriknaz Galusti Torosyan (Galstyan), Leninakan, Gharakilisa, 1916 ♦ Heriknaz Gevorgi Gevorgyan, Yonjalu, Kop, 1917 ♦ Heriknaz Gevorgi Ter-Sargsyan, Bulanagh, Kop, 1909 ♦ Heriknaz Gyulizari Harutyunyan, Kars, Zrchi, 1908 ♦ Heriknaz Hakobi Torosyan, Erzrum, Kyorpikoy, 1908 ♦ Heriknaz Haruti Hovsepyan, Alekpol, Armtlu, 1916 ♦

Heriknaz Haruti Martirosyan, Kars, Gyamrlu, 1916 ♦ Heriknaz Harutyuni Harutyunyan, Alekpol, Gheghaj, 1915 ♦ Heriknaz Harutyuni Sargsyan (Harutyunyan), Sarighamish, Armtlu, 1911 ♦ Heriknaz Harutyuni Torosyan, Shirak, Ghzlghoch, 1910 ♦ Heriknaz Hayrapeti Hayrapetyan, Turkey, Hin Bayazet, 1915 ♦ Heriknaz Hmayaki Tigranyan (Mikayelyan), Akhalkalak, Gentura, 1916 ♦ Heriknaz Hovhannesi Petrosyan, Alekpol, Ghoshavank, 1914 ♦ Heriknaz Hovhannesi Sahakyan, Pirvali, 1911 ♦ Heriknaz Hovnani Muradyan, Kars, Aljaghal, 1912 ♦ Heriknaz Karapeti Gasparyan (Karapetyan), Kars, 1913 ♦ Heriknaz Khachaturi Gevorgyan, Koghb, 1911 ♦ Heriknaz Khachaturi Makaryan, Bulanagh, Gharaghl, 1909 ♦ Heriknaz Khachaturi Poghosyan (Khachatryan), Kars, Cbni, 1909 ♦ Heriknaz Khachoyi Khachatryan, Basen, Dalibaba, 1912 ♦ Heriknaz Kirakosi Manukyan, Kars, Agrak, 1908 ♦ Heriknaz Levoni Khlghatyan, Erzrum, Derik, 1908 ♦ Heriknaz Makari Manukyan, Leninakan, Ghzlghoch, 1913 ♦ Heriknaz Mkrtchi Adamyan, Kars, Kharkov, 1912 ♦ Heriknaz Mnatsakani Zadoyan, Kars, Ghzlchakhchakh, 1915 ♦ Heriknaz Nazareti Nazaryan, Shirak, Chorpnlu, 1906 ♦ Heriknaz Nazareti Poghosyan (Kotanjyan), Kars, Kyadiklar, 1912 ♦ Heriknaz Nikoghosi Nikoghosyan, Sarighamish, Churik, 1911 ♦ Heriknaz Petrosi Vardanyan, Kars, 1914 ♦ Heriknaz Sahaki Sahakyan, Aparan, Alikuchak, 1914 ♦ Heriknaz Sargsi Simonyan, Akhalkalak, Karzakh, 1910 ♦ Heriknaz Serkoyi Hakobyan, Alekpol, Hajikhalil, 1913 ♦ Heriknaz Simoni Danielyan, Lori, Hamamlu, 1912 ♦ Heriknaz Sukiasi Manukyan, Kars, Mazra, 1910 ♦ Heriknaz Sukiasi Sargsyan (Gasparyan), Khnus, Khlut, 1914 ♦ Heriknaz Tadevosi Tadevosyan, Alashkert, Gharakilisa, 1914 ♦ Heriknaz Vanoyi Poghosyan, Shirak, Bashgyugh, 1919 ♦ Heriknaz Vardani Tadevosyan, Akhalkalak, Janjgha, 1910 ♦ Heriknaz Varderesi Baghdasaryan, Basen, Yaghan, 1912 ♦ Heriknaz Yeghiayi Nikoghosyan, Erzrum, Bayburt, 1913 ♦ Heriknaz Yeghoyi Yeghoyan, Bulanagh, Votnchor, 1914 ♦ Heriknaz Zakari Manukyan, Bulanagh, Lataran, 1908 ♦ Heriknaz Zohrabi Aghsaghalyan (Kurtanjyan), Alekpol, 1910 ♦ Herko Ghazari Badalyan (Ghazaryan), Van, Gharakilisa, 1912 ♦ Hermine Sedraki Pirghalamyan, Archesh, 1913 ♦ Hero Serobi Serobyan, Ghamrlu, Davalu, 1917 ♦ Hmayak Alekoyi Aleksanyan, Alekpol, Horom, 1912 ♦ Hmayak Arami Yeranosyan, Karin, Tetaveran, 1991 ♦ Hmayak Arshaki Andreasyan, Daralagyaz, Yelpin, 1915 ♦ Hmayak Avagi Petrosyan, Kars, Paldrvan, 1912 ♦ Hmayak Avetisi (Avetisyan) Barseghyan, Van, Mandan, 1912 ♦ Hmayak Baghdasari Baghdasaryan, Bulanagh, Kars, 1916 ♦ Hmayak Galusti Astanyan, Kars, Mazra, 1913 ♦ Hmayak Gevorgi Danielyan (Gevorgyan), Nakhijevan, 1908 ♦ Hmayak Gevorgi Khachatryan, Kars, Mec Parket, 1913 ♦ Hmayak Ghazari Gevorgyan, Yerevan, Gyozli, 1909 ♦ Hmayak Ghazari Manukyan, Manazkert, Akner, 1912 ♦ Hmayak Ghazari Sarukhanyan (Ghazaryan), Mush, Vardov, 1912 ♦ Hmayak Ghazaryan, Yerevan, 1918 ♦ Hmayak Ghukasi Hambardzumyan (Ghukasyan), Basen, Bashgegh, 1915 ♦ Hmayak Grigori Grigoryan, Van, Koch, 1912 ♦ Hmayak Grigori Vardanyan, Leninakan, Keti, 1911 ♦ Hmayak Hakobi Avetisyan, Kars, Paldrvan, 1912 ♦ Hmayak Harutyuni Sargsyan, Manazkert, Iknakhoja, 1908 ♦ Hmayak Hovhannesi Sukiasyan, Basen, Armtlu, 1915 ♦ Hmayak Karapeti Stepanyan (Karapetyan), Alashkert, Zetkan, 1909 ♦ Hmayak Karoyi Aleksanyan, Lori, Shahnazar, 1916 ♦ Hmayak Khachaturi Baghdasaryan, Nakhijevan, Diza, 1912 ♦ Hmayak Khachaturi Khachatryan (Simonyan), Van, Laman, 1908 ♦ Hmayak Khachaturi Khachatryan, Kars, 1910 ♦ Hmayak Levoni Levonyan, Van, 1917 ♦ Hmayak Markosi Markoyan, Yerevan, Gyaykilisa, 1914 ♦ Hmayak Martirosi Baghdasaryan (Martirosyan), Van, Nor gyugh, 1914 ♦ Hmayak Meliki Ter-Sargsyan, Karabagh, Nukhi, 1912 ♦ Hmayak Mkhitari Hovhannisyan, Kars, Tigor, 1913 ♦ Hmayak Mkhitari Tigranyan, Alashkert, Yonjalu, 1914 ♦ Hmayak Movsesi Martirosyan, Alekpol, Saribagh, 1913 ♦ Hmayak Musheghi Khachatryan (Musheghyan), Kars, Berna, 1913 ♦ Hmayak Musheghi Sarukhanyan, Vardo, Gundemir, 1912 ♦ Hmayak Nahapeti Harutyunyan, Khnus, Kopal, 1911 ♦ Hmayak Nazareti Torosyan, Kars, Nakhijevan, 1910 ♦ Hmayak Nikoli Kocharyan, Lori, Shnogh, 1914 ♦ Hmayak Nshani Nshanyan, Aljavaz, 1914 ♦ Hmayak Nshani Nshanyan, Van, Averak, 1915 ♦ Hmayak Nuroyi Hovhannisyan, Alekpol, Dzithankov, 1914 ♦ Hmayak Petrosi Apoyan, Sarighamish, Bashgegh, 1909 ♦ Hmayak Petrosi Avetisyan (Petrosyants), Kars, 1916 ♦ Hmayak Poghosi Gharibyan (Poghosyan), Salmast, Kyavas, 1904 ♦ Hmayak Rafayeli Azizyan (Rafayelyan), Van, Yerkrin, 1908 ♦ Hmayak Sahaki Sargsyan (Sahakyan), Van, Darman, 1907 ♦ Hmayak Sargisi Davtyan, Zangezur, Khodanan, 1910 ♦ Hmayak Sargisi Sargsyan, Ghazakh, Aghdam, 1915 ♦ Hmayak Smbati Smbatyan, Leninakan, Kaps, 1908 ♦ Hmayak Vardevani Mkrtchyan (Vardanyan), Kars, Cbni, 1910 ♦ Hmayak Yeloyi Ayvazyan, Alashkert, Zetkan, 1912 ♦ Hmayak Yervandi Yervandyan, Gharakilisa, 1919 ♦ Hnazand Arseni Gabrielyan, Kars, Bashkyadiklar, 1911 ♦ Hnazand Avetisi Tumasyan, Kars, Aksighaz, 1910 ♦ Hnazand Nikoli Hambaryan, Alekpol, Ghanlija, 1910 ♦ Hnazand Sergoyi Sergoyan, Alekpol, Bandivan, 1912 ♦ Hnazand Serobi Janoyan (Serobyan), Basen, Ishkhu, 1914 ♦ Hnazand Yeghiazari Nalbandyan, Kars, Kyurakdara, 1911 ♦ Hndik Karoyi Zakaryan, Akhalkalak, Abul, 1912 ♦ Hndyan Yeghiazari Yeghiazaryan, Kars, 1916 ♦ Hogaberd Simoni Khachatryan, Kars, Koghb, 1913 ♦ Holia (Koryun) Hovhannesi Hovhannisyan, Kars, 1917 ♦ Horom (Horomsim) Sargsi Sargsyan, Mush, Khardun, 1914 ♦ Horom (Hripsime) Yegori Yegoryan, Ghamrlu, Imanshalu, 1915 ♦ Horom Aleksani Aleksanyan, Kars, Paldlu, 1918 ♦ Horom Armenaki Armenakyan, 1915 ♦ Horom Arshaki Simonyan (Arshakyan), Sarighamish, 1916 ♦ Horom Artashi Saribekyan (Artashyan), Shirak, Syogutlu, 1914 ♦ Horom Avagi Gevorgyan, Kars, Uzunkilisa, 1914, 1911 ♦ Horom Avagi Zakaryan, Van, Khojan, 1913 ♦ Horom Avetisi Bedoyan, Basen, Gharabunghar, 1912 ♦ Horom Bagrati

Bagratyan, Kars, Cbni, 1914 ♦ Horom Danieli Sukiasyan, Kars, 1911 ♦ Horom Gevorgi Hakobyan, Kars, Khas, 1914 ♦ Horom Gevorgi Khachatryan, Leninakan, 1913 ♦ Horom Ghukasi Mkrtchyan, Leninakan, Paldlu, 1913 ♦ Horom Gyulbeki Petrosyan, Kars, Sarighamish, 1912 ♦ Horom Haruti Harutyunyan, Yerevan, 1918 ♦ Horom Haruti Sargsyan, Kars, Nakhijevan, 1912 ♦ Horom Harutyuni Minasyan, Alekpol, Atiyaman, 1908 ♦ Horom Khachaturi Khachatryan, Alekpol, Gharakilisa, 1918 ♦ Horom Khachaturi Khachatryan, Nakhijevan, Khznaberd, 1914 ♦ Horom Minasi Minasyan, Basen, Khoshgyaldi, 1913 ♦ Horom Nazari Ghazaryan (Nazaryan), Basen, Harsenkar, 1907 ♦ Horom Nikoghosi Tarzyan (Nersisyan), Pambak, Ghaltaghchi, 1915 ♦ Horom Petrosi Avetisyan, Basen, Gordakhas, 1912 ♦ Horom Sedraki Tumasyan, Leninakan, Ghazanchi, 1918 ♦ Horom Smbati Minasyan, Gharakilisa, Gyoran, 1915 ♦ Horom Smbati Smbatyan, Lori, Shahnazar, 1916 ♦ Horom Vardani Khudoyan (Vardanyan), Nakhijevan, Arinj, 1911 ♦ Horomsim Arshaki Manukyan, Kars, 1914 ♦ Horomsim Barseghi Vardanyan, Kars, Gorkhana, 1914 ♦ Horomsim Markosi Aghababyan, Alekpol, Jalal, 1912 ♦ Horomsim Simoni Muradyan (Simonyan), Kars, Sarighamish, 1915 ♦ Horomsim Yegori Mukeyan, Jalal oghli, Urut, 1918 ♦ Horomsim Yeranosi Avagyan (Ghazaryan), Erzrum, Betvan, 1912 ♦ Horomsima Khachaturi Shahinyan, Shulaver, Akhkorpi, 1914 ♦ Horomsime Hovhannesi Hovhannisyan, Ashtarak, Aparan, 1915, 1917 ♦ Horut Aleki Chorchoryan (Alekyan), Erzrum, Gomadzor, 1914 ♦ Hovak Gaspari Galstyan, Mush, Bulanagh, 1914 ♦ Hovakim Nersesi Yeghoyan, Alekpol, Gharamahmat, 1913 ♦ Hovakim Sargisi Sargsyan, Nor Nakhijevan, 1910 ♦ Hovasap Yeghoyi Yeghikyan, Mush, Hershtir, 1912 ♦ Hovhan Mkhitari Ghazaryan (Mkhitaryan), Bulanagh, Perkashen, 1909 ♦ Hovhannes (Askanaz) Sedraki Mnoyan, Kars, Bashkyadiklar, 1917 ♦ Hovhannes (Ghazari) Adami Ghazaryan, Gharakilisa, Alikhan, 1917 ♦ Hovhannes Abgari Nahapetyan (Abgaryan), Tavriz, Koyum, 1914 ♦ Hovhannes Aghabeki Matosyan, Leninakan, Ghanlija, 1915 ♦ Hovhannes Aleksani Manukyan (Aleksanyan), Erzrum, Tetveran, 1911 ♦ Hovhannes Aloyan, 1919 ♦ Hovhannes Arakeli Movsisyan, Kars, Marvik, 1909 ♦ Hovhannes Arami Aramyan, Akhalkalak, Taknali, 1916 ♦ Hovhannes Arami Papoyan, Kars, Aghuzum, 1917 ♦ Hovhannes Arami Tonoyan, Alekpol, Ghaplu, 1914 ♦ Hovhannes Arshaki Arshakyan, Alekpol, Sariar, 1915 ♦ Hovhannes Arshaki Hovhannisyan, Kars, Aghuzum, 1914 ♦ Hovhannes Arshaki Karapetyan, Kars, Teknis, 1913 ♦ Hovhannes Artyomi Stepanyan, Gandzak, Nukhi, 1914 ♦ Hovhannes Avetisi Vardanyan, Mush, Motkan, 1910 ♦ Hovhannes Azati Khachatryan, Kars, Cbni, 1909 ♦ Hovhannes Baghdasari Baghdasaryan, Ayntap, Batnots, 1912 ♦ Hovhannes Bareghami Baghdikyan (Hambardzumyan), Leninakan, Mastara, 1917 ♦ Hovhannes Bareghami Hakobyan, Leninakan, Adiyaman, 1917 ♦ Hovhannes Barseghi Barseghyan, Alashkert, Khastur, 1912 ♦ Hovhannes Daviti Nazaryan, Leninakan, Chiftali, 1913 ♦ Hovhannes Gabrieli Kocharyan, Gyokcha, Tobishen, 1910 ♦ Hovhannes Gaspari Ghazaryan, Leninakan, Hajinazat, 1918 ♦ Hovhannes Gaspari Sargsyan, Mush, Bndiner, 1920 ♦ Hovhannes Gevorgi Antonyan, Alekpol, Gharakilisa, 1912 ♦ Hovhannes Gevorgi Gevorgyan (Poghosyan), Leninakan, Yeganlar, 1917 ♦ Hovhannes Gevorgi Sergoyan, Darachichak, Meliki gyugh, 1911 ♦ Hovhannes Gevorgi Suvaryan, Basen, 1908 ♦ Hovhannes Ghevondi Nalbandyan, Kaghzvan, 1915 ♦ Hovhannes Ghukasi Santoyan, Kars, Ghzlchakhchakh, 1913 ♦ Hovhannes Ginosi Ginosyan, Shirak, Chiftali, 1918 ♦ Hovhannes Grigori Gevorgyan, Kars, Pirvali, 1912 ♦ Hovhannes Grigori Movsisyan, Kars, Mavrak, 1912 ♦ Hovhannes Grigori Potoyan, Kars, 1913 ♦ Hovhannes Grigori Sargsyan, Shamakh, Kyuylich, 1912 ♦ Hovhannes Habeti Maloyan, Leninakan, 1912 ♦ Hovhannes Hakobi (Sargsyan) Hakobyan, Nakhijevan, Khanlakhlar, 1912 ♦ Hovhannes Hakobi Hakobyan, Kars, Bashgegh, 1913 ♦ Hovhannes Hakobi Sahakyan (Hakobyan), Bitlis, Sasik, 1911 ♦ Hovhannes Hakobi Sahakyan, Van, Kerts, 1911 ♦ Hovhannes Hambardzumi Martirosyan, Kars, Aghjaghala, 1916 ♦ Hovhannes Hambardzumi Mkhitaryan, Erzrum, 1914 ♦ Hovhannes Harutyuni Ghazaryan, Kars, Bazrgan, 1915 ♦ Hovhannes Hayrapeti Harutyunyan (Hayrapetyan), Terjan, Bulk, 1912 ♦ Hovhannes Hayrapeti Mayilyan, Persia, Gharadagh, 1911 ♦ Hovhannes Hovaki Hovakyan, Shirak, Ghanlija, 1918 ♦ Hovhannes Hovhannisyan, Leninakan, 1919 ♦ Hovhannes Hovsepi Grigoryan, Nakhijevan, Ghazanchi, 1912 ♦ Hovhannes Hovsepi Israyeli Chakhoyan, Kars, 1915 ♦ Hovhannes Hunani Mukuchyan, Chanakhchi, 1917 ♦ Hovhannes Israyeli Maghakyan (Israyelyan), Basen, Gomadzor, 1911 ♦ Hovhannes Kamoyi Khachatryan, Alekpol, Ghanlija, 1913 ♦ Hovhannes Karapeti Avagyan (Karapetyan), Van, 1914 ♦ Hovhannes Karapeti Hamasyan, Alekpol, 1910 ♦ Hovhannes Karapeti Harutyunyan (Karapetyan), Basen, Arjarak, 1914 ♦ Hovhannes Karapeti Karapetyan, Mush, Taghanis, 1914 ♦ Hovhannes Karapeti Sargsyan, Van, 1908 ♦ Hovhannes Karapeti Tatosyan (Karapetyan), Nakhijevan, Znaberd, 1914 ♦ Hovhannes Khachaturi (Hambardzumi) Gevorgyan, Nakhijevan, Badamlu, 1912 ♦ Hovhannes Khachaturi Khachatryan, Mush, Harvarenj, 1919 ♦ Hovhannes Khachaturi Vardanyan, Shirak, Jajur, 1911 ♦ Hovhannes Kirakosi Kirakosyan (Abrahamyan), Manazkert, Rostomgedak, 1914 ♦ Hovhannes Knyazi Harutyunyan, Alekpol, Svanverdi, 1913 ♦ Hovhannes Lazoyi Musayelyan, Karabagh, Gharaghshlagh, 1912 ♦ Hovhannes Levoni Simonyan, Alekpol, 1914 ♦ Hovhannes Manuki Manukyan, Manazkert, 1913 ♦ Hovhannes Manuki Muradyan, Kars, Agrak, 1910 ♦ Hovhannes Martirosi Hovhannisyan, Kars, 1916 ♦ Hovhannes Martirosi Manukyan, Van, 1910 ♦ Hovhannes Martirosi Martirosyan, Manazkert, Berd, 1911 ♦ Hovhannes Martirosi Martirosyan, Nakhijevan, Khach gyugh, 1911 ♦ Hovhannes Martirosi Sahakyan, Darachichak, Ddmashen, 1912 ♦ Hovhannes Melkoni Baghdasaryan, Bulanagh,

Kop, 1912 ♦ Hovhannes Minasi Minasyan, Van, Karchkan, 1914 ♦ Hovhannes Misaki Misakyan, Kars, Sarighamish, 1914 ♦ Hovhannes Mkrtchi (Sargsyan) Nahapetyan, Leninakan, Akhkilisa, 1913 ♦ Hovhannes Mkrtchi Avagyan, Shirak, Ghazarapat, 1910 ♦ Hovhannes Mkrtchi Khachatryan, Shirak, Chorli, 1913 ♦ Hovhannes Mkrtchi Stepanyan, Alekpol, Ghapli, 1912 ♦ Hovhannes Mkrtchi Zakaryan, Alekpol, Norashen, 1912 ♦ Hovhannes Mnatsakani Ketetsyan, Akhalkalak, Gandza, 1912 ♦ Hovhannes Moskovi Gevorgyan, Leninakan, Tashghala, 1915 ♦ Hovhannes Movsesi Sahakyan (Movsisyan), Karin, Asparak, 1912 ♦ Hovhannes Movsesi Yeghiazaryan, Leninakan, Ghoshavank, 1911 ♦ Hovhannes Nazari Nazaryan, Basen, Dalibaba, 1912 ♦ Hovhannes Nazari Sahakyan, Kars, Mar-Vak, 1913 ♦ Hovhannes Nikoli Nasibyan (Nikolyan), Ghazakh, 1918 ♦ Hovhannes Nikoli Nazaryan (Nikolyan), Leninakan, Vordnav, 1916 ♦ Hovhannes Ohani (Ohanyan) Manukyan, Sasun, Aghnd, 1910 ♦ Hovhannes Papoyi Ter-Poghosyan, Erzrum, Ishkhu, 1912 ♦ Hovhannes Paroni Hovhannisyan (Paronyan), Van, Yererin, 1912 ♦ Hovhannes Petrosi Gevorgyan (Petrosyan), Etchmiadzin, Shariar, 1914 ♦ Hovhannes Petrosi Hakobyan, Akhalkalak, Dadesh, 1912 ♦ Hovhannes Petrosi Mkrtchyan (Petrosyan), Alashkert, 1912 ♦ Hovhannes Poghosi Poghosyan (Margaryan), Basen, Dalibaba, 1912 ♦ Hovhannes Sahaki Movsisyan, Kars, Bulanagh, 1909 ♦ Hovhannes Sakoyi Hovhannisyan, 1919 ♦ Hovhannes Sargisi Khachatryan (Sargsyan), Gharakilisa, Lorut, 1914 ♦ Hovhannes Sargisi Khachatryan, Shirak, Ghanlija, 1914 ♦ Hovhannes Sargsi Atoyan, Yerevan, 1917 ♦ Hovhannes Sargsi Sargsyan, Aparan, Gharakilisa, 1912 ♦ Hovhannes Saroyi Gharibyan, Alekpol, Ghazarapat, 1912 ♦ Hovhannes Saroyi Saroyan, Mec Gharakilisa, Aghbulagh, 1912 ♦ Hovhannes Sedraki Sedrakyan, Aljavaz, 1914 ♦ Hovhannes Serobi Serobyan (Hovhannisyan), Mush, Shina, 1909 ♦ Hovhannes Serobi Serobyan, Ghamarlu, Davalu, 1917 ♦ Hovhannes Sisaki Galstyan, Alashkert, Kurmupuchakh, 1917 ♦ Hovhannes Smbati Karapetyan (Hovsepyan), Leninakan, Darband, 1910 ♦ Hovhannes Smbati Ter-Hovhannisyan, Igdir, Kulap, 1912 ♦ Hovhannes Soghomoni (Abrahami) Abrahamyan, Zangezur, 1910 ♦ Hovhannes Tadevosi Hovhannisyan (Tadevosyan), Shirak, Gheghaj, 1915 ♦ Hovhannes Tadevosi Stepanyan, Leninakan, Illi, 1911 ♦ Hovhannes Tatosi Poghosyan, Pambak, Gharakilisa, 1914 ♦ Hovhannes Tatosi Tonoyan, Kars, Bashshoragyal, 1910 ♦ Hovhannes Ter-Matevosi Minasyan, Abagha, Nazaravan, 1908 ♦ Hovhannes Tonakani Stepanyan (Muradyan), Derjan, Khachgyugh, 1910 ♦ Hovhannes Torosi Mkrtchyan, Kars, Mazra, 1912, 1911 ♦ Hovhannes Torosi Torosyan, Babert, 1912 ♦ Hovhannes Vahani Hovhannisyan, Daralagyaz, Chanakhchi, 1914 ♦ Hovhannes Vahani Papikyan, Kars, 1910 ♦ Hovhannes Vardani Gasparyan, Akhalkalak, Vachyan, 1913 ♦ Hovhannes Vardani Hovhannisyan (Vardanyan), Van, 1907 ♦ Hovhannes Vardani Karapetyan (Motsoyan), Shirak, Tavshanghshlagh, 1915 ♦ Hovhannes Varosi Tiraturyan, Kars, Ughuzli, 1914 ♦ Hovhannes Verdoyi Verdoyan, Bulanagh, Kaparlu, 1913 ♦ Hovhannes Voskani Gevorgyan, Alekpol, Tashghala, 1919 ♦ Hovhannes Yeghiayi Sahakyan, Shirak, Pokr Keti, 1914 ♦ Hovhannes Yeranosi Tonoyan, Bulanagh, Kop, 1912 ♦ Hovhannes Zakari Zakaryan, Van, 1915 ♦ Hovik (Onnik) Aleksani Varosyan, Aghbulagh, 1918 ♦ Hovik Minasi Minasyan, Mush, Artonk, 1919 ♦ Hovsep (Hovasap) Hakobi Hakobyan, Mush, Bulanagh, 1910 ♦ Hovsep Aleki (Hovsepi) Hovsepyan (Grigoryan), Leninakan, Ghazanchi, 1919 ♦ Hovsep Aleki Sardaryan (Aleksanyan), Kars, Hamzakarak, 1912 ♦ Hovsep Aleksani Galstyan (Aleksanyan), Bayazlu, Ghshlagh, 1914 ♦ Hovsep Aleksani Mesropyan, Alekpol, Paltlu, 1912 ♦ Hovsep Asaturi Asatryan, Bulanagh, Sheykhaghab, 1914 ♦ Hovsep Barseghi Kyamalyan, Van, Vozm, 1917 ♦ Hovsep Barseghi Mirzoyan, Lori, Ghotur, 1914 ♦ Hovsep Gabrieli Hovsepyan, Kars, 1910 ♦ Hovsep Galusti Zakaryan, Ghamarli, Artashat, 1913 ♦ Hovsep Gevorgi Hunanyan (Gevorgyan), Akhlat, Prkhus, 1913 ♦ Hovsep Gharibi Hovsepyan, Kars, 1911 ♦ Hovsep Ghazari Muradyan, Van, Karchkan, Goms, 1912 ♦ Hovsep Hakobi Maralyan (Hakobyan), Yerevan, 1914 ♦ Hovsep Harutyuni Gabrielyan (Harutyunyan), Van, Berd, 1913 ♦ Hovsep Hovhannesi Hovhannisyan, Van, Mzhngert, 1911 ♦ Hovsep Khachaturi Gabrielyan (Khachatryan), Kars, Mec Parket, 1910 ♦ Hovsep Martirosi Sargsyan, Khnus, Gharakobri, 1909 ♦ Hovsep Meloyi Mkhitaryan (Kinjoyan), Bulanagh, Liz, 1909 ♦ Hovsep Mesropi Khachatryan, Leninakan, Babol, 1916 ♦ Hovsep Misaki Adamyan, Leninakan, Tashlanghshlagh, 1916 ♦ Hovsep Mkhitari Mkhitaryan, 1919 ♦ Hovsep Muradi Poghosyan (Muradyan), Archesh, 1911 ♦ Hovsep Muradi Sargsyan, Manazkert, Dugnug, 1913 ♦ Hovsep Muradi Umroyan (Muradyan), Ayntap, Badnots, 1908 ♦ Hovsep Poghosi Gasparyan (Poghosyan), Bitlis, Khulig, 1913 ♦ Hovsep Poghosi Poghosyan, Jalaloghli, Khotur, 1916 ♦ Hovsep Sahaki Sahakyan, Aljavaz, 1907 ♦ Hovsep Sahaki Sahakyan, Yerevan, Jarabat, 1913 ♦ Hovsep Smbati Muradyan, Khnus, Chavurma, 1908 ♦ Hovsep Stepani Atikyan, Alekpol, Tapanlu, 1909 ♦ Hovsep Vahani Sargsyan (Vahanyan), Mush, Poghorgov, 1910 ♦ Hovsep Vardani Tovmasyan, Mush, Shirvanshugh, 1909 ♦ Hovsep Yeghoyi Yeghoyan, Yerevan, Alapars, 1919 ♦ Hoyemzar Hovhani Hayrapetyan, Daralagyaz, Yerpun, 1910 ♦ Hrach (Frants) Sargsi Kerobyan, Zangezur, Jrashen, 1916 ♦ Hrach (Zarzand) Minasi Harutyunyan, Basen, Tortum, 1913 ♦ Hrach Abrahami Abrahamyan, Sarighamish, Ghoshakilisa, 1916 ♦ Hrach Aghani Muradyan, Shirak, Horom, 1914 ♦ Hrach Aleki Karapetyan (Hakobyan), Kars, 1918 ♦ Hrach Aleksani Stepanyan, Kars, 1910 ♦ Hrach Arakeli Gyunashyan, Kars, Ghzlchakhchakh, 1914 ♦ Hrach Armenaki Armenakyan, Sarighamish, 1918 ♦ Hrach Arshaki Akulyan, Kars, Araz, 1909 ♦ Hrach Arshaki Grigoryan, Kars, 1914 ♦ Hrach Artashesi Melikyan (Melkonyan), Khnus, 1909 ♦ Hrach Avetiki Safaryan, Kars, Ghzlchakhchakh, 1914 ♦ Hrach Avetisi Baboyan, Akhaltsikha, 1911 ♦ Hrach Avetisi Stepanyan, Bulanagh, Shirvanshugh, 1912 ♦ Hrach

Avetisi Ter-Poghosyan, Kars, Sarighamish, 1914 ♦ Hrach Avoyi Avoyan, Kars, 1917 ♦ Hrach Bagrati Galstyan, Kars, 1916 ♦ Hrach Daviti Poghosyan, Alekpol, Mustughli, 1914 ♦ Hrach Geghami Geghamyan, Igdir, Blur, 1916 ♦ Hrach Gevorgi Gasparyan, Shirak, Samtlu, 1912 ♦ Hrach Grigori Barseghyan, Kars, Zochi, 1914 ♦ Hrach Grigori Cicaghyan, Pokr Gharakilisa, 1914 ♦ Hrach Grigori Mkrtchyan, Alekpol, Ghanlija, 1911 ♦ Hrach Hakobi Manukyan, Kars, 1916 ♦ Hrach Hovhannesi Danielyan, Erzrum, 1915 ♦ Hrach Hovhannesi Sargsyan, Kars, 1913 ♦ Hrach Hovsepi Hovsepyan, Ghardaghuli, Ghazigetan, 1919 ♦ Hrach Hovsepi Shmoyan, Aparan, Shiragala, 1912 ♦ Hrach Hrachyan ♦ Hrach Hrapi Kurghinyan (Hrapyan), Leninakan, Syogutli, 1913 ♦ Hrach Karapeti Petrosyan (Karapetyan), Van, Avrag, 1912 ♦ Hrach Karapeti Shmoyan (Karapetyan), Kars, Nakhijevan, 1911 ♦ Hrach Levoni Serobyan, Leninakan, Ghanlija, 1914 ♦ Hrach Manuki Manukyan, Kars, Ghs, 1917 ♦ Hrach Meliki Zakaryan, Kars, Benkliahmat, 1911 ♦ Hrach Melkoni Geghamyan (Melkonyan), Alekpol, Bashaparan, 1918 ♦ Hrach Mkrtchi Papikyan (Harutyunyan), Kars, Bangliahmat, 1913 ♦ Hrach Movsesi Movsisyan, Van, Boghan, 1911 ♦ Hrach Sahaki Sahakyan (Shahbazyan), Yerevan, Zohrablu, 1914 ♦ Hrach Sahaki Sahakyan, Terjan, Shadivan, 1914 ♦ Hrach Sargisi Ghazaryan, Kars, Hamzakarak, 1911 ♦ Hrach Sargsyan, 1923 ♦ Hrach Sedraki Tashchyan, Alashkert, Gharakilisa, 1911 ♦ Hrach Sergoyi Simonyan, Alashkert, 1912 ♦ Hrach Simoni Hakobyan, Alekpol, Ghanlija, 1916 ♦ Hrach Torosi Torosyan (Hovhannisyan), Van, Gandzak, 1912 ♦ Hrach Vardani Hovhannisyan, Alashkert, Yeghntapa, 1911 ♦ Hrach Vardani Piloyan (Vardanyan), Archesh, Akants, 1911 ♦ Hrach Yeghiazari Yeghiazaryan, Kars, Terjan, 1914 ♦ Hrach Yenoki Martirosyan, Leninakan, Kaps, 1912 ♦ Hrachik Galusti Galstyan, Akhalkalak, Dadesh, 1916 ♦ Hrachik Hakobi Abrahamyan, Yerevan, 1916 ♦ Hrachik Harutyuni Harutyunyan, Kars, Ghzlchakhchakh, 1917 ♦ Hrachik Martirosi Martirosyan, Van, Skhkes, 1916 ♦ Hrachik Tatuli Tadevosyan, Kars, Bazrkyadak, 1921 ♦ Hrachya Aghasi Hakobyan, Kars, Ughuzli, 1909 ♦ Hrachya Aghasu Hovhannisyan, Kars, 1910 ♦ Hrachya Antoni Khachatryan, Leninakan, Kifli, 1915 ♦ Hrachya Armenaki Aghajanyan, Akhalkalak, 1911 ♦ Hrachya Ghevondi Avagyan, Koghb, 1913 ♦ Hrachya Grigori Baghdasaryan, Shushi, Gandzak, 1912 ♦ Hrachya Grigori Grigoryan, Alekpol, Vojaghuli, 1914 ♦ Hrachya Harutyuni Arakelyan, Kars, Gharamahmat, 1916 ♦ Hrachya Harutyuni Harutyunyan, Mush, Bntgh, 1912 ♦ Hrachya Hovhannesi Hlghatyan, Mush, Bulanagh, 1911 ♦ Hrachya Hunani Grigoryan, Kars, 1917 ♦ Hrachya Karapeti Nalbandyan, Alekpol, Khlli Gharakil., 1912 ♦ Hrachya Kirakosi Mkrtchyan, Kars, Mazra, 1914 ♦ Hrachya Martirosi Harutyunyan, Pambak, Gharakilisa, 1913 ♦ Hrachya Musheghi Poghosyan, Kars, Bashkyadiklar, 1913 ♦ Hrachya Sahaki Nikoghosyan, Pambak, Parni gyugh, 1917 ♦ Hrachya Srapioni Kostanyan (Hovhannisyan), Kars, 1913 ♦ Hrachya Yesayi Khachatryan (Khachoyan), Van, Tiramayr, 1913 ♦ Hracin Yeremi (Yeremyan) Movsisyan, Igdir, 1913 ♦ Hrahat Gaspari Poghosyan, Kars, Chrason, 1914 ♦ Hrahat Minasi Arakelyan, Erzrum, Ilija, 1910 ♦ Hransuh Manuki Stepanyan, Kars, Bagliahmat, 1914 ♦ Hrant (Gevorgi) Mukuchi Gevorgyan (Mukuchyan), Gharakilisa, 1917 ♦ Hrant Adami Adamyan, Igdir, Khalfalu, 1916 ♦ Hrant Arshaki Arshakyan, Manazkert, 1915 ♦ Hrant Aslani Kirakosyan (Aslanyan), Alashkert, Yonjalu, 1911 ♦ Hrant Avagi Avagyan, Van, Kurubagh, 1914 ♦ Hrant Avetisi Gevorgyan, Mush, Bulanagh, 1914 ♦ Hrant Avetisi Khachatryan, Surmalu, Khoskhabar, 1913 ♦ Hrant Baghdasari Vardanyan, Bulanagh, Yonjalu, 1914 ♦ Hrant Baghdasari Vardanyan, Kars, 1915 ♦ Hrant Gevorgi Gharibyan (Gevorgyan), Maku, 1912 ♦ Hrant Gyulbeki Ter-Hovhannisyan, Erzrum, Krtabagh, 1912 ♦ Hrant Karapeti Serobyan, Erzrum, Yaghan, 1912 ♦ Hrant Khachaturi Ayvazyan, Akhalkalak, Aragova, 1912 ♦ Hrant Khachaturi Khachatryan, 1916 ♦ Hrant Khachaturi Poghosyan, Mush, 1911 ♦ Hrant Khudoyi Sargsyan (Sakoyan), Van, Akhosik, 1916 ♦ Hrant Knyazi Knyazyan, Igdir, Teshir, 1914 ♦ Hrant Martirosi Yeghiazaryan, Sarighamish, Bashgyugh, 1910 ♦ Hrant Movsesi Avetisyan, Gharakilisa, 1915 ♦ Hrant Nikoghayosi Ghazaryan, Basen, Kherseveran, 1913 ♦ Hrant Nikoli Nikolyan, Alashkert, Khakhabek, 1914 ♦ Hrant Sedraki Ghazaryan, Bulanagh, Kop, 1916 ♦ Hrant Sedraki Sedrakyan, Bulanagh, Kop, 1916 ♦ Hrant Simoni Markosyan (Simonyan), Manazkert, Rostamgedak, 1914 ♦ Hranush Abgari Abgaryan, Van, Baghghala, 1910 ♦ Hranush Aghasi Aghasyan, Kars, Gorkhana, 1915 ♦ Hranush Aghasi Malkhasyan (Aghasyan), Kars, Khorghan, 1916 ♦ Hranush Aghasu Mkhitaryan, Kars, Bashshoragal, 1908 ♦ Hranush Arami Vardanyan, Shirak, Syugutli, 1912 ♦ Hranush Armenaki Avetisyan, Kars, Bayrakhtar, 1914 ♦ Hranush Armenaki Barinyan, Kaghzvan, 1911 ♦ Hranush Arseni Ayvazyan, Kars, Ortakyadiklar, 1911 ♦ Hranush Artashesi Badalyan, Kars, Gorkhana, 1912 ♦ Hranush Avagi Avagyan, Kars, 1916 ♦ Hranush Avetisi Galstyan, Kars, Cbni, 1912 ♦ Hranush Baghdasari Baghdasaryan, Leninakan, Mastara, 1915 ♦ Hranush Bareghami Hambardzumyan, Leninakan, Mastara, 1915 ♦ Hranush Galusti Barseghyan, Kars, Ghzlchakhchakh, 1913 ♦ Hranush Geghami Harutyunyan, Alekpol, Ghapli, 1913 ♦ Hranush Gevorgi Gevorgyan, Shirak, Illi, 1916 ♦ Hranush Gevorgi Gevorgyan, Surmalu, Alghzl, 1913 ♦ Hranush Grigori Grigoryan, Akhaltsikhe, 1918 ♦ Hranush Grigori Muradyan (Grigoryan), Kars, Syogutli, 1912 ♦ Hranush Grigori Tarzyan (Terzyan), Kars, 1912 ♦ Hranush Grigori Vardanyan, Kars, Ortakatiklar, 1909 ♦ Hranush Hakobi Hakobyan (Muradyan), Kars, Ortakilisa, 1917 ♦ Hranush Hakobi Martirosyan, Kars, 1918 ♦ Hranush Hakobi Navasardyan, Nakhijevan, Mazra, 1912 ♦ Hranush Hakobi Poghosyan, Baku, 1911 ♦ Hranush Harutyuni Hovhannisyan, Van, Kurupasht, 1912 ♦ Hranush Harutyuni Samvelyan, Kars, Mazra, 1914 ♦ Hranush Hovakimi Atikyan (Galstyan), Shirak, Chzghlar, 1912 ♦ Hranush Hovhannesi Hovhannisyan (Kostanyan), Alekpol,

Chlokhan, 1913 ♦ Hranush Hovhannesi Manasaryan (Hovhannisyan), Van, 1911 ♦ Hranush Hovhannesi Stepanyan (Hovhannisyan), Kars, Kyadiklar, 1908 ♦ Hranush Hovsepi Tonoyan, Mush, Yonjalu, 1914 ♦ Hranush Karoyi Mkrtchyan, Shirak, Ortakilisa, 1914 ♦ Hranush Khachaturi Khachatryan, Alekpol, Bashghala, 1916 ♦ Hranush Khachaturi Khachatryan, Kars, 1918 ♦ Hranush Khachaturi Khachatryan, Kars, Gharamahmet, 1914 ♦ Hranush Khachaturi Khachatryan, Van, 1916 ♦ Hranush Khachaturi Khanbegyan, Ardahan, 1916 ♦ Hranush Manuki Manukyan, Van, 1911 ♦ Hranush Margari Margaryan, Erzrum, Zeynal, 1910 ♦ Hranush Martirosi Ayvazyan, Sarighamish, 1912 ♦ Hranush Martirosi Gharibyan, Akhalkalak, 1915 ♦ Hranush Meleki Amirkhanyan, Lori, Gyulagarak, 1911 ♦ Hranush Meliki Amirkhanyan, Stepanavan, Gyulagarak, 1911 ♦ Hranush Meliki Melikyan, Alekpol, Ortakilisa, 1916 ♦ Hranush Misaki Harutyunyan, Kars, Ughuzli, 1918 ♦ Hranush Mkoyi Mkrtchyan, Shirak, Gheghach, 1915 ♦ Hranush Mkrtchi Mkrtchyan, Kars, Cbni, 1914 ♦ Hranush Musheghi Petrosyan, Kars, Ughuzli, 1914 ♦ Hranush Nikoli Mesropyan, Alekpol, Zarnchi, 1912 ♦ Hranush Nshani Karapetyan (Nshanyan), Van, 1909 ♦ Hranush Petrosi Asatryan, Kars, Ghzlchakhchakh, 1916 ♦ Hranush Petrosi Petrosyan, Yerevan, Mollabayazet, 1914 ♦ Hranush Sakoyi Movsisyan, Kars, Ghzlchakhchakh, 1910 ♦ Hranush Sargsi Hardinyan (Sargsyan), Leninakan, Ghzlkilisa, 1908 ♦ Hranush Sargsi Sargsyan, Kaghzvan, 1914 ♦ Hranush Sedraki Simonyan (Davtyan), Kars, Bagliahmat, 1918 ♦ Hranush Simoni Manukyan, Kaghzvan, 1912 ♦ Hranush Sirekani Sirakanyan, Kars, Gedaksatlmish, 1910 ♦ Hranush Smbati Sargsyan, Leninakan, Mec Keti, 1910 ♦ Hranush Smbati Smbatyan, Kars, Darlu, 1914 ♦ Hranush Soghomoni Melkonyan, Kars, Ghzlchakhchakh, 1911 ♦ Hranush Soghomoni Vardanyan (Soghomonyan), Dilijan, 1911 ♦ Hranush Srapioni Karapetyan, Kars, 1909 ♦ Hranush Tatosi Asoyan, Kaghzvan, 1910 ♦ Hranush Tepani Tepanyan, Leninakan, Samrlu, 1917 ♦ Hranush Tigrani Sukiasyan, Alekpol, Talin, 1913 ♦ Hranush Tigrani Tigranyan (Hovhannisyan), Sasun, 1911 ♦ Hranush Vardani Avetisyan, Surmalu, Igdir, 1906 ♦ Hranush Vardani Hambardzumyan (Vardanyan), Shirak, Ghlli-Gharakilisa, 1915 ♦ Hranush Vardevani Grigoryan, Kars, Nakhijevan, 1914 ♦ Hranush Vasili Kirakosyan (Hayrapetyan), Kars, 1914 ♦ Hranush Yeghiazari Ghazaryan, Erzrum, Bayburt, 1917 ♦ Hranush Yenoki Davtyan (Yenokyan), Yerevan, Blur, 1909 ♦ Hranush Yesayi Minasyan, Alekpol, Duzkharaba, 1916 ♦ Hranush Zakari Terteryan, Akhalkalak, Khlaver, 1913 ♦ Hrayr Yepremi Andreasyan (Yepremyan), Gandzak, 1913 ♦ Hreghen Grigori Gasparyan, Leninakan, 1917 ♦ Hreghen Margari Margaryan, Mush, Berd, 1913 ♦ Hreghen Petrosi Baghdasaryan, Alekpol, Ghoshavank, 1912 ♦ Hrip Serobi Serobyan, Basen, Yaghan, 1914 ♦ Hripsik (Horomsim) Arami Baghdasaryan, Leninakan, 1911, 1913 ♦ Hripsik Abgari (Serobi) Manukyan (Artavazdyan), Kars, Gopanlu, 1912 ♦ Hripsik Aleksani Aleksanyan, Kars, 1915 ♦ Hripsik Aleksani Chilingaryan, Jalal oghli, Vardablur, 1912 ♦ Hripsik Aleksani Karapetyan, Kaghzvan, 1916 ♦ Hripsik Amriki Martirosyan, Leninakan, Sirvanjugh, 1912 ♦ Hripsik Arami Vardanyants (Vardanyan), Alekpol, Syogutli, 1911 ♦ Hripsik Aristakesi Hovhannisyan, Manazkert, Noragyugh, 1913 ♦ Hripsik Armeni Martirosyan, Shirak, 1912 ♦ Hripsik Arseni Arsenyan, Leninakan, Bashshoragyal, 1919 ♦ Hripsik Arshaki Aghajanyan, Alekpol, 1912 ♦ Hripsik Arshaki Arshakyan, Karabagh, Shushi, 1914 ♦ Hripsik Arshaki Davtyan, Akhalkalak, Sulda, 1915 ♦ Hripsik Arshaki Hovhannisyan, Kars, Cbni, 1910 ♦ Hripsik Arshaki Khachatryan, Alekpol, Khli Gharakilis, 1913 ♦ Hripsik Artashesi Hunanyan, Akhalkalak, Aragova, 1915 ♦ Hripsik Artemi Galstyan, Igdir, Tashburan, 1909 ♦ Hripsik Asoyi Stepanyan, Kars, Bulanagh, 1917 ♦ Hripsik Avetisi Avetisyan, Etchmiadzin, Gechulu, 1916 ♦ Hripsik Baghdasari Baghdasaryan, Leninakan, Ghonakhran, 1912 ♦ Hripsik Daviti Petrosyan, Kars, Parket, 1909 ♦ Hripsik Gaspari Amirkhanyan, Kars, 1916 ♦ Hripsik Gaspari Gasparyan, Kars, Paldrvan, 1920 ♦ Hripsik Gevorgi Gevorgyan, 1914 ♦ Hripsik Gevorgi Hovhannisyan, Van, Marmet, 1911 ♦ Hripsik Gevori Khachatryan, Kaghzvan, Arjarak, 1914 ♦ Hripsik Ghukasi Ghukasyan, Nakhijevan, Bitliz, 1914 ♦ Hripsik Grigori Adamyan, Akhalkalak, Khanchali, 1910 ♦ Hripsik Grigori Grigoryan (Tovmasyan), Van, Dshogh, 1913 ♦ Hripsik Grigori Grigoryan, Baberd, Erzrum, 1914 ♦ Hripsik Grigori Grigoryan, Kars, Sarighamish, 1913 ♦ Hripsik Grigori Muradyan, Kars, Berna, 1915 ♦ Hripsik Haji Hovhannisyan, Nor Bayazet, 1911 ♦ Hripsik Hakobi Ohanyan, Kars, 1907 ♦ Hripsik Hakobi Sahakyan (Hakobyan), Kars, 1911 ♦ Hripsik Hakobyan, Kars, Bashkadiklar, 1918 ♦ Hripsik Hanoyi (Sargsyan) Yeghikyan, Bulanagh, Shekhyaghub, 1908 ♦ Hripsik Haruti Harutyunyan, Leninakan, Darband, 1919 ♦ Hripsik Harutyuni Harutyunyan, Van, 1916 ♦ Hripsik Hayrapeti Balasanyan, Karabagh, 1914 ♦ Hripsik Hovhannesi Ayvazyan, Kaghzvan, 1908 ♦ Hripsik Hovhannesi Hovhannisyan (Mkhoyan), Ardahan, Shavshar, 1914 ♦ Hripsik Hovhannesi Hovhannisyan, Kars, Karmir Vank, 1917 ♦ Hripsik Hovhannesi Karapetyan, Yerevan, Syogutli, 1910 ♦ Hripsik Hovhannesi Mkrtchyan, Shirak, Toparlu, 1915 ♦ Hripsik Hranti Asoyan, Kars, 1910 ♦ Hripsik Ispiri Tonoyan, Kars, Gedaksatlmish, 1908 ♦ Hripsik Karapeti (Karapetyan) Sahakyan, Van, 1912 ♦ Hripsik Karapeti Karapetyan, Yerevan, 1917 ♦ Hripsik Karapetyan, 1921 ♦ Hripsik Khachaturi Khachatryan, Leninakan, Ghoshavank, 1909 ♦ Hripsik Khachaturi Musheghyan, Shirak, Chtchkhlar, 1913 ♦ Hripsik Malkhasi Sargsyan, Kaghzvan, 1909 ♦ Hripsik Martirosi Margaryan, Erzrum, Ishkhan, 1910 ♦ Hripsik Martirosi Martirosyan, Bulanagh, Kharabshat, 1911 ♦ Hripsik Matevosi Baghdasaryan, Van, Berdak, 1913 ♦ Hripsik Meliki Amirkhanyan, Jalaloghli, Gyulagarak, 1917 ♦ Hripsik Minasi Khngoyan (Minasyan), Basen, Dzandzgh, 1911 ♦ Hripsik Mkrtchi Khachatryan, Kars, Sarighamish, 1913 ♦ Hripsik Muradi Shahinyan, Van, Narek, 1913 ♦ Hripsik Oniki Khachatryan, Akhaltsikha,

1916 ♦ Hripsik Papiki Papikyan, Van, Noragyugh, 1908 ♦ Hripsik Petrosi Petrosyan, Yerevan, Etchmiadzin, 1917 ♦ Hripsik Pilosi Pilosyan, Akhalkalak, Aragova, 1915 ♦ Hripsik Rafayeli Muradyan, Alekpol, Ghonakhran, 1915 ♦ Hripsik Sahaki Frangulyan, Alekpol, 1912 ♦ Hripsik Samsoni Khachatryan, Surmalu, Margar, 1914 ♦ Hripsik Sanasari Margaryan, Igdir, 1912 ♦ Hripsik Saroyi Khachatryan, Pambak, Ghshlagh, 1917 ♦ Hripsik Sedraki Avetisyn, Bagaran, 1911 ♦ Hripsik Sedraki Sardaryan, Gharakilisa, Derbend, 1918 ♦ Hripsik Serobi Sargsyan, Shirak, Tomardash, 1912 ♦ Hripsik Shmavoni Gnunyan, Kars, Bashshoragyal, 1909 ♦ Hripsik Soghomoni Soghomonyan, Sardarapat, Shahriar, 1915 ♦ Hripsik Tadevosi Manukyan, Kars, Cbni, 1912 ♦ Hripsik Tatosi Tadevosyan, Etchmiadzin, Talin, 1917 ♦ Hripsik Tigrani Hovhannisyan, Sarighamish, 1914 ♦ Hripsik Torosi Shahinyan, Akhalkalak, Vachian, 1914 ♦ Hripsik Vardani Pecikyan, Pambak, Parni gyugh, 1910 ♦ Hripsik Vardani Shahinyan, Kars, 1910 ♦ Hripsik Vardani Vardanyan, Kars, Gharamahmat, 1909 ♦ Hripsik Voskani Voskanyan, Van, Korsot, 1907 ♦ Hripsik Yeghiazari Shahnazaryan (Yeghiazaryan), Van, 1911 ♦ Hripsik Yervandi Yervandyan, Alekpol, Talin, 1914 ♦ Hripsik Zakari Petrosyan, Gandzak, 1908 ♦ Hripsime (Horom) Tovmasi Atoyan (Tovmasyan), Kars, Bangliahmat, 1913 ♦ Hripsime Aleksani Yaroyan (Minasyan), Kars, Parket, 1912 ♦ Hripsime Arseni Arsenyan, Erzrum, Terjan, 1911 ♦ Hripsime Avagi Muradyan, Pambak, Ghaltaghchi, 1918 ♦ Hripsime Avetisi Ter-Martirosyan, Van, Mavrak, 1905 ♦ Hripsime Badali Hovhannisyan, Alekpol, Mahmud, 1912 ♦ Hripsime Gaspari Amirkhanyan, Van, Khek, 1909 ♦ Hripsime Ghukasi Sahakyan, Kars, Bagran, 1913 ♦ Hripsime Hajipapi Gasparyan, Kars, 1909 ♦ Hripsime Hakobi Adamyan, Alekpol, Taknali, 1914 ♦ Hripsime Hambardzumi Torosyan (Hambardzumyan), Leninakan, Zarnji, 1915 ♦ Hripsime Harutyuni Abrahamyan (Harutyunyan), Alekpol, Bandivan, 1913 ♦ Hripsime Hovhannesi Grigoryan (Hovhannisyan), Ardahan, 1910 ♦ Hripsime Karapeti Barseghyan (Karapetyan), Sarighamish, Khoshgyaldi, 1914 ♦ Hripsime Khachaturi Khachatryan (Hunanyan), Erzrum, Terjan, 1910 ♦ Hripsime Khachaturi Khachatryan, Van, 1910 ♦ Hripsime Manuki Darbinyan, Kars, Bankliahmat, 1907 ♦ Hripsime Mkhitari Mkhitaryan, Kars, Ghzl-chakhchakh, 1917 ♦ Hripsime Mkrtchi Marukyan (Shakaryan), Akhalkalak, Karzakh, 1912 ♦ Hripsime Nikoli Poghosyan, Alekpol, Adiyama, 1916 ♦ Hripsime Nshani Hovhannisyan (Pokhanyan), Van, 1907 ♦ Hripsime Pilosi Harutyunyan, Sarighamish, Adan, 1910 ♦ Hripsime Poghosi Poghosyan, Basen, Dalibaba, 1912 ♦ Hripsime Sargsi Khachatryan, Kars, Chala, 1911 ♦ Hripsime Shahnazari Martirosyan, Borzhom, Karmir vank, 1905 ♦ Hripsime Vardani Aleksanyan, Yerevan, 1916 ♦ Hrispsik Minasi Minasyan, Leninakan, Toparlu, 1916 ♦ Hro (Hranush) Ohannesi Ohannesyan, Leninakan, Sariar, 1918 ♦ Hro Sargsi Karapetyan, Leninakan, Tomardash, 1920, 1917 ♦ Hrush (Hrach) Hovhannesi Parpuryan (Vaghashtsyan), Akhalkalak, Vachyan, 1917 ♦ Hrush Mkrtchi Mkrtchyan, Kars, Paldrvan, 1915 ♦ Hrush Poghosi Poghosyan, Yerevan, 1918 ♦ Hrush Smbati Smbatyan, Kars, Cbni, 1916 ♦ Hsakayel Avetisi Poghosyan, Alekpol, Imrkhan, 1910 ♦ Hulianne Khachaturi Stepanyan, Karabagh, Nukhi, 1913 ♦ Hulyane Geghami Avetisyan (Geghamyan), Ghamarlu, Yuva, 1911 ♦ Hunan Abrahami Abrahamyan, Alashkert, Batnots, 1909 ♦ Hunan Baghdasari Baghdoyan (Petrosyan), Leninakan, Chlokhan, 1914 ♦ Hunan Martirosi Martirosyan, Persia, Salmast, 1912 ♦ Hunan Nikoli Mkrtchyan, Akhaltsikha, Khorenia, 1912 ♦ Hunan Voskani Hovhannisyan, Shirak, Sariar, 1910 ♦ Hunan Yeghoyi Yeghoyan, Mush, Arnis, 1912 ♦ Hurher Hovsepi Stepanyan, Yerevan, Igdir, 1912 ♦ Hurian (Siranush) Antevani Manukyan, Alashkert, Amadan, 1913 ♦ Huriat Nazari Nazaryan, Khnus, Berd, 1915 ♦ Huriat Safari Gevorgyan, Bulanagh, Hamzashekh, 1912 ♦ Hurinaz Nersesi Manukyan, Bulanagh, Latar, 1914 ♦ Huryat Martirosi Igityan (Martirosyan), Mush, 1911 ♦ Hustine (Ustian) Mkrtchi Abrahamyan, Shatakh, 1911 ♦ Ibrahim Velii Valiyan, Yerevan, Japajalu, 1913 ♦ Ifo Geghami Geghamyan, Mush, Khoshgaldi, 1908 ♦ Ighab Ghukasi Ghukasyan, Leninakan, Paldlu, 1914 ♦ Igit Arshaki Sargsyan, Alekpol, Kyapanak, 1914 ♦ Igit Avetisi Simonyan, Bitlis, 1911 ♦ Igit Minasi Minasyan, Bitlis, Prkhus, 1910 ♦ Igit Muradi Muradyan (Vardikyan), Mush, Prkhus, 1911 ♦ Ignatos Karapeti Mosoyan, Basen, Chrason, 1913 ♦ Ilias Soghomoni Hovhannisyan, Mush, Vorgnots, 1911 ♦ Ilpapa Ali Akbar Mashadinyan, Yerevan, 1914 ♦ Ilya Hovhannesi Sargsyan (Hovhannisyan), Darachichak, Caghkunk, 1910 ♦ Imastun Asaturi Saroyan, Manazkert, Berd, 1912 ♦ Iran Sargsi Sargsyan, Nor Bayazet, Dalughartash, 1912 ♦ Isahak Karapeti Kyureghyan (Karapetyan), Kars, 1912 ♦ Ishkhan Arshaki Grigoryan, Zangezur, 1912 ♦ Ishkhan Baghdasari Baghdasaryan, Sarighamish, 1916 ♦ Ishkhan Caruki Muradyan, Kars, Bashkyadiklar, 1915 ♦ Ishkhan Galusti Mkrtchyan (Galstyan), Sarighamish, Bashgyugh, 1915 ♦ Ishkhan Grigori Gevorgyan, Sarighamish, 1913 ♦ Ishkhan Hovhannesi Hakobyan, Kars, Uzunkilisa, 1918 ♦ Ishkhan Hovsepi Hovsepyan, Igdir, 1916 ♦ Ishkhan Manasi Manasyan, Van, Zaran, 1913 ♦ Ishkhan Meliki Gevorgyan (Levonyan), Alashkert, Yeranos, 1913 ♦ Ishkhan Meliki Hakobyan (Melikyan), Alashkert, Iritsu, 1917 ♦ Ishkhan Mnatsakani Asatryan, Leninakan, Imirkhan, 1913 ♦ Ishkhan Musheghi Musheghyan, Kars, Bashshoragyal, 1915 ♦ Ishkhan Petrosi Hayrapetyan, Tiflis, 1916 ♦ Ishkhan Sakoyi Chkhoyan, Alekpol, Bashgegh, 1916 ♦ Ishkhan Sukiasi Hakobyan, Alashkert, Khachlu, 1912 ♦ Iskandar Gevorgi Gevorgyan, Van, Karchivan, 1913 ♦ Iskos Arshaki Hakobyan, Shirak, Khli Gharakilis, 1913 ♦ Iskuhi Galoyi Galoyan, Akhalkalak, 1915 ♦ Iskuhi Ghazari Ghazaryan, Aparan, 1914 ♦ Iskuhi Ghukasi Hakobyan (Ghukasyan), Van, Shatakh, Cican, 1913 ♦ Iskuhi Jojaghayi Mkrtchyan, Van, Kendanants, 1911 ♦ Iskuhi Khachaturi Asatryan (Khachatryan), Shatakh, Tagh, 1910 ♦ Iskuhi Khachaturi Khachatryan, Etchmiadzin, Korpalu, 1914 ♦ Iskuhi Manuki Petrosyan, Vaspurakan, 1909 ♦ Iskuhi Martirosi (Barkhudovi) Sargsyan,

Van, Archesh, 1910 ◆ Iskuhi Martirosi Matevosyan (Martirosyan), Ghamarlu, Hamamlu, 1920 ◆ Iskuhi Matevosi Yeghoyan, Akhalkalak, Khando, 1910 ◆ Iskuhi Mesropi Harutyunyan (Mesropyan), Yerznka, Gharatikin, 1909 ◆ Iskuhi Mkrtchi Mkrtchyan, Van, Mokhraberd, 1911 ◆ Iskuhi Sedraki Sedrakyan, Alekpol, Saltli, 1913 ◆ Iskuhi Ter-Karapetyan, Van, 1908 ◆ Iskuhi Tigrani Melkonyan (Tigranyan), Van, 1912 ◆ Iskuhi Yeghiazari Yeghiazaryan, Van, Kharakonis, 1913 ◆ Ispir Kachkachyan, Goghtan, 1920 ◆ Ispir Martirosi Martirosyan, Van, Nor gyugh, 1910 ◆ Israyel Arami Hovsepyan, Bulanagh, Sheykhaghab, 1914 ◆ Israyel Baghdasari Marutyan (Baghdasaryan), Bulanagh, Hamzashekh, 1908 ◆ Israyel Gaspari Gasparyan, Khnus, Berd, 1911 ◆ Israyel Gochoghlyan, Darachichak, Karvansara, 1916 ◆ Israyel Mkrtchi Tovmasyan, Leninakan, Arzaghala, 1918 ◆ Israyel Sahaki Khachatryan, Akhalkalak, Vachian, 1912 ◆ Israyel Zakari Ghazaryan, Kars, Uzunkilisa, 1914 ◆ Ivan Nikoghayosi Kirakosyan, Bulanagh, Geabol, 1913 ◆ Jandaz Baghdasari Hakobyan (Baghdasaryan), Manazkert, Tolagh Basha, 1909 ◆ Jandaz Muradi Grigoryan, Bitlis, Jamaldi, 1908 ◆ Jandaz Nazari Muradyan, Mush, Kop, 1912 ◆ Jangir Hovsepi Hovsepyan, Ghazakh, Karvansara, 1914 ◆ Janibek Aleksani Tovmasyan, Nor Bayazet, Dali-ghardash, 1913 ◆ Janibek Yeghishi Grigoryan, Bitlis, Prkhus, 1912 ◆ Janjan Tigrani Nazoyan, Bulanagh, Shahaghab, 1912 ◆ Jano Abrahami Baghdasaryan, Basen, Armtlu, 1914, 1912 ◆ Jano Khachoyi Mkrtchyan, Shirak, Taknalu, 1918 ◆ Jantas (Aghunik) Hovhannesi Torosyan (Hovhannisyan), Bitlis, Mec, 1909 ◆ Jantas Baghdasari Khachatryan (Baghdasaryan), Manazkert, 1915 ◆ Jantas Grigori Asatryan, Manazkert, Derka, 1909 ◆ Jantaz Hovhannesi Hovhannisyan, Bitlis, 1913 ◆ Javahir Aslani Amiryan, Aparan, Sangyar, 1910 ◆ Javahir Danieli Sahakyan, Kars, Gharamamat, 1912 ◆ Javahir Harutyuni Gevorgyan, Igdir, Panik, 1915 ◆ Javahir Hovhannesi Avagyan, Kars, Ghoshavank, 1910 ◆ Javahir Karapeti Poghosyan, Alekpol, Khli Gharakilisa, 1911 ◆ Javahir Kostani Kostanyan, Lori, Ghshlagh, 1914 ◆ Javahir Misaki Misakyan (Tigranyan), Igdir, Khashkhabar, 1910, 1908 ◆ Javahir Petrosi Baghdasaryan, Bulanakh, Latar, 1912 ◆ Javahir Petrosi Petrosyan, Yerevan, 1914 ◆ Javahir Sedraki Melkonyan, Bulanakh, Shekhaghut, 1912, 1911 ◆ Jazo Daviti Grigoryan, Mush, Kop, 1912 ◆ Jazo Hovaki Hambardzumyan, Bulanakh, Derik, 1913 ◆ Jehran Gevorgi Gabrielyan, Van, Aljavaz, 1914 ◆ Jeyran Azizi Ghazaryan, Akhlat, Khulik, 1914 ◆ Jeyran Hakobi Hovhannisyan, Alashkert, Ghazi, 1907 ◆ Jeyran Hovaki Hovsepyan, Kars, Ghzlchakhchakh, 1918 ◆ Jeyran Karapeti Hayrapetyan (Karapetyan), Nor Bayazet, 1914 ◆ Jeyro Mkrtichi Vasilyan (Mkrtchyan), Van, 1912 ◆ Jndo Manuki Baghdasaryan, Mush, Bulanagh, 1909 ◆ Jumshut Danieli Baloyan, Baku, 1914 ◆ Kachavan Gevorgi Khroyan, Alekpol, Ghulavert, 1918 ◆ Kachka (Vardanush) Grigori Dukhoyan, 1918 ◆ Kaghtsrik Aleki Hunanyan (Alekyan), Sardarapat, Kyalagyar, 1911 ◆ Kaghtsrik Harutyuni Harutyunyan, Leninakan, Syogutli, 1910 ◆ Kaghtsrik Meliki Melkonyan, Alekpol, Hajinazar, 1914 ◆ Kajavan Soghomoni Poghosyan, Shirak, Duzkharaba, 1914 ◆ Kakav Abrahami Abrahamyan, Alashkert, Habob, 1914 ◆ Kakav Chgnavori (Manuki) Manukyan, Karchakan, Gomar, 1912 ◆ Kakav Daviti Aleksanyan (Hambardzumyan), Kars, Bulanagh, 1916 ◆ Kakav Gaspari Martirosyan, Kars, Aghjaghala, 1913 ◆ Kakav Hambardzumi Hambardzumyan, Etchmiadzin, Uzunopay, 1918 ◆ Kakav Igiti (Tonoyan) Hovhannisyan, Manazkert, Berd, 1916 ◆ Kakav Khachaturi Ghurshudyan, Khnus, Yaghjamelik, 1909 ◆ Kakav Knyazi Margaryan, Kars, Tekniz, 1910 ◆ Kakav Movsesi Movsisyan, Bitlis, 1909 ◆ Kakav Movsesi Movsisyan, Van, Mokhraberd, 1908 ◆ Kakav Nshani Avagyan (Nshanyan), Van, Kurubash, 1908 ◆ Kakav Petrosi (Petrosyan) Khachatryan, Van, Archesh, 1909 ◆ Kakav Petrosi Petrosyan, Alashkert, Mosun, 1911 ◆ Kakav Simoni (Haruti) Simonyan (Harutyunyan), Karchkan, Urants, 1914 ◆ Kakav Tadevosi Tadevosyan, Khnus, Khrta, 1912 ◆ Kakav Torosi Aramyan (Torosyan), Van, Artamet, 1914 ◆ Kalip Muradi Manukyan, Kars, Gyarmli, 1912 ◆ Kalipse (Noyemzar) Vagharshaki Aghajanyan, Nor Bayazet, Ghshlagh, 1913 ◆ Kalipse Aristakesi Karapetyan, Kars, Pirvali, 1914 ◆ Kalipse Gaspari Karapetyan, Hin Bayazet, 1910 ◆ Kalipse Hakobi Hakobyan, Akhalkalak, Bughashen, 1916 ◆ Kalipse Hakobi Simonyan (Hakobyan), Alashkert, Khastur, 1913 ◆ Kalipse Hakobi Sukiasyan (Hakobyan), Alekpol, Bandivan, 1911 ◆ Kalipse Karoyi Ghazaryan, Alekpol, Darbandlu, 1912 ◆ Kalipse Khachaturi Hakobyan, Alekpol, Pokr Keti, 1912 ◆ Kalipse Madoyi Gogoyan (Madoyan), Leninakan, Kaps, 1911 ◆ Kalipse Margari Martirosyan, Igdir, Mush, 1909 ◆ Kalipse Poghosi Poghosyan, Alekpol, Ghaplu, 1917 ◆ Kalipse Rubeni Ghazaryan, Kars, Bashkyadiklar, 1918 ◆ Kalipse Vardani Vardanyan, Pambak, Gharaboja, 1914 ◆ Kamisar Smbati Chimshlyan (Chimalyan), Gharakilisa, Dilijan, 1917 ◆ Kamo Ayvazi Ayvazyan, Alekpol, Bashgyugh, 1912 ◆ Kamsar Beybuti Torchyan, Kars, Pirvali, 1912 ◆ Kamsar Harutyuni Papikyan, Kars, Bangliahmat, 1909 ◆ Kandukht Hakobi Khachatryan, Yerevan, Zeva, 1913 ◆ Kandukht Manuki (Khachaturi) Khachatryan, Shirak, Toros gyugh, 1914 ◆ Kandukht Stepani Stepanyan, Alekpol, Ghazarabad, 1911 ◆ Kanyak Aleksani Saroyan, Leninakan, Bash gyugh, 1917 ◆ Karapet (Shasho) Hovsepi Sargsyan, Akhalkalak, 1918 ◆ Karapet Abrahami Abrahamyan, Aljavaz, Sipan, 1913 ◆ Karapet Aleki Alekyan (Hovsepyan), Leninakan, Akhta, 1916 ◆ Karapet Andreasi Manukyan, Yerevan, Nors, 1911 ◆ Karapet Avdali Sargsyan, Bulanagh, 1916 ◆ Karapet Avetiki Khlghatyan, Alekpol, Hajinazar, 1913 ◆ Karapet Balabeki Sargsyan, Shirak, Bandivan, 1914 ◆ Karapet Daviti Davtyan, Van, Tap gyugh, 1906 ◆ Karapet Gaspari Manukyan, Erzrum, Dyuknak, 1912 ◆ Karapet Gevorgi Demirchyan, Ardahan, 1908 ◆ Karapet Gevorgi Pashayan, Akhalkalak, Satkha, 1912 ◆ Karapet Ghazari Petrosyan, Mush, Havadorik, 1901 ◆ Karapet Ghevondi Nersisyan, Van, 1909 ◆ Karapet Grigori Baghdasaryan, Erzrum, Karin, 1908 ◆ Karapet Grigori Khachatryan, Leninakan, Ghzlgoch, 1916 ◆ Karapet Grigori Shahinyan, Alekpol, 1908 ◆

Karapet Hakobi Hakobyan, Alekpol, Bozeghush, 1920 ♦ Karapet Hakobi Ohanyan, Kars, 1916 ♦ Karapet Hambardzumi Karapetyan, Sarighamish, 1913 ♦ Karapet Harutyuni Harutyunyan, Alekpol, Babrlu, 1913 ♦ Karapet Harutyuni Harutyunyan, Mush, Bostakand, 1913 ♦ Karapet Harutyuni Karapetyan (Harutyunyan), Erzrum, Karin, 1914 ♦ Karapet Hasagili Avetisyan (Hasagilyan), Alashkert, Yeghantapa, 1911 ♦ Karapet Hayrapeti Kamalyan, Kars, 1916 ♦ Karapet Hovhannesi Adamyan, Akhalkalak, 1918 ♦ Karapet Hovhannesi Hovhannisyan (Manushyan), Erzrum, Bayburt, 1910 ♦ Karapet Hovhannesi Hovhannisyan, Terjan, Kajaz, 1913, 1916 ♦ Karapet Hovhannesi Mkhitaryan, Kars, 1917 ♦ Karapet Karapeti Ter-Hovhannisyan, Van, Atana, 1908 ♦ Karapet Karoyan (Khanamiryan), 1919 ♦ Karapet Khachaturi Hovivyan, Alekpol, 1912 ♦ Karapet Khachaturi Khachatryan, Van, Aranjkos, 1912 ♦ Karapet Khachaturi Muradyan, Kars, 1909 ♦ Karapet Khachaturi Sargsyan, Aljavaz, Norshnjugh, 1913 ♦ Karapet Khachoyi Mkhoyants (Khachatryan), Kaghzvan, Changlu, 1914 ♦ Karapet Kostani Papikyan, Akhalkalak, Vachyan, 1915 ♦ Karapet Margari Poghosyan (Margaryan), Van, Aljavaz, 1910 ♦ Karapet Martini Tepanyan (Martinyan), Leninakan, Darband, 1915 ♦ Karapet Meliki Lusparonyan, Erzrum, 1912 ♦ Karapet Melkoni Malkhasyan, Bulanagh, Teghut, 1913 ♦ Karapet Mkrtchi (Vardani) Mkrtchyan, Kars, 1916 ♦ Karapet Mkrtchi Gharibyan, Leninakan, 1916 ♦ Karapet Mkrtchi Khchtyan, Leninakan, Mec Keti, 1913 ♦ Karapet Mkrtchi Mkrtchyan, Alekpol, Bozyokhush, 1916 ♦ Karapet Mkrtchi Mkrtchyan, Leninakan, Duzkharaba, 1917 ♦ Karapet Mkrtchi Palaryan, Akhalkalak, 1913 ♦ Karapet Mkrtchi Petrosyan, Alashkert, Mollasleym, 1915 ♦ Karapet Mkrtchi Yeghiazaryan, Nakhijevan, 1912 ♦ Karapet Movsesi Movsisyan, Alekpol, Khli Gharakilis, 1916 ♦ Karapet Nersesi Nersisyan, Leninakan, Pokr Keti, 1911 ♦ Karapet Petrosi Karapetyan (Petrosyan), Kars, Chermalu, 1913 ♦ Karapet Poghosi Poghosyan, Mush, Dalvorik, 1909 ♦ Karapet Rafayeli Khachatryan (Rafayelyan), Van, Khoragom, 1913 ♦ Karapet Sahaki (Sho) Karapetyan (Sahakyan), Aljavaz, Haren, 1912 ♦ Karapet Sahaki Grigoryan, Akhalkalak, Khanchali, 1913 ♦ Karapet Sahaki Ter-Poghosyan, Kars, Chala, 1914 ♦ Karapet Sargsi Harutyunyan, Van, Shatakh, 1911 ♦ Karapet Sargsi Poghosyan, Surmalu, 1912 ♦ Karapet Sargsi Sargsyan (Yeghoyan), Leninakan, Pokr Keti, 1917 ♦ Karapet Sarhati Hovhannisyan, Leninakan, Illi, 1916 ♦ Karapet Simoni Karapetyan, Kars, Voghuzli, 1914 ♦ Karapet Simoni Margaryan, Leninakan, Svanverdi, 1908 ♦ Karapet Stepani Hovhannisyan, Leninakan, Jalab, 1914 ♦ Karapet Stepani Stepanyan, Surmalu, Alighamat, 1916 ♦ Karapet Tonakani Grigoryan, Kars, 1916 ♦ Karapet Vardani Vardanyan, Kars, 1914 ♦ Karapet Yeghiazari (Yeghoyi) Yeghiazaryan (Yeghoyan), Aljavaz, Arcvi, 1913 ♦ Karapet Zakari Gevorgyan (Zakaryan), Manazkert, Rustamgedak, 1908 ♦ Karmile Gevorgi Bashkalantsyan, Van, 1913 ♦ Karmile Grigori Grigoryan, Van, 1910 ♦ Karmile Hovhannesi Hovhannisyan, Van, 1915 ♦ Karmile Iknadosi Inknadosyan, Van, 1907 ♦ Karmile Mikayeli Mikayelyan, Van, 1911 ♦ Karmile Sargsisi Andranikyan (Sargsyan), Van, 1915 ♦ Karmile Stepani Paronikyan, Van, Archesh, 1910 ♦ Karmile Stepani Paronikyan, Vaspurakan, Van, 1910 ♦ Karmile Vardani Pokhanyan, Van, 1919 ♦ Katar Bagrati Papikyan, Shirak, Ghanlija, 1917 ♦ Katar Vahani Hovhannisyan, Basen, Hasanghala, 1916 ♦ Katarine Aleki Antonyan, Alekpol, Chzghlar, 1915 ♦ Katarine Aslani Madoyan, Lori, Marts, 1908 ♦ Katarine Avetisi Katikoghlyan (Nersisyan), Akhalkalak, Gandza, 1913 ♦ Katarine Bekoyi Dilanyan, Olti, Olor, 1913 ♦ Katarine Daviti Davtyan, Ashtarak, Aparan, 1914 ♦ Katarine Gevorgi Davtyan Gevorgyan, Shushi, Aluzlu, 1909 ♦ Katarine Mikayeli Mikayelyan, Van, 1913 ♦ Katarine Misaki Yeghoyants (Misakyan), Alekpol, Arkhivali, 1911 ♦ Katarine Nazari Mkrtchyan, Kars, Kyadiklar, 1908 ♦ Katarine Sergoyi Shaboyan, Leninakan, 1912 ♦ Katarine Tovmasi Torosyan, Van, 1914 ♦ Katarine Vardani Aontsyan, Alekpol, Syogutli, 1911 ♦ Katik Abrahami (Sahaki) Sahakyan, Van, 1914 ♦ Katik Hunani Hunanyan, Nakhijevan, Gyaznar, 1915 ♦ Katinka Arestaki Yepremyan (Ter-Margaryan), Alekpol, Mastara, 1913 ♦ Katush Sergoyi Sergoyan, Leninakan, Kyapanak, 1916 ♦ Katya Hovhannesi Hovhannisyan, Alekpol, Sogyutli, 1918 ♦ Katya Hovhannesi Hovhannisyan, Kars, Zuchi, 1915 ♦ Katya Manuki Manukyan, Bayburt, Yevrik, 1913 ♦ Katya Sargsi Manushakyan, Tavrik, Paloga, 1915 ♦ Kaycak Sedraki Boyajyan (Gharagyozyan), Bayburt, Seyran, 1912 ♦ Kaycak Torosi Torosyan, Kars, Kadiklar, 1917 ♦ Kayser Igiti Kostanyan (Ghazaryan), Leninakan, Mec Alakhari, 1917 ♦ Kayzer Arami Aramyan, Van, 1915 ♦ Keghvard Mkrtchi Ignatosyan, Yerznka, 1912 ♦ Kekel Mkoyan, Jalaloghli, Uzunlar, 1917 ♦ Kerob Asaturi Hakobyan, Van, Archesh, 1912 ♦ Kerob Baghdasari Baghdasaryan, Bulanagh (Manazkert), 1914 ♦ Kerob Ghazari Harutyunyan, Sarighamish, Gedak, 1916 ♦ Kerob Hakobi Hakobyan, Kars, Paldrvan, 1914 ♦ Kerob Hambardzumi Hambardzumyan, Van, Pok, 1912 ♦ Kerob Khachaturi Khachatryan, Alashkert, 1911 ♦ Kerob Melikseti Yenokyan (Meliksetyan), Igdir, Kulap, 1914 ♦ Kerob Musheghi Simonyan, Alashkert, Berd, 1907 ♦ Kerob Papoyi Mkhitaryan, Kars, Agrak, 1911 ♦ Kerob Saghateli Saghatelyan, Manazkert, Khotalu, 1911 ♦ Khachatur (Martiros) (Hayrapeti) Arakeli Hayrapetyan, Kharberd, Sorpian, 1912 ♦ Khachatur Aghasi Hovhannisyan (Aghasyan), Nakhijevan, Khalkhal, 1912 ♦ Khachatur Aharoni Yegoryan (Aharonyan), Yelinovka, Vortakli, 1915 ♦ Khachatur Aleki Ter-Vardanyan, Akhalkalak, Khojabek, 1917 ♦ Khachatur Aleksani Harutyunyan, Nakhijevan, Shakh-mahmud, 1909 ♦ Khachatur Andraniki Hakobyan, Basen, Hekibat, 1913 ♦ Khachatur Andraniki Soghomonyan (Andranikyan), Darachichak, Fasugh, 1910 ♦ Khachatur Andreasi Nikoghosyan (Barseghyan), Sarighamish, 1911 ♦ Khachatur Arami Karapetyan, Nor Bayazet, 1914 ♦ Khachatur Arshaki Movsisyan, Alekpol, Chlokhan, 1910 ♦ Khachatur Artaki Harutyunyan, Kars, Mavrak, 1912 ♦ Khachatur Asaturi Ter-Mkhitaryan,

Bulanagh ◆ Khachatur Asaturi Ter-Mkhitaryan, Bulanagh, Yonjalu, 1909 ◆ Khachatur Avagi Mirzoyan, Zangezur, Alighuli, 1912 ◆ Khachatur Avetisi Karapetyan, Kars, Syogutlu, 1911 ◆ Khachatur Bagrati Khachatryan, Yerevan, Avan, 1911 ◆ Khachatur Barseghi Sargsyan (Barseghyan), Bulanagh, Yonjalu, 1916 ◆ Khachatur Daviti Davtyan (Harutyunyan), Van, Bltenz, 1910 ◆ Khachatur Eloyi Muradyan, Mush, Ghazi, 1909 ◆ Khachatur Gabrieli Gabrielyan, Shirak, Svanverdi, 1912 ◆ Khachatur Galusti Galstyan, Erzrum, Hoghik, 1911 ◆ Khachatur Galusti Petrosyan, Alekpol, Taknali, 1912 ◆ Khachatur Gaspari Harutyunyan, Kars, Ughuzli, 1911 ◆ Khachatur Gevorgi Gevorgyan (Grigoryan), Shirak, Klokhan, 1914 ◆ Khachatur Gevorgi Gevorgyan (Hovhannisyan), Etchmiadzin, Bashaparan, 1914 ◆ Khachatur Gevorgi Yeghiazaryan, Kars, Tazakand, 1914 ◆ Khachatur Grigori Ghazaryan (Mkhitaryan), Leninakan, Mec Keti, 1908 ◆ Khachatur Hakobi Hovhannisyan, Mush, Cghakay, 1909 ◆ Khachatur Harutyuni Hayrapetyan, Leninakan, Nor Artik, 1912 ◆ Khachatur Hayrapeti Gevorgyan (Hayrapetyan), Yerevan, Norashen, 1913 ◆ Khachatur Hovakimi (Yengibaryan) Movsisyan, Igdir, 1913 ◆ Khachatur Hovhannesi Ghazaryan, Shirak, Horom, 1913 ◆ Khachatur Hovhannesi Harutyunyan (Hovhannisyan), Leninakan, Svanverdi, 1913 ◆ Khachatur Hovsepi Martirosyan, Maku, 1912 ◆ Khachatur Hunani Hunanyan, Basen, Cholakhlu, 1914 ◆ Khachatur Karapeti Muradyan (Karapetyan), Van, Marmet, 1911 ◆ Khachatur Margari Dashikyan, Alekpol, Mastara, 1915 ◆ Khachatur Margari Yeghoyan (Margaryan), Erzrum, Khirseviran, 1912 ◆ Khachatur Markosi Tovmasyan, Sarighamish, Ghoshakilise, 1913 ◆ Khachatur Meliki Melikyan, Alekpol, Ghzlghoch, 1915 ◆ Khachatur Melkoni Hamazaspyan, Akhalkalak, Gyumurda, 1915 ◆ Khachatur Mikayeli Shahinyan, Van, 1915 ◆ Khachatur Misaki Ghazaryan (Misakyan), Alekpol, Mec Kyapanak, 1915 ◆ Khachatur Mkrtchi Ayvazyan, Leninakan, Boghazkyasan, 1912 ◆ Khachatur Mkrtchi Hovhannisyan (Mkrtchyan), Bitlis, Norshin, 1910 ◆ Khachatur Mkrtchi Mukayelyan (Mkrtchyan), Leninakan, Kyapanak, 1910 ◆ Khachatur Mkrtchi Sahakyan, Akhalkalak, 1912 ◆ Khachatur Mnatsakani Sargsyan, Alekpol, Horom, 1911 ◆ Khachatur Mukoyi Madoyan, Lori, Ghotur, 1915 ◆ Khachatur Nikoli Nikolyan, Alekpol, Ghanlija, 1914 ◆ Khachatur Ohani Harutyunyan (Ohanyan), Vayots dzor, Chanakhchi, 1914 ◆ Khachatur Poghosi Barseghyan, Basen, Hekibad, 1910 ◆ Khachatur Sakoyi Petrosyan, Shirak, Mastara, 1910 ◆ Khachatur Sargsi Serobyan, Kars, 1911 ◆ Khachatur Sargsi Stepanyan, Nukhi, Jafarapat, 1914 ◆ Khachatur Simoni Abgaryan, Erzrum, Hopviran, 1912 ◆ Khachatur Sirakani Musheghyan, Shirak, Ghazarapat, 1912 ◆ Khachatur Sirekani Ayvazyan, Etchmiadzin, 1917 ◆ Khachatur Stepani Khachatryan (Stepanyan), Yerznka, Zatgegh, 1908 ◆ Khachatur Tonoyi Avetisyan, Mush, Dashtadem, 1909 ◆ Khachatur Tonoyi Tonoyan, Leninakan, Haji Nazar, 1917 ◆ Khachatur Vardani Khachatryan (Vardanyan), Alashkert, Khtr, 1914 ◆ Khachatur Vardani Tovmasyan, Nor Bayazet, Gharangyugh, 1910 ◆ Khachatur Yeghishei Vardapetyan (Vardanyan), Akhalkalak, 1911 ◆ Khachatur Yepremi Grigoryan, Shirak, Mastara, 1907 ◆ Khachik Aleksani Carukyan, Akhalkalak, Satkha, 1910 ◆ Khachik Arami Khachatryan (Khachikyan), Leninakan, 1916 ◆ Khachik Avetiki Serobyan, Akhalkalak, Pokr Khanchalu, 1913 ◆ Khachik Badoyi Avoyan (Baghdasaryan), Leninakan, Ghzlghoch, 1914 ◆ Khachik Barseghi (Yeghiazari) Yeghiazaryan (Zhamkhoryan), Hin Bayazet, 1914 ◆ Khachik Barseghi Aghoyan, Akhalkalak, Samsar, 1911 ◆ Khachik Boghoyi Hovhannisyan, Mush, Bulanagh, 1910 ◆ Khachik Gevorgi Levonyan (Hakobyan), Bulanagh, Khoshgyaldi, 1908 ◆ Khachik Ghevondi Ghambaryan (Hambardzumyan), Basen, Ghoshakilisa, 1916 ◆ Khachik Grigori Gurgenyan (Manukyan), Alekpol, 1914 ◆ Khachik Grigori Soghomonyan (Vasilyan), Kars, 1913 ◆ Khachik Grigori Ter-Baghdasaryan, Mush, Argavank, 1908 ◆ Khachik Gurikhi Konjoyan, Terjan, Khas gyugh, 1909 ◆ Khachik Hakobi Stepanyan, Akhalkalak, Murjakhet, 1913 ◆ Khachik Hambardzumi Nikoghosyan, Basen, Arjarak, 1913 ◆ Khachik Hambari Hamboyan, Akhalkalak, 1917 ◆ Khachik Harutyuni Harutyunyan, Gharakilise, Tapanli, 1914 ◆ Khachik Hovhannesi Saroyan (Khachatryan), Alekpol, Toparlu, 1914 ◆ Khachik Khachaturi Hovhannisyan (Khachatryan), Van, 1918 ◆ Khachik Knyazi Hakobyan, Leninakan, Araz, 1914 ◆ Khachik Knyazi Hovhannisyan (Knyazyan), Leninakan, Ghasmali, 1911 ◆ Khachik Lyudvigi Sargsyan, Kars, 1910 ◆ Khachik Manuki Hambaryan, Shirak, Taknal, 1912 ◆ Khachik Manuki Papayan (Manukyan), Van, Shahbagh, 1907 ◆ Khachik Martirosi Hambardzumyan, Persia, Vina, 1917 ◆ Khachik Martirosi Shahinyan (Martirosyan), Akhlat, Prkhuz, 1909 ◆ Khachik Meliki Tumasyan, Kars, Glmir, 1915 ◆ Khachik Mesropi Mesropyan (Khachikyan), 1921 ◆ Khachik Minasi Gharibyan, Surmalu, Dashburan, 1907 ◆ Khachik Misaki Misakyan (Tovmasyan), Leninakan, Paldlu, 1914 ◆ Khachik Mkrtchi (Kolotyan) Mkrtchyan, Basen, Krtaban, 1914 ◆ Khachik Mkrtchi Hovhannisyan (Mkrtchyan), Van, Ishkhanakond, 1911 ◆ Khachik Movsesi Sargsyan, Leninakan, Toros, 1918 ◆ Khachik Nersesi Muradyan, Van, Noraduz, 1911 ◆ Khachik Ohani Abrahamyan, Erzrum, Arjarak, 1907 ◆ Khachik Petrosi Avetisyan (Petrosyan), Basen, Islam dzor, 1914 ◆ Khachik Sargsyan, 1923 ◆ Khachik Sergoyi Kharazyan, Akhalkalak, Pokr Kenturi, 1914 ◆ Khachik Smbati Hovsepyan / Khachikyan, Shirak, Pokr Keti, 1917 ◆ Khachik Smbati Karapetyan, Van, 1915 ◆ Khachik Smbati Vardanyan, Alekpol, Bozdoghan, 1915 ◆ Khachik Tadevosi Gyulbazyan, Kars, Kaghzvan, 1915 ◆ Khachik Tamuri Asatryan, Kars, 1919 ◆ Khachik Tatosi Amiryan, Gharakilisa, Gyoran, 1914 ◆ Khachik Tovmasi Tovmasyan, Bitlis, Khizan, 1910 ◆ Khachik Vardani Vardanyan, Khnus, Gharakoghb, 1914 ◆ Khachik Yenoki Martirosyan, Alekpol, Kaps, 1914 ◆ Khacho Kndoyi Temurov, Kars, Tegor, 1919 ◆ Khala Karoyi Karoyan, Nakhijevan, 1914 ◆ Khalat Gevorgi Mkhitaryan, Turkey, Yonjalu, 1911 ◆ Khalat Moskovi Hakobyan, Bulanagh, Rostomgedak,

1913 ◆ Khalat Musheghi Gevorgyan, Erzrum, Shnstan, 1914 ◆ Khamberi Nazari Yeghoyants (Nazaryan), Basen, Gomadzor, 1910 ◆ Khanaev Khachaturi Harutyunyan, Kars, Aghjaghala, 1913 ◆ Khanaev Sergoyi Sergoyan, Alekpol, Ghonakhran, 1917 ◆ Khanamir Arseni Mikayelyan, Kars, Bayrakhtar, 1912 ◆ Khanamir Avetisi Grigoryan (Stepanyan), Mush, 1913 ◆ Khanamir Gabrieli Vahanyan (Gabrielyan), Kars, Ortakadiklar, 1913 ◆ Khanamir Hovhannesi Manukyan, Alashkert, Ashkhulva, 1913 ◆ Khanan Sukiasi Sukiasyan, Leninakan, Khurtburagh, 1916 ◆ Khane Yeghishi Yeghishyan, Mastara, 1919 ◆ Khanik Hmayaki Tonoyan, Kars, Bashshoragyal, 1915 ◆ Khanperi Hovhannesi Sargsyan, Basen, Gomadzor, 1911 ◆ Khanum (Khumar) Movsesi Movsisyan (Hashoyan), Bulanagh, Machtlu, 1914 ◆ Khanum Abrahami Gogoryan, Alekpol, Illi, 1914 ◆ Khanum Armenaki Mkrtchyan, Kars, Paldrvan, 1916 ◆ Khanum Arshaki Sargsyan (Arshakyan), Nakhijevan, Jalal, 1910 ◆ Khanum Artashesi Sargsyan (Artashyan), Gharakilisa, Ghshlagh, 1911 ◆ Khanum Avdali Petrosyan, Bulanagh, Kop, 1917 ◆ Khanum Avetisi Avetisyan (Serobyan), Akhalkalak, 1915 ◆ Khanum Ayvazi Ayvazyan, Basen, Hasnkar, 1914 ◆ Khanum Baghdasari Baghdasaryan, Khnus, 1915 ◆ Khanum Beybuti Tarkhanyan, Nukhi, Mejlis, 1909 ◆ Khanum Galusti Galstyan, Nor Bayazet, Kyavar, 1914 ◆ Khanum Gerasimi Yekhtaryan, Kars, Gharajala, 1909 ◆ Khanum Gevorgi Gevorgyan, Khnus, Khuzlu, 1914 ◆ Khanum Gevorgi Poghosyan, Hin Nakhijevan, 1913 ◆ Khanum Haruti Ghazaryan, Alekpol, Khonaghran, 1916 ◆ Khanum Harutyuni Gevorgyan, Bulanagh, Kop, 1917 ◆ Khanum Harutyuni Harutyunyan, Van, 1918 ◆ Khanum Hovhannesi Hovhannisyan, Shirak, Khonakhran, 1919 ◆ Khanum Israyeli Sanosyan (Israyelyan), Erzrum, Gomadzor, 1910 ◆ Khanum Karapeti Hakobyan, Kaghzvan, 1912 ◆ Khanum Karapeti Mkhitaryan, Manazkert, Norashen, 1913 ◆ Khanum Khachaturi Petrosyan, Kars, Ughuzli, 1909 ◆ Khanum Manuki Manukyan, Van, Akants, 1914 ◆ Khanum Martirosi Davtyan, Van, Noraduz, 1910 ◆ Khanum Meliki Melikyan (Melkonyan, Alashkert, 1914 ◆ Khanum Melkoni Tumasyan, Bulanagh, Kharakhol, 1909 ◆ Khanum Mkrtchi Grigoryan, Alekpol, Duzkharaba, 1914 ◆ Khanum Moskovi Hovhannisyan, Bulanagh, Teghuk, 1913 ◆ Khanum Movsesi Aghababyan, Alekpol, Toros, 1913 ◆ Khanum Movsesi Hakobyan, Van, Soskun, 1913 ◆ Khanum Movsesi Harutyunyan, Jalal oghli, Lorut, 1915 ◆ Khanum Mukayeli Martirosyan, Leninakan, Talin, 1913 ◆ Khanum Muradi Arakelyan (Muradyan), Manazkert, Berd, 1912 ◆ Khanum Nazareti Nazaretyan, Alekpol, Toros, 1911 ◆ Khanum Nikoghosi Nikoghosyan, Alekpol, Toros, 1914 ◆ Khanum Nshani Mnoyan (Nshanyan), Kghi, Astghaberd, 1912 ◆ Khanum Sahaki Hakobyan (Sahakyan), Aparan, Damjlu, 1913 ◆ Khanum Sargsi Gharibyan, Kars, Kyadiklar, 1911 ◆ Khanum Serobi Avagyan, Nakhijevan, Yerminja, 1917 ◆ Khanum Soghomoni Harutyunyan (Soghomonyan), Alashkert, Gharakilisa, 1914 ◆ Khanum Stepani Dallakyan, Jalaloghli, Mazart, 1913 ◆ Khanum Tadevosi Chakhoyan, Kars, Sarighamish, 1910 ◆ Khanum Tadevosi Mnoyan, Akhalkalak, Ikhtila, 1914 ◆ Khanum Tigrani Tonoyan (Tigranyan), Manazkert, Rostamgedak, 1911 ◆ Khanum Zakari Grigoryan, Basen, Gomadzor, 1911 ◆ Khaser Abgari Abgaryan, Kars, Svanverdi, 1916 ◆ Khashush Khachaturi Khachatryan, Van, 1908 ◆ Khasik Badali Baghdasaryan, Alashkert, Yonjala, 1915 ◆ Khatun Avagi Petrosyan (Avagyan), Karin, Khnus, 1908 ◆ Khatun Avetisi Avetisyan, Nor Bayazet, 1915 ◆ Khatun Daviti Gharibyan, Archesh, Soskan, 1912 ◆ Khatun Hakobi Hakobyan, Bulanagh, Kop, 1912 ◆ Khatun Hovsepi Harutyunyan, Manazkert, Derik, 1911 ◆ Khatun Martirosi Martirosyan, Manazkert, 1914 ◆ Khatun Matevosi Vardanyan, Nakhijevan, Damurzndan, 1912 ◆ Khatun Nazari Nazaryan, Mush, Khnus, 1912 ◆ Khatun Sargsi Khachatryan (Sargsyan), Kharberd, Sevjugh, 1909 ◆ Khatun Simoni Minasyan, Ardahan, Chavush, 1913 ◆ Khatun Vardani Grigoryan (Vardanyan), Karin, Khnus, 1910 ◆ Khatunik Gerasimi Chakhoyan, Kars, 1911 ◆ Khazal Ghazari Ghazaryan, Bulanagh, Kharabshugh, 1913 ◆ Khazal Khachatri Khachatryan, Van, Haviz, 1913 ◆ Khazal Manuki Hakobyan (Manukyan), Manazkert, Maymus, 1907 ◆ Khazal Movsesi Movsisyan, Khnus, 1911 ◆ Khedif Muradi Muradyan (Tumasyan), Bulanagh, Yonjali, 1915 ◆ Khngenik Abrahami Khanbudyan, Igdir, Yevjilar, 1911 ◆ Khnkaber Tumasi Shishkoyan, Erzrum, Ghzlkilisa, 1910 ◆ Khnko Sedraki Sukoyan, Alashkert, Khastura, 1914 ◆ Khnkyanos Hovakimi Danielyan, Kars, Tikor, 1906 ◆ Khoren (Manuki) Andreasi Manukyan, Kars, Berna, 1917 ◆ Khoren Abeli Aghajanyan, Akhalkalak, Aragyal, 1913 ◆ Khoren Arakeli (Manuki) Terteryan (Torosyan), Kharberd, Lazvan, 1912 ◆ Khoren Arshaki Sargsyan, Shamakhi, Khanlija, 1916 ◆ Khoren Artashesi Martirosyan, Tiflis, 1910 ◆ Khoren Avoyi (Avoyan) Avdalyan, Khnus, Gharachoban, 1912 ◆ Khoren Chutikyan, 1920 ◆ Khoren Gabrieli Gabrielyan (Sargsyan), Erzrum, Chkhlnoz, 1910 ◆ Khoren Galusti Hovhannisyan, Pambak, Sarmisaghli, 1914 ◆ Khoren Gaspari Barseghyan, Shirak, Illi, 1911 ◆ Khoren Hovhannesi Hakobyan (Hovhannisyan), Erzrum, Agrak, 1914 ◆ Khoren Hovhannesi Manvelyan, Alashkert, Iritsu, 1908 ◆ Khoren Ivani Baghdasaryan, Nakhijevan, Aylapat, 1915 ◆ Khoren Khachiki Khachikyan, Erzrum, 1917 ◆ Khoren Martirosi Aharonyan, Kharberd, Khozat, 1907 ◆ Khoren Matevosi Gasparyan, Shirak, Ghzl-ghoch, 1918 ◆ Khoren Mikayeli Revazyan, Ghzlar, 1915 ◆ Khoren Minasi Minasyan, Alekpol, Samrlu, 1916 ◆ Khoren Mkrtchi (Gaboyi) Mkrtchyan, Alekpol, Keftalu, 1915 ◆ Khoren Nersesi Hovhannisyan, Akhalkalak, 1917 ◆ Khoren Nikoghosi Harutyunyan, Alekpol, Chiftali, 1909 ◆ Khoren Nshani Terteryan (Nshanyan), Terjan, Sarighaya, 1912 ◆ Khoren Petrosi (Aleki) Aleksanyan, Gharakilisa, Hajighara, 1915 ◆ Khoren Srapi Tumasyan (Srapyan), Shirak, Paltlu, 1914 ◆ Khoren Tadevosi Poghosyan, Basen, Chrasun, 1907 ◆ Khoren Tigrani Petrosyan, Kars, 1918 ◆ Khoren Torosi Torosyan, Mush, Berdak, 1918 ◆ Khoren Torosi Torosyan, Mush, Marnik, 1910 ◆ Khoren Zakari Zakaryan, Leninakan, Chiftali,

1915 ♦ Khorik Sukiasi Sargsyan, Leninakan, Khortbulagh, 1913 ♦ Khorot Ghazari Muradyan, Bitlis, Ghlat, 1911 ♦ Khorsik Gevorgi Demirchyan, Ardahan, 1914 ♦ Khosrov Aloyi Vardanyan, Alekpol, Peltikan, 1913 ♦ Khosrov Avdali Harutyunyan, Khnus, Kopala, 1912 ♦ Khosrov Danieli Manukyan, Kars, Khani, 1910 ♦ Khosrov Grigori Tonoyan, Bitlis, Khulik, 1914 ♦ Khosrov Hakobi Davtyan, Akhalkalak, Bandivan, 1912 ♦ Khosrov Hovhannesi Hakobyan, Leninakan, Armtlu, 1909 ♦ Khosrov Khoreni Abgaryan, Akhalkalak, Ghoshabek, 1912 ♦ Khosrov Levoni Petrosyan (Levonyan), Van, Amenashat, 1910 ♦ Khosrov Mesropi Avetisyan (Zakaryan), Alekpol, Norashen, 1912 ♦ Khosrov Mkrtchi Yeghoyan Mkrtchyan, Leninakan, Samarlu, 1913 ♦ Khosrov Mkrtchi Zakaryan (Mkrtchyan), Alekpol, Norashen, 1912 ♦ Khosrov Movsesi Movsisyan, Khnus, 1913 ♦ Khosrov Poghosi Poghosyan, Kars, Syogutli, 1911 ♦ Khosrov Sirekani Mkhitaryan, Kars, 1912 ♦ Khosrov Tigrani Petrosyan, Alekpol, Jlovkhan, 1911 ♦ Khosrovadukht Arshaki (Asaturi) Melkonyan, Kars, Gorkhan, 1918 ♦ Khosrovadukht Hambardzumi Babayan, Hin Nakhijevan, Shekhmahmud, 1910 ♦ Khosrovadukht Hambardzumi Karapetyan, Kars, Pirvali, 1908 ♦ Khosrovadukht Harutiki Ghazaryan, Kars, Tekniz, 1913 ♦ Khosrovadukht Hovhannesi Astvacatryan, Kars, Bashkyadiklar, 1910 ♦ Khosrovadukht Petrosi Muradyan, Kars, Tekniz, 1909 ♦ Khosrovadukht Saroyi Aristakesyan, Leninakan, Tharli, 1910 ♦ Khosrovadukht Smbati Smbatyan, Shirak, Illi, 1917 ♦ Khosrovadukht Tadevosi Hakobyan (Khojumyan), Leninakan, Svanverdi, 1910 ♦ Khosrovadukht Tigrani Tigranyan, Vagharshapat, Aghjaghala, 1918 ♦ Khosrovadukht Yeghiazari Barseghyan, Kars, Araz, 1912 ♦ Khosrovik (Khosrovadukht) Smbati Yagoryan, Kars, Uzunkilisa, 1913 ♦ Khumar Antoni Antonyan, Van, Khzhshk, 1913 ♦ Khumar Khachaturi Khachatryan, Van, Mashtak, 1908 ♦ Khumash Manuki Khosteghyan (Kostanyan), Van, Karchkan, 1908 ♦ Khunar Gevorgi Ghukasyan, Leninakan, Syogutli, 1911 ♦ Khungin Hovhannesi Sargsyan, Kars, Pirvali, 1912 ♦ Khunki Mkhitari Muradyan, Leninakan, Vojakhuli, 1911 ♦ Khurma Sahaki Hakobyan, Shamakhi, Karchevan, 1913 ♦ Khushush Avetisi Avetisyan (Choravetyan), Van, 1914 ♦ Khushush Harutyuni Harutyunyan, Van, Tiramer, 1915 ♦ Kibar Gaspari Gasparyan (Melikyan), Alashkert, Khachlu, 1912 ♦ Kibar Hakobi Harutyunyan, Basen, Armtlu, 1911 ♦ Kibo Grigori Manukyan (Grigoryan), Igdir, Musum, 1913 ♦ Kirakos Avetisi Sargsyan, Basen, Gharapunjar, 1913 ♦ Kirakos Bagrati Gharagyozyan, Akhalkalak, Mec Khanchali, 1915 ♦ Kirakos Hlghati Markosyan (Martirosyan), Khnus, Kopal, 1909 ♦ Kirakos Mkrtchi Zakaryan (Mkrtchyan), Pambak, Aghbulagh, 1914 ♦ Kirakos Ohani Grigoryan (Ohanyan), Salmast, Saramereg, 1910 ♦ Kishmish Galusti Avetisyan, Basen, Ishkhu, 1913 ♦ Kishmish Gaspari Baghdasaryan, Kars, 1909 ♦ Kishmish Gaspari Gasparyan, Karin, Khastur, 1908 ♦ Kishmish Ghazari Muradyan, Bitlis, Karmunj, 1908 ♦ Kishmish Grigori Grigoryan, Jajur, Sariar, 1914 ♦ Kishmish Hakobi Sukiasyan, Alashkert, Gharakilisa, 1910 ♦ Kishmish Hovhannesi Hovhannesyan, Lori, Sarchapet, 1910 ♦ Kishmish Karapeti Karapetyan (Nersisyan), Van, Gangvar, 1909 ♦ Kishmish Karapeti Mkhitaryan, Basen, Chrason, 1915 ♦ Kishmish Khachaturi Khachatryan, Mush, Vardenis, 1912 ♦ Kishmish Khachaturi Yeghiazaryan, Sarighamish, 1912 ♦ Kishmish Markosi Markosyan, Basen, Yaghan, 1913 ♦ Kishmish Meliki Melkonyan, Kars, 1914 ♦ Kishmish Meliki Melkonyan, Van, 1910 ♦ Kishmish Melkoni Martinyan, Mush, Arkavank, 1910 ♦ Kishmish Melkoni Movsisyan, Manazkert, Bulanlukh, 1912 ♦ Kishmish Misaki Soghomonyan, Bitlis, Tapavank, 1909 ♦ Kishmish Nikolayi Avetisyan, Kars, Dashkov, 1916 ♦ Kishmish Nikoli Davoyan, Alekpol, Boghaskasan, 1912 ♦ Kishmish Petrosi Petrosyan, Basen, Bashgyugh, 1915 ♦ Kishmish Poghosi Martirosyan (Poghosyan), Bulanagh, Kop, 1913 ♦ Kishmish Sargisi Sargsyan (Gyulbegyan), Akhalkalak, Tadesh, 1914 ♦ Kishmish Saroyan ♦ Kishmish Serobi Serobyan, Van, Archesh, 1912 ♦ Kishmish Smbati Mikayelyan, Kars, Paldrvan, 1915 ♦ Kishmish Tadevosi Chakhoyan, Kars, 1908 ♦ Kishmish Vardani Vardanyan, Bitlis, Teghut, 1909 ♦ Knar Gevorgi Gevorgyan, Kaghzvan, Tpkhis, 1918 ♦ Knar Karapeti Movsisyan (Karapetyan), Bitlis, Prkhus, 1910 ♦ Knar Manuki Manukyan, Leninakan, Khli Gharakilis, 1917 ♦ Knar Musheghi Darbinyan, Kars, 1910 ♦ Knar Sargisi Karapetyan, Kars, 1922 ♦ Knar Simoni Chobanyan (Simonyan), Akhalkalak, Khojabak, 1915 ♦ Knar Tadevosi Melikyan (Melkonyan), Kars, 1918 ♦ Knarik (Ginevard) Harutyuni Harutyunyan, Akhalkalak, Mamzara, 1911 ♦ Knarik Abrahami Marmanyan, Kaghzvan, 1910 ♦ Knarik Aleksani Frangulyan (Aleksanyan), Zangezur, Alkhatyan, 1914 ♦ Knarik Aleksani Virabyan, Kars, 1912 ♦ Knarik Arshaki Gevorgyan, Shirak, Bashshoragal, 1914 ♦ Knarik Artashi Unanyan, Akhalkalak, Aragova, 1918 ♦ Knarik Artemi Tutunjyan, Kars, 1917 ♦ Knarik Avagi Avagyan, Van, Arinj, 1909 ♦ Knarik Bagrati Petrosyan, Surmali, Panik, 1912 ♦ Knarik Dabaghyan, 1920 ♦ Knarik Daviti Davtyan (Levonyan), Akhalkalak, Tadesh, 1916 ♦ Knarik Galusti Aslanyan, Kars, Mazra, 1914 ♦ Knarik Gevorgi Gevorgyan, Erzrum, 1914 ♦ Knarik Ghazari Ghazaryan, Alekpol, 1920 ♦ Knarik Ghazari Ghazaryan, Kars, 1915 ♦ Knarik Ghazari Ghazaryan, Sarighamish, 1914 ♦ Knarik Ghukasi Vardapetyan, Akhalkalak, Pokr Gendura, 1910 ♦ Knarik Grigori Surenyan (Grigoryan), Lori, Aghkorpi, 1917 ♦ Knarik Hakobi Malkhasyan, 1915 ♦ Knarik Hakobi Mkrtchyan, Alekpol, Toros, 1917 ♦ Knarik Hambardzumi Abrahamyan, Dorbandlu, 1916 ♦ Knarik Harutyuni (Khachatryan) Jihanyan, Karin, Vozna, 1917 ♦ Knarik Harutyuni Harutyunyan, Kars, 1920 ♦ Knarik Harutyuni Petrosyan, Leninakan, Dzitankov, 1912 ♦ Knarik Hayki Topchyan, Kars, 1914 ♦ Knarik Karapeti Mshetsyan, Akhalkalak, Tadesh, 1915 ♦ Knarik Karapeti Nalbandyan, Alekpol, Khlli Gharakilis, 1915 ♦ Knarik Karapeti Serobyan (Karapetyan), Kars, 1915 ♦ Knarik Khachaturi (Arami) Khachatryan, Leninakan, 1917 ♦ Knarik Khachaturi Khachatryan, Nakhijevan, 1917 ♦ Knarik Khachaturi Muradyan (Khachatryan),

Igdir, 1915 ♦ Knarik Markosi Mkrtchyan, Kars, Hamzakarak, 1914 ♦ Knarik Martirosi Martirosyan, Akhalkalak, 1914 ♦ Knarik Mikayeli Voskanyan, Zangezur, 1915 ♦ Knarik Mkrtchi Mkrtchyan, Kars, 1914 ♦ Knarik Mukayeli Mukayelyan (Galoyan), Kars, Chala, 1917 ♦ Knarik Petrosi Petrosyan, Kars, Uzunkilisa, 1915 ♦ Knarik Sahaki Keshishyan, Sarighamish, 1911 ♦ Knarik Sahaki Minasyan, Erzrum, 1912 ♦ Knarik Sargisi Abrahamyan, Karabagh, 1913 ♦ Knarik Sargisi Sargsyan, Kars, 1914 ♦ Knarik Sargisi Sargsyan, Kars, 1916 ♦ Knarik Simoni Simonyan, Akhalkalak, Kuligam, 1914 ♦ Knarik Tigrani Grigoryan, Surmalu, Igdir, 1912 ♦ Knarik Tumasi Azizyan, Bitlis, Koshtyan, 1907 ♦ Knarik Vardani Alaverdyan, Alashkert, Berd, 1914 ♦ Knkush Grigori Khachatryan, Surmalu, Yevjilar, 1912 ♦ Knkush Mkrtchi Manukyan, Van, Alur, 1910 ♦ Knkush Stepani Hayrapetyan (Stepanyan), Surmalu, Alijan, 1913 ♦ Knyaz (Srap) Hakobi Voskanyan, Alekpol, Duzkharab, 1909 ♦ Knyaz Ghazari Movsisyan, Mush, Khut, Shen, 1911 ♦ Knyaz Meliki Sargsyan (Melikyan), Kor, 1914 ♦ Knyaz Serobi Sahakyan (Serobyan), Kars, Tikor, 1914 ♦ Knyaz Sureni Hovhannisyan, Yerznka, 1907 ♦ Kolya Avetisi Avetisyan, Bulanagh, Votnchor, 1914 ♦ Kolya Gevorgi Tumasyan (Aghasyan), Lori, Vardablur, 1915 ♦ Kolya Movsesi Sukiasyan, Kars, Araz, 1913 ♦ Kolya Nazareti Khachatryan, Kars, Berna, 1912 ♦ Kolya Vardani Mkhitaryan (Vardanyan), Zangezur, Norashen, 1914 ♦ Komitas Smbati Mikayelyan, Alekpol, Palutli, 1916 ♦ Konstantin Hlghati Martirosyan, Khnus, Kopal, 1909 ♦ Koryun (Kolya) Artashi Movsisyan, Kars, Bagliahmat, 1919 ♦ Koryun Bagrati Poghosyan, Kars, 1913 ♦ Koryun Hovhannesi Pilinjyan (Sargsyan), Kars, 1912 ♦ Koryun Karapeti Caghikyan, Kaghzvan, 1914 ♦ Koryun Martini Gevorgyan, Kars, 1914 ♦ Koryun Mokrovi Hovhannisyan (Mokrovyan), Khnus, Gharakyopru, 1913 ♦ Koryun Stepani Simonyan, Basen, Stan, 1912 ♦ Kostan Hazarapeti Hovhannisyan, Nakhijevan, Aylabad, 1913 ♦ Kostan Khachaturi Poghosyan (Tadevosyan), Kars, Ortakilisa, 1914 ♦ Kostan Martirosi Martirosyan (Madoyan), Alekpol, Daharlu, 1913 ♦ Kostan Minasi Minasyan, Bulanagh, Gabolan, 1912 ♦ Kostan Nikolayi Stepanyan (Grigoryan), Nakhijevan, Ghazanchi, 1917 ♦ Kosti Aristakesi Amirkhanyan (Vardanyan), Nakhijevan, Damrzndan, 1917 ♦ Kosti Grigori Sahakyan, Yerevan, 1917 ♦ Krist Hakobi Hachyan, Akhalkalak, 1917 ♦ Krist Hakobi Janoyan, Lori, Khotur, 1914 ♦ Krist Levoni Petrosyan, Lori, Vardashen, 1918 ♦ Krist Mikayeli Mikayelyan, Lori, Madan, 1915 ♦ Krist Simoni Simonyan, Van, Farugh, 1912 ♦ Kristine Avetisi Shirakyan, Van, 1908 ♦ Kristine Baghdasari Gabrielyan, Kars, Nakhijevan, 1909 ♦ Kristine Baghdasari Gasparyan, Van, Kem, 1911 ♦ Kristine Khachaturi Aghajanyan, Akhaltsikha, 1907 ♦ Kristine Khachaturi Davtyan (Khachatryan), Leninakan, Dzitankov, 1913 ♦ Kristine Khachaturi Hovhannisyan, Kars, Chala, 1912 ♦ Kristine Kristofori Stepanyan, Van, 1908 ♦ Kristine Manuki Hatsagorcyan (Manukyan), Van, 1909 ♦ Kristine Mkhitari Hakobyan (Mkhitaryan), Bulanagh, Teghut, 1912 ♦ Kristine Petrosi Avetisyan (Sharafyan), Mush, 1909 ♦ Kristofor Zakari Zakaryan, Yerevan, Kanaker, 1918 ♦ Kristopor Harutyuni Serobyan, Karin, Mavrak, 1905 ♦ Kristopor Ingoyi Vardanyan (Aleksanyan), Basen, Totviran, 1913, 1912 ♦ Kristopor Torosi Nersisyan, Zangezur, Angeghakot, 1912 ♦ Ksenia Paveli Smilidova, Lori, Madan, 1911 ♦ Kudrat Minasi Grigoryan (Minasyan), Van, 1912 ♦ Kyaram Danieli Manukyan, Bulanagh, Piran, 1914 ♦ Kyaram Gevorgi Gasparyan, Bulanagh, Shirvanshekh, 1911 ♦ Kyaram Khachaturi Muradyan, Manazkert, Noratin, 1912 ♦ Kyaram Khachaturi Musheghyan, Bulanagh, Agrak, 1913 ♦ Kyaram Khurbati Avetisyan, Bulanagh, Shirvanshekh, 1912 ♦ Kyaram Mkrtchi Mkrtchyan, Manazkert, Gharaghala, 1912 ♦ Kyaram Nazari Avetisyan, Erzrum, Ghara-Kyopri, 1909 ♦ Kyaram Nersesi Nersisyan, Mush, Bulanagh, 1917 ♦ Kyaram Petrosi Pertrosyan, Khnus, Kholmkhakay, 1912 ♦ Kyaram Sargisi Sargsyan, Alashkert, Mankasar, 1911 ♦ Kyaram Stepani Kocharyan (Stepanyan), Bulanagh, Sultanlu, 1912 ♦ Kyaram Tonakani Khachatryan, Manazkert, Khasmi, 1911, 1908 ♦ Kyaram Torosi Galstyan (Torosyan), Archesh, Soskan, 1912 ♦ Kyuregh Avetisi Avetisyan, Nakhijevan, Badamlu, 1916 ♦ Kyuregh Hambardzumi Grigoryan, Shirak, Bughdashen, 1911 ♦ Lala Petrosi Hovhannisyan, Shirak, Bayandur, 1918 ♦ Lala, 1922 ♦ Lalik Batkosi Batkosyan, Yerevan, 1918 ♦ Larvin (Loro) Nikoli Mkrtchyan, Alekpol, Ghazanchi, 1912 ♦ Larvin Kerobi Kerobyan, Alekpol, Shishtapa, 1914 ♦ Lena Hakobi Shakoyan (Hakobyan), Igdir, 1912 ♦ Levon Abrahami Nazaryan (Abrahamyan), Kars, 1910 ♦ Levon Aleksani Hovhannisyan, Alekpol, Kyalal, 1914 ♦ Levon Arami Tonakanyan, Kars, Ardahan, 1911 ♦ Levon Arshaki Danielyan, Kars, Cbni, 1913 ♦ Levon Arshaki Karapetyan (Ghaltaghchyan), Kars, Khani gyugh, 1913 ♦ Levon Artashesi (Zakaryan) Zadoyan, Kars, 1913 ♦ Levon Asaturi Baghdasaryan (Asatryan), Mush, Havaturik, 1909 ♦ Levon Avetisi Avetisyan, Van, 1913 ♦ Levon Avetisi Bayatyan, Nakhijevan, 1913 ♦ Levon Avetisi Shahinyan, Van, 1913 ♦ Levon Baghdasari Ayvazyan, Akhalkalak, Viranakarcakh, 1910 ♦ Levon Baghdasari Gasparyan (Baghdasaryan), Kars, 1918 ♦ Levon Barseghi Bazoyan, Basen, Yaghan, 1911 ♦ Levon Bughdosi Khachtryan, Nakhijevan, Gatababa, 1913 ♦ Levon Danieli Danielyan, Erzrum, Bayburt, 1911 ♦ Levon Danieli Safaryan, Karin, Basen, Hekibad, 1910 ♦ Levon Daviti Yepremyn (Davtyan), Lori, Damin, 1913 ♦ Levon Gabrieli Piltakyan, Akhalkalak, Aragova, 1916 ♦ Levon Gaspari Aleksanyan, Shirak, Arkhvali, 1916 ♦ Levon Gevorgi Gasparyan, Kars, Kyurakdara, 1914 ♦ Levon Ghazari Galstyan, Terjan, Prul, 1907 ♦ Levon Ghazari Sargsyan, Bulanagh, Rostomgedak, 1916 ♦ Levon Ghukasi Ghukasyan, Akhalkalak, Goman, 1914 ♦ Levon Grigori Mkrtchyan, Bulanagh, Bostakyand, 1910 ♦ Levon Grigori Papikyan (Mukayelyan), Leninakan, Khli Gharakilis, 1912 ♦ Levon Grigori Sahradyan (Israyelyan), Kars, 1910 ♦ Levon Hakobi Hakobyan, Alekpol, Tavshanghshlagh, 1917 ♦ Levon Hakobi Hakobyan, Jalal oghli, Shnogh, 1912 ♦ Levon Hakobi Janoyan, Lori, Ghotar, 1916 ♦ Levon Hakobi Vardanyan

(Hakobyan), Bitlis, Teghvut, 1912 ♦ Levon Hovhannesi Avagyan, Pambak, Gharakilisa, 1912 ♦ Levon Hovhannesi Baghdasaryan, Leninakan, Ghanlija, 1908 ♦ Levon Hovhannesi Bezhanyan, Leninakan, Goght, 1912 ♦ Levon Hovsepi Stepanyan (Ivanyan), Tifliz, 1914 ♦ Levon Karapeti Tovmasyan, Kars, Bayburt, 1912 ♦ Levon Khachaturi Barseghyan, Van, 1914 ♦ Levon Khachaturi Khachartyan, Bulanagh, Yonjalu, 1912 ♦ Levon Khachaturi Khachatryan, Erzrum, Kyoprkyo, 1911 ♦ Levon Khachaturi Khachatryan, Yerevan, 1917 ♦ Levon Khachaturi Mkhoyan, Kars, 1916 ♦ Levon Kirakosi Khachatryan, Sarighamish, Hopveran, 1909 ♦ Levon Manuki Manukyan, Van, Yeghegis, 1913 ♦ Levon Martirosi Abrahamyan, Basen, Dalibaba, 1913 ♦ Levon Martirosi Gevorgyan, Tiflis, 1914 ♦ Levon Melkoni Melkonyan (Khalatyan), Tifliz, 1916 ♦ Levon Misaki (Misakyan) Grigoryan, Leninakan, Koraghbyur, 1913 ♦ Levon Misaki Shahinyan, Bulanagh, Sheghyaghub, 1911 ♦ Levon Mkhitari Grigoryan, Kars, Hopveran, 1914 ♦ Levon Mkrtchi (Mkrtchyan) Khachatryan, Leninakan, Sariar, 1912 ♦ Levon Mkrtchi Khachatryan, Kars, Syogutli, 1910 ♦ Levon Mkrtchi Ter-Abrahamyan, Manazkert, Inknakhojan, 1912 ♦ Levon Muradi Mikayelyan, Urmia, 1910 ♦ Levon Nazareti Nazaretyan, Shirak, Toros gyugh, 1919 ♦ Levon Nazari Asatryan, Kars, Paldrvan, 1914 ♦ Levon Nikoghosi Hambardzumyan, Erzrum, Kyarboz, 1912 ♦ Levon Nikoli Ghazaryan (Asatryan), Alekpol, Ojaghul, 1911 ♦ Levon Ohanjani Safaryan, Nakhijevan, 1912 ♦ Levon Ozmanyan ♦ Levon Poghosi Karapetyan, Kars, 1916 ♦ Levon Poghosi Petrosyan, Leninakan, Shishtapan, 1910 ♦ Levon Poghosi Poghosyan, Van, Archesh, 1914 ♦ Levon Safari Safaryan (Gasparyan), Vardo, Dzaner, 1907 ♦ Levon Sahaki Hakobyan, Mush, Khvner, 1912? ♦ Levon Sergeyi Baghdasaryan, Van, Khorants, 1911 ♦ Levon Simoni Atanesyan, Leninakan, Ghazanchi, 1909 ♦ Levon Stepani Antonyan, Basen, Arjarak, 1910 ♦ Levon Stepani Davtyan, Kars, 1916 ♦ Levon Stepani Pichimyan, Akhaltsikhe, 1909 ♦ Levon Tovmasi Mkrtchyan (Tovmasyan), Van, Undzak, 1909 ♦ Levon Vardani Chilingyan, Kars, Kaghzvan, 1910 ♦ Levon Zakari Grigoryan, Manazkert, Norashen, 1914 ♦ Leyli Javadi Gevorgyan, Gyokcha, Kyarband, 1914 ♦ Lia Antoni Antonyan (Khachatryan) (Khachoyan), Alekpol, Kefli, 1913 ♦ Lia Arakeli Arakelyan, Ghamarlu, 1916 ♦ Lia Gabrielyan, Chibukhlu, 1916 ♦ Lia Geghami Ghukasyan, Leninakan, Toros, 1913 ♦ Lia Ghazari Ghazaryan, Alashkert, Khazi gyugh, 1919 ♦ Lia Grigori Gabrielyan, Kars, Uzunkilisa, 1912 ♦ Lia Hovhannesi Khachatryan, Leninakan, Bozdoghan, 1911 ♦ Lia Hovsepi Arakelyan, Yerevan, Gozlu, 1910 ♦ Lia Hovsepi Ghazaryan, Alekpol, Ghazanchi, 1914 ♦ Lian Smbati (Hayrapeti) Hayrapetyan, Aparan, Tamjli, 1916 ♦ Limonea Avrami Kaskachyan, Lori, Yaghdan, 1912 ♦ Liparit Arshaki Manukyan, Nakhijevan, Znaberd, 1910 ♦ Liparit Artashi Martirosyan, Leninakan, Horom, 1916 ♦ Liparit Baghdasari Galstyan, Shirak, Chotus, 1917 ♦ Liparit Danieli Hovhannisyan, Kars, Uzunkilisa, 1915 ♦ Liparit Grigori Baghdasaryan, Kars, Bashkyadiklar, 1913 ♦ Liparit Harutyuni Avagyan, Kars, Ghzlchakhchakh, 1912 ♦ Liparit Hovhannesi Gabrielyan, Alekpol, Boghazkasan, 1923 ♦ Liparit Hovsepi Hovsepyan, Leninakan, Sariar, 1916 ♦ Liparit Knyazi Mkoyants (Knyazyan), Alekpol, Samrlu, 1913 ♦ Liparit Levoni Abrahamyan, Leninakan, Ghonakhran, 1913 ♦ Liparit Petrosi Karapetyan, Alekpol, Bayandur, 1912 ♦ Liparit Sedraki Stepanyan, Yerevan, Changhchi, 1914 ♦ Liparit Smbati Sargsyan, Alekpol, Ghapli, 1915 ♦ Liparit Soghomoni Gevorgyan (Tumoyan), Shirak, Ghapli, 1909 ♦ Liparit Tadevosi Khachatryan, Leninakan, 1911 ♦ Liparit Vardani Gabrielyan, Leninakan, Ghoshavank, 1912 ♦ Liparit Yenoki Pilosyan, Kars, Mec Parket, 1912 ♦ Liparit Yervandi Sargsyan (Adoyents), Kars, Mec Parket, 1913 ♦ Liyay Poghosi Movsisyan, Kars, Bayburt, 1912 ♦ Liza Arshaki Manasyan, Van, Kghzi, 1915 ♦ Liza Bagrati Stepanyan, Ghazarabat, Aghin, 1913 ♦ Liza Grigori Poghosyan, Baku, Girg, 1914 ♦ Liza Karapeti Gasparyan, Kars, 1911 ♦ Liza Tatosi Mukayelyan (Tadevosyan), Yerevan, Shahab, 1913 ♦ Lizik Harutyunyan, Tifliz, 1917 ♦ Lorik Hovhannesi Hovhannisyan, Kars, Bashkyadiklar, 1914 ♦ Loris Andraniki Kopalyan (Poghosyan), Basen, Gomadzor, 1912 ♦ Loris Hovhannesi (Lazaryan) Nazaryan, Terjan, Khashgegh, 1912 ♦ Luko Torosi Karapetyan, Alekpol, Pokr Keti, 1917 ♦ Lusaber Aghaneki Manukyan, Shirak, Boghdughan, 1918 ♦ Lusaber Aristakesi Sakoyan, Kars, Hamzakarak, 1913 ♦ Lusaber Harutyuni Hambaryan (Harutyunyan), Leninakan, Ghoshavank, 1910 ♦ Lusaber Hovhannesi Shahinyan, Alekpol, Gharakilisa, 1912 ♦ Lusaber Khachaturi Khachatryan, Leninakan, Ghpchagh, 1914 ♦ Lusaber Meliki Sargsyan (Melikyan), Kars, Parket, 1912 ♦ Lusaber Mukuchi (Martirosi) Martirosyan, Leninakan, Bandivan, 1917 ♦ Lusaber Petrosi (Hovhannesi) Hovhannisyan, Leninakan, Bayandur, 1915 ♦ Lusaber Samveli Avetisyan, Igdir, Blur, 1915 ♦ Lusaber Simoni Manucharyan, Bayburt, 1912 ♦ Lusia Karpi Aslanyan, Sibir [Siberia], Irkutsk, 1905 ♦ Lusik Adami Petrosyan, Persia, Magu, 1912 ♦ Lusik Aghabeki Ghazaryan, Kars, Tekniz, 1912 ♦ Lusik Aleksani Aleksanyan, Zangezur, Akhlatan, 1914 ♦ Lusik Andreasyan, Tiflis, 1915 ♦ Lusik Arakeli Arakelyan, Khnus, 1912 ♦ Lusik Arseni Arshakyan, Bulanagh, Teghut, 1909 ♦ Lusik Arshaki Hovhannisyan, Igdir, Panik, 1915 ♦ Lusik Asaturi (Israyeli) Israyelyan, Van, Noraduz, 1908 ♦ Lusik Avagi (Harutyuni) Harutyunyan, Basen, Yeghan, 1913 ♦ Lusik Avetisi Avetisyan, Van, Salmast, 1914 ♦ Lusik Avetisi Sargsyan, Alekpol, Babrlu, 1910 ♦ Lusik Badali Badalyan, Akhalkalak, Khospia, 1915 ♦ Lusik Baghdasari Baghdasaryan, Khnus, Chaurma, 1908 ♦ Lusik Bakhshii Avagyan, Baku, 1912 ♦ Lusik Barsami Barseghyan, Leninakan, Bandivan, 1916 ♦ Lusik Barseghi Haroyan (Barseghyan), Basen, Chyuruk, 1909 ♦ Lusik Barseghi Hovhannisyan, Kars, 1908 ♦ Lusik Daviti Rostomyan, Karabagh, Shushi, 1912 ♦ Lusik Eloyi Eloyan, Bulanagh, Takarlu, 1909 ♦ Lusik Fidani (Hambaryan) Fidanyan, Leninakan, Sariar, 1909 ♦ Lusik Gabrieli Minasyan, Van, Pshavank, 1912 ♦ Lusik Galoyi Tovmasyan (Tarvandyan), Alekpol, Chorli, 1911 ♦ Lusik Galusti

LISTING OF ORPHANS 433

Abgaryan, Akhalkalak, 1916 ♦ Lusik Garegini Karapetyan (Vaghoyan), Basen, Ilkhi, 1918 ♦ Lusik Geghami Geghamyan, Yerevan, Kanaker, 1917 ♦ Lusik Gevorgi Gevorgyan, Kars, 1917 ♦ Lusik Gevorgi Gevorgyan, Tiflis, 1918 ♦ Lusik Gevorgi Gevorgyan, Tiflis, 1918 ♦ Lusik Gevorgi Khachatryan, Kars, 1919 ♦ Lusik Gevorgi Yeloyan (Gevorgyan), Alashkert, Yeghantapa, 1912 ♦ Lusik Ghazari Poghosyan, Bitlis, 1908 ♦ Lusik Ghukasi Vardapetyan, Akhalkalak, 1911 ♦ Lusik Grigori (Eroyan) Grigoryan, Basen, Alijakrak, 1910 ♦ Lusik Grigori Baghdasaryan, Aparan, Kyullija, 1912 ♦ Lusik Grigori Khachatryan, Khnus, Berd, 1913 ♦ Lusik Grigori Kyureghyan, Leninakan, Ghzlghoch, 1913 ♦ Lusik Grigori Movsisyan Harutyunyan, Lori, Uzunlara, 1912 ♦ Lusik Grigori Petrosyan (Grigoryan), Vaspurakan, Van-Khachpoghan, 1914 ♦ Lusik Grigori Yeritsyan, Akhalkalak, Satgha, 1913 ♦ Lusik Gyul-Azizi Gyul-Azizyan (Vardanyan), Van, Kendanants, 1912 ♦ Lusik Hakobi Hakobyan, Alashkert, Ahmat, 1914 ♦ Lusik Hakobi Marutyan (Hakobyan), Van, 1909 ♦ Lusik Hakobi Sahakyan, Kars, 1910 ♦ Lusik Hambardzumi Grigoryan, Alekpol, Bughdashen, 1909 ♦ Lusik Hambardzumi Khachatryan (Hambardzumyan), Alekpol, Svanverdi, 1915 ♦ Lusik Hambardzumi Mkrtchyan, Karabagh, Shushi, 1914 ♦ Lusik Harutyuni Harutyunyan, Alekpol, Salut, 1919 ♦ Lusik Harutyuni Harutyunyan, Gharakilisa, 1920 ♦ Lusik Harutyuni Manukyan, Van, Kendanants, 1910 ♦ Lusik Harutyuni Vardanyan, Daralagyaz, Azatert, 1916 ♦ Lusik Hovhannesi Arzumanyan, Van, 1915 ♦ Lusik Hovhannesi Asmatyan, Shirak, Sariar, 1913 ♦ Lusik Hovhannesi Hovhannisyan, Van, Amenashat, 1909 ♦ Lusik Hovhannesi Meltonyan, Kars, 1911 ♦ Lusik Hovsepi (Hayrapeti) Hayrapetyan (Hovsepyan), Shirak, Duzkand, 1917 ♦ Lusik Hovsepi Abrahamyan (Hovsepyan), Van, Archesh, 1913 ♦ Lusik Hovsepi Davtyan (Hovsepyan), Van, Svan, 1912 ♦ Lusik Karapeti Asatryan, Basen, Arjarak, 1911 ♦ Lusik Karapeti Gevorgyan (Grigoryan), Kars, Tekniz, 1910 ♦ Lusik Karapeti Karapetyan, Khnus, Gharachoban, 1913 ♦ Lusik Khachaturi Khachatryan, Akhalkalak, Sultan, 1917 ♦ Lusik Khachaturi Khachatryan, Kars, 1915 ♦ Lusik Khachaturi Khachatryan, Nakhijevan, Norashen, 1914 ♦ Lusik Khachaturi Margaryan, Akhalkalak, Dilif, 1910 ♦ Lusik Khachaturi Martirosyan (Khachatryan), Van, Haskibak, 1907 ♦ Lusik Khachaturi Sargsyan (Khachatryan), Ghamarlu, Davalu, 1914 ♦ Lusik Khachaturi Simonyan, Van, Shamanis, 1909 ♦ Lusik Khachaturi Vardanyan, Van, Avan, 1908 ♦ Lusik Khachoyi (Misaki) Khachatryan, Manazkert, 1917 ♦ Lusik Manuki Asatryan (Manukyan), Akhalkalak, Merenia, 1917 ♦ Lusik Manuki Safaryan (Manukyan), Vaspurakan, Katsakh, 1910 ♦ Lusik Markosi Asloyan, Nakhijevan, Gultapa, 1911 ♦ Lusik Martini Mayilyan, Baku, 1914 ♦ Lusik Martirosi Gasparyan (Madoyan), Pambak, Gyoran, 1913 ♦ Lusik Martirosi Martirosyan, Kars, Gedalu, 1913 ♦ Lusik Matevosi Yenfiratyan, Akhalkalak, Dilif, 1914 ♦ Lusik Matsaki Arshakyan, Kars, Uzunkilisa, 1918 ♦ Lusik Meliki Melikyan (Mirijanyan), Akhalkalak, Khando, 1913 ♦ Lusik Mihrani Hovhannisyan, Van, Psti gyugh, 1908 ♦ Lusik Mikayeli Karapetyan, Shirak, Ghoshavank, 1917 ♦ Lusik Minasi Gevorgyan, Alekpol, Norashen, 1914 ♦ Lusik Minasi Minasyan, Erzrum, Dali baba, 1916 ♦ Lusik Misaki Khachatryan, Kars, Tekniz, 1913 ♦ Lusik Mkhitari Hovhannisyan, Kars, Paldrvan, 1911 ♦ Lusik Mkrtchi Martirosyan, Alekpol, Ghzlghoch, 1912 ♦ Lusik Mkrtchi Melikyan (Mkrtchyan), Etchmiadzin, Ghurdughuli, 1912 ♦ Lusik Movsesi Movsisyan, Gharakilisa, Chotus, 1914 ♦ Lusik Nazari Melkonyan, Kars, Chala, 1915 ♦ Lusik Nikoli Tigranyan, Alekpol, 1914 ♦ Lusik Parsami Harutyunyan, Shirak, Armtlu, 1914 ♦ Lusik Petrosi Galstyan (Petrosyan), Kaghzvan, 1914 ♦ Lusik Petrosi Grigoryan, Van, 1914 ♦ Lusik Petrosi Petrosyan, Alekpol, Pirvali, 1914 ♦ Lusik Petrosi Petrosyan, Kars, Ghzlchakhchakh, 1916 ♦ Lusik Poghosi Poghosyan, Tifliz, 1918 ♦ Lusik Poghosi Sargsyan, Alashkert, Gharakilisa, 1908 ♦ Lusik Sahaki (Hovhannesi) Hovhannisyan, Kars, 1912 ♦ Lusik Sahaki Balasanyan (Sahakyan), Van, Artamet, 1910 ♦ Lusik Sahaki Galstyan, Khnus, Khnusberd, 1906 ♦ Lusik Sahaki Sahakyan (Ter-Poghosyan), Van, Khorgom, 1908 ♦ Lusik Samsoni Margaryan, Hin Bayazet, Arcap, 1911 ♦ Lusik Sargisi Avetisyan (Sargsyan), Alekpol, Aghin, 1918 ♦ Lusik Sargsi Avetisyan (Sargsyan), Van, Angegh, 1909 ♦ Lusik Sargsi Hovhannisyan, Ghamarlu, Yuva, 1911 ♦ Lusik Sargsi Khachatryan (Sargsyan), Khnus, 1914 ♦ Lusik Sedraki Sedrakyan, Aparan, Gharakilisa, 1916 ♦ Lusik Serkoyi Karapetyan, Leninakan, Svanverdi, 1914 ♦ Lusik Serobi (Sargsyan) Serobyan, Erzrum, 1915 ♦ Lusik Shanoyi Tovmasyan, Bulanagh, Shirvanshekh, 1910 ♦ Lusik Simoni Hovhannisyan, Nakhijevan, Chinchili, 1918 ♦ Lusik Simoni Simonyan, Akhalkalak, Sildar, 1917 ♦ Lusik Soghomoni Grishyan, Kars, Bayghars, 1916 ♦ Lusik Stepani Krdoghlyan, Leninakan, Sariar, 1912 ♦ Lusik Stepani Nersisyan, Shirak, Paldlu, 1912 ♦ Lusik Stepani Vorskanyan (Stepanyan), Kars, Gharaghala, 1914 ♦ Lusik T. Harutyuni Hovhannisyan, Bulanagh, Teghut, 1908 ♦ Lusik Tatosi Torosyan, Kars, Pokr Parket, 1914 ♦ Lusik Tigrani Ayvazyan, Akhalkalak, Goma, 1913 ♦ Lusik Tigrani Hambardzumyan, Kars, Mazra, 1914 ♦ Lusik Torosi Arzumanyan, Sharur, Khanakhlar, 1909 ♦ Lusik Torosi Khnustsyan, Terjan, Chamudara, 1918 ♦ Lusik Tovmasi Nazaryan (Tovmasyan), Van, Averak, 1913 ♦ Lusik Tovmasi Tovmasyan, Nakhijevan, 1914 ♦ Lusik Vaghoyi Melkonyan, Tifliz, 1918 ♦ Lusik Vahani Vahanyan, Alashkert, Gharakilisa, 1915 ♦ Lusik Vardani (Gaspari) Vardanyan (Gasparyan), Khnus, 1908 ♦ Lusik Vardani Danielyan, Van, Moks, 1907 ♦ Lusik Vardani Khachatryan (Vardanyan), Van, Pakhezik, 1907 ♦ Lusik Voskani Voskanyan, Alashkert, Garasu, 1913 ♦ Lusik Yeghiazari Nahapetyan, Erzrum, Khnus, 1912 ♦ Lusik Yeghoyi Gevorgyan, Van, Cvstan, 1908 ♦ Lusik Yegori Asatryan, Tiflis, 1918 ♦ Lusik Yegosi Yegoryan, Igdir, Blur, 1912 ♦ Lusik Yeremi Yeremyan, Van, 1915 ♦ Lusik Yervandi Khurshudyan, Alekpol, Horom, 1910 ♦ Lusik Yervandi Mkrtchyan, Yerevan, Nakhijevan, 1915 ♦ Lusik Zakari Shahbazyan, Alekpol, Bughdashen, 1910 ♦ Lusntag

Hovsepi Karakhanyan, Van, Mashtak, 1907 ♦ Lusvard Hakobi Petrosyan, Karabagh, Arpavut, 1909 ♦ Lusvard Karapeti Ter-Samvelyan, Bitliz, Shirvan shekh, 1907 ♦ Lutia Abrahami Tonoyan, Alekpol, Muslughlu, 1913 ♦ Lutsia Muradi Petrosyan, Leninakan, Mec Kapanak, 1912 ♦ Lyuba Dimitrii Vasilyan-Vasileva, Dilijan, 1912 ♦ Lyudvig Aleksani Khachatryan, Kars, Khani gyugh, 1909 ♦ Lyudvig Arseni Mikayelyan, Kars, Bayragh tar, 1909 ♦ Lyudvig Arshaki Sargsyan, Leninakan, Chorli, 1915 ♦ Lyudvig Baghdasari Avoyan, Basen, Chrason, 1915 ♦ Lyudvig Daviti Davtyan (Poghosyan), Leninakan, Musughlu, 1913 ♦ Lyudvig Ghazarosi Arakelyan (Ghazaryan), Basen, Boziyeghush, 1914 ♦ Lyudvig Manuki Nahapetyan (Nalbandyan), Alashkert, Khastur, 1911 ♦ Lyudvig Sargsi Sargsyan, Sarighamish, Dalibaba, 1912 ♦ Lyudvig Srapioni Martirosyan, Kars, Mavrak, 1911 ♦ Lyudvig Yeghiazari Harutyunyan (Yeghiazaryan), Bitliz, 1912 ♦ Maghak Arshaki Nazaryan (Arshakyan), Bulanagh, Yonjalu, 1914 ♦ Maghak Mkrtchi Sahakyan (Hakobyan), Alashkert, Ghazi, 1909 ♦ Magtagh Grigori Sargsyan, Leninakan, Kaps, 1909 ♦ Magtagh Martirosi Ohanyan, Aparan, Shiraghana, 1910 ♦ Magtagh Ohannesi Ohanisyan, Yerevan, Byuzakli, 1908 ♦ Magtagh Sargisi Hayrapetyan, Yerevan, Bashaparan, 1909 ♦ Magtagh Sedraki Scdrakyan, Kars, 1916 ♦ Magtagh Stepani Sahakyan (Stepanyan), Erzrum, 1911 ♦ Makar Arshaki Khachatryan, Igdir, 1914 ♦ Makar Ghazari Abrahamyan (Ghazaryan), Archesh, Irglat, 1907 ♦ Makar Hovhannesi Galoyan, Erzrum, Arjarak, 1912 ♦ Makar Sakoyi Tadevosyan, Alekpol, Ghaplu, 1914 ♦ Makar Smbati Karapetyan (Mecoyan), Leninakan, Svanverdi, 1911 ♦ Mako Gaspari Sedrakyan (Gasparyan), Van, Archesh, 1912, 1911 ♦ Makro Yesayi Yesayan, Alekpol, Mastara, 1914 ♦ Makruhi Abrahami Abrahamyan, Leninakan, Hajinazar, 1917 ♦ Makruhi Aghoyan Ashotyan, Kars, Baglamat, 1919 ♦ Makruhi Amiri Asatryan, Van, Archesh, 1910 ♦ Makruhi Artcmi Hovhannisyan, Basen, 1913 ♦ Makruhi Asaturi Grigoryan, Leninakan, Sirvan, 1911 ♦ Makruhi Aslani Gevorgyan, Van, Karchkan, 1911 ♦ Makruhi Balasani Balasanyan, Van, 1912 ♦ Makruhi Barseghi Barseghyan, Kars, Bagliahmat, 1917 ♦ Makruhi Daviti Davtyan, Van, Moks, 1910 ♦ Makruhi Daviti Gevorgyan (Davtyan), Van, 1911 ♦ Makruhi Gabrieli Sargsyan (Gabrielyan), Van, Khach-kyokhan, 1910 ♦ Makruhi Gevorgi Gevorgyan, Van, Karchkan, 1914 ♦ Makruhi Grigori Grigoryan, Alashkert, Gharakilisa, 1911 ♦ Makruhi Grigori Grigoryan, Hin Bayazet, Korun, 1913 ♦ Makruhi Grigori Grigoryan, Van, Hayots dzor, 1911 ♦ Makruhi Grigori Minasyan (Gevorgyan), Yerevan, Aparan, 1911 ♦ Makruhi Hakobi Abrahamyan, Bitlis, 1910 ♦ Makruhi Hakobi Martirosyan, Kars, Ughuzli, 1913 ♦ Makruhi Hakobi Petrosyan, Van, Hayots dzor, 1909 ♦ Makruhi Harutyuni Tumasyan, Van, Khek, 1911 ♦ Makruhi Jangili Petrosyan (Jangilyan), Van, 1909 ♦ Makruhi Karapeti Avetisyan, Van, Timar, 1909 ♦ Makruhi Karapeti Hovhannisyan (Karapetyan), Van, 1913 ♦ Makruhi Karapeti Karapetyan (Vardanyan), Persia, Perikyop, 1911 ♦ Makruhi Karapeti Sargsyan (Hajiyan), Kars, Ghzlchakhchakh, 1909 ♦ Makruhi Karapeti Sargsyan, Kars, Kyurakdara, 1912 ♦ Makruhi Margari Margaryan, Van, Blten, 1910 ♦ Makruhi Martirosi Khachatryan, Bitlis, Khoztik, 1913 ♦ Makruhi Martirosi Poghosyan, Van, Koghpan, 1912 ♦ Makruhi Mihrani Mihranyan, Van, 1912 ♦ Makruhi Muradi Melikyan (Muradyan), Van, 1910 ♦ Makruhi Musheghi Sargsyan, Kaghzvan, 1917 ♦ Makruhi Poghosi Galoyan (Gatayan), Akhalkalak, Pokr Bendura, 1913 ♦ Makruhi Poghosi Karapetyan, Khnus, 1908 ♦ Makruhi Poghosi Petrosyan, Van, Shatakh, 1909 ♦ Makruhi Poghosi Poghosyan, Van, Balkala, 1913 ♦ Makruhi Sargisi Sargsyan, Karkar, Yerkudzu, 1910 ♦ Makruhi Senoyi Arzumanyan, Akhalkalak, Khojabek, 1912 ♦ Makruhi Shaheni Shahenyan, Van, Plten, 1914 ♦ Makruhi Simoni Simonyan (Margaryan), Van, Pstik gyugh, 1912 ♦ Makruhi Simoni Simonyan, Van, Karchkan, 1914 ♦ Makruhi Tigrani Ghandilyan, Alashkert, Iritsu gyugh, 1911 ♦ Makruhi Tumasi Mikayelyan, Van, Pstik gyugh, 1914 ♦ Makruhi Voskani Voskanyan (Gasparyan), Aparan, Ilanchalan, 1912 ♦ Makrun Meliki Manukyan, Leninakan, Mec Kapanak, 1911 ♦ Maksim Piloyi Simonyan, Tiflis, 1908 ♦ Malak Avetisi Sahakyan (Nazaretyan), Kars, Nakhijevan, 1911 ♦ Malkhas Mkrtchi Barikyan (Mkrtchyan), Van, Mashtak, 1910 ♦ Mamak Harutyuni Arakelyan, Kars, Gharamahmat, 1912 ♦ Mamash Stepani Hovhannisyan, Hin Nakhijevan, Jugha, 1914 ♦ Mamasha Makari Makaryan, Nakhijevan, Yarnja, 1911 ♦ Mambre Gabrieli Khachatryan, Nakhijevan, Bagran, 1909 ♦ Mambre Harutyuni Harutyunyan, Igdir, Hay-tagh, 1915 ♦ Mamikon Adoni Grigoryan, Alashkert, Akhlali, 1913 ♦ Mamikon Babloni Zabunyan (Torosyan), Akhalkalak, Diliska, 1915 ♦ Mamikon Barseghi Adoyan, Basen, Churuk, 1912 ♦ Mamikon Barseghi Carukyan, Iti, 1908 ♦ Mamikon Daviti Khachatryan, Akhalkalak, Molit, 1911 ♦ Mamikon Gabrieli Manukyan, Kars, Berna, 1908 ♦ Mamikon Garegini Tumasyan, Akhalkalak, Vachyan, 1918 ♦ Mamikon Gokori Ghukasyan, Bandivan, 1915 ♦ Mamikon Grigori Stepanyan, Kars, 1911 ♦ Mamikon Harutyuni Aharonyan (Harutyunyan), Kars, Mec Parket, 1919 ♦ Mamikon Ispiri Tonoyan, Kars, Gedaksatlmish, 1913 ♦ Mamikon Karapeti Karapetyan (Sargsyan), Leninakan, Bashgyugh, 1918 ♦ Mamikon Margari Zakaryan, Kars, Bashkadiklar, 1909 ♦ Mamikon Misaki Misakyan, Alekpol, Tashkhala, 1913 ♦ Mamikon Movsesi Ter-Gevorgyan, Kars, Chirmali, 1911 ♦ Mamikon Panosi Ter-Markosyan (Panosyan), Van, Avan, 1906 ♦ Mamikon Sosi Arakelyan, Alekpol, Gharakilisa, 1915 ♦ Mamikon Tigrani Vardanyan, Kars, Paldrvan, 1916 ♦ Mamikon Torosi Mnoyan, Kars, Bagran, 1911 ♦ Manan (Mariam) Matevosi Matevosyan, Leninakan, Syogutli, 1913 ♦ Manas Maghaki Maghakyan, Kars, Chrason, 1914 ♦ Manas Mkrtchi Soghomonyan (Mkrtchyan), Darachichak, Farush, 1912 ♦ Manaset Meliki Harutyunyan (Melikyan), Leninakan, Illi, 1916 ♦ Manavaz Melkoni Gasparyan (Melkonyan), Manazkert, 1912 ♦ Manik Avetisi Avetisyan, Kaghzvan, Koghb, 1915 ♦ Manik Galusti Peroyan (Broyan),

Akhalkalak, Satkha, 1918 ◆ Manik Ghukasi Ghukasyan, Akhalkalak, Gyoman, 1916 ◆ Manik Grigori Grigoryan, Kars, 1920 ◆ Manik Khachiki Khachikyan, Baku, 1914 ◆ Manik Levoni Levonyan (Saponjyan), Akhaltsikhe, 1916 ◆ Manik Manuki Manukyan, Kars, 1920 ◆ Manik Mikayeli Grigoryan, Pambak, Chotur, 1918 ◆ Manik Rubeni Rubenyan (Sukiasyan), Nor Bayazet, 1914 ◆ Manik Sedraki Hakobyan (Mirzoyan), Kaghzvan, 1914 ◆ Manik Vahani Vahanyan, Akhalkalak, Karcakh, 1917 ◆ Mantash Poghosi Aroyan (Rashoyan), Shirak, Sirvangyugh, 1919 ◆ Manuk Abrahami Davtyan, Kars, Syogutlu, 1913 ◆ Manuk Asaturi Hovhannisyan, Shirak, Jajur, 1912 ◆ Manuk Galoyi Galoyan, Kars, Bayburt, 1916 ◆ Manuk Gaspari Gasparyan, Sasun, Dalvorik, 1911 ◆ Manuk Gevorgi Aleksanyan, Alashkert, Yeghantapa, 1914 ◆ Manuk Gevorgi Gevorgyan, Terjan, Briz, 1910 ◆ Manuk Gevorgi Terjyan, Kaghzvan, 1914 ◆ Manuk Ghazari Hovhannisyan (Ghazaryan), Terjan, Pris, 1908 ◆ Manuk Grigori Sargsyan, Van, Gojer, 1912 ◆ Manuk Hakobi Khachatryan, Besen, Harsnikar, 1914 ◆ Manuk Hambardzumi Hambardzumyan, Bitlis, Teghut, 1912 ◆ Manuk Haroyi Sukiasyan (Hakobyan), Kars, Cbni, 1912 ◆ Manuk Harutyuni Martirosyan (Davtyan), Kars, 1909 ◆ Manuk Hovhannesi Hovhannisyan, Leninakan, Horom, 1918 ◆ Manuk Hovhannesi Margaryan, Basen, Ishkhan, 1910 ◆ Manuk Karapeti Manvelyan (Karapetyan), Nakhijevan, Aprakonis, 1912 ◆ Manuk Khachaturi Ghazaryan, Van, Vozm, 1913 ◆ Manuk Khachiki Mkrtchyan (Khachatryan), Leninakan, Taknalu, 1916 ◆ Manuk Levoni Hovhannisyan, Ghamarlu, Chenchrlu, 1913 ◆ Manuk Maghaki Maghakyan (Grigoryan), Basen, Chrason, 1912 ◆ Manuk Mangasari Muradyan, Van, Archesh, 1911 ◆ Manuk Markosi Petrosyan, Van, Abagh, 1914 ◆ Manuk Martirosi Ohannesyan, Jalal oghli, Ghotur, 1911 ◆ Manuk Mkrtchi Mkrtchyan, Ayntap, 1911 ◆ Manuk Movsesi Movsisyan, Basen, Chrason, 1911 ◆ Manuk Poghosi Manukyan (Poghosyan), Van, Kharkin, 1911 ◆ Manuk Saribeki Saribekyan, Derjan, Chkhnlu, 1918 ◆ Manuk Sedraki Hakobyan, Sarighamish, Ghoshakilisa, 1914 ◆ Manuk Setoyi Petrosyan, Kars, Nakhijevan, 1912 ◆ Manuk Shmavoni Muradyan, Mush, Noratin, 1911 ◆ Manuk Simoni Stepanyan, Aparan, Alikuchak, 1913 ◆ Manuk Yeghiazari Yeghiazaryan (Karapetyan), Van, 1914 ◆ Manuk Yeghiazari Yeghiazaryan, Alashkert, 1913 ◆ Manush Arami Ghazaryan, Kars, Ortaghala, 1911 ◆ Manush Harutiki Aghanyan, Akhalkalak, Vachyan, 1916 ◆ Manush Martirosi Martirosyan, Kars, Kaghzvan, 1913 ◆ Manush Misaki Misakyan, Sarighamish, 1916 ◆ Manush Panosi Grigoryan, Surmalu, Aleto, 1911 ◆ Manush Sargisi Sargsyan, Shamakhi, 1911 ◆ Manush Sayati Movsisyan, Bulanagh, Gharaghl, 1908 ◆ Manushak Arseni Grigoryan, Archesh, Machar, 1908 ◆ Manushak Daviti Amirkhanyan, Pambak, Yeghaplu, 1908 ◆ Manushak Ghazari Hambardzumyan (Ghazaryan), Mush, Khasgyugh, 1915 ◆ Manushak Ghazari Poghosyan, Bashegh, Hessunk, 1910 ◆ Manushak Grigori Karoyan, Nakhijevan, Khznaberd, 1914 ◆ Manushak Hambardzumi Petrosyan, Baku, 1912 ◆ Manushak Hovasapi Azatyan, Igdir, Alighamar, 1915 ◆ Manushak Hovhannesi Simonyan, Gori, Ghzlkilisa, 1915 ◆ Manushak Hovhannisyan, Surmalu, Igdir, 1910 ◆ Manushak Hovsepi Hakobyan, Nakhijevan, Julfa, 1914 ◆ Manushak Khachaturi Tadevosyan, Kars, Ortakilisa, 1910 ◆ Manushak Manuki Manukyan, Van, 1911 ◆ Manushak Musayeli Shakaryan, Nukhi, Gyoybulagh, 1909 ◆ Manushak Nshani Avetisyan, Van, Tiramer, 1908 ◆ Manushak Sargisi Avetisyan, Kars, Tazakand, 1907 ◆ Manushak Sargisi Avetisyan, Kars, Tazakand, 1909 ◆ Manushak Serobi Serobyan (Melkonyan), Mush, 1912 ◆ Manushak Vardani Vardanyan, Alashkert, Khoshan, 1908 ◆ Manushak Vardani Vardanyan, Kars, Zrchi, 1912 ◆ Manvel Avetisi Avetisyan, Van, Kim, 1911 ◆ Manvel Nikolayi Nikolyan, Leninakan, Ghshk, 1906 ◆ Manvel Petrosi Petrosyan, Shamakhi, Madras, 1913 ◆ Manvel Petrosi Ter-Manvelyan, Ardven, 1908 ◆ Manya Antoni Rostomyan, Akhalkalak, Karzakh, 1911 ◆ Manya Arshaki Arshakyan (Badalyan), Karabagh, Shushi, 1914, 1912 ◆ Manya Artashesi Varoyan, Kars, 1908 ◆ Manya Avetisi Simonyan (Avetisyan), Leninakan, 1917 ◆ Manya Ghazari Ghazaryan, Shirak, Aghin, 1915 ◆ Manya Harutyuni Harutyunyan (Papikyan), Akhalkalak, Diliska, 1912 ◆ Manya Harutyuni Hovhannisyan, Yerevan, Darachichak, 1913 ◆ Manya Hovhannesi Hakobyan, Alekpol, Ghonaghran, 1912 ◆ Manya Hovhannesi Hovhannisyan (Sargsyan), Kaghzvan, 1907 ◆ Manya Hovhannesi Sardaryan (Hovhannisyan), Pambak, Ghaltaghchi, 1915 ◆ Manya Karapeti Muradyan (Karapetyan), Kars, 1911 ◆ Manya Khoreni Poghosyan, Igdir, Koghp, 1914 ◆ Manya Kostani Petrosyan (Kostanyan), Alekpol, 1913 ◆ Manya Mambrei Mambreyan, Yerevan, Gomadzor, 1913 ◆ Manya Margari Margaryan, 1916 ◆ Manya Mkrtchi Arshakyan, Nakhijevan, 1911 ◆ Manya Mkrtchi Arzumanyan, Nukhi, 1916 ◆ Manya Musheghi Zakaryan, Igdir, Aleklu, 1913 ◆ Manya Sahaki Sargsyan (Sahakyan), Karabagh, Shushi, 1913 ◆ Manya Sedraki Ghazaryan, Baku, Madras, 1915 ◆ Manya Smbati Grigoryan (Smbatyan), Leninakan, Duzkharaba, 1914 ◆ Manya Stepani Dzerdazkyan, Leninakan, 1923 ◆ Manya Stepani Gurgenyan, (Stepanyan), Nakhijevan, Abrakonis, 1917 ◆ Manya Tonoyi Borjoyan, Shirak, Khli Gharakilis, 1913 ◆ Manya Tonoyi Sirunyan, Leninakan, Gharakilisa, 1918 ◆ Manya Yeghishi Harutyunyan, Leninakan, 1914 ◆ Manya Zaveni (Zakari) Ter-Zavenyan, Basen, Yaghan, 1914 ◆ Manyak Gaspari Melkonyan, Igdir, Blur, 1908 ◆ Manyak Sedraki Sedrakyan, Surmalu, Alijan, 1914 ◆ Manyak Simoni Simonyan, Sarighamish, 1916 ◆ Manyak Yeghishei Saghatelyan, Akhalkalak, Vachyan, 1911 ◆ Margar Aloyi Botoyan, Mush, Bulanagh, 1910 ◆ Margar Gabrieli Gabrielyan, Kars, Dalibaba, 1912 ◆ Margar Ghevondi Papikyan, Nakhijevan, Shurut, 1912 ◆ Margar Hambardzumi Hambardzumyan, Nakhijevan, 1916 ◆ Margar Harutyuni Hayrapetyan, Nakhijevan, Aznaberd, 1915 ◆ Margar Harutyuni Melkonyan, Alashkert, 1911 ◆ Margar Harutyuni Yepremyan, Bulanagh, 1912 ◆ Margar Khachaturi Petrosyan, Van, 1902 ◆ Margar Mikayeli Makaryan

(Revazyan), North Caucasus, Ghzlar, 1911 ♦ Margar Vardani Hovhannisyan, Kars, 1915 ♦ Margar Vardani Vardanyan, Bitlis, Karp, 1910 ♦ Margarit Abgari Abgaryan, Kars, Bashshoragyal, 1913 ♦ Margarit Abrahami Danielyan, Kars, Hamzakarak, 1909 ♦ Margarit Abrahami Manukyan, Kars, Bayghara, 1908 ♦ Margarit Abrahami Sargsyan, Kars, 1910 ♦ Margarit Aghasii Vardanyan (Aghanyan), Yerevan, Aparan, 1911 ♦ Margarit Andreasi Geghamyan (Hovhannisyan), Van, Khizan, 1912 ♦ Margarit Arami Flagoryan, Basen, Yaghan, 1913 ♦ Margarit Arshaki Badalyan, Baku, 1912 ♦ Margarit Avetisi Avetisyan, Kars, Ghosyuchyugh, 1911 ♦ Margarit Avetisi Avetisyan, Khnus, Kaghkik, 1910 ♦ Margarit Avetisi Avetisyan, Tiflis, 1919 ♦ Margarit Avetisi Avetisyan, Van, 1912 ♦ Margarit Baghdasari Baghdasaryan (Musheghyan), Khnus, 1919 ♦ Margarit Danieli Maloyan, Kars, Bashshoragal, 1914 ♦ Margarit Daviti Galstyan, Mush, Vardenis, 1914 ♦ Margarit Galusti Melkonyan, Lori, Karinj, 1916 ♦ Margarit Gevorgi Gevorgyan, Van, Norashen, 1912 ♦ Margarit Grigori Grigoryan, Van, Anapat, 1908 ♦ Margarit Hakobi Gaboyan, Kars, Mec Parket, 1911 ♦ Margarit Hakobi Hakobyan, Karchkan, Koms, 1913 ♦ Margarit Hakobi Melikyan, Etchmiadzin, Tashburn, 1911 ♦ Margarit Harutyuni Dallakyan, Pambak, Hajighara, 1913 ♦ Margarit Harutyuni Poghosyan, Yerznka, Mec Akrak, 1910 ♦ Margarit Hayrapeti Hayrapetyan, Nor Bayazet, 1913 ♦ Margarit Hovhannesi Hovhannisyan, Van, 1914 ♦ Margarit Hovhannesi Hovhannisyan, Van, Karchkan, 1913 ♦ Margarit Hovhannesi Manukyan, Leninakan, Ghazarapat, 1912 ♦ Margarit Hovhannesi Petrosyan, Kharberd, Surban, 1909 ♦ Margarit Hovsepi Marutyan, Bulanagh, Hamzashekh, 1910 ♦ Margarit Kalashi Kalashyan, Kars, Gedaksatlmish, 1914 ♦ Margarit Karapeti Karapetyan, Erzrum, Keghi, 1908 ♦ Margarit Karapeti Sahakyan, Van, Boghazkyasan, 1913 ♦ Margarit Khachaturi Aleksanyan, Akhalkalak, Vachyan, 1910 ♦ Margarit Khachaturi Grigoryan, Kars, 1918 ♦ Margarit Khachaturi Khachatryan, Alekpol, Panik, 1916 ♦ Margarit Khachaturi Khachatryan, Erzrum, Bagarij, 1909 ♦ Margarit Khlaghti Karapetyan, Kars, Paldrvan, 1913 ♦ Margarit Kostani Kostanyan, Yerevan, Madan, 1917 ♦ Margarit Mikayeli Mikayelyan, Karchkan, Vanik, 1911 ♦ Margarit Mikayeli Varosyan, Leninakan, 1915 ♦ Margarit Minasi Minasyan, Kars, Bagran, 1908 ♦ Margarit Misaki Margaryan (Misakyan), Erzrum, Babert, 1909 ♦ Margarit Mkhitari Mkhitaryan, Mush, Sheykhaghab, 1910 ♦ Margarit Mkrtchi Stepanyan (Mkrtchyan), Khnus, 1913 ♦ Margarit Muradi Melkonyan, Van, 1916 ♦ Margarit Nshani Petrosyan (Nshanyan), Van, Voskepat, 1910 ♦ Margarit Patvakani Arakelyan Dallakyan, Nukhi, 1914 ♦ Margarit Petrosi Petrosyan, Van, 1910 ♦ Margarit Petrosi Petrosyan, Van, 1912 ♦ Margarit Petrosi Petrosyan, Van, Mokhraberd, 1910 ♦ Margarit Petrosi Vardanyan, Kars, Gedaksatlmish, 1910 ♦ Margarit Pilosi Hayrapetyan, Akhalkalak, Ikhtila, 1913 ♦ Margarit Saghateli Ayvazyan, Kars, Armtlu, 1911 ♦ Margarit Sahaki Baghoyan, Yerznka, 1908 ♦ Margarit Sargisi Gasparyan, Kars, Baglamat, 1913 ♦ Margarit Sedraki Sedrakyan, Bitlis, 1913 ♦ Margarit Sedraki Sedrakyan, Khnus, Kaghkik, 1908 ♦ Margarit Seyrani Mirakyan, Van, 1910 ♦ Margarit Simoni Simonyan, Sardarapat, Margar, 1909 ♦ Margarit Simoni Simonyan, Yerevan, Etchmiadzin, 1910 ♦ Margarit Stepani Carukyan (Stepanyan), Alekpol, Toparli, 1910 ♦ Margarit Tigrani Tigranyan, Kars, Paldrvan, 1917 ♦ Margarit Tovmasi Nazaryan (Tovmasyan), Van, Averak, 1910 ♦ Margarit Vahani Snkhshyan, Akhalkalak, Chandura, 1914 ♦ Margarit Yeghiazari Yeghiazaryan, Bitlis, Sasik, 1911 ♦ Margarit Yervandi Khachatryan (Poghosyan), Kars, Parket, 1912 ♦ Margarit Zakari Galstyan, Bulanagh, Bakarlu, 1913 ♦ Margo Grigori Grigoryan (Hayrapetov), Lori, Akhkorp, 1916 ♦ Margo Muradi Malkhasyan (Muradyan), Van, Noraduz, 1910 ♦ Margo Sargsi Gyozalyan, Tiflis, 1913 ♦ Margush Arami Stepanyan, Kars, 1914 ♦ Margush Harutyuni Harutyunyan, Baku, Shamakhi, 1917 ♦ Maria Hovhannesi Simonyan, Leninakan, Mahmatjugh, 1916 ♦ Maria Iraklii Khoblonozova, Lori, Madan, 1909 ♦ Maria Kirakosi Sirakanyan, Alekpol, Imrkhan, 1916 ♦ Mariam (Manya) Hovhannesi Shahnazaryan, Karabagh, Shushi, 1910 ♦ Mariam Abgari Karapetyan, Kars, Syogutli, 1911 ♦ Mariam Abrahami Khachatryan, Gharadagh, Voghan, 1914 ♦ Mariam Abrahami Margaryan (Abrahamyan), Van, Mokhraberd, 1909 ♦ Mariam Abrahami Muradyan (Abrahamyan), Van, Shatakh, 1912 ♦ Mariam Andraniki Gevorgyan, Kars, 1914 ♦ Mariam Andreasi Alamyan, Kharberd, Berd, 1910 ♦ Mariam Antoni Hakobyan, Alekpol, 1912 ♦ Mariam Antoni Petrosyan, Kars, 1914 ♦ Mariam Arakeli Galstyan, Van, Akhorik, 1910 ♦ Mariam Arakeli Tadevosyan, Nakhijevan, Noragyugh, 1913 ♦ Mariam Arami Aramyan, Leninakan, Illi, 1912 ♦ Mariam Aresi Piloyan, Akhalkalak, Azarvet, 1914 ♦ Mariam Arshaki Arshakyan, Erzrum, 1914 ♦ Mariam Arshaki Barseghyan, Akhalkalak, Karzakh, 1915 ♦ Mariam Arshaki Movsisyan, Kars, 1912 ♦ Mariam Arshaki Movsisyan, Yerevan, Nork, 1914 ♦ Mariam Artashesi Davtyan, Alekpol, Syogutli, 1911 ♦ Mariam Artashi Melkonyan, Akhalkalak, Bughashen, 1914 ♦ Mariam Artemi Khudoyan, Tiflis, 1916 ♦ Mariam Atami Kyahiyan (Harutyunyan), Terjan, Pulk, 1912 ♦ Mariam Avagi Mughseyan, Bitlis, Sparkert, 1907 ♦ Mariam Avetiki Khachatryan, Leninakan, Tapadolak, 1915 ♦ Mariam Avetiki Yayloyan, Shirak, Dzitankov, 1910 ♦ Mariam Avetisi Arzumanyan, Baku, Nukhi, 1911 ♦ Mariam Avetisi Shirakyan, Van, 1911 ♦ Mariam Baghdasari Baghdasaryan, Khnus, Khozlu, 1913 ♦ Mariam Baghdasari Baghramyan, Kharberd, Berdak, 1908 ♦ Mariam Barseghi Ayvazyan, Olti, 1913 ♦ Mariam Barseghi Soghomonyan (Barseghyan), Mush, Akrak, 1911 ♦ Mariam Beglaryan, Karabagh, Shushi, 1910 ♦ Mariam Chakhoyi Hunanyan, Kars, Gharamahmad, 1911 ♦ Mariam Chakhoyi Hunanyan, Kars, Gharamahmad, 1911 ♦ Mariam Daviti (Davtyan) Shavarshyan, Yerznka, 1915 ♦ Mariam Daviti Hovhannisyan (Davtyan), Kars, Khoshgyaldi, 1915 ♦ Mariam Daviti Karamanyan, Shamakhi, Madras, 1913 ♦ Mariam Daviti Khachatryan, Kars, 1909 ♦ Mariam Daviti Martirosyan,

LISTING OF ORPHANS 437

Kars, Bayburt, 1911 ◆ Mariam Gabrieli (Abgari) Abgaryan, Yerevan, Darachichak, 1911 ◆ Mariam Gabrieli (Abgari) Abgaryan, Yerevan, Darachichak, 1911 ◆ Mariam Gabrieli Mkrtchyan, Leninakan, 1915 ◆ Mariam Garamani Garamanyan, Vedi Basar, Rehanlu, 1914 ◆ Mariam Gaspari Galstyan, Bulanagh, Kakarlu, 1908 ◆ Mariam Gaspari Gasparyan, Shirak, Toparlu, 1916 ◆ Mariam Gaspari Torosyan, Bitlis, Vanik, 1909 ◆ Mariam Gevorgi Avetisyan (Gevorgyan), Bulanagh, Kakarlu, 1914 ◆ Mariam Gevorgi Gevorgyan, Kaghzvan, Koghb, 1914 ◆ Mariam Gevorgi Manukyan, Leninakan, Bozdoghan, 1909 ◆ Mariam Ghevondi Safaryan, Kars, Ortakilisa, 1911 ◆ Mariam Ghzari Poghosyan, Bitlis, Yersunk, 1910 ◆ Mariam Grigori Antonyan (Khachatryan), Kars, 1908 ◆ Mariam Grigori Ghazaryan, Surmalu, Molaghamar, 1910 ◆ Mariam Grigori Ghukasyan, Alekpol, Bandivan, 1913 ◆ Mariam Grigori Grigoryan, Kars, 1918 ◆ Mariam Grigori Grigoryan, Leninakan, Ghapli, 1917 ◆ Mariam Grigori Grigoryan, Van, 1915 ◆ Mariam Grigori Karapetyan, Kars, 1917 ◆ Mariam Grigori Safaryan, Van, Noragyugh, 1913 ◆ Mariam Grigori Sargsyan, Van, Bertaku, 1910 ◆ Mariam Grishi Gharibyan, Shirak, Khli Gharakislis, 1914 ◆ Mariam Grishi Manukyan, Kars, Mec Parket, 1911 ◆ Mariam Hakobi Abrahamyan (Hakobyan), Basen, Chrason, 1914 ◆ Mariam Hakobi Avetisyan, 1915 ◆ Mariam Hakobi Galstyan (Hakobyan), Van, Archesh, 1907 ◆ Mariam Hakobi Gasparyan (Hakobyan), Mush, Teshi, 1908 ◆ Mariam Hakobi Hakobyan (Yeghiazaryan), Ashtarak, Karbi ◆ Mariam Hakobi Hakobyan, Leninakan, 1917 ◆ Mariam Hakobi Hakobyan, Van, Hazar, 1909 ◆ Mariam Hakobi Manukyan, Alekpol, 1913 ◆ Mariam Hakobi Petrosyan, Alekpol, Shishtapa, 1913 ◆ Mariam Hakobi Serobyan (Hakobyan), Sarighamish, Tarkhoja, 1913 ◆ Mariam Hakobi Tonoyan, Mush, Ablbuhat, 1910 ◆ Mariam Hakobi Vardanyan, Van, Moks, 1911 ◆ Mariam Hambardzumi Avetisyan, Basen, Ishkhi, 1911 ◆ Mariam Hambardzumi Hakobyan, Basen, Kyoprkoy, 1914 ◆ Mariam Harutyuni Hambardzumyan (Taramyan), Turkey, Terjan, 1911 ◆ Mariam Harutyuni Harutyunyan, Mush, Pndikhner, 1909 ◆ Mariam Harutyuni Misakyan, Gharakilisa, 1919 ◆ Mariam Harutyuni Safaryan, Van, Psti gyugh, 1911 ◆ Mariam Hovhannesi Alekyan, Kars, Chermalu, 1910 ◆ Mariam Hovhannesi Danielyan, Yerevan, Aylabat, 1914 ◆ Mariam Hovhannesi Manukyan (Hovhannisyan), Alashkert, Batnots, 1913 ◆ Mariam Hovhannesi Martirosyan, Van, Haspilar, 1910 ◆ Mariam Hovhannesi Mesropyan, Alekpol, 1914 ◆ Mariam Hovhannesi Minasyan, Ardahan, Kars, 1914 ◆ Mariam Hovhannesi Mkrtchyan, Yerznka, 1909 ◆ Mariam Hovsepi Harutyunyan (Hovsepyan), Khnus, Berd, 1911 ◆ Mariam Hovsepi Hokhanyan (Hovsepyan), Van, Gandzak, 1912, 1911 ◆ Mariam Hovsepi Musheghyan, Akhalkalak, 1913 ◆ Mariam Hunani Hunanyan, Turkey, Kghi, 1914 ◆ Mariam Israyeli Danielyan, Kars, 1912 ◆ Mariam Ivani Ivanyan, Yerevan, 1917 ◆ Mariam Karapeti Antonyan, Kars, Sarighamish, 1907 ◆ Mariam Karapeti Antonyan, Sarighamish, 1908 ◆ Mariam Karapeti Avdalyan (Karapetyan), Basen, Hekibat, 1911 ◆ Mariam Karapeti Davtyan, Nukhi, 1916 ◆ Mariam Karapeti Igityan (Karapetyan), Mush, Yavran, 1909 ◆ Mariam Karapeti Karapetyan, Erzrum, Mamakhatun, 1911 ◆ Mariam Karapeti Karapetyan, Kars, Ghoshkilisa, 1912 ◆ Mariam Karapeti Khachatryan, Kars, 1909 ◆ Mariam Karapeti Kirakosyan, Akhalkalak, Tandzi, 1911 ◆ Mariam Karapeti Sanoyan, Van, 1910 ◆ Mariam Karapeti Vardanyan, Tiflis, 1909 ◆ Mariam Khachaturi Aghababyan, Erzrum, Ajarak, 1913 ◆ Mariam Khachaturi Arakelyan, Shirak, Aghin, 1914 ◆ Mariam Khachaturi Khachatryan (Petrosyan), Van, Norashen, 1911 ◆ Mariam Khachaturi Khachatryan, Van, Shahgaldi, 1913 ◆ Mariam Khachaturi Poghosyan (Ghazaryan), Van, Aljavaz, 1912 ◆ Mariam Khachaturi Safaryan (Khachatryan), Van, Hatij, 1911 ◆ Mariam Khachiki Sahakyan (Khachatryan), Sarighamish, Arjarak, 1913 ◆ Mariam Kirakosi Manukyan, Bitlis, Korve, 1909 ◆ Mariam Manuki Abrahamyan (Manukyan), Bulanagh, Teghut, 1908 ◆ Mariam Manuki Gasparyan, Akhaltsikhe, 1912 ◆ Mariam Manuki Melkonyan (Manukyan), Manazkert, Kharaghala, 1908 ◆ Mariam Manuki Reseyan, Kghi, Denek, 1906 ◆ Mariam Manuki Sargsyan, Van, Mokats, 1914 ◆ Mariam Manuki Sargsyan, Van, Moks, 1916 ◆ Mariam Manukyan, Pambak, Gharakilisa, 1918 ◆ Mariam Margari Margaryan, Nakhijevan, 1913 ◆ Mariam Margari Margaryan, Van, Berkri, 1914 ◆ Mariam Markosi Markosyan, Van, 1912 ◆ Mariam Martirosi Gharibyan (Martirosyan), Van, Tiramer, 1908 ◆ Mariam Martirosi Hakobyan, Akhalkalak, Janjgha, 1915 ◆ Mariam Martirosi Hakobyan, Alekpol, 1911 ◆ Mariam Martirosi Harutyunyan, Kharberd, Balishekh, 1909 ◆ Mariam Martirosi Manucharyan, Baku, 1912 ◆ Mariam Martirosi Martirosyan, Van, 1913 ◆ Mariam Martirosi Martirosyan, Van, Khachpoghan, 1915 ◆ Mariam Martirosi Sandrosyan, Akhalkalak, 1908 ◆ Mariam Matevosi Asatryan, Kars, 1910 ◆ Mariam Matosi Hakobyan (Matosyan), Bulanagh, Ortnavu, 1913 ◆ Mariam Matsaki Ghumushyan, Pambak, Gharakilisa, 1914 ◆ Mariam Meliki Melikyan (Shakaryan), Kars, Mavra, 1916 ◆ Mariam Meliki Mikayelyan, 1913 ◆ Mariam Melkoni Malkhasyan, Bulanagh, Teghut, 1912 ◆ Mariam Melkoni Shahinyan, Van, Aljavaz, 1912 ◆ Mariam Mesropi Yeghiazaryan, Bulanagh, 1911 ◆ Mariam Mheri Manukyan (Mheryan), Bitlis, Latara, 1908 ◆ Mariam Minasi Markosyan, Yerznka, Kirsna, 1913 ◆ Mariam Misaki Abrahamyan (Misakyan), Van, Aljavaz, 1911 ◆ Mariam Misaki Avetisyan, Volti, 1907 ◆ Mariam Misaki Petrosyan (Misakyan), Bulanagh, Teghut, 1914 ◆ Mariam Mkrtchi Hakobyan, Nakhijevan, Badamlu, 1912 ◆ Mariam Mkrtchi Mkrtchyan, Van, 1909 ◆ Mariam Mkrtchi Sargsyan, Bulanagh, Kakarlu, 1908 ◆ Mariam Mnatsakani Mnatsakanyan, Akhalkalak, Dadesh, 1914 ◆ Mariam Movsesi Movsisyan, Van, Eribna, 1910 ◆ Mariam Movsesi Petrosyan, Kars, 1911 ◆ Mariam Movsesi Sahakyan, Nakhijevan, Khznaberd, 1911 ◆ Mariam Movsesi Sargsyan, Erzrum, Agrak, 1909 ◆ Mariam Mukayeli Kocharyan, Leninakan, Shishtapa, 1913 ◆ Mariam Mukuchi Mkrtchyan, Alekpol, Syugutlu, 1913 ◆ Mariam

Muradi Aslanyan (Muradyan), Kars, 1911 ♦ Mariam Muradi Avetisyan, Van, Aspashen, 1909 ♦ Mariam Muradi Galstyan (Avetisyan), Van, 1910 ♦ Mariam Muradi Sargsyan, Mush, Avzat, 1913 ♦ Mariam Nazareti Sukiasyan (Nazaryan), Alashkert, Kharaber, 1910 ♦ Mariam Nazari Karapetyan, Kars, 1911 ♦ Mariam Nazari Nazaryan, Alashkert, 1916 ♦ Mariam Nazari Yasagilyan (Grigoryan), Kars, 1914 ♦ Mariam Nersesi (Geghami) Nersisyan, Van, Shahab, 1916 ♦ Mariam Nikoghosi Nikoghosyan, Kharberd, Sorbyan, 1913 ♦ Mariam Nikoli Gabrielyan, Sarighamish, 1914 ♦ Mariam Nikoli Nikolyan, Kars, Ghanlija, 1916 ♦ Mariam Ohani Ohanyan, Sasun, Sghni, 1912 ♦ Mariam Papiki Grigoryan, Van, Khachan, 1908 ♦ Mariam Petrosi (Margari) Petrosyan, Ghanlija, 1917 ♦ Mariam Petrosi Martirosyan, Bulanagh, Machtlu, 1910 ♦ Mariam Petrosi Petrosyan (Poghosyan), Kars, 1909 ♦ Mariam Petrosi Petrosyan, Aghben, Norashen, 1915 ♦ Mariam Petrosi Petrosyan, Kharberd, Avjugh, 1910 ♦ Mariam Petrosi Petrosyan, Terjan, Caghkut, 1911 ♦ Mariam Petrosi Petrosyan, Van, 1908 ♦ Mariam Piliposi Baghdasaryan (Piliposyan), Dvin, 1912 ♦ Mariam Pilosi Aslanyan, Kars, Mazra, 1912 ♦ Mariam Poghosi (Manuki) Manukyan (Poghosyan), Alashkert, 1913, 1911 ♦ Mariam Poghosi Martirosyan, Van, Voskebak, 1908 ♦ Mariam Poghosi Poghosyan, 1918 ♦ Mariam Poghosi Soghomonyan, Van, Archesh, 1913 ♦ Mariam Rafayeli Rafayelyan (Avagyan), Van, 1916 ♦ Mariam Safari Safaryan, Sasun, Tazavank, 1910 ♦ Mariam Sahaki Hovhannisyan, Igdir, 1918 ♦ Mariam Sahaki Poghosyan, Akhalkalak, Vachyan, 1916 ♦ Mariam Sahaki Simonyan (Sahakyan), Van, 1907 ♦ Mariam Sargisi Hakobyan, Khnus, Arus, 1910 ♦ Mariam Sargisi Sargsyan, Kars, 1917 ♦ Mariam Sargisi Sargsyan, Kars, 1920 ♦ Mariam Sargisi Sargsyan, Mush, Modkan, 1915 ♦ Mariam Sargisi Sargsyan, Van, 1916 ♦ Mariam Sargisi Yeganyan (Sargsyan), Kars, Alijakrak, 1909 ♦ Mariam Sargsi Mkrtchyan, Jalaloghli, Lejan, 1914 ♦ Mariam Sargsi Muradyan, Akhalkalak, Chandura, 1915 ♦ Mariam Saroyi Grigoryan, Kars, Pokr Parket, 1911 ♦ Mariam Sedraki Galstyan, Basen, Totaviran, 1914 ♦ Mariam Sedraki Kurghinyan, Akhalkalak, Dadesh, 1913 ♦ Mariam Sedraki Sedrakyan (Davtyan), Alekpol, Sariar, 1918 ♦ Mariam Sedraki Sedrakyan, Erzrum, 1915 ♦ Mariam Sedraki Tumasyan, Shirak, Paldli, 1913 ♦ Mariam Sergoyi Sargsyan, Kharberd, 1915 ♦ Mariam Serobi Hovhannisyan, Khnus, Sosan, 1915 ♦ Mariam Serobi Saroyan, Kars, Dikor, 1908 ♦ Mariam Serobi Serobyan, Khnus, Karakop, 1912 ♦ Mariam Shaheni Amroyan (Shahinyan), Van, Yezekes, 1909 ♦ Mariam Simoni Simonyan, Kars, Ghani, 1911 ♦ Mariam Smbati Karapetyan, Leninakan, Khoshavank, 1913 ♦ Mariam Smbati Smbatyan, 1918 ♦ Mariam Stepani Pashinyan (Stepanyan), Erzrum, Mamakhatun, 1908 ♦ Mariam Stepani Stepanyan, Nakhijevan, Noragyugh, 1914 ♦ Mariam Sukiasi Hakobyan, Erzrum, Arjarak, 1911, 1912 ♦ Mariam Sukiasi Sukiasyan, Kars, Beyliahmet, 1914 ♦ Mariam Tadevosi Amerikyan (Simonyan), Shulaver, 1920 ♦ Mariam Tadevosi Asatryan (Harutyunyan), Kars, Gorkhana, 1920 ♦ Mariam Tadevosi Danielyan, Alashkert, Amada, 1914 ♦ Mariam Tadevosi Madoyan, Erzrum, Herts, 1910 ♦ Mariam Tadevosi Tadevosyan, Kars, 1915 ♦ Mariam Tadevosi Tadevosyan, Kars, Zrcha, 1913 ♦ Mariam Ter-Yeghiazari Ter-Yeghiazaryan, Van, Kavash, 1913 ♦ Mariam Tigrani Danielyan (Tigranyan), Khoyt, Shenis, 1913 ♦ Mariam Tigrani Grigoryan (Tigranyan), Alashkert, Yonjalu, 1922 ♦ Mariam Torosi Ghlajyan, Balvi, Ghoshmat, 1909 ♦ Mariam Torosi Hovakimyan, Terjan, Blku, 1912 ♦ Mariam Tovmasi Avoyan (Asoyan), Kars, Mazra, 1911 ♦ Mariam Tumasi Baghdasaryan, Sasun, Hajo, 1910 ♦ Mariam Tumasi Tumasyan, Van, Lem, 1913 ♦ Mariam Vardanesi Hovhannisyan, Nakhijevan, Shekhmahmud, 1914 ♦ Mariam Vardani Grigoryan, Nor Bayazet, Ghulali, 1916 ♦ Mariam Vasili Gasparyan (Vasilyan), Sarighamish, 1914 ♦ Mariam Voskani Hovhannisyan, Alekpol, Mec Sariar, 1914 ♦ Mariam Yeghiazari Yeghiazaryan, Van, Narekavank, 1914 ♦ Mariam Yeghishi Sahakyan, Akhalkalak, Gimbirda, 1914 ♦ Mariam Yeghoyi Sargsyan (Yeghiazaryan), Alekpol, Taknalu, 1912 ♦ Mariam Zakari Khachatryan, Nukhi, 1916 ♦ Mariam Zakari Zakaryan, Van, Arinj, 1911 ♦ Mariam Zakari Zakaryan, Yerevan, 1912 ♦ Mariamik Vardani Sargsyan, Kars, 1913 ♦ Mariamik Vardani Toschyan, Erzrum, 1908 ♦ Marina Abrahami Ter-Abrahamyan, Van, Tiramer, 1912 ♦ Marina Grigori Ovoyan (Manukyan), Terjan, Priz, 1910 ♦ Marina Martirosi Hovhannisyan (Martirosyan), Alekpol, Tavshanghshlagh, 1913 ♦ Marina Sedraki Mikayelyan, Akhalkalak, Burnashet, 1913 ♦ Marine Abrahami Abrahamyan, Moka, Arinj, 1913 ♦ Marine Azizi Azizyan, Van, 1908 ♦ Marine Hovakimi Hovakimyan, Van, Noravan, 1911 ♦ Marine Manuki Sahakyan, Van, Kem, 1911 ♦ Marine Muradi Mayilbashyan, Van, 1909 ♦ Marine Sargisi Harutyunyan, Van, Khav, 1907 ♦ Marine Saroyi Sargsyan (Saroyan), Alekpol, Bakhtalu, 1915 ♦ Marinos Manuki Karapetyan (Mazmanyan), Bayburt, Lusunk, 1908 ♦ Maritsa (Mariam) Torosi Hovsepyan, Kars, Ghoshakilis, 1911 ♦ Maritsa Avetisi Avetisyan, Kharberd, 1913 ♦ Maritsa Khachaturi Khachatryan, Bitlis, 1907 ♦ Maritsa Safari Davtyan, Khnus, Gharakyopra, 1910 ♦ Marjan Baghdasari Minasyan (Baghdasaryan), Aljavaz, Noragyugh, 1908 ♦ Marjan Hakobi Poghosyan, Alekpol, 1914 ♦ Marjanik Harutyuni Hakobyan, Surmalu, Igdir, 1914 ♦ Marjanik Khachaturi Hovsepyan, Van, 1912 ♦ Marko Martirosi Manucharyan, Baku, 1916 ♦ Marko Sedraki Mkhitaryan, Etchmiadzin, 1912 ♦ Markos Ghazari Hovhannisyan, Basen, Cholakhli, 1914 ♦ Markos Stepani Abrahamyan (Stepanyan), Kars, Bagran, 1914 ♦ Markos Tigrani Grigoryan, Igdir, 1913 ♦ Markos Vardani Vardanyan, Manazkert, Berd, 1912 ♦ Marmar Agheki Aghekyan, Kars, Gorkhan, 1914 ♦ Marmar Hambardzumi Hambardzumyan, Leninakan, Zarnji, 1915 ♦ Marmar Harutyuni Baghdasaryan, Shirak, Gyuzaldara, 1914 ♦ Marmar Sardari Mkrtchyan, Alekpol, Aghin, 1912 ♦ Maro Arshaki Arshakyan (T. Hovhannisyan), Akhalkalak, Vorajalar, 1916 ♦ Maro Arshaki Tumasyan, Shirak, Talin, 1915 ♦

Maro Grigori Mukayelyan (Grigoryan), Van, Lim, 1912 ♦ Maro Hovhannesi Ghazaryan (Hovhannisyan), Van, Archesh, 1915 ♦ Maro Hovhannesi Muradyan, Van, 1908 ♦ Maro Karapeti Karapetyan, Alashkert, Gharaghala, 1905 ♦ Maro Mkhitari Vardanyan, Kars, Kyurakdara, 1909 ♦ Maro Sargisi Sargsyan, 1914 ♦ Maro Tigrani Mkrtchyan (Karapetyan), Manazkert, Gharamlu, 1915 ♦ Marta (Nardos) Torosi Asatryan, Basen, Arjarak, 1909 ♦ Marta Grigori Grigoryan, Kars, Bayburt, 1918 ♦ Marta Harutyuni Harutyunyan, Basen, Dalibaba, 1911 ♦ Marta Hovhannesi Sayadyan, Nor Nakhijevan, Chanakhchi, 1913 ♦ Marta Mahmati Mahmatyan, Yerevan, 1916 ♦ Marta Mkrtichi Paylakyan (Valadyan), Akhalkalak, Jigrashen, 1905 ♦ Marta Nshani Terteryan, Derjan, Sarghara, 1908 ♦ Marta Yeghiazari Yeghiazaryan, Kaghzvan, 1911 ♦ Martik Gevorgi Manukyan, Akhalkalak, Bankli, 1914 ♦ Martin Arshaki Martirosyan, Erzrum, 1914 ♦ Martin Artashesi Sardaryan, Kars, Gorkhana, 1913 ♦ Martin Artemi Artemyan, 1912 ♦ Martin Aslani Melkonyan (Khachatryan), Kars, Ghutni-ghshlagh, 1914 ♦ Martin Avetisi Kirakosyan, Bitlis, Baghesh, 1908 ♦ Martin Karapetyan, Akhalkalak, 1918 ♦ Martin Yepremi Martirosyan, Alekpol, Ghazarapat, 1914 ♦ Martiros (Matevos) Harutyuni Vardanyan, Basen, Archarak, 1913 ♦ Martiros Arakeli Karapetyan, Ghardaghali, Chibukhli, 1912 ♦ Martiros Arakeli Simonyan, Erzrum, Gharahasan, 1912 ♦ Martiros Askanazi Madoyan, Aparan, Shazlu, 1912 ♦ Martiros Barseghi Barseghyan, Basen, Yuzviran, 1912 ♦ Martiros Gaspari Barseghyan (Gasparyan), Basen, Cancagh, 1912 ♦ Martiros Grigori Gharibyan, Basen, Shadivan, 1908 ♦ Martiros Hakobi Hovhannisyan (Hakobyan), Alashkert, Gharabek, 1910 ♦ Martiros Hamoyi Melkonyan, Kars, Mavrak, 1918 ♦ Martiros Hovhannesi Arshakyan, Kars, Cbni, 1913 ♦ Martiros Hovhannesi Hovhannisyan, Van, Norduz, 1912 ♦ Martiros Hovhannesi Mkrtchyan, Basen, Tarkhoja, 1911 ♦ Martiros Karapeti Karapetyan, Kars, 1916 ♦ Martiros Khachaturi Khachatryan, Archesh, Kharkinor, 1913 ♦ Martiros Khachoyi Vardanyan, Kars, Ortakadiklar, 1911 ♦ Martiros Melkoni Melkonyan (Meloyan), Leninakan, Shishtapa, 1916 ♦ Martiros Mkrtchi Mkrtchyan, Bayazet, Koran, 1917 ♦ Martiros Poghosi Poghosyan, Van, Avan, 1911 ♦ Martiros Sahaki Srapyan, Ardahan, 1913 ♦ Martiros Samsoni Sargsyan (Samsonyan), Alashkert, Khayabek, 1909 ♦ Martiros Sargisi Stepanyan, Sarighamish, 1914 ♦ Martiros Sargsi Sargsyan, Kharbert, 1913 ♦ Martiros Tigrani Galstyan, Tiflis, Nor Bayazet, 1915 ♦ Martiros Vagharshaki Karinyan (Gareginyan), Kars, Burshur, 1913 ♦ Marus Antoni Tumasyan, Kanaker, 1911 ♦ Marus Arakeli Abrahamyan (Arakelyan), Alekpol, Bashgyugh, 1912 ♦ Marus Arshaki Arshakyan (Ghadimyan), Ghamarlu, Darghalu, 1920 ♦ Marus Bakhshii Avagyan, Baku, 1912 ♦ Marus Grigori Avetisyan, 1917 ♦ Marus Grigori Grigoryan, Shirak, Mec Keti, 1916 ♦ Marus Hakobi Manukyan, Tiflis, 1916 ♦ Marus Hovsepi Hovsepyan, Shirak, Shishtapa, 1917 ♦ Marus Khachoyi Khachoyan, Leninakan, Gharakilisa, 1918 ♦ Marus Levoni Simonyan (Levonyan), Leninakan, 1914 ♦ Marus Makari Hakobyan, Nakhijevan, Shekhmahmud, 1913 ♦ Marus Mekhaki Sisoyan, Tiflis, 1913 ♦ Marus Mkrtichi Hovhannisyan, Nor Bayazet, Kyavar, 1914 ♦ Marus Movsesi Babayan, Gyokcha, Kyalband, 1914 ♦ Marus Poghosi Grigoryan, Igdir, 1914 ♦ Marus Poghosi Poghosyan, Tiflis, 1920 ♦ Marus Yesayi Arakelyan (Mkrtchyan), Igdir, 1913 ♦ Marusya (Mariam) Arshaki Arshakyan, Van, 1913 ♦ Marusya Arshaki Arshakyan, Bulanagh, Yonjalu, 1918 ♦ Marusya Bagrati Maranjyan, Akhalkalak, Khanchali, 1910 ♦ Marusya Hakobi Hakobyan, Van, Shatakh, 1911 ♦ Marusya Hakobi Vardanyan (Hakobyan), Shamakhi, 1916 ♦ Marusya Harutiki Khachatryan (Avetisyan), Leninakan, Ghzlghoch, 1916 ♦ Marusya Harutyuni Sargsyan, Baku, 1914 ♦ Marusya Hayrapeti Balayan, Karabagh, Shushi, 1914 ♦ Marusya Hovhannesi Hovhannisyan (Arshakyan), Erzrum, 1911 ♦ Marusya Khachoyi Khachatryan, Akhalkalak, 1917 ♦ Marusya Sargisi Sargsyan, Alekpol, Kepanak, 1913 ♦ Marusya Sureni Muradyan, Akhalkalak, Chandura, 1914 ♦ Marusya Yashayi Karzanyan, Shushi, 1913 ♦ Maryanush Tevosi Hakobyan (Dikhtrikyan), Van, 1911 ♦ Mashinka Shirini Harutyunyan, Gandzak, Nukhi, 1914 ♦ Masho Aghabeki Dilsinyan, Pokr Gharakilis, Gilanlar, 1918 ♦ Masho Hakobi Hakobyan, 1918 ♦ Masho Khachaturi Hovhannisyan, Karabagh, 1917 ♦ Masho Mukuchi Aleksanyan, Kars, Dashkov, 1917 ♦ Matevos Aghabeki Martirosyan, Kars, Aghjala, 1914 ♦ Matevos Avetiki Avetikyan (Minasyan), Taknali, 1913 ♦ Matevos Daviti Galstyan (Davtyan), Van, Khachan, 1914 ♦ Matevos Gevorgi Gevorgyan, Van, Kurupagh, 1910 ♦ Matevos Gevorgi Harutyunyan, Kars, Syogutlu, 1914 ♦ Matevos Harutyuni Harutyunyan, Akhalkalak, Holaver, 1915 ♦ Matevos Karapeti Sargsyan (Karapetyan), Sarighamish, 1915 ♦ Matevos Serobi Davtyan (Serobyan), Leninakan, Bandivan, 1915 ♦ Matevos Smbati Ter-Grigoryan, Kars, Kidali, 1914 ♦ Matevos Yepremi Karapetyan, Kars, Gharamahmat, 1909 ♦ Matos Mkrtichi Mukuchyan, Alekpol, Ghapli, 1917 ♦ Matush Yepremi Khachatryan, Surmali, Kizrlu, 1915 ♦ Mavi Hovhannesi Yeghoyan (Hovhannisyan), Bulanagh, Hamzashekh, 1912 ♦ Mavi Kirakosi Hakobyan, Mush, Cghak, 1910 ♦ Mavi Sargsi Sargsyan, Alashkert, Yeghantapa, 1908 ♦ Mavi Vardani Barseghyan (Vardanyan), Mush, 1910 ♦ Mavik Misaki Ghazaryan (Misakyan), Khnus, Khnusaberd, 1912 ♦ Mayranush Abrahami Abrahamyan, Yerevan, 1914 ♦ Mayranush Armenaki Armenakyan (Boyajyan), Nor Bayazet, 1917 ♦ Mayranush Avagi Sargsyan, Akhta, Alapars, 1916 ♦ Mayranush Danieli Gasparyan, Van, Shatakh, 1911 ♦ Mayranush Garegini Avetisyan, Van, 1911 ♦ Mayranush Grigori Grigoryan, Ghamarlu, Hajighshlagh, 1916 ♦ Mayranush Hakobi Hakobyan, Kars, 1919 ♦ Mayranush Hambardzumi Karapetyan, Kars, Oghuzli, 1909 ♦ Mayranush Harutyuni Harutyunyan, Etchmiadzin, 1916 ♦ Mayranush Khachaturi Khachatryan, Mush, 1908 ♦ Mayranush Khachaturi Khachatryan, Van, 1914 ♦ Mayranush Khachaturi Masmyan, Nakhijevan, Nors, 1913 ♦ Mayranush Martirosi Karapetyan (Martirosyan), Van, Artamet,

1914 ♦ Mayranush Muradi Muradyan, Van, 1912 ♦ Mayranush Ohannesi Ohannesyan, Van, Shahbaz, 1913 ♦ Mayranush Simoni Karapetyan, Van, Archak, 1911 ♦ Mayranush Tigrani Karapetyan, Yerevan, 1919 ♦ Mayranush Vahani Hakobyan, Van, 1909 ♦ Mayrush Karapeti Karapetyan, Nakhijevan, Badamli, 1914 ♦ Mayrush Karapeti Karapetyan, Nakhijevan, Badamli, 1914 ♦ Mazi Grigori Aleksanyan, Handab, Koshk, 1912 ♦ Meco (Ghazar) Tigrani Ghazaryan, Akhalkalak, Karcakh, 1911 ♦ Mekhak (Mocak) Levoni Harutyunyan (Kyandrbazyan), Kars, Karmir vank, 1911 ♦ Mekhak Karapeti Baghdasaryan, Alekpol, 1912 ♦ Mekhak Sargisi Poghosyan, Akhalkalak, Karzakh, 1911 ♦ Melik Abgari Abgaryan (Hakobyan), Lori, Khotur, 1912 ♦ Melik Arami Martirosyan, Kars, Satlmish, 1914 ♦ Melik Gaspari Gasparyan (Melikyan), Alashkert, Khachlu, 1917 ♦ Melik Gevorgi Vardanyan, Shirak, Toros, 1909 ♦ Melik Grigori Khachatryan, Kars, Hamzakarak, 1910 ♦ Melik Grigori Melkonyan (Grigoryan), Leninakan, Ojaghghuli, 1911 ♦ Melik Hovhannesi Hovhannisyan, Karabagh, Paraka, 1916 ♦ Melik Mkrtchi Manukyan, Alekpol, Khmrkhan, 1910 ♦ Melik Nersesi Saghoyan (Nersisyan), Akhlat, Darvan, 1909 ♦ Melik Rashoyi Harutyunyan, Aljavaz, Aren, 1911 ♦ Melik Sargsi Arsenyan (Sargsyan), Van, Akhta, 1915 ♦ Melik Stepani Stepanyan, Darachichak, Untamal, 1918 ♦ Melik Sukiasi Hakobyan, Alashkert, Khachlu, 1912 ♦ Melik Tachati Mkrtchyan, Kars, Ughuzlu, 1913 ♦ Melik Tatosi Hovhannisyan (Tatevosyan), Darachichak, Farugh, 1911 ♦ Melik Torosi Hakobyan, Kars, Hamzakarak, 1909 ♦ Melikset Arseni Manukyan, Leninakan, Khli Gharakilis, 1912 ♦ Melikset Badali Mnoyan – Badalyan, Hin Bayazet, 1908 ♦ Melikset Harutyuni Hovsepyan, Van, 1913 ♦ Melikset Mekhaki Chtchyan, Alekpol, 1916 ♦ Melikset Movsesi Hayrapetyan (Movsisyan), Nakhijevan, Davalu, 1914 ♦ Melikset Sedraki Mikayelyan, Leninakan, Marmajugh, 1911 ♦ Melitos Ghazari Ghazaryan, Basen, Aljarak, 1917 ♦ Melkon Abrahami Melkonyan (Abrahamyan), Kars, 1912 ♦ Melkon Asaturi Hakobyan, Mush, 1911 ♦ Melkon Daviti T. Movsisyan, Manazkert, Dolaghbash, 1912 ♦ Melkon Gaspari Sisakyan (Gasparyan), Van, Tiramer, 1910 ♦ Melkon Hovhannesi Ghevoyan (Hovhannisyan), Hamamlu, Parni gyugh, 1915 ♦ Melkon Hunani Hunanyan, Van, Marmet, 1907 ♦ Melkon Martirosi Martirosyan, Van, Khosp, 1913 ♦ Melkon Misaki Hakobyan (Aslanyan), Ardahan, 1911 ♦ Melkon Mkrtchi Sargsyan, Ardahan, Shavshik, 1914 ♦ Melkon Movsesi Hakobyan, Kars, Kachan, 1912 ♦ Melkon Musheghi Petrosyan, Van, 1909 ♦ Melkon Nikoli Nikolyan, Shirak, Ghskhdagirman, 1916 ♦ Melkon Tigrani Gasparyan (Tigranyan), Van, Akhorik, 1912 ♦ Melkon Yeremi Vardanyan, Darachichak, Farush, 1912 ♦ Merto Melkoni Melkonyan, Van, Shatakh, 1908 ♦ Meruzhan Arami Hayrapetyan (Aramyan), Kars, Bayrakhtar, 1913 ♦ Meruzhan Harutyuni Yeritsyan, Akhalkalak, Mec Kendura, 1917 ♦ Meruzhan Petrosi Harutyunyan, Kars, Kyadiklar, 1912 ♦ Meruzhan Sargisi Sargsyan, Kars, Pirvalu, 1916 ♦ Meruzhan Sedraki Khachatryan, Leninakan, Teknis, 1911 ♦ Meruzhan Yeghoyi Melkonyan, Kars, Mavrak, 1916 ♦ Mesrop Garegini Gareginyan, Yerevan, Ashtarak, 1913 ♦ Mesrop Ghukasi Ghukasyan, Gandzak, Nukhi, 1914 ♦ Mesrop Hakobi Grigoryan, Akhlat, Prkhus, 1911 ♦ Mesrop Harutyuni Hovsepyan, Kars, Paldrvan, 1910 ♦ Mesrop Karapeti Harutyunyan (Karapetyan), Van, Dazviran, 1914 ♦ Mesrop Khachaturi Avetisyan, Alashkert, Amada, 1909 ♦ Mesrop Mkrtchi Mkrtchyan, Mush, Havatorik, 1913 ♦ Mesrop Parosi Stepanyan, Kars, Paldrvan, 1913 ♦ Mesrop Petrosi Manukyan, Bitlis, Teghut, 1910 ♦ Mesrop Yeghoyi Hovhannisyan, Alekpol, Ghskhdagirman, 1908 ♦ Metaksya Hovhannesi Muradyan (Hovhannisyan), Sasun, Shiniar, 1909 ♦ Mihran (Shirak) Ashoti Poghosyan, Alashkert, Berd, 1913 ♦ Mihran Baghdasari Muradyan (Baghdasaryan), Bulanagh, Gapol, 1909 ♦ Mihran Daviti Sargsyan (Davtyan), Van, Hayots dzor, 1914 ♦ Mihran Gevorgi Gevorgyan, Alashkert, Iritsu, 1914 ♦ Mihran Gharibi Hovhannisyan, Alashkert, Hamadan, 1913 ♦ Mihran Ghukasi Simonyan (Ghukasyan), Sarighamish, Armtlu, 1910 ♦ Mihran Hakobi Hakobyan, Bitlis, Yonjalu, 1914 ♦ Mihran Hayrapeti Hayrapetyan, Kharberd, 1915 ♦ Mihran Hovhannesi Hakobyan, Bulanagh, Mirbar, 1910 ♦ Mihran Karapeti Karapetyan, Alashkert, Amad, 1912 ♦ Mihran Karapeti Karapetyan, Bulanagh, Yonjalu, 1917 ♦ Mihran Khachaturi Petrosyan, Akhalkalak, Sulda, 1912 ♦ Mihran Khachaturi Yenokyan (Khachatryan), Persia, Vayrava, 1912 ♦ Mihran Khanoyi Khanoyan, Alashkert, 1918 ♦ Mihran Khnkianosi Manukyan, Sarighamish, Gharaghurut, 1909 ♦ Mihran Manuki Vardanyan (Aleksanyan), Kaghzvan, Khar, 1911 ♦ Mihran Martirosi Khalatyan, Bayazet, Arcap, 1910 ♦ Mihran Meliki Melikyan (Melkonyan), Van, Aljavaz, 1913 ♦ Mihran Meliki Melikyan, Yerevan, Ghazarapat, 1917 ♦ Mihran Minasi Panosyan, Baku, 1909 ♦ Mihran Misaki Khachatryan, Alashkert, 1916 ♦ Mihran Misaki Poghosyan, Mush, Ghasmik, 1911, 1909 ♦ Mihran Mkhitari Gevorgyan (Vardanyan), Van, Hndstan, 1911 ♦ Mihran Mkrtichi Simonyan, Manazkert, Ghasmu, 1912 ♦ Mihran Movsesi Movsisyan (Baghdasaryan), Manazkert, Rostamgedak, 1912 ♦ Mihran Movsesi Soghomonyan, Alashkert, Khastur, 1910 ♦ Mihran Musheghi Musheghyan, Alashkert, Jujan, 1914 ♦ Mihran Sargisi Mkrtchyan (Sargsyan), Van, Hatana, 1909 ♦ Mihran Sargsi Ghazaryan, Kars, Hamzakarak, 1914 ♦ Mihran Sargsyan, 1919 ♦ Mihran Sedraki Sargsyan, Alekpol, Toros, 1914 ♦ Mihran Senekerimi Nazaryan, Van, Kuel, 1911 ♦ Mihran Setoyi Carukyan, Kars, Pirvali, 1917 ♦ Mihran Seyran Harutyunyan, Khnus, Khrekopru, 1910 ♦ Mihran Vardani Movsisyan, Bulanagh, Mirabar, 1912 ♦ Mihran Yeghiazari Margaryan (Yeghiazaryan), Manazkert, Berd, 1910 ♦ Mihrdat Khachaturi Sargsyan (Khachatryan), Van, Ishkhan gom, 1911 ♦ Mikayel Abrahami Vardanyan, Bitlis, Teghut, 1909 ♦ Mikayel Aghajani Aghajanyan, Pambak, Avdibek, 1917 ♦ Mikayel Aleksani Etoyants (Yetaryan), Shirak, Khlli Gharakilis, 1913 ♦ Mikayel Antoni Mkrtchyan, Kars, Ughuzli, 1912 ♦ Mikayel Batoyi Ter-Antonyan, Basen, Arjarak, 1914 ♦ Mikayel Gevorgi Gevorgyan,

LISTING OF ORPHANS

Shirak, Ghoshavank, 1914 ♦ Mikayel Gevorgi Nikolyan, Shirak, Horom, 1914 ♦ Mikayel Hakobi Musaelyan (Baghdasaryan), Karabagh, Binaktu, 1915 ♦ Mikayel Sahaki Levonyan, Baku, Shamakhi, 1914 ♦ Mikayel Sargisi Vardanyan (Sargsyan), Alashkert, Mazra, 1913 ♦ Mikayel Sedraki Balyan, Baku, Vanashen, 1912 ♦ Mikayel Yervandi Asatryan, Karin, Karno, 1913 ♦ Mildred Msropi Avetisyan, Van, 1908 ♦ Milidan Knyazi Manukyan, Kars, Ghzlchakhchakh, 1914 ♦ Milin Gurgeni Gurgenyan, Alashkert, 1918 ♦ Minas Abgari Abgaryan, Ghamarlu, Yava, 1916 ♦ Minas Aghajani Poghosyan (Aghajanyan), Ghamarlu, Yuva, 1916 ♦ Minas Amii Markosyan, Shamakhi, Zargaran, 1913 ♦ Minas Gevorgi Melkonyan (Gevorgyan), Van, Kharakonis, 1913 ♦ Minas Gevorgi Mesropyan, Babert, Balakhor, 1910 ♦ Minas Hovhannesi Avetisyan (Hovhannisyan), Aljavaz, Asen, 1906 ♦ Minas Kirakosi Kirakosyan (Farmanyan), Volti, Chichuris, 1909 ♦ Minas Samueli Karapetyan, Ardahan, 1914 ♦ Minas Stepani Grigoryan, Kars, 1911 ♦ Minas Vardani Avetisyan, Bitlis, Khard, 1912 ♦ Minas Yenoki Gasparyan, Sharur, Dasharkh, 1908 ♦ Minas Yepremi Yepremyan, Nakhijevan, Karakhanbaylu, 1913 ♦ Minush Avagi Ter-Hovhannisyan, Leninakan, Bangliahmat, 1922 ♦ Mirali Vozmani Vozmanyan, Alekpol, Ghozlija, 1913 ♦ Miran Arami Hovsepyan, Mush, Shekhiakhab, 1910 ♦ Mirik (Sirekan) Sirakani Hambaryan, Alekpol, Psti Keti, 1916 ♦ Mirobe Levoni Zakaryan, Trapizon, 1908 ♦ Mirzo Hovhannesi Hovhannisyan, Van, 1912 ♦ Mirzo Stepani Mkhoyan (Stepanyan), Basargechar, 1914 ♦ Misak Aleksani Aleksanyan, Kars, Bazrgan, 1910 ♦ Misak Avetisi Gasparyan, Sasun, Dalvorik, 1912 ♦ Misak Ayvazi Mkrtchyan (Ayvazyan), Basen, Harsnkar, 1913 ♦ Misak Brati Janoyan, Lori, Khotur, 1913 ♦ Misak Danieli Danielyan, Alekpol, Chorli, 1917 ♦ Misak Gevorgi Melikyan, Kars, Paldrvan, 1910 ♦ Misak Ghazari Davtyan (Sukiasyan), Alashkert, Khastur, 1914 ♦ Misak Grigori Miralayan, Sarighamish, Bashgyugh, 1911 ♦ Misak Hovhannesi Ghazaryan, Bulanagh, Teghut, 1909 ♦ Misak Hovhannesi Karapetyan (Hovhannisyan), Erzrum, Kghi, 1910 ♦ Misak Hovhannesi Yeretsyan, Akhalkalak, Abul, 1911 ♦ Misak Karapeti Paspandanyan (Karapetyan), Kars, 1910 ♦ Misak Khachatryan, Leninakan, 1920 ♦ Misak Khoreni Khorenyan, Van, Aghpshat, 1909 ♦ Misak Martirosi Melkonyan, Kars, Cbni, 1914 ♦ Misak Meloyi Meloyan (Mkhoyan), Kars, 1915 ♦ Misak Mkrtchi Badalyan, Karabagh, 1911 ♦ Misak Muradi Muradyan, Khnus, Elbis, 1910 ♦ Misak Nersesi Nersisyan, Kars, 1917 ♦ Misak Sargisi Petrosyan (Sargsyan), Khnus, Berd, 1908 ♦ Misak Sargsi Manukyan, Kars, Zayim, 1913 ♦ Misak Sedraki Durgaryan, Gharakilisa, Albulagh, 1913 ♦ Misak Simoni Abrahamyan (Simonyan), Leninakan, Ghotur, 1911 ♦ Misak Yegheki Asatryan, Leninakan, Kyapanak, 1918 ♦ Misak Yeghiazari Khachatryan, Aparan, Hajibazar, 1916 ♦ Misha Dimitrii Vasilev, Kuban, Opluz, 1917 ♦ Mitko Arshaki Torosyan, Gharakilisa, 1917 ♦ Mkhitar Abrahami Abrahamyan (Harutyunyan), Nukhi, Charghat, 1915 ♦ Mkhitar Antoni Vardanyan, Kars, Paldrvan, 1909 ♦ Mkhitar Gaspari Gasparyan, Van, Koshk, 1913, 1912 ♦ Mkhitar Gevorgi Haroyan – Gevorgyan, Erzrum, Khnus, 1910 ♦ Mkhitar Gharibi Manukyan (Gharibyan), Khlat, Prkhus, 1913 ♦ Mkhitar Harutyuni Hovhannisyan, Kars, Aksighaz, 1910 ♦ Mkhitar Hovakimi Hovhannisyan, Lin, Aghin, 1912 ♦ Mkhitar Hovhannesi Eloyan, Bulanagh, Yonjalu, 1911 ♦ Mkhitar Hovsepi Simonyan (Hovsepyan), Akhalkalak, Mec Bendura, 1916 ♦ Mkhitar Karapeti Karapetyan, Mush, 1918 ♦ Mkhitar Khachaturi Poghosyan (Khachatryan), Bitlis, 1912 ♦ Mkhitar Kirakosi Ghazaryan, Bulanagh, Mirabat, 1911 ♦ Mkhitar Malkhasi (Malkhasyan) Shahinyan, Manazkert, 1910 ♦ Mkhitar Manuki Mkhitaryan (Manukyan), Van, Mokhraberd, 1904 ♦ Mkhitar Manuki Petrosyan, Akhlat, Spsadzor, 1911 ♦ Mkhitar Mkrtichi Artemyan (Mkrtchyan), Khnus, 1912 ♦ Mkhitar Saghoyi Kakoyan (Hakobyan), Basen, Armtlu, 1916 ♦ Mkhitar Sargisi Baghdasaryan, Kars, 1910 ♦ Mkhitar Sargisi Poghosyan, Akhalkalak, 1908 ♦ Mkhitar Sargsi Holoyan (Sargsyan), Basen, Archarak, 1910 ♦ Mkhitar Shaheni Manukyan (Ghazaryan), Kars, Bulanagh, 1909 ♦ Mkhitar Stepani Harutyunyan, Alekpol, Aghin, 1914 ♦ Mkhitar Vardani Melikyan (Vardanyan), Kaghzvan, Yengicha, 1913 ♦ Mkrtich (Mukuch) Sakoyi Saghatelyan, Akhalkalak, Karcakh, 1915 ♦ Mkrtich Abrahami Somunjyan, Akhalkalak, 1916 ♦ Mkrtich Aleksani Manukyan, Akhaltsikha, 1915 ♦ Mkrtich Arami Aramyan, Etchmiadzin, Oshakan, 1917 ♦ Mkrtich Arami Martirosyan, Shirak, Gyulibulakh, 1913 ♦ Mkrtich Arshaki Grigoryan, Van, Noravan, 1910 ♦ Mkrtich Arshaki Sargsyan, Shirak, Ghonaghran, 1912 ♦ Mkrtich Artashesi Poghosyan, Alekpol, Mastara, 1909 ♦ Mkrtich Badali Melkonyan (Badalyan), Van, Norduz, 1907 ♦ Mkrtich Chakhoyi Mkrtchyan, Leninakan, Gyozaldara, 1911 ♦ Mkrtich Daviti Harutyunyan, Sardarapat, 1912 ♦ Mkrtich Gaspari Gasparyan, Bulanagh, Gharaghlu, 1911 ♦ Mkrtich Gevorgi Gevorgyan, Van, Atana, 1910 ♦ Mkrtich Gevorgi Hakobyan, Leninakan, Kefli, 1911 ♦ Mkrtich Ghazari Hovhannisyan, Alekpol, Ghoshavank, 1908 ♦ Mkrtich Ghukasi Melkonyan (Ghukasyan), Khnus, Torakhan, 1911 ♦ Mkrtich Gokori Movsisyan, Basen, Krtabash, 1913 ♦ Mkrtich Grigori Grigoryan, Van, Ardam, 1913 ♦ Mkrtich Grigori Hakobyan (Jorkrtsyan), Akhalkalak, Majadia, 1914 ♦ Mkrtich Grigori Movsisyan, Kars, Mavrak, 1913 ♦ Mkrtich Grigori Zhamkochyan, Alekpol, 1922 ♦ Mkrtich Hakobi Grigoryan (Hakobyan), Van, Dshogh, 1911 ♦ Mkrtich Hakobi Hakobyan (Hovsepyan), Igdir, 1917 ♦ Mkrtich Hamayaki Stepanyan, Shirak, Khli Gharakilis, 1916 ♦ Mkrtich Harutyuni Karapetyan, Leninakan, Gheghach, 1912 ♦ Mkrtich Harutyuni Simonyan, Etchmiadzin, Byurakan, 1914 ♦ Mkrtich Harutyunyan, 1920 ♦ Mkrtich Hayrapeti Hayrapetyan, Surmalu, Panik, 1914 ♦ Mkrtich Hayrapeti Manukyan (Kamalyan), Kars, 1913 ♦ Mkrtich Hovhannesi Hovhannisyan, Van, 1913 ♦ Mkrtich Hovhannesi Melkonyan, Kars, Paldrvan, 1912 ♦ Mkrtich Hovhannesi Mnatsakanyan, Aresh, Balarkand, 1912 ♦ Mkrtich Hovhannesi Stepanyan

(Hovhannisyan), Leninakan, Kefli, 1917 ♦ Mkrtich Hovhannesi Yegoryan, Leninakan, Araz, 1914 ♦ Mkrtich Hovsepi Harutyunyan, Shirak, Svanverdi, 1910 ♦ Mkrtich Karapeti Aspaturyan, Kars, 1913 ♦ Mkrtich Karapeti Karapetyan (Hovhannisyan), Sarighamish, Aghkilisa, 1911 ♦ Mkrtich Karapeti Mkrtchyan (Karapetyan), Erzrum, Kyoprakoy, 1908 ♦ Mkrtich Karapeti Mkrtchyan, Kars, Ortakilisa, 1912 ♦ Mkrtich Khachaturi Harutyunyan, Leninakan, 1917 ♦ Mkrtich Khachaturi Khachatryan, Bitlis, Manazkert, 1914 ♦ Mkrtich Khachaturi Khachatryan, Mush, Aragh, 1921 ♦ Mkrtich Khachaturi Mkoyan, Tiflis, 1915 ♦ Mkrtich Knyazi Grigoryan, Bandivan, 1912 ♦ Mkrtich Knyazi Hovhannisyan, Shirak, Jajur, 1913 ♦ Mkrtich Madoyi Simonyan, Alekpol, Voghuzli, 1911 ♦ Mkrtich Makari Danielyan, Alekpol, Chiftali, 1910 ♦ Mkrtich Manuki Manukyan, Van, 1911 ♦ Mkrtich Manuki Petrosyan, Van, Khek, 1907 ♦ Mkrtich Manuki Poghosyan, Alekpol, Mec Keti, 1914 ♦ Mkrtich Martirosi Baghdasaryan, Alekpol, Syogutli, 1912 ♦ Mkrtich Martirosi Gasparyan, Erzrum, Dzandzagh, 1912 ♦ Mkrtich Martirosi Hovsepyan, Van, Haspstan, 1911 ♦ Mkrtich Martirosi Martirosyan, Van, 1912 ♦ Mkrtich Matsaki Kharmandaryan, Leninakan, Bashshoragal, 1912 ♦ Mkrtich Meliki Aleksanyan, Van, 1912 ♦ Mkrtich Mikayeli Movsisyan, Leninakan, Jalab, 1912 ♦ Mkrtich Mnatsakani Avetisyan, Surmalu, Igdir, 1913 ♦ Mkrtich Mnatsi Mnatsakanyan, Leninakan, Syogutli, 1916 ♦ Mkrtich Mukayeli Mkrtchyan (Mukayelyan), Van, 1912 ♦ Mkrtich Nahapeti Simonyan, Alekpol, Sirvanjugh, 1913 ♦ Mkrtich Nikoli Zakaryan, Leninakan, Sariar, 1912 ♦ Mkrtich Panosi Panosyan, Van, 1914 ♦ Mkrtich Pilosi Grigoryan, Kars, Mazra, 1910 ♦ Mkrtich Poghosi Vardanyan (Poghosyan), Van, 1908 ♦ Mkrtich Sargisi Harutyunyan (Ghevondyan), Akhalkalak, Karzagh, 1911 ♦ Mkrtich Sargisi Mkrtchyan, Basen, Kyoprkoy, 1912 ♦ Mkrtich Sargsi Sargsyan, Kars, 1915 ♦ Mkrtich Sargsi Vardanyan, Gharakilisa, Ghzlghoch, 1914 ♦ Mkrtich Sedraki Harutyunyan, Van, Hamkuberd, 1909 ♦ Mkrtich Sedraki Voskanyan, Kars, Mazra, 1915 ♦ Mkrtich Sergoyi Hakobyan, Tiflis, 1912 ♦ Mkrtich Shmavoni Yeghiazaryan (Shmavonyan), Mush, Khoshgaldi, 1912 ♦ Mkrtich Sirekani Hovhannisyan (Sirekanyan), Shirak, Ghaplu, 1914 ♦ Mkrtich Smbati Pahlavanyan, Leninakan, 1908 ♦ Mkrtich Stepani Harutyunyan, Kars, Paldrvan, 1911 ♦ Mkrtich Sukiasi Sukiasyan, Darachichak, Solak, 1913 ♦ Mkrtich Tepani Simonyan, Alekpol, Toparli, 1911 ♦ Mkrtich Tigrani Ghazaryan (Tigranyan), Van, Bltents, 1911 ♦ Mkrtich Tonoyi Poghosyan, Khnus, Khozlu, 1912 ♦ Mkrtich Tovmasi Asatryan, Sasun, Khort, 1912 ♦ Mkrtich Vaniki Hambaryan, Leninakan, Ghanlija, 1914 ♦ Mkrtich Vanoyi Madoyan, Shirak, Tavshanghshlagh, 1914 ♦ Mkrtich Varosi Martirosyan (Varosyan), Alekpol, Ghzlghoch, 1908 ♦ Mkrtich Yeghiazari (Ghazari) Ghazaryan, Shirak, Illi, 1916 ♦ Mkrtich Yeghiazari Yeghiazaryan, Bulanagh, Khoshgeldi, 1908 ♦ Mkrtich Yenoki Varosyan, Kars, 1916 ♦ Mkrtich Zakari Zakaryan, Alekpol, 1917 ♦ Mnats Mukuchi Mukuchyan (Khachatryan), Alekpol, Kalal, 1918 ♦ Mnats Nahapeti Nahapetyan, Erzrum, Totva, 1909 ♦ Mnatsakan Aleksani Aleksanyan, Alashkert, Kumlipuchakh, 1914 ♦ Mnatsakan Aleksani Gevorgyan, Pambak, Gharakilise, 1909 ♦ Mnatsakan Aleksani Vardanyan (Margaryan), Sarighamish, Shadivan, 1912 ♦ Mnatsakan Arseni Hakobyan, Leninakan, Gheghaj, 1913 ♦ Mnatsakan Baloyi Aloyan, Basargechar, 1912 ♦ Mnatsakan Barseghi Levonyan (Yatoyan), Erzrum, Basen, 1915 ♦ Mnatsakan Daviti Davtyan, Lori, Dsegh, 1914 ♦ Mnatsakan Gevorgi Gevorgyan, Alekpol, Aghbulagh, 1913 ♦ Mnatsakan Gevorgi Mirzoyan, 1919 ♦ Mnatsakan Grigori Mkhitaryan, Van, 1909 ♦ Mnatsakan Hakobi Kerobyan, Kars, Gorkhana, 1916 ♦ Mnatsakan Harutyuni Ayvazyan (Harutyunyan), Van, Taghviran, 1908 ♦ Mnatsakan Harutyuni Grigoryan, Kars, 1914 ♦ Mnatsakan Harutyuni Torosyan, Kars, Berna, 1912 ♦ Mnatsakan Hovhannesi Harutyunyan (Hovhannisyan), Leninakan, Ghoshavank, 1915 ♦ Mnatsakan Hovhannesi Hovhannisyan, Kars, Nakhijevan, 1911 ♦ Mnatsakan Hovhannesi Petrosyan, Bulanagh, 1914 ♦ Mnatsakan Karapeti Petrosyan (Karapetyan), Leninakan, Boghazkyasan, 1915 ♦ Mnatsakan Knyazi Ghazaryan, Leninakan, Ghzlghoch, 1912 ♦ Mnatsakan Meliki Baghdasaryan, Kars, Hamzakarak, 1916 ♦ Mnatsakan Melkoni Melkonyan, Kars, 1916 ♦ Mnatsakan Misaki Misakyan (Shriyan), Alekpol, Maymajugh, 1910 ♦ Mnatsakan Nersesi Sargsyan, Kars, Dolbandlu, 1915 ♦ Mnatsakan Poghosi Poghosyan, Kars, 1915 ♦ Mnatsakan Saghateli Madoyan (Saghatelyan), Leninakan, Bandivan, 1912 ♦ Mnatsakan Saroyi Maloyan (Malkhasyan), Kars, Bashshoragal, 1914 ♦ Mnatsakan Sedraki Movsisyan, Alekpol, Ghzlghoch, 1912 ♦ Mnatsakan Soghomoni Manukyan, Kyavar, Basargechar, 1914 ♦ Mnatsakan Yeghiazari Vardanyan (Yeghoyan), Kars, Bulanagh, 1914 ♦ Mnatsakan Yepremi Torosyan (Yepremyan), Kars, Dorbandlu, 1914 ♦ Mnatsakan Zakari Khachatryan, Nukhi, Jafarabad, 1909 ♦ Mobe Yusufi Yusufyan, Yerevan, 1912 ♦ Moskov Galoyi Chakhalyan (Galoyan), Kars, Aghuzum, 1909 ♦ Moskov Gurgeni Harutyunyan, Sarighamish, Gyulantap, 1915 ♦ Moskov Harutyuni Simonyan, Kars, Voghuzli, 1912 ♦ Moskov Levoni Alekyan (Levonyan), Leninakan, Syogutli, 1914 ♦ Moskov Nikoli Abrahamyan, Alekpol, Ghanlija, 1914 ♦ Moskov Petrosi Grigoryan, Bulanagh, Kop, 1915 ♦ Movses Arshaki Adamyan (Aramyan), Kars, Bayburt, 1909 ♦ Movses Gaspari Hrghatyan, Mush, Miriban, 1909 ♦ Movses Ghukasi Ghukasyan, Moks, Arinj, 1913 ♦ Movses Grigori Grigoryan, Mush, Vardov, 1910 ♦ Movses Hakobi Arakelyan (Hakobyan), Van, Hazar, 1906 ♦ Movses Hmayaki Gevorgyan, Kars, Zaim, 1910 ♦ Movses Hovhannesi Petrosyan, Bulanagh, Miribat, 1911 ♦ Movses Karapeti Gyurjyan, Khnus, Gharachoban, 1910 ♦ Movses Khachaturi Hovhannisyan, Alashkert, Mazra, 1913 ♦ Movses Marati Muradyan, Bulanagh, Machtlu, 1913 ♦ Movses Melikseti Meliksetyan, Koghb, Ghulab, 1917 ♦ Movses Melkoni Arakelyan, Vardov, Dotan, 1911 ♦ Movses Mkrtchi Mkrtchyan, Bulanagh, Khoshgeldi, 1909 ♦ Movses Stepani Stepanyan, Leninakan, Syogutli, 1914 ♦ Movses

Tadevosi Tadevosyan, Van, Khachan, 1913 ♦ Mukuch Gevorgi (Yeghoyi) Gevorgyan (Yeghoyan), Kars, Bayghara, 1918 ♦ Mukuch Hovhannesi Hovhannisyan (Tarvanyan), Akhaltsikha, 1914 ♦ Mukuch Meliki Arakelyan, Kars, Ghzlchakhchakh, 1915 ♦ Mukuch Mkhitari Mkhitaryan, Basen, Arjarak, 1913 ♦ Murad Abrahami Abrahamyan, Shatakh, Moks, 1913 ♦ Murad Arshaki Arshakyan, Bulanagh, Yonjalu, 1910 ♦ Murad Avetisi Avetisyan, Moks, Covan, 1910 ♦ Murad Daviti Vahanyan, Mush, 1912 ♦ Murad Gaspari Khachatryan (Gasparyan), Alashkert, Yeghntap, 1912 ♦ Murad Grigori Artinyan, Bitlis, Kharabshat, 1916 ♦ Murad Hakobi Hovsepyan, Bulanagh, Shirvanshekh, 1909 ♦ Murad Karapeti Muradyan, Sasun, Hazva, 1910 ♦ Murad Kerobi Kerobyan (Harutyunyan), Kars, Nakhijevan, 1916 ♦ Murad Manuki Hovakimyan, Van, 1910 ♦ Murad Melkoni Melkonyan (Shahinyan), Aljavaz, Sipan, 1913 ♦ Murad Vardani Muradyan (Vardanyan), Manazkert, Gharaghala, 1911 ♦ Murad Vardani Muradyan, Van, 1915 ♦ Murad Vardani Vardanyan, Van, Gargar, 1914 ♦ Muraz Melkoni Melkonyan, Leninakan, Ghzlghoch, 1913 ♦ Mushegh Abrahami Khachatryan, Persia, Mzkit, 1916 ♦ Mushegh Aghabeki Aghabekyan, Alekpol, Illi, 1909 ♦ Mushegh Aleksani Aleksanyan, Gandzak, 1914 ♦ Mushegh Antoni Muradyan, Basen, 1917 ♦ Mushegh Arakeli Abrahamyan (Arakelyan), Bitlis, 1907 ♦ Mushegh Arakeli Arakelyan, Ayntap, Batnots, 1910 ♦ Mushegh Arshaki Minasyan (Arshakyan), Mush, Derek, 1912 ♦ Mushegh Arshaki Sahakyan, Alekpol, Keti, 1914 ♦ Mushegh Baghdasari Ayvazyan, Manazkert, Derek, 1909 ♦ Mushegh Baghdasari Hovhannisyan, Mshu, Kost, 1910 ♦ Mushegh Baghdasari Mkhitaryan, Aljavaz, Ghaza, 1914 ♦ Mushegh Daviti Hakobyan (Davtyan), Basen, Alvar, 1912 ♦ Mushegh Davti Hakobyan (Davtyan), Bulanagh, Kharabshat, 1914 ♦ Mushegh Gaspari Gasparyan (Nanoyan), Bulanagh, Kop, 1919 ♦ Mushegh Gevorgi (Avetisyan) Avagyan, Alekpol, Ghaplu, 1912 ♦ Mushegh Gevorgi Ter-Gevorgyan, Bulanagh, Majralu, 1906 ♦ Mushegh Ghukasi Martirosyan, Bulanagh, Votnchor, 1914 ♦ Mushegh Grigori Gevorgyan, Ayntap, Batnoc, 1911 ♦ Mushegh Grigori Hakobyan (Dilbaryan), Shushi, Blegh, 1911 ♦ Mushegh Harutyuni Harutyunyan, Sasun, Hazva, 1910 ♦ Mushegh Hayrapeti Sardaryan, Vana, Kozir, 1910 ♦ Mushegh Hovhannesi Davtyan, Nor Bayazet, Gol gyugh, 1911 ♦ Mushegh Hovhannesi Hakobyan (Hovhannisyan), Bulanagh, Kop, 1913 ♦ Mushegh Hovhannesi Khachatryan, Zangezur, Tatev, 1910 ♦ Mushegh Hovhannesi Sahakyan, Van, Aljavaz, 1911 ♦ Mushegh Khachaturi Karapetyan, Mush, 1908 ♦ Mushegh Khachaturi Khachatryan (Kamalyan), Van, Spartkert, 1908 ♦ Mushegh Khachaturi Sahakyan, Bulanagh, Kop, 1909 ♦ Mushegh Kostani Aghemyan, Bitlis, Kaghzvan, 1914 ♦ Mushegh Kuchaki Kuchakyan (Tonoyan), Manazkert, Gharaghala, 1911 ♦ Mushegh Kyuchuki Kyuchukyan, Bulanagh, Gharaghl, 1912 ♦ Mushegh Manuki Avetisyan, Mush, Latar, 1910 ♦ Mushegh Manuki Terteryan, Kharberd, Lazva, 1914 ♦ Mushegh Manuki Yeghoyan (Manukyan), Kars, Gedaksatlmish, 1910 ♦ Mushegh Margari Poghosyan, Aljavaz, Norshnjugh, 1910 ♦ Mushegh Matevosi Matevosyan, Derjan, Sargha, 1910 ♦ Mushegh Mkrtchi Mkrtchyan, Mush, Noratin, 1910 ♦ Mushegh Mnatsakani Mnatsakanyan, Gharakilisa, Hamamlu, 1914 ♦ Mushegh Petrosi Baghdasaryan, Karabagh, Shushi, 1911 ♦ Mushegh Petrosi Grigoryan, Mush, 1911 ♦ Mushegh Petrosi Khachatryan, Van, Khizan, 1910 ♦ Mushegh Samsoni Mikayelyan, Kars, Ghapanli, 1909 ♦ Mushegh Yeghiazari Amiryan, Leninakan, Syogutli, 1912 ♦ Mushegh Yegori Movsisyan, Alekpol, Cholakha, 1912 ♦ Muso (Movses) Movsesi Musoyan (Movsisyan), Yerevan, 1916 ♦ Nado Mkrtchi Mkrtchyan, Bitlis, Khut, 1913 ♦ Nado Movsesi Movsisyan, Bulanagh, Kop, 1918 ♦ Nado Movsesi Movsisyan, Bulanagh, Kop, 1918 ♦ Nado Vardani Vardanyan, Sasun, Khut, 1913 ♦ Nadya Ayvazi Karapetyan, Alekpol, Duzkharaba, 1914 ♦ Nahapet Avagi Avagyan, Salmast, 1918 ♦ Nahapet Hakobi Hakobyan, Bayazet, 1910 ♦ Nahapet Hakobi Hakobyan, Nakhijevan, Nors, 1914 ♦ Nahapet Hakobi Hakobyan, Nakhijevan, Nors, 1914 ♦ Nahapet Hovhannesi Petrosyan, Etchmiadzin, Bashaparan, 1913 ♦ Nahapet Hovhannesi Petrosyan, Etchmiadzin, Bashaparan, 1913 ♦ Nahapet Movsesi Gevorgyan, Rostamgedak, 1911 ♦ Nahapet Movsesi Movsisyan (Ayvazyan), Shirak, Imrkhan, 1913 ♦ Nakhshun Ashoti Avetisyan (Ashotyan), Tpkhis, 1916 ♦ Nakhshun Baghdasari Galstyan, Leninakan, Syogutli, 1913 ♦ Nakhshun Daviti Poghosyan (Davtyan), Alekpol, Boghazkyasan, 1916 ♦ Nakhshun Gevorgi Gevorgyan, Tiflis, 1917 ♦ Nakhshun Hovhannesi Hovhannisyan, Alekpol, Dzitankov, 1914 ♦ Nakhshun Khachaturi Karapetyan, Leninakan, Mastara, 1910 ♦ Nakhshun Margari Mikayelyan (Grigoryan), Alekpol, Kaps, 1915 ♦ Nakhshun Mkhitari Serobyan, Pambak, Gharakilisa, 1915 ♦ Nakhshun Nazareti Ayvazyan, Ardahan, Shavshegh, 1910 ♦ Nakhshun Nazareti Ayvazyan, Ardahan, Shavshegh, 1910 ♦ Nakhshun Nazari Petrosyan (Nazaryan), Kars, Kyadiklar, 1915 ♦ Nakhshun Nazari Petrosyan (Nazaryan), Kars, Kyadiklar, 1915 ♦ Nakhshun Petrosi Petrosyan, Tiflis, 1915, 1913 ♦ Nakhshun Petrosi Petrosyan, Yerevan, 1920 ♦ Nakhshun Poghosi Poghosyan, Hamamlu, Vortna, 1916 ♦ Nakhshun Poghosi Poghosyan, Hamamlu, Vortna, 1916 ♦ Nakhshun Sargisi Muradyan, Alekpol, Syogutli, 1910 ♦ Nakhshun Sargsi Grigoryan (Avetisyan), Kars, Bulanagh, 1915 ♦ Nakhshun Sargsi Sargsyan, 1919 ♦ Nakhshun Sargsi Sargsyan, 1919 ♦ Nakhshun Tonoyi Khachatryan, Kars, Zaim, 1910 ♦ Nakhshun Tumasi Tumasyan, Bulanagh, 1915 ♦ Nakhshun Vasili Arakelyan, Kars, Pokr Parket, 1911 ♦ Names Baloyi Gevorgyan (Baloyan), Basen, Iskhi, 1914 ♦ Nana Gevorg Gevorgyan, Bulanagh, 1916 ♦ Nana Gevorg Gevorgyan, Bulanagh, 1916 ♦ Nanagyul Avetisi Avetisyan, Bulanagh, Yonjalu, 1914 ♦ Nanagyul Avetisi Avetisyan, Bulanagh, Yonjalu, 1914 ♦ Nanagyul Gevorgi Sargsyan (Gevorgyan), Leninakan, Ghzlghoch, 1914 ♦ Nanagyul Gevorgi Sargsyan (Gevorgyan), Leninakan, Ghzlghoch, 1914 ♦ Nanagyul Harutyuni Harutyunyan, Leninakan, Munjughli, 1914 ♦ Nanam Simoni

Simonyan, Bulanagh, Shirvanshekh, 1910 ♦ Nanan Ghazari Petrosyan, Leninakan, Illi, 1913 ♦ Nanash Vardani Ghatachyan, Erzrum, Gomadzor, 1910 ♦ Nanash Vardani Ghatachyan, Erzrum, Gomadzor, 1910 ♦ Nanik (Sarngyul) Mikayeli Martirosyan, Kaghzvan, Karabagh, 1917 ♦ Nanik (Sarngyul) Mikayeli Martirosyan, Kaghzvan, Karabagh, 1917 ♦ Nanik Tatosi Avoyan, Kars, Tikor, 1912 ♦ Nano (Nunik) Aboyan, Gharakilisa, Pambak, 1919 ♦ Nano (Nunik) Aboyan, Gharakilisa, Pambak, 1919 ♦ Nano Khachatryan, Kars, 1920 ♦ Nano Mukayeli Mukayelyan, Kars, Nakhijevan, 1915 ♦ Nano Muradi Umroyan (Muradyan), Mush, Avzut, 1910 ♦ Nano Nazari Petrosyan (Nazaryan), Kars, Nerkin Kyadilak, 1912 ♦ Nano Nazari Petrosyan (Nazaryan), Kars, Nerkin Kyadilak, 1912 ♦ Nano Simoni Manukyan, Nakhijevan, 1917 ♦ Nano Srapi Vardanyan, Kars, Kyadiklar, 1915 ♦ Nano Vardani Yeghiazaryan (Tonoyan), Bulanagh, Votnchor, 1908 ♦ Napet Sargisi Sargsyan, Akhalkalak, Vachyan, 1915 ♦ Napoleon Arakeli Shumashyan (Gyunashyan), Kars, Ghzlchakhchakh, 1917 ♦ Napoleon Gevorgi Karapetyan, Leninakan, Charnchi, 1915 ♦ Napoleon Hovhannesi Gasparyan (Hovhannisyan), Kars, Ardahan, 1912, 1910 ♦ Napoleon Hovhannesi Gasparyan (Hovhannisyan), Kars, Ardahan, 1912, 1910 ♦ Napoleon Khachaturi Ghazaryan (Khachatryan), Kars, Hamzakarak, 1918 ♦ Napoleon Levoni Hovhannisyan, Nakhijevan, Yarmkar, 1914 ♦ Napoleon Mukuchi Aleksanyan, Kars, Dashkov, 1917 ♦ Nardos Mkrtchi Gevorgyan (Mkrtchyan), Basen, Dalibaba, 1913 ♦ Nardos Mkrtchi Gevorgyan (Mkrtchyan), Basen, Dalibaba, 1913 ♦ Narduhi Grigori Gasparyan, Bulanagh, Kop, 1901 ♦ Narduhi Hmayaki Aghajanyan, Ayntap, Duragh, 1911 ♦ Narduhi Mikayeli Hovhannisyan, Bulanagh, Shirvanshekh, 1908 ♦ Narduhi Serobi Sargsyan, Mush, Denik, 1907 ♦ Narduhi Serobi Sargsyan, Mush, Denik, 1907 ♦ Nargiz Abrahami Margaryan (Abrahamyan), Van, Mokhraberd, 1912 ♦ Nargiz Abrahami Margaryan (Abrahamyan), Van, Mokhraberd, 1912 ♦ Nargiz Avagi Avagyan, Daralagyaz, Khachik, 1912 ♦ Nargiz Avetisi Nikoghosyan, Van, Ermer, 1914 ♦ Nargiz Avetisi Nikoghosyan, Van, Ermer, 1914 ♦ Nargiz Baghdasari Baghdasaryan, Bulanagh, Kop, 1914 ♦ Nargiz Barseghi Barseghyan (Badalyan), Lori, Urut, 1917, 1918 ♦ Nargiz Bayramyan (Vahramyan), Yerevan, 1916 ♦ Nargiz Hakobi Hakobyan, Bulanagh, Hamzashekh, 1909 ♦ Nargiz Harutyuni Hakobyan – Harutyunyan, Van, Mokhraberd, 1912 ♦ Nargiz Hovhannesi Khlghatyan, Mush, Tolaghbasha, 1909 ♦ Nargiz Karapeti Lalayan, Shamakhi, Vanadni, 1908 ♦ Nargiz Meliki Melikyan, Pambak, Gharakilisa, 1918 ♦ Nargiz Sargisi Sargsyan, Van, 1913 ♦ Nargiz Saroyi Sargsyan, Bulanagh, Hamzashekh, 1912 ♦ Nargiz Sedraki Grigoryan, Tiflis, 1910 ♦ Naro (Haro) Ghazari Karapetyan, Yerevan, 1918 ♦ Naro Hovhannesi Simonyan, Kars, Ghani, 1910 ♦ Naro Hovhannesi Simonyan, Kars, Ghani, 1910 ♦ Natal Hayroyi Torosyan, Karvansara, Aghdam, 1913 ♦ Natal Makari Manukyan, Leninakan, Ghzlghoch, 1912 ♦ Natal Petrosi Petrosyan, Kars, Mavrak, 1915 ♦ Natalia Arami Aramyan, Tiflis, 1918 ♦ Natalia Arami Aramyan, Tiflis, 1918 ♦ Natalia Arseni Hayrapetyan, Kars, Bashhoragyal, 1913 ♦ Natalia Avagi Abrahamyan, Leninakan, Mec Keti, 1915 ♦ Natalia Avetisi Galstyan, Kars, Cbni, 1913 ♦ Natalia Khachaturi Galstyan, Gyokcha, Tobishen, 1909 ♦ Natalia Khachaturi Hakobyan, Leninakan, Chrpli, 1909 ♦ Natalia Mkhitari Hovhannisyan, Kars, Tigos, 1914 ♦ Natalia Poghosi Gharagyozyan, Ghazakh, Dostlu, 1910 ♦ Natash Barseghi Barseghyan, Basargechar, 1913 (1917) ♦ Natash Minasi Khachatryan, Nakhijevan, 1911 ♦ Natasha Asaturi Ghazaryan (Asatryan), Gharakilisa, Bzovdal, 1916 ♦ Natasha Sahaki Aleksanyan (Sahakyan), Nor Bayazet, 1909 ♦ Nato Avoyi Avoyan (Torosyan), Khnus, Gharakilisa, 1907 ♦ Navo Vardani Vardanyan, Akhta, Alapars, 1916, 1912 ♦ Nazan Asaturi Melikyan, Leninakan, Chzghlar, 1912 ♦ Nazan Avagi Avagyan, Kars, Bayrakhtar, 1913 ♦ Nazan Avagi Avagyan, Kars, Koghb, 1914 ♦ Nazan Daviti Chirakhyan, Sarighamish, Bashgegh, 1917 ♦ Nazan Daviti Davtyan, Basen, Hekibad, 1913 ♦ Nazan Daviti Davtyan, Basen, Hekibad, 1913 ♦ Nazan Daviti Davtyan, Kars, Bayramali, 1916 ♦ Nazan Gaspari Dankuryan, Alekpol, Khlli Gharakilis, 1909 ♦ Nazan Gaspari Dankuryan, Alekpol, Khlli Gharakilisa, 1909 ♦ Nazan Gaspari Gasparyan, 1917 ♦ Nazan Gaspari Gevorgyan, Ghamarlu, Znjrlu, 1911 ♦ Nazan Gaspari Gevorgyan, Ghamarlu, Znjrlu, 1911 ♦ Nazan Grigori Melkonyan (Muradyan), Kars, Berna, 1914 ♦ Nazan Grigori Vardanyan, Kars, Berna, 1913 ♦ Nazan Grigori Vardanyan, Kars, Berna, 1913 ♦ Nazan Hajibabi Hajibabyan, Kars, Ghzlchakhchakh, 1914 ♦ Nazan Hambardzumi Arakelyan (Martirosyan), Basen, Totaviran, 1913 ♦ Nazan Karapeti Baghdasaryan, Kars, 1911 ♦ Nazan Khachaturi Khachatryan, Van, 1915 ♦ Nazan Khachaturi Vahanyan (Khachatryan), Kars, Paldrvan, 1916 ♦ Nazan Safaryan, Alashkert, 1914 ♦ Nazan Safaryan, Alashkert, 1914 ♦ Nazan Sakoyi Gevorgyan, Leninakan, Chorli, 1912 ♦ Nazan Sakoyi Gevorgyan, Leninakan, Chorli, 1912 ♦ Nazan Sargisi Sargsyan (Poghosyan), Kars, Sarighamish, 1913 ♦ Nazan Sedraki Khachatryan, Kars, Mec Parket, 1914 ♦ Nazan Sedraki Margaryan, Koghb, 1910 ♦ Nazan Shamiri Hovhannisyan, Karabagh, Alkhatia, 1910 ♦ Nazan Stepani Manukyan, Khoy, Sedamal, 1913 ♦ Nazan Zakari Harutyunyan, Khnus, Aghjamelik, 1909 ♦ Nazani Hovhannesi Hovhannisyan, Basen, Yaghan, 1915 ♦ Nazani Levoni Aslanyan, Kars, Mazra, 1910 ♦ Nazar Arakeli Martirosyan (Arakelyan), Alashkert, Zidgan, 1908 ♦ Nazar Arami Ghazaryan, Kars, Ortaghala, 1912, 1913 ♦ Nazar Gevorgi Gevorgyan, Kars, Gharaghala, 1915 ♦ Nazar Hakobi Asatryan (Hakobyan), Alashkert, Zidgan, 1906 ♦ Nazar Hovhannesi Hovhannesyan, Bulanagh, Kakarlu, 1917 ♦ Nazar Hovhannesi Hovhannisyan, Bulanagh, Kakarlu, 1917 ♦ Nazar Khachaturi Muradyan, Ashtarak, Dghr, 1912 ♦ Nazar Mkrtchi Khachatryan, Mush, Yonjalu, 1910 ♦ Nazar Nahapeti Artashyan, Etchmiadzin, Aghavnatun, 1918 ♦ Nazar Shaboyi Shaboyan, Mush, Manazkert, 1915 ♦ Nazar Zakari Torosyan, Yerevan, Akhta, 1910 ♦ Nazaret Asaturi

Harutyunyan, Mush, 1911 ◆ Nazaret Grigori Avetisyan (Elbakyan), Basen, Kilantpu, 1909 ◆ Nazaret Hovsepi Hovikyan (Hovsepyan), Mush, Sheghaghab, 1911 ◆ Nazaret Martirosi Grigoryan, Kars, 1910 ◆ Nazeli Ghazari Hakobyan, Mush, Cghak, 1893 ◆ Nazeli Hovhannesi Madoyan, Erzrum, 1912 ◆ Nazeli Khirani Khiranyan, Van, Aygestan, 1910 ◆ Nazik Adibeki Torostyan (Mkrtchyan), Igdir, Panik, 1913 ◆ Nazik Aleksani Gasparyan, Kars, Bayghara, 1912 ◆ Nazik Arami Aramyan, Alashkert, Berd, 1918 ◆ Nazik Arshaki Arshakyan, Alekpol, Tashkhala, 1914 ◆ Nazik Arzumani Nikolyan (Arzumanyan), Darachichak, Ddmashen, 1914 ◆ Nazik Arzumani Nikolyan (Arzumanyan), Darachichak, Ddmashen, 1914 ◆ Nazik Danieli Simonyan, Sarighamish, 1916 ◆ Nazik Galusti Hovhannisyan, Tiflis, Tsarski, 1913 ◆ Nazik Gaspari Sahakyan, Nakhijevan, Nors, 1911 ◆ Nazik Gevorgi Chakhoyan, Leninakan, Bashgyugh, 1913 ◆ Nazik Ghazari Ghazaryan, Basen, Ishkhu, 1917 ◆ Nazik Grigori Avetisyan (Grigoryan), Alekpol, Jajur, 1914 ◆ Nazik Hakobi Mkrtchyan, Kars, Uzunkilisa, 1914 ◆ Nazik Harutyuni Harutyunyan, Mush, Khoshgyaldi, 1910 ◆ Nazik Harutyuni Simonyan, Kars, Tazakand, 1911 ◆ Nazik Hovaki Bakhinyan, Akhalkalak, Khando, 1912 ◆ Nazik Hovhannesi Ghazaryan, Kars, Chormalu, 1914 ◆ Nazik Hovhannesi Grigoryan, Van, Khachara, 1913 ◆ Nazik Hovhannesi Kirakosyan, Nakhijevan, 1910 ◆ Nazik Hovhannesi Tonoyan, Sarighamish, 1907 ◆ Nazik Karapeti Karapetyan, Kars, Byurakdara, 1913 ◆ Nazik Khachaturi Khachatryan, Van, Norgyugh, 1912 ◆ Nazik Khosrovi Karapetyan (Sargsyan), Van, Averak, 1912 ◆ Nazik Khosrovi Karapetyan (Sargsyan), Van, Averak, 1912 ◆ Nazik Kyarami Budaghyan, Mush, Koghak, 1912 ◆ Nazik Markosi Hovsepyan (Markosyan), Van, Khachan, 1907 ◆ Nazik Markosi Markosyan, Basen, 1917 ◆ Nazik Markosi Markosyan, Basen, 1917 ◆ Nazik Meloyi Gevorgyan, Shirak, Bughdashen, 1909 ◆ Nazik Misaki Kurghinyan (Misakyan), Akhalkalak, 1916 ◆ Nazik Mkhitari Mnatsakanyan, Alashkert, Amati, 1912 ◆ Nazik Mkrtchi Nadoyan (Mkrtchyan), Akhlat, Prkhus, 1909 ◆ Nazik Mkrtchyan, 1920 ◆ Nazik Mnatsakani Nazaretyan, Alekpol, 1910 ◆ Nazik Musheghi Safaryan (Musheghyan), Erzrum, Alashkert, 1912 ◆ Nazik Nazari Poghosyan, Kars, Kaghzvan, 1913 ◆ Nazik Nazari Poghosyan, Kars, Kaghzvan, 1913 ◆ Nazik Panosi Abrahamyan, Igdir, Panik, 1912 ◆ Nazik Petrosi Arabkhanyan, Basen, Kyoprikoy, 1914 ◆ Nazik Petrosi Petrosyan, Van, 1912 ◆ Nazik Sargisi Hovhannisyan (Sargsyan), Van, 1916 ◆ Nazik Sargisi Melkonyan, Akhalkalak, 1914 ◆ Nazik Sargsi Minasyan (Sargsyan), Archesh, Soskan, 1911 ◆ Nazik Saribeki Hovakimyan, Leninakan, Svanverdi, 1911 ◆ Nazik Sedraki Setoyan, Leninakan, Sariar, 1920 ◆ Nazik Serobi Simonyan, Van, 1910, 1911 ◆ Nazik Serobi Simonyan, Van, 1910, 1911 ◆ Nazik Setoyi Melkonyan, Shirak, Gorkhana, 1917 ◆ Nazik Simoni Sahakyan, Bulanagh, Gharabashara, 1914 ◆ Nazik Simoni Sahakyan, Bulanagh, Gharabashara, 1914 ◆ Nazik Soghomoni Brutyan (Soghomonyan), Alashkert, Yeghntap, 1912 ◆ Nazik Soghomoni Soghomonyan, Alashkert, 1912 ◆ Nazik Stepani Gasparyan, Leninakan, Zjkhlar, 1911 ◆ Nazik Stepani Manvelyan, Ardahan, Shavsher, 1912 ◆ Nazik Stepani Manvelyan, Ardahan, Shavsher, 1912 ◆ Nazik Stepani Mkrtchyan, Alekpol, Svanverdi, 1911 ◆ Nazik Stepani Mkrtchyan, Alekpol, Svanverdi, 1911 ◆ Nazik Stepani Muradyan, Sarighamish, Hopviran, 1908 ◆ Nazik Tadevosi Tadevosyan, Alekpol, Jalap, 1910 ◆ Nazik Tumasi Tumasyan, Kars, 1912 ◆ Nazik Vanoyi Melkonyan, Alekpol, Alikhan, 1914 ◆ Nazik Yenoki Avetisyan, Hin Bayazet, 1910 ◆ Nazlu Yeghishi Melkonyan, Akhalkalak, Chandura, 1916 ◆ Nazuk Grigori Mkrtchyan, Kars, 1914 ◆ Nektar Garegini Mkrtchyan, Alekpol, Gharakilisa, 1913 ◆ Nektar Hovhannesi Gasparyan, Batum, Tandzut, 1909 ◆ Nektar Hovhannesi Gasparyan, Batum, Tandzut, 1909 ◆ Nerses (Norsik) Gevorgi Gevorgyan, Alekpol, Ortakilisa, 1914 ◆ Nerses (Norsik) Gevorgi Gevorgyan, Alekpol, Ortakilisa, 1914 ◆ Nerses Arshaki Arshakyan, Mush, Drmed, 1913 ◆ Nerses Arshaki Arshakyan, Mush, Drmed, 1913 ◆ Nerses Arshaki Sargsyan, Shirak, Chorli, 1912 ◆ Nerses Avetisi Avetisyan, Van, 1913 ◆ Nerses Gevorgi Simonyan, Shirak, Ghaplu, 1913 ◆ Nerses Hakobi Hovhannisyan, Yerevan, Davalu, 1912 ◆ Nerses Hakobi Hovhannisyan, Yerevan, Davalu, 1912 ◆ Nerses Hovhannesi Karapetyan, Leninakan, Toros, 1911 ◆ Nerses Kerobi Gevorgyan, Shirak, Syogutli, 1912 ◆ Nerses Levoni Hovakyan, Leninakan, Toparlu, 1913 ◆ Nerses Martirosi Martirosyan, Kars, Bashkyadiklar, 1916 ◆ Nerses Rubeni Hovakimyan, Erzrum, 1909 ◆ Nerses Soghomoni Arakelyan, Kars, Gharaghala, 1913 ◆ Nerses Soghomoni Arakelyan, Kars, Gharaghala, 1913 ◆ Nigar Avetisi Manukyan, Manazkert, Noradin, 1908 ◆ Nigar Gaspari Yeghoyan, Bulanagh, Teghut, 1907 ◆ Nigar Israyeli Tevoyan (Israyelyan), Van, Aljavaz, 1911 ◆ Nigar Mkrtchi Hovsepyan, Alashkert, Kolin, 1912 ◆ Nigar Mkrtchyan Mkrtchi, Basen, Stana, 1912 ◆ Nigar Sargisi Hakobyan, Bulanagh, Teghut, 1909 ◆ Nigar Vardani Vardanyan, Darachichak, Akhta, 1910 ◆ Nigar Vardani Vardanyan, Van, Aygestan, 1915 ◆ Nigar Vardani Vardanyan, Van, Aygestan, 1915 ◆ Nigyar Mkhitari Mkhitaryan, Bulanagh, Latar, 1910 ◆ Nigyar Vagharshaki Hovhannisyan, Manazkert, Berd, 1914 ◆ Nikala Arshaki Arshakyan, Shirak, Arkhvali, 1917 ◆ Nikala Arshaki Arshakyan, Shirak, Arkhvali, 1917 ◆ Nikar Avagi Avagyan, Van, Blur, 1908 ◆ Nikar Serobi Avetisyan, Aljavaz, Yarin, 1907 ◆ Nikoghos Balasani Harutyunyan (Balasanyan), Etchmiadzin, Kuluja, 1909 ◆ Nikoghos Balasani Harutyunyan (Balasanyan), Etchmiadzin, Kuluja, 1909 ◆ Nikoghos Barseghi Haroyan (Barseghyan), Akhalkalak, Khanchali, 1913 ◆ Nikoghos Barseghi Haroyan (Barseghyan), Akhalkalak, Khanchali, 1913 ◆ Nikoghos Grigori Sargsyan (Dadayan), Basen, Bashgegh, 1918 ◆ Nikoghos Hasakili Arakelyan, Bayburt, Ksanti, 1910 ◆ Nikoghos Hasakili Arakelyan, Bayburt, Ksanti, 1910 ◆ Nikoghos Hovhannesi Hovhannisyan, Shirak, Chiftalu, 1916 ◆ Nikoghos Sargisi Tadevosyan, Kars, 1913 ◆ Nikoghos Sedraki Khnkoyan (Sedrakyan), Sarighamish,

Gharaghlu, 1912 ♦ Nikoghos Tatosi Tatosyan (Martirosyan), Alekpol, Syogutli, 1912 ♦ Nikol Abgari Nahapetyan (Abgaryan), Salmast, Khoy, 1917 ♦ Nikol Arshaki Sukiasyan, Kars, Arazi, 1913 ♦ Nikol Gharibi Gharibyan, Aparan, Hajibaghr, 1911 ♦ Nikol Karapeti Aleksanyan, Leninakan, Paltlu, 1910 ♦ Nikol Karapeti Aleksanyan, Leninakan, Paltlu, 1910 ♦ Nikol Khachaturi Sargsyan, Alekpol, Gyuli-bulagh, 1914 ♦ Nikol Musheghi Azizyan, Bulanagh, 1912 ♦ Nikol Sargisi Grigoryan (Sargsyan), Kars, Bashgegh, 1910 ♦ Nikol Serobi Sahakyan, Kars, Gharamahmat, 1912 ♦ Nikol Voskani Ayvazyan, Nukhi, Sabatlu, 1909 ♦ Nikolay Harutyuni Topchyan, Baku, 1915 ♦ Nina Aghajani Gevorgyan, Karabagh, Tgena, 1908 ♦ Nina Anastasi Mutafalyan, Lori, Alaverdi, 1907 ♦ Nina Asaturi Hakobyan, Kars, 1919 ♦ Nina Avagi Sargsyan, Karabagh, Norashen, 1906 ♦ Nina Eriklei Similtov, Lori, Madana, 1917 ♦ Nina Grigori (Grigoryan) Mirmanyan, Tiflis, Tiflis, 1916 ♦ Nina Grigori (Grigoryan) Mirmanyan, Tiflis, Tiflis, 1916 ♦ Nina Hovsepi Ayvazyan, Baku, Baku, 1916 ♦ Nina Hovsepi Hovhannisyan, Shirak, Tapadollak, 1916 ♦ Nina Hovsepi Hovhannisyan, Shirak, Tapadollak, 1916 ♦ Nina Khachaturi Khachatryan, Kars, 1913 ♦ Nina Khachiki (Fila) Khachikyan, Tiflis, Madan, 1913 ♦ Nina Khachiki (Fila) Khachikyan, Tiflis, Madan, 1913 ♦ Nina Levoni Chikiashvili, Tiflis, 1912 ♦ Nina Manuki Manukyan, Alashkert, 1914 ♦ Nina Poghosi Poghosyan, Van, Norashen, 1910 ♦ Nina Tadevosi Cholakhyan, Alashkert, 1917 ♦ Nina Tomasi Tumasyan, Nakhijevan, Aza, 1912 ♦ Nina Tumasi Tumasyan, Nakhijevan, Aza, 1912 ♦ Nizina Grigori Ter-Poghosyan, Daralagyaz, Bashkend, 1911 ♦ Norayr Edoyi Edoyan (Ardenyan), Kars, Gorkhana, 1910 ♦ Norayr Grigori Tokmajyan, Yerznka, 1910 ♦ Norayr Harutyuni Gabrielyan (Harutyunyan), Alekpol, Horom, 1914 ♦ Norayr Kerobi Poghosyan, Basen, Dalibaba, 1910 ♦ Norayr Margari Zakaryan, Kars, Byurakdara, 1910 ♦ Norayr Melkoni Melkonyan, Van, Archcsh, 1913 ♦ Norayr Mikayeli Harutyunyan (Darbinyan), Leninakan, Dzitankov, 1912 ♦ Norayr Mkhitari Gasparyan, Kars, 1910 ♦ Norayr Mkhitari Gasparyan, Kars, 1910 ♦ Norayr Rubeni Sargsyan, Igdir, Baharlu, 1913 ♦ Norayr Rubeni Sargsyan, Igdir, Baharlu, 1913 ♦ Norik Bagrati Poghosyan, Shirak, Sariar, 1916 ♦ Norik Misaki Misakyan (Sahakyan), Bulanagh, Kop, 1914, 1915 ♦ Norik Misaki Misakyan (Sahakyan), Bulanagh, Kop, 1914, 1915 ♦ Noyem Barseghi Minasyan, Alekpol, Baytar, 1912 ♦ Noyem Grigori Khachatryan (Grigoryan), Alashkert, Amada, 1914 ♦ Noyem Hakobi Zhamkochyan, Yerevan, 1914 ♦ Noyem Harutyuni Khachatryan, Ajarak, 1914 ♦ Noyem Hayrapeti Hayrapetyan, Alashkert, Khachli, 1910 ♦ Noyem Hovhannesi (Hakob) Hovhannisyan (Hakobyan), Alashkert, 1915 ♦ Noyem Karapeti Karapetyan, Kars, 1919 ♦ Noyem Khachaturi Minasyan, Kars, Askighazi, 1909 ♦ Noyem Khachaturi Sahakyan (Khachatryan), Kars, Gedaksatlmish, 1909 ♦ Noyem Khachaturi Simonyan, Turkey, 1910 ♦ Noyem Martirosi Mkhitaryan, Mush, Janik, 1909 ♦ Noyem Martirosi Petrosyan (Martirosyan), Shirak, Ghzlghoch, 1914 ♦ Noyem Misaki Avetisyan (Heghsoyan), Alekpol, Adiyaman, 1911 ♦ Noyem Mkrtchi Asatryan, Alashkert, Gharakilisa, 1907 ♦ Noyem Simoni Gasparyan (Simonyan), Bitlis, 1910 ♦ Noyemzar Avagi Avagyan, Alashkert, Mazra, 1914 ♦ Noyemzar Avani Ghevondyan (Avanyan), Daralagyaz, Khachik, 1911 ♦ Noyemzar Gaspari Soghomonyan, Kaghzvan, 1914 ♦ Noyemzar Ghazari Ghazaryan (Mkrtchyan), Mush, Haner, 1914 ♦ Noyemzar Ghazari Ghazaryan, Bulanagh, Babul, 1912, 1914 ♦ Noyemzar Ghazari Ghazaryan, Van, Meja, 1913 ♦ Noyemzar Hakobi Hakobyan, Kars, 1908 ♦ Noyemzar Hakobi Hakobyan, Van, 1911 ♦ Noyemzar Hambardzumi Hovhannisyan (Hambardzumyan), Kaghzvan, 1912 ♦ Noyemzar Hambardzumi Hovhannisyan (Hambardzumyan), Kaghzvan, 1912 ♦ Noyemzar Hayrapeti Hovsepyan, Akhalkalak, Samsar, 1914 ♦ Noyemzar Hovhani Hayrapetyan, Daralagyaz, Yerpun, 1910 ♦ Noyemzar Hovhannesi Hovhannisyan, Mush, Ijtaku, 1912 ♦ Noyemzar Hovhannesi Ter-Vardanyan, Erzrum, 1908 ♦ Noyemzar Khachaturi Khachatryan, Van, Yasinj, 1914 ♦ Noyemzar Khachaturi Khachatryan, Van, Yasinj, 1914 ♦ Noyemzar Margari Manukyan, Hin Bayazet, 1912 ♦ Noyemzar Martirosi Malkhasyan, Bulanagh, Yonjalu, 1911 ♦ Noyemzar Mikayeli Natoyan, Pambak, Ghotur-bulagh, 1911 ♦ Noyemzar Minasi Nazaryan, Akhalkalak, Gendura, 1915 ♦ Noyemzar Minasi Nazaryan, Akhalkalak, Gendura, 1915 ♦ Noyemzar Miroyi Manukyan, Van, Asparacin, 1910 ♦ Noyemzar Mkrtchi Khachatryan, Kars, 1908 ♦ Noyemzar Mkrtchi Manukyan, Igdir, 1913 ♦ Noyemzar Mnatsakani Hovhannisyan (Mnatsakanyan), Yerevan, Khalfalu, 1915 ♦ Noyemzar Murati Kirakosyan, Sarighamish, Armtlu, 1909 ♦ Noyemzar Nazari Hovhannisyan (Nazaryan), Alashkert, Ziro, 1914 ♦ Noyemzar Nshani Manukyan, Van, 1912 ♦ Noyemzar Petrosi Petrosyan (Khanoyan), Erzrum, Kyoprikoy, 1914 ♦ Noyemzar Petrosi Ter-Petrosyan, Van, Tigris, 1908 ♦ Noyemzar Poghosi Ghazaryan (Poghosyan), Kars, Chakhmakh, 1914 ♦ Noyemzar Poghosi Ghazaryan (Poghosyan), Kars, Chakhmakh, 1914 ♦ Noyemzar Sayadi Movsisyan, Baku, Salibeglu, 1911 ♦ Noyemzar Stepani (Stepanyan) Vardanyan, Alekpol, Duzkand, 1910 ♦ Noyemzar Stepani Davtyan, Kars, 1912 ♦ Noyemzar Sukiasi Vardanyan, Alashkert, Iritsu, 1911 ♦ Noyemzar Tadevosi Avetisyan, Sarighamish, Bashgegh, 1913 ♦ Noyemzar Tigrani Khrikyan, Akhalkalak, Olaver, 1909 ♦ Noyemzar Tovmasi Shahbazyan, Van, Yerec, 1905 ♦ Noyemzar Tumasi Abgaryan, Sarighamish, Stan, 1912 ♦ Nranhat Vardani Hovsepyan (Vardanyan), Van, 1914 ♦ Nranhat Vardani Hovsepyan (Vardanyan), Van, 1914 ♦ Nshan Gaspari Gasparyan (Torosyan), Manazkert, Sipan, 1907 ♦ Nshan Ghazari Sargsyan (Ghazaryan), Van, Karchkan, 1910 ♦ Nshan Grigori Safaryan, Van, Noragyugh, 1911 ♦ Nshan Harutyuni Petrosyan, Erzrum, Jermuk, 1907 ♦ Nshan Khachaturi Sargsyan, Baku, 1909 ♦ Nshan Kostani Hakobyan, Van, Archak, 1913 ♦ Nshan Manasi Hovhannisyan (Manasyan), Van, Zarants, 1911 ♦ Nshan Manuki Manukyan, Erzrum, 1915 ♦ Nshan Manuki

Manukyan, Van, Archesh, 1916 ♦ Nshan Manuki Manukyan, Van, Atana, 1911 ♦ Nshan Movsesi Movsisyan, Terjan, 1916 ♦ Nshan Muradi Muradyan, Van, 1914 ♦ Nshan Petrosi Vardanyan, Van, Hermet, 1910 ♦ Nshan Simoni Simonyan, Alashkert, Iritsu, 1916 ♦ Nshan Sukiasi Abrahamyan, Van, Ziraklu, 1910 ♦ Nsher Hovhannesi Sahakyan, Archesh, 1913 ♦ Nshkhun Vardani Hambardzumyan (Vardanyan), Alekpol, Khli Gharakilis, 1909 ♦ Nshkhun Vardani Melikyan, Kaghzvan, 1911 ♦ Nubar Abrahami Aghamiryan (Abrahamyan), Van, Aghk, 1909 ♦ Nubar Avetisi Avetisyan, Van, Goms, 1912 ♦ Nubar Hakobi Manukyan, Van, Artamet, 1910 ♦ Nubar Hovhannesi Melkonyan, Van, 1909 ♦ Nubar Hovhannesi Melkonyan, Van, 1909 ♦ Nubar Javari Petrosyan, Van, Moks, Kaser, 1911 ♦ Nubar Manuki Karapetyan (Manukyan), Van, Khachan, 1908 ♦ Nubar Manuki Kostanyan, Van, Karchkan, 1910 ♦ Nubar Martirosi Martirosyan, Van, 1915 ♦ Nubar Melkoni Melkonyan, Van, Aljavaz, 1911 ♦ Nubar Melkoni Melkonyan, Van, Aljavaz, 1911 ♦ Nubar Muradi Muradyan, Van, Akants, 1912 ♦ Nubar Muradi Muradyan, Van, Khazam, 1912 ♦ Nubar Murati Margaryan, Hayots dzor, Hirch, 1908 ♦ Nubar Nshani Nshanyan, Van, 1915 ♦ Nubar Petrosi Barseghyan (Petrosyan), Van, Kghzi, 1912 ♦ Nubar Petrosi Barseghyan (Petrosyan), Van, Kghzi, 1912 ♦ Nubar Poghosi Muradyan, Pambak, Gharakilisa, 1913 ♦ Nubar Sargisi Hakobyan (Sargsyan), Van, Archesh, 1908 ♦ Nubar Sargisi Hakobyan (Sargsyan), Van, Archesh, 1908 ♦ Nubar Saroyi Saroyan, Van, Shadivan, 1910 ♦ Nubar Tevosi Tevosyan, Yerevan, Yuva, 1915 ♦ Nubar Tumasi Tumasyan, Vaspurakan, Kerc, 1911 ♦ Nubar Vardani Muradyan (Vardanyan), Van, Pirbadalan, 1909 ♦ Nubar Yenoki Movsisyan (Yenokyan), Yerevan, Tokhanshanlu, 1914 ♦ Nunik Abrahami Poghosyan (Abrahamyan), Sarighamish, Armtlu, 1910 ♦ Nunik Alberti Mnatsakanyan, Baku, Nukhi, 1912 ♦ Nunik Aleksani Varosyan, Alekpol, Ghzlghoch, 1915 ♦ Nunik Andraniki Baghdasaryan, Akhalkalak, Gimbirda, 1912 ♦ Nunik Arakeli Arakelyan, Kars, Kirs, 1914 ♦ Nunik Arakeli Ghukasyan (Arakelyan), Alashkert, Iritsu, 1913 ♦ Nunik Arteni Harutyunyan Alashkert, Khastur, 1912 ♦ Nunik Arteni Harutyunyan, Alashkert, Khastur, 1912 ♦ Nunik Azizi Minasyan (Azizyan), Van, Lima, 1910 ♦ Nunik Galusti Khndoryan (Galstyan) Sarighamish, Gharaghurut, 1913 ♦ Nunik Galusti Khndoryan (Galstyan), Sarighamish, Gharaghurut, 1913 ♦ Nunik Gevorgi Abrahamyan (Gevorgyan), Alekpol, Toros, 1914 ♦ Nunik Ghazari Hakobyan, Leninakan, Ortakilisa, 1909 ♦ Nunik Grigori Mikayelyan, Alekpol, Adiaman, 1912 ♦ Nunik Hakobi Ghazaryan, Kars, Tigor, 1908 ♦ Nunik Hakobi Poghosyan, Bulanagh, Yonjalu, 1913, 1911 ♦ Nunik Hakobi Poghosyan, Bulanagh, Yonjalu, 1913, 1911 ♦ Nunik Harutyuni Harutyunyan, 1915 ♦ Nunik Harutyuni Harutyunyan, 1915 ♦ Nunik Hovhannesi Galstyan, Shirak, Alekpol, 1909 ♦ Nunik Hovhannesi Mkrtchyan, Kars, Ardahan, 1911 ♦ Nunik Hovhannesi Mkrtchyan, Kars, Ardahan, 1911 ♦ Nunik Karapeti Karapetyan, Kars, Cbni, 1912 ♦ Nunik Karapeti Margaryan, Erzrum, Karabazar, 1911 ♦ Nunik Khachaturi Aleksanyan, Kars, 1914 ♦ Nunik Khachaturi Yeksuzyan, Akhaltsikha, 1910 ♦ Nunik Martirosi Petrosyan, Kars, Dolband, 1913 ♦ Nunik Mkrtchi Hakobyan, Alekpol, Ghaplu, 1911 ♦ Nunik Movsesi Maroyan, Basen, Gulantapa, 1908 ♦ Nunik Musheghi Knyazyan, Shirak, Ghapli, 1909 ♦ Nunik Nikoghosi Hovsepyan, Alekpol, Ghapli, 1911 ♦ Nunik Nikoghosi Hovsepyan, Alekpol, Ghapli, 1911 ♦ Nunik Sahaki Petrosyan, Alekpol, Ghapli, 1911 ♦ Nunik Sedraki Mirzoyan, Kaghzvan, 1921 ♦ Nunik Serobi Baroyan, Basen, Chrason, 1911 ♦ Nunik Serobi Manukyan, Kars, Kaghzvan, 1911, 1912 ♦ Nunik Tigrani Tigranyan, Basen, Hekipat, 1913 ♦ Nunik Vagharshaki Vagharshakyan, Kars, 1913 ♦ Nunik Vagharshaki Vagharshakyan, Van, 1916 ♦ Nunik Vagharshaki Vagharshakyan, Van, 1916 ♦ Nunik Vahani Sargsyan, Kars, 1918 ♦ Nunik Vardani Gasparyan (Vardanyan), Manazkert, Yekmal, 1912 ♦ Nunik Vardani Vardanyan, Leninakan, Bandivan, 1914, 1917 ♦ Nunik Varosi Tatosyan, Alekpol, Imrkhan, 1917 ♦ Nunik Varosi Tatosyan, Alekpol, Imrkhan, 1917 ♦ Nunik Yervandi Yervandyan (Poghosyan), Leninakan, Paltlu, 1918 ♦ Nunik Zakari Sahakyan, Alekpol, Tavshanghshlagh, 1911 ♦ Nunufar Aghasi Aghajanyan, Kars, 1911 ♦ Nunufar Ghazari Yeghoyan, Karabagh, 1917 ♦ Nunufar Harutyuni Hovhannisyan, 1920 ♦ Nunufar Nushikyan, Yerevan, Koghp, 1918 ♦ Nunufar Sahaki Sahakyan, Nukhi, 1917 ♦ Nunufar Vanushi Harutyunyan, Baku, Masara, 1913 ♦ Nunufar Vardani Grigoryan, Archesh, Machars, 1911 ♦ Nunush Arshaki Margaryan, Kars, 1910 ♦ Nunush Artashesi Gasparyan, Kars, 1916 ♦ Nunush Ghukasi Poghosyan, Kars, 1914 ♦ Nunush Minasi Minasyan, Nakhijevan, 1917 ♦ Nunush Minasi Minasyan, Nakhijevan, 1917 ♦ Nunush Papiki Avagyan, Shirak, Chiftali, 1915 ♦ Nunush Papiki Avagyan, Shirak, Chiftali, 1915 ♦ Nuria Sargisi Sargsyan, Akhalkalak, 1915 ♦ Nurik Moskovi Hakobyan, Mush, Yonjalu, 1910 ♦ Nushik Arami Aramyan, Van, Psti, 1914 ♦ Nushik Arshaki Hovhannisyan, Yerevan, Davalu, 1917 ♦ Nushik Asaturi Asatryan, Bulanagh, Teghut, 1912 ♦ Nushik Barseghi Arevshatyan, Manazkert, Molla-mutafa, 1908 ♦ Nushik Hakobi Hakobyan, Bulanagh, Votnchor, 1912 ♦ Nushik Hunani Samvelyan (Hunanyan), Kars, Araz, 1917 ♦ Nushik Misaki Arakelyan, Shirak, Karmir vank, 1913 ♦ Nushik Sakoyi Sakoyan, Alekpol, Ghzlkilisa, 1913 ♦ Nushik Sakoyi Sakoyan, Alekpol, Ghzlkilisa, 1913 ♦ Nushik Sargisi Sargsyan, Leninakan, Jajur, 1911 ♦ Nushik Sargisi Sargsyan, Leninakan, Jajur, 1911 ♦ Nushik Sargisi Yeranosyan, Bitlis, 1909 ♦ Nushik Sargsi Hakobyan, 1910 ♦ Nushik Serobi Sahakyan, Alekpol, Chiftali, 1914 ♦ Nushik Tadevosi Sahakyan, Igdir, 1909 ♦ Nusho Artashesi Sargsyan (Artashyan), Shirak, Mec Keti, 1915 ♦ Nusho Poghosi Ispiryan, Jalaloghli, Khotur, 1914 ♦ Nvard Abrahami Abrahamyan, Van, Sevan, 1912 ♦ Nvard Abrahami Arshakyan, Alashkert, Ghayabek, 1913 ♦ Nvard Aghasu Movsisyan, Kars, Agrak, 1914 ♦ Nvard Aghasu Movsisyan, Kars, Agrak, 1914 ♦ Nvard Aleksani Aleksanyan, Mec Gharakilis, Hajighara, 1913 ♦ Nvard Aleksani Harutyunyan,

Kars, Mec Parket, 1912 ♦ Nvard Aleksani Hovhannisyan, Kars, 1909 ♦ Nvard Aleksani Khachatryan, Bulanagh, Rostomgedak, 1914 ♦ Nvard Aleksani Sargsyan, Basen, Gomadzor, 1909 ♦ Nvard Aleksani Sargsyan, Hasanghala, Hekibat, 1911 ♦ Nvard Andraniki Hakobyan, Leninakan, Khrkh Dagirman, 1910 ♦ Nvard Arakeli Pilosyan (Arakelyan), Erzrum, Khachavank, 1916 ♦ Nvard Arshaki Harutyunyan, Alekpol, Mec Sariar, 1913 ♦ Nvard Artashesi Artashyan, Yerevan, 1918 ♦ Nvard Avdali Avdalyan, Alashkert, 1915 ♦ Nvard Avdali Avdalyan, Alashkert, 1915 ♦ Nvard Avetisi Karapetyan, Mush, Bulanagh, 1915 ♦ Nvard Avetisi Karapetyan, Mush, Bulanagh, 1915 ♦ Nvard Baghdasari Baghdasaryan, Alekpol, Sirvanshugh, 1913 ♦ Nvard Baghdasari Baghdasaryan, Alekpol, Sirvanshugh, 1913 ♦ Nvard Baghdasari Derdzyan, Basen, Bashgyugh, 1911 ♦ Nvard Baghdasari Grigoryan (Baghdasaryan), Alashkert, Ghazi, 1914 ♦ Nvard Daviti Noramiryan, Van, 1908 ♦ Nvard Gabrieli Simonyan, Kars, 1911 ♦ Nvard Galusti Galstyan, Gharakilisa, Sarmsakhli, 1921 ♦ Nvard Galusti Galstyan, Gharakilisa, Sarmsakhli, 1921 ♦ Nvard Galusti Vardanyan, Alekpol, Ghanlija, 1912 ♦ Nvard Gevorgi Gasparyan, Bulanagh, Shirvanshekh, 1907 ♦ Nvard Ghukasi Abrahamyan, Kars, Chala, 1911 ♦ Nvard Ghukasi Ghukasyan, Kars, Dolbandli, 1910 ♦ Nvard Ginosi Karapetyan, Karin, Aprunk, 1916 ♦ Nvard Ginosi Karapetyan, Karin, Aprunk, 1916 ♦ Nvard Grigori Grigoryan, Van, Archesh, 1915 ♦ Nvard Grigori Grigoryan, Van, Archesh, 1915 ♦ Nvard Hakobi Gasparyan, Leninakan, 1910 ♦ Nvard Hambardzumi Hambardzumyan, Akhalkalak, Gandza, 1914 ♦ Nvard Hambardzumi Hambardzumyan, Kars, Gomadzor, 1912 ♦ Nvard Hambardzumi Hambardzumyan, Leninakan, Ortakilisa, 1913 ♦ Nvard Haruti Papikyan, Shirak, Sariar, 1912 ♦ Nvard Harutyuni (Grigori) Harutyunyan (Grigoryan), Yuzviran, 1912 ♦ Nvard Harutyuni Asaturyan (Harutyunyan), Kars, Hamzakarak, 1914 ♦ Nvard Harutyuni Harutyunyan, Van, Kyurnents, 1910 ♦ Nvard Harutyuni Shmavonyan, Van, 1912 ♦ Nvard Hayrapeti Manukyan, Van, Hererin, 1914 ♦ Nvard Hayroyi Hlghatyan (Melkonyan), Bulanagh, Gharaghl, 1913 ♦ Nvard Hovaki Hovsepyan, Alekpol, Bozdoghan, 1911 ♦ Nvard Hovhannesi Hakobyan, Etchmiadzin, Ghardughuli, 1912 ♦ Nvard Hovhannesi Martirosyan (Ghazaryan, Kars, Chala, 1915 ♦ Nvard Hovhannesi Mkhitaryan, Manazkert, Derik, 1909 ♦ Nvard Hovhannesi Shaboyan, Sharur, Bashnorashen, 1912 ♦ Nvard Hovhannesi Shaboyan, Sharur, Bashnorashen, 1912 ♦ Nvard Karapeti Gareginyan, Van, Kyurbadaran, 1910 ♦ Nvard Karapeti Papikyan, Kars, Cbni, 1914 ♦ Nvard Karapeti Papikyan, Kars, Cbni, 1914 ♦ Nvard Karapeti Rashoyan, Mush, Poghorkov, 1911 ♦ Nvard Karapeti Rashoyan, Mush, Poghorkov, 1911 ♦ Nvard Karapeti Yeghoyan, Bulanagh, Hamzashekh, 1911 ♦ Nvard Kerobi Avetisyan (Sargsyan), Karin, 1912 ♦ Nvard Khachaturi Baghdasaryan (Khachatryan), Gharakilisa, Ghachaghan, 1915 ♦ Nvard Manuki Darbinyan, Van, 1913 ♦ Nvard Manuki Darbinyan, Van, 1913 ♦ Nvard Manuki Hayrapetyan (Gabrielyan), Akhalkalak, Agana, 1912 ♦ Nvard Margari Avetisyan (Margaryan), Erzrum, Yaghan, 1911 ♦ Nvard Martirosi Ayvazyan (Martirosyan), Sarighamish, 1914 ♦ Nvard Martirosi Ayvazyan (Martirosyan), Sarighamish, 1914 ♦ Nvard Martirosi Grigoryan, Erzrum, 1908 ♦ Nvard Martirosi Khachatryan (Martirosyan), Gharakilisa, Chotur, 1917 ♦ Nvard Meliki Adamyan, Alekpol, Duzkharaba, 1910 ♦ Nvard Meliki Nalbandyan, Van, 1908 ♦ Nvard Meliki Shakafyan, Kars, Mazra, 1911 ♦ Nvard Meliki Shakafyan, Kars, Mazra, 1911 ♦ Nvard Melkoni Melkonyan (Vardapetyan), Bulanagh, Shaghab, 1912 ♦ Nvard Mikayeli Janikyan, Van, 1911 ♦ Nvard Mikayeli Janikyan, Van, 1911 ♦ Nvard Minasi Avagyan, Chanakhchi, Chanchrlu, 1914 ♦ Nvard Mkrtchi Mkrtchyan (Burnazyan), Kars, 1914 ♦ Nvard Mkrtchi Pilosyan, Basen, Aljavaz, 1912 ♦ Nvard Mkrtchi Salamkaryan, Constantinople, 1907 ♦ Nvard Mnatsakani Movsisyan, Van, Korkot, 1913 ♦ Nvard Mnatsakani Movsisyan, Van, Korkot, 1913 ♦ Nvard Movsesi Movsisyan, Mush, Bulanagh, 1912 ♦ Nvard Movsesi Movsisyan, Mush, Bulanagh, 1912 ♦ Nvard Mukayeli Serobyan, Sarighamish, 1916 ♦ Nvard Muradi Tonoyan, 1918 ♦ Nvard Muradi Tonoyan, 1918 ♦ Nvard Nikoli Muradyan, Gharakilisa, Vortnav, 1913 ♦ Nvard Poghosi Panosyan, Van, 1907 ♦ Nvard Poghosi Panosyan, Van, 1907 ♦ Nvard Poloyi Aghajanyan (Sirunyan), Bulanagh, Kop, 1913 ♦ Nvard Sahaki Sahakyan, Khnus, 1911 ♦ Nvard Sahaki Yeghiazaryan, Van, Alrtsi, 1912 ♦ Nvard Sakoyi Sakoyan, Alekpol, Ghzlkilisa, 1915 ♦ Nvard Santuri Santuryan (Gevorgyan), Bulanagh, Hamzashekh, 1916 ♦ Nvard Sedraki Khachatryan, Bulanagh, Rostomgedak, 1907 ♦ Nvard Sedraki Sedrakyan, Khnus, Khrt, 1910 ♦ Nvard Sedraki Sedrakyan, Sarighamish, Gyulantap, 1918 ♦ Nvard Stepani Manukyan (Stepanyan), Nakhijevan, Gharakhanbegla, 1914 ♦ Nvard Stepani Margaryan (Stepanyan), Van, 1910 ♦ Nvard Stepani Margaryan (Stepanyan), Van, 1910 ♦ Nvard Tadevosi Grigoryan, Erzrum, Varduk, 1906 ♦ Nvard Tadevosi Zakaryan, Leninakan, Sariar, 1912 ♦ Nvard Torosi Hovhannisyan, Van, Gandzak, 1908 ♦ Nvard Torosi Poghosyan (Torosyan), Kharberd, Havshakar, 1910 ♦ Nvard Vahani Karapetyan, Sarighamish, Kharayorghan, 1911 ♦ Nvard Vahani Karapetyan, Sarighamish, Kharayorghan, 1911 ♦ Nvard Voskani Grigoryan, Kaghzvan, Yengija, 1909 ♦ Nver Avetisi Avetisyan, Van, Mashtak, 1911 ♦ Nver Karapeti Karapetyan, Hayots dzor, Khorgom, 1911 ♦ Oberon Hovhannesi Kirakosyan, Alekpol, Aghin, 1911 ♦ Ofelia Bagrati Ter-Harutyunyan, Igdir, 1912 ♦ Ofelia Grigori Melikyan, Krakom, 1910 ♦ Ofelia Hakobi Hakobyan, Yerevan, Daharlu, 1917 ♦ Ofelya Gevorgi Gevorgyan, Igdir, 1912 ♦ Ofik Gevorgi Arslanyan, Van, 1913 ♦ Ofik Gevorgi Yeghiazaryan (Grigoryan), Shirak, 1919 ♦ Ofik Kolyayi Poghosyan, 1920 ♦ Ofik Sahakyan (Sargsyan), 1921 ♦ Ofik Vachoyi Hovhannisyan, Leninakan, Gorkhana, 1918 ♦ Ofik Vahani Vahanyan, Alekpol, Svanverdi, 1918 ♦ Ogher Khachaturi Avagyan, Kars, Aksighazi, 1914 ♦ Ogher Sargisi Sargsyan, Kars, Gorkhana, 1919 ♦ Ogher Smbati Khachatryan, Kars, Tekniz, 1915 ♦ Ogsen Avetisi Asatryan,

Van, Berdak, 1914 ◆ Ogsen Gaspari Melkonyan, Alekpol, Shishtapa, 1914 ◆ Ogsen Melkoni Khachatryan (Melkonyan), Bayazet, 1912 ◆ Ohan Avetisi Poghosyan (Avetisyan), Leninakan, Toparli, 1915 ◆ Ohannes Gevorgi Nazaryan, Kars, Ghzlchakhchakh, 1914 ◆ Okhtanes Manuki Manukyan, Alekpol, Sirvan gyugh, 1916 ◆ Olga Hovhannesi Hovhannisyan, Kars, Ghzlchakhchakh, 1913 ◆ Olichka Feodori Avlastimov, Lori, Madan, 1913 ◆ Olichka Hovhannesi Martirosyan (Gevorgyan), Kars, Sarighamish, 1913 ◆ Olichka Margari Margaryan, Tiflis, 1916 ◆ Olichka Vanoyi Kachkova, Alaverdi, 1916 ◆ Olik Arami Aramyan, Shirak, Samrlu, 1915 ◆ Olinka Aleksani Hayrapetyan, Karabagh, Khnabar, 1915 ◆ Olinka Grigori Minasyan, Yerevan, Ghrghbulagh, 1917 ◆ Olinka Hovhannesi Hovhannisyan, Alekpol, Toros, 1918 ◆ Onik (Vano) Gaspari Gasparyan, Pambak, Gharakilisa, 1918 ◆ Onik Artashi Onikyan, 1918 ◆ Onik Hovhannesi Petrosyan, Alekpol, Ghonaghran, 1917 ◆ Onik Misakyan, Kars, 1919 ◆ Onik Saroyi Stepanyan (Saroyan), Leninakan, Imrkhan, 1915 ◆ Onik Tadevosi Harutyunyan (Melikyan), Shirak, Talin, 1916 ◆ Osan Abeli Zakaryan, Hin Nakhijevan, Gyumri, 1913 ◆ Osan Aleksani Saroyan (Aleksanyan), Leninakan, Chzghlar, 1914 ◆ Osan Grigori (Smbtai) Smbatyan, Alekpol, Bandivan, 1916 ◆ Osan Grigori Grigoryan, Leninakan, Jalap, 1914 ◆ Osan Hambarzumi Hamazaspyan, Nakhijevan, 1917 ◆ Osan Karapeti Hambaryan, Alekpol, Artik, 1912 ◆ Osan Kerobi Kerobyan, Leninakan, Sariar, 1916 ◆ Osan Meliki Galstyan, Kars, Gedaksatlu, 1911 ◆ Osan Mkrtchi Harutyunyan, Leninakan, 1912 ◆ Osan Nazari Stepanyan, Leninakan, Molla gokcha, 1909 ◆ Osan Tigrani Minasyan, Alekpol, Tavshanghshlagh, 1914 ◆ Osan Yervandi Hakoyan, Kars, Pirvali, 1915, 1912 ◆ Ovsanna Arshaki Arshakyan, Van, Alur, 1911 ◆ Ovsanna Avetisi Avetisyan, Kars, Mazra, 1919 ◆ Ovsanna Galusti Darbinyan, Akhalkalak, Ikhtila, 1915 ◆ Ovsanna Geghami Margaryan (Geghamyan), Surmalu, Tashburan, 1912 ◆ Ovsanna Hakobi Abrahamyan (Hakobyan), Kars, 1908 ◆ Ovsanna Hayki Kirakosyan, Leninakan, 1909 ◆ Ovsanna Khachaturi Israyelyan, Leninakan, Bozyekhush, 1911 ◆ Ovsanna Khachaturi Torosyan, Leninakan, Ghanlija, 1916 ◆ Ovsanna Meliki Hovakimyan, Etchmiadzin, Tashburan, 1911 ◆ Ovsanna Misaki Samvelyan, Bitlis, 1908 ◆ Ovsanna Mnatsakani Khachatryan, Kars, Bagran, 1913 ◆ Ovsanna Petrosi Grigoryan, Shirak, Svanverdi, 1916 ◆ Ovsanna Yeghiayi Karapetyan, Hin Nakhijevan, Gyuznud, 1912 ◆ Palasan Nersesi Gevorgyan, Alekpol, Bandivan, 1912 ◆ Pambakh Arshaki Arshakyan, Van, 1915 ◆ Pambukh Abgari Avetisyan, Kars, Bayburt, 1914 ◆ Pambukh Andraniki Mahtesyan, Van, Berkri, 1911 ◆ Pambukh Hayrapeti Yenokyan, Yerevan, Kulap, 1915 ◆ Pambush Karapeti Poghosyan (Karapetyan), Alekpol, Psti Keti, 1915 ◆ Pampukh Margari Margaryan, Kars, Zrchi, 1908 ◆ Pampukht Stepani Stepanyan (Mkrtchyan), Alekpol, Samrlu, 1911 ◆ Pampush Avetisi Hovsepyan (Avetisyan), Van, Moks, 1914 ◆ Pampush Gevorgi Gevorgyan, Kars, Kharkov, 1916 ◆ Pampush Khachiki Grigoryan (Khachikyan), Berkri, 1914 ◆ Pampush Petrosi Sahakyan (Petrosyan), Nor Bayazet, Noraduz, 1915 ◆ Panos Tigrani Blbulyan (Tigranyan), Bitlis, Sasik, 1908 ◆ Panpukh Fidani Gabrielyan, Basen, Yaghan, 1910 ◆ Papash Tonoyi Poghosyan, Leninakan, Gharakilisa, 1912 ◆ Papik Haruti Harutyunyan, Shirak, Taknoli, 1918 ◆ Papik Minasi Achemyan, Gharakilisa, Hamamlu, 1901 ◆ Papik Papikyan, Gharakilisa, 1919 ◆ Papik Simoni Sargsyan, Van, Lim, 1913 ◆ Papo Aleksani Papikyan, Shirak, Shyogutli, 1912 ◆ Paranci Hovaki Yermoyan, Erzrum, Mants, 1910 ◆ Parandzem Adibeki Aleksanyan, Nor Bayazet, Ghzli, 1914 ◆ Parandzem Aleki Torosyan, Yerevan, Dashburan, 1910 ◆ Parandzem Aleksani Aleksanyan, Leninakan, Bandivan, 1915 ◆ Parandzem Aleksani Caturyan, Kars, 1908 ◆ Parandzem Aleksani Hayrapetyan, Shushi, Khnabat, 1912 ◆ Parandzem Annayi Harutyunyan, Kars, Kelfalu, 1914 ◆ Parandzem Antanasi Nersisyan, Aljavaz, Karakilis, 1915 ◆ Parandzem Armenaki Yeghoyan (Karapetyan), Sarighamish, Sthan, 1916 ◆ Parandzem Arshaki Baghdasaryan, Akhalkalak, 1915 ◆ Parandzem Avetisi Avetisyan, Kars, Tigor, 1911 ◆ Parandzem Avetisi Margaryan, Yelinovis, Cho-Cho, 1914 ◆ Parandzem Barseghi Barseghyan, Nor Bayazet, Aluzalu, 1911 ◆ Parandzem Gabrieli Grigoryan, Kars, 1914 ◆ Parandzem Galusti Hovhhannisyan, Leninakan, Gharakilisa, 1909 ◆ Parandzem Garegini Martirosyan, Ijevan, 1914 ◆ Parandzem Gaspari Gasparyan, Bulanagh, Latar, 1911 ◆ Parandzem Geghami Mkhitaryan (Geghamyan), Shirak, Mastara, 1913 ◆ Parandzem Geghami Movsisyan (Geghamyan), Akhalkalak, Karcakh, 1916 ◆ Parandzem Gevorgi Martirosyan, Kars, Paldrvan, 1916 ◆ Parandzem Gharibi Manukyan, Bitlis, Prkhus, 1911 ◆ Parandzem Ghukasi Ghukasyan, Erzrum, Terjan, 1910 ◆ Parandzem Grigori Grigoryan, Alashkert, Gharakilisa, 1909 ◆ Parandzem Grigori Grigoryan, Gharakilise, Koran, 1914 ◆ Parandzem Grigori Grigoryan, Kars, Gharakilisa, 1916 ◆ Parandzem Grigori Khachatryan, Leninakan, Ghzlghoch, 1912 ◆ Parandzem Hakobi Ghalumyan (Gyulumyan), Ghazakh, Sev kar, 1913 ◆ Parandzem Hakobi Martirosyan, Kars, Ughuzli, 1914 ◆ Parandzem Hakobi Nalbandyan, Alekpol, Horom, 1910 ◆ Parandzem Hambardzumi Hambardzumyan, Shirak, Arkhivali, 1917 ◆ Parandzem Harutyuni Manukyan, Shirak, Dorbandlu, 1911 ◆ Parandzem Hovakimi Babayan, Nakhijevan, Sultanbek, 1910 ◆ Parandzem Hovhannesi Hovhannisyan, Alekpol, Khli Gharakilis, 1914 ◆ Parandzem Hovhannesi Hovhannisyan, Mamakhatun, Kot, 1911 ◆ Parandzem Hovhannesi Khachatryan, Kars, Bashkadiklar, 1909 ◆ Parandzem Hovhannesi Sahakyan, Nakhijevan, Nors, 1912 ◆ Parandzem Hovsepi Vardanyan, Kars, 1913 ◆ Parandzem Kerobi Hovhannisyan, Kars, Ghapanlu, 1911 ◆ Parandzem Khachaturi Harutyunyan, Dilijan, 1909 ◆ Parandzem Khachaturi Khachatryan, Bitlis, 1909 ◆ Parandzem Khachaturi Sargsyan, Kars, Kaghzvan, 1911 ◆ Parandzem Knyazi Grigoryan, Leninakan, Bandivan, 1912 ◆ Parandzem Manuki Manukyan (Hovhannisyan), Van, 1911, 1910 ◆ Parandzem Manuki Manukyan, Alekpol, Ortakilisa, 1914 ◆ Parandzem Martirosi

Muradyan, Kars, Kyadiklar, 1909 ◆ Parandzem Meliki Dallakyan, Lori, Akori, 1911 ◆ Parandzem Mihrani Dilanyan, Van, 1911 ◆ Parandzem Mikayeli Yepremyan, Koghb, 1912 ◆ Parandzem Misaki Ghandilyan (Misakyan), Bitlis, Prkhus, 1912 ◆ Parandzem Misaki Martirosyan (Misakyan), Kars, Zaim, 1914 ◆ Parandzem Misaki Misakyan, Kars, Ghzlchakhchakh, 1917 ◆ Parandzem Mkrtchi Kolotyan, Karin, 1912 ◆ Parandzem Mkrtchi Safaryan (Mkrtchyan), Van, 1909 ◆ Parandzem Mukoyi Muradyan, Kars, Bagliahmat, 1911 ◆ Parandzem Mukuchi Torosyan, Erzrum, Khan, 1907 ◆ Parandzem Musheghi Asoyan, Bashshoragal, 1912 ◆ Parandzem Petrosi Petrosyan, Kars, Bagaran, 1914 ◆ Parandzem Rostomi Rostomyan, Etchmiadzin, Aparan, 1913 ◆ Parandzem Sedraki Carukyan, Kars, Pirvali, 1913 ◆ Parandzem Sedraki Sargsyan, Kars, Gorkhan, 1908 ◆ Parandzem Serobi Manukyan, Kars, Ghapanlu, 1911 ◆ Parandzem Smbati Ghukasyan, Alekpol, Toros, 1915 ◆ Parandzem Stepani Harutyunyan, Caghkadzor, Undamal, 1915 ◆ Parandzem Tepani Khachatryan, Alekpol, Ghoshavank, 1910 ◆ Parandzem Vardani Gasparyan, Akhalkalak, Vachyan, 1913 ◆ Parandzem Vardani Grigoryan (Vardanyan), Gharakilise, Koran, 1914 ◆ Parandzem Yeghishi Zurabyan (Yeghishyan), Kars, Bazrgan, 1920 ◆ Parandzem Yeranosi Muradyan, Etchmiadzin, Ghznavuz, 1914 ◆ Parantsi Hovhannesi Hovhannisyan, Kaghzvan, 1910 ◆ Paravon Hovsepi Hovsepyan, Erzrum, Chifli, 1912 ◆ Pares Hambardzumi Paresyan (Hambardzumyan), Taron, Khasgyugh, 1909 ◆ Pargev Alaverdii Alaverdyan, Manazkert, Yeknakhcha, 1913 ◆ Pargev Grigori Hovhannisyan (Grigoryan), Van, 1911 ◆ Pargev Grigori Tadevosyan (Grigoryan), Surmalu, Dashburan, 1914 ◆ Pargev Grigori Yeghiazaryan, Kars, Gedaksatlmish, 1916 ◆ Pargev Hakobi Hakobyan, Alashkert, Vank, 1914 ◆ Pargev Hovnani Musheghyan, Bayazet, Kishmishtapa, 1914 ◆ Pargev Hovnani Musheghyan, Maku, Shishtapa, 1913 ◆ Pargev Hovsepi Avetisyan (Hovsepyan), Kars, Gedaksatlmish, 1916 ◆ Pargev Khachaturi Hovhannisyan (Khachatryan), Leninakan, 1914 ◆ Pargev Martirosi Martirosyan, Van, 1911 ◆ Pargev Martirosi Sukiasyan, Surmalu, Tashburan, 1909 ◆ Pargev Rafayeli Harutyunyan, Erzrum, Pulg, 1911 ◆ Pargev Sedraki Carukyan, Kars, Pirvali, 1911 ◆ Pargev Yeghiazari Yeghiazaryan, Etchmiadzin, 1914 ◆ Parijan Ghazari Zakaryan (Ghazaryan), Mush, Kharabshat, 1910 ◆ Parijan Khachaturi Kirakosyan (Khachatryan), Mush, Avrak, 1913 ◆ Parik (Paran) Hakobi Avetisyan, Leninakan, Khli Gharakilis, 1918 ◆ Parik Poghosi Poghosyan, Kaghzvan, 1919 ◆ Parkesht Movsesi Gharibyan, Surmalu, Alija, 1913 ◆ Parmeli Khachaturi Martirosyan, Van, 1910 ◆ Parnavaz Arshaki Asoyan, Alekpol, 1914 ◆ Parnavaz Ghevodnyan ◆ Parnavaz Grigori Grigoryan, Alekpol, Kyadiklar, 1917 ◆ Paron Bek Baloyi Kirobyan, Kars, Dashkov, 1916 ◆ Partez Vanoyi Vanoyan, Leninakan, Paldlu, 1914 ◆ Paruyr Adami Khachatryan, Leninakan, Talin, 1913 ◆ Paruyr Aleki Aleksanyan, Alekpol, Gharakilisa, 1914 ◆ Paruyr Andraniki Postoyan (Andranikyan), Karin, Karin, 1912 ◆ Paruyr Arami Mikayelyan, Kars, Kars, 1914 ◆ Paruyr Arshaki Avagyan, Kars, Gorkhana, 1911 ◆ Paruyr Arshaki Petrosyan, Shirak, Chorli, 1912 ◆ Paruyr Durasani Petrosyan, Shamakhi, Ghazar, 1914 ◆ Paruyr Galusti Ghukasyan, Basen, Dalibaba, 1916 ◆ Paruyr Hakobi Hakobyan, Alekpol, Bozyughash, 1916 ◆ Paruyr Hakobi Manukyan, Kars, Vortakatiklar, 1911 ◆ Paruyr Hambardzumi Nalbandyan, Erzrum, Olti, 1912, 1911 ◆ Paruyr Hovhannesi Arshakyan (Hovhannisyan), Sarighamish, Bashgyugh, 1917 ◆ Paruyr Hovhannesi Petrosyan (Hovhannisyan), Alekpol, Ghonaghran, 1915 ◆ Paruyr Hovsepi Poghosyan, Alekpol, Duzkharaba, 1912 ◆ Paruyr Margari Kelashyan, Kars, Chidmalu, 1912 ◆ Paruyr Mkrtichi Saprichyan (Hovhannisyan), Yerznka, 1911 ◆ Paruyr Mnatsakani Manukyan, Kars, Ghzlchakhchakh, 1912 ◆ Paruyr Movsesi Herkoyan, Shirak, Khlli Gharakilis, 1914 ◆ Paruyr Nikoli Ksharyan (Hovhannisyan), Alekpol, Molakericha ◆ Paruyr Pilicosi Zakaryan, Alekpol, Gharakilisa, 1911 ◆ Paruyr Poghosi Galstyan (Poghosyan), Shirak, Tiraklar, 1914 ◆ Paruyr Sedraki Poghosyan (Sedrakyan), Kars, Chala, 1914 ◆ Paruyr Tadevosi Gevorgyan, Basen, Hobviran, 1911 ◆ Paruyr Tigrani Harutyunyan, Shirak, Bayrazdat, 1913 ◆ Parzanush Aghabeki Paronyan, Pambak, Hamamlu, 1912 ◆ Paskov Vahani Hambardzumyan, Alekpol, Ghanlija, 1912 ◆ Paskovich Vahani Khachatryan, Alekpol, Ghanlija, 1914 ◆ Patvakan Armenaki Sahakyan, Ghamarlu, Kajazlu, 1914 ◆ Patvakan Gevorgi Nersisyan, Alekpol, Svanverdi, 1914 ◆ Patvakan Khachaturi Khachatryan, Kaghzvan, Chankli, 1910 ◆ Paycar Aleksani Aghasyan, Nukhi, Sabatlu, 1911 ◆ Paycar Aleksani Hovhannisyan, Persia, Shnblapat, 1913 ◆ Paycar Arami Shahbazyan (Aramyan), Alashkert, Zitkan, 1911, 1910 ◆ Paycar Armenaki Khurshudyan (Armenakyan), Khnus, Berd, 1914 ◆ Paycar Arshaki Mkrtchyan, Alekpol, Alekpol, 1913 ◆ Paycar Artashi Arshakyan, Gharakilisa, Yeghaplu, 1913 ◆ Paycar Avetisi (Manuki) Manukyan, Basen, Armtlu, 1913 ◆ Paycar Avetisi Avetisyan, 1916 ◆ Paycar Daviti Davtyan, Yerevan, Artashat, 1914 ◆ Paycar Garegini Harutyunyan, Pambak, Gharakilisa, 1914 ◆ Paycar Ghazari (Karapeti) (Karapetyan), Van, Nor gyugh, 1909 ◆ Paycar Ghazari Ghazaryan, Van, Archesh, 1915 ◆ Paycar Grigori Arakelyan, Kars, Gorkhana, 1916 ◆ Paycar Grigori Hovhannisyan (Grigoryan), Alashkert, Yeghintap, 1914 ◆ Paycar Hakobi (Margari) Torosyan (Hakobyan), Karin, Karin, 1912 ◆ Paycar Hayrapeti Darbinyan, Alashkert, Khachlu, 1911 ◆ Paycar Heranosi Harutyunyan, Alekpol, Aghin, 1914 ◆ Paycar Hovhannesi Hovhannisyan (Khachatryan), Bulanakh, 1918 ◆ Paycar Hovhannesi Hovhannisyan, Alekpol, Ghazarapat, 1917 ◆ Paycar Hovsepi Ghazaryan, Nakhijevan, Imrkhan, 1912 ◆ Paycar Kamsari Khachatryan, Ashtarak, Oshakan, 1914 ◆ Paycar Karapeti (Khachaturi) Grigoryan, Alekpol, Pirvali, 1919 ◆ Paycar Karapeti Karapetyan, Karabagh, 1917 ◆ Paycar Khachaturi Khachatryan, Alashkert, 1913 ◆ Paycar Manuki Grigoryan, Van, Archesh, 1909 ◆ Paycar Mehrabi Mehrabyan, Ghamarlu, Tkhkun, 1916 ◆ Paycar Meliki Matinyan, Erzrum, Bayburd, 1914 ◆ Paycar Melkoni

Melkonyan, Bulanagh, Rostom-Gedak, 1912 ♦ Paycar Mihrani Mihranyan ♦ Paycar Mirijani Mirijanyan, Van, Shadivan, 1909 ♦ Paycar Mnatsakani Mkrtchyan, Alashkert, Yeghntap, 1911 ♦ Paycar Petrosi (Arakelyan) Petrosyan, Moks, Avran, 1919 ♦ Paycar Petrosi Sargsyan, Van, Aljavaz, 1915 ♦ Paycar Piloyi Zakaryan, Alekpol, Pokr Gharakilis, 1916 ♦ Paycar Poghosi Abrahamyan, Van, Miginir, 1910 ♦ Paycar Poghosi Bazikyan, Van, Sekhgil, 1907 ♦ Paycar Poghosi Poghosyan, Van, Van, 1912 ♦ Paycar Poghosi Poghsoyan, Van, Mokhraberd, 1911 ♦ Paycar Sahaki Petrosyan, Shatakh, Haynan, 1911 ♦ Paycar Sahaki Sahakyan, Aljavaz, Anushaghbyur, 1913 ♦ Paycar Sargisi Karapetyan, Van, Khachan, 1913, 1912 ♦ Paycar Sargsi Sargsyan, Yerevan, Khatunarkh, 1914 ♦ Paycar Serobi Serobyan, Van, Karavan, 1913 ♦ Paycar Torosi Hardinyan (Torosyan), Basen, Hekibad, 1914 ♦ Paycar Varosi Martirosyan, Alekpol, Bughdashen, 1912 ♦ Paycar Yeghiazari Melikyan (Yeghiazaryan), Alashkert, Gharakilisa, 1911 ♦ Paycar Yeghishei Ter-Yeghishyan, Kharberd, 1908 ♦ Paycar Yeghishi Yeghiazaryan, Nakhijevan, Nors, 1912 ♦ Paycar Yeghoyi Yeghoyan, Van, 1914 ♦ Paycar Yenoki Matevosyan, Akhalkalak, Karcakh, 1911 ♦ Paylacu Aleksani Avetisyan, Erzrum, Gomadzor, 1907 ♦ Paylacu Mkrtchi Safaryan, Van, 1911 ♦ Paylacu Mkrtchi Ter-Tovmasyan, Van, Shatakh, 1909 ♦ Paylacun (Parandzem) Vahani Shahinyan, Kars, 1912 ♦ Paylak Aleksani Aleksanyan (Shamtsyan), Kars, 1914 ♦ Paylak Avetisi Khurmajyan (Avetisyan), Kars, 1913 ♦ Paylak Gaspari Muradyan, Kars, Chala, 1910 ♦ Paylak Gevorgi Gevorgyan, Kars, Araz, 1913 ♦ Paylak Habeti Habetyan, Kars, Bayrakhtar, 1917 ♦ Paylak Levoni Levonyan, Shirak, Mastara, 1916 ♦ Paylak Manuki Khanoyan (Manukyan), Yerevan, 1914 ♦ Paylak Nikoli Nikolyan, Kars, Bashshoragal, 1915 ♦ Paylak Sahaki Sahakyan, Kars, Araz, 1915 ♦ Paylak Simoni Avdalyan, Leninakan, Mahmatjugh, 1915 ♦ Paylun (Parandzem) Hakobi Khachatryan, Kars, Agrak, 1914 ♦ Paylun Habeti Sargsyan, Sarighamish, Shadivan, 1914 ♦ Paylun Hakobi Hakobyan, Van, 1910 ♦ Paylun Haruti Ghukasyan (Harutyunyan), Lori, Agarak, 1916 ♦ Paylun Harutyuni Harutyunyan, Gharakilisa, Hamamlu, 1916 ♦ Paylun Hovhannesi Hovhannisyan, Van, Kendananc, 1911 ♦ Paylun Martirosi Martirosyan, Van, 1913 ♦ Paylun Vahani Vahanyan, Basen, Gomadzor, 1912 ♦ Paylun Zakari Zakaryan, Van, 1913 ♦ Pecik Gevorgi Gevorgyan, Igdir, Tashburan, 1914 ♦ Penez Arami Melkonyan, Leninakan, Taknali, 1916 ♦ Penik Sargsi Sargsyan, Igdir, 1918 ♦ Pepel Petrosi Ghazaryan, Gharakilisa, Gyoran, 1914 ♦ Pepo Arshaki Arshakyan, Tiflis, 1919 ♦ Pepo Artushi Mkrtchyan, Bandivan, 1912 ♦ Pepo Barseghi Haroyan, Shirak, Kor aghbyur, 1915 ♦ Pepo Gevorgi Gevorgyan, Kars, Paldrvan, 1918 ♦ Pepron Avetisi Avetisyan, Kars, Dolbandlu, 1911 ♦ Pepron Baghdasari Galoyan (Baghdasaryan), Akhalkalak, 1912 ♦ Pepron Daviti Petrosyan, Kars, Mec Parket, 1913 ♦ Pepron Harutyuni Harutyunyan, Kars, Bazrgan, 1912 ♦ Pepron Hovhannesi Markosyan, Van, Bovan, 1912 ♦ Peprone Abrahami Hovsepyan, Alekpol, Dzithankov, 1911 ♦ Peprone Arshaki Poghosyan, Baghesh, 1911 ♦ Peprone Grigori Torgomyan, Akhaltsikha, 1912 ♦ Peprone Harutyuni Grigoryan, Alekpol, Bandivan, 1910 ♦ Peprone Hovhannesi Ghukasyan, Igdir, Alet, 1911 ♦ Peprone Ivani Sargsyan, Lori, Alaverdi, 1918 ♦ Peprone Mihrani Umbrejyan, Erzrum, Komi, 1912 ♦ Peprone Mkrtchi Musheghyan, Kars, Hopviran, 1913 ♦ Peprone Rafayeli Krdyan, Akhalkalak, Alastan, 1909 ♦ Peprone Sedraki Israyelyan, Leninakan, Bughdashen, 1910 ♦ Peprone Simoni Ghukasyan, Alekpol, Toros, 1910 ♦ Pepronya Galusti Poghosyan (Karapetyan), Kars, Chirmali, 1911 ♦ Pepruhi Garniki Garnikyan, Erzrum, Bayburt, 1912 ♦ Perchaluys Petrosi Achemyan, Kaghzvan, 1908 ♦ Perchanush Armenaki Ayvazyan, Ardahan, 1912 ♦ Perchanush Artushi Badalyan, Kars, Gorkhana, 1914 ♦ Perchanush Gokori Ter-Gevorgyan, Akhaltskha, 1915 ♦ Perchanush Manuki (Sahakyan) Manukyan, Alekpol, Keti, 1913 ♦ Perchanush Manuki Manukyan, Alekpol, Opers, 1918 ♦ Perchanush Mikayeli Vardanyan, Akhalkalak, Gendira, 1914 ♦ Perchanush Sedraki Abovyan, Kars, Bashshoragyal, 1910 ♦ Perchanush Simoni Gabrielyan (Simonyan), Kars, Gorkhana, 1917 ♦ Perchanush Tadevosi Vardanyan, Kars, Gedaksatlmish, 1913 ♦ Perchanush Vanoyi Vanoyan, Alekpol, Ghaplu, 1915 ♦ Percho Vahani Ulikhanyan, Kars, Ortakyadiklar, 1914 ♦ Peri Daviti Davtyan, Nukhi, Tashbulagh, 1911 ♦ Petik Ghazari Ghazaryan, Tiflis, 1918 ♦ Petik Levoni Hovhannisyan, Zangezur, 1915 ♦ Petros Aleksani (Movsesi) Movsisyan, Mush, Norashen, 1915 ♦ Petros Aleksani Hovsepyan, Akhalkalak, Ikhtila, 1913 ♦ Petros Asaturi Harutyunyan, Bulanagh, Khoshgyaldi, 1909 ♦ Petros Asaturi Karapetyan, Kars, Pokr Parket, 1911 ♦ Petros Avagi Nazaretyan, Kars, Bayraghtar, 1913 ♦ Petros Avetisi Mirakyan, Van, 1911 ♦ Petros Ayvazi Nshanyan (Ayvazyan), Van, Kharakonis, 1907 ♦ Petros Bakuri Karapetyants, Alekpol, Bayandur, 1917 ♦ Petros Ghukasi Manukyan, Basen, Gomadzor, 1914 ♦ Petros Grigori Khachatryan, Khnus, Duman, 1912 ♦ Petros Hakobi Grigoryan (Hakobyan), Van, Dshogh, 1912 ♦ Petros Hakobi Hakobyan, Kars, Kars, 1918 ♦ Petros Hazroyi Sukiasyan, Alashkert, Ghayabek, 1912 ♦ Petros Karapeti Chatalbashyan, Yerznka, 1908 ♦ Petros Khachaturi Aleksanyan, Leninakan, Chlokhan, 1913 ♦ Petros Khlghati Hovsepyan, Van, Vozm, 1913 ♦ Petros Manuki Karapetyan (Manukyan), Van, Vozm, 1912 ♦ Petros Manuki Nahapetyan, Alashkert, Khastur, 1908 ♦ Petros Mihrani (Tovmasi) Mihranyan, Shatagh, Harmshat, 1912 ♦ Petros Mikayeli Mikayelyan (Kolkayan), Shamakhi, Matraz, 1914 ♦ Petros Movsesi Gevorgyan, Basen, Krtabas, 1914, 1912 ♦ Petros Movsesi Hovhannisyan, Karin, Gomadzor, 1910 ♦ Petros Musheghi Tumasyan (Musheghyan), Akhlat, 1907 ♦ Petros Natoyi Hunanyan, Mush, Agarak, 1910 ♦ Petros Nazari Manukyan (Nazaryan), Basen, Khosrovitan, 1910 ♦ Petros Papiki Petrosyan, Van, Khachan, 1912 ♦ Petros Poghosi Rashoyan, Leninakan, Sirvangyugh, 1910 ♦ Petros Sahaki Nazaryan, Lori, Khotur, 1915 ♦ Petros Sedraki Sedrakyan, Bitlis, Kasp, 1913 ♦ Petros Simoni Harutyunyan, Alashkert, Berd, 1909 ♦ Petros

Soghomoni Soghomonyan (Kostanyan), Kars, Kyurakdara, 1912 ♦ Petros Srapi Apoyan (Margaryan), Jalaloghli, Shahnazar, 1918 ♦ Petros Stepani Petrosyan, Van, Mantants, 1909 ♦ Petros Stepani Pichimyan, Akhaltskha, Akhaltskha, 1911 ♦ Petros Tadevosi Galstyan, Shamakh, Zargaran, 1913 ♦ Petros Tigrani Harutyunyan, Shirak, Kosaghbyur, 1913 ♦ Petros Voskani Yedigaryan, Sarighamish, Shadivan, 1911 ♦ Pilos Galusti Ghazaryan, Akhalkalak, Gandza, 1914 ♦ Pilos Sargsi Sargsyan, Aljavaz, Norshnjugh, 1912 ♦ Pilos Yegori Gasparyan (Yegoryan), Alekpol, P. Arkhvali, 1914 ♦ Piruz Arshaki Arshakyan, Bitlis, 1910 ♦ Piruz Asaturi Petrosyan (Astvacatryan), Van, Alur, 1912 ♦ Piruz Ghazari Poghosyan (Ghazaryan), Alashkert, Hamat, 1908 ♦ Piruz Hakobi Arshakyan (Hakobyan), Yerevan, 1914 ♦ Piruz Martirosi Matosyan (Martirosyan), Van, Khachan, 1916 ♦ Piruz Melik-Manuchari Manukyan (Manucharyan), Yerevan, Margara, 1918 ♦ Piruz Mkrtchi Manukyan, Kars, Bulanagh, 1914 ♦ Piruz Serobi Grigoryan, Bitlis, 1912 ♦ Piruz Vardani Manukyan (Vardanyan), Akhlat, Prkhus, 1914 ♦ Piruz Vardani Vardanyan, Van, Bagavan, 1907 ♦ Piruz Zohrapi Zohrapyan, Nor Bayazet, Yeranos, 1915 ♦ Piruza Arakeli Norikyan, Terjan, Dvnik, 1907 ♦ Piruza Asaturi Hakobyan, Persia, Khoy, 1911 ♦ Piruza Ghazari Asatryan, Van, 1914 ♦ Piruza Khachaturi Khachatryan, Bulanagh, Yonjalu, 1912 ♦ Piruza Mkhitari Mkhitaryan, Alashkert, Gharakilisa, 1909 ♦ Piruza Mkrtchi Martirosyan (Mkrtchyan), Bitlis, 1912 ♦ Piruza Simoni Arzumanyan, Manazkert, Gharaghala, 1908 ♦ Piruza Yeghoyi Martirosyan, Alashkert, Mazra, 1911 ♦ Piso Hambardzumi Hovnanyan, Aparan, Bash Aparan, 1914 ♦ Plotia Galusti Martirosyan, Kars, 1912, 1910 ♦ Poghos Avetisi Arakelyan, Kars, Cbni, 1912 ♦ Poghos Barseghi Baghdasaryan, Kars, Bulanagh, 1910 ♦ Poghos Barseghi Khachatryan, Van, Psti, 1914 ♦ Poghos Gevorgi Gevorgyan, 1918 ♦ Poghos Ghazari Sargsyan, Bulanakh, Kop, 1910 ♦ Poghos Gulani Muradyan, Alchavaz, Parket, 1908 ♦ Poghos Hakobi Hovhannisyan, Alashkert, Molla seliman, 1913 ♦ Poghos Hovhannesi Hovhannisyan, Van, Dshogh, 1915, 1912 ♦ Poghos Hovhannesi Sargsyan, Alekpol, Paldlu, 1914 ♦ Poghos Karapeti Karapetyan (Hovhannisyan), Leninakan, Aghkilisa, 1912 ♦ Poghos Martirosi Tovmasyan, Akhalkalak, Varevan, 1915 ♦ Poghos Misaki Minasyan, Alekpol, Dolbandlu, 1910 ♦ Poghos Oniki Shahnazaryan, Akhalkalak, Chandura, 1912 ♦ Poghos Petrosi Mkrtchyan, Leninakan, Paldlu, 1913 ♦ Poghos Poghosi Avetisyan, Akhalkalak, Varevan, 1917 ♦ Poghos Soghomoni Harutyunyan, Kharberd, Sofyan, 1911 ♦ Poghos Tigrani Hovhannisyan, Alekpol, Chiftali, 1910 ♦ Poghos Zakari Muradyan, Ardvin, 1916 ♦ Poghos Zohrabi Mekhakyan (Misakyan), Yerevan, Davalu, 1913 ♦ Poghos, 1923 ♦ Polad Danieli Muradyan (Danielyan), Kars, Tekniz, 1915 ♦ Prak Ghazari Ghazaryan, Akhalkalak, 1917 ♦ Prak Virabi Virabyan, Surmali, Tashburan, 1915 ♦ Pyulbul (Bulbul) Hakobi Hovhannisyan, Kars, Ghzlchakhchakh, 1911 ♦ Radios Sedraki Simonyan (Sedrakyan), Yerznka, Piriz, 1914 ♦ Rafayel (Hetum) Sukiasi Hamamjyan, Erzrum, Bayburt, 1910 ♦ Rafayel Abrahami Abrahamyan, Van, Doghan, 1913 ♦ Rafayel Arshaki Hambaryan, Leninakan, Chrakhli, 1914 ♦ Rafayel Arshaki Manukyan, Yerevan, Znaberd, 1909 ♦ Rafayel Azati Galstyan, Pambak, Gharakilisa, 1917 ♦ Rafayel Hayrapeti Muradyan (Hayrapetyan), Alashkert, Ghazi, 1913, 1912 ♦ Rafayel Hovhannesi Melik-Adamyan, Nakhijevan, Agulis, 1901 ♦ Rafayel Mkrtchi Mkrtchyan, Kars, Agrak, 1914 ♦ Rafayel Pavlei Papikyan, Yerevan, Norashen, 1914 ♦ Rafayel Tigrani Harutyunyan, Kars, Sogutli, 1912 ♦ Rafayel Vardani Baghdikyan, Kars, Chala, 1912, 1911 ♦ Rafayel Vardani Grigoryan, Mec Gharakilisa, Goran, 1914 ♦ Rafik Danieli Danielyan, Mush, Khas, 1914 ♦ Raman Arshaki Ghazaryan, Tiflis, 1913 ♦ Rebeka (Rehan) Harutyuni Harutyunyan, Van, 1914 ♦ Rebeka Hakobi Sahradyan, Igdir, Dash-Buran, 1911 ♦ Rebeka Hovhannesi Sahakyan, Kars, Chirghan, 1911 ♦ Rebeka Martirosi Hovhannisyan, Van, Shatakh, 1911 ♦ Rebeka Mkrtchi Avetisyan, Van, 1909 ♦ Rebeka Tigrani Gevorgyan, Surmali, Zakarlu, 1915 ♦ Rebeka Yeghiazari Khachoyan, Van, 1909 ♦ Rehan Avagi Avagyan, Van, Urants, 1908 ♦ Rehan Avetisi Avetisyan, Van, 1910 ♦ Rehan Daviti Davtyan, 1916 ♦ Rehan Gaspari Ghazaryan, Sasun, Arpa, 1909 ♦ Rehan Gipranosi Manukyan, Kharberd, Svjugh, 1911 ♦ Rehan Grigori Grigoryan, Van, Pshavan, 1912 ♦ Rehan Hakobi Hakobyan, Khnus, Teghut, 1910 ♦ Rehan Hakobi Hakobyan, Nakhijevan, 1918 ♦ Rehan Hakobi Poghosyan, Van, Arkom, 1913 ♦ Rehan Hambardzumi Tumasyan, Khnus, Gyunush, 1910 ♦ Rehan Hovhannesi Karapetyan, Van, Kafka, 1909 ♦ Rehan Hovhannesi Yeghiazaryan, Bulanagh, Mirbran, 1909 ♦ Rehan Manuki Grigoryan, Bitlis, 1908 ♦ Rehan Manuki Manukyan, Van, Urants, 1912 ♦ Rehan Manuki Muradyan, Van, Vozm, 1909 ♦ Rehan Muradi Muradyan, Bitlis, 1907 ♦ Rehan Poghosi Poghosyan, Leninakan, Gharakilisa, 1918 ♦ Rehan Sargisi Sargsyan, Van, Ptghants, 1910 ♦ Rehan Sargsi Sargsyan, 1914 ♦ Rehan Simoni Grigoryan, Van, Berkri, 1913 ♦ Rehan Vardani Ghazaryan, Bitlis, Glak, 1908 ♦ Rehan Vardani Vardanyan, Van, Ganagh, 1907 ♦ Ripsik Sateniki Ayvazyan, Kars, 1918 ♦ Ripsime (Hripsime) Vagharshaki Nazaretyan, Alekpol, Imrkhan, 1918 ♦ Robovam Aghababi Pashinyan (Balikyan), Kars, 1911 ♦ Roza Adami Gevorgyan, Kars, Gorkhana, 1916 ♦ Roza Arami Madoyan, Bitlis, 1912, 1916 ♦ Roza Arshaki Nazaretyan, Akhalkalak, 1911 ♦ Roza Avagi Paravyan, Gharakilisa, Kzlagh, 1914 ♦ Roza Galusti Asoyan, Kars, Ghzlchakhchakh, 1914 ♦ Roza Garegini Simonyan, Van, 1917 ♦ Roza Ginosi Harutyunyan, Basen, Gomadzor, 1913 ♦ Roza Ginoyi Movsisyan, 1918 ♦ Roza Grigori Grigoryan, Kars, 1919 ♦ Roza Hakobi Khachatryan, Nor Bayazet, 1912 ♦ Roza Hmayaki Margaryan (Grigoryan), Igdir, 1914 ♦ Roza Hovaki Atoyan, Alekpol, Mecketi, 1913 ♦ Roza Karapeti Karapetyan, 1915 ♦ Roza Martirosi Avetisyan, Kars, Gyulkhidan, 1919 ♦ Roza Mnatsakani Harutyunyan, Kars, Byurakdara, 1917 ♦ Roza Mnatsi Mnatsakanyan, Alekpol, 1914 ♦ Roza Movsisyan ♦ Roza Nikoli Valesyan, Leninakan, Khlli Gharakilis, 1908 ♦ Roza Poghosi Abovyan, Van,

LISTING OF ORPHANS

Hurher, 1911 ◆ Roza Sahaki Sahakyan, Alekpol, Duzkharaba, 1916 ◆ Roza Sargisi Sargsyan, Kars, 1919 ◆ Roza Vagharshaki Vagharshakyan, Igdir, Khalfalu, 1914 ◆ Ruben Abrahami Abrahamyan, Mush, Khardos, 1913 ◆ Ruben Aleksani Sargsyan, Van, Prkhus, 1913 ◆ Ruben Armenaki Shahinyan, Mush, 1911 ◆ Ruben Avetisi Hakobyan, Mush, Baghlu, 1906 ◆ Ruben Barseghi Barseghyan, Kars, Bagliahmat, 1914 ◆ Ruben Barseghi Gasparyan, Mush, 1916 ◆ Ruben Danieli Mkhitaryan, Alashkert, Amat, 1912 ◆ Ruben Garegini Hovhannisyan, Leninakan, Ghaplu, 1914 ◆ Ruben Gaspari Avagyan, Mush, Arinjvank, 1905 ◆ Ruben Gaspari Galstyan, Gharakilisa, Chotas, 1910 ◆ Ruben Gaspari Khachatryan, Alashkert, Ghazi, 1912 ◆ Ruben Gevorgi Aghoyan, Kaghzvan, 1910 ◆ Ruben Gevorgi Militosyan, Leninakan, Vortakilisa, 1908 ◆ Ruben Gevorgi Shahinyan, Vaspurakan, Shatakh ◆ Ruben Gevorgi Tumanyan, Lori, Vardablur, 1908 ◆ Ruben Hakobi Hakobyan, Etchmiadzin, Nerkin Karkhan, 1914 ◆ Ruben Hakobi Hovhannisyan, Kars, Agarak, 1912 ◆ Ruben Harutyuni Safaryan (Harutyunyan), Kars, Uzunkilisa, 1913 ◆ Ruben Hayrapeti Gevorgyan, Mush, Votnchor, 1911 ◆ Ruben Hovhannesi Avetisyan, Shirak, Paldlu, 1917 ◆ Ruben Hovhannesi Hakobyan (Hovhannisyan), Van, Khachan, 1912 ◆ Ruben Hovhannesi Manukyan, Nor Bayazet, Basargechar, 1911 ◆ Ruben Hovhannesi Ter-Manvelyan, Mush, Votnchor, 1912 ◆ Ruben Karapeti Papoyan, Kars, Chala, 1912 ◆ Ruben Khachaturi Aghababyan, Akhalkalak, Lomators, 1913 ◆ Ruben Khachaturi Sahakyan, Leninakan, Kharkov, 1910 ◆ Ruben Khachaturi Zhmharyan, Bitlis, 1915 ◆ Ruben Khachiki Khachatryan (Khachoyan), Kars, Alashkert, 1917 ◆ Ruben Khachoyi Khachatryan, Leninakan, Ghzlkilisa, 1912 ◆ Ruben Kristi Avetisyan, Hin Nakhijevan, Jznut, 1913 ◆ Ruben Levoni Serobyan, Alekpol, Ghanlija, 1917 ◆ Ruben Lipariti Martikyan, Batum, 1913 ◆ Ruben Manuki Manukyan, Kaghzvan, Karabagh, 1914, 1915 ◆ Ruben Martirosi Manusajyan, Akhalkalak, Goman, 1912, 1910 ◆ Ruben Melkoni Melkonyan, Kop, 1918 ◆ Ruben Misaki Arakelyan, Kars, Karmir Vank, 1912, 1910 ◆ Ruben Mkhitaryan, Kars, 1918 ◆ Ruben Mkrtchi Mkrtchyan, Kars, Ghzlchakhchakh, 1914 ◆ Ruben Nahapeti Nahapetyan, Alashkert, Yonjalu, 1912 ◆ Ruben Navasardi Navasardyan, Nakhijevan, Uznaberd, 1911 ◆ Ruben Nazari Tatosyan, Van, Marmrtu, 1913 ◆ Ruben Petrosi Petrosyan, Kars, Bayburd, 1916 ◆ Ruben Petrosi Poghosyan, Alashkert, Ziro, 1907 ◆ Ruben Petrosi Rubenyan (Petrosyan), Akhlat, Khyardank, 1913 ◆ Ruben Saghateli Ayvazyan, Kars, Armtli, 1912 ◆ Ruben Sargisi Muradyan, Kars, Gharaghala, 1911 ◆ Ruben Tigrani Gasparyan (Tigranyan), Akhlat, Prkhus, 1916, 1914 ◆ Ruben Vardani Shahbazyan, Basen, 1913 ◆ Ruen Samsoni Samsonyan, Alashkert, Mankasar, 1917 ◆ Ruzan Armenaki Aghajanyan, Akhalkalak, 1908 ◆ Salvi Harutyuni Simonyan, Kars, Byurakdara, 1909 ◆ Satenik Asaturi Khachatryan, Alashkert, Mankasar, 1911 ◆ Satenik Avetisi Sargsyan, Van, 1913 ◆ Satenik Vahani Petrosyan, Leninakan, Babrlu, 1912 ◆ Satenik Varosi Varosyan, Alekpol, Ghanlija, 1914 ◆ Sedrak Harutyuni Kochoyan (Harutyunyan), Kars, Cbni, 1912 ◆ Shaghik Galusti Galstyan, Pambak, Tapanlu, 1912 ◆ Shahandukht Arami Ghazaryan, Alekpol, Alikhan, 1914 ◆ Shahandukht Saghateli Madoyan, Shirak, Bandivan, 1909 ◆ Shahen Arshaki Mkhitaryan (Arshakyan), Leninakan, Taknalu, 1913 ◆ Shahen Avagi Khlghatyan, Kars, Bashkyadiklar, 1914 ◆ Shahen Gasoyi Gasoyan, Ghamarlu, 1914 ◆ Shahen Martirosi Alashkertyan (Vardanyan), Alekpol, Ghanlija, 1911 ◆ Shahik Mkrtchi Mkrtchyan, Hin Bayazet, Korun, 1913 ◆ Shahine Margari Chiloyan (Sakoyan), Kars, Zrchi, 1909 ◆ Shahizar Aleksani Harutyunyan, Shirak, Ghazarapat, 1914 ◆ Shahnazar Movsesi Abrahamyan, Basen, Chrason, 1912 ◆ Shahno Ghazari Mnoyan, Akhalkalak, Ikhtila, 1912 ◆ Shahrista Papiki Sukiasyan (Papikyan), Basen, Krtapal, 1913, 1912 ◆ Shahzad Sedraki Sargsyan, Leninakan, Pirvali, 1915 ◆ Shahzad Sirakani Madoyan, Kars, Uzunkilisa, 1914 ◆ Shamam (Shamiram) Yenoki Tarhadyan, Persia, Salmast, 1910 ◆ Shamam Avagi Karapetyan, Van, 1911, 1909 ◆ Shamam Hovhannesi Sargsyan, Bulanagh, Kop, 1910 ◆ Shamam Poghosi Poghosyan, Van, 1915 ◆ Shamam Rubeni Damrchyan, Akhalkalak, Karcakh, 1916 ◆ Shamik Galusti Asoyan, Kars, Ghzlchakhchakh, 1915 ◆ Shamiram Aleksani Papikyan, Akhalkalak, Vachyan, 1912 ◆ Shamiram Bagrati Kostanyan, Kaghzvan, 1914 ◆ Shamiram Gevorgi Margaryan (Danielyan), Kars, Zhlrji, 1913 ◆ Shamiram Grigori Grigoryan, Ardahan, 1911 ◆ Shamiram Harutyuni Abajyan, Kars, 1913 ◆ Shamiram Ignatosi Simonyan, Akhalkalak, Vachyan, 1914 ◆ Shamiram Karapeti Melkonyan, Kars, 1912 ◆ Shari Sosii Manukyan, Bitlis, Prkhus, 1908 ◆ Shashli Simoni Simonyan, Leninakan, Bashshoragal, 1917 ◆ Shashlo Hakobi Mkrtchyan, Kars, 1918 ◆ Shavarsh Abrahami Abrahamyan, Kars, Ardahan, 1912 ◆ Shavarsh Arami Groyan, Kars, 1917 ◆ Shavarsh Avagi Mikayelyan, Kars, Bayghara, 1915 ◆ Shavarsh Avetisi Nersisyan (Gyadukoghlyan), Akhalkalak, Gandza, 1910 ◆ Shavarsh Gevorgi Amirkhanyan (Gevorgyan), Kars, Bayburt, 1913 ◆ Shavarsh Ghazari Hovhannisyan, Alekpol, Ghoshavank, 1910 ◆ Shavarsh Hovhannesi Matevosyan, Shirak, Ghaplu, 1914 ◆ Shavarsh Hovsepi Shahbazyan, Shirak, Khli Gharakilis, 1913 ◆ Shavarsh Martirosi Manusajyan, Akhalkalak, Goman, 1913 ◆ Shavarsh Srapi Harutyunyan, Leninakan, Aghin, 1916 ◆ Shavarsh Ter-Antoni Ter-Antonyan, Karin, 1915 ◆ Shavarsh Tigrani Vagharshakyan, Etchmiadzin, Khatunarkh, 1912 ◆ Shavarsh Tumasi Fidanyan, Akhalkalak, Merenia, 1916 ◆ Shavarsh Vagharshaki Kirakosyan, Leninakan, Kefli, 1910 ◆ Shavarsh Yeghoyi Ghazaryan, Kars, Chirghan, 1911 ◆ Shayino (Shushanik) Nazari Hovnanyan, Kars, Zrchi, 1910 ◆ Shigo Ghazari Ghazaryan, Kars, Tigor, 1909 ◆ Shirak Aleksani Sevoyan, Alekpol, Khlli Gharakilis, 1913 ◆ Shirik Geghami Geghamyan, 1918 ◆ Shirin Aleksani Aleksanyan, Igdir, 1913 ◆ Shmavon Abrahami Avetisyan, Shirak, Chiftali, 1912 ◆ Shmavon Arshaki Simonyan (Arshakyan) (Elbakyan), Leninakan, Ghanlija, 1915 ◆ Shmavon Gaspari Mkhitaryan (Gasparyan), Khnus, Khrt, 1912 ◆ Shmavon

Hakobi Hakobyan, Kars, Ortaghala, 1919 ♦ Shmavon Harutyuni Nazaryan, Sarighamish, Bashgyugh, 1908 ♦ Shmavon Khachaturi Vardanyan, Sarighamish, Gyulantap, 1909 ♦ Shmavon Misaki Misakyan, Yerevan, Ghlbulagh, 1910 ♦ Shmavon Mnatsakani Mnatsakanyan (Shahinyan), Kars, Gyamrlu, 1914 ♦ Shmavon Petrosi Meloyan, Kars, Paldrvan, 1913 ♦ Shmavon Sahaki Danielyan (Sahakyan), Kars, Zrchi, 1913 ♦ Shmavon Sedraki Sedrakyan, Khnus, Berd, 1911 ♦ Shmavon Yeghiazari Mkhitaryan, Mush, Ghasmik, 1909 ♦ Shnorhik Avetisi Avetisyan, Erzrum, 1912 ♦ Shnorhik Ignatosi Ignatosyan, Van, 1913 ♦ Shnorhik Karapeti Karapetyan, Van, 1912 ♦ Shnorhik Mukayeli Vardanyan (Khachatryan), Nor Bayazet, 1913 ♦ Shnorhik Vardani Vardanyan, Van, 1910 ♦ Shnorhk Hayki Ter-Harutyunyan, Van, 1914 ♦ Shoghak (Shahat) Hovhannesi Hovhannisyan, Leninakan, Hajinazar, 1916 ♦ Shoghakat (Shushik) Petrosi Petrosyan, Erzrum, Berdak, 1913, 1911 ♦ Shoghakat Aleksani Hovsepyan (Aleksanyan), Kars, 1909 ♦ Shoghakat Antoni Tumasyan, Alekpol, Paltli, 1911 ♦ Shoghakat Aslani Gevorgyan, Van, Koms, 1909 ♦ Shoghakat Avetisi Melkonyan (Avetisyan), Alekpol, Ghapli, 1915 ♦ Shoghakat Avetisi Petrosyan, Van, Archesh, 1913 ♦ Shoghakat Avetisi Tumasyan, Kars, Aksighaz, 1912 ♦ Shoghakat Gevorgi Sahakyan (Gevorgyan), Kars, Mec Parket, 1916 ♦ Shoghakat Ghukasi Lilikyan, Akhalkalak, Gandza, 1912 ♦ Shoghakat Hambardzumi Avetisyan, Kars, 1909 ♦ Shoghakat Harutyuni Harutyunyan, Nakhijevan, Yarmja, 1911 ♦ Shoghakat Harutyuni Harutyunyan, Sarighamish, Cholakhlu, 1912 ♦ Shoghakat Harutyuni Simonyan, Yerevan, Davalu, 1916 ♦ Shoghakat Hovnani Ter-Mkrtchyan, Van, Undzak, 1912 ♦ Shoghakat Khachaturi Gevorgyan, Mush, Kop, 1909 ♦ Shoghakat Khachaturi Harutyunyan, Kars, Mazra, 1908 ♦ Shoghakat Levoni Abrahamyan, Kars, 1915 ♦ Shoghakat Manuki Hambardzumyan, Shirak, Ortakilisa, 1911 ♦ Shoghakat Margari Margaryan, Alekpol, 1911 ♦ Shoghakat Margari Simonyan, Kars, Baglamat, 1915, 1912 ♦ Shoghakat Mkrtchi Darbinyan, Akhalkalak, 1911 ♦ Shoghakat Muradi Muradyan, Leninakan, Paldli, 1916 ♦ Shoghakat Petrosi Petrosyan, Alashkert, Mollalerman, 1910 ♦ Shoghakat Rubeni Ter-Hovhannisyan, Akhalkalak, Jigrashen, 1910 ♦ Shoghakat Sargisi Asatryan, Kars, Kaghzvan, 1913 ♦ Shoghakat Sargisi Petrosyan, Mush, Khoshgyaldi, 1909 ♦ Shoghakat Sedraki Sedrakyan, Tiflis, 1918 ♦ Shoghakat Seyrani Ayvazyan, Bulanagh, Kharabshat, 1912 ♦ Shoghakat Yeghishei Mnatsakanyan (Yeghishyan), Alekpol, Darband, 1914 ♦ Shogher Gaspari Gasparyan, Leninakan, Taknalu, 1915 ♦ Shoghik Aghasu Kocharyan, Akhalkalak, 1916 ♦ Shoghik Aghoyi Martirosyan, Jalaloghli, Lori berd, 1915 ♦ Shoghik Arakeli Davtyan (Arakelyan), Bulanagh, Mirba, 1908 ♦ Shoghik Arshaki Avetisyan, Kars, 1913 ♦ Shoghik Arshaki Sargsyan (Arshakyan), Alekpol, Tashghala, 1913 ♦ Shoghik Avetisi Karapetyan, Alekpol, Jalab, 1914 ♦ Shoghik Avetisi Ter-Antonyan (Avetisyan), Akhalkalak, Goman, 1914 ♦ Shoghik Galusti (Knyaz) Galstyan (Knyazyan), Kars, 1911 ♦ Shoghik Gaspari Gasparyan, Van, Ckor, 1907 ♦ Shoghik Gaspari Stepanyan (Galoyan), Leninakan, Ghanlija, 1910 ♦ Shoghik Grigori Badalyan, Alekpol, Mastara, 1917 ♦ Shoghik Grigori Grigoryan, Shirak, Pirtikan, 1913 ♦ Shoghik Grigori Movsisyan, Surmalu, Tashburan, 1911 ♦ Shoghik Hakobi Avetisyan (Hakobyan), Kars, 1916 ♦ Shoghik Hakobi Mkrtchyan, Alekpol, 1910 ♦ Shoghik Hamazaspi Mkhitaryan (Hamazaspyan), Akhlat, Khulik, 1913 ♦ Shoghik Harutyuni Harutyunyan, Akhalkalak, Poks, 1914 ♦ Shoghik Hovakimi Hovakimyan, Van, Noravan, 1910 ♦ Shoghik Hovhannesi Sargsyan, Kars, 1915 ♦ Shoghik Hovhannesi Simonyan, Leninakan, Jalap, 1910 ♦ Shoghik Hovhannesi Stepanyan, Leninakan, Ghanlija, 1914 ♦ Shoghik Hovsepi Arakelyan, Basen, Khoshgyaldi, 1908 ♦ Shoghik Karapeti Karapetyan, Van, Archesh, 1915 ♦ Shoghik Karapeti Melkonyan (Karapetyan), Sarighamish, Churuk, 1912 ♦ Shoghik Kerobi Vardanyan, Mush, Artet, 1912 ♦ Shoghik Khachaturi Abrahamyan, Baku, 1914 ♦ Shoghik Khachaturi Asatryan (Khachatryan), Bulanagh, Votnchor, 1915 ♦ Shoghik Khachaturi Hovhannisyan (Khachatryan), Van, Kendanants, 1900 ♦ Shoghik Khachaturi Mirzakhanyan, Kars, Zaim, 1916 ♦ Shoghik Khachiki Muradyan, Manazkert, Noratin, 1911 ♦ Shoghik Mesropi Baghdasaryan, Nakhijevan, Khanlar, 1911 ♦ Shoghik Misaki Hovsepyan, Alekpol, Svanverdi, 1912 ♦ Shoghik Misaki Misakyan, Yerevan, Darghalu, 1915 ♦ Shoghik Mkrtchi Mkrtchyan, Dilijan, 1913 ♦ Shoghik Movsesi Hayrapetyan, Bulanagh, Kop, 1914 ♦ Shoghik Mukayeli Mukayelyan, Gandzak, 1917 ♦ Shoghik Musheghi Khachatryan, Kars, Ughuzli, 1911, 1910 ♦ Shoghik Nazari Arshakyan (Nazaryan), Vaspurakan, Vostang, 1909 ♦ Shoghik Nersesi Tumoyan (Nersisyan), Manazkert, Voghjents, 1914 ♦ Shoghik Nikoli Yeloyan (Muradyan), Kars, 1916 ♦ Shoghik Poghosi Poghosyan, Alashkert, Berd, 1914 ♦ Shoghik Poghosi Poghosyan, Kars, 1910 ♦ Shoghik Poghosi Sargsyan, Mush, Shmshak, 1908 ♦ Shoghik Saghateli Hakobyan, Sarighamish, Armtlu, 1912 ♦ Shoghik Sargisi Sargsyan, Van, 1914 ♦ Shoghik Sosi Yesayan, Gharakilisa, Yeghabli, 1909 ♦ Shoghik Torosi Nersisyan, Sasun, Tazavank, 1913 ♦ Shoghik Tumasi Khachatryan (Tumasyan), Aparan, Hajibaghr, 1916 ♦ Shoghik Vardani Panosyan, Van, Arjak, 1908 ♦ Shoghik Yeghiazari Yeghiazaryan, Kars, Voghuzli, 1917 ♦ Shoghik Yepranosi Torosyan, Tordan, 1909 ♦ Shoghik Yepremi Harutyunyan, Nakhijevan, Voghz, 1912 ♦ Shoghik Yepremi Melkonyan, Spitak, 1917 ♦ Shogho (Shoghik) Tadevosi Khanbekyan, Akhalkalak, Mec Aragyal, 1911 ♦ Shogho Avetisi Avetisyan, Bitlis, Prkhus, 1909 ♦ Shogho Mkrtchi Mkrtchyan, Basen, Alichagrak, 1915 ♦ Shogho Smbati Smbatyan, Kars, Hamzakarak, 1908 ♦ Shohlar Grigori Goroyan, Van, Berkri, 1915 ♦ Shura Aleksani Kapityan, Erzrum, 1912 ♦ Shura Seryozhayi Karakhanov, Russia, 1919 ♦ Shushan (Dalal) Hakobi Hakobyan, Mush, Aliklpun, 1909 ♦ Shushanik Abrahami Abrahamyan, Bulanagh, Kharabshat, 1909 ♦ Shushanik Abrahami Manukyan, Kars, 1908 ♦ Shushanik Aghababi Dndoyan (Jndoyan),

Kaghzvan, 1914 ♦ Shushanik Aghabeki Ghazaryan (Aghabekyan), Kars, 1917 ♦ Shushanik Aleki Alekyan, Kars, Dashkov, 1916 ♦ Shushanik Aleksani Ayvazyan, Ardahan, Shavsher, 1908 ♦ Shushanik Aleksani Vordanyan, Akhalkalak, Abul, 1912 ♦ Shushanik Arakeli Astvacatryan, Leninakan, Sirvangyugh, 1909 ♦ Shushanik Arakeli Pilosyan (Arakelyan), Erzrum, 1911 ♦ Shushanik Arakeli Vardanyan, Kars, Jalal, 1912 ♦ Shushanik Asaturi Sahakyan, Mush, Kharabshat, 1909 ♦ Shushanik Avetisi Baghdasaryan, Kars, Bayturk, 1911 ♦ Shushanik Baghdasari Baghdasaryan, Van, 1911, 1910 ♦ Shushanik Barseghi Petrosyan, Van, Armezon, 1913 ♦ Shushanik Danieli Simonyan (Danielyan), Bulanagh, Piran, 1911 ♦ Shushanik Daviti Hakobyan (Davtyan), Van, 1913, 1911 ♦ Shushanik Gabrieli Gabrielyan, Van, 1915 ♦ Shushanik Garegini Voskanyan, Akhalkalak, Vachyan, 1912 ♦ Shushanik Gevorgi Gasparyan (Gevorgyan), Shirak, Samrlu, 1914 ♦ Shushanik Gevorgi Gevorgyan, Van, Psti gyugh, 1911 ♦ Shushanik Gevorgi Martirosyan, Basen, Ghoshakilisa, 1912 ♦ Shushanik Gevorgi Petrosyan, Igdir, 1915 ♦ Shushanik Gevorgi Pnjoyan, Alekpol, Tavshanghshlagh, 1911 ♦ Shushanik Gevorgi Smbatyan, Kars, Berna, 1914 ♦ Shushanik Gevorgi Ter-Karapetyan, Van, 1912 ♦ Shushanik Ghazari Grigoryan, Alekpol, Bayandur, 1912 ♦ Shushanik Ghazari Grigoryan, Leninakan, Duzkharaba, 1912 ♦ Shushanik Ghazari Karapetyan, Alekpol, Bayandur, 1912 ♦ Shushanik Ghazari Martirosyan, Van, Norduz, 1909 ♦ Shushanik Ghazaryan Ghazaryan, Van, Archesh, 1910 ♦ Shushanik Ghukasi Ter-Sargsyan, Kars, Mavrak, 1910 ♦ Shushanik Grigori Baghdasaryan, Shirak, Khlli Gharakilis, 1911 ♦ Shushanik Grigori Grigoryan, Leninakan, Tomarbash, 1911 ♦ Shushanik Grigori Hakobyan, Leninakan, Daharlu, 1910 ♦ Shushanik Grigori Khachatryan, Nukhi, Akhprakand, 1911 ♦ Shushanik Grigori Semrjyan, Van, 1910 ♦ Shushanik Grigori Ter-Stepanyan, Erzrum, Norma, 1913 ♦ Shushanik Hakobi Galstyan, Van, Khnus, 1910 ♦ Shushanik Hakobi Geriyan, Shamakhi, Kirk, 1911 ♦ Shushanik Hakobi Hakobyan, Kars, Nakhijevan, 1913 ♦ Shushanik Hakobi Minasyan, Kars, Ghzlchakhchakh, 1911 ♦ Shushanik Hamazaspi Ananyan, Hin Nakhijevan, Yarmja, 1912 ♦ Shushanik Hambardzumi Khachatryan, Alekpol, Svanverdi, 1916 ♦ Shushanik Haruti Heboyan, Kars, Aghjala, 1916 ♦ Shushanik Harutyuni Harutyunyan (Yepremyan), Nakhijevan, 1912 ♦ Shushanik Harutyuni Harutyunyan, Alekpol, Leninakan, 1914 ♦ Shushanik Harutyuni Harutyunyan, Bulanagh, Kop, 1913 ♦ Shushanik Harutyuni Harutyunyan, Leninakan, Illi, 1914 ♦ Shushanik Harutyuni Hovhannisyan, Leninakan, Dzitankov, 1912 ♦ Shushanik Harutyuni Torosyan, Kars, Chala, 1914 ♦ Shushanik Hovhannesi Hambardzumyan, Alekpol, Sariar, 1914 ♦ Shushanik Hovhannesi Hovhannisyan (Hakobyan), Van, 1909 ♦ Shushanik Hovhannesi Hovhannisyan, Alekpol, Ghaplu, 1909 ♦ Shushanik Hovhannesi Hovhannisyan, Dilijan, 1907 ♦ Shushanik Hovhannesi Hovhannisyan, Hin Nakhijevan, 1911 ♦ Shushanik Hovhannesi Hovhannisyan, Nakhijevan, 1911 ♦ Shushanik Hovhannesi Hovhannisyan, Van, 1914 ♦ Shushanik Hovhannesi Khachatryan, Kars, Bagliahmat, 1912, 1910 ♦ Shushanik Hovhannesi Muradyan, Persia, Salmast, 1908 ♦ Shushanik Hovhannesi Poghosyan, Alekpol, 1913 ♦ Shushanik Hovsepi Kalikyan (Hovsepyan), Van, 1907 ♦ Shushanik Israyeli Aleksanyan (Hazryan), Akhalkalak, Aragyal, 1911, 1914 ♦ Shushanik Karapeti Grigoryan (Karapetyan), Alekpol, Tavshanghshlagh, 1909 ♦ Shushanik Karapeti Hakobyan, Ghazakh, Sarhatun, 1913 ♦ Shushanik Karapeti Khachatryan, Kars, 1911 ♦ Shushanik Karapeti Serobyan, Bulanagh, Khoshgyaldi, 1913 ♦ Shushanik Kerobi Shahbazyan, Jalaloghli, Khotur, 1913 ♦ Shushanik Khachaturi Hakobyan, Alekpol, 1911 ♦ Shushanik Khachaturi Khachatryan, Kars, 1916 ♦ Shushanik Khachaturi Khachatryan, Kars, 1917 ♦ Shushanik Khachaturi Khachatryan, Kars, Bulanagh, 1912, 1911 ♦ Shushanik Khachaturi Khachatryan, Yerevan, Artashat, 1914 ♦ Shushanik Khachaturi Khanbegyan, Ardahan, 1911 ♦ Shushanik Khoreni Khorenyan (Shaghoyan), Van, Kharakants, 1910 ♦ Shushanik Kokoli Saribekyan, Alekpol, Tavshanghshlagh, 1912 ♦ Shushanik Malkhasi Danielyan, Kars, Zrchi, 1911 ♦ Shushanik Manuki Abrahamyan (Manukyan), Alashkert, Khastur, 1913 ♦ Shushanik Manuki Manukyan, Van, 1910 ♦ Shushanik Martirosi Arshakyan, Van, Shahbazi, 1910 ♦ Shushanik Matevosi Baghdasaryan (Papikyan), Akhaltsikha, 1912 ♦ Shushanik Mergeli Manukyan, Kars, 1908 ♦ Shushanik Mihrani Muradyan, Van, Abagha, 1909 ♦ Shushanik Minasi Minasyan, Alashkert, Khastur, 1915 ♦ Shushanik Minasi Minasyan, Leninakan, Kyapanak, 1915 ♦ Shushanik Mirzoyi Safaryan, Vaspurakan, Asparacin, 1908 ♦ Shushanik Misaki Misakyan, Van, 1914 ♦ Shushanik Misaki Tumanyan, Erzrum, 1909 ♦ Shushanik Mkhitari Mkrtchyan, Sarighamish, 1912 ♦ Shushanik Mkrtchi Ghazaryan, Kars, 1909 ♦ Shushanik Mkrtchi Mkrtchyan (Danielyan), Bitlis, 1911 ♦ Shushanik Mkrtchi Mkrtchyan (Hovhannisyan), Etchmiadzin, Vagharshapat, 1914 ♦ Shushanik Mkrtchi Stepanyan, Akhaltsikha, 1912 ♦ Shushanik Musheghi Knyazyan, Leninakan, Ghapli, 1910 ♦ Shushanik Nahapeti Mkoyan, Yerevan, Aparan, 1912 ♦ Shushanik Nshani Aghazaryan (Ghazaryan), Van, 1910 ♦ Shushanik Petrosi Harutyunyan, Kars, Zrji, 1910 ♦ Shushanik Petrosi Khurshudyan, Kars, 1914 ♦ Shushanik Petrosi Manukyan, Van, Pshavan, 1913 ♦ Shushanik Petrosi Sahakyan, Ghamarlu, Barghalu, 1913 ♦ Shushanik Petrosi Sargsyan, Ardahan, 1912 ♦ Shushanik Poghosi Vardanyan (Hovhannisyan), Kars, Agrak, 1912 ♦ Shushanik Sahaki Kostanyan, 1916 ♦ Shushanik Sahaki Sahakyan, Kars, 1917 ♦ Shushanik Sahaki Sahakyan, Nakhijevan, Shekhmahmud, 1914 ♦ Shushanik Sargisi Astvacatryan, Kaghzvan, 1907 ♦ Shushanik Sargisi Hambardzumyan (Sargsyan), Shirak, Chiftali, 1911 ♦ Shushanik Sargisi Kakosyan (Sargsyan), Bitlis, 1914 ♦ Shushanik Sargisi Minasyan, Leninakan, Paldlu, 1915 ♦ Shushanik Sargisi Poghosyan, Leninakan, Kaps, 1909 ♦ Shushanik Sargisi Sargsyan, Kars, 1912 ♦ Shushanik Sargisi Sargsyan, Leninakan, Chorli, 1914 ♦ Shushanik Sargisi Sargsyan, Yerevan, Mec Kyapanak, 1918 ♦

Shushanik Saroyi Avagyan (Saroyan), Alekpol, Ghpchagh, 1916, 1917 ◆ Shushanik Saroyi Petrosyan, Shirak, Alekpol, 1911 ◆ Shushanik Sedraki Ghukasyan, Kars, Chala, 1911 ◆ Shushanik Sedraki Hakobyan, Akhalkalak, 1911 ◆ Shushanik Shaheni Grigoryan (Shahenyan), Van, Arinj, 1909 ◆ Shushanik Stepani Aghajanyan, Kars, Ardahan, 1912 ◆ Shushanik Stepani Hayrapetyan, Alekpol, Gheghaj, 1912 ◆ Shushanik Sukoyi Sukoyan, Kars, Nakhijevan, 1912 ◆ Shushanik Tadevosi Tadevosyan, Kars, Mec Parket, 1914 ◆ Shushanik Tadevosi Tadevosyan, Van, Corevan, 1909 ◆ Shushanik Tatosi Khachatryan, Leninakan, Ghoshavank, 1910 ◆ Shushanik Tigrani Harutyunyan, Leninakan, Ghoshavank, 1911 ◆ Shushanik Tigrani Tigranyan, Pambak, Gharakilisa, 1915 ◆ Shushanik Torosi Ghazaryan, Kars, Bashkyadiklar, 1913 ◆ Shushanik Trdati Torosyan, Sarighamish, 1911 ◆ Shushanik Vardani Gharibyan Hovhannisyan, Kars, Bayburt, 1905 ◆ Shushanik Vardani Hakobyan (Vardanyan), Kars, Gharamahmat, 1914 ◆ Shushanik Vardani Shahbazyan, Bitlis, Margorg, 1912 ◆ Shushanik Vasili Yeganyan, Yerevan, 1909 ◆ Shushanik Yeremi Ter-Zakaryan (Yeremyan), Ardahan, 1916 ◆ Shushanik Zakari Voksuzyan, Kars, 1908 ◆ Shushik (Fatima) Gevorgi Gevorgyan, Yerevan, 1915 ◆ Shushik Abrahami Serobyan, Sarighamish, Bashgyugh, 1912 ◆ Shushik Amiri Panosyan (Laloyan), Koghb, 1911 ◆ Shushik Arami Aramyan, Leninakan, Ghanlija, 1917 ◆ Shushik Armenaki Armenakyan, Yerevan, Nork, 1915 ◆ Shushik Arshaki Tzhikyan, Van, 1909 ◆ Shushik Baghdasari Baghdasaryan, Surmalu, Khalfala, 1917 ◆ Shushik Baghdasari Baghdasaryan, Van, 1908 ◆ Shushik Elbaki Hovhannisyan, Alekpol, Ojaghuli, 1917 ◆ Shushik Geghami Geghamyan, Yerevan, Khalnafat, 1919 ◆ Shushik Gevorgi Gevorgyan, Ilkhiabi, 1919 ◆ Shushik Gevorgi Martirosyan, Sarighamish, 1911 ◆ Shushik Ghukasi Abrahamyan, Kars, Chala, 1910 ◆ Shushik Grigori Hakobyan, Kars, Bashshoragal, 1912 ◆ Shushik Hambardzumi Safaryan, Pambak, Parni, 1916 ◆ Shushik Harutyuni Tatosyan (Harutyunyan), Basen, Hasandara, 1917 ◆ Shushik Hovhannesi (Sukias) Sukiasyan, Kars, 1919 ◆ Shushik Hovhannesi Hovakyan, Erzrum, 1914 ◆ Shushik Hovhannesi Hovhannisyan, Van, 1914 ◆ Shushik Karapeti Karapetyan, Basen, Khoshgyaldi, 1917 ◆ Shushik Khachaturi Alekyan (Khachatryan), Kars, 1917 ◆ Shushik Khachaturi Khachatryan, Basen, Alijagrak, 1918 ◆ Shushik Khachoyi Movsisyan, Basen, Gomadzor, 1916 ◆ Shushik Laloyan, 1912 ◆ Shushik Levoni Levonyan, Ghamarlu, Artashat, 1917 ◆ Shushik Meliki Avdalyan (Avetisyan), Leninakan, Illi, 1917 ◆ Shushik Melkoni Melkonyan, Van, 1915 ◆ Shushik Minasi Minasyan, 1917 ◆ Shushik Misaki Barseghyan, Akhalkalak, Samsar, 1913 ◆ Shushik Movsesi Movsisyan, Kars, Ghzlchakhchakh, 1918 ◆ Shushik Nersesi Mayilyan, Baku, Ghalaga, 1916 ◆ Shushik Petrosi Aghababyan, Kars, 1914 ◆ Shushik Piloyi Harutyunyan, Kaghzvan, Kirs, 1913 ◆ Shushik Sergoyi Tadevosyan (Sardaryan), Kars, Paldrvan, 1910 ◆ Shushik Simoni Gasparyan, Kars, 1916 ◆ Shushik Sukiasi Sahakyan, Alekpol, Ghaplu, 1909 ◆ Shushik Tadevosi Grigoryan, Kars, Zrchi, 1914 ◆ Shushik Ter-Markosi Martirosyan, Ghamarlu, Artashat, 1914 ◆ Shushik Vanoyi Mkhchyan, Kars, 1915 ◆ Shushik Voskani Voskanyan, Erzrum, 1916 ◆ Shushik Yegori Hakobyan, Leninakan, Sirvanjugh, 1917 ◆ Shushik Zmoyi Melkonyan ◆ Siranush Manuki Khachatryan, Alekpol, Paldrvan, 1915 ◆ Siranush Mekhaki Poghosyan (Hakobyan), Akhalkalak, Mec Samsar, 1912 ◆ Siranush Sirekani Karapetyan, Alekpol, Sirvanjugh, 1913 ◆ Sirekan Asaturi Hambardzumyan, Olti, Agrak, 1913 ◆ Sirush Sargisi Ghazaryan, Alashkert, 1917 ◆ Sirvard Hovsepi Gharibyan, Ghamarlu, Dyugan, 1911 ◆ Sirvard Khosrovi Hakobyan, Bitlis, 1909 ◆ Smbat Nikoli Arakelyan (Nikolyan), Leninakan, Ghazanchi, 1914 ◆ Sona Avetisi Danielyan, Karabagh, Tashbgh, 1912 ◆ Suren Khachiki Sahakyan (Khachikyan), Sarighamish, Arjarak, 1910 ◆ Tachat Daviti Shahinyan, Alashkert, Yeghantapa, 1913 ◆ Tachat Grigori Kirakosyan, Kars, Pirvali, 1916 ◆ Tachat Hovhannesi Hovhannisyan, Kars, Mazra, 1917 ◆ Tachat Mnatsakani Stepanyan, Leninakan, Aghin, 1910 ◆ Tachat Petrosi Petrosyan, Van, Kghzi, 1914 ◆ Tachat Poloyi Mkrtchyan, Alekpol, Artik, 1913 ◆ Tachat Sargisi Hamalbaghyan, Ardahan, 1912 ◆ Tachat Sureni Gasparyan, Igdir, Koghb, 1915 ◆ Tadevos Aleksani Galstyan (Aleksanyan), Yerevan, Nakhijevan, 1913 ◆ Tadevos Arakeli Tadevosyan, Darachichak, Kyarvansara, 1913 ◆ Tadevos Asaturi Muradyan, Leninakan, Hajinazar, 1910 ◆ Tadevos Avagi Simonyan, Alekpol, Tavshanghshlagh, 1910 ◆ Tadevos Baghdasari Bghdoyan (Baghdasaryan), Bulanagh, Latara, 1915 ◆ Tadevos Galusti Sargsyan, Sarighamish, Yayla, 1911 ◆ Tadevos Grigori Sargsyan, Darachichak, Kaghsi, 1911 ◆ Tadevos Hambardzumi Hambardzumyan, Nakhijevan, Gyulnat, 1912 ◆ Tadevos Harutyuni Harutyunyan, Van, Ghalakh, 1913 ◆ Tadevos Harutyuni Manukyan (Harutyunyan), Kharkov, 1912 ◆ Tadevos Harutyuni Mkrtchyan, Alekpol, Bozdoghan, 1913 ◆ Tadevos Harutyuni Petrosyan (Karapetyan), Kars, Agarak, 1910 ◆ Tadevos Harutyuni Tigranyan (Sargsyan), Leninakan, Tomardash, 1915 ◆ Tadevos Hovhannesi (Tadevosi) Sahakyan, Alekpol, Ghaplu, 1913 ◆ Tadevos Hovhannesi Gevorgyan, Van, Gorcod, 1907 ◆ Tadevos Karapeti Danielyan (Karapetyan), Kars, Voghuzli, 1914 ◆ Tadevos Khachaturi Poghosyan, Van, Corcor, 1914 ◆ Tadevos Noyemzari Ghazaryan (Stepanyan), Kars, Kaghzvan, 1914 ◆ Tadevos Nshani Arzumanyan, Kars, 1911 ◆ Tadevos Sargsi Muradyan, Kars, Gharaghala, 1912 ◆ Tadevos Sedraki Manukyan (Mnoyan), Sarighamish, Gharaghurut, 1910 ◆ Tadevos Varosi Gevorgyan, Kars, Bayghara, 1910 ◆ Tadevos Yervandi Martirosyan, Kars, Melik kyok, 1912 ◆ Taguhi Arakeli Yengoyan (Arakelyan), Aljavaz, Gazukh, 1911 ◆ Taguhi Arshaki (Sargsi) Vardanyan (Martirosyan), Van, Cvstan, 1912 ◆ Taguhi Asaturi Astvacatryan, Van, Pshants, 1911 ◆ Taguhi Asaturi Vardanyan, Manazkert, Gharaghala, 1909 ◆ Taguhi Avetisi Hovakimyan (Avetisyan), Moks, Dashti tagh, 1910 ◆ Taguhi Avetisi Kirakosyan (Avetisyan), Van, 1912 ◆ Taguhi Chatoyi (Martirosi) Hovsepyan, Van, Aljavaz, 1911 ◆ Taguhi Gevorgi

Gevorgyan, Bulanagh, Khoshgyaldi, 1916 ♦ Taguhi Gevorgi Gevorgyan, Bulanagh, Kop, 1915 ♦ Taguhi Grigori Grigoryan, Van, Gandzak, 1911 ♦ Taguhi Harutyuni Harutyunyan, Van, Shitan, 1909 ♦ Taguhi Harutyuni Poghosyan, Erzrum, Yeghan, 1908 ♦ Taguhi Hovhannesi Sargyan, Gyokcha, Ushfal, 1912 ♦ Taguhi Hovsepi (Mkhitari) Hovhannisyan (Mkhitaryan), Bitliz, Koshtan, 1909 ♦ Taguhi Hovsepi Avetisyan (Hovsepyan), Leninakan, Shishtapi, 1912 ♦ Taguhi Hovsepi Hovsepyan, Van, 1910 ♦ Taguhi Karapeti Karapetyan, Bitliz, 1912 ♦ Taguhi Karapeti Karapetyan, Bitliz, 1919 ♦ Taguhi Karapeti Sargsyan, Kars, Khani gyugh, 1910 ♦ Taguhi Khachaturi Hakobyan, Kars, Kop, 1913 ♦ Taguhi Khachiki Khachatryan, Kharberd, Balishir, 1912 ♦ Taguhi Melkoni Nersisyan (Melkonyan), Alashkert, Badnots, 1910 ♦ Taguhi Movsesi Sargsyan (Movsisyan), Van, 1911 ♦ Taguhi Sahaki Muradyan, Van, Archesh, 1911 ♦ Taguhi Sargsi Petrosyan, Van, Gandzak, 1908 ♦ Taguhi Sargsi Poghosyan, Baku, Ghalakyan, 1908 ♦ Taguhi Simoni Khachatryan, Bitliz, 1909 ♦ Taguhi Simoni Manukyan, Kaghzvan, 1911 ♦ Taguhi Smbati Smbatyan (Abrahamyan), Alekpol, Jalab, 1912 ♦ Taguhi Smbati Smbatyan, Yerevan, Norashen, 1913 ♦ Taguhi Soghomoni Amroyan, Alashkert, Mazra, 1914 ♦ Taguhi Tiraturi Tiraturyan, Kharberd, Balisher, 1913 ♦ Taguhi Yeghiazari Hovhannisyan, Kars, Bashshoragyal, 1908 ♦ Tagush Amirkhani Amirkhanyan, 1914 ♦ Tagush Grigori Grigoryan, Etchmiadzin, 1916 ♦ Tagush Grigori Hovsepyan, Alekpol, Paldlu, 1915 ♦ Tagush Hakobi Hakobyan, Sarighamish, 1914 ♦ Tagush Hambardzumi Hambardzumyan, Hin Nakhijevan, 1913 ♦ Tagush Hovhannesi Torosyan (Tosunyan), Akhalkalak, Tadesh, 1918 ♦ Tagush Hovsepi Hovsepyan, Nakhijevan, 1918 ♦ Tagush Jangyuli Jangyulyan, Van, Khorgom, 1912 ♦ Tagush Nazari Davtyan, Kars, Baylamat, 1913 ♦ Tagush Stepani Mikayelyan, Alekpol, Kosaghbyur, 1915 ♦ Tagush Torosi Torosyan, Kaghzan, 1916 ♦ Talit Khachaturi Shakaryan, Kars, Mazra, 1913 ♦ Talita Hambardzumi Hambardzumyan, Kars, Agrak, 1911 ♦ Tamar Abgari Sargsyan, Alashkert, Mazra, 1912 ♦ Tamar Arseni Manukyan, Yerevan, Ellar, 1916 ♦ Tamar Ghazari Ghazaryan, Kars, 1918 ♦ Tamar Grigori Grigoryan (Karapetyan), Nakhijevan, 1917 ♦ Tamar Hakobi Gharibyan (Hakobyan), Aparan, Chamrlu, 1912 ♦ Tamar Henriki Vardanyan, Igdir, Blur, 1915 ♦ Tamar Ivani Simonyan, Tifliz, 1912 ♦ Tamar Karapeti Karapetyan, Yerevan, Norashen, 1914 ♦ Tamar Mamikoni Mnoyan, Akhalkalak, Azarvet, 1914 ♦ Tamara (Roza) Khurshudi Abrahamyan, Baku, Karabagh, 1913 ♦ Tamara Aleksani Malkhasyan, Baku, 1910 ♦ Tamara Arshaki Hakobyan (Gevorgyan), Surmalu, Bharlu, 1916 ♦ Tamara Arshaluysi (Yegosi) Arshaluysyan, Leninakan, Sirvangyugh, 1917 ♦ Tamara Artemi Grigoryan, Nakhijevan, 1912 ♦ Tamara Arzumani Safaryan, Darachichak, 1915 ♦ Tamara Gevorgi Khachatryan, Nor Bayazet, Adiyama, 1914 ♦ Tamara Grigori Badasyan, Erzrum, Kyoprikoy, 1909 ♦ Tamara Grigori Hovsepyan, Karabagh, Shushi, 1913 ♦ Tamara Hambardzumi Hambardzumyan, Mec Gharakilisa, 1916 ♦ Tamara Harutyuni Ghazaryan, Aparan, Atma, 1914 ♦ Tamara Hovhannesi Hovhannisyan, Yerevan, Mazarjugh, 1912 ♦ Tamara Hovhannesi Melik-Shakhnazaryan, Aghsabad, 1912 ♦ Tamara Hovsepi Hovsepyan, Shirak, Sariar, 1915 ♦ Tamara Karapeti Adibegyan, Hin Bayazet, Arcap, 1910 ♦ Tamara Karapeti Karapetyan, Karabagh, Shushi, 1916 ♦ Tamara Martirosi Grigoryan (Martirosyan), Van, Aljavaz, 1914 ♦ Tamara Mayili Mayilyan, Van, 1911 ♦ Tamara Mikayeli Kostanyan, Lori, Sisi madan, 1914 ♦ Tamara Misaki Hakobyan, Baku, 1910 ♦ Tamara Mkrtchi Sardaryan, Igdir, 1913 ♦ Tamara Mkrtchi Vardanyan (Mkrtchyan), Van, 1914 ♦ Tamara Mnatsakani Mnatsakanyan, Etchmiadzin, 1916 ♦ Tamara Nersesi Nersisyan, Yerevan, 1915 ♦ Tamara Petrosi (Martirosi) Alikhanyan, Karabagh, Shushi, 1912 ♦ Tamara Rostomi Mirzoyan, Nakhijevan, Gyumri, 1913 ♦ Tamara Rubeni Sargsyan, Igdir, 1916 ♦ Tamara Sargsi Misakyan, Alekpol, Sirvanjugh, 1915 ♦ Tamara Smbati Smbatyan, Nor Bayazet, 1917 ♦ Tamara Soghomoni Sargsyan, Karabagh, 1911 ♦ Tamara Stepani Arsenyan, Yerevan, Norashen, 1914 ♦ Tamara Yani Izmiryan, Lori, Madan, 1912 ♦ Tangik Avagi Avagyan, Van, Moks, 1910 ♦ Tangik Papiki Papikyan, Van, Vozm, 1910 ♦ Tanginov Srapi Ter-Margaryan (Srapyan), Yerevan, Mastara, 1912 ♦ Targyul Haruti Minasyan, Shirak, Atyaman, 1913 ♦ Targyul Igiti Vardanyan, Van, Aljavaz, 1909 ♦ Targyul Khlghati Khlghatyan, Bulanagh, Manazkert, 1909 ♦ Tarvand Muradi Muradyan, Yerevan, Agarak, 1912 ♦ Tatos Armenaki Armenakyan, Nor Bayazet, 1915 ♦ Tatos Artashi Hakobyan, Gharakilisa, Mec Parni, 1914 ♦ Tatos Khlghati Khlghatyan, Shirak, Svanverdi, 1914 ♦ Tatos Mirani Avetisyan, Yerznka, 1908 ♦ Tatsu (Tiratur) Amroyi Sahakyan, Leninakan, Shishtapa, 1917 ♦ Tatul Grigori Grigoryan (Petrosyan), Kars, Syogutli, 1910 ♦ Tatul Poghosi Manukyan, Karin, Yakh, 1911 ♦ Tatul Sargsi Muradyan, Kars, Khach, 1914 ♦ Tatul Zakari Muradyan (Sahakyan), Kars, 1908 ♦ Tatush Mamikoni Ghukasyan (Manukyan), Alashkert, Gharakilisa, 1914 ♦ Tatush Serobi Petrosyan, Yerevan, Gyozli, 1913 ♦ Tavriz Harutyuni Vardanyan, Khnus, Gobal, 1912 ♦ Tavriz Khachaturi Mkhoyan (Khachatryan), Sarighamish, Hopviran, 1913 ♦ Tavriz Mkrtchi Muradyan (Sedrakyan), Kars, Aksi-Ghaz, 1908 ♦ Tavriz Poghosi Nazaryan (Poghosyan), Kharberd, Shvchugh, 1912 ♦ Tavriz Tigrani Hovhannisyan, Aljavaz, Verin Sipan, 1908 ♦ Tazagyul Abrahami Khachatryan, Alashkert, Khoshan, 1909 ♦ Tazagyul Gabrieli Gabrielyan (Hovsepyan), Alekpol, Gharakilisa, 1912 ♦ Tazagyul Grigori Yeghiazaryan (Grigoryan), Kars, Gedaksatlmish, 1910 ♦ Tazagyul Harutyuni Grigoryan, Bulanagh, Hamzashekh, 1911 ♦ Tazagyul Sakoyi Atoyan (Vardanyan), Kars, Gorkhana, 1915 ♦ Tazagyul Saribeki Karapetyan (Ghazaryan), Gharakilisa, Sarmusaghli, 1913 ♦ Tazagyul Stepani Stepanyan, Gharakilisa, 1917 ♦ Tego Khachaturi Khachatryan, Kars, Cbni, 1916 ♦ Tego Mamikoni Gevorgyan, Yerevan, Kyurtkat, 1912 ♦ Tegush Garsevani Ivanyan (Musheghyan), Yerevan, Aghpara, 1911 ♦ Telek Zakari Zakaryan,

Hin Nakhijevan, Gyagh, 1917 ♦ Tello Hakobi Kocharyan, Pambak, Gharakilisa, 1918 ♦ Telo Margari Mkrtchyan, Alekpol, Duzkharaba, 1911 ♦ Telo Milioni Haroyan, Igdir, Orgul, 1909 ♦ Temraz Antanesi Hakobyan, Kars, Bagran, 1917 ♦ Temur Avdali Avdalyan, Yerevan, Ghara-kelfi, 1910 ♦ Tepo Barseghi Hakobyan, Alekpol, Bandivan, 1914 ♦ Tepo Sargisi Gharibyan, Kars, N. Kyadiklar, 1911 ♦ Tereza Atomi Nersisyan, Leninakan, Svanverdi, 1917 ♦ Tereza Gabrieli Grigoryan, Kharberd, Mec berd, 1912 ♦ Tereza Vardani Arakelyan, Persia, Khoy, 1910 ♦ Tereza Yeghishei Ter-Yeghishyan, Kharbert, Ghozat, 1909 ♦ Tero Mkrtchi Tonoyan, Leninakan, Ghapuli, 1913 ♦ Tevan Vardazari Petrosyan (Vardazaryan), Zangezur, Ghapan, 1913 ♦ Tevos Harutyuni Harutyunyan (Manukyan), Van, Hartak, 1912 ♦ Tevos Serobi Gasparyan (Khumaryan), Alekpol, Taknalu, 1912 ♦ Tigo Karapeti Papikyan, Kars, Cbni, 1913 ♦ Tigran Adami Grigoryan (Adamyan), Khizan, Prosh, 1909 ♦ Tigran Aleksani Sevoyan, Alekpol, Pokr Gharakilis, 1917 ♦ Tigran Avagi Nersisyan, Alekpol, Gharakilisa, 1914 ♦ Tigran Avetisi Yeghiazaryan, Nor Bayazet, Zagha, 1912 ♦ Tigran Gevorgi Arakelyan, Mush, Brkashen, 1908 ♦ Tigran Gevorgi Khachatryan, Basen, Krdabaz, 1910 ♦ Tigran Gevorgi Petrosyan (Mirzoyan), Shirak, Hajinazar, 1916 ♦ Tigran Grigori Tonoyan, Kharberd, Mets Berd, 1909 ♦ Tigran Hakobi Gevorgyan, Van, 1907 ♦ Tigran Hovhannesi Hovhannisyan, Hin Nakhijevan, Nors, 1916 ♦ Tigran Hovhannesi Hovhannisyan, Nor Bayazet, 1914 ♦ Tigran Karapeti Ter-Sargsyan, Kars, Kaghzvan, 1912 ♦ Tigran Kerobi Kerobyan, Kharberd, Chimshkacak, 1917, 1916 ♦ Tigran Manuki Khachatryan (Manukyan), Van, Moks, 1914 ♦ Tigran Martirosi Sargsyan, Khlut, Nazuk, 1913 ♦ Tigran Minasi Markosyan, Yerznka, Keron, 1914 ♦ Tigran Mkhitari Hovhannisyan, Alashkert, Koshk, 1909 ♦ Tigran Mkrtchi Minasyan (Mkrtchyan), Khnus, Khalchavush, 1912 ♦ Tigran Movsesi Hovhannisyan, Baku, Khlg, 1915 ♦ Tigran Nikoli Kotanjyan, Alekpol, Koraghbyur, 1917 ♦ Tigran Poghosi Poghosyan, Mush, Arinj, 1912, 1910 ♦ Tigran Sahaki (Sayadi) Sahakyan, Hin Bayazet, Arcap, 1914 ♦ Tigran Sandroyi Baghdasaryan, Sasun, Petar, 1911 ♦ Tigran Simoni Simonyan, 1919 ♦ Tigran Tadevosi Petrosyan, Nor Bayazet, 1914 ♦ Tigran Vahani Aghajanyan, Mush, Krdagom, 1911 ♦ Tigran Yeremi Melkonyan, Lori, Spitak, 1914 ♦ Tigranhi (Tigush) Sedraki Sahakyan, Kars, 1917 ♦ Tigranuhi Aleksani Kharmandanyan (Gevorgyan), Kars, Bashshoragal, 1911 ♦ Tigranuhi Arseni Muradyan, Surmalu, Tashburan, 1914 ♦ Tigranuhi Galusti Sukiasyan, Kars, Kaghzvan, 1913 ♦ Tigranuhi Gevorgi Khachatryan, Van, Koghb, 1910 ♦ Tigranuhi Hovsepi Barkhudaryan, Persia, Khoy, 1906 ♦ Tigranuhi Khachaturi Mkrtchyan, Yerevan, Nakhijevan, 1914 ♦ Tigranuhi Makari Zakaryan, Kars, Sarighamish, 1910 ♦ Tigranuhi Manuki Minasyan, Kars, 1911 ♦ Tigranuhi Musheghi Poghosyan, Kars, Bashkyadiklar, 1913 ♦ Tigranuhi Nshani Andreasyan, Akhalkalak, 1912 ♦ Tigranuhi Petrosi Hamalbashyan, Ardahan, 1910 ♦ Tigranuhi Sargisi Muradyan (Sargsyan), Hayots dzor, Ishkhan, 1908 ♦ Tigranuhi Stepani Baloyan, Alekpol, 1910 ♦ Tigranuhi Tatosi Melikyan, Kars, 1914 ♦ Tigranuhi Vardani Asatryan, Leninakan, Ghapli, 1911 ♦ Tigranuhi Vardani Khachatryan, Igdir, 1908 ♦ Tigranuhi Voskani Grigoryan, Kaghzvan, Yengija, 1914 ♦ Tigranush Petoyi Dilanyan (Harutyunyan), Erzrum, Volor, 1918 ♦ Tikush Artashesi Artashesyan, Ghamarlu, Yuva, 1913 ♦ Tikush Grigori Vasilyan, Kars, 1919 ♦ Tikush Hovhannesi Khachatryan, Alekpol, Ghzlghoch, 1917 ♦ Tikush Zakari (Daviti) Davtyan, Kars, 1918 ♦ Tiran Aleksandri Grigoryan, Shirak, Ghonaghran, 1911 ♦ Tiran Mkrtchi Stepanyan, Kars, 1909 ♦ Tirayr Avetisi Petrosyan (Avetisyan), Kars, Pirvali, 1915 ♦ Tirayr Hakobi Malkhasyan, Akhalkalak, Sulda, 1913 ♦ Tirayr Saroyi Arakelyan, Kars, Ghzlchakhchakh, 1915 ♦ Tiraz Vardani Tigranyan, Khnus, Duman, 1910 ♦ Tiruhi Abrahami Hovhannisyan (Abrahamyan), Yerevan, Aparan, 1917 ♦ Tiruhi Arakeli Arakelyan, Kars, Bulanagh, 1912 ♦ Tiruhi Barseghi Manukyan, Kars, Tigor, 1912 ♦ Tiruhi Gaspari Aboyan, Alekpol, 1915 ♦ Tiruhi Harutyuni Grigoryan, Sarighamish, Zalaju, 1913 ♦ Tiruhi Harutyuni Harutyunyan, Hin Nakhijevan, 1913 ♦ Tiruhi Rostami Avagyan, Yerevan, 1909 ♦ Tiruhi Vardani Karapetyan, Akhalkalak, Khospis, 1910 ♦ Tirun Baghdasari Hakobyan, Sarighamish, Chrason, 1909 ♦ Tirun Barseghi Barseghyan, Alashkert, 1918 ♦ Tirun Gevorgi Gevorgyan, Leninakan, 1916 ♦ Tirun Khachaturi Ghazaryan, Akhalkalak, Ghul-ali, 1914 ♦ Tirun Khachaturi Harutyunyan, Alekpol, Bandura, 1911 ♦ Tirun Matevosi Vasilyan, Yerevan, Nakhijevan, 1915 ♦ Tirun Nersesi Nikolyan, Kars, Kaghzvan, 1914 ♦ Tirun Papiki Sukiasyan (Papikyan), Basen, 1915 ♦ Tirun Poghosi Poghosyan, Aparan, 1918 ♦ Tirun Vahani Terteryan, Basen, Gomadzor, 1912 ♦ Tirun Vahrami Karapetyan, Ghamarlu, 1914 ♦ Titipar Tevosi Davtyan, Akhalkalak, Machata, 1911 ♦ Toik (Dukhik) Sedraki Hakobyan (Sedrakyan), Basen, Yaghan, 1912 ♦ Tonakan Galusti Davtyan (Galstyan), Erzrum, Bulk, 1909 ♦ Tonik Hakobi Gasparyan, Manazkert, Khanoghli, 1906 ♦ Tonik Sandroyi Baghdasaryan, Sasun, Gomer, 1911 ♦ Torgom Arakeli Gevorgyan, Kars, 1913 ♦ Torgom Arami Mkrtchyan (Harutyunyan), Leninakan, Gharakilisa, 1911 ♦ Torgom Armenaki Papikyan, Kars, Nakhijevan, 1912 ♦ Torgom Bagrati Galstyan, Kars, 1912 ♦ Torgom Ginosi Ghukasyan (Ginosyan), Basen, Totoviran, 1914 ♦ Torgom Grigori Hayrapetyan (Torgomyan), Van, 1911 ♦ Torgom Grigori Hovhannisyan (Grigoryan), Kars, Gharamahmat, 1915 ♦ Torgom Haruti Petrosyan (Mkoyan), Etchmiadzin, Mastara, 1910 ♦ Torgom Karapeti Karapetyan (Nahapetyan), Sarighamish, Shadivan, 1911 ♦ Torgom Khachoyi Ghazaryan, Alekpol, Dashghala, 1911 ♦ Torgom Mkrtchi Hovhannisyan, Alekpol, Duzkharaba, 1913 ♦ Torgom Mkrtchi Muradyan, Mush, Drmetr, 1914 ♦ Torgom Mkrtchi Nazaretyan, Kars, 1914 ♦ Torgom Mkrtchi Vardanyan (Mkrtchyan), Kars, 1912 ♦ Torgom Musheghi Musheghyan, Kars, Mavrak, 1916 ♦ Torgom Poghosi Movsisyan, Mush, Khasgyugh, 1912 ♦ Torgom Sargsi Ter-Sargsyan, Kars, Gyarmlu, 1915 ♦ Torgom Yeghishi

Antonyan, Alekpol, Ortakilisa, 1913 ♦ Torgom Yeghishi Ter-Melikyan, Shirak, Tekniz, 1914 ♦ Torik (Tornik) Nshani Grigoryan, Kars, Chghrghan, 1914 ♦ Torik Misaki Amiryan, Erzrum, Yaghan, 1911 ♦ Torinj (Aram) Abrahami Levonyan (Abrahamyan), Nukhi, 1914 ♦ Torman Grigori Grigoryan, Mush, Gharaghala, 1911 ♦ Tornik Benyamini Gevorgyan, Shirak, Bozdughan, 1918 ♦ Tornik Gabrieli Mkrtchyan, Van, 1913 ♦ Tornik Meliki Grigoryan, Shirak, Aghula, 1915 ♦ Toros (Tadevos) Aleksani Alekyan, Akhalkalak, Majadia, 1916 ♦ Toros Arakeli Terteryan (Koshkakaryan), Kharberd, Lazvan, 1910 ♦ Toros Hovhannesi Hovhannisyan, Erzrum, Ghachagh, 1911 ♦ Toros Hovhannesi T. Markosyan, Kharberd, 1910 ♦ Toros Karapeti Galoyan, Sarighamish, Armtlu, 1912 ♦ Toros Margari Margaryan, Van, Sivan, 1899 ♦ Toros Yenoki Shirinyan (Yenokyan) (Martirosyan), Terjan, Ghachagh, 1907 ♦ Torvant Khachaturi Manukyan, Kharberd, Sivgyugh, 1911 ♦ Tovmas (Tumas) Khachaturi Serobyan, Leninakan, Gharamahmad, 1917 ♦ Tovmas Galusti Ter-Martirosyan, Alekpol, Chrakhli, 1912 ♦ Tovmas Ghazari Nazaryan (Tovmasyan), Van, Vanik, 1907 ♦ Tovmas Serobi Margaryan (Serobyan), Aparan, Gharakilisa, 1907 ♦ Trchnak Petrosi Haykazyan, Van, Kghzi, 1909 ♦ Trdat Arshaki Ghazaryan, Surmalu, Koghb, 1916 ♦ Trdat Avetisi Vardanyan, Erzrum, Yuzviran, 1911 ♦ Trdat Martirosi Avagyan, Van, 1909 ♦ Trdat Mheri Mheryan, Bulanagh, Latar, 1914 ♦ Tsetrik Manuki Manukyan (Khojoyan), Van, Kharakonis, 1905 ♦ Tsoghik Nazareti Soghomonyan, Alekpol, Khlli Gharakilis, 1916 ♦ Tsoghik Sedraki Galstyan, Kars, Paldrvan, 1914 ♦ Tsoghik Vahani Melikyan (Melkonyan), Kars, 1917 ♦ Tsolak (Meshokyan) Misakyan, Tiflis, 1919 ♦ Tsolak Aleksani Aleksanyan, H. Nakhijevan, Ghazanchi, 1914 ♦ Tsolak Andraniki Aslanyan, Kars, 1911 ♦ Tsolak Arami Karapetyan, Alekpol, 1908 ♦ Tsolak Arshaki Arshakyan, Kars, Keti, 1919 ♦ Tsolak Avetisi Khachatryan, Bulanagh, Yonjalu, 1913 ♦ Tsolak Danieli Baghdasaryan (Danielyan), Mec Gharakilis, Alikhan, 1916 ♦ Tsolak Daviti Khachatryan, Kars, 1913 ♦ Tsolak Gevorgi Arakelyan, Pambak, Ghshlagh, 1913 ♦ Tsolak Gevorgi Grigoryan, Kars, 1910 ♦ Tsolak Hakobi Paylakyan (Hakobyan), Van, 1916 ♦ Tsolak Harutyuni Kerobyan, Leninakan, Ghortbulagh, 1917 ♦ Tsolak Hovhannesi Avetisyan (Hovhannisyan), Kars, Mazra, 1913 ♦ Tsolak Hovhannesi Khachatryan, Leninakan, Bayandur, 1911 ♦ Tsolak Ishkhani Shahinyan, Akhalkalak, Vachyan, 1915 ♦ Tsolak Javati Azatyan (Javatyan), Nakhijevan, Gyumri, 1913 ♦ Tsolak Karapeti Ghazaryan (Karapetyan), Leninakan, Bayandur, 1917 ♦ Tsolak Khachaturi Gevorgyan, Kars, 1914 ♦ Tsolak Khachaturi Khachatryan, Akhalkalak, Pokr Kendura, 1914 ♦ Tsolak Khachaturi Movsisyan, Igdir, 1907 ♦ Tsolak Kirakosi Hayrapetyan, Basen, Dalibaba, 1911 ♦ Tsolak Levoni Levonyan, Leninakan, Mastara, 1917 ♦ Tsolak Makari Arakelyan, Shirak, Bozgyugh, 1914 ♦ Tsolak Manuki Antonyan, Shirak, Ghapli, 1914 ♦ Tsolak Martirosi Papoyan (Babayan), Kars, Pirvali, 1912 ♦ Tsolak Meliki Melikyan (Mikayelyan), Basen, Yaghan, 1916 ♦ Tsolak Mkrtchi Hovhannisyan, Alekpol, Sirvanjugh, 1906 ♦ Tsolak Mkrtchi Karapetyan (Mkrtchyan), Alekpol, Sariar, 1914 ♦ Tsolak Nikoghosi Arakelyan, Yerevan, Ghznaberd, 1912 ♦ Tsolak Poghosi Poghosyan, Akhalkalak, 1916 ♦ Tsolak Sahaki Aslanyan, Kars, Bashkyadilkar, 1912 ♦ Tsolak Sedraki (Grigoryan) Sedrakyan, Van, 1915 ♦ Tsolak Shmavoi Gnunyan, Kars, Bashshoragal, 1913 ♦ Tsolak Sirekani Sirekanyan, Yerevan, Hakhzer, 1916 ♦ Tsolak Soghomoni Sargsyan, Batum, 1914 ♦ Tsolak Tadevosi Sargsyan (Tadevosyan), Kars, Bashkadiklar, 1915 ♦ Tsolak Tigrani Movsisyan, Leninakan, Araz, 1916 ♦ Tsolak Torosi Torosyan, Kars, Ortakilisa, 1912 ♦ Tsolak Vardani Avetisyan, Kars, 1913 ♦ Tsolakuhi Manuki Ghazaryan, Surmalu, Narafat, 1908 ♦ Tufo Ghazari Grigoryan, Alekpol, Duzkharaba, 1912 ♦ Tukhan (Dukhan) Margari Azulyan, Kars, Nakhijevan, 1911 ♦ Tukhik (Dukhik) Petrosi Ghazaryan, Basen, Alichakrak, 1912 ♦ Tukhik Pilosi Piloyan, Basen, Yeghan, 1914 ♦ Tulit Mkrtchi Petrosyan, Alekpol, Ghoshavank, 1913 ♦ Tuman Harutyuni Grigoryan, Kars, Gyadmlu, 1912 ♦ Tuman Karapeti Ghaltaghchyan, Kars, Ghani, 1908 ♦ Tumas Hakobi Hakobyan, Shirak, Babuli, 1911 ♦ Tumo Atoyi Konoyan, Leninakan, Duzkharaba, 1916 ♦ Turvand Hakobi Simonyan, Terjan, Berkli, 1913 ♦ Tutan Harutyuni Asatryan (Harutyunyan), Bulanagh, 1913 ♦ Tutik Petrosi Gaboyan (Nazaryan), Basen, Bashgegh, 1915 ♦ Tutush Gaspari Aleksanyan (Gasparyan), Bulanagh, Kop, 1914 ♦ Tutush Gevorgi Harutyunyan, Erzrum, Aljarak, 1912 ♦ Tutush Mikayeli Karapetyan, Kaghzvan, 1917 ♦ Tutush Soghomoni Gevorgyan, Alekpol, Ghaplu, 1913 ♦ Ukhtanis Grigori Gevorgyan, Basen, Cancagh, 1911 ♦ Umrik Hakobi Yeghiazaryan (Hakobyan), Khizan, Kharit, 1906 ♦ Unkuyz Ardeni Baloyan, Kars, Bazrgan, 1919 ♦ Ustian Gabrieli Gabrielyan, Leninakan, Gharakilisa, 1911 ♦ Ustian Grigori Badalyan (Dallakyan), Akulis, 1914 ♦ Ustian Harutyuni Vardanyan, Khnus, Gopal, 1911 ♦ Ustian Hovakimi Sahakyan, Van, 1914 ♦ Ustian Hovhannesi Shahinyan, Van, Gorcot, 1913 ♦ Ustian Khachaturi Khachatryan, Alekpol, Koraghbyur, 1914 ♦ Ustian Matsaki Sahakyan, Aljavaz, 1914 ♦ Ustian Misaki Ter-Misakyan, Bitlis, Meck, 1910 ♦ Ustian Movsesi Sahakyan, Mush, 1909 ♦ Ustian Serobi Serobyan, Tiflis, 1917 ♦ Ustian Vahani Petrosyan, Aghbak, Paghgale, 1912 ♦ Ustian Vardani Vardanyan, 1914 ♦ Ustian Vardanyan, 1912 ♦ Vachagan Arakeli Manukyan, Kars, 1915 ♦ Vachagan Arshaki Galoyan, Kars, Mazra, 1912 ♦ Vachagan Daviti Davtyan, Kars, Bulanagh, 1914 ♦ Vachagan Galusti Hovhannisyan, Igdir, 1912 ♦ Vachagan Hambardzumi Ghazaryan, Leninakan, Ghzlghoch, 1912 ♦ Vachagan Hovhannesi Nalbandyan, Mec Gharakilis, 1912 ♦ Vachagan Karapeti Khachatryan, Leninakan, 1913 ♦ Vachagan Karapeti Poghosyan, Leninakan, Khli Gharakilis, 1913 ♦ Vachagan Mambrei Khachatryan, Archesh, Akants, 1912 ♦ Vachagan Minasi Mkrtchyan, Kars, 1914 ♦ Vachagan Sahaki Nikoghosyan, Pambak, Parni, 1911 ♦ Vachagan Sargisi Sargsyan, Alekpol, Chiftalu, 1914 ♦ Vachagan Sedraki Mikayelyan, Leninakan, Mahmatjugh, 1914 ♦ Vachagan

Sedraki Sedrakyan, Shirak, Chiftali, 1916 ♦ Vachagan Serobi Gasparyan, Akhalkalak, Satkha, 1911 ♦ Vachagan Soghomoni Tumasyan, Kars, Uzunkilisa, 1913 ♦ Vachagan Tigrani Gevorgyan, Leninakan, Svanverdi, 1913 ♦ Vachagan Tipani Carukyan, Alekpol, Taparlu, 1914 ♦ Vachagan Varantsovi Tadevosyan, Kars, Ghzl chakhchakh, 1914 ♦ Vachik Geghami Geghamyan, Alashkert, 1919 ♦ Vachik Hovhannesi Hovhannisyan, Kaghzvan, Aghuzum, 1915 ♦ Vachik Petrosi Mloyan, Kars, Paldrvan, 1918 ♦ Vagharshak (Garnik) Movsesi Arakelyan, Shamakhi, 1913, 1911 ♦ Vagharshak Abeti Abetyan, Van, 1914 ♦ Vagharshak Aghajani Khachatryan, Kars, 1911 ♦ Vagharshak Aleki Hakobyan, Kars, 1909 ♦ Vagharshak Aleksani Karapetyan, Van, Chandur, 1917 ♦ Vagharshak Aleksani Petrosyan, Alekpol, Ghonaghran, 1911 ♦ Vagharshak Andreasi Sargsyan, Archesh, Ktrac kar, 1912 ♦ Vagharshak Artashesi Baghdasaryan, Kars, Shadivan, 1914 ♦ Vagharshak Asoyi Asoyan, Kars, Aksi ghazi, 1913 ♦ Vagharshak Avagi Avagyan, Leninakan, Toros, 1916 ♦ Vagharshak Baghdasari (Arakeli) Baghdasaryan, Shirak, Ghrdbulagh, 1916 ♦ Vagharshak Baghdasari Baghdasaryan, Yerevan, Darachichak, 1916 ♦ Vagharshak Barseghi Khosrovyan, Shirak, Parni, 1915 ♦ Vagharshak Caruki Simonyan, Kars, Uzunkilisa, 1918, 1921 ♦ Vagharshak Galusti Kirakosyan (Galstyan), Kars, Pirvali, 1915 ♦ Vagharshak Galusti Petrosyan, Alekpol, Taknali, 1909 ♦ Vagharshak Gevorgi Safaryan (Khachatryan), Yerevan, 1914 ♦ Vagharshak Ghevondi Azatyan, Van, Moson, 1910 ♦ Vagharshak Hakobi Avetisyan, Alekpol, Ortakilisa, 1911 ♦ Vagharshak Harutyuni Ghazanchyan, Akhalkalak, Karcakh, 1913 ♦ Vagharshak Harutyuni Harutyunyan, Basen, Alvar, 1911 ♦ Vagharshak Harutyuni Harutyunyan, Van, Moks dasht, 1909 ♦ Vagharshak Harutyuni Torosyan, Kars, Berna, 1916 ♦ Vagharshak Hovakimi Petrosyan, Akhalkalak, Sulda, 1913 ♦ Vagharshak Hovhannesi Hovhannisyan, Basen, Bashgegh, 1914 ♦ Vagharshak Hovhannesi Hovhannisyan, Basen, Yaghan, 1912 ♦ Vagharshak Hovhannesi Varosyan, Kars, Bayrakhtar, 1909 ♦ Vagharshak Karapeti Ghazaryan, Mec Gharakilisa, Yughabli, 1911 ♦ Vagharshak Karapeti Mirzoyan, Kars, Bozghara, 1913 ♦ Vagharshak Khurshudi Manukyan, Khnus, Khat, 1912 ♦ Vagharshak Martirosi Danielyan, Alekpol, Kaps, 1913 ♦ Vagharshak Martirosi Gasparyan, Kars, Hamzakarak, 1914 ♦ Vagharshak Martirosi Hakobyan, Akhalkalak, Goman, 1912 ♦ Vagharshak Martirosi Martirosyan, Mush, 1912 ♦ Vagharshak Martirosi Ohanyan, Akhalkalak, Vachyan, 1915 ♦ Vagharshak Meliki Adamyan, Kars, Begliahmat, 1908 ♦ Vagharshak Mkrtchi Andreasyan, Gharakilisa, 1916 ♦ Vagharshak Mkrtchi Davtyan, Kars, Ardahan, 1913 ♦ Vagharshak Petrosi Petrosyan, Van, 1914 ♦ Vagharshak Poghosi Hakobyan, Kars, Berna, 1910 ♦ Vagharshak Sedraki Aleksanyan, Kars, Oghuzli, 1911 ♦ Vagharshak Shabaghari Mkrtchyan, Zangezur, Khndzoresk, 1913 ♦ Vagharshak Srapi Kakoyan (Srapyan), Alekpol, Chiftalu, 1915 ♦ Vagharshak Yeghishei Vardanyan, Erzrum, 1910 ♦ Vaghinak (Vagharshak) Martirosi Petrosyan, Kars, Dorbandlu, 1910 ♦ Vaghinak Abrahami Abrahamyan, Igdir, Koghb, 1914 ♦ Vaghinak Abrahami Ghazaryan, Kars, Byurakdara, 1910 ♦ Vaghinak Antoni Khachatryan, Kars, Terjan, 1914 ♦ Vaghinak Arshaki Hambardzumyan, Kars, Zrchi, 1913 ♦ Vaghinak Artashesi Firmanyan (Margaryan), Akhalkalak, Sulda, 1912 ♦ Vaghinak Grigori Papikyan, Shirak, Khlli Gharakilis, 1914 ♦ Vaghinak Kochari Poghosyan, Igdir, 1912 ♦ Vaghinak Levoni Baloyan, Kars, Paldrvan, 1915 ♦ Vaghinak Misaki Andreasyan, Kars, 1909 ♦ Vaghinak Sirakani Martirosyan, Kars, Tekniz, 1914 ♦ Vagho Avagi Avagyan, Leninakan, Khzlkilisa, 1917 ♦ Vagho Sahaki Mkrtchyan (Sahakyan), Kars, Zrchi, 1915 ♦ Vagho Smbati Madoyan, Kars, Ortakadiklar, 1914 ♦ Vahagn Habeti Mshetsyan (Maloyan), Leninakan, 1914 ♦ Vahagn Shavarshi Grigoryan, Leninakan, Khli Gharakilisa, 1914 ♦ Vahan (Vano) Khachaturi Dolinyan, Koghb, 1909 ♦ Vahan Abrahami Davtyan, Kars, Aksighaz, 1915 ♦ Vahan Aleksandri Aleksanyan, Alashkert, Yeghantap, 1910 ♦ Vahan Aleksani Sargsyan (Aleksanyan), Nakhijevan, Karakhach, 1916 ♦ Vahan Arshaki Poghosyan, Khnus, Duman, 1912 ♦ Vahan Artashi Tavrizyan (Artashyan), Akhalkalak, Tadesh, 1916 ♦ Vahan Avetisi Sargsyan (Avetisyan), Basen, Arjarak, 1911 ♦ Vahan Daviti Davtyan, Nor Bayazet, 1917 ♦ Vahan Gabrieli Ghafaryan (Gabrielyan), Erzrum, Bayburt, 1911 ♦ Vahan Galusti Torosyan, Kars, Berna, 1908 ♦ Vahan Galusti Yesayan, Zangezur, Ghazanchi, 1914 ♦ Vahan Gevorgi Gevorgyan, Kars, Ghzlchakhchakh, 1918 ♦ Vahan Ghazari Grigoryan (Tarjumanyan), Kaghzvan, 1917 ♦ Vahan Hambardzumi Uzunyan (Hambaryan), Bulanagh, Khoshgyaldi, 1911 ♦ Vahan Karapeti Arshakyan (Karapetyan), Kars, 1917 ♦ Vahan Karapeti Papoyan, Kars, Chala, 1911 ♦ Vahan Karapeti Ter-Davtyan, Van, Moks, 1911 ♦ Vahan Kerobi Kerobyan, Basen, Hekibat, 1915 ♦ Vahan Manuki Martirosyan (Manukyan), Basen, Khordzor, 1916 ♦ Vahan Martirosi Hovhannisyan, Mush, Bostakand, 1913, 1910 ♦ Vahan Martirosi Mayilyan, Turkey, 1912 ♦ Vahan Mkhitari Hovhannisyan, Alashkert, Khastur, 1912 ♦ Vahan Mkhitari Mkhitaryan, Mush, Lorndzor, 1908, 1911 ♦ Vahan Mnatsakani Shahinyan, Kars, Gyarmlu, 1910 ♦ Vahan Muradi (Arshak) Harutyunyan (Muradyan), Bulanagh, Gharaghlu, 1912 ♦ Vahan Muradi Temoyan (Muradyan), Mush, Yonjalu, 1912 ♦ Vahan Nikoghosi Tadevosyan, Yerevan, Evjilar, 1903 ♦ Vahan Sahaki Mkrtchyan, Bulanagh, Rostomgedak, 1914 ♦ Vahan Sargisi Grigoryan, Nakhijevan, Ghazanchi, 1912 ♦ Vahan Sargisi Karapetyan, Basen, Bashgegh, 1910 ♦ Vahan Soghomoni Martirosyan, Kars, Mavrak, 1912 ♦ Vahan Soghomoni Soghomonyan, Alashkert, Gharakilisa, 1921 ♦ Vahan Soghomoni Ter-Grigoryan, Van, Aljavaz, 1912 ♦ Vahan Stepani Mejlumyan, Lori, Atan, 1916 ♦ Vahan Sukiasi Gevorgyan, Erzrum, Ughtadzor, 1909 ♦ Vahan Vardani Vardanyan, Van, Nor gyugh, 1911 ♦ Vahan Voskani Karapetyan, Kharberd, Mec Gert, 1911 ♦ Vahan Voskani Vardanyan, Alekpol, Mahmatjugh, 1912 ♦ Vahandukht Tadevosi Tadevosyan, Surmali, Khoshkhabar, 1914 ♦ Vahrad (Fahrad) Sargisi Sargsyan, Basen, 1915 ♦ Vahrad Vaghoyi Vaghoyan, Kars, 1918 ♦

Vahram Hambardzumi Hambardumyan, Van, Alur, 1911 ◆ Vahram Manuki Manaseryan (Manukyan), Van, Kendanants, 1911 ◆ Vahram Manuki Serobyan, Sarighamish, Hopviran, 1916 ◆ Vahram Meliki Melikyan, Yenzeli, 1910 ◆ Vahram Minasi Grigoryan, Akhalkalak, Mec Khanchalu, 1909 ◆ Vahram Vanyayi Shahmuradyan (Torosyan), Gyokcha, Vanashen, 1911 ◆ Vahram Yeghishei Ter-Grigoryan, Alekpol, Gharakilisa, 1917 ◆ Vahrich Aleksani Aleksanyan, Leninakan, Gharakilisa, 1919 ◆ Vahrich Arshaki Ghazaryan, Erzrum, 1908 ◆ Vahrich Artashi Gevorgyan (Tutunjyan), Kars, 1918 ◆ Vahrich Khachoyi Melkonyan, Kars, Mavrak, 1914 ◆ Vahrich Sahaki Keshishyan, Kars, Sarighamish, 1915 ◆ Valandi Arseni Hovhannisyan, Yerevan, 1915 ◆ Valandin Nshani Astvacaturyan, Van, Shaghbagh, 1910 ◆ Valik (Balik) Baghdasari Baghdasaryan, Van, 1918 ◆ Valik Arzoyi Arzumanyan, Madan, 1919 ◆ Vanik Aleksani Hakobyan (Stepanyan), Kars, 1914 ◆ Vanik Arami Misakyan (Aramyan), Erzrum, Ishkhu, 1917 ◆ Vanik Arshaki Arshakyan (Yeranakyan), Khnus, Saylun, 1914 ◆ Vanik Arshaki Ginosyan, Shirak, Taliboghli, 1914 ◆ Vanik Gevorgyan Gevorgi, 1920 ◆ Vanik Haroyi Haroyan (Harutyunyan), Basen, Arjarak, 1916 ◆ Vanik Karapeti Avagyan, Leninakan, Talib oghli, 1916 ◆ Vanik Karapeti Karapetyan (Manukyan), Basen, Bashgegh, 1910 ◆ Vanik Musheghi Poghosyan, Kars, Paldrvan, 1912 ◆ Vanik Petrosi Vardanyan (Petrosyan), Ardahan, 1917 ◆ Vanik Tevosi Dightrikyan, Van, 1916 ◆ Vano Aveti Bayatyan, Nakhijevan, 1918 ◆ Vano Badali Serobyan (Badalyan), Aparan, Gharabulagh, 1916 ◆ Vano Daviti Poghosyan (Davtyan), Alekpol, Boghazkasan, 1914 ◆ Vano Gaspari Gasparyan, Lori, Shahnazar, 1918 ◆ Vano Gevorgi Movsisyan, Tiflis, 1915 ◆ Vano Meliki Melikyan, Khnus, Kopal, 1914 ◆ Vano Mkrtchi Khachatryan (Hakobyan), Kars, Bagliahmat, 1916 ◆ Vano Nikoghosi Nikoghosyan (Mkrtchyan), Igdir, Khalfalu, 1913 ◆ Vano Vardani Mesropyan (Vardanyan), Basen, Ghoshakilisa, 1916 ◆ Vanuhi Arshaki Arshakyan, Van, 1914 ◆ Vanuhi Gaspari Khlghatyan, Van, 1908 ◆ Vanuhi Grigori Grigoryan, Nakhijevan, 1914 ◆ Vanuhi Hakobi Hakobyan, Van, 1915 ◆ Vanuhi Khachaturi Hakobyan, Van, Kerc, 1911 ◆ Vanuhi Mkrtchi Aghakhanyan (Mkrtchyan), Van, 1913 ◆ Vanuhi Mkrtchi Asatryan, Van, 1916 ◆ Vanuhi Mkrtchi Sahakyan, Van, Dashmal, 1908 ◆ Vanuhi Sargisi Sargsyan, Van, 1913 ◆ Vanuhi Vardani Poghharyan, Van, 1909 ◆ Vanush Arzumani Mnoyan, Gyokcha, Ghshlagh, 1914 ◆ Vanush Khachaturi Danielyan (Khachatryan), Igdir, 1917 ◆ Vanush Kostani Sargsyan, Darachichak, Gomadzor, 1910 ◆ Vanush Yeynati Yeynatyan (Karamyan), Daralagyaz, Vordaven, 1913 ◆ Vanya Hovhannesi Hakobyan, Sibir, Verni, 1917 ◆ Varantsov Khachoyi Khachatryan, Kars, Bulanagh, 1918 ◆ Varantsov Smbati Madoyan, Kars, Kyadiklar, 1913 ◆ Varazdat Andreasi Andreasyan, Basen, Todoveran, 1914 ◆ Varazdat Armenaki Atoyan, Kars, Mec Parket, 1911 ◆ Varazdat Arseni Ghazaryan, Kars, Bayburt, 1913 ◆ Varazdat Arshaki Khachatryan, Leninakan, Khli Gharakilisa, 1913 ◆ Varazdat Arshaki Sahakyan (Arshakyan), Leninakan, Illi, 1912 ◆ Varazdat Asaturi Davtyan, Kars, 1916 ◆ Varazdat Avetisi Hasratyan (Avetisyan), Daralagyaz, Norashen, 1912 ◆ Varazdat Avoyi Gabrielyan (Avoyan), Nakhijevan, Znaberd, 1916 ◆ Varazdat Galoyi Kostanyan, Leninakan, Mahmajugh, 1911 ◆ Varazdat Galusti Arshakyan (Galstyan), Kars, Gedaksatlmish, 1918 ◆ Varazdat Galusti Gasparyan (Galstyan), Shirak, Kyaftarli, 1917 ◆ Varazdat Geghami Nersisyan, Igdir, Shahabli, 1914 ◆ Varazdat Gevorgi Petrosyan, Leninakan, Tavshanghshlagh, 1912 ◆ Varazdat Grigori Madoyan (Grigoryan), Kars, Hamzakarak, 1916 ◆ Varazdat Hamazaspi Hamazaspyan, Alashkert, 1913, 1912 ◆ Varazdat Hovhannesi Hovhannisyan, Alekpol, Artik, 1915 ◆ Varazdat Hovhannesi Hovhannisyan, Bulanagh, Kop, 1918 ◆ Varazdat Khachaturi Martirosyan, Leninakan, Bashshoragal, 1916 ◆ Varazdat Khachaturi Petrosyan, Leninakan, Babrlu, 1914 ◆ Varazdat Margari Hakobyan (Svaryan), Van, Sevan, 1912 ◆ Varazdat Margari Sargsyan (Margaryan), Kars, Zrchi, 1914 ◆ Varazdat Martirosi Khachatryan (Martirosyan), Alekpol, Syogutli, 1912 ◆ Varazdat Misaki Avagyan, Alekpol, Dzitankov, 1914 ◆ Varazdat Misaki Sargsyan (Misakyan), Kars, Gyarmlu, 1913 ◆ Varazdat Mkrtchi Hakobyan, Alashkert, Ghaza, 1912 ◆ Varazdat Mkrtichi Mkrtchyan, Yerevan, Ghamarlu, 1915 ◆ Varazdat Papiki Mnatsakanyan, Kars, Chala, 1914 ◆ Varazdat Petrosi Petrosyan, Basen, Hopveran, 1913 ◆ Varazdat Setoyi Petrosyan, Alekpol, Kefli, 1916 ◆ Varazdat Stepani Khachatryan (Khojayan), Igdir, Ali ghzl, 1912 ◆ Varazdat Stepani Tumasyan, Kars, Shadivan, 1912 ◆ Varazdat Tigrani Tigranyan, Leninakan, Bayandur, 1916 ◆ Varazdat Torosi (Kirakosyan) Stepanyan, Leninakan, Zyufali, 1919 ◆ Varazdat Torosi Hakobyan (Torosyan), Leninakan, Chorli, 1915 ◆ Varazdat Yeghoyi Nalbandyan (Yeghoyan), Kars, Kyurakdara, 1917 ◆ Varazdat Zakoyi Psoyan, Ughuzli, 1918, 1916 ◆ Vard Aleki (Alekyan) Harutyunyan, Shirak, Syogutli, 1914 ◆ Vard Ghukasi Hovhannisyan (Ghukasyan), Leninakan, Sariar, 1914 ◆ Vard Hakobi Martirosyan, Kars, Sarighamish, 1915 ◆ Vard Hambardzumi Grigoryan, Kars, Ghzlchakhchakh, 1914 ◆ Vard Hovhannesi Nalbandyan, Kars, Byurakdara, 1912 ◆ Vard Khnkoyi Khachatryan, Alekpol, Imrkhan, 1914 ◆ Vard Knyazi Virabyan, Kars, 1911 ◆ Vard Matosi Piloyan, Alekpol, Ghanlija, 1910 ◆ Vard Nersesi Khachatryan, Leninakan, Mec Keti, 1913 ◆ Vard Poghosi Grigoryan (Poghosyan), Gharakilisa, Chotur, 1911 ◆ Vard Sahaki Grigoryan (Sahakyan), Sarighamish, Hopviran, 1914 ◆ Vard Sahaki Sahakyan, Yerevan, Tejrabat, 1913 ◆ Vard Sedraki Bozoyan, Alekpol, Horom, 1912 ◆ Vard Sirakani Matsoyan (Sirakanyan), Kars, Uzunkilisa, 1916 ◆ Vard Smbati Tazoyan (Smbatyan), Alekpol, Ghanlija, 1912 ◆ Vard Soghomoni Aleksanyan, Leninakan, Ghonaghran, 1912 ◆ Vard Stepani Stepanyan, Shirak, Mec Sariar, 1919 ◆ Vardan Abgari Khachatryan, Akhalkalak, Namzara, 1913 ◆ Vardan Arshaki Khachikyan, Shamakhi, Saghian, 1912 ◆ Vardan Arshaki Poghosyan, Leninakan, Chlovkhan, 1917 ◆ Vardan Daviti Davtyan (Arakelyan), Kars, 1911 ◆ Vardan Daviti Davtyan, Hin Nakhijevan, 1917 ◆ Vardan Gaboyi

Gevorgyan, Leninakan, Kefli, 1913 ♦ Vardan Gabrieli Hovsepyan, Kars, 1915 ♦ Vardan Galusti Mkrtchyan (Papikyan), Leninakan, Ghzlghoch, 1912 ♦ Vardan Gevorgi Sahakyan (Gevorgyan), Bitlis, Hant, 1910 ♦ Vardan Ghazari Muradyan (Ghazaryan), Van, Karchkan, 1916 ♦ Vardan Ghazari Tatosyan (Ghazaryan), Erzrum, 1914 ♦ Vardan Ghazari Tovmasyan (Ghazaryan), Kachkan, Vanik, 1913 ♦ Vardan Hakobi Aghajanyan, Kaghzvan, 1909 ♦ Vardan Hakobi Hakobyan, Akhalkalak, Vachyan, 1917 ♦ Vardan Hakobi Hakobyan, Van, Cvstan, 1912, 1911 ♦ Vardan Hakobi Harutyunyan, Tiflis, 1915 ♦ Vardan Hamazaspi Palanjyan, Kars, 1913 ♦ Vardan Harutyuni Vardanyan, Van, 1912 ♦ Vardan Hayrapeti Ayvazyan, Nakhijevan, Koghb, 1913 ♦ Vardan Hazroyi Muradyan (Hazroyan), Motkan, Korv, 1907 ♦ Vardan Hovhannesi Hovhannisyan, Van, Archesh, 1911 ♦ Vardan Igiti Simonyan, Alekpol, Arkhivali, 1914 ♦ Vardan Israyeli Khachatryan, Van, 1910 ♦ Vardan Karapeti Barseghyan, Kars, 1913, 1911 ♦ Vardan Karapeti Ghazaryan, Kars, 1914 ♦ Vardan Karapeti Hakobyan, Ardahan, 1917 ♦ Vardan Karapeti Hovhannisyan (Hambaryan), Akhalkalak, Satkha, 1912 ♦ Vardan Karapeti Minasyan, Sarighamish, Akhkilisa, 1911 ♦ Vardan Karapeti Sedrakyan, Alekpol, Ortakilisa, 1916 ♦ Vardan Khachaturi Aleksanyan, Akhalkalak, Vachyan, 1909 ♦ Vardan Khalati Safaryan, Van, Norduz, 1909 ♦ Vardan Kirakosi Avetisyan, Nakhijevan, Znjrlu, 1911 ♦ Vardan Levoni Abrahamyan, Nakhijevan, 1916 ♦ Vardan Markosi Karapetyan, Erzrum, 1912 ♦ Vardan Misaki Sedrakyan (Misakyan), Trapizon, Munda, 1912 ♦ Vardan Mkrtchi Dovlatbekyan, Tiflis, 1920 ♦ Vardan Mnatsakani Galstyan (Mnatsakanyan), Van, 1907 ♦ Vardan Ohanjani Vachoyan, Ardahan, Shavsher, 1912 ♦ Vardan Oniki Grigoryan, Sarighamish, 1918 ♦ Vardan Petrosi Shahinyan, Lori, Gharakilisa, 1914 ♦ Vardan Petrosi Sharmanyan, Baku, Kalband, 1912 ♦ Vardan Shaheni Shahinyan, Mush, 1916 ♦ Vardan Vahani Vardanyan, Van, Archak, 1910 ♦ Vardan Yegori Abrahamyan, Mec Gharakilis, Hamamlu, 1912 ♦ Vardansuh Abrahami Movsisyan, Alekpol, Taliboghli, 1913 ♦ Vardanush (Khatun) Harutyuni Banduryan, Batum, Shavsher, 1909 ♦ Vardanush (Lusin) Abrahamyan (Baloyan), Shirak, Artik, 1908 ♦ Vardanush Abrahami Abrahamyan, Khnus, Berd, 1909 ♦ Vardanush Abrahami Harutyunyan, Van, Nor gyugh, 1910 ♦ Vardanush Abrahami Mkrtchyan, Ghamarlu, Ayazlu, 1912 ♦ Vardanush Aleki Alekyan (Aloyan), Leninakan, Paldlu, 1915 ♦ Vardanush Aleki Amiryan, Erzrum, Yaghan, 1914 ♦ Vardanush Aleksani Aleksanyan, Lori, Uzunlar, 1918 ♦ Vardanush Aleksani Aleksanyan, Yerevan, Bezavlu, 1912 ♦ Vardanush Aleksani Barikyan, Kars, 1913 ♦ Vardanush Aleksani Ghazaryan, Kars, Uzunkilisa, 1912 ♦ Vardanush Aleksani Harutyunyan, Kars, Parket, 1913 ♦ Vardanush Aleksani Ispiryan, Leninakan, Horom, 1915 ♦ Vardanush Aleksani Karapetyan, Alashkert, Hamat, 1915 ♦ Vardanush Aleksani Khachatryan, Kars, Mavrak, 1911 ♦ Vardanush Antoni Hakobyan, Shirak, Ghrghdagirman, 1913 ♦ Vardanush Arami Aramyan, Leninakan, Taknali, 1916 ♦ Vardanush Arestaki Hayrapetyan, Kars, Bashkadiklar, 1915 ♦ Vardanush Armenaki Ghukasyan, Lori, Vardablur, 1914 ♦ Vardanush Arseni Ayvazyan, Kars, Ortakadiklar, 1914 ♦ Vardanush Arshaki Ghukasyan, Gharakilisa, Ghshlagh, 1914 ♦ Vardanush Arshaki Tadevosyan, Kars, 1912 ♦ Vardanush Arshaki Torosyan, Alekpol, Ghaplu, 1914 ♦ Vardanush Aslani Margaryan (Aslanyan), Alashkert, Hamat, 1913 ♦ Vardanush Avagi Adamyan, Kars, Gorkhana, 1913 ♦ Vardanush Avagi Martirosyan, Kars, Aghjaghala, 1913 ♦ Vardanush Avetisi Avetisyan, Erzrum, Ishkhu, 1912 ♦ Vardanush Avetisi Ayvazyan, Ardahan, Shavghi, 1913 ♦ Vardanush Avetisi Gevorgyan, Nor Bayazet, 1912 ♦ Vardanush Avetisi Kopoyants (Avetisyan), Mush, Kop, 1912 ♦ Vardanush Azkari Muradyan, Bulanagh, Yonjalu, 1913 ♦ Vardanush Baghdasari Hovsepyan (Baghdasaryan), Van, 1912 ♦ Vardanush Baghoyi Arshakyan, Shirak, Arkhvali, 1915 ♦ Vardanush Bagrati Galstyan, Nakhijevan, Norashen, 1914 ♦ Vardanush Bagrati Ter-Matevosyan, Kars, Byurakdara, 1913 ♦ Vardanush Barseghi Vardanyan, Kars, Marvik, 1913 ♦ Vardanush Beglari Mikayelyan (Beglaryan), Nakhijevan, Aza, 1913 ♦ Vardanush Caruki Asatryan, Kars, Uzunkilisa, 1914 ♦ Vardanush Caruki Khachatryan (Carukyan), Kars, Uzunkilisa, 1915 ♦ Vardanush Danieli Harutyunyan (Danielyan), Darachichak, Akhta, 1915 ♦ Vardanush Daviti Davtyan, 1915 ♦ Vardanush Gabrieli Gabrielyan, Basen, 1915 ♦ Vardanush Gabrieli Mkrtchyan (Gabrielyan), Igdir, Alijan, 1912 ♦ Vardanush Galusti Hovhannisyan, Kars, 1912 ♦ Vardanush Gaspari Gasparyan, Khnus, 1911 ♦ Vardanush Geghami Harutyunyan, Leninakan, Ghapli, 1915 ♦ Vardanush Gevorgi Gevorgyan, Kars, 1918 ♦ Vardanush Gevorgi Gevorgyan, Kars, Hamzakarak, 1917 ♦ Vardanush Gevorgi Gevorgyan, Van, 1910 ♦ Vardanush Gevorgi Grigoryan, Kars, 1919 ♦ Vardanush Gevorgi Hayrapetyan (Gevorgyan), Nor Bayazet, 1913 ♦ Vardanush Gevorgi Manukyan, Kars, Chala, 1910 ♦ Vardanush Gevorgi Petrosyan (Gevorgyan), Kars, 1912 ♦ Vardanush Gevorgi Semerjyan (Gevorgyan), Vaspurakan, Aljavaz, 1909 ♦ Vardanush Ghazari Ghazaryan, Van, Shushan, 1911 ♦ Vardanush Ghazari Ghazaryan, Yerevan, Davalu, 1916 ♦ Vardanush Ghukasi Karapetyan, Kars, Ortakilisa, 1914 ♦ Vardanush Gogori Piloyan, Kars, Uzunkilisa, 1914 ♦ Vardanush Grigori Grigoryan, Kars, 1914 ♦ Vardanush Grigori Grigoryan, Kars, Mavrak, 1912 ♦ Vardanush Grigori Grigoryan, Kars, Syogutli, 1912 ♦ Vardanush Grigori Hovanyan, Van, Artamet, 1910 ♦ Vardanush Grigori Khachatryan, Kars, Bagliahmat, 1914 ♦ Vardanush Grigori Manukyan, Archesh, 1909 ♦ Vardanush Grigori Sargsyan (Grigoryan), Manazkert, Rostomgedak, 1917 ♦ Vardanush Grigori Srapyan, Kharberd, Peri, 1909 ♦ Vardanush Grigori Vardanyan, Kars, 1917 ♦ Vardanush Grishayi Ghonakhchyan, Ashtarak, 1913 ♦ Vardanush Grishayi Karapetyan (Manukyan), Leninakan, 1926 ♦ Vardanush Grishi Chomaryan, Akhalkalak, 1912 ♦ Vardanush Hajipapi Tadevosyan, Erzrum, Hekipat, 1913 ♦ Vardanush Hakobi Hajyan, Akhalkalak, Gimbirda, 1916 ♦ Vardanush Hakobi Hakobyan, Kars,

LISTING OF ORPHANS

Kyurakdara, 1914 ♦ Vardanush Hakobi Khalatyan, Kars, Bashkadiklar, 1908 ♦ Vardanush Hakobi Manukyan, Alashkert, Gharakilisa, 1913 ♦ Vardanush Hakobi Margaryan, Surmalu, Igdir, 1911 ♦ Vardanush Hakobi Mkhoyan, 1919 ♦ Vardanush Hakobi Muradyan, Van, Ktrac kar, 1908 ♦ Vardanush Hamazaspi Sargsyan, Olti, 1914 ♦ Vardanush Hambari Arakelyan, Leninakan, Chorli, 1911 ♦ Vardanush Haruti Harutyunyan, Alekpol, Mec Kapanak, 1913 ♦ Vardanush Haruti Simonyan, Kars, Tazakand, 1910 ♦ Vardanush Harutyuni Davoyan, Van, Pandz, 1910 ♦ Vardanush Harutyuni Grigoryan (Harutyunyan), Kars, Bagran, 1915 ♦ Vardanush Harutyuni Grigoryan, Kars, Germlu, 1912 ♦ Vardanush Harutyuni Harutyunyan, Erzrum, Dalibaba, 1914 ♦ Vardanush Harutyuni Harutyunyan, Gharakilisa, Hamamlu, 1915 ♦ Vardanush Harutyuni Harutyunyan, Kars, Mavrak, 1916 ♦ Vardanush Harutyuni Khachatryan, Erzrum, Grihasan, 1914 ♦ Vardanush Harutyuni Zohrapyan, Akhalkalak, Namzara, 1912 ♦ Vardanush Hayrapeti Karapetyan (Hayrapetyan), Nakhijevan, 1914 ♦ Vardanush Hayrapeti Margaryan, Nakhijevan, Ghashkha, 1911 ♦ Vardanush Hayrapeti Markosyan (Hayrapetyan), Darachichak, Caghkunk, 1911 ♦ Vardanush Hayrapeti Petrosyan, Manazkert, Berd, 1914 ♦ Vardanush Hovhannesi Aghajanyan, Zangezur, Sev kar, 1915 ♦ Vardanush Hovhannesi Arakelyan, Leninakan, Pertikan, 1915 ♦ Vardanush Hovhannesi Gasparyan, Sarighamish, 1909 ♦ Vardanush Hovhannesi Hovhannisyan, Kars, Gyuleyran, 1917 ♦ Vardanush Hovhannesi Hovhannisyan, Shirak, Ghapli, 1915 ♦ Vardanush Hovhannesi Hovhannisyan, Surmalu, Koghb, 1916 ♦ Vardanush Hovhannesi Hovhannisyan, Van, 1911 ♦ Vardanush Hovhannesi Khanashyan (Stepanyan), Van, 1912 ♦ Vardanush Hovhannesi Mkrtchyan, Yerevan, Ghazanchi, 1911 ♦ Vardanush Hovhannesi Movsisyan, Yerevan, Ashtarak, 1910 ♦ Vardanush Hovhannesi Muradyan (Hovhannisyan), Alashkert, Ghazi, 1908 ♦ Vardanush Hovhannesi Sargsyan, Ban, Karchkan, 1909 ♦ Vardanush Hovhannesi Vardanyan, Leninakan, Bayandur, 1908 ♦ Vardanush Hovnani Hovhannisyan, Kars, Nakhijevan, 1916 ♦ Vardanush Hovsepi Khachatryan, Ashtarak, Hanavank, 1915 ♦ Vardanush Hunani Karapetyan, Surmalu, Baharlu, 1912 ♦ Vardanush Hunani Margaryan (Hunanyan), Alashkert, Gharakilisa, 1914 ♦ Vardanush Hunani Sargsyan, Kars, 1919 ♦ Vardanush Karapeti Astvacatryan, Tiflis, 1910 ♦ Vardanush Karapeti Avagyan (Karapetyan), Leninakan, Pokr Kapanak, 1911 ♦ Vardanush Karapeti Ghevondyan, Nor Bayazet, 1918 ♦ Vardanush Karapeti Karapetyan, Alekpol, Chlokhan, 1916 ♦ Vardanush Karapeti Karapetyan, Nakhijevan, Badamlu, 1910 ♦ Vardanush Karapeti Khloyan (Karapetyan), Kars, Chala, 1910 ♦ Vardanush Khachaturi Khachatryan, Basen, Krdabaz, 1912 ♦ Vardanush Khachaturi Khachatryan, Hin Nakhijevan, Znaberd, 1914 ♦ Vardanush Khachaturi Khachatryan, Van, Tiramayr, 1910 ♦ Vardanush Khachiki Grigoryan, Kharberd, Sorpyan, 1911 ♦ Vardanush Khnkianosi Grigoryan, Terjan, Bakasigh, 1911 ♦ Vardanush Konstantini Movsisyan, Ashtarak, 1906 ♦ Vardanush Manuki Harutyunyan (Manukyan), Kaghzvan, Karabagh, 1912 ♦ Vardanush Manuki Manukyan, Van, Belu, 1907 ♦ Vardanush Margari Shahinyan, Igdir, Aliahmat, 1907 ♦ Vardanush Martirosi Sanoyan, Van, Pstik, 1909 ♦ Vardanush Martirosi Tonoyan, Surmalu, Abaz gyugh, 1912 ♦ Vardanush Matevosi Matevosyan (Hovhannisyan), Leninakan, Ghazanchi, 1915 ♦ Vardanush Matevosi Paronyan, Akhalkalak, Sulda, 1911 ♦ Vardanush Matevosi Saroyan, Alekpol, Ghazarapat, 1914 ♦ Vardanush Mekhaki Grigoryan, Leninakan, Mastara, 1914 ♦ Vardanush Meliki Sargsyan, Kars, Ghzlchakhchakh, 1911 ♦ Vardanush Melkoni Khachatryan, Kars, 1910 ♦ Vardanush Meloyi Meloyan (Israyelyan), Van, Archesh, 1912 ♦ Vardanush Meloyi Meloyan, Kars, Voghuzli, 1915 ♦ Vardanush Misaki Harutyunyan, Nor Bayazet, Ghblagh, 1912 ♦ Vardanush Misaki Tumanyan, Erzrum, 1911 ♦ Vardanush Mkhitari Arakelyan (Mkhitaryan), Alashkert, Khoyabek, 1910 ♦ Vardanush Mkhitari Galstyan, Van, Kerc, 1912 ♦ Vardanush Mkhitari Hovsepyan, Alekpol, Mastara, 1911 ♦ Vardanush Mkrtchi Elbakyan, Sarighamish, 1909 ♦ Vardanush Mkrtchi Mkrtchyan (Avagyan), Alashkert, Berd, 1911 ♦ Vardanush Mkrtchi Mkrtchyan, Erzrum, 1912 ♦ Vardanush Mkrtchi Mkrtchyan, Khnus, Berd, 1914 ♦ Vardanush Mkrtchi Mkrtchyan, Yerevan, Samaghar, 1916 ♦ Vardanush Mkrtchi Mukayelyan, Gharakilisa, Gharalu, 1916 ♦ Vardanush Mkrtchi Nalbandyan, Shirak, Alekpol, 1907 ♦ Vardanush Mkrtchi Sargsyan, Igdir, 1914 ♦ Vardanush Movsesi Sargsyan, Kars, Uzunkilisa, 1911 ♦ Vardanush Mukayeli Antonyan, Leninakan, Mastara, 1911 ♦ Vardanush Muradi Karapetyan, Akants, 1909 ♦ Vardanush Muradi Manukyan (Muradyan), Van, Pstik, 1913 ♦ Vardanush Muradi Mkhitaryan, Kars, 1907 ♦ Vardanush Muradi Muradyan, Bulanagh, Yonjalu, 1908 ♦ Vardanush Muradi Yervandyan, Kars, Bulanagh, 1914 ♦ Vardanush Musheghi (Varduhi) Asoyan, Kars, Bashshoragal, 1912 ♦ Vardanush Musheghi Avetisyan (Musheghyan), Daralagyaz, Khachik, 1910 ♦ Vardanush Musheghi Karapetyan, Bulanagh, Gharaghli, 1914 ♦ Vardanush Nazari Ghazaryan, Bulanagh, Kop, 1908 ♦ Vardanush Nazari Javoyan (Nazaryan), Yerevan, Yelpin, 1914 ♦ Vardanush Nazari Rustamyan (Nazaryan), Mamakhatun, Terjan, 1911 ♦ Vardanush Nikolayi Hovoyan, Kars, Ardahan, 1912 ♦ Vardanush Nikolayi Poghosyan (Kotanjyan), Alekpol, Koraghbyur, 1913 ♦ Vardanush Nikoli Ter-Mesropyan, Alekpol, Zarnchi, 1914 ♦ Vardanush Nikoyi Nikoghosyan, Shirak, Ghzlkilisa, 1914 ♦ Vardanush Paputi Adilaryan, Gyokcha, Gandzak, 1911 ♦ Vardanush Petrosi Abrahamyan, Kars, Bagliahmat, 1914 ♦ Vardanush Petrosi Asatryan, Kars, Ghzlchakhchakh, 1915 ♦ Vardanush Petrosi Grigoryan, Kars, 1914, 1910 ♦ Vardanush Petrosi Harutyunyan, Gharakilisa, Hamamlu, 1911 ♦ Vardanush Petrosi Muradyan, Kars, Teknis, 1910 ♦ Vardanush Petrosi Petrosyan, Basen, Todiveran, 1911 ♦ Vardanush Poghosi Avetisyan, Nakhijevan, Nors, 1910 ♦ Vardanush Poghosi Petrosyan (Poghosyan), Tiflis, 1916 ♦ Vardanush Rubeni Sukiasyan, Nor Bayazet, 1908 ♦ Vardanush Sahaki

Mikayelyan (Sahakyan), Van, 1913 ♦ Vardanush Sahaki Sahakyan, Baku, 1916 ♦ Vardanush Sahaki Sahakyan, Kars, Aghjaghala, 1911 ♦ Vardanush Sargisi Sargsyan, Leninakan, 1910 ♦ Vardanush Sargisi Sargsyan, Leninakan, Horom, 1913 ♦ Vardanush Sargisi Sargsyan, Nor Bayazet, 1913 ♦ Vardanush Sargisi Sargsyan, Van, Shushi, 1913 ♦ Vardanush Sargisi Yengoyan (Yengibaryan), Akhalkalak, Khorenia, 1909 ♦ Vardanush Saroyi Saroyan, K.Polis, 1914 ♦ Vardanush Serobi Khachatryan, Surmali, Tashburan, 1914, 1913 ♦ Vardanush Serobi Martirosyan, Kars, Aghjaghala, 1915 ♦ Vardanush Serobi Muradyan, Bulanagh, Kop, 1911 ♦ Vardanush Serobi Serobyan, Leninakan, Syogutli, 1914 ♦ Vardanush Sharani Mnatsakanyan, Van, Akorik, 1913 ♦ Vardanush Simoni Nahapetyan (Srapyan), Basen, Aljarak, 1915 ♦ Vardanush Simoni Tonoyan, Karberd, Mazket, 1910 ♦ Vardanush Sirekani Martirosyan, Etchmiadzin, Margara, 1911 ♦ Vardanush Sirekani Sirekanyan, Baku, 1917 ♦ Vardanush Stepani Grigoryan, Van, Corcta, 1911 ♦ Vardanush Stepani Harutyunyan, Kars, Gharaghala, 1910 ♦ Vardanush Tevosi Vardanyan (Tevosyan), Yerevan, Norashen, 1912 ♦ Vardanush Vaghinaki Nazaretyan, Alekpol, Imrkhan, 1914 ♦ Vardanush Vardani Melkonyan, Bulanagh, Majtlu, 1912 ♦ Vardanush Vardani Vardanyan (Levonyan), Salmast, 1913 ♦ Vardanush Vardani Vardanyan, Baku, 1918 ♦ Vardanush Vardani Vardanyan, Van, Cvstan, 1911 ♦ Vardanush Vardani Vardanyan, Yerevan, Etchmiadzin, 1919 ♦ Vardanush Vasili Grigoryan, Kars, Uzunkilisa, 1911, 1909 ♦ Vardanush Voskani Khachatryan, Tiflis, 1912 ♦ Vardanush Voskani Voskanyan, Kars, Nakhijevan, 1914 ♦ Vardanush Yeghishei Sahakyan, Khnus, Berd, 1914 ♦ Vardanush Yeghoyi Ginosyan, Leninakan, Syogutli, 1911 ♦ Vardanush Zadoyi Abgaryan, Basen, Armtlu, 1914 ♦ Vardanush Zakari Muradyan, Ardvin, Batum, 1914 ♦ Vardanush Zakari Rafayelyan, Batum, Ardanugh, 1907 ♦ Vardenik Harutyuni Tabashyan, Van, Aygestan, 1912 ♦ Vardenik Sedraki Grigoryan, Igdir, 1911 ♦ Vardevan Hovhannesi Mkrtchyan (Hovhannisyan), Hasanghali, Tarkhoja, 1910 ♦ Vardevan Tadevosi Artenyan (Tadevosyan), Gharakilisa, Tapanlu, 1912 ♦ Vardevar Hakobi Hakobyan, Van, Aljavaz, 1911 ♦ Vardges Armenaki Ayvazyan, Kars, Ardahan, 1913, 1910 ♦ Vardges Arshaki Arshakyan, Igdir, Alighamar, 1914 ♦ Vardges Asaturi Asatryan, Alekpol, Talin, 1915 ♦ Vardges Avetisi Gevorgyan, Van, Khordzor, 1914 ♦ Vardges Azizi Ghazaryan (Azizyan), Khnus, Duman, 1914 ♦ Vardges Baghdasari Baghdasaryan, Bulanagh, 1917 ♦ Vardges Baghdasari Yeranosyan, Khnus, Saylu, 1912 ♦ Vardges Buniati Dekoyan (Tigranyan), Hin Bayazet, 1914 ♦ Vardges Galusti Galstyan, Kars, Nakhijevan, 1914 ♦ Vardges Garegini Stepanyan, Van, Poghants, 1911 ♦ Vardges Gaspari Gasparyan, Hayots dzor, Hermer, 1912 ♦ Vardges Gevorgi Martirosyan, Kars, 1912 ♦ Vardges Gevorgi Martirosyan, Kars, 1913, 1911 ♦ Vardges Grigori Grigoryan, Van, Archesh, 1913 ♦ Vardges Hovnani Ter Samvelyan, Bulanagh, Shirvanshekh, 1912 ♦ Vardges Hovsepi Hovsepyan, Van, Hayots dzor, 1912, 1910 ♦ Vardges Karapeti Hakobyan (Karapetyan), Kars, Gedaksatlmish, 1912 ♦ Vardges Levoni Khachatryan (Levonyan), Manazkert, Derek, 1912 ♦ Vardges Manuki Papikyan, Van, 1913 ♦ Vardges Meliki Aleksanyan, Van, Hasan-Tamra, 1911 ♦ Vardges Melkoni Meklonyan, Mush, Ghalaghaj, 1913 ♦ Vardges Mkrtchi Mkrtchyan, Basen, Gomadzor, 1915 ♦ Vardges Mkrtchi Ter Hakobyan, Ardahan, Shavsher, 1909 ♦ Vardges Musheghi Grigoryan, Khnus, 1912 ♦ Vardges Musheghi Musheghyan, Khnus, 1917 ♦ Vardges Petrosi Barseghyan, Van, Mokhraberd, 1909 ♦ Vardges Petrosi Hakobyan, Hin Bayazet, 1913 ♦ Vardges Petrosi Yedigaryan (Petrosyan), Van, Aljavaz, 1912 ♦ Vardges Pilosi Poghosyan, Leninakan, Toros, 1914 ♦ Vardges Rafayeli Arshakyan, Kars, Uzunkilisa, 1912 ♦ Vardges Sargisi Sargsyan (Hovhannisyan), Akhalkalak, Sulda, 1912 ♦ Vardges Sedraki Aghajanyan (Sedrakyan), Bayburt, Avarak, 1912 ♦ Vardges Sedraki Sedrakyan, Van, Avrak, 1913 ♦ Vardges Vardani Aghababyan, Alekpol, Tanagirmaz, 1914 ♦ Vardges Yeghishi Yeghishyan, Van, S. Sahak, 1911 ♦ Vardishat Agheki Aghekyan, Manazkert, 1912 ♦ Varditer Bagrati Mnatsakanyan, Yerevan, Chanakhchi, 1912 ♦ Varditer Gaspari Gasparyan, Van, Norshen, 1912 ♦ Varditer Grigori Grigoryan, Van, Karchkan, 1915 ♦ Varditer Khlghati Hakobyan (Khlghatyan), Manazkert, Noratni, 1911 ♦ Varditer Mkrtchi Mkoyan (Mkrtchyan), Leninakan, Sirvanjugh, 1914 ♦ Varditer Mnatsakani Astvacatryan, Kars, Cbni, 1909 ♦ Varditer Movsesi Movsisyan, Van, Tosp, Aljavaz, 1913 ♦ Varditer Rubeni Rubenyan, Van, 1918 ♦ Varditer Sahaki Sahakyan, Van, Aljavaz, 1914 ♦ Varditer Tatosi Aghajanyan, Kars, Bayburt, 1911 ♦ Varditer Ter-Martirosi Petrosyan, Van, Harik, 1909 ♦ Varditer Vardani Vardanyan, Van, 1913 ♦ Varditer Yeghiki Martirosyan (Petrosyan), Olti, 1913 ♦ Varditer Zadoyi Zadoyan, Van, 1910 ♦ Varduhi Abrahami Abrahamyan, Mush, Avzut, 1909 ♦ Varduhi Ayvazi Ayvazyan, Van, 1913 ♦ Varduhi Gevorgi Khudaverdyan, Van, 1905 ♦ Varduhi Gevorgi Shirinyan, Kars, Gharaghala, 1910 ♦ Varduhi Grigori Hovhannisyan, Sarighamish, Chirink, 1916 ♦ Varduhi Hambardzumi Hambardzumyan, Yerevan, Dizay, 1913 ♦ Varduhi Kostani Kostanyan, Lori, Uzunlar, 1910 ♦ Varduhi Madati Harutyunyan, Karabagh, Gandza, 1913, 1911 ♦ Varduhi Manuki Manukyan, Manazkert, Berd, 1910 ♦ Varduhi Minasi Navasardyan, Nakhijevan, Gomer, 1912 ♦ Varduhi Movsesi Petrosyan, Baku, Shamakhi, 1911 ♦ Varduhi Ohani Hovhannisyan, Van, 1908 ♦ Varduhi Sakoyi Ghazaryan, Lori, Urut, 1914 ♦ Varduhi Soghomoni Baghdasaryan, Baku, Keghshurt, 1910 ♦ Varduhi Sureni Hambardzumyan, Erzrum, Bayazet, 1913 ♦ Varduhi Varosi Martirosyan, Alekpol, Norashen, 1910 ♦ Vardunik Zakari Grigoryan Zakaryan, Nakhijevan, 1912 ♦ Vardush Abgari Abgaryan, Tpkhis, 1915 ♦ Vardush Abrahami Abrahamyan, Alekpol, Ughtapen, 1914 ♦ Vardush Aleksani Aleksanyan, Mec Gharakilis, 1908 ♦ Vardush Andoni Andonyan, Kars, Aksighaz, 1913 ♦ Vardush Arakeli Arakelyan, Alashkert, Khasdzor, 1914 ♦ Vardush Arakeli Asvaturyan, Alekpol, Shirvanjugh, 1908 ♦ Vardush Arseni Martirosyan, Sharur,

1915 ♦ Vardush Arshaki Arshakyan, Alekpol, Arkhvali, 1914 ♦ Vardush Arshaki Geghamyan, Yerevan, 1917 ♦ Vardush Avetisi Sedrakyan (Avetisyan), Bulanagh, Teghut, 1916 ♦ Vardush Bekoyi Simonyan, Shirak, Toparlu, 1916 ♦ Vardush Beniamini Hayrapetyan, Leninakan, Dyuzkand, 1920 ♦ Vardush Danieli Khachatryan, Hamamlu, Ortnak, 1914 ♦ Vardush Gaspari Davtyan (Gasparyan), Kars, Paldrvan, 1917 ♦ Vardush Gevorgi Astvacatryan, Mush, 1908 ♦ Vardush Gevorgi Gevorgyan, Basen, Yaghan, 1913 ♦ Vardush Gevorgi Gevorgyan, Leninakan, Bandivan, 1912 ♦ Vardush Gevorgi Khachatryan, Van, Koghpants, 1907 ♦ Vardush Ghazari Aroyan (Ghazaryan), Bitlis, Teghut, 1911 ♦ Vardush Grigori Galstyan, Kars, 1916 ♦ Vardush Grigori Grigoryan, Yerevan, Khatunarkh, 1912 ♦ Vardush Hakobi Mkhoyan (Hakobyan), Nakhijevan, Khulibek dyuza, 1912 ♦ Vardush Hakobi Sahakyan, Lori, Marts, 1913 ♦ Vardush Hamayaki Hamayakyan, Alekpol, Gheghach, 1915 ♦ Vardush Haroyi Vardanyan (Haroyan), Leninakan, Ghzlchakhchakh, 1914 ♦ Vardush Harutyuni Melikyan, Kars, 1914 ♦ Vardush Harutyuni Petrosyan, Yerevan, Yuva, 1912 ♦ Vardush Hmayaki Hmayakyan, Bitlis, 1912 ♦ Vardush Hmayaki Madoyan (Kirakosyan), Koghb, 1914 ♦ Vardush Hovaki Snkhchyan, Akhalkalak, Jigrashen, 1916 ♦ Vardush Hovhannesi Hovhannisyan (Mkhitaryan), Baku, 1915 ♦ Vardush Hovhannesi Hovhannisyan (Muradyan), Hin Nakhijevan, Khanakhlar, 1915 ♦ Vardush Hovhannesi Hovhannisyan, Kars, 1918 ♦ Vardush Hovsepi Hakobyan, Yerevan, 1914 ♦ Vardush Hovsepi Musheghyan, Georgia, Akhalkalak, 1909 ♦ Vardush Hovsepi Papikyan (Hovsepyan), Lori, Kurtan, 1915 ♦ Vardush Hovsepi Poghosyan, Manazkert, 1910 ♦ Vardush Karapeti Karapetyan, Kars, 1918 ♦ Vardush Karapeti Karapetyan, Leninakan, 1919 ♦ Vardush Khachaturi Hovhannisyan, Kars, Chala, 1911 ♦ Vardush Khachaturi Khachatryan, Erzrum, Basen, 1914 ♦ Vardush Khachaturi Khachatryan, Hin Nakhijevan, Norsi, 1912 ♦ Vardush Khachaturi Khachatryan, Van, Kerts, 1914 ♦ Vardush Khachaturi Stepanyan, Van, Pstik, 1915 ♦ Vardush Khachaturi Tonoyan, Alekpol, Kapanak, 1918 ♦ Vardush Khachiki Aghabekyan, Akhalkalak, Lumaturs, 1916 ♦ Vardush Khachoyi Khachatryan, Berd, 1914 ♦ Vardush Khachoyi Khachoyan, Aparan, 1918 ♦ Vardush Khachoyi Khlghatyan, Manazkert, Rostomgedak, 1914 ♦ Vardush Kostani Ter-Hakobyan, Hin Nakhijevan, Chanakhchi, 1911 ♦ Vardush Levoni Ghazaryan, Kars, 1920 ♦ Vardush Lipariti Sargsyan, Alekpol, 1912 ♦ Vardush Manuki Khachatryan, Van, Moks, 1913 ♦ Vardush Manuki Manukyan, Surmalu, Igdir, 1915 ♦ Vardush Matevosi Bagoyan (Matevosyan), Leninakan, Ghshlagh, 1914 ♦ Vardush Matevosi Voskanyan, Yerevan, Shovik, 1918 ♦ Vardush Melkoni Melkonyan, Alekpol, Syogutli, 1915 ♦ Vardush Minasi Vardanyan, Gharakilisa, 1914 ♦ Vardush Misaki Misakyan, Alashkert, Gharakilisa, 1911 ♦ Vardush Misaki Misakyan, Van, Shushan, 1916 ♦ Vardush Misaki Poghosyan (Gasparyan), Kars, Chala, 1915 ♦ Vardush Mkrtchi Hovhannisyan, Nakhijevan, Nor Bayazet, 1914 ♦ Vardush Mkrtchi Sargsyan (Mkrtchyan), Kars, Dolbandli, 1914 ♦ Vardush Mukayeli Galstyan (Mukayelyan), Leninakan, Mec Artik, 1915 ♦ Vardush Muradi Muradyan, Van, 1910 ♦ Vardush Musheghi Mkrtchyan, Bulanagh, Shirvanshekh, 1912 ♦ Vardush Nikoli Abrahamyan, Leninakan, Ghanlija, 1911 ♦ Vardush Petrosi Petrosyan, Sarighamish, 1917 ♦ Vardush Rafayeli Poghosyan (Avagyan) Kars, Pirvali, 1920 ♦ Vardush Sahaki Karapetyan, Alekpol, 1916 ♦ Vardush Sardari Ghazaryan (Sargsyan), Shirak, Syogutli, 1915 ♦ Vardush Sedraki Khachatryan, Alekpol, Ghoshavank, 1913 ♦ Vardush Serobi Petrosyan (Serobyan), Turkey, 1914 ♦ Vardush Shirini Shirinyan, 1918 ♦ Vardush Sisaki Gevorgyan (Melkonyan), Kars, Ghzlchakhchakh, 1914 ♦ Vardush Soghomoni Gasparyan, Akulis, 1913 ♦ Vardush Soghomoni Khachatryan, Kars, 1908 ♦ Vardush Soghomoni Soghomonyan, Alekpol, Chlokhan, 1915 ♦ Vardush Srapi Baghdasaryan, Zangezur, Shnatagh, 1914 ♦ Vardush Stepani Galstyan, Akhalkalak, Khojabad, 1915 ♦ Vardush Sukiasi Sukiasyan (Hakobyan), Alashkert, Khachlu, 1908 ♦ Vardush Tatosi Zhamharyan, Pokr Gharakilis, 1918 ♦ Vardush Torgomi Galstyan, Van, 1908 ♦ Vardush Voskani Grigoryan (Voskanyan), Shirak, Saribagh, 1917 ♦ Vardush Yeghoyi Yeghoyan, Van, Boghazkasan, 1910 ♦ Vardush Yepremi Yepremyan, 1917 ♦ Vardush Zakari Maghlochyan, Olti, 1916 ♦ Varich Artemi Harutyunyan, Kars, Bayrakhtar, 1911 ♦ Varich Ashoti Bagratyan, Alekpol, Bashshoragal, 1913 ♦ Varik (Zarik) Vahani Vahanyan, Alashkert, 1914 ♦ Varinka Avetisi Avetisyan (Papikyan), Jalaloghli, Berd, 1914 ♦ Varinka Ghevondi Asatryan, Yerevan, Chanakhchi, 1914 ♦ Varinka Hakobi Bagratyan (Hakobyan), Lori, Haghpat, 1912 ♦ Varinka Harutyuni Sargsyan, Mec Gharakilisa, Haydarbek, 1919 ♦ Varinka Hmayaki Aghikyan, Shirak, Ghzlghoch, 1916 ♦ Varinka Matevosi Tarkhanyan, Lori, Vardablur, 1910 ♦ Varinka Petrosi Hovhannisyan (Petrosyan), Nakhijevan, Norashen, 1914 ♦ Varinka Sahaki Khachatryan, Hin Nakhijevan, 1916 ♦ Varinka Vardani Vardanyan, Nakhijevan, 1916 ♦ Varinka Yeghishei Davtyan, Aparan, Samrlu, 1913 ♦ Varmandukht Arshaki Aghajanyan, Nakhijevan, Aylapat, 1915 ♦ Varo Grigori Badalyan, Akhalkalak, Gandza, 1913 ♦ Varo Hakobi Hakobyan, Akhalkalak, Chanchgha, 1916 ♦ Varo Hambardzumi Uzunyan, Alashkert, Khoshgyaldi, 1911 ♦ Varo Karapeti Karapetyan, Nakhijevan, Iza, 1914 ♦ Varo Tepanosi Sargsyan, Leninakan, Muslughli, 1912 ♦ Varo Tonoyi Tonoyan (Harutyunyan), Manazkert, 1914 ♦ Varos Avdali Simonyan, Bulanagh, Koghtyan, 1912 ♦ Varos Avetisi Avetisyan (Arakelyan), Kars, Dolbandlu, 1911 ♦ Varos Haykoyi Harutyunyan, Leninakan, Ghapli, 1914 ♦ Varos Meliki Melikyan, Kars, Mec Parket, 1915 ♦ Varos Sedraki Aleksanyan, Kars, Ughuzlu, 1917 ♦ Varsenik (Harutyunyan), Kars, 1920 ♦ Varsenik (Vasilisa) Nersesi Nersisyan, Shatakh, 1916 ♦ Varsenik Abrahami Abrahamyan, Van, 1909 ♦ Varsenik Abrahami Melkonyan, Kars, 1914 ♦ Varsenik Aleksani Avoyan, Leninakan, Pokr Arkhvali, 1910 ♦ Varsenik Aleksani Petrosyan, Shirak, Ghzlghoch, 1914 ♦ Varsenik Aleksani Sargsyan, Zangezur, Akhlatyan, 1918 ♦

Varsenik Andreasi Sargsyan, Yerevan, Bashaparan, 1914 ♦ Varsenik Antoni Zohrabyan, Kars, Dorbandlu, 1911 ♦ Varsenik Arestaki Gevorgyan, Kars, Ortakadiklar, 1912 ♦ Varsenik Aristakesi Aristakesyan, Van, 1914 ♦ Varsenik Armenaki Karapetyan (Armenakyan), Kars, Bashshoragal, 1914 ♦ Varsenik Armenaki Karapetyan, Alekpol, Bozyokhash, 1914 ♦ Varsenik Arseni Arsenyan, Aparan, Blkher, 1915 ♦ Varsenik Arseni Arsenyan, Baku, 1916 ♦ Varsenik Arshaki Harutyunyan, Alekpol, Sirvanjugh, 1914 ♦ Varsenik Arshaki Mihranyan, Erzrum, Karin, 1913 ♦ Varsenik Arshaki Mkrtchyan (Arshakyan), Aparan, Tamjlu, 1914 ♦ Varsenik Arzumani Arzumanyan, Karabagh, Svazgh, 1914 ♦ Varsenik Asaturi Smbatyan, Kars, 1914 ♦ Varsenik Ashoti Hakobyan, 1919 ♦ Varsenik Aslani Aslanyan, Van, Seghkes, 1915 ♦ Varsenik Avetisi Gevorgyan, Van, Kendanants, 1914 ♦ Varsenik Avetisi Karapetyan, Hin Nakhijevan, Yarmjlu, 1911 ♦ Varsenik Avoyi Markosyan (Ayvazyan), Kars, Cbni, 1911 ♦ Varsenik Ayvazi Petrosyan (Ayvazyan), Zangezur, Znaberd, 1916 ♦ Varsenik Baghdasari Baghdasaryan, Nor Bayazet, 1914 ♦ Varsenik Barseghi Tadevosyan, Alekpol, Sirvanjugh, 1913 ♦ Varsenik Danieli Grigoryan, Leninakan, Mastara, 1912 ♦ Varsenik Deniki Poghosyan, Alekpol, Chandura, 1916 ♦ Varsenik Gabrieli Karapetyan, Kars, Gorkhana, 1917 ♦ Varsenik Gabrieli Mkrtchyan, Van, 1911 ♦ Varsenik Gabrieli Stepanyan, Leninakan, Chlokhan, 1913 ♦ Varsenik Galusti Galstyan, Kars, Cbni, 1911 ♦ Varsenik Galusti Hovhannisyan, Kars, 1911 ♦ Varsenik Gaspari Gevorgyan, Kars, Hamzakarak, 1911 ♦ Varsenik Gaspari Ghazaryan, Sasun, Arpi, 1914 ♦ Varsenik Gaspari Petrosyan, Pambak, Haghpat, 1909 ♦ Varsenik Gevorgi Gevorgyan, Kars, Bagliahmat, 1917 ♦ Varsenik Gevorgi Mkrtchyan, Kars, Beyliahmat, 1912 ♦ Varsenik Ghevondi Hayrapetyan, Shamakhi, 1911 ♦ Varsenik Ghukasi Baghdasaryan, Kars, Syogutli, 1909 ♦ Varsenik Ghukasi Chakhalyan (Ghukasyan), Kars, Zrchi, 1912 ♦ Varsenik Grigori Arakelyan, Karabagh, Shekhsher, 1908 ♦ Varsenik Grigori Gevorgyan, Akhalkalak, Jigrashen, 1914, 1913 ♦ Varsenik Grigori Grigoryan, 1919 ♦ Varsenik Grigori Grigoryan, Van, 1918 ♦ Varsenik Grigori Hovhannisyan, Kars, 1918 ♦ Varsenik Grigori Hovsepyan, Dilijan, 1912 ♦ Varsenik Grigoryan (Simonyan) Grigori, Akhalkalak, Abul, 1908 ♦ Varsenik Hakobi Baghdasaryan (Hakobyan), Kars, Dolbandlu, 1911 ♦ Varsenik Hakobi Hakobyan, Kars, Bayburt, 1913 ♦ Varsenik Hakobi Hovhannisyan, Kars, Araz, 1914 ♦ Varsenik Hakobi Melkumyan, Alekpol, Chandura, 1916 ♦ Varsenik Hakobi Serobyan (Hakobyan), Yerevan, Darachichak, 1915 ♦ Varsenik Hakobi Torosyan, Kars, Berna, 1910 ♦ Varsenik Hambari Sargsyan (Hambardzumyan), Kars, Mec Parket, 1914 ♦ Varsenik Hamboyi Hambardzumyan, Kars, Kyadiklar, 1908 ♦ Varsenik Haruti Khachatryan, Basen, 1913 ♦ Varsenik Harutyuni Gasparyan, Ardvin, 1911, 1909 ♦ Varsenik Harutyuni Ghazaryan, Leninakan, Ghonaghran, 1911 ♦ Varsenik Harutyuni Israyelyan, Kars, Mazra, 1909 ♦ Varsenik Harutyuni Khachatryan, Akhalkalak, Akan, 1912 ♦ Varsenik Harutyuni Mkheyan (Harutyunyan), Mush, Bostakand, 1906 ♦ Varsenik Harutyuni Vardanyan, Van, 1911 ♦ Varsenik Hovakimi Martirosyan, Leninakan, Choplu, 1910 ♦ Varsenik Hovhannesi Haroyan, Akhalkalak, Karcakh, 1913 ♦ Varsenik Hovhannesi Hovhannisyan, Bitlis, 1914 ♦ Varsenik Hovhannesi Hovhannisyan, Kars, Bagliahmat, 1916 ♦ Varsenik Hovhannesi Hovhannisyan, Shirak, Mastara, 1917 ♦ Varsenik Hovhannesi Hovhannisyan, Van, Perka, 1915 ♦ Varsenik Hovhannesi Nazaryan, Leninakan, Bozdoghan, 1913 ♦ Varsenik Hovhannesi Poghosyan, Basen, Alijagrak, 1916 ♦ Varsenik Hovsepi Hovsepyan, Van, Cvstan, 1911, 1909 ♦ Varsenik Iskandari Hovnanyan, Van, 1914 ♦ Varsenik Karapeti Gevorgyan, Tiflis, 1914 ♦ Varsenik Karapeti Grigoryan, Kars, Ghoshavank, 1914 ♦ Varsenik Karapeti Hovhannisyan, 1914 ♦ Varsenik Karapeti Karapetyan (Khachatryan), Nakhijevan, 1909 ♦ Varsenik Karapeti Karapetyan, Akhalkalak, 1917 ♦ Varsenik Karapeti Karapetyan, Alekpol, Illi, 1913 ♦ Varsenik Karapeti Karapetyan, Nakhijevan, 1917 ♦ Varsenik Kerobi Gabrielyan, Ardahan, Tandzut, 1914 ♦ Varsenik Khachaturi Arakelyan (Khachatryan), Yerevan, Darachichak, 1917 ♦ Varsenik Khachaturi Gevorgyan, Kars, Gharamahmat, 1912, 1909 ♦ Varsenik Khachaturi Grigoryan, Kars, Paldrvan, 1909 ♦ Varsenik Khachaturi Manukyan, Darachichak, Andamal, 1912 ♦ Varsenik Khachaturi Manukyan, Surmalu, Igdir, 1910 ♦ Varsenik Khachaturi Mnatsakanyan, Darachichak, Yaji, 1913 ♦ Varsenik Khachaturi Petrosyan (Khachatryan), Kars, Chala, 1912 ♦ Varsenik Khachaturi Stepanyan, Karabagh, Nukhi, 1915 ♦ Varsenik Komisari Ghevondyan, Kaghzvan, 1916 ♦ Varsenik Levoni Arakelyan, Leninakan, Talin, 1911 ♦ Varsenik Manuki Ghazaryan, Kars, Bashkadiklar, 1913 ♦ Varsenik Manuki Mkrtchyan, Kars, Paldrvan, 1914 ♦ Varsenik Manuki Petrosyan, Mec Gharakilisa, Hajighara, 1917 ♦ Varsenik Margari Grigoryan, Van, 1908 ♦ Varsenik Margari Margaryan, Alekpol, Bozdoghan, 1915 ♦ Varsenik Martirosi (Yeghiazaryan) Harutyunyan, Van, Kharakonis, 1915 ♦ Varsenik Martirosi Barikyan, Van, Avand, 1909 ♦ Varsenik Martirosi Davoyan, Basen, Gharapunghar, 1912 ♦ Varsenik Martirosi Khachatryan, Shirak, Mec Keti, 1911 ♦ Varsenik Martirosi Kurghinyan, Kars, Jalal, 1913, 1912 ♦ Varsenik Martirosi Martirosyan, Akhalkalak, Tandzik, 1916 ♦ Varsenik Martirosi Martirosyan, Alekpol, Syogutli, 1908 ♦ Varsenik Meliki Ghazaryan, Alekpol, Syogutlu, 1910 ♦ Varsenik Melkoni Antonyan, Alekpol, Khlli Gharakilis, 1913 ♦ Varsenik Melkoni Grigoryan, Talin, 1912 ♦ Varsenik Mezhlumi Alaverdyan, Shamakhi, Geyvand, 1903 ♦ Varsenik Minasi Margaryan, Kars, 1915 ♦ Varsenik Misaki Aslanyan, Ardahan, 1908 ♦ Varsenik Mkhitari Madoyan, Sarighamish, 1914 ♦ Varsenik Mkhitari Mikayelyan, Alekpol, Koraghbyur, 1911 ♦ Varsenik Mkhitari Mkhitaryan, Van, 1917 ♦ Varsenik Mkrtchi Hovhannisyan, Sharur, Norashen, 1914 ♦ Varsenik Mkrtchi Karapetyan, Leninakan, Tavshanghshlagh, 1909 ♦ Varsenik Mkrtchi Khachatryan, Akhalkalak, 1912, 1911 ♦ Varsenik Mkrtchi Mkrtchyan, Van, Janik, 1913, 1911 ♦ Varsenik Mkrtchi Mukelyan, Jalal oghli, 1919 ♦ Varsenik Mkrtich Mikayelyan, Pambak, Gharal, 1918 ♦ Varsenik Movsesi Grigoryan, Van, Soskan, 1915 ♦ Varsenik Movsesi Nersisyan, Kars, Aksi ghazi, 1916 ♦ Varsenik Mukayeli Mukayelyan, Hin Nakhijevan, Gyumri, 1912 ♦ Varsenik Muradi Aslanyan (Muradyan), Kars, 1915 ♦ Varsenik Musheghi Hakobyan, Kars, Ghani, 1913 ♦ Varsenik Musheghi Khachatryan, Alekpol, Ghanlija, 1911 ♦ Varsenik Nersesi Mayilyan, Shamakhi, Ghalaga, 1912 ♦ Varsenik Nshani Margaryan, Kaghzvan, 1911 ♦ Varsenik Paveli Margaryan, Igdir, 1909 ♦ Varsenik Petrosi Hayrapetyan, Kars, Bashkadiklar, 1913 ♦ Varsenik Petrosi Levonyan (Petrosyan), Van, Ghzldash, 1910 ♦ Varsenik Petrosi Petrosyan, 1918 ♦ Varsenik Poghosi Grigoryan (Poghosyan), Pambak, Chotur, 1918 ♦ Varsenik Poghosi Martirosyan, Kars, Hamzakarak, 1912 ♦ Varsenik Poghosi Muradyan, Kars, 1914 ♦ Varsenik Poghosi Poghosyan, Gharakilisa, Hamamlu, 1914 ♦ Varsenik Safari Grigoryan, Kars, Paldrvan, 1910 ♦ Varsenik Sahaki Arakelyan, Erzrum, Kyoprakoy, 1908 ♦ Varsenik Sahaki Sahakyan, Alashkert, Mankasar, 1918 ♦ Varsenik Sahaki Sahakyan, Kars, Zrchi, 1914 ♦ Varsenik Samsoni Harutyunyan, Ghamarlu, 1913 ♦ Varsenik Sargisi Argoyan (Sargsyan), Kars, Paldrvan, 1912, 1911 ♦ Varsenik Sargisi Hovhannisyan, Leninakan, Psti Keti, 1912 ♦ Varsenik Sargisi Mikayelyan, Van, Hern, 1912 ♦ Varsenik Sargisi Poghosyan, Kars, Beyliahmat, 1908 ♦ Varsenik Sargisi Topchyan, Akhalkalak, Karcakh, 1910 ♦ Varsenik Sargisi Vardanyan, Aparan, Ghaznfor, 1910 ♦ Varsenik Sargsyan, Van, 1918 ♦ Varsenik Saroyi Harutyunyan, Leninakan, Gheghaj, 1911 ♦ Varsenik Saroyi Nersisyan, Shirak, Bashgyugh, 1913 ♦ Varsenik Saroyi Sahakyan, Shirak, Munjughlu, 1912 ♦ Varsenik Sedraki Ayvazyan (Avetikyan), Erzrum, Harsnakar, 1912 ♦ Varsenik Sedraki Petrosyan, Sarighamish, 1917 ♦ Varsenik Simoni Asratyan (Simonyan), Basen, Tedeveran, 1909 ♦ Varsenik Simoni Gevorgyan, Karabagh, Shushi, 1914 ♦ Varsenik Simoni Hovhannisyan, Alekpol, Chorli, 1912 ♦ Varsenik Simoni Minasyan, Ardvin, Shavsher, 1916 ♦ Varsenik Stepani Khachatryan, Kars, 1916 ♦ Varsenik Tadevosi Barseghyan, Darachichak, Caghkunk, 1911 ♦ Varsenik Tadevosi Kirakosyan, Alekpol, 1909 ♦ Varsenik Tadevosi Manukyan (Tadevosyan), Leninakan, Toros, 1915 ♦ Varsenik Tadevosi Tadevosyan, Darachichak, Rndamal, 1914 ♦ Varsenik Tatosi Harutyunyan (Tadevosyan), Bashgyugh, 1910, 1909 ♦ Varsenik Tevosi Gevorgyan, Vayots dzor, Gharakhach, 1912 ♦ Varsenik Tigrani Avagyan, Baku, Shamakhi, 1913 ♦ Varsenik Vanoyi Vanoyan, Nor Bayazet, Ghzli, 1911 ♦ Varsenik Vardani Mkoyan (Vardanyan), Darachichak, Kaghsi, 1913 ♦ Varsenik Vardani Tonyan, Shirak, Syogutli, 1912 ♦ Varsenik Vardani Vardanyan, Van, 1914 ♦ Varsenik Vardani Vardanyan, Van, 1915 ♦ Varsenik Yeghiazari Aleksandryan, Kars, Beyliahmet, 1908 ♦ Varsenik Yeghiazari Yeghiazaryan, Nakhijevan, Bist, 1914 ♦ Varsenik Yegori Arakelyan, Shirak, Bozdoghan, 1919 ♦ Varsenik Yegori Sargsyan, Kars, 1909 ♦ Varsenik Yepremi Sargsyan, Nakhijevan, Jnjrli, 1912 ♦ Varsenik Yepremi Yepremyan, Alekpol, Artik, 1916 ♦ Varsenik Yesayi Yesayan, Van, 1913 ♦ Varsham Arshaki Grigoryan, Leninakan, Ghoshavank, 1913 ♦ Varsham Artemi Hovsepyan, Gandzak, Shamakhi, 1913 ♦ Varsham Dvini Aghababyan, Akhalkalak, Lomaturs, 1914 ♦ Varsham Hovhannesi Harutyunyan, Alekpol, Ghoshavank, 1918 ♦ Varsham Mkrtchi Martirosyan (Mkrtchyan), Shirak, Bozdoghan, 1914 ♦ Varsham Stepani Poghosyan, Akhalkalak, Chandura, 1914 ♦ Varsham Yegori Tadevosyan (Khachatryan), Alekpol, Chrakhlu, 1916 ♦ Varsik (Zaruhi) Misaki Sahakyan, Manazkert, Derek, 1913 ♦ Varsik Abrahami Abrahamyan, Alashkert, 1918 ♦ Varsik Abrahami Abrahamyan, Van, 1910 ♦ Varsik Artaki Khachatryan, Yerevan, Darachichak, 1913 ♦ Varsik Barseghi Vardanyan, Kars, Sarighamish, 1911 ♦ Varsik Galusti Galstyan, Alekpol, Kapanak, 1918 ♦ Varsik Gevorgi Melkonyan, Aparan, Gharakilisa, 1910 ♦ Varsik Hamboyi Baboyan, Alekpol, Ghzlchakhchakh, 1915 ♦ Varsik Hovhannesi Tadevosyan, Ghamarlu, Artashat, 1914 ♦ Varsik Khachoyi Chopuryan, Pambak, Chotur, 1918 ♦ Varsik Mesropi Galstyan, Akhalkalak, Gandza, 1917 ♦ Varsik Minasi Minasyan, Van, 1916 ♦ Varsik Mkrtchi Mkrtchyan, Kaghzvan, 1914, 1912 ♦ Varsik Sahaki Baghdasaryan, Kars, 1915 ♦ Varsik Sahaki Sahakyan, Alashkert, Akan, 1918 ♦ Varsik Smbati Smbatyan, 1919 ♦ Varuzh Tigrani Vardanyan (Tigranyan), Kars, Chala, 1914 ♦ Varuzhan Gevorgi Torosyan, Kars, Chala, 1916 ♦ Varuzhan Nikoli Simonyan, Leninakan, Ghoshavank, 1917 ♦ Varvara Avagi Manukyan, Kars, Ghzlchakhchakh, 1912 ♦ Varvara Ghazari Ghazaryan, Van, 1914 ♦ Varvara Nazari Aleksanyan, Leninakan, Paldlu, 1915 ♦ Varvara Stepani Ispiryan (Stepanyan), Yerznka, 1910 ♦ Varya Adami Hakobyan, Akhalkalak, Mec Kachr, 1912 ♦ Varya Samveli Baghdasaryan, Shamakhi, 1913 ♦ Vasak Mkrtchi Mkrtchyan, Yerevan, Norashen, 1913 ♦ Vasil (Tigrani) Sargsyan (Avetisyan), Mush, Yershter, 1911 ♦ Vasil (Vazgen) Yenoki Avetisyan (Yenokyan), Hin Bayazet, 1914 ♦ Vasil Abrahami Vushyan (Abazyan), Ghazakh, Dostlu, 1916 ♦ Vasil Avagi Avagyan, Lori, Uzunlar, 1915 ♦ Vasil Hovsepyan, 1920 ♦ Vasil Mikayeli Mikayelyan, Tiflis, 1914 ♦ Vasil Serobi Tadevosyan, Lori, Ghotur, 1914 ♦ Vasil Zakari Gevorgyan (Shaveyan), Alashkert, Yonjalu, 1909 ♦ Vasiluhi Armenaki Hakobyan (Armenakyan), Van, Alyur, 1908 ♦ Vaso Stepani Aslanyan, Nakhijevan, Nors, 1913 ♦ Vayrat Hambardzumi Grigoryan, Basen, Alvar, 1912 ♦ Vazar (Varazdat) Poghosi Torosyan, Akhalkalak, Samsar, 1913 ♦ Vazganush (Azganush) Hakobi Yeghiazaryan, Kars, Teknis, 1914 ♦ Vazganush Torosi Torosyan, Leninakan, Svanverdi, 1912 ♦ Vazgen Abeli Virabyan, Nakhijevan, Znaberd, 1912 ♦ Vazgen Armenaki Avetisyan, Van, Kendanants, 1914 ♦ Vazgen Avetisi Sahakyan, Leninakan (1911) ♦ Vazgen Bagrati Golchanyan, Leninakan, Khlli Gharakilis, 1911 ♦ Vazgen Gevorgi Gevorgyan, Van, Parni, 1912 ♦ Vazgen Ghazari Ghazaryan, Alekpol, Bayandur, 1912 ♦ Vazgen Khachaturi Khantumanyan, Van, Archak, 1912 ♦ Vazgen Khachaturi Tokmajyan, Leninakan, Syogutli, 1913 ♦ Vazgen Khachiki Khachatryan, Van, Darman, 1908 ♦ Vazgen Martirosi Shakaryan,

Nakhijevan, 1912 ♦ Vazgen Meliki Muradyan, Kars, Bulanagh, 1914 ♦ Vazgen Mihrani Gasparyan (Mihranyan), Kars, Kaghzvan, 1913 ♦ Vazgen Minasi Yeghiazaryan, Van, Khach-poghan, 1913 ♦ Vazgen Musheghi Geghamyan (Musheghyan), Surmali, Najafal, 1911 ♦ Vazgen Sakoyi Voskanyan, Kars, Bayrakhtar, 1913 ♦ Vazgen Sedraki Muradyan, Kaghzvan, 1915 ♦ Vazgen Sedraki Sedrakyan, Van, Kendanants, 1913, 1911 ♦ Vazgen Simoni Simonyan, Van, 1913 ♦ Vazgen Stepani Yeghdaryan (Ghukasyan), Kars, Gharaghala, 1914 ♦ Vazgen Tadevosi Khachatryan, Kars, Voghuzli, 1914 ♦ Velikhan Adami Hakobyan, Kars, Ghzlchakhchakh, 1921 ♦ Velikhan Arami Tonoyan, Alekpol, Ghaplu, 1918 ♦ Velikhan Armenaki Hakobyan, Shirak, Toros, 1914 ♦ Velikhan Daviti Gevorgyan, Shirak, Duzkharaba, 1914 ♦ Velikhan Harutyuni Putikyan, Alekpol, Ghanlija, 1914 ♦ Velikhan Knyazi Margaryan, Kars, Teknis, 1916 ♦ Velikhan Mnatsakani Nazaretyan, Alekpol, Bozyoghush, 1914 ♦ Velikhan Nikoli Khachatryan, Leninakan, Kyalalu, 1916 ♦ Velikhan Sukiasi Danielyan, Alekpol, Toros, 1912 ♦ Velikhan Tonoyi Tonoyan, Akhalkalak, Delif, 1916 ♦ Vensik Grigori Mkrtchyan, Persia, Ghazvin, 1911 ♦ Vera Timofeevna, Kars, 1913 ♦ Vergin Agheki Hovhannisyan, Yerevan, Bazarjugh, 1911 ♦ Vergine Ghazari Khachatryan, Van, 1912 ♦ Vergine Hakobi (Bagrati) Gyuzalyan, Gharakilisa, Chigtama, 1910 ♦ Vergine Petrosi Petrosyan, Van, 1917 ♦ Vergine Sedraki Panosyan, Van, 1912, 1911 ♦ Vergine Soghomoni Gasparyan, Ordubad, Verin Agulis, 1913 ♦ Vergush Adibeki Manukyan, Nor Bayazet, Khul-ali, 1914 ♦ Vergush Arseni Samsonyan (Arsenyan), Nakhijevan, Khanukhlar, 1914 ♦ Vergush Asoyi Martirosyan, Shirak, Sirvanjugh, 1913 ♦ Vergush Badali Badalyan, Nakhijevan, 1914 ♦ Vergush Badali Ghazaryan, Igdir, 1914 ♦ Vergush Hayrapeti Hayrapetyan, Ghamarlu, 1915 ♦ Vergush Hazarapeti Ohannisyan, Hin Nakhijevan, 1914 ♦ Vergush Ivani Simonyan, Tiflis, 1914 ♦ Vergush Karoyi Karapetyan (Tovmasyan), Manazkert, 1914 ♦ Vergush Khachaturi Manukyan, Yerevan, Kharal, 1916 ♦ Vergush Levoni Margaryan, Aparan, 1911 ♦ Vergush Mamikoni Gevorgyan, Yerevan, Kyurdkand, 1915 ♦ Vergush Martirosi Martirosyan, Nakhijevan, 1919 ♦ Vergush Poghosi Poghosyan, Leninakan, Mastara, 1918 ♦ Vergush Sargisi Ayvazyan, Not Bayazet, 1913 ♦ Vergush Tevosi Tatosyan (Tevosyan), Alekpol, Samarlu, 1916 ♦ Verjaluys Vardani Vardanyan, Van, 1916 ♦ Vero Ghazari Vodianyan, Basen, Aliagrak, 1910 ♦ Veron Karapeti Stepanyan, Alekpol, Kyaftarlu, 1910 ♦ Veronik Aleksani Ter-Meliksetyan, Leninakan, Ghoshavank, 1917 ♦ Veronik Gevorgi Khachatryan (Gevorgyan), Mush, Yonjalu, 1913 ♦ Veronik Karapeti Manukyan, Kars, Chala, 1918 ♦ Verzhine Martirosi Martikyan (Martirosyan), Van, 1909 ♦ Verzhine Mkrtchi Mkrtchyan, Van, Shatakh, 1912, 1911 ♦ Verzhuhi Grigori Grigoryan, Darachichak, Ddmashen, 1913 ♦ Vigush Arami Aramyan, Surmalu, Khoshkhabar, 1916 ♦ Viktor Daviti Petrosyan, Kars, Mec Parket, 1913 ♦ Viktor Harutyuni Harutyunyan, Van, 1918 ♦ Viktor Samsoni Samvelyan, Karabagh, Shushi, 1909 ♦ Viktor Sergoyi Nazaryan, Alekpol, Mec Kapanak, 1915 ♦ Viktor Zakari T[er] Khachatryan (Zakary[an]), Kars, 1918 ♦ Viktoria Arami Grigoryan, Kars, 1908 ♦ Viktoria Armenaki Melikyan, Igdir, 1916 ♦ Viktoria Gabrieli Gabrielyan, Van, 1912 ♦ Viktoria Garegini Gareginyan (Khachatryan), Kars, 1914 ♦ Viktoria Grigori Dilanyan, Akhaltsikha, 1916 ♦ Viktoria Hakobi Khanamiryan, Hin Nakhijevan, 1907 ♦ Viktoria Harutyuni Terteryan, Kharberd, Khozar, 1908 ♦ Viktoria Harutyuni Vardanyan, Van, 1912 ♦ Viktoria Manuki Movsisyan, Kars, Jalal, 1909 ♦ Viktoria Minasi Hovhannisyan, Igdir, Alghamar, 1908 ♦ Viktoria Minasi Minasyan, Akhlat, Prkhus, 1906 ♦ Viktoria Misaki Misakyan, Khnus, Kopala, 1910 ♦ Viktoria Nikoghosi Nikoghosyan, Erzrum, Mamakhatun, 1908 ♦ Viktoria Soghomoni Abrahamyan, Basen, Todiveran, 1912 ♦ Viktoria Tigrani Tigranyan, Yerevan, Aghhamzalu, 1914 ♦ Viktoria Yeranosi Yaroyan, Nakhijevan, Dshogh, 1912 ♦ Vilhelm Mnatsakani Gevorgyan, Leninakan, Mastara, 1914 ♦ Vilo Movsesi Arshakyan (Movsisyan), Kars, Araz, 1916 ♦ Viray Moyiseyi Trekuzov, Novonikolayevka, 1916 ♦ Viro Gaspari Manukyan, Nor Bayazet, 1913 ♦ Volodya Aghabeki Paronyan, Mec Gharakilisa, Hamamlu, 1919 ♦ Vormez Mkrtchi Mnatsakanyan, Alekpol, Svanverdi, 1914 ♦ Vormik Abrahami Madoyan, Kars, Kyadiklar, 1915 ♦ Voskan Yesayi Yesayan, Yerevan, Ptghni, 1914 ♦ Voskehat Chitoyi Mkhitaryan (Chitoyan), Van, Kharakonis, 1904 ♦ Voskehat Danieli Ghazaryan, Erzrum, Agrak, 1912 ♦ Voskehat Grigori Nikoyan, Kars, Baglamat, 1912 ♦ Voskehat Grigori Yeghoyan, Kars, Basen, 1916 ♦ Voskehat Harutyuni Harutyunyan (Margaryan), Shirak, Ghanlija, 1913 ♦ Voskehat Hovakimi Mirzoyan, Vaspurakan, Aljavaz, 1911 ♦ Voskehat Karapeti Mkhikyan, Kharberd, Uzpag, 1911 ♦ Voskehat Matevosi Bagoyan, Alekpol, Tavshanghshlagh, 1910 ♦ Voskehat Meliki Muradyan, Alekpol, Bashgyugh, 1915 ♦ Voskehat Melkoni Tadevosyan (Melkonyan), Van, 1915 ♦ Voskehat Nazari Karapetyan (Nazaryan), Kaghzvan, Changru, 1910 ♦ Voskehat Panosi Panosyan, Van, Apnakants, 1909 ♦ Voskehat Saghateli Hovhannisyan, Baku, Bilinka, 1915 ♦ Voskehat Sargsi Sargsyan, Yerevan, Khatunarkh, 1915 ♦ Voskehat Vardani Minasyan, Nakhijevan, Alhet, 1910 ♦ Voski Avetisi Ghazaryan (Avetisyan), Van, Aljavaz, 1910 ♦ Voski Hakobi Hakobyan, Van, Khavents, 1909 ♦ Voski Hakobi Petrosyan (Hakobyan), Van, 1913 ♦ Voski Hovhannesi Sukiasyan, Basen, Armtlu, 1911 ♦ Voski Malkhasi Malkhasyan, Bitlis, Markorg, 1913 ♦ Voski Mheri Mheryan, Bulanagh, Votnchor, 1911 ♦ Voski Mkrtchi Mkrtchyan, Kaghzvan, Karabagh, 1914 ♦ Voski Poghosi Danielyan (Poghosyan), Kars, Mavrak, 1914 ♦ Voski Sargisi Sargsyan, Nukhi, 1917 ♦ Voski Vardani Vardanyan, Igdir, 1915 ♦ Voski Yeghiazari Vardanyan, Kars, Bulanagh, 1904 ♦ Vosko Arshaki Aghikyan, Shirak, Ghzlghoch, 1911 ♦ Vosko Avagi Avagyan, Yerevan, Shmali, 1914 ♦ Vosko Avetisyan ♦ Vosko Barseghi Martirosyan (Barseghyan), Van, Tosp, Tshogh, 1911 ♦ Vosko Daviti Davtyan (Aslanyan), Van, Kusnants, 1913 ♦ Vosko Ghazari Ghazaryan, Aparan, 1915 ♦ Vosko Hakobi

Hakobyan, Kars, 1914 ◆ Vosko Harutyuni Sukiasyan, Kars, Cbni, 1908 ◆ Vosko Hovhannesi Hakobyan, Kaghzvan, Gharavank, 1912 ◆ Vosko Hovhannesi Petrosyan, Kars, Ghani, 1912 ◆ Vosko Hovsepi Hovsepyan, Mush, Khoshgyaldi, 1916 ◆ Vosko Hovsepi Hovsepyan, Van, 1916 ◆ Vosko Kerobi Kerobyan, Basen, Toti, 1911 ◆ Vosko Khachaturi Sargsyan, Bulanagh, Ojaghalu, 1912 ◆ Vosko Melkoni Abelyan, Akhalkalak, Gimbirda, 1916 ◆ Vosko Misaki Khachatryan, Leninakan, Bughdashen, 1914 ◆ Vosko Musheghi Mkrtchyan (Ayvazyan), Shirak, Bashshoragal, 1910 ◆ Vosko Rubeni Aslanyan, Akhalkalak, Namzara, 1915 ◆ Vosko Sahaki Baghdasaryan, Kars, Nakhijevan, 1911 ◆ Vosko Soghomoni Stepanyan, Daralagyaz, Zncholi, 1911 ◆ Vosko Sumbati Hovhannisyan, Shirak, Illi, 1913 ◆ Vosko Yeghoyi Avetisyan, Kars, Gharamahmat, 1910 ◆ Vosko Yeghoyi Grigoryan, Mec Gharakilisa, Avdibek, 1920 ◆ Vostanik Khachaturi Gabrielyan, Van, Koghb, 1909 ◆ Vostanik Mambrei Khachatryan (Mambreyan), Van, Archesh, 1911 ◆ Vram Sargisi Sargsyan, Yerevan, 1913 ◆ Vramshapuh Manuki Gabrielyan, Basen, Bashgegh, 1913 ◆ Vramshapuh Nikoghosi Serobyan (Nikoghosyan), Kars, Gedaksatlmish, 1908 ◆ Vrasho Hakobi Hakobyan, Kars, Ghzlchakhchakh, 1919 ◆ Vrezh Aleksani Aristakesyan (Aleksanyan), Sebastia, Shapingarah[isar], 1908 ◆ Vruyr Hakobi Hurikhanyan (Manukyan), Kars, Kyadiklar, 1914 ◆ Vruyr Haruti Harutyunyan, Leninakan, Imrkhan, 1916 ◆ Vruyr Hovhannesi Harutyunyan, Yerevan, Varmazar, 1914 ◆ Vruyr Khachaturi Hovhannisyan, Kars, Chala, 1912 ◆ Vruyr Petrosi Manvelyan, Batum, Ardvin, 1909 ◆ Yaghut Arakeli Kakosyan (Melikyan), Kars, Bayghara, 1914 ◆ Yaghut Arshaki Hambaryan, Shirak, Imrkhan, 1910 ◆ Yaghut Hakobi Hakobyan, Sarighamish, 1919 ◆ Yaghut Hambardzumi Saroyan (Hambardzumyan), Kaghzvan, 1914 ◆ Yaghut Harutyuni Gevorgyan (Harutyunyan), Terjan, Aspavirak, 1909 ◆ Yaghut Hayrapeti Khachatryan, Ardahan, 1914 ◆ Yaghut Kerobi Sargsyan (Alvrsyan), Basen, Ishkhi, 1908 ◆ Yaghut Matosi Sargsyan, Erzrum, Bulk, 1910 ◆ Yaghut Melkoni Manukyan (Melkonyan), Vaspurakan, Van, 1914 ◆ Yaghut Minasi Gevorgyan, Khnus, Satkhi, 1910 ◆ Yaghut Mkrtchi Arakelyan, Manazkert, Latar, 1911 ◆ Yaghut Sukiasi Yepremyan (Sukiasyan), Sarighamish, Bashgyugh, 1908 ◆ Yaghut Vardani Vardanyan, Kars, Bagliahmat, 1915 ◆ Yalduz Abrahami Gasparyan (Abrahamyan), Yerevan, Khalachi, 1909 ◆ Yalduz Hakobi Hakobyan, Archak, Berd, 1912 ◆ Yalduz Hovhannesi Hovhannisyan, Van, Berkri gyozak, 1912 ◆ Yalduz Hovhannesi Hovhannisyan, Van, Moks, 1912 ◆ Yalduz Margari Margaryan, Van, Sevan, 1911 ◆ Yalduz Mkrtchi Mkrtchyan, Van, Khachan, 1910 ◆ Yalduz Mkrtichi Mkrtchyan, Van, Chochan, 1912 ◆ Yalduz Muradi Muradyan, Bulanagh, Kop, 1912 ◆ Yalduz Poghosi Poghosyan (Davtyan), Van, Khorgom, 1910 ◆ Yalduz Poghosi Poghosyan, Van, Perka, 1908 ◆ Yalduz Tonoyi Hovhannisyan, Manazkert, Noratin, 1910 ◆ Yalduz Vardani Karapetyan, Bitlis, Prkhus, 1908 ◆ Yango Martirosi Yervandyan, Mush, Bulanagh, 1913 ◆ Yaret (Habet) Gabrieli Nazaryan, Gharakilisa, Parni gyugh, 1919 ◆ Yazgul Ghukasi Barseghyan (Ghukasyan), Basen, Tarkhajan, 1912 ◆ Yedigar (Yedo) Arshaki Petrosyan, Kars, Dolbandli, 1912 ◆ Yedigar Margari Melikyan, Shirak, Ghli Gharakilisa, 1906 ◆ Yedigar Tevani Toneryan, Akhalkalak, Pokr Kentire, 1912 ◆ Yedo Gevorgi Aleksanyan, Basen, Gomadzor, 1910 ◆ Yedvard Hovhannesi Simonyan, Alekpol, Jalab, 1911 ◆ Yeghia Aleki Alekyan Sargsyan, Erzrum, Gomadzor, 1911 ◆ Yeghiazar Margari Margaryan (Simonyan), Van, Pstik gyugh, 1905 ◆ Yeghiazar Movsesi Harutyunyan, Erzrum, Batnots, 1909 ◆ Yeghik Papoyi Yepremyan, Yerevan, Bzhni, 1910 ◆ Yeghis Ghukasi Hovhannisyan (Ghukasyan), Van, Marmir, 1912 ◆ Yeghisab Avetisi Avetisyan, Bulanagh, Yonjalu, 1912 ◆ Yeghisabet (Yughaber) Yebrayeli Melkonyan, Leninakan, 1914 ◆ Yeghisabet Abrahami Movsisyan, Alekpol, Taliboghli, 1912 ◆ Yeghisabet Abrahami Stepanyan, Leninakan, Koraghbyur, 1912 ◆ Yeghisabet Adami Khachatryan, Erzrum, 1914 ◆ Yeghisabet Aghabeki Movsisyan, Kars, Derbandlu, 1912 ◆ Yeghisabet Aleksani Movsisyan, Leninakan, 1915 ◆ Yeghisabet Aleksani Stepanyan, Van, Pstik gyugh, 1908 ◆ Yeghisabet Arshaki Tadevosyan, Kars, 1915 ◆ Yeghisabet Artemi Grigoryan, Nakhijevan, Karchivan, 1910 ◆ Yeghisabet Asaturi Asatryan, Van, Chobanoghli, 1918 ◆ Yeghisabet Baghdasari Vardanyan, Nakhijevan, Shurud, 1913 ◆ Yeghisabet Gaspari Gasparyan, Van, Pakhner, 1910 ◆ Yeghisabet Gaspari Hovhannisyan (Gasparyan), Van, Pakhnet, 1912 ◆ Yeghisabet Gevorgi Gevorgyan, Sasun, Hazo, 1910 ◆ Yeghisabet Gevorgi Grigoryan, Kars Cbni, 1906 ◆ Yeghisabet Gevorgi Sargsyan, Kars, Kop, 1914 ◆ Yeghisabet Ghazari Melikyan, Karin, Gharaksi, 1908 ◆ Yeghisabet Ghazari Simonyan, Van, Mokhraberd, 1908 ◆ Yeghisabet Ghukasi Karapetyan, Kars, Khaszi ftlik, 1909 ◆ Yeghisabet Grigori (Yenkoyan) Grigoryan, Leninakan, Horom, 1913 ◆ Yeghisabet Grigori Grigoryan, Kaghzvan, Keti, 1911 ◆ Yeghisabet Hakobi Hakobyan, Yerevan, Ddmashen, 1912 ◆ Yeghisabet Hakobi Movsisyan, Khnus, Kharakonis, 1910 ◆ Yeghisabet Hakobi Sargsyan (Hakobyan), Van, Shushan, 1909 ◆ Yeghisabet Hambardzumi Vardanyan, Yerevan, Chnjghlu, 1911 ◆ Yeghisabet Haruti Hovsepyan, Basen, Alzar, 1910 ◆ Yeghisabet Harutyuni Harutyunyan, Van, Pakhes, 1911 ◆ Yeghisabet Harutyuni Harutyunyan, Van, Zarana, 1911 ◆ Yeghisabet Harutyuni Vardanyan, Van, Ghaymaz, 1909 ◆ Yeghisabet Hovhannesi Gharibyan, Aljavaz, 1911 ◆ Yeghisabet Hovsepi (Martirosi) Martirosyan, Kharberd, Sorpian, 1912 ◆ Yeghisabet Hovsepi Hovsepyan, Alashkert, Gharakilise, 1914 ◆ Yeghisabet Hovsepi Khachatryan, Kars, Ughuzlu, 1912 ◆ Yeghisabet Karapeti Karapetyan (Simonyan), Leninakan, 1912 ◆ Yeghisabet Karapeti Karapetyan, Kars, 1918 ◆ Yeghisabet Khachaturi Hakobyan, Yerznka, 1913 ◆ Yeghisabet Khachaturi Tonoyan, Kars, Gedaksatlmish, 1912 ◆ Yeghisabet Kirakosi Hakobyan, Erzrum, 1910 ◆ Yeghisabet Knyazi Mkrtchyan, Alekpol, Bozdoghan, 1911 ◆ Yeghisabet Knyazi Smbatyan, Khnus, 1912 ◆ Yeghisabet Manuki Budaghyan, Bulanagh, Rostom gedak, 1913 ◆ Yeghisabet Margari Margaryan, Van, 1910

♦ Yeghisabet Martirosi Hovhannisyan, Van, Koms, 1913 ♦ Yeghisabet Martirosi Martirosyan, Van, Dshogh, 1911 ♦ Yeghisabet Mihrani Yeritsyan (Mihranyan), Erzrum, Kez, 1909 ♦ Yeghisabet Mikayeli Davtyan, Akhalkalak, Alastan, 1912 ♦ Yeghisabet Mkhitari Hovhannisyan, Basen, Chrason, 1908 ♦ Yeghisabet Mkrtchi Ghazaryan (Mkrtchyan), Erzrum, Terjan, 1913 ♦ Yeghisabet Mkrtchi Khachatryan, Kars, Gorkhan, 1912 ♦ Yeghisabet Mkrtchi Safaryan, Alekpol, Dzithankov, 1911 ♦ Yeghisabet Mkrtchi Torosyan, Erzrum, Kan, 1909 ♦ Yeghisabet Mukayeli Martirosyan (Mukayelyan), Kaghzvan, Karabagh, 1910 ♦ Yeghisabet Nersesi Nersisyan, Van, Shatakh, 1913 ♦ Yeghisabet Nshani Nshanyan, Erzrum, Terjan, 1914 ♦ Yeghisabet Petrosi Petrosyan, Alashkert, Kharas, 1911 ♦ Yeghisabet Petrosi Petrosyan, Van, Harinj, 1911 ♦ Yeghisabet Poghosi (Poghosyan) Mkhitaryan, Bitlis, Norashen, 1909 ♦ Yeghisabet Poghosi Petrosyan, Van, 1910 ♦ Yeghisabet Sahaki Gevorgyan, Manazkert, Norashen, 1912 ♦ Yeghisabet Sahaki Tadevosyan, Daralagyaz, Khanlukhlar, 1914 ♦ Yeghisabet Sargsi Babayan, Karabagh, Nukhi, 1913 ♦ Yeghisabet Sargsi Harutyunyan, Persia, 1916 ♦ Yeghisabet Sargsi Sargsyan, Kharberd, Tlat, 1909 ♦ Yeghisabet Sedraki Sedrakyan, Van, 1907 ♦ Yeghisabet Simoni Mirzoyan, Moks, Norovan, 1911 ♦ Yeghisabet Stepani Stepanyan, Leninakan, Gheghach, 1914 ♦ Yeghisabet Tadevosi Chakhoyan, Alekpol, Chrakhli, 1915 ♦ Yeghisabet Tigrani Ter-Avetisyan, Kars, Jalal, 1911 ♦ Yeghisabet Tigrani Tigranyan (Kerobyan), Alekpol, Shish-tapa, 1914 ♦ Yeghisabet Vahani Sargsyan, Kars, 1911 ♦ Yeghisabet Vardani Vardanyan, Van, 1914 ♦ Yeghisabet Yeghiazari Ktakyan (Yeghiazaryan), Van, Pesandasht, 1898 ♦ Yeghisabet Yervandi Gevorgyan, Ardahan, 1909 ♦ Yeghisabet Zakari Zakaryan, Bulanagh, Khraplar, 1914 ♦ Yeghise (Yeghsan) Ter-Khachaturi Ter-Poghosyan, Lori, Shahnazar, 1912 ♦ Yeghish (Yeghya) Vaniki Hovhannisyan, Darachichak, Alapars, 1912 ♦ Yeghish Aleksani Hakobyan, Leninakan, Duzkharaba, 1910 ♦ Yeghish Gaspari Galstyan, Bulanagh, Kaparlu, 1912 ♦ Yeghish Gaspari Hakobyan, Mush, Oghunk, 1906 ♦ Yeghish Gevorgi Gevorgyan, Kars, Paldrvan, 1919 ♦ Yeghish Gevorgi Michoyan (Petrosyan), Alekpol, Haji-Nazar, 1912 ♦ Yeghish Harutyuni Mkhoyan, Shirak, Paltlu, 1914 ♦ Yeghish Khachaturi Khachatryan, Sarighamish, Changli, 1916 ♦ Yeghish Khachiki Aghababyan, Akhalkalak, Lomaturs, 1911 ♦ Yeghish Levoni Harutyunyan, Akhta, Zinjirlu, 1911 ♦ Yeghish Mkrtchi Mkrtchyan, Manazkert, Shirvanshekh, 1911 ♦ Yeghish Muradi (Mkrtchi) Muradyan, Sharur, Norashen, 1915 ♦ Yeghish Nazari (Mheryan) Mkhitaryan, Bulanagh, Gharaghshl, 1909 ♦ Yeghish Petrosi Manukyan (Petrosyan), Manazkert, 1912 ♦ Yeghish Tigrani Tigranyan, Van, 1916 ♦ Yeghishe (Karapeti) Vardani Vardanyan, Sasun, Hazva, 1914 ♦ Yeghishe Abrahami Margaryan, Sasun, Gelegyuzan, 1909 ♦ Yeghishe Aleki Varosyan, Kars, Ghzlchakhchak, 1914 ♦ Yeghishe Arami Ter-Arakelyan, Kars, 1911 ♦ Yeghishe Arshaki Davtyan, Cghak, 1912 ♦ Yeghishe Avetisi Avetisyan (Hovhannisyan), Khnus, Vardov, 1914 ♦ Yeghishe Avetisi Martikyan (Avetisyan), Bitlis, Vanik, 1907 ♦ Yeghishe Avoyi Avetisyan, Khnus, Kopal, 1912 ♦ Yeghishe Baghdasari (Tadevosi) Baghdasaryan, Kars, 1917 ♦ Yeghishe Grigori Khachatryan, Sasun, 1908 ♦ Yeghishe Hovhannesi Khanzadyan, Gharakilisa, Aghbulagh, 1915 ♦ Yeghishe Karapeti Minasyan, Kaghzvan, Agh-Kilisa, 1914 ♦ Yeghishe Khachaturi Hovhannisyan, Alashkert, Mazra, 1912 ♦ Yeghishe Manasi Aleksanyan (Manasyan), Bitlis, Teghva, 1912 ♦ Yeghishe Mikayeli Martirosyan, Shamakhi, Kyarkand, 1913 ♦ Yeghishe Misaki Tigranyan (Misakyan), Tigranakert, 1914 ♦ Yeghishe Mkhitari Mkhitaryan (Safaryan), Bulanagh, Kharablagh, 1916 ♦ Yeghishe Movsesi Gevorgyan (Movsisyan), Mush, Rostamgedak, 1913 ♦ Yeghishe Nahapeti Nahapetyan, Bayazet, 1912 ♦ Yeghishe Nikolayi Ghazaryan, Nakhijevan, Ghazanchi, 1912 ♦ Yeghishe Petrosi Barseghyan, Van, Moks, 1908 ♦ Yeghishe Rubeni Rubenyan, Nor Bayazet, 1915 ♦ Yeghishe Saghateli Zakaryan, Hin Bayazet, Musun, 1910 ♦ Yeghishe Sedraki Avetisyan, Kars, Bagran, 1910 ♦ Yeghishe Seroyi Khachatryan, Pambak, Gharakilisa, 1919 ♦ Yeghishe Vardani Mkrtchyan (Vardanyan), Sarighamish, 1915 ♦ Yeghishe Yesayi Papikyan (Yesayan), Kars, Laloy-mavrak, 1914 ♦ Yegho Mesropi Martirosyan, Yerevan, 1920 ♦ Yeghsab Hovhannesi Hovhannisyan, Alekpol, Ghazanchi, 1914 ♦ Yeghsab Levoni Hakobyan, Akhalkalak, 1910 ♦ Yeghsab Nazari Zakaryan, Alekpol, Ghpchagh, 1911 ♦ Yeghsab Sargsi Aleksanyan, Shirak, Jajur, 1913 ♦ Yeghsan Hayroyi Sahakyan, Bulanagh, Kop, 1914 ♦ Yeghsan Minasi Arshakyan (Minasyan), Kars, Mavrak, 1915 ♦ Yeghsan Zakari Hovhannisyan, Alekpol, Toros gyugh, 1914 ♦ Yeghsik Daviti Mikayelyan, Kars, Bagran, 1913 ♦ Yeghsik Khachaturi Khachatryan, Kars, Sarighamish, 1916 ♦ Yeghsik Khachaturi Shivaryan, Basen, Gomadzor, 1908 ♦ Yeghso Bagrati Stepanyan, Alekpol, Ghazarabad, 1910 ♦ Yeghso Gevorgi Gevorgyan Ghazaryan, Van, 1917 ♦ Yeghso Hakobi Hakobyan, Yerevan, 1916 ♦ Yeghso Harutyuni Mutafyan, Akhalkalak, 1911 ♦ Yeghso Hovhannesi Hovhannisyan, Kars, 1906 ♦ Yeghso Hovsepi Khachatryan, Kars, Ughuzli, 1912 ♦ Yeghso Mukoyi Gasparyan, Jalaloghli, Shahnazar, 1914 ♦ Yeghso Nersesi Nersisyan, Yerevan, Darghalu, 1915 ♦ Yeghso Sahaki Nikolyan (Sahakyan), Leninakan, Paltli, 1915 ♦ Yegor Karapeti Melkonyan (Karapetyan), Hin Nakhijevan, Znaberd, 1912 ♦ Yegor Margari Manukyan, Leninakan, Ghskhdagirman, 1911 ♦ Yegor Mkrtchi Kocharyan, Leninakan, Ghanlija, 1910 ♦ Yelen (Yelush) Yezroyi Khachatryan, Yerevan, 1917 ♦ Yelena (Eliza) Khurshudi Abrahamyan, Baku, 1915 ♦ Yelena Anushavani Carukyan, Alekpol, Ghoshavank, 1911 ♦ Yelena Erklei Khopchiyan, Pambak, Allaverdi, 1918 ♦ Yelena Harutyuni Simonyan, Kars, Ughuzli, 1918 ♦ Yelena Harutyuni Torosyan, Yerevan, 1917 ♦ Yelena Hayrikyan, 1918 ♦ Yelena Hmayaki Grigoryan, Kars, 1918 ♦ Yelena Khachaturi Rostomyan, Karabagh, Shushi, 1915 ♦ Yelena Matevosi Matevosyan, Tifliz, 1919 ♦ Yelena Musheghi Mnatsakanyan, Yerevan, Hakhveris, 1914 ♦ Yelena Smbati Petrosyan, Kaghzvan, 1918 ♦ Yelena Tadevosi Sarukhanyan,

Nakhijevan, 1917 ♦ Yelena Tatosi Movsisyan Tatosyan, Akhlat, Gesu, 1916 ♦ Yelena Yeranosi Markosyan (Yeranosyan), Nakhijevan, Diza, 1911 ♦ Yelgana Rafayeli Harutyunyan, Derjan, Bulk, 1912 ♦ Yelik Musheghi Musheghyan (Asatryan), Bulanagh, Liz, 1912 ♦ Yeliz Kurneliosi Hurikhanyan, Kars, Ortakadiklar, 1914 ♦ Yelko Arshaki Mkhitaryan (Arshakyan), Manazkert, Yegna khoja, 1913 ♦ Yelo (Arakel) Martirosi Manukyan (Martirosyan), Alashkert, Zeytkan, 1912 ♦ Yelpis Vardani Harutyunyan, Kars, Dalband, 1911 ♦ Yelush Nikitayi Khachatryan, Leninakan, 1918 ♦ Yengibar Tatosi Hakobyan, Maku, Kishmish tapa, 1914 ♦ Yenok Aleksani Aleksanyan (Shakyan [Sahakyan]), Van, Goli, 1908 ♦ Yenok Danieli Danielyan (Zakaryan), Alekpol, Hajinazar, 1914 ♦ Yenok Davtyan, Basen, 1907 ♦ Yenok Hambardzumi Mkrtchyan, Kars, Paldrvan, 1914 ♦ Yenok Harutyuni Baghdasaryan, Bitlis, Khulik, 1910 ♦ Yenok Hovhannesi Hovhannisyan, Nakhijevan, Kndonir, 1914 ♦ Yenok Israyeli Harutyunyan, Bitlis, Meck gyugh, 1903 ♦ Yenok Karapeti Hovsepyan (Karapetyan), Archesh, Gragom, 1908 ♦ Yenok Karapeti Karapetyan, Alashkert, Gharakilisa, 1912, 1910 ♦ Yenok Khachaturi Khachatryan, Gharalagyaz, Yelpi, 1912 ♦ Yenok Khosrovi Khosrovyan, Khlat, Teghut, 1908 ♦ Yenok Nersesi Sargsyan, Alashkert, Ghazi, 1910 ♦ Yenok Nshani Karapetyan, Van, Ango, 1911 ♦ Yenok Petrosi Minasyan (Petrosyan), Van, Aljavaz, 1914 ♦ Yenok Sargsi (Simoni) Simonyan, Manazkert, Tundras, 1912 ♦ Yenok Sargsi Muradyan (Sargsyan), Alashkert, Gharakilisa, 1912 ♦ Yenok Simoni (Simiki) Stamboltsyan, Akhalkalak, Tadesh, 1911 ♦ Yenok Tigrani Grigoryan, Kars, Azghighaz, 1911 ♦ Yenok Yeghoyi (Yeghoyan) Hayrapetyan, Van, Aljavaz, 1912, 1911 ♦ Yepraksi Aghani Grigoryan, Alekpol, Uzunkilisa, 1915 ♦ Yepraksi Antoni Alekyan, Leninakan, Chzghlar, 1912 ♦ Yepraksi Arshaki Madoyan, Kars, Pirvalu, 1909 ♦ Yepraksi Arshaki Ter-Markosyan, Kars, Ghzlchakhchakh, 1913 ♦ Yepraksi Asoyi Martirosyan, Leninakan, Taliboghli, 1913 ♦ Yepraksi Avagi Gevorgyan, Kars, Uzunkilisa, 1910 ♦ Yepraksi Avetiki Grigoryan, Leninakan, Illi, 1916 ♦ Yepraksi Avetisi Bteyan (Avetisyan), Sarighamish, Gharapanvar, 1911 ♦ Yepraksi Avetisi Hovhannisyan, Kars, Chala, 1913 ♦ Yepraksi Bagrati Arakelyan, Akhalkalak, Mec Gendura, 1909 ♦ Yepraksi Elbaki Harutyunyan, Kars, Gorkhan, 1914 ♦ Yepraksi Galusti Galstyan, Kars, Ghzlchakhchakh, 1915 ♦ Yepraksi Galusti Manukyan (Khachatryan), Kars, Chala, 1911 ♦ Yepraksi Garegini Avetisyan, Alekpol, Ghonaghran, 1914 ♦ Yepraksi Gevorgi Gasparyan, Shirak, Samrlu, 1913 ♦ Yepraksi Gevorgi Ghazaryan, Basen, Yeghan, 1913 ♦ Yepraksi Ghazari Avetisyan, Leninakan, Sirvanjugh, 1915 ♦ Yepraksi Ghazari Torosyan, Akhalkalak, Samsar, 1913 ♦ Yepraksi Ghukasi Ghukasyan, Kaghzvan, Khas gyugh, 1915 ♦ Yepraksi Grigori Barseghyan, Kars, Mavrak, 1915 ♦ Yepraksi Grigori Grigoryan, Alekpol, Kops, 1913 ♦ Yepraksi Grigori Grigoryan, Leninakan, Jajur, 1913 ♦ Yepraksi Hakobi Baghdasaryan, Kars, 1912 ♦ Yepraksi Hakobi Melkonyan, Akhalkalak, Chandura, 1914 ♦ Yepraksi Hambardzumi Tumasyan, Shirak, Jalab, 1910 ♦ Yepraksi Hambardzumi Vardanyan, Kars, Gharamahmat, 1909 ♦ Yepraksi Harutyuni Baghdasaryan, Leninakan, Ortakilisa, 1912 ♦ Yepraksi Hovaki Sahakyan, Akhalkalak, Jigrashen, 1911 ♦ Yepraksi Hovhannesi (Khachaturi) Vardanyan, Leninakan, Duzkharaba, 1914 ♦ Yepraksi Hovhannesi Grigoryan, Kars, Gharamahmat, 1914 ♦ Yepraksi Hovhannesi Hovhannisyan, Van, 1920 ♦ Yepraksi Hovhannesi Muradyan, Kars, Aghjaghala, 1911 ♦ Yepraksi Hovhannesi Stepanyan, Kars, 1915 ♦ Yepraksi Karapeti (Gevorgi) Gevorgyan, Kars, Jalal, 1915 ♦ Yepraksi Karapeti Karapetyan, Kars, Bayraghtar, 1912 ♦ Yepraksi Karapeti Margaryan, Leninakan, Horom, 1913 ♦ Yepraksi Karapeti Melkonyan, Bulanagh, Yonjalu, 1910 ♦ Yepraksi Khachaturi Avagyan, Kars, Ghoshavank, 1912 ♦ Yepraksi Khachaturi Sargsyan, Kars, 1915 ♦ Yepraksi Kirakosi Aghabekyan, Kars, Kyadiklar, 1913, 1910 ♦ Yepraksi Knyazi Ghazaryan, Kars, Karmir vank, 1910 ♦ Yepraksi Lyovayi Galstyan, Aparan, Ghotur, 1910 ♦ Yepraksi Madati Yesayan, Kars, Uzunkilisa, 1916 ♦ Yepraksi Martirosi Gevorgyan (Martirosyan), Gharakilisa, 1918 ♦ Yepraksi Martirosi Martirosyan, Alekpol, Chlokhan, 1916 ♦ Yepraksi Martirosi Simonyan, Kars, Kyurakdar, 1914 ♦ Yepraksi Martirosi Vardanyan, Kars, Ghzlchakhchakh, 1913 ♦ Yepraksi Mesropi Avagyan, Akhalkalak, Jigrashen, 1908 ♦ Yepraksi Misaki Baghdasaryan, Kars, Ortakyatiklar, 1911 ♦ Yepraksi Mnatsakani Avetisyan, Akhalkalak, Bash gyugh, 1911 ♦ Yepraksi Mnatsakani Harutyunyan, Kars, Kyurakdar, 1909 ♦ Yepraksi Movsesi Hovhannisyan, Alekpol, Maymajugh, 1914 ♦ Yepraksi Mukuchi Ghazaryan, Alekpol, Chrplu, 1914 ♦ Yepraksi Petrosi Baghdasaryan, Leninakan, Ghoshavank, 1916 ♦ Yepraksi Petrosi Muradyan (Petrosyan), Leninakan, Vojaghuli, 1914 ♦ Yepraksi Petrosi Papikyan, Leninakan, Gharakilisa, 1912 ♦ Yepraksi Petrosi Petrosyan, Kars, 1914 ♦ Yepraksi Petrosi Tachatyan, Alekpol, Ghoshavank, 1912 ♦ Yepraksi Sahaki Hovhannisyan, Kars, Gedaksatrmish, 1913 ♦ Yepraksi Sakoyi (Margar) Sakoyan (Margaryan), Kars, Zochi, 1916 ♦ Yepraksi Samsoni Samsonyan, Alashkert, Mankasar, 1914 ♦ Yepraksi Saribeki Saribekyan, Pambak, Urut, 1916 ♦ Yepraksi Saroyi (Stepanyan) Saroyan, Alekpol, Illi, 1913 ♦ Yepraksi Sedraki Grigoryan, Kars, Jali, 1912 ♦ Yepraksi Smbati Harutyunyan, Leninakan, Ghanlicha, 1911 ♦ Yepraksi Smbati Mkrtchyan, Kars, Teknis, 1914 ♦ Yepraksi Smbati Vardanyan, Kars, Mec Parket, 1913 ♦ Yepraksi Srabi Galoyan (Srapyan), Alekpol, Sogutli, 1916 ♦ Yepraksi Stepani Khachatryan, Alekpol, Tekniz, 1914 ♦ Yepraksi Sukiasi Yeprikyan (Sukiasyan), Kars, Bashgegh, 1914 ♦ Yepraksi Tadevosi Mkoyan (Zatikyan), Kars, Gorkhana, 1910 ♦ Yepraksi Tatosi Gevorgyan, Kars, Hopveran, 1915 ♦ Yepraksi Tatosi Sudyan (Avetisyan), Alekpol, Aghin, 1909 ♦ Yepraksi Tigrani Hakobyan, Alekpol, Sirvanjugh, 1916 ♦ Yepraksi Tigrani Saribekyan (Tigranyan), Kars, Ghzlchakhchakh, 1914 ♦ Yepraksi Tumasi Sargsyan, Alekpol, Mec Keti, 1916 ♦ Yepraksi Vanoyi Harutyunyan, Shirak, Mec Arkhvali, 1911 ♦ Yepraksi Vardani Hakobyan, Alekpol, Daharlu, 1912 ♦ Yepraksi Vardani Sargsyan, Kars, Mec

Parket, 1909 ♦ Yepraksi Vardani Vardanyan, Leninakan, Ghaplu, 1912 ♦ Yepraksi Yeghoyi Yeghoyan, Alekpol, Adiaman, 1916 ♦ Yepraksi Yegori (Yekosi) Mkrtchyan (Yekosyan), Leninakan, Samali, 1914 ♦ Yepraksi Yepremi Melkonyan, Shirak, Talin, Ghrmzli, 1909 ♦ Yepraksi Yervandi Tadevosyan (Yervandyan), Leninakan, Horom, 1914 ♦ Yepraksi Zakari (Kostani) Zakaryan, Alekpol, Jalab, 1913 ♦ Yepraksia Gevorgi Grigoryan, Kars, 1910 ♦ Yepraksia Mkhitari Grigoryan, Kars, Galmli, 1913 ♦ Yepraksia Tigrani Tigranyan, Kars, Dashkov, 1916 ♦ Yepraksya Hovhannesi Dolukhanyan, Igdir, Dashbarun, 1910 ♦ Yepraksya Khachaturi Khachatryan, Kars, Araz, 1916 ♦ Yepraksya Mekhaki Shahinyan, Yerevan, Koghb, 1916 ♦ Yepraksya Nikoli Galstyan, Shirak, Keti, 1910 ♦ Yepranos Asaturi Yeremyan, Nakhijevan, Jahri, 1913 ♦ Yeprem Arshaki Ter-Karapetyan, Kars, Berna, 1912 ♦ Yeprem Barseghi Aslanyan, Kars, Girmlu, 1911 ♦ Yeprem Habeti Shahinyan, Kars, Gyarmni, 1909 ♦ Yeprem Khachaturi Vardanyan, Basen, 1912 ♦ Yeprem Martirosi Savayan, Kars, Berna, 1910 ♦ Yeprem Meliki Shahinyan (Shahverdyan), Kars, Bashshoragyal, 1916 ♦ Yeprem Sargsi Sargsyan, Alekpol, Darbandlu, 1916 ♦ Yeran Avagi Margaryan, Gharakilisa, Yaghablu, 1917 ♦ Yeranak (Yeranuhi) Tadevosi Zakaryan, Alekpol, Mec Sariar, 1916 ♦ Yeranak Arshaki Arshakyan, Alekpol, Khlligharakilis, 1918 ♦ Yeranak Arshaki Khachatryan, Leninakan, Chorli, 1916 ♦ Yeranak Garushi Badalyan, Akhalkalak, Gandza, 1913 ♦ Yeranak Ghazari Hakobyan, Leninakan, Ortakilisa, 1910 ♦ Yeranak Grigori Harutyunyan, Alekpol, Aghin, 1915 ♦ Yeranak Haruti Harutyunyan, Alekpol, Huli, 1910 ♦ Yeranak Harutyuni Harutyunyan (Baghdasaryan), Leninakan, Byurakdara, 1918 ♦ Yeranak Harutyuni Harutyunyan, Van, Aljavaz, 1911 ♦ Yeranak Hovhannesi Hovhannisyan, Dilijan, Karvansara, 1913 ♦ Yeranak Hovsepi Hovsepyan, Daralagyaz, Ghznaberd, 1916 ♦ Yeranak Igiti (Yeranosyan) Simonyan, Leninakan, Mec Arkhvali, 1917 ♦ Yeranak Karapeti (Sargsyan) Karapetyan, Kars, Kyurakdara, 1915 ♦ Yeranak Karapeti Karapetyan, Alekpol, Mec Keti, 1918 ♦ Yeranak Karapeti Martirosyan, Van, 1910 ♦ Yeranak Ohani Hovhannisyan, Akhalkalak, Vachian, 1914 ♦ Yeranak Sakoyi (Sargis) Torosyan, Kars, Bashshoragyal 1909 ♦ Yeranak Stepani Stepanyan, Kars, Dashkov, 1917 ♦ Yeranos Torosi Daroyan (Torosyan), Lengavar, Karghlnki, 1916 ♦ Yeranuhi Abrahami Manukyan, Mush, Khastar, 1911 ♦ Yeranuhi Andraniki Mkrtchyan, Kars, Ughuzli, 1913 ♦ Yeranuhi Arshaki Movsisyan, Yerevan, Nork, 1911 ♦ Yeranuhi Daviti Davtyan, Etchmiadzin, 1911 ♦ Yeranuhi Davti Gabrielyan, Van, Kirashen, 1908 ♦ Yeranuhi Gaspari Gevorgyan, Van, Psti gyugh, 1907 ♦ Yeranuhi Gaspari Hakobyan, Van, 1909 ♦ Yeranuhi Grigori Paronyan, Akhalkalak, Majadira, 1913 ♦ Yeranuhi Hakobi Hakobyan, Alekpol, Artik, 1914 ♦ Yeranuhi Hambardzumi Abgaryan, Van, Marmet, 1910 ♦ Yeranuhi Hambardzumi Janazyan, Nakhijevan, Koghb, 1913 ♦ Yeranuhi Harutyuni Tadevosyan, Yerevan, Noragavit, 1910 ♦ Yeranuhi Hovhannesi Karapetyan (Hovhannisyan), Akhalkalak, Verin Karcakh, 1911 ♦ Yeranuhi Karapeti Simonyan, Kars, Pirvali, 1910 ♦ Yeranuhi Khachaturi Atanyan (Khachatryan), Igdir, Abas, 1910 ♦ Yeranuhi Kirakosi Barseghyan, Kars, Hamzakarak, 1910 ♦ Yeranuhi Kirakosi Tonikyan, Akhalkalak, Pokr Kendura, 1909 ♦ Yeranuhi Manuki Manukyan, Khud, Shnher, 1916 ♦ Yeranuhi Melkoni Ghazaryan, Kars, 1911 ♦ Yeranuhi Misaki Martirosyan, Van, 1907 ♦ Yeranuhi Mkrtchi Mkrtchyan, Yerevan, Aparan, 1912 ♦ Yeranuhi Nshani Karapetyan, Nakhijevan, Aylabad, 1915 ♦ Yeranuhi Petrosi Petrosyan, Van, Bozanik, 1913 ♦ Yeranuhi Poghosi (Galoyi) Tumanyan, Van, Hayots dzor, 1909 ♦ Yeranuhi Poghosi Manukyan, Akhaltsikhe, 1909 ♦ Yeranuhi Poghosi Sinaelyan, Van, 1910 ♦ Yeranuhi Sargsi Umrikyan, Bulanagh, Teghut, 1909 ♦ Yeranuhi Sukiasi Hakobyan (Sukiasyan), Alashkert, Khazlvi, 1916 ♦ Yeranushi Antoni Atoyan, Akhalkalak, Vachian, 1912 ♦ Yeranushi Hmayaki Arikyan, Kharberd, Uchbeg, 1910 ♦ Yeranushi Karapeti Momjyan, Van, 1912 ♦ Yeranushi Khachaturi Nhoyan, Alekpol, Khli Gharakilisa, 1911 ♦ Yeranyak Abrahami Avagyan, Kars, Bulanagh, 1914 ♦ Yeranyak Aleksani Karapetyan (Hakobyan), Leninakan, Bogheghush, 1917 ♦ Yeranyak Avetisi Kirakosyan, Kars, Hamzakarak, 1915 ♦ Yeranyak Karapeti Galoyan (Karapetyan), Kars, Zayim, 1913 ♦ Yeranyak Khachaturi Danielyan, Alekpol, Bozdogha, 1912 ♦ Yeranyak Mihrani Mihranyan, Van, Zaran, 1914 ♦ Yeranyak Minasyan, Leninakan, Ghapli, 1919 ♦ Yeranyak Sergoyi Sergoyan, Gharakilisa, Parni gyugh, 1917 ♦ Yeranyak Torosi Torosyan, Alekpol, Ghrtagilman, 1913 ♦ Yeraz Antoni Antonyan (Baghdasaryan), Akhalkalak, Gimbirda, 1914 ♦ Yerazik Arshaki Vardanyan, Hin Nakhijevan, Znaberd, 1914 ♦ Yerem Barseghi Barseghyan, Alekpol, Toros gyugh, 1916 ♦ Yerem Gaspari Hayrapetyan, Kars, Hamzakarak, 1910 ♦ Yerem Grigori Hakobyan, Kaghzvan, Chrakhlu, 1918 ♦ Yerem Manuki Shahbazyan, Alekpol, Toparli, 1913, 1911 ♦ Yerem Movsesi Hakobyan, Kars, Uzunkilisa, 1912 ♦ Yerem Tadevosi Sargsyan, Leninakan, Khachakilisa, 1913 ♦ Yerem Voskani Gasparyan (Voskanyan), Aparan, Ilankalan, 1913 ♦ Yerenak Arshaki Gevorgyan, Leninakan, Ghapli, 1919 ♦ Yerenak Meliki Manukyan, Alekpol, Avdibek, 1910 ♦ Yerenak Poghosi Matsakyan, Leninakan, Chotli, 1912 ♦ Yerinaz Danieli Mnatsakanyan, Kars, Ghzlchakhchakh, 1910 ♦ Yerinaz Hakobi Hovhannisyan, Kars, Akrak, 1912 ♦ Yerinaz Manuki Ghazaryan, Kars, Agrak, 1914 ♦ Yerinaz Sargsi Sargsyan (Fahradyan), Kars, Nakhijevan, 1912 ♦ Yerjanik Misaki Mnatsakanyan, Basen, Gomadzor, 1914 ♦ Yerman Sedraki Amiryan, Kars, Bashshoragyal, 1911 ♦ Yermon Grigori Melkonyan, Ghamarlu, Davalu, 1917 ♦ Yermon Matevosi Martirosyan, Alekpol, Toros gyugh, 1915 ♦ Yermon Mukuchi Avetisyan (Mukuchyan), Leninakan, Tavshanghshlagh, 1915 ♦ Yermon Vardani Vardanyan, Shirak, Julab, 1913, 1912 ♦ Yermone (Margarit) Yepremi Harutyunyan (Grigoryan), Shirak, Kaps, 1917 ♦ Yermone Hovsepi Hovsepyan, Alekpol, Bavra, 1918 ♦ Yermonya Harutyuni Grigoryan, Yerevan, 1912 ♦ Yermonya Hovhannesi Yandyan, Akhalkalak, Alastan, 1916 ♦ Yermonya Vigeni Sahakyan,

Akhalkalak, Alastan, 1913 ♦ Yermonya Voskani Zakaryan, Baku, 1914 ♦ Yermonya Yegori Ghukasyan, Alekpol, Toros gyugh, 1913 ♦ Yervand Abgari Abgaryan, Bulanagh, Kharabshar, 1915 ♦ Yervand Adami Petrosyan (Adamyan), Kars, Chala, 1915 ♦ Yervand Andraniki Karapetyan, Erzrum, 1911 ♦ Yervand Antanesi Hakobyan, Kars, Bagran, 1909 ♦ Yervand Arami Mkrtchyan (Aramyan), Kars, Uzunkilisa, 1912 ♦ Yervand Arshaki Hakobyan, Shirak, Ghlligharakilis, 1909 ♦ Yervand Arshaki Mkrtchyan, Alekpol, Ghapli, 1918 ♦ Yervand Artashi Karapetyan, Nakhijevan, 1913 ♦ Yervand Asaturi Gharibyan (Avetisyan), Daralagyaz, Keshishveran, 1914 ♦ Yervand Barseghi Mkrtchyan, Leninakan, Kyulali, 1909 ♦ Yervand Chachoyan, Akhalkalak, Aragova, 1914 ♦ Yervand Danieli Grigoryan, Kaghzvan, Khazlu, 1912 ♦ Yervand Galusti Galstyan, Kars, Aghuzu, 1916 ♦ Yervand Gevorgi Gevorgyan, Van, Noravan, 1909 ♦ Yervand Harutyuni (Gasparyan) Ghazaryan, Karabagh, Khashmachk, 1918 ♦ Yervand Harutyuni Harutyunyan, Van, Kem, 1912 ♦ Yervand Hmayaki Danielyan, Leninakan, Boghaz-Kyasan, 1909 ♦ Yervand Hovhannesi Torosyan, Erzrum, Yerznka, 1907 ♦ Yervand Karoyi Grigoryan (Papikyan), Kars, Cbni, 1914 ♦ Yervand Kirakosi Hunanyan (Hovnanyan), Kars, Zrzi, 1910 ♦ Yervand Kochari (Kochoyi) Melikyan, Manazkert, Rostomgedak, 1913 ♦ Yervand Levoni Levonyan (Khlghatyan), Manazkert, Derek, 1916 ♦ Yervand Lyudvigi Tadevosyan, Nakhijevan, 1913 ♦ Yervand Margari (Bagrati) Margaryan (Martirosyan), Leninakan, Nor Artik, 1918 ♦ Yervand Meliki Amirkhanyan, Jalaloghli, Gyulagarak, 1914 ♦ Yervand Minasi Toroyan (Minasyan), Basen, Toti, 1912 ♦ Yervand Misaki Vokhikyan, Bitlis, Polis, 1910 ♦ Yervand Misaki Yeghiazaryan, Kars, 1913 ♦ Yervand Movsesi Movsisyan, Alashkert, Iritsu, 1916 ♦ Yervand Muradi Melikyan, Kars, Paldrvan, 1913 ♦ Yervand Nadroyi Gasparyan, Bitlis, Karb, 1911 ♦ Yervand Poghosi Sedrakyan, Khnus, Yelbiz, 1914 ♦ Yervand Sahaki Nazaryan (Nazaretyan), Jalal oghli, Khotur, 1918 ♦ Yervand Smbati Navoyan (Smbatyan), Igdir, Surmali, 1918 ♦ Yervand Stepani Stepanyan, Shirak, Shahnazar, 1914 ♦ Yervand Tigrani Baghdasaryan, Bulanagh, Shirvanshekh, 1908 ♦ Yervand Yeghiazari Markosyan, Khnus, Kaghkik, 1909 ♦ Yervand Yeghishi Khachatryan, Basen, Kztavaz, 1915 ♦ Yervand Yeghishi Levonyan, Basen, Izveran, 1913 ♦ Yervand Yeghoyi Yeghoyan, Alekpol, Mullagokcha, 1914 ♦ Yesa Badoyi Badoyan, Darachichak, Makrivan, 1917 ♦ Yesayi Aghabeki Martirosyan, Kars, Aghjaghala, 1911 ♦ Yesayi Artashesi Shahinyan, Akhalkalak, Vachian, 1913 ♦ Yesayi Kirakosi Hovhannisyan, Khachen, Abakh, 1913 ♦ Yesayi Martirosi Margaryan, Van, Nabat, 1910 ♦ Yester (Etar) Gaspari Khachatryan (Gasparyan), Kars, 1913 ♦ Yester Andraniki Gevorgyan, 1919 ♦ Yester Arakeli Arakelyan, Kars, Cbni, 1916 ♦ Yester Arakeli Muradyan, Alashkert, Amada, 1911 ♦ Yester Arshaki Arshakyan, Kars, Dolbandlu, 1915 ♦ Yester Ashoti Poghosyan, Alashkert, Berd, 1913 ♦ Yester Avetisi Sahakyan (Nazaretyan), Kars, Bagran, 1912 ♦ Yester Gevorgi Markosyan, Basen, Armtlu, 1909 ♦ Yester Gevorgi Markosyan, Sarighamish, Armtlu, 1907 ♦ Yester Ghazari Ghazaryan, Alashkert, Gharakilisa, 1912 ♦ Yester Ghukasi Avagyan, Karin, Gomadzor, 1909 ♦ Yester Ghukasi Ghukasyan, Sarighamish, Gulantap, 1910 ♦ Yester Ghukasi Manukyan, Erzrum, Gomadzor, 1908 ♦ Yester Ghukasi Poghosyan (Ghukasyan), Nakhijevan, Jalal, 1914 ♦ Yester Hakobi Hakobyan, Baku, 1916 ♦ Yester Hakobi Mkrtchyan, Kars, Berna, 1912 ♦ Yester Hambardzumi Uzunyan, Basen, Khoshgyaldi, 1907 ♦ Yester Haruti Harutyunyan, Kars, Cbni, 1910 ♦ Yester Harutyuni Hovhannisyan, Kars, Chala, 1911 ♦ Yester Harutyuni Torosyan, Kars, Berna, 1912 ♦ Yester Karapeti Stepanyan, Leninakan, Kaftarlu, 1909 ♦ Yester Khachaturi Manukyan, Kars, Tegor, 1914 ♦ Yester Khachaturi Matevosyan, Shamakh, Saghia, 1912 ♦ Yester Kirakosi Meloyan (Kirakosyan), Alashkert, Khastur, 1908 ♦ Yester Manuki Grigoryan (Mkhitaryan), Kars, Ortaghala, 1914 ♦ Yester Manuki Manukyan, Kars, Kaghzvan, 1909 ♦ Yester Manuki Manukyan, Kars, Sarighamish, 1914 ♦ Yester Martirosi Martirosyan, Kharberd, Gyodap, 1912 ♦ Yester Misaki Yedigaryan, Etchmiadzin, Haytagh, 1910 ♦ Yester Mkrtchi (Mkuch) Mkrtchyan, Kars, Beglamat, 1917 ♦ Yester Mkrtchi Muradyan (Mkrtchyan), Sarighamish, Hopveran, 1911 ♦ Yester Mkrtchi Vardanyan, Van, Artom, 1912 ♦ Yester Papiki Serobyan (Papikyan), Erzrum, Gomadzor, 1907 ♦ Yester Poghosi Rashoyan (Harutyunyan), Kars, Paldrvan, 1910 ♦ Yester Sahaki Kerobyan (Sahakyan), Basen, Chrason, 1912, 1911 ♦ Yester Sargsi Martirosyan (Artashyan), 1921 ♦ Yester Tigrani Hovhannisyan, Alashkert, Mangasar, 1910 ♦ Yester Zohrabi Petrosyan, Nor Bayazet, Basargechar, 1913 ♦ Yetar (Yester) Gaspari Gasparyan (Ghaghoyan), Bulanagh, Yonjalu, 1912 ♦ Yetar Sargsi Mukayelyan (Harutyunyan), Van, Norajgh, 1908 ♦ Yetar Sukiasi Muradyan, Kars, Ortaghars, 1916 ♦ Yeto Poghosyan, Kars, 1918 ♦ Yeva Aslani Aslanyan, Van, Shatakh, 1910 ♦ Yeva Garegini Abrahamyan, Erzrum, 1916 ♦ Yeva Kostani Sargsyan, Akhalkalak, 1917 ♦ Yeva Margari Sahakyan, Basen, Yeshkh, 1910 ♦ Yeva Mekhaki Sisoyan, Kakhet, 1914 ♦ Yeva Samsoni Samsonyan, Nukhi, Gharabash, 1913 ♦ Yeva Simoni Simonyan, Motkan, Grkho, 1914 ♦ Yevgenia Arshaki Martirosyan, Kars, 1919 ♦ Yevgenia Mnatsakani Mnatsakanyan, Igdir, Hakhveris, 1910 ♦ Yevgine (Avetisi) Martirosi Avetisyan, Kars, 1917 ♦ Yevgine Abrahami Hovhannisyan, Van, 1916 ♦ Yevgine Arami Ghukasyan, Alashkert, Gharakilisa, 1911 ♦ Yevgine Asaturi Asatryan, Erzrum, Ishkhu, 1910 ♦ Yevgine Gabrieli Hunanyan, Erzrum, Dali baba, 1911 ♦ Yevgine Galusti Galstyan, Alashkert, Khoshban, 1912 ♦ Yevgine Gevorgi Balyan, Erzrum, 1915 ♦ Yevgine Ghazari Ghazaryan, Erzrum, Terjan, 1911 ♦ Yevgine Grigori Tarumyan, Batum, 1915 ♦ Yevgine Hakobi Harutyunyan, Kharberd, 1912 ♦ Yevgine Harutyuni Harutyunyan (Ghazaryan), Karabagh, Shishvan, 1912 ♦ Yevgine Harutyuni Khachatryan (Aramyan), Shamakh, Madras, 1909 ♦ Yevgine Hovhannesi Gevorgyan, Kars, Uzunkilisa, 1918 ♦ Yevgine Hovhannesi Hovhannisyan (Hovakyan), Erzrum, Archesh, 1916 ♦ Yevgine Hovhannesi Hovhannisyan,

Van, Akagh, 1915 ♦ Yevgine Hovhannesi Tatosyan, Kars, Ortakilisa, 1908 ♦ Yevgine Hovhannesi Yeghiazaryan, Karabagh ♦ Yevgine Hovhannesi Zakaryan, Erzrum 1914 ♦ Yevgine Khachaturi Soghomonyan, Igdir, Tashburun, 1914 ♦ Yevgine Margari Petrosyan (Ter-Margaryan), Leninakan, Baldlu, 1909 ♦ Yevgine Martirosi Baghdasaryan, Hin Nakhijevan, 1914 ♦ Yevgine Minasi Mirzoyan (Minasyan), Mush, Satagh, 1911 ♦ Yevgine Mnatsakani Mnatsakanyan, Van, 1916 ♦ Yevgine Nveri Nshanyan, Van, Atanants, 1910 ♦ Yevgine Petrosi Churikyan, Van, Khzhishk, 1909 ♦ Yevgine Poghosi Gasparyan, Baku, 1913 ♦ Yevgine Sahaki Sargsyan (Kerobyan), Van, Darman, 1911 ♦ Yevgine Samveli Adamyan, Akhalkalak, Namzara, 1909 ♦ Yevgine Sedraki Sedrakyan, Basen, Gomadzor, 1913 ♦ Yevgine Sedraki Torosyan, Van, 1916 ♦ Yevgine Simoni Simonyan, Van, Pighan, 1909 ♦ Yevgine Stepani Stepanyan, Akhalkalak, Samsar, 1918 ♦ Yevgine Sukiasi (Sukiasyan) (Tumasyan) (Vardanyan), Alashkert, Iritsu, 1910 ♦ Yevgine Tatosi Tatosyan, Van, Marmed, 1909 ♦ Yevgine Vagharshaki Vardanyan, Alekpol, 1912 ♦ Yevgine Vahani Stepanyan (Vahanyan), Shirak, Bandivan, 1916 ♦ Yevgine Zakari Sukiasyan, Alashkert, Gharakilisa, 1909 ♦ Yeznik Karapeti Avetisyan, Leninakan, Syogutli, 1913 ♦ Yughab Saribeki Saribekyan, Aparan, Gharakilisa, 1911 ♦ Yughaber (Khgho) Samsoni Soghomonyan, Aparan, 1917 ♦ Yughaber (Yughik) Petrosi Petrosyan, Yerevan, Molabayazet, 1917 ♦ Yughaber Abrahami Margaryan (Abrahamyan), Bulanagh, Teghut, 1911 ♦ Yughaber Aresi Piloyan, Akhalkalak, Azarvet, 1911 ♦ Yughaber Arshaki Tumasyan, Alekpol, Paldlu, 1909 ♦ Yughaber Caruki Hakobyan, Kars, Hamzakarak, 1913 ♦ Yughaber Danielyan, Yerevan, 1920 ♦ Yughaber Ghazari Sargsyan, Leninakan, Mec Sariar, 1919 ♦ Yughaber Ghukasi Mikayelyan, Alekpol, Paldlu, 1910 ♦ Yughaber Hakobi Haykyan, Leninakan, Khlli Gharakilis, 1910 ♦ Yughaber Hakobi Sargsyan, Kars, Bashgyugh, 1907 ♦ Yughaber Hakobi Vardanyan, Kars, Paldrvan, 1912 ♦ Yughaber Harutyuni Davtyan, Kars, Bagliahmat, 1918 ♦ Yughaber Harutyuni Melkonyan, Khnus, Burnaz, 1910 ♦ Yughaber Harutyuni Paronyan, Akhalkalak, Machadia, 1910 ♦ Yughaber Hovakimi Ghazaryan, Alekpol, Daharli, 1907 ♦ Yughaber Hovhannesi Gharibyan, Kars, 1911 ♦ Yughaber Hovhannesi Petrosyan, Kars, Mush, 1910 ♦ Yughaber Hovhannesi Sargsyan, 1919 ♦ Yughaber Karapeti Tonoyan, Leninakan, Jajur, 1910 ♦ Yughaber Khachaturi Kirakosyan (Khachatryan), Erzrum, Dalibaba, 1908 ♦ Yughaber Khachaturi Manukyan, Kars, Hamzakarak, 1910 ♦ Yughaber Petrosi Vardanyan, Kars, 1909 ♦ Yughaber Sedraki Hakobyan, Bashshoragyal, 1913 ♦ Yughaber Smbati Davtyan (Smbatyan), Kars, Kyurakdara, 1913 ♦ Yughaber Tigrani Tigranyan, Leninakan, Derbend, 1912 ♦ Yughaber Yeghishei Sahakyan (Yeghishyan), Mush, Khnusghala, 1910 ♦ Yughik Movsesi Hovhannisyan, Yerevan, Ghamarlu, 1914 ♦ Yusuf Hasanyan, Yerevan, 1916 ♦ Zabel Aleksani Aleksanyan, Mush, 1911 ♦ Zabel Arakeli Arakelyan (Kocharyan), Van, Aljavaz, 1910 ♦ Zabel Arseni Gabrielyan (Harutyunyan), 1914 ♦ Zabel Arshaki Dilanyan, Yerevan, Koghb, 1911 ♦ Zabel Avagi Manukyan, Leninakan, Kyapanak, 1914 ♦ Zabel Galoyi Grigoryan, Alekpol, Chlokhan, 1913 ♦ Zabel Garegini Gevorgyan, Khnus, Berd, 1913 ♦ Zabel Gevorgi Gevorgyan, Van, Koghbants, 1909 ♦ Zabel Harutyuni Harutyunyan, Van, 1916 ♦ Zabel Hovhannesi Khachatryan, Shirak, Sariar, 1910 ♦ Zabel Karapeti Azatyan (Karapetyan), Nakhijevan, Gumri, 1913 ♦ Zabel Karapeti Karapetyan, Alekpol, Jajur, 1910 ♦ Zabel Karapeti Khechbabyan, Alekpol, Gharakilisa, 1912 ♦ Zabel Khachaturi Buniatyan, Etchmiadzin, Korpalu, 1913 ♦ Zabel Kkhlani Kulanyan (Gulanyan), Erzrum, Khnus, 1906 ♦ Zabel Makari Manukyan, Alekpol, Ghzlghoch, 1907 ♦ Zabel Manuki Yeghiazaryan (Manukyan), Kars, Gedaksatlmish, 1911 ♦ Zabel Margari Margaryan, Gharakilisa, Aghbulagh, 1919 ♦ Zabel Matsaki Hayrapetyan, Alekpol, Horom, 1910 ♦ Zabel Mkhitari Mkhitaryan, Leninakan, Paltlu, 1909 ♦ Zabel Mkhoyi Mkhoyan, Alekpol, Khlli Gharakilis, 1918 ♦ Zabel Muradi Amiryan, Van, Shatagh, 1914 ♦ Zabel Muradi Muradyan, Sarighamish, Chyuruk, 1915 ♦ Zabel Nazari Galstyan, Kars, Tazakyand, 1916 ♦ Zabel Sandroyi Nazaryan (Aleksanyan), Sharur, Norashen, 1911 ♦ Zabel Sargsi Aramyan (Sargsyan), Turkey, Berd, 1909 ♦ Zabel Sargsi Bagelyan (Sargsyan), Ghamarlu, Yuva, 1912 ♦ Zabel Serobi Gasparyan, Koghb, 1910 ♦ Zabel Simoni Simonyan, Mush, Drmed, 1909 ♦ Zabel Tepanosi Poghosyan, Leninakan, Gharakilisa, 1915 ♦ Zabel Tigrani Tumasyan, Van, Khzheshk, 1909 ♦ Zabel Vahani Saroyan, Leninakan, Ghoshavank, 1915 ♦ Zabel Yeghishi Yeghisyan, Shirak, Baghirgan, 1917 ♦ Zabel Zakari Muradyan, Batumi, Ardvin, 1911 ♦ Zabighon Tigrani Ayvazyan, Leninakan, Gharakilisa, 1913 ♦ Zado Avetisi Harutyunyan, Leninakan, Ghonakhran, 1914 ♦ Zahar Tonoyi Tonoyan, 1915 ♦ Zakar Arakeli Meliksetyan (Arakelyan), Hin Nakhijevan, Karakhanaklu, 1911 ♦ Zakar Bagrati Bagratyan, Igdir, Tejeghlu, 1914 ♦ Zakar Galusti Hovhannisyan, Kars, Berna, 1909 ♦ Zakar Galusti Torosyan, Kars, Berna, 1912 ♦ Zakar Hoviki Khachikyan (Hovikyan), Bulanagh, Hamzashekh, 1916 ♦ Zakar Makari Nersisyan (Zakaryan), Nakhijevan, 1918 ♦ Zakar Mheri (Badoyi) Badoyan, Turkey, Khulik, 1912 ♦ Zakar Soghomoni Hovhannisyan, Leninakan, Chrpli, 1918 ♦ Zakar Vardani Davtyan (Vardanyan) (Piloyan), Archesh, Akants, 1913 ♦ Zakeos Gevorgi Khachatryan, Alekpol, Ghzlghoch, 1910 ♦ Zakeos Grigori Petrosyan, Leninakan, Ghzlghoch, 1913 ♦ Zakivas Khachaturi Davtyan, Leninakan, Toparlu, 1912 ♦ Zanan Badoyi Arakelyan, Akhalkalak, Mec Kendura, 1909 ♦ Zanazan Danieli Movsisyan, Kars, Bulanagh, 1909 ♦ Zanazan Harutyuni Harutyunyan (Galstyan), Astvacacin, Van, 1907 ♦ Zanazan Hovsepi Hovsepyan, Van, 1915 ♦ Zanazan Karapeti Karapetyan, Van, 1910 ♦ Zanazan Margari Hovhannisyan, Kars, 1912 ♦ Zanazan Mayasyan, Kars, 1909 ♦ Zanazan Meliki Grigoryan, Shirak, Sirvangyugh, 1914 ♦ Zanazan Mikayeli Muradyan (Mikayelyan), Shirak, Sirvangyugh, 1915 ♦ Zanazan Mirzoyi Mirzoyan, Van, 1910 ♦

Zanazan Nazari Nazaryan, Bulanagh, Rostamgedak, 1909 ◆ Zanazan Samsoni Samsonyan (Aleksanyan), Surmalu, Igdir, 1914 ◆ Zanazan Torosi Torosyan, Kars, Bagran, 1911 ◆ Zanazan Vardani (Darmoyi) Vardanyan, Van, Mashtak, 1912 ◆ Zanazan Vardani Harutyunyan (Vardanyan), Alekpol, Zurtubulagh, 1911 ◆ Zanazan Vardani Vardanyan, Van, Khachan, 1912 ◆ Zanik Smbati Manukyan, Kars, Getuklar, 1918 ◆ Zano Gevorgi Gevorgyan, Cholakhli, 1916 ◆ Zano Vardani Muradyan, Van, Gandzak, 1910 ◆ Zanuhi Sargsi Galstyan (Sargsyan), Gharakilisa, Ghazaghan, 1909 ◆ Zardar (Hayastan) Kerobi Kerobyan, Pambak, Parni gyugh, 1920 ◆ Zardar Aleksani Melkonyan, Kaghzvan, 1914 ◆ Zardar Antoni Antonyan, Gharakilisa, 1918 ◆ Zardar Aspatami Grigoryan, Van, Archesh, 1910 ◆ Zardar Avetisi Avetisyan, Van, 1914 ◆ Zardar Baghdasari Baghdasaryan (Aleksanyan), Van, Patnos, 1911 ◆ Zardar Danieli Khachatryan, Leninakan, Ghrghdagirman, 1909 ◆ Zardar Gaspari Baroyan (Gasparyan), Basen, Khoshgyaldi, 1914 ◆ Zardar Gevorgi Gevorgyan (Grigoryan), Kars, Armtlu, 1915 ◆ Zardar Ghevondi Sargsyan, Hin Nakhijevan, Poratasht, 1910 ◆ Zardar Grigori Grigoryan, Erzrum, 1914 ◆ Zardar Harutiki Kidanyan, Kars, 1913 ◆ Zardar Hayrapeti Darbinyan, Karabagh, Khozlu, 1908 ◆ Zardar Hovhannesi Poghosyan (Hovhannisyan), Van, Boghazkyasan, 1912 ◆ Zardar Hovsepi Sargsyan (Hovsepyan), Basen, Arjarak, 1912 ◆ Zardar Karapeti Karapetyan, Van, Voskebad, 1910 ◆ Zardar Karapeti Kostanyan, Alekpol, Svanverdi, 1912 ◆ Zardar Kerobi Karapetyan (Kerobyan), Gharakilisa, Parni, 1914 ◆ Zardar Melkoni Karapetyan, Basen, Jrason, 1908 ◆ Zardar Mikayeli Mikayelyan (Harutyunyan), Basen, Sanamer, 1912 ◆ Zardar Sargsi Sargsyan, Van, Norashen, 1909 ◆ Zardar Simoni Galstyan, Daralagyaz, Yelpin, 1913 ◆ Zardar Simoni Khachatryan, Manazkert, Yeknakhoch, 1912 ◆ Zardar Smbati Hazaryan, Kars, Delbandlu, 1912 ◆ Zardar Tigrani Tigranyan, Bulanagh, Khotanlu, 1909 ◆ Zardar Varosi Hakobyan, Kars, Berna, 1913 ◆ Zardarik Poghosi Zakaryan, Nukhi, Aghblki, 1911 ◆ Zare Simoni Simonyan, Bulanagh, 1915 ◆ Zargar Gevorgi Gasparyan, Nakhijevan, 1909 ◆ Zarghalam Hovhannesi Safaryan (Hovhannisyan), Kars, 1910 ◆ Zarghalam Israyeli Hakobyan, Akhalkalak, Abul, 1912 ◆ Zarik Akbari Akbaryan (Khachatryan), Leninakan, 1910 ◆ Zarik Aleki Melkonyan, Kars, Gedaksatlmish, 1908 ◆ Zarik Aleksani Aleksanyan, 1916 ◆ Zarik Arakeli Harutyunyan, Daralagyaz, Ortakand, 1909 ◆ Zarik Arami Aharonyan, Baku, 1908 ◆ Zarik Avagi Avagyan, Gharakilisa, Hamamlu, 1917 ◆ Zarik Avoyi Torosyan, Kars, Cbni, 1915 ◆ Zarik Ayvazi Sargsyan (Ayvazyan), Alekpol, Norashen, 1916 ◆ Zarik Azizi Hovhannisyan, Surmalu, Igdir, 1915 ◆ Zarik Danieli Danielyan (Muradyan), Kars, Bulanagh, 1916 ◆ Zarik Danieli Hovhannisyan, Alashkert, Chamrlu, 1913 ◆ Zarik Galusti Galstyan, Etchmiadzin, Gecharlu, 1914 ◆ Zarik Gaspari Sahakyan, Van, 1916 ◆ Zarik Gevorgi Ter-Sargsyan, Bulanagh, Yonjalu, 1914 ◆ Zarik Ghukasi Ghukasyan (Barseghyan) (Hakobyan), Basen, Tarkhosh, 1914 ◆ Zarik Grigori Harutyunyan, Erzrum, 1915 ◆ Zarik Grigori Manukyan, Kars, Araz, 1912 ◆ Zarik Hakobi Hakobyan, 1918 ◆ Zarik Hakobi Hakobyan, 1919 ◆ Zarik Hakobi Hakobyan, Darachichak, 1914 ◆ Zarik Hakobi Manukyan, Erzrum, 1912 ◆ Zarik Harutyuni Karapetyan, Kars, Zochi, 1909 ◆ Zarik Hayrapeti Poghosyan, Nakhijevan, 1914 ◆ Zarik Hovaki Hovsepyan, Leninakan, Bozdoghan, 1913 ◆ Zarik Hovhannesi Safaryan (Hovhannisyan), Alekpol, Sirvangyugh, 1916 ◆ Zarik Hovsepi Gevorgyan, Bitlis, 1909 ◆ Zarik Karapeti Harutyunyan (Karapetyan), Shirak, Boghazkasan, 1913 ◆ Zarik Karapeti Karapetyan, Kars, 1911 ◆ Zarik Kerobi Chakhoyan, Alekpol, Pokr Sariar, 1912 ◆ Zarik Khachoyi Davtyan (Ghazaryan), Gandzak, 1914 ◆ Zarik Khachoyi Hambaryan, Alekpol, Khli Gharakilis, 1914 ◆ Zarik Khosrovi Sargsyan (Khosrovyan), Van, 1913 ◆ Zarik Levoni Levonyan, Ghapan, Kavart, 1918 ◆ Zarik Manuki Manukyan, Van, Kharberd, 1915 ◆ Zarik Martirosi Davtyan, Sarighamish, Cholakhlu, 1911 ◆ Zarik Mayili Azizyan (Mayilyan), Nakhijevan, Nors, 1913 ◆ Zarik Meliki Melikyan, Alashkert, Iritsu, 1914 ◆ Zarik Mikayeli Vardanyan, Akhalkalak, Mec Gentira, 1910 ◆ Zarik Mkhitari Mkhitaryan, Bulanagh, Kharaghl, 1910 ◆ Zarik Mkrtchi Khachatryan, Nakhijevan, Jahuk, 1916 ◆ Zarik Musheghi Musheghyan, Van, Abagha, 1911 ◆ Zarik Nikolayi Tatoyan (Davtyan), Nor Bayazet, Pashakyand, 1911 ◆ Zarik Nshani Nshanyan, Van, Ghortul, 1912 ◆ Zarik Petrosi Simonyan, Erzrum, Bayazet, 1908 ◆ Zarik Safari Safaryan, Yerevan, 1914 ◆ Zarik Samsoni Samsonyan, Yerevan, Hankavan, 1916 ◆ Zarik Serobi Serobyan, Manazkert, Kasmik, 1912 ◆ Zarik Vagharshaki Sirakanyan, Akhalkalak, Mec Gendira, 1911 ◆ Zarkhalam Gevorgi Khachikyan (Khachaturyan), Alashkert, Gharakilisa, 1914 ◆ Zarman Harutyuni Harutyunyan, Alekpol, Aghin, 1912 ◆ Zarman Knyazi Manukyan, Kars, Ghzlchakhchakh, 1912 ◆ Zarmandukht Bagrati Yesayan, Yerevan, Norashen, 1914 ◆ Zarmandukht Geghami Avetisyan (Geghamyan), Ghamarlu, Yuva, 1915 ◆ Zarmandukht Karapeti Karapetyan, Yerevan, Aylabad, 1913 ◆ Zarnushan Vardani Avetisyan, Lori, Uzunlar, 1920 ◆ Zaro Daviti Khachatryan, Alekpol, Toparlu, 1913 ◆ Zaruhi (Zarik) Levoni Levonyan, Alekpol, Shazli, 1916 ◆ Zaruhi (Zarik) Movsesi Ashkheyan, Kars, Bvek, 1912 ◆ Zaruhi (Zarik) Tadevosi Manukyan, Kars, Cbni, 1911 ◆ Zaruhi Arakeli Arakelyan, Alekpol, Chroksan, 1913 ◆ Zaruhi Arakeli Arakelyan, Van, Aljavaz, 1913 ◆ Zaruhi Artashesi Ter-Nikoghosyan, Kars, 1914 ◆ Zaruhi Barseghi Dasoyan, Bulanagh, Yonjalu, 1910 ◆ Zaruhi Galusti Poghosyan, Akhalkalak, Araga, 1913 ◆ Zaruhi Gevorgi Avetisyan, Erzrum, Terjan, 1913 ◆ Zaruhi Ghazari Ghazaryan (Barseghyan), Van, Karchkan, 1909 ◆ Zaruhi Ghazari Stepanyan (Ghazaryan), Van, 1912 ◆ Zaruhi Grigori Hakobyan, Archesh, Soskon, 1909 ◆ Zaruhi Hakobi Hakobyan, Yerevan, 1916 ◆ Zaruhi Harutyuni Harutyunyan, Van, Shatakh, 1911 ◆ Zaruhi Harutyuni Petrosyan, Sarighamish, Ghoshakilisa, 1909 ◆ Zaruhi Harutyuni Zakaryan (Harutyunyan), Aparan, Mulik, 1912 ◆ Zaruhi Hovhannesi Avagyan, Baku, 1920 ◆ Zaruhi Hovhannesi Hovhannisyan, Van, Gandzak, 1910 ◆

Zaruhi Hovhannesi Sahakyan, Leninakan, Ghapli, 1913 ◆ Zaruhi Hovsepi Hovsepyan, Van, Shatakh, 1912 ◆ Zaruhi Hovsepi Nahapetyan (Hovsepyan), Van, Mokhraberd, 1910 ◆ Zaruhi Israyeli Martirosyan, Kars, Hopveran, 1913 ◆ Zaruhi Martirosi Grigoryan (Martirosyan), Kars, Bayghara, 1912 ◆ Zaruhi Melkoni Avetisyan (Melkonyan), Van, Gisane, 1910 ◆ Zaruhi Minasi Minasyan, Van, 1918 ◆ Zaruhi Mkhitari Mkhitaryan, Mush, Machtli, 1911 ◆ Zaruhi Mkrtchi Sargsyan (Mkrtchyan), Bulanagh, Takarlu, 1914 ◆ Zaruhi Muradi Tumasyan, Akhlat, Kamurj, 1909 ◆ Zaruhi Nshani Ter-Torosyan, Erzrum, Terjan, Khach, 1911 ◆ Zaruhi Petrosi Petrosyan, Erzrum, Tandzi, 1912 ◆ Zaruhi Rubeni Hovhannisyan (Rubenyan), Vaspurakan, Archesh, 1912 ◆ Zaruhi Rubeni Shahnazaryan, Bayburt, 1911 ◆ Zaruhi Sahaki Sahakyan, Tiflis, 1918 ◆ Zaruhi Sahaki Tonakanyan, Akhalkalak, Olaver, 1910 ◆ Zaruhi Sedraki Mkrtchyan, Basen, Khzviran, 1914 ◆ Zaruhi Shaheni Shahinyan, Van, Aljavaz, 1914 ◆ Zaruhi Sisaki Sisakyan, Van, Khoshab, 1911 ◆ Zaruhi Tadevosi Martirosyan, Yerevan, 1909 ◆ Zaruhi Yeghiazari Harutyunyan (Yeghiazaryan), Van, Dlul, 1912 ◆ Zaruhi Yegori Simonyan, Alekpol, Tashghala, 1914 ◆ Zaruhi Yervandi Yervandyan, Yerevan, Sardarabad, 1911 ◆ Zarzalam Petrosi Hovhannisyan, Kars, Chirgha, 1910 ◆ Zarzand Andreasi (Grigoryan) Kirakosyan, Basen, Khzviran, 1912 ◆ Zarzand Geghami Sukiasyan, Kars, Ortaghala, 1916 ◆ Zarzand Israyeli Gevorgyan, Basen, Gharaghl, 1912 ◆ Zarzand Karapeti Mkrtchyan (Karapetyan), Alashkert, Gharakilisa, 1913 ◆ Zarzand Karapeti Simonyan (Muradyan), Bulanagh, Kabul, 1912 ◆ Zarzand Khachaturi Arakelyan (Petrosyan), Bulanagh, Bostankand, 1915 ◆ Zarzand Martirosi Tonoyan, Manazkert, Khasmik, 1914 ◆ Zarzand Sedraki Vardanyan (Sedrakyan), Alashkert, 1915 ◆ Zarzand Vasili Sakoyan, Alashkert, Mankasar, 1915 ◆ Zaven (Gegham) Ghazari Ghazaryan, Kars, Ghzlchakhchakh, 1914 ◆ Zaven Avetisi Movsisyan (Avetisyan), Nakhijevan, Kznut, 1913 ◆ Zaven Gevorgi Minasyan (Gevorgyan), Samrlu, Koghp, 1916 ◆ Zaven Ghazari Sargsyan, Leninakan, Gyulibulagh, 1914 ◆ Zaven Harutyuni Arakelyan, Shirak, Mavrak, 1913 ◆ Zaven Hayrapeti Antonyan, Yerevan, 1911 ◆ Zaven Hlghati Hlghatyan, Mush, Drmed, 1913 ◆ Zaven Hovsepi Hovsepyan, Basen, Archagh, 1916 ◆ Zaven Karapeti Aslanyan, Kars, 1910 ◆ Zaven Mamikoni Zakaryan, Kghi, Lichik, 1911 ◆ Zaven Melkoni Gevorgyan, Igdir, 1915 ◆ Zaven Mnatsakani Grigoryan (Petrosyan), Kars, Ortakilisa, 1914 ◆ Zaven Nersesi Vardanyan, Van, Boshants, 1914 ◆ Zaven Petrosi Khachatryan (Petrosyan), Van, 1914 ◆ Zaven Yeranosi Avetisyan, Mush, Vardikhagh, 1912 ◆ Zaven Zadoyi Hovhannisyan, Shirak, Ghanlija, 1914 ◆ Zazik Vardani Soghomonyan, Mush, Teghut, 1909 ◆ Zebet Hakobi Movsisyan (Hakobyan), Kars, Mavrak, 1916 ◆ Zebet Sahaki Hovhannisyan, Kars, Gedikhatrmish, 1908 ◆ Zebet Stepani Gasparyan (Stepanyan), Alekpol, Paltlu, 1914 ◆ Zebetia Hovhannesi Gasparyan, Ardahan, Sasatel, 1910 ◆ Zelfo Grigori Grigoryan, Bulanagh, Khoshgeldi, 1913 ◆ Zenivar Kostani Tigranyan (Kostanyan), Akhalkalak, Karcakh, 1918 ◆ Zepyur (Khanum) Asaturi Khachatryan, Trabzon, Sheyran, 1914 ◆ Zeytun Manuki Levonyan (Manukyan), Aparan, 1915 ◆ Zhenik Ghukasi Karapetyan, Van, Vostan, 1916 ◆ Zhenik Melkoni Semerjyan, Van, 1911 ◆ Zhenya Anushavani Zhamharyan, 1921 ◆ Zhenya Armenaki (Mkrtchi) Armenakyan (Mkrtchyan), Bitlis, 1908 ◆ Zhenya Baghdasari Baghdasaryan, Karabagh, Shushi, 1916 ◆ Zhenya Ghukasi Harutyunyan, Van, Hatalan, 1912 ◆ Zhenya Hambardzumi Ghabuzyan, Gandzak, 1912 ◆ Zhenya Khachaturi Mirmiryan, Baku, 1916 ◆ Zhenya Mkrtchi Karapetyan, Van, 1909 ◆ Zhirayr Hovhannesi Hovhannisyan, Basen, Bashgyugh, 1914 ◆ Zhirayr Mkhitari Grigoryan, Sarighamish, Hopveran, 1910 ◆ Zhirayr Simoni Mtoyan, Basen, Khzveran, 1910 ◆ Zhirayr Soghomoni Sargsyan, Kaghzvan, 1913 ◆ Zhorzhik (Gevorg) Arshaluysyan, 1918 ◆ Zhorzhik Datayi Poghosyan, Tiflis, 1914 ◆ Zhorzhik Hakobi Hakobyan, Lori, Haghpat, 1919 ◆ Zhorzhik Hakobi Hakobyan, Shirak, Leninakan, 1917 ◆ Zhorzhik Karapeti Karapetyan, Kars, 1916 ◆ Zhorzhik Misaki Hakobyan, Baku, 1914 ◆ Zhorzhik Tovmasi Tovmasyan, Yerevan, Kyalar, 1915 ◆ Zhorzhik Vanetsyan, Kars, 1921 ◆ Zibet Sedraki Davtyan, Kars, Hamzakarak, 1912 ◆ Zilfo (Zarik) Aleksani Manukyan, Bulanagh, Hamzashen, 1910 ◆ Zilfo Sedraki Sedrakyan, Basen, Ishkh, 1914 ◆ Zilo Malkhasi Malkhasyan, Mush, Yekmala, 1909 ◆ Zina (Zanazan) Haruti Harutyunyan, Alashkert, Aza, 1910 ◆ Zina (Zmrut) Harutyuni Martirosyan, Kars, 1909 ◆ Zina Abgari Minasyan (Abgaryan), Ghamarlu, Yuva, 1917 ◆ Zina Galusti Chklyan (Galstyan), Leninakan, P. Gharakilisa, 1915 ◆ Zina Hayrapeti Mirzoyan, Van, 1913 ◆ Zina Hovhannesi Galstyan, Van, 1914 ◆ Zina Petrosi Petrosyan, Dilijan, 1918 ◆ Zina Smbati Nazaryan, Alekpol, Kyapanak, 1913 ◆ Zina Stepani Ayvazyan, Hin Nakhijevan, 1914 ◆ Zina Vardani Safaryan (Vardanyan), Bitlis, Prkhus, 1909 ◆ Zinaida Hakobi Nalbandyan, Leninakan, Horom, 1910 ◆ Zinavard Nersesi Nersisyan, Baku, Terek, 1915 ◆ Zine (Zmrut) Mkhitari Mkhitaryan (Melikyan), Bulanagh, Gharaghl, 1910 ◆ Zinnat Musheghi Margaryan (Musheghyan), Bitlis, Cghak, 1909 ◆ Zinotia Matevosi Shahinyan, Akhalkalak, Diliska, 1911 ◆ Zizik Garniki Hovhannisyan, Leninakan, 1920 ◆ Zizo Poghosi Poghosyan, Van, Yasen, 1913 ◆ Zmo Abgari Abgaryan, Basen, Gomadzor, 1916 ◆ Zmrukht Avetisi Nersisyan, Karin, Sarghaya, 1910 ◆ Zmrukht Gevorgi Hakobyan, Van, Aljavaz, 1911 ◆ Zmrukht Hayrapeti Hayrapetyan (Nahapetyan), Alashkert, 1912 ◆ Zmrukht Nahapeti Galoyan, Leninakan, Armtlu, 1917 ◆ Zmrukht Samsoni Ghazaryan, Kars, 1910 ◆ Zmrut Daviti Abazyan, Karin, S. Toros, 1909 ◆ Zmrut Manuki Mkrtchyan, Khnus, 1913 ◆ Zmrut Margari Margaryan, Van, Avrak, 1909 ◆ Zmrut Mkrtchi Gasparyan, Van, Archesh, 1914 ◆ Zmrut Simoni Grigoryan, Van, Aljavaz, 1914 ◆ Zmrut Torosi Torosyan, Erzrum, 1913 ◆ Zoghik Manuki Manukyan, Manazkert, Gharaghala, 1908 ◆ Zohra Avetisi Avetisyan, Van, Karchkan, 1913 ◆ Zohra Saghateli Saghatelyan, Shirak, Ghrdagirman, 1912 ◆ Zohrab (Ghazar) Sargsi Serobyan, Van, Nor gyugh, 1910 ♦ Zohrab (Zurab) Aleksani Aghayan, Leninakan, Samrlu, 1915 ♦ Zohrab (Zurab) Yenoki Yengoyan, Leninakan, 1908 ♦ Zohrab Aleksani Torosyan, Leninakan, Chlokhan, 1912 ♦ Zohrab Asaturi Petrosyan, Manazkert, 1915 ♦ Zohrab Barseghi Sahakyan, Kars, Nakhijevan, 1912 ♦ Zohrab Galusti Ghukasyan, Basen, Dalibaba, 1914 ♦ Zohrab Grigori Khachatryan, Sarighamish, 1908 ♦ Zohrab Harutyuni Galstyan (Harutyunyan), Gharakilisa, Bashgegh, 1910 ♦ Zohrab Harutyuni Harutyunyan, Kars, Jalal, 1912 ♦ Zohrab Hmayaki Hmayakyan (Avagyan), Basen, Gomadzor, 1913 ♦ Zohrab Kerobi Manukyan, Kars, Aksaghaz, 1910 ♦ Zohrab Khachaturi Aleksanyan, Alekpol, Jorkhan, 1916 ♦ Zohrab Kyarami Barseghyan, Alashkert, Ahmat, 1911 ♦ Zohrab Meliki Hovhannisyan, Sarighamish, Gilantap, 1910 ♦ Zohrab Mkrtchi Mkrtchyan, Leninakan, Samrlu, 1913 ♦ Zohrab Saribeki Ivanyan, Shirak, Parket, 1914 ♦ Zohrab Smbati Ter-Hovhannisyan, Alekpol, Illi, 1912 ♦ Zohrab Vasili Chakhoyan, Surmali, Bashgegh, 1913 ♦ Zohrik (Goharik) Nazari Nazaryan, Manazkert, Norashen, 1910 ♦ Zore (Kamalya) Sargsi Kamalyan, Manazkert, Rostomgedak, 1912 ♦ Zori Asaturi Asatryan, Manazkert, Berd, 1915 ♦ Zorya Hakobi Manukyan, Leninakan, Horom, 1912 ♦ Zoza Mkrtchi Zakaryan, Alashkert, Koshk, 1910 ♦ Zozan (Roza) Misaki Grigoryan, Khnus, Gobal, 1914 ♦ Zozan Hakobi Hakobyan, Pambak, Gharakilisa, 1918 ♦ Zozan Margari Grigoryan, Van, Hererin, 1911 ♦ Zulo Karapeti Khachatryan, Darachichak, 1911 ♦ Zulumat Martirosi Martirosyan, Van, 1914 ♦ Zumo Geghami Sakoyan, Kars, Ortaghala, 1913 ♦ Zuzan Grigori Hovhannisyan, Mush, 1914 ♦ Zvart Andraniki Vardanyan, Babert, Karavirak, 1908 ♦ Zvart Gabrieli Tonoyan, Bulanagh, 1909 ♦ Zvart Gevorgi Nazaryan, Basen, Dalbur, 1914 ♦ Zvart Harutyuni (Karapet) Harutyunyan (Karapetyan), Bayburt, Erzrum, 1911 ♦ Zvart Harutyuni Stepanyan, Kharbert, 1906 ♦ Zvart Hovhannesi Hovhannisyan, 1919 ♦ Zvart Karapeti Karapetyan, Etchmiadzin, 1916 ♦ Zvart Khachatyri Hakobyan (Khachatryan), Erzrum, 1914 ♦ Zvart Margari Margaryan, Bayazet, 1914 ♦ Zvart Martirosi Gasparyan (Martirosyan), Basen, Dzandzakh, 1911 ♦ Zvart Meliki Mesropyan, Van, 1914 ♦ Zvart Mkrtchi Davtyan (Mkrtchyan), Manazkert, Dugnuk, 1911 ♦ Zvart Petrosi Khachatryan, Alashkert, Mankasar, 1916 ♦ Zvart Sahaki Sahakyan, Van, Hayots dzor, 1916 ♦ Zvart Sargsi Hovhannisyan (Sargsyan), Manazkert, Tolaghbash, 1912 ♦ Zvart Tigrani Mkrtchyan (Kirakosyan), Turkey, Bulanagh, 1908 ♦ Zvart Vardani Vardanyan, Van, Archesh, 1913 ♦

LISTING OF AMERICAN & ARMENIAN EMPLOYEES ACCORDING TO DEPARTMENT & POSITION (Incomplete)

The men and women listed below comprised the group who converged on The City of Orphans in Alexandropol/Leninakan to shape an environment where orphans were to grow into citizens of Armenia. As diverse as the orphans they cared for, they originated in different parts and regions of the world and carried with them widely differing cultural, political, social, and religious outlooks. Only a handful understood the other's language. Since adjustments were frequently made in the responsibilities assigned to relief workers, the positions of some individuals changed over time; others held more than one position, while still others served at NER's other orphanages in the Caucasus as in Batum, Tiflis, Kars, Karakilisa, Karakala, Yerevan and Jalaloghli. The length of time individuals spent at the City of Orphans varied from a few months to several years, but all who are listed below were involved in the City of Orphans between 1919 and 1931, in one capacity or another.

Most American personnel were screened and approved by NER headquarters in New York. They were provided with guidelines that suggested the appropriate code of behavior for relief workers overseas. The guiding principles were honesty, respect and empathy. With the surge in the orphan population of Armenia in 1921, the number of personnel increased but their selection became more discerning and only personnel with qualifications in certain specialties were encouraged to apply.[1]

The local personnel of the City of Orphans, the vast majority of whom were Armenians, outnumbered the American relief workers and administrators appreciably. They were selected and hired by NER administrators in Armenia. Beginning July 1923, NER established the Sixth Section (S-6) for the hiring of local personnel, headed by the Director of Local Personnel and Industrial Relations. This department was responsible for the screening and hiring of prospective local employees, their salaries, supervision, transfer, discharge, housing and other related labor issues.[2]

The names, brief biographical data and photographs—the latter only rarely in good condition if available at all—have been culled from a large variety of primary sources. James Barton's compilation of personnel in his *Story of Near*

---

1. Barton 1930: 327; "Love of Service," *The New Near East*, September 1921: 4.
2. NAA 113/38/33/f.118.

East Relief, while helpful, does not indicate the locations where relief workers served in the Near East. Another list, in the June 13, 1924, issue of NER's periodic publication entitled *Team Work* includes for the most part the earlier group of American relief workers. A third source, Barclay Acheson's diaries of 1926 and 1927, mentions only a handful of individuals, as do Elsie Kimball's collection of letters. And, with only a rare exception or two these sources do not include the names of Armenian employees. A special effort has also been made to gather as much biographical information and photographs as possible about NER personnel from archives and newspapers. Small town newspapers in the U.S. were especially valuable in this respect.

In the list that follows, every effort has been made to include as many of the Armenian employees of the City of Orphans as were available for the simple reason that an enterprise as large as the City of Orphans with an orphan population of over 20,000 could not have been realized by American relief workers alone, who were generally administrators and who at their peak numbered no more than 55 individuals. Typically, tasks that needed to be performed, from the cleaning and maintenance of the physical plant to the care and education of orphans, were assigned to Armenian employees.

The 705 individuals listed below are grouped by the department or division where they worked and the capacity in which they served, arranged in alphabetical order. While most workers were single men and women, several of the American and Armenian workers also brought at least one family member with them. Family members, unless they held a position at the City of Orphans are not included in the total number of employees.

For the majority, biographical information is scant, except, at best, for basic data such as date and place of birth, educational background and other brief pertinent information, which have been included whenever available below their names, along with a small selection of sources where their names appear. When photographs have been available, they appear above the individual's name. Relatively more data was available for some relief workers, especially when they held higher administrative positions, or if they were well known figures. This group appears in multiple sources but only a few representative sources have been included. Finally, those employees whose specific roles or titles was not possible to determine or confirm, have been grouped at the end of the listing under the heading of "General Relief and Orphanage Workers." The notation (?) that appears in a handful of names indicates that the handwriting in the sources was illegible.

While regrettably incomplete, it is hoped that the compilation below may still project the wide range and variety of tasks that had to be performed to operate the City of Orphans from 1919–1931, and the men and women who performed those tasks—be they charwomen or shoemakers, nurses or teachers, school principals or orphanage managers, directors or hewers.

GENERAL ADMINISTRATION

DIRECTORS GENERAL

JOSEPH BEACH
MANAGING DIRECTOR GENERAL, NER CAUCASUS BRANCH
Born: Bangor, Maine
Graduate, Yale University
(RAC: NEF Photos Box 143; *Minutes of the Conservation Committee*, Feb.10,1930:5f.;NAA131/3/543/f.61)

ELMER ECKMAN
ACTING DIRECTOR GENERAL
ASSISTANT DIRECTOR GENERAL, NER CAUCASUS AREA
Home: Grand Forks, North Dakota
(*The New York Times*, November 11, 1920; *The Grand Forks Daily Herald*, May 12, 1920)

CALEB FLAGG
ACTING MANAGING DIRECTOR, NER CAUCASUS BRANCH
(NAA 39/1/17/f. 35; RAC NEF Photos Box 143; Acheson Diary 1926, Part 1: 135; Alpoyachyan 2005: 133)

VERONICA HARRIS
ASSISTANT DIRECTOR GENERAL
Home: Santa Cruz, California
(*The New York Times*, November 11, 1920; *Near East Relief (for Private Circulation)* June 11, 1921: 1; *The Reno Evening Gazette*, January 9, 1923)

B. L. HORN
ACTING DIRECTOR GENERAL, NER CAUCASUS BRANCH
TRAVELING AUDITOR FOR NER ORPHANAGES IN THE NEAR EAST AND THE CAUCASUS
Home: Athens, Ohio
(Andreasian 1977: 344; NAA 113/30/19 (Pt.1)/f. 11; *The Athens Messenger*, June 27, 1921; Paul Barsam Private Collection)

JESSE K. MARDEN
DIRECTOR GENERAL, NER CAUCASUS BRANCH
Physician and Surgeon by Training; Graduate, Dartmouth College and University of Michigan
Home: North Leominster, Massachusetts
(*The Silver Lake Record*, September 21, 1922)

GEORGE E. SMITH
ASSISTANT DIRECTOR GENERAL, NER CAUCASUS BRANCH
DIRECTOR OF GENERAL RELIEF
Born: Chicago, Illinois
Formerly, Assistant Division Superintendent, New York Central Railroad
(*The Chicago Daily Tribune*, July 1, 1923; NAA 113/30/19 (Pt.1) /f. 11)

ERNST YARROW
DIRECTOR GENERAL, NER CAUCASUS BRANCH
Born: 1876, London, England; Naturalized U.S. Citizen
Graduate, Wesleyan University; Hartford Seminary
Formerly Missionary in Van
(*The Edward W. Hazen Foundation*, 1940: 5–17; *The New Near East*, June 1923: 12)

DISTRICT DIRECTORS & COMMANDERS

HAROLD B. BARTON
DIRECTOR, NER CAUCASUS ORPHANAGES AND HOSPITALS
Born: 1885, Worcester, Massachusetts
Graduate, Harvard College; St. John's University, Shanghai, China
Member, Haskell Caucasus operations
Nephew of Clara Barton
(*The New York Times*, November 11, 1920; *The Boston Daily Globe*, September 5, 1920; *25th, 40th Reports, Harvard Class of 1910*)

MILTON D. BROWN
DISRICT COMMANDER
DIRECTOR, ORPHANAGES AND SCHOOLS IN ARMENIA
Born: 1889, Somerville, Massachusetts
Graduate, Columbia University; Carnegie Institute; Formerly in service of American Red Cross
Languages Spoken: English, French
(*The New Near East*, September 1923:17; RAC NEF Box 133; NAA 131/3/20/f. 67; *The Boston Daily Globe*, July 17, 1921; *The Patriot*, December 3, 1921)

ERNEST FOTHERGILL
ADMINISTRATIVE DIRECTOR, EXECUTIVE SUPERINTENDENT
Born: 1878, Germany; British by Birth
Businessman
Spoken languages: English, Russian, German, French
Married, Wife Nina Kopieva; Son, Christian
Arrived in Moscow 1920; Alexandropol 1921
(RAC NEF Box 133; NAA 131/3/20; NAA 113/30/19. (Pt. 1)/f. 11)

FRED MARGERUM
DISTRICT DIRECTOR
Home: Elizabethville, Dauphin County, Pennsylvania
(NAA 57/3/275/ff. 1–6 recto & verso; *Near East Relief (for Private Circulation)* May 22, 1921: 4)

JOHN D. MCNABB
DISTRICT COMMANDER
Kazachi
Home: Washington, DC
(NAA 113/38/7/f. 1014; *Team Work*, June 1924)

K. L. RANKIN
DISTRICT COMMANDER
ASSISTANT DIRECTOR OF EDUCATION FOR VOCATIONAL TRAINING & INDUSTRIES
Engineer
Born: 1898, California
Languages Spoken: English, French, German
Service in U.S. Navy, Los Angeles Harbor
(NAA 138/3/14/f. 198; RAC NEF Box 133; NAA 131/3/20/f. 82; NAA 113/30/19 (Pt. 1)/f. 11)

ADMINISTRATIVE OFFICERS

WALTER B. AMBROSE
CHIEF PURCHASING AGENT
Born: 1889, Baltimore, Maryland
Businessman
Member, American Red Cross
Arrived in Alexandropol August 1922
(NAA 131/1/104/f. 58)

CHARLES F. GRANT
GENERAL PURCHASING AGENT
Home: New York, New York
(*The New York Times*, November 11, 1920; *The New Near East*, July 1921: 17; *The Waukesha Daily Freeman*, May 9, 1921)

FRED LANGE
REGULATING OFFICER
(NAA 113/38/33/f. 110; RAC NEF Box 133)

CLARK D. MARTIN
EXECUTIVE OFFICER
Alexandropol, Constantinople, Yerevan, Batum
Born: Pine Grove, Pennsylvania
Graduate, University of Pennsylvania
Languages Spoken: English, French
(*The New Near East*, September 1923: 17; RAC NEF Box 133; *The Times Picayune*, December 3, 1921; *The Patriot*, December 3, 1921)

OFFICE OF HUMAN RESOURCES

THOMAS ODELL
ACTING SUPERINTENDENT OF LOCAL PERSONNEL AND INDUSTRIAL RELATIONS
(*News-Evedroppings-Rumors*: February 20, 1924: 3; RAC NEF Box 133)

RANDAL SWAIN
DIRECTOR OF PERSONNEL
Born: 1893, Ohio
Languages Spoken: English
Service in U.S. Navy
Arrived in Alexandropol August 1922
(NAA 131/3/20/f. 90)

ADMINISTRATIVE, CLERICAL & LOGISTICAL STAFF

SARGIS ASLANYAN
SECRETARY
(NAA 114/1/22/f. 67)

ANN DINGLEDINE
SECRETARY, DEPARTMENT OF HUMAN RESOURCES
SECRETARY TO DIRECTOR GENERAL
Born: 1892, Timberville, Virginia
Attended Business School
Arrived in Alexandropol 1923
(RAC NEF Box 133; NAA 131/3/20)

KENNETH DOWNER
ASSISTANT TO SUPERINTENDENT OF GENERAL RELIEF
(NAA 113/30/19 (Pt. 1)/f. 11)

LORENA B. EVANS
ASSISTANT SECRETARY TO DIRECTOR GENERAL
Born: Connecticut
Languages Spoken: English
Relocated to Alexandropol Fall 1923
Married to Dr. John Evans
(NAA 131/3/20/f. 81; RAC NEF Box 133)

DONA E. FARMER
SECRETARY TO ERNEST YARROW
Kazachi
Born: London, England
(*Team Work*, Volume 3, No. 6, June 1924)

ROBERT L. FERGUSON
STENOGRAPHER
Home: Jacksonville, Florida
(*The New Near East*, July 1921: 17)

P. O. FLOYD
ASSISTANT TO THE DIRECTOR
Alexandropol and Karakala
Home: Cuthbert, Georgia
(RAC NEF Box 133; *The New York Times*, August 12, 1926; *The Xenia Evening Gazette*, May 22, 1925)

JESSIE GOODRICH
SECRETARY
Home: New York
(*The New York Times*, December 21, 1920)

OLIVE GRAY
STENOGRAPHER
Home: London, England
(*The New York Times*, November 11, 1920; Elsie Kimball letter, January 16, 1920)

MARY HERALD
SECRETARY
Alexandropol, Yerevan, Tiflis
Born: 1887, New York
Languages Spoken: English
Attended Business School
Arrived in Alexandropol May 1923
(NAA 131/3/20/f. 84)

MIHRAN KHACHATRYAN
OFFICE CLERK
Kazachi Post Orphanage Department
Born: 1902
(NAA 113/38/14/f. 122)

ELSIE KIMBALL
SECRETARY TO COL. WILLIAM HASKELL AND DIRECTOR GENERAL YARROW
Born: 1887, Bennington, New York
Attended Holyoke College, Massachusetts
Languages Spoken: English
In Alexandropol 1919–1921; 1923–1925
(NAA 131/3/20/f. 71; *Near East Relief (for Private Circulation)* May 22, 1921: 4; Elsie Kimball Papers, Mount Holyoke College)

MARGUERITE MILNER
SECRETARY TO DIRECTOR GENERAL
(Elsie Kimball letter, August 3, 1923)

LILLIAN O'NEIL
SECRETARY
Born: 1891, Pittsfield
(NAA 105/1/2853/f. 153)

NONA TZERETELLI (Georgian)
ASSISTANT TO ELSIE KIMBALL
Born: 1903
(NAA 190/1/116/f. 91 verso, 92; Elsie Kimball letter, October 24, 1923)

OKSEN TEGHTSOONIAN
LOGISTICS
Born: 1896, Van
Attended American Missionary School in Van
Clerk, Hospital Manager for NER Yerevan in 1917
In charge of logistics at Alexandropol in 1920
(Oksen Teghtsoonian, 2003)

FINANCE & SUPPLIES

ROBERT S. BUCKALEW
DIRECTOR OF FINANCE AND SUPPLIES
Graduate, University of California, Berkeley
(*The Logos of Alpha Kappa Lambda*, December 1927: 12; *The Berkeley Daily Gazette*, June 4, 1928)

SAMUEL BORNE
DIRECTOR OF FINANCE
Home: Richmond Harbor, New York
Arrived in Alexandropol 1923
(NAA 131/3/20/f. 98)

ADELA H. CHICKERING
DIRECTOR OF PRODUCTION ACCOUNTING
DIRECTOR OF CHILD WELFARE
Home: Spencer, Massachusetts
(NAA 39/1/17/f. 26; RAC NEF Box 133; *The Spokesman-Review*, October 24, 1926)

LOWELL B. COLLINS
DIRECTOR OF FINANCE AND SUPPLIES
CAUCASUS AREA
(NAA 39/1/17/ff. 17, 23, 27; *The San Antonio Express*, July 21, 1931)

MARIE CYR
INDUSTRIAL ACCOUNTING,
Polygon
(RAC NEF Box 133)

VARDAN DARBINYAN
COMTROLLER
(NAA 114/1/22/f. 67)

ARTASHES GALIGYAN
TREASURER
(NAA 114/1/22/f. 67)

ANNE A. GRAY
ASSISTANT TO THE
SUPERINTENDENT OF
SUPPLIES
Home: Brooklyn, New York
(*The Berkeley Daily Gazette*, May 14, 1921; *Team Work*, Volume 3, No. 6, June 1924)

CONSTANCE HORSFORD
Home: Boston, Massachusetts
(*The Bridgeport Telegram*, May 5, 1921; *Team Work*, June 13, 1924)

ELISHA E. LATHROP
SUPERINTENDENT OF
FINANCE AND SUPPLIES
Home: Brooklyn, New York
(*Team Work*, June 13, 1924)

CHRISTIAN MURPHY
DIRECTOR OF FINANCE AND
SUPPLY
Born: New York
Graduate, Business School
Languages Spoken: English
Arrived in Alexandropol 1923
(NAA 131/3/20/f. 61; RAC NEF Box 133)

SAMUEL OCHS
SECRETARY TO DIRECTOR OF
FINANCE AND SUPPLIES
Born: 1902, New York
Arrived in Alexandropol August 1921
Languages Spoken: English
(NAA 131/3/20; RAC NEF Box 133)

RUBEN SHATVORYAN
MANAGER, DIVISION OF
FINANCE
(NAA 114/1/22/f. 68 verso)

HARRY H. STOCKFLETH
ASSISTANT TO DIRECTOR OF
FINANCE AND SUPPLY
(RAC NEF Box 133)

NANCY STROUD
SECRETARY TO DIRECTOR OF
FINANCE AND SUPPLY
Born: 1891, Garland, Texas
Attended Business School
Languages Spoken: English
Arrived in Alexandropol October 1923
(NAA 113/3/20/f. 79; RAC NEF Box 133)

HMAYAK YEKARYAN
PURSER
(NAA 114/1/22/f. 67 verso)

FORREST D. YOWELL
DIRECTOR OF FINANCE AND
SUPPLIES
Home, Beaver Falls, Pennsylvania
(NAA 113/38/33/f. 115; *Team Work*, Volume 3, No. 6, June 1924)

ACCOUNTANTS, BOOKKEEPERS & AUDITORS

TIGRAN ABAGHYAN
CHIEF ACCOUNTANT
(NAA 114/1/22/f. 67)

HAMBARDZUM AMERIKYAN
ACCOUNTANT
(NAA 114/1/22/f. 69)

HOVHANNES AYAZYAN
ACCOUNTANT
(NAA 114/1/22/f. 69)

CHARLES CLARK
ACCOUNTANT
Kazachi
Born: New York
College graduate
Languages Spoken: English
Married to Lilly Clark of Riga, Latvia
(NAA 131/3/20/f. 95; NAA 113/30/19 (Pt. 1)/f. 11)

ROSE EWALD
ACCOUNTANT
Born: 1884, Yonkers, New York
Attended Business School
Languages Spoken: English
Arrived in Alexandropol Summer 1922
(NAA 131/3/20/f. 92)

LISTING OF EMPLOYEES

ARAM GEVORGYAN
ACCOUNTANT
Born: 1885
(NAA 190/1/116/f. 90 verso)

VARDAN HOVAKIMYAN
ACCOUNTANT
(NAA 114/1/22/f. 69 verso)

YEPREM KOTOGHYAN
BOOKKEEPER
(NAA 114/1/22/f. 67 verso)

MKRTICH MATATYAN
BOOKKEEPER
Kazachi Post Orphanage Department
Born: 1902
(NAA 113/38/14/f. 122)

BLANCHE SCRIBNER
ACCOUNTANT
Home: Lansing, Michigan
(*The Charleston Daily Mail*, April 12, 1922; *Team Work*, Volume 3, No. 6, June 1924)

SHAKHPAZ SHAKHPAZYAN
ACCOUNTANT
(NAA 114/1/22/f. 68 verso)

HARUTYUN SUNETCHYAN
ACCOUNTANT
(NAA 114/1/22/f. 68)

RAYMOND K. SWANSON
SUPERINTENDENT OF FINANCE AND ACCOUNTING
Born: Minneapolis, Minnesota
Business School Graduate
Languages Spoken: English
Arrived in Alexandropol Fall 1923
(RAC NEF Box 133; NAA 131/3/20; *The Manitowoc Herald News*, December 26, 1925)

GAREGIN VARDAZARYAN
AUDITOR
Born: 1887
(NAA 190/1/116/f. 90 verso)

ROMAN ZILBERSTEIN
BOOKKEEPER
Kazachi Hospital
Born: 1896
(NAA 113/38/14/f. 121)

INTERPRETERS

EUGENE BAKHMETEV
Brother of Boris Bakhmetev, Ambassador of Russian Provincial Government to the U.S. 1917–1922
(*The New York Times*, July 22, 1920; *The Kansas City Star*, July 30, 1920)

NINA BRAILOVSKYA
(*The New Near East*, June 1922: 10)

BARGEV CHOLAKYAN
(Alpoyachyan 2005: 119)

BEATRICE (ZAPEL) DINKILYAN
Born: 1886, Constantinople, Turkey
British Citizen
Arrived in Alexandropol 1922 with Daughter Zapel to work with NER
Married, Husband in Istanbul, Son in Tiflis
(NAA 131/1/104/f. 70)

ANUSHAVAN GEVORGYAN-HARUTYUNYAN
Born: 1893, Akhuryan Village
(NAA 1191/6/1432)

TIGRAN HYUSYAN
(Alpoyachyan 2005: 118)

MANI MUSAYELYAN
Born: 1896
(NAA 190/1/116/f. 90 verso)

RUBEN SHKHYAN
Born: 1897
(NAA 113/38/14/f. 121)

PUBLICITY

ELLA JANE HARDCASTLE
Photographer
Born 1878, Niagara Falls, New York
(*The Niagara Falls Gazette*, August 6, 1954; *The Charleroi Mail*, December 19, 1924)

ORPHANAGE DEPARTMENT

ADMINISTRATORS & ASSISTANTS

MARINE ARZUMANYAN(?)
ASSISTANT TO ORPHANAGE SUPERVISOR
(NAA 113/30/19 (Pt. 1)/f. 31)

R.M. DAVIDSON
DIRECTOR
(NAA 113/30/19 (Pt. 1)/f. 11 verso; *The New Near East*, April 1922: 16)

EVELYN EASTMAN
DIRECTOR
Home: Chicago, Illinois
(*The New York Times*, August 9, 1926; Acheson Diaries 1927: 381)

OLIVIA M. HILL
ORHANAGE OUTPLACEMENT DEPARTMENT
Born: New York
In Alexandropol December 1921–1928
(NAA 131/3/20; NAA 113/30/19 (Pt. 1)/f. 11)

MAYTIE B. JOHNSON
CHILD WELFARE DEPARTMENT
Home: Burlington, Iowa
(NAA 131/3/555/f. 219; *The Spokesman-Review*, October 24, 1926)

VAHAN KARAPETYAN
ASSISTANT TO ORPHANAGE SUPERVISOR
(NAA 113/30/19 (Pt. 1)/f. 30)

MKRTICH MATATYAN
BOOKKEEPER
Kazachi Post Orphanage Department
Born: 1902
(NAA 113/38/14/f. 122)

ELIZABETH B. MAYSTON
DIRECTOR
(NAA 39/1/17/f. 16)

MARY LOUISE MORTON
ASSISTANT TO DIRECTOR OF ORPHANAGES
Born: 1885, Washington
Attended Business School
Languages Spoken: English, Some French
Arrived in Alexandropol 1923
(NAA 131/3/20/f. 55; RAC NEF Box 133; Elsie Kimball letter, October 14, 1924)

GEVORG SARGSYAN
ASSISTANT TO ORPHANAGE DIRECTOR
(NAA 114/1/22/f. 68)

VARDANUSH SHALCHYAN
ASSISTANT TO ORPHANAGE SUPERVISOR
(NAA 113/30/19 (Pt. 1)/f. 31)

MYRTLE O. SHANE
DIRECTOR
Born: 1880, Kansas
Formerly Missionary in Bitlis, Harput and Kars
In Alexandropol 1919–1922 (with interruptions)
(*The New Near East*, November 1920: 14; *Near East Relief (for Private Circulation)*, June 11, 1921: 1; *The Kansas City Star*, November 18, 1920)

DOROTHY STRATTON
DIRECTOR
Home: South Norwalk, Connecticut
(*The Spokesman-Review*, October 24, 1926; *The Monroe News Star*, January 11, 1928)

MANAGERS

HMAYAK ABRAHAMYAN
Polygon
Born: 1906
(NAA 190/1/116/f. 90 verso)

LUCINE N. AGHAYAN
Born: 1886, Kars
Languages Spoken: Armenian, Russian, Turkish, German, French, English
Formerly Supervisor, NER's Kars Orphanage #2
(Lucine Aghayan Collection, AGMI)

PARANDZEM ANANYAN
Born: 1886
(NAA 190/1/116/f. 90 verso)

SIRANUSH ASLANYAN
Born: 1907
(NAA 190/1/116/f. 90 verso)

NINA BABOVICH (Polish)
Born: 1907
(NAA 190/1/116/f. 90 verso)

YULIA BABOVICH (Polish)
Born: 1899
(NAA 190/1/116/f. 90 verso)

VARDANUSH ANDREASIAN CHERAZ
(Shown With Daughter Byurakn)
Born: 1895 Harput province
Married Vahan Cheraz in 1924
(Andreassian 1977: 184ff.; Musheghyan 1991, 2(8); Private Collection of Byuragn Cheraz Ishkhanyan)

ASHOT KHACHATRYAN
Born: 1899
(NAA 190/1/116/ff. 90, 91)

SHOGHAKAT KUBETSYAN
(NAA 113/30/19 (Pt. 1)/f. 30)

MARIAM MARGARYAN
Born: 1900, Van
Graduate, French Boarding School, Van
(NAA 681/26/1/ff. 3, 4, 5)

ARMENUHI MATOYAN
(NAA 113/30/19 (Pt. 1)/f. 30)

HRANUSH MINASYAN
(NAA 113/30/19 (Pt. 1)/f. 31)

SIRANUSH MIRZOYAN
(NAA 113/30/19 (Pt. 1)/f. 31)

TAGUHI MKRDYAN
(NAA 113/30/19 (Pt. 1)/f. 31)

HAKOB MKRTCHYAN
Born: 1898
(NAA 113/38/14/f. 122)

ANAHIT PAPIKYAN
(NAA 113/30/19 (Pt. 1)/f. 31)

YEGHISABET PETROSYAN
(NAA 113/30/19 (Pt. 1)/f. 31)

KARINE SIMONYAN
(NAA 113/30/19 (Pt. 1)/f. 30)

SHUSHANIK TER-GRIGORYAN
Born: Shushi
Daughter of Shushi Mayor
Graduate, Baku Girl's Gymnasium
Formerly Relief Worker in Armenian Orphanages and Hospitals in Tiflis, Igdir, Sanahin, Erzurum, Sarikamish, Alexandropol
(Andreassian 1977: 266; Byurakn Cheraz Ishkhanyan Private Collection)

JENYA TOROSYAN
MANAGER
(NAA 113/30/19 (Pt. 1)/f. 30)

HRACH VARDAZARYAN
MANAGER
Born: 1885
(NAA 190/1/116/f. 90 verso)

VARDANUSH YERVANDYAN
MANAGER
(NAA 113/30/19 (Pt. 1)/f. 31)

HEALTH DEPARTMENT

PHYSICIANS & SURGEONS

SAHAK ALTUNYAN
PHYSICIAN
(NAA 131/2/35/f. 9; NAA 113/30/19 (Pt. 1)/f. 31)

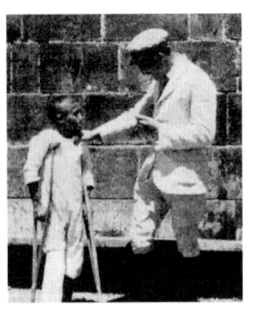

ROWLAND P. BLYTHE
CHIEF SURGEON
Kazachi
Graduate, Cornell Medical School, New York
Home: Wappinger Falls, New Jersey
(*The Cornell Alumni News. Pictorial Supplement*, October 1922; *Near East Relief (for Private Circulation)*, May 22, 1921: 4; NAA 113/30/19 (Pt. 1)/f. 11)

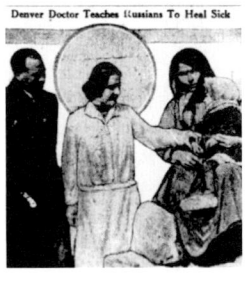

ALBERT W. DEWEY
(Standing, left)
MEDICAL DIRECTOR
Home: Denver, Colorado
(NAA 131/3/658/f. 7; *The Evening Sun*, March 13, 1929)

MABEL ELLIOTT
DIRECTOR AND ORGANIZER OF HOSPITALS AND NURSING IN ALEXANDROPOL & YEREVAN
Born: 1881, Benton Harbor, Michigan
Arrived in Alexandropol 1921
Member, American Women's Hospitals
(NAA 131/1/104/ff. 110 & verso; NAA 113/30/19 (Pt. 1)/f. 11; Mabel Elliott, 1924)

JOHN H. EVANS
CHIEF SURGEON
Born: 1877, Connecticut
Relocated from Yerevan to Alexandropol Fall 1923; NER Plenipotentiary in Alexandropol, September 1923
Languages Spoken: English
Married, Wife Lorena
(NAA 133/1/626/f. 118f.; NAA 131/3/20/f. 59; NAA 123/1/77/f. 76; RAC NEF Box 133)

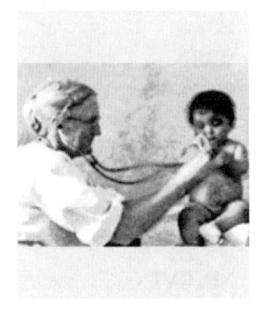

ELFIE R. GRAFF
Member, American Women's Hospitals
(NAA 113/30/19 (Pt. 1)/f. 11 verso; *Near East Relief (for Private Circulation)* October 15, 1921: 3; *400 Square Miles Covered*: 5)

BYRON M. HARMON
(*The New York Times*, July 22, 1920; *The Kansas City Star*, July 30, 1920)

(?) HARUTYUNYAN
VISITING LECTURER IN PEDIATRICS TO NURSING STUDENTS
(NAA 131/3/658/f. 7)

LISTING OF EMPLOYEES   489

JEFFERSON HAWTHORNE
PHYSICIAN
Born: 1873, Pittston, Maine
In Alexandropol from 1919 to 1920
Formerly service with British Army
1915–1919
(Leigh Hallett: 85; NAA 200/1/638/
ff. 277–279)

P. JANSEN
(*Near East Relief (for Private Circulation)*, June 11, 1921: 1)

DUDLEY C. KALLOCH
OPHTHALMOLOGIST
Born: 1884 New York, New York
Education: Bowdoin College, Brunswick, Maine; Tulane University, New Orleans, Louisiana
(*The Sewanee Alumni News*, 1952; *The Alamogordo News*, August 16, 1928; *Journal of the American Medical Association*, October 29, 1927: 151ff.)

RUSSELL B. MAIN
Home: Pine Grove, Pennsylvania
(The *New York Times*, December 21, 1920; *Near East Relief (for Private Circulation)* June 11, 1921: 1; Baldwin 1924: 149)

HAROLD M. MARVIN
Born: Florida
Formerly of Peter Bent Brigham Hospital, Boston, Massachusetts
(G. L. Richards 1923: 32–35)

ERNEST W. McCAFFREY
Born: 1869, Cambridge, Massachusetts
Languages Spoken: English
Arrived in Alexandropol Spring 1922
(NAA 131/3/20/f. 80; *The Boston Daily Globe*, May 26, 1922)

(?) MELKUMYAN
(NAA 113/38/10/f. 47)

AKOB MURATYAN
(NAA 114/1/22/f. 69 verso)

WILLIAM MURRAY
Born: 1897, Buffalo, New York
Languages Spoken: English, German, Turkish
Service as Lieutenant, U.S. Army Division, Ford Island, New York
Arrived in Alexandropol September 1923
(NAA 131/3/20/f. 88)

(?) PAPIKYAN
VISITING LECTURER ON G.U. AND DERMATOLOGY
TO NURSING STUDENTS
(Andreasian 1977: 312; NAA 131/3/658/f. 7)

ARSHAVIR PAPOYAN
VISITING LECTURER ON HYGIENE AND SANITATION
TO NURSING STUDENTS
Formerly Medical Student at Kazachi Hospital
(NAA 113/38/14/f. 121; NAA 131/3/659/f. 7)

KARAPET SARGSYAN
CHIEF PHYSICIAN
(NAA 114/1/22/f. 69; NAA 190/1/116/f. 79)

(?) SATYAN
(Nelly Musheghyan 1991, 2(8))

WALTER SISSON
CHIEF SURGEON
Married to Mary Sisson
(*The Spokesman-Review*, October 24, 1926; Acheson Diary 1926, Part 1: 188)

KHACHATUR TAMLAMYAN
(NAA 141/1/22/f. 71)

LUTVIK TER-GRIGORYAN
(NAA 131/2/35/ff. 8, 9; NAA 113/30/19 (Pt. 1)/ff. 31)

KHACHIK PARTEV TEYESYAN
(NAA 114/1/22/f. 71)

RUSSELL UHLS
OPHTHALMOLOGIST
DIRECTOR, TRACHOMA HOSPITAL
Born: 1888, Woodbine, Kansas
Married to Florence Uhls
Arrived in Alexandropol July 1921;
Languages Spoken: English
(NAA 131/3/20; NAA 113/30/19 (Pt.1)/f. 11)

CLARENCE USSHER
CHIEF SURGEON
ALEXANDROPOL AND
YEREVAN
Born: 1870
Medical Missionary in Van and
Elsewhere in Turkey
(C. Ussher, 1917; Baldwin 1925: 86;
NAA 114/1/22/ff. 10)

GALUST VOSKERICHYAN
(NAA 131/2/35/f. 7; NAA 113/30/19
(Pt. 1)/f. 31)

(?) WEBSTER
(Acheson Diary 1926, Part 1: 120)

(?) WHITE
(Elise Kimball letter, September 25, 1923)

V. YERZNKYAN
(NAA 57/3/275/ ff. 1–6; (Mihran Hovhannisyan Memoirs: 65)

DENTISTS

TAMARA MERKUROVA
(NAA 39/1/17/f. 24)

MARIAM STEPANYAN
(NAA 113/30/19 (Pt. 1)/f. 31

ZLATA TOGHENBERG(?)
(NAA 113/30/19 (Pt. 1)/f. 31)

MEDICAL STUDENTS & ASSISTANTS

ARTASHES ALEKSANDRYAN
MEDICAL STUDENT
Kazachi Hospital
Born: 1900
(NAA 113/38/14/f. 121)

SUREN CATURYAN
MEDICAL ASSISTANT
(NAA 141/1/22/f. 71)

ZOLOK(?) KHURDAYAN
MEDICAL STUDENT
Kazachi Hospital
Born: 1900
(NAA 113/38/14/f. 121)

KARAPET SHAHKHATUNYAN
MEDICAL STUDENT
Kazachi Hospital
Born: 1902
(NAA 113/38/14/f. 121)

NURSING DEPARTMENT

ADMINISTRATION

GRACE BLACKWELL
SUPERINTENDENT, NURSES
TRAINING SCHOOL,
SEVERSKI AND KAZACHI
HOSPITALS
(RAC NEF Box 133; "News-Evedroppings-Rumors," February 20, 1924: 4; NAA 113/30/19 (Pt.1)/f. 11)

ELIZABETH GILLESPIE
NURSING DIRECTOR
Home: Detroit, Michigan
Languages Spoken: English
Arrived in Alexandropol 1921
(NAA 131/3/20; *The New York Times*, November 11, 1920)

ELSIE JARVIS
NURSING DIRECTOR, NURSES
TRAINING SCHOOL
Home: Washington, DC
(*The Evening Independent*, February 2, 1927; *The Ogden Standard Examiner*, October 2, 1926; Acheson Diary 1926, Part 1: 142)

MARGARET KINNE
NURSING DIRECTOR
Born: Ovid, New York
Graduate, Syracuse University
(*The New York Times*, November 11, 1920; *The Syracuse Herald*, January 18, 1922)

LISTING OF EMPLOYEES   491

GERTRUDE H. LEGGE
DIRECTOR, NURSES
TRAINING SCHOOL, SEVERSKI
HOSPITAL
Home: Oxford, Massachusetts
Graduate, Worcester Memorial
Hospital
Served in Serbia with American
Women's Hospitals
(*The Boston Daily Globe*, May 26,
August 30, 1922; NAA 113/30/19
(Pt. 1)/f. 11)

JANET MACKAYE
CHIEF OF RED CROSS NURSES,
SEVERSKI, POLYGON
AND KAZACHI HOSPITALS
Born: 1886, Scotland; Naturalized
American Citizen
Languages Spoken: English, French
Formerly Nurse at Bellevue Hospital,
New York
In Alexandropol, 1919 to 1920; 1921
to 1929
(NAA 131/1/104/f. 45; 131/3/20; *The
Sandusky Register*, October 8, 1926,
The Oakland Tribune, November 8,
1929; RAC NEF Box 133)

EDNA F. STEIGER
DIRECTOR OF NURSING,
POLYGON HOSPITAL
Home: Williamsport, Pennsylvania
(*The Spokesman-Review*, October 24,
1926; *The Canton Daily News*, March
18, 1928)

LAURA MACFETRIDGE
DIRECTOR
EDITH WINCHESTER SCHOOL
OF NURSING,
POLYGON HOSPITAL
Born: 1889, Pennsylvania
In Alexandropol 1921 to 1929
(NAA 131/1/104/f. 61; NAA
131/3/20/f. 96; NAA 113/30/19 (Pt.
1)/f. 11)

HELEN RIORDAN
SUPERINTENDENT OF
GENERAL NURSING,
POLYGON HOSPITAL
Born: 1882, Lambertville, New York
Languages Spoken: English
Arrived in Alexandropol May 1923
(RAC NEF Box 133; NAA 131/3/20)

FLORENCE L. UHLS
NURSING DIRECTOR,
SEVERSKI HOSPITAL
Born: 1896 Fitchburg, Massachusetts
Graduate, Worcester City Hospital
Training School
Married to Russell Uhls
Arrived in Alexandropol July 1921
(*The Boston Daily Globe*, August 30,
1922; NAA131/3/20/f. 91; NAA
113/30/19 (Pt. 1)/f. 11)

INEZ WEBSTER
NURSING DIRECTOR,
POLYGON HOSPITAL
Home: Galesburg, Illinois
Graduate, Lombard College,
Galesburg, Illinois
Formerly with YMCA in France
during WWI
(*The Spokesman-Review*, October 24,
1926; *The New Near East*, September
1923:17)

NURSES

ZABEL AMIRYAN
Severski Hospital
Graduate, Severski Nurses Training
School
(NAA 154/1/60/f. 6)

LUSYA ASLANYAN
Severski Hospital
Graduate, Severski Nurses Training
School
(NAA 154/1/60/f. 6)

TIGRANUHI BARKHUDARYAN
Severski Hospital
Graduate, Severski Nurses Training
School
(NAA 154/1/60/f. 6)

MARIAM ERAMLYAN
Severski Hospital
Graduate, Severski Nurses Training
School
(NAA 154/1/60/f. 6)

ALMA FOSSOM
Born: 1886, Wallingford, Iowa
Education: St. Olaf College, City
and County Hospitals in St. Paul,
Minnesota
Brother: L. O. Fossum, NER District
Commander in Yerevan
(*The New York Times*, December 21,
1920; *Lutheran Mideast Development*)

VARDUSH GALSTYAN
Severski Hospital
Graduate, Severski Nurses Training
School
(NAA 154/1/60/f. 6)

TIGRANUHI GEVORGYAN
Polygon Hospital
(NAA 39/1/17/f. 24)

SATENIK GHAZARYAN
Severski Hospital
Graduate, Edith Winchester School
of Nursing
(NAA 154/1/60/f. 7)

ARCVIK HAKOBYAN
Severski Hospital
Graduate, Edith Winchester School
of Nursing
(NAA 154/1/60/f. 7)

ASTGHIK HAKOVBYAN
Severski Hospital
Graduate, Severski Nurses Training
School
(NAA 154/1/60/f. 6)

AZNIV HAKOVBYAN
Severski Hospital
Graduate, Severski Nurses Training
School
(NAA 154/1/60/f. 6)

YEGHIS HAKOBYAN
Severski Hospital
Graduate, Edith Winchester School
of Nursing
(NAA 154/1/60/f. 7)

MARINE HARUTYUNYAN
Severski Hospital
Graduate, Edith Winchester School
of Nursing
(NAA 154/1/60/f. 7)

ELIZABETH HOLLENBECK
Severski Hospital
Home: Washington, DC
(*Team Work*, Volume 3, No. 6, June
1924)

GOHARIK KARAPETYAN
Severski Hospital
Graduate, Severski Nurses Training
School
(NAA 154/1/60/f. 6)

(?) KHORENYAN
Severski Hospital
Graduate, Edith Winchester School
of Nursing
(NAA 154/1/60/f. 7)

MARIAM KYANDARYAN
Severski Hospital
Graduate, Severski Nurses Training
School
(NAA 154/1/60/f. 7)

TSEDIK MANUKYAN
Severski Hospital
Graduate, Severski Nurses Training
School
(NAA 154/1/60/f. 6)

VARDUSH MANUKYAN
Severski Hospital
Graduate, Severski Nurses Training
School
(NAA 154/1/60/f. 6)

VIKTOR MINASYAN
Severski Hospital
Graduate, Edith Winchester School
of Nursing
(NAA 154/1/60/f. 7)

VARDANUSH MOVSISYAN
Severski Hospital
Graduate, Edith Winchester School of Nursing
(NAA 154/1/60/f. 7)

FLORENCE L. MYERS
Home: Hinsdale, Illinois
Arrived in Alexandropol 1920
(*The Chicago Daily Tribune*, January 25, 1921)

ISABEL T. NORKEWICZ
Home: Shenandoah, Pennsylvania
(*Team Work*, Volume 3, No. 6, June 1924)

ASTGHIK NSHANYAN
Severski Hospital
Graduate, Edith Winchester School of Nursing
(NAA 154/1/60/f. 7)

TEGHDSANIK PETROSYAN
Severski Hospital
Graduate, Edith Winchester School of Nursing
(NAA 154/1/60/f. 7)

KALIPSE POGHOSYAN
Severski Hospital
Graduate, Severski Nurses Training School
(NAA 154/1/60/f. 6)

LEILA PRIEST
Born: 1892, England
British Citizen, Representing the Lord Mayor's Armenian Relief Fund
Home: Detroit, Michigan
(NAA 131/3/20; NAA 113/30/19 (Pt. 1)/f. 11; *The Sydney Morning Herald*, October 16, 1924)

HAYKANUSH SARGSYAN
Severski Hospital
Graduate, Edith Winchester School of Nursing
(NAA 154/1/60/f. 7)

LUSYA SARGSYAN
Severski Hospital
Graduate, Edith Winchester School of Nursing
(NAA 154/1/60/f. 7)

RUTH STUART
Home: Boston, Massachusetts
Formerly of the Children's Hospital, Boston, Massachusetts
(*The Boston Sunday Post*, November 23, 1919; *The Anniston Star*, October 18, 1919)

BAMBICH TER-GRIGORYAN
Severski Hospital
Graduate, Edith Winchester School of Nursing
(NAA 154/1/60/f. 6)

ANNA TER-POGHOSYAN
(NAA 114/1/22/f. 68 verso)

ELENA TER-TATEOSYAN
Severski Hospital
Graduate, Severski Nurses Training School
(NAA 154/1/60/f. 6)

ELIZABETH A. THOM
Polygon, Kars and Jalaloghli
Citizen of Canada
Home: London, Canada
(*The New York Times*, November 11, 1920 and December 21, 1920; NAA 113/30/19 (Pt. 1)/f. 11; *The Daily Illini*, June 21, 1922)

SOPHIA TOKMACHYAN
Polygon Hospital
(NAA 39/1/17/f. 24)

CHANTAZ TOROSYAN
Polygon Hospital
(NAA 39/1/17/f. 24)

KATHRYN B. TUCKER
Severski and Kazachi Hospitals
Born: 1895, New York
Graduate in Science, Columbia University
Nurse Training at Presbyterian Hospital, New York
Languages Spoken: English and French
Arrived in Alexandropol August 1923
(NAA 131/3/20; *The New Near East*, September 1923:17)

494   THE CITY OF ORPHANS

HOSPITAL SUPPORT STAFF

SMBAT AVETISYAN
MEDICAL ORDERLY
(NAA 114/1/22/f. 67)

SOKRAT AVETISYAN
HOSPITAL JANITOR
(NAA 141/1/22/f. 71)

NVARD KARASEFERYAN
SECRETARY
Polygon Hospital
(NAA 39/1/17/f. 24)

STEPAN KERAKOSYAN
ATTENDANT
Kazachi Hospital
Born: 1902
(NAA 113/38/14/f. 121)

ARAM MKRTCHYAN
HOSPITAL DOORMAN
(NAA 141/1/22/f. 71)

GEVORG MURADYAN
CLEANER
(NAA 141/1/22/f. 71)

KHACHIK PETROSYAN
GUARD AND HOSPITAL ATTENDANT
(NAA 114/1/22/f. 69 verso)

MARTIN ROMCHIKYAN
SUPERINTENDENT
Kazachi Hospital
Born: 1897
(NAA 113/38/14/f. 121)

MARGAR STEPANYAN
ATTENDANT
(NAA 141/1/22/f. 71)

HOSPITAL INTERPRETERS

HAYK ABALYAN
Kazachi Hospital
Born: 1902
(NAA 113/38/14/f. 121)

ALEXANDER KHARAZOV
Kazachi Hospital
Born: 1899
(NAA 113/38/14/f. 121; NAA 39/1/17/f. 24)

MISAK SAHAKYAN
Kazachi Hospital
Born: 1895
(NAA 113/38/14/f. 121)

PHARMACISTS

OSSEP (HOVSEP) APRESYAN
ASSISTANT PHARMACIST
Born: 1899, Kars
Citizen of Persia
Arrived in Alexandropol via Kars, 1920
(NAA 131/1/104/f. 184; NAA 113/38/14/f. 121)

TIGRAN DERDZAKYAN
CHIEF PHARMACIST
(NAA 114/1/22/f. 69)

HRAND POGHNAKYAN(?)
PHARMACIST
(NAA 113/30/19 (Pt.1)/f. 31)

RUBEN VASILYAN
PHARMACIST
(NAA 39/1/17/f. 24)

PUBLIC HEALTH

DOUGLAS C. ORBISON
SUPERINTENDENT OF PUBLIC HEALTH
SUPERINTENDENT OF ORPHANAGES
DIRECTOR OF PERSONNEL
(RAC, NEF, Box 133; "News-Evedroppings-Rumors," February 20, 1924: 3; NAA 190/1/116/f. 79)

LILA STANLEY
ASSISTANT SUPERINTENDENT OF PUBLIC HEALTH
Born: 1891, Pittsfield, Massachusetts
College Graduate
Arrived in Alexandropol November 1923
(NAA 131/3/20/f. 65)

SOCIAL WORKERS

HELEN FRANCIS DONOVAN
Born: 1895
(*Near East Relief (for Private Circulation)* May 13, 1922: NAA 862/1/832/f. 32 verso)

LISTING OF EMPLOYEES   495

EDUCATION: ACADEMIC & VOCATIONAL

ADMINISTRATION

DOROTHY FRANCIS
Born: 1886, Bedford, New York
Languages Spoken: English
Arrived in Alexandropol July 1922
(NAA 131/3/20)

BELL GREVE
Born: 1894, Cleveland, Ohio
Superintendent, Alexandropol City Orphanages
Arrived in Alexandropol August 1922
(NAA 131/1/104/f. 55; *The Encyclopedia of Cleveland History*)

JOSEPHINE STRODE
Home: Berkeley, California
(*The Berkeley Daily Gazette*, October 19, 1922)

PAULINE STRODE
Home: Berkeley, California
(*The Berkeley Daily Gazette*, October 19, 1922)

H. B. ALLEN
DIRECTOR OF EDUCATION,
NER CAUCASUS BRANCH
Home: Kent, New York
(NAA 131/3/558/f. 153)

BYRTENE ANDERSON
SUPERINTENDENT
Textile and Sewing Workshops
Home: Jacksonville, Florida
(*The Washington Post*, August 7, 1922; *400 Square Miles Covered*: 3; NAA 113/30/19 (Pt. 1)/f. 11)

CORA BEACH
DIRECTOR
Kars and Alexandropol
Home: Ogdensburg, New York
(*The New York Times*, December 21, 1920; *The Frederick News Post*, November 17, 1923; *The Syracuse Herald*, May 6, 1921)

ROY L. DAVIS
DIRECTOR OF EDUCATION,
CHURCH MINISTER,
NER CAUCASUS BRANCH
Home: Monticello, Arkansas
Graduate Erskine College, South Carolina
(NAA 122/1/399/f. 31; NAA 113/30/19 (Pt. 1)/f. 11; *The New York Times*, April 16, 1922)

VARAZDAT DEROYAN (also Varaztad Deroyan)
OVERSEER OF EDUCATION, NER 1921; ASSISTANT TO NER DIRECTOR OF EDUCATIONAL INSTITUTIONS IN THE CAUCASUS, 1922
SSRA LIAISON TO NER, 1921
SUPERINTENDENT GENERAL, NER SCHOOLS, ORPHANAGES AND HOSPITALS (1919)
Born: 1887, Van
Education at Sorbonne University; University of Berlin
Translated German and French works of Philosophy into Armenian
(V. Deroyan circa 1932; V. Deroyan 2006)

THEODORE A. ELMER
DIRECTOR OF EDUCATION
Born: 1871, Fairfield, Ohio
University Graduate
Languages Spoken: English,

Adequate Russian
Formerly of the Mission in Persia
Married, Wife in Tiflis, Children in U.S.
Arrived in Alexandropol 1920
(NAA 131/3/20/f. 64; *The New York Times Special*, April 23, 1919)

EVERETT D. GUNN
DIRECTOR, VOCATIONAL SCHOOL
Graduate, University of Kansas, 1922
Married, one child
(*The Lincoln Star*, May 11, 1930; *The Logos of Alpha Kappa Lambda*, December 1927; Polygon Vocational School, RAC NEF Bound Volumes Box 134; NAA 131/3/558/f. 233)

LEONARD HARTILL
DIRECTOR, EXPERIMENTAL AGRICULTURAL PROGRAM
Born: 1886, New York
Married to Mary Hartill, son Richard
Agronomist, Head of Department of Horticulture in Farmingdale, New York
Arrived in Alexandropol March 1922
(NAA 131/3/20; *The New York Times*, April 27 and September 1, 1922; NAA 113/30/19 in (Pt. 1)/f. 11)

MARY HARTILL
Born: 1895, New Haven, Connecticut
College Graduate; Languages Spoken: English, French, German, and Russian
Married to Leonard Hartill
Arrived in Alexandropol March 1922
(NAA 131/3/20; NAA 113/30/19 (Pt. 1)/f. 11)

PAULINE JORDAN
SUPERINTENDENT OF SCHOOL FOR THE BLIND
Home: Welchville, Maine
Graduate, New York Hospital
(NAA 113/30/19 (Pt. 1)/f. 11; *The New York Times*, November 11, 1920; *The American Journal of Nursing*, October 1920: 123; RAC NEF Box 133)

HELEN MAYS
DIRECTOR OF EDUCATION
Graduate, Columbia University
(*The Saturday Evening Journal*, October 9, 1926; *The Sandusky Register*, October 8, 1926)

SAMUEL NEWMAN
AGRONOMIST
DIRECTOR OF NER INSTITUTE OF AGRICULTURE
Arrived in Alexandropol Summer 1921; in Jalaloghli, Fall 1921
(*The Sunday Oregonian*, January 22, 1922; *The Quad City Herald*, December 30, 1921; RAC NEF Box 133; NAA 113/30/19 (Pt. 1)/f. 11 & verso)

ETHYL NEWMAN
AGRONOMIST
Arrived in Alexandropol Summer 1921; in Jalaloghli, Fall 1921
Married to Samuel Newman
(*The Malheur Enterprise*, April 22, 1922)

ERNEST PARTRIDGE
DIRECTOR OF EDUCATION
HEAD, DISCIPLINARY/ UPBRINGING DEPARTMENT
Born: 1870, Ohio
Graduate, Oberlin College; Andover Theological Seminary; Languages Spoken: English, Armenian
Married to Winona Partridge
Arrived in Alexandropol 1921
(RAC NEF Box 133; *The Journal Advance*, April 9, 1936)

LISTING OF EMPLOYEES

PAUL H. PHILLIPS
AGRONOMIST
DIRECTOR OF AGRICULTURAL
PROGRAM
Home: Cushman, Montana
(*The Spokesman-Review*, October 24, 1926; NAA 113/30/19 (Pt. 1)/f. 11 verso; *The Hamilton Evening Journal*, September 20, 1926)

MRS. PAUL PHILLIPS
AGRONOMIST
(*The Hamilton Evening Journal*, September 20, 1926; *The East Liverpool Review/Tribune*, July 27, 1926)

CAROLINE SILLIMAN
SUPERINTENDENT OF
EDUCATION
Born: 1881, Connecticut
Educator/Teacher; Former Missionary in Van
Languages Spoken: English, Turkish, Armenian

Arrived in Alexandropol September 1920
(*From God's Acre*, February 2013: 23; RAC NEF Box 133; NAA 113/30/19 (Pt. 1)/f. 11; NAA 131/1/104/f. 49)

ALFRED G. SMALTZ
DIRECTOR OF AGRICULTURE
Home: Le Mars, Iowa
Member, American Friends (Quakers) Relief and Reconstruction Mission in Samara
(*The Sioux City Journal*, November 20, 1926; Alfred G. Smaltz, 1925; Elsie Kimball letter, July 9, 1925)

GEORGE WILCOX
DIRECTOR OF EDUCATION
Born: 1890, Des Moines, Iowa
Graduate: University of Iowa; Cornell University; Columbia University Teachers' College
(*The Taylor Daily Press*, August 31, 1924; *The Lancaster Daily Eagle*, August 25, 1924; *The Journal of Educational Sociology*, December 1928, 221–231)

MARJORIE JEAN WILSON
HEAD OF DISCIPLINARY/
UPBRINGING DEPARTMENT
SUPERINTENDENT OF
WELFARE AND RECREATION
Born: Albany, New York, 1895
Graduate, St. Lawrence University, New York
Languages Spoken: English
Arrived in Alexandropol August 1923
(NAA 131/3/20/f. 87; *The Spokesman-Review*, October 24, 1926; *The New Near East*, September 1923: 17; RAC NEF Box 133)

SCHOOL PRINCIPALS & SUPERINTENDENTS

ABRAHAM AYTINYAN
PRINCIPAL, POLYGON
SCHOOL #2
Born: 1880, Shushi
(NAA 131/3/543/f. 178; NAA 131/3/543/f. 22)

GURGEN EDILYAN
PRINCIPAL, KAZACHI
SCHOOLS
Born: 1885, Ijevan
Education at universities in Leipzig, Bern, and Jenna; studied with

498   THE CITY OF ORPHANS

Wilhelm Wundt, a Founder of
Experimental Psychology in Europe
Later served as first Dean of the
Pedagogical Institute at Yerevan State
University
(NAA 122/1/422/f. 2)

GRIGOR HAKOBYAN
PRINCIPAL, SEVERSKI SCHOOL
PRINCIPAL, POLYGON SCHOOL
Born: 1905
(NAA 190/1/116/ff. 91–92; NAA
113/38/33/f. 143; NAA 131/3/558/f.
152)

HAYK HOVHANNISYAN
PRINCIPAL, KAZACHI,
POLYGON SCHOOLS
Born: 1875, Meghri
(NAA 131/3/558/f. 151; NAA
131/3/543/f. 22)

NSHAN HOVHANNISYAN
SUPERINTENDENT, POLYGON
SCHOOLS
Born: 1896, Van Province
Graduate, American Missionary
School in Van
Later moved to France, Syria and
finally Cyprus where he taught at the
Melkonian School
(Kazandjian 1950: 157f.; Aghababyan
and Sahakyan 2004: 25; NAA
122/1/422/f. 2; NAA 122/2a/14/ff.
140–142)

MAGHAK SHALJYAN
PRINCIPAL, POLYGON
SCHOOL #4
Born: 1886, Van
(NAA 131/3/543/f. 136; NAA
39/1/19/f. 10; NAA 131/3/558/f. 152)

G. SHIKAHER
PRINCIPAL, POLYGON
SCHOOL #3
(NAA 39/1/19/f. 10)

ISHKHAN SHINDYAN
PRINCIPAL, POLYGON
AGRICULTURE SCHOOL
Born: 1885, Mountainous Karabagh
(NAA 131/3/543/f. 178; NAA
131/3/558/f. 152; NAA 39/1/17/f. 24)

B. TER-HARUTYUNYAN
PRINCIPAL, POLYGON
SCHOOL #5
(NAA 39/1/19/f. 10)

**T. TER-MELIKSETIKYAN
[MELIKSETYAN?]**
PRINCIPAL, SEVERSKI
SCHOOLS
(NAA 122/1/422/f. 2)

HOVHANNES TER-MIRAKYAN
PRINCIPAL, SCHOOL #2
Polygon Pedagogical Technicum
Formerly Principal of Hovnanyan
School, Tiflis
(NAA 131/3/543/f. 178; NAA
39/1/19/f. 10; NAA 131/3/558/f. 153)

BAGRAT TUMANYAN
PRINCIPAL, POLYGON
SCHOOL #2
Born: 1873, Ijevan
(NAA 131/3/543/ff. 22, 178; NAA
131/3/558/f. 232; NAA 1387/1/301/f.
3 verso)

SUPERVISORS & HEAD TEACHERS

HASMIK ARAKELYAN
HEAD TEACHER, KAZACHI
(NAA 113/30/19 (Pt. 1)/f.30)

MIKAYEL AYVAZYAN
HEAD TEACHER, KAZACHI
POLYGON PEDAGOGICAL
TECHNICUM
Mathematics and Physics
Born: Akhaltsikh, 1882
(NAA 39/1/19/f. 11; NAA 131/3/558/f.
233; NAA 122/2a/14/f.139; NAA
131/3/558/f. 233)

GAREGIN BOTIKYAN(?)
SUPERVISOR, KAZACHI
WEAVING WORKSHOP
(NAA 113/30/19 (Pt. 1)/f. 30)

MAMIKON GASPARYAN
HEAD TEACHER, KAZACHI
SCHOOLS
Born: 1895
(NAA 113/38/14/f. 121; NAA
113/30/19 (Pt. 1)/f.30)

TACHAT GHEMOYAN
HEAD TEACHER AND DRIVER,
POLYGON SCHOOLS
Sociology
Born: 1888, Bayazet
Graduate, Gevorgyan Chemaran,
Etchmiadzin
(NAA 131/3/543/f. 178: NAA
131/3/558/f. 152)

HOVHANNES MECHLUMYAN
HEAD TEACHER,
KAZACHI, POLYGON
AGRICULTURAL SCHOOL
Mathematics, Physics, German
Language
Born: 1874, Meghri
Education, Leipzig University
(NAA 131/3/543/f. 136; NAA
1191/4/1286; NAA 113/30/19 (Pt.
1)/f. 30; *The New Near East*, July
1922: 17)

(?) MELIK-ADAMYAN
SUPERVISOR OF THE
TEACHING OF ETHICS
(NAA 122/1/399/f. 31)

STEPAN NALCHAJYAN
SUPERVISOR, KAZACHI
VOCATIONAL SCHOOL
(NAA 113/30/19 (Pt. 1)/f. 30)

DAVIT PARNASYAN
SUPERVISOR, STUDENT
SELF-GOVERNMENT
Polygon Schools
Born: 1890, Mush
Graduate, Istanbul Berberian School
Languages Spoken: French, Turkish, English
Formerly at Constantinople-Bayazet German joint-stock railroad company, Anatolia; Employed by NER 1922–1929
(NAA 1191/13/708; NAA 131/3/543/f. 178; NAA 1387/1/302/f. 5)

(?) PARUNAKYAN
SUPERVISOR, POLYGON
(Araksi Pluzyan Memoirs: 18)

PARUNAK TER-HARUTYUNYAN
HEAD TEACHER, KAZACHI AND POLYGON SCHOOLS
Born: Van
(NAA 122/2a/14/f. 139; NAA 113/30/19 (Pt. 1)/f. 30)

POGHOS TER-POGHOSYAN
HEAD TEACHER, KAZACHI
(NAA 113/30/19 (Pt. 1)/f. 30)

SIRAKAN TIGRANYAN
HEAD TEACHER, POLYGON PEDAGOGICAL TECHNICUM
Born: 1875, Alexandropol
Graduate, St. Petersburg University Department of Law; Formerly Rector, Lecturer in Law and Philosophy at Tiflis and Etchmiadzin Seminaries; a founder of Yerevan State University; Minister of Foreign Affairs, Minister of Enlightenment and Member of Parliament, First Republic of Armenia; Principal, Superintendent, NER Yerevan Schools.
(NAA 131/3/543/f. 178; NAA 131/3/558/ff. 153, 233; NAA 1191/9/1017, 1018; NAA 122/2a/14/ff. 140–142)

TOROS ZHAMGOCHYAN
SUPERVISOR, POLYGON AGRICULTURAL SCHOOL
Born: 1901, Sivaz/Sebastia
Graduate, American Anatolia College, Marzvan; American Agricultural School, Salonika, Greece
(NAA 122/4/128/f. 9; NAA 131/3/543/f. 178 and f. 232; NAA 1387/1/301/f. 3 verso)

TEACHERS & INSTRUCTORS (ACADEMIC & VOCATIONAL)

HOVHANNES ABGARYAN
POLYGON AGRICULTURAL SCHOOL, POLYGON BOYS' SCHOOLS
English Language
Graduate, American School of Van
(NAA 131/3/543/f. 136, 178)

BENYAMIN AGHOYAN
POLYGON PEDAGOGICAL TECHNICUM
(NAA 131/3/558/f. 153)

SARGIS ALEMYAN
POLYGON AGRICULTURAL SCHOOL
(NAA 131/3/558/f. 152)

GEVORG ALTUNYAN
POLYGON HIGH SCHOOL
Social Sciences
(NAA 39/1/19/ff. 10 and f. 11)

ASHKHEN ALVARDYAN
POLYGON AGRICULTURAL SCHOOL
Armenian, Mathematics, Science
Born: 1895, Van
(NAA 122/4/128/f. 16; NAA 131/3/543/f. 178; NAA 131/3/558/f. 151; NAA 1387/1/302/f. 5 verso)

VARPET [MASTER] ANDREAS
(Shown with students)
POLYGON
Pottery
Born: Mush
(*The New Near East*, March, 1922: 7)

KARAPET APINYAN
POLYGON
Armenian Literature
(Dashtents 1967: 13)

TSOLAK APRESYAN
POLYGON GIRLS' SCHOOLS
Drawing, Painting
Born: Kars
(131/3/543/f. 178)

HOVHANNES ASHOTYAN
POLYGON SCHOOLS
Language, Literature
(NAA 39/1/19/f. 11)

YENOVK ATOYAN
POLYGON
Born: 1905
(NAA 190/1/116/ff. 91 verso, 92)

HAMBARDZUM AVAKYAN
KAZACHI SCHOOLS
Born: 1899
(NAA 113/38/14/f. 121)

MKRTICH AYLAMAZYAN
POLYGON
(Mihran Hovhannisyan Memoirs: 62)

MURAD AZATYAN
POLYGON PEDAGOGICAL
TECHNICUM
Physics and Mathematics
Born: 1888, Van
(NAA 39/1/19/f. 11; NAA 131/3/558/f. 153)

GALUST AVETISYAN
POLYGON GIRLS' SCHOOLS
Mathematics, Geography
Graduate, Gevorgyan Chemaran, Etchmiadzin
(NAA 131/3/543/f. 178)

PARUYR BABAYAN
POLYGON AGRICULTURAL SCHOOL, LENINAKAN CITY SCHOOLS
Singing, Dance, Music
Born: 1868, Alexandropol
Graduate, Leningrad Imperial Music Conservatory
(NAA 122/4/128/f. 23; NAA 131/3/558/f. 232; NAA 1387/1/302/f. 5 verso)

RUBEN BABAYAN
POLYGON AGRICULTURAL SCHOOL
History
(NAA 131/3/543/f. 136)

ARTASHES BADALYAN
POLYGON GIRLS' SCHOOLS
Biology, Geography
Born: Akhalkalak
Graduate, Gevorgyan Chemaran, Etchmiadzin
(NAA 131/3/543/f. 178; NAA 122/2a/14/ff. 140–142)

GALUST BADALYAN
POLYGON TECHNICUM, POLYGON GIRLS' SCHOOLS POLYGON AGRICULTURAL SCHOOL
Mathematics
Born: 1901, Van
(NAA 131/3/543/f. 136)

GALUST BAGHALYAN
POLYGON AGRICULTURAL SCHOOL
(NAA 131/3/558/f. 232; NAA 131/3/543/f. 178)

GEVORG BAYANDURYAN
Chemistry, Accounting, Geology
Graduate, Tiflis Polytechnic
(NAA 131/3/543/f. 178)

NEKTARINEH BEKLARYAN
POLYGON, SCHOOL #2
(NAA 39/1/19/f. 18)

ARUSYAK BRINDZYAN
POLYGON AGRICULTURAL SCHOOL
Russian Language
Born: 1902, Tiflis
(NAA 131/3/543/f. 136)

PHYLLIS H. BROWN
Kazachi, Jalaloghli
Agronomy
Graduate, Vassar College, New York; Michigan Agricultural College
Languages Spoken: English, French
Naturalized U.S. Citizen
(NAA 131/3/20/f. 72: *The New Near East*, September 1923:17)

GEVORG BRUTYAN
POLYGON PEDAGOGICAL TECHNICUM
Art
Born: 1888, Alexandropol
Studied at the Oskar Schmerling School of Fine Arts in Tiflis
Founding member and President of Alexandropol Association of Painters
(A. Grigoryan, *Patma-Banasirakan Handes*, 1997: 215–217; NAA 131/3/558/f. 153; NAA 131/3/558/f. 233)

NINA BUNYATYAN
POLYGON AGRICULTURAL SCHOOL
Russian Language
Born: 1907, Kars Province
Graduate, Krasnodar School
(NAA 122/4/128/f. 7; NAA 1387/1/302/f. 5; NAA 1387/1/301/f. 3 verso)

TAMARA CHTCHYAN
POLYGON SCHOOLS
Handicrafts
Born: 1902, Kars
(NAA 122/4/128/f. 5; NAA 131/3/543/f. 22)

ARTASHES DARBINYAN
POLYGON SCHOOL
Born: 1877, Alexandropol
(NAA 122/2a/14/f.139)

VAGHARSHAK DAVTYAN
POLYGON PEDAGOGICAL TECHNICUM
(NAA 131/3/558/f. 153; NAA 131/3/558/f. 233)

SUREN DRAMBYAN
POLYGON GIRLS' SCHOOLS
Armenian Language, Mathematics
Born: 1894, New Bayazet
Graduate, Gevorgyan Chemaran
(NAA 131/3/543/f. 178: NAA 131/3/558/f. 152)

HRIPSIME GABRYELYAN
POLYGON AGRICULTURAL SCHOOL
Born: 1900, Alexandropol
Graduate, Arghutyan School, Leninakan
(NAA122/4/128/f.18;NAA131/3/558/f. 151; NAA 1387/1/301/f. 3 verso)

HAMBARDZUM GALSTYAN
POLYGON VOCATIONAL SCHOOL
History, Mathematics, Science
Born: 1890, Van
(NAA 131/3/543/f. 136)

VARDUHI GARANFILYAN
POLYGON GIRLS' SCHOOLS
Home Hygiene
Graduate, American College (City Unknown)
(NAA 131/3/543/f. 178)

JOSEFINA GASPARYAN
POLYGON
Embroidery and Sewing
Born: 1882
(NAA 190/1/116/f. 90 verso)

LEVON GHUKASYAN
POLYGON GIRLS' SCHOOLS
Mathematics
(NAA 131/3/543/f. 178)

ARTASHES GRIGORYAN
POLYGON SCHOOL #2
(NAA 39/1/19/f. 18)

NVARD GRIGORYAN
POLYGON
Sewing and Dressmaking
Born: 1886
(NAA 190/1/116/f. 90 verso)

SEDRAK GRIGORYAN
POLYGON GIRLS' SCHOOLS
Anatomy, Physics, Vegetable Gardening
(NAA 131/3/543/f. 178)

SOPHIA GRIGORYAN
POLYGON GIRLS' SCHOOLS
Russian Language
Graduate, Women's Gymnasium (City Unknown)
(NAA 131/3/543/f. 178)

BAGRAT HAKOBYAN
POLYGON
English Language
(NAA 122/2a/14/f. 139)

KHOSROV HAMBARYAN
POLYGON GIRLS' SCHOOLS
Armenian Language
Born: 1895
Graduate, Nersisyan School, Tiflis
(NAA 131/3/543/f. 178)

ANAHIT HARUTYUNYAN
POLYGON SCHOOLS
Mathematics, Armenian and Russian Languages, Science
Born: 1896, Baku
Graduate, Hripsimiants Girls' School, Baku
(NAA 122/4/128/f. 17; NAA 1387/1/302/f. 5)

KHACHATUR HARUTYUNYAN
POLYGON GIRLS' SCHOOLS
Zoology, Geography, Gardening
Born: 1883
(NAA 131/3/543; NAA 131/3/543/f. 178)

ASATUR HAYKAZYAN
POLYGON GIRLS' SCHOOLS
(Also Librarian)
Drawing
Graduate, Nersisyan Gymnasium, Tiflis
(NAA 131/3/543/f. 178)

HOVAKIM HOVAKIMYAN
POLYGON GIRLS' SCHOOLS
Social History
(NAA 131/3/543/f. 178)

SOKRAT HOVHANNISYAN
POLYGON SCHOOLS
Born: 1898, Bitlis
Graduate, Polygon School
(NAA 122/4/128/f. 19; NAA 1387/1/302/f. 5)

KARMILEH IGNATYOSYAN
POLYGON AGRICULTURAL SCHOOL
Born: 1908, Van
(NAA 1387/1/302/f. 5 verso; NAA 1387/1/301/f. 3 verso)

HEGHINE ISAHAKYAN
POLYGON SCHOOL
(NAA 131/3/558/f. 232)

HARUTYUN KARAKHANYAN
KAZACHI SCHOOLS
Born: 1896
(NAA 113/38/14/f. 121)

LUSIK (LUSNTAK) KARAKHANYAN
POLYGON SCHOOLS, POLYGON AGRICULTURAL SCHOOL
Armenian, Mathematics, Science, Singing
Graduate, Polygon School # 2
Born: 1906, Van
(NAA 122/4/128/f.1; NAA 1387/1/302/f. 5)

HOVHANNES KHACHATRYAN
POLYGON
Born: 1906
(NAA 190/1/116/ff. 91 verso, 92)

GURGEN KHAZHAKYAN
POLYGON GIRLS' SCHOOLS
Russian Language
Born: Alexandropol, 1890
Graduate, Moscow Institute
Former Army Officer (Army Unknown)
(NAA 131/3/543/f. 178; NAA 39/1/19/f. 11; NAA 122/2a/14/f. 140–142)

KARAPET KHLOYAN
POLYGON
Born: 1906
(NAA 190/1/116/ff. 91 verso, f. 92)

NIKOGHAYOS KIRAKOSYAN
POLYGON GIRLS' SCHOOLS, POLYGON PEDAGOGICAL TECHNICUM
Language and Literature
Born: 1877, Leninakan Province
Graduate, Lazaryan and Gevorgyan Chemarans
(NAA 131/3/543/f. 178; NAA 39/1/19/f. 11; NAA 131/3/558/f. 153)

OHAN KYANDARYAN
POLYGON AGRICULTURAL SCHOOL
Physics, Chemistry and Mathematics
Born: 1866, Leninakan
Graduate, Nersisyan School, Tiflis
(NAA 131/3/543/f. 178; NAA 131/3/558/f. 232)

MKRTICH LORETSYAN
(Deroyan 2008: 19)

LEVON LUSIKYAN
POLYGON BOYS' SCHOOLS, POLYGON AGRICULTURAL SCHOOL
Physics, Natural History, Chemistry
Graduate, Robert College, Istanbul
(NAA 131/3/543/f. 136; NAA 131/3/543/f. 178; NAA 131/3/558/f. 152)

VARDAN MAKSAPETYAN
Born: 1892, Van
(NAA 1191/4/34)

HOVHANNES MANUKOGHLYAN
POLYGON GIRLS' SCHOOLS
Russian Language
Graduate, Leninakan Trade School
(NAA 131/3/543/f. 178)

KRISTINE MANUKYAN
POLYGON SCHOOLS
Born: 1908
Graduate, Polygon School
(NAA 122/4/128/f. 2; NAA 1387/1/301/f. 3 verso; NAA 131/3/543/f. 22)

MANVEL MANUKYAN
POLYGON SCHOOLS
Mathematics, Science, Armenian Language
Born: 1890, Van
Graduate, Van Teachers' School, 1915
(NAA 122/4/128/f. 6; NAA 39/1/19/f. 18; NAA 1387/1/302/f. 5)

SAHAK MARTIROSYAN
POLYGON GIRLS' SCHOOLS
(Substitute Teacher)
Graduate, Aghtamar School, Van
(NAA 131/3/543/f. 178)

ABRAHAM MELIK-JANCHANYAN(?)
Ethics
Founder, Leninakan Protestant Community
Born: Persia
(NAA 122/2a/14/ff. 140–142)

SOGHOMON MELIK-SHAHNAZARYAN
POLYGON AGRICULTURAL SCHOOL
Born: 1862, Shushi
Graduate, Gevorgyan Chemaran, Etchmiadzin
Writer, Historian
(NAA 131/3/543/f. 136; NAA 131/3/558/f. 232; Khachatryan 1981: 513)

ARTASHES MELIKYAN
POLYGON
Social Sciences
(NAA 39/1/19/f. 11)

NATALYA MELIKYAN
POLYGON AGRICULTURAL SCHOOL
Russian Language
Born: 1878, Gandzak
Graduate, Tiflis Girls' Gymnasium,
(NAA 131/3/543/f. 178; NAA 122/4/128/f. 22; NAA 1387/1/302/f. 5)

ARTAK MELYAN
POLYGON
Born: Tabriz
(NAA 122/2a/14/f.139)

ARTAVAZD MIKAELYAN
POLYGON GIRLS' SCHOOL
Physics, Mathematics, Armenian Language, Geography
Born: 1895, Alexandropol
(NAA 1191/6/53; NAA 131/3/543/f.178)

GEORGE MILIKYAN
KAZACHI SCHOOLS
Born: 1897
(NAA 113/38/14/f. 121)

HOVHANNES MINASYAN
POLYGON, SCHOOL #2
(NAA 39/1/19/f. 18)

HEGHINE MIRZOYAN
POLYGON SCHOOLS
Geography, Botany, Biology
Born: 1890, Leninakan
(NAA 131/3/543/f. 178)

MAMBRE MKRYAN
POLYGON SCHOOLS AND TECHNICUM
Physics, Chemistry and Mathematics
Born: 1868, Van
Graduate, Nersisyan Chemaran, Tabriz Diocesan School,
Father of literary historian Mher Mkryan
(*Akunk*, 2011: 9; NAA 122/4/13; NAA 39/1/19/f. 11; NAA 131/3/558/f. 1530)

MKRTICH MOVSISYAN
POLYGON, SCHOOL #7
Language and Literature
(NAA 39/1/19/ff. 11, 18)

SAHAK MOVSISYAN (BENSE)
POLYGON
Agricultural School
Father of writer Soghomon Tarontsi
Born: 1867, Mush
(Alpoyachyan: 135; NAA 131/3/543/f. 136; NAA 131/3/558/f. 232)

SARGIS MUBAYEAJIAN (ATRPET)
POLYGON GIRLS' SCHOOLS
Sociology, Botany, Biology
Born: 1860, Kars
Graduate, Istanbul Lyceum
Writer well known for his novel "*Djvjik*"
(NAA 131/3/543/f. 178)

TIGRANUHI NERSISYAN
(Nelly Musheghyan 1991, 2(8))

NARIMAN NIKOGHAYOSYAN
(Preacher and Gospel Teacher)
(NAA 114/1/22/f. 71)

NARGYUL (HAYKUSH) OHANYAN
POLYGON SCHOOLS
Mathematics, Geometry
Born: 1907, Tiflis
Graduate, Leninakan Secondary School
(NAA 122/4/128/f. 11; NAA 1387/1/302/f. 5)

MAMIKON PANOSYAN
POLYGON
Art
Born: 1901, Van
Graduate, Polygon School
(Alpoyachyan 2005: 137; NAA 131/3/543/f. 136; NAA 131/3/558/f. 151; Arakelyan 2007: 18)

KARAPET PAPYAN
POLYGON PEDAGOGICAL TECHNICUM
Born: 1880, Tiflis
Graduate, Nersisyan Gymnasium, Tiflis
(NAA 131/3/543/f. 178; NAA 131/3/558/f. 153)

HAYK PEYLERYAN
POLYGON SCHOOLS
Born: 1897, Istanbul
(NAA 1387/1/302/f. 5)

OLGA ROMANOFF
(*The New Near East*, July 1922: 16f.)

ARSHALUYS SAFARYAN
POLYGON GIRLS' SCHOOLS
Drawing, Painting
(NAA 131/3/543/f. 178)

ARAKSI SAFRASDYAN
POLYGON SCHOOLS, POLYGON AGRICULTURAL SCHOOL
Armenian Language
Born: 1897, Van
Graduate, Tiflis Hovnanyan School
(NAA 122/4/128/f. 20; NAA 131/3/543/f.178; NAA 1387/1/302/f. 5 verso)

ARPYAR SAFRASDYAN
POLYGON AGRICULTURAL SCHOOL
Born: Van, 1890
Graduate, Central School, Van
(NAA 122/4/128/f. 3; NAA 131/3/543/f. 136; NAA 131/3/558/f. 151)

ARTAK SAFYAN
POLYGON SCHOOLS, POLYGON AGRICULTURAL SCHOOL
Born: 1896, Van
Graduate, Van American School
(NAA 122/4/128/f. 13; NAA 131/3/543/f. 178; NAA 1387/1/301/f. 3 verso; NAA 122/4/128/f. 13)

ASTGHIK SANASARYAN
POLYGON SCHOOLS
Graduate, Tiflis Gymnasium
Born: 1902, Alexandropol
(NAA 122/4/128/f. 8; NAA 131/3/543/f.178; NAA 39/1/19/f. 18; NAA 1387/1/302/ff. 5, 6)

MKRTICH SANOYAN
POLYGON AGRICULTURAL SCHOOL
Agronomy
Born: 1893, Leninakan
(Possibly the father of playwright and literary critic, Ruben Sanoyan in Gyumri)
(NAA 131/3/543/f. 136; NAA 131/3/558/f. 152)

SATENIK SANOYAN
POLYGON, SCHOOL #1
(NAA 39/1/19/f. 18)

ARMENAK SARGSYAN (SARMEN)
POLYGON AGRICULTURAL SCHOOL
Geography, Sociology (Also Guard)
Born: 1901, Van Province
Graduate, Polygon School
(NAA 131/3/543/f. 136; NAA 131/3/558/f. 232)

VARDAN SHAHNAZARYAN
POLYGON, SCHOOL #5
(NAA 39/1/19/f. 18)

SHAHPAZ SHAHPAZYAN
POLYGON SCHOOLS
Handicrafts
Born: 1900, Van
Graduate, Van American School
(NAA 122/4/128/f. 4; NAA 131/3/543/f.178; NAA 131/3/558/f. 151; NAA 131/3/558/f. 232)

SHAHEN SHIRAKUNI
POLYGON GIRLS' SCHOOLS
Leninakan City School
Zoology and Animal Husbandry
Born: 1896
Graduate, Leninakan City School; NER Pedagogical Training Course
NAA 131/3/543/f. 178)

ASHOT SIMONYAN
POLYGON GIRLS' SCHOOLS
(Substitute Teacher)
(NAA 131/3/543/f. 178)

MKRTICH SIMONYAN
SEVERSKI SCHOOLS
Born: 1893, Alexandropol
Graduate, Gevorgyan Chemaran, Etchmiadzin
(NAA 1191/4/1286)

SARGIS SIMONYAN
POLYGON GIRLS' SCHOOL
Armenian Language
Graduate, Gevorgyan Chemaran, Etchmiadzin
(NAA 131/3/543/f. 178)

MKRTICH SIRUNYAN
POLYGON GIRLS' SCHOOLS
Chemistry
Graduate, Tiflis Polytechnic
(NAA 131/3/543/f. 178)

GURGEN STAMBOLTZYAN
KAZACHI SCHOOLS
Born: 1898
(NAA 113/38/14/f. 121)

HAKOB TADEOSYAN
POLYGON GIRLS' SCHOOLS
Physics
Graduate, Moscow University
(NAA 131/3/543/f. 178)

ISRAYEL TER-ABRAHAMYAN
POLYGON SCHOOLS
Russian Language, Mathematics, Science, Armenian Language
Born: 1895, Kars
(NAA 122/4/128/f. 12; NAA 131/3/543/f. 178; NAA 1387/1/302/f. 5; NAA 122/2a/14/f. 139)

ALEXANDER TER-HAKOBYAN
POLYGON, SCHOOL #5
(NAA 39/1/19/f. 18)

ADAMAND TER-HARUTYUNYAN
POLYGON KINDERGARTEN, SCHOOL #1
Singing, Play
(NAA 39/1/19/ff. 9, 18)

VARDGES TER-HOVHANNISYAN
POLYGON AGRICULTURAL SCHOOL
Born: 1901
(NAA 122/4/128/f. 10; NAA 131/3/543/f. 178; NAA 131/3/558/f. 151)

ZARUHI TER-HOVHANNISYAN
POLYGON SEPTENNIAL GIRLS' SCHOOLS
Russian Language
Born: 1878, Leninakan
Graduate, Tiflis Gymnasium #1
(NAA 131/3/543/f. 178; NAA 131/3/558/f. 152)

ZAVEN TER-MATEVOSYAN
POLYGON
(NAA 122/2a/14/f. 139)

MAKRUHI TER-MARTIROSYAN
POLYGON SCHOOL, POLYGON AGRICULTURAL SCHOOL
Born: 1888, Alexandropol
(NAA 122/4/128/f. 14; NAA 131/3/543/f. 178; NAA 131/3/558/f. 151; NAA 131/3/558/f. 22)

ARMENAK TER-POGHOSYAN
POLYGON SCHOOLS
Social Sciences
Born: Van
(NAA 39/1/19/f. 11)

GRIGOR TER-POGHOSYAN
POLYGON PEDAGOGICAL TECHNICUM
Armenian Language
Born: 1870
(NAA 131/3/543/f. 178; NAA 131/3/558/f. 153)

RUBEN TER-SARGSYAN
POLYGON SCHOOLS
Engineering, Algebra
Born: 1896
Graduate, Lukashin School, Polygon School
(NAA 131/3/543/f. 178; NAA 131/3/558/f. 152)

VAHRAM TERZIBASHYAN
KAZACHI AND POLYGON SCHOOLS
Graduate, Tiflis Nersisyan School
Later philologist, literary figure, historian of the Theatre Arts, Professor of the History of Theater, Yerevan State University, Researcher at SSRA Art Institute
Born: 1899, Van
(NAA 1191/3/1656; Khachatryan, 1975: 236)

ZARUHI TIROYAN
POLYGON SCHOOL #1
(NAA 39/1/19/f. 18)

ASHKHEN TUSTRIKYAN
(Nelly Musheghyan 1991: 2(8))

HAKOB TOMASYAN
POLYGON GIRLS' SCHOOLS, POLYGON AGRICULTURAL SCHOOL
Armenian Language, Mathematics, Sciences
Born: 1892, Van
Graduate, Van American School
(NAA 122/4/128/f. 21; NAA 39/1/19/f. 18; NAA 131/3/543/f. 178; NAA 131/3/558/f. 151)

TIGRAN VANYAN
KAZACHI SCHOOLS
Born: 1900
(NAA 113/38/14/f. 121)

ASTGHIK YEKANYAN
POLYGON AGRICULTURAL SCHOOL
Graduate, Alexandropol Arghutyan School
Born: 1897, Alexandropol
(NAA 122/4/128/f. 15; NAA 131/3/543/f. 178; NAA 1387/1/301/f. 3 verso)

ISAHAK ZAKARYAN
POLYGON PEDAGOGICAL TECHNICUM
Leninakan Technicum
Geography
Born: 1891
(NAA 131/3/543/f. 178)

KHAZHAK ZAKARYAN
POLYGON PEDAGOGICAL TECHNICUM
Geography
Born: 1891
(NAA 131/3/558/f. 153)

KHOREN ZATIKIAN
KAZACHI SCHOOLS
Born: 1898
(NAA 113/38/14/f. 121)

PHYSICAL EDUCATION & SCOUT TRAINING

VAHAN CHERAZ (also TCHERAZ)
SCOUTMASTER, PHYSICAL EDUCATOR, ASSISTANT TO DIRECTOR
Kazachi
Born: 1886, Constantinople
Educated in Constantinople, France and England; Spoken languages: English, Turkish, French, Armenian, Arabic
Wife, Vardanush Andreassian; daughter Byurakn, born in Kazachi Hospital
(NAA 113/30/19 (Pt. 1)/f. 31; Andreasian, 1977; Vahan Ishkhanyan, http://www.tert.am/blog/?p=10981)

TZOLAK HAYKAZYAN
TRAINER AND LEADER, POLYGON FOOTBALL TEAM
(Also Secretary and Teacher)
Born: Van, 1904
(Alpoyachyan: 126f; Aghababyan and Sahakyan 2004: 25; NAA 1191/3/1445/ff. 15–18)

LESTER RAY OGDEN
SCOUT MASTER, POLYGON, JALALOGHLI
Born: 1887, California
Graduate, University of California, Berkeley, 1918
Arrived in Alexandropol 1921
(NAA 131/1/104; Mihran Hovhannisyan Memoirs: 48–51; Garnik Stepanyan: 511–570; NAA 113/30/19 (Pt. 1)/f. 11; *Near East Relief (Private Circulation)*, June 11, 1921: 1)

ARSEN RUBENYAN
POLYGON TRAINER
(Aghababyan and Sahakyan 2004: 14)

VLADIMIR SOLDAN
TRAINER AND LEADER, SEVERSKI FOOTBALL TEAM
(Also Engineer at Polygon and Severski)
Born: Poland
(Aghababyan and Sahakyan 2004: 24f.)

VARDAN VARDANYAN
SEVERSKI TRAINER
Physical education for girls
(Alpoyachyan 2005: 118)

CONSTRUCTION & TRADES

RUSSELL H. ANDERSON
CONSTRUCTION SUPERVISOR
Severski
Home: Bridgeboro, New Jersey
Champion athlete, Wesleyan University, Connecticut
(*The Journal of the Medical Society of New Jersey*, April 1922: 120; NAA 113/30/19 (Pt. 1)/f. 11; *The New York Times*, April 16, 1922)

CLINTON W. CROW
CONSTRUCTION SUPERVISOR
Kazachi
Home: New York, New York
(*Team Work*, Volume 3, No. 6, June 1924)

BYRON D. MACDONALD
CONSTRUCTION SUPERVISOR
Severski
Home: Dorranceton, Pennsylvania
Graduate, Wesleyan University
(*The Lowell Sun*, April 15, 1922; *The Indianapolis Star*, November 20, 1921)

PETROS MERTINYAN
MANAGER
TRADES DEPARTMENT
(NAA 114/1/22/f. 69 verso)

ARDAVAZD(?) MIKAYELYAN
ENGINEER
Polygon
(NAA 57/3/275/ff. 1–6, recto & verso)

KHACHIK MKRTCHYAN
FOREMAN
(NAA 114/1/22/f. 68)

JAMES W. VAN WART
DIRECTOR OF CONSTRUCTION ENGINEER
Kazachi
Born: 1889, Michigan
Arrived in Alexandropol early 1923
Service in U.S. Army
Languages Spoken: English, adequate French and German
(NAA 131/3/20/f. 85; NAA 113/30/19 (Pt. 1)/f. 11)

TIGRAN VOSKERCHYAN
FOREMAN
Kazachi
Born: 1898
(NAA 113/38/14/f. 121)

WHITEWASHERS

AHARON MARTIROSYAN
(NAA 114/1/22/f. 68)

GRIGOR ZHAMKOCHYAN
(NAA 114/1/22/f. 67)

TINSMITHS

BAGRAT ESHILPASHYAN
Kazachi
Born: 1902
(NAA 113/38/14/f. 121)

MANUK KAZARYAN
Kazachi
Born: 1902
(NAA 113/38/14/f. 121)

VAHAN KHANCHYAN
(NAA 114/1/22/f. 67 verso)

IRONSMITHS

AGHASI ALEKSANYAN
(NAA 114/1/22/f. 67)

HMAYAK ALEKSANYAN
(NAA 114/1/22/f. 67)

VAHAN ALEKSANYAN
(NAA 114/1/22/f. 67)

TARON HAYRAPETYAN
(NAA 114/1/22/f. 67 verso)

GEVORG MINASYAN
(NAA 114/1/22/f. 68)

SUREN SHKHYAN
(NAA 114/1/22/f. 68 verso)

ARSHAVIR PANOSYAN
(NAA 114/1/22/f. 68 verso)

CARPENTERS

AVETIS ARAKELYAN
(NAA 190/1/116/f. 70)

HARUTYUN CARUKYAN
(*Hetq*, May 31, 2010)

GURGEN NAKSHKARYAN
Kazachi
Born: 1901
(NAA 113/38/14/f. 121)

AGHASI SARGSYAN
Kazachi
Born: 1899
(NAA 113/38/14/f. 121)

MKRTICH TADEOSYAN
Kazachi
Born: 1897
(NAA 113/38/14/f. 121)

KHACHATUR ZHAMKOCHYAN
Kazachi
Born: 1902
(NAA 113/38/14/f. 121)

PLUMBERS & ASSISTANT PLUMBERS

ARTASHES KHURSHUTYAN
Kazachi
Born: 1896
(NAA 113/38/14/f. 121)

SARGIS PAGHTASARYAN
Kazachi
Born: 1902
(NAA 113/38/14/f. 121)

ELECTRICIANS

HARUTYUN ALPOYACHYAN
(ALSO LOCKSMITH, PROJECTIONIST)
Polygon
Born: 1904, Fntjak Village, Zeytun
Orphan in Antura (Lebanon) Turkish Orphanage; transferred to Salonika, graduated from NER Orphanage Agricultural School
Arrived in Alexandropol 1925, employed by NER until December 1930
(Alpoyachyan 2005; Svazlian 2000: Survivor Testimony #144)

VLADIMIR KLEBANSKI
Kazachi
Born: 1900
(NAA 113/38/14/f. 121)

SERYOZHA ORTSIEV
Polygon
(Alpoyachyan: 119)

ANATOLI POGORELSKI
Kazachi Construction Department
Born: 1895
(NAA 113/38/14/f. 121)

ZAYRMAYR TER-GHEVONDYAN
(NAA 114/1/22/f. 69 verso)

TELEPHONE LINEMAN

VARDAN ROSTOMYAN
Kazachi
Born: 1897
(NAA 113/38/14/f. 121)

SHOEMAKERS, SADDLE MAKERS AND LEATHER CRAFTSMEN

MURAT DAVTYAN
SHOEMAKER
Kazachi
Born: 1896
(NAA 113/38/14/f. 121)

ARSHAK GALSTYAN
SHOEMAKER
Kazachi
Born: 1902
(NAA 113/38/14/f. 121)

GEVORG GEVORGYAN
SHOEMAKER
Kazachi
Born: 1895
(NAA 113/38/14/f. 121)

YEREM GHAMPARYAN
SHOEMAKER
(NAA 114/1/22/f. 70)

HARUTYUN GRIGORYAN
SANDAL MAKER
(NAA 114/1/22/f. 69)

MARTIROS HARUTYUNYAN
SHOEMAKER
Kazachi
Born: 1898
(NAA 113/38/14/f. 121)

BABKEN KANKANYAN
MASTER SHOEMAKER
(NAA 114/1/22/f. 70)

HAYRAPET KULIKYAN
SADDLE MAKER
(NAA 114/1/22/f. 67 verso)

ANUSHAVAN MARTIROSYAN
SHOEMAKER
Kazachi
Born: 1902
(NAA 113/38/14/f. 121)

POGHOS MINASYAN
ASSISTANT SHOEMAKER
Kazachi
Born: 1898
(NAA 113/38/14/f. 121)

TACHAT NALBANDYAN
SHOEMAKER
(NAA 114/1/22/f. 69 verso)

ARAM OHANYAN
SHOEMAKER
Kazachi
Born: 1895
(NAA 113/38/14/f. 121)

TOVMAS VARDANYAN
MASTER SANDAL MAKER
(NAA 114/1/22/f. 69 verso)

ARMENAK YEGHYAZARYAN
LEATHER CRAFTSMAN
(NAA 114/1/22/f. 67 verso)

MKHITAR ZAKARYAN
LEATHER CRAFTSMAN
(NAA 114/1/22/f. 69)

WEAVERS

HOVHANNES AVETISYAN
(NAA 114/1/22/f. 67)

KARAPET DAVITYAN
WEAVER
(NAA 114/1/22/f. 67)

GEVORG GALSTYAN
MASTER WEAVER
(NAA 114/1/22/f. 67)

MARTIROS KARPUZYAN
WEAVER
(NAA 114/1/22/f. 67)

PETROS MANUKYAN
THREAD WEAVER
(NAA 114/1/22/f. 69 verso)

MARGAR ORMANYAN
WEAVER
(NAA 114/1/22/f. 68 verso)

HAKOVB TOVMASYAN
WEAVER
(NAA 114/1/22/f. 67 verso; NAA 122/4/128/f. 21)

KHACHIK VARDANYAN
WEAVER
(NAA 114/1/22/f. 68 verso)

WAREHOUSE & SUPPLIES DEPARTMENT

ADMINISTRATION

NIKOLAI ALBAZANOV
WAREHOUSE REGULATING OFFICER
Kazachi
Born: 1897
(NAA 113/38/14/f. 122)

FRANCIS B. APPLEBEE
WAREHOUSE ACCOUNTANT
Kazachi
(NAA 113/38/14/f. 105

WILLIAM COOK
DIRECTOR OF SUPPLIES
Born: 1881 Iowa
Attended Art Institute in Paris
Married to Jeanne in France
(NAA131/3/20)

CHARLES S. HOELZLE
EXECUTIVE SUPERINTENDENT OF WAREHOUSES
(RAC NEF Box 133, *News-Evedroppings-Rumors. Athens*, February 20, 1924: 4; NAA 113/30/19 (Pt. 1)/f. 11)

MRS. C. S. HOELZLE
SUPERINTENDENT OF MEDICAL WAREHOUSE
(*News-Evedroppings-Rumors*, February 20, 1924: 4)

LISTING OF EMPLOYEES

E. C. JOHNSTON
SUPERINTENDENT OF SUPPLIES, WAREHOUSE MANAGER
(*News-Evedroppings-Rumors*, February 20, 1924: 1, 3; Elsie Kimball letter, March 21, 1925)

WAREHOUSE STAFF

MKRTICH ACHEMYAN
MANAGER OF SUPPLIES
Kazachi
(Father of well-known theatrical director Vardan Achemyan)
(Alpoyachyan 2005: 119; Andreasian 1977: 315; Andreasian and Sofenatsi 1982: 235)

ARAM ANDREASYAN
SUPERVISOR OF WOOD SUPPLIES
Kazachi
(NAA 113/30/19 (Pt. 1)/f. 31)

HAMBARDZUM AVETISYAN
WAREHOUSE CUSTODIAN
Kazachi
Born: 1901
(NAA 113/38/14/f. 122)

NIKOLAI BURTINYAN (?)
SUPERVISOR OF MILK SUPPLIES
Kazachi
(NAA 113/30/19 (Pt. 1)/f. 31)

VAHAN DARBINYAN
SUPERVISOR
Kazachi
(NAA 113/30/19 (Pt. 1)/f. 31)

GAREGIN GHEKOYAN
WAREHOUSE CUSTODIAN
Kazachi
Born: 1896
(NAA 113/38/14/f. 122)

LIPARIT GURGENYAN
Kazachi
Born: 1902
(NAA 113/38/14/f. 122)

EVAN HAKOBYAN
Kazachi
Born: 1889
Former Army Officer (Army Unknown)
(NAA 113/38/14/f. 122)

MIKAYEL HOVHANNISYAN
ASSISTANT TO WAREHOUSE MANAGER
(NAA 114/1/22/f. 67 verso)

MNATSAKAN HOVHANNISYAN
WAREHOUSE MANAGER
(NAA 114/1/22/f. 69 verso)

KARAPET KHACHATRYAN
WAREHOUSE MANAGER
(NAA 114/1/22/f. 67)

BAGRAT MELIKSETYAN
CHIEF ACCOUNTANT
Kazachi Warehouse
Born: 1888
Former Army Officer (Army Unknown)
(NAA 113/38/14/f. 122)

SAMSON NALBANDYAN
WAREHOUSE MANAGER
(NAA 114/1/22/f. 69 verso)

GHAZAR NERKARARYAN
WAREHOUSE MANAGER
(NAA 114/1/22/f. 68)

VAHAN PALYAN
WAREHOUSE HEAD
(NAA 114/1/22/f. 68 verso)

SAHAK PETROSYAN
WAREHOUSE MANAGER
(NAA 114/1/22/f. 69 verso)

ARSHAK SAFYAN
SUPERVISOR
Kazachi
(NAA 113/30/19 (Pt. 1)/f. 31)

MIHRAN SEROBYAN
WAREHOUSE MANAGER
Orphanage #2
(NAA 114/1/22/f. 71)

MELIK SUREN SHAHNAZARYAN
Kazachi
Born: 1895
(NAA 113/38/14/f. 122)

SEDRAK SEMERCHYAN
WAREHOUSE CUSTODIAN
(NAA 114/1/22/f. 68)

AKOB TER-BARSEGHYAN
WAREHOUSE MANAGER
(NAA 114/1/22/f. 67)

ARSHAK TER-GASPARYAN
WAREHOUSE HEAD
(NAA 114/1/22/f. 68)

NSHAN TER-SIMONYAN
ASSISTANT TO DIRECTOR OF KAZACHI WAREHOUSE
(NAA 113/30/19 (Pt. 1)/f. 31)

VARDAN TER-TOMASYAN
ASSISTANT WAREHOUSE CUSTODIAN
Kazachi
Born: 1902
(NAA 113/38/14/f. 122)

ARAM TURCHINYAN
SUPERVISOR, WAREHOUSE II
Kazachi
(NAA 113/30/19 (Pt. 1)/f. 31)

ALEXANDER TUTUNYAN
Kazachi
Born: 1898
(NAA 113/38/14/f. 122)

VAHAN VARZHAPETYAN
HEAD, KAZACHI
SLAUGHTERHOUSE
(NAA 114/1/22/f. 68 verso)

VARDGES VARZHAPETYAN
WEIGHER/MEASURER
(NAA 114/1/22/f. 68)

SATENIK ZATIKYAN
POLYGON WAREHOUSE
CUSTODIAN
Born: 1891
(NAA 190/1/116/f. 90 verso)

TRANSPORTATION

DRIVERS, WHEELWRIGHTS, AND FARRIERS

YEGHYAZAR AVETISYAN
FURKON [COVERED WAGON]
DRIVER
(NAA 114/1/22/f. 67)

GURGEN DANIELYAN
WAGONER
(NAA 114/1/22/f. 67)

AYVAZ DAVITYAN
CARRIAGE DRIVER
(NAA 114/1/22/f. 67)

MARGAR DAVITYAN
WHEELWRIGHT
(NAA 114/1/22/f. 67)

PANOS GRIGORYAN
FARRIER
(NAA 114/1/22/f. 67)

HMAYAK HARUTYUNYAN
DRIVER
Polygon
(NAA 39/1/17/f. 27)

STANLEY E. HOPKINS
TRANSPORTATION SERVICE
Home: Wilkes-Barre, Pennsylvania
(*The Uniontown Morning Herald*,
December 5, 1921)

GRIGOR HOVHANNISYAN
WAGONER
(NAA 114/1/22/f. 67)

EDWARD F. MARTIN
SUPERINTENDENT OF
TRANSPORTATION
Home: Wisconsin
(*The Oshkosh Daily Northwestern*,
October 31, 1921; *Team Work*,
Volume 3, No. 6, June 1924)

AVETIS MELKONYAN
WAGONER
(NAA 114/1/22/f. 68)

OHANNES MOVSISYAN
WAGONER
(NAA 114/1/22/f. 67 verso)

HARUTYUN MURADYAN
WAGON SUPERVISOR
(NAA 114/1/22/f. 68)

GAREGIN MUSHEGHYAN
WAGONER
(NAA 114/1/22/f. 67 verso)

VAHAN PANOSYAN
COACHMAN
(NAA 114/1/22/f. 68 verso)

HAKOVB POGHOSYAN
CARRIAGE DRIVER
(NAA 114/1/22/f. 68 verso)

SIMYON PURNUTYAN
WAGON SUPERVISOR
(NAA 114/1/22/f. 68 verso)

MUSHEGH SARGSYAN
WAGONER
(NAA 114/1/22/f. 68)

POGHOS SHAHPAGHLYAN
HEAD OF TRANSPORTATION
DIVISION
(NAA 114/1/22/f. 68 verso)

VAHAN VARDANYAN
WAGONER
(NAA 114/1/22/f. 68 verso)

AVETIS ZNTOYAN
WAGONER
(NAA 114/1/22/f. 68 verso)

GARAGE & STABLES

HAKOB AMRCHYAN(?)
STABLES SUPERVISOR
Kazachi
(NAA 113/30/19 (Pt. 1)/f. 31)

SHAHEN APRIKYAN
STABLES MANAGER
(NAA 114/1/22/f. 67)

MURAD KOTOYAN
STABLES MANAGER
(NAA 114/1/22/f. 67 verso)

MANUK MOMCHYAN
MANAGER
(NAA 114/1/22/f. 69 verso)

MANUK MUROYAN
STABLES KEEPER
(NAA 114/1/22/f. 68)

HAKOVB MUSOYAN
MANAGER
(NAA 114/1/22/f. 69)

HAKOVB TAPAGHYAN
ORPHANAGE MANAGER
(NAA 114/1/22/f. 68 verso)

ALEXANDER TURCHINYAN
GARAGE SUPERVISOR
Kazachi
(NAA 113/30/19 (Pt. 1)/f. 31)

MECHANICS

WILLIAM J. CRONIN
EXECUTIVE SUPERINTENDENT, MECHANIC
Kazachi, Jalaloghli
Born: 1894, New Haven, Connecticut
College Education, two years
Arrived March 1922
Languages Spoken: English
(NAA 131/3/20/f. 94; NAA 113/30/19 (Pt. 1)/f. 11; *The New York Times*, April 27, 1922; RAC NEF Box 133)

HARRY HALL
ASSISTANT SUPERINTENDENT OF AGRICULTURE & CHIEF MECHANIC
Severski
Born: 1891, New York
Arrived in Alexandropol April 1922
Served as Sergeant in U.S. Army
(NAA 113/30/19 (Pt. 1)/f. 11; RAC NEF Box 133; NAA 131/3/20; *The New York Times*, April 27, 1922)

SECURITY

CHIEF OF GUARDS

NSHAN HARUTYUNYAN
(NAA 114/1/22/f. 69)

SARGIS MANUKYAN
(NAA 1191/3/1445/ff. 224–226)

HAYRAPET POGHOSYAN
Kazachi
(NAA 113/30/19 (Pt. 1)/f. 31)

GUARDS

STEPAN ALLAHVERDYAN
(NAA 114/1/22/f. 69)

ARSHAK ARAKELYAN
(NAA 114/1/22/f. 69)

ARAM AVAKYAN
(NAA 114/1/22/f. 69)

KHACHIK AVETISYAN
(NAA 114/1/22/f. 69)

SOKRAT AVETISYAN
(NAA 114/1/22/ff. 69, 71)

GEVORG BARSEGHYAN
(NAA 114/1/22/f. 69)

YEGHYAZAR BARSEGHYAN
(NAA 114/1/22/f. 69)

KHACHATUR DAVTYAN
(NAA 114/1/22/f. 69)

LEVON GHAZARYAN
(NAA 114/1/22/f. 70)

AVETIS HARUTYUNYAN
(NAA 114/1/22/f. 69)

HOVHANNES HAYKAZYAN
(NAA 114/1/22/f. 69 verso)

SARGIS HOVAKIMYAN
(NAA 114/1/22/f. 69 verso)

LEVON ISPIRYAN
(NAA 114/1/22/f. 69)

GAREGIN KHACHATRYAN
Kazachi Orphanage Department
Born: 1902
(NAA 113/38/14/f. 122)

HARUTYUN KHACHERYAN
(NAA 114/1/22/f. 69)

BAGHDASAR KHACHIKYAN
(NAA 114/1/22/f. 69)

ARMENAK KHIKARYAN
(NAA 114/1/22/f. 69)

ZAKAR KIRAKOSYAN
(NAA 114/1/22/f. 69)

HRANT KOMITASYAN
(NAA 114/1/22/f. 69)

ARMENAK MANUKYAN
(NAA 114/1/22/f. 69 verso)

LEVON MANUKYAN
(NAA 141/1/22/f.71)

PANOS MARASYAN
(NAA 114/1/22/f. 69 verso)

MKRTICH MARGARYAN
(NAA 141/1/22/f.71)

ARTASHES MELIK-SARGSYAN
Kazachi Orphanage Department
Born: 1898
(NAA 113/38/14/f. 122; NAA 114/1/22/f. 69)

HARUTYUN MELIKYAN
(NAA 114/1/22/f. 69 verso)

ARSHAK MELKONYAN
(NAA 114/1/22/f. 69 verso)

MIHRAN MINASYAN
(NAA 114/1/22/f. 69 verso)

VARDAN NARMANYAN
(NAA 114/1/22/f. 69 verso)

HOVHANNES NERSISYAN
(NAA 114/1/22/f. 69 verso)

STEPAN PAPAYAN
NAA 114/1/22/f. 69 verso)

POGHOS SAHAKYAN
(NAA 114/1/22/f. 69 verso)

GRIGOR SALAKYAN
(NAA 114/1/22/f. 69)

HARUTYUN SARACHYAN
(NAA 114/1/22/f. 69 verso)

SEDRAK SARGSYAN
(NAA 114/1/22/f. 69 verso)

MISAK SEFERYAN
(NAA 114/1/22/f. 69 verso)

KEMAL SHAHPAZYAN
(NAA 114/1/22/f. 69 verso)

SEDRAK SHOGHIKYAN
(NAA 114/1/22/f. 69 verso)

ARTASHES MELIK
STEPANYAN
(NAA 114/1/22/f. 69 verso)

HAMBARDZUM
SURMENYAN(?)
(NAA 114/1/22/f. 69 verso)

GAREGIN TER-KARAPETYAN
(NAA 114/1/22/f. 69)

MILITIA

GEVORG HARUTYUNYAN
(NAA 114/1/22/f. 69)

HOVHANNES MURADYAN
(NAA 114/1/22/f. 69 verso)

SEDRAK MURADYAN
(NAA 141/1/22/f. 71)

POGHOS PETELYAN
(NAA 141/1/22/f. 71)

MESSENGERS & BARBERS

AVETIS AMIRYAN
MESSENGER
(NAA 114/1/22/f. 67)

YERANOS DILANYAN
BARBER
(NAA 141/1/22/f.71)

MIKAEL GHAZARYAN
BARBER
Polygon
Born: 1886
(NAA 190/1/116/f. 90 verso)

MKRTICH KUTANYAN
MESSENGER
(NAA 114/1/22/f. 69)

MAINTENANCE & UPKEEP

LABORERS

AVETIS ASLANYAN
(NAA 114/1/22/f. 67)

GEVORG AVETISYAN
(NAA 114/1/22/f. 67)

HOVHANNES BARSEGHYAN
(NAA 114/1/22/f. 67)

SEDRAK DAVTYAN
Kazachi
Born: 1902
(NAA 113/38/14/f. 121)

NSHAN GEVORGYAN
(NAA 114/1/22/f. 67)

GENERAL KONSTANTIN M.
GHAMAZOV
(AKA GHAMAZYAN,
HAMASYAN)
LABORER
Polygon
Born: 1882
Formerly Officer in Russian Imperial
and Anton Denikin's Armies,
Lieutenant General in Army of
the First Republic of Armenia;
conflicting views about date of death.
(NAA 204/1/40/ff. 38, 71;
NAA 204/1/68 part 2/f.437;
NAA 204/1/215/ff. 1, 65; NAA
1267/1/32/f. 1; Alpoyachyan 2005:
122; Vratsian 1928: 228)

MARKOS HAKOVBYAN
(NAA 114/1/22/f. 67 verso)

RASHID HAMBARDZUMYAN
(NAA 114/1/22/f. 67 verso)

GASPAR HOVHANNISYAN
Kazachi
Born: 1902
(NAA 113/38/14/f. 121)

LEVON HOVHANNISYAN
Kazachi
Born: 1895
(NAA 113/38/14/f. 121)

AVETIS HOVSEPYAN
(NAA 114/1/22/f. 67)

SEROB KALASHYAN
Kazachi
Born: 1896
(NAA 113/38/14/f. 121)

RUBEN KAZARYAN
(NAA 114/1/22/f. 67 verso)

SEDRAK KHACHATURYAN
(NAA 114/1/22/f. 67)

DAVIT KHURSHUTYAN
Kazachi
Born: 1897
(NAA 113/38/14/f. 121)

MARTIROS KUKUNYAN
(NAA 114/1/22/f. 67)

MARTIROS MALKHASYAN
(NAA 114/1/22/f. 68)

KARAPET MANUKYAN
(NAA 114/1/22/f. 67 verso)

LEVON MANUKYAN
(NAA 114/1/22/f. 68)

GRIGOR MARTIROSYAN
Kazachi
Born: 1896
(NAA 113/38/14/f. 121)

GRIGOR MKHITARYAN
(NAA 114/1/22/f. 68)

KHACHIK MKRTCHYAN
(NAA 114/1/22/f. 68)

MANUK MRTIKYAN
(NAA 114/1/22/f. 68)

KARAPET MURADYAN
(NAA 114/1/22/f. 68)

MARTIROS MURADYAN
(NAA 114/1/22/f. 67 verso)

HAKOVB OHANNESYAN
(NAA 114/1/22/f. 68 verso)

TIGRAN PAGHEKYAN
(NAA 114/1/22/f. 68 verso)

GRIGOR PAGHTASARYAN
Kazachi
Born: 1895
(NAA 113/38/14/f. 121)

HAMBARDZUM PAPAZYAN
Kazachi
Born: 1895
(NAA 113/38/14/f. 121)

NERSES PETROSYAN(?)
(NAA 114/1/22/f. 68 verso)

NSHAN SAHAKYAN
(NAA 114/1/22/f. 68)

KHACHATUR SARIBEKYAN
Kazachi
Born: 1897
(NAA 113/38/14/f. 121)

VARDAN SERUNYAN
(NAA 114/1/22/f. 68)

KIRAKOS SHAKHPAZYAN
(NAA 114/1/22/f. 68 verso)

HARUTYUN SIMONYAN
(NAA 114/1/22/f. 68)

HAKOB SOGHOMONYAN
Kazachi
Born: 1901
(NAA 113/38/14/f. 121)

MOVSES TAKULYAN
(NAA 114/1/22/f. 67 verso)

AVETIS TOROSYAN
(NAA 114/1/22/f. 67 verso)

SERVANTS

NSHAN GHUKASYAN
Kazachi Schools
Born: 1901
(NAA 113/38/14/f. 121)

MNATSAKAN MANRIKYAN
(NAA 114/1/22/f. 69 verso)

PETROS MELKONYAN
(NAA 114/1/22/f. 68)

TIRAN MOMCHYAN
(NAA 141/1/22/f. 71)

MKRTICH SARGSYAN
DINING ROOM SERVANT
Polygon
Born: 1855
(NAA 190/1/116/f. 90 verso)

HOVHANNES ZHAMKOCHYAN
(NAA 114/1/22/f. 69)

WASHERWOMEN

REHAN AVAGYAN
Polygon
Born: 1906
(NAA 190/1/116/ff. 91 verso, 92)

YALDUZ GEVORGYAN
Polygon
Born: 1907
(NAA 190/1/116/ff. 91, 92)

ZARUHI GHAZARYAN
Polygon
Born: 1907
(NAA 190/1/116/f. 90 verso)

VARDUHI GRIGORYAN
Polygon
Born: 1908
(NAA 190/1/116/f. 90 verso)

HRIPSIMIK HAKOBYAN
Polygon
Born: 1907
(NAA 190/1/116/f. 90 verso)

SIRANUSH HOVSEPYAN
Born: 1907
(NAA 190/1/116/ff. 91verso, 92)

TAGUHI MARTIROSYAN
Polygon
Born: 1907
(NAA 190/1/116/ff. 91 verso, 92)

SATENIK MATOYAN
Polygon
Born: 1907
(NAA 190/1/116/f. 90 verso)

SHUSHANIK MIKAYELYAN
Polygon
Born: 1907
(NAA 190/1/116/ff. 91 verso, 92)

VARSENIK MOVSISYAN
Polygon
Born: 1907
(NAA 190/1/116/f. 90 verso)

LUCIK MUSHEGHYAN
Polygon
Born: 1906
(NAA 190/1/116/ff. 91 verso, 92)

S. PAPIKYAN
Polygon
Born: 1907
(NAA 190/1/116/ff. 91 verso, 92)

SHOGHIK SARGSYAN
Polygon
Born: 1907
(NAA 190/1/116/f. 90 verso)

VARINKA STEPANYAN
Polygon
(NAA 39/1/17/f. 24)

WATER CARRIERS

HRAHAT ARARKTSYAN
(NAA 114/1/22/f. 69)

MKRTICH OHANNESYAN
(NAA 114/1/22/f. 69 verso)

HEWERS

MUSHEGH ASATRYAN
(NAA 114/1/22/f. 67)

MARTIROS FRINCHYAN
(NAA 114/1/22/f. 68 verso)

SAHAK GRIGORYAN
(NAA 114/1/22/f. 67)

MARTIROS HAYRAPETYAN
(NAA 114/1/22/f. 67)

ABGAR KIRAKOSYAN
(NAA 114/1/22/f. 67)

PARGEV PARONIKYAN
(NAA 114/1/22/f. 68 verso)

SARGIS PETROSYAN
(NAA 114/1/22/f. 68 verso)

MIHRAN POGHOSYAN
(NAA 114/1/22/f. 68 verso)

PETROS SARGSYAN
(NAA 114/1/22/f. 68)

ABRAHAM SRACHYAN
(NAA 114/1/22/f. 68)

NUTRITION & CULINARY

BELLE BASS
HEAD, HOME SUPERVISION
AND NUTRITION
Polygon
Born: Rome, Georgia
Formerly served in Red Cross
and YMCA in France, Siberia and
Czechoslovakia
(*The Atlanta Constitution*, February 7, 1929; *The New Near East*, September 1923:17; RAC NEF Photos Box 143; RAC NEF Box 133)

MABEL FARRINGTON
DIETITIAN, NUTRITIONIST
Graduate, University of California
In Alexandropol 1920–1921
(*The Semi-Weekly Maui News*, January 17, 1922)

COOKS, BAKERS & BUTCHERS

VARDAN ABRAHAMYAN
BUTCHER
(NAA 114/1/22/f. 67)

ALEKSAN ANTONYAN
COOK
(NAA 114/1/22/f. 69)

HAMBARDZUM ASATRYAN
COOK
(NAA 114/1/22/f. 69)

ANDRANIK AVAKYAN
BAKER
(NAA 190/1/116/f. 62)

HARUTYUN DAVTYAN
COOK
Polygon
Born: 1907
(NAA 190/1/116/ff. 91 verso, 92)

GEGHAM GALSTYAN
BREAD BAKER
(NAA 114/1/22/f. 67)

ACHO KARAPETYAN
COOK
Polygon
Born: 1907
(NAA 190/1/116/f. 90 verso)

YEGHISABET KHACHATRYAN
COOK
Polygon
Born: 1907
(NAA 190/1/116/ff. 91–92)

MARGARITE KIRAKOSYAN
COOK, 2ND CLASS
Polygon
(NAA 39/1/17/f. 24)

PAYCAR MARTIROSYAN
COOK
Polygon
Born: 1907
(NAA 190/1/116/f. 90 verso)

SARGIS MARTIROSYAN
FLOUR KNEADER
(NAA 114/1/22/f. 68)

MIHRAN PANOSYAN
COOK
(NAA 114/1/22/f. 71)

SAVAR SAHAKYAN
COOK
(NAA 114/1/22/f. 69 verso)

HAKOB SIMSARYAN
SUPERVISOR OF OVENS
Kazachi
(NAA 113/30/19 (Pt. 1)/f. 31)

HAMBARDZUM TADEOSYAN
COOK
(NAA 114/1/22/f. 69)

SEDRAK TERLOYAN
COOK
Kazachi Post Orphanage Department
Born: 1901
(NAA 113/38/14/f. 122)

SARGIS TUMANYAN
HOSPITAL COOK
(NAA 114/1/22/f. 71)

GRIGOR VARDANYAN
FLOUR KNEADER
(NAA 114/1/22/f. 68 verso)

HMAYAK ZATIKYAN
BAKERY MANAGER
(NAA 114/1/22/f. 67 verso)

KITCHEN GARDEN WORKERS

HMAYAK DARBINYAN
KITCHEN GARDEN MANAGER
(NAA 114/1/22/f. 67)

GHUKAS GHUKASYAN
KITCHEN GARDEN EXPERT
(NAA 114/1/22/f. 68 verso)

MIKAYEL MOKATSYAN
KITCHEN GARDEN MANAGER
(NAA 114/1/22/f. 68)

AVETIS VARDANYAN
GARDENER
(NAA 141/1/22/f. 71)

DOORKEEPERS & CLOAKROOM ATTENDANTS

AVETIS GRIGORYAN
CLOAKROOM ATTENDANT
(NAA 114/1/22/f. 69)

HAYRAPET KHANCHYAN
DOORMAN
(NAA 114/1/22/f. 67)

MKRTICH MELKONIAN
DOORKEEPER
Kazachi Orphanage Department
Born: 1896
(NAA 113/38/14/f. 122)

GENERAL RELIEF & ORPHANAGE WORKERS

(Specific Positions or Ranks Unknown or Unconfirmed)

(?) ARAKELYAN
Polygon
Former Officer, Russian Army
(Alpoyachyan 2005: 122)

MESROP AVETISYAN
Polygon
(NAA 122/2a/14/ff. 140–142)

RAY C. BAKER
Polygon
Home: Clyde, Michigan
(*The Spokesman-Review*, October 24, 1926)

CLARA L. BISSELL
Home: Claremont, California
Graduate, Pomona College, California
(*The New York Times*, November 11, 1920; *The Pomona College Quarterly Magazine*, June 1922: 133)

ELIZABETH CAMPBELL
Born: 1892
Arrived in Alexandropol 1922
Formerly on the faculty of Constantinople Women's College.
(NAA 131/1/104; NAA 113/30/19 (Pt. 1)/f. 11; *New Near East (for Private Circulation)*, December 31, 1921)

CHARLES CARROLL
Polygon
Home: McGregor, Iowa
(*The Washington Post*, December 27, 1925; *The Manitowoc Herald News*, December 26, 1925; *The Spokesman-Review*, October 24, 1926)

HOWARD W. CINCH
Home: Bay City, Michigan
(*Team Work*, Volume 3, No. 6, June 1924)

LILLY CLARK
Born: 1898 Riga, Latvia
Languages spoken: English, Russian, German
U.S. citizen by marriage to Charles Clark in 1920
(NAA 131/3/20; NAA 113/30/19 (pt. 1) /f. 11)

CARL C. COMPTON
(Compton, 2008: 75f.)

J. F. DANGERFIELD
(*Team Work*, Volume 3, No. 6, June 1924)

EDWIN M. DOUGLAS
Polygon
Home: East Orange, New Jersey
(*The Spokesman-Review*, October 24, 1926)

CHRISTINA DUNBAR
(*News-Evedroppings-Rumors*, February 20, 1924: 1, 3)

RAYMOND GILLMAN
Home: Mission Hill, South Dakota
(*The New York Times*, December 21, 1920; Elsie Kimball letter, June 25, 1920)

ARTHUR B. HAMMOND
Home: Newark, New Jersey
(*The New York Times*, November 11, 1920)

LEONARD C. HUBBARD
Home: Princeton, W. Virginia
(*The New York Times*, November 11 and December 21, 1920)

PETER J. JANSEN
Home: New York, New York
(*The New York Times*, November 11, 1920)

CHRISTIAN LEYTON
Home: Framingham, Massachusetts
(*The New York Times*, December 21, 1920)

EVA MAJGULYAN (?)
Polygon
Born: 1896
(NAA 190/1/116/ff. 90–91)

ANNE M. MARLIN
Home: Pittsburgh, Pennsylvania
(*Team Work*, Volume 3, No. 6, June 1924)

LUCY MARTIN
Born: 1870, Ohio
(NAA 131/1/104)

LISTING OF EMPLOYEES

SOLON P. MASSEY
Polygon
Home: Denver, Colorado
(*The Spokesman-Review*, October 24, 1926; Acheson Diary 1926, Part 1: 148)

AZNIV MAYLAMAZYAN
Polygon
(NAA 122/2a/14/ff.140–142)

HARRISON MAYNARD
Home: Topeka, Kansas
(*The New York Times*, December 21, 1920; *The Albuquerque Journal*, March 27, 1921)

CHARLES L. MCBRIDE
Home: Chicago, Illinois
(*The New York Times*, November 11, December 21, 1920)

NELSON P. MEEKS
Born: 1896, New York, New York
Graduate, Columbia University
(*The New York Times*, November 11, 1920)

ALFRED MERRITT
Home: Tacoma, Washington
(*The Arlington Times*, December 11, 1924; NAA 113/30/19 (Pt. 1)/f. 11)

EDWIN KNOX MITCHELL, JR.
Home: Hartford, Connecticut
(NAA 105/1/2853/f. 153)

ANNETTE L. MUNRO
Home: Newton, Massachusetts
(*The New York Times*, November 11, 1920)

WILLIAM W. NELSON
Home: Topeka, Kansas
(*The New York Times*, November 11, 1920 and December 21, 1920)

LOUISE B. PAISLEY
Polygon
Home: Mount Vernon, New York
(*The Spokesman-Review*, October 24, 1926)

FRANK J. W. PEERS
Born: 1891, Topeka, Kansas
(*The New York Times*, November 11, 1920)

WALTER RICHARDS
(*The New York Times*, November 11, 1920)

SUSAN SHEDD
Niece of Curtis D. Wilbur, the 19th Chief Justice of California, and in March 1924, U.S. Secretary of the Navy)
(*The Lodi Sentinel*, September 21, 1922; *The Berkeley Daily Gazette*, May 23, 1923)

LIEUTENANT GENERAL MOVSES SILIKYAN
Born: 1862, Vardashen
Formerly decorated general in Russian and Armenian armies; accountant and salesman, Alexandropol branch of Swedish Joint Stock Company, 1922; Employed by NER 1923–1929
(NAA 119/2/1956/f. 36; NAA 1191/1/ 1124/f. 37; NAA 571/5/158/f. 17; Ruben Sahakyan, (2012), No. 2: 63–74; NAA 3/1819/29; Vratsian 1928, between pages 416–417)

CLAYTON M. SKINNER
Home: Greenfield, Massachusetts
(*The New York Times*, November 11, 1920 and December 21, 1920)

FANNIE G. STROWGER
Home: Rochester, New York
(*The Olean Evening Herald*, May 4, 1921; *Team Work*, Volume 3, No. 6, June 1924)

ADELINE M. TIPPLE
Home: New York, New York
(*The Stevens Point Daily Journal*, September 10, 1920; *Team Work*, Volume 3, No. 6, June 1924)

YEBRAKSI TONOYAN
Polygon
Born: 1908
(NAA 190/1/116/f. 90 verso)

GEORGE AND ELSIE WHITE
Home: Grinnell, Iowa
(*The New York Times*, December 21, 1920)

GRANT YORK
Home: New York
(*The New York Times*, December 21, 1920)

New Year's greetings from Hayk Hovhannisyan to H. B. Allen. (NAA 1387/1/224/f.7)
→

Near East Relief,
Office of Principal of
Primary and Normal Schools.

December 31, 1927, Polygon.

To: Mr. H. B. Allen, Director of Education,
      Near East Relief, Caucasus Area.

Dear Mr. Allen:-

Personally and on behalf of the teachers, employees and pupils of the Primary as well as of the Normal School, I have the honour to express to you and to Mrs. Allen our best wishes for Happy New-Year and wish you success and happiness in future.

Haik Hovhanessian
Principal of the Primary
and Normal Schools, Polygon.

Armenia, Leninakan

Near East Relief,
Seversky Post,

April 24th, 1926.

To: Director of the Summer Session
      Columbia University
      New York, N.Y.

We have received your preliminary announcement for which we thank you most cordially. As we are not able to attend personally the courses of the Columbia University during the Summer Session, will you please inform us whether or not "Corresponding Students" (Korrespodierende Studenten) are admitted to the Summer Session? In case of an affirmative answer, please let us know all the details in this respect.

There are three-four persons who would like to be Corresponding Students of your University.

Yours respectfully

Haik Hovhanessian, Ph.D.
Principal of the Seversky
Near East Relief Schools.

↑
Hayk Hovhannisyan's inquiry regarding participation in the summer session of Columbia University in New York. (NAA 1387/1/285/f.11)

→
Hayk Hovhannisyan's employment record. (NAA 1387/1/224/f.7)

Near East Relief
Caucasus Branch

Certificate of Employment # 4078

Leninakan
June 20, 1929

To whom it may concern

This is to certify that HOVANESSIAN HAIK was employed in the Near East Relief at Leninakan, Polygon in Education Primary SDepartment as Principal from August 24, 1922 to June 15, 1929 19

Remarks Liquidated June 15, 1929 with salary up to August 31, 1929 Reduction in force.

Not official unless stamped with official stamp.

Американский Комитет
Помощи на Ближнем Востоке

УДОСТОВЕРЕНИЕ # 4078

Ленинакан
20-го Июня 1929 г.

Сим удостоверяется, что ОВАНЕСЯН ГАЙК состоял на службе в Америкоме в Ленинакане, на Полигоне в Образовательном отделе в качестве Заведущего с 24-го Августа 1922 г. по 15-е Июня 1929 г. 19

Примечание Ликвидирован 15-го Августа 1929 г. с уплатой жалованья по 31-е Августа 1929 г. Сокращение штатов.

LISTING OF EMPLOYEES   519

APPENDIX

DIARY OF AN ANONYMOUS RELIEF WORKER

As conditions in Armenia became known after the Armistice, NER hastened to recruit large numbers of relief workers to attend to orphans and refugees at various locations in the country. The manuscript below, in the collection of the Genocide Museum and Institute in Armenia, is a 94-page long handwritten diary written by an anonymous young American woman who worked in Armenia from April 1919 to May 1920.

The first part was rewritten from memory since she had lost her original notes. On the first page of the manuscript appear the star and the words ACRNE, and a note on the top left corner which reads: *Re Written In Karaklis, A Village Conducive To Romance And Practical Expression*. There is no date given in the first section of the diary, but the events she describes suggest that she sailed from New York on February 16, 1919, on the SS *Leviathan* with a group of relief workers. Disembarking the Leviathan in France, she traveled to Marseilles in a Red Cross hospital train, from where she and her company left for Salonika, Greece. She then arrived in Constantinople on March 8, where she received an official letter assigning her to the Caucasus. She arrived in Batum about a month later, on April 1, where she connected with the British train leaving for Tiflis. From there she continued to Armenia and was in Yerevan on April 16, 1919.

She worked, at various intervals, at NER institutions in Yerevan, Karaklisa and Kars, and spent two weekends in Alexandropol. She left Armenia with the other American relief workers in May 1920 following orders from Colonel William Haskell, then the Interallied High Commissioner to Armenia and Director General of ACRNE's Caucasus Branch.

The diary entries reveal that she was trained in, and loved music. She also enjoyed dancing, singing and entertaining others, and especially liked working with children. In addition to her wish to be helpful, she sought adventure, was excited about seeing the world and meeting new people. Although her primary areas of work were Yerevan and Karakilisa, with only a short time spent in Alexandropol and Kars, the anonymous writer chronicles valuable information about NER, the everyday activities of young relief workers, the internal dynamics of NER's leadership in the field and candid observations about the refugees and children she was helping.

The manuscript has been transcribed with only minimal editing. Some of the multiple errors in syntax, spelling, grammar, capitalization and punctuation (or lack thereof), which permeate the entire manuscript, have been corrected minimally to make it more legible than it would otherwise have been. Undecipherable words are indicated by [...] and words difficult to confirm are indicated by the notation [?]. In some cases, such as proper names and names of cities she visited, corrections have been made.

I am grateful to Dr. Hayk Demoyan, Director of the Armenian Genocide Museum and Institute in Yervean, for permission to publish the manuscript *in toto*.

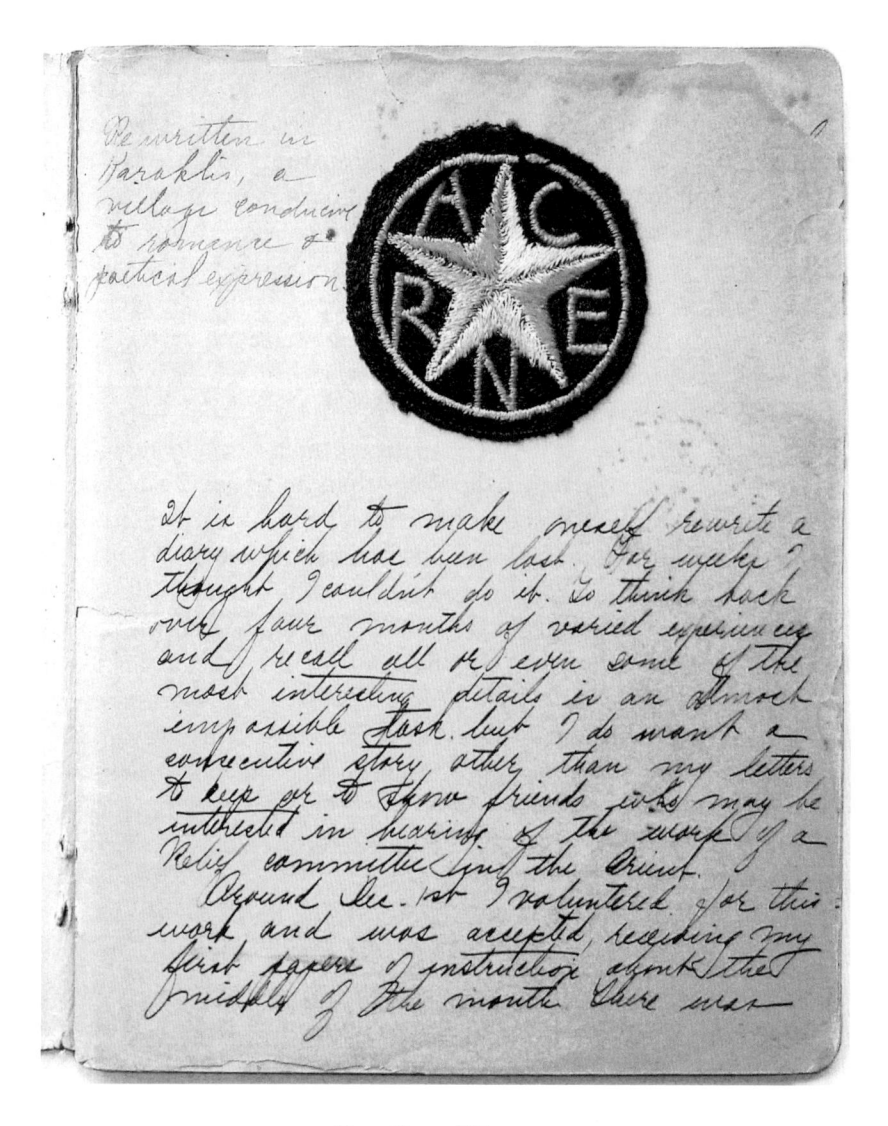

Page One of Diary

Re written in Karaklis, a village conducive to romance & practical expression

It is hard to make one rewrite a diary which has been lost. For weeks I thought I couldn't do it. To think back over four months of varied experiences and recall all or even some of the most interesting details is an almost impossible task, but I do want a consecutive story other than my letters to keep or to show friends who may be interested in hearing of the work of a Relief committee in the Orient.

Around Dec. 1st [1918] I volunteered for this work and was accepted, receiving my first papers of instruction about the middle of the month. There was much to do of course in preparation for a year or more in the Near East and it was all so much fun as had as getting a trousseau ready.

Jan. 22—I left home for New York where I stayed for almost three weeks finishing my preparations, getting uniforms etc. and having a good time in general. Lloyd Crewe [?] is such a fine friend and he was lovely to me.

Feb. 16—the grand old Leviathan sailed and at four or five in the morning I watched the goddess of Liberty emerge in all her glory from darkness through the glorious sunrise into broad daylight dazzlingly brilliant.

And what wonderful people there were on board. A better class of people could not be found. All alive with interest and ready for anything. Nearly all, except the nurses were College graduates, and clever people. I never had such a good time in my life. We had daily language classes in five languages. I landed in a Turkish class—for which language I have had no use since.

Before we left New York two of the men and myself were given charge of the musical entertainments on the ship and we had so much fun planning deck sings, concerts, and […] songs. Everyone seemed to be interested in chorus [?] work so I was given charge of it. I had about twenty voices, we were able to come each afternoon for rehearsals, and they all had lu[s]cious voices. I thought of Miss Westervelt's methods and used them to the best of my ability. At any rate the final performance was a success and after it I was asked to go to an American college in Turkey to take charge of the music there.

I came over for Relief work so did not want to accept.

Dances and disc sings were a great success. Those ship officers certainly could dance and we managed to stand up, though we slid a lot even when the boat was pitching and rolling. The K.C. man was wonderful to me, an artist himself and a good one. He did all in his power to give me a good time. Any night I was up at midnight he sent down to my room turkey sandwiches and coffee and during the journey he presented me with about twelve pounds of candy and 8 or 10 handkerchiefs.

The second night out he introduced me to an ensign who he said was one of the two finest men on board. He was too, but after that night the K. C. saw much less of me. Such a dancer—and so versatile in his tastes and abilities. He played and well—he liked everything I did. We had wonderful talks after the dances were over at ten o'clock. We stayed on deck until eleven. Then I went inside. It was a military ship and I was anxious to be very careful of all unwritten rules. Mr. Hackett was kind enough to keep me posted. Two or three afternoons were spent in posing for the K.C. who insisted on drawing my portrait. I told him to send them to my folks at home, but later in Paul's letters—oh yes he has written faithfully and has even gone so far as to get Constantinople duty for a few months, that he had even [?] led him to let him send them home. As a result they are reposing in Paul's private suite on the Leviathan or they were until he changed his boat. He was miles away from me when that happened so "what could I do"?

In France and such a scramble on a drizzly day. The Red Cross had lunch for us and in the afternoon we talked our heads off to relays [?] of boys hungry for news from home. There was a little dancing and lots of singing. How those boys disliked the French. Well the American girls need never worry. Those discussions in the papers kill me. Those boys almost ate us up they were so glad to see <u>American</u> girls. It was so all along the line through France. I lost a lot of my candy to those boys, who hadn't seen any for months, in fact all I could get at.

A sixty hour trip across France in a Red Cross hospital train, with army rations, gave us an idea of what our boys were putting up with and I was glad to share it with them. The trip was trying of course. Our men carried our trunks and the women carried the hand luggage. I didn't take my cloths off the whole journey and there was no confusion around me. I slept like a top too much to the surprise of all in the car.

Marseilles welcomed us at about one or two o'clock. We filed into the hold of the ship and took our bunks. I preferred the top deck as I knew I wouldn't be sick and I wanted to be as far away from the 150 women in the same room who might be sick, as possible. And ah—such miserable people and such a stuffy place. I stayed on deck until I couldn't stay any longer.

On the whole the trip was rather uninteresting. The tommies [British soldiers] did all in their power to make us happy and we did appreciate it. They waited on us constantly. One night they gave a show and it was very clever, songs, dances, impersonations, slight of hand stunts etc. I did meet some interesting French people. One family especially I enjoyed and they helped me with my French. The youngest girl spoke English a little and I helped her too. They kept me busy evenings singing to them. Oh, yes and a French man from the navy—painfully good looking, but ah, so frivolous and out for a good time. It was fun to have him make love to me in French. He tried it in English, but that tickled me so he gave up and tried it in French and the poor man received the shock of his life when he realized that when an American said no, she meant it. When finally the last night I was still as cold as a stove as he put it, he cornered me as I was retiring and insisted that I let him talk to me just a minute, still laughing at him and trying to tell him I was sleepy, I turned to leave. I almost screamed with laughter when I was confronted by a pistol. He thought he had me then, but when the expression of my face didn't change he was absolutely stunned. I never spent such a dramatic evening in my life. I got away from him only through a little strategy on my part. I finally eluded him and got down into the hold. When I compare him with others I feel sorry for him. He told me once that he believed life was meant for pleasure and he was out for it regardless of the other fellow, and the tragic part is that he believed God wanted it so. Our doctrines of restraint he says are all wrong. In short I should say he believed in following the line of least resistance. My what a lot he misses—

Another Frenchman, older, the Adjutant General of Land and Naval forces was so different. In fact just the opposite and so fine. Perrol [?] was his name.

There were so many interesting people on board. General Gough [General Hubert Gough]—so famous in the English battle at Cambrai was an interesting humorous talker, and he gave us some lively experiences at the front.

At night I hated to go to bed and leave such people. It was going from the "sublime to the ridiculous." Then to go down into a regular ghetto—for that is what it was—rope clotheslines were hung from bunk to bunk long and short and they were filled with much clothes—the family laundry. Why we didn't all catch Mr. Death of cold is beyond me, sleeping in that stuffy damp atmosphere.

We sailed into Salonika in the morning having passed Mt. Olympus at sunrise. It was glorious. Words fail to express such grandeur. We found we were to lay over here for three days so we went sight seeing—ten of us guided by the Frenchman Gen. Perrol. We went everywhere with him even to the customs house yards. We climbed the Acropolis, from where there was a marvelous view of the town and bay, walked through the narrow cobblestone streets passed little many colored houses with overhanging balconies the widows of which were heavily screaned [screened] that the women might see out but that men could not see in.

The whole town was sprinkled with graceful white minarets which I preferred to view from the outside rather than inside as there were 200 steps to climb and I was tired out from trying to find the softest part of each cobblestone.

After a typical Oriental dinner at a French Restaurant and no water to drink the men hired two sail boats and we went up and down the bay until just after sunset at seven o'clock where we sidled up to the big boat and climbed up the ladder, tired and starved of course.

Such filth I never hope to see. I have seen dirt since and plenty of it but as that was my first glimpse of Oriental conditions it impressed me strongly. The war had made refugees out of people and they were existing out of doors or behind walls of ruined buildings, in rags. I have seen even worse since but at the time that was terrible.

March 8th we came into Constantinople Harbor and it was beautiful, passed Leander's Tower, the Sultan's Palace and St. Sophia. The first impression however far surpassed the reality. It is not what it looks to be. It is interesting of course historically but dirty, dusty and generally orientally [sic] inconvenient. The museums and churches now Mosques and colleges were beautiful, each in a different way and all expressing very definitely the period to which they belonged. Some dusky, dull decorations, and others brilliant. All metal work hung very fancy. On the mosques the rugs or carpets, over which we walked in felt slippers, all ran in the direction of Mecca.

The bazars were fascinating places. Natives squatting on a rug in front of their wares screaming at you and others running after you in an effort to make a bargain with you, coming down in their prices over half. Such buzzing you never heard in your life; with no respect or knowledge of law and order.

Prinkips the little island [Princes' Islands] where most of us stayed was an ideal spot for a summer home, beautiful buildings were there but run down of course because of the war and occupied many of them by the one thing that spoiled the place for me—arrogant Germans, armed and free, retained until the treaty was signed. No woman went out of the hotel at night I can tell you without a body guard of armed men, and that was seldom done.

My room looked out on the sea of Marmaron [Marmara] and when we arrived it was a perfect moonlight [moonlit] night. It was a sight for the gods—those hilly Islands out over the water. You couldn't help but hear music even if there was none. I loved it.

And one day when I was writing in my diary, I had spent all morning in so doing, I received an official letter sending me to the Caucasus then considered, and rightly so, for there has been no place where there has been so much suffering, the place with the greatest need. No one will ever know the thrills I had—never—I had hoped to go there but had not ever expressed the desire fearing I would be disappointed as others were who volunteered in writing. And that night after a talk with Dr. Usher [Ussher] the one sent as our leader for that journey I watched the moon with a new and bigger interest and I knew where that same old moon would find me next time it looked down at me.

Wonderfully welcomed by the Armenians by receptions etc., at one of which I was asked to sing the Battle Hymn of the Republic, all of which was written up in the Armenian paper the next day with a flash light picture in it. I left with a few others for Deringa [Derince], our supply station where we were to get ready for the final expedition into the Caucasus.

In the meantime I had picked up a Constantinople dust bug and I was suffering with follicular tonsillitis. At Deringa, I was put to bed in sick bay—a section curtained off on the 5th floor of a warehouse there our only abode until the day before we left. I couldn't stay in bed any longer, so I got up and did what little I could do in the way of guard duty, and then finally checking on all the baggage of the personnel onto the box car in which we traveled to Constantinople, still sick.

On arriving at Constantinople we discovered we were not wanted so soon as there was no boat leaving for several days, and that the telegram was an old one to which we responded. As a result no arrangements had been made for us to sleep that night and we were piled into a dreary dismal chapel, cold as ice. The next morning I finally told the Dr. I simply could not stand it any longer. So we went to a drug store and got some silver nitrate and ferrous glicirine [glycerin]. I couldn't eat a thing and by night could [couldn't?] swallow even water. That couldn't go on so that night the ladies of the Bible House made one of the girls move out and give me her room where from then on I was properly taken care of, except that I had to swab my own throat as the Dr. was never there on time. I had a fever which made Dr. Usher [Ussher] think I ought not to try a mountain climate but I told him I never had throat trouble and that it was a bug which I had been unable to throw off, having had the "Flue" a few weeks before. Finally I reasoned him into letting me get up and go but I was still miserable.

Off at last on the "Katroucha" and in a private room with hot running water. My! How I fondled those water faucets. Sick as I was I had a good time and though I couldn't sing played the piano for the crowd and I met some interesting people both English and Australian, especially Major Hewitt and Major Checkerston [?] and Major Stoever and Macony [?].

Batouma [Batum], no place at all, and on April 1st we made rather good connections with the British train leaving for Tiflis. Bugs! Heavens—I saw them but didn't get any on me. That journey I will never forget. I couldn't eat hard [...] and bully beef to save my soul, and I got worse all the time. Dr. Harmon and Miss Farrington saved my life by bringing me some cocoa made on a steno. I appreciated it no one knows how much.

The second day—I couldn't stand it any longer so Dr. Harmon took some cotton on a hairpin and pressed so hard on the tonsils that it lanced them and then applied raw iodine. Oh! Help!—but it did the deed and the next morning I ate graham crackers and jam.

In Tiflis April 3rd Mr. Arrol [Arroll] almost fell in our necks, he was so glad to see us. He had been in Russia during the war and was keeping relief work alive with Mr. Elder—in the Caucasus. Tiflis the Paris of Russia or of the Caucasus was a modern city and I was disappointed, for they had hotels, operas stores etc. but it didn't last long for I was sent to Erivan where I stayed for months and left only because somebody overstepped his authority.

While in Tiflis I was entertained by an Armenian family, wealthy refugees on their way to Paris. They spoke French, so I could say a few things to them but I was afraid to show my ignorance even though I acknowledged it. There was an English girl—governess there, a fine woman whom I enjoyed immensely. They tried to entertain me but I always had an American business appointment at their dinner hours, and they made me late for some of them.

I couldn't realize that I was a Relief worker, those people ate and ate all day long and they knew their fellow men were suffering. The trouble was that Tiflis is a Georgian town and Oh how they hate the Armenians. More beautiful women I never saw, but I don't like them as a rule.

April 16th found me in Erivan and such a contrast. Men women and children dropping before beside and behind you from cold and starvation. Living skeletons reduced to eating the human flesh of diseased relatives, some before they were buried and others dug up afterwards and cooked for soup. Disease and filth surrounded us everywhere. I never could describe the suffering. People disfigured so from kidney trouble as a result of starvation that one could not see their features separately. All merged into a mass of something that looked as if it would squirt puss if pricked. And bugs—everyone was alive with bugs, in fact rotting away as a result of them.

Well—we plunged in in accordance with Mr. Elder's suggestions. The nurses doing the medical work—and the rest of us the orphanage work. In a few weeks I was relieved of orphanage work however and asked to take charge of the playgrounds and organize the schoolwork for the winter. The playground work was the joy of my life. In a large park which the government gave us the use of there were games, songs, both Armenian and American—gymnasium work, for both boys and girls given to them in amounts according to the physical condition of the child, increasing as it got stronger.

The Boy Scout work was getting well under way when I left. I had an Armenian translation of the U.S. scout book as a guide for them.

My work was crippled for lack of funds and I was doing the best I could out of nothing. Kindergarten supplies we had to create out of anything we could get hold of. There were not even beans to string every bean went down somebodies [somebody's] "Little Red Lane."

Then the cloud when Mr. Elder left for America. A new director. A man inhuman and his wife a dead live wire came and ruined everything. I spare anyone the details though I leave them in print. Sufficient to say that they wanted to sleep at 9:00 o'clock just when we young people were starting to play and sing, our only relaxation. As I made the noise I got the blame and when Col. [...] came down, a friend of Dr. Spaers [?] (We all resigned en masse by telegram if he was allowed to continue) and temporarily representing Haskell the new man. Miss Farrington and I were sent to Tiflis for reassignment. She too he disliked. They couldn't get us for inefficiency so could only write a flattering letter sending us to Tiflis.

In appreciation for my efforts in Erivan I received two silver engraved cups from my two lace factory managers—which by the way was another thing that I organized and ran. I have the most beautiful lace not only from the factory but from refugees passing through who came to me and as a result of personal financial help gave me lace—no use to them in rags. Pitiful!

In Tiflis I had the time of my life. The new men came in and changed things all around (they changed me 4 times) from one room to another, all over town, and finally to Karaklis [Karakilisa]—for which they were sorry afterwards. We gave a dance or rather one was given for Miss Mary and me as we were leaving town, and Cols. Rhea [second in command to Haskell] and Haskell and many others asked me why we hadn't given the dance a week ago. That I never would have left Tiflis if I had. You see I was able to play an honest to goodness fox trot for them and when there wasn't dancing I sang for them. Little as it was it was the best there was and they were cross to have sent me to a little place where I am the only young person and have no piano. I don't care myself. I rather enjoy it. I have the fiddle.

While at Erivan the "mutual admiration society" as we were called worked together neck-to-neck and we played too. We were: Miss Farrington, from Claremont Cal—Miss Kifer from Sioux City Iowa—Miss Draper from Nebraska, a Mr. Perry from Hartford Conn., Mr. Ayer from Boston, Mr. Skinner from Mass., Mr. Meeks from New York., Mr. Elder from Pennsylvania but studies and lives in Chicago—Mr—[...] from Florida but Chicago most of the time, an A.R.A man who came over with the Hoover Commission, from France.

But we have been separated. John Elder has gone home as has Mr. Ayer. Now Bob [...] has gone to France, Paris and Miss Mable Farrington has been sent to Kars—and I here, but we remain true and always will we write to each other and in the States we are all going to get together for a house party. A finer group of young people I never saw. I have been breaking my neck here at Karaklis to live up to a reputation in the new office which I have for getting in most accurate district reports. It is because of that that I am here. I love military work. It demands a certain amount of speed and absolute accuracy. I tell the world I have honed [?] on letter forms and telegrams. I have to laugh at myself running this office and doing the typewriting and taking dictation. It is long hand of course but the commander has never had to repeat yet. I would remember a whole letter first. I really enjoy the work. At night I go to bed to keep warm and then read and study Armenian and French. I have lots of fun talking to myself and I am surprised at the amount of intelligence I show and I get along with "the boss" beautifully. Already he turns letters over to me to answer.

When I think of these different experiences I almost scream with laughter. To think that it is all happening to Bobbed hair Billy—Oh yes I cut my hair as soon as I got to Erivan and it is coming in now fine after being cut several times. We did it to avoid bugs!

A letter from Erivan tells me that Perry is very ill and they are afraid of Typhus—I would have a dozen fits if anything happened to that boy. He is the third of our Erivan group to have it—one died—Miss Winchester and it cast a horrible cloud over us all.

Since the last bug—I have had three attacks of Malaria and have to take grams and grams of quinine constantly to prevent a return any time.

Giving out old clothes is a joke and yet tragic. There is appreciation of course among the recipients but Oh the dissatisfaction of some was overwhelming. You would have thought that we were tailor shops and responsible for all holes. They in rags criticizing—When I was on police duty, on horseback, and had cloths thrown at me maybe I didn't light into them.

I grant there were some impossible things given out due to the Armenian force which Miss Brown, the nurse who ran the thing, had to help her. We were sorry for that and explained to them the cause, sometimes changing garments if returned afterwards.

Police duty is tiring, but I enjoyed it, being cross one minute and smiling the next, jollying them in Armenian, just generally keeping their spirits up for they stood for hours—all day and night, so as to keep their place in line but when people are smiling and laughing they can't be cross and rough in line, so I kept up the joking and playing with the babies dirty as little rats, rather than have to quell fights with my whip which I had to do occasionally. These people are ignorant and as unruly as animals, cattle.

The first day of the ordeal my job was to check off garments or sets given out. It totaled 590—each one was sent in a group of twenty to the bath house which we are running. Each day for three days we did the same. There were at least 1500 cleaner people in town than before.

Dr. Pratt refused to give out clothes at all until the people cleaned up the town, and that means work here believe me—you see—this is a small place and things can be handled in that way. The same policy would not work in Erivan at all—the capital of Armenia with a population of 30 or 40 thousand and refugees bringing it to 90 thousand and over. Here, there are almost 2000 orphans. There—in that district there are nearly 9 thousand by now probably 10.

Dr. and Mrs. Pratt have gone to Tiflis leaving Miss Brown, Miss O'Neil and myself to hold down the place. I have to do the cooking so I will have to leave the office earlier. Mrs. Pratt fired the cook just before she left hoping to find one in Tiflis. So I have a maid only to do things. Of course I have the purchaser and yardmen but I have to supply the brains [?] for all of them. Thank heaven I can speak the language a little as I have to interpret for the family most of the time. Armenians have little or no initiative. We have to supply all of that and it means thinking for the whole town collectively and individually.

I personally won't know how to act when back in the States. I will only have to think for myself. What would it be like? What an easy life it must be.

But in the States I will miss the mountains, Ararat, Alagoz, with the sunsets and sun rises on the snow, and the moonlight—Well—it's a sight for Gods and artists and those who love nature. Life is so free here, with no artificialities. I think now of Lake Sevan the highest fresh water lake in the world I am told. A place where monks have lived and prayed and sinned for they were human—and therefore weak. We went there for two or three weekend trips in the terrible hot weather where we cast our burdens on the Lord or to the

Winds and did nothing, but swim, climb the cliffs, straight up, terrifyingly so, sometimes, and cook our meals on a primus and it tasted so good. Such moonlights I never hope to see. On top of the island of Sevan we looked out on every side over calm rippling water to the mountains partly hidden by silvery fleecy moonlit clouds. Romantic? Could it be anything else?

And the little old boat that sailed to the main land creaking and leaking, till it nearly swamped us, carried us to or fro in that moonlight. Centuries old it seemed just suited to the grey haired, bearded monks still living there alone—And how glad they were to see us. Their language was not ours, but we understood and our eyes and hearts communed in silence.

Dr. and Mrs. Pratt are back, having arrived at 1 o'clock last night. I got up of course and cooked a meal for a starving couple. They appreciated it, too. The doctor remarking that no Armenian had cooked that meal. Some compliment from him. I almost puffed up.

This a. m. Doctor asked me to start cooperative work with the children in the orphanages. Military drill, setting up exercises and other things for the children. The work I did in Erivan and enjoyed so much. I am to have two hours off from the office a day to do this work. Where I can get the time I know not, but I will do the best I can. I am crazy to get at it. Things seem to be working out all right now. I do admire this new organization, even their mistakes,—and <u>Dr. Pratt too!</u>

I had a dear letter from Major Kallogh [Kalloch] this a. m. My, how I do like that man. He is so very splendid to me. I ask the world how could I help it? And he is trying to get me back in Tiflis. Apparently they <u>all</u> miss me. It is good to be appreciated, even to the smallest degree. If I make as good in a business way as I seem to have done socially, for some reason I will be the happiest girl alive. Then I will know positively that my little share in the relief work has been worth while. They are critical, yet very fair, and I would accept their judgment on anything, as I have done from the start.

Col. Spalding, now the Personnel Dept. manager is also a fine man, a sister of his came with our party. A. C. R. N. E. all the way to Constantinople and then leaving for assignment in Turkey.

Co. Rhea is a peach—too. Capable as Chief of Staff, and socially a splendid man of about 45 or perhaps 50, tho' I very much doubt if he is that old. Fine dancer.

I could mention other fine people. Among the demobilized men Jerry Smith and Dr. Brasseau and Mr. Kinich are fine fellows. I enjoyed being with them all.

Opera is going full tilt in Tiflis and I am missing it of course. Only 50 cents a seat and the best. But I am here for relief work and I <u>must</u> forget my former life all steeped in wonderful music, for the time being. It is hard because it is such a big part of me and to be so near to real Russian Opera—on native soil and all seems too much at times. Last spring I was taken to one opera.

Letters from home telling about dinners at the club, dances and theaters etc. don't help much either. I sometimes think I will do anything or would do anything to get back to bright light and home. I have been here, working without a break of any kind, Sundays included for nearly seven weeks. I think I could stand any kind of isolation after this. Major Kallogh saves my life by coming down as often as he can, sometimes arriving at one o'clock in the morning, giving me the pleasure of cooking a meal for him. That was the most thrilling thing that had happened to me for weeks. The sunsets and the very crudeness of the place make one's imagination run along in the natural world breaking the monotony and making life easier. My fiddle does a lot to make us all happy too. I am glad for that. When the open fire is blazing I curl up in front of it and relax. When I am tired I sing and so it goes.

Halloween Major McAlpine [McAlbin] and I made fudge on a little stove and we talked until 12:30 to celebrate. I never will forget that 31st of October. On his birthday a few days later we had a Taffy pull. Such is the excitement in Karaklis.

And now it is Dec. 6th and I have been back in the traces [?] for several days, after a marvelous spree in Tiflis, for a week over Thanksgiving. Such a round of good times. Major Kallock met me at the station at noon and took me to lunch at officers' mess. In the evening he gave a lovely dinner for me at the Union Club. 10 people present and a congenial crowd. We danced between courses and all evening until into the morning. Thanksgiving Col. Rhea gave a tea dance and in the evening we went directly to Commander and Mrs. Bryans, for dinner and entertainment. Well! It continued like that until I went home. I stayed as long as I did to finish some dentist work.

Col. Lonergan—Director of Orphanages G-3 was in Karaklis while I was gone and at last realizes what a poor organization or lack of any, exists here. He was furious and is insistent upon relieving him. I expect tomorrow some sudden changes. I dread the scenes but I feel it is a wise step as no one can work with the present administration. He has no sense of organization at all and is not a big enough man in any sense of the word.

(I forgot to mention the fire that Major McAlpine and I had before I went to Tiflis. We almost burned the kitchen down trying to get something to eat after meeting the courier at 11: something. The lamp caught the ceiling and the sheerings above. Oh—such a mess—but we got it out with no damage done).

The work is fine. I love it and hope to stay a little longer. It is such a wonderful experience for me. My latest plan is to meet friends in Paris when I go home and stay for a while, studying voice and learning to speak French as well as English. I think I can do it. If I can get a position of some kind, with an American concern. I think I have friends who can help me put it through.

It is a good thing for me that I am thinking of these things. I am so thoroughly disgusted with the situation here, I almost die. No one appreciates having an outsider map out one's personal existence for them. It is simply intolerable, and I am helpless, being at an age when taking a definite stand means catty gossip. The men stand up for their rights and think me a fool for not doing the same.

I hope Bob understands the letter I wrote him today. I certainly did let off steam. He is such a peach, and I would like to help him out, but I just can't do it. He writes the loveliest, most beautiful letters.

I wanted to write the Major just about one sentence today demanding an explanation of their delay, but my pride got the better of me, since I had written him last week thanking him for the marvelous time in Tiflis, and I wouldn't write so soon after. But I don't understand. It is getting on towards 2 weeks since they realized the situation here. I suppose they don't know whom to put in their places. Patience is a virtue.

Thank the Lord Pratt is out and we are happy. Mrs. Hunter came down, a nurse, who has been to France. She is a southern girl and such a peach.

We worked like mad Sunday the day after the Pratt's departure to get the house fixed up, and now it is cozy and pretty. I have the job of being mess officer, I run the house, a lovely job, but I have good willing servants who with a bit of training will do very well. (They are all so happy to have the Pratts out of here. They treated them terribly.) I have a few things to do now that I have both the office work to do and the personnel house to run, but it is all such wonderful experience for me.

Col. Haskell and Parker came through Saturday, the latter asked me to come to Tiflis Xmas, but I said no. I have refused to go to Erivan too planning to go later as those here don't want me to leave since they aren't. We expect to have a happy time here. We have loads of snow and coasting, sleighing and riding is great. We are expecting to have bear meat for Xmas dinner.

The dolls I made patterns for are very attractive. The children will surely appreciate them.

This […] I received another cheque [?] from Monty and a personal one too. People are so wonderful to stand back of me, in that way.

Jan. 24th [1920]. What has happened since I last wrote in my diary I can't begin to tell. In the first place, I am no longer in the office but in my old and wonderful work with the little children. I am starting all of the educational work, both the industrial and the academic. It is rather slow up hill work as we have so much to do, to catch up with work which should have been done three months ago. Before I can stir one inch I have to repair buildings. Then I have to have tables made. For chairs I use the various boxes, soap and milk. It saves carpenters time as well as the wood. The military and gymnastic drills are started. I hope in a few months to be able to have things running as well as possible for this place.

Just now my mind is taken up when I am not working, by thoughts, just a little Romantic. Captain Clayton Philip Colman, by another name, has after 3 1/2 months, nearly four, of business acquaintance turned out to be a lover. He reminds me of Carl so much though he is over 6 feet tall. Stunning looking he is and just naturally dear. I never did dream of such a thing and in fact I am so surprised all of the time, as I really know him that he almost takes my breath away...I will hold on though for a few months yet, just to make sure I love him. I am so proud of him in every way I cannot see why I should hesitate a minute. We may find we love each other well enough to be married here and go home together. In fact those here think us foolish not to. I feel myself slipping decidedly, into the hands of love's fate. I wonder if anything will happen to change things. It would be romantic to be made his wife here. No one could guess how really wonderful this life is unless they had tried it. We make our own good times and we do have such wonderful ones. Everything is so beautiful here in the mountains. Philip and I have been sleighing since the very heavy snow has fallen. It is a real fairy land. After the rides to come home to a blazing fire, in the fireplace and a fine quail dinner, (yes, we live high) all we have to do is hunt and we have venison, bear, rabbit and quail etc.) Then if we like, an Armenian orchestra will come in and stay as long as you wish, playing the loveliest waltzes and an occasional two-step to which you can one step. All of the music having an Oriental inspired sound. The instruments are fascinating.

Sometimes we sit around the fire and I in fits of happiness either play the fiddle or sing, usually both alternating. Philip is in Tiflis now and he intends to bring me a piano, so that we can do still more to enjoy the evenings. A Col. [...] and his wife, most attractive people. He an Armenian, though a Russian in trayning [?] and she a Russian—are here in Karaklis. He plays the violin marvelously and she sings. You can imagine their joy when they found I could accompany. We have had such good times. Thank the Lord for my music—If I should lose all my faculties and be unable to play or sing I would feel that what I have been able to do for others' pleasure already just out here would satisfy me, or paid me for the work. The climate has cracked and warped my fiddle but I play it anyway and it isn't so bad and I enjoy it so much as if it were priceless.

Yesterday two fox skins were brought in from the hunt and they were beauties. I paid five dollars for them and it is a sin, as they cost so much in the States. If I could shoot I would get them for nothing. Mrs. Hunter is the only lady hunter in the crowd. She, Dr. Harmon and the [...] go, weekends.

Feb. 23rd, 1920

Each time that I write so much has happened in the interim I fear I will forget important things. Philip came back from Tiflis and brought me such lovely things, silver dagger, riding crop and for all a huge box of fine candy. We were and have been so happy, still waiting and wondering if we were really in love. Valentine's day a telegram changed things here, releasing Major McAlpine as District Commander and taking Philip to Tiflis and then to Alexandropol on a much bigger job. It seems that I am always separated from those I love, but this time it was done too late, for Philip promptly asked me to marry him and I promptly accepted. He stayed here a short time to finish up his work but is in Tiflis now buying silk for me and making pretty things. When my contract is up, March eighth, I will not sign up again but go on at the same rate if they wish for one month longer. Then I will stay and plan to be married giving all my attention to that. If I don't go on working I will just take all of the time to get ready perhaps being married a little sooner than I anticipated. If the Bolsheviks come we may be out of here before very long. It looks a little that way.

April 1st

And how appropriate is the day to my feelings. I don't know whether to pray or swear and then laugh or cry. It's a man of course which is the cause. Philip said he was coming to Karaklis over this weekend and he didn't show up or send a wire or letter saying why. I have been simply furious all week and today I wrote a sassy curt note demanding excuses and apologies. Something has gone wrong, but I want to know what.

We decided when I visited Alexandropol the week before that we would not be married until we get to the States. I may renew my contract for a few months and finish up the job or I may go to Paris and carry out former plans. I am just mad enough to brake [break] engagements, plans and everything say—a bad word and get out, but that would be biting off my nose to spite my face. I can save money here for a rainy day. I suppose this will all blow over in a few days and I will laugh at myself for being so blue and temperamental. Then I am all upset because they are closing up the Karaklis district. I do not know what they are going to do with me but if I don't like what they do I will leave. Philip thinks I will be sent to Alexandropol where he is but I don't know. Tonight I am not in the mood to go there but I do want a change as it is hard to accomplish anything here, for lack of buildings and local supplies. I would like to have more to work with, but after I have gotten things running nicely in some branches it is hard to leave. However we all need a change. The personnel is so small and we see others so seldom that we get very tired of each other. We get along beautifully but you do like a change for even a few days. It is wilderness and beautiful, but I long for civilization and music.

April 8th 1920

This week has been a very different proposition. Philip came for the week end and came to find out Mabel Farrington took the letter of explanation to Tiflis with her. It was her idea of going home that upset the pie and made Philip miss his train. He was furious and when he found out I had not received his letter he was wild and jumped on a train and came along. He stayed with me for two whole days leaving at 4 A.M. on Monday morning. He is coming again a week from this Sunday, again unless some one else goes home and makes P. C. lose another train. I am in a good humor but am anxious for a change of some kind, since I know this district is about to close. I would go home but I know I would not be happy but a very few weeks. Perhaps I will travel around and go to Paris for a few months. Go to London Scotland and Ireland etc. I only have about $400 aside from the $500 for transportation. I would like to stay a little longer and save some more. xxxxxxxxxxx

May 13th 1920

When will things so different stop happening to me. I feel so strange and unlike myself. As I read the last few pages of my diary I have a most peculiar heart sick feeling and yet why not. I have suffered so much. What have I done to deserve such a rebuke. Perhaps my eyes just had to be opened to some things and yet I know that drink did certain things. My Philip whom I have loved so terribly has not been himself for weeks. Alexandropol has pulled him to the depths and he has never been the same to me. Needless to say I am not engaged to him and no matter what he does now in the way of atonement (if he ever tries it) he cannot come back to me. Details I can't record, they are too painful and I am anxious to forget them all. I have suffered enough.

I spent two weekends at Alexandropol, one on route to Kars and the other a week later. I had been transferred to that station just a week having ridden down in a boxcar on the floor sleeping on hay the sole occupant of the car except for the sting friends, when Col. Weight [?] came down to take us all out of Armenia. The evening he came we knew something was wrong but they told us nothing until 7 o'clock the next morning (Sunday.) When we were around and asked to "report" to the living room as soon as possible. There we were told that we must get our baggage to be ready at 12 am and be ready to depart on the two o'clock train. Quietly and without even letting the servants know, we got out in a boxcar, straddling baggage. We carried seven days' ration with us. At Alexandropol we were to stay for 2 days where the Erivan crowds were also to report. From there a special train was to carry us to Tiflis and on through to Poti. We never got there as the Bolsheviks were there and had cut us off. At Alex. [Alexandropol] preparations were made. Beds, tables, stools, supplies, toilets were put in the cars where we were to live we knew not how long. My luggage being packed I had nothing to do but have fun, which I proceeded to do. Col. Shelby, the dearest old man (he'd kill me if he heard me say that) who always has his own horses took me out over the canyons for a 4 hour run, climb, jumping ditches boulders etc. It set me up and also kept me away from Philip. I was forced to be there and all the men realizing what I was up against put themselves out to keep me busy and away from him. They knew I had the situation in my hands and was playing a tremendous game in which thank God I won. As a result I have the fullest respect from all, both men and girls and as a consequence have better friendships. It has been a tremendous experience and I feel at least 5 years older in some ways.

That same afternoon Col. Weight and I rode again and of course I all dressed up in my riding habit had to be rolled into the river which we attempted to ford. The horse was mired and rolled over. I saw he was going to so I was prepared to roll with him as one rolls on the top of a barrel. When I got my footing I too was stuck in the quick sand and rolled, being completely immersed. Such bedraggled parties. I, dripping and the horse muddy and wet all over. I could do nothing when I finally did get out but scream with laughter. The horse then all pepped up from his cold plunge could hardly be held going home. We galloped all the way, and by the time we got home my suit was almost dry. For the next 2 days I kept hearing of the feat that I had performed.

The Col. apparently was much impressed with the way I had gotten away from the horse in the water. I confess I might have been under him. We danced all that night until 5 A.M. (I leading the Russian band pounding American rhythm into them and jabbering Armenian.)

A jollier crowd one never saw en route. We never knew when we were stopped and searched at the borders. We had been ordered to leave dutiable goods behind, rugs and furs, which I did and have been swearing mad ever since for doing so. I smuggled my lace through. Each car did its own cooking on little sheet iron stoves. Major Natty [?] is feeling very smart. One morning having been told we were to stay for an hour, put the stove along side the car. It was going full blast, hot water almost boiling, when the train pulled out. Such excitement—picture 2 men running along side carrying a burning stove almost killing themselves with laughter (to say nothing of us). Fairly throwing the stove in and then just making it themselves. That refugee trip I'll never forget. At Batum we were billeted in a school building staying only one night and long enough to see the town and have a little trot. The officers certainly know how to give you a mighty fine time. We had tea at the seaside inn or rather wine, and dined that night at the Pavilion. The next day the two men sailed on the destroyer Cole and the ladies on the cruiser, the Pittsburgh which came to save the American refugees. The first time in U.S. history that women have been on a battleship after the propeller had been turned over. We were on for 3 days, stopping at Trebizond and Samsoun [Samsun]. Two dirty but to me very attractive little Turkish towns. The navy men are and were wonderful. We slept in the Admirals and Captains cabin (Knapp and Todd). The men who were particularly nice to me were Capt. Dunn, Lieut. Dillon. Camp [?] man, Australian [...], Dr. Smith, Ensign Reed. Ah—I thought I could remember all the names but I can't. They were a splendid lot of men.

At Samsoun after we had seen the town the consul stopped us on the street and invited us to a barbecue. We went and so did the whole Pittsburgh crew including the band. The 3 of us, 2 English and 3 others were the only girls from the boat there. The N.E.R. ladies were hostesses and the wives of the tobacco men. The latter being No. Carolina people and very attractive. Such fun I never had. I led the navy band and had my picture taken so much I was nervous because if I ever commit a crime I'd never have a chance in the navy. The last day on board malaria grabbed me and I missed all the excitement—dances dinners n' everything. A fever of 104.2 is no fun and even the next morning I was terribly weak. Dr. Smith was splendid to me.

Taken ashore stranded on the island of Halki the only available accommodations in Constant. with all arrangements to make for getting out. Then the joy to find we could go to Egypt and that old Col. Shelby would come with me. He takes such wonderful care of me and enjoys himself too every minute. There are 12 of us on this little trip. We expect to go back to Constant. and start from there on a tour of Europe. I sent a box home but I am afraid it won't get there. I only hope it is still in Constant. when I return to ensure it and get a receipt which I hadn't time for.

I am on the British Transport Huntspill now en route to Alexandria. Thrilled and <u>almost</u> perfectly happy.

While in Constant. I saw Mrs. Bristol and heard all about Paul. He has been faithful. Mrs. B. is adorable. I hope to know her better some time.

I ought to say a bit about my work in Karaklis. Finally after much difficulty I literally took a building away from the Arm. Govt. and started a school for my 1st Orphanage. 600 children. The other Orphanages had their school in the respective buildings. I managed to scrape together two or three blackboards and benches. Tables were a luxury and too hard to get as it took so long to make them and we had so much construction work to do which had to come first, like beds.

The Industrial schools were going full blast. Sewing, plain and fancy—and carpenter shops.

Today the British asked the Indians to perform their religious rights [rites] in our presence a thing they never do as the ceremony is sacred but they would do anything for England her savior. I took a picture and I only hope it is good. Their music, strange to say is very like Armenian music. I wonder why. They use the whole tone scale, too. They have a queer little piano or box organ that sits either on your lap or the floor. A box about 2 ft by 8in by 8in. One long side lets down and you see it is a [...]. You play with your left hand the melody and work the [...], with your right hand.

Our Refugee Song.

I'm an American Refugee
And from Armenia bound
I'm on my way to Batoum
I hope I get there sound
I came into this country
A savior for to be
And now I'm being cleared out
A dirty refugee.
I've patches on my britches
A half a mile around
No soles upon my shoes
My feet are on the ground
A half a funt of bread a day
Is all I get from [...]
And now I'm here to tell you
? it's not enough!

Smells

There are smells that make you dizzy
"   "   "   "   "   "   mad
"   "   "   "   "   "   happy

In this land of Garabed

There are smells that set your stomach reeling

For from smells you never can be free

But the darndest smell I ever smelt yet

Is the smell of the Refugee.

May 21st 1920

Our trip on board the ship was prolonged as we were quarantined for two days, a plague of bubonic nature having been said to be prevalent in Constantinople. We came ashore on Wednesday and after getting permission from the Commandant to go to Jerusalem we set out to go to all the shops in Port Said. We landed there instead of Alexandria. I had rather an interesting time there. Col. Shelby is the biggest baby for a man that I ever saw. He gets hurt at everything I say and he almost left me and the crowd to go home alone. He finally decided to stay with us but once at Constantinople I will go alone with a girl or two. I can't stand to have people so touchy as that travelling with me. I am on my way to Jerusalem now and I cannot realize it. We stayed at the Marina Palace in Port Said and we were very comfortable. Say what you like about English men but they are not all so conservative as they try to make you think.

June 3rd

Well, we have seen Egypt and such a fascinating place it is. I would have liked to stay longer but had I done so I might not have been able to get transportation out. We went first to Jerusalem and it is a wonderful place. A beautiful sight as well as historically interesting. To see all of [the] places where the most interesting incidences in Christ's life took place was wonderful. I felt an atmosphere of the past descending upon me all of the time. So much so that I was speechless while looking at some of the old things. The realization of all that happened on the spot where I stood gripped me. What the religion of these people has meant to them. They have given all to the church and the riches that the various old churches hold is appawling [appalling?]. Millions of dollars worth of jewel bedeck the Virgin Mary. One of the most beautiful examples of this is in the church of Calvary. You see there the place where Christ was crucified and buried and rose from the dead and right along with all of the incidents concerning our religion go those of the Mohamedans. They too hold sacred many of the same spots those of course taking place in the Old Testament. They hold sacred those things which are Christian too as they consider Christ as a fine man and prophet. The beauty of Jerusalem lies in the fact that the Old town and the new are not mixed up. You see only the old life portrayed in the old town and in the new entirely modern life. As always one is surrounded with beggars, screaming "Bakshish" constantly.

Bethlehem is the dearest little village all white or rather terra cotta color. There, on Sunday morning we visited High Mass in the church which marks the stall and manger. It was so thrilling and yet peaceful and quiet. None of the disturbances of civilization. The chanting of those children's angel voices brought the tears to my eyes. As we walked down the little narrow streets I could see Mary riding her little donkey and led by Joseph. It seemed so perfectly natural and just like what was going on right then. Those humble people. How little they knew that a virgin was passing by, the destined Mother of the Divine Christ, to the Church of the Nativity. And the dead see [sea] salty and hot with nothing on its shores but a few Egyptian or Arab huts and sail boats. I waded in that sea. I have wondered so often how all of the things took place in or near this barren spot. But the Jordan River was lovely. We crawled into a rickety little row-boat and let the current carry us down stream. Personally I should not like to be baptized there as it was such a muddy stream but perhaps then it was different.

The ride to these places we made in an automobile. The [SS] Pittsburgh officers having followed us from Constantinople met us in Jerusalem and continued to stay with [us] at Cairo and Alexandria. Such a wonderful time they showed me. I never could express it. Col. Shelby has decided to leave me several times but he has not done so as yet. He comes back every time. I know why, but it is hard for me. He is so fine to me and does so much for me. It is a shame that he has such an unfortunate disposition. I feel that I never know when he will leave me. I expect this time he will do so in Constantinople. At any rate I hope that something definite will be settled.

In Cairo the interesting things were the pyramids and Sphinx, the Burrage and the mosques and museums in town. Cairo itself is modern, rather pretty, but you are not happy until you get out of town and on a camel. We climbed the pyramid by moonlight. And Oh such a view as we had. Your fortunes is told and you are tremendously thrilled. At the Burrage (beautiful gardens) you ride about on little cars and have tea in the garden somewhere. A jongler [jongleur] does tricks for you and your guid [guide] talks you to death, but you don't mind.

Alexandria is simple a modern city and cosmopolitan. There is not anything of historical interest there. And now I am on the "Field Marshal" transport on the way back to Constant. We have met some Americans in nearly every place such as the Military Attaché and his wife. We [...] some old A.C.R.N.E members too, leaving for Constant and home. Mr. and Miss Peers. At Alexandria we went out to the Pittsburgh for lunch and small dance in the afternoon they are the dearest crowd of boys. I expect to see them in London.

July 13th 1920

It is a long time since I wrote in my diary. I have not had a minute's time, with the help of my pictures however I think it will not be difficult to pick up the threads and go on.

The trip back to Constant was more or less of a bore. Col. Shelby wanted to be with me every minute and I could not see that. I don't like staying with one person eternally especially if I am not very much interested. All along the line I have felt it would have been better if I had been alone. He has such a terrible disposition. If I had it I would shoot it. He has done wonderful things for me, but never again!!!

At Constant we had to stay for about 4 or 5 days but we finally got passage on the Lord Trieste Line "Carinola" a slow boat going everywhere we wanted to go—such as Athens, Corfu and other places. (Greece is a perfectly lovely place). While in Constant we took in all of the good things. We dined at the Tacotleon [?], the Petite Champs etc. The latter a beautiful out door place with vaudeville and music. What one doesn't see there isn't worth seeing. I feel sorry for those young girls (street walkers) I can't help it even if they are bad all through. It is just as bad as it is in France.

It is horribly expensive to live in Constantinople so on the whole I was very glad to get out.

We were surprised to find that Mrs. Hunter and Dr. Harmon had been married before leaving for France. They who I watched with rather suspicious eyes all along the line, but they were very wise in saying nothing about it.

July 16th

The journey home was a fine one though trying in many ways. All of the places where we stopped were interesting but Col. Shelby got to be a terrible problem and nuisance to me. I positively dislike him now and was relieved when he left me in Paris. Though he considered himself a great help to me he was not as he has an unfortunate disposition, easily excited and a mean temper. It aggravated me to have him eternally landing on some poor servant for no reason at all especially as he knows nothing of their languages and I had to hear them and translate for him. Never again! When I was alone everything went smoothly and I had no trouble and consequently was always in a good humor.

Our stop at Salonique was made very pleasant by the Red Cross people there. Mrs.?, her name has escaped me, was the hostess and she entertained us during the day beautifully. We had been sent to the house by a Major King whom we had met in town while sight seeing. We danced and enjoyed ourselves in general. The Major and Mr. Clare [?] were to join us on the boat en route to Venice and Paris, respectively. I later disliked the major very much and was glad not to be bothered with either as they stayed rather near me and I did not like to be rude after being so beautifully entertained at their house.

At Athens we were shown about by an Americanized Greek architect who was an interesting guid [guide] as he knew the ground so well. He was glad to know I knew something about things from study and therefore opened up, being careful to leave nothing out that I would like to know. We saw the various sections of the Museum, Temple and Jupiter, Arch of Hadrian, Temple to Theseus. The King[']s Palace and grounds. The stadium, now on the sight [site] of the old, and on the Acropolis. The Parthenon Temple and ~~Thea~~ Neptune and Minerva, Temple to Victory and the museum containing statues and relics rescued from the remains of the Parthenon and other temples of the Acropolis.

At noon during the day we were in Athens we went to the National Restaurant and had a splendid meal. It tasted good because it was different from any thing we had had—and I had been craving some juicy steak. It seemed a relief to get off of the boat anyway as I had some Turkish cabin mates, who refused to have air and the porthole was kept closed in spite of all my protestations. I having either suffocated all night or slept on deck, was a bit weary. That part of the journey I did not enjoy and I was thankful when we landed in Brindisi. On Corfu there wasn't much to see but a lovely view of the bay and the fortress, an old castle and the Kaiser Bill's [Kaiser Wilhelm II] summer home, a lovely spot. The other small ports at which we stopped such as Valo, Patras and Valona were just little places of no particular interest. At Valona , however, Italy was having a little trouble with the Albanians. Several were killed and wounded and about 1000 prisoners were taken while we were there. The search lights on the battle ships played along the coast all night. We did not go ashore but anchored inside. The Corinth Canal was interesting but different.

Italy is wonderful! The trip to Naples over night tho' trying as we had to either sit up straight or recline only a little all night, was not so bad really. The stay in Naples in a beautiful hotel, Mt. Vesuvius and the scenery along the Bay of Naples was a joy worth suffering a bit for. Mt. Vesuvius itself is a glorious crater and it boiled and spil [spilled] beautifully for us. Such red fire and stream and smoke against a greenish yellow lava setting was fascinating and as I was not dizzy in the least while climbing on the cog railway, I enjoyed it all to the fullest. The only bad feature of it all is that the two pictures which I took did not turn out. Why I don't know as everything else was splendid. The view from the top of the crater of the Bay and of the Island of Capri in the distance was exquisite. Oh if everyone could stand where I stand and see it all.

I had a touch of homesickness while on the way down the Mt. as we stopped at a restaurant where an old Italian was grinding out an accompaniment to his own beautiful whistling and it sounded so lovely and I thought of Carl and his whistling and I wanted to cry a little bit. I have not seen you for so long, Alec [?]—over two and a half years. (Uncle Jim gave this man some money and I felt better for he smiled sweetly then and didn't look so pitiful with his one leg, and his eye sight failing.)

Pompeii, though exceedingly interesting got to be a bit monotonous after an hour of walking about in the ruins. There was so much sameness in it all. After one had seen an example or two of the old Greek homes, temples,

Basilicas and wine presses, one has seen most all. The theatres of tragedy, comedy, etc. were very interesting to see as one could follow Greek thought in both architecture and drama.

Rome, a grand a glorious place filled you with a feeling of strength and power as long as you were there. Everything has the appearance of such massiveness. The Coloseum [Coliseum] and the Forum, the wonderfully constructed aquiducts [aqueducts] and the Appian Way. St. Peters! What a monument to leave the world. Never in one place have I seen such grandeur. St. Pauls—St. Johns—and St. Lawrence—all gorgious [gorgeous] church [churches]—heavily inlaid with mosaics, statues and memorials of all kinds. Raphael and Michilangelo [Michelangelo] and their helpers were certainly living wonders. The Sistine Chapel in St. Peter's is enough to make you weep. Oh such delicacy in color and line, tho' massive in form, as it had to be the dimensions of the whole church and chapel being too huge. I cannot begin to give an idea of the size of St. Peter's except that all the other churches in the world have engraved slabs on the floor showing their length. The little cherubs throughout the building which look to be life size from where you may stand are the size of a big man. The figures of men are 22 feet long and over. Such is the comparative size. And everything in the purest of marble and varied stones. Piety gifts have been presented by kings and emperors to the individual chapels. Such as a lapus lazurly [lapis lazuli] altar, etc. The dome is like heaven itself must be—and oh, so far away. Imagine lying flat on your back with a brush in your hand or a chisel for years in the production of such work. It took over 250 years to build St. Peters.

Regardless of where you stand in Rome—history floods you with its real ties and you stared in awe and admiration for the men in those days who attempted and were able to finish such huge pieces of work. The massive pillars in all of the buildings such as the Pantheon of one piece. And the tombs of these men are right there for you to see. You feel as if you had known them—"For by his works ye shall judge him" and they are great.

Just lately they have begun to excavate ruins on the Palatine Hill and under a huge summer villa they have recently found the old home of Julius Caesar. I saw enough to get a very good idea of how it must have looked. They are finding other interesting places too: From both Palatine and Capitoline Hills you can get splendid views of the Forum—both of which I have, there is the Temple of Vesta—the old gate at the entrance of the city. St. Michaels tower a place reeking with historical interest and the various old bridges such as the one near which the huge old sewer opened into the Tiber. It is still there. Then on the Apian [Appian] Way is the old tomb of Caecilia Metella. Its walls being something like 15 ft. thick.

They are putting up new buildings too which are costly and magnificent. The House of Justice where both the Higher and Lower Courts meet is new and then another huge museum yet unfinished, stands out as a monument.

The bronze or gilt horse is large enough to have a banquet given in his belly for eight or ten people. Imagine the size of the rest of the white marble building. I couldn't get a picture of it as the sun was always in the wrong place, no matter what time of day I visited it. (The moving [?] pictures were not bad in Rome either).

The journey from Rome to Florence was the pleasantest of all. We were able to get our berths in a wagon lit and enjoy the night. The grand Hotel in Florence was very nice and the service was good. Something unusual for Europe. I gave the Col. a birthday dinner there and we had ice cream and cake. Yes we had champagne too. It was good.

The first day happened to be a St's Holiday and no sightseeing tours were being conducted. So we drove about the town in a carriage to kill time. The next day we saw everything. The churches and museums and the Porte [Porto] Vecchio. Donatelo's [Donatello's] singing angels—his David and his bronze doors were wonderful, also the Bambino by Dela Robia [Della Robbia] were lovely. I was tempted to buy some of the pictures, copies of the originals, which were perfectly splendid, but I couldn't carry them, as they were all too big. I did want a copy of Botticelli's Springtime or Venus and Raphael's Madonna of the Chair—as did I want copies of many of those in the Vatican at Rome—but they were all too large. But the sad part is that they were really very reasonable in price.

All of the buildings so closely connected with the Medici were fascinating. Especially the church which they built for their tombs, which half-finished was never completed. It remains just as it was, with half of the floor still uncovered with the marble slabs. And the places made for statues vacant. It is really a gorgeous thing, done in shades of green marble, mostly dark. The trimmings are of bronze and brown. You see also the gardens of the Medici, and wonder what went on there.

The old home of Dante is a very interesting place, as is the wine shop where a contemporary of Michael Angelo, an artist, who felt he was not appreciated, sold his wines thinking he at least could not be excelled in that.

Oh—miserable night! En route to Venice. We sat up all night. It was impossible to get berths. Col. Shelby and I took turns curling up on his pillow in each other's laps—trying of course but it was part of the experience and had to be done. However, after two hours of sleep we were fit for anything and we strolled up and down the square where all of the shops are, just behind the cloisters, and facing St. Marks Cathedral. There was something very restful about St. Mark's. The walls and domes though heavily inlaid with mosaics were not brilliant, but rather, subdued by age, sank into the grey background of the massive walls [...] and the pillars.

The pigeons were there as usual and I fed them. So, were the Gondola's there, and how I did love those things. We glided along at sunset and on into the night with its moon, and listened to the serenades out in the canal. Oh, what a place for a honeymoon. Venice, and Switzerland, and the Italian lakes are my idea of the place to go for such if we go out of the States.

We stayed at the Royal [...] an old palace which is historically of interest. Its walls are mosaic too. The Bridge of Sighs is the next canal or street from there. Down the Grand Canal a long way is the famous Rialto Bridge.

One day while there, we took the hotel launch to the Lido, a famous summer resort where all the aristocrats and the elite go. We went swimming and then had a wonderful dinner at the fine Hotel Excelsior. We met Col. Weight in Venice and he went over with us. He had come by way of Vienna having had quite an exciting time. He too was infatuated with Venice.

The trip to Milan was one again of comfort for we had a sleeping car. But sad to tell, the Italians care not where they put you on the train, and so anyway you fix it. I was with a man in a compartment. So, to make the best of a situation the Col. and I slept in the same compartment. We had the best and roomiest one on the car. So I went to bed while he stayed outside and then when all set, he came in and climbed up to his berth. In the morning, he rose first and went out leaving me to get dressed in peace. If you can imagine such as that in America—but I find it the usual thing in Europe so I smiled sweetly and made the best of it. The porter was not at all upset and explained to the Col. that in Europe that was quite all right. When I got to London and talked to Mina Ness I discovered that I was not alone in my experiences and that she had had similar funny ones. We laughed together over it. I did not tell cousin Rita and Robert however, as they are as simple and old fashioned as ever and would be horrified and unable to understand.

The journey from Milan through Switzerland was a joy. We went thru' by day. We had planned for that. Such scenery. It was simply superb. Delicate scenery, snow capped mountains, dainty waterfalls-surrounded with lacy greens. It was lovely to emerge from a tunnel into all the glory of a new picture. Lakes and islands with villas who[se] gardens hung out over the water. Such an atmosphere of laziness and ease as was there, beconing [beckoning] one to come and rest. My how I wanted to answer that call.

Tho' warned against the customs all along the line, we were very fortunate and got through without having our baggage even looked at. On the train a French girl was in our compartment. She was alone, and being used to travel only with her husband. She seeing [we] were Americans was very much relieved and dependid [depended] on us. She was attractive and young looking tho' thirty years old having a son ten years of age. Her husband was also relieved and was glad we were not natives of the country. As a result we took her in to dinner with us and helped her with her baggage at the customs house. I only could talk to her—so we had a jolly time. Col. Shelby as usual was jealous and I had another fight with him. He is such an old baby.

I tried to see some thing of her in Paris, as she wished to in some way repay me or us for helping her. We could not get together however so I never saw her again. I did see her very attractive sister and son however. In Paris we had a great time shopping and sight seeing. The Col. left me after 3 days. I sail on a U.S. transport as per orders. They wouldn't let me go. I was mad as they could have just as well as not. I had a glorious time alone however. I had to talk for no one but myself and I heard no rangling [rankling] with the servants or anyone else. I was independent wholly. I loved it. And all went smoothly. I went to Versailles—and met a rather interesting English lady. I went to the battle field Soissons Reims Belleau Woods—Chateau Thierry etc. And I did it on July 4th. Could it have been a better day. If only parents and relatives could see those graves—they would never ask that their sons be sent home. The[y] lie with their "pals" in a field of honor, watched over by American girls, who act as hostesses continually. The graves themselves are beautifully kept each with its white cross. Reims is a wreck, nothing but ruin and the church is a sight to be hold [behold]. However they are very quickly raising the money to rebuild the Cathedral. We stayed all night in Reims in a quaint hotel—clean and nice, no real conveniences but just what one would want to find there amongst the ruins. Lamps candles, and washbasins, etc.

Frightened to death lest I would not be able to get out of Paris with my money, I made my way to Boulogne, thinking that honesty was the best policy. And low [lo], no questions were asked and we sailed thru' untouched. The boat ride across the channel was interesting mainly because I tried to help a Swiss girl who was horribly seasick. She was appreciative and nice. I wish I could have known her better (She spoke English perfectly).

On the train from Folkston to London an American demobilized Navy officer came to my aid by offering to help me find accommodations at a hotel. I didn't want to go to my relatives immediately. We went all over London in a taxi and could find nothing, so in despair I went to Montique Square. The taxi driver said it was the nearest. but I bumped into a big dinner party there and after a little difficulty in getting by the maid I got in and ask[ed] for a pencil and paper to be given to Mrs. Ferrard [?]. At that instant cousin Mina hearing me say cousin, came to the door and pulled me in. She rushed up the stairs to cousin Margaret and came back telling me that cousin Robert was expecting me. So!! With hurried apologies I jumped into the taxi which I had kept waiting and went straight to my cousin Roberts. They were dear and welcomed me beautifully. I, having dropped my American promised to drop him a line telling him that I was safe. He was just a bit worried. I did so and all was well. I had a glorious time. I went to two plays—The Jig-Saw and One Night in Rome (Larette [Laurette] Taylor.) She was fine as usual but it seemed strange to be watching a performance of hers in London.

Westminster Abbey was the grand old palace just as was Notre Dame in Paris. Its lacy carvings were lovely and they looked really old. They are raising money to make repairs as they say it will collapse if it is not tended to at once. Of course nothing could compare with the Italian churches. But they were lovely in their way. The museum in London was interesting as was the Louvre in Paris. It completed the seeing of the various paintings and sculptural works which I had wanted to see. Venus de Milo and the Monna [Mona] Lisa at the Louvre and Turner—Constable ~~Leonardo de Vinci~~ in London. The Tower of London—and the large monument were interesting too. Historically principally.

I was fortunate in being able to see the House of Lords setting. We were told at the door that we could not get in, but the policeman saw I was anxious to get a glimpse of the interior of the house of parliament so he told cousin Rita to go on in and if we were stopped, simply to ask for the court of appeal. So with long faces we did this and got away with it. The men had on their state wigs. Something like this [*]. It look as if they had jumped out of a picture. The chapel in which Charles was condemned to be beheaded—and where the Royal funerals took place were being somewhat reconstructed, as it was so old it was dangerous. It is the tendency to make these old places appear too new, almost spoiling the old structures. An other example is the Norman Chapel in the Tower of London, which has been made to look just as it did originally. It looks too new now. The old prisons, where Raleigh and the royalty were kept still are as they used to be and therefore more interesting.

Isn't it queer how the world is changing? In England—the present young generation does not and never will agree with the old. The war has made the young people think for themselves since so many have been out of their homes for so long. There is a feeling of constraint between father and son. They never discuss the real things of life and there is therefore, no understanding. Bill, opened up to me in the week I was there more than he ever did in his life before, simply because he felt I would understand. Americans always do. He is afraid to assert himself, lest he be thrown out of the house. Imagine a grown man fearing a thing like that. He has been made to feel that such an experience would be a disgrace to him and the family. Yet inwardly he rebels and wants something bigger and freer, less conventional. Rarely, in the English houses, do the parents understand the children. Right now, that family are wondering why it is that they each feel closer to me after a week[']s acquaintance, than they do to each other. If I am not mistaken letters will soon come to the States to Aunt Constance expressing some such idea. I feel it myself so strongly. I feel them unfolding themselves to me. Why? Because I paid no attention to the crusty, quivering, thin surface, but struck at once at the things which are deepest in every one[']s heart. I made them feel that I loved them, and I tried to forget myself. Human nature is the same, the whole world over and it must respond sincerely to the almighty force of love. And they were not unusual. I knew they wouldn't be. It was a revelation to me, yet a proof of what I have always felt that everything superficial, however impregnable it may seem, is helpless in the face of sincere love. How worthwhile it is to be real, giving out the best of one[']s self continually. "Sow and ye shall reap." "Seek and ye shall find." I firmly believe that that family has learned a lesson, all unconsciously.

I was sorry to miss Mr. Dillon in London. He crossed me arriving in London about as I was leaving. I may never see him again. Perhaps it is Fate again which knows what is best for us all or shall I call it God!? I have been taken care of always. I do not even feel bitter after my experience with Philip. I am disappointed in him, but I love the world. There are too many people in it who are fine and strong, that I feel only that I perhaps after months of both mental and physical stress lost my clear sense of vision. It was an answer to prayer really, that things happened as they did for I felt incapable of seeing both sides and in my uncertainty I cried out to God to lead me! And if Philip was not the right man he must show me. I put it in his hands and as if he heard at once he sent Philip to Alexandropol, put him in the way of temptation and let me see what he would do if thrown in a similar circumstance later on. He was weak withal his strength not because he liked alcohol, but because he felt he must do as his superior officer wished. He had lost the power of juding [judging] the best for the future. He could not live up to the best that was in himself, unless I was with him every minute. It was hard for me to see this at first, but it came so suddenly after my appeal for guidance, lest I make a mistake, I could not help but realize that it was for my good. It was a bitter pill which I had to swallow, but I have learned so much by it. I believe he has too, and regrets his mistake but that chapter of my life is closed and can never be opened.

How strange that Paul is still waiting patiently for me at home loving, in spite of all that has happened and I have told him all. Could it be that God is bringing me to him safely as a result of his faithfulness. How could he be true to the memory of a few days on the ship. But time will tell—and all things do fall in the face of real love you know. The same old thing in the same old way. I wonder what will happen next to me.

On board the St. Paul and such a pleasant journey. Restful and quiet, I have not danced once. None of the people are interesting in that way. There are a few very nice girls whom I enjoyed [...] with them.

I have been so busy reading. Romola, The Last days of Pompeii and the Little Visitors, or I should say the Young Visitors, and writing in this diary, that I have had little time to speak to any one. It seems so good to have time to read again. Then too I have gone over all of my pictures and have explained them all on the back.

I cabled Paul from England as to my time of sailing as he requested. I wonder if he will be there to meet me. What a funny world! I love it though. There is so much for everyone to do that is good and helpful to others.

ENDNOTES

NOTES TO CHAPTER ONE

1 Charles Woodman and George M. Towle, *The Northern and Asiatic Defenses of Turkey*, New York, 1877: 26.
2 "The Invasion of Turkey," *The Otago Witness*, May 5, 1877, illustrated weekly newspaper popular in New Zealand in the 19th and early 20th centuries. Also see Demetrius Charles Boulger, *The Life of Gordon*, Vol. I, London, 1896: 86ff.
3 The name Lorisamenskey is most probably a permutation of Mikhail Tarielovich Loris-Melikov, of Armenian origin, who excelled in the Russo-Turkish War of 1877–78 as an officer of the Russian army for which he received the title of Count from the Tsar.
4 Ralph Meeker, "Through the Caucasus," *Harper's New Monthly Magazine*, Part I, April 1887: 716.
5 Meeker, Part II, May 1887: 912.
6 Ibid.: 923.
7 Ibid.: 922.
8 Ibid.: 918.
9 *The Washington Post*, April 9, 1905. Also in *The Charlotte Democrat*, May 11, 1877; *The Minnesota Daily Journal*, May 10, 1902; *The New Orleans Daily Democrat*, May 5, 1877; *The Wheeling Daily Intelligencer*, February 19, 1856.
10 Luigi Villari, *Fire and Sword in the Caucasus*, London, 1906: 292f. For an earlier description of the city see R. Grant Barnwell's *The Russo-Turkish War*, Toledo, 1878: 466–468. For a recent comprehensive description of the growth of Gyumri and its demographics see *Gyumri. Kaghake yev mardik* [Gyumri. City and People], Vardan Ghukasyan, et al., eds., Gyumri, 2009; Ashot Mirzoyan, "Aleksandrapol-Leninakan. Kaghakashinakan dimagic" [Alexandropol-Leninakan. Profile of City Planning], *HH GAA Shiraki hayagitakan hetazotutyunneri kentron, gitakan ashkhatutyunner* [National Academy of Sciences of Armenia Shirak Center for Armenological Research. Research Papers], 2008: 17–26.
11 "Another New Russian Railway Now on Tapis," *The Minneapolis Journal*, May 10, 1921.
12 *Gyumri* 2009: 66. Also, *Bradshaw's Through Routes to the Capitals of the World and Overland Guide to India, Persia and the Far East*, London, 1903: 77.
13 *Gyumri* 2009: 50f. On education and literacy see E. Sahakyan, "Mi kani tvyalner Andrkovkasi dprotsneri veraberyal (XX dari skizb)" [Some Data on Schools in the Transcaucasus, at the Beginning of the 20th Century], *Banber Yerevani hamalsarani* [Bulletin of Yerevan University], 1968 (3): 219–224.
14 Thomas Dann Heald, "Relief Worker's Adventures," *The Wide World Magazine*, August 1919: 288.
15 Heald (September 1919): 404.
16 Mariam V. Kirakosyan, *Petakan yev hasarakakan hastatutyunneri vorbakhnam gorcuneutyune Hayastani hanrapetutyunum, hyusisayin Kovkasum yev Andrkovkasum 1918–1920* [The Activities in Orphan Care by State and Public Institutions in the Republic of Armenia, the Northern Caucasus and the Transcaucasus], Thesis, National Academy of Sciences of Armenia and Armenian Genocide Museum and Institute (AGMI), Yerevan, 2011: 18.
17 For a discussion of early efforts in orphan care and refugees in Alexandropol and related archival documents, see Karine Aleksanyan, "Arevmtahay gaghtakannern Alexandrapoli gavarum arajin hamashkharhayin paterazmi tarinerin" [Western Armenian Refugees in the Province of Alexandropol during the Years of the First World War], *Banber Hayastani arkhivneri* [Bulletin of the Archives of Armenia], 2008 (2): 40–56 and by the same author, *Arevmtahay gaghtakanutyune Aleksandrapoli gavarum, 1914–1922. Pastatghteri zhoghovacu* [Western Armenian Refugees in the Province of Alexandropol. Compilation of Documents],

Yerevan, 2012: 125f. The establishment of large numbers of orphanages in Armenia, supported by several Armenian benevolent organizations in the Caucasus and Moscow, had been in response to an encyclical from Catholicos Gevorg V on November 22, 1914, calling on all Armenians to come to the rescue of their brethren (National Archives of Armenia (NAA) 57/3/73/f. 137). For a discussion and archival documents on benevolent organizations, number of orphanages they supported, financial difficulties and relevant correspondence, see Aleksanyan 2012; Kirakosyan 2011.

18 NAA 28/1/428/f. 21.

19 See, for example: *Ashkhatank*: May 7, 1916; June 4, 1916; June 15, 1916; July 8, 1919; July 9, 1916; July 27, 1916; September 21, 1916; September 28, 1916; March 29, 1917; April 15, 1917; April 19, 1917; May 31, 1917; June 3, 1917; June 28, 1917; December 2, 1917; April 29, 1919; July 1, 1918; July 3, 1919; July 10, 1919; May 22, 1919; June 15, 1916; July 8, 1916; *Zhoghovurdi dzayn*: September 19, 1918; October 19, 1919; November 27, 1918; *Mardkaynutyun*, May 10, 1919; *Zang*, January 12, 1919; *Van-Tosb*, No. 7, 1917; *Mshak*, No. 227, 1916.

20 *Horizon*, August 29, 1915.

21 Edilyan was appointed inspector of orphanages in June 1916, and charged with assessing the condition of orphans in the Caucasus, their basic needs, emotional states and educational prospects. Edilyan was well suited for the job. After attending schools in Ijevan and Tiflis he had attended universities in Europe—Leipzig, Bern and Jenna—to study with Wilhelm Wundt, renowned as one of the founders of experimental psychology in Europe. He would later serve as principal at the Kazachi Post and ultimately as the first dean of the Pedagogical Institute at Yerevan State University.

22 According to Edilyan, the first ten orphanages had opened between August and November 1915: Yerevan on August 3, 1915; Dilijan on August 28, 1915; Ganja on September 9, 1915; Igdir on September 20, 1915; Tiflis in September 1915; Karakilisa on October 5, 1915; Etchmiadzin in October 1915; Alexandropol on November 20, 1915; Nor Bayazet on November 20, 1915; Kars on November 21, 1915. The next four had appeared between February and June 1916: Karavansarai (Ijevan) on February 4, 1916; Akhta (Vayots Dzor) on February 20, 1916; Akhaltsikhe on June 6, 1916; and Akhalkalak on June 27, 1916.

23 Gurgen Edilyan, *Gaghtakanakan vorbanotsner* [Orphanages for the Refugees], Tiflis, 1917: 33–48. Edilyan also presented a final tally of orphans in the Caucasus by their location, gender and age group. Accordingly, by September 3, 1916, there were 53 boys and 59 girls between the ages of 1 and 3; 315 boys and 349 girls between the ages of 4 and 6; 1,028 boys and 869 girls between the ages of 7 and 10; and 1,189 boys and 981 girls aged 11 and older, for a total of 4,486 orphans, in addition to the 50 who were in the hospital in Alexandropol.

24 NAA 28/1/338/f. 18–20.

25 Regarding support provided to refugees and orphans by various organizations, expenses involved, and correspondence on related issues see NAA 57/2/1287/ff. 4–5; NAA 57/2/1306/f. 10; NAA 28/1/428/ff. 1, 9, 51; NAA 28/1/338/f. 47; NAA 28/1/347/ff. 17–20; NAA 28/1/187/ff. 21–26; NAA 28/1/637/f.13. Various aspects of refugee life are discussed in Aleksanyan 2008: 41ff.

26 Kirakossyan 2012: 19. According to data gathered by Russian Duma member Papachanov, who visited Yerevan and Alexandropol toward the end of 1915, about 40–50% of the refugees were children, among them unattached orphans.

27 NAA 57/2/1311/ff. 23–24. In an earlier request dated October 30, 1915, this time for a loan, Dr. Ashot Karayan had asked the assistance of the Holy See for the hospital for refugees he directed in Alexandropol. The hospital was located in a house owned by the Holy See, but since it had not originally been built as a hospital, the doctor explained, he and the committee had decided to make the building more suitale for the needs of a hospital and to make a few needed repairs. Of the estimated expense of 1,500 rubles needed, he explained,

> …half would be taken care of by the local committee, and the other half, by a loan from the religious authorities, not as a lump sum but by freeing the hospital from paying the monthly rent of 50 rubles until the sum is exhausted (NAA 57/2/1274/f. 80f.).

The doctor continued to say that if for any reason, the location of the hospital should change before the loan was paid in full, all new construction would be left to the religious authorities, unconditionally. In the absence of a loan, urged the doctor, the repairs would not be made, in which case "our unfortunate refugee brethren alone will suffer." But the Holy Synod in Etchmiadzin declined the loan of 750 rubles. The Holy See did suggest, however, that the local committee was in a position to undertake the necessary repairs at its own expense, but only on condition that at the end, all construction would become the property of the Holy See of Etchmiadzin (NAA 57/2/1274/f. 147).

28 NAA 57/2/1311/f. 25f.

29 Ibid.: f. 27.

30 Marine Martirosyan, "Pastatghter Hayastanum Angliakan ognutyan (Anglkom) komiteyi gorcuneyutyan masin," [Documents Pertaining to the Activities of the British Committee of Assistance (Anglkom) to Armenia] *Banber Hayastani arkhivneri*, 2005(2): 74–86; and Suren Avetisyan, "Amn-i yev Mec Britanyayi hayanpast gorcuneutyune arajin ashkharhamartits heto," [The Benevolent Armenian Philanthropic Activities of the U.S. and Great Britain following the First World War], *Banber Yerevani hamalsarani*, 137(6), 2012: 3–12.

31 ACRNE's (American Committee for Relief in the Near East) workshops, clinics and orphanages were covered in some detail in *Ashkhatank* September 23, 1917; September 30, 1917; *Van-Tosp* February 14, 1916; April 17, 1916; *The Literary Digest*, March 9, 1918; *The New Near East*, June, 1923: 12. One of the earliest to arrive in Armenia to assess the refugee situation was missionary Richard Hill, in 1915. He was followed by later groups of missionaries and relief workers in 1916 and 1917.

32 A letter from the 70-year-old father of Suren Papikyan, an Armenian student at the University of California at Berkeley described the importance of the soup kitchens for the population of Yerevan. Enclosed in the letter was a clipping from *Ashkhatank* recounting the high death toll and the rising prices of bread. Papikyan's father, in Yerevan, was thankful that his two sons were in Berkeley (the older brother was a pastor of the Armenian Protestant Church in Berkeley) since life in Yerevan was unbearable, with hundreds dying daily from typhus and starvation. The letter, published in the *Berkeley Daily Gazette* of April 14, 1920, went on to explain that

> The American relief committee has opened dining rooms or soup kitchens in twelve places [in Erivan], giving half a pound of bread to each person and some stew…If the Americans withdraw all the people will collapse and perish. I don't know how it will be next year, since there is no harvest, no seeds, no cattle with which to plow….

33 Ernest Yarrow had served as a missionary and president of the American College in Van for several years, but had retreated to Russian Armenia with other missionaries and the Armenian population of Van at the fall of Van. He was a veteran of the Spanish-American War and had later served in Siberia as a member of the American Red Cross. The story of the group is told by Jane Yarrow in *Ernest A. Yarrow. 1876–1939*, The Edward W. Hazen Foundation, 1940: 5–12. Her narrative includes valuable information about the retreat of the Yarrow family from Van in 1915.

34 According to Jane Yarrow, her husband had been chosen to lead the relief workers out of the country and decide on their exit strategy:

> The American consul at Tiflis secured permission from the Tartar chiefs for the safe passage of a special train from Tiflis to Baku on the Caspian Sea. Stranded in Baku for days by street fighting between the Russians and Tartars, this group of some forty persons managed to get food by back-door methods and subsist while Syme [Ernest Yarrow] and his committee were trying to arrange escape for our small group from a city from which the whole population would have liked to flee. A boat was finally chartered and we were secretly gotten aboard. A last-minute strike of the crew was "settled" by a long harangue of a skilled Soviet orator authorized by Syme to promise wages. We set sail on the Caspian Sea bound for Astrakhan at the mouth of the Volga…(Hazen Foundation, 1940: 8ff.).

They traveled for weeks from Astrakhan to Samara to Omsk, Krasnoyarsk, Irkutsk, Chita and Khabarovsk. The departure of the American Relief workers from Armenia was also discussed in *The Denton Record Chronicle*, April 11, 1919.

35 Oksen Teghtsoonian, *From Van to Toronto. A Life in Two Worlds*, R. Teghtsoonian and C. Teghtsoonian, eds., Lincoln, Nebraska, 2003: 91. Oksen Teghtsoonian's autobiography is a highly useful source on how assistance was initially organized, the arrival of American officers, problems that needed to be resolved in Yerevan. His recollections of events at Kazachi Post where he was based for a while are especially valuable.

36 Carl C. Compton, *The Morning Cometh, 45 years with Anatolia College*, Athens, Greece, 2008: 75f.

37 Vazgen Andreasian, *Vahan Cheraz yev ir yergn Hayastani* [Vahan Cheraz and His Song of Armenia], Beirut, 1977: 197.

38 Discussed in Kirakosyan 2011: 45f.

39 Before his short term as the Republic's fourth and last prime minister, Vratsian had held various governmental posts. He was educated at the Pedagogical and Law faculties of the University of St. Petersburg, and held leadership positions in the Armenian Revolutionary Federation.

40 Simon Vratsian, "Letter to Koboyan" in New York, January 8, 1919, *Hin tghter nor patmutyan hamar* [Old Papers for New History], Beirut, 1962: 276f.

41 NAA 200/1/125/f. 27; discussed in *Gyumri* 2009: 77.

42 NAA 127/1/2976/f. 20.

43 Karine Aleksanyan, "Aleksandrapoli gavare 1920i Turk-Haykakan paterazmi nakhoryakin" [The Province of Alexandropol on the Eve of the Turkish-Armenian war of 1920], *Haigazian Armenological Review*, 2012: 402, note 35.

44 NAA 105/1/2715/ff. 4–5,16.

45 Ibid.: ff. 40–42.

46 Melville Chater, "The Land of the Stalking Dead," *The National Geographic Magazine*, Vol. 36, No. 5, November 1919: 408. Chater also did publicity work for NER beginning in 1920, and was on the cargo ship Quequen that carried relief to the Caucasus in April 1921 (*Team Work*, June 1924).

47 Elsie Kimball Papers, Mount Holyoke College Archives and Special Collections (MS 0562, LD 7096.6, x1909, Kimball), South Hadley, Massachusetts, letter dated Nov. 25, 1919. The letter was written in Akhalkalak, where she was stationed at the time, and soon after her visit in Alexandropol. Kimball worked in Alexandropol for some years, and then in 1926 as a clerk and translator for the Georgian Manganese Company, a mining firm with offices in Tchiatouri (C'iatura), Georgia, and Moscow, Russia. She returned to the United States in 1927. She was Superintendent of Stenographers in the Law Department of Union Carbide and Carbon Corporation in New York City for twenty-one years. She died on February 28, 1972 in Mount Vernon, New York, at the age of eighty-four. For additional biographical notes see the Mount Holyoke College Archives and Special Collections Manuscript Register.

48 Chater 1919: 407.

49 For a discussion of orphanages and orphans during the First Republic of Armenia and government efforts to care for orphans, see Suren Avetisyan, *Merdzavor arevelki Amerikyan npastamatuyts komiteyi gorcuneyutyune Hayastanum, 1918–1930* [The Activities of the American Near East Relief Committee in Armenia 1918–1930], Yerevan, 2009: 80–112; Suren Avetisyan 2012: 3–12, and "Pastatghter Hayastanum amerkomi yev anglekomi gorcuneyutyan masin," [Documents Pertaining to the Activities of the American Committee and British Committee], *Banber Hayastani arkhivneri*, 2009 (2): 173–181; B. Balasanyan, "Mankatnere Hayastanum 1917–1920" [The Orphanages in Armenia 1917–1920], *Banber Yerevani hamalsarani* 1968(2): 217–220; Marine Martirosyan, "Vorb u anotevan yerekhaneri khndirnere Hayastanum" [The Problems of Orphan and Homeless Children in Armenia], Unpublished Manuscript, Yerevan 2009: 1–5; Kirakosyan 2011: 43–89; G. G. Makhmourian, "Management of the U.S. Relief and the Republic of Armenia, 1918–1920, *Lraber hasarakakan gitutyunneri* [Herald of the Social Sciences] 2008(1): 100. (http://lraber.asj-oa.am/385/1/2007-2_%28122%29.pdf).

50 NAA 205/1/619/f. 1f.
51 NAA 199/1/22/f. 77.
52 For Minutes of the meeting see NAA 205/1/566/ff. 45–48 recto & verso.
53 By early August 1919, the Catholicos had been asked to appoint priests who would provide spiritual and moral guidance to the orphans in NER's orphanages; the Holy See was happy to oblige (NAA 50/1/254/f. 95).
54 *Haraj*, December 3, 1919; *Hayastani dzayn*, December 18, 1919.
55 *Kran*, August 1, 1919; for a discussion of editorials see Kirakosyan 2011: 70f.
56 *Van-Tosp*, May 12, 1919.
57 NAA 105/1/2853/f. 153.
58 NAA 205/1/562/f. 33.
59 "Alexandropol and the Caucasus," *The Medical Work of Near East Relief*, ed. Geo. L. Richards, MD, New York, 1923: 32–34.
60 Ibid.: 33.
61 Ibid.
62 Ibid.: 34.
63 NAA 207/1/94/ff. 30–32.
64 For a full discussion of revisions and adjustments see Avetisyan 2009: 80ff and Kirakosyan 2011: 67ff.
65 NAA 205/1/750/ff. 126–129.
66 NAA 205/1/780/f. 161.

NOTES TO CHAPTER TWO

67 Leland Rex Robinson, "The Armenian Republic," *The Survey*, January 3, 1920: 344.
68 *The Memoirs of Herbert Hoover. Years of Adventure 1874–1920*, New York (5th printing), 1951: 386.
69 Haskell routinely updated the ARA and NER on conditions in Armenia and the scope of the relief work being conducted there. One of his cables, received at NER headquarters in New York outlines the status of relief work in fall 1919, and the difficulties faced in the transportation of goods to Armenia. It reads, in part:

> Haskell Tiflis, October 5, 1919. Near East, New York: No. 182. Following summarizes activities to date. Functions ACRNE assumed September 5. Army personnel arrived 15. Property funds being inventoried. Reorganization includes division of central office into five sections, comprising (1) administration; (2) investigation of actual conditions, needs; (3) operation of orphanages and hospitals and industrial work; (4) purchase, storage, transportation, distribution; (5) preparation budgets, disbursements, auditing, and exchange. Field assigned into districts and sub districts to operate from Tiflis, Batoum, Kars, Erivan, Alexandropol, and Karakilisa. Eight hundred thousand destitute, 250,000 homeless are afforded every relief possible by distribution bread, flour, wheat, and soup kitchens.
>
> …Transportation in securest trains; robberies frequent since completion withdrawal all British except from Batoum; lack train guards, and uncurbed general lawlessness constantly imperil our relief shipments outlying districts and force us to organize train guards and R. T. O. service. Poor terminal facilities Batoum additional handicap. These difficulties rapidly being overcome. Closer checking of food-stuffs distributed already made quantity available reach increased number. Organization now completed, extending operations daily; central distributing dump established Alexandropol, where hoped build some reserve for emergency, also obtained large military barracks from Armenian Government where fifty to sixty thousand refugees will be concentrated and employed on roads, public works, to reduce cost maintenance. Thirteen thousand two hundred twenty-five orphans in 49 orphanages in operation throughout Russian

Armenia, together with women, are now being employed in light industrial work which hope will be self-supporting soon as exportation manufactures from trans-Caucasia commences. Fourteen hospitals, 1,800 occupied beds, already operating; others planned. Aim our work hundred percent relief. Possible of attainment by expansion present organization. Haskell. ("Maintenance of Peace in Armenia. Hearings Before a Subcommittee of the Committee on Foreign Relations," *United States Senate, Sixty-sixth Congress, First Session, Copy of Telegram of Oct. 11, 1919, to the Secretary Of State From The American Mission, Paris:* 77).

70 See T. C. Lonergan's proposal for the temporary concentration of refugees in Armenia prior to their final repatriation in their homes, dated January 31, 1920 (NAA 205/1/634 pt. 2/f. 361–372).

71 Haskell Cablegrams to NER, Rockefeller Archive Center (RAC) NEF Box 136.

72 *Ashkhatank*, April 15, 1919.

73 Grace H. Knapp, *The Tragedy of Bitlis*, New York, 1919: 155ff.

74 According to James Barton, $11,155,426 was a contribution from NER, and $500,000 from the Red Cross. The American Relief Administration provided more than 50,000 tons of food valued at $10,630,872 from the Congressional Relief appropriation, and the Armenian government gave its notes covering this amount. By a later Act of Congress, March 1920, the U.S. Grain Corporation contributed 40,000 tons of flour, representing a governmental gift of $4,813,744. The Commonwealth Fund co-operated in a special feeding program for children through an appropriation of $750,000. Other funds and clothing were received from the American Relief Administration, the Red Cross, the Canadian Fund for Cattle and Seed Grain, Lord Mayor's Fund and Friends of Armenia (Barton 1930: 125).

75 Major Walter P. Davenport, Medical Corps, U.S. Army, "General Health Conditions and Medical Relief Work in Armenia," *The Military Surgeon*, February 1921: 139.

76 *News Bulletin*, American Committee for Armenian and Syrian Relief, July 1919.

77 Telegram dated October 11, 1919, in "Maintenance of Peace in Armenia…."

78 "Making Leftovers Both Left and Right," *The New Near East*, December 1921: 5.

79 "The Importance of the Old Clothes Bag," *The New Near East*, March 1922: Centerfold.

80 "Wardrobe for a President," *The New Near East*, December 1920: 24f.

81 NAA 50/1/127/f. 25.

82 "Col. Haskell Cables for Aid," *The New Near East*, January 1920: 10.

83 Haskell Report, August 1920 (RAC CF, Series 18, Grants, Box 12, Folder 121).

84 "Winter Conditions in the Caucasus," *The Journal of International Relations*, July 1920: 109–119. The same article also appeared in the February 1920 issue of *The New Near East*.

85 Kimball Papers, letter dated March 26, 1920.

86 Ibid.

87 Ibid.

88 Yarrow, July 1920: 111f. These included the districts of Nakhchivan, Yerevan, Kars, Karakilisa, Tiflis, Akhalkalak, and Alexandropol.

89 Yarrow, July 1920: 113f.

90 Yarrow, February 1920: 11.

91 Teghtsoonian 2003: 117.

92 Yarrow, July 1920: 115.

93 Ibid.

94 Ibid.

95 *The New Near East*, December 1920: 30.

96 Verjine Svazlian, *The Armenian Genocide: Testimonies of the Eye Witness Survivors*, Yerevan 2000: Testimony #38.

97 Yarrow, July 1920: 114f.

98 *Haraj*, December 3, 1919.

99 At its retreat, the Russian Army had left behind a number of delousers, which consisted of a large galvanized box mounted on wheels, with a revolving wire cage in which the clothes were placed. A file box under the galvanized box would reach a temperature of 145 degrees F., and after being maintained for 15 minutes, it killed adult lice and eggs. But due to the scarcity of fuel in the winter of 1920, no adequate supply of hot water had been available for bath and laundry purposes, resulting in an increase in the incidence of scabies and lice in the orphanages. See Davenport 1921: 150.

100 Yarrow, July 1920: 113f.

101 NAA 205/1/830/ff. 1–12; discussed in Aleksanyan 2012: 325–334.

102 NAA 205/1/634.2/f. 295.

103 Ibid.: f. 318.

104 Kimball Papers, letter dated May 8, 1920.

105 Ibid.

106 "Incoming cablegram N. C. 2—1276," *The Acorne*, March 27, 1920.

107 "Incoming cablegram N. C. 2—1333," Ibid., March 1920.

108 Ibid.

109 Ibid.

110 Ibid.

111 The unpublished and anonymous diary is in the collections of AGMI.

112 "Yanks Forced to Pledge Food," *The San Antonio Evening News*, May 12, 1920.

113 *The San Diego Union*, November 28, 1920; *The Kansas City Star*, November 18, 1920.

114 "Turks and Bolsheviks Keep Things Warm for E. A. Eckman in His Armenian Relief Work," *The Grand Forks Daily Herald*, May 12, 1920.

115 "Reds Shoot Brother of M. Bakhmeteff," *The Washington Post*, July 22, 1920. Dr. Byron Harmon of NER, who had left Alexandropol via Kars, had relayed the news.

116 Yarrow, February 1920: 11.

117 Davenport, February 1921: 151f.

118 NAA 205/1/855/f. 20; NAA 200/1/438/f. 11.

119 See NAA 205/1/635.2/f. 237; NAA 205/1/634/ff. 237, 238, 295 & verso, 350–351; NAA 205/1/799/f. 61; NAA 205/1/688/f. 50; NAA 205/1/873/f. 305; NAA 205/1/3/f. 250; NAA 205/1/636/f. 16.

120 NAA 205/1/634/ff. 283, 285.

121 NAA 200/1/638/ff. 88, 95, 110.

122 "Mr. and Mrs. Yarrow at Alexandropol?" *The Friend*, November 1920: 285f.

123 NAA 200/1/638/ff. 277–279.

124 Ibid.: f. 279.

125 "Barton Appointed to Relief Post," *The Boston Daily Globe*, September 5, 1920. Harold Barton, of Concord, MA, was a graduate of the Harvard College Class of 1909. Barton had lived in China for four years and served in WWI.

126 Harold Barton, *Twenty-fifth Class Report of the Harvard Class of 1909* (1934): 29ff., Harvard University Archives (HUA), HUD/309/25B/RR). Additional details of his personal life and work appeared in his Fortieth and Fiftieth Class Reports (HUA, HUD/309/40B/RR and HUD/309/50B/RR).

127 "Cable from Charles V. Vickrey," *The New Near East*, September 1920: 30. Vickrey's tour guide had been Alexandropol Mayor Levon Sargsyan to whom Vickrey wrote a note thanking him for his hospitality (NAA 105/1/2888/f. 118f). Vickrey also wrote similar "thank you" letters to Gevorg Ghazaryan, Minister of Education, and "Mr. Ohanjanian, Minister-President of Armenia" (NAA 307/1/46/f.159, and NAA 200/1/638/f 297f., respectively).

128 Teghtsoonian 2003: 125.

129 "Supplies en Route," *The New Near East*, December 1920: 25.

130 Fossum, a native of Iowa and a missionary of the Lutheran Church, served as Yerevan District Commander. He died in Yerevan in October 1920 from nervous exhaustion and convulsions at the age of 41.
131 NAA 205/1/636/f. 291.
132 NAA 57/2/1345/f. 1.
133 Eleanor F. Egan, "This To Be Said for the Turk," *The Saturday Evening Post*, December 20, 1919: 74.
134 Ibid.: 77.
135 For a description of NER orphanages in Kars see NAA 307/1/94/f. 53.
136 NAA 205/1/636/f. 284 and 288.
137 Ibid.: f. 289.
138 NAA 205/1/562/f. 33.
139 NAA 205/1/566/f. 71 & verso.
140 NAA 205/1/635/ff. 23, 3.
141 Ibid.: f. 26.
142 Ibid.
143 Ibid.: f. 17.
144 Ibid.: f. 26.
145 Ibid.: f. 17.
146 Teghtsoonian 2003: 125.
147 Ibid.: 126.
148 NAA 200/1/638/f. 250.
149 NAA 307/1/328/ff. 1–2.
150 In theory at least, the children were to be instructed in the Armenian and English Languages, Mathematics, National and General History, Natural Sciences, Armenian and General Geography, Singing, Drawing and Gymnastics, albeit at basic levels (NAA 122/1/328/f. 7).
151 NAA 307/1/46/ff. 162–164.
152 Ibid.: f. 152.
153 NAA 207/1/94/f. 52.
154 *The New Near East*, December 1920: 13; NAA 200/1/638/f. 300.
155 "How Kars Fell," *The New Near East*, February 1921: 9.
156 Svazlian 2011: Survivor Testimony #44.
157 *The New Near East*, February 19: 10; "Girl Plies Whip on Turks to Save Orphans at Kars," *The Day*, February 8, 1921.
158 Elizabeth Anderson, "Hunting Trouble in Armenia," *The Atlantic Monthly*, 1921: 695–707. Anderson had first been assigned to Dilijan in the winter of 1920 and was put in charge of two orphanages. On April 1, 1920, she received orders to move to Kars where she was appointed Director of Education and Agriculture. Just as she was getting the fields ploughed and the 5,000 children separated into classes, on May 2 she and her sister received orders to evacuate, following the May events in Alexandropol. Anderson, as other NER workers, returned to Kars on July 4, 1920.
159 Anderson 1921: 699–702.
160 "Late News from Armenia," *The Friend*, December 1919: 282.
161 Father Tigran Khoyan, *Nahatak tseghi anmahner* [Immortals of a Martyred Race], Beirut, 1983: 124.
162 "Near East Workers Remain at Posts" *The New York Times*, November 11, 1920. *The New York Times* also listed the names of the 38 American personnel in Armenia at that time and their homes in the U.S.: Ernest A. Yarrow, Director, NY; Mrs. Veronica Harris, San Diego, California; Harold Barton, Concord, Massachusetts; Elmer Eckman, Grand Forks, North Dakota; Milton D. Brown, Malden, Massachusetts; Robert L. Ferguson, Jacksonville, Florida; Arthur B. Hammond, Newark, New Jersey; Peter J. Jansen, New York City; Harrison Maynard, Topeka, Kansas; Olive Gray, London; Raymond Hillman,

Mission Hill, South Dakota; Dr. Jefferson Hawthorne, Framingham, Massachusetts; Dr. J. H. T. Mains, Grinnell, Iowa; Clark D. Martin, Pine Grove, Pennsylvania; Nelson P. Meeks, Yonkers, New York; Florence L. Myers, Hinsdale, Illinois; Myrtle O. Shane, Kansas; Clayton M. Skinner, Greenfield, Massachusetts; Elizabeth A. Thom, London (Ontario), Canada; Clara L. Bissell, Claremont, California; Frank J. W. Peers, Topeka, Kansas; Charles F. Grant, New York City; Mr. and Mrs. George De Forest White, Grinnell, Iowa; Joseph W. Beach, Bangor, Maine; Elizabeth Gillespie, Detroit, Michigan; Leonard C. Hubbard, Princeton, West Virginia; Elsie May Kimball, Mount Vernon, New York; Theodore A. Elmer, Oberlin, Ohio; Pauline Jordan, Welchville, Maine; Annette L. Munro, Newton, Massachusetts; Margaret Kinne, Ovid, New York; Elizabeth and Frances Anderson, New York City; Charles McBride; W. W. Nelson; Walter Richards; Captain J. Dangerfield, Miss [Alma] Fossum, Caroline Silliman.

163 Ibid.
164 Teghtsoonian 2003: 127.
165 Ibid.: 126f.
166 According to the report generated by Lt. Colonel T.C. Lonergan, Gen. Staff at headquarters in Tiflis, prepared on 31 January 9, 1920 (NAA 205/1/634 pt. 2/ff. 361–371), the largest number of refugees—117,000 out of a total of 333,605 on December 1, 1919— was found in Alexandropol; the second was in Yerevan with 67,000, Kars with 57,000 and Etchmiadzin with 52,000. The district of Alexandropol, in December 1919, also had the largest concentration of the native poor in Armenia.

NOTES TO CHAPTER THREE

167 For a discussion see K. Aleksanyan, "Turkiyayi tseghaspanutyan kaghakakanutyan sharunakutyunn Aleksandrapoli gavarum" [The Continuation of Turkey's Genocidal Policy in the Province of Alexandropol], *Banber Hayastani arkhivneri* (1) 2005: 18–25.
168 Kimball Papers, letter dated December 15, 1920.
169 760J.67/39: Telegram. "The High Commissioner at Constantinople (Bristol) to the Secretary of State," Constantinople, November 30, 1920—7 p.m. [Received December 1—5:25 a.m.]" *United States Department of State/Papers Relating to the Foreign Relations of the United States, 1920*: 805. (http://digital.library.wisc.edu/1711.dl/FRUS).
170 860J.01/367: Telegram, "The Consul at Tiflis (Moser) to the Acting Secretary of State. Tiflis, December 4, 1920—10 a.m." [Received December 11—10:30 a.m.] (Transmitted via Constantinople) *Foreign Relations of the United States...1920*: 806.
171 "Near East Relief Workers Leave Armenia: Sent by Kemal Pasha to Kars, where they continue to aid 7,000 orphans," *The New York Times*, December 21, 1920.
172 "Asks Turks for Protection," *The New York Times*, December 27, 1920. A similar article appeared in *The Kansas City Times* on December 27, 1920.
173 *The New York Times*, December 27, 1920; *The Kansas City Times*, December 20, 1920.
174 Two of many examples are: "Collapse of Red Rule Expected by Washington," *The New York Tribune*, October 13, 1920; "Armenia Being Sovietized," *The New York Times*, January 8, 1921.
175 "How Kars Fell," *The New Near East*, February 1921: 11.
176 NAA 114/1/22/f. 61 (in French); NAA 114/1/22/f. 62 (in Armenian).
177 *860J.48/80, No. 42*: 927. "The High Commissioner at Constantinople (Bristol) to the Secretary of State," Constantinople, February 9, 1921. [Received March 1.] *Foreign Relations of the United States...*
178 Kimball Papers, letter dated January 9, 1921.
179 "Food Intended for Orphans Is Seized by Reds," *The Albuquerque Journal*, March 27, 1921.
180 NAA 114/1/22/63 (in French); NAA 114/1/22/ff. 59–60 (in Armenian).
181 Clarence Ussher was replaced by Dorothy Sutton in mid-July 1921 (NAA 114/1/22/f. 132).

182 Oliver R. Baldwin, *Six Prisons and Two Revolutions. Adventures in Trans-Caucasia and Anatolia, 1920–1921*, New York, 1925: 86.
183 NAA 114/1/22/f. 10.
184 "Another Turn of the Kaleidoscope," *The New Near East*, January 1921: 6.
185 NAA 114/1/22/f. 8.
186 Ibid.: 13.
187 Baldwin 1924: 87.
188 "200,000 Armenians Dying," *The New York Times*, January 15, 1921.
189 NAA 114/1/22/f. 52.
190 Svazlian 2011: Survivor Testimony #37.
191 NAA 114/1/22/ff. 65–66; Ibid.: f. 56 (Armenian translation). Harcourt returned to Armenia in summer 1921, as the representative of the Lord Mayor of London and a few benevolent English societies. In Yerevan the British committee had two orphanages—where the children slept and ate but received their education in the NER orphanage in Yerevan—and two shelters. In December 1923, the British Committee ran four orphanages where 483 children found shelter; it took care of one hospital, a few workshop/schools, and conducted feeding stations in Yerevan, Ashtarak, Ghamarlu, etc., where 5,800 children and refugees received ½ funt of bread. The British Committee ended relief work in Armenia in 1926.
192 "New Plea for Armenians: 100,000 in Alexandropol Area Near Famine, Says British Foreign Office," *The New York Times*, February 17, 1921.
193 Elizabeth Thom, an NER nurse in Kars in early 1921, explained that within four weeks NER had opened "a maternity ward, nursery, medical hospital and scabies hospital," at Kars. The scabies hospital, she explained, "had once been an old armoury, and was in tumble-down shape…when the snow on the roof melted during the day, a small rain storm poured through on to our defenceless patients…" *Near East Relief (for Private Circulation)*, January 7, 1922; NAA 862/1/832/f. 2.
194 Kimball Papers, letter dated January 9, 1921.
195 Ibid.: letter dated December 15, 1920.
196 Ibid.: letter dated January 9, 1921.
197 Ibid.
198 Ibid.
199 Ibid.
200 Ibid.
201 Ibid.: letter dated January 29, 1921.
202 Ibid.
203 Araksi Pluzyan, *Im kyanki patmutyune* [The Story of My Life], unpublished manuscript in the collections of AGMI.
204 Svazlian 2000: Survivor Testimony #77; Ani Gasbaryan, "I know that One Day the World Will Condemn the Genocide," Interview with Heghine (Elena) Abrahamyan, *Hetqonline*, April 23, 2007. (http://hetq.am/eng/news/6479/i-know-that-one-day-the-world-will-condemn-the-genocide.html/).
205 *Near East Relief (for Private Circulation)*, May 14, 1921: 17.
206 Kimball Papers, letter dated April 25, 1921.
207 Ibid.
208 For a detailed account of the conflict and negotiations see Edik A. Zohrabyan, "Turk-Haykakan paterazme: Hayastani Khorhrdaynatsume" [The Turkish-Armenian War. The Sovietization of Armenia], in *Hayots Patmutyun* [The History of the Armenian People], Volume IV, Book One, V. Ghazakhetsyan, et al., eds., Yerevan, 2010: 262–276; also, Christopher J. Walker, *Armenia: The Survival of a Nation*, London, 1980: 319ff.
209 *Gyumri* 2009: 90ff.
210 NAA 144/3/110/ff. 42–43.
211 S. L. Nalbandyan 1980: 6f.

212 Baldwin 1924: 151.

213 Ibid.: 152.

214 Paxton Hibben, "Turks' Grip on Armenia," *The New York Times, Historical Section*, November 21, 1920. In support of his concerns, Hibben mentioned the stripping of the fortress of Kars of some 600 pieces of artillery by the British, and how, when two years later, Armenians had raised $1,250,600.00 "by private subscription,"

> ...and purchased in England small arms and artillery to replace that which the British had taken from them in 1918. Sixty per cent of this order reached Armenia—and in it, not a piece of artillery.

With respect to the Italians, who were selling and delivering arms and ammunition to the Turkish forces, Hibben quoted the answer of a member of the Italian Mission: "Why not?...They pay."

215 Ktrich Sardaryan, "Hayastanum sovetakan ishkhanutyunn amrapndelu ughghutyamb tsernarkvac mijotsarumnere (1921 April-Hunis)" [Methods Aimed at Strengthening Soviet Rule in Armenia, April-June, 1921], *Lraber hasarakakan gitutyunneri*, April-June, No. 3, 1986: 25; NAA 114/1/46/ff. 4–5. See also H. Abrahamyan, "Aleksandrapoli iradartsutyunneri shurj. 1920 Noyember-1921, April" [On the Events of November-April, 1920 in Alexandropol], *Lraber hasarakakan...*: 132; Artashes Boyajyan, "Alexandropol-Leninakakani gavari joghovrtagrakan drutyune 1914–1920-agan tt." [The Demographics of the Province of Alexandropol-Leninakan during 1914–1920], *Gidakan ashkhatutyunner. Shiraki hayagitakan hetazotutyunneri kendron*, XII, 2009: 125; R. J. Rummel, *Death by Government*, 2009: 232f.

216 Kimball Papers, letter dated June 18, 1921.

217 Ibid., letter dated November 6, 1921.

218 "Saved 17,000 from Starving," *The Boston Daily Globe*, July 17, 1921.

219 Baldwin 1924: 149.

220 NAA 430/1/1270/f. 1.

221 "Personal Letter from Miss Myrtle O. Shane, Alexandropol, April 22, 1921" *Life and Light for Woman. Woman's Board of Missions*, September 1921: 330.

222 Mihran Hovhannisyan, *Kensagrutyunner, kentsaghayin sovorutyunner, hishoghutyunner, yeghelutyunner* [Biographies, Traditions, Memories, Events], Hovhannisyan family collection. Among his recollections are experiences at the NER orphanages in Alexandropol and Jalaloghli recorded over 20 pages. I am grateful to the family of Mihran Hovhannisyan and to Professor Hranush Kharatyan-Araqelyan for facilitating access to the unpublished manuscript.

223 "Milton D. Brown, District Commander, Extracts of Report from Alexandropol, April 8th, 1921," *Near East Relief (for Private Circulation)*, June 11, 1921: 1ff.

224 "Medical Report from Dr. Russell B. Main, *Near East Relief (for Private Circulation)*, June 11, 1921: 2.

225 Baldwin 1924: 149. Alopecia is a designation for hair loss; anaemia for deficiency of red blood cells; cankers for spreading sores; ringworm for contagious fungal diseases of the skin, hair, or nails characterized by ring-shaped discolored skin patches covered with fluid-filled pouches and scales; oedema for swelling by fluid in body tissues usually in feet, ankles and legs; ophthalmia for severe inflammation of the eye; consumption for tuberculosis; catalepsy for a nervous condition expressed in the rigidity of posture and decrease in sensitivity to pain, regardless of external stimuli; pleurisy for inflammation of the membrane around the lungs; rickets for a disease of growing bone unique to children and adolescents; cataract for clouding of the lens inside the eye: erysipelas for acute infection of the skin; chlorosia for anemia due to iron-deficiency especially of adolescent girls that gives a greenish hue to the skin.

226 NAA 57/3/275/ff. 1–6 recto & verso.

227 Milton D. Brown, "Native Personnel of Alexandropol Near East Relief Orphanages Volunteer to Work on Half Food Ration and Without Salary," *Near East Relief (for Private Circulation)*, June 11, 1921: 2.

228 *Life and Light for Woman*, September 1921: 329.

229 RAC LSRM, Accession Number 25, series 3, Box 8.

230 "Pledges to Relief Agents," *The New York Times*, April 23, 1921; also, "Southern Russians Spare Relief Train, *The Standard-Examiner*, April 23, 1921.

231 860J.48.46 *Foreign Relations of the United States…1921*: 930. Wireless communication between Armenia and the outside world was furnished courtesy of the Italian Consul in Tiflis and the Italian Embassy in Constantinople ("Cooperation in the Caucasus," *The New Near East*, February 1922: 19).

232 "Constantinople Supply Department has forwarded four shiploads of supplies to the Caucasus since April 13th," *Near East Relief (for Private Circulation)*, June 11, 1921: 2.

233 James L. Barton 1930: 128f.

234 RAC LSRM, Accession Number 25, series 3, Box 8.

235 Cable from Jaquith in Constantinople to NER in New York, April 22, 1921, in *The Cross in The East and the Church in the West*, Near East Relief, 1921.

236 Ibid.

237 Ibid.

238 "Extracts From Letter From Erivan," *Near East Relief (for Private Circulation)*, June 11, 1921: 3.

239 Vickrey's report to Congress for the year 1921 was quoted in part in *American Medicine* 1922: 259.

240 Barton 1930: 129.

241 In his letter home at the end of April 1921, Milton Brown mentions the arrival of 6,000 children, while in his cable to New York he reports, "7,500 orphans have arrived" (Incoming Telegram, May 2, 1921, RAC LSRM Accession Number 25 Series 3 Box 8).

242 Kimball Papers, account of "Elsie White, George White's Wife," May 26, 1921.

243 NAA 57/3/511/ff. 1–20. The letter is dated December 17, 1922, Alexandropol, but his account relates to events that took place on October 29, 1920, beginning at 3 o'clock in the afternoon. For a discussion see Maro Avetisyan, "Mi pastatught Karsi hay bnakjutyan kotoraci masin" [A Document about the Massacre of the Armenian Population of Kars], *Banber Hayasdani arkhivneri*, 2006(1): 100ff. Father Goryun had stayed until October 1922, when he finally left for Alexandropol. Soviet authorities in Alexandropol imprisoned him not long after his return to the city.

244 *Life and Light for Woman*, April 22, 1921: 330f. Death rates at the Kazachi gradually decreased by the end of 1922.

245 Andreasian 1977: 344.

246 "Asks Permanent Aid for Near East," *The New York Times*, September 18, 1921. Minna McEuen Meyer, "The Largest Orphanage in the World," *St. Andrew's Cross* (Oct. 1922: 272) quotes a slightly smaller number for the first part of 1921.

247 NAA 118/1/209/ff. 104 and 105, recto & verso. Dr. Kocharyan stated at the beginning of his report dated March 1924, that NER had begun to provide information about its hospitals only in 1923. It appears that he received the figures for 1921 and 1922 retroactively.

248 "Near Famine Relieved in Transcaucasia," *The New Near East*, September 1921: 3f.

249 Varazdat Deroyan, *Misionerabaregorcakan kazmakerputyunneri ashkhatanke merdzavor arevelkum yev andrkovkasum* [The Work of Missionary-Benevolent Organizations in the Near East and the Transcaucasus], circa 1932, with an introduction by Ruben Sahakyan, Yerevan, 2008: 51.

250 *Gyumri* 2009: 92.

251 "Cable from Ernest Yarrow, September 10, 1921," *Near East Relief (for Private Circulation)*, September 10 & 17, 1921: 1.

252 NAA 131/2/35/ff. 3–18.

253 RAC LSRM Folders 104-101 Series 3, Box 9 NERelief Reports 104. "Alexandropol," NER Incoming Cablegram Jaquith to Vickrey, New York.

NOTES TO CHAPTER FOUR

254 The other commissars were: P. Makintsyan, Internal Affairs; A. Bekzatyan, Provisions and Foreign Trade; S. Khanoyan, Finance: A. Khachlyan, Labor and Social Security; A. Hovhannisyan, Enlightenment; D. Ter-Simonyan, Post-Telegraph; A. Shahverdyan, Workers/Peasants Affairs (Sardaryan 1986: 26).

255 At Myasnikyan's invitation, major intellectuals and artists returned to Armenia, among them writers Alexander Shirvanzade and Avetik Isahakyan, actor Hovannes Abelyan, architect Alexander Tamanyan, painter Martiros Saryan and others. Leading literary figure Marietta Shahinyan observed that Yerevan reminded her of the Weimar of Goethe and German intellectuals. (See Gohar Achemyan, "Hakhurn u krkot gragiduhin, Marieta Shahinyan" [The Courageous and Passionate Writer, Marietta Shahinyan], *GeghArm Monthly*, Stepanakert, reproduced in *Mitk.am*, December 29, 2013.

256 NAA 3/1/18/ff. 3,1.

257 NAA 116/3/14/f. 25.

258 861.48/1468. The High Commissioner at Constantinople (Bristol) to the Secretary of State, Constantinople, June 15, 1921. [Received July 7] No. 297, *Foreign Relations of The United States*...

259 A separate contract for wood between the Commissar of Forest and Charles F. Grant, General Purchasing agent of the NER (NAA 113/38/14/f. 55) was dated Yerevan, October, 1921, and read:

In continuation of the former contract signed by Mr. White on behalf of the NER and the Government of Armenia, the following agreement is made.

1. Forest Commissaire [sic] of Armenia is obliged to transport sufficient without spleting [sic] wood to load 750 railway wagons containing a minimum of ¼ sajin of wood each to railway stations Shahali, Pambag or Karaklis where the wood will be measured before acceptance by the committee.

2. The committee agrees to give the Commissaire of Forestry for the transportation of the above mentioned wood to the stations 2 ½ poods of flour and ten funts of soap, for each sajin on the delivery of the wood at the stations.

3. The Armenian Commissaire of Forestry obliges himself to deliver wood to the amount of 500 wagon loads, containing a minimum of 2 ¼ sajins each, before December 1st. 1921. The balance 250 wagon loads will be delivered during the month of December 1921.

4. One copy of this contract is retained by the NER Erivan and one copy will be held by the Armenian Commissaire of Forestry, Erivan.

5. The Committee agrees to pay for hundred (100) sajins of wood in advance of the work.

260 See H. Meliksetyan, *Arevmtahayeri brnagaghte yev spyurkahayeri hayrenadartsutyune Sovetakan Hayastan* [The Deportations of Western Armenians and the Return of Diasporan Armenians to Soviet Armenia 1915–1940], Yerevan, 1975: 97.

261 NAA 113/38/10/f. 42.

262 Ibid.: f. 41.

263 Aroyan was an American Armenian who had been involved in ARA's efforts in Armenia. He had later returned to Armenia representing The American Trade and Development Co. in Boston, Mass., to retrieve rugs that had been promised in lieu of payments for motor parts he had sold when in Armenia. Since he had not been able to resolve the financial issue, he wrote to Alexander Myasnikyan to explain the situation and receive his help. It was probably to enlist Myasnikyan's help that he was invited to dinner at the home of Dudley Lewis (NAA 113/38/10/ff. 45 recto & verso, 46).

264 NAA 113/38/10/f. 33. On another occasion, Dudley Lewis was given special permission by the Commissariat of Foreign Affairs to cross the border at Margara village into Turkey for an excursion to the base of Mount Ararat (NAA 113/30/19/f. 8). All military and civil authorities were asked to extend their assistance to Lewis and his party.

265 For types of assistance sent and specific amounts see Meliksetyan 1975: 79ff.

266 "Hin yev nor Hayastan" [Old and New Armenia], *Khorhrdayin Hayastan*, November 29, 1921.

267 NAA 113/38/24/f. 8.

268 Published in *Nork. Grakan, gitakan yev kaghakakan handes* [Nork. A Literary, Scientific and Political Journal], Yerevan, No. 1, November-December, 1922: 229ff.

269 The president of the Provincial Central Executive Committee in Alexandropol wrote to Fred Margerum on February 11, 1922 (NAA 138/1/14/f. 18) to thank the

> …American people, through whose efforts and assistance thousands of orphans, refugees and natives of Alexandropol were saved from the claws of starvation,

and, Fred Margerum for his

> …love and work for the little orphans, the children, for whom you were able to create bearable conditions under impossible circumstances.

Similar expressions of gratitude were also extended to NER General Secretary Charles Vickrey, a frequent visitor to Armenia in the 1920s and NER Caucasus Director General Ernest Yarrow (NAA 113/38/7/f. 29f.; NAA 112/4/758/f. 10 & verso, respectively).

270 "Transcaucasia Today," *The New Near East*, September 1922: 3.

271 *NER Annual Report to U.S. Congress for the Year Ending December 31, 1921*.

272 Esther P. Lovejoy, *Certain Samaritans*, New York, 1927: 117.

273 Mabel E. Elliott, *Beginning Again at Ararat*, New York, 1924: 207.

274 Barclay Acheson, *Plowshares and Pruning Hooks*, Chapter III, 1940: 11. A copious note taker of his activities during his travels, Acheson has left a wealth of information that throw light on the last few years of NER's operations in Armenia: the complex relationship that had developed between NER and the Soviet government of Armenia; the dynamics among the various members of NER's leadership; the internal situation at the City of Orphans and the American staff in the latter half of the 1920's. His diaries of 1926 and 1927, and his incomplete typescript for a book from 1940, are full of valuable insights and observations. His diaries, written with candor, reflect Acheson's energy and superb organizational and negotiation skills.

275 *NER Annual Report to U.S. Congress 1921*: 5–7.

276 See, for example, "Some Kiddies You Are Helping Feed," *The Ogden Standard-Examiner*, February 20, 1921; "Armenian Nation Looks to U.S. for Succor from Death," *The Herald*, April 14, 1921; "YOU are keeping them Warm!" *The Tomahawk*, February 3, 1921; "Americans should be Proud of Work by Near East Relief," "Cholera and Famine Grip Armenia; Hundreds Die," *The New York Tribune*, September 12, 1921; "Asks for Permanent Aid for Near East," *The New York Times*, September 18, 1921; "The Need," *The New Near East*, October 1921: 5.

277 "The Need," *The New Near East*, October 1921: 5.

278 *Report of the General Secretary to the Board of Trustees for 1922*.

279 John Finley, "Armenia To-Day," *The American Review of Reviews*, January 1922: 81–84.

280 John Finley, *Kindergarten-Primary Magazine*, March 1922: 100.

281 Finley, March 1922: 100.

282 Ibid.

283 Finley, January 1922: 84.

284 See *Bristol Papers*, U.S. Library of Congress, General Correspondence, Container #34.

285 Ibid.

286 Ibid.

287 *The Brewster Herald*, November 4, 1921.

288 *The Buffalo Express*, September 25, 1921.

289 *The Newark Evening News*, September 13, 1921.

290 "Worker in Far East Relief Comes Soon for Visit to Maui," *The Semi-Weekly Maui News*, January 17, 1922.

291 "Another Mercy Ship," *Team Work*, April 19, 1922, Vol.1, No.7: 2; *The New Near East*, June 1922: 20.

292 *Near East Relief (for Private Circulation)*, May 20, 1922; NAA 862/1/832/f. 33.
293 "New Jersey Relief Reaches Armenia," Special Cable to *The New York Times*, August 15, 1922.
294 "Filling the Good Ship in Newark, New Jersey," *The New Near East*, June 1922: 15.
295 "A Hardy Perennial," *The New Near East*, October 1921: 8.
296 "Understanding," *The New Near East*, October 1921: 18.
297 "Biddy Laying Share for Hungry Kiddies," *The Quad City Herald*, December 30, 1921.
298 *The New Near East*, September 1921: 7.
299 NAA 113/38/10/f. 10; NAA 113/38/2/f.75; NAA 113/38/7/f. 43 & verso.
300 NAA 114/1/22/ff. 204–205.
301 NAA 113/38/10/f. 6.
302 NAA 116/3/156/f. 91.
303 NAA 113/38/7/ff. 10–14.
304 NAA 113/38/10/f. 47.
305 NAA 114/1/122/f. 4 & verso.
306 NAA 113/38/14/f. 56. The Armenian translation of the text appeared immediately below the English, and according to the note at the bottom of the page, copies were sent to Mr. Abovyan and the president of the Cheka. A hand-written note below that says: "This is being sent to you for your information. We have already sent copies to all our sister institutions. M.D. Brown."
307 NAA 113/38/14/f. 9.
308 Ibid.: f. 8.
309 NAA 138/3/14/f. 46.
310 Ibid.: f. 50 & verso.
311 Ibid.: f. 80.
312 Ibid.: f. 52.
313 NAA 113/30/14/ff. 8ff.; NAA 113/38/27/ff. 196ff.; and NAA 122/1/112/ff. 14ff., respectively. For a detailed discussion and analysis of the various versions see Avetisyan 2009: 160ff.
314 113/38/24/ff. 17–24.
315 NAA 113/38/7/ff. 37, 38.
316 NAA 113/38/7/f. 38f. On the same day, January 13, 1923, Vickrey wrote two other letters, to A. Mravyan, identical in content to those he wrote to Lukashin (NAA 113/38/7/f. 34; 113/38/7/f. 35).
317 NAA 430/1/1280/ff. 1–6.
318 NAA 122/1/399/f. 32.
319 NAA 133/1/713/f. 4 & verso.
320 In a circular addressed to village schools, NER Yerevan Regulating Officer H. A. Maynard announced that by a government decision, missionaries were no longer allowed to work in Armenia and that they were therefore closing their work effective February 11, 1923, at which time all communication with them would have to cease. However, since the teachers had been paid for the school term in full, he hoped that the government would allow them to continue teaching to the end of the term (NAA 122/1/422/f. 7). Maynard also forwarded a copy of his circular to Mravyan, assuring him that they would no longer work in Armenia, but asked him not to close down the schools (NAA 122/1/422/f. 6).
321 Barton 1930: 132ff.
322 The agreement Barton quoted was signed by: "A. Mravian, Vice President S.S. Republic of Armenia, N. Tergazarian, Government Commissioner for co-operation with N.E.R.," on behalf of the government, and by "C. V. Vickrey, General Secretary and Member of the Executive Committee, New York, H. C. Jaquith, Member of the Administrative Committee, and Managing Director, Constantinople, Jesse K. Marden, Acting Director, Caucasus Branch," on behalf of Near East Relief.
323 NAA 113/38/10/f. 42.

324 Ibid.: f. 47.

> To: President of RevCom
>
> We are grateful for your assignment of Dr. Melkonian [Melkumyan] as Liaison Officer between the Near East Relief and your Government at Alexandropol. Dr. Melkonian was one of my most respected employees last winter at Kazachi Post and I am well acquainted with the work that he is now doing with the government.

But, he added,

> My only plea is that his present responsibilities will not be too great to interfere with his new duties with the Near East Relief.

325 NAA 113/38/14/f. 128.
326 Ibid.: f. 53.
327 Ibid.: ff. 112, 113.
328 Ibid.: f. 3.
329 NAA 122/1/422/f. 10.
330 NAA 113/38/14/ff. 105, 112, 113, 96; NAA 113/38/42/ff. 32, 158–159, 266.
331 NAA 113/38/14/ff. 50, 73.
332 NAA 113/38/30/ff. 98–105.
333 NAA 113/3/157/f. 15.
334 *The New Near East*, June 1921: 2.
335 As recounted to the author during interviews with Mrs. Khachatryan at the Hovhannes Shiraz House Museum in Gyumri on October 2013.
336 Yeranuhi Soghoyan, "Severski Vorpanotsi San, 97-amya Amalya Sukyasyan [97-year-old Amalya Sukyasyan, student of the Severski Orphanage], *Hedqonline*, May 31, 2010. (http://hetq.am/arm/news/45039/severski-orbanoci-san-97-amya-amalya-suqiasyani-husheric.html).
337 NAA 113/38/98/f. 116.
338 Ibid.: f. 113.
339 Ibid.: f. 115.
340 NAA 122/1/399/ff. 68, 72.
341 For the laws and chronology see "Iradartsutyunneri taregrutyun 1921–1941" [Annals of Events 1921–1941], National Archives of Armenia website. (http://www.armarchives.am/am/content/121/).
342 NAA 113/38/30/f. 88.
343 Ibid.: f. 86.
344 NAA 113/3/112/f. 40.
345 *The New Near East*, May 1923: 8.
346 *The New Near East*, September 1923: 9.
347 NAA 113/38/30/f. 148 ff.
348 NAA 113/38/42/ff. 299, 300.
349 Ibid.: f. 299.
350 Ibid.: ff. 302, 303, 304.
351 NER trained speakers to address national audiences in the U.S., and to that end produced speakers' manuals for guidelines. One of the manuals was entitled "Coaching and Utilizing Speakers," by Dr. William E. Doughty. Another manual, printed in 1921, was entitled "Securing Contributions from Large Givers, Trust Funds and Foundations, to be used as a supplement to the 'Community Campaigns.'" ("What Do You See?" *Team Work*, February 27, 1922, Vol. 1, No. 3: 4).
352 Volunteer committees represented a total of 2,068 counties across the country. On the State committees, serving either as honorary chairmen, active chairmen, or vice chairmen, were 41 governors, four judges, three senators, five college professors, bankers, merchants, etc. Organizations that cooperated with NER in 1921 included, but were not limited to: Protestant and Catholic Churches and Sunday Schools, The Federal Council

of Churches, Young Men's Christian Association, Young Women's Christian Association, Sunday School associations, Women's clubs and organizations nationwide, public schools and colleges, fraternal businesses, including Kiwanis, Rotary, Cosmopolitan, Lions, Masonic organizations, Odd Fellows, Elks, Knights of Columbus and Knights of Pythias, Agricultural organizations, Industrial Organizations, wholesale and retail, Armenian and Greek organizations, The Armenian Relief Fund Association of Canada, The American Red Cross. All members of governing administrative committees contributed their services without compensation, but it was deemed necessary to provide compensation to directors, doctors, nurses, or other administrators in the field, in order to command full-time service. Stipends were fixed on a purely social-service basis designed to cover only reasonable living expenses. No large salaries, or salaries in excess of a moderate living rate were paid. See *NER Annual Report to U.S. Congress 1921*.

353 H. C. Jaquith, "America's Aid to 1,000,000 Near East Refugees," *The Current History Magazine*, December 1924: 403.

354 John Dos Passos "One Hundred Views of Ararat," *Asia. The American Magazine on the Orient*, January-December 1922: 273.

355 Acheson 1940, Chapter III: 5ff.

356 Ibid.: 6.

357 *An American Report on the Russian Famine, Findings of the Russian Commission of the Near East Relief*, 1921:3f.

358 For a description of his tour, see Yarrow's letter to his mother-in-law published in *The Oneonta Daily Star*, November 2, 1921.

359 As on April 15, 1922 concerning the shortage of textile in Armenia, *Near East Relief (for Private Circulation)*, April 15, 23, 1922; NAA 862/1/862/f. 25.

360 *Near East Relief (for Private Circulation)*, May 7, 1922; NAA 862/1/862/f. 29.

361 NAA 113/38/42/ff. 326–328; for the Armenian translation see ibid.: ff. 320–324.

362 Ibid.: f. 36.

363 Some of the newspapers the proposal appeared in are: *The Elyria Chronicle Telegram*, September 13, 1924; *The Logansport Press*, October 3, 1924; *The Janesville Daily Gazette*, September 20, 1924.

364 See Inger Marie Okkenhaug, "Refugees, Relief and the Restoration of a Nation: Norwegian Mission in the Armenian Republic, 1922–1925," *Protestant Missions and Local Encounters in the Nineteenth and Twentieth Centuries*, Hilde Nielssen, Inger Marie Okkenhaug and Karina Hestad Skeie, eds., Boston, 2011: 207–232. Also see Bodil Biorn-An Unsung Heroine, (*hetq online http://hetq.am/eng/news/27216/bodil-biorn---an-unsung-heroine.html/*).

365 NAA 113/3/241/f. 2

366 Barclay Acheson, "An Emerging Russia," *The New Near East*, October 1924: 5.

367 Albert W. Palmer, "The National Council Endorsement of Near East Relief, *The Friend*, January 1924: 11.

368 George Sanford Holmes, "Rehabilitation and Reconstruction," *The New Near East*, June 1925: 17. Vickrey's answer was for the benefit of all similar inquiries:

> The part which Near East Relief had in the construction of this canal dates back several years. At that time Armenians were dying by thousands of starvation. We did not make any cash contribution to construction of the canal, although the idea and plan originated with one of our American engineers.
>
> We happened to have 7,000 tons of corn-grits given us by the American Relief Administration for the relief of starvation, and we had large quantitates of refugee clothing. Instead of giving corn and clothing to the refugees free of charge, leaving them in idleness, we did with this canal what we did with other public improvements: we gave able-bodied men an opportunity to work, for which they received in wages enough food and clothing to keep their families alive until the next harvest.
>
> In this way we not only saved many thousand lives, but brought considerable areas of otherwise arid land under irrigation, enabling these same people today to support themselves.
>
> I think most people will agree that this method of giving relief was wise and strategic.

369 *The New Near East*, June 1925: 16.
370 Acheson 1940, Chapter IV: 32.
371 Ibid.: 31.
372 Ibid.: 30.
373 Ibid.
374 Ibid.: 31f.
375 Ibid.: 33.
376 Ibid.: 34.
377 Ibid.: 34f.
378 NAA 113/38/42/f. 326f.
379 NAA 113/39/563/f. 51.
380 NAA 113/3/174/f. 46.
381 Inez Webster, "The Day in Armenia," *The New Near East*, December 1927: 9.

NOTES TO CHAPTER FIVE

382 Kimball Papers, letter dated March 2, 1920.
383 "Orphan City Houses 20,000 Builders of New Armenia," *The New York Times*, August 5, 1923.
384 Acheson 1940, Chapter III: 12.
385 NAA 114/1/22/ff. 195–197.
386 Reprinted under the title "Optimism in Darkness," *The New Near East*, November 1921: 16.
387 Andreasian 1977: 327.
388 "The Human Flower Bed," *The New Near East*, December 1921: 18.
389 On July 29, 1921, Mravyan had written Alexandropol RevKom President S. Manutzyan about transferring the Severski Post to NER, and asked for an update of ongoing negotiations with NER on the Severski.
390 NAA 114/1/22/f. 197.
391 "Alice in Hungerland," *The New Near East*, November 1921: 5.
392 *The Anaconda Standard*, September 12, 1921.
393 "Alice in Hungerland, Saturday, at Keith's," *The Washington Post*, December 11, 1921.
394 See, for example, *The Maui News*, January 31, 1922; *The Ontario Argus*, April 13, 1922; *The Ogden Standard Examiner*, December 10, 1922; *The Dakota County Herald*, December 22, 1921; *The Mohave County Miner and our Mineral Wealth*, November 18, 1921; *The Evening World*, April 28, 1922; *The New York Tribune*, December 1, 1921; *The New York Times*, December 27, 1921; *The Washington Post*, December 11, 1921.
395 *The New York Times*, December 11, 1921.
396 "Three Dollars Apiece," *The New Near East*, June 1922: 6.
397 "The Power of Children," *The New Near East*, December 1921:14.
398 "Alice of Hungerland Comes to Wonderland," *The Prescott Evening Courier*, March 21, 1922. Also see Anat Lapidot-Firilla, "Subway Women and American Near East Relief," in *Gendering Religion and Politics. Untangling Modernities*, Hanna Herzog and Ann Braude, eds., New York, 2009: 159.
399 "Rabbi Wise Asks Possession of 'Alice in Hungerland,'" *The New York Tribune*, April 28, 1922.
400 *The Evening World*, April 27 and 28, 1922; *The New York Times*, April 28 and May 16,1922; *The New York Tribune*, April 28, April 29 and May 16, 1922.
401 *The New York Times*, January 16, 1919; *The Brooklyn Eagle*, January 15, 1939.
402 Ibid., September 9, 1939.

403 Ibid., December 9, 1944.
404 Acheson 1940, Chapter III: 16f.
405 Ibid.: 17–23.
406 Ibid.: 18.
407 Ibid.
408 Ibid.
409 Ibid.:19ff.
410 Ibid.
411 Ibid.: 21.
412 Ibid.: 22.
413 Ibid. According to C. F. Rowland, Superintendent of Refugee Department in Yerevan, the Star Spangled Banner was played in Yerevan as well:

> One might almost think Ervan, Armenia, was a small transplanted section of America. The Stars and Stripes wave proudly over every one of our buildings here, and we are occupying thirty of them.
>
> The other night one of our native employees was married, and as is the custom, the marriage procession came marching down the streed led by a band. They were playing "The Star Spangled Banner!" I could hardly believe my ears, our national anthem played by a Russian military band on Soviet soil!"
>
> …The other evening I was invited to the home of a business man. One of the many toasts was "to the health of Theodore Roosevelt, the great friend of the Armenian people." Another toast was "to George Washington." *(Near East Relief (for Private Circulation)*, January 28, 1922; NAA 862/1/832/ f. 10).

414 Ibid.: 10.
415 NAA 113/38/33/f. 236.
416 Ibid.
417 I am grateful to Dr. Demoyan for forwarding the clip.
418 Lovejoy 1927: 125.
419 Ibid.
420 Ibid.
421 Ibid.
422 "Motion Picture in Behalf of Grain Appeal to be shown at The Princess," *The Rushville Daily Republican*, Rushville, Indiana, April 3, 1923.
423 *The New Near East*, May 1923: 14. For two years the inmates of the Virginia State Penitentiary sent a donation to the orphaned children of the Near East, the first contribution amounting to $120; the second was in a similar amount.
424 *The New Near East*, April 1922: 14. The short announcement identified the donor as a "negro convict in a Virginia prison."
425 The visitor was Northern California Near East Relief Committee Secretary Frank R. Buckalew of Berkeley ("America Called 'Uncle Country' By War Orphans," *The Berkeley Daily Gazette*, October 19, 1922).
426 Lovejoy 1927: 129f.
427 Ibid.: 130f.
428 Kimball Papers, letter dated September 2, 1923.
429 George L. Bowen, "A Sig Ep Invades the Interior of Soviet Russia," *The Sigma Phi Epsilon Journal*, February 1924: 89–99.
430 Ibid.: 89.
431 Ibid.: 98.
432 "Henry Allen Hopeful of Russia's Future," *The New York Times*, June 11, 1923.
433 *The New Near East*, July 1923: 3–5.
434 Ibid.: 1.
435 Ibid.: 5.

436 Ibid.
437 "To An Honorable Conclusion," *The New Near East*, December 1923: 15–17.
438 Ibid.: 15f.
439 *The New York Times*, March 12, 1925.
440 "Soviet Chiefs Laud Near East Relief Work," *The New York Times*, March 12, 1925.
441 Nansen devoted several pages of his 1928 book entitled *Armenia and the Near East*, to his visit at the NER orphanages in Leninakan (pp. 170–176). See also Fridtjof Nansen, *Betrogenes Volk*, 1929, translated into Armenian as *Khabvacjoghovurd*, by Evelina Margaryan, Yerevan 2000: 143–148.
442 Nansen 1928: 165.
443 Ibid.: 172.
444 Zvart Muradyan interview in *Aravot Daily*, October 9, 2010, when she was 97 years old. (http://www.aravot.am/2010/10/09/343651/).
445 Kimball Papers, letter dated July 29, 1925.
446 Ibid.: letter dated February 20, 1924.
447 Ibid.: letter dated December 16, 1923.
448 Ibid.: letter dated July 13, 1923.

NOTES TO CHAPTER SIX

449 In a special report prepared for the "Responsible Representative for Armenia" in Yerevan dated May 21, 1923 (NAA 113/38/33/f. 165), NER Yerevan District Commander John Evans presented the changes that had taken place in the orphan population in Yerevan between April 1 and May 18, 1923:

A. Total orphans, Erivan District, as of April 1, 1923
   a. In orphanages   3548
   b. Home placed   282
   c. Total for district   3830
B. Total orphans, Erivan District, as of May 18, 1923
   a. In orphanages   1804
   b. Home placed   567
   c. Total for district   2371
C. Total orphans disposed of, April 1st to May 18, 1923
   a. By discharge   407
   b. By transfer to Government   52
   c. By transfer to Alexandropol   646
   d. Total disposed of   1099
D. Waiting acceptance by Government, Orphanage 5   150

450 NAA 113/38/33/ff. 231–233. According to the document, dated April 21, 1923, NER agreed to also supply food rations until February 10, 1924, and asked that NER have the privilege of inspecting the condition of the orphans during that period.
451 One of the cables (NAA 113/58/27/f. 25) was sent to Alexandropol, while the second, sent the same day and in similar wording, was sent to NER's Tiflis office (NAA 113/58/27/f. 29). The cable to Alexandropol read:

> Expect to transfer, three cars boys, all ages, favus cases, Tuesday, as arranged. President Armenia requests postpone further transfers temporarily. Will comply unless advised otherwise. Wire answer. Letter follows.

452 NAA 113/38/33/f. 209.
453 Ibid.: f. 206.
454 NAA 113/38/33.

455 Ibid.: f. 204.
456 Ibid.: f. 148.
457 Ibid.: f. 149.
458 Ibid.: f. 160.
459 Ibid.: f. 156.
460 Ibid.: f. 125.
461 NAA 113/38/13/f. 57.
462 NAA 113/38/33/f. 114.
463 NAA 122/1/335/f. 34.
464 Ibid.: f. 51.
465 Ibid.: ff. 23, 28.
466 Barclay Acheson, "A Page of Polygon Patter," *The New Near East*, December 1924: 16.
467 NAA 113/38/33/f. 223.
468 Ibid.: f. 144.
469 "Welchville Woman in Near East Relief Orphanage at Severski," *The Lewiston Daily Sun*, April 26, 1922.
470 *The New Near East*, December 1923: 6.
471 Robert E. Speer and Russell Carter, *Report on India and Persia. Deputation Sent by the Board of Foreign Missions of the Presbyterian Church in the U.S. to visit these fields in 1921–1922*, New York, 1922: 559.
472 NAA 113/38/30/f. 103.
473 "1,000,000 Rubles a Day for an Armenian Child," *The New York Times*, April 26, 1922.
474 "Some Figures from Alexandropol," *The New Near East*, April 1923: 18.
475 *NER Annual Report to U.S. Congress 1921*: 17–21.
476 NAA 113/30/19.1/f. 32.
477 A type of fuel oil that becomes diesel when blended or broken down.
478 "Near Famine Relieved in Transcaucasia," *The New Near East*, September 1921: 3.
479 Report entitled *400 Square Miles Covered By Alexandropol General Relief* (RAC NEF, ACCA2009: 104 Series, Photos, Box 144). On the basis of the contents, it may be assumed that the report was most likely generated in December 1921.
480 *400 Square Miles Covered*: 2
481 Ibid.
482 Ibid.
483 Elliott 1924: 174f.
484 *400 Square Miles Covered*: 2.
485 Ibid.: 3.
486 Letter to Mrs. A. B. Caldwell of Cranford (NJ) in *Cranford (New Jersey) History*. (http://cranfordhistory.org/wp-content/uploads/2012/06/2012_06_05_12_32_41.pdf).
487 *400 Square Miles Covered*: 3.
488 Ibid.: 1. The report continues to describe NER's assistance to orphanages in the city:

> 1629 girls and 1274 boys fill six orphanages in the city itself. More children are being taken right along as they drift in from outside districts to drag their weak bodies aimlessly about from refuse heap to refuse heap in search of nourishment. They are kept here only until there are vacancies at the huge Kazatchi Post and Polygon orphanages. Thus we act as a sort of clearing house.
>
> The orphans receive daily medical inspection, and the sick are treated in the orphanage ambulatory, or if seriously ill, are sent to the city orphanage hospital. Our newly completed bath-house with its tile floor, modern tubs and shower will help keep down disease.
>
> All children receive schooling equivalent to our primary grades. Older boys and girls are being taught useful trades. The sewing classes make garments and mattress covers. Stockings received in the precious old clothes bales from America are first unraveled and then re-knit into children's sizes by the knitting classes. The shoe apprentices

make "churucks," native sandals of tanned cow-hide, and repair and re-make the worn shoes donated in America. The eagerness of these children, their quickness in "catching on", and their absorbed intentness on the work is an inspiration.

Besides these orphans, we take care of 900 needy children, virtually orphans, giving them food, medical attention, clothes and education at the "N.E.R. Home for Destitute Children."

For those orphans who remained outside orphanages, as well as to refugees, the NER provided general relief. The author described Alexandropol as

One huge refugee camp, crowded with pitiable orphans and hungry, diseased, frost-bitten wanderers from the adjacent country-side, that is Alexandropol. To keep more refugees from coming into the already congested city, relief work is now being done in 160 villages by Kazatchi Post under the direction of George E. Smith...

...food supplies are issued daily to the absolutely destitute only. There are 24,000 such, probably the most miserable derelicts in the world, in these 160 villages...

In Alexandropol proper,

...3,000 utterly destitute, together with a constant influx of pitiable objects, hardly recognizable as human beings, from villages beyond the area in which we are able to help, receive regular refugee rations. In addition, we furnish daily rations to 350 poverty patients in the governmental hospital, 121 crippled and infirm in the government infirmary, one hundred suffering children in the children's hospital and one hundred fifty employees of these institutions. N.E. R. help is the mainstay of these public charities.

489 NAA 57/3/275/ff. 1–6 recto & verso.
490 Ibid.: f. 5 verso.
491 "Items from the Caucasus," *The New Near East*, February 1922: 10; *NER Annual Report to U.S. Congress for 1921*: 22.
492 "Extracts of Letter from Dr. E. R. Graff, Caucasus Area," *Near East Relief (for Private Circulation)*, October 15, 1921: 3.
493 *The Poughkeepsie Eagle News*, June 20, 1922; "A City of Orphaned Boys," *The Charlotte News*, June 17, 1922; "American Gifts Support Village," *The Trenton Evening Times*, June 16, 1922.
494 "A City of Orphaned Boys," *The Charlotte News*, June 17, 1922.
495 Alabama House: Residence for local personnel No. I
Arizona House: Industrial School, main building
Arkansas House: Industrial School, garage work
California House: School No. 1
Carolina House: Main office building
Colorado House: Nurses' home
Connecticut House: Hospital No. II
Dakota House: Construction offices
Delaware House: Hospital No. III
Florida House: Playground building
Georgia House: Industrial school, sewing classes
Idaho House: Industrial school, power plant and water station
Illinois House: Orphanage residence No. I (350 children)
Indiana House: Trachoma orphanage No. III (350 children)
Iowa House: Central bath-building
Kansas House: Hospital No. I
Kentucky House: Industrial School, laundry work
Louisiana House: Warehouse No. IV
Maine House: Trachoma orphanage No. II (350 children)
Maryland House: Trachoma orphanage No. I (350 children)
Massachusetts House: Orphanage residence No. II (350 children)
Michigan House: Orphanage residence No. III (350 children)

Minnesota House: Orphanage residence No. IV (350 children)
Mississippi House: Teachers' residence
Missouri House: Orphanage residence No. V (350 children)
Montana House: Residence for local personnel No. II
Nebraska House: School assembly building
Nevada House: School No. II
New Hampshire House: Warehouse No. I
New Jersey House: Orphanage residence No. VI (350 children)
New York House: Orphanage residence No. VII (350 children)
Ohio House: Orphanage residence No. VIII (350 children)
Oklahoma House: Industrial school, tinsmithing, carpentry, blacksmithing
Oregon House: Industrial school, pottery making
Pennsylvania House: Orphanage residence No. IX (350 children)
Rhode Island House: Orphanage XII (350 children)
Tennessee House: Dining hall
Texas House: Orphanage residence No. X (350 children)
Utah House: Industrial school, poultry raising and gardening
Vermont House: Warehouse No. II
Virginia House: Residence for American personnel No. II
Wisconsin House: Industrial school, baking
Wyoming House: Medical laboratory and pharmacy

In addition, there was a Canada House, the name given to Orphanage No. XII, which served as a receiving station.

496 Margerum had sailed for the Caucasus on May 20, 1921 with Cora Beach, Elsie Kimball and Rowland Blythe (*Near East Relief (for Private Circulation)*, May 22, 1921: 4).

497 NAA 138/3/14/f.17f. The RevKom president responded on February 11, 1922, in a warm letter of appreciation.

498 NAA 114/1/122/f. 4 recto & verso.

499 *NER Annual Report to U.S. Congress for 1921*: 21.

500 *400 Square Miles Covered*: 5. The tuberculosis sanatorium in Dilijan was in operation in late fall 1921 and groups of children from Alexandropol were transferred there as reported by John McNabb, District Director of Karakilisa in the December 31, 1921 issue of *Near East Relief (for Private Circulation)*:

> Our Humanity Mills, the orphanages, are working full blast. Every day we take in a lot of strange, ragged little animals and in a few days make them into clean, bright-eyed kiddies.
>
> Last week a hundred tubercular children from Alexandropol spent a few days here en route to the splendid sanatorium established by Dr. Graff and Miss Pellow at Dilijan.

501 *400 Square Miles Covered*: 5.

502 *Near East Relief (for Private Circulation)*, January 28, 1922; NAA 862/1/832/f. 9.

503 Lovejoy 1927: 104. Mabel Elliott's letter read, in part:

> I have had my talk with Captain Yarrow, and after two days to consider and do some figuring, have decided to accept his proposition, which is to give up the Erivan district and take on the Alexandropol area. He asked me to get off at Alexandropol on my way back from Tiflis, and look over things, and serve on a committee to consider the problem of trachoma for the whole Caucasus area. We have decided to make Alexandropol a trachoma center.

Mabel Elliott continued to work with doctors in Yerevan where she also established a medical society in 1922:

> I have started a medical society in Erivan with our eleven local doctors and myself as members. We expect to invite in the outside doctors as guests. I am now getting a library together and fixing up a reading room…Dr. Ussher has very kindly offered to me the use of his medical library for this purpose, which makes it possible for me to

start the library immediately. I am asking Tiflis Headquarters to allow me to buy a few Russian and French medical books...

The doctors seem so pleased. Really, when one stops to think, these poor doctors are, as one of them expressed it to me, "In a veritable desert as far as any chance of keeping up with the medical world is concerned."

Also see *American Medicine*, Complete Series, January-December 1922: 188.

504 *Journal of the Medical Society of New Jersey*, April 1922: 120; Elliott 1924: 179; *NER Annual Report to U.S. Congress for 1921*: 21; "Items from the Caucasus," *The New Near East*, February 1922: 10. The first work sponsored by NER specifically directed against trachoma had been launched in Istanbul in September 1920. The hospital operated for about nine months. In May 1921, the trachoma specialist was ordered to the Caucasus. See "Trachoma in Armenia," *Report of the General Secretary to the Board of Trustees for 1924*, Appendix I E, Report by R. T. Uhls, MD, (formerly) Medical Director and Ophthalmologist, Near East Relief Caucasus Area.

505 "Would You Fight?" *The New Near East*, April 1922: 9.

506 Elizabeth Knowlton, "Hospitals in the Near East," *Hospital Management*, June 1922: 50.

507 Knowlton, "The Largest Children's Hospital in the World," *The American Journal of Nursing*, July 1922: 829f.

508 "Welchville Woman in Near East Relief Orphanage at Severski," *The Lewiston Daily Sun*, April 26, 1922.

509 Knowlton, June 1922: 50; Lovejoy 1927: 121:

Leninakan might better have been named the "trachoma city" than the "orphan city."

All the people in that country whose children had eye diseases tried to get them into the orphanages at Leninakan, where they would get food, education and proper treatment. It was not possible to tell whether a child was an orphan or not, but it was possible to diagnose trachoma, and practically all the children in the orphanages and hospitals of Leninakan had trachoma.

Of the many other diseases I will not speak...And the Americans who sent us to Armenia, the safe and clean Americans for whom I am writing, will be sickened even by reading of the things these children lived with every day.

510 *Near East Relief (for Private Circulation)*, January 18, 1922; NAA 862/1/832/f.9.

511 *Report of the General Secretary for 1924*, February 26, 1925: 58; *The New Near East*, March 1924: 9.

512 An examination of 30,000 refugees revealed that 27,000 or 90% were in the first stages of the disease (*Medical Record*, April 8, 1922: 592).

513 The report provided statistics on cases under NER care, listing the number of trachoma cases by year and their decrease over four years: On June 1, 1921 there had been 14,000 cases; on January 1, 1922, there were 9, 252 cases; on January 1, 1923, the number had been reduced to 5,140; and on January 1, 1924 the total number of trachoma cases registered at 3,163 (*Report of the General Secretary for 1924*).

514 Community campaigns were also launched on the cause and prevention of trachoma: "Today, trachoma has been eliminated from Severski Barracks except for comparatively mild cases. It is labor lost to cure these children and then place them out in homes where they will recontact the disease of which they have been cured; therefore it has become necessary to conduct educational campaigns in the communities on the cause and prevention of disease..." (*NER Annual Report to U.S. Congress for 1924*; *The New Near East*, June 1926: 7).

515 *The New Near East*, October 1923: 12.

516 Knowlton, June 1922: 50.

517 *Report of the General Secretary for 1924*: 58f.

518 Acheson, December 1924: 16f.

519 "School for the Blind to Open in Armenia," *The Daily News*, July 29, 1922; *International Record of Medicine and General Practice Clinics*, 1922: 228; "Hope for the Hopeless," *The New Near East*, January 1924: 16.

520 "Blind School in East," *The Kokomo Tribune*, August 11, 1922.

521 *The New Near East*, October 1923: 12.

522 "Schools for the Blind," *The New Near East*, September 1922: 17; *Near East Relief. Institutions and Industries*, 1925.

523 "Beginning Again at Ararat for the Blind," *The New Near East*, September 1926: 12ff. The first step had been learning the alphabet, with each letter being an individual arrangement of six dots. To make the plates stiff, heavy paper was used on a special wooden slate, which had a double band of perforated steel at the top. The operator punched the dots in the perforations with a steel punch at the proper positions. The transcription was made from right to left, and turned over to be read from left to right. An ordinary volume of print would fill several volumes in Braille.

524 *The Lewiston Evening Journal*, January 9, 1926.

525 See Zvart Muradyan's interview in *Aravot*, and a video of 8 minutes and 24 seconds where she narrates her life, published online in 2013 on the occasion of her 100th anniversary. (https://www.youtube.com/watch?v=vi2RtHnvu-U April 25, 2013).

526 Nikoghayos Tigranyan, *Oxford Music on Line*; (http://www.oxfordmusiconline.com/subscriber/article/grove/music/27954?q=Nikoghayos+Tigranian&search=quick&pos=2&_start=1#firsthit); *Aztag Daily*, December 10, 2011.

527 NAA 113/38/98/ff. 89ff.; NAA 113/39/420/f. 175.

528 Kimball Papers, letter dated June 10, 1923.

529 NAA 113/38/48/ff. 27–34.

530 Ibid.: f. 33f. Neosalvarsan, an effective treatment for syphilis had become available in 1912, but due to the considerable risk of side effects it carried, it was replaced by penicillin in the 1940s.

531 For a history of the establishment of the Boy Scout movement in Armenia, see Andreasian 1977: 253f; Raffi Papoyan, *Bardzratsir yev bardzratsru. Skautakan sharzhman taracume Hayastanum* [Rise and Raise. The Spread of the Scout Movement in Armenia], Yerevan, 1991; NAA 207/1/328/f. 34 & verso. For the development of sports and physical education in Alexandropol see Varazdat Aghababyan and Hasmik Sahakyan, *Marzakan Gyumrin. 1920–1993* [Athletic Gyumri. 1920–1993], Gyumri, 2004. According to Andreasian, physical education had been launched in 1919 through the initiative of Nshan Hovhannesyan, a school principal in the Polygon.

532 Khoyan 1983: 89.

533 Andreasian 1977: 254f.

534 Ibid.: 276, 279.

535 Vahan Cheraz had been in Armenia earlier as a volunteer fighter alongside General Andranik, and in the spring of 1915, with Soghomon Tehlirian. Tehlirian would later become the executioner of Talaat Pasha, the main architect of the deportations and massacres of Ottoman Armenians. Tehlirian was acquitted in a German court in Berlin in 1921. In late April 1918 Cheraz was in Alexandropol with the 3,000 Armenian volunteer army which had camped in the fortress and military posts of Alexandropol (Andreasian, 1977: 197). Cheraz had returned to Istanbul in 1919, but was back in Armenia in July 1920 and would stay till the end of his life, which came at the age of 41, when he was executed in the Metekh prison in Tiflis on trumped up charges of counter revolutionary activities, in January 1928. His stay had been less than 8 years, part of which he had spent in exile or in prison. From 1921 to 1923 he was intensely active at the Kazachi, when it became the nucleus from which future Armenian sports and the boy scout movement would spawn. For a full history of Cheraz's life and activities see Andreasian 1977.

536 Khoyan 1983: 128f., 138.

537 The story is told in Andreasian 1977: 303.

538 Papoyan 1991: 32.

539 The mission Cheraz assigned to his boy scouts echoed the editorial of the May 28, 1920 issue of the bi-monthly magazine, *Hye Skaut* [Armenian Scout] in Constantinople, which read in part:

> It is the anniversary of the Armenian Republic, today. Every Armenian is happy and proud. The dream of centuries is a reality today…
>
> But all expressions of this kind assume the awareness of resonsibility to shape a homeland and make it prosper…
>
> The Armenian is persecuted and tired; Armenia, ruined and deserted awaits you, your strong arm…
>
> Tomorrow, what am I saying, today, even today we hear the trumpet inviting us to the fatherland, that invitation is for us, especially you, Armenian boy scout.
>
> The work of rebuilding Armenia will begin, and when you step foot in your fatherland, from that very place, you will begin your creative work next to your older brothers…The bones of your race are before your feet, you will see the ruins of its destroyed homes, it will leave the impression of a graveyard on you.
>
> You will not dishearten…
>
> You will inspire that desolation with your song…
>
> The Armenian and Armenia await you.

540 Aghababyan-Sahakyan 2004: 30.

541 Ibid. The first unofficial football (soccer) game had taken place in Alexandropol, between the Kars and Alexandropol teams in 1916 (Aghababyan-Sahakyan 2004: 22). The matches continued for several years and became a popular sport. In 1918, the football team known as the *Mecn Vardan* [Vardan the Great] was formed, the first official football team to be formed in Alexandropol. The *Mecn Vardan* team would frequently play against the Yerevan football team by the name of *Sportagumb* (Sport Club). The first game between the two teams took place on August 8, 1920 in Yerevan and ended with the victory of the Yerevan team. The rematch was in Alexandropol; they played on the open field of the Kazachi Post, by the Russian Church. (Aghababyan-Sahakyan 2004: 23). Writing about the second match, Tigran Khoyan (Khoyan 1983: 119) describes the trip from Yerevan and the match:

> Sunday, September 26, 1920.—Today, at 3 o'clock in the morning (when it was still dark) we arrived in Alexandropol…
>
> We have brought with us from Yerevan the football team of the capital which will today play against Alexandropol's *Mecn Vardan* football team…We saw the announcements at the station and everywhere. There are no more tickets left…
>
> The game took place on the beautiful field of the Kazachi Post. The governor of Shirak, Garo Sasuni was there and presiding. There, also were the musical band of the city, well-known individuals, and a huge crowd. Yerevan won the game by a goal of 1 against 0.

542 In 1928, the textile factory organized its own football team, most of them former orphans of the City of Orphans who had found employment at the textile factory. In that year, there were other teams, as the Alexander Martuni, Lukashin, Dynamo, Pioner, etc. It is believed that football in Armenia was born in Alexandropol.

543 Father of Karen Demirchyan, who served as First Secretary of the Communist Party of Soviet Armenia from 1974–1988 and as the Speaker of independent Armenia's parliament beginning in June 1999. Karen Demirchyan was assassinated four months later in the parliament along with then Prime Minister Vazgen Sargsyan, two Deputy Speakers, and others.

544 *400 Square Miles Covered*: 2

545 Ibid.

546 Papoyan 1992: 32–46.

547 Andreasian 1977: 350.

548 Ibid.: 313.
549 Ibid.: 350.
550 Cited in Andreasian 1977: 305ff., 516.
551 "Parting From a Friend," *The New Near East*, April 1923: 15.
Milton Brown served first in Alexandropol and then in Yerevan. He later returned to Alexandropol, leaving permanently in 1925. As he was leaving the first time, in 1922, he requested permission to take with him souvenirs he had acquired while in Armenia. His letter dated March 29, 1922 to "M. Mravian, Acting President, Sovnarkom" (NAA 113/38/24/f. 1) read:

> During my two years' stay in Armenia I have purchased a few souvenirs which I would like to take to America with me. None of these things are new, having been used in my various households throughout Armenia. I would be very grateful if you would approve of the following list in order that I may have no difficulty with the customs either at Batum or Constantinople. This list would also help me to get consular invoices at Constantinople, permitting me to take these things through the New York customs. It is understood that these are my personal possessions and will under no circumstances be sold.
>
> I shall probably not leave for America for several months but from now on I shall be stationed in our Headquarters in Tiflis. M.D. Brown

The list Milton Brown submitted included: "1 chest table silver, 3 strings amber beads, 1 piece Persian embroidery, 1 Samovar, 3 Silver table jugs, 1 Silver tray, 1 Fur coat (coon skin). Rugs: 1 Turkinsky 5ft × 7ft, 1 Bokhara 3ft × 4-1/2ft, 1 Tabriz 4ft × 5ft, 1 Ispahan 2-1/2ft × 10ft, 1 Sumac 18ft × 12ft, 1 Caucasus 3ft × 6ft, 1 Caucasus 3ft × 6ft, 1 Caucasus 2-1/2ft × 6ft, 1 Armenian 5ft × 8ft, 1 Mosul 3-1/2ft × 8ft, 1 Kurdish 4ft × 6ft, 1 Kelim 10ft × 12ft." (NAA 113/38/24/f. 2).
552 NAA 138/3/14/f. 198.
553 Andreasian 1977: 356. The idea of constructing villages where orphans would settle down after they were discharged from NER orphanages was pursued by NER in the early 1920s but did not last very long. Nor was *Ariashen* ever completed.
554 NAA 113/38/33/f. 77.
555 Andreassian 1977: 360.
556 NER requested a plot of land on the shores of the Arpachai to use as summer campgrounds for groups of orphans. The land was granted in August 1924 (NAA 113/39/563/f. 49). Places were reserved for 550 children from the Polygon and 400 from the Severski for sessions that lasted 15 days. During the two-week period the children lived in large tents while the staff and the mobile hospital used the smaller tents. The boys were in charge of cleanliness and meal preparation, but a good part of their day was taken up by gymnastics.
557 Tereza Aghayan, *Hishoghutyunner tatikis Tikin Lusini masin* [Memories of My Grandmother Mrs. Lucine], Unpublished Manuscript, Lucine Aghayan Collection, AGMI.
558 Andreasian 1977: 312.
559 NAA 39/1/19/f. 19.
560 *The New Near East*, January 1925: 7.
561 Alpoyachyan 2005: 124f.
562 Ibid.: 147f.
563 Kimball Papers, letter dated January 13, 1925.
564 Alpoyachyan 2005: 129.
565 The story is told by Khachik Dashtents in *Ughtsyal aygabatsi yergiche* [The Singer of the Coveted Dawn], Yerevan 1967: 13–15.
566 Ibid.
567 Ibid: 14.
568 Alpoyachyan 2005: 124.
569 Svazlian 2000: Survivor Testimony #48.
570 Alpoyajyan 2005: 124.

571 Armen Armenyan, *60 Tari Hay bemi vra : husher* [Sixty Years on the Armenian Stage: Memoirs], Yerevan, 1954: 217.

572 Ibid.: 218.

573 Ibid.: 219.

574 Daniel Ghazaryan would later be known as a prominent composer and conductor of Armenian Children's music and theater, whose music curriculum was adopted by later generations of teachers.

575 Armenyan 1954: 220.

NOTES TO CHAPTER SEVEN

576 *Hayastani hanrapetutyan bnakavayreri bararan* [Dictionary of Inhabited Locations of the Republic of Armenia], Yerevan, 2008: 149.

577 NAA 122/1/328/f. 16.

578 NAA 207/1/328/ff. 31–40 recto & verso.

579 Ibid.: f. 32.

580 Ibid.: f. 35.

581 Madame Olga Romanoff, "Training Armenia's Daughters," *The New Near East*, July 1922: 16f.

582 Ibid: 17.

583 Ibid.

584 Ibid.

585 *The New Near East*, September 1921: 13.

586 Nina Brailovskya, "Sketches in an Armenian Kindergarten," *The New Near East*, June 1922: 10.

587 Ibid.: 11.

588 Mary Davis, "Kindergartening in the Near East, "*The New Near East*, February 1923: 17.

589 Ibid.

590 Brailovskya, June 1922: 11.

591 NAA 122/1/399/f. 31.

592 NAA 122/1/422/f. 2.

593 Ibid.

594 Ibid.: f. 5.

595 *The New Near East*, October 1923: 9.

596 A. Mravyan," Vorberi dastiyarakutyan khndire" [The Problem of Orphans' Education], *Khorherdayin Hayastan*, July 8, 1923.

597 NAA 122/1/422/f. 21.

598 *NER Annual Report to U.S. Congress for 1921*: 8. The report pointed out that the greatest need for industrial and other relief was in the Caucasus, but the whole economic life was so disorganized and tools and raw materials so lacking, that it had been hard to achieve acceptable results.

599 "Where Children Outnumber Adults," *The New Near East*, July 1922: 6. Also see Charles Vickrey, "Putting A Nation on its Feet," *Asia. The American Magazine on the Orient*, January-December 1922: 301.

600 "The Future of the Orphans," *The New Near East*, July, 1921: 3.

601 *Report of the General Secretary for 1922*.

602 See *400 Square Miles Covered*: 3.

603 Finley, March 1922: 100.

604 Acheson 1940, Chapter III: 7ff.

605 *400 Square Miles Covered*: 4.

606 Ibid: 3.

607 Ibid: 4.
608 According to a report in *The New Near East* ("To Replace the Weavers Who Died in the War," *The New Near East*, July 1922: 5), Yarrow had met Myasnikyan in early 1922, where the latter had reportedly said that due to the destruction of hand looms during the war it would be a long time before the country could manufacture cloth in pre-war quantities, and that because of the scarcity of sheep and financial inability to import raw cotton, textile manufacturing would be inadequate for at least two years or longer. Myasnikyan had also expressed pleasure that NER was teaching the ancient art of weaving in its orphanages, because it would "result in hundreds of young women in the new generation assisting in keeping the country self-supporting and will help to replace the thousands of skilled weavers who have died during the war."
609 "Near East Sewing Bees," *The New Near East*, January 1922: 16f.
610 "Woman Organizes Sewing Industry in Near East," *The New York Tribune*, August 7, 1922; "Orphan Children at Work," *The Washington Post*, August 7, 1922.
611 "Summary of Industrial Training," *The New Near East*, June 1920: 5.
612 *The New Near East*, February 1922: 5.
613 "Northwest Flour Real Life Savers," *Quad City Herald*, December 30, 1921.
614 *The New Near East*, November 1923: 9.
615 "Where Children Outnumber Adults," *The New Near East*, July 1922: 6.
616 *The New Near East*, May 1921: 14.
617 Ibid.
618 "Canned Foods in the Near East," *The Canning Age*, January 1922: 54:

> …Thanks to our tin cans, these boys turned out in the first three months 5,600 articles—soup bowls, cups, spoons, pails, basins, and water pipes. Milk is not the only canned food consumed although it is the only item purchased. Canned milk is purchased on a competitive price basis from the offices of the Near East Relief at 151 Fifth Avenue, New York City. In May, contributions came in so liberally that no bids were opened until the third week when bids were asked for 50,000 cases. The same conditions are expected through June. The children are probably the most consistent of voluntary contributors. Last October, one Philadelphia school with 2,500 pupils, gave 3,800 cans of milk in that month alone. Single cans and in carload lots they are received in all quantities.
>
> The Canners League of California has donated generously. Arrangements have been made so that the railroads of the state are transporting the goods to San Francisco free of charge…The Near East Relief carries it to the Dardanelles and Black Sea Ports…The vessels fly none but the American flag.

619 "Blacksmiths Teach Trade to Orphans in Near East," *American Blacksmith and Motor Shop*, January 1922: 282.
620 Barclay Acheson, "Our Machinery Hope of Armenia," *American Industries*, June 1922: 37–40.
621 Ibid.: 37–40.
622 "A Large Orphanage. Children Who Govern Themselves, "*Hawera & Normanby Star*, March 21, 1923.
623 Acheson, December 1924: 16.
624 Pluzyan Memoirs: 15
625 Ibid.
626 *The New Near East*, March 1924: 9.
627 "Children Save Orphanage," *The New York Times*, April 1, 1923.
628 "Serious Destruction of Relief Institutions,"*Hawera & Normanby Star*, 3 April 1923.
629 *The Barrier Miner*, April 3, 1923.
630 "Near Famine Relieved in Transcaucasia," *The New Near East*, September 1921: 3f.
631 "Hope and the First Furrow," *The New Near East*, December 1921: 7.
632 *The New Near East*, June 1923: 13. An additional 1,400 desiatines of land were put under NER's disposal around Yerevan.

633 "Agriculture in Armenia," *The New Near East*, June 1923: 12ff.

634 "Northwest Couple Braves Death to Help Armenia," *The Issaquah Press*, January 20, 1922.

635 Letter from Ethel Newman dated August 10, 1921 in "A Close-up View of Near East Relief Need Given," *The O.A.C.* (Oregon Agricultural College) *Alumnus*, December 1921: 7.

636 *The Sunday Oregonian*, January 22, 1922.

637 "Ethel Long Newman. Writes of Life in Armenia Where She Manages Great Orphanage," *Malheur Enterprise*, April 22, 1922.

638 "What Do You See?" *Team Work*, February 27, 1922: 2.

639 Hartill sailed on the SS *King Alexander* and was followed by tractor engineers Harry Hall and W. J. Cronin who sailed on the freighter SS *Sagaporak*, which carried tractors, several cases of other farm machinery and implements and varieties of seeds. The group connected in Constantinople whence they sailed to Batum ("Helping Armenia," *The Goodland Herald*, February 11, 1922).

640 "Teach Armenian Farmers: Americans Bring in Trainload of Agricultural Machinery," *The New York Times*, April 27, 1922.

641 "Hope Sprouts from Grain Seeds," *The New Near East*, September 1922: 5.

642 "Armenian Crop Doubled: American Tractors Teach a Lesson to Native Farmers," *The New York Times*, Sept. 1, 1922.

643 *Institutions and Industries* 1925: 38:

> When it is considered that Armenia used to stir its heavy soil with a plow requiring ten yokes of oxen, it will be understood what a paralysis of food production resulted from this terrific reduction in animal power. The reduction was a result of Turkish invasion and general disorganization immediately following the War. In fact, in one section, where before the War there were 2500 head of oxen and horses, there were in 1922 only 50 oxen and four horses. The natural result was that villages, in a rich grain section which sowed on an average 300 tons of grain per village before the War, were able in 1922 to sow by actual count only 174 bushels, and 1923 was only slightly better.

644 NAA 430/1/1280/ff. 7–13. Kansan agricultural expert William A. Biby's report in fall 1923 was even more enthusiastic:

> I have seen corn twelve feet high; Wheat tall enough to hide a walking man.
>
> Rich, black soil nowhere less than a yard deep; Hydraulic power possibilities enough to irrigate production beyond men's dreams.

And, Biby thought, "What a pity" that the United States turned down a mandate of potentially "the future garden spot of the world," and added:

> …I am not going to say that America made a business mistake when she turned down a mandate in Armenia, but I want to know who said that Armenia was a desert!…I am inclined to believe that the European diplomats who led us to think that the Armenian mandate was a hopeless proposition were trying to bamboozle us. If we spent on Armenia a quarter of what we have spent on the Philippines, we not only would have a self-supporting, thrifty country, but a country paying back with interest every cent we have invested there…
>
> We Americans are operating a farm project of 35,000 acres to introduce modern agriculture, backing a move to repatriate homeless farmers from Turkish Armenia on 60,000 acres of virgin prairie land, making the refugees earn relief rations by rebuilding destroyed villages, and are using gifts of American corn to restore ruined irrigation canals which will feed life-saving waters to a once-productive land (*The New Near East*, January 1923: 14ff.).

645 Agriculture in Armenia," *The New Near East*, June 1923: 13ff.

646 "Armenia Returns to the Land," *The New Near East*, June 1925: 18.

647 Ibid.

648 *Report of the General Secretary for 1922*.

649 *Institutions and Industries* 1925: 43. In 1925 the electric station was transferred to the Armenian Government. NER was reimbursed in part and retained the rights to electric service for its Farm School at that station and the use of the station for NER's instructional purposes.

650 *Institutions and Industries* 1925: 43.

651 "Quarterly Report on Near East Relief Institute of Agriculture, Stepanavan, Russian Armenia, July, August, September, 1924," Appendix III B: 41–48, by Samuel Newman, in *Report of the General Secretary for 1922*.

652 "Near East Relief Institute of Agriculture, Stepanavan, Russian Armenia," *Report of the General Secretary for 1922*, Appendix III A. The administration and faculty consisted of: "Capt. E. A. Yarrow, Director General, Near East Relief, Caucasus; Samuel E. Newman, Dean of Agriculture, Near East Relief Caucasus, Graduate of University of Idaho; Edward W. Rankin, Dean of Academy, Graduate, McCormick Seminary and Princeton University Seminary; Leon Tatadjian, Chief of Agricultural Staff, Graduate Expert from England and Germany; H. Barghagarian, B. Sc., Chief of Laboratory Dept., Chemical expert of the University of Tiflis; Peter O. Floyd, Dairying and Cotton Specialist, Cotton grower and farm manager from Atlanta, Georgia; Dean of Girls and Agricultural Adviser, Ethel L. Newman, B.Sc., Graduate, Oregon Agricultural College; Phyllis H. Brown, AB, Horticulturist and Gardening Specialist, Graduate, Michigan Agricultural College and Michigan School of Horticulture; William J. Cronin, Farm Mechanics Department, New York State Institute of Agriculture, Department Head on Agricultural Staff," and five Armenian graduates from the Polytechnic Institute of Tiflis. There were also twenty other, unnamed Armenian instructors, both academic and agricultural.

653 NAA 430/1/1292/f. 1.

654 Budget items included:

American staff salaries and maintenance	$965.00
Armenian staff salaries and maintenance	$2,815.79
Students, food and clothing	$4,879.94
Students, medical service	$126.00
Buildings and equipment, upkeep	$1,144.02
Printing and school supplies	$134.29
Transportation	$101.01
Fuel, light and water	$237.16
Telephone and cable	$5.00
*Forage, grain and stable	$70.84
Miscellaneous	$239.62
	$10,808.75

*It was expected that items such as forage, grain, etc., would later be absorbed by farm production and that the orphan-student food cost would be reduced by the production or that the present average cost of approximately $11,000 monthly will be reduced to approximately $10,000 monthly or a yearly budget of $120,000. ("Near East Relief Institute of Agriculture, Stepanavan, Russian Armenia," *Report of the General Secretary for 1922*, Appendix III A).

655 NER sent several movies on agricultural methods, one of which was filmed in California, announced *The Los Angeles Times*, January 30, 1924 in "Southland Farm Film Will Help Near East Young." The article read, in part:

> California methods of horticulture and agriculture, depicted in three reels of motion picture recently sent overseas by the Near East Relief Commission, will go far in demonstrating to more than 100,000 youths of Asia Minor countries the possibilities in lands now lying idle in a climate similar to that of the Pacific-Southwest, according to the local chapter of the relief agency.
>
> The reels are descriptive of California orange growing, bean raising and sugar beet culture and are being contributed by the Los Angeles Chamber of Commerce and the California Fruit Grower's Exchange.

> "For the present," says Mr. Vickrey, world secretary of the relief organization, "these California films are to be shown at American orphanages and schools in and around Alexandropol, Trans-Caucasus, where more than 17,000 children are being taught useful trades. Later the pictures will be shown in Greece, Syria and Palestine."

656 John Evans left his position as District Commander in Yerevan in August 1923, and transferred to Alexandropol. In a letter to "Comrade Yerznkyan," People's Commissar of Agriculture, Evans expressed his thanks and gratitude for the help and affection he was extended by members of the SSRA government (NAA 123/1/77/f. 76).

657 "Quarterly Report on Near East Relief Institute of Agriculture…," July, August, September, 1924," Appendix III.B: 95

658 Kimball Papers, letter dated October 14, 1924.

659 Ibid.

660 Ibid.: letter dated August 12, 1925.

661 Ibid.

662 *Distribution of Near East Relief Orphanages in its Schools in Armenia* (RAC LSRM, Folders 104-101, Series 3, Box 9, NERelief Reports).

663 *Institutions and Industries* 1925: 37ff.

664 *The New Near East*, October 1923: 12.

665 Madam Tsendorf was described as the wife of one of the largest stock-farmers in Tsarist Russia. She had lived in Moscow and assisted her husband in the management of seven big estates in southern Russia and had received the title of Veterinary Surgeon from the Government College in Moscow. During the revolution she had become a refugee in south Russia. When NER discovered that she was a cattle expert, she was employed in one of the farming projects in northern Armenia, from which she rose rapidly to her position as director.

666 C. D. Morris, "Madam Zonia Tsendorf, Cattle Expert," *The New Near East*, September 1922: 17.

667 "Speaker Says Conditions in Russia Better," *The Sioux City Journal*, November 20, 1926.

668 "American Battles Tartar Raiders All Day, Till Cavalry Saves Near East Relief Ranch," *The New York Times*, July 19, 1926.

669 *The Hamilton Evening Journal*, September 20, 1926.

670 *Institutions and Industries* 1925: 39.

671 Ibid.: 37.

672 Ibid.: 37ff.

673 Ibid: 39.

674 "Quarterly Report on Near East Relief Institute of Agriculture…," July, August, September, 1924, Appendix III B: 94.

675 *Institutions and Industries* 1925: 37ff.

676 Barclay Acheson, "At Djelal Oghli and Kara Kala," *The New Near East*, July 1925: 15f. The age requirement was adjusted in summer 1925 to allow boys less than 14 years of age to work.

677 "Quarterly Report, Orphanage Department, Djalal Oghlou," by Elsie Kimball, Kimball Papers, October 1, 1924.

678 "Last Year's Gardens," *The New Near East*, February 1922: 12.

679 "Hope and the First Furrow," *The New Near East*, December 1921: 7.

680 *The New Near East*, March 1924: 13.

681 Barclay Acheson, "A Model Village," *The New Near East*, October 1924: 12.

682 Clara D. Noyes, R.N., "Department of Red Cross Nursing," *The American Journal of Nursing*, July 1924: 827. In 1921, Mabel Elliott had established a nursing school in Yerevan with a class of 28 students:

> We have our training class well under way. There are 28 girls to start with. They all go to one of Mrs. Power's hospitals for an English class, and Miss Priest and Mrs. Power each have classes in nurses' courses. Then from six to eight o'clock they go to the Near East Relief night school for their lessons in ordinary studies. All these girls are from the orphanages. They are so happy in their work. It is a pleasure to see them. Miss

Priest and Mrs. Power are busy getting their uniforms in order. After three months, those who pass their examinations will be capped. (Lovejoy, 1927: 103).

683 "Czar's Old Barracks Used to Train Nurses in Near East," *The Boston Daily Globe*, August, 1922.
684 *The New Near East*, March 1924: 13.
685 *The New Near East*, January 1924: 5.
686 NAA 154/1/60/ff. 5–7.
687 The event was covered in many U.S. newspapers, with *The Daily Times* in its April 24, 1924 issue (2nd edition) reporting that a message from Moscow to NER headquarters in New York announced the dedication of the school to Edith May Winchester.
688 For the detailed curriculum in nurse training by Elsie L. Jarvis, Director of the Edith Winchester School of Nursing see NAA 131/3/642/ff. 84–89.
689 NAA 131/3/642/f. 96.
690 Mabel Smith, "Three American Nurses in Armenia," *The American Journal of Nursing*, January 1927: 38; also Clara D. Noyes, R. N., "Department of Red Cross Nursing," ibid., December 1928: 1254.
691 NAA 154/1/60/ff. 9–10.
692 *Institutions and Industries* 1925: 53.
693 "Annual Report to Congress," *The New Near East*, June 1926: 7.
694 Elsie Jarvis, "Edith Winchester School for Nurses," *The New Near East*, March 1927: 13. There was also an Eye, Ear, Nose and Throat clinic, a special eye clinic for the diagnosis and treatment of trachoma, and a pediatric care section where a limited number of patients from the outside were admitted.
695 Edna F. Steiger, "The Open Forum," *The American Journal of Nursing*, April 1927: 303:

"…as this is the first appointment of this kind with the organization, she is quite proud of her position, and is certainly a wonderful help to me. She was, as are most of our nurses, a former inmate of the orphanage and then graduated from our training school. When we see results of this kind, it helps to realize that our efforts are not in vain."

696 The story was carried in a large number of U.S. newspapers nationwide, a few examples being: "Thousands Said to be Injured, Homes in Ruins," *The Miami Daily News*, October 23, 1926; "Graphic Tale of Armenia's Death-Dealing, Destructive Quake Told by Eye-Witness," *The Miami Daily News and Metropolis*, October 26, 1926; "100,000 Made Homeless," *The Cornell Daily Sun*, October 25, 1926 and "Quakes Lasting 15 Days Alarm Armenians," November 8, 1926; "Russia: Titan Earthquake," *TIME Magazine*, November 1, 1926; "Relief Worker Tells of Death and Destruction Caused by Earthquakes," *The Reading Eagle*, October 28, 1926; "300 Armenians Buried by Quake. American Doctors Restore Peace to Terror Stricken Inhabitants. Thousands Homeless," *The Spokesman-Review*, October 24, 1926; "Scores Perish in Armenia Earthquake," *The Ludington Sunday Morning News*, Sunday, October 24, 1926; "Quake Destroys Golden Rule Orphanages," *The Alto Herald*, April 21, 1927, and others.
697 A correspondent of the Associated Press had spent two days, October 27 and 28, in the earthquake area and reported on the 29th that:

The Government and Near East Relief reports reveal that the casualties of last week's great earth shock will be higher than at first thought. In the villages of Alexandrovka, Daharlu and Karakilis alone 152 persons were buried in the ruins and 210 badly injured. If the same proportion of death prevails in the other thirty-four devastated villages, the total loss of life will exceed 1,500, as against the 600 first reported.

…Long caravans of bandaged, limping peasants make their way haltingly over the broken roads, searching for new abodes, reluctant to begin the work of restoring their ruined homes because of the continued earth shocks, which fill them with fear of a new calamity. Wagons, donkeys and horses piled high with people, furniture and bedding form a mournful cavalcade as the natives wander from one village to another in search of succor.

>Frenzied mothers were observed carrying dead babies in their arms, refusing to believe that life had left the frail bodies. Snow and bitter cold in the mountains have driven packs of famished wolves to the plains, where they have devoured the carcasses of cattle and even human bodies caught in the ruins.

698 A list of the American relief workers was published in the *The Spokesman-Review* on October 24, 1926). They were: H. B. Allen, Kent, New York; Ray C. Baker, Clyde, Michigan; Joseph W. Beach, Bangor, Maine; Charles K. Carroll, McGregor, Iowa; Adela H. Chickering, Spencer, Massachusetts; Edwin M. Douglas, East Orange, New Jersey; Everett D. Gunn, Nickerson, Kansas; Olivia M. Hill, Cresco, Pennsylvania; Elsie I. Jarvis, Washington, DC; Maytie B. Johnson, Burlington, Iowa; Laura MacFetridge, Morrisville, Pennsylvania; Solon P. Massey, Denver, Colorado; Louise B. Paisley, Mount Vernon, New York; Mrs. Paul H. Phillips, Cushman, Montana and Nampa Idaho; H. Sisson, Wauseon, Ohio; Mary C. Sisson, Philadelphia, Pennsylvania; Edna F. Steiger, New York City and Williamsport, Pennsylvania; Dorothy Stratton, South Norwalk, Connecticut; Inez Webster, Galesburg, Illinois; Marjorie Wilson, New York, New York.

699 Noyes, December 1926: 968.

700 "Orphans Aid Near East Relief," *The New York Times*, June 17, 1927.

701 Storm Adds to Horror" *The Los Angeles Times*, October 31, 1926.

702 Noyes, December 1926: 968.

703 Ibid.: 967f.; Smith, January 1927: 38ff.

704 *The New York Times*, November 4. A conference was held in Beach's office on February 22, 1927 to discuss the situation following the earthquake (NAA 154/3/6/f. 50). Present were Joseph Beach, as Chairman, Olivia M. Hill, M. B. Johnson, G. Sargsyan, Dr. Atapegyan, General Secretary of the Armenian Red Cross, and interper Hambaryan from Olivia Hill's office. The Armenian Red Cross, which had cared for thousands suffering from the damages of the earthquake, needed a supplement for March and April 1927. One of the issues that emerged concerned 3,000 blankets, which were en route from the Bible Lands Mission Aid Association of London. Sargsyan pointed out that a considerable amount could be raised if the blankets were sold and used to help the villagers. Especially since, he pointed out, villagers in Armenia preferred quilts filled with wool. He was concerned that the villagers might in any case sell them in Leninakan but receive nowhere close to the value. Joseph Beach stated that it would be difficult to explain to the committee in London such a policy and felt that a portion of the blankets at least, should actually be distributed. NER agreed to furnish a sum of money not to exceed 20,000 rubles to help the Armenian Red Cross continue its work. The work included two tea stations, a milk station for babies, and the daily feeding of adults and children. The Armenian Red Cross would then provide daily and weekly reports to NER (NAA 157/3/6/f. 48).

705 According to *The New York Times* November 18, 1926 issue, "The Soviet State Insurance organization will pay fire insurance totaling 2,500,000 rubles for houses and property destroyed during the recent earthquake in Leninakan, Armenia. This varies from the general rule, which refuses damage claims for earthquake or volcano losses."

706 "Triplets born in Quake," *The New York Times*, November 1, 1926.

707 Smith, January 1927: 38.

708 "From the Near East," *The American Journal of Nursing*, April 1927: 303.

709 George M. Wilcox, "Education in Soviet Armenia," *The Journal of Educational Sociology*, December 1928: 228.

710 NAA 131/3/558/f. 83.

711 *Institutions and Industries* 1925: 52.

712 "Orphan Teachers," *The New Near East*, September 1924: 7.

713 *The New Near East*, June 1926: 5.

714 *NER Annual Report to U.S. Congress for 1926*: 18.

715 Paul Monroe, *Educational Policy of the Near East Relief*, New York, 1924:1–24.

716 Ibid.: 11ff.

717 Ibid.: 8.

718 Ibid.: 10.
719 Pluzyan Memoirs: 18ff.
720 Monroe 1924: 16f.
721 Ibid.: 14f.
722 NAA 39/1/19/f. 1.
723 Ibid. The suggestions were summarized thus:

  1. Prof. Paul Monroe: "Little work in the classes and much work outside classes." He pointed out the natural setting sprawling around the Polygon and suggested that we take advantage of it in teaching the natural sciences. He showed us an Armenian village and suggested that we use it as a basis while teaching social sciences."
  2. Mr. Barclay Acheson: "Outdoors games, knowledge and preservation of the rules of hygiene should be an important component of the education of orphans in NER orphanages." He said, "If the students lost their physical vitality, they might become unhappy citizens. After leaving the orphanage, NER orphans should take with them much knowledge of hygiene. The Armenian village is in need of much knowledge in health."
  3. Comrade Tigranyan: "Football, games and clean air has made the students at the Polygon healthy, confident, bold." He also suggested replacing the words "orphan" and "orphanage" with "Polygon Children's workshops" where indeed much was accomplished and had more conveniences than all other vocational schools in Armenia and even within the Soviet Union.

724 Ibid.: f. 2.
725 Ibid.: ff. 5–16.
726 Ibid.: f. 19.
727 NAA 39/1/19/ff. 16, 20.
728 "Armenia and Alpha Kappa Lambda," *The Logos of Alpha Kappa Lambda*, December 1927: 12.
729 Wilcox 1928: 222 ff.
730 Ibid.: 227.
731 Ibid.: 229.
732 Ibid.: 223f.
733 *NER Annual Report to U.S. Congress for 1926*: 19.
734 Andreasian 1977: 387.
735 Deroyan 2008: 84.
736 Ibid.: 59.
737 Ibid.: 83.
738 Monroe 1924: 13.
739 Anderson, May 1921: 697.
740 Barton 1930: 253.
741 Mary Davis, "Kindergartening in the Near East," *The New Near East*, February 1923: 17. Reference to the children's excitement about native dances was also made earlier in 1921 when Severski Russian interpreter Nina Brailovskya had observed that the children enjoyed native dances, especially the "handkerchief dance":

  There is á leader who does the main dance in the center of a ring of children, who sway back and forth, clap their hands and sing a musical accompaniment. The leader throws down his handkerchief and then dances slowly around it, gradually stooping lower and lower until he picks up the handkerchief…(Nina Brailovskya, "Sketches in an Armenian Kindergarten," *The New Near East*, June 1922: 11).

742 *The Anaconda Standard*, August 2, 1925.
743 *The New Near East*, January 1925: 7.
744 "The Future of the Children," *The New Near East*, June 1923: 8.
745 Ibid.: 9.
746 "Teaching Orphans to Play," (no author cited) *The Playground*, April 1927: 60
747 Acheson 1940, Chapter III: 8f.

NOTES TO CHAPTER EIGHT

748 Barton 1930: 251ff.
749 Hon. Henry J. Allen, "New World Ideals and the Future Near East," *The New Near East*, July 1923: 4.
750 Barton 1930: 252.
751 Ibid.: 220–21.
752 I am grateful to Mrs. Anahit Dashtents Turabian for making relevant excerpts from her father's unpublished memoirs available for this book. A videotape of Dashtents's biography is available at https://www.youtube.com/watch?t=209&v=bEadmLhQ69U Yerevan, March 4, 2014. Additional information and photographs are available at http://khachikdashtents. blogspot.com, produced on the occasion of the 100th anniversary of his birth.
753 In the Hovhannisyan Family Collection.
754 Mkrtich Armen, *Skaut #89* [Scout #89], Yerevan, 1933.
755 Araksi Pluzyan Collection, AGMI.
756 Twenty-one years later Mkrtich Armen published the expanded version entitled *Karmir yev kapuyt poghkapner*, Yerevan 1954.
757 This was a much expanded version of Stepanyan's earlier publication of 1945.
758 See Gagik Khachatryan, "Leninakanyan skautanots—vorbanotsneri patkere Mkrtich Armeni 'Skaut No. 89' vepum" [Leninakan Scout Houses—The Image of Orphanages in Mkrtich Armen's Scout # 89 Novel], The Historical and Cultural Heritage of Shirak. Papers of the Eighth International Session, Gyumri, October, 2010: 245–251.
759 Svazlian 2000: Survivor Testimony #46.
760 In an interview with Nelly Musheghyan, *Haradevelu uzhe* [The Strength to Persevere], *Haykazunk*, February 1991: 2(8).
761 Mariam Badalyan, "Aharon Manukyan. Sweet Van: Genocide Survivor Has Mother's Memories To Sustain A Long Life," *ArmeniaNow*, 2007 (http://www.armeniapedia.org/wiki/Aharon_Manukyan); Tatevik Grigoryan "Akanatese. 99-amya Aharon Manukyane..." [The Eyewitness. 99-year-old Aharon Manukyan...], *Armenpress*, April 23, 2013.
762 Derenik Temirchyan, "A Great City of Little Children," *The New Near East*, June 1925: 3f.
763 Ibid.: 4.
764 "A Large Orphanage. Children Who Govern Themselves," *Hawera & Normanby Star*, March 21, 1923.
765 Lovejoy 1927: 125.
766 Ibid.: 125f.
767 Acheson, December 1924: 16.
768 Svazlian 2000: Survivor Testimony #46.
769 Mihran Hovhannisyan: 54.
770 Musheghyan, February 1991: 2(8).
771 Nalpantyan 1981: 45.
772 Andreasian 1977: 373.
773 Dashtents, *De Profundis*, Part III-D.
774 Ibid.
775 Mihran Hovhannisyan: 60f.
776 Ibid.: 66
777 Ibid.
778 In a version in Dashtents's memoirs entitled *Gyumri kaghakits. Polygon* [From the City of Gyumri. Polygon], Part II, presumably intended for incorporation in *De Profundis*.
779 Ibid.

780 Dashtents, *De Profundis*, Part III-D.
781 Ibid. Part III-E.
782 Mihran Hovhannisyan: 53.
783 Ibid.: 54.
784 Ibid.: 65.
785 Ibid.
786 Shiraz, *Mi pedur im arciv kyankits*, Yerevan, 1984: 10–13.
787 Ibid.: 10.
788 Ibid.: 11.
789 Ibid.
790 Ibid.
791 Stepanyan 2009: 515.
792 Ibid.: 515f.
793 Ibid.: 541f.
794 Ibid.: 546f.
795 Ibid.
796 Ibid.: 547f.
797 Ibid.: 549.
798 Acheson Diary 1927, Part 3: 364.
799 NAA 122/1/561/f. 14.
800 NAA 113/3/204/ff. 103–105.
801 Ibid.: f. 105.
802 NAA 113/3/664/f. 10.
803 Elliott 1924: 182.
804 Ibid.: 185.
805 "Im unker Lorike" [My Friend Lorik], *Knar Hayastani* [Lyre of Armenia], Yerevan, 1960.
806 Andreasian 1977: 255.
807 Ibid.: 319.
808 Ibid.: 343.
809 Ibid.: 310.
810 The incident is recounted by Onnik Yazmajian in his *Chgnazang, Ahazang* [Crisis, Alarm], Beirut, 1956: 199–201, cited in Andreasian 1977: 308–311.
811 L. Ray Ogden, "What Chance Has An Orphan?" *The New Near East*, March 1926: 6ff.
812 NAA 133/1/713/f. 4 & verso.
813 NAA 113/38/30/ff. 98–105.
814 NAA 113/38/42/ff. 354.
815 Ibid.: f. 365. A graduate from the Physics/Mathematics Department of St. Petersburg University, Musheghyan had returned to Armenia in 1919. In 1921, he was appointed chief of the Department of Socialist Education in the Council of Commissars, and later Deputy Commissar of Enlightenment; he played a central role in the development of the *Patkom* movement in Soviet Armenia. Musheghyan was at the same time a highly admired lecturer at the Yerevan State University in mathematics, physiology and astronomy as well as a research scientist.
816 Hamo Sukiasyan, "Patkomakan sharzhman skzbnavorume Hayastanum" [The Beginnings of the Patkom Movement in Armenia], *Pyoner Weekly*, Yerevan, 2011, No. 9.
817 "Mer yeramyake" [Our Third Anniversary], *Patkom*, No. 2, 1923: 8ff.; *Patkom*, No. 1, 1923: 33.
818 *Patkom*, No. 4 (8): 14.
819 Armen 1933: 7.
820 NAA 681/26/1/ff. 3, 4, 5.
821 Armen 1933: 46.

822 Mkrtich Armen, "Amerkomi gorcuneyutyune Hayastanum" [The Activities of the American Committee in Armenia], *Banber Hayastani arkhivneri*, 4 (31), 1971: 47–68. The author now argued that NER had fed, sheltered, and clothed thousands of orphans and refugees, and that this was made possible by the generosity of the American people. But, he insisted, there could be no doubt about the injustices and severe punishment inflicted on what had remained of the nation, and that some of the American workers dealt in their own "small businesses" by buying precious objects through the donations of old clothes by the people of America. And, Armen maintained, an organization that had been sanctioned by the U.S. government was a spy organization, unbeknownst to the people of America who had generously helped Armenia in its time of need. The NER as an organization, he further maintained, was in the region to secure the business interests of the U.S. government, especially in the oil wells of Baku, since it was believed at the time, that the Soviet Union would not last long and the U.S. would have a foothold in the Caucasus through NER. But when the Soviet Union did not collapse, the "business" idea was abandoned and NER had withdrawn. Nowhere in the article, however, does he mention the scoutmaster, Vahan Cheraz, in whose eventual demise he may have played a role.

823 *Heghnar Aghbyur* is set in a 19th century traditional town and tells the story of a certain Master Mkrtich who builds water fountains. His wife Heghnar, who falls in love with another man and betrays him, dies. Master Mkrtich, still in love with his wife, builds a fountain in her name, where the water flows only for him, and no one else.

824 Armen 1933: 126.
825 Ibid.: 132.
826 Ibid.: 133.
827 Ibid.: 215.

NOTES TO CHAPTER NINE

828 NAA 113/38/46/f. 16. Brown transmitted the substance of his discussion with Lukashin to Abovyan, Myasnikyan's appointee as SSRA liaison with NER, on September 29, 1923:

> In conversation with Mr. Lukashin yesterday we decided that all relatives applying for the discharge of children from this unit should have a letter from you as our authorization. This may prevent exploitation of the children.
>
> We shall, therefore, send all relatives to you before considering. There may be numerous requests of this sort when it is announced that we are transferring the children to Jalaloghli.

829 NAA 113/3/174/f. 60.
830 "Restoration to Normalcy" (RAC LSRM, Folders 104-101, Series 3, Box 9, NE Relief Reports 5B).
831 *The New Near East*, November 1923: 9.
832 NAA 138/3/14/f. 39.
833 NAA 113/39/563/ff. 38–40 recto & verso.
834 NAA 122/1/339/ff. 73, 75.
835 NAA 113/38/42/f. 352 f.
836 Monroe 1924: 6.
837 NAA 113/2/16/f. 22 & verso.
838 Monroe 1924: 5.
839 Ibid.: 5ff.
840 NAA 113/38/42/f. 263.
841 Ibid.: f. 352.
842 Ibid.: f. 353f.
843 Ibid.: f. 52.

844 NAA 113/3/174/f. 17 verso.
845 *Report of the Secretary for 1924*: 2ff.
846 NAA 113/3/174/f. 317.
847 Ibid.: f. 317 verso.
848 NAA 113/38/111/f. 7.
849 Ibid.: ff. 7–9.
850 NAA 113/38/98/f. 93.
851 NAA 113/1/38/f. 89.
852 NAA 113/38/98/f. 118.
853 NAA 39/1/2/f. 17.
854 *NER Annual Report to U.S. Congress for 1926*: 32.
855 Ibid.
856 *Institutions and Industries* 1925: 66.
857 NAA 113/39/563/ ff. 38–40 recto & verso.
858 Ibid.: f. 39 verso.
859 Ibid.
860 NAA 113/39/420/f. 18.
861 Acheson 1940, Chapter III: 26.
862 Ibid.: 26f.
863 *Near East Relief. Annual Report-Foreign Department, Summary*, 1925: 2.
864 Acheson Diary 1926, Part 1: 123.
865 NAA 39/1/19/f. 7.
866 NAA 1387/1/270/f. 4. For the large number of documents detailing the life and activities of Hayk Hovhannisyan while an employee at the City of Orphans, see the following representative documents at the National Archives of Armenia: 1387/1/155/f. 5; 1387/1/156/ff. 1ff.; 1387/1/157/f. 1f.; 1387/1/158/ff. 2–4; 1387/1/ 174/f. 18; 1387/1/224/f. 60; 1387/1/251/f. 1; 1387/1/252/f. 8; 1387/1/285/ff. 1, 11, 15; 1387/1/313/ff. 2, 6.
867 NAA 1387/1/270/f. 4.
868 Ibid.: f. 7.
869 NAA 1387/1/302/f. 6 verso.
870 Ibid.: f. 7.
871 Acheson Diary 1926, Part 2: 242.
872 Ibid.: 249.
873 Ibid.
874 For a sampling of documents carrying lists of orphans' names see NAA 39/1/4/ff. 1, 8–9, 16; NAA 39/1/3/ff. 1, 6, 8, 9, 11, 25, 33, 31, 35, 39; NAA 39/1/6/ ff. 12, 13, 14, 19; NAA 39/1/7/f. 6.
875 NAA 122/1/347/ff. 35, 46.
876 NAA 39/1/7/f. 9.
877 Alpoyachyan 2005: 122. Another group of children outplaced in Sukhum was accompanied by Sarmen, writes Alpoyachyan. Born Armenak Sargsyan, Sarmen was then a staff member in Leninakan but would soon move to Yerevan where he became a renowned poet.
878 Ibid.: 123.
879 NAA 39/1/6/ff. 20–23.
880 Ibid.: ff. 12, 14.
881 NAA 39/1/4/ff. 8–9.
882 NAA 122/1/347/ff. 35–46.
883 Ibid.: f. 38.
884 Ibid.
885 Ibid.: ff. 38 ff.
886 Ibid.: f. 41.
887 Ibid.: f. 44 f.

888 NAA 39/1/8/f. 10.
889 NAA 39/1/3/f. 30.
890 NAA 39/1/4/f. 6.
891 Svazlian 2000: Survivor Testimony #71.
892 NAA 39/1/5/f. 34.
893 For a few examples see: NAA 39/1/7/ff. 14–15; NAA 131/3/543/f. 172; NAA 131/3/558/ff. 169, 170.
894 NAA 113/3/664/ff. 61–63.
895 Ibid.: f. 58.
896 Ibid.: f. 57.
897 *NER Annual Report to U.S. Congress for* 1928: 1.
898 Ibid.
899 Ibid: 21.
900 Ibid. Although not mentioned in the reports, supervision of outplaced children was also conducted by Evelyn Eastman of Chicago who visited villages on horseback. During one such visit, *The New York Times* announced in August 1926, she failed to return to Leninakan ("Chicago Girl Missing in Russian Armenia," *The New York Times*, August 9, 1926). Search parties were organized, but were not successful. Then, three days later, *The New York Times* announced that Evelyn Eastman was safe and sound in Leninakan. ("Relief worker is found," *The New York Times*, August 12, 1926). She had lost her way when dense clouds settled about the mountain. Leaving her horse she had groped forward on foot hoping to reach the nearest village. She wandered the remainder of the day and all night. It was daybreak when the clouds lifted and she reached a mountaineer's hut, where she was found by a search party under Peter Floyd of Cuthbert, Georgia.
901 *NER Annual Report to U.S. Congress for 1928*: 8.
902 Acheson 1940, Chapter IV: 27.
903 Ibid.
904 Ibid.: 28.
905 Acheson Diary 1926, Part 2: 253.
906 Ibid.: 241.
907 Ibid.: 253. In general, the suggestion was to reorganize the personnel by dividing the duties of the Area directors into Supervision of Programs, which would include the Agricultural, Industrial, Recreational, Teachers Training, Nurses Training, Elementary and Orphanage programs, and Supervision of Business, which would include Budgets and Expenditures, Statistics and Records, Warehouse and Supplies, Contracts, Accounts, Transportation, and Building and Equipment.
908 Acheson Diary 1926, Part 1: 137.
909 Ibid., Part 2: 267.
910 Ibid.: 267f. Acheson does not elaborate on the reasons Yarrow caused him anxiety.
911 Ibid., Part 1: 147.
912 NAA 190/1/116/ff. 90–92.
913 Acheson Diary 1927, Part 3: 306.
914 Ibid.: 283. There was, in addition, the payroll for the American staff. Salaries of some of the American staff in 1927 were: "Miss Steiger, $175 per month; Carroll, the Finance officer, $300 per month; Eastman, Supply officer, $300 per month; Dr. Kalloch, in 1927, $250 per month." (Ibid.: 274).
915 Within NER's administration in Alexandropol was a department called The Sixth Section (S-6), or the Department of Local Personnel and Industrial Relations, whose director reported to the Director General. The section was in charge of supervising local personnel activities in all aspects—hiring, transferring, discharging, housing, social insurance, registration of personnel, accident prevention and settlement of accident claims not covered by social insurance, issuing of certificates of service, letters of recommendations, negotiations with the government, labor unions, etc. Ernest Yarrow had issued the redefinition of this department on July 6, 1923, in Alexandropol (NAA 113/38/33/f. 118).

916 NAA 113/38/33/ff. 110–111.
917 Copies were sent to: "Mr. Moravian" [Mravyan], the Director General, Mr. Partridge, Dr. Evans, and Mr. Merritt of NER.
918 Acheson Diary 1927, Part 3: 280.
919 Ibid.: 276.
920 Ibid.: 286, 288.
921 Ibid.: 272.
922 Ibid.: 312f.
923 Ibid.: 284ff., 309.
924 Ibid.: 275.
925 Ibid.: 283.
926 Ibid.: 316.
927 Ibid.: 273.
928 Acheson Diary 1926, Part 1: 120.
929 Ibid., Part 2: 245.
930 Dudley C. Kalloch, "Treatment of Trachoma By Surgical Diathermy," *Journal of the American Medical Association*, October 29, 1927: 1511ff. The article was intended for medical audiences.
931 Ibid.: 152.
932 Acheson Diary 1926, Part 1: 137.
933 Ibid.: 142.
934 *Institutions and Industries* 1925: 25.
935 "Armenian Delegates Thank America," *The New Near East*, September 1926: 8.
936 *NER Annual Report to U.S. Congress for 1926*: 26f.

NOTES TO CHAPTER TEN

937 "Near East Relief to Alter Policy," *The New York Times*, May 21, 1929.
938 Acheson Diary 1926, Part 1: 117.
939 Ibid.: 129.
940 Ibid.: 128.
941 Ibid.: 127–132.
942 Ibid.: 131.
943 Ibid.: 177.
944 Ibid.: 131.
945 Ibid.: 133.
946 NAA 113/38/111/ff. 39–41.
947 Ibid.: f. 39.
948 Ibid.: f. 41.
949 Acheson Diary 1926, Part 1: 178.
950 Ibid.: 116.
951 Ibid.: 113.
952 Ibid.: 139.
953 Ibid.
954 Ibid.: 140.
955 Ibid.: 156.
956 Ibid.: 159.
957 Ibid.: 176.
958 Ibid.: 176, 180.

959 Ibid.: 191.
960 Ibid.: 181.
961 Ibid.: 151.
962 Acheson Diary 1926, Part 2: 223.
963 Ibid.: 226.
964 NER had been sued before. On July 18, 1923, Yerevan district Commander John Evans sent a memorandum to the "Responsible Representative for Armenia" regarding a lawsuit against the NER. (NAA 113/38/33/f. 98). A certain "Simon Hakhoomian" had sued the NER for a very large sum of money, which E. Yarrow, the Director General, refused to pay and requested that either the case be thrown out of court or be postponed. The note does not provide the details of the case, but reads, in part:

> The Director General states that this case should never have come to trial, and that if it does come to trial and judgment against the NER is obtained that he will absolutely refuse to pay it, and if this should be followed by confiscation of property, he will if necessary withdraw the entire organization.

> The Director General states that if this case comes to trial it will but repeat the "Batoum Case," producing a state of antagonism and friction and serious trouble between the NER and the Government, and that for the sake of maintaining the present harmonious relations,

the Responsible Representative should in this and in similar cases see that they are not brought to court, and ended the note by repeating that the Director General deemed that:

> ...this and similar cases should never be permitted to come to trial and that the Responsible Representative should see that they did not.

In the PS, Evans added: Considering that the Director General has but very recently assumed command he perhaps has not had opportunity to prepare a defense of this case-- thus warranting postponement (NAA 113/38/42/f. 98).
965 Acheson Diary, 1926 Part 2: 233.
966 Ibid.: 233f.
967 Ibid.: 235.
968 Ibid.: 234.
969 Acheson Diary 1926, Part 1: 180, 183.
970 Acheson Diary 1926, Part 2: 240, 237.
971 Ibid.: 248.
972 Ibid.: 237f.
973 Ibid.: 260.
974 Ibid.: 253.
975 Ibid.: 126.
976 Ibid.
977 Ibid.: 225.
978 Ibid.: 255.
979 Ibid.: 248.
980 Ibid.: 248, 257.
981 Ibid.: 257.
982 Ibid: 258.
983 Andreasian 1977: 431.
984 Ibid.: 442.
985 Acheson Diary 1927, Part 3: 277.
986 Ibid.: 273.
987 Ibid.: 279. It appears from a conversation between Acheson and Ter-Ghazaryan, recorded in the August 19, 1926 entry of Acheson's diary (Acheson Diaries 1926, Part 1: 193) that the Military had occupied some of the buildings at the Kazachi. The passage reads:

> We discussed at length the way the Military has occupied some of our buildings at Kazachi, ridden through our property and otherwise misbehaved, although in reality the offenses have been small, all things considered.

988 Acheson Diary 1927, Part 3: 279.

989 "28 Relief Workers Arrested by Russia," *The New York Times*, September 29, 1927; "Near East Aides Seized by Reds," *The Los Angeles Times*, Sept. 29, 1927.

990 NAA 122/2a/14/ff. 140–142.

991 Ibid.: f. 139.

992 Ibid.

993 Acheson Diary 1927, Part 3: 290.

994 Ibid.: 289–291.

995 Ibid.: 296, 300.

996 "Not since the Near East Relief was incorporated has there been such a dire falling off in the general contributions as in the past six weeks, during which time the American flood has been doing its damaging work…" ("Near East Relief Running Low," *The Boston Daily Globe*, June 5, 1927.

997 Acheson Diary 1927, Part 3: 317–319.

998 Ibid.: 325.

999 Ibid.: 323.

1000 Ibid.: 333.

1001 Ibid.: 334.

1002 Acheson Diary 1927: 33.

1003 Ibid.

1004 Ibid.: 35.

1005 Ibid.

1006 "Armenian 'Pope' Is Secluded in Old Monastery," *The Coshocton Tribune*, January 19, 1930.

1007 NAA 131/3/543/f. 61.

1008 Ibid.

1009 NAA 131/3/543/f. 135.

1010 Ibid.: f. 137. One group consisted of 106 boys, of whom 12 were 11 years old; 35 were 12 years old; 25 were 13 years old; 17 were 14 years old; 14 were 15 years old; 3 were 16 years old. A second group consisted of 113 boys and 50 girls, where 22 were 12 years old; 48 were 13 years old; 40 were 14 years old; 27 were 15 years old; 21 were 16 years old; and 5 were 17 years old. The third group had 17 girls and 7 boys, where 3 were 13 years old; 2 were 14 years old; 12 were 15 years old; 6 were 16 years old and 1 was 17 years old.

1011 Alpoyachyan 2005: 138f.

1012 NAA 131/3/543/f. 138.

1013 *NER Annual Report to U.S. Congress for 1928*: 20.

1014 "Relative of Atlantan Aids Work of Relief in Armenia," *The Atlanta Constitution*, February 7, 1929. Part of Belle Bass's program was to divide the orphanages into units of children's homes, with one American director for each group, the other offices and chores of each unit filled by native workers. This arrangement had yielded significant savings in expenses as well as furnishing employment for the natives.

1015 "Teacher Back, Praises Reds' Education Plan," *The New York Times*, May 15, 1931. Chickering had returned to Boston on May 2, 1931, after spending five years in Leninakan. After her return to Boston, she described her experience in Leninakan in establishing the first home economics course in 1928.

1016 Acheson Diary 1926, Part 1: 114.

1017 Dry farming refers to crop production during the dry season, utilizing the residual moisture in the soil from the rainy season, usually in a region that receives 20" or more of annual rainfall. Dry farming works to conserve soil moisture during long dry periods primarily through a system of tillage, surface protection, and the use of drought-resistant seed varieties.

1018 A village in the province of Alexandropol renamed Gharibjanyan in the mid-thirties.

1019 "Agricultural School," *NER Annual Report to U.S. Congress for 1928*.

1020 Two of the school's supervisors—Elsie Jarvis of Washington, DC, and Laura MacFetridge, of Morrisville, Pennsylvania—had been members of the American Red Cross before joining NER. Nursing supervisors, however, did not work independently but reported to Dr. Albert W. Dewy, of Denver, Colorado, who was also in charge of all clinics and hospitals at the Polygon (*NER Annual Report to U.S. Congress for* 1928: 20). Dr. Dudley C. Kalloch of Tularosa, New Mexico, had left by the end of 1928, after reducing the trachoma problem from 74% to practically zero, by inaugurating a special treatment.

1021 *NER Annual Report to U.S. Congress for 1928*: 20.

1022 A small sample of these documents at the National Archives of Armenia include: NAA 39/1/3/ff. 47, 48, 51; NAA 131/3/543/ff. 105–107, 119, 121, 172; NAA 39/1/7/ff. 13, 14–15, 17, 18, 22–23, 25, 29, 42; NAA 131/3/558/ff. 148–149, 169–170, 172, 178; NAA 39/1/4/ff. 34, 35, 39, 43.

1023 NAA 131/3/558/f. 151.

1024 Ibid.: f. 154.

1025 Ibid.: f. 232.

1026 Ibid.: f. 233.

1027 NAA 113/3/664/ff. 42–47.

1028 Ibid.: f. 43.

1029 Ibid.: f. 44.

1030 Ibid.: f. 45.

1031 Acheson Diary 1926, Part 1: 174.

1032 Ibid.: 125.

1033 Ibid.: 265.

1034 *Speech Made at Board of Trustees Meeting, Tuesday, January 18, 1927 at the Pennsyulvania Hotel, New York*, (RAC NEF Acheson Diaries Box 135: 1–14).

1035 NAA 113/3/664/f. 45.

1036 Ibid.: f. 46.

1037 Ibid.: ff. 46.

1038 NAA 119/1/13/f. 46.

1039 Ibid.

1040 Ibid.: f. 47.

1041 NAA 119/1/13/f. 22.

1042 Ibid.: f. 28.

1043 NAA 122/2a/11/ff. 37–38.

1044 NAA 133/1/800/ff. 14–15 recto & verso.

1045 Ibid.: f. 17.

1046 NAA 113/3/664/ff. 7–9 recto & verso.

1047 Ibid.: f. 7 verso.

1048 Ibid.: f. 20.

1049 Ibid.: f. 13.

1050 Ibid.: f. 12.

1051 "Banvore Polygonum arkelvac e" ["Banvor" is Banned at the Polygon], *Banvor*, February 10, 1929.

1052 NAA 113/3/664/f. 53.

1053 Ibid.: f. 52.

1054 Ibid.: ff. 50–51.

1055 Ibid.

1056 Ibid.

NOTES TO CHAPTER ELEVEN

1057 James Barton's keynote speech at the February 6, 1930 Meeting of the Trustees in New York entitled, "Near East Relief—Looking Backward and Forward": 3.
1058 Minutes of the Conservation Committee, Feb. 14, 1929: 2.
1059 Ibid.: 5.
1060 Ibid.
1061 Ibid., April 12, 1929: 3.
1062 Ibid.
1063 Ibid., July 29,1929: 10ff.
1064 Ibid., November 14, 1929: 2.
1065 Ibid., Feb. 10, 1930: 5f.
1066 Ibid.
1067 *Report of Managing Director, Caucasus Area*, March 1930: 1, 4–5 (incomplete).
1068 Ibid.: 5.
1069 *The Mount Pleasant News*, May 9, 1930; *The Patoka Register*, June 27, 1930.
1070 NAA 39/1/17/ff. 41, 42.
1071 Ibid.: f. 42.
1072 Ibid.: f. 25.
1073 Ibid.: f. 39.
1074 Ibid.: f. 37.
1075 Ibid.: f. 33.
1076 Ibid.: f. 10.
1077 In a second letter to Dr. Melik-Karamyan, September 10, 1930 (NAA 39/1/17/f. 14).
1078 Ibid.: f. 31.
1079 Details of the rental agreement are outlined in NAA 154/3/7/f. 186; also see NAA 154/3/15/f. 178 on related matters.
1080 NAA 39/1/17/f. 7.
1081 Ibid.: f. 35.
1082 Ibid.: ff. 23, 24.
1083 In fact, the reduction of the American staff had begun earlier. On January 1, 1924, there were 42 American relief workers in Alexandropol; by December 31, 1925, there were 32 (RAC NEF 1925 Report Box 134: 72).
1084 NAA 39/1/17/f. 2.
1085 NAA 113/4/13/f. 7.
1086 Barclay Acheson, *Inter-State Communications*, March 10, 1931: 1–3. (RAC NEF Bound Volumes Box 134).
1087 Ibid.: 1.
1088 Ibid.: 1ff. Acheson may have been referring to the Industrial Party Trial in Moscow that lasted from November 25 to December 7, 1930. The defendants, well-known Soviet engineers and economists, were accused and convicted of involvement in a conspiracy against the Soviet government, devised by Russian émigrés in the West. The trial is considered to be the precursor of the Moscow Show Trials of the late 1930s.
1089 Ibid.: 2.
1090 Ibid.
1091 Ibid.: 3.
1092 Ibid.
1093 Ibid.
1094 "Tells of Life Under Soviet," *The Brandon Daily Sun*, May 26, 1931.
1095 NAA 113/4/13/ff. 3–4.
1096 *The New York Times*, January 9, 1922.
1097 *The New Near East*, April 1922: 5.

1098 "Santa Cruz Woman Weds Georgian Prince Abroad," *The Reno Evening Gazette*, January 9, 1923.

1099 *The Winchester Star*, April 6, 1923.

1100 Soviet Honors Ohio Doctor," *The Dansville Breeze*, February 5, 1927.

1101 *The New York Medical Journal*, October 18, 1922: 473.

1102 "Obituaries," *The American Journal of Nursing*, January 1942: 117f.; *The Daily Times*, April 24, 1924.

1103 Kimball Papers, letter dated February 3, 1926.

1104 Ibid., letter dated February 12, 1926.

1105 *The Mount Pleasant News*, May 9, 1930.

1106 Acheson's lectures were covered in U.S. newspapers nationwide. See, for example, *Oak Park Oak Leaves*, April 17, 1931 (Illinois); "Tells of Work in Far East," *The Portsmouth Herald*, September 28, 1933 (New Hampshire); "U.C. Man Reelected by Near East Group," *The Berkeley Daily Gazette*, October 28, 1933 (California); "Acheson Speaks on Progress in Social Justice," *The Cedar Rapids Coe College Cosmos*, December 9, 1937 (Iowa); "Barclay Acheson to Give Address," *Lehigh University Brown and White*, October 28, 1938 (Pennsylvania); "Noted Speaker Will Address Kiwanis Club," *The Abilene Reporter News*, October 17, 1939 (Texas); "Barclay Acheson Lecture at Club Session Friday," *The Escanaba Daily Press*, September 16, 1939 (Michigan); "Editor Draws Dictator as 'Stifler,'" *The Madison Wisconsin State Journal*, February 12, 1939 (Wisconsin); "Ex-Near East Workers Meet," *The Hutchinson News*, February 15, 1940 (Kansas).

1107 *The Oakland Tribune*, November 8, 1929.

1108 "Honor Yankee Nurse for Armenian Work," *The Oshkosh Daily Northwestern*, November 11, 1929.

1109 "Al Fresco Clinics," *The Huntington Daily News*, March 3, 1930.

1110 Tereza Aghayan, *Hishoghutyunner…*

1111 Acheson Diary 1926, Part 1: 248, 257.

1112 Vahan Cheraz's grandson Vahan Ishkhanyan, was able to retrieve the interrogation documents of his grandfather from archives in Tiflis, and has made some available on line: *"Im gndakaharvac tseghe"* [My Executed Race]. (*VahanIshkhanyan.files.wordpress.com/2014/05/23.jpg*).

1113 Alpoyachyan 2005: 158.

1114 NAA 122/2a/14/f. 139.

1115 Levon Kazanjian, *Renaissance of Van-Vasburagan*, Boston, 1950: 291ff.

1116 For details on Deroyan's life, his rich literary legacy, translations from German philosophy and subsequent arrests, see Ruben Sahakyan, "Varazdat Deroyan. Gyanke yev gorcuneyutyune" [Varazdat Deroyan: His Life and Activities], *Bulletin of the National Archives of Armenia*, (1) 2005: 153–163; Varazdat Deroyan, *Gitakan yev hraparakakhosakan ashkhatutyunner* [Scholarly and Public Affairs Writings], R. Sahakyan, ed., Yerevan, 2006.

1117 NAA 1191/4/973/Part I.

1118 Ibid., f. 22 verso.

1119 Ibid.

1120 Ibid.

1121 NAA 1191/3/1656.

1122 NAA 1191/6/1432.

1123 Interview with author, October 2012.

1124 Vahan Ishkhanyan presents rich biographical details on his mother and his grandparents, the circumstances of the arrests and execution of his grandparents in a number of online publications: *"Untanekan Alpom. Vahan Cheraz"* [Family Album. Vahan Cheraz] (https://vahanishkhanyan.wordpress.com/2014/06/10/cheraz/).

1125 "Our Flag in Russia," Letter to the Editor, *The New York Times*, December 13, 1933.

1126 Acheson, 1940, notes for Chapter X: no page numbers.

1127 Ibid.

NOTES TO CHAPTER TWELVE

1128 Marina Bazayeva, "Lyudvig Yeghiazaryan, the Armenian Genocide Survivor," *FAR* (Fund for Armenian Relief). (http://blog.farusa.org/2010/04/23/beneficiaries-potraits-lyudvig-Ayeghiazaryan-thearmenian-genocide-survivor/ April 23, 2010).

1129 H. Kharatyan-Araqelyan, *Speaking to One Another*, Yerevan, 2010: 82f.

1130 "Aharon: Mother's Memories of Sweet Van," in *Remember 24, ArmeniaNow*, Yerevan, 2007: 8.

1131 Grisha Balasanyan, "95 Years of Memories: Eye Witnesses to the 1915 Genocide," Interview with *Yepraksya Gevorgyan, Hetq*, April 24, 2010. (http://old.hetq.am/en/society).

1132 Svazlian 2000: Survivor Testimony #34; Svazlian 2011: Survivor Testimony #39.

1133 Svazlian 2000: Survivor Testimony #39.

1134 Bazayeva 2010.

1135 Ibid.

1136 *The Middleboro Daily News*, October 17, 1924.

1137 Janet MacKaye, together with Caroline Silliman and Helen Mays, had gone on vacation for a few months in 1926 (*The Hamilton Evening Journal*, October 9, 1926).

1138 Interview of Tikin Margarita by author, October 2013, Gyumri.

1139 *The Berkeley Daily Gazette*, May 23, 1928.

1140 Soghoyan, May 31, 2010.

1141 Svazlian 2000: Survivor Testimony #34.

1142 Ibid.: Survivor Testimony #46.

1143 Musheghyan, February 1991, 2(8).

1144 Mihran Hovhannisyan: 62.

1145 Ibid.: 59.

1146 Svazlian 2000: Survivor Testimony #6.

1147 Svazlian 2011: Survivor Testimony #44.

1148 Video produced on the occasion of Zvart Muradyan's 100th birthday.

1149 Ibid.

1150 Bazayeva, FARusa: 2010.

1151 Svazlian 2000: Survivor Testimony #48.

1152 Khachik Badikyan, "Hrachya Acharyane Etchmiadsnum," [Hrachya Acharyan in Etchmiadzin] *Etchmiadzin*, October-November 1996: 118.

1153 Mark Petrosyan, *Shoghik Mkrtchyan*, Yerevan, 1991: 8f.

1154 Ibid.: 24.

1155 Svazlian 2000: Survivor Testimony #38.

1156 Laura Delsere, "Armenian Genocide: I Remember Them," *Osservatorio Balcani e Caucaso*, December 1, 2010.

1157 I am grateful to Mr. Gevorg Ghazaryan for sharing the history of his family with me.

1158 I am grateful to Mr. Armen Ghazaryan for sharing his grandmothers' photographs.

1159 Tereza Aghayan, *Hishoghutyunner*... The event was also recounted to the author during an interview in October 2012 at the AGMI.

1160 Elinar Shahen, *Shaheni Hushamadyane* [Shahen's Memoirs], Yerevan, 2011: 48.

1161 Shahen 2011: 49–54. For a videotaped biography see https://www.youtube.com/watch?v=hF5IRYK_cVA, narrated by Elinar Shahen and Arpen Movsesyan.

1162 Recounted to author by Narine Khachatryan, Hovhannes Shiraz House-Museum in Gyumri, October 2012.

1163 Aghababyan-Sahakyan, 2004: 26.

1164 For a full biography see Yerevan State University website "History of the Faculty" http://ah.do.am/mer_masin/nshanavor_demq/karapetyan_tadevos_harutyuni.htm. Also mentioned by his orphanage manager, in an undated document (NAA 681/26/1/f. 5).

1165 For a full biography and list of books see Yerevan State University website "History of the Faculty" http://ah.do.am/mer_masin/nshanavor_demq/ohanyan_kirakos_ohani.htm.

1166 NAA 1191/3/1445/ff. 15–18.

1167 NAA 883/1/290; NAA 883/1/f. 509; NAA 883/1/289.

1168 In an addendum to her autobiography, entitled "Pilisopayutyune nshanakum e ser depi imastutyun" [Philosophy Means Love Toward Wisdom]. [Pluzyan Memoirs].

1169 *Grakan Teghekatu* [Literary Bulletin], Hayk Khachatryan, ed., Yerevan, 1975: 720f.

1170 Ibid.: 436.

1171 Ibid.: 23.

1172 Ibid.: 159.

1173 Ibid.: 91f.

1174 For a videotaped version of his early life as portrayed in his poem "Im hin unkernere" [My Old Companions], see https://www.youtube.com/watch?v=ZvXcMTsjJD0 narrated by Parsegh Habeckian.

1175 *Grakan Tert* [Literary Newspaper], March 10, 1937.

1176 Dashtents 1967: 15.

1177 *Grakan Teghekatu* 1975: 745.

1178 Khoyan 1983: 140.

1179 For a list of Mahari's works see Kevork B. Bardakjian, *A Reference Guide to Modern Armenian Literature, 1500–1920*, Detroit, 2000: 405f.

1180 Mentioned in Svazlian 2000: Survivor Testimony #71.

1181 *Grakan Teghekatu* 1975: 12.

1182 Maro Alazan "Im kyanki voghbergutyune," [The Tragedy of My Life]. (http://www.azg.am/AM/2005072322).

1183 For an extensive discussion on the role Zaryan and Kochar played in the persecution and annihilation of progressive writers in Armenia, see *N. Zaryan and H. Kochar, Seruntnere kneren te voch* [N. Zaryan and H. Kochar, Will the Generations Forgive Them or Not?], "Dar" Akumb Forum. (*www.akumb.com*).

1184 See Sassun Grigoryan's *Musanere chlretsin* [The Muses Were Not Silent], Yerevan, 1989 and Angin Arakelyan's *Anavart dimankarner* [Unfinished Portraits], Yerevan, 2007 for a discussion of their lives and artistic careers. For a video biography of the life of Hmayak Avetisyan see https://www.youtube.com/watch?v=7sJ3z46mpI4 narrated by Arpen Movsesyan and Anahit Avetisyan, January 27, 2013.

1185 Khoyan 1983: 128, 132, 138.

1186 Grigoryan 1989: 249–251.

1187 NAA 1191/7/670.

1188 Ghazar Avetisyan Collection, AGMI.

1189 "Armenia Dances as Moscow Plays," *The Lowell Sun*, April 12, 1938.

1190 A few of the newspapers that carried the story on the same day, October 16, 1950: *The Madison Wisconsin State Journal*; *The Janesville Daily Gazette*; *The Portland Press Herald*; *The Bluefield Daily Telegraph*.

1191 "Reds Return Bodies of Six Airmen," *The Indiana Evening Gazette*, September 25, 1958.

1192 "Soviets Say Generals Violated Airspace," *The Watertown Daily Times*, October 23, 1970; *The Montana Standard*, October 23, 1970.

SOURCES

ARCHIVES

Alexandropol Digital Archive, Gyumri Research Center, Gyumri, Armenia.

Archives of the American School of Classical Studies at Athens (Dorothy Horrax Sutton Papers).

Archives of the Near East Relief Historical Society.

Armenian Genocide Museum and Institute, Yerevan, Armenia.

Cranford New Jersey Digital Archives (Roland P. Blythe and Caldwell), Cranford, New Jersey.

Drexel University College of Medicine Archives and Special Collections Digital Resources (Women Physicians 1850s–1970s), Philadelphia, Pennsylvania.

Harvard University Archives (Harold Barton Class Reports), Cambridge, Massachusetts.

History Museum of Armenia, Yerevan, Armenia.

Houghton Library, Harvard University (ABCFM Papers), Cambridge, Massachusetts.

Matenadaran, The Museum of Ancient Manuscripts, Yerevan, Armenia.

Mount Holyoke College Archives and Special Collections Manuscripts (Elsie Kimball Papers), South Hadley, Massachusetts.

National Archives of Armenia, Yerevan, Armenia.

National Library of Armenia, Yerevan, Armenia.

National Library of Norway (Digital Photo Collection of Fridtjof Nansen), Oslo, Norway.

Rockefeller Archive Center, (NEF [Near East Foundation], LSRM [Laura Spellman Rockefeller Memorial] and Rockefeller Family Collection [RFC]), Sleepy Hollow, New York.

United States Library of Congress (Bristol Papers), Washington, DC.

University of Iowa Libraries, Iowa Digital Library (Alfred G. Smaltz, Redpath Chautauqua Collection), Iowa City, Iowa.

University of Wisconsin Digital Collections (Foreign Relations of the United States), Madison, Wisconsin.

MINUTES AND REPORTS

400 Square Miles Covered by Alexandropol General Relief. Alexandropol District Report for December 8th (RAC NEF Record Group [ACCA2009: 104] Photos, Box 144).

Agricultural Projects of Near East Relief (RAC LSRM Folders 104-101, Series 3, Box 9, NERelief Reports 4B).

An Enviable Health Record in Armenia (RAC LSRM Folders 104-101, Series 3, Box 9, NERelief Reports 12B).

Distribution of Near East Relief Orphans in its Schools in Armenia (RAC LSRM Folders 104-101, Series 3, Box 9, NERelief Reports, 10B).

Educational Policy of the Near East Relief, 1924, by Paul Monroe, Ph.D. LL.D (RAC RFC, Record Group III 2Q, World Affairs, Box 41, Folder 356).

Educational Program of Near East Relief in Armenia (RAC LSRM Folders 104-101, Series 3, Box 9, NERelief Reports 11B).

Findings of the Russian Commission of the Near East Relief. An American Report on The Russian Famine, New York, 1921.

Guiding Principles in Connection with Near East Relief Orphanage Work, April 29, 1921. Report of Special Committee of James L. Barton, Walter George Smith, Stanley White (RAC LSRM Folders 91-103, Series 3, Box 8, NERelief Reports).

Maintenance of Peace in Armenia. Hearings before a Subcommittee of the Committee on Foreign Relations, United States Senate, Sixty-sixth Congress, First Session, Copy of Telegram of October 11, 1919, to the Secretary of State from the American Mission, Paris: 77.

Medical Report by Dr. Russell B. Main, *Near East Relief (for Private Circulation)*, June 11, 1921.

The Near East and American Philanthropy. A Survey Conducted under the Guidance of The General Committee of the Near East Survey, Ross, Frank A., Fry, C. Luther, Sibley, Elbridge, New York, 1929.

Near East Relief Annual Report—Foreign Department. Summary. 1925 (RAC NEF 1925 Report Box 134).

Near East Relief. Annual Report to U.S. Congress for the Year Ending:
December 31, 1921: 67th Congress, 2nd Session, Document No. 192.
December 31, 1922: 67th Congress, 4th Session, Document No. 343.
December 31, 1923: 68th Congress, 1st Session, Document No. 111.
December 31, 1926: 69th Congress, 2nd Session, Document No. 229.
December 31, 1927: 70th Congress, 1st Session, Document No. 70.
December 31, 1928: 70th Congress, 2nd Session, Document No. 257.

Near East Situation, 1921 (RAC LSRM Folders 91-103 Series 3, Box B, NERelief Reports).

Near East Relief. Institutions and Industries by Areas, December 31, 1925 (RAC NEF, 1925 Report Box 134).

Near East Relief. Inter-State Communications, by Barclay Acheson, March 10, 1931 (RAC NEF Bound Volumes Box 134).

Near East Relief—Looking Backward and Forward, by James L. Barton. Report to the Board of Trustees and Executive Committee of Near East Relief, February 6, 1930, (RAC NEF Report by Barton to Board, February 6, 1930, Box 134, Conservation Committee).

Near East Relief. Minutes of the Conservation Committee, February 14, 1929; April 12, 1929; July 29, 1929; November 14, 1929, and February 10, 1930 (RAC NEF Box 134, Conservation Committee).

Present Situation in the Near East (RAC LSRM, Folders 104-101, Series 3, Box 9, NERelief Reports, 14B); "Restoration to Normalcy" (RAC LSRM, Folders 104-101, Series 3, Box 9, NERelief Reports 5B).

Quarterly Report on the NER Institute of Agriculture, Stepanavan, by Samuel Newman, Dean of Agriculture, July, August, September, 1924, Appendix IIIB.

Quarterly Report, Orphanage Department, Djalal Oghlou, by Elsie M. Kimball, October 1, 1924, Djalal Oghlou (Elsie Kimball Papers).

Repatriation of Refugees, January 31, 1920, by Lt. Colonel, Gen. Staff T.C. Lonergan (NAA 205/1/634 pt. 2/ff. 361–372).

Report of the General Secretary to the Board of Trustees of the Near East Relief Covering the Calendar Year January 1, 1922 to December 31, 1922, at the Annual Meeting, February 27, 1923.

Report of the General Secretary to the Board of Trustees of the Near East Relief for the Year Ending December 31, 1924, at the Annual Meeting, February 26, 1925.

Report of Managing Director, Caucasus Area, by Joseph Beach, March 1930 [Incomplete] (RAC NEF Bound Volumes, Box 134).

Report to Survey Committee of the Near East Relief, by George Stewart, Ph.D., F.R.G.S. (RAC NEF Box 133 Unnamed Folder).

DIARIES, MEMOIRS, BIOGRAPHIES, AUTOBIOGRAPHIES AND AUTOBIOGRAPHICAL NOVELS

Barclay Acheson, *Diary*, 1926 (Unpublished Manuscript/Typescript, RAC NEF Acheson Diaries, Box 135, 1926).

———, *Diary*, 1927 (Unpublished Manuscript/Typescript, RAC NEF Acheson Diaries Box 135).

———, *Ploughshares and Pruning Hooks*, 1940 (Unpublished Typescript, RAC, Acheson Book Draft [Plowshares and Pruning Hooks], Box 132, Third Carbon).

Tereza Aghayan, *Hishoghutyunner tatikis Tikin Lusini masin* [Memories of My Grandmother Mrs. Lucine] (Unpublished Manuscript, Lucine Aghayan Collection, AGMI). [Biography].

Harutyun Alpoyachyan, *Khachelutyan chambanerov* [On the Paths of the Crucifixion], Yerevan, 2005. [Autobiography].

Vazgen Andreasian, *Vahan Cheraz yev ir yergn Hayastani* [Vahan Cheraz and his Song of Armenia], Beirut, 1977. [Biography].

Anonymous Near East Relief Worker's Diary, 1919–1920. (Unpublished Diary Manuscript, AGMI, Yerevan).

Walter Aramyan, *Zarmanali tariner* [Astonishing Years], Yerevan, 1985. [Autobiography].

Mkrtich Armen, *Skaut #89* [Scout #89], Yerevan, 1933. [Autobiographical novel].

———, *Karmir yev kapuyt poghkapner* [Red and Blue Neckties], Yerevan, 1954. [Autobiographical novel].

Armen Armenyan, *60 Tari hay bemi vra: husher* [Sixty Years on the Armenian Stage: Memoirs], Yerevan, 1954. [Autobiography].

Hmayak Avetisyan, video biography narrated by Arpen Movsesyan and Anahit Avetisyan, Yerevan, January 27, 2013. [Biography]. *https://www.youtube.com/watch?v=7sJ3z46mpI4*.

Harold Barton, *Class Albums of the Harvard College Class of 1909*, Reports for 1924, 1934, 1949, and 1959 (Harvard University Archives). [Autobiographical Notes].

"Bodil Biørn—An Unsung Heroine," *Hetq*, Yerevan, 10 December 2007. [Biography].

Khachik Dashtents, *De Profundis*, Moscow, ca. 1935 (Unpublished Autobiographical Memoirs, Anahit Dashtents Turabian Private Collection, New York).

———, "Husheris het" [With My Memories], in Khachik Dashtents, *Ughtsyal aygabatsi yergiche* [The Singer of the Coveted Dawn], Yerevan 1967. [Autobiography].

———, Video Biography of Khachik Dashtents, Yerevan, March 4, 2014. *https://www.youtube.com/watch?t=209&v=bEadmLhQ69U*.

———, Biographical Notes and Photographs on the occasion of the 100th anniversary of the birth of Khachik Dashtents, May 3, 2010. *http://khachikdashtents.blogspot.com*.

Laura Delsere, "Armenian Genocide: I Remember Them," *Ossevatorio Balcani e Caucaso*, December 1, 2010 [Biographical Notes on Adel and Gurgen Faroyan].

Kachuni Gharagyozyan, *Cnndavayritses depi Ter Zor, Kachuni Gharagyozyani hishoghutyunnere* [From My Birthplace Toward Ter Zor. The Recollections of Kachuni Gharagyozyan], with an introduction by Inga E. Avagyan, Gyumri, 2004. [Autobiography].

Varazdat Harutyunyan, *Kyankis karughinerum* [At the Crossroads of My Life], Yerevan, 1999. [Autobiography].

Herbert Hoover, *The Memoirs of Herbert Hoover. Years of Adventure 1874–1920*, New York, 1951. [Autobiography].

Mihran Hovhannisyan, *Kensagrutyunner, kentsaghayin sovorutyunner, hishoghutyunner, yeghelutyunner* [Biographies, Social Habits, Memories, Events]. [Unpublished Autobiographical Manuscript, Hovhannisyan Family Collection, Armavir Marz, Armenia].

Vahan Ishkhanyan, *Ayd khoshor kapuyt achkere* [Those Big, Blue Eyes], [Biographical Notes on Vardanush and Byurakn Cheraz]. *http://www.tert.am/blog/?p=11848*.

———, Byurakn Andreasyan, *ArmeniaNow*, 2005 [Biographical notes on Byurakn Cheraz Andreasyan].

———, "Im gndakaharvac tseghe" [My Executed Race]. [Biographical Notes on Vahan and Vardanush Cheraz]. *VahanIshkhanyan.files.wordpress.com/2014/05/23.jpg*.

———, "Untanekan Alpom" [Family Album]. *Vahan Cheraz*, October 6, 2014. *http://vahanishkhanyan.files.wordpress.com/2014/06/4.jpg*.

Tatevos Karapetyan, in "History of the Faculty, Yerevan State University." [Biographical Notes on Tatevos Karapetyan]. *http://ah.do.am/mer_masin/nshanavor_demq/karapetyan_tadevos_harutyuni.htm*.

Levon Kazanjian, "Nshan Hovhannisyan," *Veracnund Van-Vaspurakani. Mshakutayin voskedar (1850–1950)* [Renaissance of Van-Vasburakan Cultural Golden Age (1850–1950)], Boston, 1950. [Biographical Notes on Nshan Hovhannisyan].

Luysi mec shogh ayn khavarum vorum aprel e 100 tari [A Great Ray of Light in the Darkness in which She Has Lived for 100 Years]. [Video Biography of Zvart Muradyan on the occasion of her 100th birthday, narrated by Zvart Muradyan, April 25, 2013]. *https://www.youtube.com/watch?v=vi2RtHnvu-U.*

Gurgen Mahari, *Yeritasardutyan semin* [On the Threshold of Youth], Yerevan, 1956. [Autobiography].

Mariam Margaryan. (Unpublished Manuscript, NAA 681/26/1/ff. 3–5). [Autobiography].

Kirakos Ohanyan, in "History of the Faculty, Yerevan State University." [Biographical Notes on Kirakos Ohanyan]. *http://ah.do.am/mer_masin/ nshanavor_demq/ohanyan_kirakos_ohani.htm.*

Mark Petrosyan, *Shoghik Mkrtchyan*, Yerevan, 1991. [Biography of Shoghik Mkrtchyan].

Araksi Pluzyan, *Im kyanki patmutyune* [The Story of My Life]. (Unpublished Autobiographical Manuscript, Araksi Pluzyan Collection, AGMI).

Armenak Sargsyan (Sarmen), *Im hin unkernere* [My Old Companions] (Video autobiographical poem by Sarmen recited by Parsegh Habeckian, January 29, 2010). *https://www.youtube.com/watch?v=ZvXcMTsj7D0.*

Elinar Shahen, *Shaheni hushamatyane*, [Shahen's Memoirs], Yerevan, 2011. [Autobiography/ Biography of Gusan Shahen].

"*Gusan Shahen*," video biography narrated by Elinar Shahen and Arpen Movsesyan, November 11, 2004. [Biography]. *https://www.youtube.com/ watch?v=hF5IRYK_cVA.*

Hovhannes Shiraz, *Yerker. Girk Arajin*, [Works. Book One], Yerevan, 1981. [Autobiographical Poems].

———, *Knar Hayastani* [Lyre of Armenia], Yerevan, 1960. [Autobiographical Poems].

———, *Mi petur im arciv kyankits* [A Feather From My Life as an Eagle], S. Aghababyan, ed., Yerevan, 1984. [Autobiography].

Garnik Stepanyan, *Mghdzavanjayin orer* [Nightmarish Days], Armen Ter-Stepanyan, ed., Yerevan, 2009. [Autobiography].

Oksen Teghtsoonian, *From Van to Toronto: A Life in Two Worlds, 1896–1987*, Robert and Christopher Teghtsoonian, eds., Lincoln, Nebraska, 2003. [Autobiography].

Nayiri Zaryan, *Paron Petrosn u ir nakhararnere* [Mr. Bedros and His Ministers], Yerevan, 1958. [Autobiographical Novel].

INTERVIEWS WITH FORMER ORPHANS OF THE CITY OF ORPHANS (By Orphan's Name)

Heghine Abrahamyan, Ani Gasparyan, "I Know that One Day the World Will Condemn the Genocide," *Hetq*, April 23, 2007.

———, Verjine Svazlian, *The Armenian Genocide: Testimonies of the Eye-Witness Survivors*, Yerevan, 2011(English Version): Survivor Testimony #77.

Nshan Abrahamyan, Verjine Svazlian, *The Armenian Genocide: Testimonies of the Eye-Witness Survivors*, Yerevan, 2000 (Armenian Version): Survivor Testimony #38.

Vardges Aleksanyan, Svazlian 2000: Survivor Testimony #46.

Azniv Aslanian, Svazlian 2000: Survivor Testimony #39.

Lucik Balasanyan, Svazlian 2000: Survivor Testimony #45.

Edward Dashtoyan, Svazlian 2011: Survivor Testimony #28.

Ghazar Gevorgyan, Svazlian 2000: Survivor Testimony #37.

Yepraksya Gevorgyan, Grisha Balasanyan, "95 Years of Memories: Eye Witnesses to the 1915 Genocide," *Hetq*, April 24, 2010. http://old.hetq.am/en/society.

Baghtasar Hakobyan, "Baghtasar: We Walked on Corpses," *Remember 24, ArmeniaNow*, April 2007: 20f.

Arusyak Hovhannisyan (Israyelyan), Nelly Musheghyan, "Haratevelu uzhe" [The Strength to Persevere], *Haykazunk*, February 1991, 2: 8.

Mushegh Hovhannisyan, Svazlian 2000: Survivor Testimony #5.

Aghasi Karoyan, Svazlian 2000: Survivor Testimony #71.

Aharon Manukyan, Mariam Badalyan, "Aharon Manukyan. Sweet Van: Genocide Survivor Has Mother's Memories To Sustain A Long Life," *ArmeniaNow*, 2007.

———, Tatevik Grigoryan, "Akanatese. 99-amya Aharon Manukyane…" [The Eyewitness. 99-year-old Aharon Manukyan…], *Armenpress*, April 23, 2013;

———, "Aharon: Mother's Memories of Sweet Van," *Remember 24, ArmeniaNow*, April 2007: 8f.

Rehan Manukyan, Svazlian 2000: Survivor Testimony #6.

Shoghik H. Mkrtchyan, Svazlian 2000: Survivor Testimony #48.

Zvart Muradyan, "Na 'tesel' e Fridhof Nansenin" [She "Has Seen" Fridtjof Nansen], *Aravot*, October 9, 2010.

Makruhi Sahakyan, Svazlian 2000: Survivor Testimony #34.

Shmavon Sahakyan, "Shmavon: The Song Survives," *Remember 24, ArmeniaNow*, April 2007: 36f.

Garnik Stepanyan, Svazlian 2000: Survivor Testimony #95.

Amalya and Armenuhi Sukyasyan, Yeranuhi Soghoyan, "Severski vorbanotsi san, 97-amya Amalya Sukyasyani husherits [From the Recollections of 97-year-old Amalya Sukyasyan, orphan at the Severski Orphanage], *Hetq*, May 31, 2010. http://hetq.am/arm/news/45039/severski-orbanoci-san-97-amya-amalya-suqiasyani-husheric.html

Manushak Ter-Stepanyan, Svazlian 2011: Survivor Testimony #91.

Lyudvik Yeghiazaryan, Marina Bazayeva, "Lyudvig Yeghiazaryan, the Armenian Genocide Survivor," *FAR* (Fund for Armenian Relief), April 23, 2010. http://blog.farusa.org/lyudvig-yeghiazaryan-the-armenian-genocide-survivor/.

OTHER INTERVIEWS, conducted by author

Tereza Aghayan (Granddaughter of Orphanage Manager Lucine Aghayan), October 2013, AGMI, Yerevan.

Byurakn Cheraz Ishkhanyan (Daughter of Vahan and Vardanush Cheraz), October 2012 and October 2013, Yerevan.

Armen Ghazaryan (Grandson of former orphans Ekaterina Mkrtchyan and Gohar Shagaryan), October 2013, Yerevan.

Gevorg Ghazaryan (Grandson of former orphans Harutyun and Heriknaz Azoyan), October 2013, Yerevan.
Narine Khachatryan (Grandniece of Hovhannes Shiraz), October 2012 and October 2013, Gyumri.
Antonina Mahari (Widow of Gurgen Mahari), October 2012, Yerevan.
Mrs. Margarita (Daughter of Azniv Hakobyan, former student of Near East Relief Worker Janet MacKaye), October 2013, Gyumri.
Raffi Papoyan (Instructor in Physical Education and Author), October 2012, Gyumri.

NEWSPAPERS

Abilene Reporter News (Abilene, Texas)
Ada Evening News (Ada, Oklahoma)
Alamogordo News (Alamogordo, New Mexico)
Albuquerque Journal (Albuquerque, New Mexico)
Alto Herald (Alto, Texas)
Anaconda Standard (Anaconda, Montana)
Anniston Star (Anniston, Alabama)
Aravot Daily [Morning Daily] (Yerevan)
Arlington Times (Marysville, Washington)
Armenian Weekly (Boston, Massachusetts)
Armenpress (Yerevan)
Ashkhatank [Labor] (Yerevan)
Ashkhatanki Droshak [Banner of Labor] (Baku)
Ashkhatavori Dzayn [Worker's Voice] (Kars)
Athens Daily Messenger (Athens, Ohio)
Atlanta Constitution (Atlanta, Georgia)
Australian Worker (Sydney, Australia)
Aztag Daily (Beirut, Lebanon)
Banvor [Laborer] (Leninakan/Gyumri)
Barrier Miner (Broken Hill, New South Wales, New Zealand)
Bastrop Advertiser (Bastrop, Texas)
Beaver County Times (Philadelphia, Pennsylvania)
Berkeley Daily Gazette (Berkeley, California)
Biddeford Daily Journal (Biddeford, Maine)
Billings Gazette (Billings, Montana)
Biloxi Daily Herald (Biloxi, Mississippi)
Bismarck Tribune (Bismarck, North Dakota)
Bluefield Daily Telegraph (Bluefield, West Virginia)
Boone News Republican (Boone, Iowa)
Boston Daily Globe (Boston, Massachusetts)
Boston Evening Globe (Boston, Massachusetts)
Boston Sunday Post (Boston, Massachusetts)
Bourbon News (Paris, Kentucky)
Box Elder News (Brigham City, Utah)
Brandon Daily Sun (Brandon, Manitoba, Canada)

Brewster Herald (Brewster, Washington)
Bridgeport Telegram (Bridgeport, Connecticut)
Brooklyn Eagle (Brooklyn, New York)
Bryan Daily Eagle (Bryan, Texas)
Buffalo Express (Buffalo, New York)
Canton Daily News (Canton, Ohio)
Carmel Standard (Carmel, Indiana)
Carroll Times (Carroll, Iowa)
Carteret Press (Carteret, New Jersey)
Cedar Rapids Coe College Cosmos (Cedar Rapids, Iowa)
Charleroi Mail (Charleroi, Pennsylvania)
Charleston Daily Mail (Charleston, West Virginia)
Charlotte Democrat (Charlotte, North Carolina)
Charlotte News (Charlotte, North Carolina)
Chicago Daily Tribune (Chicago, Illinois)
Cornell Daily Sun (Ithaca, New York)
Coshocton Tribune (Coshocton, Ohio)
Cumberland Evening Times (Cumberland, Maryland)
Daily Illini (Champaign, Illinois)
Daily News (Batavia, New York)
Daily Times (Beaver County, Pennsylvania)
Dakota County Herald (Dakota City, Nebraska)
Dansville Breeze (Dansville, New York)
Davenport Democrat and Leader (Davenport, Iowa)
Day (New London, Connecticut)
Delmarva Star (Wilmington, Delaware)
Denton Journal (Denton, Maryland)
Denton Record Chronicle (Denton, Texas)
Denver Times (Denver, Colorado)
East Chicago Times (Chicago, Illinois)
East Liverpool Review/Tribune (East Liverpool, Ohio)
El Paso Herald (El Paso, Texas)
Elkhart Review (Elkhart, Indiana)
Elyria Chronicle Telegram (Elyria, Ohio)
Escanaba Daily Press (Escanaba, Michigan)
Evening Gazette (Xenia, Ohio)
Evening Independent (Massillon, Ohio)
Evening Sun (Hanover, Pennsylvania)
Evening Times (Trenton, New Jersey)
Evening World (New York, New York)
Frederick News Post (Frederick, Maryland)
Fulton Patriot (Fulton, New York)
Goodland Herald (Goodland, Indiana)
Goshen Daily Democrat (Goshen, Indiana)
Grand Forks Daily Herald (Grand Forks, North Dakota)
Hamilton Evening Journal (Hamilton, Ohio)
Haraj [Forward] (Yerevan)
Hattiesburg American (Hattiesburg, Mississippi)

Hawera & Normanby Star (Taranaki Region, New Zealand)
Haykazunk (Yerevan)
Herald (Algiers, Louisiana)
Herald (Hayti, Missouri)
Herald (Manchester, New Hampshire)
Herald (New Orleans, Louisiana)
Hetq [Trail] (Yerevan)
Horizon (Tiflis)
Huntington Daily News (Huntington, Pennsylvania)
Huron Evening Huronite (Huron, South Dakota)
Hutchison News (Hutchison, Kansas)
Indiana Evening Gazette (Indiana, Pennsylvania)
Indianapolis Star (Indianapolis, Indiana)
Ironwood Daily Globe (Ironwood, Michigan)
Issaquah Press (Issaquah, Washington)
Janesville Daily Gazette (Janesville, Wisconsin)
Journal Advance (Gentry, Arkansas)
Kansas City Star (Kansas City, Missouri)
Kansas City Times (Kansas City, Missouri)
Khorhrdayin Hayastan [Soviet Armenia] (Yerevan)
Kokomo Daily Tribune (Kokomo, Indiana)
Kran [Sledge] (Chicago, Illinois)
Lancaster Daily Eagle (Lancaster, Ohio)
Lawrence Journal (Lawrence, Kansas)
Lehigh University Brown and White (Bethlehem, Pennsylvania)
Lewiston Daily Sun (Lewiston, Maine)
Lewiston Evening Journal (Lewiston, Maine)
Lincoln Star (Lincoln, Nebraska)
Lodi Sentinel (Lodi, California)
Logan Republican (Logan, Utah)
Logansport Press (Logansport, Indiana)
Los Angeles Times (Los Angeles, California)
Lowell Sun (Lowell, Massachusetts)
Ludington Sunday Morning News (Ludington, Michigan)
Lusartsak [Lantern] (Varna, Bulgaria)
Madison Capital Times (Madison, Wisconsin)
Madison Journal (Tallulah, Louisiana)
Madison Wisconsin State Journal (Madison, Wisconsin)
Malheur Enterprise (Vale, Oregon)
Manitowoc Herald News (Manitowoc, Wisconsin)
Mardkaynutyun [Humanity] (Alexandropol)
Martakoch [Battle Cry] (Tiflis)
Miami Daily News (Miami, Florida)
Miami Daily News and Metropolis (Miami, Florida)
Middlesboro Daily News (Middlesboro, Kentucky)
Minneapolis Journal (Minneapolis, Minnesota)
Minnesota Daily Journal (Fergus Falls, Minnesota)
Mohave County Miner and Our Mineral Wealth (Kingman, Arizona)

Monroe News Star (Monroe, Louisiana)
Montana Standard (Butte, Montana)
Mount Pleasant News (Mount Pleasant, Iowa)
Mshak [Farm Laborer] (Tiflis)
Nevada State Journal (Reno, Nevada)
New Castle News (New Castle, Pennsylvania)
New Orleans Daily Democrat (New Orleans, Louisiana)
New York Times (New York, New York)
New York Times, Historical Section (New York, New York)
New York Tribune (New York, New York)
Newark Evening News (Newark, New Jersey)
North Platte Semi Weekly Tribune (North Platte, Nebraska)
North Weld Harold-Voice (Eaton, Colorado)
Northern Star (Lismore, New South Wales, Australia)
Oak Park Oak Leaves (Oak Park, Illinois)
Oakland Tribune (Oakland, California)
Ogden Standard-Examiner (Ogden, Utah)
Olean Evening Herald (Olean, New York)
Oneonta Daily Star (Oneonta, New York)
Ontario Argus (Ontario, Oregon)
Orrville Courier Crescent (Orrville, Ohio)
Oshkosh Daily Northwestern (Oshkosh, Wisconsin)
Otago Witness (Dunedin, New Zealand)
Pacific Commercial Advertiser (Honolulu, Hawaii)
Patoka Register (Patoka, Illinois)
Patriot (Harrisburg, Pennsylvania)
Paykar [Struggle] (Yerevan)
Portland Press Herald (Portland, Maine)
Portsmouth Herald (Portsmouth, New Hampshire)
Poughkeepsie Eagle News (Poughkeepsie, New York)
Poverty Bay Herald (Gisborne, New Zealand)
Prescott Evening Courier (Prescott, Arizona)
Public Ledger (Memphis, Tennessee)
Quad City Herald (Brewster, Washington)
Reading Eagle (Reading, Pennsylvania)
Red Cloud (Red Cloud, Nebraska)
Reno Evening Gazette (Reno, Nevada)
Rushville Daily Republican (Rushville, Indiana)
San Antonio Evening News (San Antonio, Texas)
San Antonio Express (San Antonio, Texas)
San Antonio Light (San Antonio, Texas)
San Diego Union (San Diego, California)
Sandusky Register (Sandusky, Ohio)
Saturday Evening Journal (Crawfordsville, Indiana)
Scarsdale Inquirer (Scarsdale, New York)
Semi-Weekly Maui News (Maui, Hawaii)
Sheboygan Press (Sheboygan, Wisconsin)
Shelbyville Republican (Shelbyville, Indiana)

Silver Lake Record (Silver Lake, Indiana)
Sioux City Journal (Sioux City, Iowa)
Sovetakan Hayastan [Soviet Armenia] (Yerevan)
Spokesman-Review (Spokane, Washington)
Stevens Point Daily Journal (Stevens Point, Wisconsin)
Sunday Oregonian (Portland, Oregon)
Sydney Morning Herald (Sydney, Australia)
Syracuse Herald (Syracuse, New York)
Taylor Daily Press (Taylor, Texas)
Times Picayune (New Orleans, Louisiana)
Times-Reporter (New-Philadelphia, Ohio)
Tomahawk (White Earth, Becker County, Minnesota)
Topeka Daily Capital (Topeka, Kansas)
Trenton Evening Times (Trenton, New Jersey)
Troy Call (Troy, Illinois)
Uniontown Morning Herald (Uniontown, Pennsylvania)
Waco News-Tribune (Waco, Texas)
Warren Evening Mirror (Warren, Pennsylvania)
Washington Post (Washington, DC)
Watertown Daily Times (Watertown, New York)
Waukesha Daily Freeman (Waukesha, Wisconsin)
Westfield Leader (Westfield, New Jersey)
Wheeling Daily Intelligencer (Wheeling, Virginia [W. Virginia])
Willmar Tribune (Willmar, Minnesota)
Winchester Star (Winchester, Virginia)
Winslow Mail (Winslow, Arizona)
Xenia Evening Gazette (Xenia, Ohio)
Yerekoyan Yerevan [Evening Yerevan] (Yerevan)
Zang [Bell] (Tiflis)
Zhoghovrdi Dsayn [Voice of the People] (Tiflis)
Zhoghovurdi Dzayne [Voice of the People] (Constantinople)

PERIODICALS AND JOURNALS

Acorne (Edited by Near East Relief, 13, rue des Petits-Champs, Constantinople, Turkey)
Akunk [Origins] (Yerevan)
American Blacksmith and Motor Shop (Buffalo, New York)
American Industries (New York, New York)
American Journal of Nursing (New York, New York)
American Medicine (Philadelphia, Pennsylvania)
American Review of Reviews (New York, New York)
Archipelago of Holy Russia (Album of the Alexandropol Detachment, 1877–1878)
Asia. The American Magazine on the Orient (New York, New York)
Atlantic Monthly (Boston, Massachusetts)
Azat Kayl [Free Step] (Alexandropol)

Banber Hayasdani arkhivneri [Bulletin of the Archives of Armenia] (Yerevan)
Banber Yerevani hamalsarani [Bulletin of Yerevan University] (Yerevan)
Bazmavep (Venice, Italy)
California Alumni Monthly (Berkeley, California)
Canning Age (New York, New York)
Contemporary Women's Writing (Oxford, England)
Cornell Alumni News (Ithaca, New York)
Current History Magazine (New York, New York)
"Dar" Akumb Forum (Yerevan)
Education (Boston, Massachusetts)
Etchmiadzin, (Etchmiadzin, Armenia)
Friend (Honolulu, Oahu)
From God's Acre, (New Canaan, Connecticut)
GeghArm Monthly (Stepanakert, Nagorno Karabakh Republic)
Gitakan ashkhatutyunner, *HH GAA Shiraki hayagitakan hetazotutyunneri kentron* [National Academy of Sciences of Armenia Shirak Center for Armenological Research. Research Papers.] (Gyumri).
Hayastani Dzayn [Voice of Armenia] (Yerevan)
Good Housekeeping (New York, New York)
Graduate Magazine of the University of Kansas (Lawrence, Kansas)
Grakan tert [Literary Newspaper] (Yerevan)
Harper's New Monthly Magazine (New York, New York)
Hayastani gochnak [Clarion of Armenia] (New York, New York)
Haygazian Armenological Review (Beirut, Lebanon)
Haykakan gitakan hamagorcaktsutyun [Armenian Scientific Cooperation] (Yerevan)
Haykakan SSR Gitutyunneri Akademiayi teghekagir [Bulletin of the Armenian Academy of Sciences] (Yerevan)
Hayots patmutyan hartser, gitakan hotvacneri joghovacu, [Problems in Armenian History, Collection of Scholarly Papers, Institute of History, National Academy of Sciences](Yerevan)
Herald and Presbyter (Cincinnati, Ohio)
Hospital Management (Chicago, Illinois)
Hye Skaut [Armenian Scout] (Constantinople)
International Record of Medicine and General Practice Clinics (New York, New York)
Journal of the American Medical Association (Chicago, Illinois)
Journal of Educational Sociology (New York, New York)
Journal of International Relations (Worcester, Massachusetts)
Journal of the Medical Society of New Jersey (Lawrenceville, New Jersey)
Kindergarten-Magazine (New York, New York)
Life and Light for Woman. Woman's Board of Missions (Boston, Massachusetts)
Literary Digest (New York, New York)
Logos of Alpha Kappa Lambda (Berkeley, California)
Lraber hasarakakan gitutyunneri [Bulletin of the Social Sciences] (Yerevan)
Lutheran Mideast Development
Medical Record (New York, New York)
Medical Woman's Journal (Cincinnati, Ohio)

Military Surgeon (Carlisle, Pennsylvania)
Mitk.am (Yerevan)
National Geographic Magazine (Washington, DC)
Near East Relief (for Private Circulation), (Constantinople)
New Near East (New York, New York)
New York Medical Journal (New York, New York)
New York State Journal of Medicine (Lake Success, New York)
News Bulletin of the American Committee for Armenian and Syrian Relief (New York, New York)
News-Evedroppings-Rumors (For the Personnel of the N.E.R. Family), (Athens, Greece) (RAC NEF, Box 133)
Nork. Grakan, gitakan yev kaghakakan handes [Nork. A Literary, Scientific and Political Journal] (Yerevan)
O A C [Oregon Agricultural College] Alumnus (Corvallis, Oregon)
Outlook (New York, New York)
Pacific Coast Journal of Nursing (San Francisco, California)
Patkom [Young Communist] (Yerevan)
Patma-Banasirakan Handes [Historical-Philological Journal] (Yerevan)
Pedagogical Seminary (Worcester, Massachusetts)
Pilgrim Teacher Quarterly (Boston, Massachusetts)
Playground (New York, New York)
Pomona College Quarterly Magazine (Claremont, California)
Public Opinion (combined with The Literary Digest, New York, New York)
Pyoner [Pioneer] (Yerevan)
Pyoner [Pioneer] Weekly (Yerevan)
Red Cross Bulletin (Washington, DC)
Saturday Evening Post (Philadelphia, Pennsylvania)
Scribner's Magazine (New York, New York)
Sewanee Alumni News (Sewanee, Tennessee)
Sigma Phi Epsilon Journal (Richmond, Virginia)
Signs of the Times (Nampa, Idaho)
Sovetakan Mankavarzh [Soviet Pedagogue] (Yerevan)
Soviet Russia (New York, New York)
St. Andrew's Cross (Boston, Massachusetts)
Survey (New York, New York)
Team Work (New York, New York)
Time Magazine (New York, New York)
Van-Tosp (Yerevan)
VEM Hamahaykakan Handes [VEM Pan Armenian Journal] (Yerevan)
Wide World Magazine (London, England)
World Agriculture (Amherst, Massachusetts)

BOOKS

M. Abgar, *Kyanke Dashnaktsakan vorbanotsnerum* [Life in the Dashnak {Armenian Revolutionary Federation} Orphanages], Yerevan, 1931.

Varazdat Aghababyan and Hasmik Sahakyan, *Marzakan Gyumrin 1920–1993* [Sports in Gyumri, 1920–1933], Gyumri, 2004.

C. P. Aghayan, et al., eds., *Urvagcer Hayastani komunistakan kusaktsutyan* [Sketches of the Communist Party of Armenia], Yerevan, 1967.

Karine Aleksanyan, *Arevmtahay gaghtakanutyune Aleksandrapoli gavarum, 1914–1922. Pastatghteri zhoghovacu* [Western Armenian Refugees in the Province of Alexandropol. Compilation of Documents], Yerevan, 2012.

Vazgen Andreasian and Gh. A. Sofenatsi, *Andranik. Petros Marzpanyan (Pete)*, Beirut, 1982.

―――, *Hay skautin arachnorde. Hator A* [The Leader of the Armenian Scout. Vol. A], Paris 1946.

Angin Arakelyan, *Anavart dimankarner* [Unfinished Portraits], Yerevan, 2007.

Florence A. Armstrong, *History of Alpha Chi Omega Fraternity*, Menasha (Wisconsin), 1922.

Robert F. Arnove, ed., *Philanthropy and Cultural Imperialism: The Foundations at Home and Abroad*, Bloomington (Indiana), 1980.

Suren Avetisyan, *Merdzavor arevelki Amerikyan npastamatuyts komiteyi gorcuneutyune Hayastanum. 1918–1930* [The Activities of the American Near East Relief Committee in Armenia, 1918–1930], Yerevan, 2009.

Liparit Azatyan, *Hay vorbere Mec Yegherni* [The Armenian Orphans of Mec Yeghern], 3 vols., Los Angeles, 1995–2002.

M. A. Badalyan, *Askanaz Mravyane yev sovetahay dprotsi zargatsman hartsere* [Askanaz Mravyan and the Problems of the Development of the Soviet Armenian School System], Yerevan, 1985.

Oliver R. Baldwin, *Six Prisons and Two Revolutions. Adventures in Trans-Caucasia and Anatolia, 1920–1921*, New York, 1925.

Kevork B. Bardakjian, *A Reference Guide to Modern Armenian Literature, 1500–1920*, Detroit, 2000.

Michael Barnett, *Empire of Humanity: A History of Humanitarianism*, Ithaca (New York), 2011.

R. Grant Barnwell, *The Russo-Turkish War*, Toledo (Ohio), 1878.

James Barton, *The Story of Near East Relief. An Interpretation (1915–1930)*, New York, 1930.

"Greve Bell," in *The Encyclopedia of Cleveland History*.

Demetrius Charles Boulger, *The Life of Gordon*, Vol. I, London, 1896.

Bradshaw's Through Routes to the Capitals of the World and Overland Guide to India, Persia and the Far East, London, 1903.

Viscount Bryce, *The Treatment of Armenians in the Ottoman Empire*, London, 1916.

Kaley M. Carpenter, *A Worldly Errand. James L. Barton's American Mission to the Near East*, Ann Arbor (Michigan), 2011.

Carl C. Compton, *The Morning Cometh: 45 Years with Anatolia College*, Athens (Greece), 2008.

E. Danielyan, *Yeghernits prgvac hay pakhstakannere Andrkovkasum 1914–1922*, [The Armenian Refugees Saved from the Yeghern in the Transcaucasus], Yerevan, 1996.

Hayk Demoyan, *Haykakan sporte yev marmnakrtutyune Osmanyan kaysrutyunum* [Armenian Sports and Physical Education in the Ottoman Empire], Yerevan, 2009.

Varazdat Deroyan, *Gitakan yev hraparakakhosakan ashkhatutyunner* [Scholarly and Journalistic Papers], R. Sahakyan ed., Yerevan, 2006.

———, *Misioneraparekorcakan kazmagerbutyunneri ashkhatanke merdzavor arevelkum yev andrkovkasum* [The Work of the Missionary-Relief Organizations in the Near East and the Transcaucasus], ca. 1932, published in 2008 with an introduction by Ruben Sahakyan.

L. Pickett Dock, S. Noyes, E. C. F. Clement, A. Van Meter Fox, *History of American Red Cross Nursing*, New York, 1922.

Gurgen Edilyan, *Gaghtakanakan vorbanotsner* [Orphanages for the Refugees], Tiflis, 1917.

The Edward W. Hazen Foundation, *Ernest A. Yarrow, 1876–1939*, Haddam, Connecticut, 1940.

David Ekbladh, *The Great American Mission. Modernization and the Construction of an American World Order*, Princeton (New Jersey), 2010.

Mabel E. Elliott, *Beginning Again at Ararat*, New York, 1924.

Lawrence J. Friedman and Mark D. McGarvie, eds., *Charity, Philanthropy, and Civility in American History*, Cambridge (UK), 2003.

V. Ghazakhetsyan, et al., eds., *Hayots patmutyun. Girg arachin* [History of the Armenians. Book One], Vol. IV, Yerevan, 2010.

Vardan Ghukasyan, et al., eds., *Gyumri. Kaghake yev mardik* [Gyumri. City and People], Gyumri, 2009.

Sassun Grigoryan, *Musanere chlretsin* [The Muses Were Not Silent], Yerevan, 1989.

Leigh Hallett, *Images of America. Newport*, Charleston, South Carolina, 2012.

Maj. Gen. James G. Harbord, U.S.Army, *Conditions in the Near East, Report of the American Military Mission to Armenia*, April 13, 1920 (68th Congress, 2nd Session, Document No. 266).

Hayastani Hanrapetutyan bnakavayreri bararan [Dictionary of Inhabited Places of the Republic of Armenia], Center for Geodesy and Cartography of the Republic of Armenia, Yerevan, 2008.

Hanna Herzog and Ann Braude, eds., *Gendering Religion and Politics. Untangling Modernities*, New York, 2009.

Richard G. Hovhannisian, *The Republic of Armenia, Vol. I, The First Year, 1918–1919*, Los Angeles, 1971.

Hayk Khachatryan, ed., *Grakan teghekatu* [Literary Bulletin], Yerevan, 1975.

Hranush Kharatyan-Araqelyan and Leyla Neyzi, *Speaking to One Another: Personal Memories of the Past in Armenia and Turkey*, Yerevan, 2010.

Fr. Tigran, Khoyian, *Nahatak tseghi anmahner* [Immortals of a Martyred Race], Beirut, 1983.

Mariam V. Kirakosyan, *Petakan yev hasarakakan hastatutyunneri vorbakhnam gorcuneutyune Hayastani hanrapetutyunum, hyusisayin Kovkasum yev Andrkovkasum 1918–1920* [The Activities of Orphan Care by State and

Public Institutions in the Republic of Armenia, the Northern Caucasus and the Transcaucasus 1918–1920], unpublished dissertation, National Academy of Sciences of Armenia and AGMI, Yerevan, 2011.

Grace H. Knapp, Grisell M. McLaren, Myrtle O. Shane, *The Tragedy of Bitlis*, New York, 1919.

Brandon Little, "Band of Crusaders, American Humanitarians, the Great War and the Remaking of the World," *Research Reports from the Rockefeller Archive Center*, Sleepy Hollow (New York), 2007.

Esther Lovejoy, *Certain Samaritans*, New York, 1927.

Marine Martirosyan, *Vorb u anotevan yerekhaneri khndirnere Hayastanum*, [The Problems of Orphan and Homeless Children in Armenia], Unpublished Manuscript made available by author, Yerevan 2009: 1–5.

Mary Kilbourne Matossian, *The Impact of Soviet Policies in Armenia*, Leiden, 1962.

H. U. Meliksetyan, *Arevmtahayeri brnagaghte yev spyurkahayeri hayrenadartzutyune Sovetakan Hayastan. 1915–1940* [The Deportations of Western Armenians and the Return of Diasporan Armenians to Soviet Armenia 1915–1940], Yerevan 1975.

Arsen Minasyan, *Defektologyayi himunknere* [Fundamentals of Defectology], Yerevan, 1980.

A. L. Nalbandyan, *Ejer Hayastani mankatneri patmutyunits* [Pages from the History of Armenian Orphanages], Yerevan, 1980.

Fridtjof Nansen, *Armenia and the Near East*, New York, 1928.

———, *Khabvads Joghovurt* [A People Deceived] translated from the original *Betrogenes Volk*, 1929, Evelina Margaryan, translator, Yerevan, 2000.

Near East Relief, *The Cross in the East and the Church in the West*, New York, 1921.

Near East Relief, *An Investment That Will Endure*, New York (circa 1925).

Hilde Nielssen, Inger Marie Okkenhaug, Karina Hestad-Skeie, eds., *Protestant Missions and Local Encounters in the Nineteenth and Twentieth Centuries: Unto The Ends of the World (Studies in Christian Missions)*, Leiden, 2011.

Papers of the 8th International Symposium. Shirak Historical and Cultural Heritage, Gyumri, October 22–24, 2010.

Raffi Papoyan, *Bardzratsir yev bardzratsru. Skautakan sharzhman taracume Hayastanum* [Rise and Raise. The Spread of the Scout Movement in Armenia], Yerevan, 1991.

Louis Bayles Paton, ed., *Recent Christian Progress*, Connecticut, 1909.

Merrill D. Peterson, *"Starving Armenians": America and the Armenian Genocide, 1915–1930 and After*, Virginia, 2004.

Geo. L. Richards, MD, *The Medical Work of the Near East Relief*, New York, 1923.

R. J. Rummel, *Death by Government*, New Brunswick (New Jersey), 2009.

Simak, *Antsac-gnatsac orer* [Days Past and Gone], Yerevan, 1962.

Øystein Sørensen, *Fridtjof Nansen: Mannen og myten* [Fridjoff Nansen: The Man and the Myth], Oslo, 1993.

Robert E. Speer and Russell Carter, *Report on India and Persia. Deputation sent by the Board of Foreign Missions of the Presbyterian Church in the U.S. to visit these fields in 1921–1922*, New York, 1922.

Ronald G. Suny, *Looking Toward Ararat. Armenia in Modern History*, Indiana, 1993.
Nikoghayos Fadeyi Tigranyan, Oxford Music online.
Petros Tonapetyan, ed., *Dzayn Tarapelots* [The Voice of the Suffering], Paris, 1922.
Samuel Totten, ed., *Plight and Fate of Children During and Following Genocide. Genocide: A Critical Bibliographic Review. Vol. 10*, New Brunswick (New Jersey), 2014.
Ian Tyrell, *Reforming the World: The Creation of America's Moral Empire*, Princeton (New Jersey), 2010.
C. Ussher, *An American Physician in Turkey*, Boston, 1917.
Luigi Villari, *Fire and Sword in the Caucasus*, London, 1906.
Amatuni Virabyan, et al., eds., *Hay dati nviryale. Fridtjof Nansen. Pastatghteri zhovovacu (1920–1930)*. [The Devotee of the Armenian Cause. Fridtjof Nansen. A Compilation of Documents (1920–1930)], Yerevan, 2005.
Simon Vratsian, *Hayastani hanrapetutyun* [The Republic of Armenia], Paris, 1928.
———, *Hin tghter nor patmutyan hamar* [Old Papers for New History], Beirut, 1962.
Christopher Walker, *Armenia. The Survival of a Nation*, London, 1980.
Elizabeth Wilson, *The Road Ahead*, New York, 1918.
Charles Woodman and George M. Towle, *The Northern and Asiatic Defenses of Turkey*, New York, 1877.
Onnik Yazmajian, *Chgnazang, ahazang* [Crisis, Alarm], Beirut, 1956.